Testing Object-Oriented Systems

The Addison-Wesley Object Technology Series

Grady Booch, Ivar Jacobson, and James Rumbaugh, Series Editors

For more information check out the series web site [http://www.awl.com /cseng/otseries/] as well as the pages on each book [http://www.awl.com/cseng/I-S-B-N/] (I-S-B-N represents the actual ISBN, including dashes).

David Bellin and Susan Suchman Simone, *The CRC Card Book*, ISBN 0-201-89535-8

Robert V. Binder, *Testing Object-Oriented Systems: Models, Patterns, and Tools*, ISBN 0-201-80938-9

Bob Blakley, *CORBA Security: An Introduction to Safe Computing with Objects*, ISBN 0-201-32565-9

Grady Booch, *Object Solutions: Managing the Object-Oriented Project*, ISBN 0-8053-0594-7

Grady Booch, *Object-Oriented Analysis and Design with Applications, Second Edition*, ISBN 0-8053-5340-2

Grady Booch, James Rumbaugh, and Ivar Jacobson, *The Unified Modeling Language User Guide*, ISBN 0-201-57168-4

Don Box, *Essential COM*, ISBN 0-201-63446-5

Don Box, Keith Brown, Tim Ewald, and Chris Sells, *Effective COM: 50 Ways to Improve Your COM and MTS-based Applications*, ISBN 0-201-37968-6

Alistair Cockburn, *Surviving Object-Oriented Projects: A Manager's Guide*, ISBN 0-201-49834-0

Dave Collins, *Designing Object-Oriented User Interfaces*, ISBN 0-8053-5350-X

Jim Conallen, *Building Web Applications with UML*, ISBN 0-201-61577-0

Bruce Powel Douglass, *Doing Hard Time: Designing and Implementing Embedded Systems with UML*, ISBN 0-201-49837-5

Bruce Powel Douglass, *Real-Time UML, Second Edition: Developing Efficient Objects for Embedded Systems*, ISBN 0-201-65784-8

Desmond F. D'Souza and Alan Cameron Wills, *Objects, Components, and Frameworks with UML: The Catalysis Approach*, ISBN 0-201-31012-0

Martin Fowler, *Analysis Patterns: Reusable Object Models*, ISBN 0-201-89542-0

Martin Fowler, *Refactoring: Improving the Design of Existing Code*, ISBN 0-201-48567-2

Martin Fowler with Kendall Scott, *UML Distilled, Second Edition: Applying the Standard Object Modeling Language*, ISBN 0-201-65783-X

Ian Gorton, *Enterprise Transaction Processing Systems: Putting the CORBA OTS, Encina++ and OrbixOTM to Work*, ISBN 0-201-39859-1

Peter Heinckiens, *Building Scalable Database Applications: Object-Oriented Design, Architectures, and Implementations*, ISBN 0-201-31013-9

Christine Hofmeister, Robert Nord, Soni Dilip, *Applied Software Architecture*, ISBN 0-201-32571-3

Ivar Jacobson, Grady Booch, and James Rumbaugh, *The Unified Software Development Process*, ISBN 0-201-57169-2

Ivar Jacobson, Magnus Christerson, Patrik Jonsson, and Gunnar Overgaard, *Object-Oriented Software Engineering: A Use Case Driven Approach*, ISBN 0-201-54435-0

Ivar Jacobson, Maria Ericsson, and Agneta Jacobson, *The Object Advantage: Business Process Reengineering with Object Technology*, ISBN 0-201-42289-1

Ivar Jacobson, Martin Griss, and Patrik Jonsson, *Software Reuse: Architecture, Process and Organization for Business Success*, ISBN 0-201-92476-5

David Jordan, *C++ Object Databases: Programming with the ODMG Standard*, ISBN 0-201-63488-0

Philippe Kruchten, *The Rational Unified Process: An Introduction*, ISBN 0-201-60459-0

Wilf LaLonde, *Discovering Smalltalk*, ISBN 0-8053-2720-7

Dean Leffingwell and Don Widrig, *Managing Software Requirements: A Unified Approach*, ISBN 0-201-61593-2

Chris Marshall, *Enterprise Modeling with UML: Designing Successful Software through Business Analysis*, ISBN 0-201-43313-3

Lockheed Martin Advanced Concepts Center and Rational Software Corporation, *Succeeding with the Booch and OMT Methods: A Practical Approach*, ISBN 0-8053-2279-5

Thomas Mowbray and William Ruh, *Inside CORBA: Distributed Object Standards and Applications*, ISBN 0-201-89540-4

Bernd Oestereich, *Developing Software with UML: Object-Oriented Analysis and Design in Practice*, ISBN 0-201-39826-5

Meilir Page-Jones, *Fundamentals of Object-Oriented Design in UML*, ISBN 0-201-69946-X

Ira Pohl, *Object-Oriented Programming Using C++, Second Edition*, ISBN 0-201-89550-1

Rob Pooley and Perdita Stevens, *Using UML: Software Engineering with Objects and Components*, ISBN 0-201-36067-5

Terry Quatrani, *Visual Modeling with Rational Rose 2000 and UML*, ISBN 0-201-69961-3

Brent E. Rector and Chris Sells, *ATL Internals*, ISBN 0-201-69589-8

Paul R. Reed, Jr., *Developing Applications with Visual Basic and UML*, ISBN 0-201-61579-7

Doug Rosenberg with Kendall Scott, *Use Case Driven Object Modeling with UML: A Practical Approach*, ISBN 0-201-43289-7

Walker Royce, *Software Project Management: A Unified Framework*, ISBN 0-201-30958-0

William Ruh, Thomas Herron, and Paul Klinker, *IIOP Complete: Middleware Interoperability and Distributed Object Standards*, ISBN 0-201-37925-2

James Rumbaugh, Ivar Jacobson, and Grady Booch, *The Unified Modeling Language Reference Manual*, ISBN 0-201-30998-X

Geri Schneider and Jason P. Winters, *Applying Use Cases: A Practical Guide*, ISBN 0-201-30981-5

Yen-Ping Shan and Ralph H. Earle, *Enterprise Computing with Objects: From Client/Server Environments to the Internet*, ISBN 0-201-32566-7

David N. Smith, *IBM Smalltalk: The Language*, ISBN 0-8053-0908-X

Daniel Tkach, Walter Fang, and Andrew So, *Visual Modeling Technique: Object Technology Using Visual Programming*, ISBN 0-8053-2574-3

Daniel Tkach and Richard Puttick, *Object Technology in Application Development, Second Edition*, ISBN 0-201-49833-2

Jos Warmer and Anneke Kleppe, *The Object Constraint Language: Precise Modeling with UML*, ISBN 0-201-37940-6

Testing Object-Oriented Systems

Models, Patterns, and Tools

Robert V. Binder

ADDISON-WESLEY

An imprint of Addison Wesley Longman, Inc.
Reading, Massachusetts • Harlow, England • Menlo Park, California
Berkeley, California • Don Mills, Ontario • Sydney
Bonn • Amsterdam • Tokyo • Mexico City

Many of the designations used by manufacturers and sellers to distinguish their products are claimed as trademarks. Where those designations appear in this book and Addison Wesley Longman Inc., was aware of a trademark claim, the designations have been printed in initial caps or all caps.

The author and publisher have taken care in the preparation of this book, but make no expressed or implied warranty of any kind and assume no responsibility for errors or omissions. No liability is assumed for incidental or consequential damages in connection with or arising out of the use of the information or programs contained herein.

The publisher offers discounts on this book when ordered in quantity for special sales. For more information, please contact:

AWL Direct Sales
Addison Wesley Longman, Inc.
One Jacob Way
Reading, Massachusetts 01867

Visit AWL on the Web: *www.awl.com/cseng/*

Library of Congress Cataloging-in-Publication Data

Binder, Robert
    Testing object-oriented systems : models, patterns, and tools / Robert V. Binder.
        p. cm. — (The Addison-Wesley object technology series)
    Includes bibliographical references and index.
    ISBN 0-201-80938-9 (alk. paper)
        1. Object-oriented programming (Computer science)   2. Computer software—
    Testing.   I.   Title.   II. Series.

QA76.64.B56 1999
005.1′17--dc21   99-045602

Executive Editor: J. Carter Shanklin
Project Editor: Krysia Bebick
Editorial Assistant: Kristin Erickson
Production Coordinator: Marilyn E. Rash
Cover Design: Simone Payment
Design/Composition: Angela Stone, Bookwrights

Text printed on recycled and acid-free paper.

ISBN 0201809389

2 3 4 5 6 7 CRW 02 01 00 99

2nd Printing December 1999

To Judith, Emily, and David.

Thus spake the master: "Any program, no matter how small, contains bugs."

The novice did not believe the master's words. "What if the program were so small that it performed a single function?" he asked.

"Such a program would have no meaning," said the master, "but if such a one existed, the operating system would fail eventually, producing a bug."

But the novice was not satisfied. "What if the operating system did not fail?" he asked.

"There is no operating system that does not fail," said the master, "but if such a one existed, the hardware would fail eventually, producing a bug."

The novice still was not satisfied. "What if the hardware did not fail?" he asked.

The master gave a great sigh. "There is no hardware that does not fail," he said, "but if such a one existed, the user would want the program to do something different, and this too is a bug."

A program without bugs would be an absurdity, a nonesuch. If there were a program without any bugs then the world would cease to exist.

Geoffrey James
The Zen of Programming

Brief Contents

Contents

List of Figures

List of Tables

List of Procedures

Foreword

Some early enthusiastic but misguided advocates of object-oriented programming (OOP) dismissed testing in the erroneous belief that the adoption of OOP would so reduce the incidence of bugs that testing would no longer be needed. We first heard similar claims two generations ago in the context of adopting Cobol as a standard programming language. More recently, CASE failed to deliver on its promise despite clear productivity advantages. For all three, Cobol, CASE, and lately OO, if adoption of the paradigm were to increase productivity to the point where there would be no labor in code creation, all that would be left would be testing and debugging—consuming 100 percent of the labor content. As was learned over decades of sometimes bitter experience for procedural programming languages, every advance has a price. In the case of OO, the very things that lead to greater flexibility, robustness, generality, and productivity are also the things that conspire to make testing, if not more difficult, then at least more challenging.

Nearly everything we have learned about testing procedural language programs also applies to testing OO implementations. Object-oriented testing, as exposited in this book, is built on that infrastructure. However, the emphasis and effectiveness of various test techniques is different for OO. For example, one might never have reason to use either dataflow testing or finite-state machine testing for an application written in a procedural programming language: for an application that exploits what OOP has to offer, the use of these techniques is inescapable. In addition, the relative emphasis on unit and integration testing changes. In procedural languages, unit testing is of primary importance and integration testing is secondary. In OOP, the relative importance is reversed.

Object-oriented programming also brings new problems for testers, problems that are not to be found in procedural programming. Of these, polymorphism, inheritance, and dynamic binding are the most problematic—and they are at the heart of OO. Some of the early research on OO testing was distinctly pessimistic—going so far as to say "What's the use of OO? We can never test it properly, and probably never really debug it." Both the research community and astute practitioners of OOP were not willing to accept that. What has emerged from those communities' mutual concerns is an approach to testing OO software that uses new techniques and/or old techniques reworked to fit the new paradigm. This knowledge, however, for the most part, has been inaccessible to the practitioner; it lay scattered among hundreds of research papers or in the largely unpublished folklore of OOP. Binder has rectified this gap in a skillful exposition of research results tempered by the harsh realities of practice in an edifice that provides methods and techniques for OOP, while building on a solid foundation of what has been proven through decades of use in previous programming paradigms. This book, I believe, provides the missing half of OOP—the testing half.

Boris Beizer
Abington, Pennsylvania

Preface

What Is This Book About?

Testing Object-Oriented Systems is a guide to designing test suites and test automation for object-oriented software. It shows how to design test cases for any object-oriented programming language and object-oriented analysis/design (OOA/D) methodology. Classes, class clusters, frameworks, subsystems, and application systems are all considered. Practical and comprehensive guidance is provided for many test design questions, including the following:

- How to design responsibility-based tests for classes and small clusters using behavior models, state-space coverage, and interface dataflow analysis.
- How to use coverage analysis to assess test completeness.
- How to design responsibility-based tests for large clusters and subsystems using dependency analysis and hierarchic state models.
- How to design responsibility-based tests for application systems using OOA/D models.
- How to automate test execution with object-oriented test drivers, stubs, test frameworks, and built-in test.

This book is about systems engineering and software engineering as much as it is about testing object-oriented software. *Models* are necessary for test design—this book shows you how to develop testable models focused on preventing and removing bugs. *Patterns* are used throughout to express best practices for designing test suites. *Tools* implement test designs—this book shows you how to design effective test automation frameworks.

Is This Book for You?

This book is intended for anyone who wants to improve the dependability of object-oriented systems. The approaches presented range from basic to advanced. I've tried to make this book like a well-designed kitchen. If all you want is a sandwich and a cold drink, the high-output range, large work surfaces, and complete inventory of ingredients won't get in your way. But the capacity is there for efficient preparation of a seven-course dinner for 20 guests, when you need it.

I assume you have at least a working understanding of object-oriented programming and object-oriented analysis/design. If you're like most OO developers, you've probably specialized in one language (most likely C++ or Java) and you may have produced or used an object model. I don't assume that you know much about testing. You will need some background in computer science and software engineering to appreciate the advanced material in this book, but you can apply test design patterns without specialized theoretical training.

You'll find this book useful if you must answer any of the following questions.

- What are the differences between testing procedural and object-oriented software?
- I've just written a new subclass and it seems to be working. Do I need to retest any of the inherited superclass features?
- What kind of testing is needed to be sure that a class behaves correctly for all possible message sequences?
- What is a good integration test strategy for rapid incremental development?
- How can models represented in the UML be used to design tests?
- What can I do to make it easier to test my classes and applications?
- How can I use testing to achieve greater reuse?
- How should I design test drivers and stubs?
- How can I make my test cases reusable?
- How can I design a good system test plan for an OO application?
- How much testing is enough?

The material here is not limited to any particular OO programming language, OOA/D methodology, kind of application, or target environment. However, I use the Unified Modeling Language (UML) throughout. Code examples are given in Ada 95, C++, Java, Eiffel, Objective-C, and Smalltalk.

A Point of View

My seven-year-old son David asked, "Dad, why is your book so big?" I'd just told David that I'd have to leave his baseball game early to get back to work on my book. I wanted to explain my choice, so I tried to be clear and truthful in answering. This is what I told David at the kitchen table on that bright summer afternoon:

> Testing is complicated and I'm an engineer. Making sure that things work right is very important for engineers. What do you think would happen if our architect didn't make our house strong enough because he was lazy? It would fall down and we could get hurt. Suppose the engineers at GM did only a few pages' worth of testing on the software for the brakes in our car. They might not work when we need them and we'd crash. So when engineers build something or answer a question about how to build things, we have to be sure we're right. We have to be sure nothing is left out. It takes a lot of work.

As I was speaking, I realized this was the point of view I'd been struggling to articulate. It explains why I wrote this book and the way I look at the problem of testing object-oriented software. Testing is an integral part of software engineering. Object-oriented technology does not diminish the role of testing. It does alter some important technical details, compared with other programing paradigms. So, this is a large book about how testing, viewed as software engineering, should be applied to object-oriented systems development. It is large because testing and object-oriented development are both large subjects, with a large intersection. By the way—David hit two home runs later that afternoon while I was torturing the truth out of some obscure notions.

Acknowledgments

No one who helped me with this book is responsible for its failings.[1] Dave Bulman, Jim Hanlon, Pat Loy, Meilir Page-Jones, and Mark Wallace reviewed the first technical report about the FREE methodology [Binder 94].

In 1993, Diane Crawford, editor of *Communications of the ACM,* accepted my proposal for a special issue on object-oriented testing, which was published in September 1994. The contributors helped to shape my views on the relationship between the development process and testing. Bill Sasso (then with Andersen Consulting and now answering a higher calling) sponsored a presentation where questions were asked that led to development of the Mode Machine Test pattern (see Chapter 12). Bob Ashenhurst of the University of Chicago, James Weber, and the rest of the Regis Study Group raised more fundamental questions: What is a state? Why should we care about pictures?

The following year, Marie Lenzie, as editor of *Object Magazine,* accepted my proposal for a bimonthly testing column. Since 1995, writing this column has forced me to transform often hazy notions into focused, pragmatic guidance six times each year. Lee White of CASE Western Reserve University and Martin Woodward of the University of Liverpool, editors of the journal *Software Testing, Verification, and Reliability,* encouraged my work in developing a comprehensive survey, patiently waited, and then allocated an entire issue to its publication. Writing the survey helped to sort which questions were important, why they were asked, and what the best available thinking did and did not answer.

My publications, conference tutorials, and professional development seminars on object-oriented testing served as a conceptual repository and proving ground. Many of these materials, with the necessary changes, have been reused here. The cooperation of RBSC Corporation, SIGS Publications, the ACM, the IEEE, and Wiley (U.K.) is appreciated in this regard (see Sources and Credits

---

1. John Le Carre crafted this concise statement about assistance he received on *The Tailor of Panama.* I can't improve on it.

that follow for details). The real-world problems and questions posed by my consulting clients and thousands of seminar participants have been humbling and constant spurs to refinement.

The patient support of Carter Shanklin and his predecessors at Addison-Wesley kept this project alive. Boris Beizer's steady encouragement, suggestions, and acerbic critiques have been invaluable.

Several adept programmers suggested code examples or helped to improve my own: Brad Appleton (C++ in the *Percolation* pattern and elsewhere), Steve Donelow (Objective-C built-in test), Dave Hoag (Java inner class drivers), Paul Stachour (Ada 95 assertions and drivers), and Peter Vandenberk (Objective-C assertions).

Drafts of patterns, chapters, and the entire book have been reviewed by many people. I am very grateful for the reviewers' thoughtful and detailed feedback. Elaine Weyuker helped to debug my interpretation of her Variable Negation strategy presented in Chapter 6. Brad Appleton and the Chicago Patterns Study Group held two pattern writer's workshops that focused on the test design pattern template and early versions of the *Invariant Boundary* and *Percolation* patterns. Ward Cunningham commented on an early draft of the test pattern template. Several people reviewed test patterns based on their work: Tom Ostrand (Category-Partition), John Musa (Allocate Tests by Profile), and Michael Feathers (Incremental Testing Framework). Derek Hatley reviewed an early version of Combinational Logic (Chapter 6); Lee White, Regression Testing (Chapter 15); Doug Hoffman, Oracles (Chapter 18); and Dave Hoag, Test Harness Design (Chapter 19). Anonymous reviewers of an early version of the manuscript pointed out many opportunities for improvement. Brad Appleton, Boris Beizer, Camille Bell, Jim Hanlon, and Paul Stachour reviewed the entire final manuscript and provided highly useful commentary.

Finally, thanks to Judith, Emily, and David for years of support, patience, and encouragement.

Sources and Credits

Some of the author's previous publications have been reused or adapted under the terms of the copyright agreements with original publishers of *Object Magazine, Component Strategies, Communications of the ACM,* and the *Journal of Software Testing, Verification and Reliability.* See the Bibliographic Notes section in each chapter for specific citations.

The other sources, citations, and applicable permissions for the materials quoted on this book's epigraph page and chapter opener pages follow.

Epigraph Page From Geoffrey James, *The Zen of Programming* (Santa Monica: Info Books, 1988), Koan Two. Reprinted by permission of Info Books.

Chapter 2 From Lewis Carroll, *Alice in Wonderland* (Project Gutenberg etext Edition, 1994). In the public domain.

Chapter 3 From Michael A. Friedman and Jeffery M. Voas, *Software Assessment: Reliability, Safety, Testability* (New York: John Wiley & Sons, Inc, 1995), page 26. Reprinted by permission of John Wiley & Sons, Inc.

Chapter 4 Attributed to Edward A. Murphy, Jr., an engineer working on U.S. Air Force rocket-sled experiments. Sixteen accelerometers were attached to a test subject as part of the instrumentation. Each could be attached in two ways, but only one was correct. Murphy made this observation after discovering that all 16 connections were wrong. The statement was repeated by Major John Stapp at a subsequent 1949 news conference. In the public domain.

Chapter 7 From Lewis Carroll, *Through the Looking Glass* (Project Gutenberg etext Edition, 1994). In the public domain.

Chapter 8 A "ha-ha, only serious" slogan often repeated by Professor Robert Ashenhurst, University of Chicago Graduate School of Business. Printed here by permission of Robert Ashenhurst. Ashenhurst notes that, "My quote is in fact parallel to a saying by philosopher W.V.O. Quine, 'No entity without identity.' Although he was speaking in the context of ontology (part of the preoccupation of the branch called analytic philosophy), it is actually also apropos for object modeling without a change in wording, using the concepts 'entity' (= object) and 'identity' (= system id) as they are understood on the OO context."

Chapter 9 As quoted in Daniel A. Yergin and Joseph Stanislaw, *The Commanding Heights* (New York: Simon & Schuster, 1998), page 195. Reprinted by permission of Simon & Schuster.

Chapter 11 From Brian Marick, *The Craft of Software Testing: Subsystem Testing Including Object-based and Object-oriented Testing* (Englewood Cliffs, NJ: Prentice Hall, 1995), page 342. Reprinted by permission of Pearson Education.

Chapter 14 From H. Tredennick (trans.), Aristotle's *Metaphysics* (Cambridge, MA: Loeb Classical Library, Harvard University Press, 1933). Reprinted with no objection from Harvard University Press.

Chapter 15 From Eric Raymond, *The New Hacker's Dictionary* (Cambridge, MA: The MIT Press, 1991), page 205. Reprinted by permission of The MIT Press.

Chapter 17 At a White House Press Conference, December 1987, President Ronald Regan said: "Though my pronunciation may give you difficulty, the maxim is, 'doveryai, no proveryai'—Trust, but verify." See George Schultz, *Turmoil and Triumph: My Years as Secretary of State* (New York: Charles Scribner's Sons, 1993). The Russian proverb translates as the imperative "trust, but verify," which rhymes in spoken Russian. My thanks to Nadya Moiseeva, Oksana Deutsch, and Igor Chudov who verified the spelling and translation in response to a query in *soc.culture.russian.moderated.newsgroup*. In the public domain.

Chapter 18 From *The Histories* (ISBN: 0460871706, J. M. Dent) by Herodotus, translated by George Rawlinson, edited by Hugh Bowden. Copyright © 1992, J. M. Dent. Reprinted by permission of Everyman Publishers PLC.

Trademarks

Part I Preliminaries

Chapter 1   A Small Challenge

The following test design problem will help you to gauge your understanding of software testing in general and testing object-oriented software in particular. I suggest that you spend a few minutes to work the problem before looking at the solution. This exercise is adapted from Myers's classic *The Art of Software Testing*. The problem (as posed in 1978) is to devise a test plan for a program that

> reads three integer values from a card.[1] The three values are interpreted as representing the lengths of the sides of a triangle. The program prints a message that states whether the triangle is scalene, isosceles, or equilateral.
>
> On a sheet of paper, write test cases (i.e., specific sets of data) that you feel would adequately test this program. When you have completed this, turn the page to analyze your tests [Myers 79, 1].

The Java class `Triangle` (see Figure 1.3) is an object-oriented rendition of the triangle requirements.[2] `Triangle` is a subclass of the `Figure` hierarchy shown in Figure 1.1.[3] `Figure` objects support raster (pixel array) display. The methods `isscalene`, `isisosceles`, and `isequilateral` evaluate to `true` or `false` depending on the state of a `Triangle` object.

The assignment here is essentially the same: develop test cases that would adequately test class `Triangle`. Just in case you're a little hazy on your high

---

1. *Card* refers to a punched paper card, which was a common input medium at the time Myers was writing.
2. An Ada-95 implementation is used to show the differences for testing procedural and object-oriented code in [Barbey 97].
3. The class hierarchy is adapted from [Meyer 97, 467 ff].

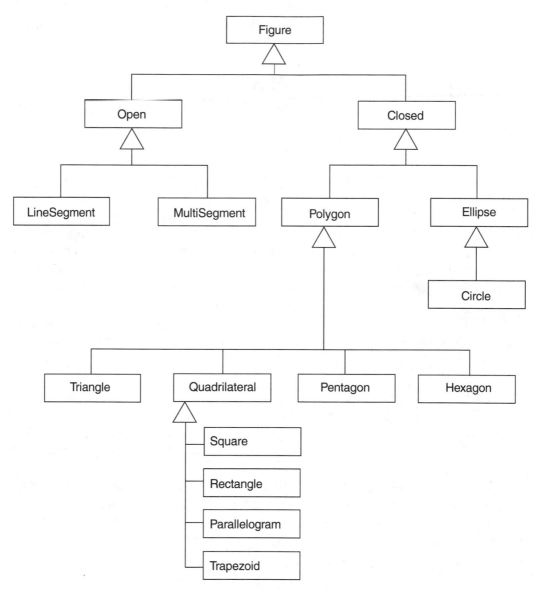

FIGURE 1.1   UML class diagram for the Figure hierarchy.

A valid triangle must meet two conditions. No side may have a length of zero and each side must be longer than the sum of all sides divided by 2. That is, let *a, b,* and *c* be the sides of any triangle:

$s = (a + b + c) / 2$

Then $s > a$, $s > b$, and $s > c$ must hold.

All sides are of equal length in an *equilateral* triangle. Any two sides are equal in an *isosceles* triangle, and all sides are unequal in a *scalene* triangle.

FIGURE 1.2   `Triangle` geometry crib sheet.

school geometry, Figure 1.2 provides a crib sheet. Purists take note: Myers's original problem gave no such information.

Table 1.1 lists Myers's test cases for the `Triangle` problem. His remarks about this exercise still ring true:

> If you are typical, you have done poorly on this test. As a point of reference, highly experienced professional programmers score, on the average, only 7.8 out of a possible 14.

Most of Myers's tests are still appropriate for the responsibilities of class `Triangle`. Test cases 1 to 24 in Table 1.1 correspond to Myers' original solution. Some of these tests are infeasible for the implementation. For example, `LineSegment` will not allow construction of a line of negative length.

But they are also woefully inadequate. Additional object-specific tests are listed in Tables 1.2 and 1.3. These tests reflect some of the unique facets of object-oriented software:

- *No method is an island.* Each method must be tested in the context of its class and its inherited features.
- *Objects preserve state.* We must test for bugs that might appear in some message sequences and states but not in others.
- *Objects keep secrets.* Encapsulation means that we rely on the methods of the class to report test results or we find another way to find out the actual results of persistent values.
- *Object behavior changes.* Dynamic binding allows an object to exhibit many distinct personalities.

```
/*   Java fragments of the Figure hierarchy */

class Polygon extends Figure {
        abstract void draw(int r, int g, int b);      /* Color closed area*/
        abstract void erase();                         /* Set to background rgb */
        abstract float area();                         /* Return area*/
        abstract float perimeter();                    /* Return sum of sides */
        abstract Point center();                       /* Return centroid pixel*/
}

/* Method implementations not shown */

class Triangle extends Polygon {
        public Triangle(LineSegment a, LineSegment b, LineSegment c) {/*ctor*/}
        public void setA(LineSegment a)      {/*  Change side a*/}
        public void setB(LineSegment b)      {/*  Change side b*/}
        public void setC(LineSegment c)      {/*  Change side c*/}

        public LineSegment getA( )           {/*  Get side a*/}
        public LineSegment getB( )           {/*  Get side b*/}
        public LineSegment getC( )           {/*  Get side c*/}

        public boolean is_isoceles()         {/*  Returns true if Isosceles*/}
        public boolean is_scalene()          {/*  Returns true if Scalene*/}
        public boolean is_equilateral()      {/*  Returns true if Equilateral*/}

        public void draw(int r, int g, int b)  {/* Triangle's implementation*/}
        public void erase();                    {/* Triangle's implementation*/}
        abstract float area();                  {/* Triangle's implementation*/}
        abstract float perimeter();             {/* Triangle's implementation*/}
        abstract Point center();                {/* Triangle's implementation*/}

};

class LineSegment extends Figure {
        public LineSegment(Point x1, Point y1, Point x2, Point y2) {/* ctor */}
        public void setx1(Point x1)    {/* Change x1*/}
        public void sety1(Point y1)    {/* Change y1*/}
        public void setx2(Point x2)    {/* Change x2*/}
        public void sety2(Point y2)    {/* Change y2*/}

        public Point getx1()           {/* Return x1*/}
        public Point gety1()           {/* Return y1*/}
        public Point getx2()           {/* Return x2*/}
        public Point gety2()           {/* Return y2*/}
};
```

FIGURE 1.3 Java classes `Figure`, `Triangle`, and `LineSegment`.

TABLE 1.1   Basic Test Cases for Class Triangle

Test Case Description	Test Case Input			Expected Output
	a	b	c	
1 Valid scalene triangle	5	3	4	Scalene
2 Valid isosceles triangle	3	3	4	Isosceles
3 Valid equilateral triangle	3	3	3	Equilateral
4 First permutation of two equal sides	50	50	25	Isosceles
5 Second permutation of two equal sides	25	50	50	Isosceles
6 Third permutation of two equal sides	50	25	50	Isosceles
7 One side zero	1000	1000	0	Invalid
8 One side has a negative length[†]	3	3	−4	Invalid
9 First permutation of two equal sides (invalid)	5	5	10	Invalid
10 Second permutation of two equal sides (invalid)	10	5	5	Invalid
11 Third permutation of two equal sides (invalid)	5	10	5	Invalid
12 Three sides greater than zero, sum of two smallest less than the largest	8	2	5	Invalid
13 Permutation 2 of line lengths in test 12	2	5	8	Invalid
14 Permutation 3 of line lengths in test 12	2	8	5	Invalid
15 Permutation 4 of line lengths in test 12	8	5	2	Invalid
16 Permutation 5 of line lengths in test 12	5	8	2	Invalid
17 Permutation 6 of line lengths in test 12	5	2	8	Invalid
18 All sides zero	0	0	0	Invalid
19 Noninteger input, a[†]	@	4	5	Invalid
20 Noninteger input, b[†]	3	$	5	Invalid
21 Noninteger input, c[†]	3	4	%	Invalid
22 Missing input a[†]		4	5	Invalid
23 Missing input b[†]	3		5	Invalid
24 Missing input c[†]	3	4		Invalid
25 Three sides greater than zero, one side equals the sum of the other two	12	5	7	Invalid
26 Permutation 2 of line lengths in test 25	12	7	5	Invalid
27 Permutation 3 of line lengths in test 25	7	5	12	Invalid
28 Permutation 4 of line lengths in test 25	7	12	5	Invalid
29 Permutation 5 of line lengths in test 25	5	12	7	Invalid
30 Permutation 6 of line lengths in test 25	5	7	12	Invalid
31 Three sides at maximum possible value	32767	32767	32767	Equilateral
32 Two sides at maximum possible value	32767	32767	1	Isosceles
33 One side at maximum possible	1	1	32767	Invalid

[†]This test is infeasible for the example implementation.

TABLE 1.2   Test Requirements for Bugs Related to Encapsulation and Persistence

	Test Cases
34	Did you test that the constructor faithfully creates the lines you've designated?
35	Did you test that only one or zero of the is-* methods is true in every case?
36	Did you try maximum and minimum values for each LineSegment parameter at least once?
37	Did you try to repeat a result?
38	Did you try to repeat a result after permuting line lengths—for example, (5, 3, 4), (4, 5, 3), (3, 4, 5)?
39	Did you try to repeat a result after sending erase?
40	Did you try to repeat a result after sending draw?
41	Did you try to repeat a result more than two times?
42	A single-point line (x1 == x2, y1 == y2).
43	Two single-point lines.
44	Three single-point lines.
45	Three lines, one side minimum length (1 pixel), other sides of maximum length.
46	Two nonintersecting single lines.
47	Two overlapping (all *x* or all *y* the same) lines of different lengths.
48	Three overlapping (all *x* or all *y* the same) lines of different lengths.
49	Two intersecting lines.
50	Two parallel lines.
51	Three lines intersecting at the same point.
52	Three parallel lines.
53	Three nonintersecting, nonparallel lines.
54	Three lines that form an interior triangle but extend beyond the intersections.
55	Three lines with two intersections (an open figure, assuming a finite coordinate space).
56	Three lines with one intersection (an open figure, assuming a finite coordinate space).
57	Three lines, each of maximum length.
58	Three lines, each of minimum length.
59	A figure with one line that lies entirely on each boundary of the *x,y* coordinate space.
60	A figure with two lines that lie entirely on each boundary of the *x,y* coordinate space.
61	A figure with three lines that lie entirely on each boundary of the *x,y* coordinate space.
62	Two lines that intersect and originate from the same boundary of the *x,y* coordinate space.

TABLE 1.3   Test Requirements Related to Inheritance and Polymorphism

	Test Cases
63	All methods defined in `Figure` inherited or overridden by `Triangle` provide a response that is consistent with the original definition.
64	All methods defined in `Closed` that are inherited or overridden by `Triangle` provide a response that is consistent with the original definition.
65	All methods defined in `Polygon` inherited or overridden by `Triangle` provide a response that is consistent with the original definition.

This book presents test models that represent objects so that we may easily design test suites, test design patterns so that test suites can be developed for many kinds of implementations, and automation design patterns to develop software that will run the test suites.

Chapter 2　How to Use This Book

There seemed to be no use in waiting by the little door,
so she went back to the table, half hoping she might
find another key on it, or at any rate a book of rules for
shutting people up like telescopes: this time she found a
little bottle on it ("which certainly was not here before,"
said Alice), and round the neck of the bottle was a
paper label, with the words "DRINK ME" beautifully
printed on it in large letters. It was all very well to say
"Drink me," but wise little Alice was not
going to do THAT in a hurry.

Lewis Carroll
Alice in Wonderland

Overview

This chapter explains the structure of this book and suggests some ways that readers may use it. Conventions, standards, and programming languages used are defined. The book's subjects are introduced by a list of frequently asked questions.

2.1　Reader Guidance

I have struggled with the problem of presenting this complex subject in an accessible way, and I believe the information in this book can be understood and applied without undue effort. This book has four main parts; each should be used and read in a different way. I don't intend that you read cover to cover. Instead, I expect (and encourage) you to jump to a subject or pattern of immediate interest, absorb the essential ideas, and apply them.

Part I: Preliminaries

Chapter 3, Testing: A Brief Introduction, explains my point of view: testing is a problem in systems engineering. Basic testing terms and concepts are defined. The limitations and capabilities of testing are summarized. Chapter 4, With the Necessary Changes, explains the kinds of bugs that object-oriented testing must target and what they imply for testing strategies.

> *Reader Guidance:* The only required reading in Part I is this chapter. If you don't know much about testing, read Chapter 3 (it's short). If you want to know why object-oriented software requires a unique testing approach, read Chapter 4 and then think about the `Triangle` problem presented in Chapter 1.

Part II: Models

Chapter 5, Models, makes the case for model-based testing. Chapter 6, Combinational Models, shows how to model and test logic relationships. Chapter 7, State Machines, shows how to develop highly effective state-based test suites. Chapters 6 and 7 present and explain testing models used in many test design patterns. I included these chapters because no other source completely explains how to apply these elegant and powerful models to testing object-oriented software. If you haven't studied decision tables and state machines previously, these chapters can help you understand why some of the test design patterns given in Part III work. The Unified Modeling Language (UML) notation is used in this book. Chapter 8, A Tester's Guide to the UML, summarizes each UML diagram and related testing strategies.

> *Reader Guidance:* Each chapter in Part II begins with a basic introduction and then works up to advanced concepts. These chapters are not required reading if your immediate goal is to design test suites. If you're in a hurry, skip Part II and go on to Part III. If you're curious about fundamental issues in testing, however, you'll find these chapters interesting. Skip the black diamonds if math gives you heartburn. If you're developing advanced test automation, Part II's concepts and techniques can be used to build effective and efficient tools.

Part III: Patterns

Part III is the "how-to" of object-oriented test design. Chapter 9, Results-oriented Test Strategy, outlines a strategy for effective and efficient testing. It also introduces and explains the notion of a *test design pattern*. All the test design techniques in this book are presented as test design patterns. Subsequent chapters present these patterns and are organized by scope: methods and classes (Chapter 10), reusable components (Chapter 11), clusters, components, and subsystems (Chapter 12), and application systems (Chapter 14). Integration and regression testing apply at all these scopes. Patterns for integration testing are consolidated into Chapter 13. Patterns for regression testing appear in Chapter 15. In each of these chapters, background material appears first, followed by the patterns.

> *Reader Guidance:* Part III is a test design handbook. Focus on the scope and kind of component in which you're interested. For example, you may want to develop a test suite for a class hierarchy. Scan the patterns in Chapter 10 and dive in when one seems to be a good fit with your application. I've tried to make each pattern self-sufficient—for the most part, you shouldn't have to read much else to be able to design a test suite when the pattern applies. If you're a first-time user of a pattern that relies on a model discussed in Part II, you may need to study the related background before you apply the pattern.

Part IV: Tools

Part IV provides the "how-to" for application-specific test automation. It motivates, explains, and gives some basic examples. Chapter 16, Test Automation, explains why object-oriented software should be developed to test object-oriented software. Chapter 17, Assertions, shows how some testing can be accomplished by code embedded in the application. Chapter 18, Oracles, presents strategies to generate expected test results and evaluate actual test results. Chapter 19, Test Harness Design, presents design patterns for automated test frameworks and components. Appendix I, BigFoot's Tootsie, is a short case study about the use of commercial-off-the-shelf testing tools.

> *Reader Guidance:* Part IV is a test implementation handbook. Focus on the scope and kind of component that would automate your test design. For example, you may want to automate the test design you've just developed for a class hierarchy. You would therefore check the test driver patterns in Chapter 19.

This book is more a reference and handbook than it is a sequential tutorial. Don't assume that you must master everything here before you can apply anything. Don't be afraid to experiment. Scan the frequently asked questions (FAQs) in this chapter. Maybe you'll see a question you've had or might have. Pick the parts you need and leave the rest for another day.

2.2 Conventions

2.2.1 Chapter Elements

Some common elements are included in each chapter. Typographic conventions are used to identify special items.

• *Epigrams*. Background, source citations, and permissions for the epigrams are given in the last section of the Preface.

• *Overview*. Each chapter opens with a brief topical summary.

• *Defined terms*. A definition of a term follows when a word or phrase is set in bold type—for example: A **bug hazard** is a circumstance that increases the chance of a bug. All definitions are collected in the Glossary. I have tried to define terms before using them. However, as testing is a large conceptual web, some forward references are unavoidable. Use the Glossary when in doubt.

• *Pattern references*. This book presents 37 test design patterns and 17 software design patterns for test automation. References to them are set in bold and italic type: State-based test models are used in ***Modal Class Test*** and ***Mode Machine Test***. All the test design patterns appear in Part III and can be located in the contents or the index. All the test automation patterns appear in Part IV and can be located by using the contents or the index. References to patterns published elsewhere are set in italics and followed by a citation: "The driver for a state-based test suite can use *Memento* [Gamma+95] to reset the environment to the pretest state."

• *Code examples*. Code examples are set in Lucida: `object.set(x)`.

• *Procedures*. Some test design and execution techniques are summarized in a Procedure for the reader's convenience. A Procedure is a list of steps used to produce a particular result. Procedures intended to be programmed are given in pseudocode.

• *Cited works*. When a specific concept has been published elsewhere or a publication has direct bearing, a citation follows the sentence that first mentions it—for example: "Testing is an integral part of the OOSE methodology [Jacobson+92]." A plus sign indicates that a publication has two or more authors. When referring to a specific page of a source (usually for a quotation), a page number follows the citation—for example: "Often we get the feeling of riding a yo-yo when we try to understand one of these message trees" [Taenzer+89, 33]. Long quotes are indented and set in a smaller type size. The References give publication details for all cited works. Web page URLs are known to be correct as of publication, but are not guaranteed indefinitely.

• *Citations in patterns.* Patterns summarize practices to which many people have contributed. Citations for these contributions appear in the pattern text as appropriate or are given in the Known Uses section of a pattern.

• *Bibliographic notes.* Each chapter concludes with notes about sources used to develop the chapter and may have a brief survey of related literature.

2.2.2 Degree of Difficulty

This book presents basic, intermediate, and advanced concepts. Advanced material may not be of interest to every reader or applicable in every circumstance. It is here for two reasons. First, I dislike technical presentations that glorify technical details for their own sake, but don't offer coherent and powerful abstractions to make sense of the details. Although they may restate an obvious practical motivation, they are silent if you ask *why* an approach should be used or *why* it works. Second, there is "nothing as practical as good theory."[1] I have used formal state machines and decision tables in every complex test design project I have developed for my clients.

Sections with advanced material are marked by paired icons inspired by ski trail signage. Figure 2.1 summarizes these markers. At least 90 percent of this book would be marked green for the intended audience: experienced developers of object-oriented software with a minimum knowledge of testing. Adding green level marks to every section would be silly, so an unmarked section is intended for the widest audience. When a different background is assumed for a section, a level marker appears on a section header. Diamonds show the beginning of an advanced section; the corresponding squares mark its end. The ending marker is omitted in footnotes. For example:

◇ 4.5.6 Level One Subject

This material assumes significant experience in object-oriented development or background as a tester. It may have applicability for language-specific test design □ and automation.

---

1. This observation was made by Kurt Lewin, a leading researcher in group psychology.

Ski Trail Degree of Difficulty		Start	End	Background	Applicability
Green	Easiest trails			Basic OO design and programming.	Wide range of testing situations. Necessary basic principles and techniques.
Blue	Moderate	◇	□	Significant experience in OO development or background as a tester.	Language-specific test design and automation.
Black	Difficult	◆	■	Some math or specialized technical knowledge. Undergraduate degree in computer science.	High-reliability applications. Nontrivial test automation.
Double black diamond	Very difficult	◆◆	■■	Highly specialized knowledge. Graduate degree in computer science or in-depth technical knowledge.	Very high-reliability applications. Provided for completeness. May support advanced automated testing.

FIGURE 2.1 Degree of difficulty markers.

◆ 4.5.6 Level Two Subject

This material assumes some math or specialized knowledge—for example, an undergraduate degree in computer science. It may have applicability to high-
■ reliability applications and nontrivial test automation.

◆◆ 4.5.6 Level Three Subject

A level three subject assumes highly specialized knowledge (e.g., a graduate degree in computer science or heavy experience in the details of a particular software technology). Double black sections are provided for completeness. They are often applicable in developing advanced test automation and in test design for very high-
■■ reliability applications.

In some chapters, ◇, ◆, or ◆◆ footnotes provide short sections of advanced material, citations, or other clarification of finer points. The purpose of these footnotes is to provide a main path for most readers. Material in marked sections is optional in the sense that you can design test suites and test automation without it. If you want to extend the techniques or explore new ideas, however, the advanced concepts may be useful.

The advanced material has its applications, of course. Black and double black material is here for the same reason that a policeman wants a shotgun in a patrol car: he or she may never have to use it, but better to carry it for 20 years unfired than to be without it when needed.

This book occasionally uses mathematical formulas to define ideas and present analytical techniques. None of the mathematics used here would be considered advanced by computer scientists or mathematicians, but it will probably be unfamiliar if you have not studied in an undergraduate program in computer science or engineering. I use mathematical notation because it is concise and unambiguous. Some analytical approaches used here have a quantitative formulation; presenting them without using the original notation is awkward and can be confusing. Many test design techniques discussed in this book are well suited to automation. The precision mathematical notation offers is useful in developing test tools.

2.2.3   Standards

This book complies with relevant standards published by the Institute of Electrical and Electronic Engineers (IEEE) and the American National Standards Institute (ANSI). Terms and formulas follow the *Glossary of Software Engineering Terminology* (610.12-1990) and the *Dictionary of Measures to Produce Reliable Software* (982.1-1988). The approaches outlined to develop and document test plans follow *Software Test Documentation* (829-1983), *Software Unit Testing* (1008-1987), and *Software Verification and Validation Plans* (1012-1986).

The UML was adopted by the Object Management Group as a standard notation for object-oriented software development in late 1997. Today, UML is supported by all leading upper-CASE tools. Where appropriate, diagrams in this book follow version 1.1 of the UML [OMG 98, Rumbaugh+99]. Chapter 8 discusses the UML from a testing point of view and summarizes the elements of the notation.

2.2.4   Object-oriented Terminology

I assume you are knowledgeable about design and programming of object-oriented software. If you are new to object-oriented development, I recommend Wilke's comprehensive and readable *Object-oriented Software Engineering:*

The Professional Developer's Guide [Wilke 93] as a companion to this book. If you're looking for a more technical discussion of conceptual foundations, I recommend Meyer's encyclopedic *Object-oriented Software Construction* [Meyer 97].

Ambiguous usage, synonyms, and homonyms are rampant in object-oriented development, so definitions of basic terms used in this book are in order. A programming language is **object-oriented** if it provides full support for encapsulation, data abstraction, inheritance, polymorphism, and self-recursion [Wegner 88, Stroustrup 88]. Ada 95, C++, Eiffel, Java, Objective-C, and Smalltalk are examples of object-oriented languages. Programming languages whose primary abstraction is module control flow—for example, C, Cobol, Fortran, Pascal, and PL/I—are **procedural** languages. Programming languages whose primary abstraction is encapsulation of modules and data are **object-based**—for example, Ada 83 and Modula.

An **object-oriented program** is an executable assemblage of objects. A **class** is a lexical unit of statements from which objects may be created. An **object** is an instance of a class created at translation time and runtime according to its class definition and the semantics of its programming language.

A class defines and implements instance variables and methods. An **instance variable** is an attribute of a class that may be implemented by using a primitive data type (e.g., integer, byte, floating point) or by defining an instance of a class.

A **method** is a lexically contiguous unit of statements that execute in response to a message. A method has a named entry point and, optionally, a list of formal parameters that constitute the **method interface**.

A **message** is a mechanism for invocation of a method, which results in binding of a specific method to the message name and binding of specific objects to message parameters. A message is **overloaded** if two or more methods may be associated with it. A class X is said to be a **client** of class Y when X defines an instance variable of type Y; Y is said to be a **server** of class X. Client objects activate methods in server objects by sending a message.

Each object of a class contains specific values for instance variables of its class. These values are typically accessed by methods of the class. A **local variable** is defined for the scope of a method's activation and is not visible outside the client class.

A **subclass** has a name and may designate a **superclass**. A subclass **inherits**, or has access to the methods and instance variables of its superclass or superclasses, if **multiple inheritance** is supported. A subclass may **override** a superclass with a method that has the same name as a superclass method, providing **method polymorphism**. It may specify its own instance variables and methods.

Class flattening makes the effects of inheritance explicit by source code expansion; a flattened class shows all of the features that it inherits [Meyer 88]. Table 2.1 lists general and language-specific terms.

2.2.5   Programming Languages and Code Examples

I have no favorite programming language. A programming language is a tool, and even a good tool cannot be the right tool for all jobs. Over the years, the pros and cons of object-oriented programming languages have been debated, ad nauseam, in Usenet news groups, conferences, articles, books, and other forums. Testing is important for application systems written in any language. Just as testing object-oriented software differs significantly from testing conventional software, important (but more narrowly focused) differences arise when testing systems written in various object-oriented languages. Any discussion of object-oriented testing would be incomplete without consideration of these programming language differences. I have tried to follow the design pattern style in dealing with these differences: the general solution followed by *idioms*—that is, language-specific considerations.

Six object-oriented programming languages are considered here: Ada 95, C++,[2] Eiffel, Java, Objective-C, and Smalltalk. All have been used on large and critical applications, and all are widely available. These languages are not exotic research tools or proprietary systems with arbitrary constraints intended to extract tribute.

This book is not about programming style, coding techniques, or the elegant use of any particular object-oriented language. I do not try to provide anything like a complete discussion of programming considerations, as thousands of such publications are already available. Instead, the code examples show basic, simple implementation for test automation strategies or provide examples for test design. Readers are encouraged to improve on and expand these examples.

The code examples are a beginning, not an end. Many of them use code fragments to illustrate a particular concept. A comment delimiter followed by an ellipsis indicates that a typical implementation would be provided at this point. The comment operator indicates that the dots are not part of the code, as shown in Table 2.2.

---

2. Where appropriate, functions are of intrinsic type `bool` and will return either `true` or `false`. Some compilers don't support `bool`, so assume the following: `typedef unsigned bool; const bool false = 0; const true = 1;`

TABLE 2.1 Object-oriented Terms and Synonyms

Term	Definition	Synonym
Abstract class	A superclass that provides common features but is not intended for direct instantiation	Deferred type (Ada 95), abstract base class (C++), deferred class (Eiffel)
Accessor	A method that does not change the state of an object	Function (Ada 95, Eiffel), `const` function (C++), get method
Argument	A formal parameter of a message	
Class variable	An instance variable that belongs to a class	Static data member (C++)
Class	A representation or implementation of a source code unit from which objects may be created	Type (Ada 95)
Class interface	The features of a class (methods and instance variables) that are visible to other classes	Argument list (C++, Smalltalk), signature (Eiffel)
Client	A class (object) that sends a message to another class (object) (possibly itself)	
Cluster	A group of classes that support some common purpose, but that may not have explicit intragroup interfaces	Group of types in a package (Ada 95)
Feature	A method or an instance variable	
Inheritance	Inclusion of superclass features in a subclass	
Instance variable	An object or primitive data type that is defined in a class	Object (Ada 95), data member (C++), entity (Eiffel), attribute
Instantiation	The creation of an object from a class	Declaration (Ada 95), construction (C++), creation (Eiffel)
Message	A static or dynamic activation of a method	Call (Ada 95, C++, Eiffel)
Method	A source code unit defined within the scope of a class that is translated into a callable executable	Member function (C++), routine (Eiffel), operation
Modifier	A method that can change the state of an object	Procedure (Ada 95, Eiffel), set method
Object	A source code unit created from a class with a unique identifier; occupies memory and is executable	
Parameterized class	A class that can take a type parameter	Generic type (Ada 95), template class (C++), generic class (Eiffel)
Self	A variable that provides the object identifier of the object in which it is used	`this` (C++ and Java), `current` (Eiffel)
Server	A class (object) that responds to a message sent by a client	
Subclass	A class that obtains features by inheritance	Derived type (Ada 95), derived class (C++), heir class (Eiffel), descendant class
Superclass	A class from which other classes inherit features	Base type (Ada 95), base class (C++), ancestor class (Eiffel), parent class

TABLE 2.2 Style for Code Ellipsis

	Code Ellipsis
Ada 95	`Procedure foo(X: Integer) is -- ...`
C++	`void foo(int x) { /* ... */}`
Eiffel	`foo (x:INTEGER) is -- ...`
Java	`void foo(int x) { /* ... */}`
Objective-C	`-(void)foo:(int)x { /* ... */}`
Smalltalk	`foo: x "..."`

2.2.6 Testing Tools

A **test tool** is a software application that supports testing. As of this book's pub-lication, roughly 1000 test tools of all kinds were offered commercially, of which approximately 100 have features specific to object-oriented software written in the six languages mentioned previously. I refer to these products as **COTS** (commercial-off-the-shelf) **tools**. Even if you own every COTS tool, you will have to write some software to test your application. This is an **application-specific tool**. Part IV discusses the design and implementation of application-specific tools.

I have used many COTS tools. The Appendix, BigFoot's Tootsie: A Case Study, is a brief report on a 1997 project that integrated several products to support full life-cycle testing. Outside of this chapter, I mention a particular commercial-off-the-self tool only if it provides a unique feature that illustrates a point.

- Tool offerings change rapidly. New products appear frequently and ex-isting tools are revised and improved. Comments cast in type would therefore become quickly obsolete.

- Each tool has strengths and weaknesses compared with its competi-tors. Thus it would be unfair to focus on just a few tools. Presenting a balanced summary based on experience and lab evaluation lies out-side the scope of this book. Even a full discussion could deal only in generalities.

- Even a good lab report would be incomplete and possibly misleading. My experience in developing customized test automation environments has shown that tools must be matched to the situation. The same prod-uct often performs very well in one circumstance and poorly in another.

Human and technical factors are just as important as specific features in determining success. I discuss some of these considerations in the companion to this book, *Managing the Testing Process for Object-Oriented Systems* [Binder 2000].

A wealth of current information on test tools can be found on the Internet. Newsgroups and newsgroup search engines offer another source of data. In addition, several consulting organizations (but not mine) publish guides to testing tools. Test tool vendors demonstrate their products at many conferences. Buyer's guides appear from time to time in publications like *Software Development* and *Dr. Dobbs Journal.*

2.2.7   Humility Department, or Bug Reports Cheerfully Accepted

My first book, published in 1985, took nearly five years to write. It was reviewed by several diligent and hawk-eyed programmers who identified many technical problems. I checked and rechecked the text many, many times. The resulting pile of typescript went to a copy editor who found errors in grammar, general composition, and so on. Changes were duly made. I found and corrected a few more lurking technical bugs along the way. This process was repeated as the manuscript was typeset. Finally, page proofs arrived so that I could produce an index. I once again read the text and excised a few more problems. The book went to press. Several months later, I received the first copy and, with great anticipation, quickly thumbed through it. On the first page that I happened to open, I saw a glaring technical error.

Nearly 15 years later, this book was produced by a similar process. Three times as many reviewers read the draft. They found roughly 1500 items needing improvement, clarification, and outright bugs. The same kind of dedicated editorial work identified style and composition errors. I put all of these bugs in (not intentionally, of course). They did not sneak in while my screen saver was running; they resulted from the limits of my ability and the tyranny of time. All found bugs have been corrected to the best of my ability. Despite this thorough testing and debugging, I am sure that some bugs remain. I encourage you to report any bugs you find in this book via the Addison-Wesley Web site at

http://www.awl.com/cseng/otseries

An errata sheet will be posted there, and necessary corrections will be made in subsequent editions. If you submit a bug report, please indicate the edition and press run number (located on the copyright page) as well as the section number and the page number. "Bugs" include errors in fact, incorrect code examples, misstatements, and typos. Bug reports shouldn't be used for general questions, flames, suggestions, and letters to the editor. Please just send this kind of commentary by snail mail or e-mail care of the publisher.

All this has parallels to software testing. Testing is necessary to remove the bugs that will occur in any large software system. Prevention is still the best cure, but even world-class best practices cannot prevent all bugs. Although absolute perfection can never be attained, I've learned to welcome the help that a good, ongoing test process provides as a writer, a software developer, and a software tester.

2.3   FAQs for Object-oriented Testing

The FAQ format originated to make discussion on Internet news groups more efficient. Instead of explaining what each chapter contains, answers to typical testing questions are used as a concise guide to chapters and sections where detailed answers are found.

2.3.1   Why Test Objects?

Why bother with testing? Doesn't object-oriented programming prevent bugs by reuse and modularity?

Object-oriented code is no less bug-prone than any other kind of code, because it is generated by the same brand of gray matter that produces all software. The object-oriented paradigm has its own little shop of horrors. See Chapter 4, With the Necessary Changes. Testing is necessary to produce high-quality OO applications.

Won't testing interfere with iterative, incremental object-oriented development? Isn't testing a crusty old idea from structured/waterfall methodologies?

Testing has been a part of software development since the earliest computers, and it is accepted by leading practitioners as a necessary part of object-oriented development. For example, the Extreme Programming approach takes as its slogan, "Continuous integration, relentless testing." Booch and Jacobson recommend comprehensive testing at all scopes [Jacobson+92, Booch 96, Jacobson+99]. The Catalysis approach recommends extensive testing [D'Souza+98]. Chapter 9,

Results-oriented Test Strategy, explains how testing fits with object-oriented development.

Isn't automated testing of use cases through the graphical user interface (GUI) enough? Why do I need to do more testing of my classes and application programming interfaces (APIs)?

This kind of testing usually does not reach all of the places that bugs can hide in your classes and objects. See Section 10.1, Class Test and Integration.

Isn't testing inconsistent with a commitment to quality? If programmers were more careful, testing wouldn't be necessary.

Only testing can find some bugs. Testing is necessary to achieve high-quality software and can result in very high-quality object-oriented code. Even in development methodologies that eschew unit testing in favor of proof-of-correctness, testing is relied on to find integration- and system-scope bugs [Deck 97]. See Section 3.4, What Can Testing Accomplish? and Section 4.5, An Object-oriented Testing Manifesto.

What's all the fuss about testing object-oriented code? A black box is a black box, and we already know how to test it.

Most of what we know about software testing in general can be applied to object-oriented code. But these general approaches are not adequate to achieve highly effective testing of object-oriented code. Object-oriented code is subject to different bug hazards—if we use general testing models, we can easily miss OO-specific bugs. Object-oriented development produces object-oriented models, and designing tests from these models must use object-oriented techniques.

The design of test drivers and interpretation of code coverage analysis must be object-oriented—ideas from other paradigms are mostly irrelevant. For more about these differences, see Chapter 4. Every test design pattern defines the bugs it targets, as discussed in Section 4.1. Chapter 9 explains how results-oriented testing replaces the "boxes." Chapters 17 and 19 explain technical differences for test automation.

Component-based development seems to be replacing low-level object coding. Why should I care about objects and object-oriented testing?

Component-based development (using composable binary executables with an API supported by a development environment and often a class framework) is an increasingly popular development approach [Szyperski 98]. Nevertheless, the millions of C++, Java, and Smalltalk programmers and the billions of lines of code they've written won't go away anytime soon. Components are typically integrated with object-oriented applications and written in an object-oriented language, even if they use a procedural or object-based "glue" like Visual Basic.

The real problem is crafting an effective test design strategy for pure component applications, mixed applications, and pure object-oriented applications. Testing pure component applications calls for a combination of good integration planning and development of use case tests. *Class Association Test*, *Round-trip Scenario*, *Controlled Exception Test*, *Mode Machine Test*, and *Extended Use Case Test* patterns will work well to develop responsibility-based tests. Component integration can be accomplished with *Top-down Integration*, *Layered Integration*, *Client/Server Integration*, *Distributed Service Integration*, or *High Frequency Integration*.

Testing the mixed or pure object-oriented code that goes into a component is no different than testing object-oriented code for any other application. If you are a component producer and you write your components in C++, Java, or Smalltalk, the test approaches in this book will apply. You must also try to anticipate how your components will be used and test them accordingly, as suggested by *New Framework Test* and *Popular Framework Test*.

2.3.2   Test Design

What does <some testing term> mean?

See the Glossary. Approximately 500 terms are defined there.

At what scope should I test—class, cluster, subsystem, or system?

At all scopes, if you can. Each scope presents bug hazards that testing at a higher scope can't easily reach. A cluster of interdependent classes is typically the smallest practical testable unit. See Chapter 9, Results-oriented Test Strategy.

How can I design black box test suites for object-oriented code?

The book doesn't discuss "boxes," but instead focuses on responsibility-based testing as a primary strategy. Most of the 37 test design patterns in the book are responsibility-based. See Chapter 9.

How can I design white box test suites for object-oriented code?

The book doesn't discuss "boxes," but instead focuses on responsibility-based testing as primary strategy. *Abstract Class Test*, *Parameterized Class Test*, and *Controlled Exception Test* are all implementation-based. See Chapter 9.

How much testing should I do for methods, classes, class clusters, application systems, and components of reusable libraries?

Every test design pattern has a feature and/or implementation coverage goal stated in the Exit Criteria section. Code coverage analysis is discussed in Section 10.2.2. Section 4.4 surveys several proposals for coverage.

What is the effect of encapsulation on bugs and testing?

Encapsulation helps by preventing bugs common in programs written in languages with global storage and weak data scoping, so we don't have to design tests to find them. However, it can make testing harder and can help to hide bugs. See Sections 4.2.2 and 19.4.

Can we trust the reports of an untested object about its state?

No. Some verification is required. See Section 19.4.1.

What is the effect of inheritance on bugs?

Deep inheritance is the single best predictor of bugs in object-oriented code. See Section 4.2.3.

What is the effect of inheritance on testing?

With a few exceptions, inherited code should be retested. Drivers can be designed to achieve some automatic reuse of superclass test suites. See Sections 4.2.3, 10.4, and 19.4.1.

To what extent should inherited features be retested in a subclass?

Generally, complete retesting is prudent. See Sections 4.2.3 and 10.4.

What is the effect of polymorphism on bugs and testing?

Although polymorphic messages have many advantages, runtime binding can obscure and fragment control relationships, leading to bugs. We do not have any good coverage models of dynamic binding. See Section 4.2.4. *Polymorphic Message Test*, *Polymorphic Server Test*, and *Percolation* can reveal bugs that are often related to polymorphic code.

What is state-based testing?

State-based testing exercises an implementation to see whether it produces the correct response for different use case and message sequences. A state machine model can represent both control responsibilities and the class interface that implements them. Test suites that are very effective at finding control bugs can be generated from these models. See Chapter 7, State Machines.

How do I design state-based test suites?

Develop a state model of the implementation and use the N+ test strategy, described in Section 7.4.3. *Modal Class Test*, *Quasi-modal Class Test*, *Modal Hierarchy Test*, and *Mode Machine Test* use this strategy and show how to apply it at different scopes.

How can I test my tests?

Test designs and application-specific tools are susceptible to the same bugs as application designs and implementations. A QA process for test deliverables is discussed in the companion book, *Managing the Testing Process for Object-Oriented Systems* [Binder 2000]. Technical considerations for assertions are discussed in Verification of Built-in Test, Section 17.5.1, and similar issues for expected results are discussed in Chapter 18, Oracles.

2.3.3 Test Design for Methods and Classes

How can I test method scope input/output relationships?

Use *Category-Partition* to identify and enumerate the input/output relationships.

How can I test a method that implements complex business rules or selection logic?

Use *Combinational Function Test* to model the rules and select input combinations.

How can I test a recursive method?

Use *Recursive Function Test* to try all of the special cases of recursive control.

How can I test usage of a polymorphic server?

Use *Polymorphic Message Test* to verify that messages are sent correctly.

Which test points should I use to find bugs that place my objects in a corrupt state?

Use *Invariant Boundaries* to model the domain of the class and select a few critical test points.

How can I test a class that accepts any sequence of messages?

Use *Nonmodal Class Test* to generate message combinations of set and get messages for critical test points.

How can I test a class that implements a statechart or state machine?

Use *Modal Class Test* to reveal all basic state control bugs.

How can I test a class whose behavior changes for some states?

Use *Quasi-modal Class Test* to model conditional transitions and reveal all basic state control bugs.

How can I test collection and container classes?

Use *Class Association Test*. This pattern lists several strategies for collections.

In what order should coding and testing at method/class scope be performed?

Use *Small Pop* and *Alpha-Omega Cycle* to plan the initial order of development and testing.

How can I test a polymorphic server hierarchy?

Use *Polymorphic Server Test* and *Percolation* to verify that the server gives a correct and consistent response for all bindings.

How can I test a class hierarchy that implements a hierarchy of state machines or statecharts?

Use *Modal Hierarchy Test* to develop a flattened state model and generate a test suite that will reveal all basic state control bugs.

How can I test clients and servers linked by dynamic binding (polymorphism)?

Use *Polymorphic Message Test* to test clients and *Polymorphic Server Test* to test servers. *Percolation* shows how to implement a built-in test for the server. Implementing design-by-contract assertions in clients and servers will catch many bugs due to polymorphism. See Section 17.3, Responsiblity-based Assertions.

How can I measure test coverage of classes and objects?

Every pattern has a coverage goal stated in the Exit Criteria section. Section 4.4 surveys several coverage models. Test coverage analysis is discussed in Chapter 10.

2.3.4   Testing for Reuse

I'm a producer of reusable components. How can I test these components without knowing how they will be used?

The reuse producer's strategy is discussed in Section 11.1.2, The Role of Testing in Reuse.

I'm a consumer of reusable components. How can I be sure that a reused component works correctly?

The reuse consumer's strategy is discussed in Section 11.1.3, Reusing Test Suites.

I'm a consumer of reusable components. How can I be sure that a reused component hasn't caused other objects in my system to break?

Chapter 15, Regression Testing, presents regression testing patterns that should be applied after instantiating new components from reusable components.

How can I design a test suite for an abstract class or an interface?

Use *Abstract Class Test* to design a testable implementation.

How can I design a test suite for a C++ template class or other parameterized class?

Use *Generic Class Test* to choose parameter combinations and develop reusable test suites.

How can I test a newly developed framework, before framework applications have been developed?

Use *New Framework Test* to design a testing application and a test suite that checks reusability.

How can I test changes to a widely used framework?

Use *Popular Framework Test* to reveal feature interaction bugs.

2.3.5   Test Design for Subsystems and Application Systems

How can I test the implementation of class associations, multiplicities, and navigation constraints?

Use *Class Association Test* to systematically exercise all dimensions of an association.

How can I test the end-to-end implementation of a use case or scenario?

Use *Round-trip Scenario Test* to systematically exercise all object-interaction paths within a scenario.

How can I test exception handling?

Use *Controlled Exception Test* to generate all exceptions and systematically exercise exception handlers.

How can I test a system with a distributed control strategy?

Use *Mode Machine Test* to synthesize an application scope state machine and then produce a test suite that reveals all basic state control bugs. Use *Distributed Services Integration* to establish basic operability.

How can I test all application scope input/output relationships?

Use *Extended Use Case Test* to define testable use cases. Then develop tests to exercise all operational relationships in the extended use case model.

How can I verify that all basic operations on problem domain objects in a system have been tested?

Use *Covered in CRUD* to analyze the operations on problem domain objects and identify untested operations.

How can I allocate system test effort to maximize operational reliability?

Use *Allocate Tests by Profile* to assign relative frequencies to extended use cases. Then allocate testing effort in proportion to frequencies.

2.3.6   Integration Testing and Order of Development

What are the main problems in integration of object-oriented systems? What is an effective test and integration strategy given the iterative approach preferred for object-oriented development?

Some integration must be achieved even before unit testing can be performed, because all methods and objects of a class or small cluster must be minimally workable to support testing. *Small Pop* and *Alpha-Omega Cycle* explain how to integrate at unit scope.

Integration can be difficult. It is usually hard to get some objects into the states required by the test design. Some objects may not have been developed yet. As scope increases, the dependencies and structure of the implementation under test should be analyzed to plan an order of development. Judicious use of stubs and careful dependency analysis make for the fewest obstacles in reaching a stable implementation. Chapter 13, Integration, discusses these problems. Chapter 19, Test Harness Design, explains how to implement stubs and drivers to obtain sufficient control.

Can the daily build process apply to object-oriented testing?

Yes. This approach and other repetitive build and test strategies can be effective. *High-frequency Integration* presents considerations for use.

Should I try to test everything at the same time?

Probably not. This approach can work in some situations, but it is more often a lot of trouble. *Big Bang Integration* discusses the try-it-all approach and its limitations.

Can I use code dependencies to plan integration?

Yes. Start with classes that have the fewest dependencies. Test these classes, then the classes that depend on the first group, and so on. This approach is presented in *Bottom-up Integration*.

When should I integrate by control hierarchy?

If a control object or clear control hierarchy exists, you can start with classes at the apex of control. You stub the immediate servers and test, then replace the stubs. You test this configuration, and so on. This approach is presented in *Top-down Integration*.

When should I integrate by collaborations and scenarios?

If several independent collaborations exist in a cluster, you can start with classes that implement one of those collaborations. The classes supporting each collaboration are coded and tested, and so on, until all collaborations have been covered. This approach is presented in *Collaboration Integration*.

Which integration approach makes sense when the virtual machine and the system infrastructure are being developed with the application?

If the application virtual machine and the infrastructure are developed in parallel with the application, the virtual machine can also be used as a test harness. *Backbone Integration* explains how to plan a development sequence of application and infrastructure components.

How can I integrate the components of a layered architecture?

A layered architecture can be approached from a top-down or bottom-up perspective. *Layered Integration* explains how to plan a development sequence of layers.

How can I integrate the components of a client/server architecture?

Some components of a client/server architecture can be built and tested in parallel and then integrated by end-to-end scenarios. *Client/Server Integration* explains how to plan a client/server development sequence.

How can I integrate the components of a distributed architecture?

Many components of a distributed architecture can be built and tested in parallel and then integrated by end-to-end scenarios. Node-to-node dependencies must be considered. *Distributed Services Integration* explains how to plan a sequence of nodes, processes, and internode messages.

I've developed a GUI with objects. How do I test it?

Try to test individual classes or clusters as you go. Use the test design patterns in Chapter 10 that best fit your application. *Top-down Integration* or *Bottom-up Integration* will probably work as an overall approach. Implement these tests with an application-specific, class scope driver—for example, *Incremental Testing Framework*. When all objects work as a system, run tests designed from *Extended Use Case Test* for the use cases supported by this GUI. If your GUI environment (e.g., Java AWT/Beans, X-Windows, or Microsoft Windows) is supported by a COTS capture-playback tool, you can implement the use case tests in its scripting language. Hint: Develop the use case test suite *before* you start coding. Develop and run the class and method scope test cases *before* or *immediately after* you code each method or refactor a class.

2.3.7 Regression Testing and Iterative, Incremental Development

Why is regression testing important for object-oriented development?

Changes often break working code—and iterative and incremental development makes a lot of changes. Clearly, we cannot make much progress if changes break code that previously worked. Without regression testing, unseen bugs will accumulate, until suddenly nothing works in what was once thought to be a stable system.

Also, just as all forms of testing promote reuse with tangible evidence of reliability, so too does regression testing. A regression test suite that can be rerun by a consumer provides a convincing demonstration that a component "works out of the box." Chapter 15, Regression, explains how regression bugs occur and presents testing strategies to find them. *Incremental Testing Framework* offers straightforward automation for regression testing at class/cluster scope.

Can I achieve good regression testing without automated testing?

No. Chapter 15 explains why such an effort is a fool's errand. Part IV shows how to develop the necessary test automation.

When should I rerun all of my tests?

As often as you can. This strategy is the safest regression testing approach, as *Retest All* explains.

I don't have enough time to rerun all of my tests. Can I use risk to choose which tests to rerun?

Considerations for risk-based regression testing are presented in *Retest Risky Use Cases.*

I don't have enough time to rerun all of my tests. Can I choose which tests to rerun by frequency of use?

Considerations for frequency-based regression testing are presented in *Retest by Profile.*

I don't have enough time to rerun all of my tests. Can I choose which tests to rerun based on which code has changed?

An approach for code dependency and change analysis to choose a regression test suite is presented in *Retest Changed Code.*

I don't have enough time to rerun all of my tests. Can I determine which classes and objects can't be affected by changes to exclude some tests?

An approach for code dependency and change analysis to choose a regression test suite is presented in *Retest Within Firewall.*

2.3.8 Testing with UML Models

What is the UML?

The Unified Modeling Language is a graphic notation for object-oriented systems. It has become a de facto standard. It includes 10 diagram types that are summarized in Chapter 8, A Tester's Guide to the UML.

How can UML diagrams be used for testing?

The responsibilities and architecture of the system under test can be represented in UML models. If the models are complete, consistent, and correct, they provide a rich source of test design information. Testers can develop their own models using the UML. Chapter 8 summarizes testing strategies for each diagram and provides complete cross references of UML diagrams and test design patterns.

What are the limitations of UML models for testing?

Many elements of the UML are indifferent to testability. These problems are identified in the Testability Extensions sections in Chapter 8. The UML does not provide explicit support for combinational logic and domain definition, which are essential for test design. As a practical matter, the models (whether using UML or not) produced for many systems need much work before test cases can be developed from them. General problems in modeling are discussed in Chapter 5, Test Models.

Can I test my UML models?

You can apply a wide range of verification and validation techniques to UML models, but testing is not one of them. You test code by executing it. You verify models by checking them (see Chapter 5). If the models are developed with a tool that makes them executable, then your model is a program written in a high-level iconic language, which you can test. Automated model checking is an advanced topic outside the scope of this book.

Can other object-oriented analysis and design (OOA/D) notations be used for test design?

Yes. The information in any representation can be used to develop a test suite. Section 8.11, Graphs, Relations, and Testing, presents a general analytical technique that can be applied to any kind of OOA/D model. Chapter 5, Test Models, explains what is required for a testable model. OOA/D methodologies are more alike than they are different. With a little reinterpretation, all of the comments about the UML will apply to any other OOA/D model. For example, the test design patterns that apply to a UML statechart also apply to an OMT dynamic model, a Fusion ObjectChart, a ROOM statechart, and so on.

Can test case inputs be automatically generated from a UML representation?

Yes, but it isn't easy. This requires that (1) no testability problems appear in the model, (2) the model resides in a CASE tool with a well-designed repository, and (3) a usable API to access the repository is available. In my experience, these conditions are satisfied only after a significant investment of time and money. The CASE tools available in 1999 are much worse than those available in 1989, so this task is an uphill battle. The application models must be complete and consistent. Additional properties must be added to basic UML representation. The testability requirements for each diagram are discussed in Chapter 8. A case study about such an environment appears in the Appendix. The Object Constraint Language (OCL) shows promise in resolving some of these problems.

Can the expected results for a test case be automatically generated from a UML representation?

In general, no. The fundamentally difficult problem of producing expected results is discussed in Chapter 18. Some research systems have been developed to explore using specifications as oracles. They require formal specifications, which could be housed as a UML extension.

How can I develop test cases from Activity Diagrams?

Chapter 8 presents a generic test strategy for Activity Diagrams. *Combinational Function Test* and *Round-trip Scenario Test* show how Activity Diagrams can be used as test models. Chapter 6 shows how an Activity Diagram can represent a decision table.

How can I develop test cases from Class (Static Structure) Diagrams?

Chapter 8 presents a generic test strategy for Class Diagrams. *Class Association Test* shows how to use class diagram associations to develop a test suite that will find association implementation bugs. *Abstract Class Test* and *Generic Class Test* show how to test specific kinds of classes.

How can I develop test cases from Component Diagrams?

Chapter 8 presents a generic test strategy for Component Diagrams. These models may be useful for dependency analysis to plan integration testing. They can support any of the regression testing patterns discussed in Chapter 13.

How can I develop test cases from Deployment Diagrams?

Chapter 8 presents a generic test strategy for Deployment Diagrams. These models may be useful for dependency analysis to plan integration testing. They can support any of the regression testing patterns discussed in Chapter 13.

How can I develop test cases from Collaboration Diagrams?

Chapter 8 presents a generic test strategy for Collaboration Diagrams. *Topdown Integration, Collaboration Integration,* and *Controlled Exceptions* show how to develop a test suite from a Collaboration Diagram.

How can I develop test cases from Package Diagrams?

Package Diagrams do not represent testable responsibilities. No test design is applicable.

How can I develop test cases from Sequence Diagrams?

Chapter 8 presents a generic test strategy for Sequence Diagrams. ***Round-trip Scenario Test*** shows how to develop a test suite from a Sequence Diagram.

How can I develop test cases from statecharts?

Chapter 7, State Machines, has an extensive discussion of statecharts, including detailed checklists for developing testable UML statecharts. These modeling guidelines are incorporated in the FREE model, also presented in Chapter 7. ***Modal Class Test*** and ***Quasi-modal Class Test*** show how to develop a test suite from a class scope statechart. ***Modal Hierarchy Test*** shows how to develop a test suite for a hierarchy of class statecharts. ***Mode Machine Test*** shows how to synthesize a system scope statechart from component statecharts. A system scope, state-based test suite can be produced from this model.

How can I develop test cases from use cases and Use Case Diagrams?

Use Case Diagrams have little use for test design. Chapter 8 presents a generic test strategy for these diagrams. UML use cases are not testable per se. Chapter 8 presents extended use cases, which are testable. The ***Extended Use Case Test*** pattern explains how to develop a comprehensive test suite for an extended use case. ***Round-trip Scenario Test*** is related, as a use case typically involves several scenarios. Extended use cases fit in well with software reliability engineering test strategies. ***Allocate Tests by Profile*** shows how quantitative analysis of use case frequency can boost test efficiency.

2.3.9　Test Automation

A test automation system can be just as complex and even larger than the system under test. Part IV deals with the design of test automation.

What roles can built-in test play?

Chapter 17, Assertions, explains how assertions can be designed and implemented. ***Percolation*** shows how to use assertions for automatic retesting as a polymorphic server hierarchy is extended and used. ***Built-in Self-test*** shows how a test driver can be packaged with a class.

How can design-by-contract and the Liskov substitution principle be used to design and implement test cases?

Chapter 17 explains how to design assertions that implement invariants, preconditions, and postconditions that conform to these design goals. *Percolation* can be used to automate this checking throughout a class hierarchy.

Should the tested implementation be identical to the released implementation?

This equivalence is generally preferable, but sometimes it may be easier to test by accepting some minor differences. The pros and cons of shipping built-in test code are discussed in Section 17.5, Deployment. A *Drone* driver tests a class composed from the class under test, but includes removable test code.

How can expected test results be generated and evaluated?

Chapter 18 explains four types of oracles and discusses the design considerations for comparators, which evaluate test results. Generation of expected results is hard. This chapter catalogs the best available solutions, but no "royal road" to expected results exists.

Do any special considerations apply in evaluating objects after a test run?

Yes. Because objects are complex, composite data structures, the reliable comparison of objects must deal with the complexities and nuances of object structure and semantics. These problems are discussed in Section 18.3, Comparators.

How can inheritance and objectification be used to improve test case and test driver reusability?

Chapter 19 shows how this goal can be accomplished by using *Percolate the Object Under Test, Test Case/Test Suite Method*, and any of the test driver patterns.

How can I set the pretest state of the implementation under test, its inputs, and its servers? How can I then gain access to its resultant state, test outputs, and its servers for test evaluation?

The stub and driver patterns in Chapter 19 provide several solutions to this problem. The simplest involves the use of a *Private Access Driver*. The most complex relies on the *Fresh Objects* framework.

How can I make tests easy to rerun and reuse?

Reusability of superclass test suites is improved with *Percolate the Object Under Test.* The *Incremental Testing Framework* provides a simple and effective framework to develop and run a large test suite of test objects, all of which share the same interface.

How can test drivers test an object of any class in a hierarchy?

Percolate the Object Under Test shows how to define the object under test and the driver interfaces so that the object can be passed from one driver to another.

How can I make it easy to rerun superclass tests on a subclass?

Reusability of superclass test suites is improved with *Percolate the Object Under Test*.

When should test cases (test suites) be implemented as a method?

Grouping test cases and test suites into methods is procedural abstraction. As most test suites are highly procedural, this is often a good approach. *Test Case/Test Suite Method* discusses it.

How can a test driver be used to test exceptions?

Catch All Exceptions shows how a test driver can be developed to cause and catch all exceptions. This approach can be combined with *Controlled Exception Test* when the exceptions are difficult to control.

When should test cases (test suites) be implemented as objects?

Grouping test cases and test suites into objects uses whole-part abstraction. Test suites are often a functional hierarchy, so this can be a good approach. *Test Case/Test Suite Class* discusses it.

How can a stub implementation of a server object be used to ease testing?

Server Stub shows how a stub can provide necessary control over server objects of the class under test.

How can a proxy implementation of a server object facilitate testing?

Server Proxy shows how a proxy stub can provide necessary control over server objects of the class under test.

How can I develop a common interface for all test drivers?

Test Driver Superclass presents a common interface and responsibilities for all test drivers. This abstract class can be implemented by any test driver class.

When should a test driver hierarchy be symmetric to the hierarchy of classes under test?

Symmetric Driver is the simplest driver hierarchy. It can be used for many kinds of testing, but is limited to using the public class interface.

When should test drivers be implemented as a subclass of the class under test?

Subclass Driver solves some problems of controllability and observability, but is effective in only a few situations.

How can a test driver defeat encapsulation to gain controllability and observability?

Private Access Driver solves all problems of controllability and observability, but depends on language-specific mechanisms that increase coupling between the driver and the class under test.

How can interface extension features (for example, Java interfaces) be used for testing?

Test Control Interface shows how language-specific mechanisms can improve controllability and observability with minimal coupling between the driver and the class under test.

When should I use mixin inheritance to implement a test driver?

Drone shows how to use multiple inheritance to produce a testable mixin class. This approach solves most problems of controllability and observability, and it results in minimal coupling between the driver and the class under test.

Can a driver be implemented as part of an application class?

Built-in Self-test locates the driver within an application class. This approach eliminates all problems of controllability and observability within the scope of the class, but it results in maximal coupling of the driver and the class under test.

How can I build a test executable to be run from a command line or console?

Command Line Test Bundle explains how to generate an executable test bundle that includes the test driver, the implementation under test, and other test components.

Is there a simple test driver framework that supports rapid iterative incremental development?

Incremental Testing Framework uses a whole-part model to organize and run test objects. Implementing test cases is straightforward.

How can a driver gain a high degree of control over an entire system of objects whose structure changes as the application executes?

Fresh Objects uses registration and a common built-in test interface. All test-controllable objects must respond to the test interface, and registration is implemented with a master test control object. This approach provides the highest degree of test control.

2.4 Test Process

Object-oriented development tends toward shorter incremental cycles. With testing added, object-oriented development can be characterized as "design a little, code a little, test a little." Process issues include the decision regarding when to do test case design, the integration strategy, and the extent of retesting for inherited features.

- When should testing begin?
- Who should perform testing?
- How can testing techniques help to prevent errors?
- How are testing activities integrated into the software process model?
- How can testing facilitate reuse?
- To what extent should reusable test suites be considered a necessary part of a reusable component library?
- What is an effective test and integration strategy given the iterative approach preferred for object-oriented development?
- How much effort should be used to test?

None of these issues is considered in this book. Instead, they (and many more) are discussed in the companion volume, *Managing the Testing Process for Object-Oriented Systems* (Binder 2000).

Chapter 3   Testing: A Brief Introduction

> How strange it is to say that testing a program and never
> having it result in a failure is a problem, but indeed that is
> exactly what we are saying.
>
> *Friedman and Voas*

Overview

The chapter presents a point of view on software testing. Basic terms
are defined and linked to chapters and sections where they are discussed. The general limits and uses of testing are discussed.

3.1   What Is Software Testing?

I view software testing as a problem in systems engineering. It is the design and
implementation of a special kind of software system: one that exercises another
software system with the intent of finding bugs. Tests are designed by analyzing the system under test and deciding how it is likely to be buggy. In turn, test
design provides the requirements for the test automation system. This system
automatically applies and evaluates the tests. It must be designed to work with
the physical interfaces, structure, and the runtime environment of the system
under test. Manual testing, of course, still plays a role. But testing is mainly
about the development of an automated system to implement an application-
specific test design.

Effective testing cannot be achieved without using abstraction to conquer
the astronomical complexity of typical software systems. Test design must be

based on both general and specific models. General models offer a systematic and repeatable means to generate test suites. Combinational logic (Chapter 6) and state machines (Chapter 7) provide the general models used in this book. You can view these models as reusable functions, to which application-specific relationships are input. In addition, application-specific test models must be developed to represent the required behavior of the system under test. A testable OOA/D model of the application can be used, if one is available. If not, application-specific test models must be developed. Chapter 8 discusses application-specific modeling. The test generation algorithm of the general model produces the application test suite as an output. This output serves as the input to the test automation system, which in turn evaluates a test run as pass or no pass. The design of test automation presents its own challenges, which are sometimes exotic. Figure 3.1 shows these relationships.

Test design requires solving problems similar to those encountered in the analysis, design, and programming of an application system. Test models are developed to represent responsibilities. Because tests must be executable, however, the equivocal abstraction that greases the wheels of analysis and design is not acceptable.

Test design involves several steps:

1. Identify, model, and analyze the responsibilities of the system under test.
2. Design test cases based on this external perspective.
3. Add test cases based on code analysis, suspicions, and heuristics.
4. Develop expected results for each test case or choose an approach to evaluate the pass/no pass status of each test case.

General solutions to recurring test design problems are presented as test design patterns in this book.

After design is complete, the tests are applied to the system under test. Unless manual testing is indicated, a test automation system must be developed to run the tests. This system may be either simple or complex. It may be implemented with general-purpose test tools (scripting, coverage analyzers, and so on), by coding application-specific test drivers and stubs, and by adding test code to the application. A test automation system typically will start the implementation under test, set up its environment, bring it to the required pretest state, apply the test inputs, and evaluate the resulting output and state.

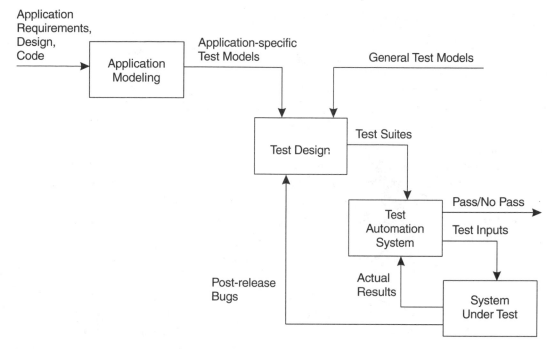

FIGURE 3.1   A systems engineering view of testing.

Test execution typically follows several steps:

1. Establish that the implementation under test is minimally operational by exercising the interfaces between its parts.

2. Execute the test suite; the result of each test is evaluated as pass or no pass.

3. Use a coverage tool to instrument the implementation under test. Rerun the test suite and evaluate the reported coverage.

4. If necessary, develop additional tests to exercise uncovered code.

5. Stop testing when the coverage goal is met and all tests pass.

Some of these steps are not always necessary or feasible, but we must nevertheless be able to run a test suite and evaluate results. Part IV provides 17 design patterns for test automation. Test design and execution are best carried out in parallel with application analysis, design, and coding. This can also follow coding, although this sequence is problematic for many reasons.

There are some things that testing is not:

- Testing is not cut-and-fit improvement of a user interface or requirements elicitation by prototyping.
- Testing is not the verification of an analysis or design model by syntax checkers or simulation.
- Testing is not the scrutiny of documentation or code by humans in inspections, reviews, or walkthroughs.
- Testing is not static analysis of code using a language translator or code checker (e.g., `lint`). Specifically, getting a clean compile is not in any sense passing a test.
- Testing is not the use of dynamic analyzers to identify memory leaks or similar problems.
- Testing is not debugging, although successful testing should lead to debugging.

All the preceding activities are important in preventing and removing software bugs. But they are not testing. At least one element of testing is missing: design, execution, or evaluation. Some writers have characterized testing as including all these and more. I reject this view. As a result, this book does not discuss other important software engineering approaches necessary to achieve high quality.

3.2 Definitions

The definitions in this section establish basic ideas needed to discuss testing. Many more definitions appear in subsequent chapters, and all definitions from the book are collected in the Glossary.

Software testing is the execution of code using combinations of input and state selected to reveal bugs.[1] Some definitions of testing include other verification and validation activities, but here testing is limited to running an implementation with input selected by test design and evaluating the response. A **component** refers to any software aggregate that has visibility in a development environment—for example, a method, a class, an object, a function, a module, an executable, a task, a utility subsystem, an application subsystem. Compo-

---

1. Several comprehensive introductions to software testing are available (see the Bibliographic Notes section). This section is limited to definitions that make the usage clear and support the subsequent chapters. Terms follow applicable IEEE/ANSI standards: IEEE 610.12, IEEE 829, and IEEE 982.1, unless otherwise stated.

nents include executable software entities supplied with an application programmer interface. See Section 12.1.1, What Is a Subsystem?

The **scope** of a test is the collection of software components to be verified. Since tests must be run on an executable software entity, scope is typically defined to correspond to some executable component or system of components. The code being tested is called the **implementation under test (IUT)**, **method under test (MUT)**, **object under test (OUT)**, **class under test (CUT)**, **component under test (CUT)**, **system under test (SUT)**, and so on. Software testing is typically categorized by the scope of the IUT and test design approach. Scope is traditionally designated as unit, integration, or system (see Figure 3.2).

The scope of a **unit test** typically comprises a relatively small executable. In object-oriented programming, an object of a class is the smallest executable unit, but test messages must be sent to a method, so we can speak of method scope testing. A test unit may consist of a class, several related classes (a cluster), or an executable binary file. Typically, it is a cluster of interdependent classes. Test design at class, cluster, and component scope is discussed in Chapters 10, 11, and 12, respectively.

The scope of an **integration test** is a complete system or subsystem of software and hardware units. The units included are physically dependent or must cooperate to meet some requirement. Integration testing exercises interfaces among units within the specified scope to demonstrate that the units are collectively operable. For example, testing the use cases implemented by a subsystem cannot begin until interprocess communication among executable processes (each composed of many objects) works well enough to run tests based on these use cases. Integration testing begins early in the programming of object-oriented software because a single class is typically composed of objects of other classes and inherits features from superclasses. Integration testing is discussed in Chapter 13.

The scope of a **system test** is a complete integrated application. Tests focus on capabilities and characteristics that are present only with the entire system. The boundary of the system under test typically excludes the virtual machine that supports it and other application systems to which it has direct or indirect interfaces. System scope tests may be categorized by the kind of conformance they seek to establish: functional (input/output), performance (response time and resource utilization), stress or load (response under maximum or overload). System testing is discussed in Chapter 14.

Testing is **fault-directed** when the intent is to reveal faults through failures; it is **conformance-directed** when the intent is to demonstrate conformance to required capabilities. These goals are not mutually exclusive. Many test design

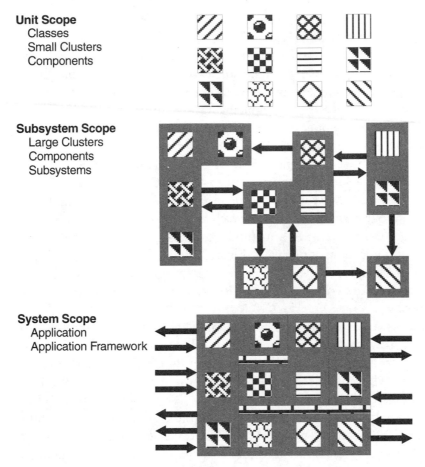

Unit Scope
  Classes
  Small Clusters
  Components

Subsystem Scope
  Large Clusters
  Components
  Subsystems

System Scope
  Application
  Application Framework

FIGURE 3.2   Relationship of unit, integration, and system tests.

techniques achieve both. Unit and integration testing are typically more fault-directed. System testing is typically more conformance-directed.

Confidence is the subjective assessment of the likelihood of unrevealed bugs in an implementation. Here, "confidence" is used in the everyday sense of a qualitative judgment based on available information. Testing provides information that can increase or decrease our confidence. When a responsibility test suite passes and achieves appropriate coverage, we may have increased confidence that the IUT will perform without failure. Confidence can be quantified when testing is conducted under certain controlled conditions [Hamlet+90]. An estimated **failure rate** is the probability that failure will occur after a certain period of usage [Friedman+95, Lyu+96, Musa 98]. Quantitative techniques for establishing statistical confidence have been developed that are applicable to object-oriented systems; these techniques are not discussed here. This book uses the qualitative sense of confidence, unless noted otherwise.

A **test case** specifies the pretest state of the IUT and its environment, the test inputs or conditions, and the expected result. The **expected result** specifies what the IUT should produce from the test inputs. This specification includes messages generated by the IUT, exceptions, returned values, and resultant state of the IUT and its environment. Test cases may also specify initial and resulting conditions for other objects that constitute the IUT and its environment. An **oracle** is a means to produce expected results. Some automated oracles can also make a pass/no pass evaluation. Oracles are the subject of Chapter 18.

A **test point** is a specific value for test case input and state variables. A test point, which may be used in many test cases, is selected from a domain. A **domain** is a set of values that input or state variables of the IUT may take.[2] **Domain analysis** places constraints on input, state, and output values to select test values. A **subdomain** is a subset of a domain.

Some well-known heuristics for test point selection include equivalence classes, boundary value analysis, and special values testing [Myers 79]. An **equivalence class** is a set of input values such that if any value is processed correctly (incorrectly), then it is assumed that all other values will be processed correctly (incorrectly). An equivalence class does not refer to "class" as a programming language construct from which we may instantiate objects. Tests with boundary and special values are based on the assumptions that bugs are likely when input or state values are at or very near to a minimum or maximum. These techniques are examples of a general strategy called **partition testing**. A **partition** divides the input space into groups, which are hoped to have the property that any member of the group will cause a failure, if a bug exists in the code related to that partition. Although partition testing approaches have some practical advantages, the selection of partitions has no necessary relationship to the conditions necessary to reach a bug—in essence, they are guesses [Hamlet+90]. Section 10.2.4, Domain Testing Models, explains the improvements that domain analysis makes on heuristic input selection.

---

2. The testing usage of *domain* derives from the mathematical definition of domain: the set of inputs accepted by a function. It is not to be confused with: (1) an "application domain," which refers to a general class of user problems (e.g., international banking, avionics, word processing, and so on) [Kean 97], (2) a "problem domain," which is any collection of ideas related by some human purpose, (3) the domain component of an IP address, or (4) the value set of an attribute in database theory [Date 82]. The use of "domain" in the testing sense predates these definitions [Howden 76]. The UML definition of domain includes both definitions (1) and (2).

A **test suite** is a collection of test cases, typically related by a testing goal or implementation dependency. A **test run** is the execution (with results) of a test suite(s). A **test plan** is a document prepared for human use that explains a testing approach: the work plan, general procedures, explanation of the test design, and so on. See Section 9.4, Documenting Test Cases, Suites, and Plans.

The IUT produces **actual results** when a test case is applied to it. These results include messages generated by the IUT, exceptions, returned values, and the resultant state of the IUT and its environment. A test whose actual results are the same as the expected results is said to **pass**; otherwise, it is a **no pass**. A no pass test reveals a bug and is therefore a successful test, even though the actual results are typically an application failure.

A **test driver** is a class or utility program that applies test cases to an IUT. A **stub** is a partial, temporary implementation of a component. It may serve as a placeholder for an incomplete component or implement testing support code. A **test message** is the code in a test driver that is sent to a method of the object under test. Two or more test messages that follow one another make up a **test sequence**. A **test script** is a program written in a procedural script language (usually interpreted) that executes a test suite(s). A **test harness** is a system of test drivers and other tools to support test execution. Chapter 19 discusses stubs, test cases, and test drivers.

A **failure** is the manifested inability of a system or component to perform a required function within specified limits. It is evidenced by incorrect output, abnormal termination, or unmet time and space constraints. A software **fault** is missing or incorrect code. When the executable code (translated from faulty statements) is executed, it may result in a failure. An **error** is a human action that produces a software fault. Errors, faults, and failures do not occur in one-to-one relation. That is, many different failures can result from a single fault, and the same failure can be caused by different faults. Similarly, a single error may lead to many faults. These categories are generally useful, but somewhat ambiguous. Readers interested in greater precision may find the orthogonal defect classification model useful [Chillarege 96].

An **abend** is an abrupt termination of a program and is synonymous with "task abort," "application crash," or "system crash."[3] An abend often produces a memory dump—for example, the "blue screen of death" generated by Microsoft operating systems.

---

3. *Abend* is IBM jargon for abnormal end. It is pronounced "ab-end," to rhyme with "the end."

An **omission** is a required capability that is not present in an implementation. For purposes of testing, an omission must be defined with respect to required capabilities. Testing can reveal omitted capabilities. However, systems are often disappointing, dangerous, or deficient because important requirements have not been identified and therefore cannot be implemented. Omitted requirements are a serious problem, but not one that testing should address. Discovering omitted requirements during testing is possible, but only if a tester is lucky enough to notice that something is odd or absent. Better ways exist to prevent omitted requirements [Gause+89, Thayer+90, Leveson 95].

A **surprise** is code that does not support a required capability. Surprises may be either benign or malignant. Figure 3.3 shows how the relationship between requirements and the implementation relate to faults, omissions, and surprises. Object-oriented applications often contain many surprises. Large-grained reusable components, for example, may implement capabilities that are irrelevant for a specific application, but that cannot be removed. This irrelevant code becomes a surprise in the reusing application. If the unused reused code can be safely deactivated or avoided, this inclusion is usually not a problem. As systems evolve, however, surprises can become bugs.

A **bug** is an error or a fault. The first recorded usage of "bug" to describe a problem in computing was made by Grace Hopper in 1945 when a moth became lodged in a computer relay, causing the program to halt [Hopper 81]. Figure 3.4 shows a photograph of this moth taped into the log book with

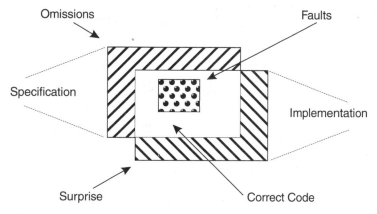

FIGURE 3.3   Faults, omissions, and surprises.

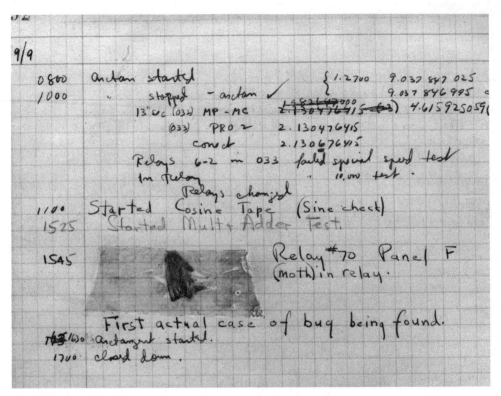

FIGURE 3.4 Hopper's bug.

Hopper's ironic note: "First actual case of bug being found." Dijkstra argues that "bug" is actually a corrupting euphemism:

> We could, for instance, begin with cleaning up our language by no longer calling a bug "a bug" but by calling it an error. It is much more honest because it squarely puts the blame where it belongs, viz., with the programmer who made the error. The animistic metaphor of the bug that maliciously sneaked in while the programmer was not looking is intellectually dishonest as it is a disguise that the error is the programmer's own creation. The nice thing of this simple change of vocabulary is that it has such a profound effect. While, before, a program with only one bug used to be "almost correct," afterwards a program with an error is just "wrong" . . . [Dijkstra 89, 1403].

Similarly, others deprecate "bug" because it connotes a malevolent being like a gremlin or leprechaun, who sabotages the developer's efforts. However, "bug" is widely used. I use "bug" unless the finer distinction of error or fault is needed. I do not think this usage will lead to irresponsible software development practices among professionals. Developers who believe that bugs result from evil forces beyond their control or who rely on small shades of meaning as a fig leaf for incompetence are beyond hope anyway.

Debugging is the work required to diagnose and correct a bug. *Testing is not debugging. Debugging is not testing.* Debugging typically occurs after a failure has been observed or when a developer identifies a fault by inspection or automatic code analysis. It includes the analysis and experimentation necessary to isolate and diagnose the cause of a failure, the programming to correct the bug, and testing to verify that the change has removed the bug.[4] The observed failure may result from testing (which is desirable) or the intended use of a system (which is undesirable). In contrast, testing is the process of devising and executing a test suite that attempts to cause failures, increasing our confidence that failures are unlikely.

Because the number of possible tests is infinite for practical purposes, rational testing must be based on a **fault model**. This is an assumption about where faults are likely to be found. An **interesting test case** is one that has a good chance of revealing a fault. Fault models for object-oriented programming are discussed in Chapter 4. Each test design pattern has an explicit fault model.

A **test strategy** is an algorithm or heuristic to create test cases from a representation, an implementation, or a test model. A **test model** represents relationships among elements of a representation or implementation. It is typically based on a fault model. **Test design** produces a suite of test cases using a test strategy. Test design is concerned with three problems: identification of interesting test points, placing these test points into a test sequence, and defining the expected result for each test point in the sequence. **Test effectiveness** is the relative ability of testing strategy to find bugs. **Test efficiency** is the relative cost of finding a bug.

Strategies for test design are responsibility-based, implementation-based, hybrid, or fault-based. **Responsibility-based test design** uses specified or expected responsibilities of a unit, subsystem, or system to design tests. The notion of responsibility is discussed in Chapter 9. For example, a test case for the trigonometric function $\tan(x)$ could be prepared from its mathematical definition, whatever the algorithm design or implementation language. It

---

4. Considerations for object-oriented debugging are developed in [Purchase+91]. Smalltalk-specific techniques are presented in [Rochat+93, Hinke+93], and C++ techniques in [Thielen 92, Davis 94, Spuler 94, Ball 95]. A survey of debugging research for procedural code appears in [Agrawal+89]. A general debugging strategy for IBM mainframe code can be found in [Binder 85].

is synonymous with "specification-oriented," "behavioral," "functional," or "black box" test design.

Behavioral testing is the generally preferred term for testing that is not based on implementation-specific information [Beizer 95]. In the context of object-oriented software, however, *behavior* usually refers to a sequence of responses that an object may produce or, more generally, to its "dynamic model." Black box testing usually means that an external view of the IUT is analyzed to develop tests, but it can also describe tests derived from analysis of implementation interfaces or imputed class functionality. To avoid confusion and to make the basis for testing clear, I characterize testing as responsibility-based or implementation-based.

Implementation-based test design relies on source code analysis to develop test cases. It is synonymous with "structural," "glass box," "clear box," or "white box" test design. The term "white box testing" was probably chosen to suggest the opposite of black box testing. As a white box is just as visually opaque as a black box, clear box or glass box is occasionally used as a rubric for implementation-based testing.

An approach is said to be **formal** if its fault-revealing capability has been established by mathematical analysis or **heuristic** if it relies on expert judgment or experience to select test cases. **Hybrid test design** blends responsibility-based and implementation-based test design and is sometimes called gray box testing. **Fault-based testing** purposely introduces faults into code (mutation) to see if these faults are revealed by a test suite [Morel+92, Friedman+95]. Although not widely used, this approach has been studied in detail. This book does not present any application of fault-based testing. General test design strategies are the subject of Part II, Models. Scope and structure specific test design is the subject of Part III, Patterns.

An **exhaustive test suite** requires that every possible value and sequence of inputs be applied in every possible state of the system under test, thereby exercising every possible execution path. This approach results in an astronomical number of test cases, even with trivial programs. Exhaustive testing is a practical impossibility. Software testing is therefore necessarily concerned with small subsets of the exhaustive test suite.

The completeness of a test suite with respect to a particular test case design method is measured by coverage. **Coverage** is the percentage of elements required by a test strategy that have been exercised by a given test suite. Many coverage models have been proposed and studied [Ntafos 88, Beizer 90, Kaner +92, Roper 94, Zhu+97]. For example, **statement coverage** is the percentage of all source code statements executed at least once by a test suite. The coding constructs that make up statements differ for the various programming languages. In C++, Java, and Objective-C, an expression terminated by a semicolon is a statement. A predicate statement results in a conditional transfer of control (if-then, loop control, case, and so on). A **branch** is one of several statements that can immediately follow a predicate statement. **Branch coverage** requires that every branch be exercised at least once. When the term "coverage" is used without quantification, 100 percent is usually understood; for example, "This test suite achieves branch coverage for member function *x*" means that 100 percent branch coverage has been achieved. Coverage of object-oriented code is discussed in Section 10.2.2, Implementation-based Test Models.

3.3   The Limits of Testing

We know from experience that any nontrivial software system will have bugs. We cannot know, in advance, exactly what combination of execution sequence, state, and input will cause a failure (excluding mutation, sabotage, and any other willfully incorrect coding). Clearly, passing a single test is not enough to show the absence of bugs. Output may depend on an internal state and typically only a small part of the code in an implementation is used for any given input. So, just because f(x) returns a correct result when x = 123, we cannot assume that it does so for all values of x or even for the *same* value of x when run in different circumstances (this consideration is the nub of the infamous Y2K problem). Even passing many tests for many different values of x does not *necessarily* mean that f(x) will perform correctly for the values that we do not test.

3.3.1   The Input/State Space

The number of input and output combinations for trivial programs is surprisingly large. It is astronomical for typical programs and beyond comprehension for typical systems. Consider the class Triangle described in Chapter 1. If we limit points to integers between 1 and 10, there are 10^4 possible ways to draw a line. Considering three lines at a time, we have $10^4 \times 10^4 \times 10^4 = 10^{12}$ possible inputs of three lines, including all invalid combinations.[5] Suppose you

---

5. A line rendering is defined by two end points, each consisting of an *x* and *y* coordinate. If we limit the *x* and *y* axis to values from 1 to 10, we get $10 \times 10 = 100 = 10^2$ possible *x*, *y* coordinates at each end. Including lines of no length (both end points are the same), we have $10^2 \times 10^2 = 10^4$ possible ways to draw a line.

are a *very* fast and tireless tester: you can run and check 1000 line tests per second, 24 hours per day, 365 days per year. You could test every possible input in $10^{12}/10^3 = 10^9$ seconds. At 3.154×10^7 seconds per year, this effort would take $10^9/3.154 \times 10^7 = 3.171 \times 10^2$, or a little more than 317 years. Thus if you had started testing around 1683 and assuming no system crashes and debugging, you'd be nearly finished now.

This case is actually a gross oversimplification. Assuming a typical raster display of 786,432 pixels (1024 × 768), a line can be drawn in $786,432^2$ ways (all possible pixel pairs). With three lines, $786,432^6$ possible test cases exist, (roughly 2.36574×10^{35}). If you ran tests nonstop, 24 hours per day, you'd need roughly the estimated age of the universe to test every possible three-line combination. Clearly, we can never test all inputs, states, or outputs.

3.3.2 Execution Sequences

Branching and dynamic binding result in a very large number of unique execution sequences for any given program. Simple iteration increases the number of possible sequences to astronomical proportions. Consider the following code fragment:

```
for ( int i = 0; i < n; ++i) {
    if ( a.get(i) == b.get(i) )
          x [ i ] = x [ i ] + 100;
    else
          x [ i ] = x [ i ] / 2;
}
```

Figure 3.5 models statement execution sequences of this loop as a flow graph (the details of flow graphs and path modeling are discussed in Section 10.2.2). If we count entry–exit paths without regarding iteration, there are only three: (1) the loop is skipped, (2) the loop is entered and the first branch is taken, and (3) the loop is entered and the second branch is taken. In terms of the nodes in the flow graph:

1. Loop Header, exit

2. Loop Header, Conditional, +100

3. Loop Header, Conditional, /2

Each possible iteration of the loop, however, doubles the number of possible paths. For example, with two iterations, there are the following five paths:

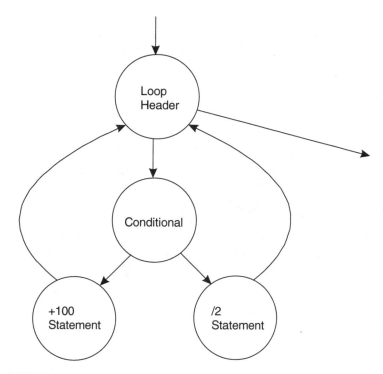

FIGURE 3.5 Flow graph for a simple loop.

1. Loop Header, exit
2. Loop Header, Conditional, +100, Conditional, +100
3. Loop Header, Conditional, +100, Conditional, /2
4. Loop Header, Conditional, /2, Conditional, +100
5. Loop Header, Conditional, /2, Conditional, /2

That is, the number of possible paths is $2^n + 1$ (for $n > 0$). If you had started testing just after the Big Bang (about 18 billion years ago) and all went well, you'd be working on $n = 36$ today.[6] Table 3.1 shows some of the arithmetic. Any day now . . .

---

6. The Big Bang is estimated to have occurred between 12 and 18 billion years ago. Assuming the largest value, 1.8×10^9 years, and testing at 1×10^3 paths/second, 3.154×10^7 seconds per year, we have 1.8×10^9 years $\times 3.154 \times 10^7 = 5.6772 \times 10^{16}$ seconds since the Big Bang. If testing started just after the Big Bang and ran at 10^3 paths per second, we could exercise $5.6772 \times 10^{16} \times 10^3$ paths, or 5.6772×10^{19} paths. At what loop value, n, would we run out of time? Solving for n, $2^n = 5.6772 \times 10^{19}$. Reducing gives $\log(2^n) = \log(5.6772 \times 10^{19})$. Then $n \log(2) = 19 \log(5.6772) = n\, 0.30103 = 19 \times 0.754134$. So $n = 3.321928 \times 19 \times 0.754134 = 35.89559$.

TABLE 3.1 Paths Due to Iteration

Number of Iterations	Number of Paths
1	3
2	5
3	9
10	1025
20	1,048,577
60	1,152,921,504,606,847,200

3.3.3 Fault Sensitivity and Coincidental Correctness

The ability of code to hide faults from a test suite is called its **fault sensitivity** [Friedman 95]. From a testing perspective, the best kind of bug is one that causes a failure every time it executes. If all bugs were so cooperative, we could guarantee bug-free code by designing a test suite that executed every line of code at least once. As we will see in Chapter 10, developing a test suite that will exercise each line of code at least once is relatively easy. Unfortunately, most bugs will not cooperate: they hide (no failure is produced) even when buggy code executes.

Coincidental correctness obtains when buggy code can produce correct results for some inputs. Suppose x + x is incorrectly coded instead of x * x. When x is 2 in a test suite, this code hides the bug: it produces a correct result from buggy code. Although only a little more testing is required to reveal this bug, simple errors can result in very pernicious fault hiding. Consider the following code fragment (adapted from Friedman 95, 34):

```
int scale(int j) {
    j = j - 1;      // should be j = j + 1
    j = j/30000;
    return j;
}
```

Out of 65,536 possible values for j, only six will produce an incorrect result: −30001, −30000, −1, 0, 29999, and 30000. We could do near-exhaustive testing of this code, covering 99.9908 percent of all input values, and still not reveal the bug.

The effects of inheritance and polymorphism provide many opportunities for coincidental correctness. Consider the following Java fragment:

```
public class Account extends Object {
   protected Date lastTxDate, today;
   // . . .
   int quartersSinceLastTx( ) {
           return (90 / daysSinceLastTx( ));
   }

   int daysSinceLastTx( ){
           return (today.day() - lastTxDay.txDate + 1);

           // Correct - today's transactions return 1 day elapsed
   }
}
public class TimeDepositAccount extends Account{
   // . . .
   int daysSinceLastTx( )  {
           return (today.day( ) - lastTxDay.txDate);

           // Incorrect - today's transactions return 0 days
elapsed
   }
```

This code is correct for an Account object and can be coincidentally correct for a TimeDepositAccount object. No faults would be revealed when methods quartersSinceLastTx( ) and daysSinceLastTx( ) are tested on an Account object, even when we include a test case where the last transaction has occurred on the current day. When the last transaction occurs on the current day, however, a TimeDepositAccount object will fail with divide by zero exception, but an Account object will not. Bugs of this kind are more likely with deeper and wider class hierarchies. Furthermore, because quartersSinceLastTx is inherited with no change, we might be tempted to skip retesting it when we develop the subclass.

Much of the test design presented in this book is motivated by the wide span of implicit dependencies in object-oriented programming languages. The test design strategies in Part III provide techniques to exercise a class systematically and shine a light into the deep crevasse of coincidental correctness resulting from polymorphism and inheritance.

3.3.4 Absolute Limitations

The kinds of bugs that testing can reveal are limited by some fundamental properties of software systems:

- In advocating proof of correctness, Dijkstra observed that "Program testing can be used to show the presence of defects, but never their absence!" [Dahl+72]. Proof of correctness is equivalent to exhaustive testing. A proof shows by analysis whether a program must produce correct results for all possible inputs. Exhaustive testing of a correct program will produce a pass on every input. As the preceding examples illustrate, however, exhaustive testing is usually impossible.[7] Because an exhaustive test cannot always be achieved, testing cannot always prove correctness (although it may be able to sometimes).

- Automating certain aspects of test design is provably impossible. No system can be completely self-descriptive, so situations arise where the system cannot produce an answer about itself.[8] While this limitation has no significance for practical test design, it may be a consideration for advanced test automation. The case for this conclusion has been well made elsewhere [Manna+78] and cannot be easily summarized, so it will not be discussed here.

- Testing must use requirements (that is, some model of required capabilities) as a point of reference. It cannot directly verify requirements. Spurious tests may be produced if requirements are incorrect or incomplete.

- Implementation-based testing cannot reveal omissions as missing code cannot be tested.

- We can never be sure that a testing system is correct. That is, bugs in test design, an oracle, or test drivers can produce spurious test results [Manna+78].

- Devising an oracle is difficult and sometimes impossible [Weyuker 82]. Without trusted expected results to compare with actual results, pass/no pass evaluation is dubious. This problem and some solutions are discussed in Chapter 18.

3.4 What Can Testing Accomplish?

Testing is complex, critical, and challenging. No "right way" exists that works every time and no "silver bullet" can solve every test design or quality problem.

---

7. Computer scientists would say exhaustive testing is **intractable**: while it may be possible in trivial cases, even moderately complex programs require prohibitively large quantities of storage or computation.

8. Computer scientists call such problems **undecidable**: it can be shown that no algorithm exists that can perform the required computation in every possible case.

The primary role of software testing is to reveal bugs that would be too costly or impossible to find with other verification and validation techniques. A secondary purpose is to show that the system under test complies with its stated requirements for a given test suite.

Testing is not a substitute for preventing faults by good software engineering. Instead, it should focus on areas where it is most effective and be complemented with other known-good software engineering practices. It is not the technique of choice for preventing or identifying all kinds of bugs. For example, testing rarely identifies missing requirements, but it can reveal interactions and special cases that might cause a system to crash. It does not make sense to try to "test quality into a system." Testing should not be the first step in bug prevention, nor should it be used as a final toxic waste filter. Figure 3.6 lists bug categories for which testing is the best technique.

How well or poorly testing activities are harmonized with a software process significantly affects testing effectiveness. Testing is most effective when test development begins at the outset of a project. Early consideration of testability, early test design, and implementation of tests as soon as possible provide a powerful bug prevention approach. This effect can improve application design by forcing closer consideration of the implications of requirements and specifications. Early decisions (or their absence) about architecture, detail design, and coding practices can make testing easier and cheaper, or harder and dearer.

Finally, from a software product perspective, effective testing is necessary to produce reliable, safe, and successful systems. Although quantitative data on testing and object-oriented systems are sparse, several reports show that testing can lead to very high quality. After systematic testing at class and cluster scope was adopted, system test defects in an Eiffel and C++ telecommunication application were reduced by a factor of 70. The total development effort was cut by half [Murphy+94]. Other reports indicate that effective testing in object-oriented development can contribute to very low defect rates. Their results can be compared by using function points to normalize system size.[9]

- The test process used to develop the ICpack 201 library (50 classes and 1200 Objective-C methods) was a significant factor in achieving 0.0121

---

9. The number of major post-release bugs and size of the system in lines of code are given in each report. The system size in function points was estimated by using the language to function point conversion factor given in [Jones 97b]. Table 3.2 shows the reported values, factors, and normalized bug rates. Details of function point models for object-oriented systems are developed in [Caldiera+98].

Type of Bug	General Cause	Applicable Validation and Verification		
		Early Validation	Static Verification	Testing
Lacks usability	Poor user interface design	✓		
Missing capability	Elicitation error	✓		
	Specification omission		✓	✓
Incorrect capability	Elicitation error	✓		✓
	Specification error	✓	✓	✓
Side effects and unanticipated, undesirable feature interaction	Elicitation error		✓	✓
	Specification error		✓	✓
	Programming error		✓	✓
	Configuration/integration error			✓
Inadequate performance, real-time deadline failure, synchronization deadlock, livelock, and so on	Elicitation error	✓		✓
	Specification error	✓	✓	✓
	Inappropriate target		✓	✓
	Inefficient algorithm		✓	✓
	Inefficient programming		✓	✓
	Infeasible problem		✓	✓
	Programming error		✓	✓
	Configuration/integration error			✓
Incorrect output	Specification error		✓	✓
	Programming error		✓	✓
	Configuration/integration error		✓	✓
Abend	Programming error		✓	✓
	Configuration/integration error			✓

Key: ✓ = Useful, ▢ = Typically most effective

FIGURE 3.6   Bugs that testing can catch.

TABLE 3.2 Reported Postrelease Bug Rates after Testing Some OO Systems

Language	LOC	LOC/FP Factor [Jones 97b]	Estimated Function Points	Major Post-release Bugs	Bugs/FP	Source
C++	75,000	55	1364	7	0.0051	[Boisvert 97]
Objective-C	12,000	29	414	5	0.0121	[Love 92]

delivered defects per function point. Testing was the primary verification technique [Love 92].

- Systematic testing at class, cluster, and system scope of a 75 KLOC C++ cellular support application resulted in 0.0051 delivered defects per function point. No other verification techniques were used [Boisvert 97].

Even allowing a factor of 10 for the estimating error, these rates compare favorably with benchmarks for "best in class" development organizations, which Jones reports as an "average less than 0.025 user-reported defects per function point" in the first year after release [Jones 97a, 44]. Jones' rate includes all defects and presumably would be lower if only major defects were considered. These reports show that effective object-oriented testing can make a major contribution to achieving world-class quality.

3.5 Bibliographic Notes

Hundreds of books and thousands of papers have been published on testing. The principles presented in Glenford Myers' *Software Reliability* [Myers 76] and *The Art of Software Testing* [Myers 79] are more than 20 years old but continue to be applicable. Both are readable and practical guides to software testing and quality. They are relevant if you mentally substitute present-day equivalents for the occasional references to obsolete technology. In a technology that churns as much as software, such durability is rare. Chapters 1 and 2 of *Software Testing Techniques* [Beizer 90] explain the test design problem in down-to-earth terms without trivializing. The presentation of test design technique that follows is unmatched in synthesizing research and practice (through 1989) and maintaining a relentless focus on test effectiveness. Kaner et al. provide a comprehensive discussion of the practical and procedural aspects of testing desktop applications [Kaner+92]. Roper's *Software Testing* is a compact, readable survey [Roper 94]. Marick's *Craft of Software Testing* offers a meticulous, detailed test design approach of special interest to C and C++ developers [Marick 95]. Beizer's *Black Box Testing* [Beizer 95] is a focused presentation of essential implementation-independent test design strategies and covers research and practice through 1994.

Friedman and Voas's *Software Assessment* [Friedman +95] provides an insightful quantitative analysis of the problems in using testing as a means to achieve high-quality software. The *Handbook of Software Reliability Engineering* [Lyu 96] is a landmark in testing and software engineering.

Several comprehensive surveys of testing approaches have been published. An early survey of verification, validation, and testing techniques appears in [Adrion+82]. Comparative surveys of testing approaches appear in [De-Millo+87, White 87, Ntafos 88]. Morell and Deimel's SEI curriculum module on testing offers a concise and readable introduction to testing research literature. The annotated bibliography is especially useful [Morell+92]. My own survey covers object-oriented testing techniques, testing strategies for abstract data types, and approaches to automated model validation published through 1994 [Binder 96i]. The survey of testing coverage models in [Zhu+97] summarizes research reports published through 1996.

Chapter 4   With the Necessary Changes: Testing and Object-oriented Software

If there are two or more ways to do something, and one of those ways can result in a catastrophe, then someone will do it.

Edward A. Murphy, Jr.

Overview

Testing is a search for bugs, so identifying bug hazards is essential for effective testing. This chapter surveys research and experience reports about bug hazards in object-oriented programming. The idea of a fault model is presented. Several code-coverage models are reviewed and some language-specific hazards are discussed. The chapter concludes with tenets and prescriptions for effective object-oriented testing.

4.1   The Dismal Science of Software Testing

Testing is a bug hunt. To find the quarry, we must know where to look. In software, this means we must examine the ways in which good languages can go wrong. The catalog of bug hazards that follows lays a foundation for effective testing. It is not a general critique of the object-oriented programming paradigm. Just as reading a medical book on various forms of disease can be unpleasant, you may find the following discussion unpleasant. And just as reading only a book on disease would give you a warped view of health, you should not conclude that the following catalog of problems is a definitive assessment of object-oriented programming. It is not.

4.1.1   I'm Okay, You're Okay, Objects Are Okay

On a personal level, you should not conclude from reading this chapter that you have made a bad career choice or are morally depraved because you design, program, or test object-oriented code. Nor should you conclude that I view object-oriented programming as a kind of mass hysteria, its advocates as charlatans, and its practitioners as incompetent twits. Likewise, you should not conclude that I am a retro techno-crank, obsessed with trashing object-oriented programming.

A curious kind of tribalism seems to be part and parcel of the social psychology of software development. For many people, being proficient in some technical skill is not enough: one must also become a true believer, taking the view that one's technology of choice is vastly superior and that practitioners of different approaches are misguided, at best. I have seen this attitude regarding hardware, analysis and design methodologies, operating systems, programming paradigms, and, of course, programming languages. It leads some people to think that "If you ain't with us, you agin' us." I'm not against any of the languages discussed here. I am a proponent of effective testing, which means that we must consider what can go wrong. Clearly, this analysis must be based on facts, not tribalism.

It could be argued that most, if not all, of the problems described in this chapter result from developer error. That is, if a programmer fails to use a language as it was intended, then the bug hazard is the fact that human effort generates most code, one keystroke at a time.

People make mistakes in the creation of all things. But the media that we use to express thoughts and craft artifacts limit the context of the mistake. I cannot fall down the stairs in the middle of a football field. I cannot make grammatical errors in French, Russian, or Japanese when I am writing in English. I cannot apply insufficient torque to a cylinder head bolt with a hammer. I cannot incorrectly and invisibly alter the program counter to a different instruction address in most high-level programming languages. I cannot (easily) create a single module that is a rat's nest of gotos sprawling over thousands of lines of code in any object-oriented language.

However, I can easily create subclasses that are inconsistent with their superclasses, each of which will pass many possible tests. I can easily create a maze of "spaghetti inheritance" rife with lurking bugs, but which compiles and seems to work. I cannot do these things (and others described in this chapter) in procedural languages. There can be no bugs without programmers, but the kinds of bugs we can produce are directly a result of the programming language in use.

This chapter inventories reported bug hazards in object-oriented programming languages. It is an expanded and updated version of one section from my 1996 survey of object-oriented testing [Binder 96i]. The survey summarized about 150 published research and experience reports. I had no control over what the authors of these reports studied. Some subjects received much attention, others less. This unevenness necessarily resulted in lopsided representation for some subjects. Nevertheless, this information remains the best available basis for establishing fact-based fault models. Lopsidedness should not be interpreted as a critique. For example, you should not interpret the fact that several reports on Objective-C mention initialization problems as meaning that (1) only Objective-C has this bug hazard or (2) I am singling out Objective-C for criticism or ridicule.

The perfect programming language has yet to be developed, and may never be. Object-oriented languages solved problems inherent in procedural languages that led to mountains of truly ugly and buggy code. The strengths of the object-oriented paradigm have been recited elsewhere, many times. For example, the analysis given by Wilke [Wilke 92] and Meyer [Meyer 97] is cogent, comprehensive, and balanced. The absence of this recitation in this chapter does not mean that the problems discussed here negate these advantages, either in fact or in my opinion. Rather, I do not feel anything would be added by repeating them yet another time.

4.1.2 The Role of a Fault Model

Testing presents fundamental and fascinating conundrums. Given that we can never hope to exercise all possible inputs, paths, and states of a system under test, which should we try? When should we stop? If we must rely on testing to prevent certain kinds of failures, how can we design systems that are both testable and efficient? How can we craft a test suite that exercises enough message and state combinations to demonstrate failure-free operation but that remains small enough to be practical?

While we can be certain there are unknown bugs in any nontrivial software system, we never know exactly where they are (if we did, we wouldn't need to test). The number of places to look is infinite for practical purposes, so any rational testing strategy must be guided by a **fault model**. A fault model answers a simple question about a test technique: *Why* do the features called out by the technique warrant our effort? This operational definition identifies relationships and components of the system under test that are most likely to have faults. The answer to the question may be based on common sense, experience, suspicion, analysis, or experiment.

A **bug hazard** is a circumstance that increases the chance of a bug. Such hazards arise for many reasons and in many situations. For example, type coercion in C++ is a bug hazard because the actual conversion depends on complex rules and on declarations that may not be visible when working on a particular class. Once identified, a bug hazard provides the basis for a fault model.

Software testing strategies are effective to the extent that their fault model is a good predictor of faults. Two general fault models and corresponding testing strategies exist:

- *Conformance-directed testing* seeks to establish conformance to requirements or specifications. Tests are designed to be sufficiently representative of the essential features of the system under test. Conformance testing relies on a **nonspecific fault model**: any fault suffices to prevent conformance. The **sufficiency** of the testing model with respect to system requirements is crucial to establish conformance. Conformance-directed testing need not consider potential implementation faults in detail, but must establish that a test suite is sufficiently representative of the requirements for a system.

- *Fault-directed testing* seeks to reveal implementation faults. It is motivated by the observation that conformance can be demonstrated for an implementation that contains faults. Searching for faults is a practical and prudent alternative to conformance [Myers 79]. Because the combinations of input, state, output, and paths are astronomically large, efficient probing of an implementation requires a **specific fault model** to direct the search for faults.

The choice of a fault model suggests a **test strategy**. A test strategy yields a test suite when applied to a representation or implementation. Conformance-oriented techniques should be **feature sufficient**: they should, at least, exercise all specified features. Fault-oriented techniques should be **fault efficient**: they should have a high probability of revealing a fault.

A well-formed fault model should explain why relative sufficiency or efficiency obtains for its associated testing technique. Either a convincing argument or strong evidence that a particular kind of probing has a good chance of revealing a fault is needed. **Error-guessing** relies on developer knowledge and surmise to imagine how a particular implementation could go wrong [Myers 79]. **Suspicions** are common-sense inferences—for example, code written by an inexperienced programmer is more likely to be buggy [Hamlet 90]. Fault models may be extrapolated from failure analysis. For example, some studies (discussed in the next section) have shown that deep inheritance hierarchies are more likely to be buggy than shallow hierarchies. Test strategies often rely on an assumption that a particular kind of construct is more prone to error (e.g., evaluation of boundary values in decision segments). By trying all such constructs, we will therefore find all faults of this type. For example, the data flow fault model makes this kind of assumption:

> Just as one would not feel confident about the correctness of a portion of a program which has never been executed, we believe that if the result of some computation has never been used, one has no reason to believe that the correct computation has been performed [Rapps+85, 367].

A fault model may also be based on an argument (or evidence) about the kinds of errors that are likely to be made and the kind of faults they cause. For example, the functional testing fault model is based on a correlation of faults and functions:

> Studies of program faults revealed that they are often associated with embedded subfunctions, or special functional aspects of a piece of code. The studies indicated that if these subfunctions had been separately considered in the construction of test cases, then the chance of discovering faults would have risen dramatically [Howden+93, 3].

4.1.3   Fault Models for Object-oriented Programming

The object-oriented programming paradigm presents a unique blend of powerful constructs, bug hazards, and testing problems. This is an unavoidable result of the encapsulation of operations and variables into a class, the variety of ways a system of objects can be composed, and the compression of complex runtime behavior into a few simple statements. Each lower level in an inheritance hierarchy creates a new context for inherited features; correct behavior at an upper level in no way guarantees correct behavior at a lower level. Interaction between message sequence and state is often subtle and complex. For example, consider a class composed by multiple inheritance, with six superclasses in each contributing hierarchy and many polymorphic methods. At best, the developer must spend considerable effort to ensure that all superclass methods perform correctly in the subclass context and that no undesirable interactions occur among methods. Polymorphism and dynamic binding dramatically increase the number of execution paths. Static analysis of source code to identify paths (a bedrock technique of procedural testing) is of little use. Encapsulation can create obstacles that limit the visibility of the implementation state.

The issue of reusability and the proper role of testing in object-oriented development raise further questions. Components offered for reuse should be highly reliable; extensive testing is warranted when reuse is intended. Neither inheritance nor compositional reuse, however, reduces the need for retesting.

Object-oriented technology does not in any way obviate the basic motivation for software testing. In fact, it poses some new challenges. Despite its similarity to testing procedural systems, object-oriented testing has significant differences. Although the use of object-oriented programming languages may reduce some kinds of errors, they increase the chance of others. Methods often consist of just a few lines of code, so control-flow bugs are less likely. Encapsulation prevents bugs that result from global data scoping and intermodule side effects in some procedural languages. Nevertheless, no compelling reason (let alone evidence) exists to suppose that developers of object-oriented programs are any more immune to errors than are developers writing in procedural languages. Coding errors (misspelling, misnaming, wrong syntax) are probably as likely as ever. In addition, some essential features of object-oriented languages pose new fault hazards:

- Dynamic binding and complex inheritance structures create many opportunities for faults due to unanticipated bindings or misinterpretation of correct usage.
- Interface programming errors are a leading cause of faults in procedural languages. Object-oriented programs typically have many small components and therefore more interfaces. Interface errors are more likely, other things being equal.
- Objects preserve state, but state control (the acceptable sequence of events) is typically distributed over an entire program. State control errors are likely.

As testing is a search for bugs, focusing on these bug hazards is good testing strategy. This chapter surveys research and experience reports to identify the bug hazards of the object-oriented programming paradigm.

4.2 Side Effects of the Paradigm

4.2.1 What Goes Wrong?

Although many code-based metrics have been developed for object-oriented programming, not much empirical analysis has been published about the relationship between object-oriented code and bugs. A study on reuse found that newly written code was 48.8 times more likely to be buggy than code reused without any change (Table 4.1) [Basili+96a]. This rate for new code bugs is consistent with a report on development of a C++ system for a medical electronics application. "On average, a defect was uncovered for every 150 lines of code, and correspondingly, the mean defect density exceeded 5.1 per 1000 lines" [Fiedler 89].

TABLE 4.1   Average Bugs per KLOC and Reuse [Basili+96a]

Extent of Reuse	Faults per KLOC
Verbatim reused code	0.125
Code slightly modified	1.500
Code extensively modified	4.890
No reuse, newly written code	6.110

Studies have been conducted using the Metrics for Object-Oriented Software Engineering (MOOSE)[1] proposed by Chidamber and Kemerer [Chidamber+94]. Two studies found a strong correlation between bugs and certain code structures measured by these metrics [Basili+96b, Briand+98]:

- Classes that send relatively more messages to instance variable and message parameter objects are more likely to be buggy.

---

1. The MOOSE metrics are Depth of Inheritance Tree (DIT), Number of Children (NOC), Coupling Between Objects (CBO), Response For Class (RFC), Lack of Cohesion in Methods (LCOM), and Weighted Methods per Class (WMC).

- Classes with greater depth (number of superclasses) and higher specialization (number of new and overridden methods defined in a class) are more likely to be buggy.
- No significant correlation was found between classes that lack cohesion (number of pairs of methods in a class using no attribute in common) and the relative frequency of bugs.

Both studies were conducted on small C++ systems (up to 30 KLOC). The structure metrics that were good bug predictors appeared to be better bug predictors than lines of code. The later study also evaluated approximately 50 proposed variants on the original six MOOSE structure metrics and found no significant differences in predictive power [Briand+98].

In a study of a 133 KLOC (thousand lines of code) C++ telecommunications application developed using the Shlaer/Mellor OOA/D, classes that "participated in inheritance structures were three times more defect prone" than those that did not [Sheppard+97].

An earlier study of two medium-sized commercial systems written in Classic Ada (an object-oriented variant of Ada 83) found that the MOOSE metrics, taken together, were better predictors of maintenance cost (including debugging) than lines of code [Li+93]. A similar relationship is noted in [Fielder 89], although complexity and size are reported there as equally good predictors: "The number of defects found seemed to be related to the composite (total) complexity of all of the class member functions and more directly to the number of noncomment source statements (NCSS) contained in the source and include files."

Summarizing data gathered as of 1996 from 150 development organizations and 600 projects using object-oriented technologies, Jones concludes:

> (1) The OO learning curve is very steep and causes many first-use errors. (2) OO analysis and design seem to have higher defect potentials than older design methods. (3) Defect removal efficiency against OO design problems seems lower than against older design methods, which is a significant observation if confirmed. (4) OO programming languages seem to have lower defect potentials than procedural programming languages. (5) Defect removal efficiency against programming errors is roughly equal [to] or somewhat better than removal efficiency against older procedural language errors [Jones 97, 292].

The available quantitative evidence indicates that heavier usage of structures intrinsic to the object-oriented programming paradigm is a good predictor of bugs. Testing requires a more specific fault model, however. The following survey of qualitative fault models and experienced-based analysis provides the details underlying this requirement.

4.2.2 Encapsulation

Encapsulation refers to the access control mechanisms that determine visibility of names in and among lexical units. Access control hides some names, typically to prevent unnecessary client dependencies to a server's implementation (e.g., making a class interface visible but not its implementation). It makes others visible, typically to simplify access (e.g., making superclass instance variables visible to subclasses). This supports information hiding and modularity. It helps to prevent problems with global data access common to procedural languages. Visibility in a particular system is determined by language defaults and the declarations as coded.

Although encapsulation does not directly contribute to the occurrence of bugs, it can present an obstacle to testing. Testing requires accurate reporting of the concrete and abstract states of an object and the ability to set state easily. Object-oriented languages make it difficult—if not impossible—to directly set or get the concrete state. The C++ friend function was developed to solve this problem [Stroustroup 92]. Ada 95 child packages play a similar role.

The interaction of encapsulation and testing is illustrated by a bug in an integer set class that was part of a commercial C++ class library [Hoffman+95].

```
class IntSet {
public:
    // operations on single sets
    Intset();
    ~Intset();
    IntSet& add(int);        // Add a member
    IntSet& remove(int);     // Remove a member
    IntSet& clear(int);      // Remove all members
    int     is_member(int);  // Is arg a member?
    int     extent();        // Number of elements
    int     is_empty();      // Empty or not?

    // operations on pairs of sets ...
};
```

A precondition of add(ix) is that ix is not already present in the set. If this condition is present and an add message is sent, the Duplicate exception is thrown. To test the Duplicate exception, add(1)was invoked twice. On the second call, the exception was thrown correctly, but the duplicate value was incorrectly added to the encapsulated implementation of the set. A subsequent

message, remove(1), was accepted without an exception. No further testing was done and the bug escaped detection. The bug was found (and fixed)
when it was noticed that two remove(x) messages were required before
is_member(x) would return false after two add(x) messages.

Chapters 17, Assertions, shows how to develop test code that is part of a
class's implementation. This strategy can overcome obstacles to observing the
state of an object. Chapter 19, Test Harness Design, presents several test automation patterns to deal with the obstacles to controllability that result from
encapsulation.

4.2.3 Inheritance

Inheritance is essential in the object-oriented programming paradigm [Wegner
87, Stroustroup 88]. It supports reusability by allowing shared and different elements of a common entity to be represented. It also supports definitions of
type and subtypes, allowing for efficient extensibility [Meyer 97]. Unfortunately, it may be abused in many ways [Armstrong+94]. In discussing how inheritance can support reuse, Weide notes

> [A] concrete component's implementation must understand the implementation de-
> tails and subtle representational conventions of all its ancestors in order to imple-
> ment that component correctly. Unless care is taken, it is possible to introduce
> components that seem to work properly yet, by manipulating their ancestor's inter-
> nal data representations, violate subtle and implicit conditions that the ancestors re-
> quire for correctness [Weide+91, 51].

Inheritance weakens encapsulation, creating a bug hazard similar to global
data in procedural languages. It can be used as an unusually powerful macro
substitution for programmer convenience, as a model of hierarchy (either problem or implementation), or as a participant in an implicit control mechanism
for dynamic binding. It is not unusual to see all three purposes at work in a single class hierarchy. This overloading can lead to undesirable side effects, inconsistencies, and incorrect application behavior. Deep and wide inheritance
hierarchies can defy comprehension, leading to bugs and reducing testability.

Inheritance can be used to implement specialization relationships or as a
programming convenience. Implementation specialization should correspond to
problem domain specialization. Reusability of superclass test cases is predicated
on this kind of correspondence. In most cases, convenience subclasses will not
reflect a true specialization relationship. As such, it is unlikely they can be ex-
cused from testing by testing their superclass, even when a lexical excuse can be

found. Fault models and test strategies for inheritance are presented in Section 10.5, Flattened Class Scope Test Design Patterns.

Incorrect Initialization and Forgotten Methods

Inheritance in Objective-C can make it difficult to understand source code [Taenzer+89]. A subclass at the bottom of a deep hierarchy may have only one or two lines of code, but may inherit hundreds of features. Without the aid of a class flattener, the interaction of these inherited features is difficult to understand. In Objective-C, all superclass instance variables are visible in subclasses. This approach creates fault hazards similar to unrestricted access to global data in procedural languages (you can avoid this problem by using accessor/modifier methods instead of statement-level access).

Initialization can easily go awry. Objects are created by the new method. The new method is often inherited and uses a class-specific `initialize` method to actually set subclass instance variable values. Determining how `initialize` is used in a subclass requires examination of the superclass that defines new. The `initialize` message must be sent to super, not self. Now, suppose new is refined and does not send `initialize` to self. Super's `initialize` will not execute, providing incorrect inherited behavior. The compounding effect of polymorphism is discussed later.

When subclasses are composed using many levels of inheritance, proper usage of upper-level features may become obscured. In Objective-C, this approach creates a bug hazard. Cox notes ". . . longstanding bugs have persisted because nobody thought to verify that deeply inherited methods, particularly easily forgotten object-level methods like copy and `isEqual:`, were overridden to adapt to the peculiarities of the subclasses" [Cox 88, 46].

These problems are not limited to Objective-C, but can occur in Smalltalk and Java for the same reasons. Classes that are subclassed from any large, deep framework (e.g., Microsoft's C++ MFC) are also susceptible to these problems.

Testing Axioms

A formal analysis of adequate testing of object-oriented programs is presented in [Perry+90]. Requirements for adequate testing are developed by interpreting Weyuker's software testing axioms (see *Testing Axioms* in Chapter 9) for object-oriented programs. Perry and Kaiser's basic result is that intuitive conclusions about test adequacy can be wrong (Berard agrees with these conclusions [Berard 93]).

- Similar functions can require different tests to achieve coverage. For example, a responsibility-based test suite that is adequate for a superclass method may not be adequate when the method is inherited and overridden. This situation arises because a test suite that is adequate for one implementation of a specification is not necessarily adequate for a different implementation of the same specification (antiextensionality axiom).

- Adequate testing of a client does not necessarily result in adequate testing of its servers. For example, suppose a client uses only a few methods of a server object. Even if we try to use the client as a test driver for the server, we cannot exercise all of the server's methods. This situation arises because a test suite that is adequate for a program that calls subroutines is not necessarily adequate for the individual subroutines (antidecomposition axiom).

- Different contexts of usage may require different tests to achieve coverage. For example, a test suite that covers a superclass method may not be adequate for this method in a subclass. This situation arises because test suites that are individually adequate for subroutines are not necessarily collectively adequate for a system that calls these subroutines (anticomposition axiom).

Overriding is typically used to provide superclass/subclass interface consistency while allowing for a different subclass implementation. An overriding method in a subclass can be implemented by a different algorithm, different functionality, or both. The test suite for the overridden method will almost certainly not be adequate for the overriding method.

Changes to a subclass can conflict with unchanged inherited features or unmask superclass faults. Retesting of these unchanged features in the new context is therefore warranted. An exception to this rule occurs with a "pure extension" subclass for which there are "new instance variables and new methods and there are no interactions in either direction between the new instance variables and methods and any inherited instance variables and methods" [Perry+90, 17].

A detailed analytical procedure to identify the dependencies that determine the scope of retesting is presented in *Retest Within Firewall*.

Inheritance Structure

A class hierarchy may represent a network of problem domain relationships or share implementation features by some kind of factoring scheme. Attempting to achieve both in a single class hierarchy may lead to bugs [Purchase +91]. Although inheritance can implement type/subtype relationships, this requires care. A "subtype relationship is a relationship between specifications, while a subclass relationship is a relationship between implementation modules" [Leavens 91]. Inheritance may easily be used as code-copying convenience, independent of any relationship between the superclass and subclass specifications.

If an implementation relies on inheritance, its specification-based test suite for inherited features may be reusable, reducing the test effort for a subclass. With the superclass tested, it is necessary to test the subclass against both its own specification and that of its superclass. The subclass is expected to respond to inherited messages in the same way that the superclass does, but with its own data state. Thus the implementation of the superclass may suggest how a subclass might fail. For example, suppose that a subclass is derived from a linked list superclass. The relative values of items for insert and delete operations are unlikely to be affected by faults in the linked list. But suppose the superclass is an ordered tree. In such a case, the relative order matters for correct operations and suggests a testing strategy.

Irregular type hierarchies will lead to incorrect polymorphic message bindings. As Jacobson argues, "We have at least two reasons for an inherited operation not to function in a descendant: (1) If the descendant class modifies instance variables which the inherited operation assumes certain values for, (2) If operations in the ancestor invoke operations in the descendant" [Jacobson+92, 321].

Inheritance will support "accidental reuse," which can lead to bugs [Marick 95, 360]. Suppose class X is developed for an application system, but is not designed to be reused—it may have hard-coded assumptions or application-specific performance optimizations. The class has been tested and works without problems in its original application system. Subsequently, however, class Y is subclassed from X and used in a new application. The superclass methods of X, now inherited in Y, may produce unanticipated, buggy behavior in the new context, even if the subclass works without trouble.

Multiple Inheritance

With multiple inheritance, a class inherits (directly) from two or more parent classes, which may contain features with the same names. Perry and Kaiser note that multiple inheritance "unfortunately cause[s] very small syntactic changes to have very large semantic consequences" [Perry+90, 18]. Multiple inheritance presents many bug hazards [Smith+90, Purchase+91, Moreland 94, Chung 94, Ball 95].

- Suppose Z is a subclass of classes X and Y, and method m is present in both superclasses. Z originally uses X.m but is changed to use Y.m. Z must then be retested. It is likely that the test suite for Y.m will not be appropriate for the new Z.m.

- An incoming selector may match two or more methods from different superclasses, resulting in incorrect binding and unanticipated interaction among inherited features.

- Repeated inheritance occurs when a common superclass appears in a multiple inheritance hierarchy. For example, suppose classes B and C are derived from superclass A, and class D is derived from B and C. This strategy can lead to multiple symbolic addresses for a single object, aliasing, and inadvertent "self" assignments. If methods and instance variables are not explicitly qualified by class, name clashes can occur and result in unexpected behavior in virtual functions. Pure virtual functions may be renamed and redefined. Public and private inheritance, abstract classes versus concrete classes, and the visibility of superclass data members compound these bug hazards.

- Scoping rules can result in different bindings when superclass methods are used in the context of a subclass. Any code change that involves binding precedence rules requires retesting of superclass methods in the subclass context. A test suite that was adequate for a superclass is therefore not guaranteed to be adequate in a subclass. Similarly, a test suite that was adequate for a baseline configuration may not prove adequate in a new configuration, even if the requirements and interface of the classes have not changed.

Abstract and Generic Classes

An abstract class provides an interface without an implementation [Woolf 97]. Abstract and generic classes are unique to object-oriented programming languages and provide important support for reuse [Meyer 97]. Abstract classes are supported in all six languages considered in this book. Besides the foregoing inheritance bug hazards, they present several specific problems [Thuy 92, Overbeck 94, Barbey 97].

- We must develop an instantiation to test an abstract class. This process may be complicated if a concrete method uses an abstract method. *Abstract Class Test* presents a fault model.

- A generic class accepts a type parameter(s) that designates a primitive type or class to be substituted for unbound type declarations. The primary bug hazard is unanticipated or incorrect interaction between a type specified as a parameter and the generic class. Firesmith argues that a generic class "may never be considered fully tested" [Firesmith 93b]. Overbeck's testing model demonstrates that generic classes must be instantiated to be tested and to show the limits on reduction of testing for subsequent instantiations [Overbeck 94b]. *Generic Class Test* presents a detailed fault model.

4.2.4 Polymorphism

Polymorphism is the ability to bind a reference to more than one object. In **static polymorphism,** the binding occurs at translation time. For example, Ada 95 types, subtypes, derived types, operators, derived operators, derived subprograms, subprograms from generic instantiations, static types, and tagged types can be bound to two or more objects. C++ templates are another example. The compiler can check the resultant binding and complain when it finds inconsistencies.

Dynamic polymorphism replaces explicit compile-time binding and static type checking by implicit runtime binding and runtime type checking. The semantics, syntax, and mechanisms involved in implementing this type of polymorphism differ for each programming language. Method polymorphism uses **dynamic binding** to select a method to be assigned to a message. The specific method bound to a message is determined when the message is sent. In contrast, static binding assigns a receiver method to a message at compile time. The same polymorphic message can be bound to any sequence of receivers. Each programming language offers its own flavor of dynamic binding and method polymorphism. There are often subtle variations between compilers of the same language.

Polymorphic server classes reduce the size and lexical complexity of client code. The client/server interface is decoupled, facilitating reuse. The method that receives a polymorphic message is determined at runtime by code generated by the language translator. In turn, the argument signature of the message selects the receiver. Sending a polymorphic message is similar to using a case structure to select the receiver of a message, in which each predicate examines the argument signature. Where a case statement includes a hard-coded set of choices, however, the choices for binding are determined by the structure of the server class at runtime. This mechanism greatly simplifies client interfaces to polymorphic servers and eases maintenance and reuse.

For example, in C++, the **virtual function call** implements method polymorphism. A client sends a message to a server object `fig`, whose class hierarchy is shown in Figure 4.1.

```
void render(Shape &fig ) {
        fig.zbuffer(x,y,z);      // Hide/reveal fig on z axis
        // . . .
}
```

The object `fig` may be a `Shape`, `Circle`, or `Triangle`. The virtual function `zbuffer` can be bound to `Shape::zbuffer()`, `Circle::zbuffer()`, or `Triangle::zbuffer()`. The declared base class (`Shape`) is mapped to the object class at runtime. This approach is termed "calling `zbuffer` through the base."

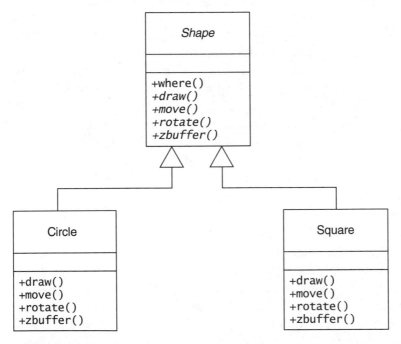

FIGURE 4.1   Shape hierarchy.

Although polymorphism can be used to produce compact, elegant, and extensible code, problematic aspects are identified by many sources [Smith+90, Purchase+91, Thuy 92, Wilde 92, Jacobson+92, Meyer 92, Wilke 93, Jüttner 94a, Jüttner 94b, McCabe+94, Ponder+94, Moreland 94, Barbey 97]. Subclassing is not necessarily identical to subtyping, so dynamic binding that relies on an irregular class hierarchy can produce undesirable results. Nevertheless, bugs are possible even with well-formed subtypes and formal specification. Suppose superclass method x has been verified. Later, a subclass overrides method x. The correctness of subclass x is not guaranteed because its precondition or postconditions may not be the same as those of superclass x. "Even if the preconditions and postconditions were textually identical, the assertions might have different meanings for each type [class]" [Leavens 91, 78].

Each possible binding of a polymorphic message is a unique computation. The fact that several bindings work without failure does not guarantee that all bindings will work. Object polymorphism with late binding can easily result in messages to the wrong class. It may be difficult to identify and exercise all such bindings.

- Polymorphic, dynamically bound messages can result in hard-to-understand, error-prone code. Such code results in delocalization of plans [Soloway+88] and the yo-yo problem (discussed later).
- Changes can be made to a polymorphic server without regard to clients, assuming that the interface will be correct. If the usage requirements of the server change even a little, an unchanged client may fail.
- Polymorphic message code is deceptively simple. The actual behavior of polymorphic messages is determined by many variables not visible in the source code. A developer may find it difficult to imagine all possible interactions under all possible bindings, which create a bug hazard. Even when polymorphic server code is placed side-by-side with a client, imagining just how the server will respond to a particular message can prove challenging. Furthermore, it may be difficult to view the server.
- Unless the server class hierarchy is carefully designed, it can produce strange results for some messages. "What is to prevent a redeclaration from producing an effect that is incompatible with the semantics of the original version—fooling clients in a particularly bad way, especially in the context of dynamic binding? Nothing of course" [Meyer 92, 47]. The Liskov substitution principle and Meyer's design-by-contract

approach can prevent these problems, but require sophistication and discipline to implement (see Section 10.5, Flattened Class Scope). Server hierarchies designed without regard to these principles are likely to cause client code to fail.

* A message may be bound to the wrong server, if even minor coding errors appear in the client message.

Polymorphic Message Test may be applied to clients; *Polymorphic Server Test* may be applied to server hierarchies. *Percolation* may be used to implement self-checking polymorphic servers or to serve as a checklist for design and code reviews.

The name overloading and yo-yo problems are not limited to Objective-C programs, but can occur in Smalltalk and Java programs for the same reasons. Classes that are subclassed from any large, deep framework (e.g., Microsoft's C++ MFC) are also susceptible to these problems.

Dynamic Binding

Dynamic binding shifts responsibility for correct operation to the server at runtime. As server classes are often developed and revised independently of clients, the understanding of the server's contract implemented by a client can become inconsistent. A client may assume or require a method not provided by the server, misuse an available method, or construct an interface signature incorrectly.

> It is obvious that the scope for subtle errors with polymorphism is enormous. A debugging agent, unaware of how the + method is overloaded, may have false confidence in a bugged variant after other incarnations pass prescribed tests. Complex polymorphic relations can serve to confuse the implementor, debugging agent, and maintainer alike by, for example, obscuring the point of origin of the bug [Purchase+91, 16].

An experience report on work to rehost a Smalltalk compiler calls this problem a kind of "Catch-22 . . . operations performed are determined [at runtime] from the variable types, and the variable types are deduced [at runtime] from the operations" [Ponder 94]. Methods are typically small (a few lines of code). Many classes may use the same method name. Understandability suffers and a bug hazard results.

Such systems are also sensitive to subtle naming errors. In a dynamically searched type [class] hierarchy there is a large pool of available procedure names, increasing the chances that a mistyped procedure call will invoke the wrong procedure [Ponder 94, 36].

The Yo-Yo Problem

An analysis of reusability suggests many fault hazards due to the message binding mechanisms employed in Objective-C [Taenzer+89]. As classes grow deeper and application systems become wider, the likelihood of misusing a dynamically bound method increases.

> Often we get the feeling of riding a yo-yo when we try to understand one of these message trees. This is because in Objective-C and Smalltalk the object *self* remains the same during the execution of a message. Every time a method sends itself a message, the interpretation of that message is evaluated from the standpoint of the original class. . . . This is like a yo-yo going down to the bottom of its string. If the original class does not implement a method for the message, the hierarchy is searched (going up the superclass chain) looking for a class that does implement the message. This is like the yo-yo going back up. *Super* messages also cause evaluation to go back up the hierarchy [Taenzer+89, 33].

Figure 4.2 illustrates this problem using five classes. C1 is a superclass, C2 is its subclass, and so on. In this example, the implementation of method A uses B and C, B uses D. Messages to these methods are bound according to the class hierarchy and the use of `self` and `super`. "The combination of polymorphism and method refinement (methods which use inherited behavior) make it very difficult to understand the behavior of the lower level classes and how they work" [Taenzer+89, 33].

Table 4.2 shows the difference between lexical message structure and a dynamic trace that can result from it. Suppose an object of class C5 accepts message A. C5's A is inherited from C4, so the search for A begins at C4.A. C4.A is a refinement, so C3.A is checked for an implementation. C3.A likewise refers to C1.A, where the implementation is found and executed. C1.A now sends message B to itself, causing B to be bound to `self` (an object of class C5); the search for B therefore begins back at C5. An implementation of B is found in C3. C3.B sends B to `super` (C2). C2.B executes, sending D, which is again bound to `self` (C5). The search for D continues up to C2, where D is implemented. C2.D executes for the C5 object, which then sends message C to `self` (still C5). The search

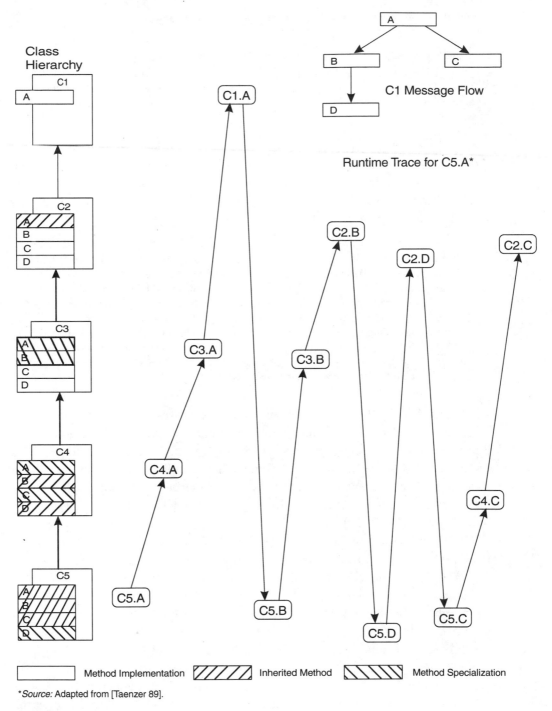

FIGURE 4.2   Trace of yo-yo execution.

Class
Hierarchy

C1 Message Flow

Runtime Trace for C5.A*

☐ Method Implementation   ▨ Inherited Method   ▨ Method Specialization

*Source: Adapted from [Taenzer 89].

TABLE 4.2   The Yo-yo Problem

Class	Method A	Method B	Method C	Method D
C1	Implements Sends self to B and C			
C2		Implements Sends self to D	Implements	Implements Sends self to C
C3	Refines Sends super to A	Refines Sends super to B		
C4	Refines Sends super to A		Refines Sends super to A	
C5				Refines Sends super to A

for C5.C is resolved at C4.C, which sends it to super (C3). Because C3 does not implement method C, C2.C is checked. The implementation C2.C is executed on self (an object of class C5).

Taenzer et al. traced messages in an eight-level class hierarchy and found that a message passed up and down through 58 methods before coming to rest.

4.2.5   Message Sequence and State-related Bugs

The packaging of methods into a class is fundamental to the object-oriented paradigm. As a result messages must be sent in some sequence, raising an issue: which sequences are correct? Which are not? A state-based fault model suggests how state corruption or incorrect behavior can occur. Chapter 7 discusses state models, state faults, and state-based test design in detail. State-based test design patterns are developed in Chapters 10 and 12. State-based testing derives test cases by modeling a class as a state machine. A state model defines allowable message sequences. For example, an Account object must have sufficient funds (be in the *open* state) before a withdrawal message can be accepted. If the withdrawal message causes the balance to become negative, the message causes a transition from the *open* state to the *overdrawn* state. Thus state-based testing focuses on detecting value corruption or sequentially incorrect message responses.

Message Sequence Model

A proposal to generate test cases by an unspecified automatic source code "search" is based on the observation that objects preserve state and typically accept any sequence of messages [Smith+92]. Four generic bugs that would result in corrupt state are identified:

1. *Interroutine conceptual*: Incorrect design resulting in methods with overlapping responsibilities.
2. *Interroutine actual*: State may be corrupted under certain message sequence patterns.
3. *Intraroutine actual*: State is corrupted due to an incorrect algorithm in a method and incorrect output or abend.
4. *Intraroutine conceptual*: An overriding implementation is omitted or implements an incorrect contract.

Equivalent Sequences

Certain activation sequences of class methods may be expected (specified) to yield identical results. In this situation, the inability of a pair of objects under test to produce equivalent results is deemed a failure. The fault model here is nonspecific: many kinds of faults could cause this kind of failure. The approach is conceptually simple, however, and can be readily automated.

The ASTOOT (A Set of Tools for Object-Oriented Testing) approach is based on "checking whether sequences of operations which, according to the specification, should yield the same state, actually do" [Doong 94].

Member functions that should support associative evaluation are considered fault-prone if "defects have been discovered by applying associativity rules ·to member functions. That is, if string s1 is null, and string s2 is not null, s1 > s2 should yield the same results as s2 < s1" [Fiedler 89].

Smith suggests that an automated "search" of the class under test could yield "identity" sequences [Smith+92]. An identity is an arbitrarily long sequence of messages that should result in no net change to an object. The test compares the initial and final state of the object under test for equality. The mechanics of the search and the test are not described.

Implications of Cooperative Design

Cooperative client/server classes increase the likelihood of state control bugs [Binder 94b]. When used as a server, a cooperative class assumes that the client will not issue incorrect message sequences or send messages with incorrect content [Meyer 92]. Servers rely on clients to implement some or all of the server's state control. In contrast, a defensive design holds the server responsible for carrying out correct operations and enforcing correct usage of itself under all circumstances. A defensive server is thus tolerant of client faults.

In contrast to procedural languages, preservation of state over the course of successive activations is an essential feature of object-oriented programming. State control must be implemented by message sequences. With cooperative design, state control is a shared responsibility, requiring correct implementation of a single idea in two or more separate software components. If the server is heavily used, many clients must correctly implement the server's state control rules.

State control faults will be predominant in object-oriented systems for several reasons. In object systems, overall control is implemented by many interfaces among small components. The resulting delocalization of plans [Soloway 88] reduces intellectual tractability, increasing the likelihood of bugs.

- Cooperative control is a popular implementation approach opening up new opportunities for control bugs in proportion to its use.
- Cooperative control is inherently complex, increasing the likelihood of control bugs when it is used.

For example, suppose that a client of an object sends a message putting the object into state x. Message p is illegal in state x, but a different client could easily send message p while the server is in state x.

Observability of State Faults

Tests applied to a member function individually "are not adequate for detecting errors due to interaction between member functions through an object state" [Kung+94]. For example, suppose a flag f is incorrectly set in member function a. Member function b uses f to determine an output. It is argued that branch coverage of a and b alone would not reveal this fault, as the incorrect output from b occurs only after a particular sequence of a and b. On the other hand, it is suggested that modeling the class as a state machine and acheiving n-switch cover [Chow 78] would reveal this fault.

Nonspecific State Faults

Many state-based testing approaches are conformance-oriented and therefore rely on a nonspecific fault model. In these approaches, no analysis addresses the specific kind of errors or faults likely to cause the failures that demonstrate nonconformance. Instead, they simply seek to demonstrate that the IUT conforms to its specification. The ASTOOT approach uses the fact that a faulty implementation may not produce the same state after accepting functionally equivalent but operationally different sequences [Doong 94]. Similarly, some sources adapt (partially) Chow's state-based conformance technique, which is known to reveal certain kinds of control faults [McGregor 93a, McGregor 93b, Hoffman 95]. The OOSE (Object-Oriented Software Engineering) methodology calls for a transition cover of class state models, but does not provide a fault model [Jacobson+92].

4.2.6   Built-in Low-level Services

The general features of object-oriented programming languages are supported by many built-in services. These services are typically automatically generated by the language translator.[2]

• *Default services.* Many compilers will generate default constructors, default destructors, default copy constructors, and default accessors if not explicitly coded. Most developers think that because they didn't code them, they don't need to test them.

• *Conversions.* Problems similar to type conversion with primitive data types (e.g., casting floats to integer) can occur in converting superclass objects to subclass objects, and vice versa. As the type of a referent is not determined until runtime with dynamic binding, changes to a server class can cause unchanged client code to fail. Considerations are discussed in Section 18.3.7, Type/Subtype Equality.

• *Garbage collection.* Garbage collection typically works without problems, but problems can develop under high loads.

• *Object identity.* An object-oriented language must provide a unique identity for every object with a runtime scope [Wegner 87]. This identity is rarely a concern of the application programmer, unless object-level operations like copy and equal must be implemented for a subclass. Barbey notes that "identity is not always defined, or observable in object oriented languages, and an oracle may be difficult to build" [Barbey 97, 80]. Relevant considerations are discussed in Section 18.3.7, Type/Subtype Equality.

4.2.7   Bug Lists

The mapping among errors, faults, and failures is complex. As noted earlier, the same general kind of failure can result from many different faults. The same

---

2. Thanks to Camille Bell for pointing out the problems with default services, conversion, and memory management.

TABLE 4.3   Errors and Failures

Process	Error	Scope				Failure
		A	S	C	M	
Requirements definition	Perceptual: Inadequate problem analysis. Communication failure.	x	x	x		Application problem not solved.
Design	Inadequate problem analysis. Specification error.		x	x	x	Requirements or specification not met.
	Abstraction: Inadequate knowledge of OO design techniques. Premature hierarchic factoring or leveling.		x	x		Poor class structure, bad factoring, inheritance hierarchy sprawling, inconsistent.
	Algorithmic: Specification misunderstood. Implementation incorrect.			x	x	Incorrect method output.
	Inadequate reuse knowledge. Reuse component or hierarchy misunderstood. Incorrect use of polymorphic protocol.	x	x	x		Unexpected, undesired behavior in reused components.
Implementation	Misuse of reuse component, ad hoc extensions of inheritance.			x	x	Incorrect method output.
	Semantic: Inadequate programming knowledge or misuse of target environment services.			x	x	Abend due to type mismatch with late binding.
	Syntactic: Inadequate programming knowledge, typographic error.			x	x	Incorrect output, abend.
Runtime	Inadequate knowledge of application or target services.			x	x	Runtime exceptions, message search failures.

Key: A = application, S = subsystem/cluster, C = class, M = method

general kinds of errors can produce many different faults. Nevertheless, it is instructive to look at these elements separately.

The relationship between errors and failures is represented in Purchase's bug taxonomy [Purchase+91]. This taxonomy was developed to frame a discussion of debugging support for object-oriented code. Bugs are categorized according to process (the activity in which a bug is introduced), failure (the observable incorrect behavior or state), and error (the developer mistake that led to the fault).[3] This classification indicates the circumstances in which bugs are created and how they are manifested. Table 4.3, which is based on this

---

3. Purchase and Winder's categories were *history* (process), *deviation* (failure), and *mind set* (error).

taxonomy, shows the scope at which these bugs are typically revealed during testing.

Faults lie between errors and failures. While there are an infinite number of particular faults, a short list of general fault types can be compiled. Tables 4.4, 4.5, and 4.6 list fault types at the method, class, and cluster scopes, respectively. These lists are composites that reflect my own experience and three published fault taxonomies: a list of dynamic binding bugs used in a white box testing strategy for a Lisp-based object-oriented language [Trausan-Matu 91]; a list of generic bugs that involve instance variables, methods, messages, classes, inheritance, clusters, and externally driven object interactions [Firesmith 92]; and design bugs related to abstraction, modularity, and hierarchy that could be detected by a static analyzer [Hayes 94].

These bug lists can be used as checklists for design or code reviews and in the development of test plans. They are not a complete and consistent bug taxonomy, however. Considerable effort would be required to review the

TABLE 4.4   Method Scope Fault Taxonomy

Method Scope		Fault
Requirements		See class scope fault taxonomy (Table 4.5)
		Requirement omission
		Incorrect or missing transformation
Design	Abstraction	Low cohesion
		Responsibilities overlap or conflict with local or superclass method
	Refinement	Feature override missing
		Feature delete missing
	Encapsulation	Overuse of friend/protected mechanisms
		Naked access
	Modularity	Excessively long method
		Method contains no code
		Excessively large instance variables
		Method has low cohesion
	Responsibilities	Incorrect algorithm
		Algorithm inefficient
		Invariant violation
		Exception not thrown
		Exception not caught

Method Scope		Fault
Implementation	General	Message sent to object without corresponding method
		Unreachable code
		Contract violation (precondition, postcondition, invariant)
		Message sent to wrong server object
		Message parameters incorrect or missing, resulting in wrong or failed binding
		Message priority incorrect
		Message not implemented in the server
		Formal and actual message parameters inconsistent
		Syntax error
	Algorithm	Inefficient, too slow, consumes too much memory
		Incorrect output
		Incorrect accuracy, excessive numerical or rounding error
		Persistence incorrect—wrong object saved, or save not done
		Does not terminate
	Exceptions	Exception missing
		Exception incorrect
		Exception not caught
		Incorrect catch
		Exception propagates out of scope
		Exception not raised
		Incorrect state after exception
		Missing object (referred to, but not defined)
	Instance variable define/use	Unused object (defined, but no reference)
		Reference to undefined or deleted object
		Corruption/inconsistent usage by friend function
		Missing initialization, incorrect constructor
		Incorrect type coercion
		Server contract violated
		Incorrect or missing unit (e.g., grams vs. ounces)
		Incorrect visibility/scoping
		Incorrect serialization, resulting in corrupted state
		Insufficient precision/range on scalar type

TABLE 4.5   Class Scope Fault Taxonomy

Class Scope		Fault
Requirements		Requirement omission: missing use case, and so on
		Problem domain object not identified
		Incorrect scope of effort, system boundaries
		Incorrect or inappropriate level of abstraction used
		Incorrect state model
		Association missing or has incorrect multiplicity
Design	Abstraction	Redundant allocation of responsibilities; the same method appears in several subclasses without being defined in a common superclass
		Design of top-level objects and protocol; poor class structure, nonorthogonal protocols; inheritance hierarchy sprawling, inconsistent
		Association missing or incorrect
		Incorrect type parameter(s) specified for a generic class
		Inheritance loops—for example, with classes A, B, and C, A hasSuper C, B hasSuper A, C hasSuper B
	Refinement	A subclass incorrectly redefines a superclass method
		Wrong feature inherited
		Subclass method to override missing
		Subclass method to nullify superclass method missing
		Hierarchy does not conform to LSP
		Incomplete specialization, missing methods or variables
		Deferred resource not provided by subclass of deferred superclass
		Dead-end or cycle in hierarchy
		Incorrect multiple inheritance
		Improper placement of class
	Encapsulation	Public interface to class not via class methods
		Implicit class-to-class communication
	Modularity	Overuse of friend/protected mechanisms
		Private/protected method not used
		Object not used
		Excessively large number of methods
		Too many instance variables
		Module, class, method, instance variable not used
		Module contains no classes
		Method contains no code

Class Scope	Fault
Responsibilities	Class contains no methods
	Class contains no instance variables
	Excessively large instance variable
	Excessively large module
	Incorrect state model
	Contract inconsistent
	Incorrect specification of concurrency
	Invariant violation possible
	Association missing or incorrect
Implementation	Incorrect method under multiple inheritance, due to synonyms, naming error, or misuse of name resolution
	Incorrect constructor or destructor
	Incorrect parameter(s) used in generic class
	Abstract class instantiated
	Syntax errors
	Association not implemented
Process	Class documentation inconsistent with its implementation
	Class doesn't meet applicable design or code standards
	Incorrect version/build used

categories and produce a taxonomy that complies with the *IEEE Standard Classification for Software Anomalies,* for example.

4.3 Language-specific Hazards

Most of the foregoing general bug hazards are present in the six languages discussed in this book, with obvious exceptions. For example, multiple inheritance bugs cannot occur in Java, Objective-C, or Smalltalk because these languages do not support multiple inheritance. Specific problems noted by users of these languages provide additional insight. The absence of sections on Ada 95, Eiffel, and Objective-C does not imply anything in particular about these languages, other than that I am not aware of published reports that detail hazards specific to these languages.

TABLE 4.6   Cluster/Subsystem Fault Taxonomy

Cluster/Subsystem Scope		Fault
Requirements		Requirement omission
		Incorrect abstraction
		Incorrect state model
		Association missing
Design	Encapsulation	Implementation data structure incorrectly exported
		Incorrect export of feature
		Incorrect package visibility
		Class contains nonlocal method
		Public method not used by object users
		Message/object mismatch
		Incorrect environment interface
	Modularity	Missing component
		Inconsistent component
		Low cohesion among components
Implementation		Incorrect priority
		Incorrect serialization
		Message sent to destroyed object
		Inconsistent garbage collection
		Incorrect message/right object
		Correct exception/wrong object
		Wrong exception/right object
		Incorrect resource allocation/deallocation
		Concurrency problems
		Inadequate performance
		Deadlock

4.3.1   C++

Stanley Lippmann, who with Bjarne Stroustrup was a lead developer of the C++ language, reflected on its difficulties in a recent interview.

> DR DOBBS JOURNAL: You worked at AT&T Bell Labs, in a research environment. You are now at Disney. Have you learned anything about the language now that you are yourself a user, working in "the real world" with other users of the language?
>
> STANLEY LIPPMANN: Actually it was a major insight to me. I think of it as a sort of Fairfield symmetry, if you will. I worked with Bjarne, Andy Koenig and other really

smart people. We all understood the language reasonably well and when it was complicated, we understood why it was complicated—to accommodate C, for example. When I moved to Disney, I found myself working with PhDs in graphics and mathematics who were, again, wonderfully smart, but they didn't understand C++. They would actually program, if you will, "naively." I was suddenly stunned by how difficult C++ can be and by how it can become an obstacle to people getting their work done [Dr Dobbs 98].

Sakkinen notes that C++ "inherits" some deficiencies of C. Understanding the behavior of arrays, constructor/destructors, and virtual functions requires consideration of complex special cases and counterintuitive behavior [Sakkinen 88]. "C++ is a powerful language that facilitates writing clear, concise, efficient, and reliable programs. However, its many features can be bewildering to the uninitiated, and injudiciously used, they can lead to programs that are confusing, bloated, slow, and bug-ridden" [Shopiro 93, 211]. Reed observes that "Most C++ bugs are due to unsafe features of the language: pointer problems, memory problems, uninitialized values, improper casts, improper union usage" [Reed 93].

The memory leak problem is not a problem exclusive to C++. Nevertheless, some of my clients estimate that half of their C++ failures are caused by memory leaks. The use of assertions in base classes, constructors, and destructors is recommended to reveal memory allocation and pointer corruption faults [Thielen 92, Spuler 94, Stout 97]. (See Chapter 17, Assertions.)

Fiedler notes that the object under test may be used as an input parameter to itself. Suppose `s1` is a string. Then `s1.append(s1)` may reveal pointer faults or insufficient isolation of self-referents [Fiedler 89]. Incorrectly duplicated instance variable names (pointer aliases) are easily made errors that can prove difficult to detect. Aliasing occurs when "an object, or part of it becomes globally accessible. As a result, it is possible to change the state of an object without calling any of its routines" [D'Souza 94, 34].

A list of 50 C++ "gotchas" provides a detailed catalog of easily made errors [Cargill 93]. These bugs typically result when the developer fails to consider the implication of some subtle C++ semantics. For example, in the following code fragment, only `Base::~Base` is called upon the deletion of `Derived`. Because the destructor for `Derived` is not activated, its allocated memory becomes garbage (this situation can be prevented by declaring the base destructor as virtual). Simple class extensions can lead to hard-to-find bugs. Similar problems occur when a member function is added to a base class that overrides a function of the same name defined at the file scope. Derived class objects will not be bound to the global function, possibly resulting in a failure [Reed 94].

```
// Wrong destructor called, scoping bug
class Base {
public:
    ~Base();
...
}

class Derived : public Base {
public:
    ~Derived();
...
}

void client::code()
{
    Base *p = new Derived;
    ...
    delete p;
    ...
}
```

Firesmith, Davis, and Moreland report similar kinds of common C++ bugs:

- (1) Misuse of friend functions, misuse of private, protected, and public scope, and incorrect type casts resulting in conflicting access or unexpected binding; (2) References in a base class to a derived class; (3) Pointers, arrays, unions, and casts (type conversions) that defeat type-safe usage; (4) Omission of virtual declarations in polymorphic superclasses; (5) Ambiguities in overloading public and private members; (6) Assignment taking place other than at initialization; (7) Overloading that ignores returned types; (8) Incorrect object references (size and address) [Firesmith 93b].
- (1) Absence of input parameter range checking; (2) Using an incorrect this pointer; (3) Using an incorrect object pointer for a virtual class; (4) State corruption due to bugs in constructor, destructor, or invalid array references [Davis 94].
- (1) Local names that hide global names; (2) Overloading and defaulting that are similar in appearance but have very different semantics; (3) Implicit type coercion with overloaded operators [Moreland 94].

4.3.2 Java

A list of 36 Java "gotchas" details inconsistent and surprising results [Green 98]. For example,

- A superclass method or variable name can be overridden in a subclass or shadowed. A shadowed superclass instance variable is declared in the subclass with the same name, but subclass references prefix the superclass name to the instance variable name. The resultant binding is resolved in one of four ways: static method, instance method, static variable, or instance variable.
- Some syntax similar to C++ is used, but with subtle differences. Developers who are accustomed to the C++ semantics are likely to misuse these constructs.
- The + operator invokes either addition (scalars) or concatenation (strings). Java determines the operation based on the operand type, "but humans can be easily fooled."

Java applets are susceptible to portability bugs and platform-specific differences in each Java Virtual Machine (JVM). A portability bug causes the applet to fail (or run) on some JVMs but not on others. This bug may appear in the applet, a particular JVM, or both. Applet bugs result from nonstandard or incorrect Java code. Enough variation exists among JVMs to warrant testing applets on different JVMs [Hayes 97]. Some of these differences result from the Java language specification, which does not define a specific thread scheduling policy, legal size of file names, or number of pixels on the screen. Different physical clients using the same JVM may see different behavior (bugs) due to varying link speeds and differences in firewalls and security configuration.

4.3.3 Smalltalk

Johnson has compiled a list of "classic" Smalltalk bugs [Johnson 97]. Table 4.7 provides an abbreviated version of this list. Interested readers are encouraged to locate the original version on the Web. This list suggests how some of the essential features of the Smalltalk object model have the unintended consequence of being bug hazards.

Silverstein notes that Smalltalk applications have several intrinsic bug hazards [Silverstein 99]. In addition to the problems noted earlier regarding polymorphism and violations of the superclass contract, "weak typing permits sloppy use of interfaces." Initialization bugs arise when a subclass neglects to override a superclass method (#copy), omits initialization code, or uses #new (lazy initialization). Despite built-in garbage collection, unreleased instances can lead to memory leaks. Bugs can be introduced during application

TABLE 4.7   Johnson's Classic Smalltalk Bugs

	Bug	Cause
1	Modifying elements of variable-sized collection classes	Superclass copy methods do not support subclass extensions. When new instance variables are added to a collection subclass, corresponding code to copy these variables must be written.
2	Using add: as if it returns a collection	Mutable collections use add:, which returns its argument, not the receiver collection.
3	Changing collection while iterating over it	Modifying a collection while iterating through its elements will cause elements of the collection to be moved. Elements might be missed or handled twice.
4	Copy of a collection is modified, but original is not	A modifiable copy of a collection is instantiated, but the modifications are not also made to the original.
5	Missing ^	Incorrect object returned.
6	Incorrect instance creation method	Incorrect object returned, incorrect usage of new, super new init, and so on.
7	Assigning to classes	A class will accept an assignment, causing the class to be corrupted.
8	Use of become:	After become: executes, the specified variable names are the same, but point to different objects. This process can wreak algorithmic havoc. Semantics of this operation differ among Smalltalk implementations.
9	Recompiling in Smalltalk/V	Smalltalk/V will accept references to undefined objects without complaint.
10	Opening windows	Smalltalk/V and the older versions of Smalltalk-80 do not return a window object to the sender when a new window is opened. Clients' attempts to use the object returned by the open window will fail.
11	Incorrect use of blocks	Block scoping (binding) of temporary variables and precedence rules can defeat the programmer's intent.
12	Cached menus	Menus are often defined in a class method, where they are created. The creation message does not necessarily result in initialization, however.
13	Incorrect cascaded messages	The omission of parentheses in a cascaded message statement causes the first message's result to be overwritten (instead of returned) to the next message.
14	Using class methods to implement a singleton object	Class methods used to implement global variables are easy to misuse and often cause maintenance problems.
15	Redefining = but not redefining hash	A redefinition of hash is required to produce the correct object identity.

packaging as a result of name overloading—for example, with the `#add:` and `#do:` methods.

> Collaboration and distribution of behavior increase dependencies between objects. Coupling between objects implies that a fix for one problem may cause a new problem—sometimes in an unanticipated area. This most often happens when fixes are applied late in a development cycle when there is little time to think about the broader implications of changes or perform extensive regression testing [Silverstein 99].

Besides recommending early class testing, integration testing, and regression testing, [Skublics+96] advocates roughly 100 specific design and coding guidelines. Many of these guidelines imply a bug hazard to be avoided. For example, guideline 98, "Do not override the identity == or ~~ operations," is given because failing to carry out this action can "change the fundamental behavior of the Smalltalk system" [Skublics+96, 79].

4.4 Coverage Models for Object-oriented Testing

Coverage is an operational definition for a complete test suite. A fault model suggests a coverage goal, as we want to exercise all elements that are likely to be buggy. For example, if a fault exists, it must be exercised to be revealed, so achieving statement coverage satisfies this simple fault model. Statement coverage is defined as the percentage of all executable source code statements in a program that have been exercised at least once by a test suite. The details of code coverage are discussed in Section 10.2.2, Implementation-based Test Models.

Many researchers and practitioners call for "thorough" testing without reference to any explicit coverage criteria. In the absence of a commonly understood operational definition of "thorough" testing (e.g., 100 percent branch coverage), the only meaningful interpretation of a "thorough" test suite is that it has satisfied someone's curiosity.

4.4.1 Code Coverage and Fault Models

The scope of retesting under inheritance established in [Perry+90] is widely, if sometimes reluctantly, accepted. It defines a general scope of testing, but does not advocate a specific coverage based on a probable fault model (see Section 4.2.3). Nevertheless, this analysis has had a significant influence on subsequent work; it is discussed in [McGregor 92, Smith 92, Harrold 92, Murphy 92,

Jacobson+92, Klimas 92, Berard 93, Coleman+94, Graham 94, D'Souza 94, Turner 95, Barbey 97]. As Perry's result requires complete testing, at least one technique has been developed to reduce the number of method-specific tests required for derived classes [Harrold+92]. A survey of abstract data type coverage definitions appears in [Binder 96a]. A coverage model for intraclass control and data flow is presented in The Class Flow Graph: A Class Scope Coverage Model section, in Chapter 10 (pages 389–396).

Optimistic Scope

An optimistic view of inheritance argues that it will reduce the testing necessary in derived classes, provided that the base classes are "thoroughly" tested [Cheatham+90]. Testing of base classes is similar to unit testing of modules in procedural languages. Unit testing may begin "as soon as a class is implemented. If the class is not a derived class, the unit testing is equivalent to unit testing in a traditional system. . . . If the class being tested is a derived class, the parent class should be thoroughly tested first. Then the derived class can be tested in conjunction with the base class" [Cheatham+90].

The assertions made in Cheatham's paper reflect an optimistic appraisal of the benefits of object-oriented development. Many of them are contradicted by later results. Message passing and inheritance influence how much testing will be needed. With unaltered inheritance, "little additional testing [of a derived class] is needed. At most the interface should be retested." An overridden or unique method "must be tested as a new member function." The meaning of "thoroughly tested" is not discussed and the assertions about testing scope are not supported.

It is speculated that reuse of "thoroughly" tested classes may reduce unit testing by 40 to 70 percent. System testing should also be eased because requirements are more readily mapped into implementation (compared to procedural implementations), but "further study is needed."

Method Scope Branch Coverage

Several variants of branch coverage [Myers 79] and basis-path coverage [McCabe 76] have been used or advocated. "Test cases are created to execute each decision path in the code. . . . except for paths that contained code for exception handling, test cases were written to ensure complete path coverage of each member function" [Fiedler 89].[4]

---

4. It is likely that by "complete path coverage" Fiedler means 100 percent branch coverage, and not all entry–exit paths.

Jacobson calls for testing each "decision-to-decision path" (a path between two predicates) at least once, noting that exercising pairs of decision paths may be useful (but time-consuming) [Jacobson+92]. Berard adds interrupts and exceptions: "Enough test cases must be written so that we can be reasonably assured that all statements are executed at least once, all binary decisions take on a true and false outcome at least once, all exceptions are raised at least once, and all possible interrupts are forced to occur at least once" [Berard 93, 259].

Coverage for a Classless Language

Two adequacy criteria are given for testing programs written in mXRL, a classless LISP-based object-oriented language [Trausan-Matu+91]: component (similar to statement coverage) and message (similar to branch coverage). "In addition to the testing of procedural components, in OOP we have to define also procedures for testing the correctness of inheritance paths." Adequate testing of a class requires the following: (1) all statements in each method must be exercised, (2) all locally defined (not inherited) attributes "must be accessed," and (3) each feature obtained by a one-step inheritance link must be used at least once. It is asserted (without substantiation) that, compared with procedural testing, "Due to code sharing by inheritance, the amount of tests corresponding to the statement adequacy criterion may be significantly reduced."

Branch coverage for mXRL is similar to covering "all the different possibilities of code activation (i.e., branches)." Message coverage requires (1) exercising all branches in methods, (2) sending all "the possible different types of messages" that an object can accept, (3) sending a given message to all objects that accept the particular message, (4) exercising all inheritance links, including implicit (multilevel) inheritance links, and (5) exercising all possible exits from methods composed by multiple inheritance.

ICpak Test Suite

The coverage goals set and met for testing of the Objective-C ICpak class library considered the effects of inheritance and dynamic binding. Each subclass was tested to demonstrate that "every method in all its superclasses was executable and gave correct results."

> With an object-oriented language one must verify that: all inherited methods used by a class are correct, all arguments that are subclasses of the specified argument type are correct, all methods by the same name perform the same logical operation, [and] the documentation is accurate and sufficient for an isolated user to use all the components [Love 92, 193].

Coverage Checklist

Classes are not testable per se, but class testing is crucial for reuse. Consequently, "testing should be thorough . . . completely unit testing a single instance completely unit tests its corresponding class" [Firesmith 92, Firesmith 93b]. Concrete, abstract, deferred, and generic classes are all subject to unique bugs. Generic classes (e.g., C++ templates) "may never be considered fully tested."

> Changes to superclasses may have unexpected effects on the class to be tested. Changes to a superclass may therefore obsolete test results and require significant regression testing, especially if configuration management and detailed analysis do not rule out impacts on the class to be tested. . . . The primary purpose of classes and inheritance is reuse. For this reason, initial testing should be exhaustive [sic] and include stress testing [Firesmith 93b].

Whereas the "testing of objects is application-specific, the testing of classes should be more general because the developer of a class cannot know in advance how the instances of that class may be used on future projects." Firesmith argues that a complete class test suite requires the following:

- Every operation is executed.
- All message parameters and exported attributes are checked using equivalence class samples and boundary values.
- Every outgoing exception is raised and every incoming exception is handled.
- Every variable attribute is updated.
- Every state is achieved.
- Every operation is executed in each state (correctly where appropriate, prohibited where inappropriate).
- Every state transition is exercised to test assertions.
- Appropriate stress, performance, and suspicion tests are performed.

Incremental Class Testing

Harrold et al. suggest that a minimal set of inherited C++ derived class features to be tested can be determined automatically [Harrold+92]. Testing of base and derived classes is therefore monitored. The selection criteria is argued to be consistent with [Perry+90], but aims to reduce or reuse base class tests. A "thorough" test suite is manually prepared and applied to each base class, then each derived class is flattened. Required test cases for derived classes are determined by

> incrementally updating the [testing] history of the parent class to reflect the differ-
> ences from the parent. Only new attributes or those inherited, affected attributes
> and their interactions are tested. The benefit of this technique is that it provides a
> savings both in the time to analyze the class to determine what must be tested and
> in the time to execute test cases [Harold+92, 78–79].

A new feature is "thoroughly" tested at the first level at which it appears. If a derived class has a new feature, it is "thoroughly" tested in the context of its defining class. "We first test base classes using traditional unit testing techniques to test individual member functions in the class." Server methods are stubbed out. The specific test case design technique is not discussed, nor is an operational definition of a "thoroughly" tested class provided.

Decision rules for setting the scope of derived class tests are presented. For a new or untested feature in a derived CUT, a complete test suite is developed. Intraclass and interclass integration tests are prepared. A new data member is tested by "testing [the CUT] with member functions with which it interacts."

For inherited features, "very limited retesting" is needed, since it is argued that the specification and implementation are assumed to be identical. Integration testing is indicated by the anticomposition axiom if the CUT interacts "with new or redefined variables, or accesses the same instances in the class's [sic] representation as other member functions."

For redefined features, reusing the test cases prepared from specifications may be possible, but new program-based test cases become necessary. Conditions under which method-specific tests need not be repeated for inherited methods are presented.

It is argued that this approach can significantly reduce the number of tests needed to verify inherited features while still meeting Perry's adequacy axioms. This approach is referred to as Hierarchic Incremental Testing (HIT) in several subsequent reports.

Class Interface Data Flow Coverage

Zweben models a class interface with a graph whose nodes represent "define" and "use" methods. The define/use ADT operations developed through this data flow test strategy may be applied to classes [Zweben+92]. (See Chapter 10 for more on the data flow model.) With the flow graph, test sets can be identi-

TABLE 4.8   Method Define/Use Coverage

Code Coverage Criterion	Corresponding Class Interface Coverage
All statements	All operations
All branches	All feasible edges
All paths	All paths
All uses	All uses
All definitions	All definitions
All DU paths	All DU message sequences

fied that provide covers corresponding to various data flow coverage criteria (Table 4.8).

A similar approach synthesizes a data flow model from a class interface and advocates coverage based on several variations of set (define) and get (use) sequences [Parrish 93]. As the flow graph may contain infeasible edges due to conditional flow, coverage may be unobtainable. A "weak class graph" is defined where conditional edges are treated as a single edge (a "weak" edge), assuring that at least one of the conditional edges can be covered.

Polymorphic Bindings

Dynamic binding presents a coverage problem. Based on experience developing a 3 MLOC C++ system, Thuy argues that exercising a single binding of a polymorphic server is "insufficient: the coverage is complete only when all the redefinitions of the called method have also been exercised" [Thuy 92]. This approach, however, could require a large number of test cases, which may be difficult to identify.

McCabe proposes a component-directed strategy to deal with the large number of tests needed to cover polymorphic servers [McCabe+94b]. Each class in the system under test is tested separately by a driver. The class test suite must (1) provide basis-path coverage, (2) exercise all intraclass uses of class methods, and (3) exercise each overloading of a polymorphic server at least once. When a class passes these tests, it is considered "safe." It is argued that tests for a client of safe server classes need not retest polymorphic bindings encapsulated in the servers. It is also asserted that regression testing for clients of safe classes is unnecessary in some circumstances. If the implementation of a safe class changes (but not the interface or behavior), no retesting of the client is needed. No empirical or analytical support is provided for these assertions.

4.5 An OO Testing Manifesto

Effective object-oriented testing must address both technical and process issues. Several observations can be made:

- The hoped-for reduction in object-oriented testing due to reuse is illusory.
- Inheritance, polymorphism, late binding, and encapsulation present some new problems for test case design, testability, and coverage analysis.
- To the extent that object-oriented development is iterative and incremental, test planning, design, and execution must be similarly iterative and incremental.
- Regression testing and its antecedents must be considered a sine qua non for professional object-oriented development.

So, while nearly all of what we know about testing procedural and abstract type software applies, testing object-oriented software has significant differences. Effective testing of object-oriented software must be guided by three basic tenets (supporting propositions for each tenet follow the list):

1. *Unique bug hazards*. Test design must be based on the bug hazards that are unique to the object-oriented programming paradigm. These techniques must be augmented with applicable established test design practices.
2. *Object-oriented test automation*. Application-specific test tools must be object-oriented and must offset obstacles to testability intrinsic to the object-oriented programming paradigm.
3. *Test-effective process*. The testing process must adapt to iterative and incremental development and mosaic modularity. The intrinsic structure of the object-oriented paradigm requires that test design consider method, class, and cluster scope simultaneously.

Unique Bug Hazards

The object-oriented programming paradigm is significantly different from the procedural, functional, or abstract type paradigms. It is error-prone in unique ways. Effective test design of object-oriented software must rely on fault models that recognize these hazards.

1. The interaction of individually correct superclass and subclass methods can be buggy. These interactions must be systematically exercised.

2. Omitting a subclass override for a high-level superclass method in a deep inheritance hierarchy is easy. Superclass test suites must be rerun on subclasses and constructed so that they can be reused to test any subclass.

3. Unanticipated bindings that result from scoping nuances in multiple inheritance and repeated inheritance can produce bugs that are triggered by only certain superclass/subclass interactions. Subclasses must be tested at flattened scope, and superclass test cases must be reusable.

4. Poor design of class hierarchies supporting dynamic binding (i.e., polymorphic servers) can result in failures of a subclass to observe superclass contracts. All bindings must be systematically exercised to reveal these bugs.

5. The loss of intellectual control that results from spaghetti polymorphism (the yo-yo problem) is a bug hazard. A client of a polymorphic server can be considered to have been adequately tested only if all server bindings that the client can generate have been exercised.

6. Classes with sequential constraints on method activation and their clients can have control bugs. The required control behavior can be systematically tested using a state machine model. Testing that is not designed to exercise control systematically cannot be expected to reveal these bugs.

7. Subclasses can accept illegal superclass method sequences or generate corrupt states by failing to observe the state model for superclass. Where sequential constraints exist, subclass testing must be based on a flattened state model.

8. A generic class instantiated with a type parameter for which the generic class has not been tested is almost the same as completely untested code. Each generic instantiation must be tested to verify it for that parameter.

9. The difficulty and complexity of implementing multiplicity constraints can easily lead to incorrect state/output when an element of the composition group is added, updated, or deleted. The implementation of multiplicity must be systematically exercised.

10. Bugs can easily hide when a set method computes a corrupt state, the class interface does not make this corrupt state visible, and the corruption does

not inhibit other operations. Define/use method sequences must be systematically exercised to reveal this kind of bug.

11. Mosaic modularity and the resulting delocalization of plans are intrinsic to the object-oriented programming paradigm. Control relationships at a scope beyond the class are obscured. OOA/D control abstractions at this scope are weak, offering only fragmentary models. This bug hazard calls for systematic testing based on integrated control models at this scope.

Object-oriented Test Automation

The structure of a test automation system must be shaped by the abstractions of the system under test and by its implementation dependencies.

1. The encapsulation and mosaic modularity intrinsic to object-oriented languages decrease controllability and observability. Any given implementation under test consists of many small objects, which contain many small objects, which contain many small objects, and so on. Their class interfaces typically do not support all of the state set/get requirements of systematic testing. Test automation countermeasures are required in proportion to encapsulation and scope of testing.

2. The absence of design for testability in large systems can greatly reduce testing effectiveness. Not only do controllability and observability suffer, but code dependencies can also force testing to be conducted at a larger (and less effective) scope than might otherwise have been prudent. Design for testability must be considered at all stages of development.

3. Test drivers and test suites should correspond to the inheritance, cluster, and package structure of the system under test. This tactic improves test suite maintainability and test suite reuse.

4. Design-by-contract implemented with assertions is a straightforward and effective approach to built-in test. Not only does this strategy make testing more efficient, but it is also a powerful bug prevention technique.

5. As of publication, no COTS tools support coverage analysis at any scope beyond the method and static call-pair. This is woefully inadequate for testing object-oriented code. I hope object-specific coverage analyzers will become available in a few years. Meanwhile, existing coverage tools must be used.

Test Process

The work of testing must be orchestrated to complement the technical constraints and opportunities of the object-oriented paradigm and the structure of the system under test.

1.   Although a class is the smallest natural unit for testing, class clusters are the practical unit for testing. Testing a class in total isolation is typically impractical. Methods are meaningless apart from their class, but must be used individually to exercise class responsibilities. Method testing must consider the class as a whole. As a result, the test design must be method-specific but based on cluster-scope responsibilities. Tests must be applied in a sequence determined by implementation dependencies. At this scope, testing must combine aspects of unit and integration testing.

2.   Test design techniques must use available OOA/D models at class, cluster, and use case level. Test models developed to compensate for missing, incomplete, or incorrect requirements and design models should follow known-good practices for OOA/D. This approach allows the same test design strategies to be used in either circumstance.

3.   Human checking of design and code work-products may be less effective (compared with procedural code). In procedural systems, static verification (walkthroughs or inspections) has been shown to be more effective and efficient in removing certain kinds of faults than testing [Basili+87]. However, object-oriented source code can be harder to comprehend for at least three reasons: (1) the yo-yo problem, (2) dynamic binding, and (3) cooperative distributed control strategies. Given these obstacles to comprehension, static techniques may miss bugs, requiring more testing to achieve comparable quality.

4.   The test strategy for producers of reusable components is different from the reuse consumer's test strategy as well as from testing of software that is not intended for general reuse. These strategies are discussed in Chapter 11.

5.   Although unfounded expectations about the magical charms of object-oriented programming have diminished in recent years, hope springs eternal. Some developers ignore or disparage known-good software engineering practices, including testing. This attitude must be confronted and corrected.

6.   Class testing must be closely tied to class programming. Object-oriented unit testing proceeds in a shorter cycle than the corresponding activities in procedural development. The development process must facilitate short code/test

cycles. Not all test activities will follow this pattern, however. Subsystem integration and system test cannot be performed until some or all components are in hand. These test activities will continue to be final steps in object-oriented development.

Just as some aspects of object-oriented design and programming have proved to be difficult, so are some aspects of testing object-oriented systems. However, if we are to master the paradigm and realize its promise, these challenges must be met.

4.6 Bibliographic Notes

This chapter includes material adapted from [Binder 94a, Binder 95b, Binder 96i, Binder 97c].

For an in-depth comparative analysis of programming language paradigms, see [Watt 90]. An extensive list of research reports on bug rates, complexity measurement, and effort estimation can be found at *Object-Oriented Metrics: An Annotated Bibliography,* maintained by the Empirical Software Engineering Research Group, Department of Computing, Bournemouth University, United Kingdom, at

http://dec.bournemouth.ac.uk/ESERG/bibliography.html

PART II Models

Part II develops analytical tools necessary to develop test models for a broad range of test design problems. The models are produced using combinational logic, state machines, and UML diagrams. In each chapter, basic ideas are reviewed and extended to classes, objects, and object-oriented systems. Criteria for complete and correct models are presented, and test generation algorithms are presented and compared.

- Chapter 5, Test Models, introduces modeling for test design.
- Chapter 6, Combinational Models, presents combinational test models that represent the relationship between input conditions and output actions. Test points are selected by analyzing relationships that control output actions instead of attempting to pick test points for each variable individually.
- Chapter 7, State Machines, shows how to develop testable state models. Basic state machines, state models for object-oriented components, and state-based testing strategies are presented.
- Chapter 8, A Tester's Guide to the UML, focuses on UML, which has become a de facto standard for object-oriented development. A generic test strategy for graphs and relations is presented, which is used to identify generic test requirements for each UML diagram. The symbols and semantics of each diagram are summarized.

The UML diagrams and the models considered in Chapters 6 and 7 can support a wide range of test design techniques. Combinational logic and state machines have been mainstays of test design since the dawn of the digital age. They are used directly and indirectly in nearly all of the test design patterns presented in Part III. The UML provides a means to represent nearly all of the basic entities that form the object-oriented landscape and is a direct input for approximately half of the test design patterns.

Nearly all of what is stated here in UML terms can be applied to any OOA/D approach, including Booch [Booch 91], Catalysis [D'Souza+98], CRC Cards [Cunningham+86], Embley-Kurtz [Embley+92], Fusion [Coleman+94], Object Behavior Analysis [Goldberg+95], OML [Firesmith+98], OMT [Rumbaugh+91], OOSE [Jacobson+92], and ROOM [Selic+94], to name a few.

Chapter 5   Test Models

Overview

We cannot test without first understanding what the implementation under test is supposed to do. The complexity of software requires development of models to support test design. A test designer must use, augment, and revise available models to design tests. Often, we need additional test models. This chapter frames general problems in developing test models for object-oriented implementations.

5.1   Test Design and Test Models

5.1.1   Why Testing Must Be Model-based

Testing can be viewed as a search problem. We are looking for those few input and state combinations that will reach, trigger, and propagate bugs out of trillions and trillions which will not. Brute force is impotent at this scale. Testing by poking around is a waste of time that leads to unwarranted confidence. Instead, our search must be systematic, focused, and automated. It must be *systematic* if we are to ensure that every targeted combination is tried. If it is not, size and complexity will defeat even the most meticulous tester. It must be *focused* if we are to take advantage of available information about where bugs are likely to be found. The number of places they are not is vast in proportion to where they are. It must be *automated* if we are to produce and run the greatest number of consistent and repeatable tests.

Model-based testing achieves all three objectives. Models support systematic enumeration of input and state combinations. Although we cannot usually generate every input and state combination of the implementation under test (IUT), we can achieve this goal for a model of the IUT. A useful testing model focuses on combinations that are likely to be buggy. Although this focus is usually no more than an educated guess, it is much better than flailing away. The number of tests that can be run with automation remains minuscule in comparison with the input and state space, but it is huge in comparison with the number of tests that can be run manually. Automated testing replaces the tester's slingshot with a machine gun. The model paints the target and casts the bullets.

5.1.2   What Is a Model?

A model captures essential relationships but is easier to develop or analyze than the system under study. Physical models have long been used in engineering and architecture to develop and test designs. More recently, mathematical and conceptual models have been used to design and explore many subjects through simulation and visualization. A model has four main elements: subject, point of view/theory, representation, and technique.

• *Subject*. A model must have a well-defined subject. For example, models of airframes, buildings, forest fires, bridges, weather, and economics have been developed. In testing, we are interested in models of the IUT that will help us select effective test cases.

• *Point of view/theory*. A model must be based on a frame of reference and principles that can guide identification of relevant issues and information. Software testing models typically express required behavior and focus on aspects of structure or elements suspected to be buggy. They must establish the information necessary to produce and evaluate test cases.

• *Representation*. A modeling technique must have a means to express a particular model. This may be a wire frame image for a CAD model of an automobile body, a blueprint for a building, or equations for a mathematical model. Many software testing models use graphs.[1] General test strategies for graph models are discussed in Chapter 8. Perhaps the most common form of

---

1. The graphs used in these test models are simple circle and arrow drawings, not x,y coordinate graphs, bar graphs, pie graphs, and so on.

a test model is a checklist. Examples include Myers's equivalence class criteria [Myers 79], Hamlet's suspicions [Hamlet+90], and Marick's test requirement catalogs [Marick 95].

- *Technique.* Models are complex artifacts. The skill and artisanship of the modeler matters. Some modeling approaches have an extensive literature covering style and heuristics—the hundreds of books on OOA/D are only one example. Other approaches are more esoteric. I have tried to avoid repeating what has been well said elsewhere and to develop examples that are understandable and scalable.

5.1.3 The Role of Models in Testing

Validation, verification, and testing focus on relationships among software artifacts.[2]

Informal or semiformal requirements[3]—for example, Unified Modeling Language (UML) diagrams.

A representation meta-model—for example, the Object Constraint Language (OCL) syntax.

A formal representation—for example, the OCL expressions that define a class contract.

An implementation—for example, a Java package.

The observable behavior of an implementation.

- *Model validation* attempts to establish confidence in the sufficiency of a formal abstract component with respect to its informal behavioral requirements. This advanced subject is not considered in this book.

- *Verification* attempts to show that implementation is correct with respect to its representation, without executing it. This effort may be either informal (using a checklist) or formal (constructing a proof). Except for

---

2. This analysis is adapted from the Weide's abstract data type verification approach in [Weide 91].

3. Webster defines the difference between formal and informal methods to be the "underlying discipline and degree of formality. . . . [Informal methods] tend to have well-defined syntax but no clear semantics. [Semi-formal methods have] some sort of basic theory, epistemology or pragmatic or operational semantics. [Formal methods have] mathematical precision, in the sense of proof or model theory, or axiomatic or denotational semantics" [Webster 87, 7–8].

the modeling checklists provided in Chapters 6 and 7, this subject is not considered here.

• *Consistency checking* evaluates a representation as an instance of its meta-model. Software engineering models have two levels. A **meta-model** is the definition of a modeling technique: symbols used in its notation, rules for using these symbols, concepts associated with symbols, and compositions of symbols. An **instance-model** is a representation constructed using the technique defined by the meta-model. Often, "a model" means an instance-model concerning a specific application. This relationship is similar to that between a programming language and a program written in that language, or between a class and an object of that class. The discussion here concerns meta-models, not instance-models. The subject of consistency checking is not considered here.

• *Responsibility-based testing* evaluates whether observable behavior conforms to the representation. The main purpose of the test models in Part II is to support the patterns for responsibility-based test design presented in Part III.

• *Implementation-based testing* evaluates observable behavior with respect to a test model derived from an implementation. This approach plays an important but secondary role in testing. Implementation-based test design approaches are discussed in Part III.

• *Product validation* evaluates conformance of observable behavior to requirements. Testing based on use cases and other system scope requirements is discussed in Chapter 14.

Each technique can make a unique contribution to defect prevention and removal. Figure 5.1 suggests the relationships that exist among these models.

5.1.4   Cartoons or Test-ready Models?

Bezier characterizes test models as an intellectual lever:

> [W]hat shall we, as testing practitioners do? As with all models, we ignore the complexities that can invalidate the model and use what we can apply with ease. After all, models for testing are intended to give us insights into effective test case design—they're intuition joggers—so it doesn't matter that they're imperfect as long as the resulting tests are good [Beizer 90, 130–131].

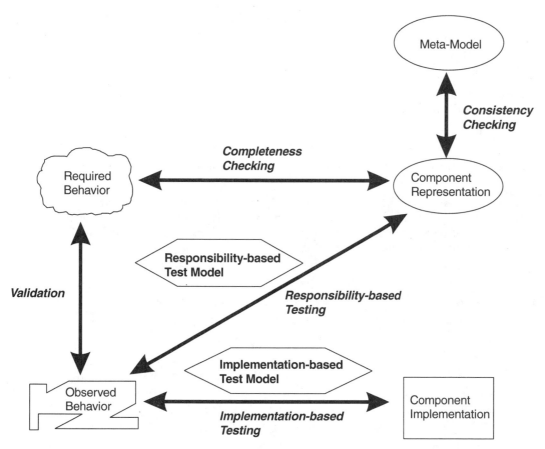

FIGURE 5.1   The relationship of models, testing, and validation.

A **test-ready** model contains enough information to produce test cases for its implementation automatically. Although automated test case generation may not be practical (or desirable) in all situations, a test-ready model must have sufficient detail to perform this task. We cannot produce a test-ready model with an OOA/D technique that lacks a means to express information necessary for testing. Even the use of a testable OOA/D technique by itself does not guarantee a test-ready result.

Analysis and design models can be used in two ways for testing. First, they can provide the information necessary for a test model or, if they are test-ready, they can serve as a test model. Second, they can be used to develop an oracle

or, if they are formal and have sufficient information, they can be used as an oracle (see Section 18.2.5, Organic Oracles).

Most OOA/D methodologies provide a loose graphical syntax and symbol
set. This is accompanied by minimal guidance for impressionistic rendering of
behavior and structure that happen to come to the designer's attention. These
are **cartoons**: they do not demand complete information, consistent usage, or
useful integration with other facets of a model. Cartoons are useful for sketching, refining, and documenting solutions, but they are not test-ready: they lack
content and consistency necessary to produce executable test cases.

> A minimal expectation for specifications is that they should be consistent: an in-
> consistent specification is one from which some statement and its negation can both
> be derived; such a specification necessarily allows any property to be derived and
> thus fails to say anything useful at all [Rushby 97, 4].

Test cases can be manually prepared from cartoons, but the tester must
make interpretations to do so. Cartoon behavior models are a necessary result
of OOA/D methodologies that lack a formal and consistent meta-model. Cartoon OOA/D methodologies and models pose several obstacles to testing:

- They are ambiguous (or tolerate ambiguity) in critical elements like
  states, events, actions, and transitions. The partial information in a
  cartoon model permits many possible interpretations.
- They are incomplete, in that no explicit definition exists for the necessary components of a well-formed behavior model.
- They are fragmentary, in that elements of the model are only loosely
  integrated with one another. The OMT approach [Rumbaigh+91] is
  notably egregious in its multiplicity of disconnects [Bourdeau 95].

Present-day computer-aided software engineering (CASE) tools for OOA/D
contribute to this problem. Nearly all CASE implementations of methodologies
are incorrect, distorted, and incomplete. Faced with notational ambiguity and
user indifference, CASE implementers devise arbitrary work-arounds. The
result is, with a few exceptions, "tools" that are barely adequate for rendering
annotated sketches and pose hard-coded obstacles to developing test-ready
models.

The criterion for model testability is that we can devise and program an algorithm that will produce ready-to-run test cases with only the information in

the model. The model should support both manual and automated test generation. A testable model must meet the following requirements:

- It is a complete and accurate reflection of the kind of implementations to be tested. The model must represent all features to be exercised.
- It abstracts detail that would make the cost of testing prohibitive.
- It preserves detail that is essential for revealing faults and demonstrating conformance.
- It represents all events (of the state model) so that we can generate these events, typically as messages sent to the IUT.
- It represents all actions (of the state model) so that we can determine whether a required action has been produced.
- It represents state so that we have an executable means to determine what state has (or has not) been achieved.

For example, a testable representation of state requires that guarded transitions have an explicit syntax, allow interval-triggered transitions, and provide an unambiguous and testable definition of state. Formal models and notation can express certain types of processing very succinctly and leave little or no room for varying interpretation. Formal and semi-formal representation are both amenable to automation; they can therefore be queried, verified, and searched with speed and accuracy. Nevertheless, informal models remain popular because of their practical nature.

Although meeting the requirements for a testable model might seem to be asking a lot from many practitioners, it is really no different from what must be done to test any software system. One must decide which inputs to use and specify a means to judge whether the response is acceptable. Although highly skilled testers, like professional musicians, can improvise test cases at the keyboard, they rely on an internalized test-ready model. Part II presents models that can be internalized, if you are so inclined. Although the combinational and state models have a mathematically formal basis, they do not require any quantitative skill beyond that needed to write good code. If you can formulate requirements as well-structured objects, then you can use the test models in Part II. In addition, these models can be implemented in test software, providing leverage for the testers' creativity.

5.1.5 Consequences

In promoting the use of rigorously formal abstract data models to support testing, Barbey noted:

> Formal specifications are more effective sources for test sets than analysis and design models, because formal specifications are easily mapped to the unit under test, and do not require extra work to gather the information. This self-containment makes it easy to generate test sets automatically. It is also easier to infer the expected results from a formal specification than from analysis and design models. To obtain the formal specification, it is, however, often necessary to go through some informal modeling steps like the Fusion analysis and design phases, and the formal specifications can be a possibly refined summary of these models. Specifications need not be formal. They can be written in natural language. However, the advantage of formal specifications is that it is easier to check their completeness and their consistency [Barbey 97, 68].

Table 5.1 suggests the consequences of choosing a modeling approach [Binder+92]. The desirable attributes are adapted from the IEEE standard for software requirements specifications [IEEE 830]. If an approach can interfere with meeting an objective, it is termed an obstacle. If it does not influence the

TABLE 5.1   Effects of Formal and Informal Test Methods

Test Model Characteristic	Effect of Informal Approaches	Effect of Formal Approaches
Unambiguous	Obstacle	Enabling
Complete		
No omissions	Neutral/Enabling	Neutral
Minimal	Neutral/Enabling	Neutral
Problem-oriented	Neutral/Enabling	Neutral
Verifiable	Obstacle/Enabling	Enabling
Feasible	Obstacle/Enabling	Neutral/Enabling
Consistent		
Absence of conflicts	Obstacle	Enabling
Structural errors	Obstacle	Enabling
Behavioral errors	Obstacle	Enabling
Protocol errors	Obstacle	Enabling
Modifiable	Neutral/Obstacle	Enabling/Obstacle
Traceable	Enabling/Neutral	Neutral/Enabling
Usable later	Enabling	Neutral/Enabling

process, it is termed neutral. If it eases an objective, it is termed enabling. If circumstances can significantly influence the outcome, then the most likely outcome is given first.

Informal methods are neutral or enabling for validation. They tend to reflect the user's point of view, making it easier to identify omissions. On the other hand, users may have blind spots, which informal approaches may reinforce. Formality may obscure usability, cost, or effectiveness of a proposed feature or function. In these circumstances, the apparent precision of an abstract model can be mistakenly equated with operational correctness.

With respect to verification, informal methods are obstacles or neutral and formal methods are enabling. Informal representations are often ambiguous, redundant, and inconsistent. They are not easily subjected to computable checks. Neither formal nor informal methods alone can achieve all goals. Even when both approaches are combined, support for completeness remains neutral. It is not possible to tell if the user's goals and expectations have been fully elicited, represented, and modeled from solution space representations alone.

5.2 Bibliographic Notes

The case for model-based testing is argued in [Beizer 90, Beizer 95]. The role of models in software engineering and surveys of approaches are provided in [Thayer+90, Davis 93]. Webster presents criteria for characterizing formality of software engineering models, classifies about 50 meta-models as formal or informal, and outlines the consequences of their use [Webster 87]. An analysis of the relationships between informal narrative requirements and formal models appears in [Binder+92]. The analysis of cartoons and model testability is adapted from [Binder 96b, Binder 96i].

An insightful comparison of structured and object-oriented modeling techniques is presented in [Fichman+92]. A framework for comparative analysis of OOA/D appears in [Monarchi+92]. An introduction to object-oriented modeling techniques can be found in [Wilke 94] and a detailed comparative survey in [Graham 94]. See the Bibliographic Notes for Chapter 8 for UML sources.

Chapter 6   Combinational Models

Overview

Many applications must select output actions by evaluating combinations of input conditions. Such requirements can appear at method, class, cluster, subsystem, and use case scope. Combinational logic provides an effective test model for these kinds of condition-action relationships. This chapter explains several forms of combinational logic and shows how they may be used to develop test models. Model verification techniques and six strategies for producing test cases are presented. The considerations for choosing a test generation approach are discussed.

6.1 How Combinational Models Support Testing

A combinational test model uses a decision table to represent the implementation under test (IUT). Modeling with decision tables is straightforward—definitions, procedures, and examples are provided in following sections. Decision tables have been used in many software engineering methodologies and in all major types of applications (including data processing, embedded real-time, scientific, and knowledge-based applications). They are an ideal representation for a test model for several reasons:

- They provide a straightforward representation of requirements where a particular response or response subset is to be selected by evaluating many related conditions. Nearly every application system has at least a few capabilities that can be modeled in this way.

- When such capabilities are required, combinational test models are effective for revealing bugs in their implementation and their specification.
- They can support test design at any scope, from method to system.
- They can be used for implementation or responsibility-based test design.
- They support manual or automated generation of test cases.

The large body of knowledge about combinational logic for hardware design and test provides a rigorous mathematical foundation for testing software systems with decision tables. Software testing strategies based on combinational logic were first published in the 1970s. These software approaches have incorporated hardware test strategies in varying degrees and even made some significant improvements (see the Bibliographic Notes section for a brief survey).

Decision tables support several test design patterns. *Combinational Function Test* shows how they apply at method scope. *Extended Use Case Test* can produce a test suite at any scope for which a use case can be defined. The basic strategy can be applied with many other patterns when the IUT can be modeled with combinational logic. The basic steps to software testing with combinational logic models are as follows:

1. Model the implementation or capability under test with a decision table.
2. Validate the decision table model.
3. Derive the logic function (optional).
4. Choose a test suite generation strategy.
5. Generate test cases.

Each step can be accomplished in several ways. This chapter presents techniques that will work for all small to medium-small models and may also prove useful for some large to very large models. Certain advanced techniques that are appropriate to large and very large models are beyond the scope of this book.

This chapter provides

- A concise guide to developing test models with decision tables.
- A brief review of the applicable math for developing the logic function.
- Guidelines for model validation.
- Several heuristic and formal test generation strategies.
- Considerations for choosing an approach.

6.2 How to Develop a Decision Table

6.2.1 Basic Approach

A decision table is indicated as a test model when the implementation under test has the following characteristics:

- One of several distinct responses is to be selected according to distinct cases of input variables.
- These cases can be modeled by mutually exclusive Boolean expressions on the input variables.
- The response to be produced does not depend on the order in which input variables are set or evaluated.
- The response to be produced does not depend on prior input or output.

If the implementation under test meets these criteria, then a decision table model will be useful for testing. The tester may be given this information as part of the system specification or may need to develop a testing model. Many strategies exist for deriving decision tables. The basic approach involves these steps:

1. Identify the decision variables and conditions.
2. Identify the resultant actions to be selected or controlled.
3. Identify which actions should be produced in response to particular combinations of conditions.
4. Derive the logic function for the model to validate its completeness and consistency.

The analytical process is the same whether testing takes place at class, cluster, or system scope. This analysis is typically iterative—conditions suggest outcomes, outcomes suggest conditions, and so on. As with most test design approaches, simply developing the model often uncovers omissions, ambiguities, and bugs. Several COTS tools are available for decision table modeling and verification.

6.2.2 Components and Structure

A **decision table** has two parts: the condition section and the action section. The **condition section** lists conditions and combinations of conditions. **Decision variables** are inputs or environmental factors referenced in the condition section. A **condition** expresses a relationship among decision variables that must be resolvable to true or false. Each unique combination of conditions and actions (represented as a single row or column) is a **variant**. When all of the individual conditions in one variant are true, then the corresponding action should be produced.

The **action section** lists responses to be produced when corresponding combinations of conditions are true. Any number of resultant actions may be specified, and any combination of actions may be associated with any particular condition variant. Resultant actions are determined by the current values of the decision variables—past inputs/outputs do not affect which action may result.[1] The order in which inputs arrive and are evaluated is irrelevant. The action selected is independent of input order and the order in which conditions are evaluated. This is like a simple spin lock, shown in Figure 6.1, which will open when the correct number is dialed in, no matter which dial is set first, second, or third.

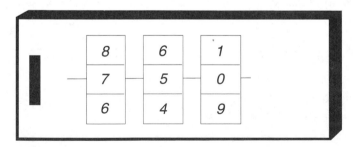

FIGURE 6.1 Spin lock.

---

1. Although the current state or other "memory" can be modeled as a decision variable, it is usually more effective to model sequential behavior with a state machine (see Chapter 7).

The decision table typically does not include a detailed specification for the process, algorithm, or implementation of the actions. Nevertheless, testability and error prevention are eased when a testable specification for each action exists. Each combination of conditions must be unique, but actions may appear more than once.

Small tables are easier to use. A fully expanded table of n decision variables has 2^n variants. Although the full size may be masked by implicit variants, adding one decision variable doubles the size of the truth table; removing one variable halves the size of the truth table. Sometimes large tables can be partitioned and tested separately.

TABLE 6.1   Insurance Renewal Decision Table

| Variant | Condition Section | | Action Section | | |
	Number of Claims	Insured Age	Premium Increase ($)	Send Warning	Cancel
1	0	25 or younger	50	No	No
2		26 or older	25	No	No
3	1	25 or younger	100	Yes	No
4		26 or older	50	No	No
5	2 to 4	25 or younger	400	Yes	No
6		26 or older	200	Yes	No
7	5 or more	Any	0	No	Yes

Source: Adapted from an example in [Weinberg 78].

6.2.3   The Auto Insurance Renewal Model

The requirements for processing the annual renewal of a hypothetical auto insurance policy are modeled with the decision table shown in Table 6.1 This decision table represents business rules used to cancel or renew a policy, determine the premium increase for a renewal, and optionally send a cancellation warning letter if several claims have been made. The decision variables are the present age of the insured person and the number of claims made by the insured in the last year. The actions are the premium increase amount, generation of a warning letter, and renewal or cancellation of the policy. The implicit logical operator between the conditions is *and*; all conditions in the row must be true for the corresponding action to be taken. Variants (rows) are interpreted as follows:

- If the insured had no claims in the last year and is age 25 or younger, the increase is $50. No letter is sent (variant 1).
- If the insured had no claims in the last year and is age 26 or older, the increase is $25. No letter is sent (variant 2).
- If the insured made one claim in the last year and is age 25 or younger, the increase is $100. A warning letter is sent (variant 3).
- If the insured made one claim in the last year and is age 26 or older, the increase is $50. No letter is sent (variant 4).
- If the insured made two, three, or four claims in the last year and is age 25 or younger, the increase is $400. A warning letter is sent (variant 5).
- If the insured made two, three, or four claims in the last year and is age 26 or older, the increase is $200. A warning letter is sent (variant 6).
- If the insured made five or more claims in the last year, the policy is canceled. There is no increase and no warning (variant 7).

Decision tables may be column-wise; that is, each condition set/action set may be given vertically instead of horizontally. Table 6.2 shows an equivalent column-wise decision table.

Conditions and actions may also be represented as a **decision tree** (Figure 6.2). Some research indicates that trees may be easier to understand [Subramanian+92]. There is no essential informational difference. Decision tables are more readily implemented as data structures used in test automation.

TABLE 6.2   Insurance Renewal Decision Table Column-wise Format

		Variant						
		1	2	3	4	5	6	7
Condition Section	Number of claims	0	0	1	1	2 to 4	2 to 4	5 or more
	Insured age	25 or younger	26 or older	25 or younger	26 or older	25 or younger	26 or older	Any
Action Section	Premium increase ($)	50	25	100	50	400	200	0
	Send warning	No	No	Yes	No	Yes	Yes	No
	Cancel	No	No	No	No	No	No	Yes

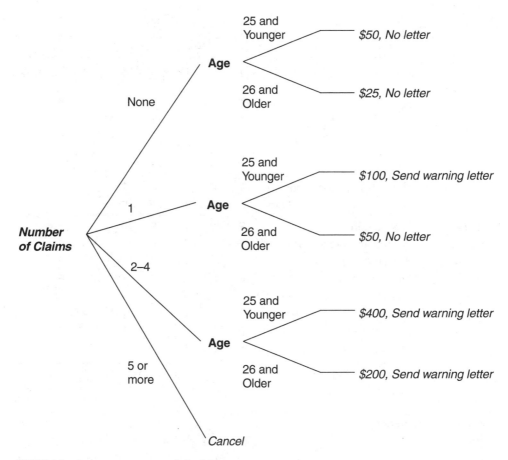

FIGURE 6.2   Insurance renewal decision tree.

The systematic enumeration of variants in a decision table means that you are less likely to overlook or omit a case. Conversely, the ease with which a decision tree can hide variants makes errors more likely. The tabular format is therefore a better choice.

6.2.4 Don't Care, Don't Know, Can't Happen

A decision table with n conditions can have at most 2^n variants, although there are usually fewer than 2^n variants. For example, six conditions appear in the insurance table for $2^6 = 64$ possible variants, but there are only seven **explicit variants**. Each action must be produced by at least one variant. If more than one combination of conditions can result in the same action, then explicit variants

TABLE 6.3   Insurance Renewal Decision Table, Truth Table Format

	Decision Variable	Condition	Variant						
			1	2	3	4	5	6	7
Condition Section	Number of claims	0	T	T	F	F	F	F	F
		1	F	F	T	T	F	F	F
		2–4	F	F	F	F	T	T	F
		5 +	F	F	F	F	F	F	T
	Insured age	25 or younger	T	F	T	F	T	F	DC
		26 or older	F	T	F	T	F	T	DC
Action Section	Premium Increase = 0		F	F	F	F	F	F	T
	Premium increase = 25		F	T	F	F	F	F	F
	Premium increase = 50		T	F	F	T	F	F	F
	Premium increase = 100		F	F	T	F	F	F	F
	Premium increase = 200		F	F	F	F	F	T	F
	Premium increase = 400		F	F	F	F	T	F	F
	Send warning		F	F	T	F	T	T	F
	Cancel		F	F	F	F	F	F	T

Key: F = false, T = true, DC = don't care

must be provided for these combinations. The decision tables shown in Tables 6.1 and 6.2 abstract the truth values for each condition combination. Table 6.3 shows each explicit variant and the truth values associated with each condition.

A variant that can be inferred but is not given is an **implicit variant**. For the insurance renewal table, there are 54 implicit variants. Implicit variants result from valid abbreviations (don't care and type-safe exclusions) or incorrect modeling (can't happen and don't know).

In a decision table, a **don't care** designates a condition that, for a particular variant, may be either true or false without changing the action. The variant is selected (or suppressed) regardless of the truth value of the don't care condition(s). This legitimate shorthand avoids enumeration of truth values with the same outcome.[2] Don't care entries simplify table specification. For example,

---

2. A don't care in the context of logic (hardware) design has a somewhat different meaning. Boolean variables represent input or output lines, which can carry a signal of logical one or zero. A don't care can refer to (1) a signal value that cannot be produced (it is physically impossible), (2) an input line for which the circuit output is independent of its signal value given values on all other input lines, or (3) an output line where either value is acceptable. A truth table with don't cares is said to be *incompletely specified.*

when more than four claims have been filed, the age of the insured is a don't care condition—the policy will be canceled at any age. That is, we do not need to specify both conditions for age because the action is the same in either case. In the boiler control example (see Table 6.4 on page 135), *IgnitionEnable* cannot be true when *NormalPressure* is false. So when *NormalPressure* is false, the values of *CallForHeat, DamperShut,* and *ManualMode* are all don't cares.

A variant with don't care decision variables can correspond to several implementation cases:

1. The inputs are necessary, but have no effect for a particular variant. They cannot be omitted or suppressed, but are (should be) irrelevant for values that correspond to the variant. For example, arguments in a method interface cannot be omitted, but they may not be used in all cases. Some programming languages support short-circuit predicate evaluation; so while the variables in an expression cannot be omitted, they are sometimes ignored. For example, given a predicate

   ```
   if ((w > x)||(w > (y/z)))
   ```

   When w > x, the evaluation of the expression to the right of the || is skipped, so y and z can be considered don't cares.

2. The inputs may be omitted, but have no effect if supplied for some particular input values. For example, suppose a command has three variables a, b, and c. When a = 999, no values for b and c are necessary. If b and c are given, they are treated as comments. So when a = 999, b and c are don't cares.

3. A **type-safe exclusion** arises when several conditions are defined for a nonbinary decision variable, which can hold only one value at a time. For example, the number of claims cannot be simultaneously 0 and 3— if one value obtains, all others are necessarily excluded. We need not enumerate excluded combinations. For example, it would not make sense to model a variant where the insured's age is both younger and older than 25. A type-safe exclusion is implicit for binary (Boolean) variables.

Thus only the mutually exclusive cases of type-safe exclusion should be considered "impossible." A specification using don't cares as a shorthand need not (and probably should not) make assumptions about what is and is not "impossible." The can't happen and don't know fallacies often arise from unwarranted assumptions about so-called impossible situations.

A **can't happen** condition reflects an assumption that some inputs are mutually exclusive, that some inputs cannot be produced by the environment, or that the implementation is structured so as to prevent evaluation. Can't happen conditions are *not* the same as type-safe exclusions or don't care conditions. Suppose that each condition defined for a certain number of claims (0, 1, 2 to 4, 5 or more) was implemented by a separate variable that could be set independently. One might be tempted to assume that an inconsistent setting of these variables "can't happen" and conclude that there is no need to specify or test the corresponding variants. However, can't happen conditions do occur because of programming errors or unanticipated effects of changes in hardware and software configurations. The appropriate response to a can't happen is typically *not* the first action that chances to fire. This kind of assumption is a chronic source of bugs.[3] The failure of the guidance software in the Ariane 5 rocket and its subsequent destruction and uninsured loss of $363 million resulted from this kind of error [Jézéquel+96b].

A **don't know** condition reflects an incomplete model. The applicability of a condition or a desired outcome may be unknown for many reasons. For instance, original documentation for the system under test may be unavailable. The requirements for a variant may be incomplete or "to be determined." In decision tables, a don't know condition may hide within a decision variable with an unspecified boundary. For example, the insurance decision table tells us nothing about what to do if the insured age reaches some improbable value (e.g., 3 or 300). Although unspecified, something will happen when implementation reaches the gap left by the don't know condition.

Effective testing strategies have been developed for legitimate don't care conditions. We can usually rely on type-safe mechanisms with confidence. However, a can't happen condition is a dubious assumption promoted to a certainty (e.g., a developer concludes that it *can't happen* that an auto insurance policy will be issued for a person older than 100). A "don't know" is similar: "I *don't know* what should happen if we get a 100-year-old insured, so I just won't specify the result." Of course, *something* will happen if a 100-year-old insured is evaluated for renewal—and it is unlikely that this accidental result will be appropriate. A can't happen or don't know is nearly always a specification

---

3. For example, a common programming error occurs in nested if expressions. When the first predicate in a nested if-else expression excludes all x less than 100, then it "can't happen" that x is less than 100 in the nested predicates.

bug with several relatives in the implementation. The tester's first response should be to insist on a specification free of can't happen and don't know conditions. The typical solution is to define a default action to be produced when none of the explicit variants applies. If this is impractical, then testing that exercises these undefined cases is warranted.

6.2.5 Decision Tables in OO Development

Decision tables can be used to model or specify requirements at any scope of an object-oriented system. The responsibilities modeled in a decision table need not correspond to a single case statement. For example, decision tables can model implementation control flow relationships (see Chapter 10) and provide an implementation-independent model of class responsibilities. They may require many object collaborations. Yet whatever the implementation scope, the same decision table model may be used for testing.

At method scope, a decision table can model a nested if or case construct (the `switch` expression of C++, Java, and Objective-C, the `Case` statement in Ada 95, the Eiffel `elseif` and `inspect` instructions, and the block selector in Smalltalk).

At class scope, a class responsibility based on distinct cases or enumerations can be modeled by a decision table—for example, a method that assigns a carrier to a shipment based on weight, size, material type, and maximum transit time, or a method that renders a graphic object based on parameters for illumination model, transparency, and output device. The insurance renewal responsibility could be implemented at class scope with a persistent Java class `AutoPolicy`: as the following fragment shows.

```
class public AutoPolicy {
    AutoPolicy(Date insuredDOB);
    public void      makeClaim();
    public void      annualRenewal();
    public Money     getPremiumRate();
    public bool      isCanceled();
    public bool      isActive();
}
```

When a new insurance policy is issued, an `AutoPolicy` object is created that holds the insured person's date of birth, policy anniversary date, premium rate, and the number of claims made (initially zero.) When a `makeClaim` message is sent, the program increments the number of claims. When the `annualRenew` message is sent, the object evaluates the insured's age and number of claims. If the policy is renewed, it increases the premium rate. If not, the premium rate is set to zero, and isCanceled will respond true. In some situations, a warning letter may be generated.

Decision tables are necessary to produce testable use cases, which can then be used to develop tests at subsystem and system scope. *Extended Use Case Test* uses decision tables to define relationships among use case variables. This model supports systematic production of tests for each use case.

Although decision tables are widely found in software engineering analysis and design models, I know of no OOA/D technique that makes explicit use of them. The UML Activity Diagram decision notation can be employed to represent a decision tree, which is equivalent to a decision table. Figure 6.3 shows how the insurance renewal requirements would be represented in the UML. The preceding comments about the limitations of a decision tree as a combinational test model apply here.

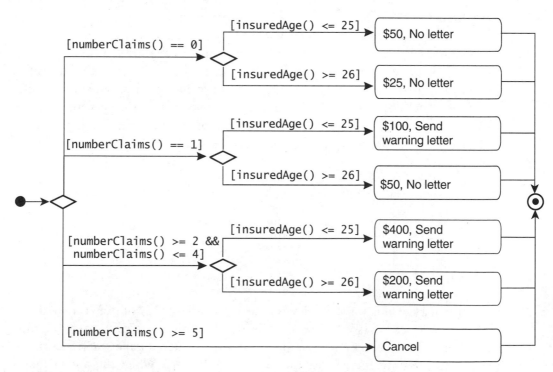

FIGURE 6.3 UML Activity Diagram representation of decision table.

6.3 Deriving the Logic Function

◇ 6.3.1 Boolean Expressions

Boolean algebra is a mathematical system of operations on variables that are either true (value 1) or false (value 0). It is named for its originator, the nineteenth-century mathematician George Boole. The **Boolean operators** are • (and), + (or),[4] ⊕ (exclusive or), and ~ (not). The *and* operator is customarily omitted, so AB is read as "A and B." Negated variables are traditionally denoted by an overbar: $\overline{A}$ is read "not A," $\overline{AB}$ is "not (A and B)," $\overline{A+B}$ is "not (A or B)," and so on. The inline *not* operator ~ is used here because it is more easily parsed. Parentheses denote scope when ~ applies to two or more variables. A **Boolean formula** is composed of Boolean operators and Boolean variables. A **Boolean equation** asserts equality of two formulas.

Nearly all programming languages implement some form of Boolean variables, operations, and formulas. For example, an expression containing the Java logical *and* operator **&&** evaluates as true only if both its operands evaluate as true. A **logic function** (also Boolean function or switching function) maps from n Boolean input variables to m Boolean output variables. Output values are determined by binding truth values to input variables and then applying the function's formula.

A **truth table** enumerates all possible input and output values for a Boolean function; given n Boolean input variables, there are always 2^n rows in its truth table. The function is the essential definition; the table is its enumeration. Table entries may be represented as rows or columns (rows are used here). Each row is an **input vector**. An **input vector number** is the decimal integer equivalent to the input vector bit pattern: 0000 is vector 0, 1001 is vector 9, and so on.

A **combinational** function, system, model, circuit, or other component has only one state—the present values of its inputs. It does not include any representation of previous input or output and therefore can produce only output determined by combinations of current input. Digital circuits that implement Boolean functions are called **combinational logic**.[5] Formulas and corresponding truth tables for several basic combinational functions are given in Figure 6.4.

---

4. In programming and mathematics the Boolean *or* is used in the same sense as the everyday meaning of "and/or"—either x or y, or both x and y—as in "Stop if the light is red or there is a moose in your way." This meaning is not the same as the sense that requires a mutually exclusive choice, as in "Do you want decaf or regular?"

5. A combinational circuit does not contain feedback loops or data registers, so it can react to only current inputs. This type of circuit is typically implemented with *nand* components, which are logically equivalent to *and, or,* and *not* logic components.

Boolean Function	Gate Name/ Symbol	Propositional Calculus	Set Operation	C++/Java Logical Operator Expression	Bitwise Truth Table		
					A	B	Z
Or $Z = A + B$	Or	Disjunction $A \vee B$	Union $A \cup B$	Logical Or a || b	0	0	0
					0	1	1
					1	0	1
					1	1	1
And $Z = AB$	And	Conjunction $A \wedge B$	Intersection $A \cap B$	Logical And a && b	0	0	0
					0	1	0
					1	0	0
					1	1	1
Exclusive Or $Z = A \oplus B$	Xor	Exclusive disjunction $A \veebar B$	— $(A \cup B) \cup (A \cap B)'$	— (!a && b) || (a && !b)	0	0	0
					0	1	1
					1	0	1
					1	1	0
Not ~A	Inverter	Negation $\neg A$	Complement A'	Not !a	0		1
					1		0
— $Z = \sim(AB)$	Nand	| (Sheffer Stroke) $\neg (A \wedge B)$	— $(A \cap B)'$	— !(a&&b)	0	0	1
					0	1	1
					1	0	1
					1	1	0
— $Z = \sim(A + B)$	Nor	↓ (Peirce Arrow) $\neg (A \vee B)$	— $(A \cup B)'$	— !(a||b)	0	0	1
					0	1	0
					1	0	0
					1	1	0
— ~AB Z	Inhibitor	— $\neg A \wedge B$	Difference $A' \cap B$ $A - B$	— !a && b	0	0	0
					0	1	1
					1	0	0
					1	1	0

FIGURE 6.4   Equivalent logic expressions.

Table 6.4 shows an example of a four-variable truth table that models the control action to enable or disable ignition of a boiler. The four inputs (*NormalPressure*, *CallForHeat*, *DamperShut*, and *ManualMode*) are binary and can be represented with Boolean variables *A*, *B*, *C*, and *D*, respectively. *NormalPressure* is true if the pressure in the boiler is within safe operating limits. *CallForHeat* is on when a thermostat senses that the ambient temperature has fallen below the set point. *DamperShut* is on when the exhaust duct is closed (the duct must be open before igniting the burner). *ManualMode* is true when manual operation has been selected to override automatic control. The single output *IgnitionEnable* is also binary; it is represented by *Z*. The logic function for this table is

$$Z = A(B{\sim}C + D)$$

TABLE 6.4   Boiler Control Truth Table

Input Vector Number	NormalPressure A	CallForHeat B	DamperShut C	ManualMode D	IgnitionEnable Z
0	0	0	0	0	0
1	0	0	0	1	0
2	0	0	1	0	0
3	0	0	1	1	0
4	0	1	0	0	0
5	0	1	0	1	0
6	0	1	1	0	0
7	0	1	1	1	0
8	1	0	0	0	0
9	1	0	0	1	1
10	1	0	1	0	0
11	1	0	1	1	1
12	1	1	0	0	1
13	1	1	0	1	1
14	1	1	1	0	0
15	1	1	1	1	1

Truth Value Interpretation

Truth Value	NormalPressure	CallForHeat	DamperShut	ManualMode	IgnitionEnable
0	No	Off	No	No	On
1	Yes	On	Yes	Yes	Off

This function means the ignition is enabled when either (1) the boiler is at *NormalPressure, CallForHeat* is on, and *DamperShut* is not true (*AB~C* is true), or (2) the boiler is at *NormalPressure* and *ManualMode* is on (*AD* is true). This function could be directly implemented as follows:

```
if (  (normalPressure && callForHeat && !damperShut) ||
      (normalPressure || manualMode) ) {
    ignitionEnable = true;
}
else {
    ignitionEnable = false;
}
```

6.3.2 Truth Tables versus Decision Tables

Although the terms *decision table* and *truth table* are often taken to mean the same thing, they are not interchangeable. As we will see, the appropriate testing strategy differs. A truth table is a special case of a decision table, in that all cells in a decision table must be resolvable to true or false. Boolean variables are limited to 1 or 0, which may represent true or false, yes or no, on or off, and so on. Boolean formulas and truth tables are directly applicable when we can represent the factors of interest by a binary variable. However, we often want to model more complex conditions and output actions. Decision variables and output actions may be arbitrarily complex variables defined from arbitrarily complex types and combined in arbitrarily complex predicate expressions.

6.3.3 Elements of Boolean Expressions

An occurrence of an individual variable in a formula is a **literal**. A string of literals connected by the *and* operation is a **product term**. A formula in **sum-of-products** form consists of product terms related by *or* operators (summing). Any Boolean formula may be rewritten in sum-of-products form by applying the laws of Boolean algebra given in Figure 6.5. These laws are similar to those used in basic algebra to manipulate formulas. For example, we can rewrite the boiler formula $A(B~C + D)$ in sum-of-products form by applying the distributive law:

$$A(B~C + D) = AB~C + AD$$

$A + A = A$ $AA \quad = A$	Idempotent
$A + 1 = 1$ $A + 0 = A$ $A \bullet 1 = A$ $A \bullet 0 = 0$	Identity
$(A + B) + C = A + (B + C)$ $(AB)C \qquad = A\,(BC)$	Associative
$AB \quad = BA$ $A + B = B + A$	Commutative
$A + (BC) \qquad = (A + B) \bullet (A + C)$ $A\,(B + C) \qquad = AB + AC$ $(A+B) \bullet (C+D) = AC + AD + BC + BD$	Distributive
$A + {\sim}A = 1$ $A \bullet {\sim}A = 0$ ${\sim}{\sim}A \quad = A$ ${\sim}1 \qquad = 0$ ${\sim}0 \qquad = 1$	Complement
${\sim}(A+B) = {\sim}A{\sim}B$ ${\sim}(AB) \quad = {\sim}A + {\sim}B$	De Morgan's Laws
$A + AB \qquad = A$ $A\,(A+B) \qquad = A$ $A+({\sim}AB) \qquad = A + B$ $AB + AC + B{\sim}C = AC + B{\sim}C$	Absorption

FIGURE 6.5 Laws for reducing Boolean formulas.

The rewritten formula has two product terms: $AB{\sim}C$ and AD. Each term in a sum-of-products formula is a sufficient condition for a true output and is called an **implicant**. When any product term is true, the output variable must also be true (1). For example, when $AB{\sim}C$ is true ($A = 1$, $B = 1$, and $C = 0$), then $Z = 1$ regardless of D. When AD is true ($A = 1$, $D = 1$), then $Z = 1$ regardless of B or C.

A **minterm** is a formula with a literal for each variable in a function that evaluates to true for that function. Minterms can be obtained by inspecting a truth table or by expanding the terms of a sum-of-products formula. For example, the term $AB\sim C$ does not include a literal for D and $\sim D$, so the minterms for $AB\sim C$ are

$$AB\sim CD$$
$$AB\sim C\sim D$$

Similarly, expanding AD gives

$$ABCD$$
$$AB\sim CD$$
$$A\sim BCD$$
$$A\sim B\sim CD$$

The same minterm may result in more than one product term—for example, $AB\sim CD$. Thus, for the logic function defined by $AB\sim C + AD$, there are five minterms:

$$AB\sim CD$$
$$AB\sim C\sim D$$
$$ABCD$$
$$A\sim BCD$$
$$A\sim B\sim CD$$

The set of all minterms is exactly the set of truth table rows that evaluate to true (compare the preceding minterms to Table 6.4).

A **cube** is a compressed, partial truth table. Suppose that for some rows of a truth table, certain variables do not affect the output value of the function. These rows may be compressed by replacing the truth value of the nonaffecting variables with a wild card. The cube is written as an input vector with wild cards followed by a vertical bar and the output value. For example, the four cubes of the boiler control table are as follows:

$$110x \mid 1$$
$$1xx1 \mid 1$$
$$0xxx \mid 0$$
$$10x0 \mid 0$$

The wild card x indicates that the corresponding variable may be either 1 or 0 without changing the output value (slashed zero $\emptyset$ is also used). In the first cube, the input vectors 1101 and 1100 both evaluate to 1. Variable D is said to be a **don't care** for the first cube but not for the second.

A cube is a **prime implicant** if (1) all outputs for the cube are true (it must be an implicant) and (2) the cube is not a subset of any other cube. For example, consider the boiler control logic function $Z = AB{\sim}C + AD$. Both terms are implicants and both terms are cubes, so they may be satisfied by more than one input vector. The input set for the first term is

$$AB{\sim}C = 110x = \{1101, 1100\}$$

and the input set for the second term is

$$AD = 1xx1 = \{1001, 1011, 1101, 1111\}$$

Term 1 is not a subset of term 2; term 2 is not a subset of term 1. Both terms are therefore prime implicants. Identification of prime implicants is the first step in specifying the logic function. **KV matrices** (discussed later) are a straightforward technique for identifing them.

There are many equivalent formulas for the logic function of a truth table. We can easily express a function as a sum of all the minterms. For example, the boiler control model may be written as

$$Z = AB{\sim}CD + AB{\sim}C{\sim}D + ABCD + A{\sim}BCD + A{\sim}B{\sim}CD$$

But as we have already seen, identical behavior is specified by

$$Z = AB{\sim}C + AD$$

Both formulas are equivalent in that they yield the same result for all inputs. **Logic minimization** refers to techniques used to derive compact but equivalent Boolean expressions that have been studied and used extensively in development of digital logic hardware.[6] In software testing, logic minimization has several uses.

- A minimal expression can be covered with fewer tests.
- Automatic test generation algorithms can run faster.
- Derivation of a minimal expression may reveal omissions or inconsistencies in the specification.
- Working with a small expression is easier than a large truth table.

Table 6.5 lists some techniques for logic minimization.

- Boolean functions of a few variables may be derived by inspection.
- The individual terms corresponding to each row in a truth table may be transformed into a minimized sum-of-products formula using a KV matrix. A brief overview of this method follows.

TABLE 6.5 Maximum Number of Variables in Logic Minimization Techniques

Initial Development	Logic Minimization Technique	Approximate Upper Limit on Number of Boolean Variables
—	Inspection	3
1950s	KV matrix	5
1970s	Cause–effect graph	8
1950–1960s	Quine-McCluskey method	9
1960s	Starner-Dietmeyer	14
1980s	Exact minimization	20–25
1980s	Heuristic minimization	20–25

Source: Adapted from [Devedas 97].

---

6. Logic designers use several logic minimization techniques to solve the trade-offs in gate-level implementation of a Boolean function. Each Boolean operator typically corresponds to a logic gate consisting of several components (e.g, transistors). Each occurrence of a literal in the formula typically corresponds to an input line (a wire) for a gate. Generally, the number of gates determines the number of components. The design that results in the lowest manufacturing cost is often the one with the fewest gates, rather than the fewest inputs (literals). Each level (an intermediate gate) increases the circuit delay, providing another design constraint. Minimizing delay, however, typically does not minimize the number of gates or simplify the gates needed.

- Cause–effect graphs and Boolean algebra can be used to derive functions for small to medium-size problems. The upper limit depends on the analyst's ability to manipulate lengthy Boolean formulas. This technique is presented later in this chapter.

- For six or more variables, automated implementations of the Quine-McCluskey algorithm (a maximum of 9 variables) or the Starner-Deitmeyer algorithm (a maximum 14 variables) are effective. Many tools are available to support these algorithms—some are available gratis on the World Wide Web.

- Advanced exact and heuristic logic minimization algorithms can deal with functions having as many as 25 variables [Devadas 97].

◇ 6.3.4 Karnaugh-Veitch Matrix

The **Karnaugh-Veitch matrix** (also known as the KV matrix, Karnaugh map, or Karnaugh-Veitch chart) is the basis of a straightforward graphical technique to derive a minimal logic function. This approach is effective for Boolean functions with five or fewer variables. Specific matrices that correspond to the number of input variables being analyzed are used. Figure 6.6 shows the KV matrices for two, three, and four input variables. In a KV matrix, each row and column represents a variable or a pair of variables. Each cell represents the output value for one input vector. The cells in the matrices on the left side of Figure 6.6 show the input vector for the cell; matrices on the right side show the input vector number. Note that the left-to-right, top-to-bottom order of bit values is not strictly increasing.

The minimal logic function for a truth table is identified by locating adjacent cell groups that have a 1 (true) output. Each group becomes a term in the function. We'll use the boiler control model to illustrate. The steps are shown in Figure 6.7.

1. Select the KV matrix that corresponds to the number of input variables. The boiler control model has four input variables, so we use the four-variable KV matrix.

2. Set up the initial matrix. Write a 1 in the cell for each corresponding implicant. The implicants for the boiler control model are input vectors 9, 11, 12, 13, and 15.

Cells Show Input Vector   **Cells Show Input Vector Number**

Two-Variable KV Matrix

	A 0	A 1
B 0	Z(00)	Z(10)
B 1	Z(01)	Z(11)

Z = F(AB)

	A 0	A 1
B 0	0	2
B 1	1	3

Three-Variable KV Matrix

	AB 00	01	11	10
C 0	Z(000)	Z(010)	Z(110)	Z(100)
C 1	Z(001)	Z(011)	Z(111)	Z(101)

Z = F(ABC)

	AB 00	01	11	10
C 0	0	2	6	4
C 1	1	3	7	5

Four-Variable KV Matrix

	AB 00	01	11	10
CD 00	Z(0000)	Z(0100)	Z(1100)	Z(1000)
01	Z(0001)	Z(0101)	Z(1101)	Z(1001)
11	Z(0011)	Z(0111)	Z(1111)	Z(1011)
10	Z(0010)	Z(0110)	Z(1110)	Z(1010)

Z = F(ABCD)

	AB 00	01	11	10
CD 00	0	4	12	8
01	1	5	13	9
11	3	7	15	11
10	2	6	14	10

FIGURE 6.6   KV matrices.

3. Find the largest group of adjacent 1 cells. Adjacent cell groups are formed by the following rules:

- An adjacent group is 2, 4, or 8 cells. Groups are formed from numbers of cells that are powers of two: 2, 4, 8, 16, and so on.
- An adjacent group is formed horizontally or vertically. Groups are not formed on any diagonal.
- In a matrix of three or more variables, an adjacent group may wrap around the right and left edges. For example, an adjacent group could be composed of the left column and the right column.
- In a four-variable matrix, an adjacent group may wrap around the right and left edges or around the top and bottom edges. For example, an adjacent group could be composed of the top row and bottom row.
- Groups may overlap.

1. Set up Initial tableau: write 1 in the cell for each corresponding implicant.

AB

	00	01	11	10
00			1	
01			1	1
11			1	1
10				

CD

2. Find largest adjacent group; transcribe product term for this group.

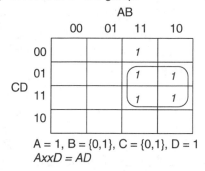

AB

	00	01	11	10
00			1	
01			1	1
11			1	1
10				

CD

$A = 1, B = \{0,1\}, C = \{0,1\}, D = 1$
$AxxD = AD$

3. Find next largest adjacent group; transcribe product term for this group.

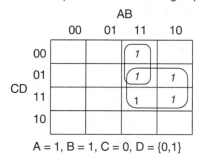

AB

	00	01	11	10
00			1	
01			1	1
11			1	1
10				

CD

$A = 1, B = 1, C = 0, D = \{0,1\}$

4. No more groups. Minimal logic function is the sum of the product terms.

$$Z = AB{\sim}C + AD$$

FIGURE 6.7 KV matrix for boiler control.

For the boiler control example, the largest adjacent group is the square four-cell block corresponding to vectors 13, 9, 15, and 11.

4. Transcribe the product terms for this group. The product term is transcribed one variable at a time by considering the truth values for each cell's row and column.

- If the group covers only 0 values for a variable, a negated literal is transcribed.
- If the group covers only 1 values for this variable, the literal is transcribed.
- If the group covers both 0 and 1 values for this variable, no literal is transcribed.

For the boiler control example, the square block group covers cells where $A = 1$ (A is transcribed), $B = \{0,1\}$ (B is not transcribed), $C = \{0,1\}$ (C is not transcribed), and $D = 1$ (D is transcribed). The resulting term is AD.

Steps 2 and 3 are repeated until all valid groups have been identified and transcribed. In the boiler control model, only one more group exists: the pair for vectors 12 and 13. This group covers cells where $A = 1$, $B = 1$ (we transcribe AB), $C = 0$ (we transcribe $\sim C$), and because $D = \{0,1\}$ we do not transcribe D. This results in the second term $AB\sim C$. The minimal logic function is the sum of the product terms—in this case,

$$Z = AB\sim C + AD$$

Often, many valid ways exist to draw adjacent groups for any given truth table. KV matrices for one to five variables, examples of edge-wrapping groups, and a discussion of five- and six-variable matrices, as applicable to software testing, may be found in [Beizer 90]. KV matrices are covered in most elementary texts on digital logic, such as [Devadas 94 and Comer 95].

◆ 6.3.5 Cause–Effect Graphs

A **cause–effect graph** may be useful for identifying and analyzing the relationships to be modeled in a decision table [Myers 79]. I first encountered cause–effect graphs in 1982 and was initially put off by their "spaghetti and meatball" appearance. After developing several cause–effect models, however, I now think they provide an effective technique for analyzing and representing logic relationships.

A node is drawn for each cause (decision variable) and effect (output action). The cause and effect nodes are placed on opposite sides of a sheet. A line from a cause to an effect indicates that the cause is a necessary condition for the effect. If an effect has only a single cause (line), then that cause is also a sufficient condition to produce the effect. If a single effect has two or more causes (lines), the logical relationship of the causes is annotated by symbols for logical *and* ($\wedge$) and logical *or* ($\vee$) placed between the lines. A cause whose negation is a necessary condition is shown by the logical *not* ($\sim$) imposed on the line. A single cause may be necessary for many effects; a single effect may have many necessary causes. Intermediate nodes may be introduced to simplify the graph. Figure 6.8 shows a cause–effect graph for the insurance renewal example.

Cause–effect graphing can offer benefits for the initial development of a specification and for test design when no decision table is available. It requires systematic consideration of decision variables, conditions, and actions. The an-

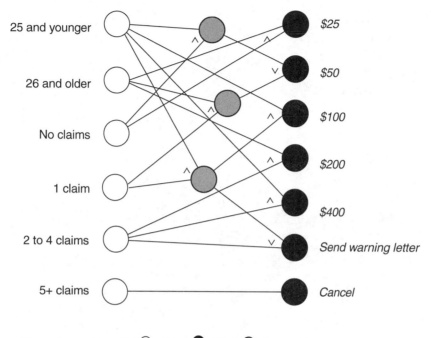

Key: ∧ = And, ∨ = Or, ~ = Not; ○ = Cause, ● = Effect, ◉ = Intermediate

FIGURE 6.8   Insurance renewal cause–effect graph.

alyst may get visual clues about missing or incorrect relationships. A consistent, simple notation to record an evolving model is used. However, the general limitations of graphical techniques apply: As the complexity and scope of the modeled behavior increases, the graphs become busy and eventually intractable.

Boolean functions can be derived from a cause–effect graph. One function (a truth table) exists for each effect. If several effects are present, then the resulting decision table is a composite of several truth tables that happen to share decision variables and actions. It is usually easier to derive the function for each effect separately. These functions may then be overlaid to produce a single decision table for all effects.

Direct transcription of a cause–effect graph onto a column-wise decision table is summarized in Procedure 1. A more detailed example is presented in [Myers 79]. Direct transcription by inspection can be difficult and error-prone. An alternative is to transcribe Boolean formulas from a cause–effect graph and then rewrite them in sum-of-products form. This approach works for any arbitrarily complex cause–effect graph.

Define and label a row in the condition section for each cause.

1.   Define and label a row in the action section for each effect.
2.   For each effect node:

        If there are one, two, or three causes for the effect:

                Try transcribing by inspection.

     fi

        If there are four or more causes for the effect:

        Transcribe node-to-node formulas from the graph.

                Write the formula for the effect and its predecessors.

                For each intermediate node:

                        Write the formula for the intermediate node and its predecessors.

             rof

        Derive the complete Boolean formula.

                Replace intermediate variables by substitution until the effect formula contains only cause variables.

                Factor and rewrite the effect formula into sum-of-products form using the Boolean laws (see Figure 6.5).

     fi

  rof

3.   Generate variant entries.

     For each effect formula:

        For each product term:

            Expand into a minterm

        rof

        Discard duplicate minterms.

        Generate a variant column for the minterm.

        Transcribe the truth values to the column.

     rof

Procedure 1   Transcribe Cause–Effect Graph to Decision Table

The first step in formula transcription is to write out the formula for each effect and intermediate node. The node name becomes the left side of the expression. The upstream node names and corresponding logical operators form the right side of the expression. These formulas are then reduced to a single sum-of-products formula by algebraic substitution and the rewrite laws given in Figure 6.5. A derivation of the sum-of-products function from the cause–effect graph in Figure 6.9 follows. Although this graph is not intimidating, the resulting formula is moderately complex.

1. *Transcribe node-to-node formulas from the graph.* Write the equation for effect Z and its predecessors P and R:

$$Z = PR \qquad (1)$$

Write the equation for intermediate node P and its predecessors:

$$P = A + {\sim}Q \qquad (2)$$

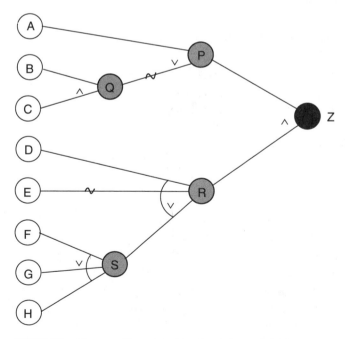

FIGURE 6.9   Cause–effect graph with eight variables.

Write the equation for intermediate node Q and its predecessors:

$$Q = BC \tag{3}$$

Write the equation for intermediate node R and its predecessors:

$$R = D + \sim E + S \tag{4}$$

Write the equation for intermediate node S and its predecessors:

$$S = F + G + H \tag{5}$$

2. *Derive the complete Boolean formula in sum-of-products form.* Substitute Equation (2) for P and Equation (4) for R:

$$Z = (A + \sim Q)\ (D + \sim E + S) \tag{6}$$

Substitute Equation (3) for Q, and Equation (5) for S:

$$Z = (A + \sim(BC))\ (D + \sim E + (F + G + H)) \tag{7}$$

Factor product $\sim(BC)$ using De Morgan's law:

$$Z = (A + \sim B + \sim C)\ (D + \sim E + F + G + H) \tag{8}$$

Expand the implied products using the distributive law:

$$
\begin{aligned}
Z = {}& AD + A\sim E + AF + AG + AH +{} \\
& \sim BD + \sim B \sim E + \sim BF + \sim BG + \sim BH +{} \\
& \sim CD + \sim C \sim E + \sim CF + \sim CG + \sim CH
\end{aligned}
\tag{9}
$$

The Boolean formula for the graph in Figure 6.9 is given by Equation (9). The fully enumerated truth table (not shown) would contain 2^8 variants.

Myers also provides a notation to model external constraints among causes. *Exclusive* causes are mutually exclusive but not required. If any is present, only one may be true; both may be false. *Inclusive* causes require that at least one must be true; all may be true. *Singleton* causes require that at least one but no more than one be true. Constraints are shown by dashed lines [Myers 79].

   Modeling constraints apart from the decision table may be useful if it simplifies the testing problem. Constraints can also be modeled by adding a term for the constraint to the function. This representation explicitly incorporates external constraints and decision variables into the model. For example, to model an exclusive constraint on variables X and Y, $\sim(XY)$ is added to the formula. $X + Y$ is added to model an inclusive constraint, and $X \oplus Y$ (exclusive *or*) to model a singleton constraint. (The expansion of $X \oplus Y$ is $\sim XY + X \sim Y$). Adding explicit constraints does not change the relative size of the test suite, as it does not increase the number of variables. Because it is easy to make a mistake in complex algebraic substitution, the resulting formula should be verified ■ (Figure 6.10).

A	B	C	D	Z = AB~C + AD	
0	0	0	0	0	@OR(@AND(+A2,+B2,@NOT(+C2)),@AND(+A2,+D2))
0	0	0	1	0	@OR(@AND(+A3,+B3,@NOT(+C3)),@AND(+A3,+D3))
0	0	1	0	0	@OR(@AND(+A4,+B4,@NOT(+C4)),@AND(+A4,+D4))
0	0	1	1	0	@OR(@AND(+A5,+B5,@NOT(+C5)),@AND(+A5,+D5))
0	1	0	0	0	@OR(@AND(+A6,+B6,@NOT(+C6)),@AND(+A6,+D6))
0	1	0	1	0	@OR(@AND(+A7,+B7,@NOT(+C7)),@AND(+A7,+D7))
0	1	1	0	0	@OR(@AND(+A8,+B8,@NOT(+C8)),@AND(+A8,+D8))
0	1	1	1	0	@OR(@AND(+A9,+B9,@NOT(+C9)),@AND(+A9,+D9))
1	0	0	0	0	@OR(@AND(+A10,+B10,@NOT(+C10)),@AND(+A10,+D10))
1	0	0	1	1	@OR(@AND(+A11,+B11,@NOT(+C11)),@AND(+A11,+D11))
1	0	1	0	0	@OR(@AND(+A12,+B12,@NOT(+C12)),@AND(+A12,+D12))
1	0	1	1	1	@OR(@AND(+A13,+B13,@NOT(+C13)),@AND(+A13,+D13))
1	1	0	0	1	@OR(@AND(+A14,+B14,@NOT(+C14)),@AND(+A14,+D14))
1	1	0	1	1	@OR(@AND(+A15,+B15,@NOT(+C15)),@AND(+A15,+D15))
1	1	1	0	0	@OR(@AND(+A16,+B16,@NOT(+C16)),@AND(+A16,+D16))
1	1	1	1	1	@OR(@AND(+A17,+B17,@NOT(+C17)),@AND(+A17,+D17))

FIGURE 6.10   Spreadsheet for checking the boiler control truth table.

6.4 Decision Table Validation

A decision table should be validated before it is used to design or generate a test suite. It should be testable, complete, consistent, and free of technical errors. The modeled capability should also be reviewed. Such checks often reveal errors and omissions before a test suite is developed and run, increasing the effectiveness and efficiency of combinational test suites.

- *Content checklist.* A decision table model that meets the conditions listed in Table 6.6 will ease testing and encourage early prevention of errors. Besides their use in checking the model, many criteria on this list can be used to develop test cases for the IUT. These criteria are noted as *testable.*

- *Logic function checking.* Making an error when manually transcribing or rewriting truth tables and formulas is easy. Some simple first-order checking can catch some of these errors and may uncover omissions and contradictions. A personal computer spreadsheet may be useful to automate logic checking.

    For example, a simple spreadsheet checker for the boiler function $Z = A(B{\sim}C + D)$ is given in Figure 6.10. One column is used for each variable $(A, B, C, D, \ldots)$ and the function Z. One row is used for each input truth value combination and result. Each cell in the function column contains the formula, evaluated by using the truth values in that row. This calculation produces the truth value of the function at all points. The input variables are entered as constants to enumerate the truth table rows for input variables. The formula is entered for the first row, checked, and then copied to the remaining rows. Text labels can be used to display descriptive names for conditions and actions (On/Off, Yes/No, and so on).

    Spreadsheets are simple to use and readily available. Several tools that support decision table development and verification are commercially available, and some research and promotional tools can be obtained free of charge via the Web. Additional techniques for formula validation are discussed in [Beizer 90].

- *Reasonability review.* A decision table should be scrutinized for omissions and inconsistencies besides being checked for technical consistency. Validation is more difficult: It is essentially a different point of view on the problem of developing the requirements and specification. For example, an early version of the boiler control example allowed the ignition to be enabled in manual mode when normal pressure was not true. This error would have allowed an

TABLE 6.6   Decision Table Checklist

1. Action selection is independent of the order of variant evaluation. Changing the order of variant evaluation has no effect on the correctness of the table or on which action will result for any variant (testable).

2. Action selection is independent of the order of condition evaluation. Changing the order of condition evaluation has no effect on the selection of the correct variant (testable).

3. Action selection is independent of prior actions. Any action may be (1) first, (2) followed by any action, including itself, and (3) last (testable).

4. Each variant is mutually exclusive. If the conditions for a variant are met, no other variant will be selected (testable).

5. If no explicit variant condition is satisfied by an input vector, either the default action is selected or the implementation will do nothing in an acceptable manner (testable).

6. Each variant is unique. If several actions are to result from one variant, multiple actions are defined—the variant is not repeated.

7. Each action has a testable specification. This specification is incorporated by reference. Unspecified actions must be unambiguous and self-explanatory.

8. All specified output actions are observable; a test harness or a tester can unambiguously determine their presence or absence and their resultant value.

9. All specified decision variables are controllable; a test harness or a tester can enter or generate any combination of decision variables for which an explicit variant exists.

10. A domain specification is given for each nonbinary decision variable—for example, InsuredAge: integer, 16 to 85; NumberClaims: integer, 0 to 10.

11. The domains of a nonbinary decision variable are adjacent or, if not adjacent, the gap is consistent with system requirements and common sense. For example, suppose that the two age groups in the insurance problem were defined as 16 to 24 and 26 to 85. There is a gap, in that 25-year-olds are not defined.

12. An explicit Boolean formula is given for a decision table whose logic function is not a simple *and* product of the decision variables (ABC . . . x).

13. The resultant action for the function has been independently verified for all input cases.

14. The action specified for a variant with a don't care is acceptable for all possible truth values of the don't care conditions (testable).

15. If the table has implicit variants, there is a designated default action (testable).

16. The designated default action is appropriate for all implicit variants.

17. Implicit variants for type-safe exclusions are based on trusted type checking or a nonvolatile configuration.

18. If a type-safe exclusion or can't happen condition is present, attempt to identify at least one circumstance where the assumed exclusions would not hold (testable).

19. Scrutinize all can't happen conditions: reject, revise, or replace with an explicit default action.

20. Scrutinize all don't know conditions: reject, revise, or replace with an explicit default action.

unsuspecting operator to light the fire under a boiler that is about to explode. In the revised version, we can see that an over-pressure boiler cannot be lit. Qualitative analysis of requirements for these kinds of problems can prevent many kinds of bugs [Gause+89, Leveson 95].

6.5   Test Generation

With a verified decision table, truth table, or logic function in hand, we can develop a test suite using any of the following strategies:

- All-Explicit variants.
- All-Variants, All-True, All-False, All-Primes.
- Each-Condition/All-Conditions.
- BDD-Determinants.
- Variable Negation.
- Nonbinary Variable Domain Analysis.

In this section, we consider what kind of faults are likely and then present each strategy. A comparison of cost and effectiveness concludes this section.

6.5.1   Fault Model

What kind of faults can we anticipate in an implementation of a decision table? Some common coding errors that would lead to decision table bugs include the following:

- Incorrect value assigned to a decision variable.
- Incorrect or missing operator in a predicate.
- Incorrect or missing variable in a predicate.
- Incorrect structure in a predicate (e.g., dangling else, misplaced semicolon).
- Incorrect or missing default case.
- Incorrect or missing action(s).
- Extra action(s).
- Structural errors in the decision table implementation: falling through (a missing `break` statement in a C++ `switch` expression), incorrect value computed for an index or action selector.

- Missing or incorrect class or method signature when variants are implemented by dynamic binding to an object that represents the decision variable or output action.

- Generic errors: wrong version, incorrect or missing specification item, ambiguous requirements.

In addition, any of the design errors suggested by this checklist would result in an incorrect implementation.

In testing hardware, the **stuck-at-one** or **stuck-at-zero** fault model is often used for combinational logic [Fujiwara+85, Abramovici+90, Devedas 97]. Stuck-at faults occur when a physical defect (a short or open) causes the input to a gate to remain at logical one or zero, whatever the actual input. In a circuit with n inputs there are $2n$ possible stuck-at faults, since a line may be either okay, stuck-at-one, or stuck-at-zero. There are $3^n - 1$ possible combinations of stuck-at faults. An advantage of the stuck-at fault model is that it is possible to automatically generate a test suite that will reveal all modeled faults.

Although the stuck-at model has been effective for hardware testing, it is not a good model of likely software faults [Weyuker+94]. Would competent programmers be likely to make the kinds of errors that are usefully modeled by stuck-at faults? Table 6.7 shows the coding blunders that correspond to stuck-at faults. For the stuck-at model to be effective, these errors would have to be common and hard to find by inspection. Because these coding errors are so glaring, it is unlikely that they will be made and if made they can easily be found by inspection. Although incorrect value assignments are less obvious, they do not favor a *single* incorrect Boolean evaluation. Stuck-at behavior would also obtain if Boolean predicate variables are incorrectly assigned single truth values or non-Boolean predicate variables are incorrectly assigned values that *always* evaluate to the same truth value. As with hardware, these faults would not produce incorrect output for all values of the stuck variable.

TABLE 6.7 Stuck-at Faults in Software

Correct Expression	Stuck-at-Zero	Stuck-at-One
!(p && !(p && q))	!(FALSE && !(p & q))	!(TRUE && !(p & q))
!(p && !(p && q))	!(p && !(FALSE & q))	!(p && !(TRUE & q))
!(p && !(p && q))	!(p && !(p & FALSE))	!(p && !(p & TRUE))
!(p && !(p && q))	!(p && FALSE)	!(p && TRUE)
!(p && !(p && q))	FALSE	TRUE

Since the simple stuck-at model is not a good bet, testing of combinational logic in software must be based on coverage of combinational relationships. The following test strategies provide varying degrees of this coverage.

6.5.2 All-Explicit Variants

The All-Explicit variants strategy requires decision variable test points such that each explicit variant is produced at least once. This is equivalent to the All-True strategy for binary decision variables. For example, one test case would be developed for each of the six explicit variants in the insurance renewal model. If a default action is defined, it is also tested. This approach is appropriate for decision tables with nonbinary variables, provided that decision variable boundaries are systematically exercised. If the implicit variant result from type-safe exclusions, it can provide acceptable variant coverage. The All-Explicit approach is very weak if can't happen conditions or undefined domain boundaries result in implicit variants. The test suite should therefore be augmented with test cases selected by domain analysis on the decision variables as explained in Section 6.5.7.

6.5.3 All-Variants, All-True, All-False, All-Primes

These four approaches are grouped together because they apply directly to a truth table and its logic function. They can result in significantly different test quantity and effectiveness.

- *All-Variants*. Every variant in the table is tested once. The number of tests (2^n) rises exponentially with the number of variables. Testing all variants may be feasible with smaller tables (seven or fewer variables). The most costly and most comprehensive form of testing possible, it is typically infeasible for large tables.

- *All-True*. Every variant in the table that produces a true outcome is tested. This approach is equivalent to testing all minterms of the function. If important behavior follows from the false actions (as in the boiler control model), this test strategy is inappropriate.

- *All-False*. Every variant in the table that produces a false outcome is tested. This approach is equivalent to testing the complement of all minterms of the function. If important behavior follows from the true actions (as in the boiler control model), this test strategy is inappropriate.

- *All-Primes*. Each prime implicant (i.e., each product term in a minimal sum-of-products form) of the function is tested at least once. As don't care conditions typically exist for these terms, the test suite selected by this strategy is a subset of the All-True strategy. If important behavior follows from the untested true or false actions (as in the boiler control model), this test strategy is inappropriate.

The weakness of the All-True, All-False, and All-Primes strategies lies in what they exclude. That is, they can easily fail to reveal bugs in critical behavior. Table 6.15 on page 172 lists the number of tests that would be produced for the boiler and insurance examples under each test strategy. Because the insurance renewal example combines several functions, the All-Primes size is not given.

6.5.4 Each-Condition/All-Conditions

The Each-Condition/All-Conditions strategy is based on a heuristic used to reduce the number of tests for expressions involving *and* and *or* operators in cause–effect graphs [Myers 79]. The test suite is composed of test cases such that each variable is made true once with all other variables being false, and one test case where all variables are true (*and* logic) or false (*or* logic). This heuristic bets on the independence of condition evaluation and the absence of faults that would mask an error. These heuristics are suggested in Myers's discussion of cause–effect graphs and in Marick's C++ predicate checklists [Marick 95, 42–50]. Marick demonstrates that it is unlikely that skipping the All-True case in an *or* expression will miss predicate coding faults.

The *or* heuristic may be applied to effects, intermediate nodes, or expressions with one or more *or* operators. The test where all variables are true is skipped, and each variable is made true only once. For example, to test the logic function $P + Q + R$ that controls action S, we would have the four tests shown in Table 6.8.

TABLE 6.8 Tests for Multivariable Or Logic

P	Q	R	Action S
False	False	True	Yes
False	True	False	Yes
True	False	False	Yes
False	False	False	No

The *and* heuristic is applied to any effect, intermediate node, or expression with one or more *and* operators. The test where all causes (variables) are false is skipped, each variable is made true only once, and the all-true result is exercised. For example, to test *PQR* that controls action *S*, we would have four tests shown in Table 6.9.

True singletons are variants with only one true value; three exist in *P* + *Q* + *R*. For a sum-of-products formula of *m* terms, there will be *m* true singletons. A **no-true** variant contains only false values; a **no-false** variant contains only true values. The *or* heuristic yields one no-true and *m* true singleton variants. With *n* variables, there are *n* true singletons, instead of n^2. The *and* heuristic yields one no-false and *n* true singleton variants. The same pattern applies for any number of variables.

The default logic function of a decision table is to apply an *and* to each condition in a row. The Each-Condition/All-Conditions strategy yields a compact test suite for a decision table with a default logic function: if *n* conditions exist, there will be *n* + 1 tests. If implicit conditions arise because of boundary values and default actions, however, this strategy is inappropriate because it will not exercise these boundaries.

This heuristic can be generalized to any logic function in sum-of-products form to produce a compact test suite. We simply apply the *and* logic pattern to each term. For example, consider the boiler control function

$$Z = AB\sim C + AD$$

For term *AB~C*, we need four variants:

1. $A\sim B\sim\sim C$ = 0   (101*x*)
2. $\sim AB\sim\sim C$ = 0   (011*x*)
3. $\sim A\sim BC$ = 0   (000*x*)
4. $AB\sim C$ = 1   (011*x*)

TABLE 6.9   Tests for Multivariable *And* Logic

P	Q	R	Action S?
False	False	True	No
False	True	False	No
True	False	False	No
True	True	True	Yes

For term *AD*, we need three variants:

5. $A \sim D$ = 0 $(1xx0)$
6. $\sim AD$ = 0 $(0xx1)$
7. AD = 1 $(1xx1)$

The number of tests increases linearly with the number of product terms, so this approach can provide a compact test suite for larger tables.[7] After test vectors are identified, values must be assigned to the don't care variables. Such assignment may be done randomly or by suspicion. If possible, scramble the truth values in don't cares from one test case to the next. The next two strategies provide an explicit approach to deal with don't care values.

◇ 6.5.5 Binary Decision Diagram Determinants

A **binary decision diagram** (BDD) is a compact representation of a truth table that can be used to produce an implementation-independent test suite [Abramovici+90]. Many advanced logic verification and model-checking strategies have been developed for BDDs [Bryant 94]. The following technique can be worked by hand for small to medium-sized models. Generation of a BDD requires a truth table. Here, the procedure to generate a BDD test suite is illustrated using the boiler control truth table.

1. *Construct a BDD from the truth table.*
   - Draw a full decision tree for the truth table. Figure 6.11 shows the decision tree for the boiler control truth table given in Table 6.4. Nodes represent Boolean variables. A left branch in a BDD always represents the 0 (false) value. Right branches always represent the 1 (true) value. Each leaf node represents the resultant value (Z) for the conditions on the root-to-leaf paths.
   - Reduce the decision tree to a BDD.
     – Working from left to right, replace leaf nodes with equivalent constants or variables and prune the branches.

---

7. If there are m product terms p_i, $i = 1, m$, and the number of literals in each term is $L(p_i)$, then the total number of tests in an Each-Condition/All-Conditions test suite for a logic function is $e = m + \sum L(p_i)$

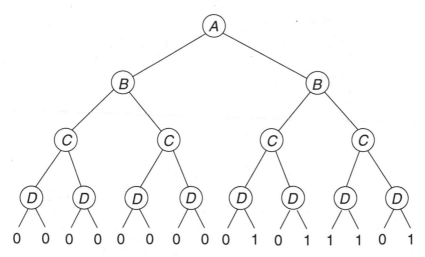

FIGURE 6.11   Binary decision tree for the boiler control truth table.

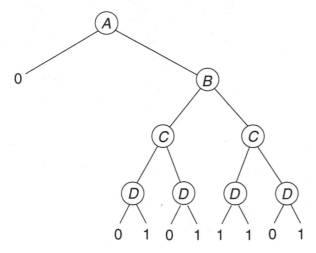

FIGURE 6.12   First reduction of boiler decision tree.

- The first eight results are determined by the value of A. This entire branch is pruned, leaving a single result of 0 under the 0 branch of A. The resulting diagram is shown in Figure 6.12.
- The next two result pairs are determined by D. The D branch above them is pruned and replaced with a result node indicating that the value is equal to D. The resulting diagram is shown in Figure 6.13.

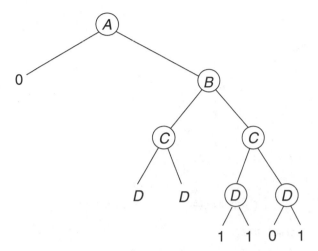

FIGURE 6.13   Second reduction of boiler decision tree.

- The far right result nodes are always equal to *D*. These branches are pruned back to the 1 branch under *C* and replaced with a result node indicating the value is equal to *D*. The 0 branch for *C* is always equal to 1. The *D* leaves are pruned and replaced with a 1. The result is shown in Figure 6.14.
- No more simplifications can be made, so the BDD is complete.

If the result node is the negation of a fixed value or sensitized variable, it is shown by a dot on the line leading to the result.

2.   *Map the BDD into a BDD determinant table.* The test suite is derived by transcribing the BDD into a BDD determinant table. A **BDD determinant** is a root-to-leaf path in the BDD; one row in the table corresponds to each path.[8] One column exists for each decision variable and the result variable. Determinant variables are one of three types:

1)   The branches of a variable node have fixed truth values. The truth values are transcribed under the variable's column.
2)   Some variables do not appear on a path. Don't care variables (*x*) are transcribed for variables that do not appear on a path.
3)   The result is sensitive to (determined by) a single variable. The variable name is transcribed.

---

8. Some terms used by Abramovici et al. [Abramovici+90] are not used here to avoid overloading.

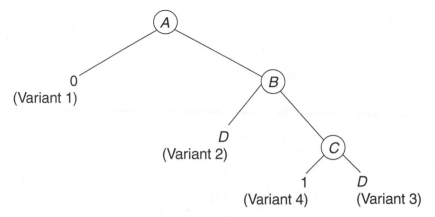

FIGURE 6.14   Boiler control binary decision tree.

Using the BDD for the boiler control model (Figure 6.14), we work from left to right. The first path shows $A = 0$ and a result of 0. The first row in the table shows $A = 0$, $Z = 0$, and x (don't care) for B, C, and D. The next path shows $A = 1$, $B = 0$, $C = 0$, and $Z = D$. Z is sensitive to D here, so D is entered as the test value and the result. The same analysis is applied to remaining paths. Table 6.10 shows the completed BDD determinant table for the boiler control model. The BDD determinants are collectively equivalent to a complete specification of the function. Exactly one row exists for every possible combination of fixed, don't care, and sensitive variables. Every pair of rows differs in at least one fixed variable. To generate the test suite, all combinations of sensitive variables for each row are assigned. The BDD test suite for the boiler control is given in Table 6.11.

The BDD test strategy does not dictate how to assign values to don't care variables. Truth values may be assigned to these variables randomly or based on suspicions about the implementation. Scramble the truth values assigned to don't care variables in each variant if possible.

TABLE 6.10   Boiler Control BDD Variant Table

BDD Variant	A	B	C	D	Z
1	0	x	x	x	0
2	1	0	x	D	D
3	1	1	1	D	D
4	1	1	0	x	1

TABLE 6.11 BDD Test Suite for Boiler Control

BDD Variant	A	B	C	D	Z
1	0	*x*	*x*	*x*	0
2	1	0	*x*	0	0
2	1	0	*x*	1	1
3	1	1	1	0	0
3	1	1	1	1	1
4	1	1	0	*x*	1

◇ **6.5.6 Variable Negation**

The BDD determinant strategy does not explicitly exercise the don't care terms of a variant. A fault that involves a don't care variable for a particular term might not be revealed when we test that term. The *variable negation* strategy [Weyuker+94] is designed to reveal faults that would otherwise hide in a don't care.

Variable negation requires a specification given as a sum-of-products Boolean formula.[9] It produces a test suite that will contain the following:

- One variant for each product term such that this variant makes the product term true but makes no other product term true (it is possible that no such variant exists). Variants that meet this criterion are called *unique true points*.

- One variant for the term that results when each literal in each product term is negated such that the function (Z) evaluates to 0 (false) for the negated term. Variants that meet this criterion are called *near false points*.

Depending on the logic function in question, several variants may meet these criteria. Variants that meet them are referred to as *test candidate sets*. These sets may have zero, one, or many variants. A test suite is produced by generating test candidate sets for each product term and then choosing test cases from all test candidate sets.

---

9. The basic variable negation strategy is considered here. Weyuker et al. define several versions of variable negation that produce larger test suites.

In this section, the production of a basic variable negation test suite is illustrated using the boiler control model. Variants are referred to by their input vector number. The boiler control function is

$$Z = AB\sim C + AD$$

We begin by selecting a unique true point for the first product term: a variant that makes $AB\sim C$ true and does not make any other product term true. Only variant 12 satisfies both criteria (variant 13 makes $AB\sim C$ true, but also makes AD true). The first test candidate set is {12}.

We now select test points by negating each literal in the term, one at a time. Table 6.12 shows the negation combinations for literals in the first term.

For the second product term, we first need a unique true point for AD (one that makes AD true but does not make any other product term true). Variants 9, 11, 13, or 15 make AD true, but we rule out 13 because it also makes $AB\sim C$ true. So, the test candidate set 5 is {9, 11, 15}. Next, the near false points of AD are identified by negating each literal in the term and checking its Z value. This procedure gives the last two test candidate sets (Table 6.13).

To select a test suite, we take at least one variant from each test candidate set. This may be accomplished by constructing a variant/candidate set matrix and selecting values by inspection, as shown in Figure 6.15. The variants of

TABLE 6.12   Variable Negations for the First Product Term

Product Term Negations			Variants Containing This Negation	Test Candidate Set: Variants Containing This Negation, where Z = 0	Candidate Set Number
A	B	~C			1
A	B	C	14, 15	14	2
A	~B	~C	8, 9	8	3
~A	B	~C	4, 5	4, 5	4

TABLE 6.13   Variable Negations for the Second Product Term

Product Term Negations		Variants Containing This Negation	Test Candidate Set: Variants Containing This Negation, where Z = 0	Candidate Set Number
A	D			5
A	~D	8, 10, 12, 14	8, 10, 14	6
~A	D	1, 3, 5, 7	1, 3, 5, 7	7

each candidate set are marked in the corresponding cell. Test case variants are selected until at least one variant from each candidate set has been chosen. Because one variant may satisfy several test conditions, the number of tests can be less than the number of test candidate sets. Figure 6.15 shows the selection of a basic variable negation test suite for the boiler control specification. The test suite consists of the variants 5, 8, 11, 12, 14, and 15. Note that the test suite composed of variants 1, 4, 8, 9, 10, 12, and 14 also includes all test candidate sets.

Weyuker et al. use random selection for the basic variable negation strategy. Other selection algorithms (including selection of a minimal set of test variants) are discussed in [Weyuker+94]. If the test suite is selected by inspection, test designers can substitute suspicion or any other form of good engineering judgment for random selection.

Variable negation is highly effective because it includes the All-Primes strategy and exercises variables whose effect is masked in All-Primes. It is a clever approach. Combinations of don't care values (near false points) are selected so

Variant	Test Candidate Set							Test Case?
	1	2	3	4	5	6	7	
0								
1							✗	
2								
3							✗	
4				✗				
5				✗			✗	✓
6								
7							✗	
8		✗				✗		✓
9					✗			
10						✗		
11					✗			✓
12	✗							✓
13								
14		✗				✗		✓
15					✗			✓

FIGURE 6.15 Matrix for selecting test cases from variable negation test candidate sets for boiler control logic function.

that any bug hiding their evaluation will be revealed. This unmasking is accomplished by embedding the don't care testing in variants that evaluate to false, allowing the effect of variables not in the product term to become visible. The developers of the variable negation strategy report that, on average, only 10 percent of the All-Variants test suite is needed to meet the basic variable negation criteria. This amount represents a significant reduction in the size of the test suite for large truth tables. Variable negation turns out to be highly effective at finding combinational logic bugs. When this type of test suite was applied to implementations of several large Boolean formulas with bugs simulated by mutation, at least 98 percent of the faults were revealed. The kind of faults that the strategy cannot detect has been unambiguously established, so one could easily add tests to compensate for them. See [Weyuker+94] for details of the approach and the mutation-based evaluation.

6.5.7   Nonbinary Variable Domain Analysis

The domain testing strategy (Chapter 10) may be applied directly to nonbinary decision table variables. Each variant with nonbinary decision variables defines a subdomain. For example, several distinct subdomains appear in the insurance renewal problem. Assuming that the age must be between 16 and 85 and that no more than 10 claims would ever be paid, we have seven subdomains:[10]

- Exactly 0 claims, age 16–25
- Exactly 0 claims, age 26–85
- Exactly 1 claim, age 16–25
- Exactly 1 claim, age 26–85
- Two, 3, or 4 claims, age 16–25
- Two, 3, or 4 claims, age 26–85
- Five to 10 claims, age 16–85

Note that each subdomain corresponds exactly to the conditions that define the variant. Although subdomains need not always map exactly to variants, the test designer should investigate any lack of congruence between the variants and decision variable subdomains.

---

10. As given, the insurance renewal table was silent about upper and lower bounds—an example of a specification omission bug. Clearly, these bounds should be specified. If not, strange situations are implicitly allowed: for example, the renewal of a three-year-old with zero claims.

The minimal domain test strategy is to pick one on point and one off point per boundary [Jeng+94, Beizer 95]. In the insurance renewal model, three or four boundaries exist for each variant (number of claims—exact or bracketed bounds, minimum age, maximum age). As the decision variable subdomains are often adjacent, an off point for subdomain *A* is often an on point for subdomain *B*. This overlap can reduce the quantity of test cases. A complete domain test suite for the insurance renewal requirements is given in Figures 6.16 through 6.22. For each variant, the on and off points of the boundaries of each variable are given in a Domain Test Matrix (see Chapter 10 for details). Several of these boundaries are adjacent. For example, there is no gap between the age groups. This means that test cases identified for one variant (typically an off-point test case) are also test cases for another variant. These overlapping test cases are indicated with "V*n*" in the Expected result cell and are not counted in the total number of tests. They can be dropped from the test suite without losing any test effectiveness for domain bugs.

An expected result of "Accept" means the test case inputs should be processed and produce the indicated output. An expected result of "Reject" means the test case inputs should not be processed and an appropriate error response should be produced. the other expected result values have been taken from the decision table.

			Test Cases					
Variant 1 Boundaries			1		2	3	4	5
Number of Claims	== 0	On	0					
		Off (above)		1				
		Off (below)			−1			
	Typical	In				0	0	0	0
Insured Age	>= 16	On				16		
		Off					15	
	<= 25	On						25
		Off							26
	Typical	In	20	20	20			
Expected result			Accept	V3	Reject	Accept	Reject	Accept	V2
Premium increase			50	100		50		50	25
Send warning			No	Yes		No		No	No
Cancel			No	No		No		No	No

FIGURE 6.16   Domain test cases for insurance renewal Variant 1.

Variant 2 Boundaries			Test Cases					
			6		7	8	9	10
Number of Claims	== 0	On	0					
		Off (above)		1				
		Off (below)			−1			
	Typical	In				0	0	0	0
Insured Age	>= 26	On				26		
		Off					25	
	<= 85	On						85	
		Off							86
	Typical	In	32	49	64			
Expected result			Accept	V4	Reject	Accept	V1	Accept	Reject
Premium increase			25	50		25	50	25	
Send warning			No	No		No	No	No	
Cancel			No	No		No	No	No	

FIGURE 6.17   Domain test cases for insurance renewal Variant 2.

Variant 3 Boundaries			Test Cases					
			11			12	13	14	
Number of Claims	== 1	On	1					
		Off (above)		2				
		Off (below)			0			
	Typical	In				1	1	1	1
Insured Age	>= 16	On				16		
		Off					15	
	<= 25	On						25	
		Off							26
	Typical	In	19	19	19			
Expected result			Accept	V5	V5	Accept	Reject	Accept	V4
Premium increase			100	400	400	100		100	50
Send warning			Yes	Yes	Yes	Yes		Yes	No
Cancel			No	No	No	No		No	No

FIGURE 6.18   Domain test cases for insurance renewal Variant 3.

			Test Cases						
Variant 4 Boundaries			15			16		17	18
Number of Claims	== 1	On	1						
		Off (above)		2					
		Off (below)			0				
	Typical	In				1	1	1	1
Insured Age	>= 26	On				26			
		Off					25		
	<= 85	On						85	
		Off							86
	Typical	In	55	55	55				
Expected result			Accept	V6	V2	Accept	V3	Accept	Reject
Premium increase			50	200	25	50	100	50	
Send warning			No	Yes	No	No	Yes	No	
Cancel			No	No	No	No	No	No	

FIGURE 6.19   Domain test cases for insurance renewal Variant 4.

			Test Cases							
Variant 5 Boundaries			19		20		21	22	23	
Number of Claims	>= 2	On	2							
		Off		1						
	<= 4	On			4					
		Off				5				
	Typical	In					3	3	3	3
Insured Age	>= 16	On					16			
		Off						15		
	<= 25	On							50	
		Off								26
	Typical	In	23	17	22	21				
Expected result			Accept	V3	Accept	V7	Accept	Accept	Accept	V6
Premium increase			400	100	400	0	400	400	400	200
Send warning			Yes	Yes	Yes	No	Yes	Yes	Yes	Yes
Cancel			No	No	No	Yes	No	No	No	No

FIGURE 6.20   Domain test cases for insurance renewal Variant 5.

Variant 6 Boundaries			Test Cases							
			24		25		26	27	28	29
Number of Claims	>= 2	On	2							
		Off		1						
	<= 4	On			4					
		Off				5				
	Typical	In					3	3	3	3
Insured Age	>= 26	On					26			
		Off						50		
	<= 85	On							85	
		Off								86
	Typical	In	83	27	36	44				
Expected result			Accept	V4	Accept	V7	Accept	Accept	Accept	Reject
Premium increase			200	50	200	0	200	200	200	
Send warning			Yes	No	Yes	No	Yes	Yes	Yes	
Cancel			No	No	No	Yes	No	No	No	

FIGURE 6.21 Domain test cases for insurance renewal Variant 6.

Variant 7 Boundaries			Test Cases							
			30		31	32	33	34	35	36
Number of Claims	>= 5	On	5							
		Off		4						
	<= 10	On			10					
		Off				11				
	Typical	In					6	7	8	9
Insured Age	>= 16	On					16			
		Off						15		
	<= 85	On							85	
		Off								86
	Typical	In	58	18	43	29				
Expected result			Accept	V5	Accept	Reject	Accept	Reject	Accept	Reject
Premium increase			0	400	0		0		0	
Send warning			No	Yes	No		No		No	
Cancel			Yes	No	Yes		Yes		Yes	

FIGURE 6.22 Domain test cases for insurance renewal Variant 7.

6.5.8 Additional Heuristics

The testable criteria in the decision table checklist can be incorporated into a test suite. Here are several additional heuristics to consider:

- A correct implementation of a decision table should produce the same results regardless of the input sequence, so try varying the order of the input variables. Condition evaluation is typically hard-coded in a case or switch construct and may assume a particular order of input.
- Scramble the test order. If variants 1, 4, 12, and 15 are to be tested, apply the tests in a different order—for example, 4, 15, 1, 12. Do not use the same order in every test run.
- Implicit variants resulting from type-safe exclusions or can't happen conditions can often be tested by purposely corrupting inputs, removing assumed conditions, or similar forms of "cheating."

6.6 Choosing a Combinational Test Strategy

As with any test approach, we must trade increased cost roughly proportional to the number of tests to obtain increased confidence in the tested implementation. The number of tests for a decision table is directly related to the number and complexity of decision variables. With nonbinary variables, the number of tests is related to the complexity of the domain of each nonbinary variable. Table 6.14 summarizes the relative test suite size for the following strategies.

TABLE 6.14 Decision Table Test Suite Size

Test Strategy	Test Size, Binary Decision Variables	Test Size, Nonbinary Decision Variables	Test Power
All-Variants	2^n	$2^n \bullet 4n$	100%
Basic Variable Negation[†]	$0.1 \bullet 2^n$	$0.1 \bullet 2^n \bullet 4n$	97%
Each Condition/All-Conditions	$m + \sum L(p_i)$	$(m + \sum L(p_i)) \bullet 4n$	?
All BDD Determinants	d	$d \bullet 4n$	?
All-True	t	$t \bullet 4n$	?
All-False	f	$f \bullet 4n$	?
All-Primes	m	$m \bullet 4n$	?
All-Explicit	x	$x \bullet 4n$	?

[†]Coefficients are the average reported in [Weyuker+94].

- *All-Variants* tests all 2^n variants. Every variant producing an incorrect result will be exercised. This strategy gives the most comprehensive (and largest possible) test suite.

- A basic variable negation test suite averages 6 percent of the All-Variants test suite and found at least 97 percent of the simulated faults in large ($n > 6$) tables [Weyuker+94].

- A BDD determinant test suite will have d variants, where d is the number of uniquely determined outcomes in the BDD. The All-Variants set results if all don't care variables are expanded from the BDD determinant variants. We assume that each BDD variant with don't care values is tested only once.

- An Each-Condition/All-Conditions test suite will have e variants, which is a linear function of the complexity of the logic formula.

- An All-True test suite will have t variants, where t is the number of minterms or total number of variants with true outcomes.

- An All-False test suite will have f variants, where f is the number of minterms or total number of variants with false outcomes. In all cases, $t + f = 2^n$.

- An All-Primes test suite will have m variants, where m is the number of prime implicants for the function.

- An All-Explicit test suite will have x test cases, where x is the number of explicit variants in the decision table.

Except for variable negation, no research or reported experience has yet established the fault-revealing power of these strategies. We cannot assume that the quantity of tests produced necessarily correlates with test effectiveness. Figure 6.23 shows how these strategies can be ordered according to the kind of variants that they include. The All-True and All-False are subsets of All-Variants. Minimum variable negation, BDD determinant, and Each-Condition/All-Conditions strategies guarantee the selection of some true and some false variants. Overlap will occur among variants selected by these strategies, but the shared elements will vary with each function. The All-Primes strategy is a subset of All-True because it requires only one true test per term but not any other variants. It is not necessarily a subset of minimum variable negation and BDD determinant, as neither of those strategies requires All-Primes. No precise criterion specifies which variants become explicit, so the All-Explicit variant strategy cannot be placed in the hierarchy. An explicit variant table could be constructed to correspond to any or none of these sets. The number of

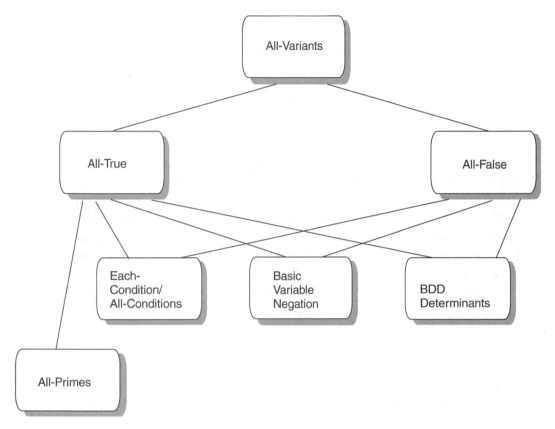

FIGURE 6.23 Inclusion hierarchy of combinational test strategies.

test points for the boiler control and insurance renewal examples is given in Table 6.15.

To what extent will nonbinary decision variables increase the size of the test suite? Assume that each nonbinary decision variable has two boundaries in each variant. For example, in the insurance renewal model, one of two ranges applies to age in each variant: 16–25 or 26–85. The size of the basic 1x1 domain testing strategy is $2b$, where b is the number of boundaries [Beizer 95]. Assuming two boundaries for each nonbinary decision variable and n decision variables, the number of tests T is

$$
\begin{aligned}
T &= 2b \times 2 \times n \\
  &= 2 \times 2 \times n \\
  &= 4n
\end{aligned}
$$

TABLE 6.15   Size of All-X Test Suites

	Boiler Control	Insurance Renewal
All-Variants	16	64
All-True	5	7
All-False	11	57
All-Primes	2	*See text*

Under these assumptions, nonbinary variables increase the size of the test suite by $4n$. The number of domain tests may be reduced significantly if the domains are adjacent (e.g., the on points for domain a are off points for domain b).

Several practical observations can be drawn from this analysis. The relative size of the decision table under test represents a good indicator for the appropriate test strategy. As with any test planning problem, the potential effect of a failure should be considered in budgeting for the extent of testing. Suppose a small function has 6 or fewer variables, a medium-sized function 7 to 11 variables, and a large function 12 or more.

- For small tables with nonbinary decision variables, the explicit variant strategy augmented with 1×1 domain tests is prudent and feasible.
- For small and medium-sized tables, All-Variants is a prudent and feasible approach.
- For small to large tables, Each-Condition/All-Conditions can be used to manually produce a compact test suite. The number of tests increases in linear proportion to the complexity of the function. A sum-of-products formula must be developed first.
- For medium-sized tables, the BDD determinant strategy can provide a comprehensive test suite that can be produced manually. The BDD can be derived from a truth table without any algebraic manipulation. The diagrams become manually intractable for medium-sized or larger tables, however.
- For large tables, the variable negation strategy is the clear choice. It is highly effective and produces a small test suite. Manual test generation for a large table is possible, but would be difficult. Algorithms and tools for variable negation test generation are sketched in [Weyuker+94].
- All-Primes or All-Explicit should be considered the minimum quick-and-dirty strategy for any size table.

6.7 Bibliographic Notes

As many introductory and advanced treatments of Boolean algebra and combinational logic have been published, only a minimum review of topics necessary to support test modeling is provided here. Chapter 10, Logic-Based Testing [Beizer 90], provides a concise tutorial on Boolean algebra and combinational logic.

Boolean algebra and combinational logic have been used in hardware design and test since the late 1940s [Gill 62, Kohavi 78, Fujiwara+85, Abramovici+90, Devadas 94, Comer 95]. Hardware fault models and functional testing strategies for combinational testing are discussed in [Fujiwara+85], [Abramovici+90], and [Comer 95]. The binary decision diagram test strategy is adapted from [Abramovici+90]. A tutorial, discussion of representation and algorithms, and survey of applications for binary decision diagrams appear in [Bryant 92]. Devadas presents an integrated approach to the automated design and verification of combinational logic [Devadas 94, Devadas 97].

A comprehensive treatment of the development and validation of decision tables for data processing is given in [CODASYL 78]. The use of decision tables to model requirements is discussed in [DeMarco 79], [Hurley 83], and [Yourdon 89]. Decision tables are an integral part of the Hatley-Pirbhai control model for embedded real-time systems. An analytical process to derive and model combinational logic is presented in [Hatley+87]. Practical techniques for qualitative analysis of requirements are presented in [Gause+89], [Thayer+90], and [Leveson 95]. The use of decision tables for client/server development is discussed in [McClintock 97].

The use of decision tables for software testing is discussed in [Goodenough+75] and [Tai 87]. The cause–effect graph technique was developed by William Elmendorf at IBM in the early 1970s. The approach, and a technique to generate a decision table from cause–effect graphs, is presented in [Myers 79]. Richard Bender's SoftTest tool implements this strategy [Bender 98]. Validation and testing strategies for decision tables are presented in [Beizer 90]. Strategy, test suite generation, and effectiveness of variable negation are presented in [Weyuker+94]. A catalog of tests for Boolean expressions containing three to five variables is provided in [Marick 95]. Domain analysis is discussed in Chapter 10.

Chapter 7   State Machines

"I know what you're thinking about," said Tweedledum:
"but it isn't so, nohow."

"Contrariwise," continued Tweedledee, "if it was so,
it might be; and if it were so, it would be; but as it
isn't, it ain't. That's logic."

"I was thinking," Alice said very politely,
"which is the best way out of this wood: it's getting
so dark. Would you tell me, please?" But the
little men only looked at each other and grinned.

Lewis Carroll
Through the Looking Glass

Overview

Object-oriented software is well suited to state-based testing. This chapter explains how to develop testable state models and state-based test suites, which may be applied at any scope. The discussion of state-based test design begins with a review of the basic state machine model and how it has been adapted to model object-oriented software. The FREE state model is defined to provide a testable state model for object-oriented systems. A fault model shows how implementations can fail to conform to a state machine specification. Test model development is discussed, with checklists for verification. The N+ test design strategy is presented with a detailed example. An analysis of the power and limitations of state-based test suites concludes this chapter.

7.1 Motivation

The packaging of instance variables and methods into a class is fundamental to object-oriented programming. The resulting interactions, dependencies, and constraints on message sequence are collectively called **behavior**.[1] Although the number of message sequences and instance variable value combinations is infinite for practical purposes, a state machine can nevertheless provide a compact and predictable model of behavior. State machines are an effective, fundamental technique for design and test of complex behavior.

> I understand every two-state finite-state machine because, including the good and bad ones, there are only eight of them. There are about eighty possible good and bad three-state machines, 2700 four-state machines, 275,000 five-state machines, and close to 100 million six-state machines, most of which are bad. We learned long ago, as hardware logic designers, that it paid to build explicit finite-state machines for even very small machines [Beizer 90, 391].

Object-oriented systems often distribute the responsibility for correct behavior over several classes, a cluster, a subsystem, or an entire system. Behavior bugs are likely because of this complex and implicit structure. Behavior may be modeled by state machines at any scope: class, cluster, component, subsystem, or system allowing state-based testing to be applied at any scope. Detail must decrease when state machines are developed for larger scope, but the same relationships and notation apply.

This chapter serves two purposes. First, it presents the state-based testing strategy used in several Part III test design patterns, avoiding repetition. Second, it collects ideas necessary to perform state-based testing on object-oriented systems. The modeling and test design approaches presented here are based on well-established theory and practice. However, no single source integrates and presents this subject in support of object-oriented testing. To preserve connections to this body of knowledge, I have used many footnotes. The notes avoid bogging down the mainline presentation—skip them if you're not interested.

---

1. In object-oriented analysis, design, and programming, *behavior* refers to the sequences of message responses that an object can make. In computer science and software engineering, *behavior-based testing* refers to testing from implementation-independent requirements. The more narrow, object-oriented sense is used here.

7.2 The Basic Model

7.2.1   What Is a State Machine?

A **state machine** is a system whose output is determined by both current and past input. The effect of previous inputs is represented by a state. In contrast, as noted in Chapter 6, the output of a combinational system is determined by current input only. For example, the thumb wheels on a luggage lock may be set in any sequence to open it. Just as the luggage spin lock in Figure 6.1 suggests a combinational system, the combination lock in Figure 7.1 suggests a state machine.[2] To open a combination lock, one must dial in specific values in a specific sequence. Although both locks retain the previous input, the sequence of these inputs determines the combination lock's response. Similarly, although most classes retain some representation of previous messages, only certain

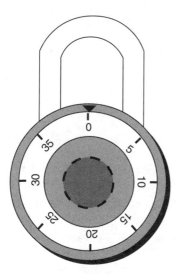

FIGURE 7.1   Combination lock.

---

2. A combinational system takes its name from the formal meaning of *combination* in mathematical logic. A combination lock takes its name from the everyday sense of *combination* as a collection of things or numbers; in this context, it could be called a sequential lock.

classes are sensitive to the sequence of past messages. A state machine can model the behavior of such classes.[3]

State machines are an engineering application of mathematical models known as **finite automata**.[4] Theoretical aspects of automata have been studied extensively. Finite automata were first applied to the design of switching circuits in the 1950s and continue to serve as essential tools for design and testing of digital logic. State machines were applied to software design problems beginning in the 1960s and became routinely used in software engineering methodologies by the late 1970s. They are now incorporated in the UML.

A state machine is an abstraction composed of events (inputs), states, and actions (outputs). A system is said to exhibit **state-based behavior** when identical inputs are not always accepted and, when accepted, may produce different outputs. State machines are also called sequential systems, which are said to have *sequential behavior*. A state machine has four building blocks:

- **State**. An abstraction that "summarizes the information concerning past inputs that is needed to determine the behavior of the system on subsequent inputs" [Hopcroft 79, 13].
- **Transition**. An allowable two-state sequence. A transition is caused by an event. It may result in an output action and must specify an accepting state and a resultant state.
- **Event**. An input or an interval of time.[5]
- **Action**. The result or output that follows an event.

A transition takes a system from one state to another. The **initial state** is the state in which the first event is accepted. The model specifies the initial state—it does not need to be entered by a transition. A transition has a pair of states:

---

3. The **basic model** is a deterministic, incompletely specified Mealy machine with guarded transitions (these attributes are explained later in the chapter).

4. In mathematics, an automaton is a model of systematic and repetitive computation. These models are termed finite because they compute with a fixed number of states. The state machines discussed are Mealy-type *deterministic finite automata*. Nondeterministic models are useful for theoretical analysis, but are not relevant for our purposes. The large body of theoretical results for finite automata is not discussed here. See this chapter's Bibliographical Notes section for sources on automata theory.

5. *Event* is used in a general, abstract sense here. This term has many implementation-specific definitions—for example, in the java.awt framework or Microsoft's ActiveX controls. These implementation-specific "events" may correspond to the general sense of an event. Just as often, the term is used as a shorthand for a complex set of capabilities. Thus, the activation of one of these "events" does not necessarily map to an event in a state machine, or vice versa.

the **accepting state** and the **resultant state,** which may be the same. A machine may be in only one state at a time. The **current state** refers to the active state. A transition is made from the current state to a resultant state. The **final state** is one in which the machine stops accepting events.[6] Every unique input/output pair that a state machine can produce has a unique sequence of prior inputs.

The mechanism of a state machine has several steps:

1. The machine begins in the initial state.
2. The machine waits for an event for an indefinite interval.
3. An event presents itself to the machine.
4. If the event is not accepted in the current state, it is ignored.
5. If the event is accepted in the current state, the designated transition is said to **fire**: the associated output action (if any) is produced and the state designated as the resultant state becomes the current state. The current and resultant state may be the same.
6. The cycle is repeated from step 2, unless the resultant state is the final state.

The basic state machine model has a simple repertoire:

- The process by which events are generated, sequenced, or queued for recognition is not a subject of the model.
- Events are recognized singly. Transitions fire one at a time.
- No events other than those defined in the model are recognized.
- The machine can be in only one state at a time.
- The current state cannot change except by a defined transition.
- The model is static: no state, event, action, or transition may be removed by execution of the machine. No new states, events, actions, or transitions may be introduced by the execution of the machine.
- The details of the process, algorithm, or implementation by which an output is computed (an action) is not a subject of the model.
- No definite interval is associated with any aspect of the model. The firing of a transition (the presentation of an event, its acceptance, and the production of its action) does not consume any specific amount of time.

---

6. A less restrictive definition of "final state" is used in formal models: a *final state* is any state that is reached after accepting a complete set of input events. The machine does not stop accepting input after reaching this state.

Some authors characterize a machine as having cycles or a "clock," where each cycle or clock tick corresponds to one transition. Except in some advanced models, no time unit is associated with such a cycle.

A valid state model must also follow rules of construction (see Table 7.5 later in the chapter). It is, of course, up to the analyst to devise a model that correctly represents the behavior of the system under study.

Figure 7.2 suggests the basic problem associated with modeling state-based behavior. This simple mechanism can model very complex control requirements

Input is externally
determined in time
and sequence.

Output is determined
by current input
and system *state.*

a,b,a,a,a,a,c,d,a, . . .

x,y,z,z,z,z,z,y,x,x, . . .

How are states, inputs, and outputs related? What's in the box?

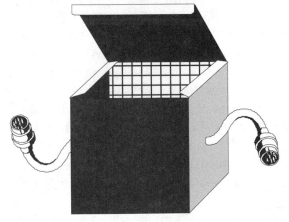

FIGURE 7.2   An external view of "behavior."

and sequentially constrained application behavior. A few examples include the folllowing:

- The behavior of GUI widgets in JavaBeans, MS/Windows, Unix X-Windows, OS/2 Presentation Manager, NeXT UI Builder, and so on.
- The life cycle and behavior of business objects (classes): order, customer, stock item, warehouse slot, and so on.
- Communication devices: network interface cards, ISDN routers, modem controllers, telephone handsets, hand-held wireless, and so on.
- Device drivers with retry, restart, or recovery.
- Command syntax parsers. State machines and syntax have an elegant, well-understood relationship.
- Long-lived database transactions.
- Motion control systems: avionics, automotive cruise control, robotic motion, and so on.

7.2.2 State Transition Diagrams

A **state transition diagram** is a graphic representation of a state machine. Nodes represent states. Arrows (directed edges) represent transitions. The annotations on the edges represent events and actions. Three popular variants are shown in Figure 7.3: traditional (as used in many computer science texts), structured analysis [Ward 85, Hatley 87], and statechart notation (rounded rectangles) as adapted by the UML.

The three diagrams in the upper part of Figure 7.3 illustrate how identical behavior is modeled in these variants. States are numbered 1, 2, 3, . . . and denoted by S_i. Events are denoted $A, B, C, . . .$ and actions are denoted $X, Y,$ and Z. Predicates in event guards (discussed later in this chapter) are denoted by p and q. The null action, Φ (phi), denotes a transition that does not produce an action.

The diagrams in the lower part of Figure 7.3 model an automatic refilling mechanism for a liquid tank. In this example, the liquid level is monitored by a float. The *float low* event occurs when the system senses a drop in the liquid level. This event is recognized only when the valve is shut. The transition causes a supply valve to open, and the tank begins to refill. When the float sensor indicates a full liquid level and the valve is open, the action to close the valve is generated. All of the diagram variants model the same behavior, and the allowed sequences of input/output are identical in all three.

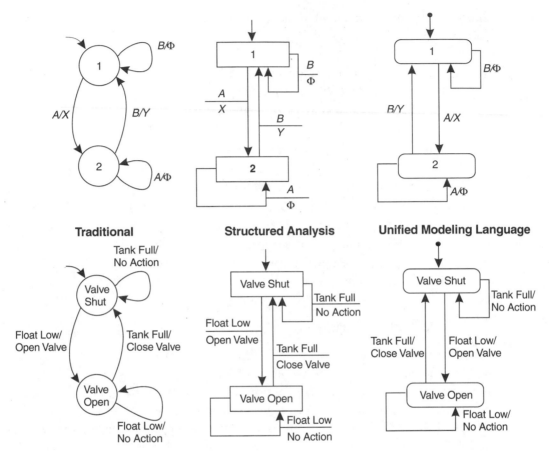

FIGURE 7.3 State transition diagram notation.

7.2.3 Some Properties of Finite State Automata

Some properties of formal automata have practical implications for testing. For example, formal models require an explicitly specified transition for every possible event/state pair. A model in which any such pair is undefined is said to be an **incomplete specification**. Nearly all software engineering state models, however, allow incomplete specification because typically only a few of all possible event/state pairs are of interest. Although this is a convenient modeling shorthand, we will see that we cannot ignore unspecified event/state pairs in testing.

Any two states are **equivalent** if all possible event sequences applied to these states result in identical output action sequences. That is, if we start in either equivalent state and apply all possible combinations of events up to and including those that result in a final state, we cannot tell from which state we started by comparing output actions. The notion of equivalence can be extended to any set of states. A **minimal state machine** has no equivalent states. A model with equivalent states is at best redundant, and probably incorrect or incomplete in some more serious way.

A state S_i is **reachable** from another state S_j when a legal event sequence takes the machine from S_j to S_i. When some state is said to be reachable without specifying a starting state, the initial state is assumed—for example, "*Player2_Next* is reachable" means that this state is reachable from the initial state. **Reachability analysis** is concerned with determining which states are reachable. In practice, nonreachable states arise for several reasons.

- *Dead state.* Once the machine enters a dead state, it effectively ceases to operate. No paths lead out of a dead state, so no other state is reachable from it.
- *Dead loop.* Once the machine enters a dead loop, no states outside of the loop may be reached. Such a loop typically prevents a transition to a final state.
- *Magic state.* A magic state has no inbound transition but provides transitions to other states. In effect, it is a pathological or extra initial state.

A dead state or dead loop is appropriate in some rare circumstances (for example, in the controller of a smart bomb), but is nearly always an error.[7] A magic state is always an error. Examples of these problems are given in the state model checklist (see Table 7.5, page 238).

7.2.4 Guarded Transitions

Consider a partial state model for class `Stack` shown in Figure 7.4. The behavior of `Stack` suggests three states: *empty, loaded,* and *full.* The methods `push` and `pop` are modeled as events. These methods behave differently at the limits of a stack's size. Sending `pop` to an *open* stack results in an *empty* stack

---

7. The Hamlet-like soliloquy of "Bomb" in the Dan O'Bannon sci-fi film *Dark Star* (1973) suggests some consequences of active, but supposedly terminal states. A self-destruction device ("Bomb") is activated aboard a deep-space freighter, but the control; software argues with itself about the wisdom of immolation.

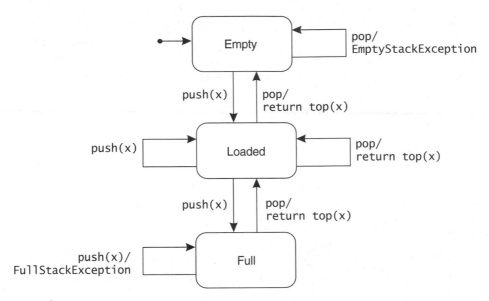

FIGURE 7.4   State machine model of Stack without guards.

when the popped item was the only item in the stack. Sending push to a *loaded* stack results in a *full* stack only if the stack contains one less item than the maximum allowed before the push. In all other cases, push and pop result in the *loaded* state. This model is ambiguous: it does not specify which transition must result for a push or pop accepted in the *loaded* state. Adding an *almost empty* or *almost full* state to our model would not help, because the same ambiguity would occur for transitions on these states.[8]

The required behavior for *loaded* may be unambiguously specified by adding a guard to these transitions. A **guard** is a predicate expression associated with an event. A **guarded transition** cannot fire unless (1) the system is in the accepting state for this transition, (2) the guarded event occurs, and (3) the guard predicate evaluates to true. In Figure 7.5, guards have been added to the Stack model. They specify behavior when the stack is almost empty or almost full.

Some OOA/D notations use a separate node to represent guards, such as a diamond [Page-Jones 95] or dot [Harel 97]. Use of this notation complicates the tree-generation algorithm used to produce a test suite, however, and it is not

---

8. Formally, a model in which the same event/state pair produces two or more transitions is a *nondeterministic finite automaton*. Guards may be represented in formal models as *transition system parameters* [Arnold 94].

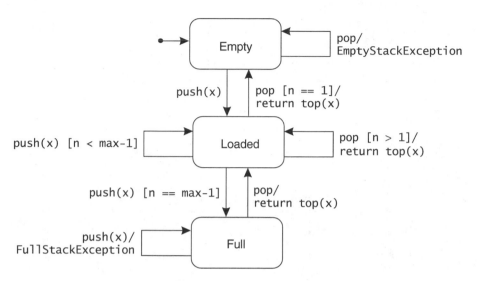

FIGURE 7.5 State machine model of Stack with guards.

used in FREE model. In UML, the guard expression is given in brackets following the event name:

event-name argument-list '[' guard-condition ']' '/' *action-expression*

A transition without an explicit guard is equivalent to a transition with a guard of [TRUE]. Similarly, an event not accepted in a certain state is equivalent to a transition with a guard of [FALSE] for that event. These annotations are redundant in a diagram, but can prove useful in automated analysis of the state model [Allen 95].

Analysis models are often silent or ambiguous about the definition, scope, and source of guard variables. This ambiguity must be resolved to test an implementation. We will discuss this issue in Section 7.3.2.

7.2.5 Mealy and Moore

The two main variants of state models differ in how they model output actions. In a **Mealy machine**, a transition may have an output action and any output action may be used in more than one transition [Mealy 55]. No output action is associated with state—states are passive. The machines depicted in Figures 7.3, 7.4, 7.5, and 7.6 are Mealy-type machines. In a **Moore machine**, transi-

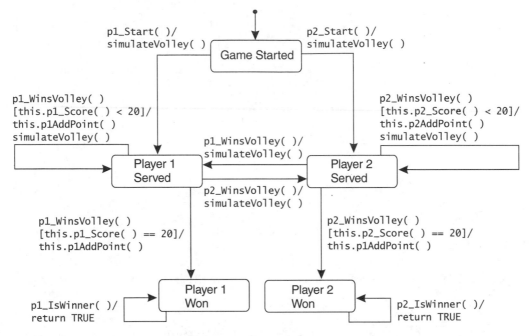

FIGURE 7.6 Mealy model of a two-player game.

tions do *not* have an output action [Moore 56]. Instead, an output action is associated with each state, that is, states are active. Every output action has at least one corresponding state. Mealy and Moore models are mathematically equivalent, in that any behavior that can be modeled with one can be modeled with the other. Algorithms have been developed to translate either to the other [Gill 62, Hopcroft 79]. In practice, the Mealy model is generally preferred.[9]

Suppose we are developing a video game that simulates two-player games like racquetball, handball, squash, or ping-pong. Each player has a start button and a reset button. All of the games follow similar rules:

---

9. The Mealy model is preferred for engineering design [Mealy 55, Gill 62, Kohavi 78, Ward 85, Hatley+87, Harel 88, Abramovici+90, Devadas 94, Comer 95] and testing [Chow 78, Sidhu 89, Beizer 90, Fujiwara 91, Holzmann 91, Beizer 95]. Many OOA/D approaches use Mealy models [Jacobson+92, Cook+94, Selic+94, Harel+97]; only [Shlaer+92] explicitly prefers the Moore model. The UML uses a hybrid form, whose problems are discussed later.

- The game starts.
- The player who presses the start button first gets the first serve. The button press is modeled as the *Player 1 Start* and *Player 2 Start* events.
- The current player serves and a volley follows. One of three things ends the volley:
  - If the server misses the ball, the server's opponent becomes the server.
  - If the server's opponent misses the ball, the server's score is incremented and the server gets to serve again.
  - If the server's opponent misses the ball and the server's score is at game point (another point to win), the server is declared the winner. In this example, a score of 21 wins, so 20 is game point.

The responsibility for these rules could be implemented in a class Two-PlayerGame, as the following Java fragment shows:

```
class TwoPlayerGame extends Object {
    private int      p1_score,p2_score;
    public           TwoPlayerGame( )  {/* Constructor */ }
    public  void     p1_Start( )       {/* P1 serves first */}
    public  void     p1_WinsVolley( )  {/* P1 ends the volley */}
    private void     p1_AddPoint( )    {/* Increase P1's score */}
    public  boolean  p1_IsWinner( )    {/* True if P1's score is 21 */}
    public  boolean  p1_IsServer( )    {/* True if P1 is server */}
    public  int      p1_Points( )      {/* Returns P1's score */}
    public  void     p2_Start( )       {/* P2 serves first */}
    public  void     p2_WinsVolley( )  {/* P2 ends the volley */}
    public  void     p2_AddPoint( )    {/* Increase P2's score */}
    public  boolean  p2_IsWinner( )    {/* True if P2's score is 21 */}
    public  boolean  p2_IsServer( )    {/* True if P2 is server */}
    public  int      p2_Points( )      {/* Returns P2's score */}
}
```

Figure 7.6 shows a Mealy machine that represents the basic protocol of two-player racquet games. Its events and actions correspond to methods in the TwoPlayerGame class. This model illustrates the use of guarded transitions, showing how multiple actions may be represented for a single transition. Although the state model represents the control for the simulation, it does not account for how the trajectory of the ball is simulated, how the players position themselves, animation rendering, sound effects, and so on. This model does represent all possible sequences in which players may exchange the role of server and conditions for determining a winner.

Note that the machine in Figure 7.6 is incompletely specified—that is, transitions are not given for all possible pairs of events and states. For example, no transition for the p1_Start() event is shown for the *Player 1 Served* state. It is assumed that this event is "ignored" while the system is in the *Player 1 Served* state. A **legal event** is explicitly allowed; all of the transitions in Figure 7.6 result from legal events. The necessary convention for state transition diagrams is that any event/state pair not shown is an **illegal event**. That is, if an event occurs for which no explicit transition exists in the current state, the state does not change and no output action is produced. However, ignoring an event is no less behavior than accepting the event and producing a transition. We will see later how to test this implicit behavior and suggest some approaches to safe implementation of illegal events.

Figure 7.7 depicts an equivalent Moore model of the two-player game. This machine responds to the same events with the same output actions represented in the Mealy model. The behavior of the two models is identical and, in this sense, they are equivalent. However, because an output action can be represented *only* by a state in a Moore model, the number of states is greater and the transition graph is more complex. A Mealy model will result in a simpler tran-

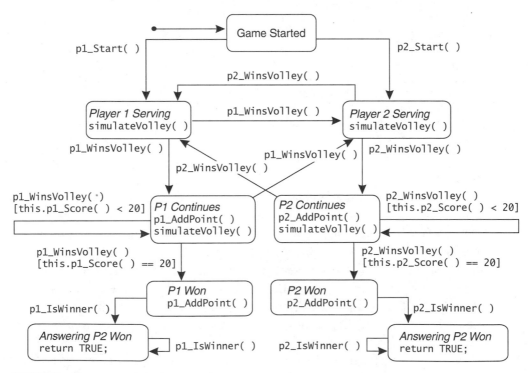

FIGURE 7.7   Moore model of a two-player game.

sition diagram if the same output action occurs on two or more transitions. In a Moore machine, every unique action/state pair must be represented with a state. If several output actions are used in different combinations, each combination requires a unique state. Moore used this form because he was interested in only externally observable behavior. "In particular, Moore asked what can be said about a circuit when one knows nothing about it except what may be inferred by performing experiments involving only the input and output terminals of the circuit" [Mealy 55, 1046].

Mealy notes that stored values constitute the essential difference between sequential and combinational logic. To exclude stored values from a sequential model is to exclude this essential difference, which turns out to be the reason that the externally focused Moore model is typically more complex. When applied to software, the stored state of a Mealy machine can be precisely defined by state invariants, providing an unambiguous, implementable, and testable definition of state (this issue is discussed in detail below). Put simply, Moore is more.

7.2.6 State Transition Tables

State transition diagrams are useful for models with a relatively small number of states. Drawing and using a large state transition diagram is difficult and error-prone, even with good CAD or CASE tools. In my experience, models with 20 or more states are graphically intractable. For large models (hundreds of states), automated support is necessary. State transition tables provide a compact representation and ease systematic examination and use of the model.

State machines may be represented in one of several tabular formats. In the **state-to-state** format, rows represent accepting states and columns represent resultant states. Figure 7.8 shows a state-to-state transition table for the two-player game. In the **event-to-state** format, each event in the model has a row; each state occupies one column. Figure 7.9 shows the event/state table for the two-player game. Both formats divide a transition cell in two parts: event and action in the state-to-state format, action and resultant state in the event-to-state format. The **expanded state-to-state** format separates these items, resulting in a larger, but more explicit table (Figure 7.10). The expanded form enumerates separately the **transition function** (the mapping of event/state pairs to resultant states) and the **output function** (the mapping of event/state pairs to output actions).

Resultant State/Event/Action

Current State	Game Started	Player 1 Served	Player 2 Served	Player 1 Won	Player 2 Won
Game Started		p1_start() simulateVolley()	p2_start() simulateVolley()		
Player 1 Served		p1_winsVolley() [p1 score < 20] this.p1_addpoint(), simulateVolley()	p2_winsVolley() simulateVolley()	p1_winsVolley() [p1 score == 20]	
Player 2 Served		p1_winsVolley() simulateVolley()	p2_winsVolley() [p2 score < 20] this.p2AddPoint(), SimulateVolley()		p2_winsVolley() [p2 score == 20]
Player 1 Won				p1_IsWinner() return TRUE	
Player 2 Won					p2_IsWinner() return TRUE

Event   Action   State

FIGURE 7.8 State-to-state transition table.

Event	Guard	Current State/Action/Next State				
		Game Started	Player 1 Served	Player 2 Served	Player 1 Won	Player 2 Won
p1_start()		*simulateVolley()* **Player 1 Served**				
p2_start()		*simulateVolley()* **Player 2 Served**				
p2_WinsVolley()	DC		*simulateVolley()* **Player 2 Served**			
	p2_Score < 20			*this.p2AddPoint(), simulateVolley()* **Player 2 Served**		
	p2_Score == 20			*this.p2AddPoint()* **Player 2 Won**		
p1_WinsVolley()	DC			*simulateVolley()* **Player 1 Served**		
	p1_Score < 20		*this.p1AddPoint(), simulateVolley()* **Player 1 Served**			
	p1_Score == 20		*this.p1AddPoint()* **Player 1 Won**			
p1_IsWinner()					*return TRUE* **Player 1 Won**	
p2_IsWinner()						*return TRUE* **Player 2 Won**

Event   *Action*   **State**

FIGURE 7.9 State transition table: paired event/state format.

191

Current State — Output Action

Event	Guard	Game Started	Player 1 Served	Player 2 Served	Player 1 Won	Player 2 Won
p1_Starts		simulateVolley()				
p2_Starts		simulateVolley()				
p2_WinsVolley()	DC		simulateVolley()			
p2_WinsVolley()	p2_Score < 20			this.p2AddPoint() simulateVolley()		
p2_WinsVolley()	p2_Score == 20			this.p2AddPoint()		
p1_WinsVolley()	DC			simulateVolley()		
p1_WinsVolley()	p1_Score < 20		this.p1AddPoint() simulateVolley()			
p1_WinsVolley()	p1_Score == 20		this.p1AddPoint()			
p1_IsWinner					return TRUE	
p2_IsWinner						return TRUE

Current State — Resultant State

Event	Guard	Game Started	Player 1 Served	Player 2 Served	Player 1 Won	Player 2 Won
p1_Starts		Player 1 Served				
p2_Starts		Player 2 Served				
p2_WinsVolley()	DC		Player 2 Served			
p2_WinsVolley()	p2_Score < 20			Player 2 Served		
p2_WinsVolley()	p2_Score == 20			Player 2 Won		
p1_WinsVolley()	DC			Player 1 Served		
p1_WinsVolley()	p1_Score < 20		Player 1 Served			
p1_WinsVolley()	p1_Score == 20		Player 1 Won			
p1_IsWinner					Player 1 Won	
p2_IsWinner						Player 2 Won

Event Action State

FIGURE 7.10 State transition table: separate event/state format.

The various formats contain the same information but emphasize different aspects to the reader. Each cell represents a possible transition. Legal transitions are represented by writing the event and corresponding action in the cell. An empty cell means that no transition is defined for the corresponding event and state.

7.2.7   Limitations of the Basic Model

The basic model has several limitations as a practical software engineering tool and for testing object-oriented implementations.[10]

First, *it is not specific for object-oriented systems*. An object-oriented interpretation of generic events, actions, and states is needed to represent aspects of object-oriented implementations relevant for test design. This issue is discussed later in this chapter.

Second, *it has limited scalability*. Basic state models do not scale well. Even with the assistance of a good CASE or CAD tool, it is difficult to draw or read a diagram with more than 20 states. Tabular representations can help, but may also become manually intractable for large machines. With a large number of states (several hundred), trying to give meaningful names to states will most likely be futile.*

Scalability is usually accomplished by partitioning or hierarchic abstraction, but the basic model does not offer any such mechanism. By the end of the 1980s, most of the hundreds of published software engineering methodologies that included state machines also allowed these machines to be placed in some kind of hierarchy. Harel's **statechart** model was one such approach [Harel 87]. The statechart technique has been adapted by many OOA/D approaches, including the UML, and is discussed in Section 7.2.8.

---

10. A purely abstract limitation of finite automata is that they cannot model certain problems with arbitrarily long input. The "memory" of a finite state automata is provided by its states. As the number of states is fixed, problems that require "remembering" an arbitrarily large number of inputs cannot be modeled by a finite state automata (for example, parsing for unmatched parentheses or palindromes in arbitrarily long strings). This result is related to some fundamental insights in the theory of computing as it helps to define (very abstractly) what "general-purpose computing" means [Hopcroft 79, Krishnamurthy 85]. The practical significance of this limitation is actually positive: the behavior of a state machine (correctly implemented) is predictable. State machines are well suited to modeling deterministic control of objects that can handle arbitrarily large qualities of inputs and persistent values. This limitation has no practical implication for testing.

* Thanks to James Hanlon for this observation, based on his experiences with the ESS-5 switching system.

Third, *concurrency cannot be modeled*. Only a single state may be active, so the basic model cannot accommodate two or more simultaneous transition processes [Murata 89, Harel 88]. A single machine cannot directly represent concurrency—that is, the aggregate behavior of two or more independent processes (for example, tasks running on separate computers in a client/server system). A basic state machine can recognize events only one at a time. Only one state may be designated as the current state. Although modeling each process with its own machine is possible, a loose collection of communicating state machines does not help in analyzing or testing aggregate system behavior. Not much can be said with certainty about the behavior of such a collection unless a good deal of additional information is available to answer questions about allowable sequences of interaction.

Concurrency can be modeled with a **product machine.**[11] The states of a product machine are combinations of the states of two or more basic machines [Brand+83, Holtzman 92, Arnold 94]. For example, in a system with two identical components, each having the possible states *on* and *off*, the product machine has four states: *on_on, on_off, off_on,* and *off_off*. Although some states of a product machine may be irrelevant or unreachable, the number of states in a product machine can be quite large, even with small component machines. A product machine formed from three 10-state machines has 1000 states. Product machines, reduced as much as possible, play a key role in automated testing of telecommunication protocols [Holzmann 91]. The test model used in *Mode Machine Test* is a product machine.

7.2.8 Statecharts

Statecharts were developed to model the control requirements of complex reactive systems [Harel 87, Harel 88]. They use a graphic shorthand to avoid enumeration of all states. However, the aggregate behavior is that of a product machine. Statecharts extend the basic model in several ways to overcome the basic machine's scalability and concurrency limitations.

Consider a traffic light control system. The traffic light has five states: *Off* (no light is lit), *Red* (the red light is lit), *Green* (the green light is lit), *Yellow* (the yellow light is lit), and *Flashing Red* (the red light strobes at a fixed interval). The events *RedOn, YellowOn, GreenOn,* and *FlashingRedOn* cause the

---

11. Models of concurrent behavior include Petri nets [Murata 89] and Hoare's Communicating Sequential Processes [Hoare 85]. The basic model can be viewed as a special case of a Petri net.

corresponding state to be entered. The event *PowerOn* starts the system, but does not turn on a light. The system does a self-test and, if no faults are recognized, the *NoFault* condition becomes true. When a *Reset* event occurs and the *NoFault* condition holds, the *RedOn* event is generated. If a fault is raised in any state, the system raises a *Fault* event and returns to the *Off* state. The model specifies the permissible sequence of colors: green, yellow, red, and so on.

Figure 7.11 shows a basic state machine model for this system. Figure 7.12 shows an equivalent statechart. The behavior of these two models is identical, but the statechart is graphically simpler and easier to read. In a statechart, a state may be an aggregate of other states (a **superstate**) or an atomic, singleton state. In the basic transition diagram, one transition arrow must exist for each transition having the same event, same resultant state, but different accepting states. This may be represented in a statechart with a single transition from a superstate.

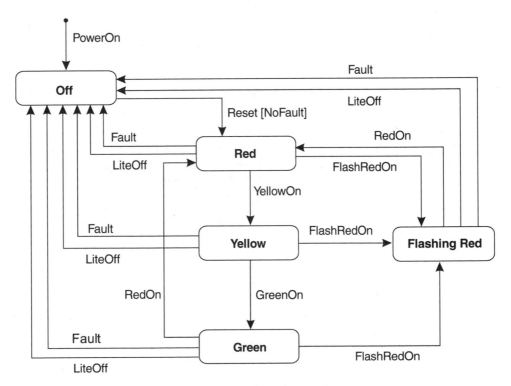

FIGURE 7.11   State transition diagram for traffic light.

For example, the two superstates in Figure 7.12, *On* and *Cycling*, show how such transitions are simplified:

- Superstate *On* represents that the system is either *Cycling* or *Flashing Red*.
- Superstate *Cycling* groups the states *Red, Yellow,* and *Green* because they share common transitions.
- *Off* is the initial state, reached by the *PowerOn* event.
- The event *FlashingRedOn* fires the transition *Red–FlashingRedOn, Yellow–FlashingRedOn,* or *Green–FlashingRedOn,* depending on which state is active.
- The event *Reset* fires *Off–On,* but only if *NoFault* is true. This is a guarded transition.
- The event *Reset* fires *Off–RedOn,* because *RedOn* is marked as the only default state with both superstates *On* and *Cycling.*
- The unlabeled transition inside the *Cycling* state shows that *Red* is the default state of *Cycling.*

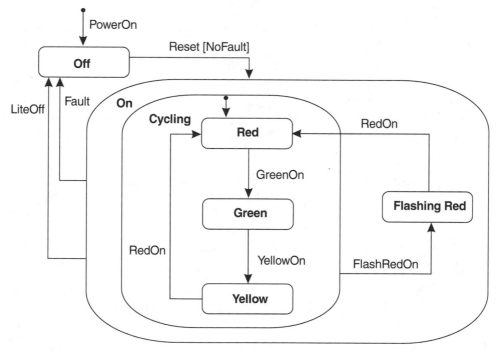

FIGURE 7.12   Statechart for traffic light.

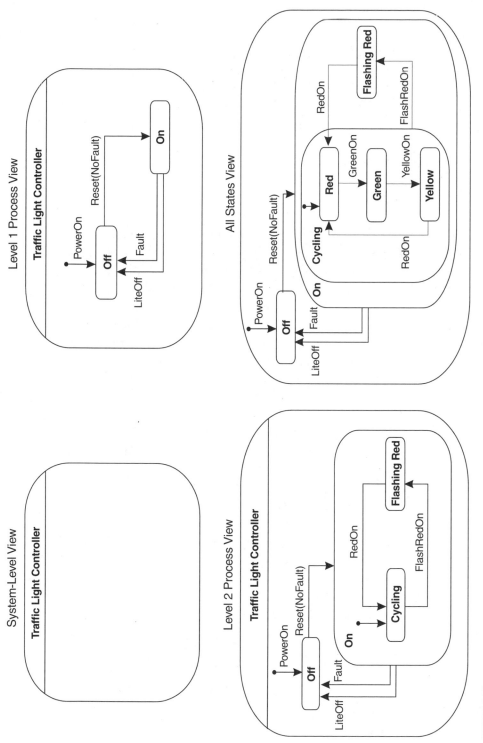

FIGURE 7.13 Nested statechart.

Statecharts can represent hierarchies of single-thread or concurrent state machines. An aggregation of states is a superstate, and the model within an aggregation is a *process*. The entire model is also a process, corresponding to the entire system under study. The traffic light model has three processes: the Traffic Light system, the *On* process, and the *Cycling* process. There are two superstates: *On* and *Cycling*.

Because all transitions among superstates appear at the boundary of the superstate, a statechart may be redrawn to suppress process details. Figure 7.13 shows the four levels possible for the traffic light system: the system-level process, the off and on processes (level 1), the off, on, and cycling processes (level 2), and all substates. Of course, the system-level view could be used as another process in a larger system model—of a six-way intersection, for example. States may be nested in any number of levels. Substate process diagrams are typically shown on separate sheets in large systems. Decomposition rules are similar to those used for data flow diagrams [DeMarco 79].

States enclosed in an undivided box are mutually exclusive, indicating that the system may be in exactly one of these states at a time. This is termed an *XOR decomposition* and represents the same state-at-a-time behavior used in the basic model. The Traffic Light Controller uses only this kind of decomposition.

Suppose we wish to model the collective behavior of two or more independent but related processes. In statecharts, concurrent (simultaneously active) states are represented by divided superstates This is termed an *AND decomposition*. That is, one state or superstate in each partition is active. An arbitrary number of simultaneously occurring states can be represented in this manner. Statecharts can thus represent systems with concurrent, independent states.

Consider the behavior of two automotive control systems: Cruise Control and Antilock Brake Control. These systems share a common event (*Brake-Applied*), but are otherwise independent. The model shown in Figure 7.14 is an oversimplification of actual motion control systems, but illustrates how statecharts represent concurrency. The behavior represented in the individual Cruise Control and Antilock Brake Control transition diagrams follows the same rules as the basic model. The transition from the *Moving* to *Stopped* state is shown only once, but may be taken from any of the six primitive states.

- The *Moving* state consists of two orthogonal processes: *Cruise Control* and *Antilock Brake Control*.

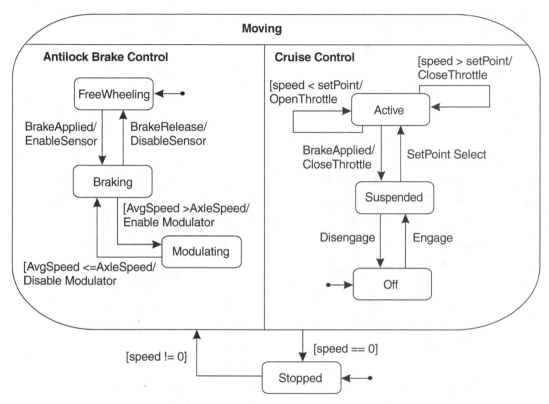

FIGURE 7.14 Automotive control statechart with orthogonal states.

- To be in the *Moving* state means that both substates *Cruise Control* and *Antilock Brake Control* are active (note the two default arrows).
- The substates of *Cruise Control* (*Off, Suspended, Active*) are mutually exclusive, as are the substates of *Antilock Brake Control* (*Freewheeling, Braking, Modulating*).

Figure 7.15 depicts an equivalent basic state model. While the statechart shows concurrent behavior implicitly, the explicit product machine must include a state for every possible combination of individual states. The number of states in the product machine is bounded by the product of the number of states in each component machine. The number of states in a statechart is the number of primitive states plus the number of enclosing processes. Both models rep-

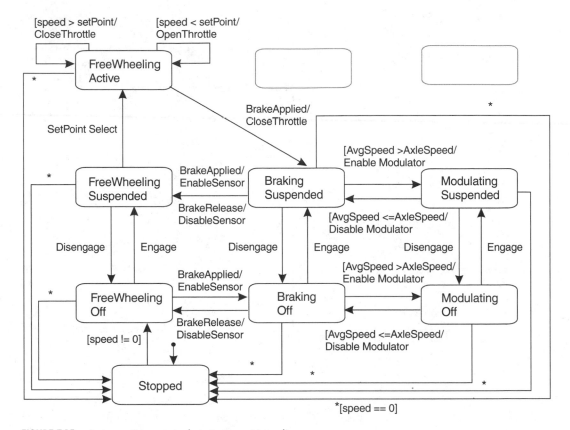

FIGURE 7.15   Automotive control state transition diagram.

resent equivalent behavior. For large systems, however, the suppression of detail achieved by statecharts is a powerful modeling tool.

Harel summarizes: "Statecharts = state diagrams + depth + orthogonality + broadcast communication" [Harel 88]. That is, statecharts incorporate all of the semantics of state diagrams from the basic model. *Depth* suggests the simplification achieved by hierarchic nesting of states. *Orthogonality* refers to the modeling of two or more independent control strategies. *Broadcast* means that all machines are visible to each other: an output action of any process may be sent to and consumed by another process.

Some semantic problems of statecharts arise from the assumption that transitions consume zero time. The response interval of the model is always shorter than the shortest interval between external events. This can lead to strange be-havior. For example, suppose the response to an event is to disable the process that produces it. As this response is assumed to consume zero time, the event effectively negates itself. Other subtle ambiguities pose similar problems [Hong 95b, Allen 95].

7.2.9 State Machines and Object-oriented Development

Statecharts have been adapted by most OOA/D methodologies and the UML.[12] Although the features dropped and added vary, the diagrams are mostly recog-nizable from one technique to the next. When using statecharts developed under different methodologies or under the same methodology on different CASE tools, however, testers should not assume any equivalency of content or semantics. Harel has developed his own interpretation of statecharts for object-oriented implementations, which includes all of the original statechart seman-tics [Harel 97]. Table 7.1 lists some key differences between UML statecharts and Harel's object-oriented flavor of statecharts. This book uses the UML in-terpretation of statecharts with the testability extensions called for by the FREE model.

Many OOA/D models refer to the orthogonal compartments of a superstate as representing "concurrent" behavior. When applied to a model of a class or object, this is a misnomer.[13] The term carries over from Harel's original model-ing of independently executing control processes as orthogonal (that is, inde-pendent and asynchronous) superstates. Unless the orthogonal compartments represent threads within a multithreaded task, separate processes in a multi-programming operating system, or processes on separate processors in a dis-tributed system, they are not concurrent—at least not in any commonly used sense. To call this situation concurrency, we would also have to say that all bits in any combination of two or more bits of memory are in concurrent states, which is a distinction without difference. Because some application models must deal with true concurrency, however, you should verify which kind of con-currency is meant.

---

12. Some OOA/D techniques using statecharts include Booch OOD [Booch 91], Object Modeling Technique (OMT) [Rumbaugh+91], Objectory (OOSE) [Jacobson+92], Embley-Kurtz [Embley+92], Objectcharts [Coleman+92], Fusion [Coleman+94], Syntropy [Cook+94], ADM4 [Firesmith 94], Real-time Object-Oriented Modeling (ROOM) [Selic+94], Object Behavior Analysis [Goldberg+95], and OML [Firesmith 98].

13. Harel observes, "Concurrent objects and orthogonal states are quite different" [Harel 97, 37].

TABLE 7.1 UML Statechart versus Harel Statechart

	UML Statechart [OMG 98]	Harel Statechart [Harel 97]
Basic semantics	Hybrid	Mealy
Event content	Message parameters, <<signal>> mapping	Any digital or analog signal of interest
Composite events	Not allowed, unless represented as parameters of a single message	Arbitrary number of external signals
Built-in operations	after, when, entry, exit, do, history	history, entered(s), exited(s), true(condition), tr!(c) (make true), fs!(c)
Interpretation of "concurrency"	Global visibility of variables defined in the "context" of the statechart and public within the scope of the modeled component	Processes that execute independently; does not model a collection of variables (objects) in the same memory space as concurrent processes
Broadcast event	Not defined, but can be modeled by messages on actions	Built-in broadcasting across boundaries of all processes
Implicit mechanism	Class (as server) with unspecified client	Nonspecific
Process	Not defined; the scope of a state or superstate is a class or method	An "XOR" group or superstate
Transition components	Limited to message semantics	Any combination of states, transitions, guards, and labels
History	Shallow and deep semantics	Built-in function
Scope/ownership of guards	Guards are visible to implicit client unless specified otherwise	As implied by the object-model diagram
Ordering of actions	Default is single-thread synchronous message calling sequence; multithread semantics may be modeled	Default is asynchronous; message passing is assumed to be queued
Transition interval	Indefinite nonzero interval	Instantaneous atomic

State machines may be implemented in many ways. The simplest strategy is to hard-code the table structure using `switch` and `ifelse` expressions. This is error-prone and difficult to maintain, especially for large machines [Auer 97]. A better tack is to represent the machine in a data structure that corresponds to one of the tables discussed in Section 7.2.6 [Cargill 92].

The *Objects for States* pattern provides another approach [Beck 94]. In this pattern, the current state is represented by a pointer to a state object. The application class implements state transition responsibilities by sending a message to the object that represents the current state. The application object passes itself in the message to the state object to provide access.

Martin's *Three-Level FSM* pattern separates an application into a three-class hierarchy [Coplien 95]. Responsibilities that have no sequential constraints are implemented in the root class. The state machine is implemented in the first subclass. Responsibilities that are to be sequentially controlled are implemented in the bottom subclass. The second-level class uses an *Objects for States* object to implement the state machine.

Many design patterns in the Gang of Four collection deal with behavior, including *State, Chain of Responsibility, Interpreter,* and *Mediator* [Gamma+95].[14] In the *State* pattern, each state subclass is flyweight singleton object, as suggested by the *Objects for States* pattern. The state machine is represented with a root abstract base superclass, which defines a method interface for each event in the machine. Each state is represented with a subclass that inherits this interface and implements the necessary actions for the event/state pair. The intent of *State* is to "allow an object to alter its behavior when its internal state changes. The object will appear to change its class" [Gamma+95, 305]. The problem addressed by *State* is not implementation of a state machine, but rather the organization of distinct, but related behaviors. Sane and Campbell show how composite state machines can be implemented with this pattern. The approach conforms to type substitutability and is efficient, using "exactly one table-lookup and one addition to dispatch events on derived state machines, no matter the depth of derivation" [Sanet 95, 17]. Schmidt's *Reactor* pattern applies *Objects for State* to design servers that must respond to asynchronous events arriving from many loosely coupled clients [Coplien 95].

Dyson and Anderson have developed six patterns for implementation of state-based behavior, which result in a cluster of objects to implement a state machine. These patterns address questions such as how state-dependent behavior can be implemented (*State Object*), where state instance variables should be located (*State Member*), how the number of state objects can be reduced (*Pure State*), how the controller can have a small interface (*Exposed State*), how transitions can be implemented (*State-Driven Transitions*), how controlled objects can be shared by several machines (*Owner-Driven Transitions*), and how the right initial state can be obtained (*Default State*) [Dyson+98].

---

14. The "Gang of Four" refers to the four authors of *Design Patterns*: Gamma, Helm, Johnson, and Vlissides.

Douglass presents and discusses many patterns for embedded system control, at a high and low level, with examples of effective table-driven implementation of state machines [Douglass 98].

7.3 The FREE State Model

The Flattened Regular Expression (FREE) state model was developed to provide a testable model of class behavior. The class under test is flattened [Meyer 88] to represent the behavior of inherited features. Behavior is modeled using definitions of state, event, and action that support the development of effective test suites. Every state machine has an equivalent regular expression—hence the name and the acronym. The FREE state model has restrictions and definitions not found in the UML, but it can nevertheless be expressed using the UML. A UML model that follows the FREE conventions will be testable. If not, the test designer will need to resolve the ambiguities and omissions that the UML tolerates or risk designing a test suite of uncertain effectiveness.

Object state at method activation and deactivation is the focus of the FREE state model. States result from the computation done by a method. An outbound message to a server object is modeled as an action associated with a transition. If an accessor method accepts an inbound message, the transition must loop back on the state in which it was accepted. If a modifier method accepts an inbound message, the transition may loop back on the state for which it was accepted or switch to a different state.

7.3.1 Limitations of OOA/D Behavior Models

Although OOA/D cartoons may be useful for preliminary analysis and design, they are inadequate for testing. Some formal models define state in terms of preconditions, postconditions, and state invariants [Schuman 87, Cook+94]. These approaches are not afflicted with the deficiencies of cartoon models, but lack certain features useful for testing. A usable object-oriented state model must answer several questions:

- How are states defined and what do they represent for class specifications? For class implementations? For objects?
- How are events and responses defined? What do they represent?
- How is control represented?

A *testable* model has sufficient information to allow automatic generation of test cases. We can devise and program an algorithm that will produce ready-to-run test cases with only the information in the model. This requires a model that meets the following criteria:

- It is a complete and accurate reflection of the kind of implementations to be tested. The model must represent all features that should be tested.
- It allows for abstraction of detail, which, if modeled explicitly, would make the cost of testing prohibitive.
- It preserves detail that is essential for revealing faults and demonstrating conformance.
- It represents all events to which the IUT must respond. A message, exception, or interrupt can be produced to test each event.
- It represents all actions such that we can generate a program to decide whether some action has been produced.
- It defines state so that the checking of resultant state can be automated.

An unambiguous and testable definition of state is the most important feature. Guards should be expressed in an executable syntax. Although executability is the key consideration, manual test production should not be precluded. A behavior model expressed as a UML statechart can meet these requirements, if it follows the FREE definitions and conventions.

7.3.2 States

A State Is a Value Set

From a control perspective, a state is simply a placeholder useful for specifying legal sequences. The nebulous definition of state that suffices for most OOA/D modeling also views state as a placeholder.[15] However, we cannot

---

15. Most OOA/D definitions of state are untestable: they cannot support an executable determination of exactly what state an object is in. The UML defines state as "a condition during the life of an object or an interaction during which it satisfies some condition, performs some action, or waits for some event. An object remains in a state for a finite (non-instantaneous) time" [Rational 97b, 104]. Harel's view that "states (or state configurations) can be viewed as abstract situations in an object's life cycle or as temporary object invariants" is closer to a testable definition [Harel 97, 37]. In contrast, Meyer's state is unambiguous: "The state of an object is defined by all its fields (the values of the class attributes for this particular instance)" [Meyer 97, 36].

have confidence in the results of a state-based test suite without the ability to decide whether a test case has (or has not) produced the expected state. Although determination of state by manual inspection may suffice in some circumstances, an executable definition is unequivocal and can be evaluated at machine speed. It is necessary for effective automated testing. Our state model must allow us to write code that can answer the question, "Is the object in state *x*?"

But just what is an object state? The phrase "state of an object" is often used to mean "a particular member of a class's combinational value set" or just "the current contents of an object."[16] Consider the class TwoBit, which contains only two one-bit variables. The domain of each instance variable is 0, 1. The complete enumeration of instance variable values is 00, 01, 10, and 11. We might be tempted to say that only four states are possible in this two-bit object, but this view is much too granular for practical testing. It leads to models with trillions of states, even in simple classes. Instead, state can be defined as a set of instance variable value combinations that share some property of interest. The states of a class are subsets of the set of all possible combinations of instance variable values. These subsets are limited to the acceptable results of computations done by methods and are grouped according to the way in which they determine acceptable message sequences. A state is therefore a relationship among instance variable values that can be coded as a Boolean expression in the object-oriented programming language of the implementation under test. Because such Boolean expressions are executable and can express any relationship of interest, they meet our requirement for an unambiguous and executable definition of state.

For example, suppose the Boolean and operation is implemented in our two-bit class. We would be interested in the states true and false. The combinational set formed by the true state contains only one member (11). The false set contains three members (00, 01, 10). The state true is bit_1 == 1 and bit_2 == 1; false is not true.

Class Account with three instance variables provides a more interesting example:

---

16. Some writers refer to the current value of the instruction register and program counter as the *program state* and use *data state* to mean the content of storage manipulated by a program. In these terms, the FREE model focuses exclusively on data state.

```
Class Account {
private:
    AccountNumber    number;        // Six digit account id
    Money            balance;       // Current balance
    Date             lastUpdate;    // Days since last transaction.
    // . . .
};
```

Suppose the balance is limited to ±$10,000.00 and that after five years of no activity (1825 days) the account is considered inactive and cannot accept any transactions. The state space for `Account` can be represented with a three-dimensional chart. Each dimension enumerates an instance variable domain, as shown in Figure 7.16. This view has 3,650,182,500,000 "states." Suppose, however, that differences in sequential behavior depend only on whether the account is overdrawn, inactive, or neither. Then only three states are of interest, as shown in Figure 7.17. Each of the 3.65 trillion value combinations falls in one of these three states.

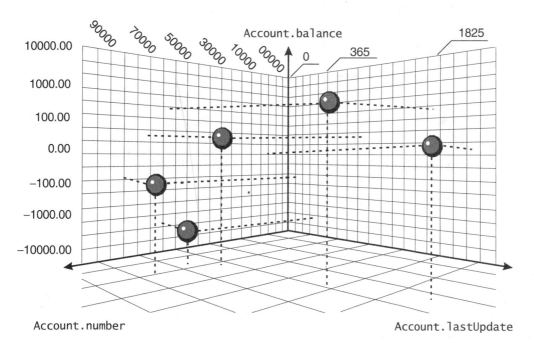

FIGURE 7.16   Primitive view of a state space.

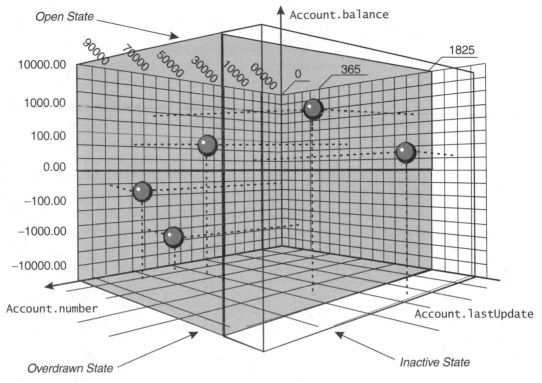

FIGURE 7.17   Abstract view of a state space.

State Invariants

Just as all valid instance values of a class may be expressed with a class invariant, a valid state may be expressed with a **state invariant**. (See Chapter 17 for more on the implementation of class invariants and state invariants.) An invariant can be implemented as a predicate expression, which means that state can be easily checked. For example,

```
assert(state1_Invariant());
// . . .
bool state1_Invariant() {
    return ( (x == 0) && remoteSession->isOpen() );
}
```

State invariants are directly related to the class invariant and method post-conditions. A state invariant must define a subset of the values allowed by the class invariant.[17] That is, it must be the same or stronger than the class invariant. If only one state is defined, the class invariant and this state variant must be equivalent. The postconditions and the invariant should provide a complete definition of all states. Methods whose postcondition contains or operators thus may compute more than one state. The number of states is equal to the number of unique non-disjoint postcondition expressions and partial expressions—for example, in Eiffel, `ensure a or b` counts as two expressions (states). Every unique postcondition in a class has at least one corresponding state. A method whose postcondition expression has n logical *or* operators can compute $n + 1$ states.

In a FREE state model, each state is defined by an executable state invariant. We can write these state definitions easily enough and thereby support state-based testing. If we implement a state machine with the *State* pattern, then the invariants may be coded within the subclasses that represent the states. In some applications, a single state variable may suffice.

◇ **Scope and Granularity**

The meaning of class or object state varies depending on its visibility, scope, and granularity. An **instance variable domain** is the set of discrete values (states) that may be represented by an instance variable. A **combinational value set** is the set of all possible combinations of instance variable values. **Visibility,** which is the basic subject of a state model, may be *abstract* (the external, public interface) or *concrete* (the internal implementation).[18] **Scope,** which is the level of abstraction, may be *bounded* (only abstract values of state variables are considered) or *recursive* (all levels of abstraction are flattened until only primitive data types remain). **Granularity,** which is the unit of definition for a state may be *aggregate* (states may consist of an arbitrary number of members of the combinational value set) or *primitive* (each member of the combinational value set is viewed as a state). States may be categorized with these concepts.

◆ 17. Formally, a state is a set of value vectors. One vector element exists for each instance variable in the class of interest. The vectors are members of the set formed over the class state space *S,* which is the Cartesian product of the legal values of each instance variable. Thus, before and after the execution of any atomic operation, an object will contain a value vector. Well-formed states are disjoint but do not necessarily cover the entire value enumeration set. If the class invariant and a complete postcondition are written in sum-of-products form, then each minterm (expressions joined by an *and* operator, see Chapter 6) is a state invariant.

18. See [Meyer 97] for an in-depth discussion of concrete and abstract state.

- *Concrete state*. A state defined over the combinational value set visible to the implementation.
- *Abstract state*. A state defined over the combinational value set visible to class clients by the class interface.
- *Recursive state*. A state defined over a combinational value set obtained by expanding (recursively) each instance variable in a class. Also called "object flattening" [Jacobson+92], "the collection of associations for that object" [Martin+92], or "complex objects" [Siepmann+94].
- *Bounded state*. A state defined over a combinational value set defined by local instance variables; that is, no recursive expansion is applied.
- *Primitive state*. A state defined by a value that can be represented with a low-level data type, which does not contain any expandable definitions.
- *Aggregate state*. A state defined by subsets of some combinational value set.

These states can be defined for both the immediate and flattened view of a class. Three distinct kinds of state variables are possible:

- *Representation*: the state variables are defined in an OOA/D model.
- *Abstract*: state variables remain limited to variables and objects visible to clients of the class under test.
- *Concrete*: state variables remain limited to those visible to the class's implementation. Typically, all abstract variables are visible to the implementation as well.

Table 7.2 summarizes the relative number of states as a function of model granularity. The difference between the most granular and the most abstract model is roughly ten orders of magnitude. The test development strategy generally remains the same for each case, but the resulting test suite typically has significant differences. Although there are some applications for fine-grained models, they generally lead us away from an efficient test model.

An abstract/aggregate state model derived from an OOD representation is ideal for class-level testing. This type of model provides a testable definition. It subsumes the fine-grain view and can be expanded to represent concrete state as necessary.

- A representation-based test suite avoids the tautological fallacy of code-based testing. Yet attempting to test only with a representation may be

TABLE 7.2   State Space Size by View

Visibility	Scope	Granularity	Number of States	Use
Concrete	Allocation	Binary	2^B	None
	Recursive	Primitive	$\Pi\, d(p_i)$, all i	Debugging
		Aggregate	$\Pi\, n(s_j)$, all i	Debugging
	Bounded	Primitive	$\Pi\, d(p_i)$	Debugging/Testing
		Aggregate	$n(s_j)$	Debugging/Testing
Abstract	Bounded	Primitive	$\Pi\, d(r_i)$	Testing
		Aggregate	$n(S_j)$	Testing

Where

B = The number of bits in the maximum amount of storage that can be allocated of the system under test for instance variables.

$d(p_i)$ = The number of discrete values representable in the ith primitive data type. For example, $d(p_i)$ for an unsigned small int = 2^{16} = 65,536.

$n(s_j)$ = The number of discrete aggregate states representable in the jth primitive object.

$d(q_k)$ = The number of discrete values representable in the kth instance variable defined in the object under test.

$n(s_j)$ = The number of discrete states in an aggregated concrete state model j, defined over all instance variables in the object under test.

$d(r_i)$ = The number of discrete values representable in the ith variable in the interface to the object under test.

$n(S_j)$ = The number of discrete states in an aggregated abstract state model j, defined over all public variables in the interface to the object under test.

impractical. In many circumstances, no representation is available. If one has been produced, it may not be test-ready; the information may be insufficient, or ambiguous, or it may leave necessary details to the developer's discretion. Even if pains have been taken to produce a test-ready representation, the model often becomes inconsistent with the actual implementation interface.

• Testing from a concrete/primitive model has drawbacks. All class features (local, inherited, and private) are considered in developing a concrete class state model. The state space can become huge, so that even a very large number of test cases may not achieve adequate state coverage. Effectiveness can suffer because the relationship of concrete states to external class features may be obscure. Explicit consideration of concrete state is at odds with information-hiding strategies. Reusability of test cases based on concrete state violates the open-closed design principle [Meyer 97].

The view of `Account` shown in Figure 7.16 (single points) is a concrete/bounded/primitive state space. In contrast, the bounded point sets in Figure 7.17 are aggregate states. An aggregate, abstract model is practical for testing. Others are usually not, due to the size of the state space and the typical lack of testability.

No Hybrids Allowed

Earlier, we noted that the Mealy model (event and action on transition, static state) is generally preferred over the Moore model (event on transition, action on state). Some OOA/D approaches, including Embley-Kurtz [Embley+92], Booch OOD [Booch 91], and OMT [Rumbaugh+91] obliterate this distinction and allow both forms in a hybrid state diagram. The UML carries this mutation forward [OMG 98]. The resulting hybrid has all the disadvantages of the Moore model, causes additional testing headaches, and does not in any way improve the model's ability to represent or analyze class behavior.

In the Moore model, state is a placeholder abstraction that does not correspond to a value set.[19] Instance variable values, however, still must map into behaviorally significant states. The hybrid does not provide a testable definition of state because actions are not readily modeled with invariants. Instead, it invites errors. Suppose that a method may compute two or more different, behaviorally significant states. The hybrid therefore represents an action(s) sandwiched between two states. In any case, the test designer must untangle the hybrid to select message sequences and check resultant state.

In short, the UML hybrid is error-prone and effort-intensive. Hybrid states are therefore not allowed in a FREE model.

7.3.3 Transitions

A **transition** is a unique combination of (1) state invariants (one for the accepting state and one for the resultant state), (2) an associated event, and (3) op-

---

19. A Mealy-type state can always be defined by an assertion that can be executed on an instance variable. These variables can always be resolved to a register, a cache, main storage, or secondary (low speed) storage that has a persistent value. A Moore-type state represents a computation in process. To assert a Moore state, we would have to write assertions on the program counter; that is, we would have to assert which units of code corresponded to the state. This ability is not supported by any of the languages discussed here. Even if it were, we still could not decide pass/no pass results of a test run by simply checking the instruction register or an instruction trace. Moore states are therefore practically and theoretically untestable. The problems that result from relying on the externally visible actions or a Moore model are discussed in Section 7.4.4.

tional guard expressions. An action may or may not be associated with a transition. The accepting and resultant states may be the same. Each transition results from an event and produces zero or more actions. Only one state may result from any particular transition.[20]

An **event** is either (1) a message sent to the class under test, (2) a response received from a server of the class under test, or (3) an interrupt or similar external control action that must be accepted by the class under test. It represents any kind of stimulus that can be presented to an object: a message from any client, a response to a message sent to the virtual machine supporting an object, or the activation of an object by an externally managed interrupt mechanism. Thus an object may change state (accept an event) without receiving a message from an external client if it encapsulates the interface to an event source.

A **guard** is a predicate expression associated with an event. If a guard references the instance that is the subject of the state model (`self`), it may designate only methods that remain visible in the assumed context of the model. That is, if the model describes behavior visible to clients, then the guard may not reference any private methods. If the model is concrete (defined on varibales visible to the implementation), then the guard may reference all methods visible within the scope of the implementation. Evaluation of the guard may not have any side effects.

An **action** is either (1) a message sent to a server object or (2) the response provided by an object of the class under test to its client. It represents the response that a class may produce for an event: messages to server objects, calls, RPCs, and so on. The structure of complex output actions (with loops and conditionals) may be modeled with regular expressions. Because actions are not states, the Moore formulation of states and transitions cannot be expressed in a FREE model.

7.3.4 Alpha and Omega States

For some test design problems, the common notion of initial and final states is problematic. If a constructor can create initial states that have different behavior, then a single initial state may not suffice to model class behavior. Two special states are defined: α (**alpha**) and ω (**omega**).[21] These states simplify testing of multiple constructors, exception handling, and destructors.

◆ 20. Formally, a transition is a partial function on S.
21. If Greek letters give you heartburn, use a instead of α and z instead of ω.

The α state is a null state representing the declaration of an object before its construction.[22] It differs from an initial state, which is the first state that an object takes after being constructed or initialized. An alpha state may accept only a constructor, new, or a similar initialization message. This message is modeled as an **alpha transition**. For example, this approach allows explicit modeling of the three-way C++ constructor idiom: default constructor, copy constructor, and parameterized constructor. Each constructor is modeled with an alpha transition.

The ω state is reached after an object has been destructed or deleted, or has gone out of scope. It may differ from an explicitly modeled final state. The omega state allows for explicit modeling and systematic testing of destructors, garbage collection, and other termination actions. It is reached by explicit or implicit destructors, which are an **omega transition**. In many implementations, a destructor is accepted in any state. Here, an omega transition applies to every state. Modeling the omega state is optional. If the omega transition is built into the implementation language and the application programmer cannot change its behavior, then it need not be explicitly modeled but should be tested.

Alpha and omega states are shown with small circles labeled as α or ω. Some care must be taken when using these states on flattened statecharts, as discussed later in this chapter.

The UML initial state (solid dot) is smaller than the alpha state, but can be used to represent different concepts (e.g., default state marker). The alpha state and the UML initial state are not interchangeable. The same goes for the UML final state (bulls eye). The UML initial and final markers may be used to designate default states in a statechart that represents a FREE model, but should not be used in lieu of alpha and omega states. Make the alpha and omega states explicit when the IUT warrants them.

◆ 22. The state space S is partitioned by the β (beta) and γ (gamma) sets. They cover the state space and are disjoint: $S = β \cap γ$ and $S - β = γ$. β is the set of legal states reachable from the α state. There are three cases of interest. An empty β set corresponds to a pathological class that does nothing. A singleton β obtains when a class has no sequential constraints on method activation (a nonmodal class). The *n*-ary case obtains when two or more states are needed to represent sequential constraints, as in a modal, unimodal, or quasi-modal class. The set of all illegal states γ is the complement of β. Any vector or set of vectors that is not a member of β is a *corrupt state*. The union of β and γ is the set of all possible combinations of instance variable values—that is, the set S.

7.3.5   Inheritance and Class Flattening

Flattening the Class Hierarchy

Inheritance must be considered to decide the prudent extent of (re)testing for a subclass. The state model of a root superclass need not consider inherited features because there are none. Subclass behavior, however, is determined by both inherited and local features. If sequential constraints exist on two or more levels, the behavior (i.e., the state machine) of the lower levels is a composite of these levels. Our testing model would be incomplete without a representation of inherited behavior. To obtain this model for subclasses, the class hierarchy is flattened.

Statecharts are well suited to representing a flattened view of behavior. A subclass state space results from two factors. The superclass state space is inherited to the extent that superclass instance variables are visible. The subclass adds state space dimensions to the extent that it defines or overrides instance variables. An orthogonal extension adds new states while preserving superclass states. A well-formed[23] and testable modal class hierarchy should conform to the following type substitutability principles:

- A subclass may accept a superclass event in more states than the superclass. That is, a superclass state can be partitioned into substates.
- A subclass may define new states, but these must be orthogonal to the superclass states. The inherited superclass state space must not be spindled, folded, or mutilated by the extensions.
- The effect of superclass private variables must be orthogonal for states formed by private and protected variables. In other words, the effect of superclass private variables on the superclass state space must be additive.

The slogan "Require no more, ensure no less" summarizes these principles. That is, compared with the superclass, a subclass's method preconditions

---

23. This discussion draws on the type-conformance rules used in Syntropy [Cook+94] and Liskov and Wing's principles of subtyping [Liskov+94]. The requirements of a well-formed class hierarchy and relative strength and weakness of invariants are further discussed in Chapter 17. Briefly, subclass state invariants should be the same or more restrictive (stronger) with respect to inherited instance variables. The preconditions of overriding methods should be the same or less restrictive (weaker) than the overridden preconditions, and the postconditions of overriding methods should be the same or stronger than the overridden postconditions. A subclass can have states that do not exist in any superclass because it can declare its own variables, and therefore may add new states.

should not be more restrictive and its postconditions should not be less restrictive. The Venn diagram in Figure 7.18 suggests state value sets that conform and do not conform to these rules.

Inheritance may be used in many ways to produce subclass behavior. The following cases illustrate how inheritance can be used to implement subclass behavior. They show that although the statechart for a given subclass may be simple, its actual behavior can be complex and explained only by a flattened model. Clearly, inheritance may be used in many other conforming and nonconforming ways. These examples follow the type substitutability rules.

• *Orthogonal composition.* Figure 7.19 shows an example of subclass behavior resulting from orthogonal composition. Each subclass inherits all of the nonprivate superclass features without redefinition and defines some new local features.

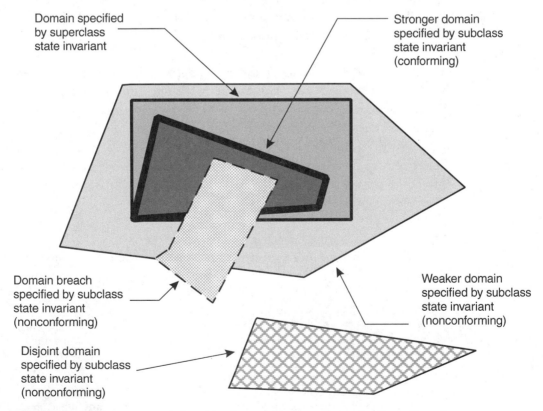

Domain specified by superclass state invariant

Stronger domain specified by subclass state invariant (conforming)

Domain breach specified by subclass state invariant (nonconforming)

Weaker domain specified by subclass state invariant (nonconforming)

Disjoint domain specified by subclass state invariant (nonconforming)

FIGURE 7.18 Conformance relationships between superstate and substate invariants.

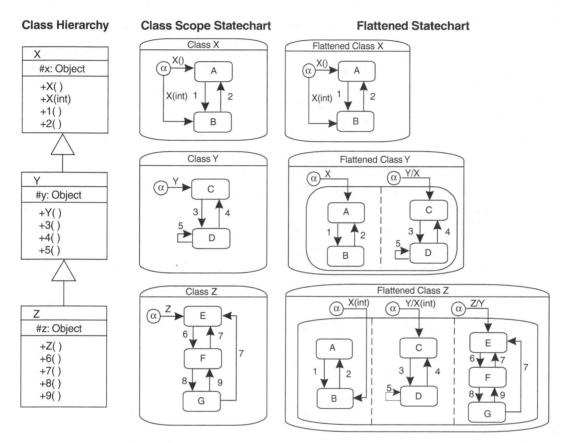

FIGURE 7.19   Flattened view of orthogonal composition.

- *Concatenation.* Figure 7.20 shows an example of subclass behavior resulting from concatenation. Concatenation involves the formation of a subclass that has no locally defined features other than the minimum requirements of a class definition. Mixin classes are an example of concatenation.

- *State partitioning and substate addition.* Figure 7.21 on page 219 provides an example of subclass behavior resulting from partitioning a superclass state. All superclass behavior for the state is preserved, and some new behavior is implemented. The new behavior is a result of partitioning the superclass state *C* and adding a new state *J*. This requires overriding some superclass methods.

- *Transition retargeting.* Figure 7.22 on page 220 shows an example of subclass behavior that results from partitioning a superclass state and changing

Class Hierarchy   **Class Scope Statechart**   **Flattened Statechart**

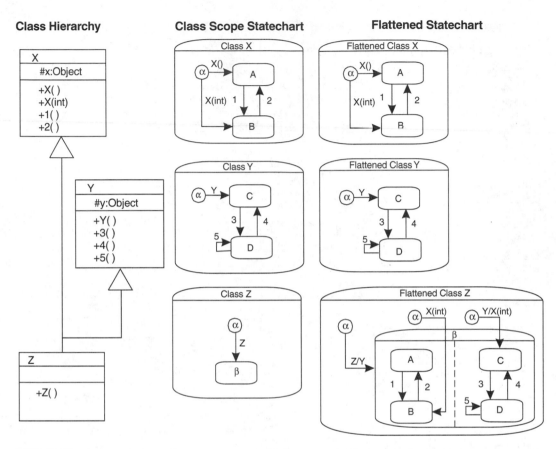

FIGURE 7.20   Flattened view of type concatenation.

the resultant state of some events. An object of class Z will reach substate *H* on event 4. *H* is a substate of *C*, which is reached when event 4 is accepted by an object of class Y. This requires overriding some superclass methods. Note that the postcondition and state invariant for the overriding method should be the same or more restrictive than those of the superclass.

• *Transition splitting.* Figure 7.23 on page 221 gives an example of superclass transitions redefined by guards. An object of class Z will reach substate *H* on event 4. *H* is a substate of *C*, which is reached when event 4 is accepted by an object of class Y. This requires overriding some superclass methods.

Multiple alpha transitions are used to model constructor behavior. Subclass constructors typically percolate up the hierarchy (see *Percolation*) so a complete

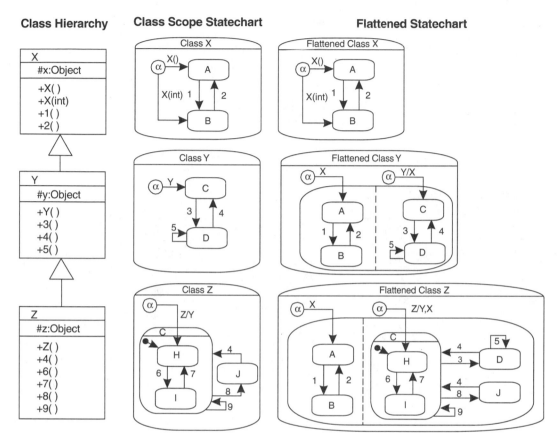

FIGURE 7.21   Flattened view of superstate partitioning.

flattened model must show the chain of events that happens upon construction of a subclass. Each class in the hierarchy has an alpha state. The transition from the subclass's alpha state to its initial state has the subclass constructor as its event. The typical percolation of constructors is represented by the action of sending the constructor message to its immediate superclass, for example, super new. When multiple alpha states appear, the first transition to fire is the one whose event must arrive from outside the scope of the statechart. This transition should involve the constructor message for the lowest-level subclass. The action on this transition becomes the event on the alpha transition for the next class up, and so on, until the root-level class is reached.

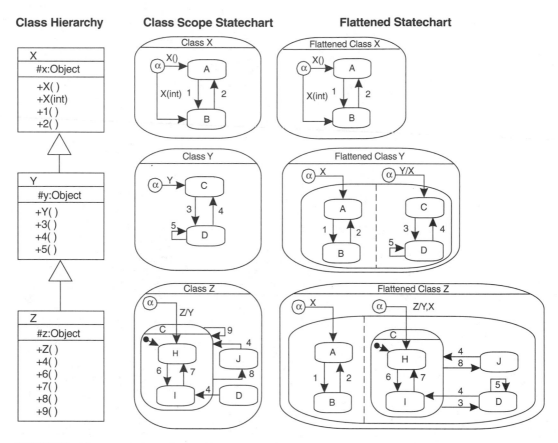

FIGURE 7.22   Flattened view of transition retargeting.

Expanding the Statechart

A statechart is an effective graphic technique to maintain intellectual control over a complex system. Although a statechart corrals the complexity beast, it cannot alter its basic nature. It is a model—not magic. Complex behavior cannot be reduced or eliminated by representing it as a statechart. Instead, we must pay for the reduction in graphic complexity by relying on the implicit semantics of the statechart. This may obscure subtle errors.

For example, suppose that the implementation incorrectly enters the last active substate upon accepting a transition that, on the statechart, enters a superstate. The implicit specification is that the initial state should obtain after accepting this transition. Testing the transition without checking the resultant

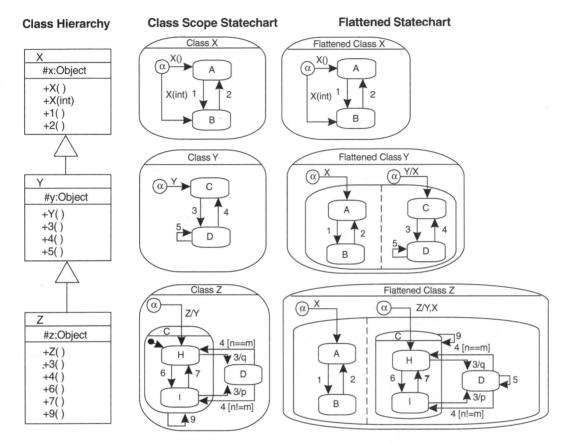

FIGURE 7.23   Flattened view of transition splitting.

state will not reveal this bug. It is possible to exercise the transition and still miss the bug if you conclude that the transition "works" after the event is accepted when the initial state just happens to be the current state. Testing from an expanded model will reveal these kinds of bugs, just as it will reveal garden-variety bugs.

Even if we manage to avoid bugs due to misinterpretation, we must expand the statechart's implicit state machine to generate a complete test suite. Implicit behavior is no less a requirement than explicit behavior. If we test only the transitions and states that have an explicit arrow or box in the statechart, we will not exercise any of the implied behavior. Clearly, such a test suite could not be considered adequate.

Although it carries more information than a local subclass model, a flattened statechart only begins to suggest the behavior that actually obtains in a subclass. Statecharts do their job well. They hide complexity, which is useful for design and efficient communication among developers. This does not decrease the actual complexity of behavior, however, and therefore does not decrease the scope of adequate testing. The resulting behavior of a flattened class is the product machine formed from the orthogonal machines in the flattened statechart. The **flattened transition diagram** shows (in gory detail) the complete behavior of the class under test. Its preparation involves three steps:

1. The flattened state model for the class under test is prepared, following a process similar to those shown in Figures 7.19 to 7.23 (pages 217–221).

2. Implicit transitions to and from each superstate within each orthogonal compartment must be expanded. For example, if we began with the level 2 model of the traffic light shown in Figure 7.13 (page 197), we would get the state transition diagram shown in Figure 7.11 (page 195).

3. The orthogonal compartments are translated into a single product machine, as shown in Figures 7.11 and 7.12 and in Figures 7.19 and 7.24. Algorithms for computing a product machine may be found in [Hopcroft 79], [Lewis 81], [Brand 82], and [Holzmann 91].

For example, Figure 7.24 shows the product machine for the flattened view of subclass Z as derived by orthogonal composition (Figure 7.19, page 217). This machine fully represents the explicit behavior of subclass Z. The expansion can be performed by hand with patience and persistence. If it is to be applied routinely, however, this task should be automated.

Flattening is not always necessary.

• You wish to test at subclass scope only and do not want to exercise any inherited features. This effort is a legitimate first step in verifying the behavior of a newly developed subclass. After you have confidence in the subclass, however, a full test suite of the subclass with its inherited features should be designed and run.

• You cannot develop a full model of the superclass(es), for any reason: information is unavailable, not enough time, and so on. Cross your fingers and hope for the best.

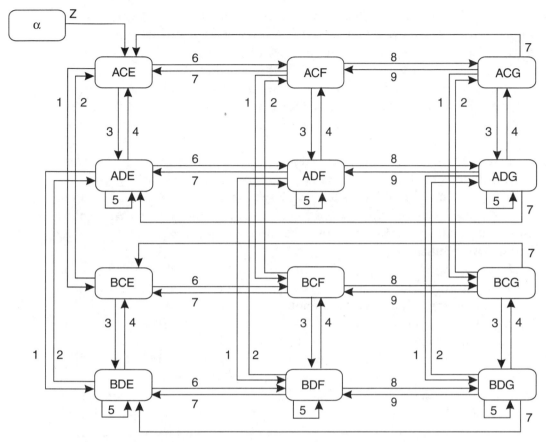

FIGURE 7.24 Expansion of flattened view of orthogonal composition.

7.3.6 Unspecified Event/State Pairs

Software engineering state machines are typically incompletely specified: many event/state pairs are to be "ignored." In a typical state model, only a few of the defined events are accepted in each state. For example, in the Traffic Light Controller, the *RedOn* event is accepted only in the *Off, Yellow,* and *FlashingRed* states. If *RedOn* occurs in the *Red* or *Green* states, however, some kind of exception should be raised. An unspecified event/state pair may mean that the implicit transition is illegal, ignored, or "impossible." It may also be a specification omission. When an event occurs and no transition is specified for it in the current state, the typical assumption is that no action results and the state remains unchanged. This assumption is more than a convenient short-hand. "Ignoring" an event in a certain state may be critically important.[24]

An **illegal event** is an otherwise valid event (message) that should not be accepted given the current state of the IUT. If it is accepted, an **illegal transition** results. An illegal transition occurs when the IUT, in some valid state, accepts a message that is not explicitly specified for that state. Similarly, a guarded transition should fire when we send a message that satisfies the guard. Yet what happens when the guard is false? An incomplete specification is often associated with failures when illegal events are presented to the implementation under test. A **sneak path** is the bug that allows an illegal transition or eludes a guard. Just as each illegal transition implies a possible sneak path, each guarded transition has a set of conditions under which the transition should not fire. An explicit exception-handling mechanism should be specified for illegal events, providing a complete specification.

I am not aware of any published OOA/D methodology that calls for an explicit specification of the response to an undefined event/state pair.[25] Although this simplifies modeling, silence and ambiguity in a specification often lead to bugs. Nothing prevents a client from issuing a message (event) that is not specified for the current state. The implementation under test will make *some* response, and this response should be tested to be sure it is acceptable. If the implementation incorrectly accepts an illegal event and executes a method, the results are unpredictable and probably undesirable. Illegal event handling implements (or fails to implement) implicit constraints on state-based behavior. Like any other application feature, it should be tested. To be tested, it must be modeled.

A further complication can arise with truly concurrent states. Suppose several independent processes are running. What happens when an event occurs that is legal for one current state but not for another, and the output control actions are inconsistent? "Conflicts will inevitably arise . . . when two or more active states wish to respond in different and mutually exclusive fashion to a given event" [Allen+95, 2].

---

24. Illegal events do not exist (by definition) in formal automata. Formal models require a completely specified machine: every possible event/state pair must have an explicit transition. An incomplete specification means that some event/state pair has not been specified (it does not refer to other kinds of omissions).

25. Allen and de Champeaux reach the same conclusion [Allen+95]. They use an extension for statecharts that assumes Harel concurrency semantics and provides an explicit specification of "not expected" and "partially expected" events. All events are assigned one of seven responses. Extended semantics are defined for an event dispatching and queuing mechanism to control the presentation of events to the statechart.

Excluded behavior is implicit in an incompletely specified state model. The typical interpretation is "don't allow any events that aren't explicitly represented" or "ignore events that aren't explicitly represented." Explicit and implicit behaviors are equally important. Two kinds of implicit behavior are important for testing: the response to illegal events and the response to events when the guard expression is false.

Complete behavior testing should exercise both explicit and implicit behavior.

The Response Matrix

The FREE model requires a response specification for all event/state pairs so that all event responses may be tested. As we have seen, the explicit response may be documented with a UML statechart. Implicit responses are specified with the **response matrix**. The response matrix in Figure 7.26 corresponds to the state transition diagram in Figure 7.25.

The response matrix is a modified form of the event/state table. This matrix lists all events. Each unguarded event has a row; each guarded event has one

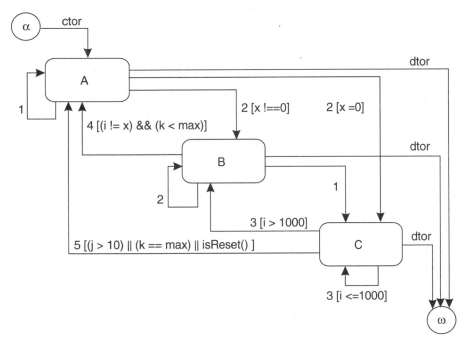

FIGURE 7.25   Guarded and implicit transitions.

Events and Guards				Accepting State/Expected Response					
				α	A	B	. . .	C	ω
ctor				✓	6	6	6	6	6
Event 1				✗	✓	✓	. . .	2	6
Event 2	x == 0								
	DC			✗	✗	✓	. . .	2	6
	F				✓	✗	✗		
	T				✓	✗	. . .		
Event 3	i <= 1000								
	DC			✗	2	2	. . .	✗	6
	Off			✗	2	2	. . .	✓	✗
	On			✗	2	2	. . .	✓	✗
Event 4	i != x	k < max							
	DC	DC		✗	2	✗	. . .	2	6
	F	F				1	. . .		
	F	T				2	. . .		
	T	F				2	. . .		
	T	T				✓	. . .		
Event 5	i > 10	k == max	isReset()						
	DC	DC	DC	✗	2	5	. . .	✗	6
	F	F	F				. . .	5	✗
	F	F	T				. . .	✓	✗
	F	T	F				. . .	✓	✗
	F	T	T				. . .	✓	✗
	T	F	F				. . .	✓	✗
	T	F	T				. . .	✓	✗
	T	T	F				. . .	✓	✗
	T	T	T				. . .	✓	✗
dtor				✗	✓	✓	. . .	✓	2

Key: T = true, F = false, DC = don't care; for Action codes, see Table 7.3
▢ Not applicable   ⊠ Excluded   ☑ Explicitly specified transition

FIGURE 7.26   Canonical response matrix for Figure 7.25.

row for each truth value combination of its guard and an additional column for each predicate within its guard. The truth table of the guard expression is enumerated in these predicate columns. In contrast, unguarded events do not have any predicate columns. Each state has a column, including alpha and omega. The cell located at the intersection of an event/guard row and state column designates whether the event is legal. A check mark indicates an explicitly specified transition. If necessary, the check mark can be replaced with a pointer to the desired action or other useful notation.

If an event has guards, then there is a row for each unique event/guard combination. If an event is guarded in some transitions but not in others, then include an additional don't care row.

Cells that do not correspond to explicit legal transitions represent illegal transitions. Each illegal cell holds a number that designates the response to be produced when an illegal event occurs. Table 7.3 lists several possible responses. Allen describes a similar, more elaborate approach to illegal events [Allen+95]. Cells with an "X" are mutually exclusive. For example, if an event is simply not accepted in a state, then any guard rows that apply to other states are excluded. The "X" is also applied to guard cells that are ignored with an unguarded event.

The response matrix corresponds to the flattened view of the class under test. Attempting to produce a response matrix without a flattened model may be difficult and confusing.

TABLE 7.3   Response Codes for Illegal Events

Response Code	Name	Response
0	Accept	Perform the explicitly specified transition
1	Queue	Place the illegal event in a queue for subsequent evaluation and ignore
2	Ignore	No action or state change is to be produced, no error is returned, no exception raised
3	Flag	Return a nonzero error code
4	Reject	Raise an `IllegalEventException`
5	Mute	Disable the source of the event and ignore
6	Abend	Invoke abnormal termination services (e.g., core dump) and halt the process

Designing Responses to Illegal Events

The response matrix defines the expected response for test cases that exercise illegal event handling. The response to an illegal event has two parts. First, an appropriate error message or exception should be produced (unless the absence of a response is truly acceptable). Second, the abstract state of the object should remain unchanged after rejecting the illegal event. The concrete state may change because of necessary error handling.

Illegal events pose interesting design questions. Some methodologists argue that an object should accept any possible sequence of messages, implying that well-designed classes should have few, if any, illegal transitions. Generic, low-level, framework classes (e.g., stack, queue, or string) are typically designed this way, but "anything goes" is rarely appropriate for classes that represent application entities having a life cycle or that implement application control strategies.

What should the response to an illegal event be? The defensive school argues that server objects should monitor for illegal events and respond appropriately [Booch 91, Weide 91]. The cooperative school argues that client objects have the responsibility to use servers correctly and therefore require little if any defensive coding [Meyer 97]. Cooperative servers should check for illegal messages during integration testing. Compared with cooperative systems, defensive classes are easier to test because the state control strategy is localized in the server. In a cooperative system, state control for any given server may be distributed over all client/server relationships in which a server participates. With polymorphism, it may be difficult to identify (let alone test) all such relationships. (See Section 17.3.7 for a discussion of defensive and cooperative design.)

Some shops follow a standard approach to exception handling, although the particulars of illegal message handling are often crafted by each developer. An exception may be raised, the message may be treated as a no-op, some form of error recovery may be attempted, or the application may invoke an abnormal termination service. Some responses to illegal messages are annoying at best and possibly dangerous because the illegal message is processed but results are unpredictable: incorrect output, hidden state corruption, and/or unexpected abnormal termination. In any case, the tester needs to decide the expected response to illegal messages so that the actual response can be evaluated.

7.4 State-based Test Design

7.4.1 How State Machines Fail

It is not enough to have correct input/output mapping for a particular input/output pair when sequential control requirements exist as well. An implementation must also be faithful to the constraints of the specified state machine. For example, if a Traffic Light is *Green*, switching to *Red* is incorrect. Even if the red light becomes lit in response to the *RedOn* message, the system is buggy. That is, the light must always switch to *Yellow* before *Red* in a correct system. Understanding how an implementation can fail to observe these constraints provides a focus for test design and a benchmark against which to evaluate test design strategies.

Control Faults

A control fault allows an incorrect sequence of events to be accepted or produces an incorrect sequence of output actions. Although an infinite number of faulty implementations exist for any given specification, there are relatively few general kinds of control faults.[26] Compared with the specification, a buggy implementation will have one or more incorrect responses:

- A missing or incorrect transition (the resultant state is incorrect, but not corrupt)
- A missing or incorrect event (a valid message is ignored)
- A missing or incorrect action (the wrong thing happens as a result of a transition)
- An extra, missing, or corrupt state (behavior becomes unpredictable)
- A sneak path (a message is accepted when it should not be)
- An illegal message failure (an unexpected message causes a failure)
- A trap door (the implementation accepts undefined messages)

These faults may occur individually or in any nightmare combination. Table 7.4 shows relationships among these faults. Not all combinations are possible.

---

26. There are sa^{es} of possible implementations for a machine with s states, e events, and a actions [Sidhu+89]. For example, with only 5 states, 2 events, and 2 actions, there 10 billion possible implementations. Fortunately, compact testing strategies are very effective at revealing incorrect implementations.

TABLE 7.4   State Control Faults

Event	Action	Resultant State	Error Description
OK	OK	OK	Normal transition
		Wrong	Incorrect state
		Corrupt	Corrupted state
	Wrong/ undefined	OK	Incorrect action
		Wrong	Incorrect action, wrong state
		Corrupt	Incorrect action, corrupt state
	Missing	OK	Missing action
		Wrong	Missing action, incorrect state
		Corrupt	Missing action, corrupt state
Reject Legal	DC	Same	Missing transition, no side effect
		Defined	Missing transition, side effect
		Corrupt	Missing transition, corrupt state
Accept Illegal	Defined for this machine	Same	Sneak path, no side effect
		Defined	Sneak path with side effect
		Corrupt	Sneak path to corrupt state
	Undefined	Same	Sneak path, no side effect, incorrect output
		Defined	Sneak path with side effect, incorrect output
		Corrupt	Sneak path to corrupt state, incorrect output
Accept Undefined	Defined for this machine	Same	Trap door to action
		Defined	Trap door to action, side effect
		Corrupt	Trap door to action, corrupt state
	Undefined	Same	Trap door with incorrect output
		Defined	Trap door with incorrect output and side effect
		Corrupt	Trap door with incorrect output to corrupt state

For example, omitting an event means that no corresponding incorrect action will exist. Figures 7.27 through 7.34 illustrate several of these faults.

- *Missing transition.* The implementation does not respond to a valid event/ state pair. For example, player 2 loses the volley, but continues as server (Figure 7.27).

- *Incorrect transition.* The implementation behaves as if an incorrect resultant state has been reached. For example, after player 2 misses, the game resets (Figure 7.28).

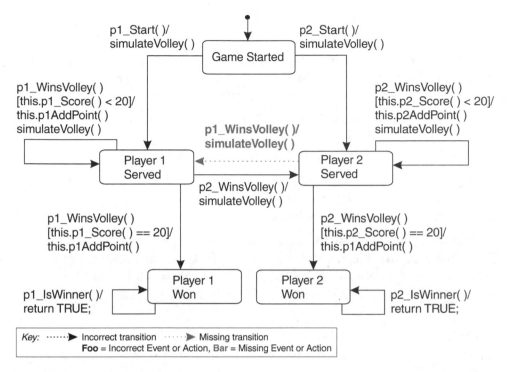

FIGURE 7.27 Missing transition.

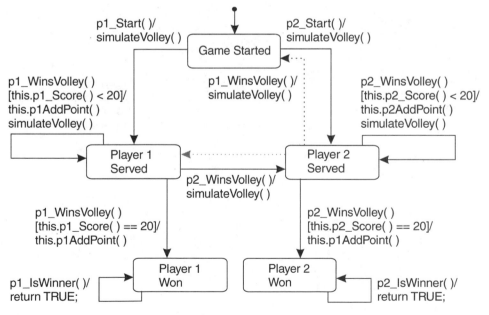

FIGURE 7.28 Incorrect transition/resultant state.

- *Missing action.* The implementation does not produce any action for a transition. For example, suppose the output action after player 1 starts is omitted. No volley is generated and the system will wait forever (Figure 7.29).

- *Incorrect action.* The implementation produces the wrong action for a transition (this case is different from incorrect output from the action). For example, after player 2 misses, player 2 is declared the winner (Figure 7.30).

- *Sneak path.* The implementation accepts an event that is illegal or unspecified for a state. For example, when player 2 is serving, player 2 can win if his or her start button is pressed (Figure 7.31).

- *Corrupt state.* The implementation computes a state that is not valid. Either the class or state invariant is violated. This state can result from a variety of coding and design errors or bugs in the virtual machine. For example, if player 1 is serving at game point and player 2 misses, the game crashes and can't be restarted (Figure 7.32, page 234).

- *Illegal message failure.* The implementation fails to handle an illegal message correctly. Incorrect output is produced, the state is corrupted, or both.

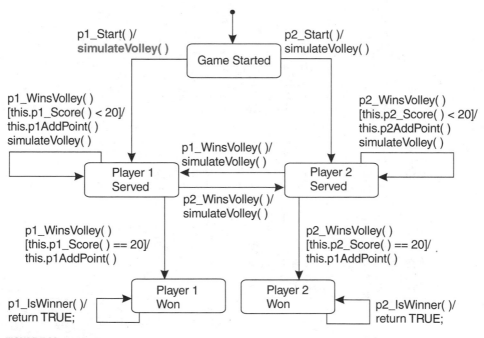

FIGURE 7.29   Missing action.

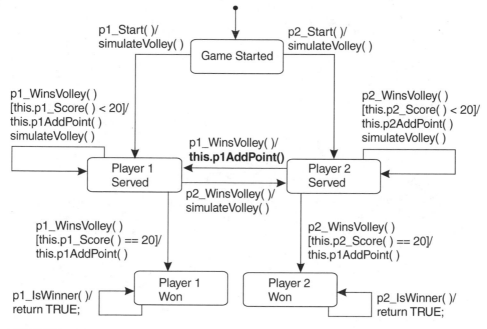

FIGURE 7.30   Wrong action.

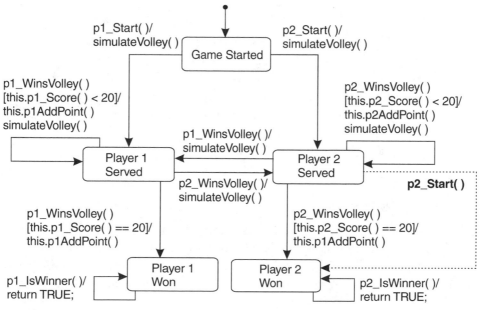

FIGURE 7.31   Sneak path.

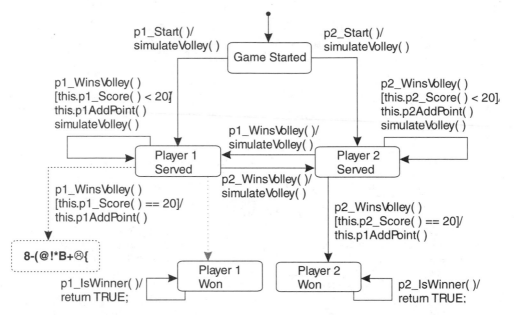

FIGURE 7.32   Transition to corrupt state.

For example, if player 1 presses the Player Select button after serving, the game crashes and can't be restarted (Figure 7.33).

• *Trap door.* The implementation accepts an event that is not defined in the specification. For example, when player 1 is serving, player 1 can win any time by pressing the Scroll Lock key (Figure 7.34). A trap door can result from: (1) obsolete features that were not removed when a class was revised; (2) inherited features that are inconsistent with the requirements of a subclass; (3) "undocumented" features added by the developer for debugging purposes; or (4) sabotage for criminal or malicious purposes.

Incorrect Composite Behavior

Misuse of inheritance with modal classes can lead to state control bugs. Unless care is taken during design and implementation, a subclass can easily conflict with the sequential requirements for one or several of its superclasses. Bugs that result from the interaction of superclasses and subclasses are not likely to be

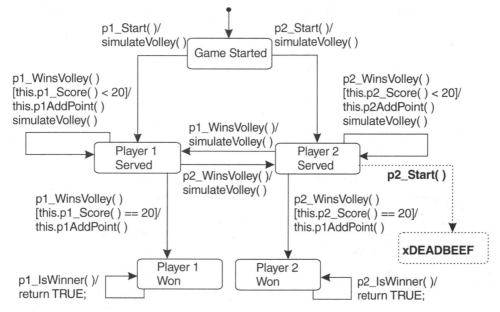

FIGURE 7.33   Sneak path to corrupt state.

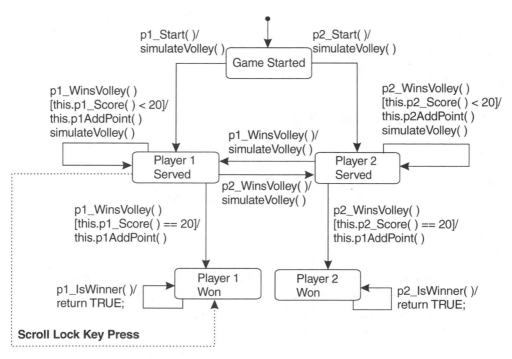

FIGURE 7.34   Trap door/extra transition.

revealed if testing is limited to the local scope of the class. These bugs include the following problems:

- The subclass method (event) to override a superclass method (event) is missing or incorrect.
- The subclass extension of state (its locally defined instance variables) conflicts with a superclass state or states (see Figure 7.18 on page 216).
- The subclass fails to retarget a superclass transition and instead switches to an incorrect or unrefined superclass state.
- The order of evaluation in guards and preconditions is incorrect or is sensitive to the order of evaluation (in effect, the guards behave as if an extra state exists).
- The evaluation of a guard produces a side effect in the subclass that is not present in the superclass.
- Default name scope resolution results in guard parameters being bound to different (wrong) subclass or superclass methods in a subclass.

These bugs will typically manifest themselves as control failures or corrupt state failures. The presence of hard real-time deadlines and true concurrency in transition conditions complicates behavior and multiplies the opportunities for error. Design errors leading to incorrect behavior are generally more difficult to find than implementation errors. Using the verification checklists at design time is an effective way to prevent design errors.

7.4.2 Developing a Testable Model

Not all implementations are well suited to state-based testing. The discussion of class modality in Chapter 10 outlines what kind of model is appropriate. When the responsibilities of the implementation under test include sequential behavior, then effective test design depends on the development of a complete, consistent, and correct state model.

When and How

Ideally, a tester can begin work with a testable OOA/D model that matches the build version of the IUT. Testers who receive untestable representations will need to close the testability gap. It is, of course, better to avoid this gap by producing testable models from the outset. However, the testability of meta-models or instance models is often moot. The model presented for testing may be incomplete, out-of-date with respect to the implementation under test, or simply not developed. In this situation, the tester must create a model of intended behavior.

A test model must correctly represent requirements and accurately reflect the implementation under test. Development of a test model recapitulates analysis/design and usually calls for some reverse engineering of the IUT.

Pragmatic guidance for developing state models is available from many sources. General approaches for state-based testing [Beizer 90, Marick 95, Beizer 95] are useful, but are not expressed in object-oriented terms. Nearly all OOA/D approaches use state models and offer state modeling guidance. The reader is cautioned, however, that most of the sources are satisfied with cartoons. ROOM [Selic+94] and Syntropy [Cook+94] are notable exceptions and can be expressed in UML. The FREE conventions and extensions will ensure that the resulting models are testable.

State Model Validation

A state model should be complete, consistent, and correct before it is used to produce a test suite. Besides technical analysis, state models should be scrutinized for omissions and inconsistencies. Qualitative analysis of requirements can prevent many kinds of bugs. The following checklists support both technical and qualitative verification. For the most part, they may be applied at any implementation scope: class, cluster, component, subsystem, or system. Some subjects—for example, inheritance—do not apply at all scopes.

- The *structure checklist* shown in Table 7.5 gives criteria for correct construction.
- Weak, ambiguous, or inappropriate state names are often symptoms of misunderstood behavior or requirements. The *state name checklist* (Table 7.6) describes kinds of state names that are often symptoms or causes of trouble.
- The *guarded transition checklist* (Table 7.7) gives criteria for checking the logic and structure of guarded transitions.
- The criteria in the *flattened machine checklist* (Table 7.8) require the state machines in a class hierarchy to be free of level-to-level conflicts, to provide consistent behavior for users of any class in the hierarchy, and are suitable targets for reuse of superclass test suites.

TABLE 7.5   State Model Checklist, Part 1: Structure

---

1. The Model Is Structurally Complete and Consistent.

   1.1 One state is designated as the initial state and has only outbound transitions (this may be the α state).

   1.2 At least one state is designated as the final state and has only inbound transitions (this may be the ω state). If not, assumptions about termination should be made explicit.

   1.3 There are no equivalent states. Algorithms for detecting equivalent states are given in [Hopcroft 79] and [Beizer 90].

   1.4 Every state is reachable from the initial state.

   1.5 The final state is reachable from all other states.

   1.6 Every state, excluding the initial state, is reachable from every other state. That is, there are no "one-shot" states. Algorithms to check reachability are provided in [Hopcroft+79] and [Marick 95]. Nonreachable states can also be found with the round-trip path algorithm (see the following).

   1.7 Every defined event and every defined action appears in at least one transition.

   1.8 Except for the initial and final states, every state has at least one incoming transition and at least one outgoing transition.

   1.9 The events accepted in a particular state are unique or differentiated by mutually exclusive guard conditions (the same event may not appear on more than one transition for any given state).

  1.10 The state machine is completely specified. Every event/state pair has at least one transition specifying that the event is (1) explicitly accepted, producing an explicit action; (2) explicitly rejected and handled by an explicit exception mechanism, resulting in a defined state; or (3) implicitly rejected and handled by an explicit exception mechanism, resulting in a defined state.

- The *robustness checklist* (Table 7.9, page 241) suggests capabilities that are necessary for safe and correct behavior under failure modes and degraded operating conditions.

I strongly recommend proactive use of these checklists. Use them to inspect and review OOA/D behavior models, implementations, and any state models that you develop for test design. A state model that meets the conditions in the checklist will encourage early prevention of errors and ease testing. Cook and Daniels note, "we also require that all sequences of messages accepted by the super-type will be accepted by the sub-type and leave it in a corresponding

TABLE 7.6   State Model Checklist, Part 3: State Names

1. **State Names.** Poorly named states are often a symptom of incomplete or incorrect design. The tester should recommend that a poorly named state in a design document be reworked (this approach is cheaper and easier than debugging code) or take it as a good indicator of buggy implementation.

   1.1 State names are meaningful in the context of the application. If there are so many states that it becomes impractical to provide unique meaningful names, consider creating a hierarchic state model.

   1.2 When in doubt, keep it out. A state is a kind of placeholder used to decide what to do next. There are many "states" that we don't care about: if a state is not necessary to control sequence, leave it out.

   1.3 Do not use "Awaiting x" or "Waiting for x" as state names. A state machine is infinitely patient—waiting for input is built-in. In many cases, "wait" states are superfluous. A state machine abstracts input/output operations—you don't usually need to model a state for "getting input," "writing output," and so on.

   1.4 Mealy-type and Moore-type states are not mixed in the same model.

   1.5 Mealy-type states have a passive name.

      1.5.1 *Best:* descriptive adjectives—hot, cold, on, off, high, low, active, inactive, full, empty, open, closed, minimized, maximized, rotated, exploded.

      1.5.2 *Good:* past tense verb phrase (verb ends with *-ed*) related to the output action that preceded the state—generated x, selected x, displayed x.

      1.5.3 *Fair:* a gerund noun phrase (verb ending in *-ing* used as an adjectival noun) that suggests the process associated with a state—running, timing, climbing, cruising, displaying.

      1.5.4 *Bad:* a gerund verb phrase—generating x, selecting x, displaying x.

   1.6 Moore-type states have an active name (better still, recast the model as a Mealy machine).

      1.6.1 *Best:* a gerund verb phrase (verb ends with *-ing*)—generating x, selecting x, displaying x, where x is the associated action.

      1.6.2 *Good:* a gerund noun phrase (*-ing* verb used as an adjective) that suggests the process associated with a state—heating, cooling, running, timing, climbing, cruising, sensing, reading, writing, sending, receiving.

      1.6.3 *Bad:* a static description—hot, cold, on, off, high, low, active, inactive, full, empty, open, closed, minimized, maximized, rotated, exploded.

   1.7 State names do not express or suggest irrelevant information.

      1.7.1 No name repeats the state variable invariant—$100 < x < 1000$.

      1.7.2 No name uses process descriptors for associated actions—compute x, display x, transmit x, enable x, disable x.

      1.7.3 No name uses input descriptors—sensor value, mouse click, user parameters.

TABLE 7.7   State Model Checklist: Guarded Transitions

3. Guarded Transitions.

   3.1 The entire range of truth values that may result from a guard expression must be covered in the set of conditions for transitions on this state (for example, there are two outcomes for [$a==b$], four outcomes for [$(a==b)$&&$(c!=d)$]. See Figure 7.26.

   3.2 Each guard condition is mutually exclusive of all other guards for a transition; that is, only one guard may be true for any possible value of the predicate variables.

   3.3 The guard variables for an abstract state model are either exported by the class under test or required in all implementations of clients of the class under test.

   3.4 The guard variables for a concrete class state model are defined by the implementation of the class under test—that is,i.e., self or this.

   3.5 A guard with three or more variables is modeled with a validated decision table.

   3.6 The evaluation of the guard expression does not produce any side effects in the class under test.

TABLE 7.8   State Model Checklist: Well-Formed Subclass Behavior

4. Subclass Behavior Is Well-Formed.

   4.1 The subclass does not remove any superclass states: All transitions accepted in the superclass are accepted in the subclass.

   4.2 The subclass does not weaken the state invariant of any superclass state.

   4.3 The subclass does not breach the state invariant of any superclass state.

   4.4 The subclass either strengthens a superclass state invariant or inherits (uses) it as is.

   4.5 The subclass may add an orthogonal state defined with respect to instance variables introduced in the subclass.

   4.6 All guards on superclass transitions are the same or weaker for the subclass transition.

   4.7 All inherited output actions are consistent with the subclass's responsibilities. In particular, verify that name-scope sensitive or dynamic binding of intraclass messages is correct.

   4.8 All inherited accessor events are appropriate in the context of the subclass.

   4.9 Messages sent to objects that are variables in a guard expression do not have side effects on the class under test.

  4.10 Messages sent to objects that are variables in a guard expression do not have side effects on the class under test.

TABLE 7.9 State Model Checklist: Robustness

---

4. The Model Specifies Robust Behavior.

4.1 There is an explicit specification for an error-handling or exception-handling mechanism for events that are implicitly rejected. In effect, the machine is completely specified.

4.2 The state of the implementation will not be incorrectly changed, corrupted, or otherwise undefined as a result of an illegal message. The illegal event mechanism either preserves the last good state, resets the class to a valid state, or performs a safe self-destruction.

4.3 For each action, there are no side effects or exceptions that would corrupt or change the resultant state(s) associated with this action.

4.4 Explicit exception, error logging, and recovery mechanisms are specified for violations of preconditions, postconditions, and invariants.

4.5 Explicit exception, error logging, and recovery mechanisms are specified for events that are missing (*A, C* instead of *A, B, C*) or late (*C* must arrive no later than 50 microseconds after *B*, but does not).

4.6 A timeout interval is specified for each state. Explicit exception, error logging, and recovery mechanisms are specified for each timeout.

4.7 The major and minor failure modes of the target environment for the system under test are cataloged. An explicit exception mechanism is specified for each failure mode.

4.8 A resultant state, fail-safe terminal state, or fail-soft terminal state is specified for each failure mode.

4.9 If the system is restartable from any other state than the initial state (e.g., fail-safe or fail-soft state), the restart mechanism is modeled as part of the state machine and defines a path to a viable normal state.

Items 4.6 through 4.9 are discussed in detail in [Leveson 95].

state. In our experience, designing this level of conformance is an excellent discipline for implementing reliable software" [Cook+94, 215].

Circumstances may warrant disregarding some of these guidelines. Often, a tester must test an implementation that violates these rules. In this situation, one should still develop a good model, even if the subject is poorly constructed. Discrepancies revealed by this analysis may serve as strong indicators of buggy code, even if making "cosmetic" corrections is impractical.

7.4.3 The N+ Test Strategy

The N+ strategy integrates elements of advanced state-based testing, UML state models, and testing considerations unique to object-oriented implementations. It builds on generic state-based testing strategies in the following ways:

- It uses a flattened state model.
- All implicit transitions are exercised to reveal sneak paths.
- The implementation must have a trusted ability to report the resultant state.

An N+ test suite that is passed achieves N+ coverage. Achieving N+ coverage will reveal all state control faults, all sneak paths, and many corrupt state bugs. Because it exercises the IUT at flattened scope, it will reveal subcontracting bugs and superclass/subclass integration bugs. If more than one alpha transition is present, this type of testing will reveal faults on each alpha transition. It will reveal faults in all omega transitions. It can suggest the presence of a trap door if used with a code coverage analyzer.

The steps to generate an N+ test suite are as follows:

1. Develop a FREE model of the implementation under test.
   - Validate the model using the checklists.
   - Expand the statechart.
   - Develop the response matrix.
2. Generate the round-trip path test cases.
3. Generate the sneak path test cases.
4. Sensitize the transitions in each test case.

The FREE model is not an absolute necessity. One can begin at step 2 with any other testable model of behavior that provides the same information. This procedure may be applied to develop a test suite for any implementation of sequential behavior.

The N+ test strategy is demonstrably more powerful than simpler state-based strategies. The simpler strategies require less analysis, however, and will produce smaller test suites. The cost/benefit trade-offs of this approach are considered at the end of the chapter.

The ThreePlayerGame Example

ThreePlayerGame is a subclass of TwoPlayerGame. It reflects the rules for cut throat, a three-player version of racquetball. A player may score only when serving. The server volleys against two other players, in no particular order. The two nonserving players compete for the opportunity to return the ball, in an effort to win the volley and become the server. The rest of the two-player rules apply. A Java fragment for this game that subclasses TwoPlayerGame follows (the superclass appears on page 187):

```
class ThreePlayerGame extends TwoPlayerGame {
    private   int       p3_score;
    public              ThreePlayerGame( )    {/* Constructor*/ }
    public    void      p3_Start( )           {/* P3 serves first */}
    public    void      p3_WinsVolley( )      {/* P3 ends the volley */}
    private   void      p3_AddPoint( )        {/* Add 1 to P3's score */}
    public    boolean   p3_IsWinner( )        {/* True if P3's is 21 */}
    public    boolean   p3_IsServer( )        {/* True if P3 is server */}
    public    int       p3_Points( )          {/* Returns P3's score */}
}
```

Our first order of business is to develop a FREE model for ThreePlayer-Game. Figure 7.35 shows the class hierarchy and corresponding statecharts.[27] Alpha and omega states are added to the TwoPlayerGame statechart. The class scope model of ThreePlayerGame simply inherits all of the behavior of TwoPlayerGame and then adds symmetric transitions for the new behavior. The statechart is shown in the lower part of Figure 7.36. Expansion of the statechart yields the flattened transition diagram shown in Figure 7.36. Figure 7.37 on page 246 gives the corresponding response matrix. The codes in the response matrix correspond to the actions listed in Table 7.3. The conformance and sneak path test suites appear in Tables 7.10 (pages 251–252) and 7.11 (pages 254–255). Next, we explain how they were developed.

Generate the Round-trip Path Tree

With a testable state model in hand, the next step is to transcribe the **transition tree** from the transition diagram.[28] This tree includes all round-trip paths:

---

27. I've used a C++ destructor to show how an omega transition is modeled. This would not be part of a Java implementation.

28. This procedure is adapted from Chow's *W-method* [Chow 78]. The W-method requires (1) a complete state machine model (all states have events and actions), (2) a minimal state model (there are no redundant or unnecessary states), (3) an initial state, and (4) no unreachable states. A verified FREE model meets these conditions.

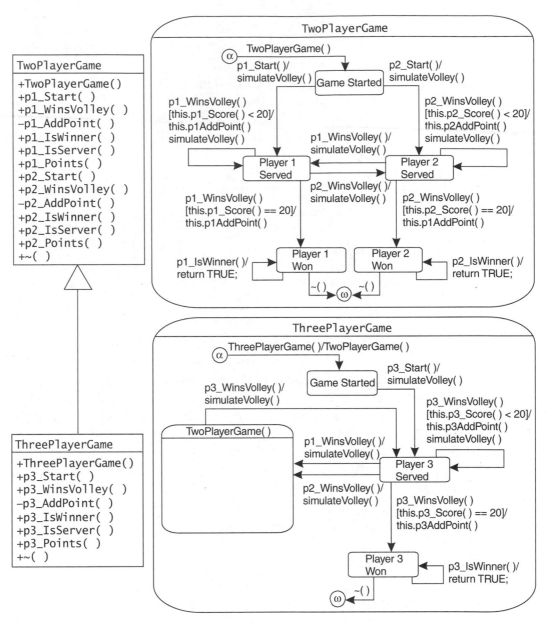

FIGURE 7.35   ThreePlayerGame class hierarchy and statecharts at class scope.

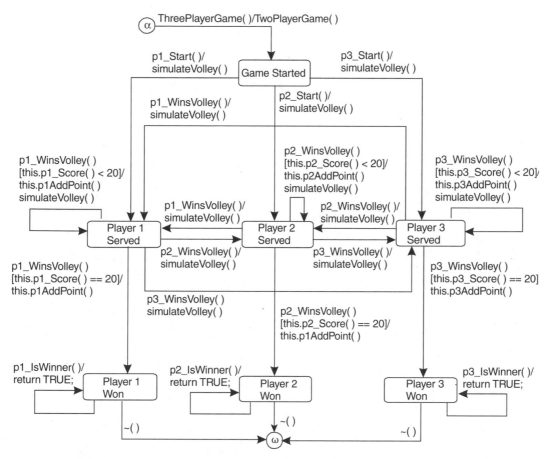

FIGURE 7.36 Flattened transition diagram, `ThreePlayerGame`.

transition sequences that begin and end with the same state and **simple paths** from the initial to final state. A **path** is a sequence of transitions: state$_p$, event$_i$, state^q, event$_j$, state$_r$, . . . A simple path contains only one iteration of a loop, if a loop is present in some sequence.

The initial state is transcribed as the root node of the tree. This is an α state if one has been specified. An edge is drawn for every transition out of the initial node, with nodes being added for resultant states. A leaf node (one with no exiting transitions) is marked as *terminal* if the state it represents has already been drawn, is a final state, or is the ω state. No more transitions are

Events and Guards			Accepting State/Expected Response								
			α	Game Started	Player 1 Served	Player 2 Served	Player 3 Served	Player 1 Won	Player 2 Won	Player 3 Won	Started ω
ctor			✓	6	6	6	6	6	6	6	6
p1_Start				✓	4	4	4	4	4	4	6
p2_Start				✓	4	4	4	4	4	4	6
p3_Start				✓	4	4	4	4	4	4	6
p1_WinsVolley	p1_score < 20	p1_Score == 20									
	DC	DC		4		✓	✓	4	4	4	6
	F	F			6						
	F	T			✓						
	T	F			✓						
	T	T									
p2_WinsVolley	p2_score < 20	p2_Score == 20									
	DC	DC		4	✓		✓	4	4	4	6
	F	F				6					
	F	T				✓					
	T	F				✓					
	T	T									
p3_WinsVolley	p3_score < 20	p3_Score == 20									
	DC	DC		4	✓	✓		4	4	4	6
	F	F					6				
	F	T					✓				
	T	F					✓				
	T	T									
p1_isWinner				✓	✓	✓	✓	✓	✓	✓	6
p2_isWinner				✓	✓	✓	✓	✓	✓	✓	6
p3_isWinner				✓	✓	✓	✓	✓	✓	✓	6
Other Public Accessors				✓	✓	✓	✓	✓	✓	✓	6
dtor				✓	✓	✓	✓	✓	✓	✓	6

FIGURE 7.37 Response matrix for ThreePlayerGame.

traced out of a terminal node. This procedure is repeated until all leaf nodes are terminal. The structure of the tree depends on the order in which transitions are traced. I prefer to work clockwise from the top of each state. This procedure gives a breadth-first traversal of transitions in each state.[29] A depth-first traversal is also possible. Graph algorithms for both approaches are well established. A tree produced by depth-first generation will have fewer, longer test sequences.

When transcribing a guarded transition, at least two test transitions are necessary. First, we must model each *true* combination. If several conditional variants can make the guard true, then we should transcribe one transition for each variant. Three cases are relevant:

- The guard is a simple Boolean expression or contains only logical *and* operators—for example, [x == 0] or [(x == 0) && (z != 42)]. One test transition is transcribed.

- The guard is a compound Boolean expression containing at least one logical *or* operator—for example, [(x == 0) || (z != 42)]. Two or more test transitions must be transcribed. One transition is required for each predicate combination that yields a *true* result. The preceding guard has two combinations: *true/false* (x == 0), (z == 42) and *false/true* (x != 0), (z != 42). If transitions for these logical variants are already explicitly specified for the state at hand, then only one test transition making is transcribed. See section 6.5.4, Each-Condition/ All-Conditions.

- The guard specifies a relationship that occurs only after repeating some event—for example, [counter >= 100000]. Here, the test sequence requires at least the number of iterations to satisfy the condition (or the ability to force an equivalent condition). The transition is graphed with a single arc annotated with an asterisk (*).

---

29. As each test sequence starts with a fresh object, the order in which the sequences are applied is irrelevant (assuming no environmental nondeterminism or side effects). Both strategies will produce all of the round-trip paths. In either case, we visit all states and trace all of their transitions. Tracing of a state stops when it has already been traced or is final. A trace ends only when a state already traced appears (thereby making the round-trip). All states are traced, so all round-trips for all states are traced. Formal analysis of the isomorphism between these graphs and any resulting implication for test effectiveness is an interesting problem, but beyond our scope.

Second, we must model at least one *false* combination. Tests to cover each guard's *false* variants are developed as part of the sneak path test suite. Strategies to model and test *true/false* variants are considered in Chapter 6.

Sometimes, all variants of the guard predicate are explicit. For example, the two transitions

```
pop [n > 0] / return top
pop [n < = 0] / return null
```

cover all logical variants of the relationship between n and 0. No additional transitions are necessary. Procedure 2 summarizes production of the transition tree.

Figure 7.38 shows the transition tree for the ThreePlayerGame. Each test case begins at the root node and ends at a leaf node. There are 15 such paths. The expected results are the sequence of states and actions which correspond to the events on the test sequence. Again, we assume a trustworthy means to determine which state is obtained.

The test cases are completed by identifying method parameter values, expected state, and exceptions (if any) for each transition. We run the test by setting the object under test to the initial state, applying the sequence, and then checking the resultant state and response.

The message sequences transcribed from the test tree always begin with the initial state. Starting with a fresh object in its initial state and repeating the test sequences is a good practice. Starting from a noninitial state would require a sequence to reach that state (or a state-set method). If a sequence is used, then the test run depends on the setup sequence. This coupling will create additional work (and new opportunities for test bugs) as the implementation and test suite are revised. If a transition path fails when we have started from the same known state and repeated previously tested transitions, then the last transition is likely to have reached the buggy code.

The round-trip-path test suite can detect several important classes of bugs: incorrect or missing transitions, incorrect or missing responses on a transition, missing states, and some corrupt states. If all tests pass, we have shown that the class under test conforms to the explicit behavior model.

1. The initial state is the root node of the tree. Use the α state if multiple constructors produce behaviorally different initial states.

2. Examine the state that corresponds to each nonterminal leaf node in the tree and each outbound transition on this state. At least one new edge will be drawn for each transition. Each new edge and node represents an event and resultant state reached by an outbound transition.

    a. If the transition is unguarded, draw one new branch.

    b. If the transition guard is a simple predicate or a complex predicate composed of only AND operators, draw one new branch.

    c. If the transition guard is a complex predicate using one or more OR operators, draw a new branch for each truth value combination that is sufficient to make the guard TRUE.

3. For each edge and node drawn in step 2:

    a. Note the corresponding transition event, guard, and action on the new branch.

    b. If the state that the new node represents is already represented by another node (anywhere in the diagram) or is a final state, mark this node as terminal—no more transitions are drawn from this node.

4. Repeat steps 2 and 3 until all leaf nodes are marked terminal.

**Procedure 2   Produce a Transition Tree from
a State Transition Diagram**

1   ThreePlayerGame( )
2   p1_Start( )
3   p2_Start( )
4   p3_Start( )
5   p1_WinsVolley( )
6   p1_WinsVolley( )[this.p1_Score( ) < 20]
7   p1_WinsVolley( ) [this.p1_Score( ) == 20]
8   p2_WinsVolley( )
9   p2_WinsVolley( ) [this.p2_Score( ) < 20]
10 p2_WinsVolley( ) [this.p2_Score( ) == 20]

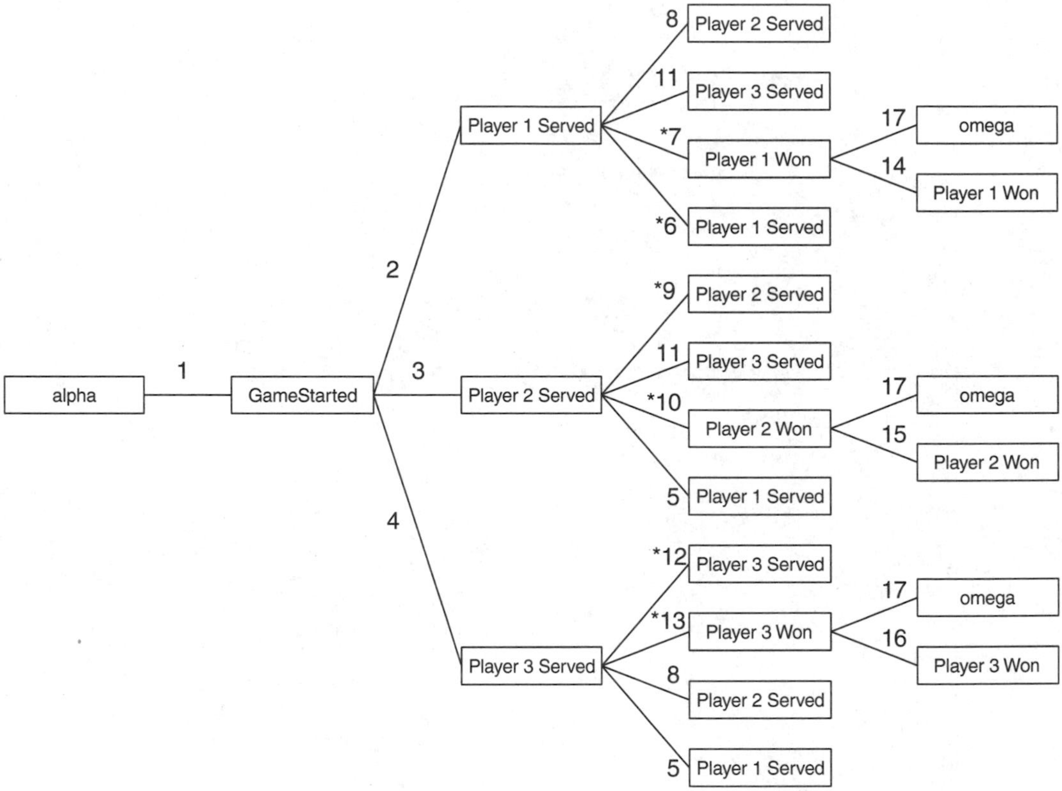

11 p3_WinsVolley( )
12 p3_WinsVolley( ) [this.p3_Score( ) < 20]
13 p3_WinsVolley( ) [this.p3_Score( ) == 20]
14 p1_IsWinner( )
15 p2_IsWinner( )
16 p3_IsWinner( )
17 ~( )

FIGURE 7.38   Transition tree for ThreePlayerGame.

TABLE 7.10   Conformance Test Suite for `ThreePlayerGame`

	Test Case Input		Expected Result	
TCID	Event	Test Condition	Action	State
1.1	ThreePlayerGame			GameStarted
1.2	p1_start		simulateVolley	Player 1 Served
1.3	p2_WinsVolley		simulateVolley	Player 2 Served
2.1	ThreePlayerGame			GameStarted
2.2	p1_start		simulateVolley	Player 1 Served
2.3	p3_WinsVolley		simulateVolley	Player 3 Served
3.1	ThreePlayerGame			GameStarted
3.2	p1_start		simulateVolley	Player 1 Served
3.3	*		*	Player 1 Served
3.4	p1_WinsVolley	p1_Score == 20		Player 1 Won
3.5	dtor			omega
4.1	ThreePlayerGame			GameStarted
4.2	p1_start		simulateVolley	Player 1 Served
4.3	*		*	Player 1 Served
4.4	p1_WinsVolley	p1_Score == 20		Player 1 Won
4.5	p1_IsWinner		return TRUE	Player 1 Won
5.1	ThreePlayerGame			GameStarted
5.2	p1_start		simulateVolley	Player 1 Served
5.3	*		*	Player 1 Served
5.4	p1_WinsVolley	p1_Score == 19	simulateVolley	Player 1 Served
6.1	ThreePlayerGame			GameStarted
6.2	p2_start		simulateVolley	Player 2 Served
6.3	*		*	Player 2 Served
6.4	p2_WinsVolley	p2_Score == 19	simulateVolley	Player 2 Served
7.1	ThreePlayerGame			GameStarted
7.2	p2_start		simulateVolley	Player 2 Served
7.3	p3_WinsVolley		simulateVolley	Player 3 Served
8.1	ThreePlayerGame			GameStarted
8.2	p2_start		simulateVolley	Player 2 Served
8.3	*		*	Player 2 Served
8.4	p2_WinsVolley	p2_Score == 20		Player 2 Won
8.5	dtor			omega

continued

TABLE 7.10 (continued)

	Test Case Input		Expected Result	
TCID	Event	Test Condition	Action	State
9.1	ThreePlayerGame			GameStarted
9.2	p2_start		simulateVolley	Player 2 Served
9.3	*		*	Player 2 Served
9.4	p2_WinsVolley	p2_Score == 20		Player 2 Won
9.5	p2_IsWinner		return TRUE	Player 2 Won
10.1	ThreePlayerGame			GameStarted
10.2	p2_start		simulateVolley	Player 2 Served
10.3	p2_WinsVolley		simulateVolley	Player 1 Served
11.1	ThreePlayerGame			GameStarted
11.2	p3_start		simulateVolley	Player 3 Served
11.3	*		*	Player 3 Served
11.4	p3_WinsVolley	p3_Score == 19	simulateVolley	Player 3 Served
12.1	ThreePlayerGame			GameStarted
12.2	p3_start		simulateVolley	Player 3 Served
12.3	*		*	Player 3 Served
12.4	p3_WinsVolley	p3_Score == 20		Player 3 Won
12.5	dtor			omega
13.1	ThreePlayerGame			GameStarted
13.2	p3_start		simulateVolley	Player 3 Served
13.3	*		*	Player 3 Served
13.4	p3_WinsVolley	p3_Score == 20		Player 3 Won
13.5	p3_IsWinner		return TRUE	Player 3 Won
14.1	ThreePlayerGame			GameStarted
14.2	p3_start		simulateVolley	Player 3 Served
14.3	p2_WinsVolley		simulateVolley	Player 2 Served
15.1	ThreePlayerGame			GameStarted
15.2	p3_start		simulateVolley	Player 3 Served
15.3	p1_WinsVolley		simulateVolley	Player 1 Served

Sneak Paths: Illegal Transitions and Evading the Guard

Passing the round-trip test suite shows that the IUT does not contain the bugs discussed earlier in its implementation of the explicit behavior model. However, this only shows conformance to explicitly modeled behavior. We must also show that implicitly excluded transitions are correctly handled; that is, the response (or the absence of a response) should be as specified and no incorrect or corrupting change of state should occur. A sneak path may have been coded to serve as a trap door for any number of purposes, including theft or sabotage.

The sneak path procedure may be skipped for a completely specified machine. This test suite is necessary only for machines that are incompletely specified (not all event/state pairs are explicit). The round-trip test suite will cover *all* transitions in a completely specified machine, including those to be "ignored." However, it is common practice to develop incompletely specified state models. Statecharts (classic and UML) purposely suppress complete specification. Separating conformance and sneak path test has practical benefits, as test drivers for explicit and implicit behavior can be significantly different. The interface to the IUT should support exercising of all explicit behavior. Implicit behavior may correspond to exceptional inputs, environmental failure modes, or other events that are not easily or directly tested using the IUT interface. The sneak path driver may be more closely coupled with the implementation. Separating the drivers can reduce test suite breakage as the IUT changes over time.

A sneak path is possible for each unspecified transition and for all situations in which the predicate of a guarded transition evaluates as FALSE. To confirm that no sneak paths exist, we attempt each state's illegal events. Although this process may seem tedious, it offers two distinct advantages. First, because we have established conformance, we need only to check for sneak paths from each state—we do not need to worry about sneak paths traversing two or more states. Second, this process is guaranteed to reveal all sneak paths.

The sneak path test suite is developed from the response matrix. We will have one test case for each nonchecked, nonexcluded transition cell, called a **possible sneak path**. The test procedure is as follows:

1. Place the IUT in the corresponding state. This may be accomplished in several ways. If it takes a long or unstable message sequence to reach the desired state (e.g., 1,000,000 message sends), then a built-in test method that forces the desired state may be necessary. The conformance suite has

sequences that will reach all states. Any conformance suite test sequence whose final resultant state is the same as the sneak path state can be used. Since the conformance sequences have been debugged and the IUT has passed them, they are trustworthy and a quick way to place the IUT into any desired state. Reusing conformance suite sequences has some minor disadvantages, however. The sneak path suite depends on it, so changes in the conformance suite may require changes in the sneak path test suite. In addition, repeating passing sequences means that you give up any chance of revealing additional bugs with these setup sequences.

2. Apply the illegal event by sending a message or forcing the virtual machine to generate the desired event.

3. Check that the actual response matches the specified response.

4. Check that the resultant state is unchanged. Sometimes, a new concrete state may be acceptable.

If the response and resultant state are as expected, the test passes. These steps are repeated for each possible sneak path. Table 7.11 shows the sneak path test suite for the ThreePlayerGame.

TABLE 7.11   Sneak Path Test Suite for ThreePlayerGame

	Test Case			Expected Result	
TCID	Setup Sequence	Test State	Test Event	Code	Action
16.0	ThreePlayerGame	Game Started	ThreePlayerGame	6	Abend
17.0	ThreePlayerGame	Game Started	p1_WinsVolley	4	IllegalEventException
18.0	ThreePlayerGame	Game Started	p2_WinsVolley	4	IllegalEventException
19.0	ThreePlayerGame	Game Started	p3_WinsVolley	4	IllegalEventException
20.0	10.0	Player 1 Served	ThreePlayerGame	6	Abend
21.0	5.0	Player 1 Served	p1_start	4	IllegalEventException
22.0	10.0	Player 1 Served	p2_start	4	IllegalEventException
23.0	5.0	Player 1 Served	p3_start	4	IllegalEventException
24.0	1.0	Player 2 Served	ThreePlayerGame	6	Abend
25.0	6.0	Player 2 Served	p1_start	4	IllegalEventException
26.0	1.0	Player 2 Served	p2_start	4	IllegalEventException
27.0	6.0	Player 2 Served	p3_start	4	IllegalEventException
28.0	7.0	Player 3 Served	ThreePlayerGame	6	Abend
29.0	2.0	Player 3 Served	p1_start	4	IllegalEventException

TABLE 7.11 (continued)

	Test Case			Expected Result	
TCID	Setup Sequence	Test State	Test Event	Code	Action
30.0	7.0	Player 3 Served	p2_start	4	IllegalEventException
31.0	2.0	Player 3 Served	p3_start	4	IllegalEventException
32.0	4.0	Player 1 Won	ThreePlayerGame	6	Abend
33.0	4.0	Player 1 Won	p1_start	4	IllegalEventException
34.0	4.0	Player 1 Won	p2_start	4	IllegalEventException
35.0	4.0	Player 1 Won	p3_start	4	IllegalEventException
36.0	4.0	Player 1 Won	p1_WinsVolley	4	IllegalEventException
37.0	4.0	Player 1 Won	p2_WinsVolley	4	IllegalEventException
38.0	4.0	Player 1 Won	p3_WinsVolley	4	IllegalEventException
39.0	9.0	Player 2 Won	ThreePlayerGame	6	Abend
40.0	9.0	Player 2 Won	p1_start	4	IllegalEventException
41.0	9.0	Player 2 Won	p2_start	4	IllegalEventException
42.0	9.0	Player 2 Won	p3_start	4	IllegalEventException
43.0	9.0	Player 2 Won	p1_WinsVolley	4	IllegalEventException
44.0	9.0	Player 2 Won	p2_WinsVolley	4	IllegalEventException
45.0	9.0	Player 2 Won	p3_WinsVolley	4	IllegalEventException
46.0	13.0	Player 3 Won	ThreePlayerGame	6	Abend
47.0	13.0	Player 3 Won	p1_start	4	IllegalEventException
48.0	13.0	Player 3 Won	p2_start	4	IllegalEventException
49.0	13.0	Player 3 Won	p3_start	4	IllegalEventException
50.0	13.0	Player 3 Won	p1_WinsVolley	4	IllegalEventException
51.0	13.0	Player 3 Won	p2_WinsVolley	4	IllegalEventException
52.0	13.0	Player 3 Won	p3_WinsVolley	4	IllegalEventException
53.0	12.0	omega	any	6	Abend

Event Path Sensitization

If a test sequence exercises one or more guards, then we must find input values that will satisfy all of these guards. If the output of an event in the sequence is used in a subsequent guard, the analysis can become complex. Values (or states) necessary for conditional expression must be determined by analysis. We can use the same approach taken to identify inputs that satisfy the source code entry–exit path conditions. See Section 10.2.3, Path Sensitization.

Built-in Test Support

Built-in test to support state-based testing focuses on state set and state get functions. Effective state-based testing cannot be done without the ability to determine which state has resulted from a test sequence. The simplest state-get function evaluates the state invariant and returns a Boolean variable indicating whether an object is in that state. Other techniques are described in Chapter 17.

Depending on the IUT, it may be hard or easy to reach the state for which a test sequence calls. If the class interface exports methods that are sufficient to set the state, then these methods may be called in an expression that sets a certain state. However, having direct access to the implementation is often necessary (and simpler). (See Chapter 17.)

Checking the Resultant State

Effective state-based testing cannot be done without the ability to determine what state has resulted from a test sequence. The resultant state can be determined in three ways.

State Reporter Methods   Implementing a method in the IUT to report state is the most reliable technique to determine resultant state. The simplest state-get function evaluates the state invariant and returns a Boolean variable indicating that an object is or is not in that state. Other techniques are described in Chapter 17, Assertions. For example, the following C++ fragment suggests the interface for state reporter functions that could be implemented in class `ThreePlayerGame`.

```
bool isGameStarted( )     {/* ... */}
bool isPlayer1Served( )   {/* ... */}
bool isPlayer2Served( )   {/* ... */}
bool isPlayer3Served( )   {/* ... */}
bool isPlayer1Won( )      {/* ... */}
bool isPlayer2Won( )      {/* ... */}
bool isPlayer3Won( )      {/* ... */}
```

After each event, the appropriate state reporter is asserted. Assume that the `int winner( )` function returns the number of the player who wins the volley and that we are able to control the simulation of the volley. For example, we could verify the sequence where player 1 serves, player 2 serves, and then player 3 serves.

```
/* Test setup precedes this sequence */

assert(isGameStarted());          /* check initial state */

out.p1_start();                   /* send the test event */
/* volley simulated */
assert(winner() == 1);            /* check the expected action */
assert(out.isPlayer1Served());    /* check resultant state */

assert(out.p2_WinsVolley());      /* send the test event */
/* volley simulated */
assert(winner() == 2);            /* check the expected actions */
assert(out.isPlayer2Served());    /* check resultant state */

assert(out.p3_WinsVolley());      /* send the test event */
/* volley simulated */
assert(winner() == 3);            /* check the expected action */
assert(out.isPlayer3Served());    /* check resultant state */
```

Assuming that the state reporter methods are correct, then this sequence will reveal an incorrect or corrupt state.

Test Repetition   If you cannot implement state reporter methods, Beizer recommends a simple heuristic to reveal corrupt states: repeat the test sequence and compare the actions [Beizer 95]. An implementation can reach a corrupt or incorrect state, but still accept events correctly and produce correct actions. A corrupt state may cause an observable failure on a subsequent event. If we repeat an identical sequence starting from a corrupt state, we probably will not get exactly the same actions. Comparing the actions produced by the first and second sequence can reveal some corrupt states. The incremental design and test implementation effort to repeat a test sequence typically is small. Beizer reports that this technique is effective for revealing corrupt state bugs that would otherwise hide.

For example, suppose that no state reporter methods were available for ThreePlayerGame. We would amend the previous sequence by (1) saving each output action, (2) repeating the test sequence, and (3) comparing the action pairs.

```
/* Test setup precedes this sequence */

assert(isGameStarted());              /* check initial state */
out.p1_start();

/* volley simulated */                /* First repeatable action */
assert(winner() == 1);
action1 = 1;
```

```
assert(out.p2_WinsVolley());
/* volley simulated */
assert(winner() == 2);
action2 = 2;

assert(out.p3_winsVolley());
/* volley simulated */
assert(winner() == 3);
action3 = 3;

assert(out.p1_winsVolley());           /* Begin repeated sequence */
/* volley simulated */
assert(action1 == winner());           /* Compare previous action */

assert(out.p2_WinsVolley());
/* volley simulated */
assert(action2 == winner());           /* Compare previous action */

assert(out.p3_winsVolley());
/* volley simulated */
assert(action3 == winner());           /* Compare previous action */
```

Note that we do not directly check the resultant state, so this technique is not as reliable as a complete set of verified state reporter methods. It is a practical alternative where state reporter methods are not available and cannot be easily implemented.

State Revealing Signatures   Confidence that no incorrect or corrupt states have occurred without using state reporter methods requires a much higher cost of test design and execution. Many state-based testing techniques were developed for systems in which direct determination of resultant states was not feasible for technical, economic, or proprietary reasons [Gill 62, Holzmann 91]. The only way to determine what state has resulted was to identify and apply a signature sequence. Advanced state-based testing techniques determine a signature and interleave it with other transition tests. These sequences can increase the size of an n-switch suite by a factor of three. Design of these sequences requires specialized, advanced analysis and cannot guarantee that all corrupt or incorrect states will be revealed. The N+ cover supported by a simple built-in test provides the same degree of testing power at one-third of the cost. The design of signatures is beyond the scope of this book (see [Gill 62, Chow 78, Sidhu+89, Fujiwara+91, and Bernhard 94]).

The difficulty and cost of using signatures motivated nearly universal acceptance of standard built-in test in VLSI [Maunder+92]. It is common practice to add similar capabilities for protocol verification [Holzmann 91]. Built-in test greatly reduces the need to identify and apply signatures to identify invalid states. Objects can be just as opaque, but with a little attention to software design-for-testability, states can be made observable without compromising encapsulation, efficiency, and good design.

◆ 7.4.4   Relative Power and Limitations

Nearly all of the lessons learned about state-based testing of hardware and telecommunications apply to object-oriented software testing. The power of state-based testing has been established for these technologies using the same Mealy-type state machine we use to model class behavior. With reinterpretation, we can bring the full power of these strategies to bear on object-oriented software. The major test design strategies for state-based testing are as follows.

- Piecewise
- All transitions
- All transition k-tuples
- All round-trip paths
- M-length signature
- Exhaustive

Figure 7.39 shows the test power hierarchy for each of these strategies. In this subsumption hierarchy, a test suite that meets the criteria for a higher strategy also meets the criteria for a lower hierarchy.[30] The piecewise and exhaustive strategies are useful to define the bounds of the testing spectrum but are not viable testing strategies.

Piecewise

Piecewise coverage obtains for a test suite that exercises specification pieces of a certain kind at least once all states, all events, or all actions. These strategies are not directly related to the structure of the state machine that controls behavior, so they are only accidentally effective at finding behavior faults. It is possible to visit all states and miss some events or actions, to exercise all events without visiting all states or producing all actions, or to produce all actions

---

30. This hierarchy and the following discussion are based on results reported in [Chow 78], [Sidhu+89], [Fujiwara+91], and [Bernhard 94]. Bernhard provides a concise survey of research in state-based protocol testing [Bernhard 94].

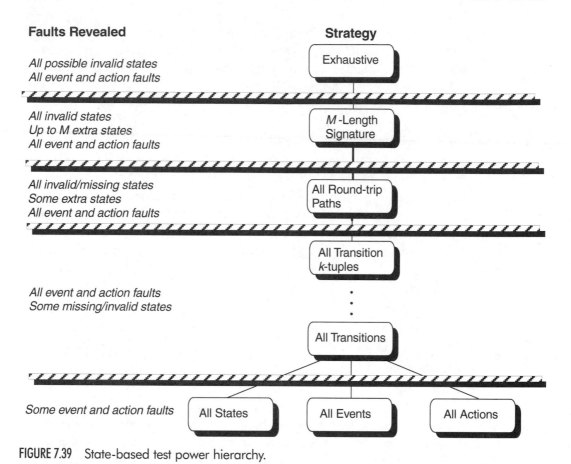

FIGURE 7.39   State-based test power hierarchy.

without visiting all states or accepting all events. A piecewise test suite can easily miss incorrect or omitted event/action pairs. An incorrect or invalid resultant state may be revealed—but only by coincidence.

Suppose an implementation of Account has a corrupt state fault; once overdrawn, it never accepts another withdrawal transaction, even if the balance exceeds zero. In effect, the transition from overdrawn to open is missing. We could easily satisfy any piecewise criteria and miss this fault. Piecewise testing should never be considered adequate coverage for any state machine.

All Transitions

All-transition coverage is obtained if every specified transition is exercised at least once. This necessarily exercises all states, all events, and all actions. No particular sequence is required, and any sequence that exercises each transition once will suffice. Although incorrect or missing event/action pairs are guaranteed to be revealed, this technique cannot show that an incorrect state has resulted. Unless the machine is completely specified, it cannot reveal the presence of extra transitions (sneak paths).

All *n*-Transition Sequences

All *n*-transition coverage obtains when every specified transition sequence of *n* events is exercised at least once.[31] We can begin to catch some incorrect or corrupt states with these sequences but a corrupt or incorrect state can still hide.

All Round-trip Paths

All-round-trip-path coverage is obtained when every sequence of specified transitions beginning and ending in the same state is exercised at least once. The shortest round-trip path is a transition that loops back on the same state. The longest round-trip path depends on the structure of the machine. The set of all round-trip paths is also known as an *n*-switch cover, in that it must include all other transition sequences for $k \leq n$ (pairs, triples, and so on).[32] Any sequence that goes beyond a round trip must be part of a sequence that belongs in another round trip. Thus, a test suite that achieves all-round-trip-path coverage will reveal all incorrect or missing event/action pairs.

This approach can reveal some incorrect or invalid states, but it cannot guarantee that all faulty implementations with more than *n* invalid states will be revealed. Suppose that the implementation enters a corrupt state that mimics correct behavior for the first 10 events it accepts, but the system crashes on the eleventh event. For this reason, the N+ strategy relies on a state inspector.

M-Length Signature

Most hardware and protocol strategies assume the implementation under test is **opaque**—that is, there is no direct means to determine its current state. Designing tests to reveal event and action bugs in an opaque implementation is

---

31. Transition sequences are called a *switch* [Chow 78]. An *x-switch* designates the number of transitions in a switch minus 1. A transition cover is a 0-switch, a transition pair cover is a 1-switch, and so on. The all-transitions cover is a 1-transition cover. Sequences are also called *k*-tuples: a 2-tuple cover includes all pairs ($k = 2$), a 3-tuple cover includes all triples ($k = 3$), and so on.

32. The *n*-switch is discussed in [Chow 78]. The set of round-trip paths is referred to as the *P-set* there.

straightforward, but determining when a corrupt state has resulted is more difficult. In fact, short of exhaustive testing, many corrupt state scenarios can escape detection under a strictly black box approach. Research on improving these approaches has focused on efficient test strategies for finding corrupt states. This problem spurred development of hardware built-in tests. The difficult part of black box, state-based testing is determining whether a correct state has obtained. From a control perspective, a correct state means that no illegal transitions are allowed. A corrupt state can easily hide if the implementation has more corrupt states than the number of states in the specification. Corrupt states can mimic a correct response and may give an incorrect response (thereby revealing a bug) only after some long sequence. A **state signature** can be used to determine the current state of an IUT if no direct means is available to do so. A state signature consists of a sequence of output actions that are unique for a particular starting state. The sequence of events that should produce the signature (a **distinguishing sequence**) is selected by analyzing the IUT's specification. Then, to determine whether the IUT is in some state, we apply the distinguishing sequence for that state. If this process yields the expected signature, we have confirmed that the system was in the expected state. If not, we have shown that it was not in the expected state at the start of the sequence.

If it is assumed that the implementation does not have any corrupt states, then we can always find a signature that is n-1 transitions long.[33] If the implementation has corrupt states, however, a bogus state can potentially produce a correct signature. We must try a sequence long enough to get beyond any possible number of corrupt states. But how long? If we guess the number of corrupt states to be no more than M, then a signature can be produced that is guaranteed to find up to that number of corrupt states, but no more. In object-oriented testing, this additional effort can be avoided with some simple and inexpensive design-for-testability.

7.4.5 Choosing a State-based Test Strategy

As with any test approach, increased test cost typically buys fewer bugs and increased confidence in the tested implementation. The following analysis is pro-

---

33. The analysis to identify a distinguishing sequence is developed in [Gill 62]. The *W-set*, which distinguishes for a fixed number of extra states, is presented in [Chow 78]. This approach (the *W-method*) is reviewed and the *Wp-method* is presented in [Fujiwara+91]. The Wp-method is equal in power to the W-method and can reduce the total size of the test suite in some circumstances. Bernhard offers three ways to accomplish similar reductions [Bernhard 94].

TABLE 7.12 Size of State-based Test Suite by Strategy and Size of IUT

Representative IUT				All Transitions		N+		W-Method	
	n	k		(1)	(2)	(1)	(2)	(3)	(4)
3Player	7	9	Test Cases	21	32	63	63	63	63
			Messages	21	32	147	284	441	3087
Small	10	15	Test Cases	50	75	150	150	150	150
			Messages	50	75	500	1125	1500	15000
Med	15	30	Test Cases	150	225	450	450	450	450
			Messages	150	225	2250	6750	6750	101250
Large	30	100	Test Cases	1000	1500	3000	3000	3000	3000
			Messages	1000	1500	30000	150000	90000	2700000

Key: n = number of states, k = number of events
(1) Assumes average number of events per test case = $k/2$.
(2) Assumes average number of events per test case = $k/3$.
(3) Worst case minimum, approximately $n^2 \times k$ [Chow 78].
(4) Worst case maximum, approximately $n^3 \times k$ [Chow 78].

vided as practical engineering approximation of test cost/benefit to help plan your test effort.[34]

The cost of state-based testing has two parts: time and resources for each test case and for each test message (event) used in a test case. The design, setup, and post-test cost per test case rarely depends on the number of events (messages) in the test cases. The cost per message within a test case includes the storage and execution of the message and development of the message. Per-message costs can be high if each test message is hand-coded. Tester effort, execution time, and storage increase at least proportionally with the size of the test model. The size of the test model has two parameters: the number of states n and the number of events k.

Cost, expressed as the size of the test suite for several strategies and representative models, is shown in Table 7.12.[35] Figure 7.40 shows the relative fault-

---

34. For a detailed mathematical analysis of state-based test size and power, see [Chow 78], [Sidhu+89], [Fujiwara+91], and [Bernhard 94]. A complete economic and technical analysis of testing is beyond our scope.

35. The average path length and ratio of explicit to implicit transitions are provided for illustration purposes only. They are consistent with my experience, but are not based on empirical study.

Fault Class	Fault Revealing Power of Some State-based Testing Strategies						
	Observable					Opaque	
	Each Event Once	Each State Once	Each Action Once	All Transitions	N+ Cover	All Transitions	W-Method [Chow 78]
Guard fault	1			1	✓	1	1
Missing transition	3			✓	✓	✓	✓
Sneak path (Extra transition)				2	✓	2	✓
Incorrect action (wrong or missing)				✓	✓	✓	✓
Incorrect resultant state				✓	✓		✓
Missing state		✓		✓	✓		✓
Corrupt resultant State ("extra state")				✓	✓		5
Trap door (extra event)	4			4	4	6	6

Key: Blank = This fault class is not targeted, ✓ = All faults of this class will be revealed.

1. Other published strategies (see Bibliographic Notes) do not consider guards.
2. Guaranteed only if model is completely specified.
3. Guaranteed only if events and transitions are one-to-one.
4. Not certain to reveal. Requires post-test, call-path coverage analysis.
5. Will reveal up to *m* corrupt (extra) states.
6. Opaque assumption precludes coverage analysis.

FIGURE 7.40   Power comparison, state-based testing strategies.

finding power of state-based testing strategies. What does this analysis tell us about the four strategies discussed earlier?

- *Piecewise*. Forget about any of the piecewise strategies if you are serious about testing. As Figure 7.40 shows, they are almost worthless in terms of their fault-revealing power. They also cost only a little less than an all-explicit-transitions test suite, which will find a much broader range of bugs.

- *All-explicit-transitions*. An all-explicit-transitions test suite consists of at least one test message for each explicit transition in the test model. It will reveal a broad range of bugs at a cost roughly proportional to the density of the explicit state machine. The number of test cases equals the number of transitions. This number can be counted for a given machine, but only the upper and lower bounds can be formulated in general. If the SUT is completely specified, this number is $k \times n$. Assuming an incomplete specification and no testing of implicit transitions, the number of tests is approximated by the number of transitions per state. Explicit systems tend to be sparse, so estimating that, on average, one-third of the events are accepted in any given state is not unrealistic. This assumption gives $kn/3$ as the total number of test cases or, assuming half are used on average, $kn/2$. The total number of test messages is the same, assuming one event per transition. This strategy, however, ignores implicit behavior. The flip side of the one-third assumption is that two-thirds of the implementation transitions remain unexercised, leaving an exposure to sneak paths and buggy exception handling.

- *All-transitions.* All-transitions coverage will reveal a broad range of bugs at a cost roughly proportional to the size of the entire state machine. It requires every transition in every state, for a total of kn test cases. The total number of test messages is the same, assuming one message per transition.

- *N+.* An N+ test suite requires every transition in every state, for a total of kn test cases. Each test case brings the IUT from the initial state to a leaf state, so the number of messages depends on the length of this sequence. Because no sequence can be longer than the number of events, the average number of messages per test case can be estimated as $k/2$. The total number of test messages on average is then $k^2n/2$. Compared with all-transitions, the additional messages in the N+ test sequence will reveal more corrupt state and incorrect transition bugs.

- *Opaque.* The cost of the W-method underscores the necessity of making the state of the IUT observable. The W-method assumes an opaque IUT and appends a distinguishing sequence to every test case in the transition cover. As Chow notes, although the W-method suite is often smaller, the minimum number of test cases under a worst case assumption is roughly kn^2 and the maximum is kn^3. With a small system, the incremental cost of the state signature messages will be negligible. With a large system, the number of messages increases exponentially. Strategies have been developed to reduce the size of W-method test suite for opaque systems [Fujiwara+91, Bernhard 94].

I suggest that you consider the following in making your cost/confidence decision:

- Design for testability: Keep your state machines small and simple. Avoid deep hierarchies of machines.

- Design for testability: If you distributed a state model across several levels of a class hierarchy, follow the guidelines for a well-formed hierarchy. This approach will allow you to reuse state-based superclass test suites in your subclasses.

- Design for testability: Provide simple and trustworthy methods to set and report state.

- If you cannot achieve an all-transitions coverage due to time or cost constraints, be aware that any lesser extent of testing can miss serious transition bugs.

- Try to quantify the *incremental* cost to achieve an N+ cover before assuming that it is too high. If you can afford all-transitions coverage, the incremental effort may be a small percentage of this effort. If you can automate at least part of the test generation and execution, getting to this higher level of coverage may require little more than developing a small amount of additional test code.

Effective state-based testing is not cheap, but it is warranted when the responsibilities of the IUT require the control complexity of a state machine. The piecewise and all-explicit-transitions strategies omit tests of many basic behaviors and should not be considered as adequate. The all-transitions strategy is the minimum acceptable for responsible testing of a state machine. The N+ strategy brings an increase in fault-finding power roughly comparable to its increased cost.

7.5 Bibliographic Notes

Thousands of papers and hundreds of books have been published on the theory, application, and testing of automata. The few mentioned here do not reflect anything like a complete survey of the subject.

State Machines in Object-oriented Development

The use of state machines in OOA/D approaches is surveyed and compared in [Monarchi+92], [Graham 94], and [Odell 95]. Meyer defines the notion of concrete and abstract state and class flattening, but does not discuss a state transition model [Meyer 88]. [Schuman+87] presents a Z-based approach that models object state with invariants. An object-oriented approach to modeling reactive systems appears in [Järvinen 90]. The Booch OOD adaptation of statecharts is presented in [Booch 91], and a similar approach is developed in [Embley+92].

The Fusion Objectchart model is presented in [Coleman+92] and [Coleman+94]. State models are used in Object Modeling Technique (OMT) [Rumbaugh+91], OOSE [Jacobson+92], the Shaler-Mellor methodology [Shaler+92], and the Martin-Odell approach [Martin+92].

The effect of inheritance on state is sketched in [McGregor 93a]. A more rigorous treatment is provided in [Overbeck 92] and [Cook+94]. The role of "history" constraints (in effect, a state transition) for subtype specifications is developed in [Liskov+94]. A notion of state as the expansion of object associations ("recursive state") is developed in [Siepmann+94]. The ROOM methodology uses an executable form of statecharts [Selic+94]. Cook and Daniels' Syntropy approach shows how class state models can be unambiguously integrated with class and method specifications [Cook+94]. Pragmatic discussions of state models and their implications of object state-space is presented in [Page-Jones 95] and [Fowler 97]. Harel reinterprets statecharts for object-oriented development in [Harel 97]. UML statecharts are defined in [OMG 98] and [Rumbaugh+99].

State-based Testing of Object-oriented Implementations

The basic elements of the FREE model and the N+ test strategy appeared in [Binder95a, Binder 95c, Binder 95d, Binder 96h, and Binder 97a]. Implementation-based state test models for C++ programs are presented in [Turner+95, Hoffman+95, and Kung+93]. All three analyze data member usage to identify value sets that are modeled as states. Transition semantics differ. Hoffman uses a reduced implementation of the model as an automated oracle. McGregor et al. use statecharts to model behavior visible to clients of a class and argue that piecewise coverage is acceptable [McGregor+93a]. All of these approaches use variations of Chow's algorithm to identify test message sequences [Chow 78].

State Machines in Software Engineering

State machines have a long history of use in software analysis and design. A comparative survey of many such techniques can be found in [Davis 93]. The Ina Jo [Kemmerer 85] and SREM [Alford 85] modeling languages use explicit, formal state models and were applied to the development of ballistic missile guidance systems, among other things. A state machine hierarchy for user interface design is developed in [Wasserman+85]. State machines are a key part of structured techniques for analysis and design [Ward+85, Hatley+87]. The System Description Language (SDL) makes extensive use of simple and product form state machines, and has been widely adopted for the design and testing of telecommunications systems [Turner 93]. Statecharts were first presented in [Harel 87] and [Harel 88] and were reinterpreted for object-oriented development in [Harel+97]. They have been the subject of many research papers. Leveson presents design considerations to reduce risks and the use of state models to analyze safety properties [Leveson 95].

State-based Software Testing

A pragmatic and complete introduction to state-based test design can be found in [Beizer 90] and [Beizer 95]. Considerations for test design with statecharts are developed in [Marick 95]. State-based testing has been extensively studied and applied for telecommunication software. The W-method and *n*-switch cover were developed to test software switching systems [Chow 78]. Empirical studies of the size and fault-finding ability of state-based testing strategies appear in [Sidhu+89] and [Fujiwara+91]. Holzmann provides a comprehensive and highly readable discussion of state-based verification [Holzmann 91]. The January 1992 issue of *IEEE Software* magazine focuses on verification of telecommunication protocols. Bernhard provides a concise comparative synopsis of formal state-based testing models [Bernhard 94]. The main results presented in this paper are three sequence selection algorithms that have the same fault-revealing power as the W-method but require significantly shorter signature sequences.

State-based Hardware Testing

State models are a fundamental tool for the design and test of digital logic circuits. See, for example, [Kohavi 78, Fujiwara 86, Abramovici+90, Devadas 94, and Comer 95].

Mathematical Theory

The Moore [Moore 55] and Mealy [Mealy 56] papers are seminal in automata theory. Gill's extensive application-oriented study of the formal properties of state machines remains useful [Gill 62]. Many computer science textbooks present finite state automata in the context of computing theory—for example, [Lewis+81, Hopcroft+79]. Extensions to formal models that represent product machines and guards are developed in [Arnold 94]. A formal analysis of the reduction in the state space in product machines owing to statechart abstractions is developed in [Drusinsky 94].

Chapter 8 A Tester's Guide to the UML

No realization without representation.
Robert Ashenhurst

Overview

This chapter considers the Unified Modeling Language (UML) from a testing perspective. The notation and semantics of each UML diagram are summarized. Considerations for developing test-ready UML diagrams are discussed. For some diagrams, testability extensions are presented. The chapter also gives a generic test strategy for graphs and relations that is used to identify generic test requirements for each UML diagram.

8.1 Introduction

8.1.1 The UML as a Test Model

At its most abstract, test design is the identification, analysis, and demonstration of relationships that must hold for the system under test. A test model captures these relationships. This model should be unambiguous, related to probable faults, and support automated production of compact test suites. As the preceding chapters have shown, combinational logic and state machines are powerful and testable models that meet these requirements.

The Unified Modeling Language (UML) is a notational syntax for expressing object-oriented models. It merges the OOA/D notations developed by

Booch [Booch 91], Jacobson et al. [Jacobson+92], and Rumbaugh et al. [Rumbaugh+91]. It has become a de facto standard for object-oriented modeling. Hundreds of publications about developing UML models are available, so we need no discussion of modeling technique here.

The UML is not a methodology. It does not prescribe technique, results, or process. It purposely places few restrictions on usage of the notation. As with natural languages, this flexibility allows both precision and muddle. Developing a rigorous application model with the UML is possible. However, fragmentary, incomplete, inconsistent, and ambiguous models are easily produced without violating any of the UML's requirements.[1]

If a model is produced at all during object-oriented development, it is likely to be a collection of UML diagrams. UML models are an important source of information for test design that should not be ignored. This chapter presents three main test development techniques:

- It summarizes the elements of UML diagrams and explains how these elements can be used for test design.
- It shows how to develop UML models with sufficient information to produce test cases.
- It presents general test requirements for each diagram, which can be used to develop application-specific test cases.

The chapter concludes with an advanced section that explains the graph relation test design model used to generate the generic test requirements.

8.1.2 Relational Testing Strategy

Lines between UML symbols represent an instance of a general relationship recognized within the UML. For example, an association line between two class symbols can show that an instance of one class depends on the other. Application-specific models are constructed from these built-in relationships. For example, an association line between the class Person and the class Dog shows that an instance of Dog may not exist unless a corresponding instance of Person is also present.

---

1. There are general and specific elements of the UML that I believe represent fundamentally bad choices for a software engineering notation. Despite these limitations, the UML can support development of test-ready models. Work-arounds for most of these problems are suggested in this chapter and elsewhere.

Such built-in relationships have corresponding generic test requirements that can be identified by applying a relational test strategy to each UML diagram. The mathematics of this approach are discussed at the end of the chapter, which explains the columns labeled *R*, *S*, and *T* in each set of generic test requirements.

You can develop a test suite for an application modeled with UML diagrams in two ways. First, you can interpret the generic test requirements for your application and develop the indicated tests. For example, we would test implementation of the existence dependency by trying to establish it, and then trying to create inconsistent instances—for example, a Dog with no human owner. Second, you can apply the related test design pattern. Figure 8.1 summarizes the intersection of the UML and the test design patterns in this book.

The generic test requirements can also serve as a test design and execution checklist. You use the following criterion to compare your test suite and your application model:

> For each UML diagram representing requirements of the SUT and for each application-specific instance of a UML relationship type that appears in that diagram, at least one actual test achieves the generic test requirements for an implementation instance of that application-specific relationship.

If nothing else, this analysis will establish traceability from each element of your application model to the implementation under test and your test suite. This exercise nearly always reveals omissions and inconsistencies.

8.2   General-purpose Elements

8.2.1   Organization and Annotation

General-purpose elements of the UML are used to organize diagrams and express details.

Package Diagrams and Packages

A *package* is a group of UML diagrams and diagram elements of any kind, including other packages. A *package diagram* shows the organization of packages. A large model is typically organized as a hierarchy of package diagrams. A package does not necessarily correspond to an Ada 95 or Java package or to any other implementation scoping mechanism (although it may). The symbol for a package is a large rectangle with a small box in the upper-left corner,

Test Design Pattern		Use Case	Class	Sequence	Activity	State-chart	Collaboration	Component	Deployment
Method scope	Category-Partition	☆		☆	☆		☆		
	Combinational Function	☆		☆	☆				
	Recursive Function			☆			☆		
	Polymorphic Message		☆	☆			☆		
Class scope	Invariant Boundaries	☆☆	☆☆	☆☆			☆		
	Nonmodal Class			☆					
	Modal Class					★			
	Quasi-modal Class					☆			
Class scope integration	Small Pop								
	Alpha-Omega Cycle		☆☆						
Flattened class scope	Polymorphic Server		☆	☆			☆		
	Modal Hierarchy		☆	☆		★	☆		
Reusable components	Abstract Class		☆☆						
	Generic Class		☆☆						
	New Framework	☆☆	☆☆	☆	☆	☆	☆	☆	☆
	Popular Framework	☆☆	☆☆	☆	☆	☆	☆	☆	☆
Subsystem	Class Associations		★						
	Round-trip Scenario			★	☆	☆	☆		
	Controlled Exception			☆	☆	☆	☆		
	Mode Machine				☆	★			

Integration	Big Bang	☆	☆	☆		☆	☆
	Bottom-up			☆		☆	☆
	Top-down		☆	☆		☆	☆
	Collaborations		☆	★		☆	☆
	Backbone	☆	☆			☆	☆
	Layers	☆	☆			☆	☆
	Client/Server	☆	☆			☆	☆
	Distributed Services	☆	☆			☆	☆
	High-frequency	☆	☆			☆	☆
Application scope	Extended Use Cases	★	☆			☆	☆
	Covered in CRUD	★				☆	☆
	Allocate Tests by Profile	★				☆	
Regression test	Retest All					☆	☆
	Retest Risky Use Cases	☆	☆				☆
	Retest by Profile	☆				☆	☆
	Retest Changed Code	☆				☆	☆
	Retest Within Firewall			☆		☆	☆

★ Pattern explicitly based on this diagram, ★ Pattern may be useful for testing elements of this diagram, ☆ Diagram may be useful when using this pattern

FIGURE 8.1 UML diagrams and test design patterns.

suggesting a file folder. The package name appears in the tab (if the content is displayed) or in the content box if the content is suppressed.

Packages may be marked as public, protected, or private. A dashed arrow shows that one package depends on another package. A solid line with an unfilled triangle on the end indicates inheritance.

Each element of a model is "owned" by only one package. The ownership relationship is a tree. Packages, however, can refer to ("depend on") any other package. They are the basic unit of organization for configuration control, storage, and access control.

Keywords and Stereotypes

UML *keywords* are labels that distinguish representation elements that use the same symbol. Keywords are reserved; that is, these terms are predefined for all UML models. For example, the classifier symbol—a rectangle with compartments—can be used to represent a type, a class, a meta-class, or an object. A label bracketed with guillemets defines the kind of classifier as a «type», «class», «metaclass», or «object». A *stereotype* is a user-defined keyword.

Expressions, Constraints, and Comments

An *expression* is a string from an executable language that can be evaluated to produce a result. A *constraint* is a predicate expression on model elements. It is shown as text enclosed in braces—for example, {x == y && !isEmpty}. A constraint expresses a relationship within the system under study. Although the interpretation of predefined UML constraints is fixed, the syntax and interpretation of user-specified constraints are user-defined. Constraints may be written in natural language, mathematical expressions, code, or Object Constraint Language (OCL). A constraint written in natural language is a called a *comment*.

Notes

A *note* is shown as a box with a dog-eared corner. It may be connected to another diagram element or it may be free-standing. The note contains a textual description.

Element Properties

The *properties* of an element can be displayed enclosed in braces and designated by a *tag* expression—for example, { LastRevDate=1999021, VersionId=0.2 }.

FIGURE 8.2   General UML symbols.

Many properties are suppressed in typical presentation diagrams. Figure 8.2 shows a package diagram and a note.

The *UML Specification* states that a line between a diagram element may be composed of one or more segments and that "A connected sequence of segments is called a path" [OMG 98, 3-52]. That is, a UML "path" is simply a line between two graph elements. The term *path* has a long-established, well-defined, and different meaning in graph theory, testing, and computer science. In this book, the graph-theoretic sense of **path** is used: a set of nodes and edges for which an unambiguous property holds. The UML also uses "node" as a diagram element that represents a processor (see Section 8.10, Deployment Diagram). In the following discussion **node,** is used in the graph-theoretic sense: the elements of a graph that are connected by edges. An **edge** is an abstract connection between abstract nodes, and a **line** refers to one or more contiguous line segments rendered on a diagram.

8.2.2 Object Constraint Language

The OCL is a modeling language that can express relationships and properties of modeled elements [Warmer+99]. It is based on Syntropy [Cook+94] and aims to make the power of specification languages like Z accessible to software developers who do not have a mathematical background. OCL uses keywords that have been chosen for their understandability without sacrificing any precision. The meta-model for the UML is expressed in OCL.

OCL can be used to define (as a constraint or expression) basic relationships that are not easily shown with UML graphs:

- Class and type invariants
- Type invariant for stereotypes
- Preconditions and postconditions on operations (methods)

- All forms of guards
- Specification of the result of a computation in a nonprocedural manner[2]

Perhaps the most interesting application of OCL is to express the navigation of a class model. Navigation expressions define how a network of class relationships is traversed. They are similar to SQL, not in syntax, but in concept.

OCL can be used to express all of the state invariants discussed in Chapter 7 and the method and class assertions covered in Chapter 17. A UML application model that correctly and consistently uses OCL to define class contracts is probably test-ready. OCL expressions can be used in the *Invariant Boundary*, *Nonmodal Class Test*, *Modal Class Test*, and *Mode Machine Test* patterns. This language presents many intriguing possibilities for test automation.

8.3 Use Case Diagram

8.3.1 Notation and Semantics

A **use case** is an abstraction of a system response to external inputs. It accomplishes a task that is important *from a user's point of view.* "When a user uses the system, she or he will perform a behaviorally related sequence of transactions in a dialogue with the system. We call such a special sequence a use case" [Jacobson 95a]. Use cases are the dominant form of system-level requirements specification in object-oriented development: "the collection of use cases is the complete functionality of the system" [Jacobson+92]. Use cases are said to "drive" the unified development process[3]—they are used as the primary representation of system requirements [Jacobson+99]. Use cases can represent many kinds of system requirements:

- Functional requirements
- Allocation of functionality to classes (objects)
- Object interaction and object interfaces

---

2. OCL is a declarative language; that is, none of its operations may change the state of the modeled system. Operations are modeled by what must be true after the operation is completed. The computation or transformation that achieves this condition cannot be expressed.

3. The unified development process is a development methodology proposed by the primary authors of the UML—Booch, Rumbaugh, and Jacobson.

- User interfaces
- User documentation

In addition, use cases can be applied to analyze and define related design problems:

- Determination of development increments
- Establishment of traceability
- Conceptualization and prototyping
- Determination of system boundaries
- Development resource and effort sizing
- Architectural partitioning

A use case focuses on only those features visible at the external interfaces of a system. It represents a dialog between the system and external **actors**. An actor need not be human. Use cases, for example, may describe interactions with other computer systems and electromechanical sensors and actuators. A **use case instance** defines particular input values and expected results. A use case is composed of **operations**. An operation is a particular sequence of messages exchanged among objects, initiated by an external input. An operation causes a particular path to be traced through a sequence diagram. An **event trace** is a path allowed by the structure of a **sequence diagram**. The UML use case model has several key elements and is a simplified form of the OOSE use case [Jacobson+92] (some OOSE use case elements dropped from the UML use case reappear in the UML Scenario Diagram).

○ *actor*   Any person or system submitting or receiving information to or from the system under test.

○ *system boundary*   An abstraction of the implementation interface that accepts and transports external inputs and system outputs. It includes sources producing messages accepted by blocks in the SUT and sinks that accept messages generated by blocks in the SUT. It may be a virtual machine, such as a GUI subsystem that is used by an application system.

○ *use case instance*   A use case with specific values specified for the use case parameters and the state of the SUT.

Figure 8.3 depicts the overall system relationships represented by a use case. The collaboration among components that support a use case may be

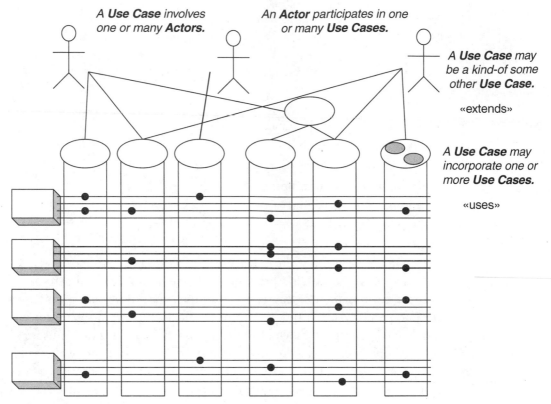

A **Use Case** involves one or many **Actors**.

An **Actor** participates in one or many **Use Cases.**

A **Use Case** may be a kind-of some other **Use Case.**

«extends»

A **Use Case** may incorporate one or more **Use Cases.**

«uses»

A **Component** supports one or many **Use Cases.**

A **Use Case** is implemented by one or many **Components.**

FIGURE 8.3   Use case relationships.

represented by a Sequence Diagram (see Section 8.5). Figure 8.4 shows a Use Case Diagram for the cash box example.

8.3.2 Generic Test Model

Table 8.1 lists the basic elements of the Use Case Diagram. Table 8.2 lists test criteria suggested by applying the relational test requirements (see Table 8.16 on page 310) to use case relationships. *Extended Use Case Test* is the primary test design pattern to develop application-specific tests. Figure 8.1 lists other test design patterns that use information presented in a Use Case Diagram and use case narratives.

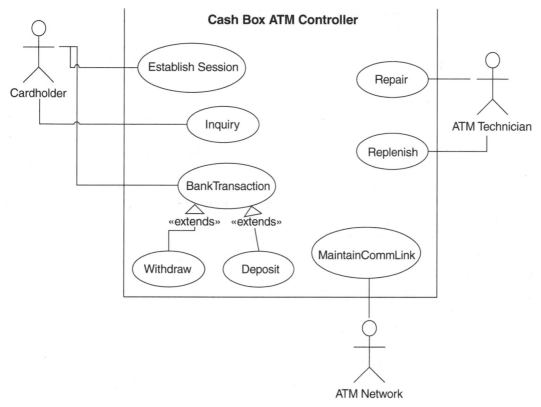

FIGURE 8.4   Use Case Diagram, cash box example.

8.3.3 Testability Extensions

A system specified with use cases provides some of the information necessary for system testing. Jacobson suggests four general kinds of tests that can be derived from use cases: (1) tests of basic courses, or "the expected flow of events," (2) tests of odd courses, or "all other flows of events," (3) tests of any line-item requirements traceable to each use case, and (4) tests of features described in user documentation traceable to each use case [Jacobson+92]. Equivalence class partitioning [Myers 79] is suggested for test design. Essentially the same test strategy is recited in [Jacobson+99]. From a testing perspective, this is good as far as it goes. But some key questions are unanswered.

TABLE 8.1   Use Case Diagram Elements

	Diagram Element	Symbol	Represents
Nodes	Actors (A)	Stick figure	Any external input source or response sink: external systems, human users, electromechanical sensors and actuators, and so on
	Use case (U)	Oval	A collection of interactions that accomplishes a user-defined task
	System	Box	A system that supports a use case
Edges	A communicates with U	Arrow	Links actors with use cases
	U1 extends U2	Generalization	U1's behavior is added to U2
	U1 uses U2	Generalization	U2's behavior is used by U1

TABLE 8.2   Generic Use Case Test Requirements

Relationship	R	S	T	Test	Test Requirement[†]
Actor communicates with Use Case	DC	Yes	DC	24	Every use case Every actor's use case
Use case 1 extends Use Case 2	No	No	Yes	2	Every fully expanded extension combination
Use case 1 uses Use Case 2	No	DC	Yes	17	Every fully expanded uses combination

[†]Entries to be read as "At least one test case that exercises <test requirement>."

How do I choose test cases?

Equivalence class partitioning is a deprecated test model (see Chapter 10). Even if it were not, UML use cases lack two necessary elements of test design. First, domain definitions for input and output variables are not a part of the UML. (This problem is not limited to the UML—with the exception of Fusion [Coleman+94], no other OOA/D approach requires explicit domain definitions for use case variables.) Second, testable specification of input/output relationships and the conditions that determine the basic and alternate flows are likewise absent in the UML.

In what order should I apply my tests?

Jacobson et al. are silent on the order in which to apply use case tests. Typical systems have hundreds of use cases from which tens of thousands of test cases can be developed. Sequential constraints and dependencies among the test cases are typically present and must be observed to conduct testing.

How do I know when I'm done?

Jacobson et al. argue that all use cases and each of their equivalence classes should be tested at least once. This goal is ambiguous because a wide range of test suites could be produced to satisfy this test strategy, because a wide range of artifacts can satisfy the requirements of use case and equivalence class specifications.

A use case describes interactions but does not tell us how often the interaction occurs or specify what the content of the interaction will be. *Use cases, as defined in UML, OOSE, and other object-oriented methodologies, are necessary but not sufficient for system test design.* We must determine the following additional items:

- The domain of each variable that participates in a use case
- The required input/output relationships among use case variables
- The relative frequency of each use case
- Sequential dependencies among use cases

Extended use cases provide this additional information and may be prepared with any OOA/D technique that calls for use cases. Operational variables are analyzed to construct an operation relation. Relative frequencies are developed by constructing an operational profile. This approach allows systematic generation of test cases, ensuring that field reliability is maximized for a given testing budget.

Operational Variables

The modeling of operational variables is illustrated with the Establish Session use case for an automatic teller machine (ATM) given in Chapter 6. Its instances differ by the amount of the transaction, the state of the customer's account, the state of the card, the number of times that the customer enters a wrong PIN, how much cash is contained in the ATM, the state of the ATM, and other factors. These factors are **operational variables**.

Operational variables may vary from one use case instance to the next use case instance and are used to construct specific test cases. They can be identified as follows.

1. *System boundary inventory.* Operational variables are typically visible at the system boundary—for example, the objects visible in the View component of an MVC application or the widgets constituting the GUI of the system under test. This inventory is not sufficient, however, because constraints or relationships among variables, key characteristics of the user or environment, and state information can be missed by a simple inventory.

2. *Use case instance inventory.* We could simply dream up (or observe) some arbitrary number of use case instances and then use them as test cases. This approach is weak from a testing point of view, because we cannot be sure that the resulting test suite will exercise all relations represented by the system's use cases.

3. *Operational variable definition.* Operational variables are inputs, outputs, and environmental conditions that (1) result in significantly different actor behavior; (2) abstract the state of the system under test (e.g., an ATM state of out of service, out of cash, ready, and so on); and (3) result in a significantly different system response.

The Operational Relation

Once operational variables have been defined, logical relationships among operational variables are modeled with a decision table yielding the **operational relation** (see Chapter 6). This supports systematic generation of test cases. When all of the conditions in a row are true, the corresponding action is to be produced. The operational relation supports systematic selection of test cases. At minimum, every row should be made true once and false once. If any operational variable specifies a range, tests that probe the boundaries of the range should be added. Chapter 6 discusses strategies for developing test suites from combinational models.

"Robustness analysis" is suggested as an initial validation of use cases [Jacobson+92, Rosenberg+99] but does not require testable content. It has been my experience that the analysis required to produce extended use cases is very effective at finding omissions, inconsistencies, and other requirements bugs. Validation techniques applicable to the operational relation are discussed in Chapter 6.

8.4 Class Diagram

8.4.1 Notation and Semantics

A Class Diagram (also Object Diagram, Static Structure Diagram) represents relationships among *classifier elements*. Class Diagrams can serve many purposes. They typically represent the entities and relationships of interest for a particular application and document the structure of the classes in a library, framework, or application. Figure 8.5 shows a Class Diagram for the cash box example.

Most classifier elements are represented by a box with *compartments*. The kind-of classifier may be designated with a keyword (e.g., «interface»).

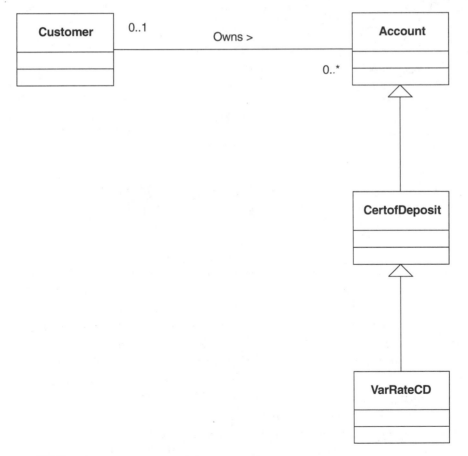

FIGURE 8.5   Class Diagram, cash box example.

TABLE 8.3   Class Diagram Elements: Nodes

	Diagram Element	Symbol	Represents
Nodes	Type	Class box «type»	A role or entity; may have attributes but no operations
	Class	Class box (name, operation, and attribute compartments)	An implementation class
	Interface	Class box or small circle	Abstract class, Java interface, Objective-C Protocol
	Parameterized class	Class box with parameter box	C++ template class, Eiffel generic, and so on
	Meta-class	Class box «metaclass»	An implementation meta-class
	Association class	Class box	An association as a class
	Object	Object box (name and attribute compartments); the name is underlined and of the form <u>ClassName:ObjectName</u>	An instance of a class
	Composite object	Object box with object boxes in the attribute compartment	The attributes of a composite object as a graph, allowing relationships to be shown
	Utility	Class box «utility»	A group of global variables and procedures

Table 8.3 lists the various classifiers. Several basic relationships and their variants may be represented in a Class Diagram.

Association

An **association** between two classes means that both must implement a mutual constraint or dependency. For example, in the cash box ATM controller, we need to represent accounts and customers. Figure 8.5 shows the Customer-Owns-Account relationship, including a classifier box for the Customer and Account classes and an association line to show the Owns relationship.

An association models a constraint that must be realized in the implementation. It does not necessarily represent the class or object structure of the implementation that realizes this constraint. A *role* is a verb phrase that suggests the nature of the modeled relationship. The subject and object of the verb phrase are the classifiers connected by the association line. Usually, this relationship can be read as a declarative sentence in either the active or passive voice. For example, the association role *owns* yields "customer owns account" (active voice) or "account is owned by customer" (passive voice).

Multiplicity parameters appear at the ends of the association line. These parameters define how many instances of one class may be associated with an instance of the other class. The multiplicity parameters in Figure 8.5 imply that (1) a customer is not required to own an account, (2) an account is owned by only one customer or has no owner, and (3) a customer may own many accounts.

Pair-wise multiplicity associations are common. In this situation, paired multiplicity parameters appear at both ends of the association line. Each pair defines the minimum and maximum number of instances for the class nearest this pair, defined with respect to any single instance of the class nearest the pair. A multiplicity parameter pair is interpreted by assuming that we have a single instance of one class and then reading the minimum and maximum number of instances for the other class. For example, reading from left to right, Figure 8.5 asserts that any given instance of a customer may own no account (0) or any number of accounts (*). Reading in the opposite direction (right to left), we see that an account may have no owner (0) or at most one owner.

Aggregation

Aggregation relationships identify classifiers that are constituent parts of another classifier (a "container"). For example, the instance variables of classes are typically objects of other classes. The class of the instance variables may be shown by an aggregation relationship. Two kinds of aggregation may be represented.

- Simple *aggregation* is shown by a line with an unfilled diamond at the container end. This indicates that the constituent classifier is created and destroyed independently of the container classifier.
- *Composition* is shown by a line with a filled diamond at the using end. This indicates that the constituent classifier is created and destroyed with the container classifier.

Both roles and multiplicity may be specified for aggregation relationships. Aggregation may be drawn as classifiers connected with an aggregation line or as a composite object (an object box enclosing other object boxes in the attribute compartment).

Generalization

Generalization relationships identify classifiers that share common elements. For example, a superclass generalizes a subclass; that is, the subclass is a specialization of the superclass that shares the elements of the superclass. Generalization is shown by a line with an unfilled triangle whose apex points to the more general classifier.

Generalization may represent abstract generalization/specialization of types and implementation inheritance of a class hierarchy. When it is used to represent an implementation hierarchy, we assume the scoping and semantics of the implementation language.

8.4.2 Generic Test Model

Table 8.3 lists the basic elements included in a Class Diagram. Relationships are listed in Table 8.4. Table 8.5 on page 288 lists test criteria suggested by applying the relational test requirements (see Table 8.17 later in the chapter) to relationships. *Class Association Test* is the primary test design pattern employed to develop application-specific tests. Figure 8.1 lists other test design patterns that use information presented in a Class Diagram.

8.5 Sequence Diagram

8.5.1 Notation and Semantics

A Sequence Diagram represents how a sequence of messages exchanged among objects can accomplish some result of interest. Sequence Diagrams are typically used to design the collaboration necessary to implement a use case. Generally, vertical lines represent objects and horizontal lines represent messages sent from one object to another. Time progresses from top to bottom—if message `foo` appears above message `bar`, then `foo` is sent before `bar`. An end-to-end path is called an *interaction*.

The nodes in a Sequence Diagram represent runtime properties of executable components and provide some drafting convenience features:

• *Objects*. An object box designates an object that participates in an interaction. The object may be a composite; for example, it can represent a component, an entire subsystem, or an interface to an external system.

TABLE 8.4   Class Diagram Elements: Edges

	Diagram Element	Symbol	Represents
Edges	Association (binary)	Undirected line with ornaments	A required pair-wise property between instances of the classifier
	Association (*n*-ary)	A large diamond with association lines	An association among instances of three or more classifiers
	Association Path	Undirected dashed line	Connects an association class to an association line
	Or association	Undirected dashed line {or}	Indicates that exactly one of the spanned associations holds for any given set of classifier instances
	Association Qualifier	Box with attribute(s) names, between an object and an association line	The attributes that identify instance-pair subsets of an association; similar to the key of a database or file.
	Aggregation	Line with a small, unfilled diamond at the container end	The contained classifier is a part of the container classifier and may be created and destroyed independently of the container
	Composition	Line with a small, filled diamond at the container end	The contained classifier is a part of the container classifier and is created and destroyed along with the container
	Generalization	Line with an unfilled triangle at the general end	The specialized classifier is a kind of the general classifier (e.g., a subclass of a superclass)
	Dependency	Dashed arrow	A physical or logical reference such that changing the target classifier may require changing the source classifier
	Link	Line between two objects	A list of object references; an instance of an association
	Realizes	Dashed line with a solid triangular arrowhead	Indicates an implementation class for a type

TABLE 8.5   Generic Test Requirements for Class Diagrams

Relationship	R	S	T	Test	Test Requirement[†]
Association (binary)					Application-specific. See **Class Association Test**.
Association (*n*-ary)					Application-specific. See **Class Association Test**.
Association path					Tested as part of its association.
Or association	N	Y	N	4	Each association singularly (accepts). Two or more associations (rejects).
Association qualifier					Tested as part of its association.
Aggregation	DC	N	N	19	Independent creation and destruction of the container and the component.
Composition	DC	N	Y	20	Sequential creation and destruction of the container and the component. An attempt at independent creation and destruction of the container and the component fails.
Generalization	N	N	Y	2	Each superclass classifier is exercised in the context of every subclass classifier.
Dependency	DC	N	N	10	Application-specific.
Link					Tested as part of its association.
Realizes	N	N	N	1	Each behavior of the type in the implementation class.

[†]Entries to be read as, "At least one test case that exercises <test requirement>."

• *Object lifeline*. The lifeline is a dashed vertical line that connects the object box to an activation interval for the object. An **X** at the bottom of a lifeline marks the explicit or implicit destruction of the object.

• *Object activation*. An activation is shown by a narrow rectangle overlaying the lifeline. At the object scope, the activation represents placing an executable instance of the object on the runtime stack. When an object is running (i.e., on the top of the runtime stack), the corresponding area of the activation box may be shaded. When the object has been context-swapped (i.e., not on the top of the runtime stack), the activation box is unfilled.

• *Conditional branch*. As a drawing convenience, a conditional segment within the scope of a method activation can be shown by a parallel activation box attached to the original activation by dashed lines. This does *not* represent a new activation record on the runtime stack.

- *Recursive activation.* An activation that results from a recursive call is shown by a single, short activation box that partially overlays the initial activation box. A looping arrow distinguishes this box from a loop box. Note that the sending method and the receiving method must be the same. The implementation semantics of recursion are language- and compiler-specific.

The edges in a Sequence Diagram represent generic properties of runtime *procedure calls:*

- *Suspend/resume procedure call.* A solid line with a filled arrowhead represents a message, function call, remote procedure call, interprocess communication call, and so on. Control is transferred from the currently active method to the receiver of the call. Recipient visibility to the call parameters is established. No return arrow from the receiver to the sender is needed, but a dashed arrow may be used.

- *Nonblocking procedure call.* A solid line with a half-open arrowhead represents a message, function call, remote procedure call, or interprocess communication call that does not suspend activation of the sender. The receiver of the call is activated when the message is received. Visibility is established for the call parameters. A dashed arrow must be used to show the return (if any) to the sender.

- *Conditional procedure calls.* Solid lines leaving the same point on the activation box indicate that only one of two or more possible procedure calls will be sent. The condition that selects each call may be written near the line, in brackets.

- *Procedure call loop.* Iteration is shown by a box that overlays the lifeline box. The predicate for a conditional or a loop appears in brackets, near the lower part of the loop box. A loop box does not have entry/exit arrows; a recursive activation box does.

- *Procedure call delay.* Flat procedure call arrows represent calls whose sending time is inconsequential to the model. If the transmit time of a call is significant, then the arrow is drawn with a downward slope.

Figure 8.6 shows a Sequence Diagram for the Start New Session use case in the cash box example.

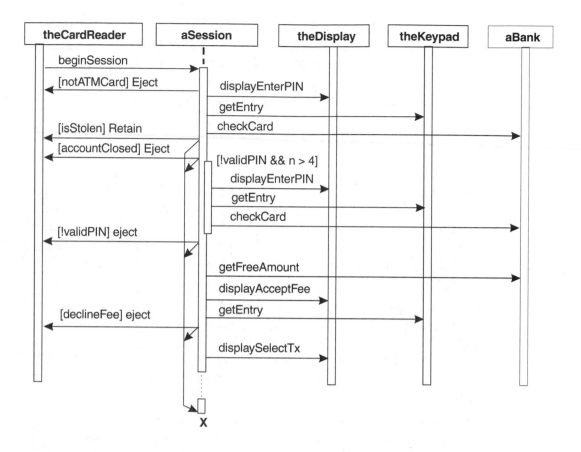

FIGURE 8.6   Sequence Diagram, cash box example.

8.5.2 Generic Test Requirements

The relationship between use case instances and Sequence Diagrams is shown in Figure 8.3. Table 8.6 lists the graph elements of Sequence Diagrams. Table 8.7 lists the generic test requirements suggested by applying the relational test strategy (see Table 8.17 later in the chapter). These test requirements confirm that basic testing practice should apply to Sequence Diagrams: all end-to-end paths should be identified and exercised. This is equivalent to the requirement to identify and exercise all transitive relations formed by the variations on client-sends-message-to-server. *Round-trip Scenario Test* is the primary test

TABLE 8.6   Sequence Diagram Elements

	Diagram Element	Symbol	Represents
Nodes	Object and Object Lifeline	Object Box over vertical dashed line	An object, component, or subsystem
	Object Activation	Narrow Rectangle	The presence or absence of an object instance during a scenario
	Conditional Branch	Short Narrow Rectangle connected by dashed lines to an Activation box	Conditional code segment within a method; diagraming convenience
	Recursive Activation	Short Narrow Rectangle, overlaying an Object Activation box, pointed to by a looping arrow	Recursive activation
Edges	Suspend/Resume Procedure Call	Solid arrow	A message that suspends activation of the sender
	Nonblocking Procedure Call	A solid line with a half-open arrowhead	A message that does not suspend activation of the sender
	Conditional Procedure Calls	Solid lines leaving the same point on the activation box	Only one of the indicated procedure calls will be sent
	Procedure Call Loop	A narrow rectangle that partially overlays an Object Activation box	The condition that selects each call may be written near the line, in brackets
	Recursive Call	Loop arrow to a Recursive Activation box	Recursive call
	Procedure Call Delay	A downward-sloping arrow	Significant message transmit time

TABLE 8.7   Sequence Diagram Test Requirements

Relationship	R	S	T	Test	Test Requirements[†]
Client calls Server (suspend/resume)	Y	N	Y	11	Client calls Server and returns.
Client calls Server (nonblocking)	N	N	Y	2	Client calls Server and returns. Server continues execution.
Client may call Server 1, 2, . . .	N	N	Y	2	Client calls Server 1, 2, . . .
Client repeats call to Server	Y	N	Y	11	Client repeats call to Server.
Client recursively calls Client	Y	N	N	10	Client recursively calls Client.
Client call delayed to Server	N	N	N	1	Client calls Server.

[†]Entries to be read as, "At least one test case that exercises <test requirement>."

design pattern to develop application-specific tests. Figure 8.1 lists other test design patterns that use information presented in a Sequence Diagram.

8.5.3 Testability Extensions

A Sequence Diagram unfolds message paths in the time dimension, which provides a useful representation for conceptualizing how a collaboration will be accomplished. However, it is a poor model for developing tests of their control flow. Where a properly constructed flow graph will show all possible activation sequences, a Sequence Diagram is *required* to show only a *single* collaboration. For example, the implementation of a use case may require several scenario diagrams. A complete model of the use case's implementation would require an overlay composed of all of these diagrams. This fragmentation creates opportunities for errors and makes it difficult to decide when a complete test suite has been developed.

Sequence Diagrams pose some additional problems:

- Representing complex control is difficult. The notation for selection and iteration is clumsy and supports possibly conflicting interpretations. This poses more problems for test design, as it will be difficult to decide when all paths in a Scenario Diagram have been covered.
- The distinction between a conditional message and a delayed message is weak (a line angles down for both; a conditional message has a predicate string). A conditional delayed message could be noted by showing the same time for both messages.
- Dynamic binding and unique superclass/subclass behavior cannot be represented directly. A Sequence Diagram depicts a single collaboration. The binding of a message to a different class (even within the same hierarchy) must be shown on a separate sheet or with an object lifeline for each level in the polymorphic server hierarchy.

A likely result is that a Sequence Diagram will not accurately represent a complex control implementation. Test design should not be done without reverifying the content of the model and analyzing the actual structure of the implementation to assess interfaces, paths, and other features. The *Round-trip Scenario Test* pattern shows how to derive a composite control flow graph from a Sequence Diagram. It allows established control flow test models to be used as test models.

8.6 Activity Diagram

8.6.1 Notation and Semantics

An Activity Diagram represents sequences in which *activities* may occur. The model borrows ideas from flow charts, state transition diagrams, industrial engineering work flow graphs, and Petri nets.[4] It is described as a flow chart that can represent two or more threads of execution. Strangely, an Activity Diagram includes no activities—the entire diagram is considered to represent a single activity. Instead, it is composed of *action states,* each of which is a collection of happenings that achieves a result of interest. When an action state finishes, one or more successor action states begin. Several action states may run concurrently. In effect, an action state is a process, not a state.

The Activity Diagram is typically used for modeling human work flow and the interaction of this work flow with a software system. It may be associated with a use case or a class. Because it supports all of the elements of a basic flow graph, this type of diagram can be used to develop test models for control flow-based techniques. Developers who are limited to using a CASE tool that supports only UML can still produce these diagrams by using a subset of the Activity Diagram.

- The Activity Diagram may be used to represent decision tables (see Chapter 6). It can therefore support test development using the **Combinational Function Test** and **Extended Use Case Test** patterns.
- The Activity Diagram can be used to create a composite control flow graph for a collection of Sequence Diagrams. This use supports **Roundtrip Scenario Test** (see Chapter 12).
- The Activity Diagram can be used to create a control flow graph at method scope. This application may be useful to analyze paths for coverage.

The nodes in an Activity Diagram represent processes and process control:

- *Action state.* A collection of happenings that are of interest. This is labeled with a descriptive phrase and represented by a horizontal capsule.

---

4. Activity Diagrams are remarkably similar to the SREM system diagrams [Alford 85], which also represent multiple threads of control.

- *Decision.* A diamond shows there are at least two successor nodes, but only one is to be reached after the antecedent action state terminates.
- *Synchronization point.* A thick bar shows that the successor action state(s) is activated only when all predecessor states (or state) terminate. It can be thought of as an *and* gate: its successor nodes are activated only when all of its predecessor nodes have terminated. A synchronization point with two or more predecessors is called a *merge;* one with two or more successors is called a *fork.*
- *Object box.* See the discussion of the object box in the Sequence Diagram discussion, Section 8.5.1.
- *Signal receiver.* It shows that the successor action state(s) is activated only when the designated signal is received. It is shown as a rectangle with a triangular notch in either side.
- *Signal sender.* It shows that the designated signal is emitted when the predecessor action state terminates. It is shown as a rectangle with a triangular point in either side.
- *Swim lanes.* These lanes indicate a group to which action states may belong. They are shown by vertical lines that form areas into which action states may be placed. Swim lanes do not represent behavior.

The edges in an Activity Diagram show which activities may follow one another and, optionally, which objects may participate in an activity.

- *Control flow.* A solid arrow shows a predecessor/successor relationship. Control flow may be omitted when messages (dashed arrows) link the same action states.
- *Message flow.* A dashed arrow shows that messages are sent between an action state and an object.·
- *Signal flow.* A dashed arrow links signal receipt and signal sending nodes.

Figure 8.7 shows an Activity Diagram for the cash box example. This diagram shows a fragment of the user behavior that occurs when a customer makes a deposit. The user must prepare the deposit envelope and insert it into the open depository slot. The slot automatically closes if no deposit is inserted after a certain interval.

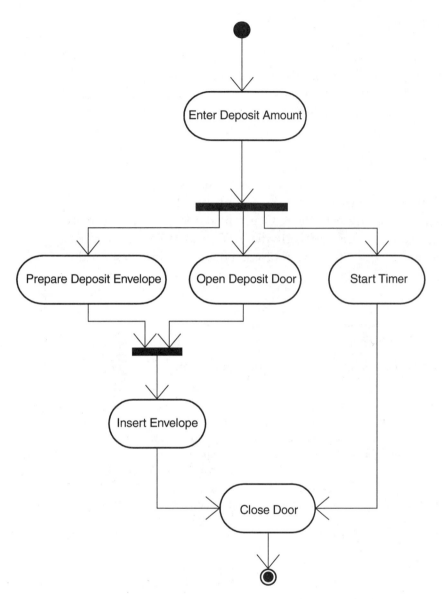

FIGURE 8.7   Activity Diagram, cash box example.

8.6.2 Generic Test Model

Table 8.8 lists the graph elements of Activity Diagrams. Table 8.9 lists test criteria suggested by applying the relational test requirements (see Table 8.17, page 312) to Activity Diagram relationships. The test requirements are applied to all pairs of nodes that can participate in a given relationship. None of the test design patterns in this book use the Activity Diagram as a basic test model. Figure 8.1 lists test design patterns that can use information presented in an Activity Diagram.

If an Activity Diagram supports concurrent action states (at least one "fork" synchronization bar exists), then the testing problem becomes more complex. Complete testing strategies for concurrent models are an advanced subject beyond the scope of this book. If the IUT modeled by an Activity Diagram warrants testing, the test strategies for product machines described in Chapter 7 may be useful.

TABLE 8.8 Activity Diagram Elements

	Diagram Element	Symbol	Represents
Nodes	Action State	Horizontal Capsule	A process
	Decision	Diamond	Only one of several successors may be next
	Swim Lane	Parallel vertical lines	A group of related processes
	Synchronization Point	Thick Bar	All predecessors must terminate before the successor can start
	Object	Object Box	An object, component, or subsystem
	Signal Receiver	Notched Rectangle	The successor cannot be started until the signal is received
	Signal Sender	Pointy Rectangle	A signal is sent before the successor starts
	Initial Action State	Filled Circle	Predecessor to first action state
	Final Action State	Bull's Eye	Final action state
Edges	Control Flow	Solid Arrow	Predecessor/successor relationship
	Message Flow	Dashed Arrow	Message sent to/from an object
	Signal Flow	Dashed Arrow	A pair of sender/receiver nodes

TABLE 8.9   Activity Diagram Test Requirements

Relationship	R	S	T	Test	Test Requirements[†]
Action 1 precedes Action 2	D	D	Y	26	Action 1 is followed by Action 2.
Action depends on Synch Point	N	N	N	1	Synch Point is followed by Action.
Action 2, 3, . . . may follow Action 1	D	D	N	25	Action 1 is followed by Action 2. Action 1 is followed by Action 3. . . .
Action depends on Signal	N	N	N	1	Action is reached after Signal.
Synch Point follows Action	N	N	N	1	Synch Point is reached after Action.

Key: Action = Action State
[†]Entries to be read as, "At least one test case that exercises <test requirement>."

8.7 Statechart Diagram

A statechart represents sequential control requirements for a class, subsystem, or system. Statecharts are discussed in detail in Chapter 7. The UML definition of a statechart provides most of the information necessary for state-based testing, but permits the development of nontestable constructs and ambiguities. The FREE state model is consistent with all requirements of UML statecharts and remedies these problems. It is also discussed in detail in Chapter 7. In addition, Chapter 7 provides the following model validation checklists:

- State name
- Guarded transition
- Flattened machine
- Robustness

As Figure 8.1 shows, FREE statecharts are the primary test model for *Modal Class Test*, *Modal Hierarchy Test*, and *Mode Machine Test*.

8.8 Collaboration Diagram

8.8.1 Notation and Semantics

A Collaboration Diagram represents interactions among object roles. The diagram shows *one* instance of an interaction, in which objects take on the *roles* necessary to perform the computation. Although the diagram can be used to represent the structure of an implementation, this is not its primary purpose. The diagram is abstract (it does not require binding to specific objects) and is a slice of the modeled scope.[5] A Collaboration Diagram may be used to specify the implementation of a method, all methods in a class, or a use case. This type of diagram may also depict the participants in design patterns. Figure 8.8 shows a Collaboration Diagram for the cash box example.

A node is a *collaboration role*. Such a node can represent any object of a class that may fulfill the role. These nodes do not represent specific objects, however. They may be simple or composite. A *ClassifierRole* is depicted via a classifier box. An *AssociationRole* is shown as a line between two classifiers and may be ornamented with the items described in a Class Diagram. A *multiobject* is a collection. Links to a multiobject are indicated with a filled diamond ornament on the link. Messages to multiobjects assume an iterator to attach the message to a member of the collection. A multiobject is shown as two stacked rectangles. An *active object* is visible to the runtime environment as a task, process, or thread. It is designated by a classifier box with a heavy border.

Edges are *links*. They are shown with solid, undirected lines and represent that visibility is required from one role to another. The sending of messages and related control mechanisms is represented by a small arrow near the link. Because the links allow more than one message to be sent, execution paths cannot be traced directly from links.

An *interaction* is a call path within the scope of a collaboration. A *message flow* represents a message sent from one object to another and is shown by a short arrow parallel to the link that supports the message. Several types may be used:

- *Procedure call.* For example, a C++ function call or a Java message with typical suspend/resume activation semantics. It is shown by a solid line with a filled arrowhead, where the arrow points to the server object.
- *Flat flow of control.* Shows execution sequence at statement scope. It is shown by a solid line with an open arrowhead. The arrow points to the successor object.
- *Asynchronous flow of control.* Indicates an "asynchronous" call or other nonblocking mechanism (the recipient and the sender execute concurrently). The arrow points to the server object.

---

5. At the method scope, a slice is a subset of the method statements. It may be defined by many criteria—for example, all statements that are needed to support an entry–exit path or all statements that can influence a given statement [Tip 95].

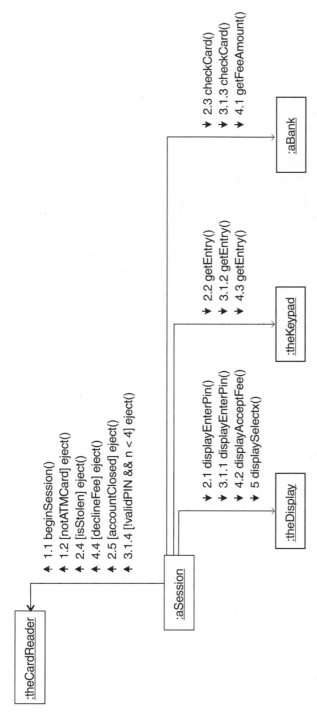

FIGURE 8.8 Collaboration Diagram, cash box example.

Each message may be labeled. Message labels can specify the predecessor call hierarchy, conditional execution, and iteration. All elements of the message are optional.

```
<message label> ::=
    <predecessor guard-condition>
    <sequence-expression>
    <<return-value> := <message-name> <argument-list>>
```

The `<predecessor guard-condition>` is a predicate evaluated within the scope of the predecessor object. If the predicate is true, then the message is sent. If not, then the message is not sent. The return expression specifies the sender's variable, which will become bound to the result of the designated message.

The `<sequence-expression>` denotes the predecessor messages using number-dot notation. The left most number denotes a step within the scope of the first method. A dot (period) separates the next level of control—that is, the scope of control for a second method called from the first method. Problems with this notation are discussed in Section 8.8.3.

Roles and links may be ornamented with *creation/destruction markers* that specify their scope of persistence.

8.8.2 Generic Test Model

Table 8.10 lists the graph elements of Collaboration Diagrams. Table 8.11 lists test criteria suggested by applying the relational test requirements (see Table 8.17) to Collaboration Diagram relationships. ***Collaboration Integration*** is the primary pattern for developing application-specific tests. Figure 8.1 lists other test design patterns that use information presented in a Collaboration Diagram.

8.8.3 Testability Extensions

The Collaboration Diagram is problematic as a test model for the following three reasons:

1. It represents only one slice of the IUT and can support coverage analysis of only this slice (see Chapter 9 for details of coverage analysis). In most circumstances, however, we are interested in testing and covering the entire implementation. A composite Collaboration Diagram would be necessary to

TABLE 8.10   Collaboration Diagram Elements

	Diagram Element	Symbol	Represents
Nodes	Object Role	Classifier Box	An object, component, or subsystem
	Multiobject	Stacked Classifier Box	A collection of the same kind of objects
	Active Object	Classifier Box with heavy border	An object that runs as an independent process, task, or thread
Edges	Link	Solid line	Visibility required between two object roles
	Procedure Call	Line with filled arrowhead	Suspend/resume message sent to a role
	Flat Control Flow	Line with open arrowhead	Predecessor/successor relationship within a method
	Asynchronous Control Flow	Line with open half-arrowhead	Nonblocking message sent to a role

TABLE 8.11   Collaboration Diagram Test Requirements

Relationship	R	S	T	Test	Test Requirements[†]
Role is linked to Role	D	D	D	NA	Not testable per se.
Statement 1 precedes Statement 2 (Flat Control Flow)	N	N	Y	2	Statement 1 and Statement 2.
Client sends message to Server (Procedure Call)	D	N	Y	20	Client sends message to Server and returns.
Client may send message to Server (Conditional Procedure Call)	D	N	Y	20	Client sends message to Server and returns. Client does not send message to Server.
Client repeats message to Server (Iterative Procedure Call)	D	N	Y	20	Client repeats message to Server and returns.
Client sends recursive message to self (Recursive Procedure Call)	Y	N	N	10	Client recursively calls self.
Client makes Nonblocking Procedure Call to Server (Asynchronous Control Flow)	N	N	Y	2	Client sends message to Server and returns. Server receives message.

[†]Entries to be read as "At least one test case that exercises <test requirement>."

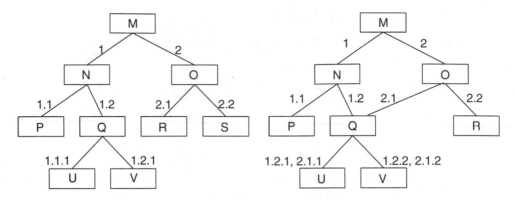

FIGURE 8.9 Overlapping sequence expressions in a Collaboration Diagram.

develop a complete test suite for the implementation. Testing only the slices represented by one or several Collaboration Diagrams does not accomplish anything for the untested slices.

2. Although [OMG 98] states that a sequence expression has "an implicit predecessor [which] need not be explicitly listed," unless the objects visited by an interaction form a tree,[6] each message must explicitly designate its prefix. Consider the call paths in Figure 8.9 (boxes represent methods, lines are messages.) The hierarchy on the left is a tree, so only one root-to-leaf path exists for every leaf level node in the graph. If we label the tree according to the `<sequence-expression>` scheme, we can trace all possible call paths: 1, 1.1, 1.2, 1.2.1, 1.2.2, 2, 2.1. Now consider the hierarchy on the right. It differs only in that object O also sends a message to object Q. It is not a tree, however, because more than one root-to-leaf path exists through O. The links Q-U and Q-V reveal the problem. If N sends a message to Q, these links should be labeled 1.2.1 and 1.2.2. If O sends a message to Q, these links should be labeled 2.1.1 and 2.1.2. So, unless the call hierarchy of collaborations is restricted to a tree, all of the predecessor prefixes must appear on each link. If they are not shown, the predecessor is ambiguous.

3. One dot level must be added for each object that participates in an interaction. For example, if a dozen objects participate, a complete `<sequence-expression>` list will look something like this:

---

6. A tree is a graph that has no cycles and for which the number of nodes equals the number of edges plus 1.

4, 4.2, 4.2.18, 4.2.18.6, 4.2.18.6.8, 4.2.18.6.8.5, 4.2.18.6.8.5.13,
4.2.18.6.8.5.13.2, 4.2.18.6.8.5.13.2.5, 4.2.18.6.8.5.13.2.5.5,
4.2.18.6.8.5.13.2.5.5.3, 4.2.18.6.8.5.13.2.5.5.3.9.

The addition of iteration, exceptions, and recursion complicates the picture.

The Collaboration Diagram presents many design bug hazards and is, by
definition, an incomplete representation of its implementation. Even if all tests
in a test suite that has been developed from several Collaboration Diagrams
pass, the tester should still ask, "Is that all there is?" Covering a collaboration
typically will not achieve coverage of the IUT, unless the Collaboration
Diagrams provide a complete representation of all slices.

The Collaboration Diagram represents highly abstract, implementation-
independent requirements (roles) and implementation-specific details (call
paths, statement level flow, return values, and so on). A likely result is a confusion about abstraction and implementation, leading to poor design decisions
or detail design omissions. Tests for implementations developed from and documented by Collaboration Diagrams should be designed using some other
model, such as a class or cluster state model.

8.9 Component Diagram

8.9.1 Notation and Semantics

A Component Diagram shows the dependency relationships among components,
physical containment of components, and interfaces and calling components,
using dashed arrows from components to interfaces on other components. A
component is an implementation entity, including source code units, binary code
(the output of a translator), and linked, loadable executable files.

- The symbol for a component is a rectangle with two small boxes on
  one side. The component name and type are underlined and placed
  either within the component symbol or near to it.
- The symbol for an interface is a small, unfilled circle attached to the
  component box.
- Compiler dependencies are shown by dashed arrows. A language-
  specific mechanism may be designated with a stereotype.

- The usage of interfaces and call dependencies is indicated with dashed arrows between components and the interfaces they use.

Figure 8.10 shows a Component Diagram for the cash box example.

8.9.2 Generic Test Model

Table 8.12 lists the graph elements of Component Diagrams. Table 8.13 lists test criteria suggested by applying the relational test requirements (see Table 8.17 on page 312). The generic test requirements confirm that basic testing practice should apply to Sequence Diagrams: all call paths should be identified and exercised.

Component Diagrams are useful for integration planning. The dependency analysis outlined in Chapter 13, for example, can be developed from a sufficiently detailed Component Diagram. Figure 8.1 lists other test design patterns that can use the information presented in Component Diagrams.

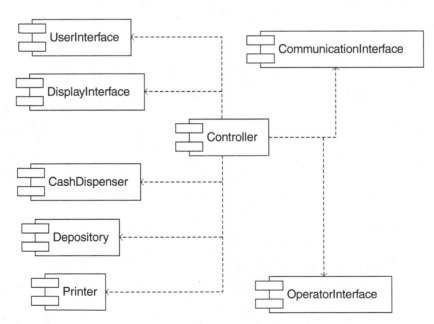

FIGURE 8.10   Component Diagram, cash box example.

TABLE 8.12   Component Diagram Elements

	Diagram Element	Symbol	Represents
Nodes	Component	Rectangle with two small box extensions on one side	A software entity visible to the target environment
	Interface	Small unfilled circle	A symbolic identifier visible to target environment thst supports activation and parameter passing
Edges	Message Flow	Dashed arrow	Message sent to/from a component
	Source Code Dependency	Dashed arrow	Components cannot operate without one another

TABLE 8.13   Component Diagram Test Requirements

Relationship	R	S	T	Test	Test Requirements[†]
Component sends message to interface	D	N	Y	20	Client sends message to server and returns
Component depends on component	D	D	D	27	Application-specific

[†]Entries to be read as "At least one test case that exercises <test requirement>."

8.10   Deployment Diagram

8.10.1   Notation and Semantics

A Deployment Diagram represents hardware, software, and network architecture.

- A Deployment Diagram *node* is a processor; it is not a node in the graph-theoretic sense. Nodes include all kinds of computer systems and may represent manual or mechanical processors. The symbol for a node is a box with dropping sides, suggesting a perspective drawing. The name and type of the node may appear as underlined text.

- Nodes are connected by *communication associations,* indicated by a solid line (no arrow). A stereotype may be used to designate particulars of the interface and channel.

- Component instances and objects that run on a node are shown by placing them in the node box. Software components in a Deployment Diagram must be executable units (entities that are visible to the

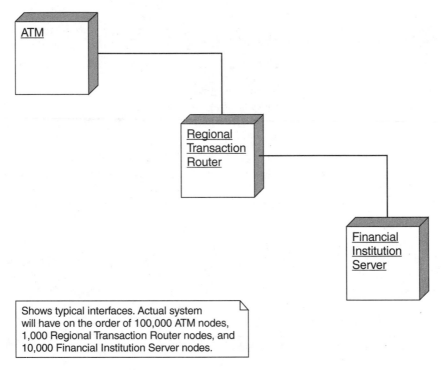

FIGURE 8.11 Deployment Diagram, cash box example.

execution and scheduling mechanisms of the target environment). Source code entities do not appear. The Component Diagram rules for components are also applied in Deployment Diagrams.

- A dashed-arrow dependency indicates that a node (or node type) can support a component (or component type). Stereotypes specify additional information; for example, the «becomes» stereotype shows that a component moves from one node to another.

Figure 8.11 shows a Deployment Diagram for the cash box example.

8.10.2 Generic Test Model

Table 8.14 lists the graph elements of Deployment Diagrams. Table 8.15 lists test criteria suggested by applying the relational test requirements (see Table 8.17). Deployment Diagrams are useful for integration planning. The dependency analysis outlined in Chapter 13, for example, can be developed from a

TABLE 8.14   Deployment Diagram Elements

	Diagram Element	Symbol	Represents
Nodes	Node	Rectangle with dropped sides	A processor
	Component	Rectangle with two small box extensions on one side	A software entity visible to the target environment
	Interface	Small unfilled circle	A symbolic identifier visible to the target environment that supports activation and parameter passing
Edges	Communication Association	Solid line	A communication channel
	Component Dependency	Dashed arrow	The node(s) on which a component may run

TABLE 8.15   Deployment Diagram Test Requirements

Relationship	R	S	T	Test	Test Requirements[†]
Component runs on Node	D	D	D	27	Component can be loaded and run on each designated host Node
Node communicates with Node (Communication Association)	D	D	D	27	Open, transmit, and close communication for each remote component

[†]Entries to be read as "At least one test case that exercises <test requirement>."

sufficiently detailed Deployment Diagram. Figure 8.1 lists other test design patterns that can use Deployment Diagrams.

◆ 8.11 Graphs, Relations, and Testing

A **graph** represents relationships among things by using two simple constructs: **nodes** and **edges**. Nodes are connected to other nodes by edges. This idea supports a wide range of mathematically rigorous models.[7] The nodes and edges of

---

7. The extensive body of mathematical knowledge about graphs is called *graph theory*. See the Bibliographic Notes section for some introductory sources. Formally, a graph is a set of vertices V and a set of edges E. An edge is a pair of vertices. I use *node* instead of *vertex*, because the content of a node matters in software engineering models. A vertex is simply an undifferentiated dot. A graph is a set of pairs of nodes (two nodes connected by an edge). Binary (pair-wise) relations on sets can be represented and analyzed with graphs, and vice versa.

a graph represent a relation, which is another simple but powerful mathematical concept. UML diagrams can be viewed as graphs (in this mathematical sense) that represent many significant relationships and therefore provide a rich source of information for test design. The basic mathematical properties of graphs and relations can yield tests to check whether the IUT is consistent in its implementation of these relationships [Beizer 90, Beizer 95]. This strategy allows the same analysis to be applied to all UML diagrams and thereby simplifies the job of testing from these representations. Although it is applied only to UML diagrams here, the same analysis can be developed for any other graphic modeling technique and, with the necessary changes, for any quantitative modeling formalism.

A **relation**, in the mathematical sense, is a set such that some property holds among members of that set. It is a "set-theoretic formalization of practical notion" [Mac Lane 86, 131], which is the basis of the relational data model and relational databases [Date 82]. In the UML, relations are represented with associations. Because the UML meta-model defines associations among UML elements, two levels of relations exist in any UML model: intrinsic relations among UML elements and application-specific relations among classifiers that represent the system under development.

For example, the classes of a framework that send messages to themselves can be enumerated by a relation defined by the requirement that at least one statement in the class has the form `this.foo( )`. Classes that are clients and servers can also be defined. For example, if class A declares an instance variable of type B, and class C declares one of type D, then the relation has two instances: A, B and C, D.

Any property can define a relation: whole-part, is-a-kind-of, adjacent-to, person-knows-system, and so on. A relation can be defined for any number of elements of a set. A *binary relation* is defined based on pairs. The mathematical shorthand for a binary relation is xRy, which is read "relation R holds for all pairs of x and y." For example, the mathematical expression $x = y$ asserts that the equality relationship holds for all pairs of x and y. The programming predicate expression (x == y) can be used to identify x,y pairs that do (and do not) satisfy this relation. If a relationship is not permitted, we write $\sim xRy$. A binary relation can be thought of as a table with two columns. Each row in this table is a member of the set defined by the relation.

Certain general kinds of relations are useful for test design:

• A **reflexive relation** is one where the property of interest holds when applied to each individual entity. For example, consider the relation *person-*

recognizes-person. This relation is reflexive, assuming that a person can recognize himself. Jill recognizes Jill—that is she recognizes herself. In a graph, an edge that exits and enters the same node (a loop on a single node) often represents a reflexive relation. If the members of a reflexive relation are depicted as a table, every cell in the diagonal must be part of the relation (see Figure 8.12). A relation that does not allow self-reference is **nonreflexive**.

- A **symmetric relation** is one where for any pair of entities, the right and left sides can be exchanged and the property of interest still holds. For example, consider *person-recognizes-person*. If all the persons in question know one another, the relationship is symmetric. That is, if Jack recognizes Jill, then Jill recognizes Jack. In a graph, a pair of edges going in opposite directions, a bidirectional arrow, or an undirected line is often used to depict a symmetric relation. If the members of a symmetric relation are shown as a table, the upper and lower triangles will be mirror images (see Figure 8.12). A relation that does not allow transposition is **nonsymmetric**.

- A **transitive relation** is one where the property of interest holds when, for any two pairs of entities that share a common entity, the relationship also holds for both pairs. For example, consider the relation *person-isTallerThan-person*. If Jack is taller than Jill, and Jill is taller than Jane, then Jack must also be taller than Jane. In a graph, a path formed by several successive directed arrows may represent a transitive relation. A relation that does not allow transitivity is **nontransitive**.

Table 8.16 lists the corresponding set expressions. The modeler can define a relation so that any or all of these properties hold, do not hold, or are irrelevant. For example, the relation x *precedes* y is nonreflexive (an x cannot precede itself), nonsymmetric (if x precedes y then y cannot also precede x), and transitive (if x precedes y and y precedes z, then x must also precede z). If a property is irrelevant, then instances that would satisfy either case must be allowed. That is, suppose that we do not care whether an x is reflexive: a class may or may not send messages to itself; a state may or may not have a transition back to itself, and so on. In other words, either situation is permitted.

For any given relation, we can ask which of the three properties is required, excluded, or irrelevant. The answers lead directly to a simple but effective test suite. That is, the general requirement implies a test requirement. A correct implementation will accept inputs (or states) that are consistent with the relation; it will reject inputs or states that are inconsistent with it. The test requirement

a Reflexive Relation		a	b	c
	a	✓		
	b		✓	
	b			✓
a Symmetric Relation		a	b	c
	a		✓	✓
	b	✓		✓
	c	✓	✓	
a Transitive Relation		a	b	c
	a		✓	✓
	b			✓
	c			

FIGURE 8.12 Tableau for reflexive, symmetric, and transitive relations.

TABLE 8.16 Formal Properties of Relations

Property	Requirement
Reflexive	$(x,x) \in R$ for every $x \in S$
Nonreflexive	$(x,x) \notin R$ for every $x \in S$
Symmetric	If $(x,y) \in R$ then $(y,x) \in R$ for every $x,y \in S$
Nonsymmetric	If $(x,y) \in R$ then $(y,x) \notin R$ for every $x,y \in S$
Transitive	If $(x,y) \in R$ and $(y,z) \in R$, then $(x,z) \in R$ for every $x,y,z \in S$
Nontransitive	If $(x,y) \in R$ and $(y,z) \in R$, then $(x,z) \notin R$ for every $x,y,z \in S$

A binary relation R is a subset of the Cartesian product (cross-product) of some set S, $R \subseteq S \times S$. Variables x, y, and z are elements of S, denoted $x \in S$, and so on. A pair of elements is denoted (x,y).

is simple: Identify test inputs to show that the acceptable case is allowed and that the unacceptable case is rejected.

- When reflexivity is required, any x that would make xRx true should be accepted.
- When reflexivity is excluded, any x that would make xRx true should be rejected.
- When reflexivity is irrelevant, some x should be accepted such that xRx is true and some x should be accepted such that xRx is false.

- When symmetry is required, any x and y that would make (xRy and yRx) true should be accepted.
- When symmetry is excluded, any x and y that would make (xRy and yRx) true should be rejected.
- When symmetry is irrelevant, some x and y should be accepted such that (xRy and yRx) is true. Also, some x and y for which (xRy and yRx) does not hold should be rejected.
- When transitivity is required, any x, y, and z that would make (xRy and yRz and xRz) true should be accepted.
- When transitivity is excluded, any x, y, and z that would make (xRy and yRz and xRz) true should be rejected.
- When transitivity is irrelevant, some x, y, and z that would make (xRy and yRz and xRz) true should be accepted. Also, some x, y, and z for which (xRy and yRz and xRz) does not hold should be accepted.

Table 8.17 summarizes the test requirements for combinations of these relationships. Entries in the table are interpreted as follows:

- *Yes.* The relationship requires this property for all entity pairs.
- *No.* The relationship excludes this property for any entity pair.
- *DC* (*don't care*). The relationship allows entity pairs that comply or do not comply with this property.
- *Accept.* When the IUT is presented with a test case that makes the test condition true, it is expected to accept the test inputs.
- *Reject.* When the IUT is presented with a test case that makes the test condition true, it is expected to reject the test inputs: an error message should be produced, an exception is thrown, the inputs are ignored, and so on.

The generic test model developed for each diagram type is also a basis for traceability (see Chapter 9). For example, one generic test requirement for use cases is that at least one test case is developed for each use case. This is also a traceability requirement. If a test strategy calls for this test, then traceability should be established and monitored between these items.

TABLE 8.17 General Test Conditions for Relations in a Graph

| | General Requirements | | | Test Conditions | | | | | |
| | Reflexive? | Symmetric? | Transitive? | Reflexivity | | Symmetry | | Transitivity | |
	xRx	xRy & yRx	xRy & yRz & xRz	aRa	bRb	aRb & bRa	aRb & !aRb	ARB & bRb & aRc	cRd & dRf & !cRf
1	No	No	No	reject	reject	reject	accept	reject	accept
2	No	No	Yes	reject	reject	reject	accept	accept	reject
3	No	No	DC	reject	reject	reject	accept	accept	accept
4	No	Yes	No	reject	reject	accept	reject	reject	accept
5	No	Yes	Yes	reject	reject	accept	reject	accept	reject
6	No	Yes	DC	reject	reject	accept	reject	accept	accept
7	No	DC	No	reject	reject	accept	accept	reject	accept
8	No	DC	Yes	reject	reject	accept	accept	accept	reject
9	No	DC	DC	reject	reject	accept	accept	accept	accept
10	Yes	No	No	accept	accept	reject	reject	reject	accept
11	Yes	No	Yes	accept	accept	reject	reject	accept	reject
12	Yes	No	DC	accept	accept	reject	reject	accept	accept
13	Yes	Yes	No	accept	accept	accept	reject	reject	accept
14	Yes	Yes	Yes	accept	accept	accept	reject	accept	reject
15	Yes	Yes	DC	accept	accept	accept	reject	accept	accept
16	Yes	DC	No	accept	accept	accept	accept	reject	accept
17	Yes	DC	Yes	accept	accept	accept	accept	accept	reject
18	Yes	DC	DC	accept	accept	accept	accept	accept	accept
19	DC	No	No	reject	accept	reject	accept	reject	accept
20	DC	No	Yes	reject	accept	reject	accept	accept	reject
21	DC	No	DC	reject	accept	reject	accept	accept	accept
22	DC	Yes	No	reject	accept	accept	reject	reject	accept
23	DC	Yes	Yes	reject	accept	accept	reject	accept	reject
24	DC	Yes	DC	reject	accept	accept	reject	accept	accept
25	DC	DC	No	reject	accept	accept	accept	reject	accept
26	DC	DC	Yes	reject	accept	accept	accept	accept	reject
27	DC	DC	DC	reject	accept	accept	accept	accept	accept

Note: x, y, and z denote variables for the relation; a, b, c, d, e, and f denote specific test case values; ! denotes logical *not*; & denotes logical *and*.

312

8.12   Bibliographic Notes

Hundreds of articles and dozens of books interpret the UML and provide guidance for its use. The primary source for the UML is the *OMG Unified Modeling Language Specification* [OMG 98]. This document can be downloaded from the OMG Web site. The authors of the UML explain its concepts and organization in [Rumbaugh+99]. Fowler's *UML Distilled* [Fowler 97] provides a concise introduction. D'Souza and Wills show how to use the UML to support a comprehensive pattern–based modeling strategy that targets implementation with frameworks and components [D'Souza+99]. Douglass presents embedded system design techniques with UML [Douglass 98].

The use of relations and graphs for test design is discussed in [Beizer 90] with a useful reprise in [Beizer 95]. Most introductory texts on discrete mathematics outline the notion of a relation and the reflexive, symmetric, and transitive properties—for example, [Hopcroft+79] and [Lewis+81]. A rigorous analysis (double black) of the role of relations in testing is developed in [Gourlay 83]. Graph theory has been studied extensively. West's *Introduction to Graph Theory* [West 96] is a popular textbook that provides an extensive bibliography. It is limited to undirected graphs, however. Directed graphs and their applications are covered in [Deo 76].

Part III Patterns

Part III presents test design patterns for results-oriented testing of classes, subsystems, and application systems. Taken as a whole, these patterns are a broad solution to the problem of test design in object-oriented development. Taken at any particular scope, they offer stand-alone solutions for developing and executing scope-specific test plans.

Test design patterns are presented at three main scopes: class, subsystem, and application system. Object-oriented software is unique in its potential for reuse. Chapter 11 therefore focuses on testing of reusable components.

- Chapter 9, Results-oriented Test Strategy, provides the necessary background for understanding the use of test design patterns.

- Chapter 10, Classes, presents test design patterns for methods, classes, and flattened classes. Although these techniques are applicable to class clusters, each focuses on the behavior of a single class in the cluster. Code coverage and domain analysis for object-oriented systems is presented.

- Chapter 11, Reusable Components, presents test design patterns for object-oriented software artifacts designed for reuse. The testing issues unique to several kinds of reusable artifacts are considered and resolved, including class, subsystem, and system scope components.

- Chapter 12, Subsystems, presents test design patterns for subsystems. Several distinct kinds of subsystems occur in object-oriented systems. Clusters, build groups, and process groups are considered.

- Chapter 13, Integration, presents test design patterns for integration. These patterns show how to choose the order and scope of component testing to achieve a stabilized system.

- Chapter 14, Application Systems, presents test design patterns for application systems. An application system is a collection of subsystems that cooperate to support a feature set intended for a user or customer.

- Chapter 15, Regression Testing, presents test design patterns for choosing how much of an existing test suite should be rerun after changing part of a system. Regression testing at class, subsystem, and system scope is considered.

Chapter 9   Results-oriented Test Strategy

It doesn't matter whether a cat is black or white
so long as it catches mice.

Deng Xiaoping

Overview

This chapter provides a topical introduction to Part III. It introduces ideas used in all the test strategies of Part III: results-oriented testing and the test design pattern. Considerations for producing professional test plan documentation are discussed.

9.1 Results-oriented Testing

Effective testing must show that the component parts of the implementation under test (IUT) are sufficiently operable and must exercise the observable behavior of the IUT. Test strategies have traditionally been scope-specific (unit, integration, or system) and either "white box" or "black box" techniques. Although these categories have been proved useful in certain contexts, they are not well suited to object-oriented systems. The white box/black box dichotomy is at odds with harnessing responsibility-based and implementation-based testing. The distinction between unit and integration testing leads to an unnatural division of work for object-oriented software development. We cannot test a class without integration of its servers, a cluster head without its collaborating objects, or a system without its subsystems.

○ **Results-oriented testing**   orchestrates test techniques for effectiveness. Instead of being cast as incompatible opposites or narrow technical specialities, scope-specific test design and execution techniques are organized into a coherent whole.

Taking a hybrid approach to testing is not a new idea. For example, Richardson's "partition analysis" produces a test suite from both a specification and its implementation. Test points are selected from a set formed by the cross-product of the subdomains of both specification language paths and code paths [Richardson+85]. Beizer observes, "Functional tests can, in principle, detect all bugs, but would take an infinite time to do so. Structural tests are inherently finite, but cannot detect all errors, even if completely executed. The art of testing, in part, is in how you choose between structural and functional tests" [Beizer 90, 11]. Marick recommends careful consideration of the IUT to develop test requirements followed by code coverage analysis to "evaluate and improve the tests" [Marick 95].

Results-oriented testing is a point of view:

Design test cases using scope-appropriate responsibility-based patterns. Develop *efficient* test suites: try to exercise many responsibilities and component interfaces with just a few test cases. If the components of the implementation under test are not trusted, choose an integration cycle based on code dependencies to control introduction of untrusted parts. Develop and execute the test suite according to this cycle. Determine responsibility coverage by analysis and implementation coverage by instrumentation. Stop testing when the modeled responsibilities and part interfaces have been covered.

Testing at any given scope should be preceded by integration of lower scope components. Implementation-based test design techniques are typically useful for integration test design. Consequently, class scope test patterns support subsystem testing and subsystem test patterns leverage class testing. In turn, subsystem test patterns support application system testing and application system strategy leverages subsystem test patterns. All the test strategies discussed in Part III combine responsibility testing and antecedent integration cycles.

Test design patterns present practical solution strategies focused on specific, recurring test design problems. They present the test approaches for all scopes. Each test design pattern addresses the basic problem of test design: Given an implementation to test, how should you develop a test plan that, when successfully executed, achieves adequate testing?

The scope of the implementation under test determines which test and integration approaches can be effective. As a result, test models must be tailored for observable behavior at a specific scope.

The overall strategy of results-oriented testing is the same at any scope. Figure 9.1 shows these steps. The sequence of steps depends on the implementation. **Parts** are software components at the next lower level of abstraction. For example, the parts of a method are statements and expressions. The parts of a class are methods. The parts of a cluster are classes, and so on. An integration cycle shows that the parts of the implementation under test work well enough. In some situations, no integration cycle is needed. In others, many integration cycles may be required before all parts of the implementation cooperate sufficiently.

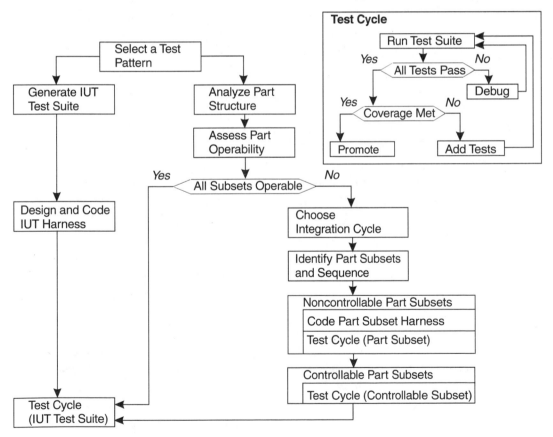

FIGURE 9.1   Steps in results-oriented testing.

The extent to which the responsibilities of the IUT can be exercised is limited by the extent to which the IUT's parts interoperate without failure. The **operability threshold** is an explicit, demonstrable criterion for part inter-operability. It can be defined in many ways:

- In a compiled language, a clean compile and link is produced for a class, and an object of the class is instantiated.
- In an interpreted language, the syntax checker makes no complaints, and an object of the class is instantiated.
- A memory leak detector cannot find any leaks.
- The "daily build" procedures and associated smoke tests pass and run to completion [McConnell 94].
- The IUT can be put through a minimal duty cycle without failures. For example, this cycle might include normal startup, acceptance of a few typical inputs, followed by normal shutdown; alternatively, it might involve running daily, weekly, and monthly transaction-processing cycles.
- All tests in an integration test suite pass.
- All tests in a regression test suite pass.

An operability threshold should be defined for each scope and integration cycle. Although their appropriate indicators are project, application-, and environment-specific, effective responsibility testing of the IUT cannot be performed until the operability threshold is passed.

Achieving effective and efficient testing for iterative incremental development and the typical architecture of object-oriented systems is a complex problem. Results-oriented testing is a way to frame questions so that rational decisions about trade-offs can be made. The primary steps are as follows:

1. Select a test design pattern appropriate to the scope of the implementation under test. If no responsibility model exists, develop one. If the available model is incomplete or not testable, it must be elaborated.

2. Assess the operability of the parts. Parts are deemed acceptable by virtue of vendor certification, part testing, or the implicit certification of field use. It will typically take longer to reach the part–interface operability threshold if you begin with many suspect parts. Skipping testing at smaller scopes is a common response to schedule pressure. Unfortunately, testing at broader scope is subsequently often hampered by inoperable parts. (This delay is a disguised blessing, as we can reach an

operability threshold with buggy parts, leading to a false confidence. Parts that refuse to run at least provide unambiguous information about operability.)

3. Select a scope-appropriate test pattern and design the test suite accordingly. Add test cases for parts and interfaces that are suspect. Strive for elegant test designs—try to exercise part interfaces with the same test cases that exercise scope-wide responsibilities.

4. Develop the appropriate test driver/harness for the implementation and its parts. Two kinds of integration drivers are commonly used. First, when parts are controllable from the IUT's interface, the test suite is partitioned to exercise selected collections of parts. The driver for the IUT serves double duty: it exercises part interfaces and scope-wide responsibilities. Second, when untrusted parts are not controllable from the test interface, part-specific drivers must be constructed for some parts.

5. Execute the test suite according to the suggested integration cycle. The goal is to have the parts working well enough to allow scope-wide responsibility testing. If the parts are mostly new, reaching this goal is typically a slow and frustrating process. If the parts are mature and stable, the operability threshold will be reached quickly. When no parts are missing or uncooperative, the full repertoire of the IUT can be exercised.

6. Continue the test/debug cycle until your coverage and stability goals are met.

Test design cannot be accomplished without testable models. A good model is necessary to gain intellectual control over complex systems. Yet even a good model is passive. We therefore need to join the model with a strategy that orchestrates the application of test cases. An ideal strategy would provide an elegant solution to the complex and often contradictory forces that shape test design and test planning.

- An effective test suite must show that responsibilities are met without failure in an adequate number of cases.
- An effective test suite must show minimal interoperability among all required interfaces within the implementation under test.
- An effective test suite must be structured so that scope-specific bugs are found by scope-specific testing, rather than being revealed during subsequent testing at a broader scope.

9.1.1 The Role of Responsibility-based Test Design

Class Responsibilities

The notion of **class responsibility** was first used as a metaphor to introduce a point of view for analysis and design of object-oriented systems [Cunningham+86]. In this anthropomorphic view, design is approached by thinking of ways to orchestrate the behavior of objects. This process is facilitated by imagining that objects act as if they are independent (human) agents. These agents *collaborate* to accomplish a general system requirement. Each is thus *responsible* for knowing about certain things, responding to requests from other agents, and making requests of other agents [Wirfs-Brock 90]. A common classroom exercise involves having each student play the role of an object and simulate the execution of the system in response to input.

The anthropomorphic point of view is the software engineering equivalent of training wheels——the sooner disposed of, the better. It leads to over-simplification and the projection of personal bias onto digital artifacts whose actual behavior is better understood by combinational logic than by wishful thinking. The anthropomorphic metaphor suggests a kind of equivalence between persons and software that is ludicrous per se. I am deeply suspicious of any point of view that trivializes human consciousness and its categorical responsibilities. (The fallacy and perils of software anthropomorphism are articulated in [Weizenbaum 76].)

Nevertheless, the term "responsibility" remains firmly fixed in the jargon of object-oriented development. It means any public service offered by a class that can be defined without regard to a particular implementation. It replaces "functionality" as a general handle on the things that a software entity can do. At class scope, aggregate responsibilities are called the **class contract**. Although tainted with anthropomorphism, the notion of a class contract is formalizable and operational [Meyer 88, Meyer 97]. A class contract is defined by assertions at method and class scopes, inherited assertions, and exceptions.

- Each server method has a precondition assertion that checks the message sent by the client. Meeting the precondition is the client's responsibility.

- Each server method has a postcondition assertion that checks the resultant state of the object and the response to be provided to the client. A postcondition assertion defines what the server promises to provide after completing any request. Meeting this criteria is the server's responsibility.

- Each class has an invariant that defines all valid combinations of instance variable values for the class. The invariant is checked at the same point as the precondition and postcondition. Meeting the variant is the server's responsibility.
- A subclass's contract must be consistent with the contracts of all of its superclasses. Thus a subclass object can be substituted for superclass objects without causing failure or requiring special case code in clients.
- The extent to which a server expects clients to handle exceptions is part of the class contract. An exception occurs when an object cannot meet its contract (a contract exception) or the runtime environment reports an anomaly to the application process (an environment exception).

Meyer's design-by-contract model does not consider sequential activation constraints. This omission is not a problem for nonmodal classes, but it does leave a significant gap for modal classes. The problem may be remedied with assertions that define the state model. Chapter 17 provides a detailed discussion of this issue.

A responsibility is usually stated as a simple verb phrase and implemented by a method or a particular sequence of methods. The following are examples of responsibilities:

- Return the last item in a list (list class).
- Add a new item to a list (list class).
- Report the current balance of an account (account class).
- Apply a debit transaction (account class).
- Dispatch messages received by a *Facade* class [Gamma+95] to objects in the corresponding subsystem.

Why Test from Responsibility Models?

A well-formed responsibility defines a capability implemented by a public method (or sequence of public methods) in a class that has a complete set of contract assertions. Contract assertions provide an operational definition of responsibilities and establish the conditions for correct execution. In practice, responsibilities are often implicit, ill formed, and incomplete. Very little useful testing may be conducted with poorly defined responsibilities. If the designers or developers have not finished the job, then the tester must construct a test-ready responsibility model. The alternative is to guess at responsibilities or to fall back on implementation-based testing. Neither of these tacks will lead to an effective test suite.

Model-based responsibility testing is the approach of choice for test suite development. Implementation-based testing does not focus on capabilities important to designers, customers, and users. Without a succinct definition of class responsibilities, discerning bugs and features may be difficult. Implementation-based tests can easily miss important capabilities or make incorrect assumptions about the intended use of the system under test. Responsibility-based testing focuses on features and functions that are typically visible to users or customers. In contrast, implementation-based testing often reflects the immediate parochial concerns of developers.

Responsibility-based testing has technical advantages. A single responsibility (or model of a responsibility fault) can represent a very large number of specific physical implementations and physical faults. Testing from responsibility models brings the well-known advantages of modeling: separation of concerns, tractability, and relative ease of change. Software testing would be a hopeless task if we could not use test models. Implementation-independent models can be applied to different implementations and reduce coupling between an implementation and its test plans. Model-based testing supports testing of systems that are very complex, poorly understood, or too costly to study in detail. Ideally, our development representation and test model will be identical. Otherwise, we will need to map cartoon representations into testable models. Without a representation, a testable model is produced by reverse engineering.

Although testing primarily focuses on finding faults in an IUT, it can also find bugs in requirements and specifications. The production of a test model often reveals omissions and inconsistencies before a single test case is run.

9.1.2   The Role of Implementation-based Test Design

Implementation-based test cases are developed by examining source code. In contrast, responsibility-based test cases are derived from requirements, object models, use cases, and so on. Implementation-based testing is also known as structural, white box, clear box, or glass box testing. It has several important applications:

- Code coverage analyzers use implementation-based testing models. Code coverage analysis is a necessary part of effective testing. Therefore, one needs to understand implementation-based testing to use coverage information.

- Analysis of source code may be necessary to decide how to achieve a coverage goal or to determine that additional coverage is truly impossible for a particular implementation.
- Test planning for exception handlers typically requires source code analysis.
- Source code is often the only source of information we have about an implementation.
- Some code-based test generation can be automated. This allows automatic generation of smoke tests that can be used to verify minimal executability.
- Many implementation-based techniques and ideas can be reinterpreted for responsibility-based testing

Although implementation-based testing techniques are a necessary part of the tester's toolbox, they should not be the primary basis for testing. Test suites developed by implementation analysis alone typically have significant limitations:

- Implementation-based testing requires code analysis skills and knowledge of application-specific implementation techniques.
- An effective test plan for a large subsystem or application system cannot be developed by code analysis. Requirements and use cases typically cannot be "reverse-engineered" from source code.
- Available code-based testing tools are useful, but not ideal.
- Object-oriented code coverage metrics are guidelines; they are not absolutes (except for branch coverage).
- Even if a code-based test suite achieves high coverage, it cannot prove the absence of faults, validate requirements, or test missing functions.
- *Code-based testing is tautological!* That is, an implementation-based test can only show that the code does what it does. This is *not* necessarily what it is supposed to do.

Implementation-based testing is problematic when it results in the exclusion of responsibility-based testing. The typically low complexity of methods is offset by the typically high complexity of associations between a client and its servers. Although white box testing alone is a logical fallacy, analysis of the parts that have (and have not) been exercised by responsibility tests is more effective than a one-sided approach [Fiedler 89, Offutt+95, Horgan+96]. Thus, the appropriate role for implementation-based testing is to support testing at a given scope. We use coverage to provide feedback about our responsibility-based techniques. In effect, we use implementation-based test techniques to test our test suites, not the implementation.

9.1.3   Integration in Object-oriented Development

Integration testing is not a separate "phase" in object-oriented development, but rather occurs throughout a project. Chapter 13 covers integration planning and test design. Such testing should be done whenever new components are added to a system, at any scope. For example, integration testing applies when several new subclasses are added to a class cluster (class/cluster scope), or when the stub implementation for a complex server subsystem is replaced by complete implementation.

Integration testing is not the same as the process sometimes called "intergration": the steps of merging—generating a set of specific versions of software components using a configuration management system—and building—generating an executable system by compiling and linking the result of merging. In contrast, the purpose of integration testing is to exercise the resulting executable to assess its operability.

The primary goal of integration testing is to stabilize a system so that responsibility-based testing may proceed smoothly. Software systems are composed of thousands of individual components. Integration testing searches for failures caused by intercomponent faults within the scope of interest. In contrast, responsibility testing focuses on the externally visible behavior of a software entity. Testing at any scope requires minimally operable components, so completion of integration testing is a necessary precondition. In conventional development, integration testing is usually a prelude to system testing. Traditional approaches to integration testing follow the physical structure of the system under test: tasks, module call paths, processes, interprocess communication, jobs, and so on. Incremental, iterative approaches to integration have been used since the dawn of large projects [Brooks 75, Baker 75].

The distinction between integration and unit testing is not as clear-cut in object-oriented development as it is in procedural implementations. Object-oriented languages and development environments are well suited to incremental development. Each increment requires some degree of integration testing, especially when existing class libraries are heavily reused. Integration testing in object-oriented development is often dictated by the use structure of classes in the system under test. Intercomponent verification of object-oriented implementations begins earlier than comparable verification of conventional systems.

9.1.4 Harnessing Responsibility and Implementation

A **scope** is a level in a hierarchy of responsibilities and parts. **Parts** are the software elements at the next lower level of abstraction, with respect to the implementation under test. For example, the parts of a class are its methods. The parts of a method are statements and expressions. **Suspect** parts have not shown sufficient reliability; **okay** parts have shown sufficient reliability. A **trusted** part has shown very high reliability.

A results-oriented testing strategy must consider the following conditions:

- The appropriate test approach depends on the scope of the implementation under test—a class, one of the many kinds of object-oriented subsystems, or an entire application system.

- A test suite should focus on the responsibilities of the implementation under test as a whole, not on its parts. Tests based on suspicions about probable faults in part interfaces, however, can and should be included.

- Effective testing at any scope requires minimal interoperability among okay parts. This requirement is satisfied when parts cooperate well enough that the whole may be tested without excessive thrashing because of buggy parts. If the parts do not work or cannot exchange messages, we have no hope of running our tests. We cannot begin to test a subsystem that contains objects of a class so buggy that it causes a crash on every other input. If interoperability has not been previously established, some form of integration testing is a necessary precursor.

- If the interoperability of the parts has not been established, then we must begin by trying a few of the parts. Often, only a few parts are interoperable when we are ready to begin testing. Physical dependencies among these parts constrain the order in which newly completed parts may be exercised. These dependencies define an **integration cycle**. Applying some whole-scope, responsibility-based test cases during an integration cycle is usually possible.

- Results-oriented testing has two coverage goals: coverage of the test model and coverage of the interfaces among parts. We want to adequately exercise modeled responsibilities and, in so doing, exercise all

Typical OOA/D Responsibility Model	Scope		
	Class	Subsystem	Application System
Narrative Requirements			✓
User Documentation			✓
Use Cases		✓	✓
Application Object Model	✓	✓	
System Architecture Model		✓	✓
Object Interaction Diagram		✓	✓
Class Interface	✓		
Class State Model	✓	✓	
Method Specification	✓		

FIGURE 9.2   Testing uses of OOA/D representations.

parts and interfaces called out in our integration model. Figure 9.2 suggests how some typical OOA/D representations may be used to support testing. The parts and interfaces defined by an implementation fault model can be instrumented (although doing so may not always be practical). Implementation-based test models provide a model for coverage by focusing our attention on interfaces that are critical for correct part-to-part interoperation. If we have exercised these interfaces and the responsibility of the IUT, then we have done adequate testing.

Just as a road map is not an itinerary, this overview of results-oriented testing is not a complete test plan. The specific conditions of a particular project must be considered and addressed for a complete strategy.

9.2 Test Design Patterns

9.2.1 What Is a Pattern?

A **pattern** is a generalized solution to a specific, recurring design problem. Patterns were first used to describe constellations of structural elements in buildings and towns. For example, the *Half-hidden Garden* pattern considers how to frame a view of a garden so that onlookers have a sense of well-being and positive anticipation [Alexander 79]. A pattern explains insights that have led to generally recognized good practices. A pattern has a **context**, which consists of the circumstances that determine its applicability. **Forces** are constituent parts of the context that may occur in varying degrees.

In the early 1990s, some designers of object-oriented systems began to express certain stereotypical relationships of classes and objects following the style of architectural patterns [Coplien+95]. These **software design patterns** capture the essence of proven solutions to recurring software design problems. For example, the *Model-View-Controller* pattern suggests that three kinds of components should be used to provide an interactive display of stored values: classes that contain the stored information (the Model), classes for the user interface (the View), and classes that mediate interaction between the user interface and the content (the Controller) [Gamma+95].

Patterns are not the best way to explain or present all subjects. They make an implicit rhetorical assertion: If the conditions expressed in the context and forces hold, then the solution strategy is a very good approach to solving the problem. Patterns are therefore not a good vehicle for the following purposes:

- Comparing and contrasting several solutions in a balanced, analytical manner
- Presenting a general model, theory, or point of view
- Defining terms and placing them in a conceptual system
- Presenting a lengthy and complex system of ideas

This is why a good deal of this book does *not* use patterns.

Critics of patterns note that best practices and the insights that support them can be (and have been) expressed in many other ways. For example, the use of named generic solutions for software design predates the interpretation of design patterns for software (see the Bibliographic Notes section). Nevertheless, patterns are an improvement over ad hoc or idiosyncratic description. They encourage articulation and refinement of reusable solutions and offer a common point of view for their development and evaluation. The popularity of software design patterns mushroomed in the mid-1990s. To date, hundreds of patterns have been identified and published. In large part, this interest can be explained by the fact that patterns are pragmatic, simple, and reflect a professional consensus about good design.

9.2.2   Patterns and Testing

A **pattern template** is a list of subjects (sections) that comprise a pattern. Several templates for software design patterns have been developed. The "Gang of Four" (GoF) template is used for patterns that describe constellations of classes that solve common software design problems of relatively small scope [Gamma+95]. The Siemens template is similar and includes a section to discuss component structures of relatively large scope [Buschmann+96]. Patterns for test automation and built-in tests presented in this book use the GoF design template. Variants of the GoF pattern have been used to describe both test drivers and test case design [Firesmith 96, McGregor+96]. Design of test cases and test suites, however, must consider questions not relevant for software design.

The subjects, organization, and presentation of testing strategies described by Beizer [Beizer 95] can be considered a pattern template for test design, suggesting the subjects that a test design pattern should address. Each of Beizer's six chapters on generic testing strategies follows the same outline: (1) relations and the model, (2) technique, (3) application indicators, (4) bug assumptions, (5) limitations and caveats, and (6) automation and tools.[1] Beizer's outline covers the essential questions that any test design approach must address. Each chapter is a pattern for test design.

Siegel's "Test Models" for object-oriented development are similar in that the same subject outline is used for many testing problems: (1) overview, (2) leadership (general conditions and goals), (3) structure (a model of the things to test), (4) dynamics (how to generate things that the model tests), (5) example, and (6) road map (a graphic summary of the model) [Siegel 96]. Siegel's test models are less elaborate than Beizer's outline, but can also be considered as an approximation of a test design pattern.

9.2.3   Test Design Pattern Template

Figure 9.3 summarizes and compares software design pattern templates and the test subject outlines. Subjects in the same row address similar content. The three design pattern templates do not consider some subjects relevant for test design and include some that are irrelevant for testing. The testing outlines do not address design pattern subjects useful for testing and lack some items necessary for a proper pattern. The *test design pattern template* includes test

---

1. The six design chapters are: Control-Flow Testing, Loop Testing, Data-Flow Testing and Transaction-Flow Testing, Domain Testing, Syntax Testing, and Finite-State Testing.

Siemens Template [Buschmann+96]	GoF Template [Gamma+95]	PLOOT Template [Firesmith 95]	Beizer's Outline [Beizer 95]	Siegel's Outline [Siegel 96]	Test Design Template	
Name	Name	Name	Chapter Title	Name	Name	
	Classification	Category				
a.k.a.	AKA					
Problem. The problem addressed, forces considered.	Intent. What does it do? What is the rationale? What issues does it address?	Summary/Problem. "How to test an x."	Synopsis	Overview	Intent	
			Bug Assumptions		Fault Model	
Context. Applicable situations.	Applicability. Problems that can be resolved with this pattern.	Context. Situations where useful.	Typical Applications	Leadership	Context	
		Applicability. Necessary conditions for use.				
Example. A design problem that this pattern can solve.	Motivation. An example problem solved with the pattern.	Solution. What to do.	The Model	Structure	Strategy	Test Model
			The Technique	Dynamics		Test Procedure
Structure. Class Diagram	Structure. Class Diagram.	Structure. Class Diagram.				
Solution. The design rationale in CRC cards.	Participants. Classes used.	Participants. Classes used.				Oracle
Dynamics. Object Interaction Diagram.	Collaboration. How/why the collaborations work.				Automation	
Implementation. Coding guidelines.	Sample Code.		Automation and Tools			

FIGURE 9.3 Comparative analysis of pattern templates and test pattern template.

continued

Siemens Template [Buschmann+96]	GoF Template [Gamma+95]	PLOOT Template [Firesmith 95]	Beizer's Outline [Beizer 95]	Siegel's Outline [Siegel 96]	Test Design Template
Example resolved. Additional considerations.	Implementation. Additional tips, language-specific issues, example implementation.				Entry Criteria
					Exit Criteria
Consequences. Benefits and liabilities.	Consequences	Risks/Benefits	Caveats and Limitations	Road Map	Consequences
Known Uses	Known Uses	Known Uses			Known Uses
Variants	Related Patterns	Related Patterns			Related Patterns
See Also					

FIGURE 9.3   Continued.

outline subjects and the general pattern. It adapts the software design template to fit the specific needs of test design. It supports results-oriented test design by harnessing both responsibility-based and implementation-based testing for the same goal.

The sections of the test design template are described next. They represent questions for the pattern writer, whose answers should articulate the insights, assumptions, and mechanics of the test design pattern.

Test Design Template

Name

The name is a word or phrase that identifies the pattern and suggests its general approach.

Intent

What kind of test suite does this pattern produce? This answer should be a succinct statement, no more than two sentences.

Context

What test design problem does this pattern solve? When does this pattern apply? To what kind of software entities? At what scope(s)? This section addresses the initial problem of test design: Given some implementation, what is an effective test design and execution strategy? It corresponds to the "motivation," "forces," and "applicability" sections of design patterns.

Fault Model

What kind of faults does this pattern target and why will it hit them? A fault model is critical for effective testing. Myers's principle that "A good test case is one that has a high probability of finding an error. A successful test case is one that detects an as-yet undiscovered error" [Myers 79, 16] suggests that effective testing must focus on finding the few faults that hide in mostly good code. Testing that is not guided by a fault model is less efficient than random testing [Hamlet+90]. A fault model provides this focus.

The "what" part of the fault model may be formal, as are the fault models in Chapters 6 and 7, or it may be based on experience and practical considerations (that is, heuristic). Both are effective and necessary. Beizer's "bug assumptions" blend formal and heuristic models [Beizer 95]. The point of view described by a tester of Windows NT is an excellent example of a practical heuristic:

> Somesgar puzzled over ways to crash a program, but he reserved his hardest thinking for the question, Where should I look for weaknesses? When preparing tests in advance of the Comdex release he tried to assume the mentality of applications writers who would receive NT: "What sorts of things will a software developer do with an early release? He wants to make progress on app. He knows a great deal

about writing code and will be curious about the deep insides of NT. What are the things he won't be able to work around? What ever those things are, they have to be right" [Zachary 94, 155].

Poston termed this kind of informal analysis as looking for "most-probable errors" [Poston 87]. Hamlet calls for using **suspicions**, which are common-sense indicators that some component or code is more likely to be buggy [Hamlet+90]. The patterns in this book blend formal and heuristic models.

This section must also explain why a test suite produced by the test model meets the necessary conditions for revealing the targeted faults.[2] For a test case to succeed and reveal a fault, three things must happen:

1. The fault must be **reached**. The test input and state of the system under test must cause the code segment in which the fault is located to execute.

2. The failure must be **triggered**. A fault does not always produce incorrect results when it is reached. The test input and state of the system under test must cause the code segment in which the fault is located to produce an incorrect result.

3. The failure must be **propagated**. The incorrect result must become observable to the tester or an automated comparator.

The fault model section must explain how the test suite will reach the targeted faults, how it can cause a failure to be triggered, and how a failure will be propagated to become observable.

Strategy

How is the test suite designed and implemented? The Test Model section defines a representation for the responsibilities and implementation that are the focus of test design. The Test Procedure section defines an algorithm, technique, or heuristic by which test cases are produced from the model. The Oracle section defines the algorithm, technique, or heuristic by which actual results to a test case are evaluated as pass/no pass. The Automation section discusses automated approaches to test suite generation, test run execution, and test run evaluation. The appropriate extent of manual testing is discussed and applicable

---

2. Fault execution (reaching), infection (triggering), and propagation are necessary and sufficient conditions for a failure [Morell 90, Voas+91]. A detailed analysis of propagation is presented in [Richardson+93]. These conditions are called the "ideal fault conditions" in [Marick 95] and the "fault/failure model" in [Friedman+95].

test automation design patterns are noted. Table 9.1 on page 338 lists the patterns for test automation presented in Part IV of this book.

The strategy is typically presented by example. The concrete result of applying a test design pattern is an uninteresting, possibly cryptic collection of input/output vectors. Instead of a commentary on test vectors, this section presents a step-by-step application of the test model to a suitable example and comments on the resulting test suite.

Entry Criteria

What are the preconditions for using this pattern? An implementation should not be tested before it is, as a whole, **test-ready**.[3] Achieving this condition has three beneficial effects. First, it reduces time lost because the IUT is too buggy to test. Second, it reduces waste of testing resources on bugs that can be more easily revealed and removed by an antecedent process, typically testing at a smaller scope. Third, it reduces the number of bugs that will escape from a given scope of testing. As test scope increases, the extent to which individual components can be exercised decreases. For example, when testing at use case scope, we typically do not attempt to achieve statement coverage on each component that supports the use cases. Instead, we try to achieve coverage of all intercomponent message paths in the use case. We cannot hope to achieve individually adequate coverage when we are testing at higher scope. If lower scope testing is inadequate or skipped, many bugs probably will not be revealed by higher scope testing, even if it is comprehensive. Therefore, meeting the entry criteria will improve both efficiency and effectiveness of testing.[4]

Exit Criteria

What conditions must be achieved to meet this pattern's test goals? This section defines the results necessary to achieve an adequate test with this pattern. Which modeled responsibilities must be exercised? What is the implementation coverage requirement? An explicit coverage goal for both features and code is required to comply with the IEEE testing standards for test documentation [IEEE 829] and unit testing coverage [IEEE 1008].

---

3. The term "test-ready" was coined by Bob Poston. As an adjective, it means that test design or test execution may proceed without interference caused by missing or incomplete specifications and/or implementations. A **test readiness assessment** is a formal process activity defined in the SEI Capability Maturity Model that determines the test-readiness of a work product [SEI 93].

4. Studies indicate that testing effectiveness reaches a plateau related to test scope [Horgan 96].

Consequences

What are the disadvantages and advantages of using this pattern? This section is an essential part of the pattern. It discusses the costs, benefits, risks, and general considerations for using this pattern.

Known Uses

What are the known uses of this test design pattern? What are the known uses of test models and strategies incorporated in this pattern? What are the efficiency and effectiveness of this pattern or similar strategies, as established by empirical studies?

Related Patterns

What other test design patterns are similar or complementary? Does this pattern support or require use of another pattern?

9.2.4 Test Patterns in This Book

The 37 test design patterns in this book reflect varying degrees of established software testing practice. The Known Uses section in each pattern summarizes published experience reports and research results. When possible, I discuss applications made by my consulting clients. Some useful testing strategies are presented as patterns, even if reports on a wide range of experience are lacking. Pattern purists might complain that such usage is necessary to establish a pattern. Where this applies, I accept the criticism. I use the pattern template express to test strategies that I believe to be valuable, however, even if I cannot provide a pedigree. The reader is invited to apply and report results.

9.2.5 Using Test Design Patterns

The test design patterns presented in this book are summarized in Table 9.1. These patterns are compatible with most test processes. No essential differences

TABLE 9.1 Test Design Patterns Presented in This Book

Method Scope	Category–Partition	Design a test suite based on input/output analysis.
	Combinational Function	Design a test suite for behaviors selected by combinational logic.
	Recursive Function	Design a test suite for a recursive function.
	Polymorphic Message	Design a test suite for a client of a polymorphic server.
Class Scope	Invariant Boundaries	Identify test vectors for complex domains.
	Nonmodal Class	Design a test suite for a class without sequential constraints.
	Modal Class	Design a test suite for a class with sequential constraints.
	Quasi-modal Class	Design a test suite for a class with content-determined sequential constraints.
	Transitive Operations	Design a test suite for methods that are transitive.
Class Scope Integration	Small Pop	Order of code/test at method/class scope.
	Alpha-Omega Cycle	Order of code/test at method/class scope.
Flattened Class Scope	Polymorphic Server	Design a test suite for LSP compliance of polymorphic server hierarchy.
	Modal Hierarchy	Design a test suite for hierarchy of modal classes.

Reusable Components	Abstract Class	Develop and test an interface implementation.
	Generic Class	Develop and test an implementation of a parameterized class.
	New Framework	Develop and test a demo application of a new framework.
	Popular Framework	Test changes to a widely used framework.
Subsystem	Class Associations	Design a test suite for implementation of class associations.
	Round-trip Scenario	Design a test suite for aggregate state-based behavior.
	Controlled Exception	Design a test suite to verify exception handling.
	Mode Machine	Design a test suite for implementation of stimulus–response scenarios.
Integration	Big Bang	Try everything at the same time.
	Bottom-up	Integration by dependencies.
	Top-down	Integration by control hierarchy.
	Collaborations	Integration by cluster scenarios.
	Backbone	Hybrid integration of subsystems.
	Layers	Integration for layered architecture.
	Client/Server	Integration for client/server architecture.
	Distributed Services	Integration for distributed architecture.
	High-frequency	Build and test at frequent regular intervals.
Application Scope	Extended Use Cases	Develop testable use cases, design a test suite to cover application input/output relationships.
	Covered in CRUD	Exercise all basic operations.
	Allocate by Frequency	Allocate system test effort to maximize operational reliability.
Regression Test	Retest All	Rerun all tests.
	Retest Risky Use Cases	Rerun tests of risky code.
	Retest Profile	Rerun tests by frequency of use.
	Retest Changed Code	Rerun tests for code that depends on changes.
	Retest Within Firewall	Rerun tests for code affected by changes.

arise in the basic tasks of testing when one uses a test pattern. Instead, test patterns simply frame and focus the issues that must be resolved to accomplish any kind of testing. Patterns support results-oriented testing; that is, a scope-appropriate responsibility model of the implementation under test is needed. It is assumed that the IUT runs well enough to allow testing to continue. The basic steps for using a test pattern are as follows:

1. Early in the development process, select test patterns that correspond to the scope and structure of the system under development and its parts.

2. Develop a test model for the implementation under test.

3. Orchestrate your development and testing work so that the test suite will be applied to an implementation that meets the minimum operability threshold, as suggested in the Entry Criteria section.

4. Generate the test suite by applying the test model.

5. Develop the test automation implementation. The Test Automation section should suggest a basic plan of attack.

6. Run and evaluate the tests. If the exit criteria's recommended coverage is not achieved, revise the test suite as needed.

A pattern is more general guidance than it is a cookbook. Patterns should not be interpreted dogmatically ("The example doesn't look like my application, so I can't apply it," or "I've coded tests for some pattern before and the IUT meets this pattern, so I can just recode the same tests for the new app."). Be sure to read and consider the entire pattern before you try to apply it. Weigh the pros and cons listed in the Consequences section. Then decide if you are ready (review the entry criteria) and whether you can achieve the Exit Criteria with available resources.

9.3   Documenting Test Cases, Suites, and Plans

The concrete result of applying a test design pattern is a test suite. Many different test patterns must be used to develop a complete test suite for a typical application system. A test plan explains how these test suites will be used and what is necessary to support the testing process. A test plan is often a voluminous document and should be organized to be usable, understandable, and maintainable. The complete contents of a plan are spelled out by IEEE Standard 829.

9.3.1   IEEE 829 Documentation

IEEE Standard 829 provides a complete table of contents for documenting a test suite; items listed in this outline include Test Plans, Test Specifications, Test Cases, Test Procedures, Test Item Transmittal Forms, Test Logs, Test Incident

Reports, and Test Summary Reports. IEEE Standard 1088 outlines a process for developing inputs, outputs, tasks, test results, and test status reports for unit testing.

Each item, section, and subsection should have an identifying number. The date prepared and revised, authors, and approvals should be given. The degree of formality can be tailored to suit your process. The standard calls for several main documents and recommends four main steps:

1. *Prepare a test plan.* Explain the approach and necessary resources and incorporate (by reference) all test deliverables into the plan. A test plan defines scope of testing—that is, features to be tested and excluded from testing and completion criteria. It defines the general approach, test design and execution deliverables, suspend/resume criteria, environmental needs, responsibilities, staffing and training, schedule, risks and contingencies, and approvals.

2. *Design the test suite.* Define features/functions to test, as well as pass/no pass criteria. Designate the test suites to be used for each feature or component.
   2.1 Define a test suite hierarchy. Organize it by test goals, use cases, or components.
   2.2 Develop procedures for running the tests.
   2.3 Prepare the test cases by applying a test design pattern. Define items to be tested; establish traceability to requirements, detail design, and documentation for users, operators, and installers. Specify the input, output, environment, procedures, and inter-case dependencies of each test case, as suggested by Figure 9.4. The items to be developed for each test case will be determined by the interface of the IUT and the testing tools in use. Example test cases appear in nearly all of the test patterns.

3. *Test the components.*
   3.1 Run the test suite.
   3.2 Check and classify the results of each test case:
     3.2.1 Pass: Actual results meet expected results.
     3.2.2 No pass: Failure observed.
       – Implementation fault
       – Design fault
       – Undetermined fault
     3.2.3 Unable to execute test case.
       – Bug in test specification or test data
       – Bug in test procedure
       – Bug in test environment or test tools

```
===================================================================
Test Id              |
Description          |
                     |
Component Under Test
        Type         |
        Name         |
SET UP ------------------------------------------------------------
*|Antecedent Test Id|
*|Message
*|     Name         |
*|In Arguments
 *|    Name         |
 *|    Type         |
 *|    Value        |
INPUT--------------------------------------------------------------
IUT State
        Invariant   |
IUT Messages
*|      Name         |
 *|In Arguments
 *|    Name         |
 *|    Type         |
 *|    Value        |
EXPECTED RESULT ---------------------------------------------------
IUT Resultant State
        Invariant    |
Returned Objects
*|      Type         |
*|      Name         |
*|      Value        |
Out Arguments
*|      Name         |
*|      Type         |
*|      Value        |
Out Bound Messages
*|      Name         |
*|      Type         |
*|      Value        |
Console/Std Out Messages
*|                   |
Exception
*|      Name         |
===================================================================
```

Key: *| = An item that is repeated for each parameter.

FIGURE 9.4   Test case schema.

4. *Prepare a test summary report.* Note the components and interfaces tested, the version of the IUT, the version of the operating system, database management system, and other key environment components. Document no pass tests and summarize the test suite results. Evaluate the operability of the IUT for further testing or general release. Summarize the testing process—what went well and what didn't. Obtain any necessary review and approvals.

Table 9.2 summarizes the main sections of an IEEE 829 plan. The sections provide a place to answer basic questions about your test process: who, what, when, where, and how. As with any standard, the test documentation called for

TABLE 9.2   Thumbnail of an IEEE 829 Test Plan

IEEE 829 Subject	Content
Test Plan Identifier, Test Items, Features to Be Tested, Features Not Tested	These sections define the scope of the system under test. If the IUT is not entirely new or is an incomplete incremental release, it is important to specify which features or components are *not* to be tested.
Approach	Provide an overview of the technical testing strategy and the test process.
Item Pass/Fail Criteria	In general, how will pass/no pass results be evaluated?
Suspend/Resume Criteria	What is the operability threshold? Under what circumstances will testing be suspended if this threshold is not met?
Test Deliverables	This section summarizes and incorporates by reference the overall test plan, individual test designs and test case specifications, procedure specifications (the things a tester must do to run each test), and the tangible results of testing. The test plan for a typical system often includes tens of thousands of test cases and hundreds of test runs.
Testing Tasks	A work breakdown structure for the testing project.
Environmental Needs	Defines the necessary test automation, hardware/software, test lab setup, and so on.
Responsibilities	Defines who owns each part of the test process.
Staffing and Training Needs	What kind of skills will be needed? Will the testers/developers need training on test design, tools, environments, and so on?
Schedule	Dates for beginning, milestones, completion, and so on.
Risks and Contingencies	What can go wrong? What are the assumptions? What can be done if major problems occur?
Approvals	Determine who must approve and review the plan.

by IEEE 829 should be tailored to the needs of your project. Planning consid-erations are discussed in detail in the companion volume to this book, *Managing the Testing Process for Object-Oriented Systems* [Binder 2000].

An IEEE 829 plan is well suited to an HTML document. I like to use a base page that lists all of the major subjects. Links are coded to other HTML pages or files that provide the details. Sometimes, linking it directly into the test case files and test run logs is possible.

Figure 9.4 shows a schema for representing the test case specifications for object-oriented code. This schema includes (at a class interface level) all neces-sary items to specify a test case. This example consists of a flattened test case. The structure of a test suite is given in the BNF model presented in Section 19.6, A Test Implementation Syntax.

9.3.2 Traceability

Traceability is a simple, common-sense bookkeeping practice that can prevent a wide range of problems (see Figure 9.5). Establishing traceability means recording and analyzing the antecedent and successor of development work products. Traceability is required by many software engineering standards [Thayer+90, SEI 93] and is recommended by the Unified Development Methodology [Jacobson+99].

In testing, we often need to know which software component implements a given specification item and which specification item implements a given requirement. For example, if each use case can be traced to a system test case, then we can determine whether every use case has been tested. With trace-

	Test Case 1	Test Case 2	Test Case 3	Test Case 4	Test Case 5	Test Case 6	. . .	Test Case n
Use Case 1				✓				
Use Case 2		✓						
Use Case 3	✓				✓			✓
Use Case 4						✓		
Use Case 5								
. . .								
Use Case m		✓						✓

FIGURE 9.5 Traceability matrix.

ability, we can quantify the extent to which a test suite has covered modeled relationships. Without this information, developing complete and accurate test plans for even a small system is practically impossible.

Each test case should be linked to an entity or relationship exercised by that test case.

- Every modeled entity should be traceable to at least one test case. For example, if a use case does not have a corresponding test suite, we should develop a test suite or drop the use case.
- Every modeled relationship should be traceable to at least one test case. For example, if use case *A* extends use cases *B, C,* and *D,* we should have corresponding test cases (*B–A, C–A,* and *D–A*) or the extension should be dropped.
- Each test case should be traceable to a modeled entity or relationship. For example, if no use case exists for a test case, is the test case inappropriate or has the test case revealed a missing or undocumented requirement?

As a practical matter, the linkage between a test case and a model element may be breached for many reasons. Test cases may have been developed without using an OOA/D model. It may be that no model exists or an existing model is obsolete or incomplete. Even in this situation, knowing that the test cases have been developed without a documented antecedent is useful.

The larger and more complex a project, the greater the risk of an omission. Traceability prevents omissions (where something "slips through the cracks") during development. It offsets the risk of requirements instability and iterative development ("scope drift," "creeping elegance") by making the impact of changes more visible. Finally, accurate traceability is useful for debugging, maintenance analysis, and setting the scope of regression testing.

The traceability relationships can be represented as a matrix (Figure 9.5), and are typically implemented with several linked tables. Traceability can be automated with low-cost desktop programs (spreadsheets or personal databases) and is supported in some CASE and CAST tools.

9.4 Bibliographic Notes

Testing and Development Strategy

Several approaches have been proposed to answer the questions of timing and scope of integration testing in object-oriented development. A comprehensive step wise increasing scope approach is outlined in [Jacobson+92]. Integration plays a key role in an overall test strategy reported by a unit of Siemens AG [Juttner+94]. Effective integration may be accomplished by successively focusing on a scope that follows the functional hierarchy of a system [Siegel 94, Siegel 96]. Marick's subsystem testing approach includes many elements of the results-oriented strategy [Marick 95]. Testing considerations in development of OOA/D models are discussed in [D'Souza+99]. The Unified Development Process [Jacobson+99] reprises the general approach in [Jacobson+92] and specifies test-specific tasks and work products. See the Bibliographic Notes section in each chapter of this book for scope-specific approaches.

Software Design Patterns

Expressions of generic, reusable, formalized software designs predate software patterns. Larry Constantine was intrigued by similarities in effective systems in the late 1960s and worked to identify the essential properties that made them so. He identified generic module structures that became the basis of structured design: the transform center, the mosque, and the transaction center. The associated principles of coupling and cohesion were developed to factor module design further [Yourdon+79, Page-Jones 88]. Other examples include the ANSI/SPARC three-level schema for database systems, the essential analysis heuristics for transformation of requirements into event categories and data flow diagrams [McMenamin+84, Ward+85], the use of representations of generic solutions (clichés) to generate code in the Programmer's Assistant [Waters+85].

A wide range of software and process patterns are presented in [Coplien+95]. The Gang of Four book is readable and stylistically consistent [Gamma+95]. It presents many small scope patterns and discusses the development and use of patterns. A detailed technical analysis is offered in [Pree 95]. Research at Siemens Corporation has resulted in several large-scale design patterns, presented in [Buschmann+96]. Process considerations for testing can be addressed by existing process patterns; three process patterns that consider testing appear in [Coplien+95].

Chapter 10   Classes

Overview

This chapter presents test patterns for results-oriented testing at class scope. Class test design must consider method responsibilities, intraclass interactions, and superclass/subclass interactions. Implementation-based testing concepts necessary to support results-oriented class testing are developed, including code coverage and class scope integration. Four method scope test patterns and five class scope test patterns are presented. These patterns correspond to constraints placed on message sequences. Considerations for testing inherited features are discussed in detail. Two patterns for test design at flattened scope are presented to solve the problem of superclass/subclass integration.

10.1   Class Test and Integration

This chapter describes how to test classes, one at a time. It usually isn't practical to test just one class in isolation, so the IUT includes the superclasses and server objects of the class under test. Testing, however, usually focuses on one class.

10.1.1   What Is Class Scope Testing?

Individual classes and **small clusters** are the focus of class scope testing. A small cluster includes several classes that are so tightly coupled that testing constituent classes in isolation is impractical. Many class scope design patterns produce a small cluster [Gamma+95]. The **cluster head** is a single class that uses the others as instance variables or as message parameters. A small cluster can be treated as a single class if the cluster head uses all the constituent class's capabilities and the constituents are not used outside the cluster. A small cluster can also result from cyclic dependencies (where each class uses the other's) so that the classes cannot be tested in isolation. The test strategies described here can be applied to the cluster head. We revisit this problem in Chapter 12, Subsystems.

Class scope testing must weave several threads of test design and test execution.

- We test classes by sending messages to methods one at a time. In this respect, class testing is like testing a single conventional module. Five test patterns to design method scope, responsibility-based tests are presented. At method scope, integration planning is simple, even trivial, and integration can be measured by various code coverage approaches. Coverage analysis provides an important tool for assessing test completeness.

- Although we test one method at a time, methods cannot exist apart from a class. Class tests must exercise the cooperation of all methods in a class. In this respect, class testing is like testing an abstract data type or a module with multiple entry points. Five test patterns for designing class scope, responsibility-based tests are presented. These test patterns focus on exercising method interactions. At class scope, integration planning must consider the order in which methods are developed and tested. The alpha-omega cycle provides a basic approach. Class scope integration may be guided with the class flow graph.

- A class is a composite of the features it defines and inherits. It cannot be considered adequately tested unless its superclass features have been exercised in the context of the subclass. This problem is unique to object-oriented software. A key test design question is the extent to which superclass methods should be tested in a subclass context. Two patterns for test design at flattened scope are presented. These patterns show how method- and scope-level test patterns can be applied to a flattened class.

These test strategies are summarized in Table 10.1. Although all elements of all three scopes must be brought together to test a class, we consider them

TABLE 10.1 Elements of Class Testing Strategy

Scope of Implementation Under Test	Typical Responsibility Model	Parts that Must Be "Integrated"	Typical Automation	Elements of Integration Stratgey				
				Prerequisite Part Coverage	Typical Integration Cycle	Integration Coverage Model	Responsibility Coverage
Method	Pre/post	Statements	Class harness	NA	Small Pop	Control flow	Per pattern
Class	Extended contract	Methods, some servers	Class harness	Branch or better	α/ω cycle and test package regression	Class scope FREE flow graph	Per pattern
Flattened class	Flattened extended contract	Inherited methods, some servers	Class harness	N+ (subclass)	α/ω cycle and test package regression	Flattened class free graph	Per pattern

separately to make clear the considerations at each scope. The general approach for class scope testing is outlined in Procedure 3 and suggested by the cartoon in Figure 10.1.

10.1.2 Why Test at Class Scope?

Class scope testing corresponds with the classical definition of unit testing: exercising a relatively small software component, usually via a driver, in isolation. Thorough testing at class scope is not just an abstractly good idea. In fact, it can provide significant improvements in quality and productivity compared with testing classes a little or not at all.

- Many bugs are likely to go undetected if class scope testing is minimal or skipped. System-level testing cannot exercise components to the same degree as class scope testing. Hence, bugs that could have been removed can escape into general release.

- Trying to exercise a class through its clients is usually like trying to pick up a dime with boxing gloves. Client classes typically don't use all the features of server classes and typically do not exercise the full repertoire of the features they do use. It is difficult or impossible to get enough control for effective testing of server classes by using an application client as a driver.

- The longer the time between creation of a bug and its debut as a failure, the higher the cost of correction. Debugging during system test is difficult and slow. It is also wasteful for bugs that could have been removed earlier. Debugging after deployment is costlier still; deployed bugs can have catastrophic consequences.

- Effective class scope testing reduces schedule risk and improves productivity. A project team can test many classes in parallel, but subsystem or system testing typically reduces the number of tests that can be run in parallel. The turnaround time for class testing is typically a few hours. With large systems, the system test cycle (build, setup, run, evaluate, debug, and rebuild) can take weeks.

- It is reasonable for developers of client classes to expect reliable operation of server class objects. It is poor practice, at best, to foist testing on to developers of client classes.

1. Make a preliminary estimate of the work needed to develop and execute a test suite for the class under test. Consider inheritance, complexity, dependence on other classes (think stubs), and your testing budget. Set your test goals accordingly.

2. Design and code a test driver. If the class is moderately complex, begin with an alpha-omega skeleton in the driver. Build the test package (driver, CUT, and stubs) and run it. After the alpha-omega tests pass, design and code additional responsibility tests.

   Tester Tip: Step 2 does not have to precede test design, but beginning with an alpha-omega driver can help to assess how buggy (reliable) the class is and how hard (easy) it is to test. You can fine-tune your testing strategy accordingly.

3. Select a class scope test pattern: nonmodal, quasi-modal, or modal.

4. Select test design patterns for each method: **Category-Partition**, **Combinatorial**, **Recursive**, etc. Use **Invariant Boundaries** to choose test values.

5. Arrange method test cases according to the sequence called for by the class scope pattern. You will probably have to add or change some method scope tests to satisfy the class scope strategy.

6. Build the test package (driver, CUT, and stubs). When all tests pass, instrument the CUT and evaluate coverage your test suite has achieved. If the coverage is insufficient, develop more tests.

Procedure 3   Responsibility-based Testing Process

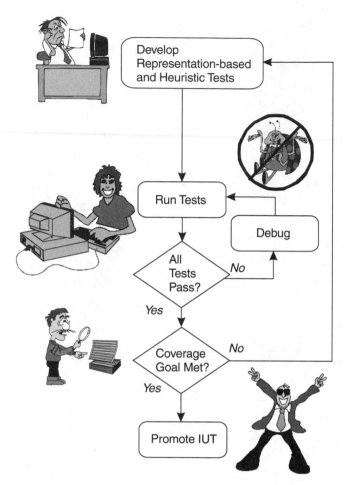

FIGURE 10.1   Model, cover, promote.

Generally, any bug in a class will be present in all objects of that class. Thus, we do not need to test every object to verify a class. Object-specific bugs are possible if an object is clobbered by a runaway pointer or its class contains self-modifying code. Class scope testing does not target these kinds of bugs, but cluster and subsystem scope testing can reveal them. Testing a class instance (an object) can verify a class in isolation. When objects of tested classes are used to create a cluster, a framework, or an application, however, they must be tested as a whole before the system of objects can be considered verified.

10.1.3 Who and When

Class scope testing is typically the responsibility of the class developer, who designs the test suite, codes the test harness, runs the tests, and evaluates the results. The developer must also choose an integration strategy: In what order will classes with dependencies be coded and tested? Several variations are possible:

- Little, if any, class-level testing is done. The MPR case study (discussed in Section 10.1.4) is typical of the negative consequences of this tactic. The no-class-testing approach is common in spite of its clearly negative effects.
- All classes are reviewed, but only some classes are tested. Each class is manually reviewed as a team effort. Classes for which confidence cannot be established by analysis or that have high risk factors are tested. The other classes are not subjected to testing [Love 92].
- Tests are designed and coded for every class before or during class development. The notion of "test before code" has been used with success since the 1970s [Hetzel 88] and is a tenet of the V-model development process [Thayer+90]. This approach has proved effective for object-oriented development [Rettig 91, Taylor 92, Jacobson+92, Beck 94, Bosman 96, Skublics+96, Gamma+98].
- Two people work on development and testing of the same class at the same time. One focuses on designing and coding tests, while the other designs and develops application code. Users of this approach report gains in productivity and quality that offset the increased cost of double-teaming [Siegel 96].

Designing for testability should be considered as classes are being developed. Specifications should be test-ready and requirements for built-in tests should be considered.

10.1.4 A Case Study: MPR Teltech

The consequences of inadequate class testing can be high cost and low quality. In contrast, effective class testing reduces cost and improves quality. The testing experiences in the Trouble Advisor for Customer Services (TRACS) system illustrate the importance of adequate class scope testing.

TRACS is a network management system used to monitor traffic and outages on telephone central office switches connected by trunk lines [Murphy+94]. The user interface is implemented in C++ with the balance being written in Eiffel. The system, which runs on a Unix platform, is required to have 7×24 availability. The application and its testing strategy evolved over subsequent releases spanning several years. The initial test strategy focused on unit testing of class clusters. At first, the effort for individual class unit testing was considered unjustified. Test cases were derived from functional narrative requirements and applied at a cluster level. Because these tests were performed on the entire cluster, little explicit integration testing was done. A proprietary automated tool executed tests, saved them, and supported test reuse for regression testing.

This approach was problematic. As clusters grew, many class interfaces were not exercised by the reused test suite even though new tests had been added to exercise new functionality. The focus on the cluster of classes led to skipping code reviews. In turn, this practice allowed many garden-variety defects (for example, using a variable before initialization) to escape early detection. Defects remained hidden in layers of clusters. The cost of late discovery and correction compared with early discovery was very high.

To address these problems, the testing approach was revised. Individual class unit testing was begun, using a "gray box" approach. The test tools were refined to support class and cluster testing. An OOA specification was developed per cluster and used to derive more effective test cases. In addition, a complete cluster test plan was prepared (meeting nearly all the documentation requirements in IEEE 829). These test plans were inspected. The changes provided significant improvements:

- On average, defects found in system testing were reduced by a factor of 70 to 1.
- The total development effort was cut by half.
- Latent defects in existing classes were revealed and corrected.

Process metrics showed that the approach was effective:

- An average of 5 defects per class were revealed by automated class-level testing.
- Five to 30 percent of class development time was used for testing.
- Five to 20 percent of cluster development time was used for testing.

10.2 Preliminaries

10.2.1 Class Scope Integration

The purpose of class scope integration is to demonstrate that the CUT is ready to test. Then, responsibility testing can proceed without interference from gross coding errors. Developing and testing code in small increments usually eases debugging, as the cause of a failure can be traced usually to the newest code. Integration of superclass features is considered in Section 10.5, Flattened Class Scope Test Design Pattern. We will look at two approaches for reaching the operability threshold: the Small Pop and the alpha-omega cycle.

Small Pop

A *Big Bang* integration cycle attempts to reach the operability threshold for a subsystem by exercising all untrusted components simultaneously (see Chapter 13). Preparatory integration is simply skipped. A Small Pop takes the same tack at class scope. While Big Bang integration is usually ineffective at subsystem or system scope, a Small Pop may be the most expedient route to class scope testing. It is effective when responsibility-based testing and debugging are unlikely to be impeded by simple coding problems, as in the following cases:

- The class under test is small and simple.
- All or most of the servers of the class under test are known to be stable by testing or usage.
- All or most of the inherited features are known to be stable by testing or usage.
- Few intraclass dependencies exist.

A Small Pop will be inefficient if many dependencies exist among class methods or the methods are more buggy than not. An alpha-omega cycle is usually a better approach in this case. Paradoxically, a Small Pop may be the only possible tack for classes with a very high degree of intraclass coupling.

The process is simple. The entire class is developed, without any intermediate checking of operability. A test driver is written that implements a test suite designed using any appropriate test pattern. A test package is built and run when the class compiles. The test suite is run and the class is debugged as needed.

Alpha-Omega Cycle

Alpha and omega are the two placeholder states that bracket the life cycle of any object (see Alpha and Omega States, Chapter 7). The alpha state represents the object declaration before it is constructed. The omega state represents the carcass of an object after it has been deleted or destructed. No tests are attempted for objects in these states.

The alpha-omega cycle takes the object under test from the alpha state to the omega state by sending a message to every method at least once. An alpha-omega cycle test suite shows that all methods in a class are minimally operable. Passing this cycle means that the class under test is ready for more extensive testing. Elements of the alpha-omega cycle are outlined in [Graham+94, Overbeck 94, Firesmith 95, and Firesmith 96].

An alpha-omega test suite exercises simple methods first. No attempt is made to achieve even statement coverage or to exercise all responsibilities. That effort comes later, after the class is working well enough to support more extensive testing. An alpha-omega cycle has six basic steps. The test driver sends one message to each of the following kinds of methods in the order specified:

1. New or constructor method
2. Accessor (get) method
3. Boolean (predicate) method
4. Modifier (set) method
5. Iterator method
6. Delete or destructor method

Within each of these steps, private methods are exercised first, followed by protected methods, and finally public methods. As public methods typically depend on private and protected methods, obstacles can arise when a buggy private or protected method interferes with a test of public method. Exercising public methods after private and protected methods can avoid some of these obstacles. Reordering the basic sequence to accommodate other class-specific dependencies may be necessary, however.

One-pass integration assumes that all or most of the class is developed. If the class is to be developed in increments, the same approach can be followed. The test driver is developed in tandem with increments of class functionality. Test messages may be added to the driver as methods are added to the class. If the entire class interface is developed but some methods are implemented as stubs, then the corresponding test messages may exercise the stub or be deferred until completion of the stub.

The alpha-omega cycle is also a useful approach for incremental development. Methods can be designed and coded in alpha-omega order: constructors first, then accessors, then Booleans, and so on. A test driver that implements this cycle provides a skeleton that can be easily expanded with pattern-based test cases. That is, the alpha-omega test suite supports incremental development of test suites and incremental development of classes.

10.2.2   Implementation-based Test Models

The Role of Code Coverage

A code coverage model calls out the parts of an implementation that must be exercised to satisfy an implementation-based test model. Coverage, as a metric, is the percentage of these parts exercised by a test suite. For example, a test suite that causes every statement to be exercised at least once provides "100 percent statement coverage" or simply "statement coverage." Hundreds of coverage models have been used, published, and analyzed since the late 1960s. Nearly all support implementation-based testing. With the exception of the class flow graph, no significant new code coverage models have been proposed or developed for object-oriented software. The method scope code coverage models reviewed here either are supported by commercially available coverage tools for our six languages or illustrate important testing concepts. Some coverage proposals for object-oriented code are summarized in Section 4.4, Coverage Models for Object-oriented Testing.

In testing theory, coverage is defined by an **adequacy criterion**, which specifies the elements of an IUT to be exercised by a test strategy [Weyuker 88]. A test suite is **adequate** if all the elements to be exercised have been exercised. Test strategy x is said to **subsume** some other strategy y if all elements that y exercises are also exercised by x. For example, branch coverage is said to subsume statement coverage, because exercising all branches necessarily exercises all statements. The **subsumes hierarchy** is an analytical ranking of coverages. No generalizable results about relative bug-finding effectiveness have been established that correlate with this ranking. Because nothing conclusive can be inferred about the number and kind of bugs that remain, reaching a coverage goal does not imply anything like fitness for use. A coverage lower in this hierarchy does not indicate that a higher criterion is necessarily better at finding bugs for a particular application and vice versa.[1]

---

1. Testing researchers do not agree on the implications of the subsumes relationship. See the Bibliographic Notes section for a partial list of papers on this issue.

For reasons explained in chapter 9, the proper role of code coverage analysis is to provide an integration model for responsibility-based testing.

Do not use a code coverage model as a test model. Do not rely on code coverage models to devise test suites. Test from responsibility models and use coverage reports to analyze test suite adequacy.

Covering some aspect of a method or class is *never* a guarantee of bug-free software. However, code analysis and code coverage continue to play important roles in results-oriented testing.

- Coverage reports can point out a grossly inadequate test suite.
- Coverage reports can suggest the presence of surprises.
- Coverage reports can help to identify implementation constructs that may require implementation-based test design or the development of special stubs and drivers.

Perhaps the most important use of code coverage analysis is to mitigate unavoidable blind spots. Both developers and independent testers are consistently unable to devise high-coverage test suites by responsibility analysis alone. Test suites thought to be excruciatingly complete often do not achieve more than 60 percent statement or branch coverage. For example, a study conducted by the vendor of one popular C++ coverage analyzer found that an extensive functional test suite developed for an aerospace application exercised only 40 percent of the branches at member function scope.

Horgan describes an experiment that shows a similar effect [Horgan+96]. This experiment was conducted on two complex, widely used utility programs: TEX and AWK. These programs were developed by leading figures in computer science and programming (Donald Knuth and Brian Kernighan, respectively) and used for many years by thousands of demanding users. The C source code and test suites for both programs are freely available. Although the test suites reflected careful analysis of functionality and significant field debugging, apparently neither had been verified by coverage analysis. Horgan instrumented both systems and ran the published test suites. The coverage results are shown in Table 10.2. Neither test suite achieved statement coverage, and only about two-thirds of the branches were covered (see the Data Flow Coverage section on pages 384–389 for an explanation of c-use and p-use coverage). In large systems, 100 percent coverage is often unattainable due to infeasible paths, dead

TABLE 10.2 Coverage Achieved by Functional Testing Alone

System Under Test	Percent Coverage Achieved by Developer's Functional Test Suite			
	Segment	Branch	p-use	c-use
TEX	85	72	53	48
AWK	70	59	48	55

Source: Adapted from [Horgan+96, 544].

code, and exception handling. Ten to 15 percent is a typical allowance for such anomalies in complex and mature systems. (In large, complex systems, an average of 80 to 85 percent branch coverage can be achieved [Grady 92, 171].) Thus, even with an infeasibility allowance and the benefit of significant field usage, the published functional test suites did not exercise all aspects of the code. These results do not reflect poorly on the ability of Knuth, Kernighan, or any other developer or tester, but rather show how difficult it is to test a complex system without explicit feedback.

Coverage analysis is of academic interest without a coverage analyzer. Code coverage tools instrument class source code by parsing it to insert trace code. When an object of an instrumented class executes, the inserted trace statements produce a trace file. After the test run, the trace file is processed to produce a coverage report. The coverage report shows which parts of the instrumented class have been executed for all test runs that are logged to the same trace file.

- The parts instrumented are determined by the coverage model supported by the coverage tool.
- All commercially available coverage tools worth considering count segments and branches at the method scope. Some tools trace client–server messages and support additional method scope coverage models. As of the publication of this book, no tools were available that supported coverage analysis at the class scope or flattened class scope.
- Unless superclasses of the class under test have been instrumented, coverage analysis tells us little, if anything, about which inherited features have or have not been exercised.
- Abstract or stubbed methods (an interface without an implementation) have no parts. Here, some tools report 0 percent coverage, others 100 percent.

A coverage analyzer is an essential part of the tester's toolkit. Manual instrumentation is error-prone and very time-consuming. In contrast, automatic instrumentation and rebuilding usually take just a few seconds. Instrumentation is typically done on a copy of the source of the class under test. Debugging changes are made to the uninstrumented code. A copy of this source is instrumented and the test suite is rerun. The instrumented source code is typically discarded or archived.

A Code Coverage FAQ

Before discussing coverage models supported for our six languages by commercially available coverage analyzers, a few basic points about coverage should be made. The details of coverage criteria are discussed in following sections.

Is 100 percent coverage the same as exhaustive testing?

No. Exhaustive testing is impossible, except in trivial cases. An exhaustive test suite requires that all paths be exercised for all possible inputs and states. If loops are present, each iteration can be considered as a separate path, so the number of paths becomes astronomically large, even in simple programs (see Section 3.3, The Limits of Testing). Typical coverage measurements are based on very small subsets of exhaustive testing.

Is branch (decision) coverage the same as path coverage?

No. A test suite that exercises each branch once does not guarantee that all entry–exit paths are exercised. Nor does it mean that all possible paths in the presence of iteration have been exercised. The number of entry–exit paths required for branch coverage is usually small compared with the total number of entry–exit paths. In a few special cases, branch and path coverage are the same. See the Branch Coverage section later in this chapter.

Is statement coverage or basis-path coverage the same as path coverage?

No. See the preceding answer.

Can path coverage be achieved?

Maybe. Path coverage requires that (1) you have enough time to identify and test all entry–exit paths (a method with just tens of statements can have hundreds of paths), (2) you treat each loop as a segment with several special cases, and (3) all paths are feasible.

Is every path in a flow graph testable?

It depends. In well-structured code, most entry–exit paths can be executed. Just because we can trace a path on a flow graph does not mean that the corresponding sequence of statements is feasible, however. The problem of path feasibility is discussed in Section 10.2.3, Path Sensitization.

Is less than 100 percent coverage acceptable?

It depends. Infeasible paths, dead code, and exception handling can prevent 100 percent coverage, of any kind. Ten to 15 percent is a typical allowance for such anomalies in complex and mature systems. This allowance shouldn't be used as a quantitative copout—don't give up unless you're sure a true roadblock prevents execution of an uncovered segment, branch, or path.

Can I have high confidence in a test suite if I don't measure coverage?

No. Missing a branch or segment is easy even if you have developed a fiendishly clever responsibility-based test suite (see Table 10.2 and the discussion of Horgan's experiment).

Does achieving 100 percent coverage for x and passing all tests mean that I have bug-free code?

No. Many bugs can hide from test suites that achieve high coverage. See pages 396 through 399, Once More with Feeling: The Dark Side of Code Coverage.

When can I stop testing?

The minimum recommended code coverage for each test design pattern is given in its corresponding Exit Criteria section. In practice, some unusual conditions may develop. In the following list, coverage refers to 100 percent coverage for the test model of choice—at a minimum, method scope branch coverage.

- *Coverage is achieved, but some tests do not pass.* The job isn't done until all tests pass *and* coverage is achieved. Promoting the IUT or releasing the code without correcting all bugs is acceptable if (1) the known bugs are noncritical (cosmetic errors in GUI formatting, for example) and (2) you include a known bug list with the release documentation.
- *All tests pass, but coverage isn't achieved.* More tests should be developed to achieve coverage, unless truly infeasible paths exist (see Section 10.2.3, Path Sensitization) or the cost of the additional tests is prohibitive.

- *Coverage is not achieved and some tests do not pass.* You may be in a situation where you cannot change the code. Some bugs can prevent coverage—if you can't change the code, then you can't achieve coverage. Try to find test cases that will bypass the bugs and produce higher coverage.

- *Coverage is achieved and all tests pass, or you've decided additional coverage is not warranted or feasible.* You're almost done. The instrumentation needed to measure coverage can sometimes cause spurious failures or mask real faults. Be sure that all bug fixes really work. Always plan to make a final rerun of the entire coverage-achieving test suite on an uninstrumented implementation.

- *Coverage is achieved and all tests pass on uninstrumented code.* Congratulations—you've performed adequate testing.

Method Scope Code Coverage Models

The Control Flow Graph.
A **predicate** expression contains a condition (or conditions) that evaluates to true or false. Predicates are used in control statements: if, case, do while, do until, for, and so on. One **condition** corresponds to each Boolean operator in a predicate expression. A predicate with multiple conditions is called a **compound predicate**. The evaluation of a predicate expression typically results in transfer of control to one of several code **segments**. A segment is one or more lexically contiguous statements with no conditionally executed statements. That is, once a segment is entered, all statements in the segment will execute (this assumes continuity of the runtime environment—we do not worry about power failures or similar catastrophic problems). The last statement in a segment must be another predicate, a loop control, a break, a goto, or method exit. The last part of a segment includes the predicate or exit expression that selects another segment but does not include any of a subsequent segment's code.

Figure 10.2 shows part of a Java class `CircularBuffer`. A circular buffer works like a tape loop. Messages are recorded sequentially until the limit of the buffer is reached. Then, the next message is written over the oldest message. The buffer can hold a fixed number of the most recent messages. The method `displayLastMsg` displays the *n* most recently added message, in reverse order of addition. If the buffer is empty, no messages are displayed. If *n* is greater than the number of available messages, all messages are displayed. The method assumes that a pointer to the last message is maintained as messages are sent to the buffer. The code for `displayLastMsg` and part of the class `CircularBuffer`

```
class CircularBuffer {
        int lastMsg,      // index of last message
            np,           // number of messages printed
            msgCounter;   // number of messages logged
  final int SIZE = 1000;  // Size of the message buffer

  String[] messageBuffer = new String[SIZE];

  // . . . other methods
```

Line		Segment
1	`public int displayLastMsg(int nToPrint) {`	A
2	`  np = 0;`	A
3	`  if ( ( msgCounter > 0)` `&& (nToPrint > 0 ) ) {`	B
4	`    for (int j = lastMsg;` `( (j != 0) &&` `(np < nToPrint) );` `--j) {`	C, D, E
5	`      System.out.println(messageBuffer[j]);`	
6	`      ++np;`	F
7	`    }`	
8	`    if ( np < nToPrint ) {`	G
9	`      for (int j = SIZE;` `( (j != 0) &&` `(np < nToPrint) );` `--j) {`	H, I, J
10	`      System.out.println(messageBuffer[j]);`	K
11	`        ++np;`	
12	`      }`	
13	`    }`	L
14	`  }`	
15	`  return np;`	
16	`}`	

FIGURE 10.2   Code segments in `displayLastMsg`.

appears in Figure 10.2. The segment labels correspond to the node labels in Figure 10.3.

All code coverage models typically use some form of a **control flow graph** [Hecht 77]. This graph shows which program segments may be followed by others. Figure 10.3 shows the control flow graph for `displayLastMsg`.

- A segment is represented by a node in the control graph (a circle). Nodes may be named or numbered by any useful convention. Uppercase letters are used here.
- A conditional transfer of control is a **branch**. A branch is represented by an outbound edge in a control graph. A directed edge (arrow) shows

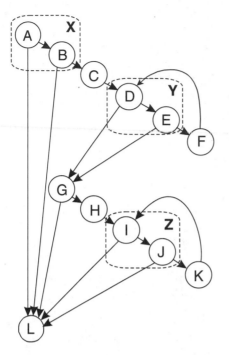

FIGURE 10.3   Control flow graph for displayLastMsg.

that another segment can be reached from another segment. The arrow does not correspond to any particular statement.

- The entry point of a method is represented by the **entry node**, which is a node with no inbound edges. The exit point of a method is represented by the **exit node**, which is a node with no outbound edges.

A path is composed of segments connected by arrows. An **entry–exit path** is a path from the entry node to the exit node. A path is denoted by the nodes that comprise the path. Loops are represented by segments within parentheses, followed by an asterisk to show that this group may iterate from zero to *n* times. These strings are **path expressions** [Beizer 90]. Paths may be traced through a control graph in many ways. Considering iteration, there are 22 entry–exit paths in displayLastMsg. The left column in Figure 10.4 shows these paths. Of course, if each possible iteration is considered, the number of entry–exit paths is infinite for practical purposes (see Section 3.3, The Limits of Testing).

		Path Conditions by Node							
		A	B	D	E	G	I	J
Entry/Exit Path	Branch Coverage	msgCounter > 0	np < nToPrint	j != 0	np < nToPrint	np < nToPrint	j != 0	np < nToPrint
1	AL	XL	F	DC	DC	DC	DC	DC	DC
2	ABL	XL	T	F	DC	DC	DC	DC	DC
3	ABCDGL	XCYGL	T	T	F	DC	F	DC	DC
4	ABCDEGL	XCYGL	T	T	T	F	DC	DC	DC
5	ABC(DEF)*DGL	XC(YF)*YGL	T	T	T/F	T/DC	F	DC	DC
6	ABC(DEF)*DEGL	XC(YF)*YGL	T	T	T/T	T/F	F	DC	DC
7	ABCDGHIL	XCYGHZL	T	T	F	DC	T	F	DC
8	ABCDGHIJL	XCYGHZL	T	T	F	DC	T	T	F
9	ABCDGH(IJK)*IL	XCYGH(ZK)*ZL	T	T	F	DC	T/F	T/DC	T
10	ABCDGH(IJK)*IJL	XCYGH(ZK)*ZL	T	T	F	DC	T/T	T/F	T
11	ABCDEGHIL	XCYGHZL	T	T	T	F	T	F	DC
12	ABCDEGHIJL	XCYGHZL	T	T	T	F	T	T	F
13	ABCDEGH(IJK)*IL	XCYGH(ZK)*ZL	T	T	T	F	T	T/F	T/DC
14	ABCDEGH(IJK)*IJL	XCYGH(ZK)*ZL	T	T	T	F	T	T/T	T/F
15	ABC(DEF)*DGHIL	XC(YF)*YGHZL	T	T	T/F	T/DC	T	F	DC
16	ABC(DEF)*DGHIJL	XC(YF)*YGHZL	T	T	T/F	T/F	T	T	F
17	ABC(DEF)*DGH(IJK)*IL	XC(YF)*YGH(ZK)*ZL	T	T	T/F	T/DC	T	T/F	T/DC
18	ABC(DEF)*DGH(IJK)*IJL	XC(YF)*YGH(ZK)*IJL	T	T	T/F	T/DC	T	T/T	T/F
19	ABC(DEF)*DEGHIL	XC(YF)*YGHZL	T	T	T/T	T/F	T	F	DC
20	ABC(DEF)*DEGHIJL	XC(YF)*YGHZL	T	T	T/T	T/F	T	T	F
21	ABC(DEF)*DEGH(IJK)*IL	XC(YF)*YGH(IJK)*ZL	T	T	T/T	T/F	T	T/T	T
22	ABC(DEF)*DEGH(IJK)*IJL	XC(YF)*DEGH(IJK)*IJL	T	T	T/T	T/F	T	T	T

Key: T = Condition must be true, F = Condition must be false, DC = Condition is a don't care for this path (cannot be reached), / = Conditions at loop entry and loop exit

FIGURE 10.4 Paths in displayLastMsg.

365

Two kinds of explicit *n*-way branching constructs exist. A case and multiple if-else expressions must be modeled with a node for each predicate, one for the conditional action and one for the default action, as shown in Figure 10.5. The default action has no condition. It has the same effect as the last else block in a multiple if-else expression. An unconditional transfer to the statement following the case statement is made after an action has been selected. C++, Java, and Objective-C carry forward the C switch expression. A switch uses an integer argument as an index to target actions within the scope of the switch (a computed goto). A break or other unconditional transfer is typically used to bracket the action. The action syntax allows the programmer to fall through to the next action (and thereby invites bugs). Figure 10.6 shows the structure of a flow graph for the switch expression. Ada permits any discrete type to be used as the argument for a Case statement and will produce a compile error if a corresponding action is not coded.

Multiple exit points are legal in our six languages and commonly used. For example,

```
int foo(int x) {
    if (a==b) return ++x;
    if (x==y) return --x;
    return x;
}
```

I model multiple exit points with a node for each return, as the return may have a right-side expression that evaluates and adds a common exit node for the method. An edge is drawn from each return node to the common exit node. This additional node makes it easier to trace entry–exit paths and does not affect coverage bookkeeping. Most automated coverage analyzers treat multiple exit points in this manner.

Short Circuit Boolean Evaluation.   **Short circuit Boolean evaluation** (also known as lazy evaluation) is generated for compound predicate expressions by many language translators. At runtime, each predicate expression operand is incrementally evaluated. When a sufficient condition to branch is reached, the branch is taken without evaluating the remaining conditions. Short circuit evaluation is useful when an operand may take on an undefined or illegal value. It reduces CPU time compared with always evaluating the complete predicate. The programmer must place the possibly undefined operand to the right of the determining operand or place the most frequently sufficient operand to the left to take advantage of CPU cycle reduction.

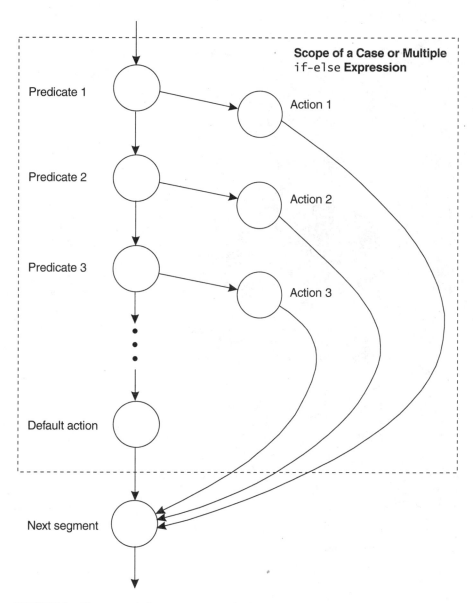

FIGURE 10.5   Flow graph for case or multiple if-else statements.

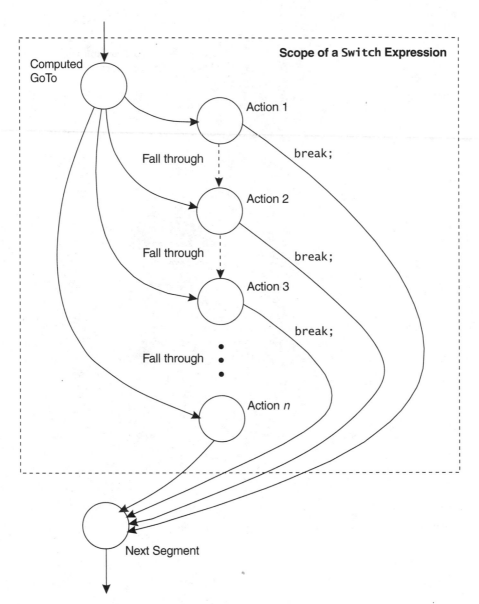

FIGURE 10.6   Flow graph for a switch statement.

All the programming languages considered in this book support compound predicates. For example, each condition in the three compound predicates of displayLastMsg is represented as a separate segment in Figure 10.7. The dashed boxes shown around the nodes in Figure 10.3 indicate that they occur in the same statement. Compound predicates should be modeled separately. All true-false combinations in a compound predicate can be analyzed, and the effects of short circuit Boolean evaluation are made explicit.

C++, Java, and Objective-C use C semantics: short circuit Boolean evaluation is automatically applied to all multiple-condition Boolean expressions. Expression evaluation stops when the left-side operand of an || operator is true, and the true branch is taken. Evaluation stops when the left-side operand of an && operator is false, and the false branch is taken. For example:

```
if ( (x != 0) && ((y/x) > 0) ) fred.foo(x);
```

When x is not zero, y/x is not evaluated and execution continues with the next statement. This approach prevents a divide-by-zero exception when x is zero. Message foo is sent only when both parts of the predicate are true.

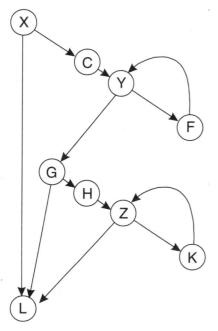

FIGURE 10.7   Aggregate predicate control flow graph for displayLastMsg.

Ada 95 does not automatically generate short circuit evaluation, but provides the AND THEN and OR ELSE short circuit operators. These operators specify evaluation order and termination. The right-side operand of an AND THEN operator is evaluated only when the left-side operand is true. Evaluation terminates at the first false left-side operand, and the false branch is taken. The right-side operand of an OR ELSE is evaluated only when the left-side operand is false. Evaluation terminates at the first true left-side operand, and the true branch is taken. For example,

```
if X /= 0 AND THEN Y/X > 0 then
    Foo(X)
end if;
```

Because one writes either

```
if (a=b) or else  -- Short ct evaluation
   (x=y and is_empty( ) );

if (a=b) or        -- full evaluation
   (x=y and is_empty( ) ) );
```

It is always clear when short circuit evaluation is performed.

Eiffel provides AND THEN and OR ELSE operators, which follow Ada semantics. The implies keyword provides a similar capability.

```
(not x = 0 ) implies ((y/x) > 0 )
```

Smalltalk implements short circuit Boolean evaluation with the block messages and:aBlock and or:aBlock. The messages can be sent only to a Boolean operand. When the receiver of and:aBlock is true, aBlock is evaluated and *anded* with the receiver. When the receiver is false, aBlock is not evaluated and the entire expression is false. When the receiver of or:aBlock is true, aBlock is not evaluated, and the expression evaluates as true. When the receiver is false, aBlock is evaluated and *ored* with false.

```
x ~= 0 and: [y/x > 0]
    ifTrue: [fred foo: x ]
```

Statement Coverage.   **Statement coverage** is achieved when all statements in a method have been executed at least once. This is also known as C1 coverage, line coverage, segment coverage, or basic block coverage. Segment and basic block coverage count segments instead of individual statements. Using segments as the unit avoids some reporting distortion. Suppose a method has two segments, **P** and **Q**. **P** has one statement and **Q** has nine statements. Ten percent statement coverage is achieved by executing **P** and 90 percent statement coverage by executing **Q**. Although the proportion of statements exercised is correct, the numbers do not reflect the number of additional tests needed. Under segment coverage, 50 percent coverage is reported for exercising either segment, suggesting that the test suite is halfway to achieving segment coverage. If we can find one entry–exit path that includes all segments, we can realize 100 percent statement coverage with a single test case (there is no guarantee that such a path will exist). Path 12 of `displayLastMsg`, ABC(DEF)*DGH(IJK)*IL is such a path. Loops need be iterated only enough to reach all statements in the loop body.

The simplicity of statement coverage is appealing, but both blatant and subtle bugs can hide from a test suite that achieves this type of coverage.

- Suppose the predicate in node **B** is incorrectly coded as `msgCounter =>` `0`. Any test suite that did not force the message counter to be zero at least once would miss this error. A large number of test suites could provide statement coverage without meeting this condition.
- Because all statements in a loop body can be reached with a single iteration, the loop is covered in one pass. It is unlikely that a single pass will reveal common loop control bugs.
- Statement coverage can typically be achieved without exercising all true-false combinations of a simple predicate, let alone a compound predicate.
- With some code structures, statement coverage also achieves branch coverage. For example, we must take both branches to reach all statements in `foo`.

```
int foo(int x) {
   if (a == b){
       ++x;
   }
   else {
       --x;
   }
   return x;
}
```

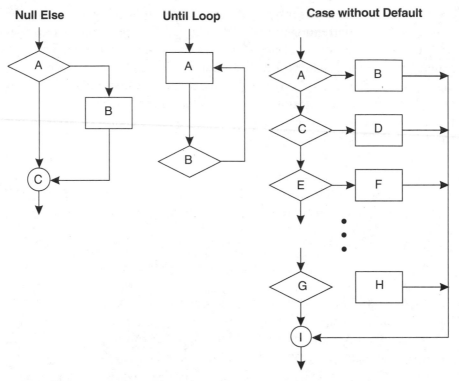

FIGURE 10.8   Structures requiring branch coverage.

However, all statements in a **null else, until loop,** and **case** without default structures can be reached without exercising all branches.[2] Figure 10.8 shows these circumstances. With a **null else,** path **ABC** provides statement coverage without exercising the branch on path **AC.** For example, statement coverage of foo( ) is achieved by setting x and y equal. When the condition is false, however, the code generates an incorrect pointer and crashes.

```
void foo( ) {
    char* c = NULL;
    if (x == y) {
        c = &aString;
    }
    *c = "test code";
}
```

2. Thanks to Rob Schultz for pointing out the statement/structured coverage issue.

In the **until loop**, path **AB** provides statement coverage without exercising any loop iterations. In the **case**-without-default structure, statement coverage is provided by a test suite exercising paths **AB**, **ACD**, **ACEF**, and **ACEFG**. The **GI** branch from the last predicate is omitted. All these instances are legitimate structured programming constructs that could hide bugs from a statement coverage test suite.[3]

Making a case for less than 100 percent statement coverage is difficult. Clearly, if a bug exists in a statement and that statement is not executed, we have almost no chance of revealing that bug. Statement coverage is the minimum required by IEEE software engineering standards [IEEE 1008] and was IBM's corporate standard for nearly 30 years. As the preceding examples show, however, it is a very weak criterion and should be viewed as the barest minimum.

Branch Coverage.   **Branch coverage** is achieved when every path from a node is executed at least once by a test suite. It is also known as decision coverage, all-edges coverage, or C2 coverage. Branch coverage improves on statement coverage by requiring that each branch be taken at least once (at least one true and one false evaluation). It treats a compound predicate as a single statement, however. A predicate expression with n conditions has at most 2^n combinations of true-false outcomes. Branch coverage requires that only two be exercised. We get credit for the path taken out of the predicate, no matter which condition leads to the branch. In effect, the branch coverage graph of `displayLastMsg` looks like Figure 10.7. The compound nodes {**A,B**}, {**D,E**}, and {**I,J**} are treated as if they are single nodes **X**, **Y**, and **Z**, respectively.

How many paths must be covered to achieve branch coverage? With no loops and D two-way branching nodes, branch coverage requires no more than $D + 1$ paths. It also may be achieved for graphs with loops in fewer than $D +$

---

3. A structured program is one whose control flow graph is reducible to a single-entry, single-exit node. The reduction is accomplished by replacing basic control structures (sequence block, iteration, selection) with a single-entry, single-exit block until only one block remains. If nonstructured control paths are present, then the graph cannot be so reduced. Nonstructured control always results from branching into or out of the span of control of a loop or a selection block. In such a situation, more than one entry or exit path appears in a block, and it cannot be reduced. A flow graph of unstructured code will have at least one intersecting (crossing) flow line (for example, see the spaghetti loop in Figure 10.11).

1 paths. For example, in `displayLastMsg`, branch coverage can be achieved in three paths:

1   XL

5   XC(YF)*YGL

13   XC(YF)*YGH(ZK)*ZL

In this example, we can take the loop entry branch and the loop exit branch on the same path.

Like statement coverage, branch coverage does not place any particular constraint on the number of iterations. It can often be achieved by several different path sets, and each path set may be activated by many different test values.

Branch coverage is an improvement over statement coverage because each outcome of a predicate expression must be exercised at least once. Nevertheless, it has its own blind spots.

- Short circuit evaluation means that branch coverage may be achieved for compound predicates without exercising all of the conditions. For example, in the C++ or Java method

```
int foo(int x) {
    if (a==b || (x==y && isEmpty( ) ) ) {
    ++x;
    }
    else {
       --x;
    }
    return x;
}
```

the `++x` branch is taken when `a==b`, whatever the value of `x`, `y`, and `this.isEmpty()`. The `--x` branch will be taken when `a!=b` and `x!=y`, whatever is returned by `this.isEmpty()`. Thus branch coverage may be achieved without ever exercising `this.isEmpty()`.

- Branch coverage ignores the implicit paths that result from compound predicates. The control flow graph that results from the full expansion of `displayLastMsg` has 22 entry–exit paths, compared with 11 for the aggregate model.

- Branch coverage does not ensure that all entry–exit paths execute: only 3 of 11 possible paths were required for `displayLastMsg`. This blind spot can affect the covering test suite even in very simple methods with simple predicates. For example, branch coverage for the method

```
int foo(int x) {
    if (a==b) ++x;
    if (x==y) --x;
    return x;
}
```

can be achieved with two tests: {a = 0, b = 0, x = 0, y = 0} and {a = 0, b = 1, x = 0, y = 1}. In fact, there are four entry–exit paths: true-true, true-false, false-true, false-false. Each path performs a significantly different computation. On the true-true path, x is unchanged but altered by both branches; it is incremented by one on true-false; it is decremented by one on false-true; and it remains unchanged and untouched on false-false.

Multiple-condition Coverage.   Branch coverage does not require exercising each condition in a compound predicate or all true-false combinations of a compound predicate. Many common bugs can therefore hide from a branch-covering test suite. Myers analyzes three alternative coverage models to exercise these relationships [Myers 79]. *Condition coverage* requires that each condition be evaluated as true and false at least once. It does not require testing all possible branches, as it is possible to skip a branch and still exercise all conditions. Condition coverage can therefore miss nodes, possibly leaving us with less than complete statement coverage. *Branch/condition* coverage improves on this approach by requiring that each condition be evaluated as true and false at least once and that each branch be taken at least once. With complex compound predicates, however, branch/condition coverage does not guarantee that all true-false combinations of conditions are exercised.

   Multiple-condition coverage requires that all true-false combinations of simple conditions be exercised at least once. There are at most 2^n true-false combinations for a predicate statement with n simple conditions. If multiple-condition coverage is achieved, then all statements, branches, and conditions are necessarily covered. This type of coverage does not guarantee path coverage. If all conditions in a method are cast into a truth table, multiple-condition coverage is the same as All-Variants coverage (see Chapter 6, Combinational Models). Practical obstacles might prevent us from realizing multiple-condition coverage:

• Reaching all condition combinations may be impossible due to short circuit evaluation.

- Mutually exclusive conditions spanning several predicate expressions may preclude certain combinations.
- Although we usually do not need 2^n test cases for multiple-condition coverage, more test cases are usually required compared with a statement or branch coverage test suite.

Some coverage tools will report the extent to which all true-false combinations of compound predicates have been activated, but usually they cannot determine which omitted combinations are infeasible. Several true-false combinations based on the structure of *or* and *and* operators in a compound predicate expression may prove useful if multiple-condition coverage is infeasible (see Chapter 6).

Object Code Coverage.   **Object code coverage** is measured by instrumentation inserted in the object code generated by the compiler, rather than in the source code. This coverage is required for certification of some safety-critical applications. Performance-profiling tools typically work at this level and can provide object segment or object branch coverage analysis as a side effect.

The results of an object coverage analyzer can be difficult to interpret. Optimizing compilers, for example, produce object code whose structure can differ significantly from the structure of the source code. Many compilers for RISC machines will inline function calls to increase the effectiveness of instruction caching and to avoid call overhead. Fixed-count loops may be unrolled, and so on. If the inlined functions have loops or branches, the object code may include many more branches than the source. C++ and Objective-C macros can result in unexpected branches and other anomalies.

This coverage shares all of the general strengths and weakness of source code coverage but imposes the additional burden of interpreting coverage analysis on object code. No evidence suggests that achieving object code coverage reveals more bugs than source code coverage.

The Basis-Path Model.   The basis-path testing model (also known as structured testing) calls for testing of C different entry–exit paths. C is a metric of program complexity, $C = e - n + 2$, where e is the number of edges and n is the number of nodes in the control flow graph for the IUT. The formula, which is derived from graph theory, is called the **cyclomatic complexity metric** [McCabe 76]. It has been restated as the C metric for single-entry, single-exit program complexity [IEEE 982.1]:

$$C = e - n + 2$$

Nearly all code coverage analyzers generate this metric, so discussion of its significance is warranted.

No research study has yet to show an unambiguous relationship between C, the number of defects, and maintenance cost. Although some studies [McCabe+89] have found a significant correlation between defects in procedural code and C, the metric does not provide significantly better information about potential trouble than counting lines of code [Gill 91, Kan 95]. A C of 10 or higher does not necessarily indicate bug-prone code.

Available studies of object-oriented code do not show significant correlation of defects and C (see Section 4.2.1, What Goes Wrong?). At method scope, C does not usually provide much more information than counting lines of code [Li 93]. Methods with more than six lines of code typically account for less than 10 percent of all methods in a system [Lejter 92, Li 93, Wilde 93, Lorenz 94]. If the C of a method is 10 or higher, the class and the method may be poorly designed or may be a special case where unusual size or complexity is warranted. If there are many methods where C > 10, a general design or process problem is indicated.

The C metric does convey some unequivocal information, however:

- C is equal to the number of bounded regions plus 1 in a flow graph. Thus C may be calculated by inspection—that is, count the number of enclosed areas in a graph and add one.
- C is equal to the number of branch nodes plus 1, assuming two-way branches.
- Branch coverage will require no more than C entry–exit paths, but may be achieved with less than C paths. A proof of this result is given in [Prather 87], demonstrated earlier, and shown in Bertolino's C++ study [Bertolino 97].
- At least C unique entry–exit paths exist in total, but there may be many more.

The **basis-path test model** requires coverage of C different entry–exit paths [McCabe 76, McCabe+89]. A test suite is developed by finding C distinct entry–exit paths and producing test cases by path sensitization. Traditionally, it has been suggested that the longest entry–exit path be included in this test suite. Basis-path coverage is achieved when C distinct entry–exit paths have been exercised.

The basis-path testing model has been widely used and analyzed [McCabe+89, Beizer 90]. It has been applied to C++ applications [Fiedler 89, McCabe+94, Bertolino 97]. It is problematic, however, as Figure 10.9 illustrates. The C of graph I is 3, requiring three entry–exit paths for basis-path coverage. However, there are four distinct entry–exit paths (left edges, right edges, cross left to right, and cross right to left). This discrepancy increases with the number of predicates in series. The C of graph II is 7, but 16 distinct entry–exit paths exist. The unreliability of the basis-path model has at least two consequences:

- Branch coverage may be achieved with less than C paths, in some methods. For example, branch coverage of graph II in Figure 10.9 can be achieved in four entry–exit paths compared with the seven paths required by C. Branch coverage on the aggregate model of `displayLastMsg` can be achieved in three entry–exit paths, compared with five required for basis-path coverage.
- It is possible to select C entry–exit paths and achieve *neither* statement coverage nor branch coverage. A "basis-path cover" for graph II in Figure 10.9 requires seven unique entry–exit paths. The following set of seven paths meets this criterion:

ABDE GKMQS
ABDE HKNQS
ABDE GKNQS
ABDE HKMQS
ACDE GKMQS
ACDE HKNQS
ACDE GKNQS

This set does not achieve branch coverage: the branches **DF, FI, FJ, LO,** and **LP** are not exercised. It also does not achieve statement coverage: the segments **F, I, J, L, O, P,** and **R** are not exercised.

Thus the basis-path criterion can be satisfied without meeting the barest minimum generally accepted standards of code coverage.

Although the effect of compound predicates has been noted for the basis-path approach [McCabe 76, Myers 77, McCabe+89], it is often ignored in computing the C metric. Most coverage tools compute C using compound predicates as single nodes (individual conditions within the predicate are not considered). The expanded C value cannot be correctly determined without taking into

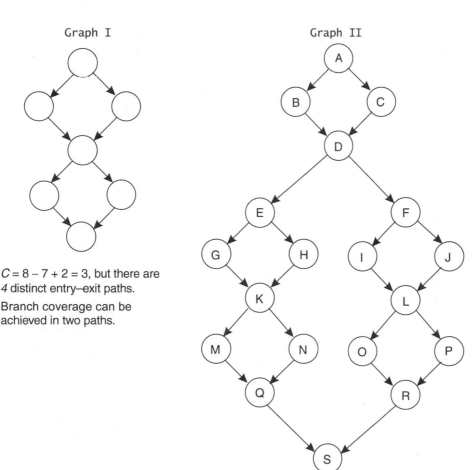

Graph I

$C = 8 - 7 + 2 = 3$, but there are 4 distinct entry–exit paths.

Branch coverage can be achieved in two paths.

Graph II

$C = 24 - 19 + 2 = 7$, but there are 16 distinct entry–exit paths.

Branch coverage can be achieved in four paths.

FIGURE 10.9 C metric versus branch coverage and entry–exit paths.

account the specific structure of the *and* and *or* operators that connect the conditions in a predicate (it is not a simple matter of *anding* the conditions as suggested in [McCabe+89]). For the aggregate predicate model of displayLastMsg, C is five, or less than half the actual aggregate entry–exit paths, and less than one-fourth of the expanded entry–exit paths. For the expanded predicate model, C is eight, or less than one-third of the actual expanded entry–exit paths. In any case, a C value cannot be interpreted correctly without knowing whether it counts individual conditions or aggregate predicates.

Like statement coverage, the basis-path model is appealing because it is simple and pragmatic. So, despite its limitations, many coverage tools compute this metric and some report C coverage. I discourage the use of the basis-path model for two reasons. First, as the examples show, it is unreliable as a coverage criterion and the distinction between simple and compound predicates is often confused in practice. Second, effective testing should not use any implementation-based test model as the primary test design approach, including the basis-path model.

Covering Iteration.   Loops pose some unique test problems. Each canonical loop structure has a different control graph, as shown in Figure 10.10. A loop can

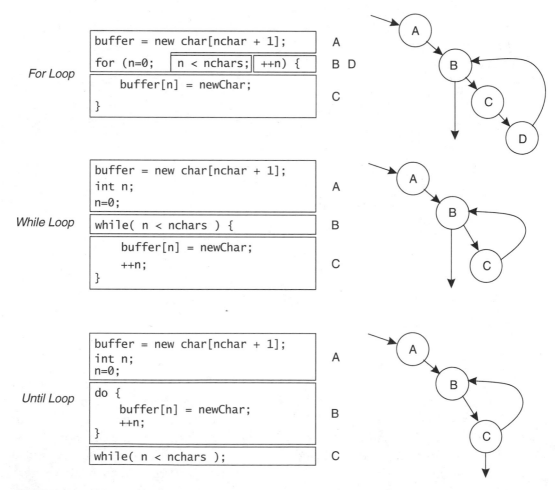

FIGURE 10.10   Flow graphs for canonical loop structures.

be thought of as a path with several special cases. A minimum test suite of a loop with variable iteration control bypasses the loop (zero iterations) and exercises it with an iteration [Marick 95]. Two iterations are the minimum needed to detect data initialization/use faults [Frankl 88]. More extensive coverage focuses on loop control boundary conditions because they are a frequent source of control faults. Loops with fixed iteration control—for example,

```
for(j=0; j<999; ++j) {/* ... */
```

can be executed only a fixed number of times and may be modeled as a single segment.

When a method contains more than one loop, the relationships among loops should be exercised. Coverage requirements depend on the number and relationship of loops in the method, as shown in Figure 10.11.

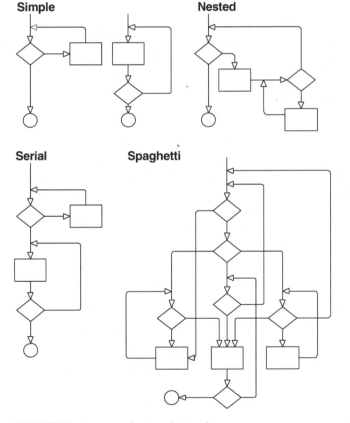

FIGURE 10.11   Loop-to-loop relationships.

• *Simple loops*. A simple loop is either a for, do-while, or repeat-until form with a single entry and a single exit. The minimum test is two iterations. A more comprehensive test suite will exercise the domain boundary of the loop control variable. Figure 10.12 lists the iteration values that should be tested. Note that "holes" in the control variable domain (excluded values) create additional boundary conditions.

• *Nested loops*. A nested loop is a simple loop contained in another simple loop. If we repeat inner range tests every time we step to an outer loop, we get many tests. For example, with the five basic loop test cases, we would have 25 test cases for two nested loops, 125 test cases for three nested loops, and so on. Beizer's loop strategy reduces the multiplicative growth to additive growth: 12 test cases for two-level loops, 16 with three-level loops, and 19 with four-level loops [Beizer 90]. Procedure 4 summarizes the test case design steps. Table 10.3 on page 384 indicates which loop controls vary and which are held constant.

• *Serial loops*. Two or more loops on the same control path are serial loops. If any define/use data relationships exist between the loops, treat them as if the loops were nested. Use data flow analysis to determine test cases. If no define/use relationships exist between the loops, test cases can be designed without the complication of setting up the control variables of both loops in a single test case.

Value for Loop Control Variable		Loop Control Value Sets	
		Minimal	Full
Minimum − 1	*		✓
Minimum (possibly zero)	*	✓	✓
Minimum + 1		✓	✓
Typical			✓
Maximum − 1			✓
Maximum		✓	✓
Maximum + 1	*		✓
Excluded interior point	**		✓
Excluded boundary values	**		✓

Key: * = May not be feasible, ** = Not required in most loops

FIGURE 10.12   Loop control value sets.

1. Find the shortest or simplest path to the loop. The input and state required for this path (up to the loop) will be required for each of the loop tests.

2. Test focus begins at the innermost loop and proceeds to the outer-most loop.

3. For each variable-iteration focus loop:
    a. For each loop control case (min, min + 1, typical, max − 1, max):
        i.   Determine the input/state values needed to drive focus loop control to the control case.
        ii. Determine the input/state values needed to drive nonfocus loop controls to the nonfocus cases of (minimum, typical, or maximum).
        iii. Add excluded values and out-of-range checks if indicated.

        Rof

    b. Add the loop conditions to the partial path conditions—you may have to choose a different path to the loop to achieve the loop to control conditions.

    Rof

4. Set up a test that will run all loops to maximal control case.

Note to OO Purists: Okay, you never use loops, but iterate over an object, possibly with polymorphic bindings to accomplish nesting. Substitute *iterator* for *loop*.

Procedure 4   Testing Nested Loops

TABLE 10.3   Nested Loop Test Strategy

	Loop Test Focus			
	Inner Loop	Middle Loop	Outer Loop	All Loops
Inner Loop variable	Full Set	Hold at Typical	Hold at Typical	Hold at Maximum
Middle Loop variable	Hold at Minimum	Full Set	Hold at Typical	Hold at Maximum
Outer Loop variable	Hold at Minimum	Hold at Typical	Full Set	Hold at Maximum

Note: Full Set values are given in Figure10.12.

• *Spaghetti loops.* A spaghetti loop has more than one entry or exit point. Nested spaghetti loops contain very complex control flow paths. Spaghetti loops should be rejected outright and returned to the developer for correction—do not waste your time testing this junk. Spaghetti code is a dangerous black hole and you are not doing anyone a favor by passing it along. If, under duress, you are forced to test a spaghetti loop, design an equivalent single-entry/single-exit loop (this approach is possible with even the worst spaghetti code [Ashcroft 71]). Develop your test cases from this design adding tests for every weird path you can imagine.

Testing a path with loops such as **ABC(DEF)*DGH(IJK)*IL** requires input and state values that will reach the loops and exercise each of the appropriate loop control focus cases. Techniques for code-based test value selection are discussed in Section 10.2.3, Path Sensitization. Chapter 17 discusses how loop invariants can be used to increase loop testability.

Data Flow Coverage.   The data flow coverage model is based on the observation that computing is a sequence of actions on instance variables. If a bug exists in such a sequence and that sequence is not executed, testing has almost no chance of revealing that bug. An access sequence (a data flow path) is constrained by control paths. The data flow test model seeks to identify and exercise these sequences. It has been the subject of advanced theoretical analysis and several studies of effectiveness (see the Bibliographic Notes section). The following synopsis presents pragmatic aspects of the technique, adapted to object-oriented programming.

Method scope data flow can be modeled for primitive or object instance variables. The content of objects must be accessed via the object interface, but the same principles apply equally well. Some common access-related bugs include the following:

- Using an undefined or uninitialized variable.
- Assigning a value to a variable more than once without an intermediate reference.
- Sending a modifier message to an object more than once without an intermediate accessor message.
- Deallocating or reinitializing a variable before it is constructed or initialized.
- Deallocating or reinitializing a variable before it is used.
- Using incorrect values in the signature of a polymorphic message, resulting in incorrect binding.
- The container problem: Deleting a collection object, thereby leaving its members orphaned and unaccessible. This problem is more likely to arise with C++ code and less likely when automatic garbage collection is performed, as it is in Java and Smalltalk.

The data flow model recognizes three basic instance variable access actions:

- *Define* actions occur in a message or statement that changes the concrete state of an instance variable: an initialization method, a constructor, a modifier method, an assignment statement, an input/output operation, or a side effect. This is abbreviated as a **D** action.

- *Use* actions occur in a message or statement that gets the value of an instance variable without changing it. This is abbreviated as a **U** action. Two kinds of uses have been identified. *Computation use* (c-use) applies when an instance variable occurs on the right side of an assignment statement or as a call-by-value argument. Access to an object may be provided by an accessor method, copy method, direct reference, and so on. *Predicate use* (p-use) obtains when an instance variable occurs in a predicate expression. A p-use is said to occur on the *edges* between the referencing node and the successor nodes. In effect, it includes the node that contains the predicate and all its immediate successor nodes, even if the successor nodes do not reference the variable.

- *Kill* actions include any message, statement, or side effect that causes an instance variable to be deallocated, released, undefined, or otherwise no longer visible within its original scope. These are abbreviated as a **K** action. Deallocation is a side effect of leaving activation scope in the six languages considered in this book. Temporary variables are created upon method activation or as loop control variables are automatically killed when the activation scope is exited. In C++, the application programmer is responsible for or can control most (but not all) deallocation at member function scope. Automatic garbage collection is necessary to support automatic deallocation, but is not considered part of the **K** action.

Table 10.4 shows valid and invalid sequences of **D**, **U**, and **K** actions. The semantics and memory management model of a particular translator determines how a given expression is classified as a Define, Use, or Kill action.

A data flow path must lie on a control flow path. It comprises a sequence of segments that begins with a Define action and ends at (but does not include) a subsequent Define or Kill action. Data flow paths may be as short as the Use action on the right side of an assignment statement and the Define action on the left side: `a = a + 1`, or `fred.foo(fred)`. They may also span a complete entry–exit path or any shorter subpath. For example, consider the member function `bar(int* x)`, which creates and destroys a `List` object `fred`.

```
1    void bar(int* x) {
3    MyClass fred;      // Define action: constructor
                        // initializes fred.
                        // Lines 4-7 don't access fred
8    fred.set(x);       // Define action: fred is changed
                        // Lines 9-13 don't access fred
14   y = fred.get( );   // Use action: first element of
                        // the list is return
                        // Lines 15-18 don't access fred
19   ~fred( );          // Kill action: fred is dead.
                        // Explicit dtor used to illustrate
                        // kill action.

20   }
```

The data flow paths for the `fred` object in `bar( )` are as follows:

3–8   A **DD** path. The definition created at line 3 is used at line 8 and superseded by another definition.

8–14   A **DU** path. The definition created at line 8 is used at line 14.

8–19   A **DK** path. The definition created at line 8 is killed at line 19.

TABLE 10.4 Valid and Buggy Define/Use/Kill Action Pairs

Action Pair	Example		Comment
	First action	Next Action	
-D	`<entry>`	`Object foo = Object(42);`	OK, typical ctor.
	`<entry>`	`foo.set(42);`	OK, if foo ctor'd in another function.
DU	`foo.set(42);`	`fum = foo;`	OK.
K-	`~Foo( );`	`<exit>`	OK.
KD	`~Foo( );`	`Object foo = Object(42);`	OK, but odd.
	`~Foo( );`	`foo.set(42);`	Incorrect – access after dtor'd.
UD	`bar.set(foo);`	`foo.set(42);`	OK.
UK	`x = foo.get( );`	`~Foo( );`	OK.
UU	`bar = foo;`	`if (fum == foo)`	OK.
DD	`Object foo = Object(0);`	`foo.set(42);`	Not necessarily a fault but probably unintended or redundant.
	`foo.set(42);`	`Object foo = Object(42);`	
-U	`<entry>`	`bar.set(foo);`	OK, if foo ctor'd in another function.
U-	`bar.set(foo);`	`<exit>`	OK.
D-	`foo.set(42);`	`<exit>`	Probably a fault if foo is used at method scope. OK if foo is used at class scope.
DK	`foo.set(42);`	`~Foo( );`	Probably a fault.
-K	`<entry>`	`~Foo( );`	OK if foo is defined and used at class scope. Possibly a fault if foo is used only at method scope.
KK	`~Foo( );`	`~Foo( );`	A fault.
KU	`~Foo( );`	`bar.set(foo);`	A fault.

Note: foo is an object of class Foo, set() and get() are methods of Foo.
Source: Adapted from [Beizer 90].

The line numbers show the beginning and ending lines of the data flow subpath for the fred object. They are subpaths of the single entry–exit path. Because all statements in this version are executed unconditionally, any activation of bar( ) will cause all data flow subpaths to be taken. Data flow paths for x and y could be developed by the same analysis.

Now suppose a predicate is coded at line 7.

```
1    void bar(int* x) {
3    MyClass fred;         // Define action: constructor
                           // initializes fred
                           // Lines 4-7 don't access fred
7    if ( x > 0 ) {        // Predicate
8    fred.set(x);          // Define action: fred is changed
     }                     //
                           // Lines 9-13 don't access fred
14   y = fred.get();       // Use action
                           // Lines 15-18 don't access fred
19   ~fred( );             // Kill action: fred is dead.
                           // Explicit dtor used to illustrate
                           // Kill action
20   }
```

The data flow paths for fred are now more interesting. The uppercase letter designates the path and is followed by beginning and ending line numbers.

I (3–8)   A **DD** path. The definition created at line 3 is used at line 8 and superseded by another definition when x is greater than zero.

J (3–8)   A **DU** path. The definition created at line 3 will be used when x is less than or equal to zero.

K (8–14)   A **DU** path. The definition created at line 8 is used at line 14, but only if line 8 is used.

L (3–14)   A **DU** path. The definition created at line 3 is used at line 14, but only if line 8 is skipped.

M (3–19)   A **DK** path. The definition created at line 3 is killed at line 19, if it has not been superseded by executing line 8 because x is greater than zero.

N (8–19)   A **DK** path. The definition created at line 8 is killed at line 19. Line 8 is reached only if x is less than or equal to zero.

Clearly, some of these subpaths are mutually exclusive within any single activation of bar( ). At least two separate activations would be required to exercise both paths: bar( ) has two entry–exit paths, **A** (x greater than zero) and **B** (x less than or equal zero). Entry–exit path **A** achieves data flow paths **I, K**, and **M**. Entry–exit path **B** achieves data flow paths **J, L**, and **N**. Thus a test suite that exercises entry–exit paths **A** and **B** also exercises all define-use paths in bar( ).

Several variations of data flow coverage have been proposed and ranked [Frankl+88, Frankl+93]. The *all-uses* criterion is recommended for practical applications. It requires that *at least one* DU path be exercised for every definition-use pair. If several control flow paths lead from a definition to a use, only one must be taken to achieve all-uses coverage. This level of coverage has been found effective. The relative effectiveness of branch and data flow testing on procedural code has been described as follows:

> While all-uses was not always more effective [at finding bugs] than [branch coverage] and [random testing], in most of those cases where it was more effective, it was *much* more effective. In contrast, in those cases in which [branch coverage] was more effective than [random testing], it was usually only a little bit more effective [Frankl+93, 78].

The algorithms for identifying data flow paths are adapted from compiler algorithms. These techniques are well established but difficult to work by hand [Rapps+85, Harrold+94]. Aliasing (in which different variables point to the same object) causes problems in tracing data flow.

The manual data flow analysis technique given in Procedure 5 does not require elaborate tabulation or quantitative searching. Rather, it requires the ability to draw and then erase lines of different colors. It is effective for small methods: roughly C of 10 or less, six or fewer instance variables. *Nonmodal Class Test* uses the data flow model at the interface level. A discussion of data flow modeling at the class scope using the class flow graph follows.

◇ The Class Flow Graph: A Class Scope Coverage Model

Test design at the class scope must produce method activation sequences to exercise intraclass (intermethod) control and data flow. The modal testing patterns use responsibility-based models to exercise class scope interactions but these test suites cannot guarantee that all intraclass paths will be activated. If the implementation contains *surprises*, then we could easily fail to exercise some intraclass paths.

A method flow graph models how states are computed. It does not show how the graphed method is related to other methods. A state transition diagram models those states that are reachable from any given state by messages sent to methods. Such a model can provide the missing linkages among class methods. The class flow graph is constructed by joining these graphs, providing a model of all intraclass control flow paths.

1. Prepare a control flow graph for the method under test.

2. Tabulate all **D, U,** and **K** actions by instance variable, by node.
   See Table 10.4.

3. Select a color for each instance variable. Use erasable ink on an easily
   erased sheet—water-soluble markers on presentation transparencies
   work well. Erasing (step 5) can be done with a damp cloth.

4. For each instance variable:
   a. Use the color for the current instance variable.
   b. Draw a solid circle at each node with a **D** or **K** action.
   c. Draw an open circle at each node with a **U** action.
   d. For each D action:
      i. For each **U** action:
         Look for a definition-clear subpath from the **D** to the **U** action
         (there might not be one). Trace this path in the current vari-
         able's color. Try to keep the line near the control flow path.
         Rof
      Rof
   Rof

5. By inspection, choose an entry–exit path with lots of **DU** paths.
   a. Add this entry–exit path to your test suite.
   b. Erase all DU subpaths (drawn in step 4) along this entry–exit
      path.
   c. Repeat step 5 until there are no more **DU** paths to erase.

6. Sensitize the test paths.
   a. Use any sensitization technique.
   b. Discard infeasible paths.

Procedure 5   Data Flow Paths by Erasing

The class flow graph is a class scope, code-based model for path analysis. It shows how paths in each method may be followed by paths in other methods, thereby supporting intraclass path analysis. The class flow graph is constructed from the FREE class state model and flow graphs for each method. It represents all possible intraclass (intermethod) control flow paths. If no sequential constraint exists for method activation, the exit node of each method is effectively connected to the entry node of every other method, including its own. If sequential constraints are present, fewer intermethod exit-to-entry paths will exist.

The basic construction of the class flow graph is illustrated with class X, which has three methods: X.a, X.b, and X.c. Figure 10.13 shows the individual flow graphs. Figure 10.14 illustrates the state model for class X. It includes three active states (I, II, and III) and the α and ω states. State α is a placeholder that facilitates graph construction; it corresponds to the declaration of an object (as opposed to its definition). Similarly, state ω corresponds to the post-destruction object. Explicit nil states allow consistent representation of constructors and destructors in the testing model. A single constructor is assumed here for simplicity.

Because state is the result of method activation, we can substitute method graphs into state transitions. The flow graphs are embedded in the state model to suggest how each state is computed (see Figure 10.15). Figures 10.16 and 10.17 suggest how transitions are accomplished by method activations. Figure 10.16 removes the state diagram annotation and represents all possible paths among method segments. Figure 10.17 on page 395 shows the effect of removing redundant nodes, yielding the class flow graph. This is a graph model of the entire class that has all the properties of ordinary flow graphs and can be used to evaluate any control flow, path-based coverage model. Procedure 6 on page 397 summarizes its construction.

The graph of a method appears once for each transition in which it occurs. A method graph may be repeated—for example, as in the graph of method X.c. Replacing the repeated graphs with a single graph of the method with edges to and from the corresponding state nodes is possible, but complicates entry–exit bookkeeping. If X.c is activated from state I, then that activation must return to state I, and not to state II or III. If the graphs for X.c were merged, then there would be no way (using only nodes and edges in the graph) to ensure that the activation proceeded correctly. An automated representation of the graph could dispense with the redundant nodes if it provided the necessary entry–exit bookkeeping.

The class flow graph can support many coverage models, just as a method scope flow graph does. We can achieve branch coverage of the class flow graph

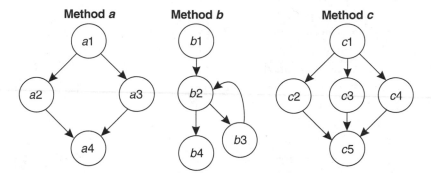

FIGURE 10.13   Method scope flow graphs.

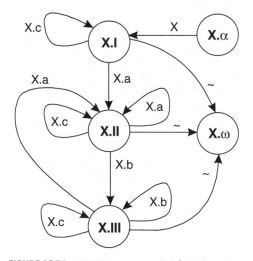

FIGURE 10.14   FREE state model for class X.

if (1) all method scope tests achieve branch coverage and (2) the transition tree is covered. This approach will also achieve statement coverage for the class under test. This level of coverage will be achieved by all class scope, responsibility-based test patterns.

When the linkage among method paths is considered, the number of paths increases significantly. A path from the alpha to the omega node is called an **alpha-omega path**. If we limit loops to zero or one iteration, then 144 distinct

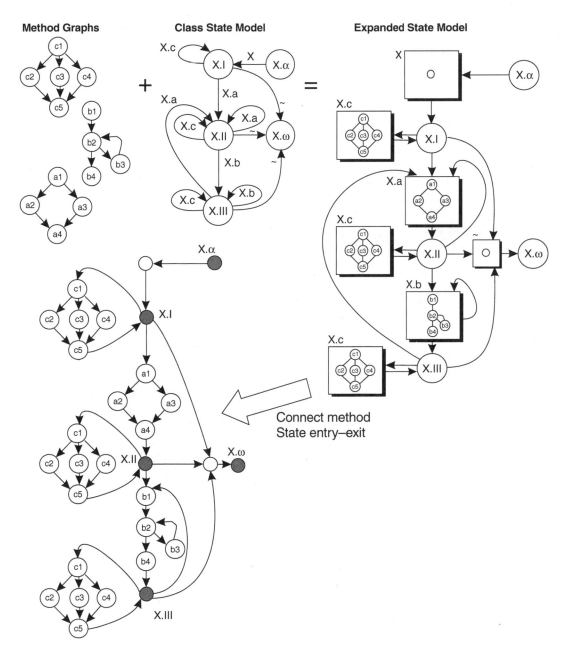

FIGURE 10.15   FREE flow graph construction.

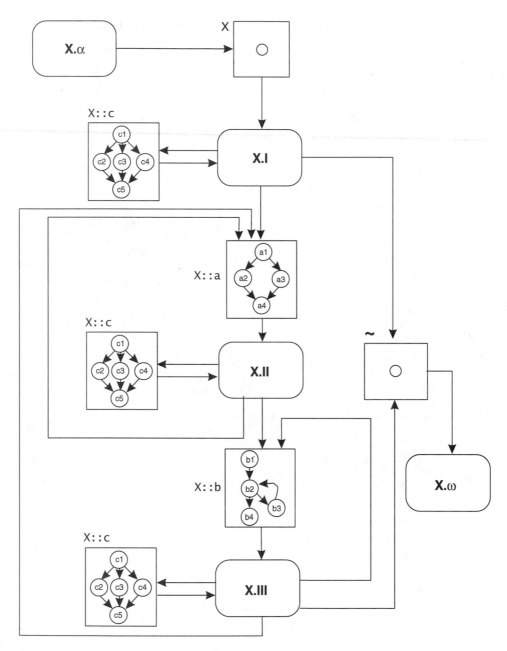

FIGURE 10.16   Method graphs replace state transitions.

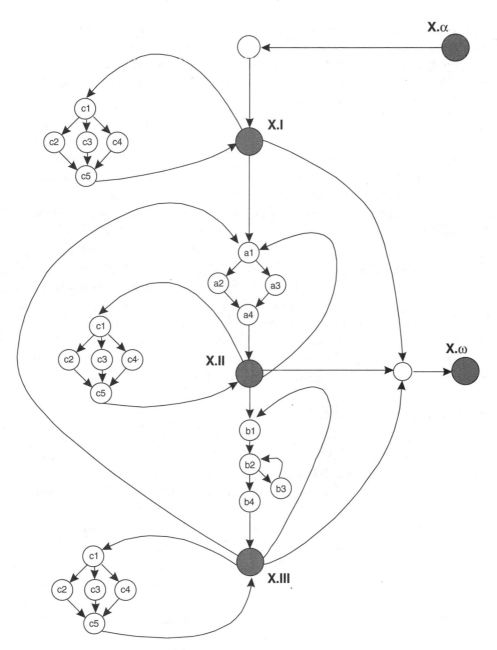

FIGURE 10.17 Resultant class flow graph.

alpha-omega paths are possible in the graph of class X shown in Figure 10.17.[4] The responsibility test suite probably will not exercise some feasible alpha-omega paths at the class scope. If a coverage analyzer could instrument and report alpha-omega coverage, it might be practical to try to achieve this goal, but no such tool exists as of this writing. Nevertheless, the class flow graph can still be used as an analytical tool.

- Identify the longest or weirdest alpha-omega path by inspection.
- Identify alpha-omega paths by inspection that might be inconsistent with class responsibilities or that might lead to corrupt states.
- Identify alpha-omega paths by inspection that might cause performance problems.

These paths should be added to your test suite.

Effective and practical class scope code coverage models are still a research topic. An approach has been proposed that would use interprocedural, data flow algorithms developed for compiler optimization to identify intraclass path sets. It assumes that the class under test has no constraints in terms of the message sequence, so a test driver is used to generate random message sequences until the data flow path set has been covered [Harrold+94].

Once More with Feeling: The Dark Side of Code Coverage

The relationships among code coverage models have been formally analyzed by many researchers (see Bibliographic Notes section). This analysis has placed code coverage models in a hierarchy. If all paths in coverage model *A* are necessarily included in coverage model *B*, then a test suite that achieves coverage *B* must also achieve coverage *A*. For example, if a test suite achieves branch coverage, it must also achieve statement coverage. This is the **subsumes** relationship.[5] All-paths (exhaustive) coverage is the most inclusive testing level. Although this theoretical ideal can be met only in trivial cases, it clearly includes all other possible paths. Within all paths, all-define-use data flow paths subsumes all-use data flow paths, which subsumes all-branches, which subsumes all-statements. The relationships among several intermediate coverage models

---

4. Note that the C metric for the entire graph is 16 and the sum of the C metric for all class methods is 9. The problematic aspects of the C metric as a testing model are compounded at the class scope.

5. Formally stated, "Criterion C1 subsumes criterion C2 if, for every program P and specification S, every test set that satisfies C1 also satisfies C2" [Frankl+93, 776].

1. Develop a FREE state model for the CUT.

2. Develop a flow graph for each method in the CUT.

3. Copy the state transition diagram to a new sheet. Provide space around the transition edges to insert method flow graphs.

4. For each transition in the state transition diagram:
   a. Delete the transition edge.
   b. Paste the graph of this transition's method into the class flow graph near the midpoint of the deleted transition edge.
   c. Add an edge from the accepting state node to the method graph's entry node.
   d. Add an edge from the method graph's exit node to the resultant state node.

   Rof

5. Revise to reduce visual clutter.

Procedure 6   Class Flow Graph Construction

of theoretical interest between all-uses and all-branches have also been established. Because coverage does not necessarily correlate with the location of bugs, however, the subsumes hierarchy provides no unequivocal information about bug-finding ability and coverage. Bugs that hide from arguably more comprehensive coverage models can be found by less stringent models. Some bugs can hide even when very stringent coverage is achieved.

> Coverage is a useful tool for finding code that a responsibility-based test suite hasn't touched, but achieving any coverage goal is never a guarantee of the absence of bugs.

We conclude our review of method scope, code-based coverage with two examples of bugs that can easily hide from high-coverage test suites.

The responsibility of the give_change method is to compute the number of dollar bills, quarters, dimes, and nickels to be returned when a purchase is made from a vending machine. The following code contains a simple, dumb mistake in the last line that turns out to be a very pernicious bug. The constant should have been 5 rather than 10. No coverage, including all-DU-paths, will find this bug unless values for deposit and price are such that at least one nickel should be returned. However, this bug could be found by a single test case that included revealing values of deposit and price.

```
void Depository::give_change(int price)
{
    int n_100, n_25, n_10, n_5;
    if ( deposit <= price ) {
        change_due = 0;
    }
    else {
        change_due = deposit - price;
        n_100      = change_due / 100;
        change_due = change_due _n_100;
        n_25       = change_due / 25;
        change_due = change_due _ n_25;
        n_10       = change_due / 10;
        change_due = change_due _ n_10;
        n_5        = change_due / 10;  // Coding Bug
    }

    // . . .
}
```

Brian Marick reports a second example of a coverage-resistant bug. The following method is part of a controller class to dispatch events in an embedded aircraft control application.

```
void flight_control_event_handler(event e)
{
    switch(e)
    {
        // ...
        case RAISE_LANDING_GEAR:
        landing_gear_motor(lgm_turn_on_until_raised);
        break;
    // ...
    }
}
```

Again, no form of coverage, including all-DU-paths coverage, will reveal the bug: What happens if the plane is still on the ground when the event_handler message is sent with the RAISE_LANDING_GEAR event value? Unless prevented by a mechanical fail-safe, the fuselage will be dropped to the tarmac.

10.2.3 Path Sensitization

Path sensitization is the process of determining argument and instance variable values that will cause a particular path to be taken. Path sensitization is undecidable; no algorithm can solve this problem in all cases. Instead, it must be solved heuristically. For small, well-structured methods, this task is usually not difficult. It becomes increasing more difficult as size and complexity increase. Even when the analysis is straightforward, however, it can be quite difficult to get the instance variables and arguments into the desired state. Solutions for this problem are discussed in Chapter 19.

If you start with a responsibility-based test suite and select inputs by domain analysis, Category-Partition, or a similar approach, most of your path sensitization work is already done [Prather 87, Jeng+94]. All that remains is to find test values to exercise a few more paths to meet the coverage goal. You can use existing test cases to find values for these missing paths.

1. Consider the existing test suite. Have you overlooked any test value or feature combinations?

2. Try to find a test case that follows part of a missing path. Identify the branch where the existing test case diverges from the missing path. Then change enough of the input to cause the opposite branch to be taken. Apply this same analysis until you reach the exit of the missing path.

3. If no existing path seems close, list the predicates for the missing path.

4. If possible, avoid paths where predicates use values computed on the path. If a variable is changed and then used in a predicate, reverse data flow tracing may be needed to establish test case values.

5. Begin with the conditions at the *end* of the missing path. Pick values that satisfy these conditions. Repeat this analysis for each prior branch in the missing path until you reach the entry node. You may find it just as easy to work from the entry node forward. In either case, you will search for a set of values that satisfies all constraints on the missing path.

You may encounter a path that cannot be executed. At least six causes lead to infeasible paths:

• *Short circuit evaluation and complex predicate expressions.*

• *Contradictory or mutually exclusive conditions.* For example, in the expression

```
if ( (x > 2) || (x < 10) ) { /* ... */ }
```

only three conditions can be obtained: x cannot be simultaneously less than 3 and greater than 9, so the false-false case is impossible. The false-false branch of this predicate can never be taken.

• *Mutually exclusive, redundant predicates.* For example, in the code fragment

```
if (x==0) {
  perpetual( );
}
else {
  free( );
}

// Code follows which does not change
// the value of x

if (x!=0) {
  motion( );
}
else {
  lunch( );
}
```

the paths `perpetual( )` ... `motion( )` and `free( )` ... `lunch( )` are impossible for any given value of x. Because the predicates could be merged, you may have found a bug—or at least a questionable piece of code.

- *Unstructured code.* Such code is acceptable (if necessary) for exception handling or exiting a case or loop expression (for example, with the `break` statement in C++). Any other kind of unstructured code is unacceptable, including upward-branching gotos or branches that enter or exit a loop body without first activating the loop control.

- *Dead code or code detours.* Sometimes a problem or incomplete segment is left in the source with an unconditional predicate to enforce a detour—perhaps as the result of a desperate 3:00 A.M. patch. If you are lucky, a comment explains the programmer's intent. Often, the detour looks just like the rest of the code.

- *"This should never happen."* Experienced programmers are often justifiably suspicious about supposedly impossible conditions. Sometimes one sees a predicate that should never be true under all conceivable operating conditions, followed by an error message and program halt (a good place for an assertion). You may not be able to reach this segment without forcing an exception or corrupting a value.

An infeasible path should be viewed with some suspicion. Although it may be necessary, it is just as often an indication of a coding error or an ill-considered design. As a practical matter, infeasible paths are only an occasional nuisance in well-structured small methods.

10.2.4   Domain Testing Models

Testing cannot be accomplished without selecting test values. Domain analysis is a straightforward and effective way to select test values.[6] It provides the test model for ***Invariant Boundaries*** and can be used to select test values for nearly all other test design patterns.

A few definitions are needed before we consider how domain analysis works and how we should use it. Any subset of all possible inputs for an IUT

---

6. Because *domain* is commonly used in many different senses, the distinction noted in Chapter 3 bears repeating: The testing usage of *domain* is derived from the mathematical definition of *domain:* the set of inputs accepted by a function. It is not to be confused with: (1) an "application domain," which refers to a general class of user problems (e.g., international banking, avionics, word processing and so on) [Kean 97], (2) a "problem domain," which is a collection of ideas related by some human purpose, (3) the domain component of an IP address, or (4) the value set of an attribute in database theory [Date 82]. The use of *domain* in the testing sense predates these definitions [Howden 76]. The UML definition of *domain* includes both (1) and (2).

is called a **partition. Partition testing** strategies define a rationale for choosing partitions and selecting values from partitions. Most, but not all, testing approaches can be considered partition testing.[7]

We can define partitions in many ways. For example, path sensitization results in a partition that contains at least one combination of input values necessary to execute a particular path. Myers's **equivalence class partitioning** is a well-known partition identification strategy [Myers 79]. An equivalence class (in Myers's usage) is a partition defined so that if any single test value from the partition passes (or does not pass), then all other values in the partition are expected to pass (or not pass). Experience has shown that boundary conditions often prove troublesome. Thus, when an equivalence class spans a range, values are chosen that lie at edges of the equivalence class. Myers called his heuristic for choosing these values **boundary value analysis**. The idea is generally effective, but does not provide specific guidance for choosing the equivalence classes and boundary values. In contrast, the domain testing model [White+78] provides a specific, complete, and unambiguous technique for choosing both.

The application-specific definition of partitions is crucial to testing effectiveness. Partitions should be defined so as to reveal bugs [Hamlet+90]. Because we cannot be certain where bugs will lie, however, any partition definition is necessarily a guess. It may be a good or bad guess. A good guess is one based on a fault model. Domain testing uses an explicit fault model whose effectiveness (and limits) has been established by years of rigorous analysis.[8] This research has confirmed the general value of heuristics like that developed by Myers and has shown how others (e.g., simply trying all combinations of maximum and minimum values) are ineffective. It has also established how to select a small, efficient, and effective set of test points. Once a domain is defined, **domain selection criteria** are applied to choose test points. Jeng and Weyuker's simplified criteria [Jeng+94] are used here.

Although Myers's equivalence class heuristic has been applied to object-oriented systems [Firesmith 92, Turner+95, Graham+94, Siegel 96, Jacobson+92], these test suites suffer from the general inadequacies of the heuristic. Even available domain testing models, however, would be incomplete. Research

---

7. Examples of nonpartition testing include generation or selection of test inputs by a pseudorandom algorithm (in effect, a single partition) and mutation testing, where a test suite itself is evaluated by adding bugs to code.

8. Roughly a dozen key research papers have analyzed, refined, and extended this approach since the publication of White and Cohen's paper [White+78]. A summary of this research and issues in advanced domain analysis can be found in [Beizer 90] and [Beizer 95].

on domain analysis has been confined to primitive data types: integer, floating-point, string, and Boolean. Although such studies are still useful in object-oriented systems when primitive data types are commonly used, application of domain models to complex data types (classes) has not been considered. For object-oriented implementations, both externally determined inputs (e.g., message parameters) and the state of the object under test must be considered in defining a partition. This section reviews the basic domain testing approach and shows how to apply it to objects.

Domain Analysis

A **domain** is the set of all inputs to the IUT. A **subdomain** is a partition of the domain defined by **boundary conditions**, which are Boolean expressions on the input variables of the implementation under test. At the class scope, the operands in a boundary condition are message parameters and instance variables. Boundary expression operands can also be specified at higher levels of abstraction by using OCL types or any other testable abstraction. A subdomain is similar to a state, in that it is a set of variable value combinations. Unlike a state, however, a subdomain does not necessarily determine sequential behavior.

The domain testing fault model is that the IUT has incorrectly implemented a boundary. For example, suppose that a collection class is supposed to hold a maximum of 4096 items. The IUT allows 4095 items, but rejects 4096 because an incorrect relational operator was coded: (n < 4096), instead of (n<= 4096). Figure 10.18 shows four general kinds of domain faults.

A domain test suite is developed by **domain analysis**:

1. Identify constraints for all input variables (boundaries).
2. Select test values for each variable in each boundary.
3. Select test values for variables not given in the boundary.
4. Determine expected results for these inputs.

The results are represented in the **domain matrix**, which will be explained shortly. This procedure can be applied to any set of variables, at any scope (see *Invariant Boundaries* and *Nonmodal Class Test* for more examples). Suppose we want to develop test cases for the parameters of the following C++ function:

```
void aFunction(int x, float y, Stack aStack) { /* . . . */ };
```

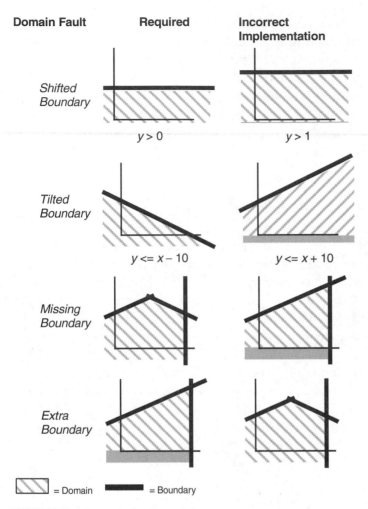

FIGURE 10.18   Domain fault model.

The float type is assumed to provide precision to six decimal digits. The specification for aFunction requires that input parameters meet this assertion:

```
assert(  (y >= 1.0 ) &&      // condition 1
         (x <= 10 ) &&       // condition 2
         (y <= 10.0) &&      // condition 3
         (x > 0 ) &&         // condition 4
         (y <= 14.0 - x) &&  // condition 5
         (! aStack.isFull)   // condition 6
);
```

Each condition defines a boundary, as shown in Figure 10.19. The effect of condition 6 is not shown in this drawing. It would add another dimension with two values: true, aStack.isFull(), and false, !aStack.isFull().

On, Off, In, and Out

All domain testing selection criteria use on points and off points [White+78]. An **on point** is a value that lies on a boundary. An **off point** is a value not on a boundary. An **in point** is a value that satisfies all boundary conditions and does not lie on a boundary. An **out point** is a value that satisfies no boundary

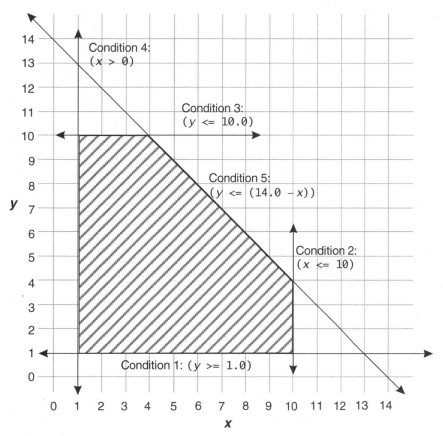

FIGURE 10.19   Input domain of aFunction.

condition and does not lie on any boundary. The kind of boundary must be considered to choose on and off points correctly.

- An **open boundary** condition is defined by a strict inequality operator— for example, a > b or c < 500. The on point of an open boundary in- cludes the boundary value, but makes the boundary condition false. Condition 4 (x > 0) is open and the on point is 0.
- A **closed boundary** condition is defined by an operator that includes strict equality—for example, a >= b or c == 500. An on point of a closed boundary includes the boundary value and makes the condi- tion true. For example, 10.0 is the on point of (y <= 10.0). An off point of a closed boundary condition makes it false—for example, a value of 10.00001 for condition 3—and must lie outside the domain. Boundaries defined by Boolean variables, membership functions, state invariants, and strict equality (==) are also closed.

That the on and off points of a closed boundary are in different places than those of an open boundary may seem somewhat counterintuitive. The COOOOI mnemonic [Beizer 90] helps to remember the off point rule. If the boundary is Closed, an Off point is *Outside* the domain. If the boundary is Open, an Off point is *Inside* the domain.

I express boundary conditions as assertions, which yields a similar mne- monic. If the asserted boundary is Closed, an Off point makes the assertion *False*. If the asserted boundary is Open, an Off point makes the assertion *True*. This yields the mnemonic COFOOT for the off point rule: closed, off, false; open, off, true. On and off points for conditions 1, 2, 3, and 4 are given in Table 10.5.

◇ Boundary Conditions with Two or More Variables

If a boundary condition uses two or more variables, then on and off points can be found by solving the related equation. Generally, if there are k independent variables (variables on the right side), there are k on points. For example, con- dition 5 involves two variables. We find the on points by solving the equation implied by this condition. Plug in any combination of independent variables (x in this example) that makes the assertion (boundary equation) true without making any other condition false. Try the midpoints of the independent vari- able(s) first.

TABLE 10.5   On and Off Points for aFunction

	Condition	Off Point Rule	On Point	Off Point
1	y >= 1.0	Closed, Off, False	1.000000	0.999999
2	x <= 10	Closed, Off, False	10	11
3	y <= 10.0	Closed, Off, False	10.00000	10.00001
4	x > 0	Open, Off, True	0	1
5	y < = 14.0 - x	Closed, Off, False	7.000000	7.000001
6	!aStack.isFull	Closed, Off, False	32676	32767

$$y = 14.0 - x$$
$$y = 14.0 - 7$$
$$y = 7, x = 7$$

Any value for x in the range 5 to 10 will work, but values outside this range violate another boundary.

Only one off point is used. We find it by choosing a centroid point[9] for the independent variable(s), solving with this value, and then changing the solution just enough to cause the condition to become false. We change this solution by the minimum possible to make the condition false while holding the values of independent variables constant. Here, we add 0.00001, the smallest possible increment for y. The off point values are $y + 0.00001 = 7.00001$ for $x = 7$.

Modeling the Domain of Objects

Finding off, on, in, and out points for primitive data types is straightforward, as the preceding examples show. But what about complex types—that is, classes?

Input domains of object-oriented implementations typically include objects that are instances of complex data types. Clearly, a domain model for object-oriented software must include objects. The foregoing techniques do not apply, however, when domain boundaries are defined with complex classes. We cannot focus on a single variable of such objects; instead, we must consider at least all the server objects' interface variables. This approach would lead to many test values, instead of just one on-off pair. Even if we did elaborate these pairs,

---

9. The centroid of two points is a point midway between high and low, in the center of the triangle formed by three points, and so on.

we would not necessarily focus on the values of the object (its abstract states) that matter most for correct functioning of the client class.

From a domain perspective, some classes are essentially the same as primitive types. For example, a Money object has one abstract state (a valid amount) and many concrete primitive states (each amount within the legal range). Thus Money is a scalar type whose domain boundaries can be modeled in the same way as primitive types.

Other classes are not so simple. A state abstraction can be used to bridge the gap between objects and primitive data types. We can model the required and excluded state(s) of any object with an abstract state invariant, which is a function that evaluates a state invariant expression and returns *true* or *false*. Similar functions commonly appear in class interfaces (e.g., isOpen(), isClosed(), and so on). An abstract state is defined only for objects visible at the class interface (see Section 7.3, The FREE State Model, for a detailed discussion of abstract state and state invariants.) We can include the abstract state invariant(s) for complex objects in the domain model by treating each state invariant as a domain boundary. Checking for the required state reduces to checking a Boolean boundary condition. This approach respects the encapsulation of constituent objects, simplifies test design, and focuses test design on relationships that determine the behavior of the class under test. It targets faults where an incorrect action is triggered by an incorrect evaluation of abstract state: For example, the IUT could fail to observe this condition if a guard check was missing or branched the wrong way.

For example, the input domain of aFunction requires that aStack is not full. This situation is modeled by the abstract state invariant function !aStack.isFull(). Objects of class Stack may be in one of three states: *empty*, *loaded*, or *full*. The abstract state invariants are as follows:

empty	(Stack.size( ) == 0)
loaded	(Stack.size( ) > 0 && Stack.size( ) < MAXSTACK)
full	(Stack.size( ) == MAXSTACK)

On and off points for each state are determined by choosing test values for the object that should satisfy the boundary condition state invariant.

• *Abstract state on points.* An **abstract state on point** is a state such that the smallest possible change in any state variable would produce a state change. For the same reasons that we select on points at the edge of a primitive type boundary, we should select state values that border on another state. For example, in the *loaded* state with 32,766 items, adding one more item results in the *full* state. Alternatively, popping the last item results in the *empty* state.

- *Abstract state off points.* A **focus state** is the state specified in a domain boundary. An **abstract state off point** is a valid state that (1) is not the focus state and (2) differs from the focus state by the smallest change that results in a different state. For example, suppose that the focus state is *loaded*. If the number of elements is zero or the maximum, then Stack cannot be in the loaded state. That is, we could move the object to the *loaded* state by adding the smallest possible increment of Stack.size in either case. The off state of *empty* is *loaded*; the off-states of *loaded* are *empty* and *full*; the off state of *full* is *loaded*. This approach assumes that server classes are robust and will not permit self-corruption. If this assumption is unwarranted, corrupt state off points can be added to the list.

- *Abstract state in points.* An **abstract state in point** is any value combination that places an object of the class in a given abstract state and is not an abstract state on point.

Table 10.6 shows these points for Stack, expressed as the number of items in the stack and assuming MAXSTACK = 32767.

Excluding classes with a single abstract state, any state must have at least one other resultant state, there are always two or more ways to define on and off points for abstract states. Which should we use? If we require trying all possible on and off points, there will be twice the number of transitions in the state model of (each) complex object as in the input domain. Our fault model, however, is that the IUT fails to use the required state correctly. Thus any wrong

TABLE 10.6 In, On, and Off Points for Stack

State	Possible Transitions	In Point	On Point	Off Point
Empty	Loaded	0	0	1
Loaded	Empty	1 < x < 32766	1	0
	Full	1 < x < 32766	32766	32767
Full	Loaded	32767	32767	32766

state will do. Instead of picking all possible on and off points, we can therefore pick one of each. Like any criteria, this set can miss bugs. If higher confidence is warranted, then one on point and one off point for each transition should be identified and included in the test suite.

Finally, the following details should be considered to develop a complete model:

- The abstract state invariant model applies to polymorphic instance and message variables. Boundaries are specified for the most abstract class that is accepted by the IUT. If an object of a specific class is required, a condition should be added to check the type. In Java this task can be accomplished by using reflection methods in the assertion; in C++, it can be realized via RTTI services.
- The complete input domain of a method is defined by the method's flattened preconditions and the flattened class invariant. See the discussion of the pattern in *Percolation* (Chapter 17) for the analysis to develop flattened assertions.
- A client class may place additional restrictions on the server object's state invariant. These restrictions, as expressed in the client's invariant (not the server's invariant), are the focus of testing for the client. For example, although a `Stack` object may contain from zero to 32,767 items, we might require that a particular `Stack` object can have at most 4096 items. This situation would be modeled by a client-specific boundary condition—for example, `Stack.size( ) < MyMAXSTACK`.
- Abstract state invariants (for a client) are not defined in terms of the implementation invariants of the server classes.

The One-by-One Selection Criteria

The 1×1 ("one-by-one") domain testing strategy calls for one on point and one off point for each domain boundary. Earlier domain selection techniques required time-consuming analysis, sometimes produced many test cases, were limited to programs containing only linear boundary conditions (or that could be so interpreted) and required variables defined over continuous domains. The 1×1 criteria drops these restrictions, but is generally as effective as these techniques and more efficient [Jeng+94]. With the addition of the abstract state model and selection criteria developed earlier, 1×1 is applicable to the full range of data types used in object-oriented programming.

The selection rules for on and off points are straightforward.

- *One on point and one off point for each relational condition.* One of each type of point is selected for each boundary condition having a relational operator. These points are to be as close as possible.[10] With *n* relational boundary conditions, the test suite will have 2*n* test cases.

- *One on point and two off points for each strict equality condition.* If a boundary condition requires strict equality on a scalar type—for example, (x == 10)—then two off points are required to reveal incorrect operator bugs. For example, suppose that the condition is incorrectly implemented as (x >= 10). Test points of 10 (on) and 9 (off) would not reveal this bug, as both will produce the expected result. An additional off point of 11 is needed to reveal the bug. Again, the points should be as close as possible. Sometimes, the second off point may be infeasible. With *e* strict equality boundary conditions, there will be 2*n* + 3*e* test cases.

- *One on point and one off point for each nonscalar type.* The boundaries of unordered data types like strings, Booleans, enumerations, and complex numbers are closed and binary. That is, the variable either conforms to the condition or it does not. The on point is a value that makes the condition true and the off point makes it false. Test values are chosen to meet inclusion conditions, not relative magnitude. The analysis used to develop abstract state test points may be applied. The difference between on and off values should be minimized. For example, choose the on and off points for a string type so that they differ by only a single character.

- *One on point and at least one off point for each abstract state invariant.* When an object of a complex type participates in an input domain, its bound-

---

10. With primitive scalar types, "as close as possible" must be interpreted for the IUT. It is generally ±1 for integers. It is the smallest supported decimal fraction for fixed decimal types and scaled integers. With floating-point numbers, the picture is more complex, as both magnitude and precision must be considered. Hardware implementation matters, as does the compiler's treatment of available hardware formats [Goldberg 91]. For example, the ANSI C standard requires a minimum magnitude of $1.0E{-}37$ to $1.0E{+}37$. Usually, at least six decimal digits of precision are supported. The ANSI C++ standard requires that this level be met or exceeded and requires the compiler to define its limits in the standard library <limits>. Assuming the minimum C standard, then, the smallest increment of a float type is $1.0E{-}37$. Note that some decimal types (e.g., the OpenStep NSDecimal class) are implemented in software as floating-point numbers.

TABLE 10.7   Adjacent Domains

	Boundary Condition	On	Off
1	$p >= 20$	20	19
2	$p < 20$	20	21

aries are modeled as abstract state invariants. The condition for the invariant is made true once (the on point) and false once (the off point).

• *One on point and one off point for nonlinear boundaries.* Although advanced domain modeling techniques have been developed to choose values for nonlinear boundaries, 1×1 testing does not require special analysis to choose nonlinear on-off pairs.

• *Don't repeat identical tests for adjacent subdomains.* Adjacent subdomains share boundaries, so it may be possible to test two or more boundaries with a single test. Table 10.7 shows a simple example. Instead of four test points (19, 20, 20, 21), only three are necessary (19, 20, 21). The output action for condition 1 is expected for inputs 20 and 21; the action for condition 2 is necessary for input 19. A more extensive example of adjacent subdomains appears in Section 6.5.7, Nonbinary Variable Domain Analysis.

The Domain Test Matrix

Although the on and off points in Table 10.5 meet the 1×1 selection criteria, more work is needed before they can be used as test cases. Expected results and in point values for the other variables must be supplied. The **domain matrix** provides a convenient representation for development of the complete test suite. Figure 10.20 shows how variables, conditions, on/off/in points, and test cases are arrayed within it.

Each column of values is a test case. Only one on or off point appears in a test case. These values fall on the diagonal of the matrix. In points are generated for all other variables in each test case. They are chosen after the on or off point is determined. In points can be developed by guessing, by analyzing the situation, or by using a pseudorandom selection algorithm. Try to avoid repeating in point values, as they will increase the chance of revealing an unexpected bug. Figure 10.21 shows the complete test suite for `aFunction` in a domain matrix.

The table below represents the Domain Matrix shown in Figure 10.20.

Variable/ Condition Type			Test Cases																	...	T-5	T-4	T-3	T-2	T-1	T
			1	2	3	4	5	6	7	8	9	10	11	12	13	14	15	16	17							
x1	c11	On																								
		Off																								
	c12	On																								
		Off																								
	...	On																								
		Off																								
	c1m	On																								
		Off																								
	Typical	In																								
x2	c21	On																								
		Off																								
	c22†	On																								
		Off																								
		Off																								
	...	On																								
		Off																								

†Strict equality conditions require two off points.

FIGURE 10.20 Domain Matrix.

continued

413

Test Cases

Variable/Condition Type		1	2	3	4	5	6	7	8	9	10	11	12	13	14	15	16	17	...	T-5	T-4	T-3	T-2	T-1	T
c2m	On																								
	Off																								
	Typical In																								
...																									
xn	cn1 On																								
	Off																								
	... On																								
	Off																								
	cnm On																								
	Off																								
	Typical In																								
Expected Result																									

Key: ☐ = Test value required, ▨ = No test value

FIGURE 10.20 *Continued.*

414

Variable	Boundary Condition	Type	1	2	3	4	5	6	7	8	9	10	11	12
										Test Cases				
x	>0	On	0											
		Off		1										
	<= 10	On			10									
		Off				11								
	Typical	In					2	3	4	5	6	7	8	9
y	> = 1.00000	On					1.00000							
		Off						0.99999						
	<= 10.00000	On							10.0000					
		Off								10.0001				
	y <= 14.0 −x	On									7.00000			
		Off										7.00001		
	Typical	In	7.97320	1.78386	8.11532	6.14728							3.33333	5.11205
aStack	!isFull( )	On											32766	
		Off												32767
	Typical	In	25	18432	4096	1	2	732	32718	9183	3718	20501		
Expected Result			x	✓	✓	x	✓	x	✓	x	✓	x	✓	x

Key: x = IUT rejects this input, ✓ = IUT accepts this value and produces correct output; Stack values are size of stack.

FIGURE 10.21 Domain Matrix for aFunction.

415

10.3   Method Scope Test Design Patterns

Although a method cannot be tested apart from its class, test cases are applied by sending messages to methods. Testing a class requires exercising all of its methods, and a class test suite is therefore necessarily composed of method tests. The design of method scope tests is fundamental to testing object-oriented software. In some situations, we may want to develop tests only for individual methods. Thus method scope test design becomes necessary.

10.3.1   Functional Cohesion

A method implements a fragment of a class contract. The responsibility of a single method is called its *function*. "Function" is used here in a mathematical sense: a well-defined input/output relationship. This abstraction supports test suite development and does not refer to a specific programming language construct. A method may implement one or more functions. The unity of purpose (or lack thereof) among two or more functions is termed **functional cohesion.**

Functional cohesion is a qualitative classification of commonality of purpose among parts of a software module [Yourdon+79]. Strong cohesion results when all parts of a module support a common goal. Weak cohesion results when the parts of a module serve several unrelated goals, have a vague or ambiguous reason for inclusion, or serve goals unrelated to the software requirements. Cohesion is also referred to as *module strength*.

The object-oriented programming paradigm encourages functional cohesion in methods, but can easily lead to strange dependencies. *Connascence* extends the idea of independence for the additional dimensions of object-oriented programing [Page-Jones 92, Page-Jones 95]. Classes A and B are connascent if at least one change could be made to A that would necessitate a change to B so as to preserve overall correctness. Eliminate any unnecessary connascence and then minimize connascence across encapsulation boundaries by maximizing connascence within encapsulation boundaries. The law of Demeter encourages a similar result by defining undesirable interclass usages and argument references [Lieberherr 89].

10.3.2   Method Scope Integration

At method scope, the parts that must interoperate are statements. Method scope integration therefore focuses on relationships among statements. Getting a clean compile is the first operability threshold.[11] Because our code must rely on many implicit, dynamic relationships among statements, we must have some assurance that these relationships have been exercised. In theory, we cannot be sure that all such relationships are correct in all possible cases without formal proof or exhaustive testing. In practice, we must settle for more modest goals. Code coverage analysis provides feasible, nonarbitrary criteria for method scope integration.

10.3.3   The Patterns

Four method scope test design patterns are presented next. They correspond to the general kind of function performed by a method.

* *Category-Partition.* This test pattern may be used on any method or testable function at any scope.
* *Combinational Function Test.* This test pattern is appropriate for methods that implement complex selection algorithms, business rules, or similar case-based logic.
* *Recursive Function Test.* This test pattern is appropriate for methods that call themselves to implement a search, evaluate a self-referencing formula, or rely on a similar algorithm.
* *Polymorphic Message Test.* Use this pattern to augment the test suite for a client of a polymorphic server.

The specific steps in method scope test case design and execution are listed in Procedure 7.

Classes are not the only unit of compilation in C++, Objective-C, and Ada 95. These hybrid languages retain the ability to define non-object-oriented modules: functions in C++ and Objective-C, subprograms (packages, procedures, functions, and operators) in Ada 95. Method scope test design patterns and integration are applicable to these conventional modules as well.

---

11. Most compilers, interpreters, and IDEs have error-checking capabilities that are usually not activated with their default settings. A clean compilation here means that, besides no fatal translation errors, no warnings are produced when all checking options are enabled. If warning messages appear, correct the offending code or make sure that warnings can be safely ignored before running your tests.

1. Set, as needed, the parameters of the test message, class variables, global variables, and the virtual machine to the desired pretest state.

2. Set the object under test to the desired pretest state. (This step may involve sending messages to the OUT and possibly its server objects. Consider stubbing server classes if this step is too difficult.)

3. Send the test message from the driver to the MUT.

4. Code the driver to make as many post-test checks as possible—don't stop after the first no pass condition is found.

   a. Compare the values returned from the MUT to the expected result. If the returned values are not as expected, record it as a no pass test.

   b. Compare the state of the OUT to the expected state. If the state is not as expected, record it as a no pass test.

   c. If call-by-reference or call-by-result semantics are used, compare the state of the test message parameters to the expected state. If the parameters are not as expected, record it as a no pass test.

   d. Catch all exceptions. If an exception is expected, determine that it is correct. If no exception is expected or an incorrect exception is raised, record it as a no pass test.

   e. If an assertion violation is expected, determine that it is correct. If no assertion violation is expected, record it as a no pass test.

   f. If necessary, compare the resultant state of class variables, global variables, and the virtual machine to the expected values. If not as expected, record it as a no pass test.

5. If any no pass condition occurs, diagnose and correct the problem. Try to rule out an incorrect test first. Rebuild the test package with the corrected CUT and corrected test driver. Rerun the test package to verify that the fix is correct and has not introduced any new bugs.

Testing Tip: Don't forget to log the time you spend (this effort will help calibrate future test budgets). Track the results of no pass tests, note any bugs found, and be sure to retest bug fixes.

Procedure 7   Basic Method Scope Test Procedure

Category-Partition

Intent

Design method scope test suites based on input/output analysis.

Context

How can we develop a test suite to exercise the functions implemented by a single method? A method may implement one or several functions, each of which may present a different level of cohesion. Even cohesive functions can have complex input/output relationships. A systematic technique to identify functions and exercise each input/output relationship is needed.

The Category-Partition pattern is appropriate for any method that implements one or more independent functions. For methods or functions that lack cohesion, the constituent responsibilities should be identified and modeled as separate functions. This approach is qualitative and may be worked by hand. It provides systematic, implementation-independent coverage of method scope responsibilities.

If the method selects one of many possible responses or has many constraints on parameter values, consider using the *Combinational Function Test* pattern.

Fault Model

The Category-Partition pattern assumes that faults are related to value combinations of message parameters and instance variables and that these faults will result in missing or incorrect method output. Offutt and Irvine found that a Category-Partition approach revealed 23 common C++ coding blunders [Offutt+95]. Faults that are manifested only under certain sequences or that corrupt instance variables hidden by the MUT's interface, however, may not be revealed by such tests.

Strategy

Test Model

The Category-Partition pattern was first introduced as a general-purpose, black box test design technique for software modules with parameterized functions

[Ostrand+88]. Development of a method scope Category-Partition test suite is illustrated with the C++ member function `List::getNextElement( )`. This member function returns successive elements of a `List` object. A position in a list of m elements is established at the nth element by other member functions. A call to `getNextElement( )` returns the element $n + 1$. Successive calls to `getNextElement( )` return the elements $n + 2$, $n + 3$, and so on. If no position has been established by a previous operation or if the previous position no longer exists due to an intervening change or delete, a `NoPosition` exception is thrown. An `EmptyList` exception is thrown if the list is empty.

Test Procedure

The test suite is produced in seven steps, as summarized in Procedure 8.

1. Identify the testable functions of the MUT.   A well-designed method implements only a few cohesive functions, which are typically suggested by its name and parameters. A method may implement several functions. Other functions may be side effects of the primary function. For example, the current position of a `List` object may be incremented as a side effect of returning the next element. A poorly designed or poorly named method may support several unrelated functions or may produce obscure side effects. In any case, the tester must tease out all of the independently testable functions in the MUT. A function is considered independently testable if it meets three criteria:

- It can be invoked by setting message parameters to particular values and sending a message to the method.
- Its output can be observed by inspecting the values returned by the method, indirectly by using other class methods, or by using an invasive inspector.
- Its output can be differentiated from the output of another function or an incorrect function.

Clearly, testability is improved when methods are explicitly designed and coded to be testable functions.

The primary function of `getNextElement( )` is to return the next element in the list. It has two secondary functions: (1) to keep track of the last position and wrap it from last to first, and (2) to throw the `NoPosition` and `EmptyList` exceptions if appropriate. Each of these functions may be controlled and observed independently.

2. Identify the input and output parameters of each testable function.   At method scope, method interface arguments and abstract class state(s) determine the function's response. Class variables, globals, and system environmental variables should be modeled, if they can influence the output or may be changed by the function call. For example, the inputs for `List::getNextElement( )` are the position of the last referenced element and the list itself. The outputs are the element returned

1.   Identify the functions of the MUT.

2.   Identify the input and output parameters of each function.

3.   Identify categories for each input parameter.

4.   Partition each category into choices.

5.   Identify constraints on choices.

6.   Generate test cases by enumerating all choice combinations.

7.   Develop expected results for each test case using an appropriate oracle.

Procedure 8   Method Scope Category-Partition Test Design

by the member function and the incremented position cursor. None of these test parameters appears in the formal argument list of the member function.

3. Identify categories for each input parameter. Categories do not overlap and must result in distinctly different output. A **category** is a subset of parameter values (1) that determines a particular behavior or output and (2) whose values are not included in any other category. Categories are conceptually similar to Myers' equivalence classes [Myers 79] and Marick's C++ test requirements [Marick 95]. Table 10.8 shows the categories for the getNextElement( ) parameters.

4. Partition each category into choices. A **choice** is a specific test value for a category. Any reasonable criteria may be used to make choices. Choices for primitive types can be selected by suspicions, past bugs, or the *Invariant Boundaries* pattern.

Table 10.9 shows choices for the getNextElement( ) parameters. These choices reflect the premises of the basic domain fault model: (1) the implementation of boundary conditions is error prone and (2) if a function works correctly in one nonboundary situation, it usually works correctly for all nonboundary situations. To increase the variation in our test suite, in-range values for m and n are chosen by a random number generator. Redundant input for choices Full, Maximum Size, and Last positions have been dropped.

Choices should include both legal and illegal values, as shown for get-NextElement( ), so as to exercise error and exception handling. "A well-defined partition should include some input classes that consist solely of error inputs" [Balcer+89, 211].

5. Identify constraints on choices. Some choices may be mutually exclusive or inclusive. With getNextElement( ) parameters, for example, an undefined position pre-

TABLE 10.8 Categories for getNextElement( )

Parameter	Category
Position of the last referenced element	nth element Special cases
State of the list	m-elements Special cases

TABLE 10.9   Categories and Choices for `getNextElement( )`

Parameter	Category	Choices
Position of the last referenced element	nth element	$n = 2$ n = some $x > 2$, $x <$ Max n = Max
	Special cases	Undefined First Last, $n <$ Max
State of the list	m-elements	m = some $x > 2$, $x <$ Max
	Special cases	Empty Singleton Full (m = Max)

cludes a response for all states of a `List`. This exclusion is implemented by the `NoPosition` exception. Exclusions can be structural or practical. See Section 6.2.4, Don't Care, Don't Know, Can't Happen, for a discussion of exclusions. Choices or combinations of choices can be excluded for practical reasons—for example, the time, cost, or complexity of generating or evaluating a combination is prohibitive.

6. Generate test cases by enumerating all choice combinations.   The test cases are identified by generating the cross-product of all the choices. Mutually inclusive or exclusive choices will result in some test cases being dropped from the cross-product set. With categories of 6 and 4 choices, there are 24 = 6 × 4 test cases. Table 10.10 shows the test suite formed by the cross-product of `getNextElement( )` choices.

7. Develop expected results for each test case using an appropriate oracle.   Table 10.10 gives the expected results for each `getNextElement( )` test case. These values were determined by analysis and manually simulating the method.

Automation

A Category-Partition test suite may be implemented with any of the API test Harness patterns presented in Chapter 19. It is particularly well suited to *Incremental Testing Framework* because it offers a systematic, yet simple way to design method scope test cases.

TABLE 10.10   Test Suite for getNextElement( )

	Function Parameters/Choices		Expected Result		
Test Case	Position of the Last Referenced Element	State of the List	Returned	Exception	Position of the Last Referenced Element
1	undefined	empty	null	NoPosition	undefined
2	undefined	singleton	null	NoPosition	undefined
3	undefined	$m = \text{rand}(x)$	null	NoPosition	undefined
4	undefined	full	null	NoPosition	undefined
5	first	empty	null	ListEmpty	undefined
6	first	singleton	first		first
7	first	$m = \text{rand}(x)$	second element		second element
8	first	full	second element		second element
9	$n = 2$	empty	null	ListEmpty	undefined
10	$n = 2$	singleton	null	NoPosition	undefined
11	$n = 2$	$m = \text{rand}(x)$	item $n + 1$		item $n + 1$
12	$n = 2$	full	item $n + 1$		item $n + 1$
13	$n = \text{rand}(x)$	empty	null	ListEmpty	undefined
14	$n = \text{rand}(x)$	singleton	null	NoPosition	undefined
15	$n = \text{rand}(x)$	$m = \text{rand}(x)$	item $n + 1$		item $n + 1$
16	$n = \text{rand}(x)$	full	item $n + 1$		item $n + 1$
17	Max	empty	null	ListEmpty	undefined
18	Max	singleton	null	NoPosition	undefined
19	Max	$m = \text{rand}(x)$	item $n + 1$		item $n + 1$
20	Max	full	item $n + 1$		item $n + 1$
21	Last	empty	null	ListEmpty	undefined
22	Last	singleton	null	NoPosition	undefined
23	Last	$m = \text{rand}(x)$	first item		first item
24	Last	full	first item		first item

Entry Criteria

✓ Small Pop.

Exit Criteria

✓ Every combination of choices is tested once. Suppose we have 3 choices for variable *a*, 7 choices for variable *b*, and 2 choices for variable *c*. A full test suite then requires $3 \times 7 \times 2 = 42$ test cases.

✓ If the method under test can throw exceptions for incorrect input or other anomalies, the test suite should force each exception at least once. The inclusion of "illegal" values or combinations in the choices should exercise all exceptions. If they do not, add tests to force all exceptions.

✓ Executing the test suite should exercise at least all branches in the method under test. Verify this coverage by checking for method scope branch coverage.

Consequences

The Category-Partition pattern is a general-purpose, nonquantitative, and straightforward technique. It does not require advanced analysis or automated support. Nevertheless, identification of categories and choices is a subjective process. Skilled and novice testers may identify different categories and choices. Individual blind spots may reduce effectiveness. Bugs that are manifested only under certain sequences of messages to other methods or that corrupt instance variables hidden by the MUT's interface may not be revealed.

The size of a Category-Partition test suite is the product of the number of choices, minus the number of combinations excluded by constraints. It can result in many test cases for even moderately complex methods. For example, suppose a function has seven parameters: three formal arguments, two significant class variables, and two significant encapsulated attributes. If we follow the weak 1×1 domain selection to define both categories and choices (one on point and one off point for each parameter), we have $2^7 = 128$ test cases.

If the parameters have more than two interesting choices, we could easily generate thousands of test cases. This number may be practically infeasible. The *Invariant Boundaries* pattern may be used to produce a smaller test suite whose size is a sum of the number of choices plus one, rather than the product.

With proper attention to interface details, a superclass Category-Partition method test suite may be reused to test an overriding subclass method. For example, the getNextElement( ) test suite could be repeated for List subclasses such as PersonList, EmployeeList, and ProgrammerList, or it could be used to test a List template instantiated with type parameters like integer, string, float, date, and money. The level of reusability depends on the extent to which the class contract follows the LSP for subclasses and parameterized types.

Known Uses

Elements of the Category-Partition pattern appear in nearly all black box test design strategies—for example, [Myers 79, Marick 95, Beizer 95]. An automated test tool for procedural code that supports Category-Partition approach is presented in [Balcer+89]. A Z-based approach to automating the Category-Partition model is presented in [Laycock 92].

A study of manually developed Category-Partition test suites for a small C++ system found 55 out of 75 inserted faults. The inserted faults were selected to represent common C++ coding errors. Of 20 faults not found by the Category-Partition test suite, 19 were memory leaks and 1 was masked by a test tool initiation sequence [Offutt+95].

Combinational Function Test

Intent

Design a test suite for behaviors selected according to combinations of state and/or message values.

Context

When a method selects one of many distinct actions based on many combinations of message parameters and instance variables, how can we choose input combinations to exercise the selection logic adequately? Other methods in the class may accept distinct cases or values for the decision parameters. The MUT delegates to other classes according to combinations of these values. For example,

- In class `Shipment`, the `assignCarrier` method determines which carrier to use for a shipment based on the shipment's weight, size, material type, and maximum transit time.
- In class `ShadedPolygon`, the `render` method delegates to one of several rendering algorithms based on parameters for an illumination model, transparency, output device, and response time constraint.
- A Boolean accessor method returns true or false based on object state, and this response is determined by checking value combinations of three or more instance variables.
- A method implements a business rule modeled by a decision table or decision tree. For example, a credit-scoring model is used to select customers to generate junk mail solicitations.

Fault Model

Common coding errors that lead to faults in an implementation of combinational responsibilities include the following:

- Incorrect value assigned to a decision variable.
- Incorrect or missing operator in a predicate.
- Incorrect or missing variable in a predicate.

- Incorrect structure in a predicate (dangling else, a misplaced semicolon, and so on).

- Incorrect or missing default case.

- Incorrect or missing action(s).

- Extra action(s).

- Structural errors in a decision table implementation: falling through (a missing or incorrectly scoped `break` statement in a C++, Java, or Objective-C `switch` expression), or computing an incorrect value for an index or action selector.[12]

- An incorrect type or incorrect value in an object that represents a condition or action that can result in a binding that produces an incorrect action. This situation can happen when variant conditions or actions are implemented as polymorphic methods instead of using a case or switch construct.

- Generic errors: wrong version, incorrect or missing specification item, ambiguous requirements, and so on.

Chapter 6 provides an extensive discussion of combinational faults. Some of the coding errors on this list can be found with tools like `lint`, code checkers, or compilers used with all warnings enabled. Many others, however, can escape this first line of defense, so testing is necessary.

Strategy

Test Model

Combinational functions may be modeled with a decision table. Chapter 6 provides a detailed discussion of decision table modeling and test generation. A **decision table** has **conditions** and **actions.** When all the conditions on one row of the decision table are true, the corresponding action is taken. Each unique set of conditions and actions (represented as a single row or column) is called a **variant.**

---

12. One of AT&T's infamous network outages of the early 1990s (January 15, 1990) was caused by a miscoded C `switch`: "there was a long 'do . . . while' construct, which contained a 'switch' statement, which contained an 'if' clause, which contained a 'break,' which was intended for the 'if' clause, but instead broke from the 'switch' statement" [Neumann 90]. The same code ran on most of the computers in the network. When the failure was first produced, it triggered recovery processing in the failing computer, which caused other computers to execute the same buggy code. The failure propagated to most of the computers in the network. The outage lasted nine hours, prevented more than 50 million calls from connecting, and cost AT&T $60 million [Peterson 95].

- The condition section lists the input combinations that result in different actions. The decision variables are the message arguments set by the client, the state of the object under test at method entry, class variables, global variables, and input arriving in the form of interrupts and exceptions.

- The action section represents the expected response of the method under test. An action may include a single point value returned by the method, a message(s) sent to another object, and the resultant state of the object under test. An action may be defined by any combination of these elements.

- The condition and action cells may contain only Boolean-type expressions. They may hold a point value expression such as `true`, `false`, `x == 1` or they may define a set of values, such as `(( x > 1 && (x < 100) && (x != 42))`.

- A separate functional variant is used for each combination of input variable values that results in a different action.

Table 10.11 shows a decision table that represents the requirements for the `Triangle` class presented in Chapter 1.

Test Procedure

At least one test should be developed for each action. If the decision variables are non-Boolean, then tests should be added to exercise their boundary conditions.

The determination of triangle type performed by class `Triangle` can be modeled as a combinational function. It meets our criteria for a combinational function: The order of inputs are irrelevant for determining the type and nontrivial Boolean relationships between input and output. The conditions in the `triangle` classification decision table can be used to select domain values, as shown in Table 10.12.

Automation

The test suite for a combinational function may be implemented with any of the API Test Harness patterns presented in Chapter 19. Test suites may be automatically produced from combinational test models. Several commercial tools provide this capability. A research system is described in [Weyuker+94].

If some or all of the decision variables are encapsulated by the class under test, try to vary the sequence in which modifier methods are used to create the test cases. For example, if the decision variables are x, y, and z, then use

TABLE 10.11   Decision Table Test Model for Reporter Methods in Class Triangle

	Variant										
	1	2	3	4	5	6	7	8	9	10	11
Condition											
a > 0	T	T	T	T	T	T	T	T	F	T	T
b > 0	T	T	T	T	T	T	T	T	T	F	T
c > 0	T	T	T	T	T	T	T	T	T	T	F
a + b > c	T	T	T	T	T	F	T	T	DC	DC	DC
a + c > b	T	T	T	T	T	T	F	T	DC	DC	DC
b + c > a	T	T	T	T	T	T	T	F	DC	DC	DC
a = b	T	T	F	F	F	DC	DC	DC	DC	DC	DC
b = c	T	F	T	F	F	DC	DC	DC	DC	DC	DC
a = c	T	F	F	T	F	DC	DC	DC	DC	DC	DC
Action											
isIsoceles( )	F	T	T	T	F	F	F	F	F	F	F
isScalene( )	F	F	F	F	T	F	F	F	F	F	F
isEquilateral( )	T	F	F	F	F	F	F	F	F	F	F

Key: DC = don't care, T = true, F = false

setx( ), sety( ), and setz( ) for the first run, use setz( ), setx( ), and sety( ) for the second run, use sety( ), setx( ), and setz( ) for the third run, and so on. The number of possible sequences increases exponentially with the number of such methods, so attempting all sequences may not be practical. The *Shuffled Define-Use* algorithm presented in **Nonmodal Class Test** can be adapted to generate these sequences.

Entry Criteria

   ✓ Small Pop. Method scope branch coverage typically establishes minimal executability.

Exit Criteria

   ✓ Produce every action at least once.

   ✓ If the method under test can throw exceptions for incorrect input or other anomalies, the test suite should force each exception at least once.

TABLE 10.12   Test Cases for Triangle Reporter Methods in Class `Triangle`

Variant		Test Case			Expected Result		
		a	b	c	`isEquilateral()`	`isIsosceles()`	`isScalene()`
Equilateral	1	1	1	1	T	F	F
	1	33	33	33	T	F	F
	1	100	100	100	T	F	F
Isosceles	2	3	2	2	F	T	T
	3	40	5	40	F	T	T
	4	100	100	99	F	T	T
Scalene	5	2	3	4	F	F	T
	5	6	3	4	F	F	T
	5	99	98	100	F	F	T
Not a	6	24	1	25	F	F	F
triangle	7	99	42	1	F	F	F
	8	2	1	1	F	F	F
	9	0	20	20	F	F	F
	10	16	0	16	F	F	F
	11	8	8	0	F	F	F
		0	0	0	F	F	F
		null	3	3	F	F	F

✓ The test suite for a combinational function should exercise at least every branch in the method under test. If all specified actions have been produced, an unexercised branch suggests a surprise action or test case omission. If a case (switch) statement is used, be sure that each case is covered (some coverage analyzers do not correctly interpret the number of branches in a case statement).

✓ Polymorphic binding is often used instead of a case statement to select an action. In this situation, branch coverage will not be meaningful. Instead, be sure that each possible binding is exercised at least once.

See Chapter 6 for more extensive responsibility coverage criteria.

Consequences

The Combinational Function Test pattern will reveal faults that result in an incorrect action in response to a test message. Faults that are manifested only under certain sequences of messages to other methods or that corrupt instance variables hidden by the MUT's interface may not be revealed. Variations in setup message sequences can be developed to offset this limitation.

Articulation of a decision table often reveals design errors and omissions, especially when no explicit specification was used to develop the method under test. Modeling and test generation are easy tasks with small decision tables. Automated support is useful with four to six decision variables and is necessary with seven or more variables. Advanced strategies and their fault-finding ability are analyzed in Chapter 6.

Known Uses

Combinational logic has been applied to hardware testing for more than 40 years and to software systems in many forms [Myers 79, Beizer 90, Weyuker +94, Marick 95]. Combinational logic selection techniques have been embedded in several commercially available testing tools. See also the Bibliographical Notes section in Chapter 6.

Recursive Function Test

Intent

Design a test suite for a method that calls itself, recursively.

Context

A recursive method sends messages to itself. Although any recursive algorithm has an equivalent loop, testing a recursive function is not equivalent to testing a loop. Recursion bugs can easily hide from low-coverage testing. How can we have high confidence that a responsibility implemented with a recursive method is correct?

The Recursive Function Test pattern is appropriate for methods that call themselves. Recursion is supported in Ada 95, C++, Eiffel, Java, and Objective-C. It is typically used for traversing treelike data structures and evaluating formulas defined in terms of themselves.[13] For example, computation of a factorial may be accomplished by recursive evaluation.

```
int factorial(int n) {

   assert(n >= 0);                     // Precondition

   if (n == 1) {
      return 1;                        // Base case
   }
   else {
      int fact = n * factorial(n-1);   // Recursive case

      assert (fact > 0);               // Postcondition
      return fact;
   }
}
```

The mechanics of a recursive method are implicit. The method must check the *base case* condition on each activation. When the base case condition is false, the method changes the argument values and calls itself again. Each call

---

13. The term "recursion" seems to have a certain cachet. It is often misused as an adjective meaning any repetitive human activity or software control structure. A function, method, or control structure is recursive only if it is self-referent and defines a base case. The LISP programming language was developed to study recursive functions. The formal definition of recursive functions is one of the basic results of computer science [Lewis+82, Krishnamurthy 85].

results in a new activation record, which is pushed onto the runtime activation stack. The activation record contains the state of the method at entry and other values necessary to support the call/return context swap. In effect, the set of values needed to evaluate the recursive function is stored in the activation stack. This is the *descent phase*.

When the base case condition is true, the method does the simplest calculation or assignment for the function and returns this value. A normal exit is taken, and the method does not call itself again. The most recent activation record is popped from the stack, causing the base case value to be bound to the function reference in the last call. The recursive case code segment executes, resulting in the value of the function evaluated on the base case to be bound to the next returned value. The call stack is popped in this manner until control returns to the client of the recursive method. This last return provides the value to be computed by the recursive algorithm. This is the *ascent phase*.

Fault Model

Recursive methods typically fail when unusual argument values are sent, insufficient stack space prevents a complete descent, or the base case is not reached or detected. Corruption of an unrelated object or a stack overflow exception is often the manifested failure. Typical recursion bugs include the following:

- Execution continues when the precondition (implicit or explicit) is violated for an undefined or illegal starting value.
- Execution continues when the precondition (implicit or explicit) is violated during the descent phase. A bug in the recursing expression could hide from the first m calls, and only be activated on call $m + 1$.
- The base case expression is omitted.
- The base case or recursive case expressions implement an incorrect algorithm.
- The base case condition is miscoded. It contains a wrong operator(s) (for example, = = instead of >=), or wrong operand(s).
- Incorrect or missing arguments are returned by the base case.
- Incorrect arguments appear in the recursive case message, or arguments are missing from it.
- Execution continues when the postcondition (implicit or explicit) is violated during the ascent phase.

- No explicit error or exception code exists or, if present, it does not correctly respond to exceptional conditions, such as stack overflow (an Ada 95 storage error).

A method that uses recursion to traverse a data structure (either an object or composite of primitive types) can fail in several ways:

- The method fails to recognize a corrupt data structure (e.g., broken pointers) or fails to handle an exception thrown by the object being traversed.
- The method incorrectly initializes or corrupts the data structure.
- The algorithm does not correctly traverse the data structure when it is instantiated with a boundary case (e.g., zero links on a node).
- The method's algorithm is inappropriate for the data structure.

Recursive calls may have space and time faults as well:

- The method's algorithm allows a recursion depth that exceeds available runtime memory or does not properly deal with varying runtime resources.
- The algorithm has nonlinear runtime, causing a real-time deadline to be missed under certain loading conditions and/or depth of recursion.

Strategy

Test Model

The test model for a recursive function should define the base case, the recursive case, the preconditions for the initial call, all descent-phase calls, and all ascent-phase bindings. It should be adapted from trusted algorithms (if available) as the implementation may be buggy. The test suite complements the fault model and should contain the following test cases:

- Attempt to violate the precondition in the initial call and at least once in the descent phase.
- Attempt to violate the postcondition at least once during an ascent phase.
- Test boundary cases on depth: zero, one, and maximum.
- Attempt to force all exceptions in the server objects or the environment on which the method depends.

- Use domain analysis to choose argument values for methods with multiple arguments: {0,0}, {1,1}, {a < b}, {a > b}, {a == b}, {a== max, b==max}, and so on. See section 10.2.4, Domain Testing Models, for details. The *Category-Partition* pattern may also be used to select such values.

- Use domain analysis on argument values and data structure states for recursive methods that traverse complex data structures (objectifed or naked). Use the *Invariant Boundaries* or *Category-Partition* pattern to identify interesting states of the data structure.

A trusted (but different) implementation of the same algorithm is the ideal oracle for a recursive function. If no trusted implementation exists, expected results must be worked by hand or simulated.

Automation

The test suite for a recursive method may be implemented with any of the API test harness patterns presented in Chapter 19. If a trusted implementation of the algorithm written in a different language exists, consider writing an object wrapper for it so that the expected result can be automatically produced and compared by the driver.

Entry Criteria

✓ Small Pop. Method scope branch coverage typically establishes minimal executability.

Exit Criteria

Statement or branch coverage can be achieved for many recursive methods with only two tests. Because most of the preceding bugs could easily hide from a branch cover, a more extensive test suite is indicated. The test suite should include at least one test for each of the following:

✓ Null case: zero recursions
✓ Singleton case: one recursion
✓ Maximal case: recursion to greatest allowed or feasible depth
✓ Attempted violation of the initial call precondition
✓ Attempted violation of the descent-phase precondition

✓ Attempted violation of the ascent phase postcondition

✓ *Invariant Boundaries* defined for values of multiple arguments and/or the states of data structures traversed by the algorithm

✓ Worst-case runtime given system load and maximum depth, if this method is to be used in performance-sensitive applications

Consequences

A test suite that provides the suggested coverage typically will not require more than two dozen test cases. This pattern will reveal faults that result in incorrect function evaluation for a given test message and state. Faults that are manifested only under certain sequences of messages to other methods or that corrupt instance variables hidden by the MUT's interface may not be revealed.

Known Uses

Some of these testing strategies are part of the oral tradition of LISP programming. General conditions for correct recursion are discussed in [Manna+78].

Polymorphic Message Test

Intent

Develop tests for a client of a polymorphic server that exercise all client bindings to the server.

Context

When a method under test sends messages to overridden methods of a polymorphic server, these messages may be bound to one of several subclasses in the server class hierarchy.

Although a polymorphic message is a single statement, it is an interface to many different methods. Just as we would not have high confidence in code for which only a small fraction of the statements or branches had been exercised, high confidence is not warranted for a client of a polymorphic server unless all the message bindings generated by the client are exercised. How can we verify that a client is using the polymorphic server class correctly and is constructing the message arguments that determine the method to be bound correctly?

Fault Model

Consider the C++ class `CertificateOfDeposit`, which is derived from `Savings`, which is in turn derived from `Account`.

```
class Account {
    virtual void listTransactions();
    // ...
};

class Savings: public Account  {
    virtual void listTransactions();
    // ...
};

class CertificateOfDeposit: public Savings {
    virtual void listTransactions();
    // ...
};
```

The virtual member function `listTransactions( )` is implemented in each class. Clients of `Account` need declare only the base class, but can operate on an object of any class in the hierarchy.

```
void reportHistory( Account *acct )
{
    // ...
    acct->listTransactions( );
    // ...
}
```

The compiler generates code that accomplishes the same result as the following multiway branch statement.

```
#include "Account.h"

extern void error( const char*, /* ... */ );

enum { ACCOUNT, SAVINGS, CERTDEPOSIT };

void reportHistory(Account *acct)
{
    // ...
    // List transactions by type of account
    switch( acct->accountType( ) )
    {
        case ACCOUNT:
            acct->listTransactions( );
            break;

        case SAVINGS:
            ((Savings*)acct)->listTransactions( );
            break;

        case CERTDEPOSIT:
            ((CertDeposit*)acct)->listTransactions( );
            break;

        default:
            error ("Invalid Account Type", acct->accountType( ) );
            break;
    // ...

}
```

Although the bugs associated with multiway branching (see *Combination Function Test*) are neatly avoided, a client can misuse a polymorphic object in at least three ways.

First, the client fails to meet all preconditions for all possible bindings of the server object. Even if a server class's preconditions are well formed,[14] its clients

---

14. A class hierarchy is well formed if it complies with the Liskov substitution priciple [Liskov+94, Martin 96]. See Chapter 17 for details.

can fail to meet a precondition for one or several subclasses. For example, suppose the minimum withdrawal for a MoneyMarketAccount object is $500.00, but any amount may be withdrawn from an Account object. A buggy client of Account would attempt to send a withdrawal message for less than $500.00 to a MoneyMarketAccount object. If the server class is not well formed, then it is more likely that errors will occur in design and coding of its clients.

Second, an unanticipated binding occurs because of unanticipated name resolution or incorrect construction of a pointer. The following code fragment shows how a buggy index calculation could result in a message being sent to the wrong object:

```
class Account {
    virtual void debit() {/* ... */};
}

class TimeDeposit: public Account {
    virtual void debit() {/* ... */};
}

class DemandDeposit: public Account {
    virtual void debit() {/* ... */};
}

Customer::report( ) {
    Account* accountList[MAXACCTS];

    int ix = tdIndex( );  // Compute an index
    accountList[ix] = new TimeDeposit;
    // ...
    ix = ddIndex( );      // Compute another index
    accountList[ix] = new DemandDeposit;
    // ...
    ix = tdIndex( );      // Select a DemandDeposit account
                          // Bug: wrong function used
    accountList[ix]->debit( );
    // ...
}
```

Third, the implementation of a server class is changed or extended. Although its clients have been tested and are unchanged, the client code is rendered inconsistent because of the server revision.

Each binding must be exercised to reach all possible interface faults. Sending any faulty message will suffice to activate an interface fault. Failure propagation will be achieved if an exception is produced, a server precondition is violated, or a result is produced that is inconsistent with the responsibilities of the MUT. The postcondition for the MUT (if present) may also propagate the failure.

The Polymorphic Message Test pattern focuses on bugs in a client's use of polymorphic servers. For a discussion of bugs in the server, see **Polymorphic Server Test**. The general fault hazards posed by polymorphism are discussed in Chapter 4.

Even if a statement that sends polymorphic messages is reached, a fault in it will not be triggered unless the faulty binding is present. Therefore it is necessary to exercise all such bindings to guarantee that incorrect client usage will be revealed.

Strategy

Test Model

The fault model requires that each possible binding of each polymorphic message in the MUT be exercised at least once. This situation may be modeled by expanding the method flow graph so that each polymorphic message is represented as a multiway branch. Figure 10.22 illustrates how an extended control flow graph is prepared.

Test Procedure

1. Determine the number of candidate bindings for each message sent to a polymorphic server object. Three bindings appear in the example.

2. Expand the segment with a multiway branch subgraph for each segment that has a polymorphic message.

3. Add two nodes for each binding: a branch node (representing the runtime binding logic) and a sequential node (representing the message send and return). The exit path of this node goes to the collector for the expanded graph.

4. Add a final, catch-all node to represent a runtime binding error. Reaching this node will test how the MUT responds to a runtime binding exception. For example, in a Smalltalk client, this node represents getting the "does not understand" message. The exit path of this node goes to the collector for the expanded graph.

Responsibility-based test design proceeds as for any other method.

Client

```
void reportHistory(Account *acct) {
  if !acct->isOpen( ) {
    acct->listTransactions( );
  }
  else {
    acct->debit(amount);
  }
}
```

Server

```
// class fragments

class Account {
  virtual void debit( );
  virtual void listTransactions( )
};

class TimeDeposit: public Account {
  virtual void debit( );
  virtual void listTransactions( )
};

class DemandDeposit: public Account
  virtual void debit( );
  virtual void listTransactions( )
};
```

Explict Flow Graph
of reportHistory( )

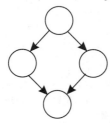

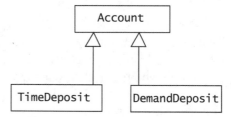

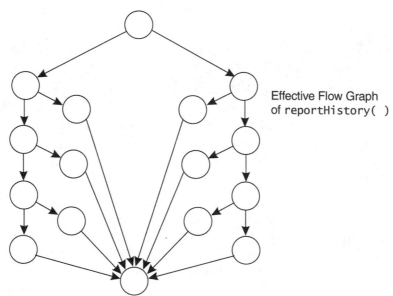

Effective Flow Graph
of reportHistory( )

FIGURE 10.22   Flow graph expansion for polymorphic messages.

Automation

It may be necessary to use stub methods in the server class to control the server's response. Any other appropriate class scope test driver may be used. Chapter 17 explains how we can reveal many bugs in a client by implementing contract assertions in a polymorphic server class. *Percolation* provides comprehensive checking of all bindings.

As this book goes to press, I am not aware of any commercially available coverage analyzers that will report the extent to which polymorphic bindings have been exercised. A partial solution is to instrument the server class so it writes a log record on entry to each method in the hierarchy.

Entry Criteria

  ✓ Small Pop. Method scope branch coverage typically establishes minimal executability.
  ✓ The server class should be either stabilized or stubbed before the interface tests are run. An attempt to verify client messages with a buggy server will not be effective.

Exit Criteria

  ✓ Achieve branch coverage of the extended message flow graph. That is, each binding to a polymorphic server should be exercised at least once.

Consequences

A test suite that covers the extended message flow graph will reveal many bugs in the client's usage of the server. This approach does not focus on other kinds of bugs and should therefore be used with an appropriate responsibility-based pattern. As all levels of the server class are exercised, some server bugs may also be revealed.

This pattern requires analysis of the server class hierarchy to determine all possible bindings. If the server class source or documentation is not available, this task cannot be done. Exercising all bindings will require more time and effort than simply achieving branch coverage.

Known Uses

McCabe's "Safe" strategy [McCabe 94] calls for exercising each polymorphic "call site" *once* after exercising all bindings of a server via a driver. Firesmith's *Delegation* pattern [Firesmith 96] suggests a similar approach.

10.4   Class Scope Test Design Patterns

Testing methods in isolation is neither practical nor prudent because intraclass interaction is not tested. Within a class, all instance variables are typically visible to all methods of the class. Intraclass visibility can contribute to errors just as global storage does in procedural languages. If we limit our testing to method scope, we can easily miss faults related to intraclass usages.

Method interactions are a common source of faults. A faulty method can be activated without a failure, masking production of an incorrect value or incorrect side effect. Subsequent activation of another method may result in a failure. Side effects and fault masking are thus likely sources of error [Hoffman 93, D'Souza+94]. Exercising methods in various sequences is necessary to reveal intraclass bugs.

10.4.1   Class Modalities

If all classes were alike, it might be enough to devise tests based on either message sequence or state. Some classes are designed to accept any message in any state, but others limit sequence based on past messages or current content. Consequently, effective testing must recognize these differences and support focused generation of test cases. The concept of *class modality* provides a testable characterization of these differences in state-based behavior. Modality is the result of constraints on both content (domain) and message sequence. Class behavior is an abstraction of the responses that objects of a class may make. A response is determined by the particular content of an object and a message, the prior sequence of messages accepted, or both. Class modality is therefore a general pattern of behavior. Modality is determined by the kind of constraints on message sequence or instance variable content.

Categorizing classes in terms of modality helps to focus on the most likely faults. The FREE state model provides a testable definition of a class domain integrated with the sequential constraints on class behavior from which we can easily generate a test sequence. Domain testing can be applied to classes and objects as integral wholes, instead of their composite parts. *Invariant Boundaries* provides a systematic technique for selecting state-based test cases for classes with undifferentiated sequential behavior. Four modalities are of interest for testing:

1. A *nonmodal* class does not impose any constraints on the sequence of messages accepted. For example, an object of a `DateTime` class will ac-

cept any interleaving of modifier/get messages. Classes that implement basic data types are often nonmodal.

2. A *unimodal* class has constraints on the acceptable sequence of messages, despite content. For example, an object of class TrafficSignal can accept the modifier message RedLightOn only after accepting a YellowLightOn message, GreenLightOn only after RedLightOn, and YellowLightOn only after GreenLightOn. Classes that provide application control are typically unimodal.

3. A *quasi-modal* class imposes sequential constraints on message acceptance that change with the content of the object.[15] For example, objects of class Stack will reject a push message if the stack is full, but accept it otherwise. Many container and collection classes are quasi-modal.

4. A *modal* class places both message and domain constraints on the acceptable sequence of messages. For example, an object of class Account will not accept a withdrawal message if the balance in an account is less than or equal to zero; a message to freeze the Account is accepted if the Account is not closed and not frozen. Classes that represent problem domain entities are often modal.

Table 10.13 shows how state constraints differ for the various modalities. Different kinds of state faults are therefore possible (or impossible) in each

TABLE 10.13 Domain and Sequence Constraints Define Class Modalities

State Constraint		Class Modality	
Domain	Sequence	Type	Example
No	No	Nonmodal	DateTime
No	Yes	Unimodal	TrafficLight
Yes	No	Quasi-modal	Stack
Yes	Yes	Modal	Account

15. The alliteration to Quasimodo (*The Hunchback of Notre Dame*, Victor Hugo) is accidental. A quasi-modal class behaves as if it is modal, but its method sequence constraints are indirectly related to the content of the object. For example, the number of items in a stack rather than the content of the items controls the behavior of a stack. The specific content of a stack is irrelevant for a test model. Instead, the parameters that describe the content are the focus of the test model. In contrast, the content of a modal class directly controls behavior and is therefore the focus of the test model.

modality. The concept of modality allows us to focus on most probable faults. For example, nonmodal classes cannot have sequence faults because all sequences are allowed. These classes are purposely designed to respond to all methods despite prior messages or current instance values. This is often true of framework or foundation classes. In contrast, classes that represent the application domain or implement control responsibilities typically have sequential constraints.

A test suite constructed from the FREE class state model is simply a sequence of messages and resultant states with expected values. These test suites can reveal all control faults in a modal class (missing or incorrect transition, incorrect response, incorrect resultant state). No control errors are possible in a nonmodal class, so our state specification is of no help in selecting a test sequence. In fact, if we follow the control-based test sequence, we end with what is effectively a brute-force enumeration of all possible message sequences of length 2. This approach is not likely to be an effective test strategy. A test pattern is presented for each modality in this section.

10.4.2 The Patterns

The following patterns apply at class scope, for any superclass or subclass:

- *Invariant Boundaries*. Identify test cases for complex domains.
- *Nonmodal Class Test*. Design a test suite for a class without sequential constraints.
- *Modal Class Test*. Design a test suite for a class with sequential constraints.
- *Quasi-modal Class Test*. Design a test suite for a class with content-determined sequential constraints.

Invariant Boundaries

Intent

Select test-efficient test value combinations for classes, interfaces, and components composed of complex and primitive data types.

Context

We must supply values for all variables in the scope of the IUT and subsequently run a test (or accept default or coincidental values). How can we model relationships among variables to support efficient and effective selection of test values?

At class scope, the valid and invalid combinations of instance variable values may be specified by the class invariant (see Section 17.3, Responsibility-based Assertions). The class invariant typically refers to instance variables that are instances of primitive and complex data types (e.g., integers and application-specific classes). The basic domain testing model is useful for scalar numeric types. With the extensions described in Section 10.2.4, Domain Testing Models, it can be applied to all data types supported in object-oriented languages.

The Invariant Boundaries pattern may be applied at any scope for which an invariant can be written:[16]

- It can be used for implementation-based testing at method or class scope. The implementation invariant is used.

- It can be used for responsibility-based testing at method or class scope. The variables visible at the class interface are used to form an implementation-independent invariant.

- It can be used for responsibility-based testing at subsystem and application system scope. The variables can be configuration parameters, system states, inputs, or outputs, and an invariant can be composed to define their relationship.

---

16. An *invariant* is a Boolean expression that specifies the required range or states of variables. These expressions can be written for the variables visible at any scope. Development of system scope invariants as part of analysis models is discussed in [Cook+94] and [D'Souza+99].

This pattern produces a set of test cases that may be used by another test approach. It will generate test cases for objects composed of objects and primitive data types (integer, floating point, string, and so on). It does not consider input/output relationships or message sequence.

Fault Model

Domain-based test models are motivated by the observation that faults are often related to domain boundary conditions (see Section 10.2.4, Domain Testing Models). Unusual but possible combinations of instance variable values are also a common source of trouble. This pattern assumes that unusual combinations of instance variable values will reveal bugs.

The Invariant Boundaries pattern targets bugs in the implementation of constraints needed to define and enforce a domain formed by several complex boundaries. Subclass invariants are often implicit or accidental, leading to misinterpretation and misuse. *Percolation* gives the requirements for well-formed, flattened invariants.

All invariant boundaries are exercised by this pattern. If an invariant boundary fault exists, we must include a test case that reaches the faulty boundary code. Once reached, the fault will be triggered if the boundary test value hits the incorrect boundary implementation. The 1×1 domain selection criteria will trigger all domain faults, except in the unusual case that the incorrect boundary passes through both on and off points [Jeng+94]. All other kinds of domain bugs (see Figure 10.18) will be triggered. Typically, input domains are related to different output actions. Triggering a domain bug typically produces an incorrect action, revealing the bug. If the boundaries of the IUT are not always related to distinctly different actions, invariant assertions can be coded to increase testability.

Although Ada 95's built-in checking, Eiffel's support for design-by-contract, or the use of assertions in other languages can prevent many domain bugs, these mechanisms cannot prevent incorrect code. Other things being equal, the chance of mistakenly coding $x > 1$ instead of $x > 0$, for example, is about the same in any language. Domain testing will find such bugs, as long as the correct boundary is known to the test designer.

Strategy

Test Model

An Invariant Boundaries test suite is developed in three steps:

1. Define the class invariant, as discussed in Section 17.3, Responsibility-based Assertions.

2. Develop on points and off points for each condition in the invariant using the 1×1 domain model.

3. Complete the test suite by developing in points for the variables not referenced in a condition and represent the results in a domain matrix.

Steps 2 and 3 are detailed in Section 10.2.4, Domain Testing Models.

1. Define the Class Invariants.   We will illustrate the development of an Invariant Boundaries test value set with the Java CustomerProfile class.

```
class CustomerProfile {
    Account account1 = new Account();
    Account account2 = new Account();
    Money creditLimit = new Money();
    short txCounter;
    //...
}
```

For simplicity, assume that account1, account2, creditLimit, and txCounter are instance and interface variables. Each Account object has a complex state model (Account is discussed in *Modal Class Test*). The abstract states of Account are *open*, *overdrawn*, *frozen*, *inactive*, and *closed*. The Money class is a scalar data type that represents fixed-point decimal numbers in the range plus or minus 999,999,999,999.99. The txCounter instance variable is a non-negative integer value of the Java primitive type short (a 16-bit signed integer). The class invariant is

```
assert(
    ( txCounter >=0 && txCounter <= 5000 )                 &&
    ( creditLimit > 99.99 && creditLimit <= 1000000.00 )   &&
    ( (!account1.isClosed( ) || !account2.isClosed( ) )
);
```

This invariant represents business policy that places a limit of 5000 transactions per customer, creates a credit limit of $1,000,000.00, requires both accounts to be in a valid state, and keeps at least one account open. It has six conditions.

2. Develop On and Off Points.   The variables creditLimit and txCounter are scalar, so the on and off points are easily identified. The test model uses abstract states of Account objects, not the domains of Account instance or interface variables. The abstract state of instance variables like account1 and account2 is relevant for modeling this behavior; the instance variables encapsulated within Account are not. Objects of class `Account` may be in one of five states: *open*, *overdrawn*, *frozen*, *inactive*, and *closed*. The on and off points for abstract states of `Account` are determined as follows:

- *Abstract state in points.* An abstract state in point is any value combination that places an object of the class in a given abstract state. Any set of abstract values that places an object in one of these states is an in point. For example;

open	balance = 345,119.76
overdrawn	balance = −932.03
frozen	isFrozen
inactive	Last transaction was six years ago
closed	Terminal state

- *Abstract state on points.* For the same reasons that we select on points for a primitive data type, we select state values that border on another state. An abstract state on point is a state such that the smallest possible change in any of its abstract state variables will result in a state change. For example, suppose that the balance of the account is −$0.01—that is, *overdrawn* by one cent. The object could be moved to the *open* state by adding the smallest possible increment in `balance`, $0.01. The abstract state on points for the focus states of `Account` are as follows:

open	balance = 0.00
overdrawn	balance = −0.01
frozen	isFrozen
inactive	Last transaction occurred five years and one day ago
closed	Terminal state

- *Abstract state off points.* Suppose the focus state is *open*. If we change the balance of an `account` object to −$0.01, it becomes overdrawn by one cent. That is, the object could be moved to the *open* state by adding the smallest possible increment in `balance`, $0.01. The abstract state off points for *open* are as follows:

overdrawn	balance = −0.01
frozen	isFrozen
inactive	Last transaction occurred five years and one day ago
closed	Terminal state

TABLE 10.14   On and Off Points for the `CustomerProfile` Invariant

Condition	On Point	Off Point
`txCounter >=0`	0	−1
`txCounter <= 5000`	5000	5001
`creditLimit > 99.99`	99.99	100.00
`creditLimit <= 1000000.00`	1000000.00	1000000.01
`!account1.isClosed( )`	True	False
`!account2.isClosed( )`	True	False

The off points for *overdrawn, frozen, inactive,* and *closed* are determined in the same way. Table 10.14 summarizes the on and off points for the `CustomerProfile` example.

- *On and off points for boundaries with two or more variables.* When a boundary is defined in terms of two or more other variables, each of these variables must be considered in choosing on and off points. Suppose a new requirement for `CustomerProfile` results in the following two-variable condition:

`(creditLimit >= (txCounter * 100) + 100)`

The on points are obtained by solving the equation implied by this condition:

$$\text{creditLimit} \geq (\text{txCounter} \times 100) + 100$$

The equation is solved for the highest and lowest values of *txCounter,* 0 and 5000:

$$creditLimit_{lowon} = (0 \times 100) + 100 = 100.00$$
$$creditLimit_{highon} = (5000 \times 100) + 100 = 500,100.00$$

Only one off point is used. It is obtained by choosing a centroid point[17] for the independent variable(s), solving with this value, and then changing the solution just enough to cause the condition to become false. For

---

17. The centroid of two points is a point midway between high and low, in the center of the triangle formed by three points, and so on.

creditLimit, the midpoint of the independent variable is 2500. Solving with 2500, we get

$$creditLimit_{midpoint} = (2500 \times 100) + 100 = 250{,}100.00$$

This solution is changed by the minimum possible to make the condition false. Here, we add 0.01 to creditLimit:

$$creditLimit_{off} = creditLimit_{midpoint} + 0.01 = 250{,}100.01$$

Table 10.15 shows the complete set of test points for the two-variable condition.

3. Develop Test Cases. Completing the domain matrix provides the complete Invariant Boundaries test suite CustomerProfile, as shown in Figure 10.23. The on and off points were developed as outlined above. The in points were chosen by inspection in less than two minutes.

Automation

The generation of an Invariant Boundaries test suite may be automated, given sufficiently detailed variable domain definitions. Several test data generation tools are commercially available. In points may be generated (or selected) by a random generation approach. All leading spreadsheets have such functions, providing effective, low-cost test vector generators. For example, the @RAND-BETWEEN(x,y) function in the Corel Quattro spreadsheet was used to generate the in points for the test cases in Figure 10.23. The x and y values are the in point ranges (e.g., for txCounter, $x = 1$, $y = 4999$). This test vector generator requires just a few minutes to set up. The in points for much larger test suites can be produced with little additional effort.

Entry Criteria

✓ A validated invariant is available or can be developed for the IUT.

This pattern is to be used to provide test values for a test suite designed with another pattern. The entry criteria for that pattern will also apply.

TABLE 10.15   On and Off Points for Multi-Variable CustomerProfile Condition

	On Point 1	On Point 2	Off Point
txCounter	0	5000	2500
CreditLimit	100.00	500100.00	250100.01

Boundary			Test Cases											
Variable	Condition	Type	1	2	3	4	5	6	7	8	9	10	11	12
txcounter	>=0	On	0											
		Off		–1										
	<= 5000	On			5000									
		Off				5001								
	Typical	In					3500	8	99	1037	4523	3102	3208	2839
creditLimit	> = 99.99	On					99.99							
		Off						100.00						
	<= 100000.00	On							100000.00					
		Off								100000.01				
	Typical	In	8327.62	99999.99	1024.02	732.86					783.98	1706.19	11205.00	87612.72
account1	!isClosed( )	On†									open			
		Off†										closed		
	Typical	In	open	OD	frozen	inactive	open	OD	frozen	inactive			open	OD
account2	!isClosed	On†											open	
		Off†												closed
	Typical	In	open	open	OD	frozen	inactive	open	OD	frozen	inactive	open		

†See definition of on and off points for Boolean variables and states.

FIGURE 10.23 Domain matrix for `CustomerProfile`.

Exit Criteria

✓ A complete set of domain tests has been developed. There is one on point and one off point for every general boundary condition as well as one on point and two off points for every strict equality boundary condition.

This pattern is used with another test approach. The coverage considerations for that pattern will apply.

Consequences

The strengths and limitations of domain testing have been established by rigorous analysis: except for a few unusual circumstances, all domain bugs will be revealed. The 1×1 domain testing model is more efficient and effective than heuristic selection of test inputs. However, it does not provide extensive checking of input/output correctness, control logic, or sequential constraints.

Developing the invariant can be time-consuming if the IUT uses many objects for which the valid ranges or states are unknown. Often, developers have a general idea of the invariant, but have not explicitly considered all the variables or relationships. This vagueness presents a testing opportunity, in that bugs are often associated with ambiguous understandings.

Once the invariant for the IUT has been developed, an Invariant Boundaries test suite can be developed in less than an hour for many systems. The number of test cases grows linearly with the number of conditions in the invariant.

Known Uses

Domain testing is a bedrock, widely used testing technique [Beizer 90, Roper 94, Beizer 95]. The data generation strategies employed by many commercially available testing tools use some variant of domain analysis. An early version of this pattern appears in [Binder 96h]. Siegel discusses some general considerations for application of the domain model to object-oriented code [Siegel 96].

Nonmodal Class Test

Intent

Develop a class/scope test suite for a class that does not constrain message sequences.

Context

Nonmodal classes are often said to "accept any message in any state." Any operation may follow any other (excluding construction/destruction). For example, an object of a `DateTime` class will accept any interleaving of modifier/accessor messages. Classes that implement basic data types are often nonmodal.

A nonmodal class imposes few constraints on message sequence but usually has a complex state space and a complex interface. Few or no message sequences are illegal; most message sequences are legal. How, then, can we select message combinations that are likely to reveal faults in nonmodal behavior?

Fault Model

Sequential constraints on messages are not imposed, so the state control model is trivial. Therefore state-based testing (see **Modal Class Test**) is inappropriate. Nevertheless, many sequence-related bugs are possible.

- A legal sequence is rejected.
- A legal sequence produces an incorrect value.
- Methods that report abstract state are inconsistent.
- A legitimate modifier message is rejected.
- An illegal modifier argument is accepted, resulting in a corrupt state.
- An accessor method has an incorrect side effect that alters or corrupts object state.
- An incorrect computation causes the class invariant to be violated.
- Some modifier/accessor methods implement an inconsistent view of abstract state.

For example, a `DateTime` object might incorrectly throw an exception when the `setHour` message is sent twice in succession to the same value.

TABLE 10.16   Nonmodal Behaviors Tested by the Shuffled Define-Use Algorithm

Test	Behavior Tested	Pass	No Pass
define-operation	Define operation.	On point is accepted.	On point is rejected.
define-operation	Define operation.	Off point is rejected.	Off point is accepted.
define-exception-corruption	Define exception handler.	No change in state after an exception.	State is corrupted after an exception.
use-exception test	Use operation.	Operation returns normally.	An exception is thrown.
use-correct-return	Use operation returns same value as input to the define operation.	Use and define values are the same.	Use and define values are not the same.
use-corruption	Use operation does not corrupt the state of the OUT.	State of the OUT unchanged after a use operation.	State of the OUT is changed after a use operation.

Strategy

Test Model

Six tests that target nonmodal bugs are described in Table 10.16. The test design problem is to generate interesting define-use sequences in which to apply these tests. The test strategy for a nonmodal class is as follows:

1. Develop a set of test cases (that is, a domain matrix) using *Invariant Boundaries*.
2. Select a message sequence strategy: define-use, random, or suspect.
3. Set the OUT to a test case from the domain matrix.
4. Send all accessor messages and verify that the returned and resulting values are consistent with the defining value.
5. Repeat steps 3 and 4 until all sequences have been exercised.

Although a nonmodal class does not constrain interleaving modifier and accessor messages, test messages must be sent in some sequence. We wish to choose sequences that will reveal a nonmodal fault, if one exists. Figure 10.24 shows a generic define-use model for a modal class. Sequences may be selected in several ways:

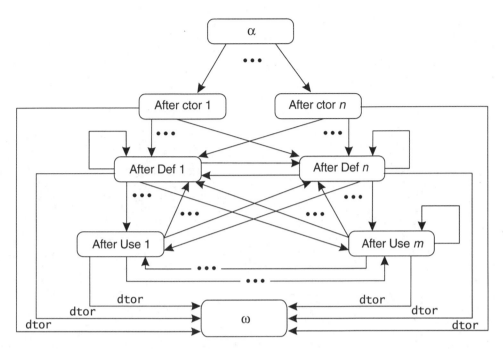

FIGURE 10.24 Generic interface data flow state model.

- *Define-use sequence.* A define-use sequence consists of a definition method followed by all of the use methods. The algorithm to generate a test suite of pair-wise define-use messages is given in Procedure 9.

- *Random sequence.* The sequence of accessor and modifier calls is assigned randomly. A pseudorandom algorithm shuffles tests, producing the test suite used in Procedure 10 on page 460. The sequences generated by this algorithm are repeatable if the same randomizing seed is used. The algorithm shuffles (randomizes the order of a fixed and finite set) the sequence of the modifier methods for each instance variable and the sequence of the accessor methods that report the resultant state.

- *Suspect sequence.* If a sequence is suspect for any reason, try it. For example, we may suspect that `DateTime` operations involving a leap year or February 29 may fail.

The Shuffled Define-Use algorithm listed in Procedure 9 combines the define-use strategy with randomized sequence generation. It generates all define-use method pairs and tests all the behaviors listed in Table 10.16. A

```
ShuffledTestDriver( ){

    // Set seed value here to allow repeatable test sequence
    seed = aBigPrimeNumber

    // Java Reflection or similar capability used to obtain method
    // names in the CUT
    MethodList DefiningMethodList = reflect.setMethods(CUT)
                                    // includes all ctors
    MethodList UsingMethodList = reflect.methods(CUT)
                                    // includes all get methods

    // Generate a shuffled list of the CUT's define methods
    ShuffledDefineList = DefiningMethodList.Shuffle(seed)

    For each method in ShuffledDefineList:
        // Execute the define sequence for the focus test point
        Set the OUT to the in points of the current test vector.
        Set the OUT to the focus point of the current test vector.

        // Check the result of the Define Sequence for this test vector
        If the focus test point is a closed off point or an open on point
            // Expect the define message for this test point is rejected
            If the expected exception is generated
                Mark this define-exception test as pass
                // Expect rejected message does not change state
                If the post-test state of the OUT is unchanged
                    Mark this define-exception-corruption test as pass
                Else
                    Mark this define-exception-corruption test as no-pass
                Fi
            Else
                Mark this define-exception test as no-pass
            Fi
        Else
            // The test point is a closed on point or is an open off point
            // Expect this define operation with current test vector
            // is accepted and correctly applied
            // New object value has been defined - now try all get methods
            // Now generate a shuffled list of the CUT's use methods
            // A different sequence is generated for each define operation
```

```
            ShuffledUseList = UsingMethodList.shuffleList()
            For each method in the ShuffledUseList
                Send the use message to the OUT
                If an exception is generated
                    // Expect all use sequences allowed
                    Mark this use-exception test as no-pass
                Else
                    Mark this use-exception test as pass
                    If the returned object(s) are
                    equivalent to the input test vector
                    // Expect use method reports same value
                        Mark this use-correct-return test as pass
                        If the post-test state of the OUT is
                        equivalent to the input test vector
                        // Expect use method does not change state
                            Mark this use-corruption test as pass
                        Else
                            Mark this use-corruption test as no-pass
                        Fi
                    Else
                        // Use method returned an incorrect value
                        Mark this use-correct-return as no-pass
                    Fi
                Fi
            Rof
        Fi
    Rof
End ShuffledTestDriver
```

Procedure 9   Shuffled Define-Use Algorithm

```
// Fragment of class MethodList

ShuffledList(int seed)
    Int         index
    Float   randomValue

    j = rand(seed)    //throwaway first value

    For i = 1, unshuffledList.listSize( ),++i
        UnshuffledList.index [i] = i
        UnshuffledList.randomValue[i] = rand()
    Rof

    //Sort ascending on random value
    ShuffledList = unshuffledList.sort( )

    Return shuffledList

End
```

Procedure 10   Shuffle Algorithm

different use sequence is generated for each define method. The pseudorandom sequences can be repeated by using the same seed.

Here we illustrate the development of a nonmodal set suite with the DateTime class. It encapsulates a representation of a single date and time and provides operations on this representation. No capabilities are provided to automatically increment the value in real or relative time. In addition, serialization is not a responsibility of this class. Any operation may follow any other (excluding construction/destruction). A nonmodal class has only one abstract state. A DateTime object has one abstract state (any valid date and time) and many concrete primitive states (each date and time increment that may be represented). For DateTime objects, these variables are year, day, hour, and minute. The class interface for a Java implementation of class DateTime follows:

```
class DateTime {
    void      DateTime(int sec, int min,
                       int hr, int day,
                       int year, int zone
              )                      { /* ... */ }
    void      setSec(int sec)        { /* ... */ }
    void      setMin(int min)        { /* ... */ }
    void      setHour(int hr)        { /* ... */ }
    void      setDay(int day)        { /* ... */ }
    void      setYear(int year)      { /* ... */ }
    void      setZone(int zone)      { /* ... */ }
    int       getSec( )              { /* ... */ }
    int       getMin( )              { /* ... */ }
    int       getHour( )             { /* ... */ }
    int       getDay( )              { /* ... */ }
    int       getYear( )             { /* ... */ }
    int       getZone( )             { /* ... */ }
    bool      equal(DateTime dt)       { /* ... */ }
    DateTime  subtract(DateTime dt)  { /* ... */ }
    DateTime  add(DateTime dt)       { /* ... */ }
}
```

Variable definitions are given in Table 10.17. Table 10.18 shows the corresponding invariant conditions. The resulting test cases are shown in Figure 10.25. The on and off points (shaded boxes) were determined by inspection. The in points were generated by using a random number function of a popular spreadsheet. If some values present special cases or are suspect for any reason, add test cases for them. With DateTime, these cases might be 00:00:00 and 23:59:59 hours on any date or the time/date combinations 23:59:59, December 31, 1999, and 00:00:00, January 1, 2000.

TABLE 10.17 Variable Domains for `DateTime`

Variable	Type	Minimum	Maximum
Second	Integer	0	59
Minute	Integer	0	59
Hour	Integer	0	23
Day	Integer	0	366
Year	Integer	1900	65363
Zone	Integer	1 (1 = GMT)	24

TABLE 10.18 On and Off Points for the `DateTime` Invariant

Boundary Condition	On Point	Off Point
`second >=0`	0	−1
`second <= 59`	59	60
`minute >= 0`	0	−1
`minute <= 59`	59	60
`hour >= 0`	0	−1
`hour <= 23`	23	24
`day >= 0`	0	−1
`day <= 366`	366	367
`year >= 1900`	1900	1899
`year < 32768`	32768	32767
`zone > 0`	0	1
`zone =< 24`	24	25

The basic test strategy is to set the object under test to a test vector value with a modifier, verify that the modifier has produced a correct state, and then try each accessor to see that it reports the state correctly without buggy side effects.

1. Pick a test vector.
2. Set the OUT to the test vector values using a constructor or modifier methods

Test Case	second	minute	hour	day	year	GMT
1	0	47	16	104	18684	21
2	−1	23	16	70	21769	11
3	59	14	6	116	13166	10
4	60	13	10	317	14309	9
5	24	0	18	321	31148	22
6	48	−1	3	358	3852	20
7	52	59	16	143	26370	11
8	6	60	9	69	28871	18
9	24	22	0	254	27316	18
10	32	40	−1	15	29438	9
11	8	55	23	83	31110	16
12	19	4	24	17	16202	9
13	27	8	4	1	32530	17
14	38	42	18	0	11437	5
15	26	38	19	366	24000	15
16	57	51	3	367	24139	6
17	22	15	4	330	1900	6
18	15	17	12	49	1899	14
19	30	28	19	119	32767	12
20	14	9	16	8	32768	14
21	29	24	19	337	30420	1
22	18	29	14	130	32249	0
23	5	55	9	304	8435	24
24	55	7	18	355	29697	25

Key: ☐ = In point, ▨ = On/off point

FIGURE 10.25 Invariant boundaries test set for DateTime.

3. If the test vector is an off point, the OUT should throw an exception without corrupting or changing the state of the OUT.

4. If the test vector is an on point, verify that the OUT is placed in the expected state with a trusted inspector.

5. Send a message to each accessor method and compare the reported value with the expected value.

6. Verify that the resultant class state is unchanged using a trusted inspector.

The algorithm for this approach is summarized in Procedure 9 (see pages 458–459).

Automation

As the ***Invariant Boundaries*** pattern generates off points (i.e., illegal states), the test driver must check for exceptions. A nonmodal test suite may be implemented with any of the API Test Harness patterns presented in Chapter 19. Systems that automate interface data flow test strategies are described in the Known Uses section for this pattern.

Entry Criteria

✓ Verify minimal operability by running an alpha-omega cycle on the class under test.

Exit Criteria

✓ The responsibilities of a nonmodal class may be considered covered if all define-use method pairs have been exercised and an object of the class under test has taken on the values in each of the ***Invariant Boundaries*** test cases at least once.

✓ Achieve branch coverage or better on each method in the class under test.

A higher level of confidence can be obtained by developing a class flow graph to identify any uncovered alpha-omega paths. Add message sequences to exercise these paths.

Consequences

Developing a pair-wise define-use driver for a class typically takes a day or two but rarely more than a week. Studies on interface define-use testing of abstract data types have shown the approach to be effective [Jalote 89, Zweben 92].

The define-use test model described here does not explicitly generate any method sequence longer than a define-use pair, or a sequence of $n = 2$. The size of a define-use test suite grows exponentially with n. That is, the number of tests is m^{n+1} where m is the number of methods in the class under test.

The limits of paired operation testing can be mitigated if the test harness implements a trustworthy state comparator (see Chapter 18) or the class under test checks method postconditions or the class invariant (Chapter 17).

Known Uses

The SITE system generates a test suite of pair-wise ADT operation combinations [Jalote 89]. Considerations for application of Jalote's approach to C++ are sketched in [Smith 92]. A detailed analysis of interface data flow testing for ADTs and an experience report appear in [Zweben 92]. A system that automatically generates Ada operation pairs is described in [Parrish 93a], and a similar approach for C++ is outlined in [Parrish 93b]. Some theoretical considerations for the application of data flow models to class interfaces are developed in [Parrish 94]. ADT-based approaches are presented in [Barbey 97] and [Chen+98].

The nonmodal test strategy [Binder 96h] was used to design test suites for the visualization subsystem of the U.S. Environmental Protection Agency's Models-3 air quality modeling package. When applied to container classes in this system, the developer responsible for testing visualization components reports that nonmodal test suites were "effective for verifying the contract, occasionally finding contract defects and very good at finding holes in contracts" (Todd Plessel, private communication, May 1999).

Quasi-modal Class Test

Intent

Develop a class scope test suite for a class whose constraints on message sequence change with the state of the class.

Context

A quasi-modal class has sequential constraints that reflect the organization of information used by the class. The specific content does not imply any sequential constraint. Container and collection classes are often quasi-modal. The Smalltalk collection class hierarchy is shown in Figure 10.26. Similar hierarchies are available in libraries and development environments of many systems. For example, a `Stack` object has the same behavior for any content or order of items in the stack, but its behavior differs when the stack is empty, holding some items, or full. A `push` message can be accepted an arbitrary number of times, but is rejected when a stack is full. No combination of stacked values will result in different behavior unless one of these special cases obtains. The state or class invariant should express these structural relationships.

Effective testing must distinguish between content that determines behavior and content that does not affect behavior. With quasi-modal classes, meta-parameters and meta-parameter relationships determine behavior. Specific values are often irrelevant. For example, we are more likely to find bugs by testing transitions involving an empty or full stack than by testing randomly selected stack items and stack sizes.

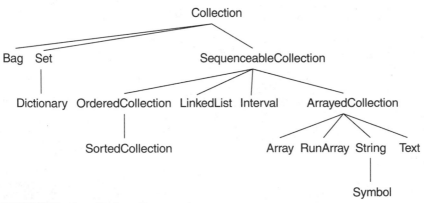

FIGURE 10.26   Smalltalk collection classes.

To test such a quasi-modal class, we must focus on this structure. If we do not, the test suite will not fully exercise behavior constraints. For example, an astronomical number of collection element permutations exist, but only a few of them have significant implications for behavior. A test model should focus on these special cases. The modal and nonmodal test models do not provide this focus.

Fault Model

Quasi-modal class failures occur when invariants related to all members of a collection are not observed. For example, consider the IntSet class provided in an early version of a commercial C++ class library [Hoffman 92].

```
class IntSet {
public:
    // operations on single sets
                IntSet();
                ~IntSet();
    IntSet&add(int);       // Add a member
    IntSet&remove(int);    // Remove a member
    IntSet&clear(int);     // Remove all members
    int    is_member(int);      // Is arg a member?
    int    extent();            // Number of elements
    int    is_empty();     // Empty or not?

    // operations on pairs of sets ...
};
```

A precondition of add(x) is that x is not already in the set. If this action is attempted when x already exists, the duplicate exception is thrown. To test the duplicate exception, the message add(123) was sent to an IntSet object twice, in succession. The second message caused the duplicate exception to be thrown, but the duplicate value was incorrectly added to the set. This problem went unnoticed until two remove(123) messages were accepted before is_member(123) returned false. This fault would have been revealed by applying the first paired operation test shown in Table 10.25.

Strategy

Test Model

Procedure 11 summarizes the steps for developing a quasi-modal test suite. Collections share the same behavior when empty, holding (neither empty nor full), or full. Figure 10.27 illustrates the generic state model for this behavior. The parameters and parameter relationships that determine behavior are the state variables of interest.

1. Design (or at least plan) method scope tests and collection-specific operation sequences. Add these tests to the test suite as you go.

2. Demonstrate minimal operability with an alpha-omega cycle. Implement just enough of the method scope tests to achieve the cycle.

3. Develop a FREE state model for the class under test. Characterize the state by constraint parameters (not by content); treat each constraint parameter as a state variable.

4. Generate the transition tree.

5. Elaborate the transition tree with a full expansion of conditional transition variants.

6. Tabulate events and actions along each path to form test cases.

7. Develop test data for the path by using **Invariant Boundaries** on message events and actions.

8. Run the conformance test suite until all tests pass.

9. Develop a sneak path test suite. Add all illegal transitions for all states and define the expected exception.

10. Run the sneak path test suite until all tests pass.

11. If any method scope tests have not yet been implemented, add them to the test suite and rerun until all tests pass.

Procedure 11   Test Plan for a Quasi-modal Class

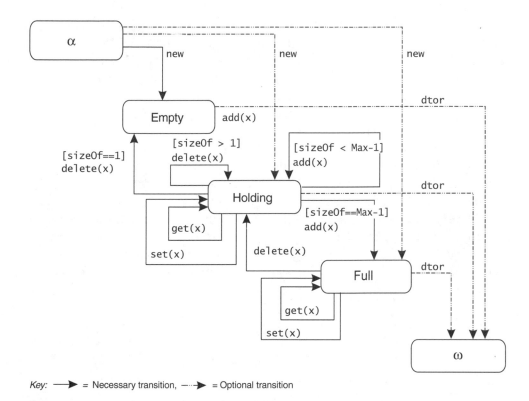

Key: ⟶ = Necessary transition, ⇢ = Optional transition

FIGURE 10.27 Generic state model for quasi-modal class.

The Quasi-modal test model has three parts:

- A state model of the generic collection behavior. The test suite is produced by applying the N+ algorithm discussed in Chapter 7 to the generic model. The generic model is tailored to the overall behavior of the class.

- An *Invariant Boundaries* set for the parameters and parameter relationships that determine behavior. For example, with Stack, the parameters of interest are the maximum size and the current number of stack elements. These parameters can typically be found by examining preconditions, postconditions, and class invariants.

- An operation-pair model of specific container behavior. Collections typically place additional constraints on pairs of operations. For example, an item with the same value cannot be added twice to a set, but can be added an arbitrary number of times to a stack.

Generic Collection Behavior Model. Figure 10.27 shows the generic state model for collection behavior. The states are defined in Table 10.19. The special states α (alpha) and ω (omega) are placeholders used to make the full creation/destruction cycle explicit and to model the effect of multiple initial states or constructors. The generic events are defined in Table 10.20.

The transitions shown with dashed lines in Figure 10.27 are supported in some collections. The typical behavior of a collection constructor is to create an empty collection. However, convenience initialization methods may return a prepopulated collection. A conservative behavior model might not allow the destruction of a nonempty collection, as this action may result in the "container" problem (elements of a collection persist after the container is deleted, but cannot be referenced). If any other objects are holding references to the elements, an attempt to use the reference typically results in a failure. This potentially hazardous behavior may, however, be the most efficient way to implement the release of a container. Figure 10.28 shows the corresponding transition table.

TABLE 10.19 Generic Quasi-modal States

State	Definition
α (alpha)	The object is defined, but not declared.
Empty	The collection has zero members.
Holding	The collection has at least one member but not more than the maximum number of members.
Full	The collection has the maximum number of members.
ω (omega)	The garbage (null) state.

TABLE 10.20 Generic Quasi-modal Events

Event	Definition
new	Create and initialize a new instance (a constructor).
add(x)	Add element x to the collection.
set(x)	Change the value of existing element x without removing it from the collection. This operation is typically defined for keyed collections (e.g., dictionaries or hash tables), but may not be defined for other collections.
get(x)	Return a copy of the reference to element x without changing the collection.
delete(x)	Remove element x from the collection.
dtor	Destroy the collection. This operation may be automatic (Smalltalk) or programmer-defined (C++).

Accepting State	Event (method)	Resultant State				
		α (alpha)	Empty	Holding	Full	ω (omega)
α alpha	new		OK			
	add(x)					
	set(x)					
	get(x)					
	delete(x)					
	dtor					
Empty	new					
	add(x)			OK	OK	
	set(x)					
	get(x)					
	delete(x)					
	dtor					OK
Holding	new					
	add(x)			OK	OK	
	set(x)			OK		
	get(x)			OK		
	delete(x)		OK	OK		
	dtor					
Full	new					
	add(x)					
	set(x)				OK	
	get(x)				OK	
	delete(x)			OK		
	dtor					
ω omega	new					
	add(x)					
	set(x)					
	get(x)					
	delete(x)					
	dtor					

Note: Shaded blocks indicate illegal transition. Multiple white blocks in a row indicate conditional transitions.

FIGURE 10.28   Full transition table for generic collection state model.

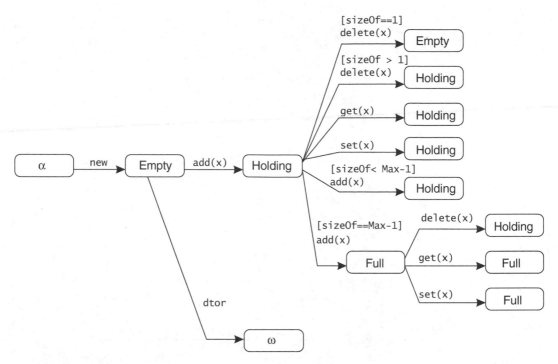

FIGURE 10.29   Transition trees for quasi-modal state model.

The transition tree for the generic collection model shown in Figure 10.29 was developed by using Procedure 12. Note that the conditional transitions have been expanded to include their full logical complement. Fourteen of the 24 possible transitions are illegal. Consequently, the sneak path tests (for each illegal message/state pair) should be applied. The expected result is that an exception is thrown and the state of the collection remains unchanged.

Interesting Operation Sequences.   After validating the behavior required by the generic state model, collection-specific behaviors should be tested. Table 10.21 shows the test points selected by applying the ***Invariant Boundaries*** strategy to the defining parameters of Stack: minimum number of elements and maximum number of elements. Suggested operation test sequences follow for some common collections.

- *Sequential collections.* A sequential collection contains a variable number of items. Items can be accessed only sequentially and may be added

1. The initial state is the root node of the tree. Use the α state if multiple constructors produce behaviorally different initial states.

2. For each nonterminal leaf node in the tree, count the number of outbound transitions for the state that it represents. Draw an edge and new node for each outbound transition. Each new edge and node represent an event and resultant state reached by an outbound transition.

3. For each edge and node drawn in step 2:

   a. Copy the corresponding transition event/action to the new edge.

   b. If the state this node represents is already represented by another node (anywhere in the diagram) or is a final state, this node is *terminal*—no more transitions are drawn from this node.

4. Repeat steps 2 and 3 until all leaf nodes are terminal.

Procedure 12   Produce a Transition Tree from a State Model

TABLE 10.21   Interesting Combination Values for Stack Parameters

Test Point	Number of Elements	Maximum Number of Elements	Condition	Type
1	min − 1	rand(x)	Error	Off
2	min	rand(x)	Empty	On
3	min + 1	rand(x)	Loaded	On
4	rand(x)	rand(x)	Loaded	On
5	max − 1	rand(x)	Loaded	On
6	max	rand(x)	Full	On
7	max + 1	rand(x)	Error	Off
8	rand(x)	min − 1	Error	Off
9	rand(x)	min	Error	Off
10	rand(x)	min + 1	Loaded	On
11	rand(x)	rand(x)	Loaded	On
12	rand(x)	max − 1	Loaded	On
13	rand(x)	max	Loaded	On
14	rand(x)	max + 1	Error	Off

only to the end. Examples include strings, buffers, and tape files. Paired operations to test error-prone behavior are shown in Table 10.22.

- *Ordered collections.* In an ordered collection, elements are added, accessed, and removed using some ordering scheme: stack, queue, tree, list, and so on. All of the sequential test patterns can be applied (with the necessary changes in expected results). Paired operations to test error-prone behavior are shown in Table 10.23.

- *Keyed collections.* Some collections (e.g., `Dictionary` in Smalltalk) provide a unique identifier for each member of a collection. Application classes that provide file or database wrappers may also rely on keyed access. Keyed collections must provide a wide range of paired operations. Faults often occur in item-to-item processing. Table 10.24 lists revealed basic (single) operation tests. Paired operations to test error-prone behavior are shown in Tables 10.25, 10.26, and 10.27.

- *Multiple collection operations.* Operations may be defined that use collections as operands. This type of definition is common practice in C++. Suppose there are two collections, A and B, both objects of collection class `Gaggle`. Nonpaired operations on `Gaggle` should be verified first. Next, A and B are instantiated and populated to set up the tests

TABLE 10.22   Sequential Collection, Variable-Length Operand Test Cases

Collection Operation	Size of Message Argument, x	Collection State	Expected Result
add(x)	Single element	Empty	Added
	Single element	Not empty	Added
	Single element	Capacity −1	Added
	Single element	Full	Reject
	Several elements, sufficient to overflow	Not empty	Reject
	Several elements	Capacity −1	Reject
	Null element	Empty	No action
	Null element	Not empty	No action
set(x)	Several elements, sufficient to overflow by 1	Not empty	Reject
	Several elements, sufficient to reach capacity	Not empty	Accept
	Several elements, sufficient to reach capacity −1	Not empty	Accept
	Null element	Not empty	No action
	Several elements, fewer than in collection	Not empty	Accept, check cleanup

TABLE 10.23   Ordered Collection, Operation Position Sensitivity Test Cases

Collection Operation	Message Argument	Target Element Position	Collection State	Expected Result
All operations	Single item	First	Not empty	Accepted
	Single item	Last	Not empty	Accepted
delete(x)	Single item	Not present	Empty	Rejected
	Single item	First	One element	Accepted
	Single item	Any	Full	Accepted

TABLE 10.24 Keyed Collection, Basic Operation Test Cases

Collection Operation	Message Argument Value	Target Item	Expected Result
add(x)	Any	Not present	Accept
get(x)	Any	Not present	Reject
set(x)	Any	Not present	Reject
delete(x)	Any	Not present	Reject
add(x)	Any	Present	Reject
get(x)	Any	Present	Accept
set(x)	Any	Present	Accept
delete(x)	Any	Present	Accept

TABLE 10.25 Keyed Collection, Key-Sensitive Paired Operation Test Cases

Collection Operation	Key Value of x	Key Value of y	y in Collection	Expected Result
add(x), add(y)	Any	Same	No	Second rejected
get(x), get(y)	Any	Same	No	Accepted
set(x), set(y)	Any	Same	Yes	Accepted
delete(x), delete(y)	Any	Same	Yes	Second rejected
add(x), add(y)	Any	Different	No	Accepted
get(x), get(y)	Any	Different	No	Rejected
set(x), set(y)	Any	Different	Yes	Accepted
delete(x), delete(y)	Any	Different	Yes	Accepted

indicated in Tables 10.28 and 10.29. The indicated operations test size-dependent processing (not the semantics of the operation).

Automation

Procedures 9 and 10 present algorithms that may be adapted to implement testing according to this pattern. A test suite may be implemented with any of the API Test Harness patterns presented in Chapter 19.

TABLE 10.26 Keyed Collection, Collation Order Sensitivity Test Cases

Collection Operation	Key Value of x	Key Value of y	Expected Result
add(x), add(y)	Highest	Highest	Second rejected
get(x), get(y)	Highest	Highest	Accepted
set(x), set(y)	Highest	Highest	Accepted
delete(x), delete(y)	Highest	Highest	Second rejected
add(x), add(y)	Lowest	Highest	Accepted
get(x), get(y)	Lowest	Highest	Accepted
set(x), set(y)	Lowest	Highest	Accepted
delete(x), delete(y)	Lowest	Highest	Accepted
add(x), add(y)	Highest	Lowest	Accepted
get(x), get(y)	Highest	Lowest	Accepted
set(x), set(y)	Highest	Lowest	Accepted
delete(x), delete(y)	Highest	Lowest	Accepted
add(x), add(y)	Lowest	Lowest	Second rejected
get(x), get(y)	Lowest	Lowest	Rejected
set(x), set(y)	Lowest	Lowest	Accepted
delete(x), delete(y)	Lowest	Lowest	Second rejected

TABLE 10.27 Keyed Collection, set and get High-Low Sensitivity Tests

Collection Method	Value of Argument x	Target Item	State of Collection	Expected Result
set(x)	Lowest	Not present	Empty	Rejected/exception
		Not present	Several higher elements	Rejected/exception
	Highest	Not present	Empty	Rejected/exception
		Not present	Several lower elements	Rejected/exception
	Lowest	Present	Empty	Changed
		Present	Several higher elements	Changed
	Highest	Present	Empty	Changed
		Present	Several lower elements	Changed
get(x)	Lowest	Not present	Empty	Rejected/exception
		Not present	Several higher elements	Rejected/exception
	Highest	Not present	Empty	Rejected/exception
		Not present	Several lower elements	Rejected/exception
	Lowest	Present	Empty	Gotten
		Present	Several higher elements	Gotten
	Highest	Present	Empty	Gotten
		Present	Several lower elements	Gotten

TABLE 10.28 Keyed Collection, set and get High-Low Sensitivity Tests

Collection Method	Value of Argument x	Target Item	State of Collection	Expected Result
add(x)	Lowest	Not present	Empty	Added
		Not present	Several higher elements	Added
	Highest	Not present	Empty	Added
		Not present	Several lower elements	Added
	Lowest	Present	Empty	Rejected/ exception
		Present	Several higher elements	Rejected/ exception
	Highest	Present	Empty	Rejected/ exception
		Present	Several lower elements	Rejected/ exception
delete(x)	Lowest	Not present	Empty	Rejected/ exception
		Not present	Several higher elements	Rejected/ exception
	Highest	Not present	Empty	Rejected/ exception
		Not present	Several lower elements	Rejected/ exception
	Lowest	Present	Empty	Deleted
		Present	Several higher elements	Deleted
	Highest	Present	Empty	Deleted
		Present	Several lower elements	Deleted

TABLE 10.29 Aggregate Collection Operator, Size Sensitivity Test Cases

Collection Operation	Size of Collection A	Size of Collection B	Expected Result
All operations	0 (empty)	0 (empty)	Operation-specific
	0 (empty)	N	Operation-specific
	N	M	Accept
All operations requiring same size A and B	N	N	Accept
	N	$N + 1$	Reject/exception
	$N + 1$	1	Reject/exception

$N > 1, N \neq M$

Entry Criteria

✓ Verify minimal operability by running an alpha-omega cycle on the class under test.

Exit Criteria

✓ Achieve at least branch coverage on each method in the class under test.

✓ A Quasi-modal Class Test suite will provide N+ coverage. It requires a test for each root-to-leaf path in the expanded transition tree and a full set of sneak path pairs. See the discussion of state-based coverage in Chapter 7 for more details.

✓ A higher level of confidence can be obtained by developing a class flow graph to identify any uncovered alpha-omega paths. Add message sequences to exercise these paths.

Consequences

The Quasi-modal Class Test pattern has the following requirements:

• A testable behavior model is available or can be developed.
• The class under test is state-observable—that is, we have trustworthy built-in tests or feasible access to the CUT so that we can determine the resultant state of each test run.
• A suitable test driver is available.
• Some servers of the class under test may require stubs to provide sufficient control of CUT state.

The test generation procedure has been mathematically proven to be able to reveal (1) missing transitions, (2) missing or incorrect action, and (3) incorrect or invalid resultant states [Chow 78]. This technique will find all sneak paths, bugs in sneak path exception handling, and value-determined faults (e.g., incorrect responses to a full container) that are associated with a modeled conditional transition. It does not explicitly focus on incorrect output or incorrect values that are within the bounds of valid state (e.g., 2 + 2 = 6).

Nevertheless, bugs can hide from pair-wise operations [Zweben 92]. An interface define-use test suite revealed 11 of 12 bugs in an ADT implementation of a LinkedList. It missed a bug where the Insert operation failed to change the back pointer correctly. Thus, when an object in a pretest state of

```
{node=001, prevNode=nil, nextNode=003}
{node=003, prevNode=001, nextNode=nil}
```

was sent the message `insertNode(002)`, the post-test state was

```
{node=001, prevNode=nil, nextNode=002}
{node=002, prevNode=001, nextNode=003}
{node=003, prevNode=001, nextNode=nil}
```

Although the node was inserted, the back pointer in the existing node following the new node was not changed correctly. This fault could be activated by a sequence like `insertNode(x)`, `insertNode(x)`, `nextNode(x)`, `previousNode(x)`. This cycle would not be generated, however, by a define-use sequence (it requires two successive definitions). This bug would have been found if the test harness implemented a trustworthy state comparator or the class under test checked method postconditions or a class invariant.

The ASTOOT system [Doon+94] automatically generates and evaluates define-use sequences of an arbitrary length. Its developers found that its bug-finding power dropped off as longer sequences were used. The available research indicates that pair-wise define-use testing is a viable compromise between effectiveness and size/complexity of a test suite.

Known Uses

Similar test strategies are described in [Beizer 90] and [Marick 95]. A similar code-based test approach is presented in [Hoffman 95]. ADT-based approaches are presented in [Barbey 97].

Related Patterns

The *Paired Test Scenario* recites some elements of the ASTOOT testing strategy [Firesmith 96].

Modal Class Test

Intent

Develop a class scope test suite for a class that has fixed constraints on message sequence.

Context

A *modal* class has both message and domain constraints on the acceptable sequence of messages. For example, an object of class Account will not accept a debit message to withdraw funds if the balance in an Account is less than or equal to zero. A freeze message is accepted if the Account is not *closed* and not *frozen*. Classes that represent problem domain entities are often modal, as are classes that provide application control [Jacobsen+92]. A class cluster that implements the *State* pattern [Gamma+95] is probably modal.

Suppose that the responsibilities of a class constrain message sequences. Interactions between message sequences and states are often subtle and complex—and therefore error-prone. When message sequences are constrained, we need to verify for all valid states that (1) messages that are to be accepted in these states are accepted, (2) messages that are illegal in these states are rejected, (3) the resultant state for accepted and rejected messages is the correct state, and (4) the response to each test message (messages sent to servers of the class under test and the response to the test message) is categorically correct. Categorical correctness means that the response matches the expected message(s) and that parameter values fall within nominal ranges.

Fault Model

A class can fail to implement its state model in five ways:

1. Missing transition: a message is rejected in a valid state.
2. Incorrect action: the wrong response is selected for accepting state and method.
3. Invalid resultant state: the method produces the wrong state for this transition.
4. A corrupt state is produced.
5. A sneak path allows a message to be accepted when it should have been rejected.

Faults		Possible Cause		
		Lexical	Dynamic	General
Transformation	Missing	✓	✓	†
	Incorrect	✓	✓	†
	Extra	✓		Programmer creativity
State Transition	Missing	✓	✓	The SUT cannot produce a required sequence
	Incorrect	✓	✓	Same as missing or extra
	Extra	✓	✓	A "sneak path" allows an unspecified sequence
Output Action	Missing	✓	✓	†
	Incorrect	✓	✓	†
	Extra	✓		Programmer creativity
State	Missing	✓	✓	†
	Incorrect	✓	✓	Incorrect method statement(s), incorrect client usage
	Extra	✓		Programmer creativity

†Many causes; see bug taxonomy in [Beizer 90].

FIGURE 10.30   Summary of state faults and possible causes.

For example, suppose the Account class becomes stuck in the *frozen* state (an unfreeze message does not unfreeze it) or a close message is accepted when an Account object is in the *overdrawn* state. Figure 10.30 summarizes state faults. See Section 7.4.1, How State Machines Fail, for a detailed discussion of state faults.

Strategy

Test Model

The behavior of a class (or a head of a modal cluster) under test is represented with a FREE state model. States are defined so as to represent sequential constraints and each state is represented with a state invariant. All methods and encapsulated interrupts are represented as events. All outbound messages and returned message values are represented as actions. Section 7.3, The FREE State Model, provides details.

With a testable state model in hand, the N+ test suite is developed.

1. Generate the augmented transition tree from the state model, including all explicit round-trip paths, combinational expansions of any guarded transitions, and sneak path expansion for each state.
2. Sensitize each transition path by picking interesting test cases and determining the expected result for each test case.

Procedure 13 summarizes the test design (see section 7.4.3, The N+ Test Strategy, for details). The Java Account class is used to illustrate this design.

```
class Account extends Object {
    private Money  currentBalance;
    private int    accountNumber;
    private Date   lastActivity;

    public void   open( )
          {/* Create an account */}

    public Money  balance( )
          {/* Report current balance */}

    public void   credit(Money creditAmt)
          {/* Add amount to balance */}

    public void   debit(Money debitAmt)
          {/* Subtract amount from balance*/}

    public void   freeze( )
          {/* Suspend customer transactions */}

    public void   unfreeze( )
          {/* Allow customer transactions */}

    public Money  settle( )
          {/* Force zero balance */}

    public void   close( )
          {/* Terminate all activity */}

}
```

The state space for Account can be represented with a three-dimensional model. Each dimension enumerates the instance variable domain. A group of points in this state space corresponds to an aggregate state, as shown in Figure 10.31.

1. Design (or at least plan) method scope tests for each method.   We'll add these tests as we go.

2. Demonstrate minimal operability with an alpha-omega cycle. Implement just enough of the method scope tests to achieve the cycle.

3. Develop a FREE state model for the class under test.

4. Generate the transition tree.

5. Elaborate the transition tree with a full expansion of conditional transition variants.

6. Tabulate events and actions along each path to form test cases.

7. Develop test data for the path by using **Invariant Boundaries** on message events and actions.

8. Run the conformance test suite until all tests pass.

9. Develop a sneak path test suite. Add all illegal transitions for all states and define the expected exception.

10. Run the sneak path test suite until all tests pass.

11. If any method scope tests have not yet been implemented, add them to the test suite and rerun until all tests pass.

Procedure 13   Test Strategy for Modal and Unimodal Classes

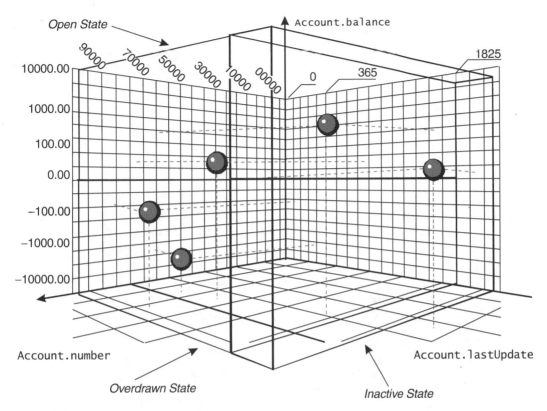

FIGURE 10.31   Aggregate state model.

1. Conformance Tests.   The first step in test case design is to prepare the transition tree. Figure 10.32 depicts the state model for Account. *Open* is the initial state of Account; it becomes the root node. For each transition out of the root state, a branch is drawn to a node that represents the resultant state. This step is repeated for each resultant state node unless either the resultant state already appears in an ancestor node or the resultant state is a final state. A node is marked as **terminal** if the state it represents has already been drawn or is a final state. No more transitions are traced out of this branch. This procedure is repeated until all nodes have been marked as terminal.

Next, transition test sequences are transcribed from the tree. Each full and partial branch in the tree (an **event path**) becomes a test case. Procedure 12 summarizes these steps. Figure 10.33 shows the transition tree for Account. The first 10 branches are terminated by reaching an ancestor state. The last two branches are terminated by reaching *closed*, the final state.

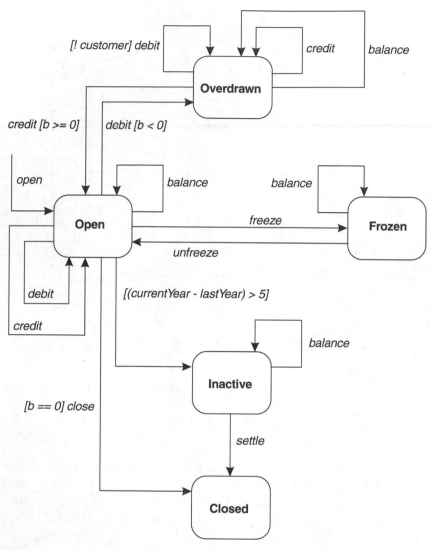

FIGURE 10.32   State transition diagram for class `Account`.

2. Conditional Transition Tests. During conformance testing, we want a conditional transition to fire when we send a message that meets its condition. But what happens when the condition is not true? Each conditional transition may have excluded transitions, so each conditional transition is analyzed to identify additional test cases.

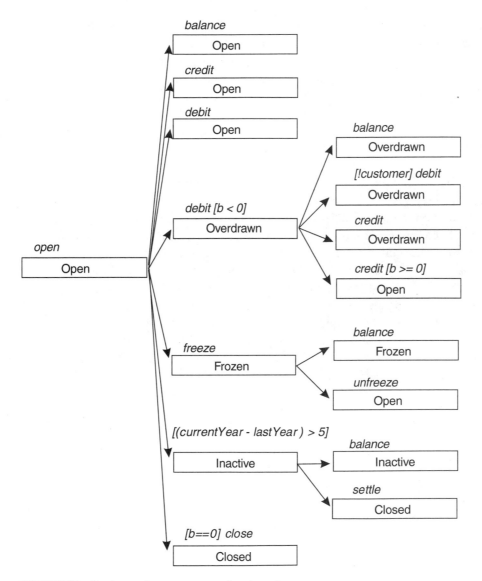

FIGURE 10.33   Basic conformance tree for class Account.

- For each conditional transition, we develop a truth table for the variables in the condition.
- We develop an additional test case for each entry in the truth table that is not exercised by the conformance tests.
- This test is added to the transition tree.

The initial conformance test suite may have already covered some or all condition transition outcomes. For example, two transitions are possible for credit messages in the *overdrawn* state: none (the account remains overdrawn) or back to *open* (the account balance becomes positive). Looking at the conformance transition tree, we find that all possible conditions (`balance < 0.00`) and (`balance >= 0.00`) are exercised.

A customer `debit` message sent to an *overdrawn* Account should be rejected (only fee debits are accepted in this state). The conformance test suite does not require trying this excluded condition, so we need to add a test.

To be accepted in the *open* state, the `close` message requires that `balance == 0.00`. We can make this condition false in two ways: `balance < 0.00`, or `balance > 0.00` Both are valid states (*overdrawn* and *open*, respectively). If `balance < 0.00`, however, we cannot be in the *open* state. The only feasible conditional variant is open/close with `balance > 0.00`. The other variant (`balance < 0.00`) is exercised in the sneak path test overdrawn/close. We therefore need to add one test case: open/close with `balance > 0.00`.

Unless we can derive the variant expansion by inspection, we should develop a truth table to enumerate of the conditions. Such a table is shown in Table 10.30. An additional test case is developed for each entry in the truth table that is not exercised by the conformance and sneak path suites. If the condition variables involve ranges, we should test boundary conditions. This analysis is identical to identifying test cases for conditional expressions (if-then, while, . . .).

TABLE 10.30   Conditional Transition Variants, Class `Account`

State	Message	Condition	Nest State
Overdrawn	Credit	Post: Balance < 0	Overdrawn
Overdrawn	Credit	Post: Balance < 0	Overdrawn
Open	Debit	Post: Balance < 0	Overdrawn
Open	Debit	Post: Balance > 0	Open
Open	—	Post: currentDate – lastDate > 5 years	Inactive
Open	Closed	Pre: Balance = 0	Closed

The temporal condition presents an interesting problem. The specification calls for an *open* Account to become *inactive* when five years pass with no activity. It does not provide an external operation to check the time elapsed since the last transaction, although the class encapsulates some mechanism to monitor time. We will not want to wait five years to complete our testing, so we will need to simulate a five-year interval and check the resultant state (resetting the system calendar may suffice). As a range is involved, we should try boundary conditions: one second less than five years and five years exactly. The conformance test would use one second more than five years (time granularity—seconds, minutes, and so on—depends on the implementation.)

The *closed* state is peculiar. Once it is entered, an Account object still exists, but cannot accept any messages. Although the model calls for this behavior, the tester should verify that this state is not a specification error. Test case design provides an opportunity to verify specifications and requirements both by applying common sense and by exercising the implementation.

Figure 10.34 shows the transition tree for Account with the additional conditional transition tests.

3. Illegal Transitions and Sneak Paths.   A test suite developed from the transition tree can demonstrate that the CUT correctly implements its behavior model. This demonstration is generally not sufficient for robust classes, however. Instead, we also should verify that the CUT does not allow any excluded behavior. An **illegal transition** is present when the CUT, in some valid state, accepts a message that is not explicitly specified for that state. An **illegal message** is an otherwise valid message that should not be accepted given the current state of the class; if accepted, an illegal transition results. A **sneak path** is a bug that allows an illegal message to be accepted, resulting in an illegal transition. For each specified state, a sneak path is possible for each message not accepted in that state. To test for sneak paths, we send illegal messages. For example, with Account, the settle message may be accepted only when an Account is in the *inactive* state. (If settle is accepted in the *overdrawn* state, an arbitrarily large overdraft could be cleared without a deposit or charge-off). One of our sneak path test cases must therefore send the settle message to an *overdrawn* Account. Figure 10.35 shows all possible sneak paths for class Account.

To confirm that no sneak paths exist, we set the CUT to a particular state and attempt each illegal message. The expected response has two parts: (1) the message should be rejected and (2) the state of the object should be unchanged after rejecting the illegal event.[18] For example, in the *open* state, the messages

---

18. See Chapter 17 for a discussion of error and exception handling.

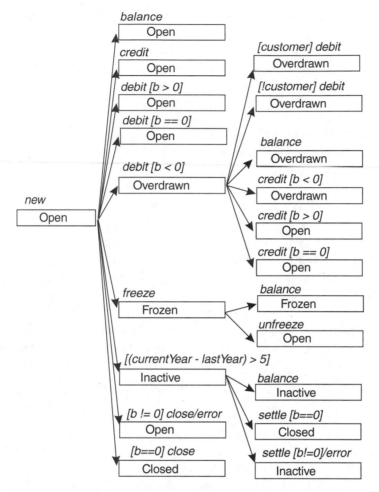

FIGURE 10.34 Expanded conformance tree for class Account.

open, unfreeze, and settle are not accepted. Although this process may seem tedious, it has two distinct advantages. First, because we have established conformance, we need to check only for sneak paths from each state—we need not worry about sneak paths traversing two or more states. Second, this process is guaranteed to reveal all sneak paths.

Illegal transitions pose interesting design questions. Some methodologists argue that an object should accept any possible sequence of messages, implying that well-designed classes should have few, if any, illegal transitions. This guidance is flawed at best, because it ignores modal classes. Although "any message

Events	States				
	Open	Overdrawn	Frozen	Inactive	Closed
Open	PSP	PSP	PSP	PSP	PSP
Credit	✓	?	PSP	PSP	PSP
Debit	?	?	PSP	PSP	PSP
Balance	✓	✓	✓	✓	PSP
Freeze	✓	PSP	PSP	PSP	PSP
Unfreeze	PSP	✓	✓	PSP	PSP
Settle	PSP	PSP	PSP	✓	PSP
5 years	✓	PSP	PSP	PSP	PSP
Close	?	PSP	PSP	PSP	PSP

Key: ✓ = Valid transition, PSP = Possible sneak path, ? = Conditional transition

FIGURE 10.35   Possible sneak paths in state/event matrix, class `Account`.

in any state" is appropriate for nonmodal classes, it is rarely appropriate for classes that model the problem domain or implement application control strategies (Jacobson's control objects, for example).

When illegal transitions are possible, how should the system handle illegal messages? The defensive school argues that illegal message handling is best done by the server. The cooperative school argues that clients have the responsibility to use servers correctly, but servers can check for illegal messages during integration testing. Compared with cooperative systems, defensive classes are easier to test because the state control strategy is localized in the server. In a cooperative system, state control for any given server is disbursed over all client/server relationships in which a server participates. With polymorphism, it may be difficult to identify (let alone test) all such relationships.

In any case, the tester needs to determine the expected response to illegal messages so that the actual response can be evaluated. Some shops follow a standard approach to exception handling, but the particulars of illegal message handling are often crafted by the individual developers. Several safe and effective ways have been developed to implement illegal message handling. An exception may be raised, the message may be treated as a no-op, or some form of error recovery may be attempted. In addition, questionable responses to illegal messages are possible: default runtime or operating system exception handlers may be assumed or, even worse, the illegal message is processed but results are unpredictable, including state corruption and abnormal termination. Finally, a sneak path may have been coded to serve as trap door for any number of purposes, including theft or sabotage. Illegal message handling implements these implicit constraints on state-based behavior. Like any other application feature, it should be tested.

4. Event Path Sensitization. The final step of test design is to transcribe transition test sequences from the transition tree. Each full and partial branch in the tree becomes a test case. To complete the test plan, we identify method parameter values, expected state, and exceptions (if any) for each transition. The test is run by setting the object under test to the initial state, applying the sequence, and then checking the resultant state and response. Table 10.31 shows the test runs transcribed from the `Account` transition tree. Values (or states) necessary for conditional expression must be determined by analysis. We can use the same ap-

TABLE 10.31 Conformance Test Suite for Class Account

	Test Run/Event Path			Expected
Run	Level 1	Level 2	Level 3	Terminal State
1	New			Open
2	New	Balance		Open
3	New	Credit		Open
4	New	Debit [b > 0]		Open
5	New	Debit [b == 0]		Open
6	New	Debit [b < 0]		Overdrawn
7	New	Debit [b < 0]	[customer] debit/error	Overdrawn
8	New	Debit [b < 0]	[!customer] debit	Overdrawn
9	New	Debit [b < 0]	Balance	Overdrawn
10	New	Debit [b < 0]	Credit [b < 0]	Overdrawn
11	New	Debit [b < 0]	Credit [b > 0]	Open
12	New	Debit [b < 0]	Credit [b == 0]	Open
13	New	Freeze		Frozen
14	New	Freeze	Balance	Frozen
15	New	Freeze	Unfreeze	Open
16	New	[cY − lY > 5]		Inactive
17	New	[cY − lY > 5]	Balance	Inactive
18	New	[cY − lY > 5]	settle [b != 0]/error	Inactive
19	New	[cY − lY > 5]	settle [b == 0]	Closed
20	New	[b != 0] close		Open
21	New	[b == 0] close		Closed

proach taken to identify path conditions for source code. Table 10.32 shows the specific test cases for test run 10.

The expected sequence and content of the test runs can be produced manually. If a trusted implementation of the state machine exists, it may be used to generate expected results by running the test suite and recording its output.

The development of test sequences for conditional transitions and sneak paths have been shown as separate, explicit steps in the Account example for clarity. However, the entire test model can be represented in a single table. Chapter 7 shows how to represent all behavior and generate a complete test suite with the response matrix.

Automation

A modal test suite may be implemented with any of the API Test Harness patterns presented in Chapter 19. Built-in test capabilities are recommended for modal classes, such as the ability to set the CUT to a state and the ability to report both abstract and concrete states. Systems that automate the modal test strategies are described in the Known Uses section for this pattern.

TABLE 10.32 Test Cases 1 and 2, Class Account

	Test Data Item	1	2.1	2.2
Test Values	State	α	α	Open
	account_Id			0000001
	balance			0.01
	last_date			<today>
	Message	new	new	balance
	account_Id			
	amount	5000.00	0.01	
	last_date			
Expected Result	State	Open	Open	Open
	account_Id	0000001	0000001	0000001
	balance	5000.00	0.01	0.01
	last_date	<today>	<today>	<today>
	Returned Value			
	account_Id			
	balance			0.01
	last_date			
	Outbound Messages			
	Exception			

The state specification can be constructed so as to allow automatic generation of required sequences, thereby avoiding a complex, hard-coded set of messages in the driver [Holzmann 91]. Chapter 17 describes how state-based testing can be implemented with a built-in sequence checker. Controllability may also be accomplished with server stubs.

We have assumed that the state of an object under test can be determined. This task may be done by method activation trace (where activation is equated with state), state-reporting capability in the CUT, or built-in test reporting in the CUT. Chapter 19 details several approaches for state reporting. Advanced test design for testing without state reporters is discussed in Chapter 7.

The most conservative (and potentially time-consuming) test strategy uses three steps:

1. Run the conformance test suite.
2. Run the sneak path test suite.
3. Run the conditional variant test suite.

The input variables and encapsulated values would change for each test case. This strategy increases the chance of revealing bugs by maximizing complexity and variety among test values.

A compromise strategy calls for initializing the CUT once, and then using the state produced by the previous test as an input to the next test where possible. The three-step process would still be followed.

A quick strategy could further reduce setup time. Conditional variant tests could be merged with conformance tests. Sneak path tests should not be performed until all conformance tests pass, as they assume conformance has been established. This strategy results in a two-phase approach. The purpose of testing is, of course, to find and repair bugs, but repairs often create new bugs. After correcting a bug, the entire test suite should be rerun.

Entry Criteria

✓ Verify minimal operability by running an alpha-omega cycle on the class under test.

✓ If critical method/scope functions exist, they should be tested before running the modal suite because leaf–node tests cannot be reached until all the predecessor tests have passed.

Exit Criteria

✓ Achieve at least branch coverage on each method in the class under test.

✓ A full modal class test suite provides N+ coverage. It requires a test for each root-to-leaf path in the expanded transition tree and a full set of sneak path pairs. See the discussion of state-based coverage in Chapter 7 for details.

✓ A higher level of confidence can be obtained by developing a class flow graph to identify any uncovered alpha-omega paths. Add message sequences to exercise these paths.

Consequences

The Modal Class Test pattern has the following requirements:

- A testable behavior model is available or can be developed.

- The class under test is state-observable—that is, we have trustworthy built-in tests or feasible access to the CUT so that we can determine the resultant state of a test run. Some servers of the class under test may require stubs to provide sufficient control of CUT state.

- A suitable test driver is available.

The test generation procedure has been mathematically proven to be able to reveal (1) missing transitions, (2) missing or incorrect action, and (3) incorrect or invalid resultant states [Chow 78]. This technique will find all sneak paths, bugs in sneak path exception handling, and value-determined faults (e.g., incorrect response to a full container) that are associated with a modeled conditional transition. This technique does not explicitly focus on incorrect output or incorrect values that are within the bounds of valid state (e.g., 2 + 2 = 6).

A modal test suite exercises the explicit and implicit behavior required of a class. Such a test suite is not necessarily complete, as classes typically implement functionality not described by the behavior model. For example, suppose that we are testing a class that uses ray tracing to illuminate a shaded polygon. We need to devise additional tests for the method(s) implementing the ray-tracing algorithm. These tests can be interlaced in the state-based sequence. For classes that have no illegal transitions, there are no sneak paths to test.

Known Uses

The Modal Class Test pattern was published in [Binder 95c, Binder 95d, Binder 95h] and has been successfully adopted by several development organizations. An experience report on application of Modal Class Test in a safety-critical application appears in [Brown+95]. The test strategy was also found to be effective for testing Smalltalk financial applications [Murphy 95].

Kirani's Sequence Checker provides a built-in test capability that will detect pair-wise operation faults on classes, but does not guarantee that all potentially faulty sequences will be applied [Kirani 94]. A similar test strategy was researched for five years and reported in [Hoffman 95]. Another adaptation of Chow's algorithm is mentioned in [McGregor+93a].

Related Patterns

The *Transition Trees* pattern recites some elements of the Modal Class Testing strategy [Firesmith 96]. The test suite produced by the *Every Kind of Event in Every State* pattern [Firesmith 96] is subsumed by a Modal Class Test test suite.

10.5   Flattened Class Scope Test Design Patterns

10.5.1   The Trouble with Superclasses

Suppose you have just developed a subclass. Its superclass has been tested to your satisfaction. Now, how much testing is needed for the subclass? Clearly, methods that appear in the subclass and the interaction among these methods should be tested. But what about the features inherited from the superclasses?

- Should you retest inherited methods?
- Can you reuse superclass tests for inherited and overridden methods?
- To what extent should you exercise interaction among methods of all superclasses and of the subclass under test?

The promise of inheritance is that known-good superclasses can be reused with confidence and that inherited test suites will be effective for subclasses. Just because a superclass has been shown to be reliable by testing or extensive usage, however, does not guarantee equal reliability in its subclasses. Separately reliable methods can fail when used in a subclass owing to interactions that occur only in that context. Likewise, questionable uses of inheritance can lead to subclass failures. Inherited features cannot be trusted in all circumstances and typically require retesting in the context of the subclass. This section analyzes the testing implications of inheritance and provides several patterns to design test suites for flattened scope. The typical process is summarized in Procedure 14.

Some Definitions

Mechanism. Inheritance is implemented by three basic mechanisms. **Extension** is the automatic inclusion of superclass features in a subclass. The superclass method implementation and interface are inherited. Some languages support name qualification to distinguish features that have the same name in both superclasses and subclasses. **Overriding** is the definition of a subclass method with the same name and message arguments as a superclass method. The interface is the same, but the method typically has a different implementation. Overriding supports polymorphic classes and abstract superclass methods. **Specialization** is the definition of methods and instance variables that are unique to a subclass.

1. Begin with the highest-level superclass in the system under test. If you are working with a trusted umbrella (framework or development environment), the root class in the system under test will be a subclass of an existing class.

2. Test the application root class in the hierarchy under test. Develop and run a class scope test plan.

3. Test refined/new methods in subclasses.

4. Perform intraclass tests. The scope of intraclass testing under inheritance is discussed in the preceding section. If the class under test uses nontested classes or nontested features of the class under test, it may be useful to provide a stub implementation of these features.

5. Continue with the next lower subclass.

Procedure 14   Superclass/Subclass Integration

Flattening. A **flattened** class makes all inherited features explicit. The term comes from Eiffel development environments, which typically include a class flattener utility. The idea of flattening is shown in Figure 10.36.

- The class scope of A includes methods A.1, A.2, and A.3. A.2 is an abstract method. A.3 is private and cannot be inherited. The flattened scope and class scope are the same.
- Class B is a subclass of A. It inherits A.1 by extension and provides an implementation for A.2's interface with B.2. Methods B.4 and B.5 are locally defined specializations. B.6 is private. The class scope of B is B.2, B.4, B.5, and B.6. Its flattened scope is A.1, B.2, B.4, B.5, and B.6.
- Class C is a subclass of B. Class C inherits A.1 and B.4 by extension and defines an overriding implementation for method 2 (C.2) and B.5 (C.5). Methods C.7 and C.8 are locally defined specializations. The class scope of C is C.2, C.4, C.7, and C.8. Its flattened scope is A.1, C.2, C.4., C.5, C.7, and C.8.

The inheritance semantics of each language (and sometimes of each compiler) determines the flattened scope of a given class.

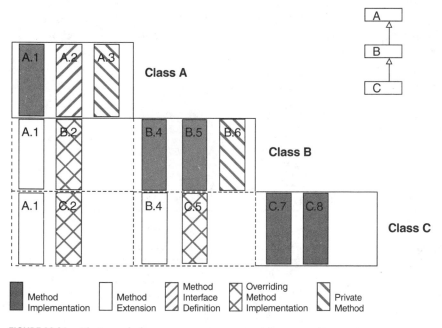

FIGURE 10.36   Flattened class scope.

Representation Versus Convenience. Inheritance can be used to represent relationships or it can serve as a programming convenience. Representation inheritance is the use of inheritance such that classes correspond to relationships in the application problem. Reusability of superclass test cases is predicated on this kind of correspondence. Convenience inheritance is the use of inheritance to grab code with little or no regard to the implicit relationships among the application entities represented.

Figure 10.37 depicts a convenience class hierarchy from the StepStone Objective-C class library [Cox 88]. These classes exhibit general-purpose collection behavior and support task scheduling that takes advantage of certain collections. `ArrayBasedCollection` and `ListBasedCollection` provide reusable methods to support application-specific subclasses. The structure means that a `Set` cannot contain anything that cannot be contained in an `Array`. `OrderedCollection` and `Queue` have first-in, first-out, add/remove behavior in common. The structure of the code only hints at this relationship, as they are symmetrically placed. The two do have differences: a `Queue` object can contain only `QueueMember` objects but any kind of object may be placed in an `OrderedCollection`. A `QueueMember` object can be a member of only one `Queue`; an `OrderedCollection` member can belong to more than one collection.

`Semaphore` is used to control access to a nonsharable resource. One `Semaphore` object is defined for a resource. The tasks waiting for the resource are represented as members of a `Queue`. In the original design, the `Semaphore` class contained an instance of `Queue`. Performance profiling showed that the

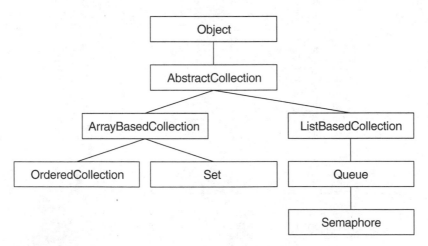

FIGURE 10.37   Implementation convienence hierarchy.

messaging overhead between these objects was significant. The hierarchy was recoded with Semaphore as a subclass of Queue, giving Semaphore access to Queue's methods and instance variables without any message overhead.

Although like-named classes in each hierarchy are much the same, the test strategies differ. A convenience hierarchy tends to inhibit the use of superclass tests because the subclasses are not usually simple subtypes. Their behavior often diverges in unusual ways. As hierarchies are modified for convenience purposes, it becomes more difficult to ensure that inherited methods are adequately exercised in a subclass. For example, although the relocated Semaphore passed all of its own tests in its new location, no testing exercised the methods now inherited from Queue.

Figure 10.38 shows a representation hierarchy for the same classes. This hierarchy more accurately reflects the relationships among the classes [Cox 90]. Semaphore inherits from Object. Collections are subdivided by access behavior, not by the underlying implementation data structure.

Inheritance-related Bugs

As always, testing should be guided by the kind of bugs that are likely. The following are some common inheritance-related bugs.

• *Incorrect Initialization.* Superclass initialization is omitted or incorrect. Deep hierarchies may lead to initialization bugs. For example, in Objective-C or Smalltalk, the new method is often inherited and uses a class-specific initialize method to set instance variable values. Determining how initialize is used in a subclass requires examination of the superclass that defines new.

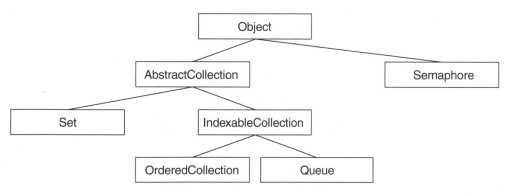

FIGURE 10.38   Representation hierarchy.

The `initialize` message must be sent to `super`, not `self`. Suppose that `new` is refined and does not send `initialize` to `self`. Super's `initialize` will not be executed.

• *Inadvertent Bindings.* Incorrect bindings can result from misunderstood name-scoping rules. For example, C++ scoping rules make private base data members invisible in a derived class. Nonprivate base data members are invisible if a derived data member has the same name as the base data member and no scope operator is applied. The binding of names under multiple inheritance introduces more subtleties.

• *Missing Override.* A subclass-specific implementation of a superclass method is omitted. As a result, that superclass method might be incorrectly bound to a subclass object, and a state could result that was valid for the superclass but invalid for the subclass owing to a stronger subclass invariant. For example, `Object`-level methods like `isEqual` or `copy` are not overridden with a necessary subclass implementation [Cox 88].

• *Naked Access.* A superclass instance variable is visible in a subclass and subclass methods update these variables directly. This can be done in C++, Java, or Objective-C, where any public or protected base class data member will allow naked access. Naked access creates the same problems as unrestricted access to global data. Changes to the superclass implementation can easily induce subclass bugs or side effects. Subclass bugs or side effects, in turn, can cause failures in superclass methods. The testing implications for implementations with naked access are simple. If a superclass is changed, we should retest both the superclass and its subclasses. If we change the subclass, we should retest both the subclass and the superclass features used in the subclass.

• *Square Peg in a Round Hole.* A subclass is incorrectly located in a hierarchy. For example, a developer locates `SquareWindow` as a subclass of `RectangularWindow`, reasoning that a square is a special case of a rectangle.[19] Methods in `SquareWindow` assume that all four sides of a window have an equal number of pixels. The inherited methods of `RectangularWindow`, however, allow different pixel lengths in adjacent sides. Suppose that `RectangularWindow::resize(x,y)` is inherited by `SquareWindow`. It allows different lengths for adjacent sides, which causes `SquareWindow` to fail after it has been resized. This situation is a design problem: a square is not a kind of

---

19. Thanks to Robert Martin for suggesting this example.

rectangle, or vice versa. Instead, both are kinds of four-sided polygons. The corresponding design solution is a superclass `FourSidedWindow`, of which `RectangularWindow` and `SquareWindow` are subclasses.

• *Naughty Children.* A subclass either does not accept all messages that the superclass accepts or leaves the object in a state that is illegal in the superclass. This situation can occur in a hierarchy that should implement a subtype relationship that conforms to the Liskov substitution principle (see Chapter 17).

• *Worm Holes.* A subclass computes values that are not consistent with the superclass invariant or superclass state invariants. The state space of lower classes of a well-formed class hierarchy must not expand on superclass state space.

• *Spaghetti Inheritance.* Top-heavy multiple inheritance and very deep hierarchies (six or more superclasses) are error-prone, even when they conform to good design practice. The wrong variable type, variable, or method may be inherited, for example, due to confusion about a multiple inheritance structure.

• *Gnarly Hierarchies.* A subclass creates new holes, boundaries, or intersections that are inconsistent with the superclass domain. Misuse of inheritance can lead to "domain shift" [Marick 95]. These new constraints may be required by subclass semantics or result from an error. If required, they may be implemented incorrectly. For example, `Base::foo( )` accepts any integer, but `Derived::foo( )` accepts only even integers.

• *Weird Hierarchies.* Inheritance is abused as a kind of code-sharing macro to support hacks without regard to the resulting semantics. A weird hierarchy takes convenience inheritance to a ridiculous extreme. For example, suppose that the class `HeavyTruck` has a persistence method `save` that appears useful to the developer of a new class `Bathtub`. `Bathtub` is made a subclass of `HeavyTruck` to "reuse" the `save` method. Testers are advised to reject this kind of programming abomination as categorically unfit.

• *Fat Interface.* A subclass inherits methods that are inappropriate or irrelevant; that is, it has a **fat interface** [Stroustroup 92a]. For example, suppose that class `Money` is a subclass of class `BigDecimal`, which provides a method to convert Booleans to decimals. The designer does not specify a method to coerce `BooleanToMoney` because it is nonsense. The `BooleanToNumber` message is still accepted by `Money` objects, with unpredictable results. Such situations are really design problems (see Square Peg in a Round Hole). If they cannot be avoided, then nonsense methods should be overridden with a no-op or other safe implementation. The *Protocol Hierarchy* pattern offers a design solution for this problem [Lakos 96].

These and other inheritance-related bugs can be found by testing at flattened class scope. This list can be put to even better use as a checklist for design, inspections, or desk checking. As always, prevention is preferable to debugging.

10.5.2   Test Strategy for Flattened Classes

What is the scope of an adequate test suite for a flattened class? To answer this question, we consider:

- The extent to which we can assume that individually correct superclass components do and do not guarantee correct behavior when reused in a subclass (Testing Axioms).
- The kind of testing that can be achieved by inheriting superclass test suites (Inheriting Class Test Suites).

◆ Testing Axioms

Composability of objects is an article of faith that motivates the mosaic modularity of the object-oriented paradigm. A composable class "favors the production of software elements which may then be freely combined with each other to produce new systems, possibly in an environment quite different from the one in which they were initially developed" [Meyer 97, 44]. The rationale is that correct systems may be obtained by "applying the rule of composition at every stage of the construction process: My product will meet its specification if each of its subcomponents meet theirs and if I assemble them correctly" [Cox 88, 44]. Composability has proven elusive, at best. Object-oriented languages do not inherently guarantee composable components, even when great care is taken to design composable interfaces [Lieberherr 92].

While composability and the ways that object-oriented languages and frameworks support it is generally a good thing, the presumption of composability has fostered several incorrect perceptions [Binder 95b], including the notion that reuse by inheritance reduces the need for subclass testing.

It has been shown with mathematical certainty that whatever degree of composability one obtains in a software system, one cannot assume that individually correct parts necessarily result in a correct whole.[20] Weyuker's testing axioms establish limits on the transferability of code coverage for test suites applied to modular systems [Weyuker 88]. Perry and Kaiser interpreted these axioms for subclass testing [Perry 90].

- The **antiextensionality** axiom states that a test suite that covers one implementation of a specification does not necessarily cover a different implementation of the same specification. A responsibility may be implemented in many ways. Thus, even if methods `Base::insertNewElement` and `Derived::insertNewElement` have identical responsibilities, test cases that cover `Base::insertNewElement` do not necessarily cover `Derived::insertNewElement`.

- The **antidecomposition** axiom states that the coverage achieved for a module under test is not necessarily achieved for modules that it calls. A test suite that covers a class or a method does not necessarily cover the server objects of that class or method. Thus, a test suite that achieves any kind of coverage of `Account` guarantees nothing about coverage of classes `Money` or `Date`, objects of which are servers of `Account`.

- The **anticomposition** axiom states that test suites that are individually adequate for segments within a module are not necessarily adequate for the module as a whole.[21] Thus, a collection of test suites that individually achieve method scope coverage x do not necessarily provide coverage x of all intraclass paths. Individual method scope test suites do not guarantee that all class interactions will be tested, at either class scope or flattened class scope. Just as we cannot be confident in a class that has passed only method scope tests, we cannot be confident in a subclass that has passed only subclass scope testing, even if both superclass and subclass methods have already passed their own test suites. This is perhaps the most important result of the testing axioms, providing a formal justification for testing at class scope and flattened class scope.

---

20. I use "correct" in the formal sense here. Exhaustive testing is equivalent to proof of correctness. The composition result of testing axioms must hold for exhaustive testing and therefore hold for correctness established by proof. Suppose some modules have been shown to be correct by exhaustive testing. Let these modules compose a system. By antidecomposition and anticomposition, composition is not a sufficient condition for a correct system. Because exhaustive testing is equivalent to proof, even a system composed of analytically proven modules cannot be assumed to be correct as a system.

21. Here an adequate test suite simply means one that meets a minimally acceptable coverage criterion—for example, statement coverage [Weyuker 88].

Some Subclass Development Scenarios

The testing axioms suggest how much testing is implied by the structure of inheritance. But what kind of testing is necessary? The implications of these rules for subclass testing can be shown by considering several development scenarios involving subclasses.

1. *Superclass modifications.* Suppose we change some methods in class Base. Clearly, we should retest the changed methods and the interaction among changed and unchanged methods in Base. But what about an unchanged subclass Derived, which inherits from Base? By anticomposition, the changed methods from Base should also be exercised in the unique context of the subclass.

2. *Subclass modifications.* Suppose we add or modify subclass Derived, without changing its superclass Base. By antidecomposition and anticomposition, we should retest methods inherited from Base, even if they were not changed. For example, suppose that we develop class Account, test it, and add it to our class library (Figure 10.39). Later, we develop CertOfDeposit as a subclass of Account. Unfortunately, we overlook the fact that both initBalance() and numberCD() change acct_bal. We would not find this error unless we retested *both* numberCD() and the inherited, previously tested initBalance() in class CertOfDeposit.

3. *Reuse of the test suite for an overridden superclass method.* Suppose we add a subclass method Derived::foo that overrides superclass method Base::foo. Clearly, the new method should be tested. Would the superclass test cases for Base::foo necessarily achieve the same coverage for the method Derived::foo? No, not necessarily (by antiextensionality). If the domains and paths in Derived::foo are only slightly different, the superclass test cases will probably not provide the same coverage. Additional test cases will probably be needed at lower levels of the hierarchy.

4. *Overriding a superclass method used by a superclass method.* Overriding a subclass method can easily produce indirect effects on inherited methods, even when the inherited superclass method is untouched. Suppose we develop classes Account and CertOfDeposit, test them, and then add both to our class library (see Figure 10.40). Account::rollOver( ) uses Account:: yearEndAmt( ) and is inherited by extension in CertOfDeposit. Later, we override Account::yearEndAmt( ) with CertOfDeposit::yearEndAmt( ), resulting in CertOfDeposit::yearEndAmt( ) being used by the inherited Account:: rollOver( ). Although we have not changed code in Account::rollOver( )

```
class Account {
  Money acct_bal;     // current balance

  // . . .

  void initBalance(Money amt)  {
    // Set current balance to parameter
    acct_bal = amt;
  }

  // . . .
};
```

```
class CertOfDeposit : public Account {
  // . . .

  void numberCD(int shares)  {
    // Set current balance to
    // share value * shares
    acct_bal = shares * cdValue;
  }

  // . . .
};
```

FIGURE 10.39 Correct superclass code causes subclass to fail.

it will now behave differently. Strange as it may seem, we cannot assume that rollover( ) is correct for CertOfDeposit simply because it was previously correct and no explicit changes have been made. Nor can we assume that reusing the test cases for Account::rollOver( ) will give the same coverage for rollover( ) in CertOfDeposit. If we later add a third subclass VarRateCD that implements a VarRateCD::yearEndAmt( ), the same retesting of rollover( ) is indicated again—this time in the context of a VarRateCD object.

5. *Addition of a new subclass method.* Suppose an entirely new method is added to a subclass. Subclass methods typically uses other inherited class features, but everything else is defined locally. A method scope test suite should be developed, and the class scope test suite should be revised to exercise the new method in an interesting sequence.

```
class Account {
  // . . .
  rollOver()  // Year end transaction, reset YTD totals
  // . . .
  yearEndAmt()  // Calculate balance-based 1099 amount
  // . . .
}
```

```
class CertOfDeposit: public Account {
  // . . .
  yearEndAmt()  // Calculate fixed rate 1099 amount
  // . . .
}
```

```
class VarRateCD : public CertOfDeposit {
  // . . .
  yearEndAmt()  // Calculate variable rate 1099 amount
  // . . .
}
```

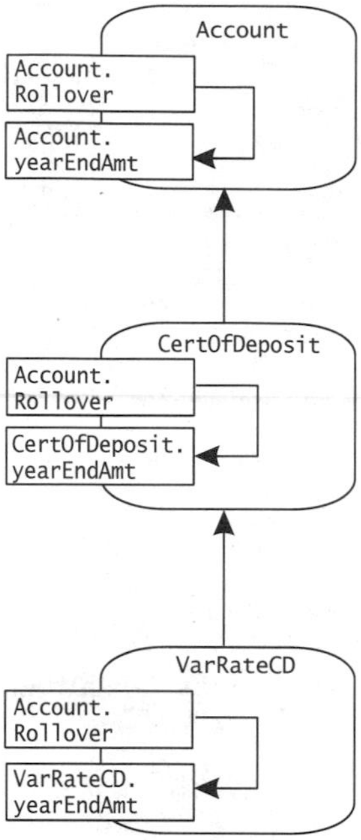

FIGURE 10.40 Overloading results in new context.

6. *Change to an abstract superclass interface.* Suppose an abstract superclass and several overriding subclass methods have been developed. The superclass method interface is changed. We must then retest all subclasses, even if they have not changed.

Multiple inheritance shares these problems and offers additional opportunities for error. Figure 10.41 suggests how classes that work correctly on their own can be combined to produce incorrect results. Because a name clash occurs, default scoping rules will determine which base class method is bound to the derived class. The resulting behavior can be quite a surprise.

Inheritance does not generally reduce the volume of test cases or the prudent scope of testing. Instead, the number of interactions to be verified is multiplied at each lower level of a hierarchy. Although some early research recommended skipping superclass method scope tests on subclass,[22] this step is advisable only under very limited conditions. In particular, if the hierarchy

22. The argument for skipping superclass tests on a subclass appears in [Harrold+92] and [McGregor+94] and is referred to as Hierarchic Incremental Testing (HIT).

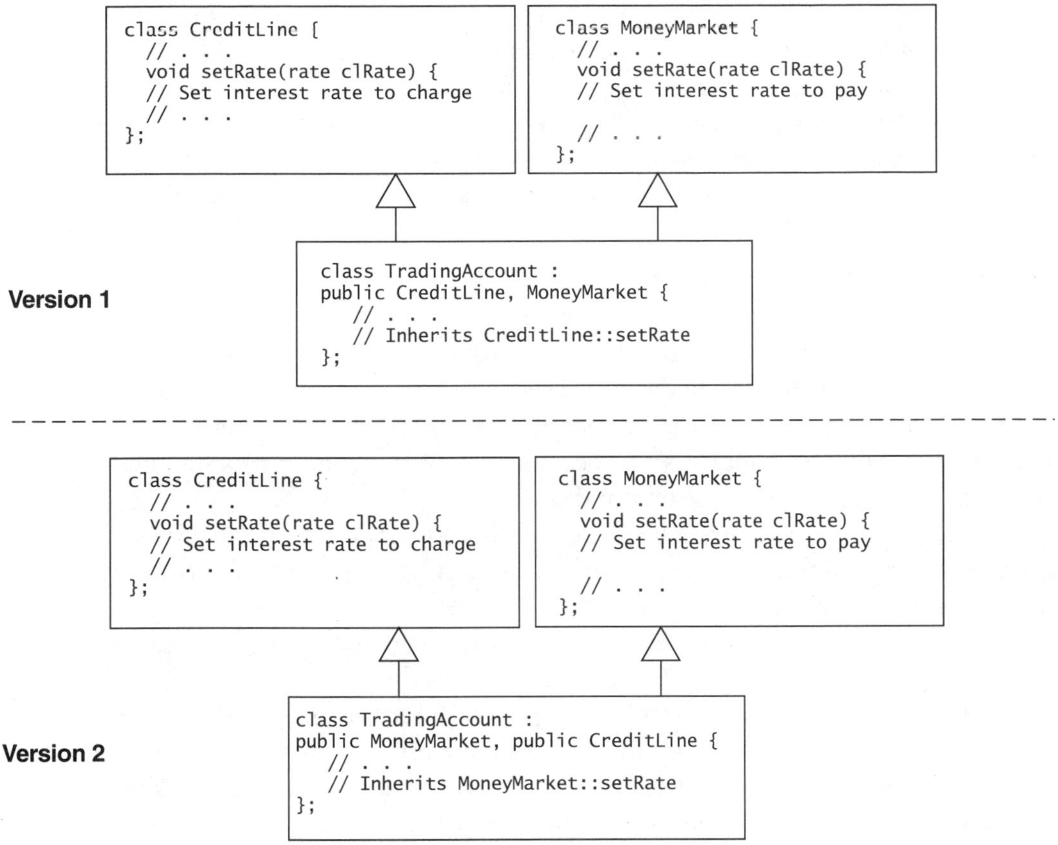

```
class CreditLine {                          class MoneyMarket {
    // . . .                                    // . . .
    void setRate(rate clRate) {                 void setRate(rate clRate) {
    // Set interest rate to charge             // Set interest rate to pay
    // . . .
};                                                  // . . .
                                            };
```

```
                    class TradingAccount :
                    public CreditLine, MoneyMarket {
                        // . . .
                        // Inherits CreditLine::setRate
                    };
```

Version 1

- -

```
class CreditLine {                          class MoneyMarket {
    // . . .                                    // . . .
    void setRate(rate clRate) {                 void setRate(rate clRate) {
    // Set interest rate to charge             // Set interest rate to pay
    // . . .
};                                                  // . . .
                                            };
```

```
                    class TradingAccount :
                    public MoneyMarket, public CreditLine {
                        // . . .
                        // Inherits MoneyMarket::setRate
                    };
```

Version 2

FIGURE 10.41   Multiple inheritance results in new contexts.

under test is a polymorphic server, skipping any of the superclass tests for a subclass is a bad idea. Such a hierarchy should conform to the LSP, so repeating superclass tests is an effective way to reveal subclass LSP conformance bugs. The designers of the ASTOOT system use this strategy to verify type/subtype consistency [Doong+94].

For example, suppose that the bug previously sketched in Square Peg in a Round Hole (page 502) has been coded. The subclass now fails to strengthen the invariant so that height always equals width for a Square derived from a Rectangle. If we blithely assume that the Rectangle methods are correct in this new context and skip retesting, this bug would probably escape. If we rerun the Rectangle tests on a Square object, however, the first attempt to resize a Square object using a Rectangle method will probably reveal the bug.

Retesting can be safely skipped only when (1) there is no possible data flow or control flow from or to the superclass and subclass methods, or (2) the subclass is null and simply renames the superclass. Both of these cases are unusual and result from questionable coding. In short, all polymorphic superclass tests should be repeated for their subclasses. This need not be an onerous task if your testware is designed to support subclass retesting as shown in Chapter 19.

Inheriting Class Test Suites

Inheritance can ease rerunning a superclass test suite on a subclass object. Superclass test suites may be inherited in a hierarchy of test driver classes that parallels the class hierarchy under test. Design considerations and patterns for such test drivers are presented in Chapter 19. Note, however, that running a superclass test suite on a subclass object is only a partial solution for the additional testing load imposed by inheritance.

To exercise interactions between superclass and subclass methods, the subclass driver must implement additional test cases. These test cases cannot be inherited and may conflict with inherited test cases.

If the superclass test suite exercises private methods, these tests will not work in the context of the subclass.

If the class hierarchy under test is designed to conform with the Liskov substitution principle (LSP), then rerunning all superclass test suites is an effective means to check LSP conformance. A hierarchy is LSP-conforming if a subclass object performs correctly when substituted for a superclass object in a superclass client. Applying a superclass test suite to a subclass object provides a systematic exercise of this capability.

If a subclass is not intended to be LSP-conforming, then the value of its superclass test suite is less clear. The superclass test suite can result in a no-pass test run, but the developer can claim that the subclass is correct because users are not expected to send some superclass messages to subclass objects. This situation is often a legitimate compromise to solve a maintenance or performance problem, but is just as often an excuse for sloppy design. In either case, the superclass test suite is of limited use.

10.5.3   The Patterns

A class should have unique responsibilities at each level of a hierarchy (if not, no subclass is needed). The test suite must be changed accordingly. Each subclass provides a new context and new paths for interaction of local and inherited features. Although rerunning superclass method scope test cases in a subclass is useful, this is not sufficient to test superclass/subclass interactions. The goals for testing a flattened class are simple:

- Retest superclass methods only to the extent necessary to gain confidence that inherited features work correctly in the context of the subclass.
- Reuse superclass test suites as much as possible.
- Extend class test suites with test cases that are effective for the kind of bugs that accompany inheritance.

Setting the scope of testing for a flattened class is, like most testing problems, a question of making the best use of available testing time. The preceding analysis shows that, in most circumstances, testing the interaction of superclass and subclass features is warranted in addition to testing subclass specializations. The elements of testing strategy at flattened class scope then consist of the following items:

- Consider the superclass. Suppose that your application class inherits from a trusted development environment like a Smalltalk system, a Java Development Kit, or Microsoft's foundation classes. In this case, you can view the testing problem more as a problem of integrating your code with a trusted system. On the other hand, if your superclasses do not warrant this level of confidence, it is prudent to retest superclass features in the context of the subclass. Table 10.33 outlines the scope of testing in this case.
- Use the pattern to design tests that extend the subclass class test suite scenarios.
- Implement additional test cases by concatenating or interleaving them with the existing subclass test suite.
- Run the flattened class test suite. If a superclass test suite is available, then it should be run as a regression test, but not as the primary vehicle for exercising the subclass.
- Use built-in tests. In particular, consider implementing the *Percolation* pattern (see Chapter 17).
- The integration strategy is much the same as at class scope.

TABLE 10.33   Decision Rules for Scope of Flattened Class Testing

	Type of Subclass Method		
	Extension	Overriding	Specialization
Should this method be included in the class scope and flattened scope inter-action testing?	Yes[1]	Yes	Yes
Prudent extent of retesting of this method in the subclass context.	Minimal[2,3]	Full[4]	Full
Reuse superclass method tests.	Yes	Probably[5]	NA
Develop new subclass method tests.	Maybe[3]	Yes	Yes

NA = Not applicable.

1. By anticomposition (individual method test cases are not sufficient to test method interactions).
2. Method scope tests do not need to be repeated [Harold+92].
3. New test cases are needed when inherited features use locally defined features as a result of names being bound to subclass features instead of superclass features.
4. By antiextensionality (different implementation of the same function requires different tests).
5. Superclass test cases are reusable to the extent that the superclass and subclasses comply with the Liskov substitution principle.

- Flattened code coverage can be achieved by instrumenting the super-class code before the subclass test package is built. Most coverage analyzers instrument only one level at a time.

All of the patterns in this chapter can be applied to subclasses. The final two patterns introduced here concentrate on testing at flattened class scope. Inherited features are explicitly considered in the test design.

- *Polymorphic Server Test.* Design reusable test suite for an LSP-compliant polymorphic server hierarchy.
- *Modal Hierarchy Test.* Design test suite for hierarchy of modal classes.

Polymorphic Server Test

Intent

Design a test suite at flattened class scope that verifies LSP compliance for a polymorphic server hierarchy.

Context

The hierarchy under test contains overridden methods and is nonmodal. If the server class is modal, use the *Modal Hierarchy Test* pattern.

The structure of overriding methods in a polymorphic class hierarchy controls how superclass methods are assigned to subclass objects. An overriding method must respect the constraints of methods that it overrides to provide a consistent and correct response. Reuse is facilitated if such a class is trustworthy.

An attempt to verify a server in the context of every client is an impossible task. Instead, how can we exercise the overridden methods in a polymorphic hierarchy with a driver to verify that a correct and consistent response is produced for all bindings for all clients?

Fault Model

Any of the fault classes described earlier in the Inheritance-Related Bugs section can result in an incorrect or inconsistent response to an overridden method.

Clearly, such a fault cannot be reached unless each overridden method is exercised for each class of object to which it may be bound. The trigger typically consists of a method used in a new context. The preceding discussion of testing axioms suggests how different contexts can trigger or bypass a failure. Assertions designed according to the *Percolation* pattern are effective propagation amplifiers.

Faults in clients are not the target of this pattern (see *Polymorphic Message Test* for an approach to testing clients of a polymorphic server). The general fault hazards posed by polymorphism are discussed in Chapter 4.

Strategy

Test Model

The fault conditions require that each polymorphic method be exercised in its defining class and all subclasses that inherit it. The test suite checks for conformance with the Liskov substitution principle: Clients of a polymorphic server can substitute any subtype without causing a failure. With these test suites in hand, the solution to this testing problem is obtained by structuring test suites and test drivers.

For example, a C++ member function that includes a Base& (or const Base&) parameter may be passed a reference to any object of a class derived from this base class. If the derived class object does not conform to LSP, the base class test suite may reveal this fault. In effect, superclass test cases can be applied to testing derived class(es). We can verify that the "is-a" relationship holds and that derived classes correctly implement the base class interface and its contracts.

Automation

Consider the C++ Account hierarchy.

```
class Account {
    // ...
    virtual void debit( );
    virtual void listTransactions( );
    // ...
};

class Savings: public Account  {
    // ...
    virtual void debit( );
    virtual void listTransactions( );
    // ...
};

class CertificateOfDeposit: public Savings {
    // ...
    virtual void debit( );
    virtual void listTransactions( );
    // ...
};
```

Suppose we have developed a corresponding set of test drivers for the virtual (polymorphic) functions of the class.

```
void PolyTestAccount( Account& acctUnderTest )
{
    // ...
acctUnderTest.debit( );
acctUnderTest.listTransactions( );
    // ...
}
```

```
void PolyTestSavings( Account& saveAcctUnderTest )
{
    // ...
    savingsAcctUnderTest.debit( );
    savingsAcctUnderTest.listTransactions( );
    // ...
}

void PolyTestCertificateOfDeposit(Account& cdAcctUnderTest )
{
    // ...
    cdacctUnderTest.debit( );
    cdacctUnderTest.listTransactions( );
    // ...
}
```

Each test driver implements a test suite designed to exercise the derived class's responsibilities implemented by polymorphic functions. To verify that these responsibilities are correctly implemented under all bindings, we package the test suite into callable drivers according to the polymorphic interface.

```
int main ( ) {

    Account acctUnderTest = new Account( );
    Savings saveAcctUnderTest = new Savings( );
    CertificateOfDeposit cdacctUnderTest = new
    CertificateOfDeposit( );

    PolyTestAccount(acctUnderTest);

    PolyTestSavings(acctUnderTest);
    PolyTestSavings(saveAcctUnderTest);

    PolyTestCertificateOfDeposit(acctUnderTest);
    PolyTestCertificateOfDeposit(saveAcctUnderTest);
    PolyTestCertificateOfDeposit(cdAcctUnderTest);

    return 1;

}
```

An actual driver will probably do other things not shown in this example: reset the state of object under test between calls, generate reports, and so on. See Chapter 19 for a discussion of test drivers and considerations for inherited test suites.

This structure binds each polymorphic method implementation to an object of all of its superclasses and reuses superclass test suites. The drivers test only the polymorphic functions, as we cannot expect a superclass to respond to messages that are unique to a subclass. The balance of the subclass interaction tests must be packaged in a different test driver, or the test driver must be able to determine which messages to send based on the class of the object under test.

Entry Criteria

✓ An alpha-omega cycle is developed from the subclass up.

✓ All superclasses pass their test suites.

Exit Criteria

✓ Every superclass method is exercised in the context of every subclass object once.

Consequences

The main benefit of a Polymorphic Server Test test suite is that it establishes high confidence in the reusability of polymorphic servers. It will reveal faults that prevent LSP conformance and may reveal other inheritance-related faults. Input/output and sequential behavior faults are not the target of this pattern, so the test suite should not be considered complete by itself. In fact, any appropriate test pattern may be used to design additional tests to cover the balance of the server's responsibilities. Inherited superclass test suites cannot test the subclass state model. If the subclass's state model is a proper subset of the superclass's state model, then the superclass's modal test suite can likely be recoded for use on the subclass.

This pattern requires the design and development of test drivers that parallel the polymorphic structure of the class under test. Test suites for method, class, and flattened class scope responsibilities should be implemented in separate test suites.

Known Uses

McCabe's "Safe" approach requires that each interface be exercised once and argues that systematic testing of all possible server bindings is not necessary [McCabe+94]. Firesmith [Firesmith 95] and McGregor [McGregor 94c] outline similar strategies for state-based testing under inheritance.

Related Patterns

Clients of a verified server should use Polymorphic Message Test to verify that their usage is correct (no amount of server testing can verify that any client is correct). The *Percolation* pattern for built-in tests will greatly facilitate initial detection of bugs and subsequent regression testing when used with this pattern. Assertions developed for *Percolation* are applicable to this kind of hierarchy.

Modal Hierarchy Test

Intent

Design a flattened class scope test suite for a hierarchy of modal classes.

Context

Suppose that the class under test is a subclass of a modal class. The subclass must conform not only to its own state model, but also to the superclass state model. How can we design a test suite that validates the flattened state model? This question is applicable for subclasses of a modal class or modal subclasses.

Fault Model

The state-based faults and failures that can occur at flattened scope include all those that can occur at class scope. In addition to the state faults that may occur at class scope, a subclass can introduce state-based failures if the superclass state control requirements are not observed.

- A valid superclass transition is rejected.
- An illegal superclass message transition is accepted.
- An incorrect action is produced on a superclass transition.

The requirements to obtain the correct relationships among superclass and subclass states are complex given the various ways that inheritance may restrict, redefine, or expand a state space. A subclass is often implemented by adding its own instance variables. In effect, these variables increase the number of dimensions in the state space.

In an LSP-compliant modal subclass, all behavior of the superclass must be respected. Thus, if methods are overridden, the overridden methods must be accepted in the same states, must produce the same actions, and result in the same states. An overridden method may produce states that are a subdivision or an extension of a superclass state, but cannot change the superclass state. Classes can be modal without being LSP-compliant, however. A superclass may have faults that are revealed only in the context of subclass usage.

Strategy

Test Model

The test model is the same as that employed for *Modal Class Test*. In this pattern, however, the state machine must reflect the states and events of the flattened class. The relationship of the superclass and subclass state machines makes a considerable difference in the test approach of choice. Table 10.34 presents the relevant considerations. The development of a flattened state machine model is discussed in Section 7.3.5, Inheritance and Class Flattening. A complete example is provided in the `ThreePlayerGame` example introduced in Section 7.4.3.

Automation

Inherited superclass test suites cannot test the subclass state model. If the subclass's state model is a proper subset of the superclass's state model, then the superclass's modal test suite can likely be recoded for use on the subclass. Use *Percolation* for built-in tests to increase confidence and ease debugging of modal subclasses. See Chapter 19 for a discussion of test drivers and considerations for inherited test suites.

Entry Criteria

✓ An alpha-omega cycle should be developed from the subclass up.

✓ All superclasses pass their test suites.

Exit Criteria

The exit criteria for the Modal Hierarchy Test pattern are the same as those for *Modal Class Test*, but at flattened scope.

✓ Achieve at least branch coverage on each method in the class under test.

✓ A full modal class test suite provides N+ coverage. It requires a test for each root-to-leaf path in the expanded transition tree and a full set of sneak path pairs. See section 7.4.6, Choosing a State-based Test Strategy, for details.

✓ A higher level of confidence can be obtained by developing a class flow graph to identify any uncovered alpha-omega paths. Add message sequences to exercise these paths.

TABLE 10.34 Testing Strategies for Modal Subclasses

Superclass State Model		Subclass State Model	Flattened Subclass's State Model	LSP Compliance Possible?	Test Approach
Partitioned	Reduced	Extended			
No	No	No	Same.	Yes	Rerun superclass test suite as regression.
No	No	Yes	New state invariant conditions for new subclass instance variables. Super's state invariant conditions same.	Yes	Revise subclass model/test suite. Rerun superclass test suite as regression.
No	Yes	No	At least one super state invariant weakened. Probable bug.	No	Revise subclass model/test suite. Superclass test suite may result in an anomaly.
No	Yes	Yes	New state invariant conditions for new subclass variables. At least one super state invariant weakened. Probable bug.	No	Revise subclass model/test suite. Superclass test suite may result in an anomaly.
Yes	No	No	At least one super state invariant subdivided and strengthened.	Yes	Rerun superclass test suite as regression.
Yes	No	Yes	At least one super state invariant subdivided and strengthened. New state invariant conditions for new subclass variables.	Yes	Revise subclass model/test suite. Rerun superclass test suite as regression.
Yes	Yes	No	At least one super state invariant subdivided and strengthened. At least one super state invariant weakened. Probable bug.	No	Revise subclass model/test suite. Superclass test suite may result in an anomaly.
Yes	Yes	Yes	At least one super state invariant subdivided and strengthened. New state invariant conditions for new subclass variables. Probable bug.	No	Revise subclass model/test suite. Superclass test suite may result in an anomaly.

Note: Number of events cannot be reduced, because we assume methods cannot be subtracted.

Consequences

Modal percolation testing requires development of a flattened scope state model. See *Modal Class Test* for additional considerations.

Known Uses

Firesmith [Firesmith 95] and McGregor [McGregor 94c] outline similar strategies for state-based testing under inheritance.

10.6   Bibliographic Notes

Coverage and Implementation-based Testing

Implementation-based testing is surveyed in [Ntafos 88], [White 87], and [Zhu 96]. Beizer's exposition of implementation-based testing is definitive [Beizer 90]. [Deo 74] is a standard text on graph theory. See [Beizer 90] for details of path expressions. Myers' levels of predicate coverage are still applicable [Myers 79].

The basis path approach is presented in [McCabe 76] and [McCabe+89]. The basis-path testing model (also known as structured testing) and its problems have been analyzed extensively [Myers 77, Beizer 90, Henderson 92].

Data flow testing strategies have been explored since the mid-1970s [Adrion 82]. Several papers established the basic approach [Rapps+85, Frankl+88]. Beizer discusses its application for implementation-based testing [Beizer 90] and black box testing [Beizer 95]. Parrish and Zweben provide a concise summary of research papers on data flow testing [Parrish+95]. An analysis of data flow across module interfaces in conventional languages that considers global storage, recursive activation, and resolution of formal and actual parameter names appears in [Harrold 91].

The relationship among implementation-based coverage strategies has been formally analyzed by many researchers [Frankl+88, Clarke+89, Frankl+93, Parrish+95]. Critiques of this concept appear in [Hamlet+90] and [Hamlet 97].

White and Cohen's conference paper on domain testing [White+78] was later published as [White+80].

Domain testing has been studied for many years. Beizer provides a concise and thorough presentation of this subject, with citations of key research results [Beizer 95]. The same ground is covered, albeit in more detail, in [Beizer 90].

Method Scope Test Design

The primary source for the Category-Partition testing approach is [Ostrand +88]. Roper provides a concise survey of conventional testing techniques [Roper 94]. The use of recursion in object-oriented programming is nicely presented in [Jézéquel 96a]. See the bibliographic notes in Part II for more on the development of test models.

Class Scope Test Design

A comprehensive survey of class and method scope test approaches appears in [Binder 96i.] The modal class pattern first appeared in [Binder 95c] and [Binder

95d]. The concept of class modality was first published in [Binder 96h] and appeared with minor revisions in [Binder 97a], including a domain-based test value selection approach.

The class flow graph model was presented in [Binder 95a]. Implementation data flow at class scope is considered in [Harrold+94] and [Chang 96]. See the Known Uses sections under each pattern for related reports.

Flattened Class Scope

The notion of class flattening is defined in [Meyer 88] and supported in most Eiffel development environments. Pragmatic guidance for design of class hierarchies can be found in [Page-Jones 95]. Meyer's discussion of design and implementation considerations for inheritance provides a useful analysis of programming convenience, good class design, and general problems in taxonomies [Meyer 97].

Chapter 11   Reusable Components

<hr>

*. . . users are the true experts in all the imaginative ways
the library can be misused, because the original
developers know too much about correct use.*

Brian Marick

Overview

This chapter focuses on components that support reuse by source
code augmentation: abstract classes, generic classes, and application
frameworks. Reuse mechanisms are reviewed and the contribution of
testing to promoting reuse is considered. The chapter introduces four
test design patterns that explain how to select a test instantiation and
apply other test design patterns to the test instantiation. These four patterns identify additional testing necessary to achieve high confidence
for each kind of reusable component.

11.1   Testing and Reuse

11.1.1   Reuse Mechanisms

Although reuse has been a goal of software development from the earliest days
of computing, object-oriented languages have been explicitly designed to facilitate reuse through inheritance, dynamic binding, and generic types. With skillful design and hard work (also known as "iterative development"), classes can
be produced that will be useful for many applications. A **component** is a stand-
alone software artifact that may be used in multiple contexts. A **consumer** uses

a component developed by a **producer**. The mechanism of reuse differs according to the binding time of the reusable component. Reuse may be accomplished by **source code augmentation, translation-time binding,** or **link-time/runtime interfaces**. A **component toolkit (component development environment)** is a collection of programming utilities that support reuse of a certain component library.

Translation-time reuse is supported by macro substitution, inheritance, and composition.[1] Problems with macros have limited their role in reuse. A class declaration that specifies a superclass accomplishes reuse by inheritance. An instance variable declaration that specifies a class accomplishes reuse by **composition**. Classes that support composition are often provided as **class libraries** whose members share some common attribute—for example, data structures like lists, queues, stacks, and sets. Classes in the library typically can be used independently. Several commercially available class libraries are in wide use, such as the C++ offerings from Rogue Wave and Rational.

A **foundation class library** supports translation-time reuse by inheritance. Foundation classes typically provide a broad range of related capabilities. The OpenStep Foundation Kit, the class library included in Smalltalk development environments, Microsoft Foundation Classes, and the Java Foundation Classes are examples of commercially available foundation class hierarchies. With these classes, the consumer develops subclasses to implement application-specific responsibilities.

Executable components support link-time/runtime reuse. Consumers must use a predefined API to send a message (call the services) of an executable component; they typically do not have access to source code. Some commercially available component libraries have become quite popular, including Sun's JavaBeans and Microsoft's ActiveX (COM/DCOM). Test patterns for producers of executable components are presented in Chapter 12. Test patterns for consumers of executable components are presented in Chapters 13 and 14.

An **abstract class** (or abstract superclass or abstract base class) exports method interfaces that do not have an implementation within the abstract class. An abstract class often serves as the root class of a polymorphic hierarchy. It supports dynamic (runtime) polymorphism by providing a common, yet decoupled, interface for an arbitrary number of overriding subclass method implementations. Although we cannot instantiate an object of an abstract class, we can declare an instance of an abstract class. Instances of concrete subclasses

---

1. In yet another example of gratuitous jargonization, the corresponding UML terms are generalization (inheritance) and aggregation (composition).

are dynamically bound to this symbolic name, allowing any subclass object to accept messages for methods defined in the abstract class.

A **generic class** requires a type parameter that binds generic instance variables and operations to a specific type (class), providing static (translation-time) polymorphism. Generic classes are well suited to implementing data types whose general behavior is nearly identical—for example, collection classes. Generic classes are supported in Ada 95 (generic types), C++ (template classes), and Eiffel (generic classes.) The C++ Standard Template Library offers an excellent example of how generic classes can support reuse. Using translation-time binding improves efficiency and type safety, and it avoids problems with comparable implementations using inheritance and runtime polymorphism. Some flexibility is lost, however [Carroll+95, Meyer 97]. The semantics of abstract and generic classes vary among languages. Because genericity requires strong translation-time type checking, it is not supported in languages like Java, Objective-C, and Smalltalk.[2] Table 11.1 compares support for abstract and generic classes.

A **framework** is an implementation of a reusable, domain-specific design.[3] It provides a partial application system. Frameworks are often a realization of several large-scale design patterns and many small-scale patterns [Coplien+95, Buschmann+96, Martin+98]. The consumer must specialize and develop additional code before the framework becomes a working system. With a **white box framework**, consumers typically develop implementations for abstract classes provided in the framework and additional application-specific code. After refinement and stabilization, a white box framework may become a **black box framework**, in which composition plays a larger role.

The general structure of reusable components is influenced by language-specific mechanisms. Speaking from the Smalltalk perspective, Johnson summarizes how language reuse mechanisms support black box frameworks: "Use inheritance to organize your component library and composition to combine

---

2. Objective-C and Smalltalk support reuse with inheritance and dynamic binding. For example, OpenStep Foundation Kit collections (e.g., `NSSet`, `NSArray`, and `NSDictionary`) are subclasses of `NSObject`. In each, the type (class) of collection elements is coded as `NSObject`. The actual class of an element object is bound at runtime, in contrast to translation-time or link-time binding of strongly typed languages.

3. When the reuse community and framework developers speak of a domain, they are not using the testing sense of domain (see Section 10.2.4, Domain Testing Models). Instead, they mean "a group or a set of systems or functional areas, within systems, that exhibit similar functionality. . . . Domain engineering . . . is the process of defining the scope (i.e., domain definition), analyzing the domain (i.e., domain analysis), specifying the structure (i.e., domain architecture development), building the components (e.g., requirements, designs, software code, documentation) for a class of subsystems that will support reuse" [Kean 97].

TABLE 11.1 Language Support for Abstract Classes, Generic Classes, Interface Extensions

	Abstract Class	Generic Class	Loosely Coupled Extension
Ada 95	Abstract type	Generic procedure Generic package	Not supported
C++	Class with at least one pure virtual function	Template class Template function	Not supported
Eiffel	Deferred class—a class with at least one deferred feature	Generic class	Not supported
Java	Abstract class Abstract method	Not supported	Interface
Objective-C	Not explicitly supported but abstract class is a common idiom; protocol and category definitions may be used with similar effect	Not supported	Protocol, category
Smalltalk	Not explicitly supported, but abstract class is a common idiom	Not supported	Not supported

the components into applications. Essentially, inheritance will provide a taxonomy of parts to ease browsing and composition will allow maximum flexibility in application development" [Johnson+98, 482]. Templates are preferred in C++ [Carroll+95]. Ada 95 supports reuse with a (very) strong static typing and a required interface specification. Reusable packages have a single specification and multiple bodies (implementations) with similar high-level behavior, but exhibit differences at lower levels. For example, all Queue packages implement operations to add and remove queue members, but have implementations that are bounded or unbounded, sequential or concurrent, and so on [Booch 90].

11.1.2   The Role of Testing in Reuse

Reuse is a general solution to chronic software development problems: high development time and cost, unacceptably frequent failures, low maintainability, and low adaptability. Much of the promise of object-oriented technology is predicated on its explicit support for reuse. In a study of C++ development using OMT analysis and design, reuse reduced design errors by a ratio of 49:1 and reduced coding errors by a ratio of 26:1, for development of a new component by reusing one without any changes. A corresponding 100:1 reduction in rework and debug time was observed [Basili+96a].

Although simple in principle, development of object-oriented components that are in fact reused is surprisingly difficult. A reusable component must be designed to support a broad range of applications. Potential consumers must know that components are available, be able to identify components that could support the system under development, and be persuaded they are better served to buy than to make. Dependability is the final barrier.[4] Consumers typically expect high dependability in components offered for reuse. A reused component must operate as advertised for a wide range of applications and provide appropriate fault tolerance. A buggy component will eliminate any benefit that might otherwise be obtained.

The most important and obvious contributions of testing to reusability are that bugs are removed and dependability is increased. But component testing supports reuse in other important ways. Component design is often improved when testability and test design are considered during development. Beyond revealing bugs, testing can also show that a component implementation is awkward, inelegant, or difficult to use. The source code of a component test suite can be used to show how to use a component, with tests documenting the component's applicability and technical requirements for consumers. Passing a test suite offers tangible evidence of dependability, instead of asking consumers to trust in the producer's proficiency. Executable test suites delivered with the component can help consumers to verify quickly that their application is correct. In this way, effective producer testing leads to more reliable components, enhances component documentation, improves design-level robustness and reusability, and encourages consumer reuse. In contrast, inadequate testing will likely result in the release of buggy components and provide none of the secondary benefits. Producer credibility lost due to buggy components is hard to regain. Consumers will reject buggy components and view subsequent offerings from a producer with suspicion.

This chapter focuses on test strategies for components that support reuse by source code augmentation: abstract classes, generic classes, and application frameworks. Components that support reuse by translation-time binding or link-time/runtime interfaces may be tested with strategies summarized in Table 11.2. The producer of a class that supports translation-time reuse by inheritance or aggregation should apply the appropriate class test pattern. The producer of an executable that supports link-time/runtime reuse should apply a

---

4. **Dependability** is the extent to which *"reliance can justifiably be placed on the service [a system] delivers*. The service delivered by a system is its behavior *as it is perceptible* by its user(s); a user is another system (human or physical) interacting with the former" [Laprie's italics] [Laprie+96, 29].

TABLE 11.2   Scope of Producer Testing for Components Supporting Translation and
Runtime Reuse

Reusable Component	Scope of Test Instantiation	Testable Responsibilities	Producer's Test Scope
Library class	Test instance	Contract	Class/flattened class
Foundation hierarchy	Test instances Application-specific subclasses	Contract Application anticipation	Class/flattened class
Executable component	Test instance	Contract Application anticipation	Executable source code

class or a subsystem test pattern appropriate for the scope and responsibilities
of the component source code.

Augmentation components exist in a kind of software limbo. They are designed to supply a significant part of an application class, subsystem, or system.
Because they do little (if anything) as written, however, the producer cannot test
them until they are instantiated. Identifying these test instance(s) is the central
problem in testing components that support reuse by augmentation. The producer's first task in test design is to identify a representative instantiation(s).
Then, a test pattern that corresponds to the scope and responsibilities of the instance is used to develop a test plan. Table 11.3 compares producer testing
strategies for components that support reuse by source code augmentation.

Instantiation means something different for each kind of component. An
abstract class instantiation is a subclass that provides an implementation of the
abstract class interfaces. A **generic class instantiation** is the class that results
when a type parameter is provided in a declaration or a definition. The test design patterns for abstract and generic classes suggest ways to identify suitable
test instantiation.

TABLE 11.3   Producer's Test Strategy for Components Using Source Code Augmentation

Reusable Component	Test Instantiation	Testable Responsibilities	Producer's Test Scope
Abstract class	Overriding subclass method implementation	Class contract	Class/flattened class
Generic class	Type parameter	Class contract	Class/flattened class
Application framework	Application implementation	Framework use cases Association invariants	System

A **framework instantiation** is a system of subclasses that realizes one possible implementation of the framework. Frameworks often evolve from insights about design solutions that can work in more than one context [Johnson+98]. As the framework evolves, the appropriate focus of producer testing shifts. The two test design patterns for frameworks bracket this evolution:

- *New Framework Test* applies to initial and early versions.
- *Popular Framework Test* applies to a framework that has become widely used.

Table 11.4 contrasts producer test design patterns for each stage. These patterns are applicable to a system of classes intended to support application development by extension (frameworks) and to class hierarchies that offer a generic programming infrastructure (foundation class libraries). Although foundation classes are typically usable as is, they can also benefit from a

TABLE 11.4 Comparison of Strategies for Producer Testing of Frameworks

	New Framework	Popular Framework
Context	Predecessor application exists.	Framework is in wide use.
Fault model	Design errors and omissions. Control bugs. Representational integrity not maintained. Reusability obstacles.	New feature bug. New feature breaks old feature. New feature breaks old application.
Strategy	Use case and association-based. Demo app instantiation. Predecessor as possible oracle.	Feature interaction tests: mix, anti-requirements, brute force. New feature use cases. Profile shift. Regression test selection. Existing applications as oracle.
Entry criteria	Component tests pass. Testable system scope model.	New component tests pass. Testable new feature model. Changes analyzed.
Exit criteria	Per applicable test design pattern(s). CRUD coverage.	Per applicable test design pattern(s). Regression complete.
Automation	Capture/playback or embedded harness.	Capture/playback or embedded harness.
Consequences	May find some design errors and some reuse problems. Moderate to high confidence if predecessor can be used as an oracle. Extensive testing not cost-effective.	High confidence if regression testing is used. Extensive testing can be cost-effective. Half-life of regression test suite.

framework testing strategy. A foundation class hierarchy is typically designed to support extensive subclassing. The problems in devising tests of this capability are similar to those associated with testing a framework. The differences in strategy for producers and consumers is further discussed in the companion book, *Managing the Testing Process for Object-Oriented Systems,* chapter 3 [Binder 2000].

The producer does not need to choose between the two strategies, but should shift the emphasis in testing as a framework evolves from its first release to widespread use. The availability of an application instantiation of the framework and the most probable kind of bugs dictate the differences.

11.1.3   Reusing Test Suites

Reuse need not be limited to code. Table 11.5 suggests how producer and consumer test suites can be reused for mutual benefit. The producer's test suite could be examined and rerun by the consumer so as to establish the dependability of the reusable asset. Because consumers generally need to test their integration of a reusable asset, the producer's test suite could be extended to parallel application extensions. In turn, producer implementations could provide a rich source for controlled testing by producers. As consumers will always subject systems to unanticipated conditions, producers could benefit by using consumer test suites and extensions in subsequent product releases.

Despite the complementary nature of producer/consumer testing, I am not aware of any commercially available class library or framework that is shipped with its test own suite.[5] Some reusable assets provide built-in tests in the form

TABLE 11.5   Opportunities for Test Suite Reuse

	Producer's Class Library Test Suite	Producer's Framework Test Suite	Consumer's Application System Test Suite
Consumer reuse of test suite	Integration test (requires extension for consumer features)	Integration test (requires extension for consumer features)	Regression test
Producer reuse of test suite	Regression test	Regression test	System test

---

5. Brad Cox has advocated this concept. A "specification language" composed of "test procedures" would be provided with each component. The test procedure runs the consumer's instantiation to see if it complies with an associated specification, or "gauge" [Cox 90]. Objective-C assertions were suggested as an implementation of test procedures [Cox 91].

of assertions. For example, Microsoft Foundation Classes include approximately 3600 assertions in 61,000 lines of C++. The greatest barriers to more extensive test reuse are probably legal and economic. When the value of reusable test suites is recognized and marketed, however, they will become as commonplace as installation documentation. Intracompany producers and consumers of reusable assets may have fewer barriers to test reuse. In these situations, both will benefit from a cooperative testing strategy that delivers lower cost and higher dependability. Approaches to reusing test suites for generic classes and frameworks are outlined in the respective Consequences sections.

11.2   Test Design Patterns

This section presents four patterns that may be used by producers to increase the dependability of their reusable components.

- *Abstract Class Test.* Design a test instantiation and a test suite for an abstract class.
- *Generic Class Test.* Design test instantiations and test suites for a generic class.
- *New Framework Test.* Design a test suite and the test instantiation from the generic requirements for a new framework.
- *Popular Framework Test.* Design a test suite and the test instantiation for a framework that has become widely used. Cover new features and perform compatibility testing.

Abstract Class Test

Intent

Develop a test implementation of and a test suite for an abstract class interface.

Context

An abstract class cannot be instantiated and cannot therefore be tested as written. Instead, it may be tested by developing a subclass that implements all of the unimplemented superclass methods. A test suite is designed for the entire hierarchy by using a pattern that corresponds to this test instantiation. As an abstract class can implement methods and instance variables and may have a contract specification, the test design should address both the abstract class and the test instantiation. For example, the following code fragments show examples of abstract classes.

In Ada 95,

```
package Account is

    type Account_Type is abstract tagged limited private;

    procedure Credit (Account : in out Account_Type;
                      Amount  : in      Money)
    is abstract;

    procedure Debit  (Account : in out Account_Type;
                      Amount  : in      Money)
    is abstract;

    function Balance (Account : Bank_Account_Type)
         return Money
    is abstract;

    -- . . .

end Account_Package;
```

In C++, an abstract class is any class that contains at least one pure virtual function.

```
class Account {
public:
            Account()                    { }
    virtual ~Account()                   { }
    virtual Money balance()              = 0;
    virtual void credit(Money& amount)   = 0;
    virtual void debit(Money& amount)    = 0;
};
```

In Eiffel, an abstract class includes at least one deferred feature.

```
deferred class
    Account
feature
    balance MONEY is
            deferred
            end
    credit(amount: MONEY) is
            deferred
            end
    debit(amount: MONEY) is
            deferred
            end
end
```

In Java, this class is designated as abstract or has at least one method designated as abstract.

```
abstract class Account {
    abstract Money balance ( );
    abstract void credit (Money amount);
    abstract void debit (Money amount);
}
```

Fault Model

Abstract classes do not present many fault hazards beyond design errors and simple coding errors. Common design errors include incomplete or inconsistent identification of common responsibilities, incorrect or incomplete representation of responsibilities in the interface, definition of instance variables that should have been deferred, and missing capabilities [Carroll+95, Meyer 88].

Strategy

A subclass must be developed to test the abstract class with an implementation for each abstract method. Then, a specification-based test suite may be developed for the contract of the flattened subclass using the applicable method and class scope test design patterns. *Polymorphic Server Test* may be used to develop a test suite for the hierarchy. The specific responsibilities of the abstract class under test will determine which tests are appropriate.

Test cases should be developed for each subclass method that implements an abstract (unimplemented) superclass method and run on a subclass object. An abstract superclass may also implement some methods. Test cases may be developed for and run on the superclass method, and then they may be reused for each subclass. Integration testing should be done at flattened scope for each subclass of the abstract class. If a concrete superclass method sends a message to an abstract method of `self`, then deferring testing of this method until implementation of a subclass is completed may be the most practical approach.

The *Subclass Driver* is appropriate as a class scope driver. The CUT (both the abstract class and the implementation) should be instrumented for method scope branch coverage.

Entry Criteria

✓ An abstract class may be tested when it is compiled.

Exit Criteria

✓ The test instantiation should achieve the coverage recommended for the test pattern applied. Method scope branch coverage is the recommended minimum.

Consequences

The development of the test subclass and its test suite may reveal design errors or reusability problems. The resulting test suite may provide useful documentation for consumers of the abstract class, even if it is not usable as part of an application system. See also the Consequences section for the applicable class test design pattern.

Known Uses

Using formal analysis, Overbeck's contract testing model shows that abstract classes must be instantiated before they can be tested [Overbeck 94a]. Marick recommends a gray box approach based on analysis of derived class features [Marick 95]. Firesmith notes that subclass drivers are frequently used to exercise abstract classes [Firesmith 96].

In a report on the test strategy used in a large C++ system, Thuy concludes that a concrete method in an abstract class that uses an abstract method of its class must be tested in an instantiation of the abstract class. "In order to simplify the test management, it is preferable to test all these methods in the same unit test using a derived concrete class which redefines none of them, if such a one exists. If not, one should find a minimal set of concrete derived classes that cover all these methods" [Thuy 92].

Generic Class Test

Intent

Develop a test implementation of and a test suite for a class that requires a type parameter.

Context

This pattern applies to any **generic class**: a C++ template class, an Eiffel generic class, or an Ada 95 generic. In Ada, type parameters are typically defined for a package or a procedure, rather than for an individual type. The declaration to produce an object of a generic class requires the generic class, a **type argument**, and other declaration elements. The type argument consists of a name of a class or primitive data type. The compiler generates a new class by substituting the type argument for occurrences of the **type parameter** defined in the generic class. In the following discussion, G refers to the generic class under test. A, B, and C refer to type parameters. The resulting objects are a, b, and c, or roughly a = new G(A), b = new G(B), and c = new G(C).

The behavior of a generic class results from its implementation and the behavior of a specific type parameter. Generic classes must be instantiated with a type parameter and tested with that type binding. Thus, not only must we test the responsibilities of the generic class, but we must also answer the following questions:

- Given that a generic typically accepts many different type parameters, which type parameters should we test?
- Which additional tests are indicated to show that the generic can be reused with confidence?
- How many possible type arguments should we test?

Fault Model

As generic classes require strong type checking, the compiler will enforce minimal compatibility with the public methods of the specified type. We do not need to test for bugs that will be caught by translation-time type checking. A class or type provided as a type argument for a generic that passes the compiler's type checking is **accepted** by the generic class. For example, a C++ compiler will reject a type argument for which isFull() is not part of the public interface of the class specified for T1.

```
template<class T1> class G {
private:
    T1 foo;
public:
    bool checkFull( ) { return foo.isFull( ); }
};
```

An Ada 95 generic declaration can restrict type parameters to certain built-in types. For example, `Discrete_Type` or `Abstract_Type` may allow `Any_Type`.

Generic classes are at risk for several kinds of faults that do not occur in other classes: type-dependent faults, type-specific faults, and multiple type interaction faults. They are also at risk for all other kinds of class scope faults.

Type-dependent Faults

A well-designed generic class should provide uniform behavior for all accepted types [Carroll+95, Meyer 97]. The general fault model is that an unintended interaction occurs between the implementation and some accepted class. Dependencies arise when the generic sends messages to the object of an accepted class and the results of these messages determine intramethod or intraclass control flow or data flow. Accepted classes typically vary in the following ways:

- The range and precision of scalar types in arguments and returned values (signed integer, unsigned integer, float, double, complex, decimal, and so on)
- Deep versus shallow implementation of copy, delete, and test for equality operations
- Initialization assumptions and the behavior of constructors
- Computational side effects
- Use of static variables and class variables
- Memory requirements and allocation/deallocation behavior
- Speed of computation, memory access, and input/output
- Thread safety

If an accepted class is polymorphic, then these fault hazards exist for every possible binding of the accepted class. For example,

```
template<class T1> class G {
public:

// . . .

    void swap(T1& lhs, T1& rhs) {
      T1 temp    = lhs;
      lhs        = rhs;
      rhs        = tmp;
    }

// . . .

};
```

A generic class may have multiple type parameters. Potentially, some combination of accepted classes may cause faults. Consequently, passing a test suite for one or several instantiations of a generic cannot guarantee that some other untested instantiation is bug-free. For a type-dependent fault to be reached, we must instantiate it with fault-causing accepted classes and then exercise all code that depends on these classes. The failure will be triggered when the OUT and the fault-causing accepted object are in states that are sensitive to the fault. The additional conditions for reaching, triggering, and propagating the fault are the same as the fault model assumed for the responsibilities of the CUT.

Type-specific Faults

A type-specific feature of a generic is intended to support some subset of accepted classes. Its presence may indicate a poor design or vulnerability to faults. For example, G accepts types A and B, but method G.5 is allowed only for a type A instantiation. Type C is accepted, but must be rejected by G (Table 11.6). The

TABLE 11.6   Generic Class with Type-specific Behavior

Methods on Class G	Type A	Type B	Type C
G	OK	OK	Not allowed
1	OK	OK	
2	OK	OK	
3	OK	OK	
4	OK	OK	
5	OK	Not allowed	
6	Not allowed	OK	

type-specific fault model is that an unintended interaction occurs between the type-specific implementation and some accepted class. Such a fault will be reached when the implementation is bound to this specific type parameter and all code that depends on that type parameter(s) is exercised. Reaching, triggering, and propagation conditions are then the same as for the type-dependent case.

If a generic implements type-specific behavior, then some generic messages/methods may be inconsistent with the special-case type argument; the special-case messages/methods must almost certainly be inconsistent with other type parameters. Thus, an additional bug hazard is present in either case if the response is unspecified, corrupting, or spurious. To reach such a fault, we must instantiate the CUT with an accepted class and attempt operations that are excluded or disallowed for the particular instantiation. Reaching, triggering, and propagation conditions are the same as the type-dependent case.

Side Effects

In many C++ compilers, instantiation of a template causes the object code (binary executable) of the instantiating type to be repeated. This repetition can lead to code bloat and runtime failures related to insufficient memory, response time, and so on.

Strategy

Single Type Parameter

The test suite has three parts: type-independent tests, type-specific tests, and type overloading tests. The following steps will allow later tests to reuse earlier tests.

1. Choose a representative type parameter. Select a type parameter that exercises all class responsibilities or at least the largest number of responsibilities. Table 11.7 shows the basic test strategy.

2. Select applicable method and class test patterns and develop test suites accordingly. For example, *Category-Partition* and *Nonmodal Class Test* would be appropriate patterns for the responsibilities of a generic container class.

3. Run the test suite on an instantiation of the representative type, debug it, and revise it to achieve the appropriate coverage.

TABLE 11.7 Test Suite for Generic Class

Test Case	Test Message	Expected Result
1	a = new G(A)	Construct object
2	a.1	Per G.1 contract
3	a.2	Per G.2 contract
4	a.3	Per G.3 contract
5	a.4	Per G.4 contract
6	a.5	Per G.5 contract
7	a.6	Exception
8	b = new G(B)	Construct object
9	b.1	Per G.1 contract
10	b.2	Per G.2 contract
11	b.3	Per G.3 contract
12	b.4	Per G.4 contract
13	b.5	Exception
14	b.6	Per G.6 contract
15	c = new G(C)	Exception

4. Determine how many additional type-dependent instantiations should be tested.

   • Design and develop type-dependent tests. For example, suppose that the class accepts int or float as a type parameter. Some boundary tests will probably be different; for example, the test cases developed with *Invariant Boundaries* for an int type parameter might include on and off points of 32,767 and 32,768, but the float on and off points might be 1.234567E+99 and 1.234567E+100.

   • If polymorphic classes are accepted, then instantiate the CUT with the base class. The test driver should then bind each subtype to the OUT and rerun the entire test suite for that instantiation (see the Test Automation section for a coding technique to implement this step). Polymorphic bindings cannot be made to a C++ template class that implements only =, ==, and != operators and does not use formal parameters of T* or T& in its public interface. If either of these conditions is not met, then each possible subtype should be instantiated and tested.

5. Determine how many additional type-specific instantiations (if any) should be tested.

- Consider the contract of each method and the class invariant. Develop your own contract model if one is not provided (see Chapter 17). If different instantiations require different invariants, preconditions, or postconditions, then test for each type that has a unique contract. Repeat the entire test suite for each type, even if it differs by a single predicate operand.

- If the CUT is modal for any type, consider the state machine for each type. Develop a *Modal Class Test* test suite. If different type parameters require different behavior, then test for each type that has a unique state machine. Repeat the entire test suite for each type, even if it differs by a single transition.

- If the CUT implements explicitly type-specific features, develop a test suite for each such type (*Category-Partition* may be useful). The test suite should attempt all operations on an instantiation of each type. First, design type-specific tests, instantiate the CUT with the corresponding type, and run the test cycle. Next, send messages that are not defined for the instantiated type. A robust design should respond with a well-behaved complaint. A buggy design will crash or produce spurious results.

- Test for robustness by attempting to instantiate the CUT with an accepted, but unallowed type parameter. A robust class should respond with a well-behaved complaint. A buggy class will crash or produce spurious results.

6. If the class exports overloadable operations (e.g., we can compare the members of an int List to members of a float List for equality), then develop a test for each possible combination, as suggested in Table 11.8.

TABLE 11.8 Representative Tests for Generic Class Overloaded Operations

First Operand Type	Second Operand Type		
	int	float	double
int	G(int) == G(int)	G(int) == G(float)	G(int) == G(double)
float	G(float) == G(int)	G(float) == G(float)	G(float) == G(double)
double	G(double) == G(int)	G(double) == G(float)	G(double) == G(double)

Two or More Type Parameters

In principle, a generic class may have any number of type parameters. Multiple-parameter template classes are common in the STL and other commercial class libraries. In some cases, multiple type parameters are a good alternative to multiple inheritance. Multiple type parameters can be used in many ways.

```
template <class T1, class T2> class Map {
    // Maps elements of a collection of T1 with a key of T2
};

template <class T1, class T2> class Matrix {
    // T1 is type of Matrix: big, small, square ...
    // T2 is type of Elements: double, LongFloat, complex ...
};

template <class T1, class T2, class T3> class Triple {
    // Singleton object containing three objects
    // of any three classes
};
```

A multiple-parameter generic class presents a more complex testing problem, as we must now exercise combinations of types. Additional fixed type parameters, such as

```
template <class T1, int maxSize> class Buffer { /*...*/ };
```

do not pose the same challenges.

The preceding considerations apply for choosing types for the individual type parameters. The test design problem involves the selection of combinations of the individual types that are valid for each parameter. Classes like Map and Matrix are likely to have dependencies between the usage of the two types; that is, the behavior of one type will affect the behavior of the other by data flow or control flow. Thus, we should test as many type combinations as time permits. A single test suite can be developed for one pair and reused for all other pairs if no type-specific behavior exists.

- Select the types that will be used most frequently—for example, SquareMatrix and LongFloat. Develop a test suite for this pair. Perform testing and debug until all tests pass. Instrument the CUT and check for branch coverage.
- Replace the secondary parameter (e.g., double), revise a copy of the test suite, and repeat.

- This cycle is repeated until all combinations have been tested and pass with acceptable branch coverage.

In contrast, the `Triple` class does not suggest any dependencies among the types (but examine the source code to make sure none exists.) We test parameter combinations. For example;

- The three most likely types: A, B, and C
- All permutations of the most likely: ACB, BCA, BAC, CAB, and CBA
- Three of the same type
- The abstract base class for three polymorphic classes, and bindings of their subclasses

We can develop additional cases by error guessing and analysis of the class's contract. The number of combinations for classes with three or more interacting parameters can be selected by orthogonal arrays [Mandl 85] or advanced software-oriented combinational selection techniques [Cohen+97].

Automation

It makes sense to implement the test driver for a generic class as a generic class that accepts the same type parameters as the class under test. For example,

```
template<class T1> class TestG {
private:
    G<T1> objectUnderTest;
public:
    void test001( ) { /*. . .*/ }
    void test002( ) { /*. . .*/ }
    // . . .
};
```

Because most of the type-independent test cases can be reused, it makes sense to develop the test driver progressively. We can base the implementation of the test suite on any appropriate driver pattern (see Chapter 19). For type-independent testing, change the type parameter, rebuild, and rerun the test suite.

1. Develop the G(A) test suite, including all type-independent tests. Run and debug the test suite and the CUT.

2. Substitute type parameter B and rerun the test suite. All tests should pass. Make sure to compare the coverage reports—they should be identical.

3. Develop type-specific test cases, one type at a time, and then run the tests and debug. Rerun the entire type-independent test suite each time you change the CUT.

4. Develop and run transitive operation tests, if appropriate. This effort will require the instantiation of multiple instances of G: G(A), G(B), and so on.

The CUT should be instrumented for method scope branch coverage.

If the CUT accepts polymorphic classes, common test cases can be factored out and reused for each such type. For example, consider the set of accepted classes in Figure 11.1. Assume that the function commonTestG( ) implements all general responsibility test cases for class G. The code for a test driver of G follows:

```
a0 = new G(A0);
if (!commonTestG(a0)) {cerr << "No pass; G fails for A0"<<endl;}
a1 = new G(A1);
if (!commonTestG(a1)) {cerr << "No pass; G fails for A1"<<endl;}
a2 = new G(A2);
if (!commonTestG(a2)) {cerr << "No pass; G fails for A2"<<endl;}
```

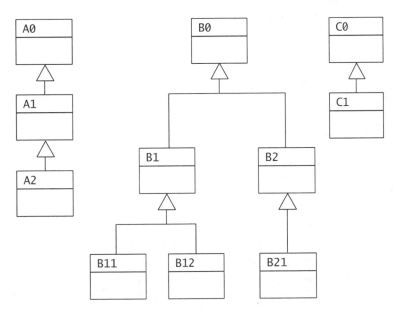

FIGURE 11.1   Structure of classes acccepted by a generic.

```
b0 = new G(B0);
if (!commonTestG(b0)) {cerr << "No pass; G fails for B0"<<endl;}
b1 = new G(B1);
if (!commonTestG(b1)) {cerr << "No pass; G fails for B1"<<endl;}
b11 = new G(B11);
if (!commonTestG(b11) {cerr << "No pass; G fails for B11"<<endl;}
b12 = new G(B12);
if (!commonTestG(b12)) {cerr << "No pass; G fails for B12"<<endl;}
b2 = new G(B2);
if (!commonTestG(b2)) {cerr << "No pass; G fails for B2"<<endl;}
b21 = new G(B21);
if (!commonTestG(b21)) {cerr << "No pass; G fails for B21"<<endl;}
c0 = new G(C0);
if (!commonTestG(c0)) {cerr << "No pass; G fails for C0"<<endl;}
c1 = new G(C1);
if (!commonTestG(c1)) {cerr << "No pass; G fails for C1"<<endl;}
```

This simple idiom reuses the test suite and simplifies instantiation of the type. Type-specific tests are easily added as A0TestG( ), A1TestG( ), A2TestG( ), B0TestG( ), and so on.

Entry Criteria

✓ All of the accepted classes identified as types for testing should have passed their individual test suites before you attempt to use them to instantiate the generic class under test. If they have not, bugs in the accepted classes will complicate testing and debugging of the generic CUT.

✓ Meet entry criteria for the applicable test pattern (e.g., *Category-Partition* or *Modal Class Test*) applied to the generic CUT. This effort typically involves a *Small Pop* integration.

Exit Criteria

✓ Attain 100 percent branch coverage or better (e.g, multicondition coverage) on every tested instantiation of the CUT. Code coverage can reveal type-specific parts of the implementation. Carefully review any differences in coverage of the same test suite on type-independent test cases. For example, suppose you cannot achieve 100 percent branch coverage, but have designed and passed an N+ test suite for a modal class. If the coverage is not blocked by an exception or dead code, you may need to develop type-specific test cases. If coverage is not identical for identical test suites applied to different type instantiations, make sure that the differences can be shown to be correct.

✓ Achieve any additional exit criteria for the applicable test pattern (e.g., *Category-Partition* or *Modal Class Test*) applied to the generic CUT.

Consequences

The fact that a generic class has passed tests with several type parameter instantiations does not guarantee that it is bug-free for all other type instantiations. A subsequent type may be buggy or present a different contract than those tested. It may also throw an exception that is not caught or have sequential constraints that tested types do not have.

The prerequisites, costs, and benefits are generally the same as they are for the test design pattern that applies to the responsibilities of the class under test.

Publishing a list of known-good types as part of the generic class's documentation would increase consumer confidence and promote greater reuse. With a little extra effort, the producer's test suite could be shipped/released with the generic class. When the consumer wishes to instantiate the class with an untested type parameter, he or she could simply substitute the untested type parameter in the test suite, as shown earlier. If the test suite passes, the consumer can have high confidence in this new instantiation. If the test suite does not pass, the consumer should perform problem determination with the producer. The consumer's passed test run could be provided to the producer, who can then include it in the next release of the class.

Known Uses

Using formal analysis, Overbeck shows that generic classes must be instantiated to be tested and that testing with one instantiation does not guarantee anything about the dependability of other type instantiations [Overbeck 94a, Overbeck 95]. This result follows from the anticomposition and antiextensionality axioms [Weyuker 88, Perry+90]. Marick recommends a gray box approach for C++ templates, concluding that each new instantiation should be tested to exercise unique or different features of the instantiating type [Marick 95].

In a report on the test strategy used in a very large C++ system, Thuy identifies two cases where only a single instantiation of a generic was tested. In the first case, the generic did not use methods exported by the type parameter class. In the second case, the untested type parameter was a subclass and an instantiation of the generic with the superclass was adequately tested. If the generic did not use any methods overridden by the type parameter subclass, then a new instantiation was not tested. Otherwise, each new type instantiation was tested [Thuy 92].

Related Patterns

At least a few of the method and class scope test design patterns (Chapter 10) will apply. The specific responsibilities of the generic class under test will determine which patterns are appropriate.

New Framework Test

Intent

Develop a test implementation of and a test suite for a framework that has few, if any, instantiations.

Context

Several reports on framework development mention that testing is difficult, but do not provide any details [Sparks+96, Codine+97]. A producer developing the initial or early release of a framework needs a test suite to validate its design and implementation. The framework may have been developed from a requirements model for which there is no antecedent application system or it may have been generalized from an existing system. The test suite and the test instantiation must be developed from the generic requirements for the framework.

This pattern is applicable to a system of classes intended to support development of specific applications by extension (frameworks) and to class hierarchies that offer a generic programming infrastructure (foundation class libraries).

A framework may be developed in (at least) two ways. First, a **model-based framework** is developed to support a family of application systems that share a common set of classes. Typically, a class model is used to represent a complex, broad scope—for example, the manufacturing operations of a plant, the start-to-finish business cycle for multiple financial products and services, or the subsystems and control strategies in an avionics suite. A model-based framework implements the classes in this model. Typically, no direct implementation antecedent exists. The framework-based applications may replace a legacy system, however.

Second, a framework may be developed by generalizing an antecedent application system. To produce a **generalized framework** one follows the *Patterns for Evolving Frameworks* [Johnson+98]. The producers believe that the overall strategy of an existing successful application system can be applied elsewhere. The design task involves separating the general parts from the application-specific parts and providing additional features to ease reuse. The framework evolves by undergoing further refinement. The scope of the producer's testing problem does not differ much for a domain model framework, although it may be possible to use the predecessor system to ease test design and execution. In either case, the framework responsibilities and the implementation under test will be new.

Fault Model

Frameworks make three general promises:

- They are a (nearly) complete and consistent representation of the salient aspects of the problem domain as classes and associations.
- They provide basic capabilities to create, read, update, and delete objects of these classes and the associations among them.
- They enforce sequential control necessary for required behavior.

Additionally, they may support infrastructure services, such as storage management, various forms of fault tolerance, idioms for iteration and searching, and distributed object strategy.

Each individual component of a framework is at risk for many kinds of bugs. In addition, a framework derived from a domain model is at risk for system scope bugs. It has not had wide usage and the producer is necessarily limited in the extent to which interaction of the framework and an application can be exercised. The newness of this stage of a framework suggests the likely kinds of bugs:

- *Design omissions.* An essential behavior or representation is incomplete or missing.
- *Representational integrity bugs.* The framework is responsible for maintaining the association constraints among objects in the domain model. For example, every `Order` object must be associated with one and only one `Customer` object, but a `Customer` object need not have an associated `Order`. Due to its newness, the framework is likely to allow association constraints to be broken.
- *Control bugs.* Frameworks typically use an inverted control strategy. The framework classes are receptors for external events, activating application objects, which return control to a framework object.
- *Infrastructure bugs.* Infrastructure code is typically complex and difficult.

Strategy

Test Model

The test suite should be developed from the framework's analysis and design models. A testable instantiation, the **demo app,** must be designed and devel-

oped. The use case model should include all use cases that developers can identify for the entire framework. The demo app should provide a minimal implementation of each use case. Test design can be accomplished with the test design
patterns presented in Chapters 10, 12, 13, and 14.

- Use *Extended Use Case Test* to develop tests for each use case.
- Use *Class Association Test* to develop tests for each association.
- If the control strategy has sequential constraints, model it as a state machine and develop a test suite to achieve N+ coverage (see Chapter 7).
  Organize the use case and association tests as leaves on a transition
  tree. If there is no explicit system control strategy, organize the use case
  and association tests around expected usage cycles.

The most attractive use of a predecessor system is as an oracle. Figure 11.2
suggests how the predecessor system may be used.

- The demo app must implement features that are the same or nearly the
  same as those of the predecessor system.

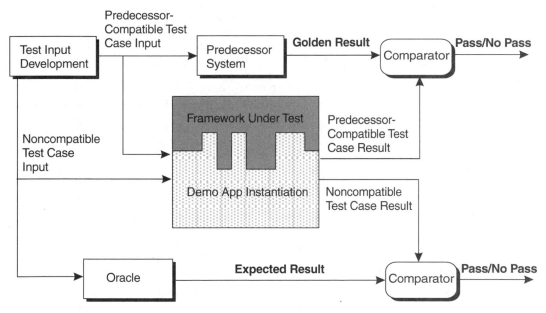

FIGURE 11.2 Predecessor application as framework oracle.

- The demo app does not need to implement all features of the predecessor system.

- The demo app can implement features not found in the predecessor system. A different kind of oracle will be needed to evaluate the test results of these features.

If a test suite was developed for the predecessor system, it may be possible to salvage some of its test cases for use on the demo app instantiation. Because test suites are typically brittle, however, it is likely that this effort will be of limited value. More likely, the test design for the predecessor will provide some insights into how to design the tests for the demo app.

The infrastructure support of the framework should be exercised as well. Because the demo app will probably not be sufficiently large or complex to stress the infrastructure, stress testing should be deferred until the first full-scale use of the framework. As this process is likely to be difficult, the consent and cooperation of the initial consumer should be obtained.

Automation

The test suite may be implemented with a capture/playback script or a test harness, as required by the external interface for the demo app. Asserting the contract of the framework classes can provide a powerful verification tool (see Chapter 17).

Entry Criteria

Frameworks are typically developed in increments. Before you attempt to test a demo app instantiation, several things should have happened:

✓ A testable system scope model should be available. Develop and evolve this model in parallel with framework development.

✓ All component classes and subsystems in an increment should have passed individually adequate test suites. If you must skip or reduce adequate testing of individual components and subsystems, use *Risk-based Allocation* [Binder 2000] to plan the testing effort.

✓ A system scope test harness should have been installed, tested, and stabilized.

✓ The test environment (mirroring the target environment) should have been installed, tested, and stabilized.

Accomplishing these tasks before beginning to test at system scope will improve testing efficiency. Skipping any of these steps often results in wasted effort due to increased rework and diminished test effectiveness.

Exit Criteria

The framework should be released to reuse consumers when the producer has shown that it can support application development. The producer's test suite should meet the exit criteria for the test design patterns used to develop the demo app test suite.

✓ At least one test for each row in the use case's operational relation, meeting the *Extended Use Case Test* exit criteria

✓ At least one minimal test of every association in the class model, meeting the *Class Association Test* exit criteria

✓ CRUD (create, read, update, delete) coverage as defined in *Covered in CRUD*

✓ Control model coverage: transition coverage for a state machine or branch coverage on all sequence diagrams

Consequences

The prerequisites, costs, and benefits with the *New Framework Test* pattern are generally the same as those in the applicable test design pattern.

The cost of testing is directly proportional to the number of use cases and class associations. My own experience is that it takes an average of five working days to design, implement, and execute the tests for one use case (*Extended Use Case Test*) or one class association (*Class Association Test*). Under optimal conditions for a simple use case or association, this effort can consume as little as a half-day. Under adverse conditions with a complex subject, the cycle can consume as much as a month.

Achieving the suggested coverage shows that the framework is usable and minimally reliable, given the scope of the demo app. Meeting the coverage goal establishes the dependability of the framework and typically reveals many minor bugs. The producers can have higher confidence if the predecessor system can be used as an oracle. Although the demo app may reveal some superficial problems in reusability, it does not follow that more extensive consumer instantiations will necessarily experience the same level of dependability. The early instantiations of full application systems can be expected to reveal more bugs and reusability problems as they draw on and extend the framework. Consequently, producers should monitor and analyze the results of application instantiations. This analysis can suggest how to design test suites for subsequent releases of the framework.

You might be tempted to release the framework after individual component and subsystem tests pass, as an alternative to testing with a demo app. The first consumers will then discover system scope bugs and reusability problems in the features that their applications use. If they are willing to accept this risk and can support interleaved debugging of the framework and their applications, this strategy can be an effective test approach. It entails considerable risk, however. Consumer usage may be limited to a feature subset, leaving some features untested. Subsequent consumers may have significantly different usage patterns, resulting in an eruption of new bugs and reuse obstacles in a system that was thought stable. Explaining this discrepancy to disgruntled consumers may be hard for the producers. Many other unpleasant scenarios can follow for both producer and consumer. For example, if the framework turns out to be more buggy than expected and the consumer's progress is blocked, the consumer may abandon the framework and seek some kind of redress from the producer. This kind of adverse outcome can kill the process of building credibility and a favorable reputation, both of which are necessary to achieve widespread use of a framework.

Known Uses

A framework development process used at Nortel relies on the use of a *verification prototype,* which is similar to the demo app. "Clearly, waiting for the applications to be built prior to testing the framework is not a viable approach. A verification prototype of the framework provides a context for application teams to build rapid prototypes of their applications. These prototypes not only serve to test out application designs, but can also be used for the purposes of framework testing" [Cherry 96].

I have worked with several clients to apply this pattern. It is effective, but some obstacles can arise. Clients are sometimes reluctant to commit resources to developing the demo app because it isn't a "real" system. It is "real" testware, however, and can be justified on these grounds. Framework development usually involves frequent refactoring, so the demo app must be kept current, requiring more work and communication. The demo app should be small enough to test easily, but large enough to exercise high-quantity or high-complexity features of the framework. This balance can be hard to achieve, especially if the higher-end features are not part of earlier increments.

Related Patterns

After several iterations, elements of the *Popular Framework Test* will become appropriate.

Popular Framework Test

Intent

Develop a test suite for a framework that has many application-specific instantiations.

Context

Several reports on framework development mention that testing is difficult, but do not provide any details [Sparks+96, Codine+97]. When a producer develops an enhanced version of a widely used framework, a test suite is needed to validate the new features and to identify potential compatibility problems. In addition, the test suite and the test instantiation must be developed for new features and compatibility testing must be performed.

A **popular framework** is a framework that has become widely used within an organization or by customers of a commercial software provider. This pattern is therefore applicable to a system of classes intended to support development of specific applications by extension (frameworks) and to class hierarchies that offer a generic programming infrastructure (foundation class libraries).

Fault Model

Each component of a framework is at risk for many kinds of faults. Component-specific faults are discussed in the corresponding test pattern. The framework itself is also at risk for faults discussed in *New Framework Test*. As a framework becomes more mature and gains wider acceptance, fewer failures caused by these kinds of faults will be seen. However, failures from three new fault classes become more likely: feature interactions, compatibility bugs, and latent bugs.

1. A **feature interaction** is a behavior or side effect produced when two or more features are used together. These effects may be either desirable or undesirable. For example, a residential telephone service offers both call forwarding (automatically transferring an incoming call to another number) and call screening (automatically rejecting a call from a telemarketer or specific numbers designated by the customer). Suppose that when call forwarding is enabled, a call from a blocked number is forwarded. When call screening is enabled, call forwarding cannot be enabled. These are undesirable feature interactions. A desirable interaction would be that an incoming call from a screened number is

not forwarded. Feature interactions often occur when new features are added to an existing system. The early developers cannot foresee all possible extensions, and the later developers may be unaware of the potential for interaction. The incremental decentralized development approach often used for frameworks creates many opportunities for undesirable feature interactions.

2.   A **compatibility bug** occurs when a revision to the framework breaks a previously working feature. For example, a new feature may be inconsistent with an old feature, or a new feature may break an unchanged application rebuilt with the new framework code. "Managing the propagation of changes made to a framework so (re-)users of that framework are not adversely affected remains an essential problem in the development of frameworks. Today, code inspection is the only available strategy for estimating the impact of a class modification. The result is that subtle conflicts with significant consequences are often detected only during the testing phase, if at all" [Codine+97, 74].

3.   A **latent bug** is one that has been dormant in the framework, perhaps since its first release. Usage patterns of application instantiation have not caused the buggy code to be reached or, if reached, have not triggered the fault. Suppose that a new instantiation of the framework can reach and trigger failures. The dependability for this new instantiation may be much worse than that observed for the known instantiations.

Finally, new features are at risk for the same kind of bugs as are other systems.

Strategy

Test Model

Each class of bugs has a related test approach.

Feature interaction testing may be approached in three ways. First, the test suite for the version of the FUT may exercise some new feature interactions, some of which may be buggy. Such a test suite includes test cases for unchanged features, drops test cases for obsolete features, and adds test cases for new features. Second, additional feature interaction tests may be identified from **anti-requirements**. Anti-requirements are system behaviors that must *not* occur. The test attempts to devise feature interactions that can defeat the anti-requirements. Third, if time permits, feature combinations may be automatically generated and applied to the FUT.

A regression test suite should be run (see Chapter 15). In contrast to a new framework, a popular framework will have many instantiations to draw on for test support. If the producer has access to the application instantiations developed for the framework, they may be used to support regression testing. Compatibility testing can use existing instantiations that have test suites. The next increment of the framework is instantiated with an application that has stabilized for the previous release. Just attempting to build the system will reveal upward code-level compatibility problems. If the system can be built, running the instantiation test suite will identify compatibility problems.

If a consumer makes a significantly different instantiation of the FUT, latent bugs may cause a rash of failures. Try to develop information about the shifts in usage patterns and allocate your testing effort accordingly.

Test cases for new features should be developed using the *Extended Use Case Test* and *Class Association Test* patterns.

The infrastructure support of the framework should be exercised as well. In contrast to the context of *New Framework Test*, an instantiation may be available that is sufficiently large and complex so that a heavy load will be effective in revealing infrastructure bugs.

Automation

The test suite may be implemented with a driver suited to the external interface of the demo app. Assertions in the framework classes (see Chapter 17) can provide a powerful development tool. Figure 11.3 suggests how the current instantiations of the framework can be used to test a new release of the framework.

Entry Criteria

Achieving the following conditions before system scope testing of an incremental framework release will improve testing efficiency and effectiveness:

- ✓ A testable system scope model should be available. Develop and evolve this model in parallel with framework coding.
- ✓ All new and changed component classes and subsystems should have passed individually adequate test suites. If you must skip or reduce adequate testing of individual components and subsystems, use *Risk-based Allocation* [Binder 2000] to plan the testing effort.
- ✓ A system scope test harness should be installed, tested, and stabilized.
- ✓ The test environment (mirroring the target environment) should be installed, tested, and stabilized.

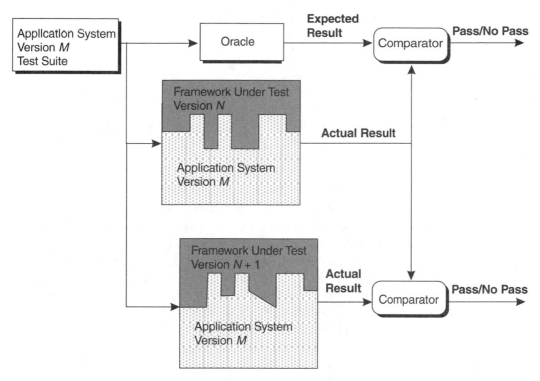

FIGURE 11.3 Application-based regression test of popular framework.

✓ Optional: You have built at least one actual consumer instantiation of the current release.

✓ You have conducted an analysis of the new and changed features.

Exit Criteria

The exit criteria are the same as those for a new framework. The framework should be released to reuse consumers when the producer has shown that it can support application development. The producer's test suite should meet the exit criteria for the test design patterns used to develop the demo app test suite.

✓ At least one test for each row in the use case's operational relation, meeting the *Extended Use Case Test* exit criteria

✓ At least one minimal test of every association in the class model, meeting the *Class Association Test* exit criteria

✓ CRUD coverage, as defined in *Covered in CRUD*

✓ Control model coverage: transition coverage for a state machine or branch coverage on all sequence diagrams

Consequences

Most of the consequences described in **New Framework Test** apply to new feature testing in a popular framework. The use of an actual application instantiation (or, better still, several instantiations) for testing will reveal many compatibility bugs before the system is released to its users. Even if the producer decides not to fix the compatibility bugs, consumers can still be informed about what is obsolete or not supported. Problem resolution costs can be avoided by checking incident reports against the obsolete list first. The cost of the version-to-version compatibility testing strategy is directly related to the extent of change. If many changes are included and only a small part of the prior instantiation and its test suite are usable, the cost of revising the old test suite may be excessive.

As the framework begins to stabilize (i.e., fewer changes are made to it), two things will happen. First, the rate of test decay will decrease. That is, fewer of the prior release's test cases will be broken by changes in features, system interfaces, and implementation. Fewer new tests will therefore have to be written and fewer tests will have to be revised or removed. Consequently, the average cost per test will drop, that is, testing efficiency will increase. Simultaneously, the **pesticide paradox** may appear [Beizer 90]. The existing library of test cases will have revealed all bugs that it can. Nevertheless, some residual bugs will remain, like mutant insects that have become resistant to a pesticide. A new application instantiation with a significantly different usage profile can trigger these bugs. As a result, a new instantiation may have a much higher failure rate, even when the framework has passed an extensive test suite and is stable for existing instantiations. Both producers and consumers should attempt to assess the similarity (or difference) between new and existing instantiations before making assumptions about their dependability.

Known Uses

Although most frameworks are tested in some manner, I am not aware of published reports on similar testing strategies. Love describes the process used to develop the Stepstone class libraries, which was quite effective and supported multiple releases for many different platforms [Love 92]. This approach include many elements of the Popular Framework Test strategy.

I have worked with several clients to apply this pattern. These engagements have had several elements in common. They began when I was asked to recommend a testing approach. The client had already spent a year or two on framework development, but the framework was not meeting expectations for dependability. The absence of systematic testing was suspected to be the culprit, and often it turned out to be a primary problem. Retrofitting an effective test process was possible, but expensive compared with establishing the test process from the outset. In either case, with sufficient time, training, and testware development, very high levels of dependability could be achieved.

11.3   Bibliographic Notes

Some material in this chapter first appeared in [Binder 96g].

Programming language support for software reuse is not a new idea. Subroutines in conventional languages, operating systems, databases, and utility programs have supported reuse since the 1960s. Support for reuse was an explicit design goal for Ada 83, leading to packages and generic types. These features are carried forward in Ada 95. Much has been written about design approaches and process strategies to accomplish reuse. A survey of reuse approaches appears in [Krueger 92]. Tracz's pragmatic discussion of reuse is both entertaining and informative [Tracz 95]. General considerations for facilitating reuse in object-oriented development are discussed in [Goldberg+95]. Lim offers a systematic management guide to achieving reuse [Lim 98].

Wiede presents an extensive analysis of technical considerations in object-based and object-oriented reusability [Weide+91]. The design of abstract classes is articulated in the *Abstract Class* design pattern [Wolfe 97]. Design and programming approaches to enhance reusability of C++ abstract classes and template classes are presented in several sources [Carroll+95, Meyer 88, Meyer 97]. An analysis of the relative merits of generics and inheritance is offered in [Meyer 97].

Object-oriented frameworks have been widely discussed and used. Johnson's article on class libraries and frameworks is a classic [Johnson+88]. The October 1997 issue of *Communications of the ACM* includes a dozen short articles and experience reports from leaders in development and application of frameworks. The Catalysis OOA/D methodology uses the UML and gives explicit consideration to identification of frameworks, abstract classes, and generic classes [D'Souza+99]. Framework scope patterns are presented in nearly every book on software design patterns.

Chapter 12   Subsystems

> One man's ceiling is another man's floor.
>
> *Anonymous*

Overview

A subsystem is composed of several classes and is a logical or physical part of an application system. This chapter presents several patterns for test design at subsystem scope. *Class Association Test* checks for anomalies in the implementation of class associations. *Round-trip Scenario Test* covers stimulus–response paths in a sequence diagram. *Controlled Exception Test* suite can verify client/server exception handling. *Mode Machine Test* verifies aggregate, externally visible, state-based behavior.

12.1   Subsystems

12.1.1   What Is a Subsystem?

For our purposes, a subsystem is any testable collection of classes, objects, components, and modules. It may consist of a small cluster of a few classes or a large hierarchy of source code directories with thousands of classes containing millions of lines of code. A subsystem has the following characteristics:

- It is executable and testable as a whole. Whatever its size, a subsystem must be executable to be testable. Thus some interesting groupings of components are not subsystems.
- It has parts that can be tested in isolation. Although some components are subsystems, and vice versa, if any composite part of a component is removed, it ceases to be executable. In contrast, at least some parts of a subsystem can be executed (tested) in isolation.
- It implements a cohesive set of responsibilities. This characteristic makes it a candidate for responsibility testing and, as a side effect, establishes a clear scope of effort. This provides a natural organization of test suites and corresponding division of labor.
- It does not provide all of the functionality of the application under test.

Subsystems may be implemented in many ways.

- *Small cluster.* A small cluster is composed of several tightly coupled classes. Testing its constituent classes in isolation is therefore impractical. A small cluster can also result from cyclic dependencies (each class uses the other) so that the classes cannot be tested in isolation. The **cluster head** is a single class that uses the others as instance variables or as message parameters. We can treat a small cluster as a single class, as long as the cluster head uses all the constituent class capabilities and the constituents are not used outside the cluster.

- *Pattern participants.* The implementation of a software design pattern can often be tested as a subsystem. Although patterns are too abstract to allow production of test cases, their implementation is often testable as a subsystem. For example, although many specific test approaches can be used to devise a test suite for a specific *Model-View-Controller* (MVC) implementation [Krasner+88], we cannot derive tests directly from the MVC pattern. A pattern does not provide enough information to select test values or a sequence of messages.

- *Developer subclasses.* The developer's subclasses are considered the cluster, excluding their symbiotic dependencies with, for example, a Smalltalk environment, NeXT App Kit, JDC, or MFC.

- *Family of Ada 95 packages.* In Ada 95, a collection of software components can share a namespace, hide their names from other subsystems, and provide a single interface.

- *Large cluster.* A large cluster is a group of related classes or related clusters. The content of a large cluster can be set for project management reasons as the scope of design, programming, and testing work that can be handled by a single person or it can correspond to the major components of system architecture.

- *Build group.* A build group is a collection of software components processed by a linkage editor to generate an executable. It may be a binary component with its own API or a group of classes with a single class as an API (as in the *Facade* pattern [Gamma+95]).

- *Task group.* A task group is a collection of build groups that is linked as an executable process or a collection of build groups that generate processes that do something interesting.

Usually, class scope test patterns can be applied to a small cluster. Sometimes, however, a cluster is headless—that is, the cluster classes assume the presence of one another and rely on a common client to function as the cluster head. For example, the classes Node and Edge might be designed to support a Graph class. We cannot do much by testing Node or Edge separately. Instead, the test driver must either supply many responsibilities of a Graph class or use an actual Graph class as a proxy driver for Node and Edge.

The classes of a library and a framework also form a kind of subsystem. They are discussed in Chapter 11.

Because testing focuses on executable entities, a testable subsystem must correspond to an aggregation of components that is visible as a whole. Subsystems may be defined for other purposes. In the UML meta-model, a *Subsystem* type is a subtype of the UML types *Package* and *Class*. A UML *Package* does not necessarily correspond to an executable implementation entity, such as an Ada 95 package or a Java package.

12.1.2 Why Test at Subsystem Scope?

We are often interested in verifying an implementation that is larger than a class or small cluster, but smaller than an entire application system. The interest in testing at this scope can arise for many reasons.

- It is a precondition for testing at system scope.
- It is a practical necessity. Partitioning an application into subsystems is typically necessary to keep scope and complexity at a manageable level.

Subsystem development and testing can progress in parallel, reducing elapsed development time.

- It supports internal releases during incremental, iterative development. As successive chunks of functionality are developed, they must be combined and tested. Each chunk is typically a subsystem. A subsystem should be tested before other developers work on it.
- Use cases can model requirements for any subsystem with a public interface. It makes sense to test these use cases at subsystem scope, as they might be difficult to test at system scope.
- Some classes and other components have been bundled for historical or commercial reasons and thus must be tested as a whole.
- Some subsystems must be shown to work before additional funding will be committed to a project.
- The testing budget or schedule is limited or reduced. There is not enough time to test each class or small cluster. Testing at subsystem scope ensures that all smaller components will receive at least a perfunctory exercise, compared with no testing at all for some of them.
- The dependability requirements of some subsystems are much higher than those of other subsystems, and more extensive testing is indicated.
- The target environment of a subsystem is unique or different or must be simulated apart from the rest of the application system.

12.2 Subsystem Test Design Patterns

A subsystem test plan must answer two key questions; (1) What features and capabilities should be tested? (2) How should the test plan and test suites be organized? As with class scope testing, both the structure of the subsystem and the nature of the responsibilities determine the appropriate testing approach. The key problem of subsystem testing lies in developing a testable model of aggregate behavior. The patterns discussed in this chapter solve that problem.

- *Class Association Test* shows how to design a test suite that will exercise the associations defined in a class or object model.
- *Controlled Exception Test* shows how to design a test suite that will exercise exception handling.

- ***Round-trip Scenario Test*** shows how to design a test suite that will cover all event–response paths in a sequence diagram.
- ***Mode Machine Test*** shows how to model the aggregate state behavior of a cluster and develop a state-based test suite.

Table 12.1 shows relationships among elements of a subsystem testing strategy. Each of the following patterns assumes that the subsystem under test has reached an operability threshold—it can be run with ease and is mostly free of bugs that could have been revealed by testing the components separately. The problem of orchestrating the content and order of tests for the constituent parts of a subsystem is considered in Chapter 13.

TABLE 12.1 Elements of Subsystem Testing Strategy

Scope of Implementation Under Test	Typical Responsibility Model	Parts to Be Integrated	Integration Strategy				
			Typical Automation	Prerequisite Part Coverage	Typical Integration Cycle	Integration Coverage Model	Integration Coverage
Cluster	Mode machine	Root client and its servers, upper-bounded	Class harness	Per component strategy	Stubs, incremental uses/threads	Collaboration Diagram, mode tree	Call paths M+
Facade	Extended contract (facade), mode machine	Classes in build group	Class harness	Per component strategy	Stubs, incremental uses/threads	Sequence Diagram	N+ of facade, M+
Binary component with API (developed, not reused)	Extended contract, XUC/SD	Classes in build group, components, VM	Component harness	Per component strategy	Incremental uses/threads	Sequence Diagram	N+ (API), M+, SD branch
Build group generating process with IPC or UI interfaces	XUC/SD, mode machine	Classes in build group, components, VM, Hw	Interface-coupled harness	Per component strategy	Stubs, Incremental uses/threads	Sequence Diagram	SD branch, M+
Process group using IPC, UI	XUC/SD, mode machine	Constituent processes, components, other apps, VM, Hw	Interface-coupled harness	Per component strategy	Various tree walks	Sequence Diagram	SD branch M+
"Component"† GUI application	XUC/SD	Binary components with API	Capture/playback	Vendor certification	Big Bang	Sequence Diagram	SD branch

Key: IUT = Subsystem—Stand-alone executable, possibly not able to do anything interesting; XUC = Extended Use Case (see Chapter 14); SD = Sequence diagram; N+ = Conformance + Sneak Path coverage, Class State Model; M+ = Conformance + Sneak Path coverage, Mode Machine Model

†For example, ActiveX or JavaBeans

Class Association Test

Intent

Design a test suite to verify the implementation of required associations among classes.

Context

Classes are typically responsible for maintaining associations with other classes. The associations in a class diagram partially define requirements for valid instance combinations in the system under test (and by implication, combinations that are not allowed). See Section 8.4, Class Diagram.

The Class Association Test pattern is applicable when the system under test must correctly implement the relationships represented in a Class Diagram. This diagram is a rich source of requirements information. Relationships occur in many forms, including association, aggregation, whole-part, is-a, subtype, aggregation, and recursive inclusion. Typical application systems have a complex network of relationships. Pair-wise associations with multiplicity constraints are common. For most medium-sized business applications, the class model includes 100 to 200 classes and 200 to 500 relationships. If we tried to model each association as a state variable and then enumerate all possible combinations of associations as states, we would soon face an astronomical number of states. The transition network would be larger still. How can we choose a practical test suite that will exercise the implementation of all association constraints implied by the class model? This pattern provides a systematic approach to transform association multiplicity parameters into test cases. The 1×1 domain testing model is adapted to produce an efficient and effective test suite. The resulting test suite will reveal typical bugs in the implementation of associations.

For example, suppose that we are developing a dog license registration system for the town of Dogpatch.[1] Figure 12.1 shows the Class Diagram representing the required relationships of dogs, owners, and ownership. Now suppose that the neighboring town of Kaynine requires that every person must own at least two dogs, but no more than 14. In a master stroke of government, the Kaynine city council insists that every dog be owned by one and only one

---

1. Adapted from Meilir Page-Jones' infamous person-owns-dog problem [Page-Jones 95] which asked: what classes will best implement this requirement? which class should implement a method `numberOfDogsOwned( )`?

FIGURE 12.1   Class model, Dogpatch policy.

FIGURE 12.2   Class model, Kaynine policy.

person. These restrictions on same association roles are represented with multiplicity constants shown in Figure 12.2.

Fault Model

An association between two classes means that both must implement a mutual constraint or dependency. The multiplicity parameters in Figure 12.1 imply that a Dogpatch resident is not required to own a dog, a dog is owned by only one person or has no owner, and a person may own as many dogs as he or she likes. The person-owns-dog requirement can be implemented with at least four different collaborations:

- Two classes: `Person` and `Dog`
- Three classes: `Person`, `Dog`, and `PersonDogOwnership`
- Three classes: `Person`, `Dog`, and `DogOwningPerson` (with `Dog` and `Person` instance variables)
- Four classes: `Person`, `Dog`, `DogOwner`, and a mixin `DogOwningPerson`

Without commenting on the relative advantages of these approaches, it is clear that each relies on subtle assumptions shared over several objects. In a typical system, hundreds of such relationships exist. Developers often use any or all these approaches, increasing the likelihood of requirements misinterpretation and coding errors. Furthermore, associations must typically be made persistent—that is, written to and retrieved from nonvolatile storage media. This goal may be accomplished in many ways. Even if a mature database management system (DBMS) is used the additional design and coding to achieve persistence is not trivial.

In short, implementing associations requires complex code with many bug hazards, which explains its status as a chronic problem. The relationship update and delete anomaly problem was a large part of the motivation for relational databases [Date 82]. Association implementations are susceptible to several kinds of faults:

- *Incorrect multiplicity.* The implementation rejects a legal combination or accepts an illegal combination. For example, a buggy implementation would insist on at least one dog for every person in Dogpatch or allow dogless persons in Kaynine. Table 12.2 lists corrupt instance combinations for the Dogpatch relationships.

- *Update anomaly.* The link that associates several instances of one class with a single instance of another class necessarily carries some redundant information. In the worst case, all information is copied for each link (every dog instance also has a complete instance of a person). When a person owns five dogs, five identical instances of person must be created. When one instance is changed, all linked instances must be changed as well. An update

TABLE 12.2 Some Possible Association Instances, Person Owns Dog

Number of Instances of a Person Who Owns an Instance(s) of Dog	Number of Instances of Dog Who Is Owned by an Instance(s) of Person	Person Owns 0..m Dog(s)	Dog Is Owned by 1..1 Person
0	0	OK	OK
No dog-owning persons are represented in the system under test.	1	OK	Corrupted state
	*	OK	Corrupted state
	M	OK	Corrupted state
1	0	OK	OK
At least one dog-owning person is represented in the system under test.	1	OK	OK
	*	OK	OK
	M	OK	OK
M	0	OK	Corrupted state
Several dog-owning persons own the same dog in the system under test.	1	OK	Corrupted state
	*	OK	Corrupted state
	M	OK	Corrupted state

anomaly is a fault that results in inconsistent values. For example, suppose four of the five instances are correctly changed, but one is not.

- *Delete anomaly.* What happens to the owned objects if the owning object is deleted? For example, suppose a person who owns eight dogs leaves Dogpatch. We would probably remove the object for that person, but what about the eight dog objects? Should they be automatically removed? Whatever the requirement, the implementation must find and remove (or change) each relationship. The implementation may be simple or convoluted, depending on the design, and may yield inconsistent results.

- *Missing link.* It is possible that some, but not all, of the links that implement an association are created or that some become corrupted. For example, a pointer from a collection of dogs is established to a person, but the pointer from the person to the dog collection is not established.

- *Wrong link.* All of the links that implement an association are created, but are incorrect or inconsistent. For example, a pointer from a collection of dogs is established to the person object for Bob Binder instead of Marge Pack.

These faults can be reached by exercising the code that implements the association constraint. This code will lie on a path that will be executed when boundary values of the constraints are input (see Section 10.2.4, Domain Testing Model). If the constraint code is reached and multiplicity boundaries are used, the assumed faults should be triggered, if they exist. The failure may be observable if the implementation under test includes built-in integrity checking (but it may be incorrect in the same way the association constraint code is incorrect, so propagation is not guaranteed). Alternatively, no integrity checking code might exist. The test harness must check the post-test state of the implementation for violations of constraints. This goal may be accomplished in many ways, including using query and reporting functions of the IUT.

The Class Association Test pattern does not directly target logic faults, computational faults leading to incorrect output, sequential behavior constraints, or performance problems.

Strategy

Test Model

Tests of association constraints could be devised by imagining likely (and unlikely) scenarios or by examining use cases for the application. For example,

- Person buys dog.
- Dog runs away.
- Person sells dog.
- Person dies, and dog inherits person's estate.
- Dog dies.

Reflecting on unusual circumstances often yields good test cases. This approach, however, is neither systematic nor repeatable.

Multiplicity Test Sets. Multiplicity parameters specify boundary conditions for the acceptable mappings between two objects. Table 12.3 lists the nonspecific multiplicities that are legal in the UML and gives several examples of legal, fixed-interval multiplicities, including the 2..14 Kaynine multiplicity. Each multiplicity has two boundary conditions: one for the minimum and one for the maximum. If the minimum and maximum are identical (e.g., 1..1), then a single strict equality boundary condition will suffice.

The notation A:n(B) is shorthand for "For each instance of type A, the number of type B must be . . ." For example, A:n(B) $\leq$ 24 is read "For each instance of type A, the number of type B must be less than or equal to 24." A and B are replaced by the names of the classes (types) that participate in the association under test; for example, Person:n(Dog) $\geq$ 14 is read "For each instance of Person, the number of Dogs must be less than or equal to 14."

TABLE 12.3 Canonical Boundary Conditions for Legal Multiplicities

Multiplicity of A to B	Boundary Conditions	
*	A:n(B) $\geq$ 0	A:n(B) $\leq$ M
0	A:n(B) = 0	
1	A:n(B) = 1	
42	A:n(B) = 42	
0..0	A:n(B) = 0	
0..1	A:n(B) $\geq$ 0	A:n(B) $\leq$ 1
0..24	A:n(B) $\geq$ 0	A:n(B) $\leq$ 24
0..*	A:n(B) $\geq$ 0	A:n(B) $\leq$ M
1..1	A:n(B) = 1	
1..24	A:n(B) $\geq$ 1	A:n(B) $\leq$ 24
1..*	A:n(B) $\geq$ 1	A:n(B) $\leq$ M
2..14	A:n(B) $\geq$ 2	A:n(B) $\leq$ 14
42..4096	A:n(B) $\geq$ 42	A:n(B) $\leq$ 4096

TABLE 12.4   Multiplicity Boundary Conditions for Dogpatch Policy

Associations		Boundary Conditions	
Person owns dog	0..*	Person:n(Dog) ≥ 0	Person:n(Dog) ≤ M
Dog has owner	0..1	Dog:n(Person) ≥ 0	Dog:n(Person) ≤ 1

Associations are bidirectional, so testing in one direction is not sufficient. Each binary association has four boundary conditions (we can simplify the conditions for zero-distance intervals with a single condition.) This is illustrated by the association boundary conditions for the Dogpatch requirements (Table 12.4). We apply the 1 × 1 test strategy to these conditions and cast the results in the domain matrix (see Section 10.2.4, Domain Testing Models). This provides test cases for these conditions, as shown in Figure 12.3. Table 12.5 and Figure 12.4 provide the same analysis for the Kaynine requirements.

Some off points may be impossible to generate. For example, no reasonable interpretation of −1 person instances is possible. Such "impossible" situations do happen however, and it is worth trying to find some way to provide them as input.

Analysis and design models often leave the multiplicity maximum value unspecified, as in 1..*. Modeling fantasies cannot change the fact that storage is

Variable/Condition/Type			Test Cases							
			1	2	3	4	9	10	11	12
Number of Dogs	Person:n(Dog) >= 0	On	0							
		Off		−1						
	Person:n(Dog) <= M	On			M					
		Off				M+1				
	Typical	In					2	42	5329	256
Number of Persons	Dog:n(Person) >= 0	On					0			
		Off						−1		
	Dog:n(Person) <= 1	On							1	
		Off								2
	Typical	In	1	1	1	1				
Expected Result			✓	✗	✓	✗	✓	✗	✓	✗

FIGURE 12.3   Domain matrix for Dogpatch policy.

TABLE 12.5   Multiplicity Boundary Conditions for Kaynine Policy

Associations		Boundary Conditions	
Person owns dog	2..14	Person:n(Dog) ≥ 2	Person:n(Dog) ≤ 14
Dog has owner	1..1	Dog:n(Person) = 1	

Variable/Condition/Type			Test Cases						
			1	2	3	4	5	6	7
Number of Dogs	Person:n(Dog) >= 2	On	2						
		Off		1					
	Person:n(Dog) <= 14	On			14				
		Off				15			
	Typical	In					3	8	13
Number of Persons	Dog:n(Person) ==1	On					1		
		Off						0	
		Off							2
	Typical	In	1	1	1	1			
Expected Result			✓	✗	✓	✗	✓	✗	✗

FIGURE 12.4   Domain matrix for Kaynine policy.

finite. By accident or conscious choice, a fixed upper limit *always* exists for the maximum. It may be large, or it may be surprisingly small. Nevertheless, some value must be chosen for the upper bound. If the actual physical limit is very large (say, 2^{64}), try testing with the largest practical quantity. For example, you may be able to copy the largest number of instances in another database. Try this test again when you are doing system scope stress tests. It may prove easier to instantiate a very large collection because stress testing typically requires high-quantity inputs.

Testing for Update/Delete Bugs. Besides verifying that multiplicity constraints are correctly implemented, we can test for update/delete bugs. A common bug is that only one instance is changed but all instances should have been modified. To test for this bug, we could set up a dog owner, Ms. Marge Pack, with an address of 123 Oak Street and five dogs (Spot, Fluffy, Fido, King, and Sparky). Then we design tests to attempt inconsistent instances, as follows.

- To test for an update bug, we change Ms. Pack's address to 456 Pine Street, then list the addresses of all dogs owned by Ms. Pack (assuming that such a function is provided by the system under test). After the change is made, the addresses for Spot, Fluffy, Fido, King, and Sparky should be 456 Pine Street. If not, we have revealed an update bug.

- To test for a delete dependency bug, we delete Ms. Pack from the system. If this operation is allowed, no trace of Spot, Fluffy, Fido, King, or Sparky should remain—no information about them should be available after Ms. Pack has been deleted. Some systems do not allow the deletion of an instance that has dependent instances. Here, we attempt the delete operation, but expect that it will be rejected.

- To test for a delete side-effect bug, we delete all of Ms. Pack's dogs from the system. We expect that Ms. Pack will still be reported as a non-dog-owner residing at the same address. Then we attempt to delete Ms. Pack from the system. After both delete operations, the expected result is confirmed if we cannot produce any information about Ms. Pack and the five dogs.

Wrong and Missing Links.   The multiplicity tests will reveal many bugs that allow incorrect or missing links. Requirements for mutual exclusion provide additional in point combinations. Keyed collections are typically used to implement associations (these classes should be individually tested with **Quasi-modal Class Test**). The test sets in Table 12.6 give example key values for collections

TABLE 12.6   Suggestive Test Instantiations for Inclusive/Exclusive Multiplicity

Instances of Customer			Instances of Employee			Multiplicity Constraint on Customer/Employee Relationship				
						Mutex	1:1	0:1	0:M	1:M
Baker	Smith		Jones	Wilson		OK	CS	OK	OK	CS
Baker	Jones		Baker	Jones		CS	OK	OK	OK	OK
Baker	Jones		Jones	Smith		CS	CS	OK	OK	CS
Jones	Smith		Baker	Jones		CS	CS	OK	OK	CS
Baker	Smith		Baker	Jones	Smith	CS	CS	OK	OK	CS
Baker	Jones	Smith	Baker	Smith		CS	CS	OK	OK	CS
Baker	Jones	Smith	Jones	Jones	Jones	CS	CS	CS	OK	CS
Jones	Jones	Jones	Baker	Jones	Smith	CS	CS	OK	OK	CS
Smith	Wilson		Smith	Wilson	Wilson	CS	CS	CS	OK	OK
Baker			Baker	Baker	Jones	CS	CS	CS	OK	OK

Key: Mutex = Mutually exclusive; CS = Corrupt state

A and B. The same values will be valid or invalid, depending on the association constraint. The assumed association is A to B. If a B-to-A association also exists, it can be tested with the same set. The example shows how these constraints would be applied to groups of customers and employees.

We should not be satisfied with running these tests for a single instance of Person. Instead, a large number of Persons should be loaded. The multiplicity/anomaly test suites should be rerun on some or all of the larger object base.

Automation

Anomaly and multiplicity testing may be combined. In particular, we can increase testing by interleaving anomaly tests with maximum-value multiplicity tests.

The subsystem under test may be exercised via an API driver interface. If the system has a GUI, the GUI may provide sufficient control to exercise the associations. If the associations are embedded within a larger system, exercising all of them may prove difficult.

If the instances of collection classes are stored using a DBMS (relational, object-oriented, and so on), setting up test cases with a database loader utility is usually easier than entering them through the user interface.

Entry Criteria

✓ Each class in the scope of the model has passed an alpha-omega cycle.

✓ Keyed collections are typically used to implement associations. These classes should have been individually tested with *Quasi-modal Class Test*.

Exit Criteria

✓ Each multiplicity on point test passes (the input is accepted, the correct output is produced, and the resultant states of the objects are not corrupted).

✓ Each multiplicity off point test passes (the input is rejected, the appropriate error message is generated or an exception is raised, and the resultant states of the objects are not corrupted).

✓ A deletion anomaly test passes.

✓ An update anomaly test passes.

✓ All tests for mutual exclusion pass.

Consequences

With n associations in the subsystem under test, there will be at most $8n$ basic multiplicity test cases (two test cases for each minimum and maximum boundary on the A:B association and two for each minimum and maximum boundary on the B:A association). Zero-interval multiplicities like 1..1 will reduce the total number of tests. For a typical system containing several hundred associations, this would require several thousand test cases.

Class Association Test requires a model of the class associations in the subsystem under test. To apply this approach to an existing application system that does not have an object model, a partial object model may be extracted by a source code analyzer. A source code analyzer typically can identify the presence of a reference between classes and objects but cannot determine multiplicity constraints. If the implementation uses dynamic binding or several levels of indirection to implement constraints, the association may be completely obscured.

Achieving sufficient control of the system under test may prove difficult, especially for maximal value testing, if the database is intended to hold a very large number of instances. In this situation, backloading the database to some full state may be necessary. A systematic and effective testing strategy based on an arbitrarily large object model is an open problem.

Pair-wise testing will be effective if no association loops are present—consider, for example, classes Customer, Order, and Product, and associations Customer-Places-Order, Order-Uses-Product, and Product-AdvertizedTo-Customer. We can test pairs of relationships in a long chain of relationships as long as no dependencies force us to consider n-way relationships. To test an n-way dependency network, we can exercise each pair in the dependency network while holding the other relationships fixed.

Known Uses

The Syntropy approach to model verification [Cook+94] exercises many conditions (on an analysis model) that *Class Association Test* exercises on an implementation.

Round-trip Scenario Test

Intent

Extract a control flow model from a UML Sequence Diagram and develop a path set that provides minimal branch and loop coverage.

Context

The message structure of the subsystem under test can be represented by a Sequence Diagram (see Section 8.5, Sequence Diagram). A Sequence Diagram is often (but not necessarily) associated with a use case. It shows how a sequence of messages is intended to service a single user input or external event. The path begins with an externally generated event and ends with the production of a response that satisfies this event.

For example, the Sequence Diagram in Figure 12.5 shows what happens when a customer inserts a card into a hypothetical automatic teller machine (ATM). Several things are checked: (1) that the card is an ATM card and not another kind of charge card, (2) that the card is not stolen, (3) that the customer has a valid bank account for the card, and (4) that the customer has a correct personal identification number (PIN). The customer gets three chances to enter the PIN. If the customer's bank is not affiliated with the ATM provider, the customer is asked whether he or she will accept a service charge for using the ATM. If the customer declines, the session ends and the card is returned to the customer. If the customer accepts the fee or no fee is charged, the customer may then select a banking transaction. Subsequent interactions are not shown in this example.

Clearly, these conditions allow for many different scenarios, each of which should be tested. But what are they? A scenario corresponds to a different path through the Sequence Diagram, so we could try to trace paths on the diagram.

A **round-trip scenario** is a complete stimulus–response path on a Sequence Diagram. A Sequence Diagram typically includes many such scenarios. How can we ensure that all scenarios are tested?

Fault Model

A scenario is one path through a Sequence Diagram. Each object or subsystem interface that participates in the scenario must be physically correct and must provide a correct implementation of its responsibilities. In addition, the overall

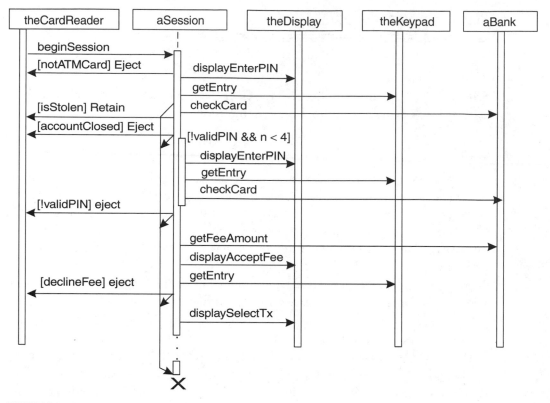

FIGURE 12.5 Sequence Diagram for ATM Establish Session Use Case.

design to produce the response must be correct. The following bugs can occur in a scenario implementation:

- Incorrect or missing output
- Acceptance of incorrect selection or object
- Action missing on external interface
- Missing function/feature in a participant
- Correct message passed to the wrong object
- Incorrect message passed to the right object
- Message sent to destroyed object
- Correct exception raised, but caught by the wrong object
- Incorrect exception raised to the right object

- Incorrect usage of target environment services
- Incorrect or ineffective memory allocation/deallocation, resulting in an abend or degraded performance
- Unbalanced or incorrect serialization of server resources (e.g., a single client can lock a shared remote object for an arbitrarily long interval)
- Unnecessary polling
- Task deadlock
- Priority inversion, leading to process starvation
- Inadequate performance

If a bug exists, it must lie on at least one round-trip path through the Sequence Diagram. To reach the bug, that path must be taken. The test model calls out all round-trip paths to ensure that these bugs are reached. Once reached, gross interface bugs are more likely to be triggered than performance, exception, or memory bugs. Exception testing may be more effective at revealing these bugs. When triggered, these kinds of faults usually result in visible failures [Arnold+94].

Strategy

Test Model

The Sequence Diagram is a good source of subsystem (and system) scope requirements. For a narrow slice of the system, it provides an abstract view of implementation.

- Sequence Diagrams often strike a good balance between too little or too much detail.
- They can model interfaces to large clusters or other subsystems, maintaining focus on the subsystem under test.

Although such diagrams are useful for analysis and design, they are not ideal test models.

- They do not provide a good representation of repetitive, recursive, or conditional sequences.
- It is usually impossible to determine every possible message binding at an object level. A Sequence Diagram typically suppresses many control and interface details.

- Like Collaboration Diagrams, they are only one fragment of all behavior required for a use case or the subsystem under test.

- Conditional and delayed messages are not clearly distinguished.

- Dynamic binding and unique superclass/subclass behavior cannot be represented.

- Tracing flows on a Sequence Diagram produces a visual mess.

The information in the Sequence Diagram can be transformed into a flow graph, which is a highly testable model. Each node in a flow graph represents a chunk of unconditional processing—once entered, all components of a segment are executed. Arrows show which block may follow another (see Section 10.2.2, Implementation-based Test Models). In essence, the test model uses a relation that is most easily analyzed as a simple directed graph. The general strengths and weaknesses of this approach have been extensively studied and are well established.

Drawing an equivalent control flow graph will probably reveal ambiguities and omissions in the Sequence Diagram. The latter diagrams are often rough sketches that favor artistic license over engineering precision. If part of the Sequence Diagram seems vague, you have found either a bug or a behavior that the coder will improvise. Like nearly all test design techniques, this approach can find bugs even before running a single test.

Test Procedure

The test procedure includes the following four steps:

1. Translate the Sequence Diagram into a Flow Graph.   The analysis that follows deals with iterated or conditionally executed message segments. A Sequence Diagram with no iterated or conditional messages has only one path (in this case, skip to step 3). Figure 12.6 shows the flow graph derived from the ATM Sequence Diagram. Rectangles in this figure indicate segments; flattened hexagons are decisions. Each arrow leaving a hexagon represents a branch. The flow graph is constructed by identifying conditions, segments, and branches.

- Each message or group of consecutive messages becomes a segment (box). A conditional action (either a branch or iteration control) ends a segment.

- Each bracketed condition becomes a decision (hexagon). The *true* path goes right. The *false* path goes down. Because Sequence Diagrams can obscure the behavior of complex conditions [Lange 97], you should

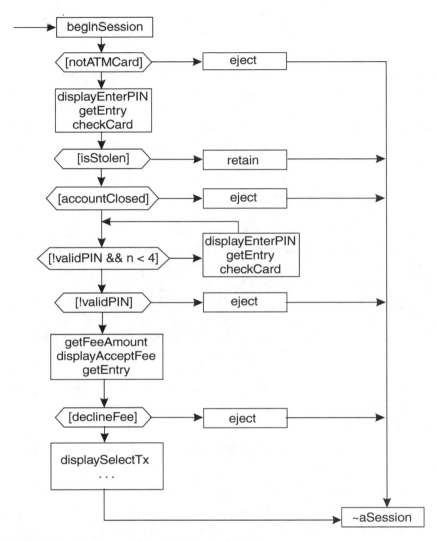

FIGURE 12.6 Flow graph for ATM Sequence Diagram.

examine the scope of the conditional—where would an *else* or *endif* appear? Are the conditionals nested? What is the complete predicate? Is part of it suppressed for simplicity?

- Each bracketed loop condition becomes a decision node. Note that the position of the loop predicate is important—it is evaluated before the loop body (as in while and for loops) or after (until loops).

The blocks and decisions are connected by tracing the flow through the Sequence Diagram.

2. Identify Paths to Test from the Flow Graph.   Any scenario will reach all segments in the graph if the graph does not contain any loops or branches. Loops and branches result in many possible entry-to-exit paths. Depending on the structure, the number of paths can easily reach astronomical numbers, even in systems with just a few nodes (see Chapter 10). We will employ a simple and effective approach that provides decision/iteration coverage. Every branch is taken at least once (decision coverage), and each loop is used in at least three ways: bypass the loop or do the minimum number of iterations, do only one iteration, and do the maximum number of iterations.

We do not need advanced analysis or special tools to develop test cases that meet these goals. Instead, using several colors of markers to draw paths will suffice. It helps to have a copier to make extra copies of the flow graph so you can—pardon the expression—iterate.

First, identify the entry-to-exit paths so that all decision branches are taken at least once (a decision branch is an arrow that is emerging from a hexagon). Each path traced becomes a test case. In this step, we bypass loops, if possible.

1. Choose the longest or most complex entry–exit path and color this path (paths are not colored here due to the cost of color printing).

2. Choose a new color.

3. Trace an entry–exit path by taking a branch that hasn't been colored yet.

4. Repeat steps 2 and 3 until all decision branches have been colored.

5. Make a table containing a row for each path. Copy the conditions that must hold for each path into the table. For example, suppose that the condition is [a == b]. The *true* path condition is [a == b] and the *false* path condition is [a != b].

Figure 12.7 shows the resulting paths. Table 12.7 shows the path condition table. These paths exercise the loop bypass condition, so two more tests are needed to meet iteration coverage: one iteration and the maximum or high iterations.

6. Pick any path that leads to the loop entry.

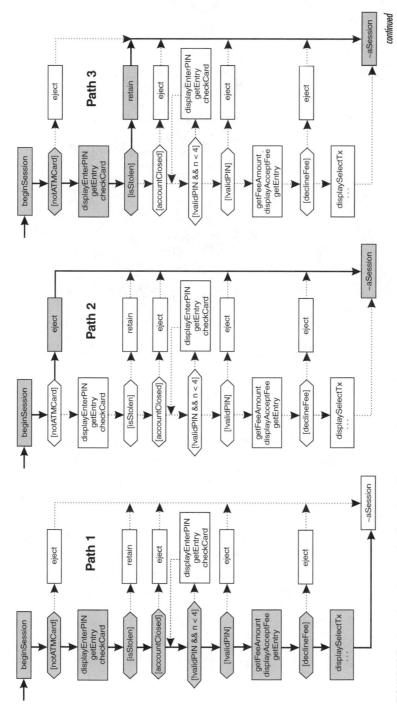

FIGURE 12.7 Nonlooping paths for ATM Sequence Diagram.

585

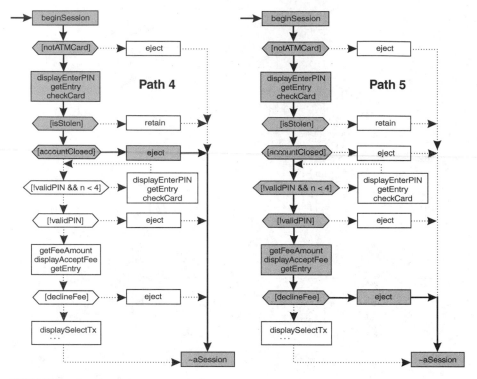

FIGURE 12.7   *Continued.*

7. Copy the path conditions, up to the loop entry to your table. Revise the condition for the loop predicate to allow one iteration. If you can, append different exit paths after the loop exit.

8. Pick another path that leads to the loop entry, if there is one (no such path appears in this example).

9. Copy the path conditions up to the loop entry to your table. Revise the condition for the loop predicate to allow the maximum iteration. If you can, append different exit paths after the loop exit. In our example, the maximum iteration (three incorrect PIN entries) ends the session.

Figure 12.8 shows the two entry–exit paths that exercise these loop conditions. The corresponding path conditions are given in Table 12.7. Each branch

TABLE 12.7 Round-trip Scenario Test Cases/Test Path Conditions for Establishing Session Sequence Diagram

Path	Comment	Path Conditions
1	Longest path, all false Bypass loop	!notATMCard, !isStolen, !accountClosed, validPIN, !declineFee
2	Branch 1 true Bypass loop	notATMCard
3	Branch 2 true Bypass loop	!notATMCard, isStolen
4	Branch 3 true Bypass loop	!notATMCard, !isStolen, accountClosed
5	Branch 4 true Bypass loop	!notATMCard, !isStolen, !accountClosed, validPIN, declineFee
6	Same as path 1 up to the loop Loop once	!notATMCard, !isStolen, !accountClosed, !validPIN && n==1, !validPIN && n==2, !declineFee
7	Same as path 1 up to the loop Loop max times	!notATMCard, !isStolen, !accountClosed, !validPIN && n==1, !validPIN && n==2, !validPIN && n==3, !validPIN

(an arrow emerging from a decision node) should appear in at least one path. A branch may appear in several tests. Each loop should iterate zero times (bypassed, if possible), once, and its maximum number of times.

3. Identify Special Cases. Sequence Diagrams rarely include two significant details: bindings to polymorphic servers and exception-handling paths. Exception handling is just as much a part of an application as its other functionality. Use *Controlled Exception Test* to develop test cases to exercise the exception handling associated with the implementation under test.

The yo-yo problem suggests a kind of bug not targeted in the fault model. Suppose that a client sends a message to a polymorphic server, which in turn sends a message to another polymorphic server. The end of the message call path is reached after the activation of five polymorphic servers. Further, suppose that each server is six subclasses deep—that is, we have $6^5 = 7776$ message paths. Clearly, a bug could lurk on any of these paths, but it is a practical impossibility to identify—let alone exercise—all of these paths. A test suite

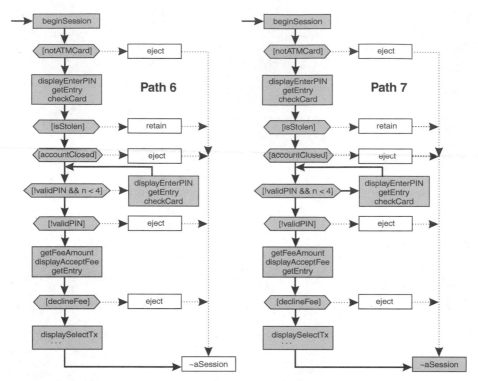

FIGURE 12.8   Looping paths for ATM Sequence Diagram.

providing round-trip coverage will probably hit at least one of each polymor-phic binding, but can easily miss bugs related to other bindings.

A practical (but weak) compromise is to do individual verification of poly-morphic servers and polymorphic messages before scenario testing. Suppose, however, that objectA sends message foo to objectB, which sends message bar to objectC, which sends message fum to objectD. Assume that foo, bar, and fum can be bound to any superclass. Now suppose that we have tested all bind-ings of objectB with objectC and all bindings of objectC with objectD. A message from objectB1.foo may still result in a failure when the thread reaches objectD4.fum. That is, pair-wise verification does not preclude *n*-way bugs.

We can take some practical steps to reduce the risk that bugs can hide in such combinations.

• Identify circumstances that (1) *must not occur* and (2) involve poly-morphic objects that do not have a direct interface. These cases should correspond to situations that are hazardous (e.g., an ignition source is enabled and a flammable material is present), illegal (e.g., the same person is registered to vote in more than one precinct), or strange (e.g., an empty truck is dispatched on a delivery run).

- Identify constraints that (1) *must always be observed* and (2) involve polymorphic objects that do not have a direct interface. For example, the current color of the traffic lights in a four-way intersection must be the same for opposite lights, the total open balance of all accounts for a single customer must not exceed a certain amount even if all balances are under their credit limit, and so on.

Develop test cases for the "must" and "must-not" scenarios. Attempt to initiate each "must-not" scenario. Also, attempt to reach a state that violates each "must" constraint. The **Category-Partition** pattern may be useful in developing the test suite for these special cases.

4. Identify Inputs and States Needed to Cause a Particular Path to Be Taken.   A path is followed when all the path conditions are met. Test cases define the specific input and state needed to satisfy the path conditions. To identify test case values, look at the predicates on each path. Work from the first predicate, picking input and state values that satisfy the particular path condition. Then, do the same for the next path condition, continuing until you have worked through all the conditions for the path. You may find it easier to work backward, beginning with the last path condition. Usually many sets of values will satisfy the conditions for a path. The discussion of path feasibility in Chapter 10 applies here.

For example, a test case for path 6 requires that we insert a valid ATM card associated with an open account at the customer's bank, enter one incorrect PIN, enter the correct PIN, and enter "yes" to accept the transaction fee. Some paths are infeasible because contradictory conditions prevent the end of the path being reached. If this happens, simply discard that path. Table 12.7 lists the path conditions for our test suite.

Finally, complete your test suite by determining the results expected for each test case. This task can be done by simulating the action of each path.

Automation

The resulting test suite can be implemented with a GUI scripting language or in an API test driver. See Chapter 19.

Entry Criteria

If the subsystem under test has been built from mostly untested objects, you will probably spend a significant amount of time fixing component-level problems before you can begin to test for scenario bugs. You can avoid this delay with adequate component scope testing.

✓ The objects, components, or subsystems participating in the scenarios should have passed at least a minimal test suite or have been sufficiently reliable in actual use.

Exit Criteria

Round-trip scenario coverage is achieved under the following circumstances:

✓ Every branch in a derived flowchart is taken at least once.
✓ Each loop is bypassed or iterated for the minimum number of iterations.
✓ Each loop is iterated once and then exited.
✓ Each loop is iterated for the maximum number of iterations.

Consequences

The Round-trip Scenario Test approach requires an accurate Sequence Diagram for the system under test. The effort for test design and execution should be roughly proportional to the complexity of the Sequence Diagram.

The minimum number of test cases depends on the structure of the implementation, as explained in Section 10.2.2, Implementation-based Test Models. Additional tests will be required to cover errors and exceptions that are not explicitly modeled.

The round-trip path heuristic will suffice for most practical problems and is far more effective than testing by poking around. You can apply any of the path selection techniques discussed in Chapter 10 to the flow graph as well.

The test model does not address the expansion of paths resulting from polymorphic bindings and does not explicitly address faults related to particular combinations of dynamic binding. Instead, a heuristic approach is taken.

Known Uses

Informal scenario-based testing is commonly used in object-oriented development [Firesmith 92, Arnold+94, Murphy+94, Jorgenson+94]. This flow graph approach was first published in [Binder 98a].

Related Patterns

Extended Use Case Test shows how to develop a responsibility-based test suite for all scenarios in a Sequence Diagram. Use *Controlled Exception Test* to develop test cases for exceptions in this scenario. The senders of messages to polymorphic servers should be exercised with *Polymorphic Message Test* and the servers with *Polymorphic Server Test*.

Controlled Exception Test

Intent

Design a test suite that will exercise exception handlers and provide a systematic means to generate all exceptions.

Context

Exception-handling code is typically packaged with a client, but a server controls the exception. A server's ability to raise exceptions can be adequately tested as part of the server's responsibility testing. Exercising a client's exception-handling code is often difficult, however, unless we can control all servers that can throw exceptions to a client. The difficulty of activating exception handlers is a frequent barrier to coverage of well-structured code. How can we control application servers and the target environment to achieve adequate coverage of a client's exception-handling code?

The Controlled Exception Test pattern applies to implementations expected to handle application-specific exceptions or exceptions raised by the target environment.

- Computational exceptions (arithmetic exceptions, underflow/overflow)
- I/O errors (device not ready, parity check)
- File errors (empty, overflow, missing)
- Main storage management (allocate, deallocate, garbage collection)
- Task management (process start, suspend, resume, terminate, inter-process communication)

Target environment exceptions typically result from incorrect or invalid usage of the virtual machine (VM) or violation of a server's contract when using utility subsystems such as an object request broker, operating system, network file/directory service, DBMS, GUI, or data communication interface.

Fault Model

Designing safe and effective exception handling is difficult. Correct and reliable implementation typically depends on arcane technical details of the target environment(s) and the programming language(s) in use [Arnold+94]. For example, nearly 1000 different exceptions can be raised by popular versions of the Unix operating system. Thus even well-designed and carefully crafted exception handling is more error-prone than application code. Several general kinds of faults can occur:

- An exception is improperly passed from a server to a client.
- An exception propagates out of scope.
- An application-specific exception handler is missing or incorrect.
- An exception is ignored and results in an immediate process/task abend.
- An exception is ignored and results in a mysterious failure in unrelated code.
- An exception handler creates an adverse side effect.
- The implementation under test does not meet target environment requirements for recognizing and handling exceptions.
- The recovery attempted by an exception is incorrect or incomplete.
- The exception structure loops; that is, the exception handler retries an operation without limitation.
- The wrong exception is thrown owing to a control flow bug or incorrect name.
- The wrong catch block is activated, possibly because of an incorrect name resolution/scoping error or incorrect build/configuration error.

If any of these faults exist, they can be reached only by activating the code that handles the exception. This requires that the exception condition be produced and that the components in the application or target environment throw or raise the necessary exception. Generating the exception will trigger any gross faults (missing or wrong exception). If the exception handler is complex, its buggy code may not be reached or triggered unless high coverage is achieved for the handler code. Propagation depends on many details of both the application and its runtime environment. If the implementation under test does not produce error messages, task termination, or similar behavior, the test harness must check the post-test state of the implementation for violations of constraints. Adding special instrumentation to monitor each exception source and handler may be necessary.

This pattern does not directly target faults in logic or computation leading to incorrect output, sequential behavior constraints, or performance problems.

Strategy

Test Model

Many exceptions simply generate an error message and terminate execution. However, the behavior of an application-specific exception handler can be quite complex if it attempts restart or recovery. With complex behavior, we need an appropriate test model. Consider using a state machine or combinational logic as a test model. With irregular behavior, the **Category-Partition** approach may be appropriate.

Exceptions must be triggered to test the exception-handling response of the implementation under test. It is usually (and should be) difficult to trigger virtual machine exceptions through the interface to the implementation under test. Triggering application-specific exceptions directly may be easier. Exception testing can be accomplished in three ways: activation, inducement, and simulation.

In *exception activation,* exceptions are activated through input and state values supplied by test cases. This approach typically requires analysis of the server's source code to select paths and test values that will trigger the desired exception. If the server is not part of the application system, this may be difficult or impossible.

In *exception inducement,* exceptions are induced by directly manipulating the implementation under test or the target environment. Target environment exceptions can be induced in many ways:

- *Mistune.* Cut down the available storage, disk space, and so on to 10 percent of normal, for example. Saturate the system with compute-bound tasks. This can force resource allocation/deallocation exceptions.
- *Cripple.* Remove, rename, disable, delete, or unplug necessary resources.
- *Pollute.* Selectively corrupt input data, files, or signals using a data zap tool.
- *Run* the system under test under a debugger and alter the object code or data to fake an error.

Make a completely separate copy of the source code under test. Alter the copy to force exceptions. Ensure that the corrupted source code remains under configuration management control as a separate configuration item (not just a revision of the original source). Do not make update-in-place changes to the source code under test.

Exception inducement typically requires time-consuming manual setup, is nonrepeatable unless the entire runtime environment can be controlled, and runs the risk of creating additional bugs.

In *exception simulation*, exceptions are simulated by using controllable wrappers for virtual machine services. The API for the virtual machine of the system under test is replaced by an API with an identical interface but a controllable implementation. The tester can select which exceptions to return through the VM API interface. This approach allows for repeatable, controllable testing. The test wrapper can perform the following checks when the call comes in or before it is returned to the IUT:

- Check the call order.
- Check parameters.
- Call the original function.
- Set the return value.
- Throw an exception.
- Change output parameters.
- Call the original function with modified parameters.
- Use system calls.
- Use selectively (based on call site and function called).
- Link the original function with the test.

Automation

Stubs (see Chapter 19) are also commonly used to simulate application-specific exceptions. The test cases should implement **Catch All Exceptions** and the exception wrapper can be implemented with **Server Proxy**. In effect, the server wrapper becomes the test driver. In an Ada 95 test stub, `raise` can generate all target environment and application exceptions explicitly.

Command-line scripts can be developed to generate anomalous conditions to trigger exceptions. Application-specific exceptions can be generated by stubs. Systematic control of target environment exceptions can be obtained with a shapable library of exception wrappers. In effect, the exception wrapper serves as a partial test driver.

Figure 12.9 shows how a wrapper class can be used to simulate exceptions that should be caught by `robustClient` (the IUT). The IUT sends message `foo` to `robustServer` and implements catch blocks for the three exceptions that `robustServer` can throw after `foo` has been sent. Suppose `robustServer` cannot be directly controlled or that these exceptions are difficult to induce. The

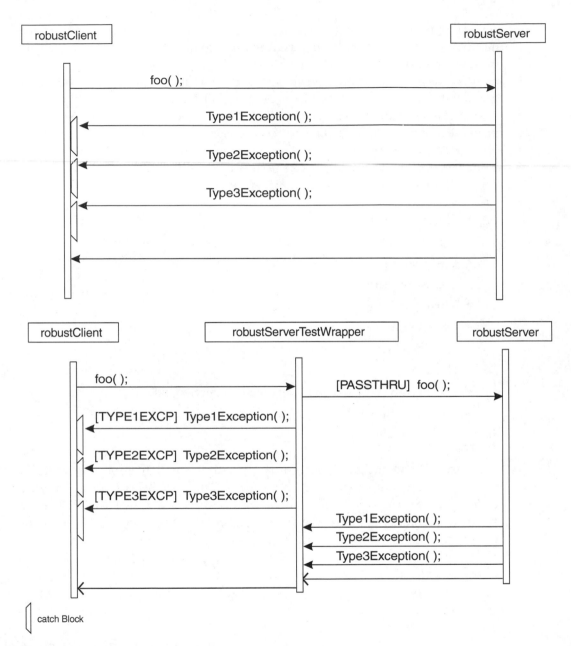

FIGURE 12.9   Exception wrapper.

tester implements a wrapper class robustServerTestWrapper, which exports the same interface as robustServer. This library for this class is compiled in place of the normal library for robustServer. The wrapper class allows messages to be passed to robustServer as well as throwing its exceptions to the IUT. Pass-through mode is useful if robustServer must be used to establish test input conditions. The IUT is compiled with robustServerTestWrapper and a test driver. The test driver activates the IUT, which sends foo to the test wrapper object, which generates each exception to be caught by robustClient. The test driver evaluates pass/no pass for the exception handling tests.

If the exception handlers in the IUT are expected to attempt restart or recovery processing, assertions can be used to check the postrecovery state. This is often the easiest way to check the results of the recovery code.

Several COTS tools that generate driver code to test exception handling are available for Ada 95, C++, and Java.

Entry Criteria

✓ It usually makes sense to do exception testing after responsibility testing of the server and client has been completed.

Exit Criteria

✓ Each server exception should be raised at least once, and each handler in the IUT should be activated at least once.

✓ If the handler is nontrivial, coverage appropriate for the responsibilities of the exception handler is achieved (e.g., if the handler can be modeled as a state machine, N+ coverage is obtained for its state model).

✓ If the exception has a long percolation chain, each link should be traversed at least once.

Consequences

Design of an exception-handling test suite requires a technical understanding of which exceptions can be raised by the target environment and which application-specific exception strategy applies. Target environment exceptions are usually well documented,[2] but application-specific exception handling typically goes undocumented and remains embedded in the code. The developer/

---

2. For example, Chan and Lee's documentation of Java Class Libraries' exceptions is quite good [Chan+97].

development team must therefore assist in developing the test plan. If exceptions are designed for testability from the outset, this problem is reduced.

In some situations, testing exception handling in an isolated test environment may not be possible. Testing exceptions in an operational system or a test system that is running in a live environment may be difficult and dangerous. Setting up the test to force the exception may be difficult, as is repeating the test under identical circumstances. If the system under test is live or running in an environment that supports other live application systems, exception testing can be disruptive and possibly dangerous.

Known Uses

Exception testing has been routinely done as part of stress testing [Beizer 84, Beizer 90]. The use of stubs to simulate returning of error codes and exceptions is also a long-standing practice [Page-Jones 88, Beizer 90, Firesmith 95].

The *QC/Sim* tool Centerline provides automated support for the wrapper approach to simulation for C++ and Unix implementations.

The *Cantata* call interface instrumentation testing system provides the ability to "wrap" calls made from the IUT with source code instrumentation similar to that used for coverage analysis. Wrapper function calls are inserted immediately before and after the original call. The wrappers support tracing the order in which calls are made, the parameters passed to each call, and returned values (see Figure 12.9). They can modify parameters passed to the target function, alter the return value or "output" parameters passed back to the software under test, or throw an exception instead of returning a value [Dorman 97].

Mode Machine Test

Intent

Develop a test suite for subsystem/scope behavior by analyzing component behavior.

Context

The Mode Machine Test pattern is useful for testing subsystems (systems) whose behavior is sequentially constrained: the same sequence of external events does not always produce the same response. A modal subsystem includes a dominant control object [Jacobsen+92], implements a state pattern (see Section 7.2.9, State Machines and Object-oriented Development), or has a similar control strategy. Chapter 7 provides a detailed discussion of state machines and system behavior.

This pattern produces a test suite that helps solve several hard testing problems: identification of end-to-end threads, unambiguous determination of external sequences necessary to test a thread given a certain constellation of class states, and unambiguous determination of external sequences necessary to place an object in a given state. It can be used to create a comprehensive test suite for reactive application systems or subsystems.

The Dr Fizz vending machine is used to illustrate development. This hypothetical coin-operated vending machine is controlled by microprocessor-based software (Figures 12.10 and 12.11). Although vending machine examples are pedestrian and even cliché, the elements of this control cycle are present in many large, complex application systems—for example,

- Inventory control systems that allocate orders to warehouses.
- Automotive antilock brake control, dispensing braking cycles to wheels when a spin or slip-angle threshold is crossed.
- Exposure control in financial trading systems, where electronic funds transfers are dispensed based on both customer demand and available supply of collateral funds. This behavior can be tested using a state machine model and the following test procedure.
- Onboard weapon fire-control systems used to launch missiles from aircraft, ships, and tanks.

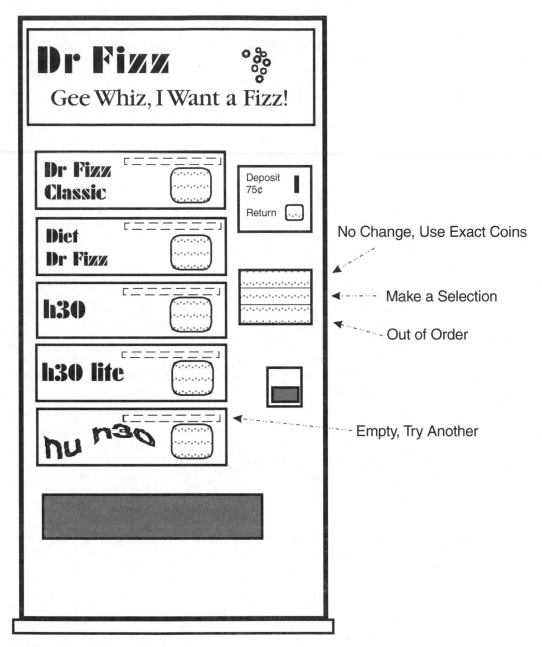

FIGURE 12.10   Dr Fizz marketing view.

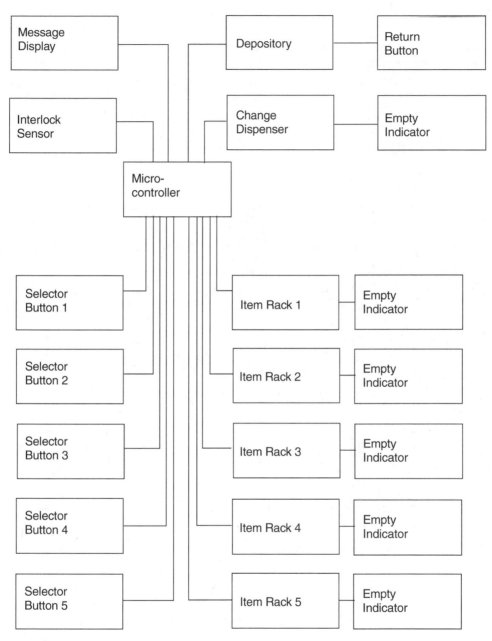

FIGURE 12.11   Dr Fizz Block Diagram.

Fault Model

The state of an application subsystem consists of the collective state of its objects, or *mode*. When sequences of external events are constrained, a correctly functioning subsystem must (1) accept legal events, (2) reject events that are illegal in these states, (3) produce a correct resultant state for accepted and rejected events, and (4) produce a correct action for each test event message (messages sent to servers of the class under test and the response to the test message).

A subsystem implementation can have five kinds of control faults:

- Missing transition: an event is rejected in a valid state
- Incorrect action: the wrong action is produced for an accepting state and event
- Invalid resultant state: the IUT enters the wrong state for a transition
- The production of a corrupt state
- A sneak path that allows an event to be accepted when it should have been rejected

See Chapter 7 for a detailed discussion of the state fault model.

If a state fault exists in the subsystem's control implementation, it cannot be reached unless all event/state sequences are exercised. The N+ test model exercises all of these sequences. The complex triggering conditions are not addressed by this fault model. All the preceding faults, except for an invalid state, should propagate because they involve externally visible events and/or actions. Incorrect resultant states must be checked by using built-in tests, or by applying a state signature sequence.

Strategy

Test Model

Mode Machine Test produces a state-based model of subsystem behavior that can generate an N+ test suite. Tests based on use cases, scenario traces, or association analysis may be added to this test suite as well. Subsystem behavior is modeled as a mode machine, and an N+ test suite is generated to exercise state control. The test model is developed in the following steps:

1. Identify the dominant control object for the subsystem under test and develop its state model.
2. Identify the external events and actions of the subsystem under test.

3. Map the external events onto the dominant control object (the mode machine).

4. Develop a modal test suite for this state model.

The test generation procedure is the same as that used in the modal class pattern.

1. Identify the Dominant Control Object.   The control responsibilities of a system include startup, all normal stimulus–response cycles, errors and exceptions, failure modes, and normal shutdown. A state-based control model is appropriate if only some event sequences are allowed. We can usually identify the dominant control object by inspecting the system-level statechart and subsystem collaboration diagrams.

Figure 12.12 shows the collaboration diagram for the Dr Fizz system. This system uses a simple control strategy: the `dfController` object runs in an endless loop that polls each object. Events are signaled to `dfController` by returning a value from a server object, followed by the institution of the appropriate action.

Although each server of the controller class exhibits state-based behavior, none overrides the behavior of `dfController` (see Figure 12.13). The `dfController` class is the dominant control object in the Dr Fizz example. The class state models for the server objects appear in Figures 12.14 through 12.20. Although all of the classes in the Dr Fizz system are modal, overall system behavior remains the responsibility of the controller class, whose state model is shown in Figure 12.20 (page 611).

This example uses some simplifying assumptions. Each item has the same price. The design is not customer-friendly: the machine will accept deposits when the changer is empty and will dispense products without returning change.

2. Model External Events and Actions.   If we were concerned with testing only the dominant control class, we could develop a test suite using the modal class pattern. In fact, we wish to test an entire subsystem. Consequently, the events and actions of interest are those occurring at the subsystem boundary. The mode machine is a model that integrates the external events and actions with the dominant control model. Some external stimuli for the system under test may not be represented in the state machine of the dominant object. Because we are testing state-based control through external stimuli, these events must be incorporated with the dominant control model.

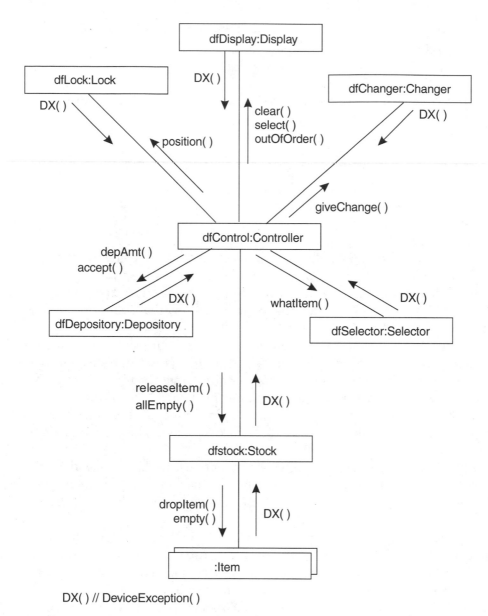

DX( ) // DeviceException( )

FIGURE 12.12   Dr Fizz Collaboration Diagram.

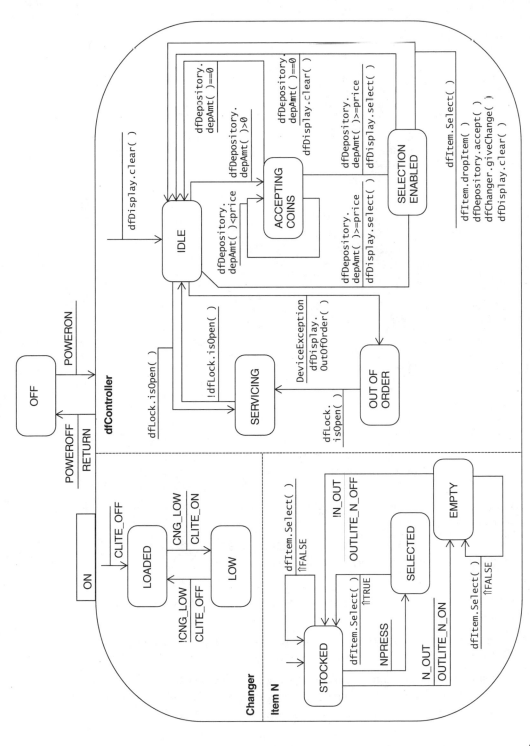

FIGURE 12.13 Dr Fizz system behavior model.

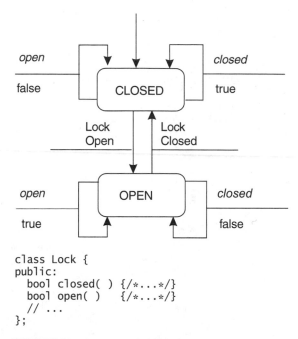

```
class Lock {
public:
  bool closed( ) {/*...*/}
  bool open( )   {/*...*/}
  // ...
};
```

FIGURE 12.14 State model for class Lock.

The boundary of the system under test defines the events and actions of the mode machine. Application systems typically rely on services provided by an operating system and other application systems.

- Control passes from the environment to the application, and then back to the environment.
- An *external event* is a message (or other mechanism) that activates a method or exception handler in the SUT.
- An *internal event* is a self-triggered behavior. It usually results from monitoring an interval or necessary response to the absence of an expected event.
- An object that recognizes or accepts an external event is called a *receptor*.
- A *response* is a message generated by the SUT for which the server is either (1) not part of the SUT or (2) part of the SUT, but does not produce any subsequent nonresponse messages.

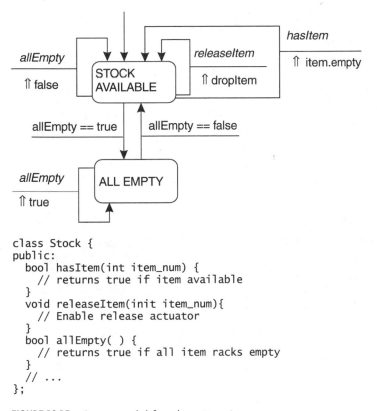

```
class Stock {
public:
  bool hasItem(int item_num) {
    // returns true if item available
  }
  void releaseItem(init item_num){
    // Enable release actuator
  }
  bool allEmpty( ) {
    // returns true if all item racks empty
  }
  // ...
};
```

FIGURE 12.15 State model for class Stock.

- An object that produces a response is called an *emitter.*
- A *mode transition* is the collective effect of a chain of state transitions, beginning with an external event and ending with the production of at least one response.

Although an exact mapping among external events, receptors, emitters, and control objects can be developed [Binder 94c], we focus on an engineering approximation.

If the control object does not recognize most of the external events, a control cluster or possibly a significant design omission may exist. If there is general correspondence, the next step is to map each external event onto the control object.

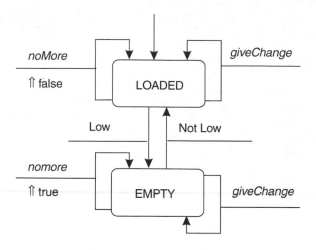

```
class changer throws DeviceException{
public:
  void giveChange(int vhng_amt){/*...*/}
  bool nomore( ){/*...*/}
  // ...
};
```

FIGURE 12.16   State model for class `Changer`.

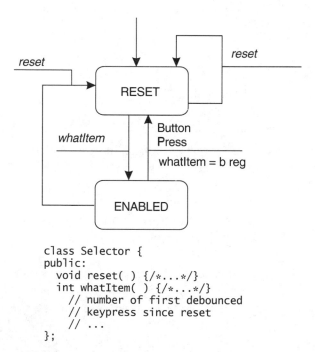

```
class Selector {
public:
  void reset( ) {/*...*/}
  int whatItem( ) {/*...*/}
    // number of first debounced
    // keypress since reset
    // ...
};
```

FIGURE 12.17   State model for class `Selector`.

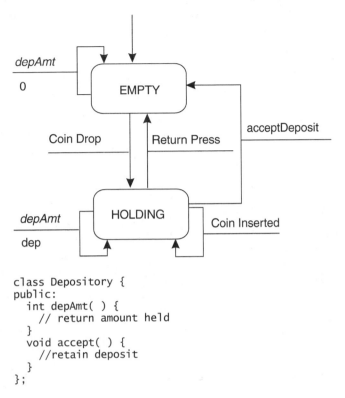

```
class Depository {
public:
  int depAmt( ) {
    // return amount held
  }
  void accept( ) {
    //retain deposit
  }
};
```

FIGURE 12.18   State model for class Depository.

- The external event is represented in the dominant control object. No change is necessary.

- The external event has a corresponding event in the dominant control object. The external event replaces this event in the mode machine model.

- The external event does not have a corresponding event in the dominant control object, and the event is consumed by a component that has an "orthogonal" state. No change is necessary. These events will be considered when we develop the sneak path matrix.

- We can drop transitions in the dominant control object that have no external visibility from the model—the select wait loop, for example. An externally invisible transition is one that does not have a corresponding external event or external action.

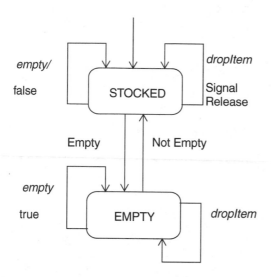

```
class Item {
public:
  bool dropItem( ) {
    // Sends release signal
    // Return false if can't drop
  }
  bool empty( ) {
    //returns true if item empty
  }
  // ...
};
```

FIGURE 12.19   State model and interface for class `Item`.

- The dominant control object has events that do not have any corresponding external event. Although these events are carried forward in the mode machine, exercising them using only an external interface to the system under test may be difficult. Their presence may indicate extra code—that is, a surprise.

Table 12.8 lists the events for the dominant control object. Figure 12.21 on page 612 shows the mapping of external events to the dominant control object in the Dr Fizz system. The only external event that does not correspond to a software event is `lowChanger`. The hardware produces the "Use Exact Change" message; a simple electromechanical switch turns this light on and off. This independent behavior is represented by an "orthogonal" state in the mode machine.

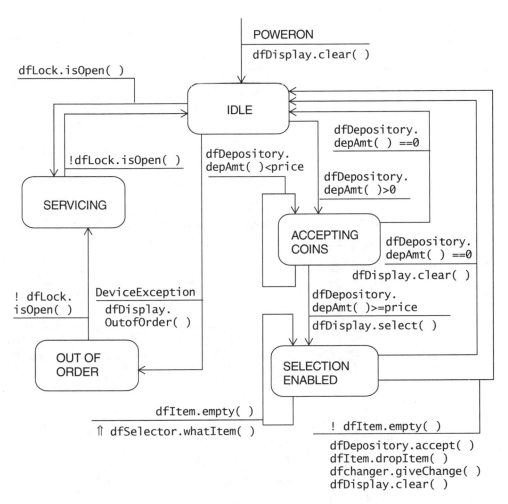

FIGURE 12.20   State model for controller class.

Figure 12.22 shows the external events mapped onto the dominant control object's statechart. It shows the mode machine for the Dr Fizz system, from which we produce the test suite.

3. Develop an N+ Test Suite.   An N+ test suite is composed of five kinds of tests: conformance, guarded transition expansion, iterator expansions, implicit transition expansion, and sneak paths (see pages 613–617).

TABLE 12.8 Events Recognized by the Dominant Control Object

Event	Note
dfDisplay.clear( )	Sent to display interface.
dfLock.isOpen( )	dfLock object responds with True or False.
DeviceException	All objects can throw this exception, which is caught by dfController.
dfItem.selected( )	dfItem object responds with True or False after positioning by iterator.
dfDepository.depAmt( )>=price	dfDepository.depAmt( ) returns current deposit amount as an integer representing the number of cents in the depository. The relational operator is evaluated in dfController.
dfDepository.depAmt( )==0	
dfDepository.depAmt( )<price	

Component	External Event	External Response	Response Allocated to	
			Hardware	Software
Power	POWERON	Initial state actions	✓	
	POWEROFF	None	✓	
All	DEVICEFAULT	"Out of Order" lit	✓	✓
Changer	LOW	"Exact Change" lit	✓	
	!LOW	"Exact Change" off	✓	
Lock	OPEN	See state model	✓	✓
	CLOSED	See state model	✓	✓
Depository	COIN_DROP	See state model	✓	✓
	RETURN_PRESS	Release deposited coins	✓	
Item N	NOUT	"Please Select Another" off	✓	
	!NOUT	"Please Select Another" lit	✓	
Selector N	NPRESS	See state model	✓	✓

Note: N = 1 . . 6—there are six item racks with identical behavior.

FIGURE 12.21 Dr Fizz system events.

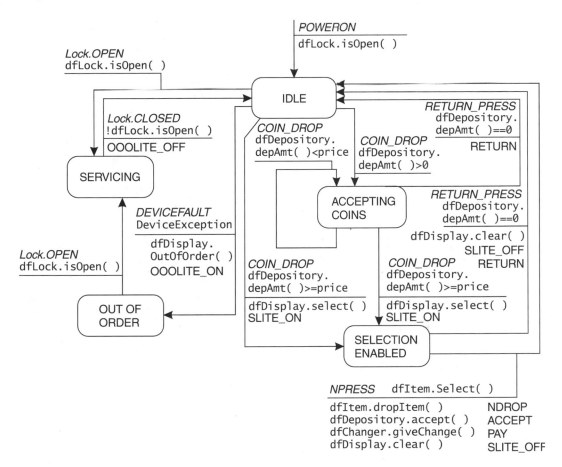

FIGURE 12.22   Mode machine for Dr Fizz system.

1. *Conformance tests* are identified by tracing a transition tree from the state model. Each root-to-node path in the tree represents a test case for a legal sequence of events. The state obtained after this sequence must be the expected state. The initial state consists of the root node of the tree. We draw an edge for every transition out of the root state to a node that represents the resultant state. If a node represents a state that has already been drawn or is a final state, then it is terminal—no more transitions are considered from this node. We repeat this procedure until all leaf nodes are terminal. Figure 12.23 depicts the transition tree for the Dr Fizz mode machine.

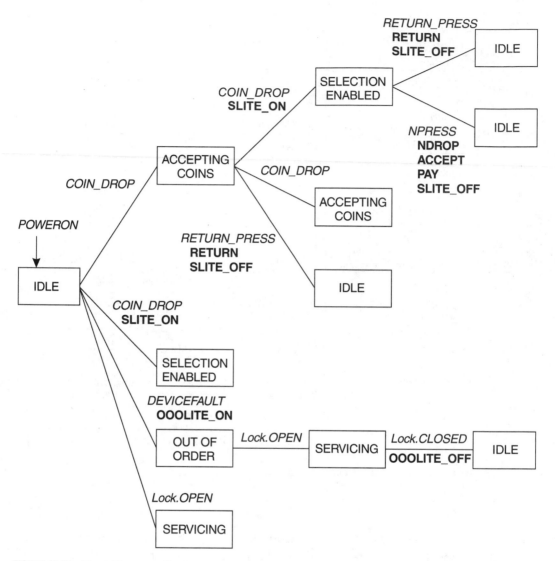

FIGURE 12.23   Transition tree for Dr Fizz mode machine.

Next, we transcribe transition test sequences from the tree. Each full and partial branch in the tree becomes a test case. Events are assumed to be implemented by calls using an enumeration parameter to designate the event. Table 12.9 lists the conformance tests.

2.   In *guard expansion*, we test the full set of Boolean outcomes for each guard on each state. A guard with *n* conditions has 2^n outcomes; that is, we re-

TABLE 12.9   Dr Fizz Conformance Tests

Test	Test Run/Event Path				Expected Terminal State	Expected Exception
1	POWERON				IDLE	None
2	POWERON	COIN DROP			ACCEPTING COINS	None
3	POWERON	COIN DROP	COIN DROP		SELECTION ENABLED	None
4	POWERON	COIN DROP	COIN DROP	RETURN PRESS	IDLE	None
5	POWERON	COIN DROP	COIN DROP	NPRESS	IDLE	None
6	POWERON	COIN DROP	COIN DROP		ACCEPTING COINS	
7	POWERON	COIN DROP	RETURN PRESS		IDLE	None
8	POWERON	COIN DROP			SELECTION ENABLED	None
9	POWERON	DEVICEFAULT			OUT OF ORDER	None
10	POWERON	DEVICEFAULT	LOCK OPEN		SERVICING	None
11	POWERON	DEVICEFAULT	LOCK OPEN	LOCK CLOSED	IDLE	None
12	POWERON	LOCK OPEN			SERVICING	None

quire that each guard combination of conditions be made true once and false once. In this example, the COIN DROP transition is guarded. When the total deposited amount is less than the price, the system should remain in the AC-CEPTING COINS state. When the total deposited amount is equal to or greater than the price, the system should transition to SELECTION ENABLED. Both outcomes are exercised from the IDLE state: test run 2 requires a deposit of less than the price, test run 8 requires a deposit greater than or equal to the price. The COIN DROP event is also accepted in the ACCEPTING COINS state. The transition to SELECTION ENABLED requires that the deposit be greater than or equal to the price. The logical complement (deposit less than price) is required for test run 6. No other guarded transitions exist, so no guard expansion is necessary for this system.

3. *Iteration expansion.* The machine contains six item subsystems, but the test model simplifies this by showing common behavior for all *n* objects. The complete test plan must identify each such case. We can accomplish this goal by expanding test run 5. Table 12.10 shows the iteration expansion tests.

4. *Implicit transition expansion.* Statecharts provide a graphic shorthand for events accepted in every state. For example, the POWEROFF event appears

TABLE 12.10   Dr Fizz Iteration Expansion Tests

Test		Test Run/Event Path			Expected Terminal State	Expected Exception
5.1	POWERON	COIN DROP	COIN DROP	1PRESS	IDLE	None
5.2	POWERON	COIN DROP	COIN DROP	2PRESS	IDLE	None
5.3	POWERON	COIN DROP	COIN DROP	3PRESS	IDLE	None
5.4	POWERON	COIN DROP	COIN DROP	4PRESS	IDLE	None
5.5	POWERON	COIN DROP	COIN DROP	5PRESS	IDLE	None
5.6	POWERON	COIN DROP	COIN DROP	6PRESS	IDLE	None

only once, but is accepted in every state of the system. To test this behavior, we must attempt this event in each of our five states. We may construct the test runs by adding this event to a test run that reaches each of the five states. Table 12.11 lists the implicit transition expansion tests.

5. *Sneak path analysis.* Although conformance tests will show that explicit, legal state transitions are correctly implemented, they cannot reveal whether incorrect sequences are rejected by an appropriate response and do not produce a corrupted state. **Modal Class Test** sneak path tests simply attempt every illegal event in every state. In a system with orthogonal states, the illegal transitions of the mode machine include all system events. The sneak path event list includes all events explicitly referenced in the mode machine and *all* other external events accepted by the system under test. The possible sneak paths are identified by the sneak path matrix (simply a table of all events and modes). Any event that is not explicitly allowed in the mode machine becomes a possible sneak path. Figure 12.24 shows the system sneak path matrix. Sneak path test

TABLE 12.11   Dr Fizz Transition Expansion

Test		Test Run/Event Path			Expected Terminal State (Before POWEROFF)	Expected Exception
13	POWERON	POWEROFF			IDLE	None
14	POWERON	COIN DROP	POWEROFF		ACCEPTING COINS	None
15	POWERON	COIN DROP	COIN DROP	POWEROFF	SELECTION ENABLED	None
16	POWERON	DEVICEFAULT	POWEROFF		OUT OF ORDER	None
17	POWERON	DEVICEFAULT	LOCK OPEN	POWEROFF	SERVICING	None

Events	States				
	IDLE	ACCEPTING COINS	SELECTION ENABLED	OUT OF ORDER	SERVICING
POWERON	✕	✕	✕	✕	✕
POWEROFF	✓	✓	✓	✓	✓
COIN DROP	✓	✓	PSP	PSP	PSP
RETURN PRESS	PSP	✓	✓	PSP	PSP
1PRESS	PSP	PSP	✓	PSP	PSP
2PRESS	PSP	PSP	✓	PSP	PSP
3PRESS	PSP	PSP	✓	PSP	PSP
4PRESS	PSP	PSP	✓	PSP	PSP
5PRESS	PSP	PSP	✓	PSP	PSP
6PRESS	PSP	PSP	✓	PSP	PSP
DEVICEFAULT	✓	PSP	PSP	PSP	PSP
LOCK.OPEN	✓	✓	✓	✓	PSP
LOCK.CLOSED	PSP	PSP	PSP	PSP	✓
LOW	PSP	PSP	PSP	PSP	PSP
!LOW	PSP	PSP	PSP	PSP	PSP
1OUT	PSP	PSP	PSP	PSP	PSP
2OUT	PSP	PSP	PSP	PSP	PSP
3OUT	PSP	PSP	PSP	PSP	PSP
4OUT	PSP	PSP	PSP	PSP	PSP
5OUT	PSP	PSP	PSP	PSP	PSP
6OUT	PSP	PSP	PSP	PSP	PSP

Key: ✓ = Valid transition, PSP = Possible sneak path, X = Infeasible

FIGURE 12.24   Dr Fizz sneak path matrix.

cases are developed by identifying a call sequence whose last call is illegal. There is one test run for each "PSP" entry in the sneak path matrix. Tables 12.12 through 12.16 (pages 618–622) show the sneak path tests for each state.

These 95 test cases complete the N+ test suite for the Dr Fizz system. Input values and expected results for each test step can be developed as for *Modal Class Test*.

TABLE 12.12   Dr Fizz Sneak Path Tests for Idle State

Test	Setup Sequence	Sneak Path Test State	Illegal Event	Expected Exception	Expected Resultant State
17	POWERON	IDLE	RETURN PRESS	None	IDLE
18	POWERON	IDLE	1PRESS	None	IDLE
19	POWERON	IDLE	2PRESS	None	IDLE
20	POWERON	IDLE	3PRESS	None	IDLE
21	POWERON	IDLE	4PRESS	None	IDLE
22	POWERON	IDLE	5PRESS	None	IDLE
23	POWERON	IDLE	6PRESS	None	IDLE
24	POWERON	IDLE	DEVICEFAULT	None	IDLE
25	POWERON	IDLE	LOCK.OPEN	None	IDLE
26	POWERON	IDLE	LOCK.CLOSED	None	IDLE
27	POWERON	IDLE	LOW	None	IDLE
28	POWERON	IDLE	!LOW	None	IDLE
29	POWERON	IDLE	1OUT	None	IDLE
30	POWERON	IDLE	2OUT	None	IDLE
31	POWERON	IDLE	3OUT	None	IDLE
32	POWERON	IDLE	4OUT	None	IDLE
33	POWERON	IDLE	5OUT	None	IDLE
34	POWERON	IDLE	6OUT	None	IDLE

The development of test sequences for conditional transitions and sneak paths have been shown for clarity, as separate, explicit steps in the Dr Fizz example. However, the entire test model can be represented in a single table. Chapter 7 shows how to represent all behavior and generate a complete test suite with the response matrix.

Automation

A modal test suite may be implemented with any of the API Test Harness patterns presented in Chapter 19. Built-in test capabilities are recommended for each modal class, including the ability to set the CUT to a state and the ability to report both the abstract and concrete state of the CUT.

The discussion of runtime sequence checking in Section 17.3.5 sketches a built-in sequence checker. The state specification can be represented so as to allow automatic generation of required sequences, thereby avoiding complex, hard-coded messages in the driver [Holzmann 91].

TABLE 12.13 Dr Fizz Sneak Path Tests for Accepting Coin States

Test	Setup Sequence		Sneak Path Test State	Illegal Event	Expected Exception	Expected Resultant State
35	POWERON	COIN DROP	ACCEPTING COINS	1PRESS	None	ACCEPTING COINS
36	POWERON	COIN DROP	ACCEPTING COINS	2PRESS	None	ACCEPTING COINS
37	POWERON	COIN DROP	ACCEPTING COINS	3PRESS	None	ACCEPTING COINS
38	POWERON	COIN DROP	ACCEPTING COINS	4PRESS	None	ACCEPTING COINS
39	POWERON	COIN DROP	ACCEPTING COINS	5PRESS	None	ACCEPTING COINS
40	POWERON	COIN DROP	ACCEPTING COINS	6PRESS	None	ACCEPTING COINS
41	POWERON	COIN DROP	ACCEPTING COINS	DEVICEFAULT	None	ACCEPTING COINS
42	POWERON	COIN DROP	ACCEPTING COINS	LOCK.CLOSED	None	ACCEPTING COINS
43	POWERON	COIN DROP	ACCEPTING COINS	LOW	None	ACCEPTING COINS
44	POWERON	COIN DROP	ACCEPTING COINS	!LOW	None	ACCEPTING COINS
45	POWERON	COIN DROP	ACCEPTING COINS	1OUT	None	ACCEPTING COINS
46	POWERON	COIN DROP	ACCEPTING COINS	2OUT	None	ACCEPTING COINS
47	POWERON	COIN DROP	ACCEPTING COINS	3OUT	None	ACCEPTING COINS
48	POWERON	COIN DROP	ACCEPTING COINS	4OUT	None	ACCEPTING COINS
49	POWERON	COIN DROP	ACCEPTING COINS	5OUT	None	ACCEPTING COINS
50	POWERON	COIN DROP	ACCEPTING COINS	6OUT	None	ACCEPTING COINS

TABLE 12.14 Dr Fizz Sneak Paths for Selection Enabled State

Test	Setup Sequence		Sneak Path Test State	Illegal Event	Expected Exception	Expected Resultant State
51	POWERON	COIN DROP	SELECTION ENABLED	COIN DROP	None	SELECTION ENABLED
52	POWERON	COIN DROP	SELECTION ENABLED	DEVICEFAULT	None	SELECTION ENABLED
53	POWERON	COIN DROP	SELECTION ENABLED	LOCK.CLOSED	None	SELECTION ENABLED
54	POWERON	COIN DROP	SELECTION ENABLED	LOW	None	SELECTION ENABLED
55	POWERON	COIN DROP	SELECTION ENABLED	!LOW	None	SELECTION ENABLED
56	POWERON	COIN DROP	SELECTION ENABLED	1OUT	None	SELECTION ENABLED
57	POWERON	COIN DROP	SELECTION ENABLED	2OUT	None	SELECTION ENABLED
58	POWERON	COIN DROP	SELECTION ENABLED	3OUT	None	SELECTION ENABLED
59	POWERON	COIN DROP	SELECTION ENABLED	4OUT	None	SELECTION ENABLED
60	POWERON	COIN DROP	SELECTION ENABLED	5OUT	None	SELECTION ENABLED
61	POWERON	COIN DROP	SELECTION ENABLED	6OUT	None	SELECTION ENABLED

TABLE 12.15   Dr Fizz Sneak Path Test Cases for Out of Order State

Test	Setup	Sequence	Sneak Path Test State	Illegal Event	Expected Exception	Expected Resultant State
62	POWERON	DEVICEFAULT	OUT OF ORDER		None	OUT OF ORDER
63	POWERON	DEVICEFAULT	OUT OF ORDER		None	OUT OF ORDER
64	POWERON	DEVICEFAULT	OUT OF ORDER		None	OUT OF ORDER
65	POWERON	DEVICEFAULT	OUT OF ORDER		None	OUT OF ORDER
66	POWERON	DEVICEFAULT	OUT OF ORDER		None	OUT OF ORDER
67	POWERON	DEVICEFAULT	OUT OF ORDER		None	OUT OF ORDER
68	POWERON	DEVICEFAULT	OUT OF ORDER		None	OUT OF ORDER
69	POWERON	DEVICEFAULT	OUT OF ORDER		None	OUT OF ORDER
70	POWERON	DEVICEFAULT	OUT OF ORDER		None	OUT OF ORDER
71	POWERON	DEVICEFAULT	OUT OF ORDER		None	OUT OF ORDER
72	POWERON	DEVICEFAULT	OUT OF ORDER		None	OUT OF ORDER
73	POWERON	DEVICEFAULT	OUT OF ORDER		None	OUT OF ORDER
74	POWERON	DEVICEFAULT	OUT OF ORDER		None	OUT OF ORDER
75	POWERON	DEVICEFAULT	OUT OF ORDER		None	OUT OF ORDER
76	POWERON	DEVICEFAULT	OUT OF ORDER		None	OUT OF ORDER
77	POWERON	DEVICEFAULT	OUT OF ORDER		None	OUT OF ORDER

Entry Criteria

The operability threshold for a modal cluster has been met.

- ✓ Each component class or cluster has met the exit criteria for the applicable test pattern. Leaf-node tests cannot be reached until all predecessor tests have passed.
- ✓ Each cluster has met minimal operability requirements. For example, the classes under test have passed the appropriate class scope test suite.

Exit Criteria

A full modal class test suite provides N+ coverage. See the discussion of state-based coverage in Chapter 7 for details.

- ✓ There is a test for every root-to-leaf path in the expanded transition tree and each sneak path pair. These test sequences pass.

TABLE 12.16   Dr Fizz Sneak Path Tests for Servicing State

Test	Setup Sequence		Sneak Path Test State	Illegal Event	Expected Exception	Expected Resultant State
78	POWERON	LOCK_OPEN	SERVICING	COIN DROP	None	SERVICING
79	POWERON	LOCK_OPEN	SERVICING	RETURN PRESS	None	SERVICING
80	POWERON	LOCK_OPEN	SERVICING	1PRESS	None	SERVICING
81	POWERON	LOCK_OPEN	SERVICING	2PRESS	None	SERVICING
82	POWERON	LOCK_OPEN	SERVICING	3PRESS	None	SERVICING
83	POWERON	LOCK_OPEN	SERVICING	4PRESS	None	SERVICING
84	POWERON	LOCK_OPEN	SERVICING	5PRESS	None	SERVICING
85	POWERON	LOCK_OPEN	SERVICING	6PRESS	None	SERVICING
86	POWERON	LOCK_OPEN	SERVICING	DEVICEFAULT	None	SERVICING
87	POWERON	LOCK_OPEN	SERVICING	LOCK.OPEN	None	SERVICING
88	POWERON	LOCK_OPEN	SERVICING	LOW	None	SERVICING
89	POWERON	LOCK_OPEN	SERVICING	!LOW	None	SERVICING
90	POWERON	LOCK_OPEN	SERVICING	1OUT	None	SERVICING
91	POWERON	LOCK_OPEN	SERVICING	2OUT	None	SERVICING
92	POWERON	LOCK_OPEN	SERVICING	3OUT	None	SERVICING
93	POWERON	LOCK_OPEN	SERVICING	4OUT	None	SERVICING
94	POWERON	LOCK_OPEN	SERVICING	5OUT	None	SERVICING
95	POWERON	LOCK_OPEN	SERVICING	6OUT	None	SERVICING

Consequences

The mode machine provides an explicit, unambiguous basis for three kinds of testing. Development of a mode machine test suite from an analysis or design model is an effective, early verification of subsystem behavior. The mode machine may be used for integration testing over many scopes of integration. It explicitly supports the development of thread-based integration test cases. In addition, it identifies actors and servers for simulation.

The mode machine provides an explicit means to identify and test system-level sneak paths. A scenario (use case) is composed of one or more threads. There is an explicit link between scenarios and the implementation. Scenario coverage can be unambiguously analyzed in terms of state coverage.

The mode machine can be used to derive integration sequence. Each event–response path is a thread. The mode machine model can be used to exercise all global states of the system. In turn, the modal class test design technique can be applied to the mode machine model. This effort will produce a conformance test suite, conditional transition tests, exception tests, and sneak path tests at the scope of the model.

Known Uses

System scope, state-based testing has been used to verify telecommunications protocols for more than 20 years [Holzmann 91, Auer 97]. The ROOM methodology results in an executable specification that supports simulation of object state-control models [Selic 94]. The mode machine model was used to develop cluster scope testing of embedded software in products manufactured by a leading medical electronics company [Brown+95].

Related Patterns

Modal Class Test applies the same technique at class and class cluster scopes.

12.3 Bibliographic Notes

Class Associations

The Class Associations test strategy first appeared in [Binder 97e]. Pragmatic, yet rigorous guidance on modeling associations can be found in [Cook+94] and [Page-Jones 95].

Sequence Diagrams

Jacobson offers a good explanation of Sequence Diagrams [Jacobson+92]. The limits of these diagrams as a practical tool for implementation tracing are discussed in [Lange 97].

Exception Handling

Leveson discusses general requirements for exception handling for safety-critical systems [Leveson 95]. A concise analysis of exception-handling design appears in [Meyer 97]. Design of exceptions for Eiffel implementations is presented in [Jézéquel 96a]. Barnes presents a basic design for Ada 95 exceptions [Barnes 96]. Effective and reusable C++ exception design is developed in [Carroll+95].

Statecharts and the Mode Machine

The mode machine model was developed to answer questions about the application of state-based class testing to object-oriented subsystems that were raised at a presentation given to Andersen Consulting in 1993. This approach was cast into a mathematically formal model that allowed algorithmic synthesis of the model. Six months later, this formal approach was presented to the Regis Study Group [Binder 94c], and it was subsequently used by several RBSC clients. This required detailed, accurate, and complete state models for all classes in the system under test. A meticulous and persistent analyst could synthesize a mode machine for a small system of classes by hand; without automation, however, synthesis of larger systems was intractable. Synthesis is unnecessary in practice because most reactive systems have a single, explicit control model, which typically resides in a single object or tightly coupled cluster. The pattern presented here therefore focuses on testing reactive subsystems with a dominant control object or control cluster. Pragmatic, yet rigorous, guidance on modeling the behavior of a system of objects can be found in [Cook+94] and [Selic+94]. Harel's discussion of statecharts for object-oriented systems identifies some errors made by OO methodologists and presents a crisp example of a statechart model of a C++ implementation of a reactive system [Harel 97].

Chapter 13   Integration

Overview

Integration test design is concerned with several primary questions. Which components and interfaces should be exercised? In what sequence? Which test design patterns are appropriate? This chapter begins by considering the role of integration testing in object-oriented development. Next, a simple dependency analysis technique and considerations for testing at several scopes are presented. Nine integration test patterns provide design and execution strategies.

13.1   Integration in Object-oriented Development

13.1.1   Definitions

A **system** is composed of **components**. Systems of software components can be defined at any physical scope. A component is itself a system of smaller components, as suggested by Table 13.1. For example, a class is a system whose components are methods and server objects, a cluster is a system of classes, an application system is composed of executables, and so on. In this chapter, *system* and *component* are used in this generic sense.

Remarks about a system or a component should be understood to apply at any scope, unless a particular scope is explicitly stated.

TABLE 13.1   Scope versus Focus of Integration Testing

Component (Focus of Integration)	System (Scope of Integration)	Typical Intercomponent Interfaces (Locus of Integration Faults)
Method	Class	Instance variables Intraclass messages
Class	Cluster	Interclass messages
Cluster	Subsystem	Interclass messages Interpackage messages
Subsystem	System	Interprocess communication Remote procedure call ORB services OS services

With this abstraction, integration patterns can be applied at many scopes. This concept is crucial for effective integration test design.

A **stable system** has sufficient dependability to support system scope testing. The threshold for stability usually reflects practical considerations—it varies from project to project and often changes within a project. An **increment** is a subset of system components that typically (but not necessarily) has a corresponding subset of requirements. Increments are typically progressive; the second increment includes and depends on the first, and so on. The last increment becomes the delivered (shipped) system. A **delta** is a change to component within the scope of an increment.

A **smoke test** is designed to pass if the implementation under test can be run at all. Expected results are not specified for a smoke test—a no pass occurs if the IUT crashes, and the system passes if any other result is obtained. A **test configuration** is a defined and versioned set of drivers, stubs, and a build of the system under test. The activities that begin and end with the development and execution of a test configuration are a **stage**. **Integration coverage** is achieved when the testing meets the exit criteria for an integration pattern.

A **call path** is a sequence of messages, function calls, remote procedure calls, interprocess communication messages, and so on, which is possible as a result of intercomponent interfaces. A **call trace** is an actual set of calls made along some call path. A **call pair** refers to a client and server that have a call between them.

A **stub** is a partial implementation of a component (see Section 19.3, Test Control Patterns). A **proxy** is a component that provides an interface but simply delegates all incoming messages to another object. A **driver** is a class, main program, or external software system that applies test cases to the component under test (see Section 19.4, Driver Patterns).

Sometimes, the process of selecting and merging specific versions of source and binary files for translation and linking within a component and among components is called "integration." Here, activity is referred to as **build generation**. A **build** is the executable(s) produced by a build generation process. Build generation is a necessary precursor to integration testing and may include smoke tests. It is supported by configuration management planning, tools, and practices. However, it is not integration testing.

13.1.2 Integration Testing Is Essential

Software systems are built with components that must interoperate. Three basic kinds of testing are needed to show that components are minimally interoperable: tests of individual components, tests of the system resulting from the federation of components, and tests of component interoperation. **Integration testing** is a search for component faults that cause intercomponent failures. An integration strategy must answer three questions:

- Which components are the focus of the integration test?
- In what sequence will component interfaces be exercised?
- Which test design technique should be used to exercise each interface?

In contrast, component scope testing is a search for intracomponent faults, and system scope testing is a search for faults that lead to a failure to meet a system scope responsibility. Most interoperability faults are not revealed by testing a component in isolation, so integration testing is necessary. System scope testing cannot be done unless components interoperate sufficiently well to exercise system scope responsibilities. The primary purpose of integration testing is to reveal component interoperability faults so that testing at system scope may proceed with the fewest possible interruptions.

Testing theory explains why integration testing is necessary.[1] According to the *antidecomposition* axiom, a test suite that achieves coverage at system scope

---

1. These are two of the testing axioms developed in [Weyuker 88]. An *axiom* is a trusted basic principle. An *adequate* test suite achieves at least statement coverage. These axioms were reinterpreted for object-oriented code in [Perry+90]. See Testing Axioms, Chapter 10.

does not necessarily result in the same coverage for its components (i.e., server objects and called modules). Testing at system scope cannot guarantee that components have been covered. For example, achieving statement coverage of a `main()` program can also achieve statement coverage of its components only when there is no branching, iteration, or dynamic binding in any of its components. According to the *anticomposition* axiom, coverage at system scope is not necessarily achieved by rerunning component test suites that have achieved component coverage. That is, adequate testing of components is not equivalent to adequate testing of a system of components. For example, suppose statement coverage of all components called by `main()` and all statements in `main()` can be achieved by taking one of two paths within `main()`. Although all components have been covered, `main()` includes an untested path. Testing that is adequate for a system of components therefore requires testing at component scope, component interaction scope, and system scope.

Distinct but complementary strategies for build generation and integration testing have been used since the early 1970s. They follow the physical structure of the system under test: module call paths, interprocess communication, or job streams, and support incremental development (see the Bibliographic Notes section for a brief survey). A key lesson learned is that incremental integration is the most effective technique: add components a few at a time and then test their interoperability. Trying to integrate most or all of the components in a system at the same time is usually problematic.

- Debugging is difficult because the bug may be in any interface.
- Last-minute patches are often necessary, resulting in low-quality fixes that may not undergo adequate testing.
- The testing is usually not systematic, so interface bugs can escape detection.

In contrast, incremental testing has several advantages. Interfaces are systematically exercised and shown to be stable before unproven interfaces are exercised. Buggy interface code will be reached, if not triggered. Observed failures are most likely to come from the most recently added component, so debugging is more efficient. Although conceptually simple, incremental development requires discipline and commitment. A sequence of components must be identified using careful analysis of component dependencies. Next, testing must be planned and managed to follow these dependencies. Automated configuration management support for build generation is necessary, as are repeatable, automated test suites. Some integration patterns require a stub or driver for every component to be integrated, adding to the items that must be included under version control.

Experience in object-oriented development has shown that these strategies are still applicable, but instead of one technique dominating, an eclectic approach is necessary [Jacobson+92, Jüttner+94a, Jüttner+94b, Arnold+94, Murphy+94, Bosivert 97]. Integration testing is a process in object-oriented development, rather than an event or phase. Barbey argues that all forms of object-oriented testing involve integration testing:

> [Because] methods are not efficient basic test units, and the structure of object oriented systems does not allow a recursive decomposition that takes all behavioral aspects into account, there is no basic unit testing for object oriented software, but there are many kinds of integration unit testing [Barbey 97, 74].

Thus integration testing in object-oriented development begins early, takes place at all scopes, and is repeated in each development increment:

- Within a class
- Within a class hierarchy
- Between a client and its servers
- Within a cluster of related classes
- Within a subsystem
- Within an application system

Testing of a class integrates its methods. Testing of a subclass integrates the superclass methods. Testing of a cluster integrates participants in its collaborations. Clearly, each development increment requires integration of the components in the scope of the increment. Figure 13.1 gives an overview of integration patterns by scope.

Integration testing is closely tied to system architecture and to the process used for development. The architecture organizes a large system into manageable components and subsystems. Beyond technical considerations, it serves many purposes, including risk management, scheduling, and verification. Architecture and process have a symbiotic relationship as well. For example, parallel development becomes easier when partitioning reduces interface coupling. Booch argues that integration is central to object-oriented development. "The macro process of object-oriented development is one of *continuous integration*. . . . At regular intervals, the process of *continuous integration* yields

Scope of Implementation Under Test (the "System")	Typical System Responsibility Model	Integration Strategy										Integration Coverage Model	Integration Exit Criteria
		Typical Components to Be Integrated	Integration Patterns										
			BB	BU	TD	CL	CK	LY	ST	MS	HF		
Cluster	Mode machine	Root client and its servers, upper-bounded	✓	✓	✓	✓						Protocol graph, Collaboration Diagram M Tree	Call paths, M+
Facade	Extended contract (facade), mode machine	Classes in build group		✓	✓	✓					✓	Collaboration Diagram Round-trip Scenario test	N+ of facade, M+
Binary component with API (developed, not reused)	Extended contract, XUC/SD	Classes in build group, components, VM	✓	✓	✓	✓						Round-trip Scenario test	N+ (API), M+, SD branch
Build group, executable with IPC or UI interface	XUC/SD, mode machine	Classes in build group, components, VM, HW				✓	✓	✓	✓		✓	Round-trip Scenario test	SD branch, M+
Process group using IPC, UI	XUC/SD, mode machine	Constituent processes, components, other applications, VM, HW				✓	✓	✓	✓		✓	Round-trip Scenario test	SD branch, M+
"Component" application with UI	XUC/SD	Binary components with API				✓		✓	✓		✓	Round-trip Scenario test	SD branch
Client/server	XUC/SD	Client applications and platforms, server applications and platforms, middleware, and platforms							✓		✓	Round-trip Scenario test	SD branch
Reactive/ embedded	Mode machine	Real-time kernel, processes, hardware					✓	✓	✓		✓	M Tree	M+
Wide area network	XUC/SD	Node applications and platforms, middleware and platforms						✓	✓	✓	✓	Round-trip Scenario test	SD branch

Key: XUC = Extended Use Case (see Chapter 14); SD = Sequence Diagram; N+ = Conformance + Sneak Path Coverage; Class State Model; M+ = Conformance + Sneak Path Coverage, Mode Machine Model; HW = Hardware

FIGURE 13.1   Overview of integration strategy.

executable releases that grow in functionality at every release . . . . It is through these milestones that management can measure progress and quality, and hence anticipate, identify, and then actively attack risks on an ongoing basis" [Booch 96, 75].

Because integration test plans are typically based on intercomponent implementation dependencies, analysis of the component architecture is required. If this architecture is not specified, then the integration test design must wait for completion of some (or, in the worst case, *all*) of the components. The process of integration test design often reveals errors, omissions, and ambiguities in the requirements and architecture—another reason to begin architectural design as soon as possible and to make testability a design goal.

Iterative, incremental object-oriented development increases the leverage of integration testing. Poorly planned integration testing will be costly and ineffective, while timely and focused integration testing will yield high efficiency. An integration test plan must answer several basic questions:

- What are the major and minor development increments?
- Which component interfaces will be the focus of integration? Which subsystems?
- In what sequence will components and their interfaces be exercised?
- Which stubs and drivers must be developed?
- Which test design patterns should be used?
- When can integration testing be considered complete?

Flexibility is important because a component may not be ready at a time that coincides with a strictly technical order of integration. In any event, the integration test patterns should be tailored to suit the requirements and constraints of a particular project. Key considerations in the design of an integration test plan include the following:

- Scope of an increment and dependencies of the components.
- Testability. As the number of components increases, it becomes harder to control and observe an individual component. How can we balance decreasing testability with increasing scope?
- Component stability. Table 13.2 offers a volatility spectrum. It usually makes sense to postpone integration of highly volatile components and begin with stable components.
- Test environment stability.

TABLE 13.2   Relative Component Volatility

Component Type	Relative Volatility
Object representing a real-world entity (e.g., Customer)	Low
Long-lived information structures	Low
Get-able object attributes	Medium
Sequences of behavior (state model)	Medium
Interface to target environment	High
Class functionality	High

Source: Adapted from [Jacobson+92, 76 ff].

This chapter provides analytical tools to solve the technical dimension of integration test design. The corresponding resource allocation and control problems are discussed in *Managing the Testing Process for Object-Oriented Systems* [Binder 2000].

13.1.3   Dependency Analysis

Components typically depend on each other in many ways. Dependencies are necessary to implement collaborations and achieve separation of concerns. Some dependencies are accidental or unavoidable side effects of a particular implementation, programming language, or target environment. Class and cluster scope dependencies result from explicit binding mechanisms, including the following:

- Composition and aggregation (the use of classes to define instance variables)
- Inheritance
- Global variables
- Calls to an API
- Server objects (instance variables or proxies)
- Objects used as message parameters
- Pointers to objects used as message parameters
- Type parameters given for declarations of generic classes
- Static and dynamic name scoping

Similar intercomponent dependencies occur at subsystem and system scopes. Components explicitly depend on each other when they exchange messages, perform remote procedure calls, or use interprocess communication services. In addition, many kinds of implicit dependencies arise: communication through persistent storage, sequential activation constraints, timing constraints, and so on. Integration testing does not focus on implicit dependencies. Instead, it concentrates on explicit dependencies to show minimal interoperability. Explicit dependencies often dictate the sequence of testing.

Most approaches to cluster scope integration use dependency analysis to support bottom-up testing. Explicit intercomponent dependencies typically correspond to interfaces that should be exercised by an integration test suite. A model of explicit dependencies can be used to plan a testing sequence. For example, the class diagram for the FinancialService cluster (Figure 13.2) shows

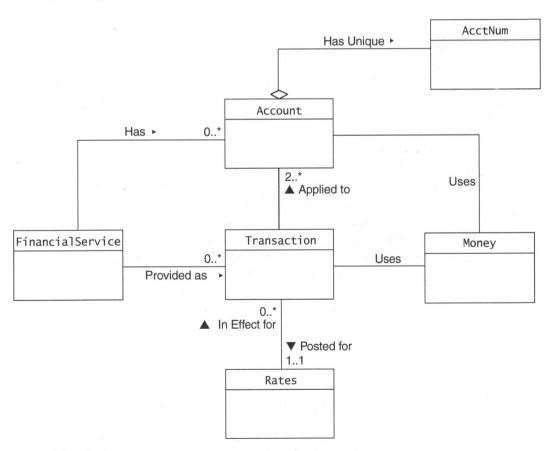

FIGURE 13.2   Class Diagram, FinancialService cluster.

some basic dependency information, but an order of testing is not immediately apparent. Suppose we have the following C++ classes:

```
Class FinancialService  {
    /* Represents a financial service including several accounts */};

Class Transaction {
    /* Represents a service transaction */};

Class Account {
    /* Account */};

Class Rates {
    /* Exchange Rates in effect */};

Class Money {
    /* Basic data type */};

Array {
    /* Generic class used to contain rates */};

AccountNum {
    /* Basic data type */};
```

Clearly, we must use `Transaction` and `Account` objects (or stubs) to test `FinancialService`, but what about `Money` and `Rate`? Suppose the usage of the generic class `Array` was not given on the Class Diagram because it was considered an "implementation detail."

Figure 13.3 shows the dependency tree for the `FinancialService` cluster. The diagram does *not* depict an inheritance hierarchy or a single message interface. Instead, an arrow represents a client-uses-server relationship. The root of the dependency graph is a client class that is not used by any other classes in the cluster under test. In practice, there may be several roots. Leaf classes do not use any other class in the cluster under test. They would be tested first in a bottom-up integration. The root is level 0.

With a small cluster, a dependency tree can be developed by inspection. Alternatively, the dependency tree can be derived from a **topological sort** of dependency relationships. Formally, a topological sort is an ordering of a directed graph such that all predecessors of every node are listed before the node itself. That is, no item appears until all of its predecessors have been listed. The topological sort can be applied at any scope. Suppose that the preceding components were subsystems implemented as Unix processes, each of which runs on a different processor. Instead of translation-time binding, suppose that the depend-

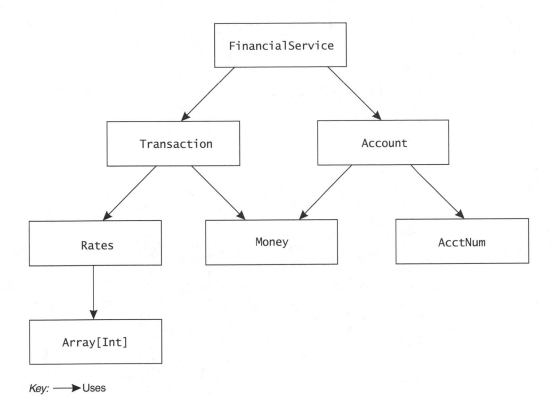

Key: ──▶ Uses

FIGURE 13.3   Dependency tree for the FinancialService cluster.

encies corresponded to remote procedure calls. The general dependencies and the tree would be the same.

The output of compilers, linkers, and loaders often provides a good deal of dependency information. Dependency analyzers are commercially available for many languages and target platforms. Note, however, that many of these tools cannot analyze dependencies that traverse network nodes, virtual machines, and operating systems.

The Unix tsort command-line utility will produce a topological sort of components. This ubiquitous utility can be easily used to produce a dependency analysis.[2] Table 13.3 indicates how tsort can be used to develop the

2. The tsort utility was developed to check forward and self-referent declarations, because C language processors will reject these dependencies. For details, do man tsort on your Unix platform. If you do not have access to a Unix machine, try a Web search for "topological sort." You will probably find several shareware implementations that will run on your platform. Failing this, the same search will probably yield several algorithms that you can code.

TABLE 13.3   Using `tsort` for Root-first Dependency Analysis

	tsort Input file	tsort Output
Relationship	*X* Uses *Y*	Root First
Simple Case	FinancialService Transaction FinancialService Account Transaction Rates Transaction Money Account Money Account AccountNum Rates Array	FinancialService Account Transaction AccountNum Money Rates Array
Multiple Roots	FinancialService Transaction FinancialService Account Transaction Rates Transaction Money Account Money Account AccountNum Rates Array Customer Customer	Customer FinancialService Account Transaction AccountNum Money Rates Array
Uses Cycle	FinancialService Transaction FinancialService Account Transaction Rates Transaction Money Account Money Account AccountNum Customer Account Money Customer Rates Array	FinancialService Transaction Rates Array tsort: cycle in data tsort: Account tsort: Money tsort: Customer Customer Account AccountNum Money

dependency tree for the FinancialService cluster. First, each pair of dependencies is identified. The dependencies are given the form *X* uses *Y*. The FinancialService uses Transaction dependency is given in the input file as FinancialService Transaction. Running tsort gives the output on the right of Table 13.3. As expected, the root class appears first. The remaining classes are then listed in uses order. To transcribe this list to a tree, use the first class as root, and draw an edge for each dependency on it. Add nodes for the dependent classes. Next, draw edges for each dependency on these classes. Add nodes for the classes at this level. Fan-in is likely, as one class may be used by several others. Continue tracing classes and dependencies until all classes in the sorted list have been transcribed.

The second part of Table 13.3 shows how multiple root clusters are handled. Suppose we add a class Customer. Customer now appears before any classes that use it. The dependency graph is produced in the same manner.

A **cycle** is a loop in a directed graph. For example, suppose class *A* uses class *B*, *B* uses *C*, and *C* uses *A*. Consequently, one class cannot be exercised without the other two. The topological sort relation is not defined for a cycle. Cycles are identified by tsort, but not sorted, as shown in the lower part of Table 13.3. Participants of a cycle must be tested as a group or decoupled with a cycle-breaking stub.

Figure 13.4 shows the dependency levels in FinancialService. A level can be considered as the root of a subtree. That is, the root and all of its dependent components may be tested as a unit. This information is essential for developing the sequence of integration.

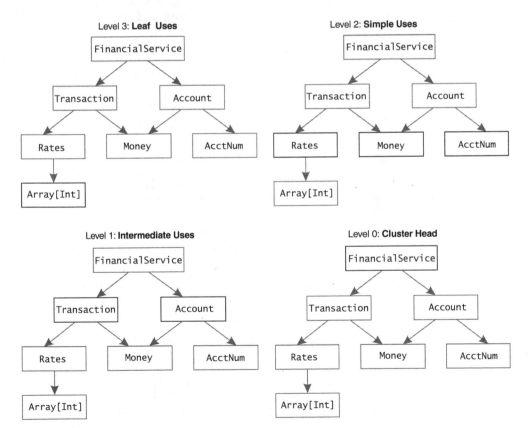

FIGURE 13.4   Dependency levels in the FinancialService cluster.

TABLE 13.4   Using `tsort` for Leaf-first Dependency Analysis

	tsort Input file	tsort Output
Relationship	*X* Is-used-by *Y*	Leaf First
Simple Case	Transaction FinancialService Account FinancialService Rates Transaction Money Transaction Money Account AccountNum Account Array Rates	Array AccountNum Money Rates Account Transaction FinancialService
Multiple Roots	Transaction FinancialService Account FinancialService Rates Transaction Money Transaction Money Account AccountNum Account Array Rates Customer Customer	Array Customer AccountNum Money Rates Account Transaction FinancialService
Uses Cycle	Transaction FinancialService Account FinancialService Rates Transaction Money Transaction Money Account AccountNum Account Customer Customer Account Customer Customer Money Array Rates	Array AccountNum Rates tsort: cycle in data tsort: Money tsort: Account tsort: Customer Customer Money Account Transaction FinancialService

If dependencies are modeled as *X is-used-by Y* (instead of *X uses Y*), `tsort` will output the class list in the opposite order, as shown in Table 13.4. The *is-used-by* form approximates the sequential order of testing: classes with no dependencies are listed first; the root class is listed last. Note that we may obtain the `tsort` input for a leaf-first sequence by swapping the names in each dependency pair. Cycles and multiple roots are handled in the same manner.

13.1.4   Integration Faults

Integration testing can reveal component faults that cause failures when components interact. For example, a study of faults in a large C system found that nearly two-thirds were interface-related; that is, a function call or its parameters had a design or coding bug [Perry+87]. Typical interface bugs include the following:

- Configuration/version control problems.
- Missing, overlapping, or conflicting functions.
- An incorrect or inconsistent data structure used for a file or database.
- Conflicting data views/usage used for a file or database.
- Violations of the data integrity of a global store or database.
- The wrong method called due to coding error or unexpected runtime binding.
- The client sending a message that violates the server's preconditions.
- The client sending a message that violates the server's sequential constraints.
- Wrong object bound to message (polymorphic target).
- Wrong parameters, or incorrect parameter values.
- Failures due to incorrect memory management allocation/deallocation.
- Incorrect usage of virtual machine, ORB, or OS services.
- Attempt by the IUT to use target environment services that are obsolete or not upward-compatible for the specified version/release of the target environment.
- Attempt by the IUT to use new target environment services that are not supported in the current version/release of the target environment.
- Intercomponent conflicts: thread X will crash when process Y is running, for example.
- Resource contention: the target environment cannot allocate resources required for a nominal load. For example, a use case may open up to six windows, but the IUT crashes when the fifth is opened.

Because many capabilities require the cooperation of several components, some people argue that all bugs that appear at system scope are integration bugs. I take a narrower view, which corresponds to the focus of integration as a dress rehearsal for system testing.

13.2   Integration Patterns

This section presents nine integration test suite test design patterns:

- *Big Bang Integration.* Attempt to demonstrate system stability by testing all components at the same time.
- *Bottom-up Integration.* Interleave component and integration testing by following usage dependencies.
- *Top-down Integration.* Interleave component and integration testing by following the application control hierarchy.
- *Collaboration Integration.* Choose an order of integration according to collaborations and their dependencies. Exercise interfaces by testing one collaboration at a time.
- *Backbone Integration.* Combine *Top-down Integration*, *Bottom-up Integration*, and *Big Bang Integration* to reach a stable system that will support iterative development.
- *Layer Integration.* Incrementally exercise interfaces and components in a layered architecture.
- *Client/Server Integration.* Exercise a loosely coupled network of components, all of which use a common server component.
- *Distributed Services Integration.* Exercise a loosely coupled network of peer-to-peer components.
- *High-frequency Integration.* Develop and rerun an integration test suite test hourly, daily, or weekly.

Figure 13.5 shows a generic dependency tree that will be used to show successive configurations.

The integration patterns are mostly independent of scope. Each is a general approach indicated when certain relationships hold among components. Some are better suited to a particular kind of architecture than others, however. For example, *Bottom-up Integration* works well for a class cluster or small subsystem. *Client/Server Integration* and *Distributed Services Integration* are appropriate for a larger system of components and distributed objects. Figure 13.1 on page 632 summarizes the relationship between scope and integration patterns.

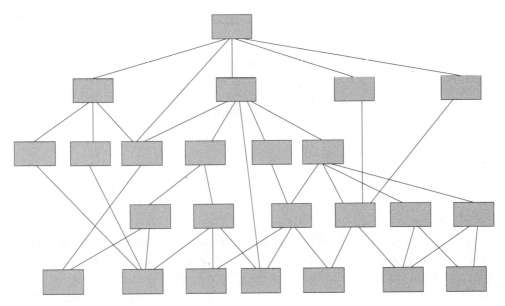

FIGURE 13.5 Generic dependency tree.

13.2.1 Scope-specific Considerations

Classes

At class scope, the system is the class under test. The components to be integrated are CUT methods, superclass methods, instance variables, and parameters in messages received and sent by the CUT. Dependency analysis was outlined in Section 13.13. Testing of class responsibilities is so closely coupled to class integration that it does not make much sense to treat the two as separate test design problems.

- Bottom-up intraclass integration is accomplished by the alpha-omega incremental development/integration strategy outlined in Chapter 10. Briefly, methods are coded and tested roughly in an order based on dependency: constructors, accessors, predicates, modifiers, iterators, and finally destructors.
- Big Bang intraclass integration is accomplished by the Small Pop development/integration strategy outlined in Chapter 10. Briefly, all methods are coded and testing begins with the appropriate class scope pattern.

- Collaboration integration of a modal class may be accomplished with *Modal Class Test*.
- Integration of superclass features can be accomplished with *Polymorphic Server Test* and *Modal Hierarchy Test*.
- There is no direct analog to *Backbone Integration*, *Layer Integration*, *Client/Server Integration*, or *Distributed Services Integration* at class scope.

Attempting to test a class in isolation is often an exercise in futility. To accomplish complete isolation testing would require that we replace all servers of the class under test with controllable stubs. This course of action turns out to be too difficult [Siepmann+94, Jüttner+95, Firesmith 96, Dorman 97]. Even if we implement the stubs, orchestrating the necessary response from the set of stubs for each test case is difficult at best. As a result, most class testing takes place in a cluster of classes. Nevertheless, responsibility-based test design may focus on one class at a time, even though the class is embedded in a cluster.

Clusters

At cluster scope, the system is the cluster under test. The components to be integrated are server objects used by the CUT. The testing of cluster responsibilities is less coupled to integration, so it makes sense to consider an integration strategy to be a master plan for the orchestration of pattern-based responsibility tests. "In general, it is not possible to do the integration testing according to only one of [inheritance, aggregation, and message passing] without a lot of tedious stubbing. Therefore, one needs a flexible mixed strategy" [Jüttner 94c, 13].

- *Bottom-up Integration* is the most widely used technique.
- *Top-down Integration* is possible if one class is the head of the cluster. For example, a cluster that implements the *Facade* pattern [Gamma+95] could be developed with the *Facade* class first and stubs for the subsystem classes. In subsequent increments, the stubs are replaced with a complete implementation. A single test driver would exercise the cluster via the *Facade* interface.
- Collaboration integration of a modal class may be accomplished with *Class Association Test*, *Round-trip Scenario Test*, or *Mode Machine Test*.

- If the class under test catches exceptions, *Controlled Exception Test* may be useful.
- There is no direct analog to *Client/Server Integration*, *Distributed Services Integration*, or *Backbone Integration* integration at the cluster scope.
- Overall, *Big Bang Integration* is not recommended unless just a few new components are being added to a stable system, as is the case in maintenance. This pattern is useful in some limited situations for development.

Procedure 15 summarizes steps for cluster integration.

Subsystem/System Scope

The scope of an implementation under test is often larger than of a single class or small cluster. We should test interactions above cluster scope but below system scope.

- Incremental development requires that successively larger sets of functionality be integrated. Increments may correspond to one subsystem or multiple subsystems.
- Stand-alone subsystems present for historical or commercial reasons must often be integrated with newly developed object-oriented subsystems.

At subsystem and system scopes, the goal of integration testing is achieving a sufficiently stable system so that responsibility testing at system scope may proceed smoothly. System and subsystem integration testing should verify the following:

- Physical configuration audit: Did the build generation use the right component versions?[3]

---

3. Configuration audits are required upon completion of "acceptance testing" for compliance with the IEEE/ANSI Standard for Software Configuration Management Plans [IEEE 1042]. In addition to this final audit, the same checks can prevent configuration bugs both before and after system scope integration. An informal review to be sure that "nothing has slipped through the cracks" will probably suffice for six or fewer developers. As the sizes of the system and the project team increase, so does the chance of configuration bugs and therefore the importance of the audit.

1.   Select an integration pattern for the cluster under test.

2.   Generate the test configuration.
     2.1 Turn assertion checking on.
     2.2 Turn instrumentation off.
     2.3 Build the cluster or thread.

3.   For each test:
     3.1 Set the system to the required mode.
     3.2 Apply the thread input: manual, script, or simulator.
     3.3 Compare the expected output to the actual output.
     3.4 Record observed failures and assertion violations.
     3.5 Diagnose and repair faults.

4.   Turn assertion checking off.

5.   Instrument the system under test using a testing tool.

6.   Rerun all your tests. No failures should be produced.

7.   Evaluate call pair coverage. If insufficient, develop additional tests to cover and repeat.

Procedure 15   Cluster Integration

- Functional configuration audit: Did the build generation use the right family of components?
- Environmental configuration audit: Will the build generation run on the specified target environment(s)? Does the system demand too much from the hardware and software resources of the target environment? Does the SUT run on all versions of operating systems, virtual machines, DBMS, and so on for which compatibility is required?
- Demonstration of minimal interoperability of components: Will *A* talk to *B*? Will *B* run with *C*? Does *X* get to *Y*?

At a minimum, a subsystem/system integration test suite should accomplish the steps outlined in Procedure 16. The sequence and content of specific test cases may be determined from the applicable pattern. Dependencies among the subsystem and its responsibilities are primary factors in determining the appropriate integration test pattern.

- ***Bottom-up Integration*** works well for small to medium systems.
- ***Top-down Integration*** works for almost any scope or architecture.
- ***Collaboration Integration*** works for almost any scope or architecture.
- ***Layer Integration*** applies to layered architectures.
- ***Client/Server Integration*** is appropriate for client/server architectures.
- ***Distributed Services Integration*** is appropriate for decentralized networks containing peer-to-peer nodes.
- ***Backbone Integration*** is well suited to small to medium systems and especially useful for embedded applications.
- ***Big Bang Integration*** is useful in a few limited circumstances.
- ***High-frequency Integration*** can be applied at almost any scope or architecture.

Once the integration exit criteria are met, your application is ready to support system scope testing.

1. Set up infrastructure.
    1.1 Configure environment.
    1.2 Create/initialize files.
    1.3 Connect input/output devices. Establish minimal handshaking.
    1.4 Compile, link, build, make, or assemble the entire system from a
        single library under configuration management control.

2. Verify executability.
    2.1 Run all batch job streams to completion with minimal input.
    2.2 Bring up all tasks in an online system. Navigate all menu paths.
        Perform normal shutdown.
    2.3 Bring up all tasks in an embedded system. Accept normal signal
        inputs; produce all output at nominal values. Perform normal
        shutdown.

3. Verify minimal cooperative functionality.
    3.1 Run through primary end-to-end threads: use case variants, all
        CRUD paths.
    3.2 Run through all cycles: on/off, polling loop, hourly, daily, weekly,
        monthly, and so on.

Procedure 16   High-level Integration Plan

Big Bang Integration

Intent

Demonstrate stability by attempting to exercise an entire system with a few test runs.

Context

The Big Bang Integration pattern brings together all components in the system under test without regard for intercomponent dependency or risk. A system scope test suite is applied to demonstrate minimal operability. Big Bang Integration is indicated in some situations:

- The SUT is stabilized and only a few components have been added or changed since the last time it passed a system scope test suite.
- The SUT is small and testable, and each of its components has passed adequate component scope tests.
- Big Bang Integration may be the only feasible approach for a monolithic system. When components are so tightly coupled that they cannot be exercised separately, it is a practical impossibility to build and test component subsets. This is a common result in unstructured systems developed with conventional programming languages (e.g., Basic, Cobol, Fortran, assembly language), object-oriented implementations with poor design or no design, or the accretion of ad hoc maintenance in either case. See *Big Ball of Mud* [Yoder+97].

If these conditions are not present, Big Bang Integration typically creates more problems than it solves. It is a common recourse under schedule pressure, but this is usually as effective as trying to put out a fire with gasoline.

Fault Model

The Big Bang fault model is ambiguous and opportunistic. The hope is that the system will "run" and thereby demonstrate that system testing can begin.

Strategy

Big Bang Integration dispenses with incremental integration testing. The entire system is built and a test suite is applied to demonstrate minimal operability at system scope. Figure 13.6 suggests this configuration. In contrast, all of the other integration patterns presented in this chapter start by building a few components, testing their interoperability, adding a few more, testing their interfaces, and so on, until all interfaces have been exercised.

The test suite for a Big Bang Integration pattern may be developed at system scope by using an appropriate responsibility-based test design pattern. Use the oracle for this pattern.

Entry Criteria

✓ All components have passed component scope testing.

✓ The virtual machine to be used in the test environment is stable.

✓ A physical, functional, and environmental audit has been conducted and has not found any anomalies that would interfere with integration testing.

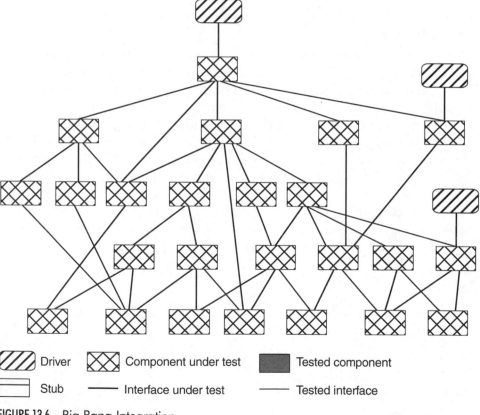

FIGURE 13.6   Big Bang Integration.

Exit Criteria

✓ The test suite passes.

Consequences

Big Bang Integration is usually ill advised. "In its purest (and vilest) form, big-bang testing is no method at all—'Let's fire it up and see if it works!' It doesn't of course" [Beizer 84, 160]. A common result is that there are so many interface bugs that the system barely runs, defeating the Big Bang Integration tests and making it hard to know where to look to diagnose a failure. "The name is somewhat misleading: the anticipated bang is all too often a fizzle" [Lakos 96, 162].

Big Bang Integration has two main disadvantages. First, debugging can be difficult because you receive fewer clues about fault locations. With incremental integration, the most recently added component is likely to be buggy, has triggered a failure in another component, or allowed the propagation of a pre-existing failure. In contrast, every component in a Big Bang Integration is equally suspect. Second, even if the SUT passes, many interface faults can hide and waylay subsequent system scope testing.

Under favorable circumstances, Big Bang Integration can result in quick completion of integration testing. Few (if any) integration drivers or stubs are developed. It may be possible to demonstrate sufficient stability with a few test runs. The favorable circumstances are: (1) a small, well-structured system whose components have received adequate testing, (2) an existing system where only a few changes have been made, and (3) a system constructed by reusing trusted components. If the integration comes off without difficulty, the effort for the test setup and the test run is incurred only a few times. If more than three bang-fix-bang cycles are required, Big Bang Integration was a poor choice.

Known Uses

Big Bang Integration has been attempted in countless projects and is discussed in [Myers 76, Myers 79, Beizer 84]. Subsystem Big Bang Integration is used in *Backbone Integration*.

Bottom-up Integration

Intent

Demonstrate stability by adding components to the SUT in uses–dependency order, beginning with components having the fewest dependencies.

Context

The Bottom-up Integration pattern achieves stepwise verification of the interfaces between tightly coupled components. It interleaves component scope testing and integration of a system of components. Components with the least number of dependencies are tested first. When these components pass, their drivers are replaced with their clients; another round of testing then begins.

Bottom-up Integration is often used to support unit scope testing in the iterative and incremental development of a subsystem's components. That is, you test each component as it is coded and then integrate it with already-tested components. The composition dependencies of the implementation under development reflect the path of least resistance. Bottom-up development is well suited to a system of components with robust and stable interface definitions.

If you can (or must) defer end-to-end, system scope exercising of the components until all components have been developed, bottom-up development is indicated. This can occur for several reasons: components developed by teams that have limited opportunity for communication, time and space separation, contractual requirements, departments separated by rigid bureaucracies, third-party development, and so on. In this situation, it is critical that component responsibility and interface definitions are stable. Architectural changes in the middle to late stages will typically require significant reworking and re-testing.

Bottom-up development can provide an early assessment of a component that must implement a critical requirement. For example, such a component might have to meet strict time or memory constraints, correctly perform complex searching, catch a wide range of exceptions, or implement a low-level device interface with complex state behavior.

Fault Model

See Section 13.1.4, Integration Faults.

Strategy

Test Model

Develop a dependency tree, as outlined in Section 13.1.3, Dependency Analysis. The responsibility test suite for each component may be developed with any appropriate test design pattern. In addition to exercising the responsibilities of the component, however, attention must be paid to exercising subcomponents. The scope of the test suite for each driver is limited to the component under test. That is, the driver does not attempt to exercise intercomponent interfaces. Instead, the driver exercises the component that implements intercomponent interfaces, thereby exercising the interfaces.

Test Procedure

Bottom-up Integration works by moving from the leaves of the dependency tree to the root. If the tree contains n levels, there are n stages.

1. In the first stage, leaf-level components are coded. Test drivers are coded for the leaf-level components, and the leaf level is tested by these drivers (Figure 13.7).
2. Components on the next higher level are coded. These components use (send messages to or pass as arguments) objects that were tested during

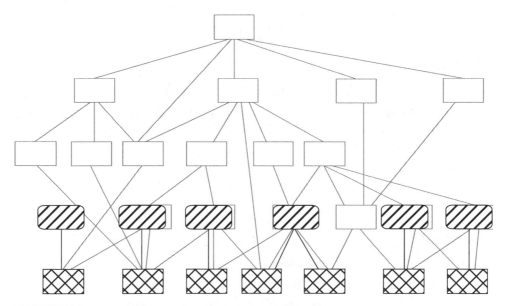

FIGURE 13.7   Bottom-up Integration, first-stage configuration.

the previous stage. The succession of stage configurations is shown in Figures 13.8, 13.9, and 13.10.

3. The entire system is exercised using the root-level component, as shown in Figure 13.11.

The actual integration test cases should be developed with an appropriate responsibility-based test design pattern. Use the oracle for this pattern.

Automation

Bottom-up Integration requires one driver for each component or component that is a root of a subtree in the dependency relationship. A bottom-up driver should correspond to an independent component or set of components. Although testing several components with a single driver may be possible or necessary, you should avoid combining the test suites for components that can be tested by individual drivers into a single driver. This approach favors the reuse of the drivers and reduces test driver maintenance. Test drivers must be revised as the classes under test are revised, especially if refactoring occurs. The inherently higher coupling of multicomponent drivers suggests that more effort can be expected to maintain them.

Verify that each successive test configuration is checked in and under version control before you begin development of a new configuration. In most cases, a design change or bug fix will require revising and rerunning tests for configurations that have already passed. If the configurations have not been saved, this effort can be difficult with just the current configuration.

Entry Criteria

- ✓ The virtual machine to be used in the test environment is stable.
- ✓ The components to be integrated in each stage are minimally operable. That is, each meets the exit criteria for the related component scope tests.
- ✓ A physical, functional, and environmental audit has been conducted and has not found any anomalies that would interfere with integration testing.

Exit Criteria

- ✓ Each driven component meets the exit criteria for its test pattern.
- ✓ The interface to each subcomponent has been exercised at least once.
- ✓ Integration testing is complete when all root-level components pass their test suites.

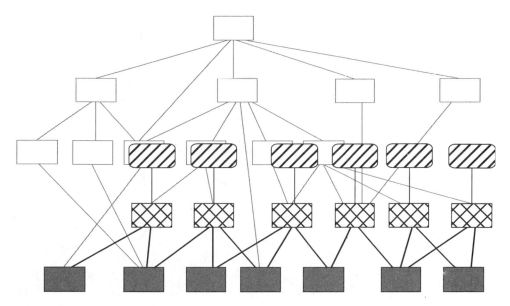

FIGURE 13.8   Bottom-up Integration, second-stage configuration.

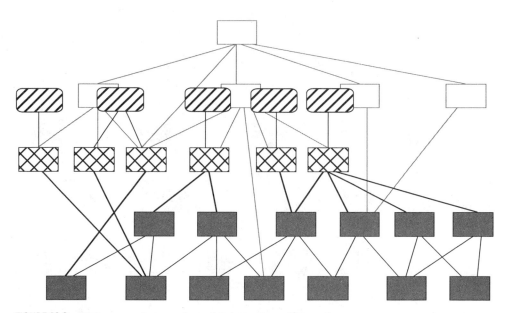

FIGURE 13.9   Bottom-up Integration, third-stage configuration.

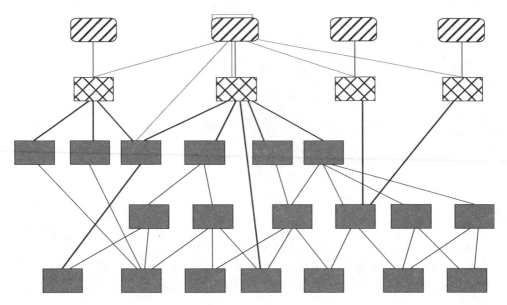

FIGURE 13.10   Bottom-up Integration, fourth-stage configuration.

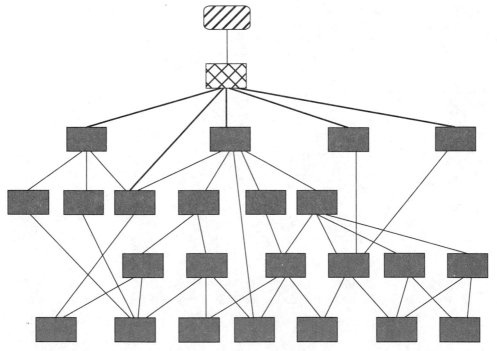

FIGURE 13.11   Bottom-up Integration, final configuration.

Consequences

Disadvantages

Driver development is the most significant cost of Bottom-up Integration. The code size of the resulting test harness can easily be twice that of the system under test. Use of this pattern in conventional development assumed that drivers consisted of "throwaway" code and identified this characteristic as a weakness [Myers 76, Myers 79]. In fact, this cost may be offset if drivers are designed to be reusable and to promote reuse of the tested component [Gamma+98]. Several COTS testware products promise to generate all or part of the driver code.

If a fix, revision, or enhancement is made to a previously tested component, the test configuration in which this component was first tested should be revised accordingly and rerun. Subsequently, the change must be propagated through successive test configurations. This process can prove error-prone, costly, and time-consuming.

A bottom-up driver does not directly exercise intercomponent interfaces. Instead, interaction testing is limited to collaborations implemented in the component that is the root of the subtree under test. This may or may not constitute adequate testing of component interactions. If the components are intended for reuse, then an application-independent test suite of component interactions should be employed.

As the upper levels of the dependency tree are reached, getting lower-level components to return values or throw the exceptions necessary to get complete coverage often proves difficult. This may require stubs to generate the desired conditions.

Bottom-up Integration postpones checking critical control interfaces and collaborations until the end of the development cycle. Operability of the highest level of control and component interoperability are not demonstrated until the root component replaces the last driver. If component interfaces are defined on the fly or are unstable, the first indication of problems will come not when the inconsistent components are "integrated," but rather when the component that uses them is exercised.

Advantages

Bottom-up testing and integration may begin as soon as any leaf-level component is ready. Initially, work may proceed in parallel. That is, several developers can work independently on subtrees. Bottom-up Integration does not limit testability (unlike *Top-down Integration*) because code coverage of the root of the subtree under test can typically be achieved with a suitably constructed test suite and driver. Although this pattern reduces stubbing, stubs may still be needed to break a cycle or simulate exceptions.

The Bottom-up Integration pattern is well suited to responsibility-based design, as only component interfaces are exercised. In contrast, *Top-down Integration* requires analysis of both client and server components to develop server stubs.

Known Uses

Bottom-up Integration is discussed in several sources [Myers 76, Myers 79, Yourdon+79, Beizer 84]. It is recommended for use with clusters [Cheatham 90, Lieberherr+92, Graham+93, Graham 94, Turner+95].

Integration by Contract

A detailed analysis of cluster scope integration testing is presented in [Overbeck 94a]. This approach does not consider specific techniques to identify sequences, state values, or input values. Instead, test design is based on the relationship between client and server classes with all possible variations on inheritance.

Two basic test suites are the building blocks of the approach. A class unit test (*self-test*) is passed if, for all methods of a CUT: (1) message input/output are correct as specified, (2) every server class of the CUT is used properly, and (3) all intraclass operation sequences are correct. The second basic test suite involves a client X and a server Y (X *contract-test* Y). X passes the contract-test suite when: (1) X passes the self-test suite, (2) X always meets Y's preconditions, and (3) X uses Y's output correctly.

Six cases for application of these two basic test suites are considered:

- Self-test of a base class
- Self-test of a single subclass
- Contract test of two base classes
- Contract test of the base client and subclass server
- Contract test of the subclass client and base server
- Contract test of two subclasses

The extent of the test suite varies in each case.

To integrate an arbitrarily large system, an order of integration must be established. The self-test and contract-test patterns are then applied according to the order of integration:

. . . if we self-test every class in the system, contract-test every client-server relationship between one client and one server, and contract-test every client-server relationship between multiple clients of a single server, we know that the complete system works correctly [Overbeck 94a, 87].

The question is, how do we accomplish this with minimal reliance on stubs? A contract test cannot be passed when the usage structure of classes is cyclic (*X* uses *Y*, *Y* uses *Z*, *Z* uses *X*). Stubs are necessary to break a cyclic usage between classes, but they increase the cost of testing. An incremental strategy may be used to deal with cycles and reduce the total number of test cases.

1. Find a class, *C*, whose superclasses and server classes have passed self-testing.
   1.1 Self-test *C*.
   1.2 Contract test all of *C*'s servers.
   1.3 Repeat these steps until no more *C* is left untested.

2. If any classes remain, there must be a cycle. Find a minimal set of classes, *S*, that have passed step 1 and which contain a cycle.
   2.1 For each client in *S*, contract test it with all unit-tested servers.
   2.2 If there are cycles in *S*, find the smallest set of classes that could break the cycle. Develop and unit test stubs for each such class.
   2.3 Test the stubbed class set.
   2.4 Replace the stubs with the original classes, and contract test the resulting client and servers.

Testing systems by this process ensures that

All classes have been self-tested, all client–server relationships between two classes have been contract-tested, and all client–server relationships between multiple clients and a single server have been contract tested. Assuming the preconditions for self-testing and contract-testing, such systems are considered to be correct [Overbeck 94a 116].

"Safe" Approach

The "safe" approach provides a strategy for dealing with the potentially large number of tests needed to cover bindings of polymorphic server classes [McCabe+94]. Each class in the system under test is tested separately by a driver. For a class under test to be considered "safe," a driver must execute a test suite that meets three goals:

- Branch coverage is obtained for each method in the CUT.
- All server object methods used by the CUT are called at least once, and each possible binding for a polymorphic server object is used at least once.
- If the CUT exports polymorphic methods, the driver must exercise, at least once, each possible binding of each method.

A class is considered "safe" when it meets all three criteria and all of its server classes are also safe. This requirement dictates a bottom-up (uses) order of integration.

McCabe et al. argued that clients of safe servers need not re-exercise bindings of the server's servers. This decision limits the scope of unit-level integration for a class under test to its immediate servers, thereby avoiding a potentially very large set of bindings for integration.

McCabe et al. also assert that regression testing for clients of safe classes is unnecessary in some circumstances. "A change to the implementation, not the interface, of an existing method within a system requires only that the changed method be tested . . . When a Safe class is extended through derivation and inheritance, it only needs to be tested in the weakest sense" [McCabe+94, 25]. Because the interface is the same and client usage of this interface has already been tested, client uses do not need retesting. Instead, a driver is used to run a test suite on the new implementation. As a result, it is not necessary to retest each client usage of the interface in an application system. It is argued that this approach is a practical necessity when widely used server classes are changed.

Object Relations

A class developer must usually consider questions like, "To test this class, what other classes must be tested?" Kung et al. propose a program representation called the *object relation diagram* (ORD) to answer such questions [Kung+93]. The ORD contains a node for each class and an edge for each inheritance, aggregation (instance variable), and association (message parameters and friends). Some order (of class integration) supposedly exists that can "eliminate" test drivers or method stubs. This order can be discovered by analysis of the ORD.

If the ORD is acyclic, a stubless test order can be obtained from the ORD by a topological sort (see Section 13.1.3, Dependency Analysis). Cycles happen frequently, however. A strategy for testing without stubs is outlined. It is asserted that all cycles must contain at least one association (a "proof" for this condition is noted but not given; it is easy to imagine counterexamples of cycles without associations). The strategy calls for "eliminating" one association from the cycle, but does not explain how this goal is accomplished. Once the cycle is broken, bottom-up testing may be performed. When the bottom-up testing is complete, the association may be reintroduced and tested.

Three Dependencies

A four-step process for C++ integration is outlined in [Lee 94]:

1. Map the relationships among system components: inheritance, friends, message passing, function calls, and the main program.
2. Test components as follows:
   2.1 Root objects: those instantiated from a base class with no friends that receives no messages from other classes.
   2.2 Other classes that have "the fewest inheritance, friend, and message passing relationships" and do not participate in any recursive relationships.
   2.3 Repeat, choosing classes with higher coupling until all classes meeting these criteria have been tested.
3. Test classes with recursive relationships. Begin with classes having "the fewest [recursive] relationships with other untested classes." Stub the untested classes. Repeat until all recursive classes have been tested.
4. Test the main program.

Top-down Integration

Intent

Demonstrate stability by adding components to the SUT in control hierarchy order, beginning with the top-level control objects.

Context

Top-down Integration achieves stepwise verification of the interfaces among components that operate under a common control strategy. This control strategy dictates the order of development, integration, and testing. Top-down Integration interleaves component scope testing and integration of a system of components.

Suppose you are developing a system following an iterative and incremental approach. The control structure of the system can be modeled as a tree in which the top-level components have control responsibilities.[4] Jacobson calls these components *control objects*. Control objects typically implement essential and nontrivial control strategies and therefore present relatively high risk. Top-down Integration focuses on these components first, making the demonstration of system scope end-to-end operability a high priority.

Because Top-down Integration exercises the control objects first, deferred or concurrent development of the controlled components is possible. Consequently, this pattern is also useful in several variants of incremental development, even if control integration is trivial or low risk.

- *Incremental development.* Each increment adds another layer under the control layer.
- *Concurrent hardware/software development.* High-level control components can be designed, coded, and tested while hardware or subsystem interfaces are designed and developed.
- *Concurrent software development.* High-level control components can be designed, coded, and tested while a virtual machine or subsystem interfaces are designed and developed.

---

4. Applications of hierarchic control in object-oriented development are described in *Manager* [Sommerlad 98], *Recursive Control* [Selic 98], and *Bureaucracy* [Riehle 98]. Douglass provides several implementation control patterns at the architectural, "mechanistic," and class scope [Douglass 98].

- *Framework development*. Reusable frameworks often implement a general control strategy while using abstract base classes to defer application-specific details. The first increment of a framework can exercise the control strategy. In fact, a framework's abstract base classes provide an ideal interface for stub development. Subsequent increments can exercise use case and domain model responsibilities. See *New Framework Test*.

Fault Model

See Section 13.1.4, Integration Faults.

Strategy

Test Model

The apex of control may be represetned in a Collaboration Diagram, Sequence Diagram, or Statechart of the system under test. A responsibility test suite may be developed with any appropriate test design pattern. If a system scope state machine model has been (or can be) developed, the cluster that implements the state machine will probably be at the top of the hierarchy. In this case, the test suite is developed by applying *Modal Class Test* or *Mode Machine Test*. If there are no sequential constraints on the collaborations, the test suite should be developed based on system scope responsibilities using *Collaboration Integration*, *Round-trip Scenario Test*, or *Covered in CRUD*.

Test Procedure

Model the control hierarchy as a dependency tree. Next, develop a staged plan for implementation and testing. Then, design a responsibility-based test suite at system scope.

1. Develop and test the component(s) at the highest level of control first. Implement the servers of this component as stubs or proxies. Figure 13.12 shows the first top-down configuration.
2. Continue in a breadth-first swath at each level, replacing the server stubs with a full implementation and stubbing the next lower level of servers. The configurations found at successive stages of Top-down Integration are shown in Figures 13.13, 13.14, and 13.15.
3. Continue in this manner until all servers in the system under test have been implemented and exercised. Figure 13.16 shows the final-stage configuration.

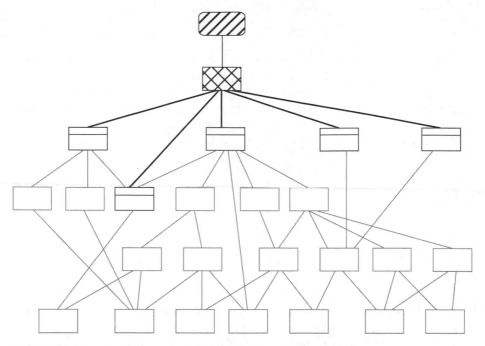

FIGURE 13.12   Top-down Integration, first-stage configuration.

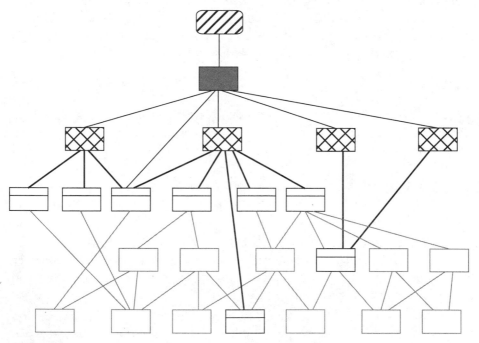

FIGURE 13.13   Top-down Integration, second-stage configuration.

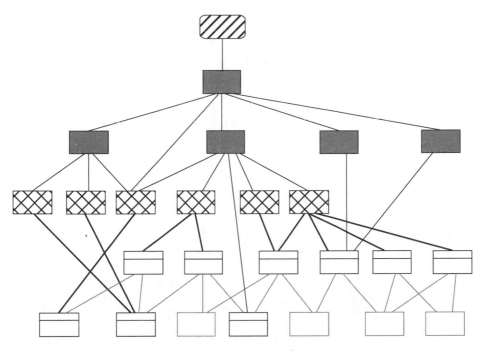

FIGURE 13.14 Top-down Integration, third-stage configuration.

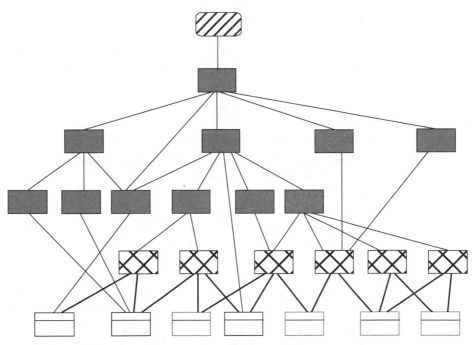

FIGURE 13.15 Top-down Integration, fourth-stage configuration.

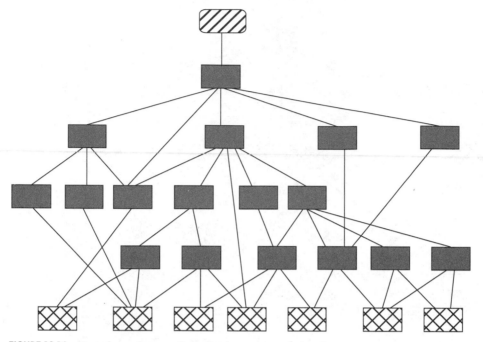

FIGURE 13.16 Top-down Integration, final-stage configuration.

The test suite for a ***Top-down Integration*** may be developed at system scope by using an appropriate responsibility-based test design pattern. Use the oracle for this pattern.

Automation

This pattern requires a single driver for the control apex. A stub is needed for each component in the layer below the current focus of integration.

Verify that each successive test configuration is checked in and under version control before you begin developing a new configuration. A design change or bug fix will likely require revising and rerunning tests for configurations that have already passed. If the earlier configurations have bnoteen saved, this step can be difficult with just the current configuration.

Entry Criteria

✓ The virtual machine to be used in the test environment is stable.

✓ The components to be integrated in each stage are minimally operable. That is, they should meet the exit criteria for the related component scope tests.

✓ A physical, functional, and environmental audit has been conducted and has not found any configuration anomalies that would interfere with integration testing.

Exit Criteria

✓ Each driven component meets the exit criteria for its test pattern.

✓ The interface to each subcomponent has been exercised at least once. Coverage analyzers will instrument and analyze call-pair traces, detailing exactly which interfaces have and have not been exercised.

✓ Integration testing is complete when a build that includes all leaf-level components passes the system scope test suite.

Consequences

Disadvantages

Stub development and maintenance are the most significant costs associated with Top-down Integration.

* Because stubs provide a necessary part of each test, setting up a test requires that a large number of stubs be coded to provide the desired response. Complex test cases can require recoding of stubs for each test case. As the number of stubs increases for a test configuration, it becomes more difficult to maintain the necessary control and consistency.

* An unforeseen requirement in a lower-level component may necessitate last-minute changes to many top-level components, breaking part of the test suite. If a fix, revision, or enhancement is made to a previously tested component, the test configuration in which this component was first tested should be revised accordingly (driver and stubs) and rerun. Then, the change must be propagated through successive test configurations. This process can be error-prone, costly, and time-consuming.

* The stubs are necessarily implementation-specific and likely to be brittle.

It may be difficult to exercise lower-level components sufficiently. The distance between the testing interface and the components being integrated increases with each successive level. This progression usually results in a loss of test control over lower-level components that are integrated at the end of the cycle. Because attaining high coverage when the component is a long distance from the driver may be difficult or impossible, a low coverage report may be difficult to interpret or remedy.

The interoperabilty of all components in the SUT is not tested until the last component replaces its stub and the test suite passes.

Advantages

Testing and integration may begin early—when the top-level components are coded. The first-stage test exercises all high-level component interfaces and can provide an early demonstration of end-to-end functionality.

The cost of driver development is reduced. Component-specific drivers typically use hard-coded test cases and are tightly coupled with a component interface. This setup limits driver and test suite reuse. In contrast, although the driver for a top-level component shares the same problems, there is only one driver to maintain, instead of a driver for every subtree. Typically, the test cases can be reused to drive lower-level tests. As lower-level components are added and tested, upper-level components are exercised again, providing regression testing. Because, many stubs are typically needed (compared with *Bottom-up Integration*), this reduced cost of driver development may be offset by the higher cost of stub development.

Initially, components may be developed in parallel. Several developers can work independently on different levels of components and stubs. Implementation of low-level, device-dependent components can be deferred. This flexibility may be useful if the target environment is under development or likely to change.

If the lower-level interfaces are undefined or likely to change, then Top-down Integration can avoid commitment to an unstable interface.

Known Uses

Top-down Integration is discussed in several sources [Myers 76, Myers 79, Yourdon+79, Beizer 84]. This pattern has been widely used. The exploratory development style followed by Extreme Programming often corresponds to Top-down Integration [Anderson+98]. Fred Brooks observes:

> Some years ago, Harlan Mills proposed that any software system should be grown by incremental development. That is, the system should first be made to run, even though it does nothing useful except call the proper set of dummy subprograms [stubs]. Then, bit by bit, it is fleshed out, with the subprograms in turn being developed into actions or calls to empty subs in the level below. . . . Nothing in the past decade has so radically changed my own practice, or its effectiveness. One always has, at every stage in the process, a working system. I find that teams can grow much more complex entities in four months than they can build [Brooks 87, 15].

Related Patterns

Modified Top-down Integration follows the same integration sequence, but requires that the components be tested under a driver before they replace a stub [Myers 76]. This approach avoids the major disadvantage of a pure top-down approach—the increasing difficulty of testing lower-level components.

Collaboration Integration

Intent

Demonstrate stability by adding sets of components to the SUT that are required to support a particular collaboration.

Context

Integration by collaboration exercises interfaces between the participants of a collaboration and organizes integration according to collaborations. A system typically supports many collaborations. Their sequence may be selected according to dependencies, sequential activation constraints, or both. Integration is completed when all components and interfaces have been exercised, which may not require testing every collaboration. Indications for integration by collaborations include the following:

- The system under test has clearly defined collaborations that can cover all components and interfaces in its scope.
- Demonstrating a working collaboration as soon as possible is important, possibly because of technical risk or criticality of a collaboration(s).
- Credible demonstration requires more than just a pass through the top of the control hierarchy. For example, all participants of a processing thread in a sensor-controller-actuator path or a search function with critical performance objectives must be exercised to demonstrate basic interoperability.

Fault Model

See Section 13.1.4, Integration Faults.

Strategy

Test Model

The components included in a collaboration are selected by membership in a processing thread, an event–response path, or critical performance objectives. If there are no sequential constraints on the collaborations, the test suite should be developed for system scope responsibilities using *Collaboration Integration*, *Round-trip Scenario Test*, or *Covered in CRUD*.

Test Procedure

1. Develop a dependency tree for the system under test. Map collaborations onto the dependency tree until all components and interfaces are covered.

2. Choose a sequence in which to apply the collaborations. There are several possible heuristics for choosing a sequence.
   - Begin with the simplest and finish with the most complex.
   - Begin with the collaboration that requires the fewest stubs or that minimizes stubs for other collaborations.
   - Develop a state machine that models sequential constraints on collaborations. Each collaboration should correspond to a transition. Develop the transition tree and test collaborations by traversing the tree.
   - Test in order of risk of disruption for system testing. Consider the relative effects on the progress of system testing of a showstopper bug in each collaboration. Test the most influential collaborations first, stopping when the interfaces and components are covered.

3. Develop the test suite for the first collaboration. If possible, design the test driver to support additional collaborations and more extensive system testing. Figure 13.17 depicts a first configuration.

4. Run the test suite and debug until the first collaboration test passes. Revise your test design as necessary. Continue until all collaborations have been exercised. Figure 13.18 depicts a second configuration. Figure 13.19 illustrates the final configuration (all components and interfaces exercised).

The test suite for Collaboration Integration may be developed at system scope by using an appropriate responsibility-based test design pattern. Use the oracle for this pattern.

Automation

This pattern requires a single driver coupled to the interface for the collaboration. In applications with a GUI, this driver is typically a widget or sequence of widgets. Stubs are required for untested components that do not participate in a collaboration. As each collaboration is tested, the relevant stubs are replaced.

Verify that each successive test configuration is checked in and under version control before you begin developing a new configuration. A design change

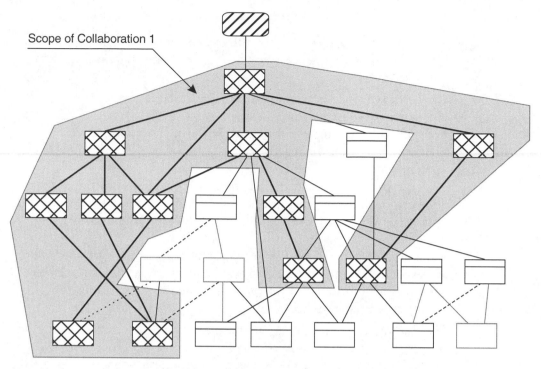

Scope of Collaboration 1

FIGURE 13.17   Collaboration Integration, first configuration.

or bug fix will likely require revising and rerunning tests for configurations that have already passed. If the earlier configurations have not been saved, this step can be difficult with just the current configuration.

Entry Criteria

- ✓ The virtual machine to be used in the test environment is stable.
- ✓ The components of the collaboration are minimally operable. That is, they should have met the exit criteria for the appropriate component scope test pattern.
- ✓ A physical, functional, and environmental audit has been conducted and has not found any anomalies that would interfere with integration testing.

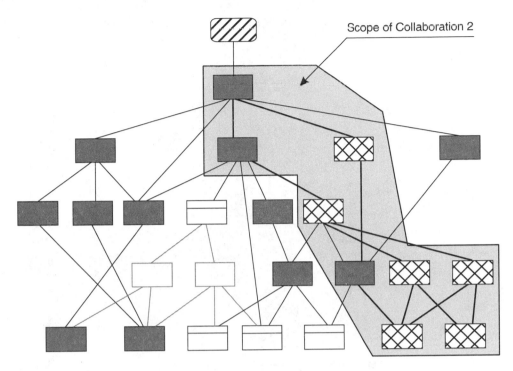

FIGURE 13.18   Collaboration Integration, second configuration.

Exit Criteria

✓ Each tested collaboration meets the exit criteria for its test pattern.

✓ All component and intercomponent messages in the system have been exercised at least once (this step does not necessarily require all collaborations to be tested, just as statement coverage does not require all paths to be covered). Coverage analyzers will instrument and analyze call-pair traces, detailing exactly which interfaces have and have not been exercised.

Consequences

Disadvantages

The disadvantages of integration by collaboration are as follows:

• Intercollaboration dependencies may be subtle and may not have been modeled.

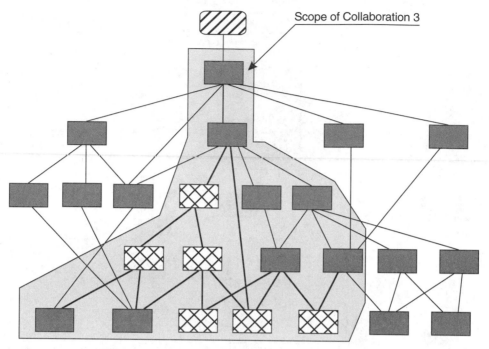

Scope of Collaboration 3

FIGURE 13.19   Collaboration Integration, final configuration.

- The exit criteria are similar to statement coverage. Exercising all components and interfaces without exercising all collaborations may be possible, missing some interface bugs.
- Participants in a collaboration are not exercised separately. In effect, this pattern is a scenario-wise *Big Bang Integration*.
- Some initial collaborations may require many stubs.
- Exercising lower-level components sufficiently may be difficult. The distance between the testing interface and the components being integrated can be long enough to make it difficult to set up test cases.
- The specified collaborations may be incomplete. A Collaboration Diagram depicts a call path or family of call paths that are feasible for the implementation under test and relevant to the application. All feasible paths need not be modeled.
- Collaborations do not focus on peculiarities of component interfaces, environment dependencies, and exception handling. A collaboration

test suite may therefore miss bugs that are load-sensitive, arise from component interactions, and so on.

- Unless several developers share development of collaboration components, it is unlikely that much overlap can be achieved.

Advantages

The advantages of integration by collaboration are as follows.

- Interface coverage may be obtained with a few test runs. It may not be necessary to exercise all collaborations to achieve integration coverage, if a few collaborations exercise all the interfaces.
- The testing focuses on end-to-end functionality, so collaboration test cases will probably be useful for system scope testing. A Collaboration Integration test suite can often be reused and expanded for system testing.
- A Collaboration Integration test suite is minimally coupled to components of a collaboration because it uses a single test interface. If the collaboration components churn due to requirements instability or bug fixes, then this lower coupling can reduce test suite breakage.
- Testing and integration may begin when the components in the first collaboration are coded. As a result, end-to-end capability can be demonstrated later than it would in *Top-down Integration*, but sooner than in *Bottom-up Integration*.
- The pattern minimizes driver development costs, for the same reasons as with *Top-down Integration*. As lower-level components are added and tested, upper-level components are exercised again, providing regression testing.

Known Uses

OOSE Integration Strategy

A coherent approach to integration testing is used in the OOSE methodology [Jacobson+92]. Integration occurs several times during development and should (ideally) be performed in the target environment. The initial process is essentially *Bottom-up Integration*:

When a block has been tested, you test it together with another block. When these two are working together, you add another, and so on. When all appear to work, we can consequently change to black-box testing . . . [Jacobson+92, 324–325].

Next, integration testing is organized by use cases because they "explicitly interconnect several blocks and classes" [Jacobson+92, 327]:

> . . . integrate one use case at a time . . . The requirements model forms again a powerful tool here; as we test each use case, we check that the objects communicate correctly [and check] user interfaces . . . the requirements model is verified by the testing process [Jacobson+92, 327].

Besides normal usage patterns, "odd courses" for use cases are tested and use cases identified from requirements and user documentation. Integration by use cases is also suggested in [Firesmith 92] and [Graham 94].

Atomic System Functions

Conventional structural integration strategies do not work well for object-oriented systems, which rely on dynamic binding [Jorgenson+94]. Without a "main program, there is no clearly defined integration structure. Thus there is no decomposition tree to impose. . . testing order of objects."

> The shift to composition (especially when reuse occurs) adds another dimension of difficulty to object-oriented software testing: it is impossible to ever know the full set of "adjacent" objects with which a given object may be composed [Jorgenson+94, 33].

Integration can be accomplished by thread identification. A thread begins with an externally generated event (a user keypress, for example). In response, some sequences of messages are generated by objects. This sequence traces a path over the network of method interfaces in the system under test. The end of the sequence is the "event quiescence" message, which typically causes some response to be sent to the system's environment (a message is displayed to the user).

This end-to-end thread is an "atomic system function" (ASF). It provides a basis for integration testing by composition. The test approach requires identification and execution of ASFs. ASFs may be identified either from a suitable representation or by analysis of source code.

Siemens

Integration plays a key role in an overall test strategy reported by a unit of Siemens AG [Jüttner+94c]. The strategy has two main steps. First, intraclass integration testing is performed with server objects stubbed out. The order of integration follows the order of inheritance: base classes first, refined and new derived member functions second, followed by interleaved sequences of inherited, new, and redefined member functions.

Integration by uses (definition of class variables, message sending, and so on) follows. It requires code analysis. The steps are as follows:

1. Inventory and classify all uses in the system under test. A simple use involves two objects; a complex use involves several objects. A cyclical use involves objects that use each other.

2. For each simple use, devise at least one test that exercises the use.

3. For each nonsimple use, devise at least one test. Monitor simple uses covered by complex uses to see whether any simple uses are tested as a side effect.

4. For cyclical uses, break the cycle with a stub. Test the parts of the cyclic use separately, then test the whole cyclic use. This process continues until all uses have been tested.

As use-based tests are performed, message traces are recorded as an object communication diagram. This diagram is then compared with the specified object communication diagram. Differences are employed to devise additional test cases. Additional object-to-object relationships in the OOA/D model can be used to select more tests. Only one test case is developed for each such facet of the model.

This integration strategy promotes classes from unproven to proven, one at a time. Within the scope of the system under test, objects are identified as either proven or unproven. Testing proceeds by examining each unproven object with trusted components. When the tests pass, the object under test is added to the proven group. When an unproven object uses other unproven components, the unproven objects are stubbed out to allow unambiguous results for the object under test.

The same degree of testing is applied to modified classes as is performed for entirely new classes. When only the implementation changes (the interface and specification remain constant), regression testing becomes easier when we use the unchanged version to produce expected results. Encapsulation is seen as helpful, as it prevents side effects. Inheritance, however, increases the complexity of test planning and execution.

Medtronics Integration Process

A four-step process is used at Medtronics to test object-oriented software used in safety-critical applications [Brown+95]. After formal Fagan-style code inspections on each class (step one), **Big Bang Integration** is done at cluster scope (step two). The goal is to exercise each public member function once and demonstrate a minimal level of functionality. The primary goal of the third step is to verify relationships among classes in a cluster or subsystem and exercise safety-related functionality. This is accomplished using the FREE test model, applied at cluster scope. At cluster scope, the transitions correspond to collaborations. System scope testing is done by an independent test group (the fourth step.)

Related Patterns

"Umbrella" and "depth-first" integration [Yourdon+79] are special cases of Collaboration Integration. In an umbrella, components included in an increment are selected according to their membership in a processing thread, an event–response path, or time-critical performance objectives. The components in a depth-first increment correspond to a root-to-leaf subtree of the dependency tree or control hierarchy. Successive increments correspond to subtrees. This approach may be useful if the collaborations require other collaborations. For example, in a simulation, several collaborations may be required to set up a model. Once the model is established, the simulation may be run in several ways. Each setup and test run corresponds to a collaboration, which in turn corresponds to a root-to-leaf subtree.

The "wave-front" approach defines a development increment as including only collaborations that can be tested with the fewest number of stubs. The goal is to define the scope of an increment by collaborations that are "sufficient for all dependent classes to achieve their negotiated level of behavior" [McGregor+94].

Backbone Integration

Intent

This pattern combines elements of *Top-down Integration*, *Bottom-up Integration*, and *Big Bang Integration* to verify interoperability among tightly coupled subsystems.

Context

Embedded system applications and their infrastructure (e.g., a real-time executive kernel or **backbone**[5]) are often developed at the same time.

- The application system cannot operate without the backbone.
- The backbone provides services that are essential for running tests and the application.
- Attempting to stub the entire backbone would be impractical or would require very complex stubs. The stubs would be either too costly or of dubious fidelity.
- The high-level control strategy can be exercised with stubs for the upper and middle levels.
- The middle level consists of several clusters that have loose intercluster coupling, but tight intracluster coupling.

At first glance, it might seem that this situation presents a Catch-22 testing problem: How can the application be run if the backbone is incomplete? In fact, "the backbone is the best possible test engine. The stragety is to create a backbone that permits further testing. The focus of testing moves from the deep infrastructure outward to the application components and functionality."[6] Backbone Integration verifies interoperability in a system that has a distinct locus of control, relies on many services of a complex virtual machine, and uses several independent clusters to implement the balance of system responsibilities.

Fault Model

See Section 13.1.4, Integration Faults.

---

5. *Backbone* as an integration metaphor is due to [Beizer 84].
6. Boris Beizer, private communication, March 1999.

Strategy

Test Model

Backbone Integration combines elements of *Top-down Integration*, *Bottom-up Integration*, and *Big Bang Integration*. The test design problem is to first identify the components that support application control, the backbone, and application subsystems. The sequence of testing is based on this analysis.

- The top and possibly the second level of control are tested top-down, using *Mode Machine Test*, *Round-trip Scenario Test*, or *Collaboration Integration*. Interfaces to the backbone and other subsystems are replaced with proxies or stubs.
- The application subsystems are developed bottom-up using test design patterns indicated by the component responsibilities.
- The backbone components are tested in isolation under a driver and test design appropriate to their specific responsibilities.

The tested components (subsystems) are then big banged. The big bang test suite should include all control tests developed for the control component. Additional tests should be developed to cover scenarios implemented by application-specific subsystems.

Test Procedure

This backbone strategy interleaves several basic integration patterns.

1. Do adequate testing on each backbone component, in isolation. Use drivers and stubs as needed, as suggested in Figure 13.20. Achieve the exit criteria for the applicable test pattern.
2. Perform *Top-down Integration* on the application control components, as suggested in Figure 13.21. The resulting test suites/drivers should be designed to be reusable/rerunnable for subsequent integration.
3. Big bang the backbone: load it, accept nominal input, and shut it down. Repeat this cycle several times.
4. Exercise the big banged backbone under a driver. Use an appropriate subsystem design: *Mode Machine Test*, *Round-trip Scenario Test*, or *Collaboration Diagram*. Figure 13.22 shows the configuration for steps 3 and 4.

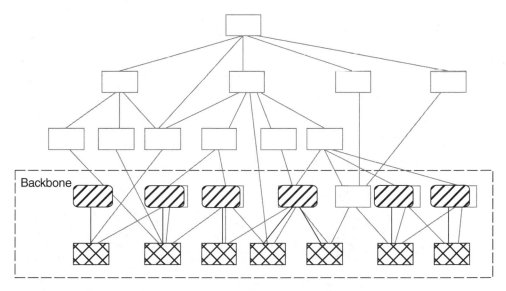

FIGURE 13.20   Backbone Integration, step 1.

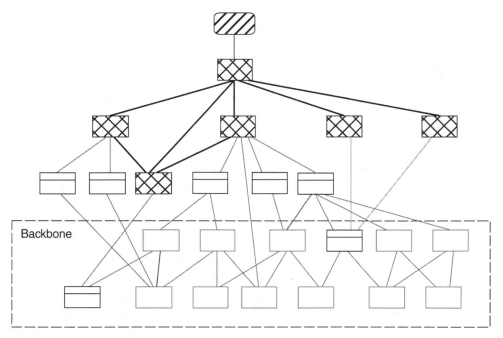

FIGURE 13.21   Backbone Integration, step 2.

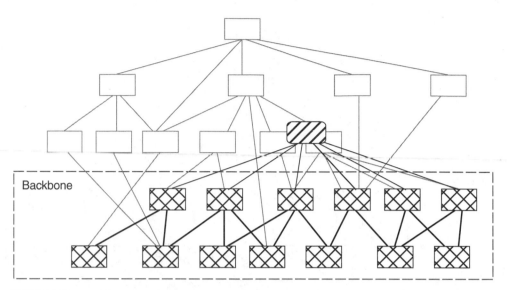

FIGURE 13.22 Backbone Integration, steps 3 and 4.

5. Rebuild the control subsystem with the backbone. Big bang the control components and the backbone; use the control test suite to exercise the interactions.

6. Use the top-down approach on the next level. Remove stubs for second-level components and implement the interfaces. Expand the control test suite to reach all newly implemented components and rerun the tests. Figure 13.23 shows the configuration for steps 5 and 6.

7. Use the top-down approach on the leaves. Remove stubs to any remaining subsystems and implement the interfaces. Expand the control test suite to reach all newly implemented components and rerun the tests. Rerun the control test suite, expanded to reach all backbone interfaces, as suggested in Figure 13.24.

These steps complete the first cycle. **High-frequency Integration** may be appropriate for subsequent cycles. Under incremental development, more capabilities will be added to each configuration. As these capabilities are added, the test suite should be revised and rerun.

The test cases for Backbone Integration may be developed at system scope by using an appropriate responsibility-based test design pattern. Use the oracle for this pattern.

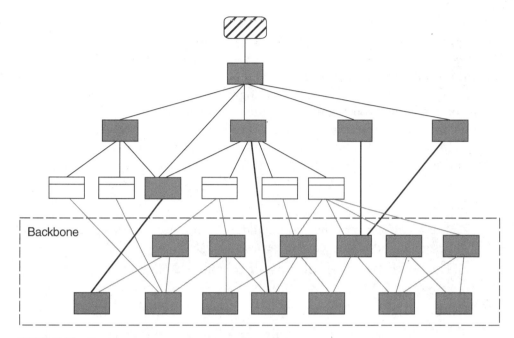

FIGURE 13.23   Backbone Integration, steps 5 and 6.

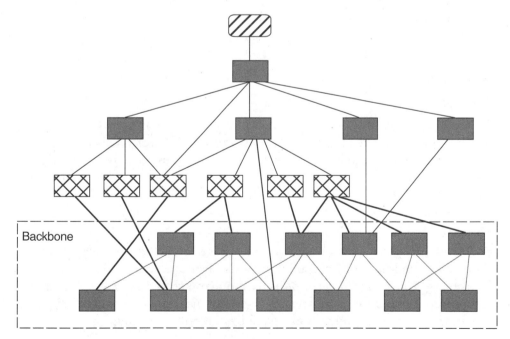

FIGURE 13.24   Backbone Integration, step 7.

Automation

This pattern requires drivers and stubs for the integration pattern applied to each configuration: stubs for clients of the control component, drivers for the application cluster components, and so on.

Verify that each successive test configuration is checked in and under version control before you begin developing a new configuration. A design change or bug fix will likely require revising and rerunning tests for configurations that have already passed. If the earlier configurations have not been saved, this process can be difficult with just the current configuration.

Entry Criteria

✓ The architecture of the system and all component interfaces have been designed and passed careful review.

✓ The backbone and application are roughly the same size and complexity.

Exit Criteria

✓ All components meet the exit criteria for the applied test pattern.

✓ Each intercomponent interface has been exercised at least once. Coverage analyzers will instrument and analyze call-pair traces, detailing exactly which interfaces have and have not been exercised.

✓ The complete increment passes a system scope test suite.

Consequences

Disadvantages

A careful analysis of system structure and dependencies is necessary. Backbone Integration requires development of both stubs *and* drivers. This approach assumes that the conditions for a successful Big Bang are acheived by adequate testing of the backbone components. If this prerequisite is not met, the problems discussed under *Big Bang Integration* are likely.

Advantages

Backbone Integration mitigates the disadvantages of *Top-down Integration* and *Bottom-up Integration* by curtailing their use at the point at which they lose effectiveness. *Top-down Integration* is used only on the upper control levels and *Bottom-up Integration* is restricted to the application subsystems. *Big Bang Integration* of the backbone is preceded by component testing.

An alternative to testing with a backbone is to develop a backbone simulator. Although this approach is common for embedded systems, simulators are often low-fidelity approximations of the backbone. Testing on a simulator can identify bugs that are a result of the simulator but miss bugs that the simulator cannot trigger. Using the actual backbone avoids these problems and the development cost of a simulator.

Integration begins on the early side of the midpoint in development. Minimal system operability will be demonstrated roughly halfway, reducing the risk of a big fizzle at the end of the cycle. Development and testing of components and subsystems may proceed in parallel until the first major integration.

Known Uses

The development of Windows NT can be characterized as a Backbone Integration followed by *High-frequency Integration* [Zachary 94]. Backbone Integration is a good fit for developing the "executable architecture" to be produced in the design phase in Booch's macro process [Booch 96].

DataVision CAD System

A hierarchical, incremental integration strategy was successful for DataVision's computer-aided design (CAD) system implemented with 1 MLOC of C++ [Thuy 92]. Early integration testing was effective, but had to deal with incomplete components. The alternative—waiting for all components to be in hand (*Big Bang Integration*)—was unacceptable. It would have required the entire system to be available and running, implying integration late in development. Debugging at this stage is difficult and time-consuming.

A hierarchical approach to both design *and* testing was therefore followed. The lowest level was a *package* of classes (any cohesive logical or physical group): a kind of high-level module. Public member functions provided the package interface. Packages were organized into libraries and engines. There were fewer than 10 engines for the entire DataVision system. Dependencies that crossed component boundaries were a significant problem. A dependency exists when each of two or more classes cannot function without a full implementation of the other.

> . . . It is difficult and extremely costly to test a component really independently of the components it depends on. That implies replacing those components by stubs, for which the reliability is not guaranteed and for which the costs and delays are very high. It is on the other hand possible and acceptable to test a component when those it depends on have themselves been tested. [This can be done if there are no dependence cycles, so] *there must be no large scale dependence cycle* [sic] [Thuy 92, 4-T-1-5].

Dependencies among components (at any level) complicate integration testing. Thus, dependencies and side effects should be removed, if at all possible. Thuy notes that if dependencies are unavoidable between components at a given level, they should be contained within a single higher-level component.

Related Patterns

Myers's *Sandwich* integration calls for a combination of Top-down and Bottom-up Integration, with the final configuration meeting in the middle [Myers 76]. The backbone strategy is similar, but requires more testing of components in isolation [Beizer 84].

Layer Integration

Intent

Layer Integration uses an incremental approach to verify stability in a layered architecture.

Context

Layer Integration verifies interoperability in a system that can be modeled as a hierarchy that allows interfaces only between adjacent layers. That is, the top layer does not send messages to the bottom layer, and vice versa. Instead, the top layer sends messages to the middle layer and the middle layer sends messages to the bottom layer. (For examples of this architecture, see *Layers* [Buschmann+96] and *Recursive Control* [Selic 98].)

Fault Model

See Section 13.1.4, Integration Faults. The layered model is popular for device interfaces and device drivers in embedded systems. Typically, propagation of a message through the layers must meet a hard, real-time deadline. Inadequate performance in a layered application is often a critical failure.

Strategy

Test Model

Layer Integration combines elements of *Top-down Integration* and *Bottom-up Integration*. The test design must identify the layers and determine which integration pattern applies to each layer. Test design and sequence of testing within a layer follows this pattern.

- The top layer and possibly the second layer are tested top-down, using *Mode Machine Test*, *Round-trip Scenario Test*, or *Collaboration Integration* to exercise control with stubs implementing the lower layer.
- The middle layer is developed bottom-up, using a test design appropriate to its specific responsibilities.
- The primary components of the bottom layer are tested in isolation, using a test design appropriate to its specific responsibilities.

All the control threads already tested for the top layer should be rerun when each lower-level test suite is added. The test suite should exercise all collaborations that traverse all layers.

Test Procedure

Layer Integration may be top-down or bottom-up. A top-down approach takes the following steps:

1. Test each layer in isolation. Use drivers as needed. Achieve the exit criteria for the pattern of choice. Figure 13.25 depicts layer isolation test configurations.
2. Perform **Top-down Integration** of layers. The resulting test suites/ drivers should be designed to be reusable/rerunnable for subsequent integration.
3. Use a top-down approach on the next layer. Remove stubs to second-level subsystems and implement the interfaces. Expand the control test suite to reach all newly implemented components and rerun the tests.

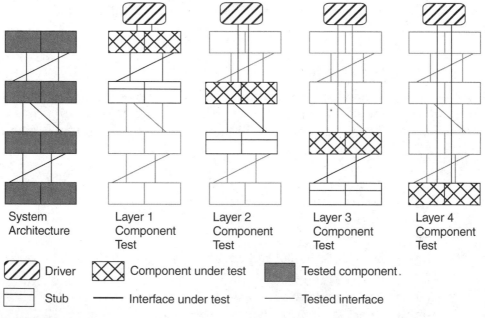

FIGURE 13.25 Layer Integration, architecture and component test configuration.

4. After the interfaces in each layer have passed, remove any stubs and implement the interfaces to the next layer.

Figure 13.26 gives the test configurations for a ***Top-down Integration*** approach. A ***Bottom-up Integration*** approach would reverse the order, beginning with the lowest-level layer and working toward the top.

The test cases for Layer Integration may be developed at system scope by using an appropriate responsibility-based test design pattern. Use the oracle for this pattern.

Automation

This pattern requires drivers and stubs for each layer. The driver for the top layer should be designed so that it can exercise the entire system.

Verify that each successive test configuration is checked in and under version control before you begin developing a new configuration. A design change or bug fix will likely require revising and rerunning tests for configurations that have already passed. If the earlier configurations have not been saved, this process can be difficult with just the current configuration.

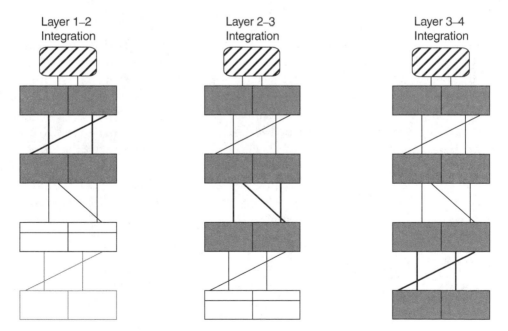

FIGURE 13.26   Layer Integration, top-down configurations.

Entry Criteria

✓ The virtual machine to be used in the test environment is stable. If the virtual machine is under development, consider *Backbone Integration*.

✓ The components of the collaboration are minimally operable. That is, they should have met the exit criteria for the appropriate component scope test pattern.

✓ A physical, functional, and environmental audit has been conducted and has not found any anomalies that would interfere with integration testing.

Exit Criteria

✓ Each driven component meets the exit criteria for its test pattern.

✓ Each collaboration that traverses two or more layers has been exercised once. Coverage analyzers will instrument and analyze call-pair traces, detailing exactly which interfaces have and have not been exercised.

Consequences

The advantages and disadvantages of Layer Integration are similar to those of *Top-down Integration* (for the top-down variant) and *Bottom-up Integration* (for the bottom-up variant). The bottom-up variant requires drivers for each layer and reduces the number of stubs needed. The complete behavior cannot be demonstrated until the top layer has been integrated. Nevertheless, the proximity of drivers to the layer under test will impose the fewest obstacles.

The top-down variant requires stubs for lower layers but only a single driver. If the stack of layers is needed as a subsystem, this approach can provide a working interface for integration to the clients of the top layer at the earliest possible date. Nevertheless, the viability of the stack is not demonstrated until the lowest layer is integrated. Because layered applications are often used in time-critical applications, this delay may pose a risk in that the performance of the stack will not be demonstrated until the end of the integration cycle.

Known Uses

Scope-specific applications in object-oriented development are discussed later in this chapter. Protocol stacks are a widely used layered application. Holzmann provides an excellent overview of state-based testing strategies for such stacks [Holzmann 91].

Client/Server Integration

Intent

Demonstrate the stability of the interactions among clients and servers. Begin by testing clients and servers in isolation, then use controlled increases in scope until all interfaces have been exercised.

Context

The Client/Server Integration sequence achieves stepwise verification of the interfaces between client components that are loosely coupled to a single server component. Concurrent development and testing are possible.

   The system under test is a variant of a client/server architecture. Unlike in the top-down situation, no single locus of control exists. Servers react to client messages, and clients react to messages from the system's environment. Each component of the system has its own control strategy. Components that have a single locus of control may be integrated using *Bottom-up Integration*, *Top-down Integration*, or *Collaboration Integration*.

Fault Model

See Section 13.1.4, Integration Faults.

Strategy

Test Model

The test plan must identify clients and servers. Client/server interaction may be modeled with any appropriate test design pattern. Both *Extended Use Case Test* and *Round-trip Scenario Test* will apply. In a two-tier star, the basic integration strategy is to exercise client–server pairs. In a three-tier star, we exercise client–server and server–server configurations, followed by client–server–server configurations.

Test Procedure

Each client is tested with a stub for the server. The server is tested with stubs for all client types. Next, pairs of clients are tested with the actual server. The server may retain some stubs for other clients. Finally, all stubs are removed and the individual use case tests are replayed.

Figure 13.27 depicts generic two-tier star. With a large system, it may not be practical to integrate every unique client individually. Instead, client groups can be identified. Members in a client group should have similar server interfaces. A two-tier client/server star integration follows a three-step procedure for each client group:

1. Representative client + server stub
2. Server + client stub
3. Representative client + server

Figure 13.28 shows the configurations that correspond to these stages.

Client/Server Integration can also be applied recursively to three-tier or *n*-tier client/server architecture. Figure 13.29 illustrates a generic three-tier star.

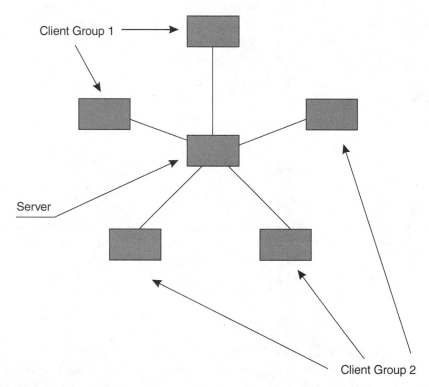

FIGURE 13.27 Generic star client/server architecture.

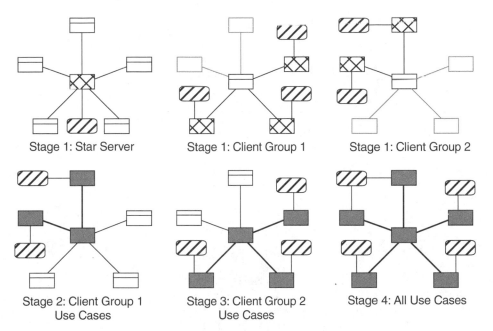

FIGURE 13.28   Client/Server Integration, stages and configurations.

For example, the procedure for a three-tier client/server star integration using an object request broker is roughly as follows:

1. Client group + ORB
2. Server + ORB
3. Client group + ORB + server proxy
4. Server + ORB + client proxy
5. Client + ORB + server (repeated for client groups)

The test cases for a Client/Server Integration may be developed at system scope by using an appropriate responsibility-based test design pattern. Use the oracle for this pattern.

Automation

The interface of the component under test will determine the kind of driver used (GUI capture/playback, API, and so on). Test scripts developed for a stage should be designed to support two kinds of reuse. First, they should be repeatable to support regression testing upon the integration of more components.

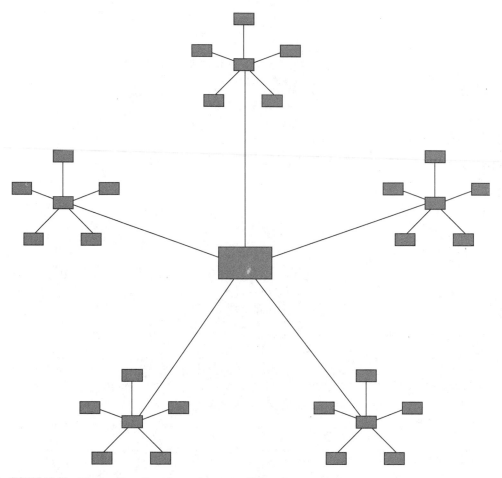

FIGURE 13.29   Three-tier client/server star architecture.

Second, they should be extensible so that system scope tests may be added after the final integration testing is completed.

Verify that each successive test configuration is checked in and under version control before you begin developing a new configuration. A design change or bug fix will likely require revising and rerunning tests for configurations that have already passed. If the earlier configurations have not been saved, this process can be difficult with just the current configuration.

Client/server systems are often multiplatform-based. For example, they may use mainframe MVS servers, AIX servers, Windows clients, Solaris servers, Java clients running on any Java Virtual Machine, and so on. A primary goal of

Client/Server Integration testing should be to reveal and correct interoperability problems. Multiplatform integration requires a controllable test environment that spans all platforms in the target environment. Typically, however, debugging and testing tools are platform-specific. Thus it may be difficult to perform controlled testing and debugging of system threads that span several platforms.

The initial test configuration can be a simplified version of the target environment. Integration should not be considered complete, however, until all test suites pass when run in a test environment that uses the same architecture, middleware, and network operating system as the target environment. For example, suppose that the target environment for the SUT is a three-tier architecture supporting international e-commerce. Passing a test suite on a simplified two-tier approximation of the target environment may be a useful first step, but it should not be considered an adequate integration test of the application and the target environment. An **isomorphic** test environment replicates the structure of the architecture and the capabilities of the target environment, if not its scale.

Careful planning for integration test support is important. Choose one platform to support your testing effort. Next, place your primary test repository on this platform. Then, develop reliable interfaces from your test repository to the test tools on each platform. If you have not already set up and tested this kind of environment, allow extra time during integration testing to do so. Besides typical testing tasks, this effort often requires defining, loading, and synchronizing databases, securing access across gateways, bridges, and routers, and establishing name control. The coordination of production and test environment typically becomes correspondingly more complex. A robust, multiplatform configuration management system is indispensable.

Entry Criteria

✓ The virtual machine to be used in the test environment is stable. If the virtual machine is under development, consider *Backbone Integration*.

✓ The components of the collaborations to be tested are minimally operable. That is, they should have met the exit criteria for the appropriate component scope test pattern.

✓ A physical, functional, and environmental audit has been conducted and has not found any anomalies that would interfere with integration testing.

✓ A multiplatform test tool suite has been installed and shown to work.

✓ A multiplatform version control system has been installed and is being used.

Exit Criteria

✓ Each driven component meets the exit criteria for its test pattern.

✓ The interface to each subcomponent has been exercised at least once. Coverage analyzers are of limited use because they typically cannot instrument call-pair traces over the scope of an entire system, but are instead limited to the scope of the client or server process or a virtual machine running on a platform. Nevertheless, some effort should be made to establish coverage of each end-to-end path.

✓ The test suite passes in a test environment that is isomorphic with respect to the target environment.

Consequences

The disadvantages of Client/Server Integration are in the cost of driver and stub development. Testers cannot exercise end-to-end use cases until midway or late in the testing cycle.

The advantages of Client/Server Integration are that it avoids the problems of *Big Bang Integration*. The order of client and server integration usually has few constraints, so integration can be sequenced according to priority or risk. A Client/Server Integration test suite provides a basis for system scope testing— drivers and test cases can typically be reused and extended. The approach supports controllable, repeatable testing.

Known Uses

The integration experience of Mead Data Central (MDC) illustrates Client/ Server Integration [Arnold+94]. MDC offers an online, computer-aided research product for legal, financial, medical, news, and business topics. The system must provide rapid search response times, high availability (24×7, except for a short daily downtime window), accurate and repeatable results, and timely print delivery. The target environment incorporates IBM mainframe systems under the MVS operating system plus many Unix systems.

Testing was integrated with design and programming. Unit (class) white box testing was a developer responsibility. A test package was developed for each class, shortly after the definition of the class interface. Each developer was required to produce test components with the application class code. The test package included a driver for the class (with embedded test cases) and a file containing expected output.

Early definition of public interfaces permitted early development of test-driver interfaces. Successive class versions tended to have more similarities than differences. This consistently eased automation of the generation and execution of regression tests. The scope of unit testing was a C++ class or class cluster. No particular strategy for unit test was reported. On completion of unit testing, several levels of integration testing were performed:

- Single Unix process
- Intraplatform thread (e.g., several Unix processes)
- Interplatform thread (e.g., PC/Unix/MVS)

Integration tests were devised by choosing external inputs that corresponded to specific threads of execution.

Arnold et al. identified several key lessons learned from testing this system [Arnold+94]. Class unit testing is relatively easy because test tools work well with individual classes. Unit testing can therefore concentrate on compliance to specifications.

- Individual methods tend to have simple behavior, so they are testable.
- Because the class interface is typically defined before the implementation is developed, the corresponding test drivers can be developed in parallel.
- Test drivers developed for higher-level classes can usually be reused with a few changes for lower-level classes in the same hierarchy.
- Test drivers can "grow" along with the application classes, thus enabling iterative and incremental development.

On the other hand, unit testing could sometimes be problematic. Some class-level obstacles to testability were identified:

- Complex behaviors and component parts
- Attempts to reuse code outside of the contexts envisioned by the designer
- Use of non-OO software for implementation with side effects due to diminished or nonexistent encapsulation

Integration testing (at all levels) was difficult. The compounded effect of differences at all levels proved challenging.

- The effectiveness of available commercial test tools diminishes on large systems (thousands of components).

- Inconsistency across class libraries is problematic. The only way to remove these inconsistencies is by adhering to standards enforced by design and code reviews. Problems noted in this implementation included different approaches to encapsulation and implementation of overloaded operators for collection classes.

- Many commercial classes were not thread-safe. That is, they were not explicitly reentrant, and control of resources under concurrency was not addressed or was incorrect.

- Debugging and testing tools are platform-specific. It was therefore difficult to perform controlled testing and debugging of threads that crossed platforms (e.g., MVS and Unix).

- Impedance mismatch occurs between OO design and client/server architecture. Available client/server interfaces or APIs may be inconsistent with typical OO class architecture.

- The DCE and C++ exception semantics are different. It was difficult to perform controlled testing of exception handling.

Recent test tool offerings have reduced the severity of these problems, but adequate integration of a large client/server system remains challenging.

Distributed Services Integration

Intent

Demonstrate the stability of interaction among loosely coupled peer components. Begin by testing some nodes in isolation, then use controlled increases in scope until all interfaces have been exercised.

Context

Distributed Services Integration is indicated when the system under test includes many components that run concurrently with no single locus of control and where there is no single hierarchy of servers.[7]

Fault Model

Integration testing is not concerned with all the ways in which a distributed system may fail, but rather concentrates on those preventing effective execution of system scope testing. The list developed in Section 13.1.4, Integration Faults, covers many general kinds of problems that can occur.

Integration faults in distributed systems are often related to incorrect binding of servers and clients. Leslie Lamport provides a qualitative hint of the kind of faults that can occur in distributed systems: "A distributed computing system is one in which your machine can be rendered unusable by the failure of some other machine you didn't even know existed" [*Communications of the ACM,* June 1992].

Strategy

Test Model

Integration testing of a distributed system is concerned with verifying that interfaces among remote hosts are minimally operable. Finding a test suite that gives adequate confidence in the aggregate behavior of a distributed system is a much more difficult problem.

---

7. Concurrent, distributed, and decentralized software systems have been in use since the early 1960s. Although some advocates of object-oriented technologies make much of "topless" architecture, with the exception of ADA 95, general-purpose object-oriented programming languages do not provide built-in support for distributed processing. Indeed, it is only in the last five years that object request brokers and distributed object models have become widely adopted and only by using ORBs and related middleware.

The worst case for interface verification is that every node is connected to every other node and that each interface is unique—for example, with nodes A, B, and C, the interfaces are AB, BA, BC, CB, CA, and AC. If there are n nodes, then there are $n(n-1)$ interfaces. If the directionality of the interface is irrelevant in all cases, then there are $(n(n-1))/2$ interfaces. The scope of testing is therefore proportional to the number of interfaces that must be operable to support system testing.

As there is no single locus of control, there are many sequences in which component interfaces may be tested. Here are a few options:

- *Risk-driven.* Begin with interfaces and components that are most likely to be problematic. Flushing out expensive or possibly catastrophic problems earlier will reduce the risk that a major problem will necessitate a schedule slip or cancellation at the last minute. The initial focus targets interfaces that depend on components, objects, middleware, or other resources that (1) are individually unstable or unproven, (2) have not been shown to work together before or are known to be unstable, (3) implement complex business rules, (4) have a complex implementation (e.g., are 10 times the code size of all other components), or (5) have been subject to high churn during development.

- *Risk-averse.* Begin with interfaces and components that are least likely to be problematic. Attempt to demonstrate minimal operability as soon as possible. If expensive or possibly catastrophic problems emerge later, the minimal capabilities can be shipped. The initial focus is on interfaces that depend on components, objects, middleware, or other resources that (1) are individually stable and proven, (2) have been shown to work together before or are known to be stable, (3) implement simple business rules, (4) have a low implementation complexity or size, or (5) are being reused with no change.

- *Dependency-driven.* Begin with interfaces and components that can be exercised in isolation or that depend on the fewest other components. Establish their operability. Next, identify use cases that this set supports or nearly supports. Incorporate the additional components to support these use cases and run minimal use case tests. Continue in this manner until all interfaces have been exercised.

- *Priority-driven.* Begin with interfaces and components that are required to demonstrate high-priority capabilities (not a priority as relates to real-time task scheduling, but rather system features that must be demonstrated to obtain project funding, for example). Establish operability of these high-priority features. Next, select other feature sets or interface sets that will exercise all other interfaces with the fewest tests.

The content of test cases for Distributed Services Integration may be developed at system scope by using an appropriate responsibility-based test design pattern. Internode collaborations may be modeled with any appropriate test design pattern. Both *Extended Use Case Test* and *Round-trip Scenario Test* will probably apply. Use the oracle for the applicable pattern.

Test Procedure

Although the general goals and strategy for integration testing of distributed and nondistributed systems are much the same, controlling and observing components on remote hosts can be time-consuming and difficult. When several different operating systems (or versions of the same OS) are added to the mix, there are often significant interoperability problems.

When a test does not run for a distributed system (as frequently happens), we want to find the cause quickly. Did it fail because of a test environment configuration problem? A testware bug? A test case bug? Or (we hope) a bug in the IUT? The following principles will help in making this determination:

• *Partition your test suite into separately executable test suites that are host/node-independent and host/node-dependent.* All test suites must be automated and fully repeatable.

• *Develop a configuration specification for each typical remote host site.* A typical remote host configuration represents a class of possible remote hosts. During integration testing it is rarely necessary to exercise every physical instance of a remote host, of which there may be tens of thousands. Nevertheless, each kind of host with a significantly different hardware/software platform and significantly different allocation of application components should be considered a distinct configuration. Develop scripts that will reset each typical remote host into a known stable state and that will set the IUT components allocated to this host into a known stable state. These scripts should be separately executable.

• *Verify that the testware that implements your test harness will run on all typical remote hosts.* Attempt to install and run it on each remote host in your test environment. As simple as this process sounds, it is often a full-time job for several people, taking several months. Do not underestimate the difficulty of configuring your test environment.

• *Debug your test suite and testware on the simplest possible configuration, first.* Try to exercise the basic distributed object interfaces on a single machine or a stable, homogeneous client/server configuration. This will ease debugging and result in a baseline test suite. Once your baseline test suite is stable for this configuration, you are ready to test additional hosts/nodes.

• *Add typical remote hosts **one at a time** to the test configuration.* Generate the IUT in a known stable state on each additional host and attempt to rerun the host-independent baseline test suite. Then run host-dependent tests. Add host-specific tests as you go, but do not bundle them with the stable baseline.

• *Stop when you have exercised all targeted interfaces and typical remote host types.* The goal of integration testing is to establish an IUT and test environment that is sufficiently stable to support system scope testing. Integration testing should not attempt to verify all functionality, distributed fault tolerance, or performance under nominal and stress loads. It may be useful to identify a minimum spanning tree [Deo 74] for the logical network interfaces.

For example, consider the architecture of the IUT shown in Figure 13.30. Six typical remote hosts are modeled. Some have locally controlled interfaces (a

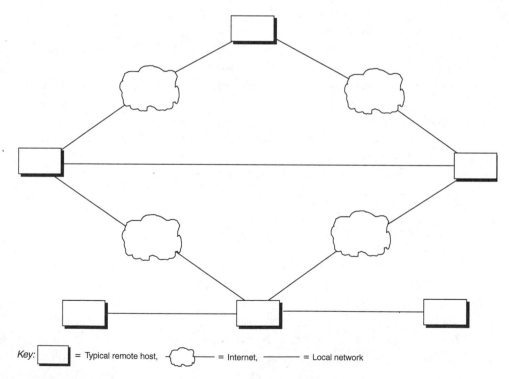

Key: ☐ = Typical remote host, ⌇◯⌇—— = Internet, ———— = Local network

FIGURE 13.30 Example distributed architecture.

solid line); others use the Internet (cloud). The one-at-a-time progression is suggested in Figure 13.31. Note that some stubs may be necessary. This diagram also includes a single driver, which shows that tests are controlled from one platform. Additional testware and drivers will probably be needed for each remote host, but are not shown to simplify this diagram. At stage 6, all typical remote hosts have been verified, but some interfaces may not have been exercised. Test cases should be added to cover any untested interfaces among remote hosts.

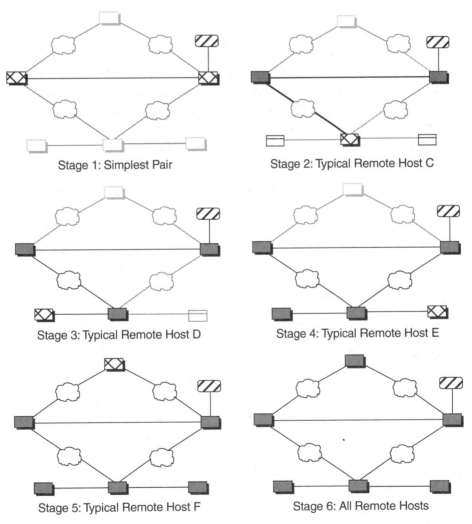

FIGURE 13.31   Stages and configurations for integration of distributed remote hosts.

Automation

The considerations for client/server test automation discussed in *Client/Server Integration* apply. The interface of the component under test will determine what kind of driver can be used (GUI capture/playback, API, and so on). Test scripts should be designed to support two kinds of reuse. First, they should be repeatable to support regression testing as more components are integrated. Second, they should be extensible so that system scope tests may be added after the final integration testing is completed.

Several COTS tools are available that can generate an exact binary image of an entire hard disk on a remote host. These utilities, which were originally developed to support automated software installation, are also useful for setting a remote host to a known stable state before running a test suite.

CORBA implementations using an ORB typically can enable filters that will write a log as services are requested and fulfilled.

Verify that each successive test configuration is checked in and under version control before you begin developing a new configuration. A design change or bug fix will likely require revising and rerunning tests for configurations that have already passed. If the earlier configurations have not been saved, this process can be difficult with just the current configuration.

Entry Criteria

- ✓ The virtual machine to be used in the test environment is stable. If the virtual machine is under development, consider *Backbone Integration*.

- ✓ The components of the collaborations to be tested are minimally operable. That is, they should have met the exit criteria for the appropriate component scope test pattern.

- ✓ A physical, functional, and environmental audit has been conducted and has not found any anomalies that would interfere with integration testing.

- ✓ A multiplatform test tool suite has been installed and shown to work.

- ✓ A multiplatform version control system has been installed and is being used.

- ✓ The typical remote host configurations have been specified, installed, and tested.

- ✓ The testware of choice has been installed and configured on each remote host.

Exit Criteria

✓ The responsibility-based exit criteria meet the requirements of the test patterns used to develop test case content. Because integration testing does not require completely exercising all features, the extent of the responsibilities used for integration test design should be limited to a practical minimum.

✓ The interface to each component on each typical remote host is exercised at least once. Source code coverage analyzers are of limited use because they typically cannot instrument call-pair traces over the scope of an entire system; instead, they are limited to the scope of the client or server process or a virtual machine running on a platform. Nevertheless, some effort should be made to establish coverage of each end-to-end path.

✓ The test suite passes in a test environment that is isomorphic with respect to the target environment.

Consequences

The disadvantages of Distributed Services Integration are in the cost of driver and stub development and establishing the entire test environment. Testers are not able to exercise end-to-end use cases until midway to late in the testing cycle. Establishing a stable test environment populated with typical remote hosts can be difficult, expensive, and time-consuming.

The advantages of Distributed Services Integration are that it avoids the problems of *Big Bang Integration*. The order of client and server integration usually has few constraints, so integration can be sequenced according to priority or risk. A Distributed Services Integration test suite provides a basis for system scope testing—drivers, test cases, and the test environment can typically be reused and extended. The approach supports controllable, repeatable testing.

Known Uses

Elements of this pattern can be found in many reports on testing of large systems [Arnold+94, Vines 98].

High-frequency Integration

Intent

Integrate new code with a stabilized baseline frequently to prevent integration bugs from going undiscovered and to prevent divergence from the working, stabilized baseline.

Context

Rapid iterative incremental development can result in missing or conflicting capabilities. The system under development might pass a minimal integration test suite, but new code is being rapidly developed. If a large volume of code is produced without checking for such problems, making the necessary changes late in a project is usually difficult and expensive. Frequent integration can prevent the unnoticed festering of such problems. The following conditions are necessary for beginning a High-frequency Integration regime:

- A stable increment is available; and some subset of the system under development can be run without trouble. This point of stability may be reached very early with just a few classes using a *Top-down Integration* pattern.

- Most meaningful functional increments can be produced within the frequency interval. That is, if the integration frequency is daily, it makes sense to size development increments to code that can be produced in one day by one programmer.

- The test suite is developed in parallel with code and kept current. The development of the integration test suite cannot be deferred. Instead, it must be available for the first integration cycle and maintained for each succeeding cycle.

- High-frequency Integration must be automated. There must be a reliable means for running and rerunning the integration test scripts. This goal can be accomplished with commercially available GUI capture/playback tools, development of test driver classes, or more exotic test harnesses.

- A configuration management tool must be installed and routinely used. Without effective configuration management, the proliferation of versions in high-frequency development will become unmanageable.

Fault Model

See Section 13.1.4, Integration Faults. The implicit fault model is that new code will most likely be buggy.

Strategy

Test Model

Tests may be developed using any appropriate system scope test pattern: ***Collaboration Integration, Round-trip Scenario Test, Covered in CRUD***.

McConnell argues for "smoke tests" that "exercise the entire system from end to end. It does not have to be exhaustive, but it should be capable of exposing major problems. The smoke test should be thorough enough that if the build passes, you can assume that it is stable enough to be tested more thoroughly" [McConnell 96, 143]. These tests should correspond to collaborations.

The scope of the build effort and the integration must include all components undergoing active development. If some developers do not participate the value of high frequency diminishes to the extent that the excluded code contains critical interfaces with the rest of the system.

It should be noted that getting a clean compile, a clean link, and passing various static analyzers is not testing. High-frequency compiling and linking is not High-frequency Integration. The IUT must be loaded and test suites must be executed. Expected and actual results must be compared.

Test Procedure

High-frequency Integration has three main steps.

First, the developers produce code deltas to be integrated and associated test suites. They perform the following tasks:

- Write or revise the code, working on a private branch.
- Write or revise a test suite for the code.
- Desk check, review, or inspect the changed component.
- Desk check, review, or inspect the test suite.
- Run all forms of static analysis and resolve all errors. Check in the changed component so that the configuration management system will search for conflicts with other versions or change packages. Run any other applicable source code analyzers.
- Compile and build the changed code.
- Run the test suite. Use a memory leak detector, if applicable.

- When the component passes all tests, check in the revised code and test suite to the development integration branch.

Second, the build tester aggregates the developer changes and runs an integration test suite:

- At an agreed-on regular interval, the person responsible for running the integration stops accepting deltas and builds a new system. If assertions have been developed (see Chapter 17), they should be enabled.
- When the build is completed successfully, the test suites are run. This testing will include smoke tests, newly developed tests, and as many existing test suites as time permits.

Third, the results are evaluated. McConnell comments: "Fix any problems immediately! If the build team discovers any errors that prevent the build from being tested (that break the build), it notifies the developer who checked in the code that broke the build, and that developer fixes the problem immediately. Fixing the build is the project's top priority" [McConnell 96].

An effective High-frequency Integration process will have a workable resolution for the following process issues:

- Who is responsible for maintaining the existing test suite? As the system evolves, some test suites will become obsolete. Some will be "broken" because the IUT interface will change, but the functionality will not.
- What is the build cycle? What is the deadline for accepting a change?
- Who may run the build and the integration test? Under what circumstances?
- What follow-up actions are taken when the build fails due to a link error or a test does not pass? To which version will the system revert? How will problem determination be done and how will a person or organization be assigned the task of correcting the problem?

The test cases for High-frequency Integration may be developed at system scope by using an appropriate responsibility-based test design pattern. Use the oracle for this pattern. Smoke tests typically do not require an oracle or evaluation, because if the IUT runs to normal termination, the smoke test is considered passed.

Automation

The daily build is often run overnight by script or batch job—for example, a Unix `cron(1)` job. The entire test suite (and the merge and build commands) must be automated to support frequent repetition. The ability to report a no pass test and continue is necessary for this kind of testing. Because the test suites often run unattended overnight, the ability to continue after a no pass result or crashed application is critical. Thus, the test tools must be able to rerun existing tests as well as newly developed tests.

Verify that each successive test configuration is checked in and under version control before you begin developing a new configuration. A design change or bug fix will likely require revising and rerunning tests for configurations that have already passed. If the existing configurations have not been saved, this process can be difficult with just the current configuration.

Entry Criteria

Several conditions should be achieved before attempting a High-frequency Integration process.

- ✓ The virtual machine to be used in the test environment is stable.
- ✓ An automatically repeatable test suite has been developed for the build and the test harness to execute it has been developed and tested.
- ✓ High-frequency Integration may begin when there are enough components to integrate. Typically, this stage corresponds to one complete collaboration or completion of the high-level control objects.
- ✓ The components are under automated configuration management control and a successful build can be generated from this configuration.
- ✓ Clear, unambiguous criteria and procedures for adding a component to the build have been established, verified, and communicated to all interested parties.
- ✓ A cutoff time for the cycle is established. It should be at the same time (hour, day, week) to set the rhythm that is essential to this pattern.

Once the process has started, the procedure for adding components to the build must be followed by all developers.

- ✓ The submitted component should pass a component scope test suite.
- ✓ The submitted component must adhere to the configuration control procedures for the build.

✓ The submitted component must adhere to the established procedures for check-in, timeliness, and so on. If the procedures do not work, change them. Do not, however, dilute their effectiveness by waiving them on an ad hoc basis.

Exit Criteria

High-frequency Integration ceases when the development increment is completed and the SUT passes the integration suite for the last increment. Two possible cases exist.

✓ The High-frequency Integration test suites have been designed to achieve integration coverage. That is, the build tests include tests that would be developed using *Top-down Integration, Bottom-up Integration, Collaboration Integration, Client/Server Integration*, and so on. If the final test suite also meets the exit criteria for such a pattern, then the SUT is ready for system testing.

✓ The High-frequency Integration test suites have been designed to demonstrate minimal interoperability, but have not attempted to achieve integration coverage. Because the SUT has been exercised, it may actually be a simple matter to achieve an appropriate integration coverage. *Collaboration Integration* coverage will probably work best. When these exit criteria are met, then the SUT is ready for system testing.

Consequences

Disadvantages

High-frequency Integration requires a commitment to developing and maintaining both source code and a test suite (this requirement is also an advantage). The extra effort is why most users of this pattern stick to simple test suites. These test suites have questionable effectiveness, especially if the test suites are produced by developers who must pay a significant penalty when they "break" the build.

Attempting High-frequency Integration will reveal problems in both the process and procedures, as well as the IUT. The initial cycles are not apt to go smoothly. Identify and resolve any process problems quickly. The painful evolution of the now-fabled daily build process for Windows NT provides an instructive case study in such evolution, which spanned three years [Zachary 94].

A test suite that passes all or most of the time suggests that the *Pesticide Paradox* may be in effect [Beizer 90]. A test suite that passes has eliminated all bugs that it can, but certainly not all bugs. If no explicit adequacy criteria have been established for high-frequency testing, a long string of successful builds may lead to unwarranted confidence. The test suite used for High-frequency Integration should be revised to keep pace with new functionality developed for the IUT. Chapter 15 discusses considerations for test suite maintenance.

Advantages

High-frequency Integration offers significant advantages.

- It requires a commitment to developing and maintaining both source code and a test suite. The production of test suites and the production of code are of equal importance. This is an effective bug prevention strategy.

- Gross errors, omissions, and incorrect assumptions are often revealed early. The process "exposes the real (vs. the imagined) dependency tree" [McCarthy 95, 112].

- Because the most recent additions to the build are most likely to be associated with failures, debugging is usually easier.

- The entire development team is focused on producing a system that works, instead of working on a system. This approach will improve morale, as the team can see tangible results early.

- Although some stubs may be necessary, none are explicitly required. This approach avoids brittle and finicky test code.

- Development and integration testing can overlap to a high degree if the test suite includes more than simple smoke tests.

Known Uses

Rettig's Group

An "incremental glass box" testing process for Smalltalk development integrated new code as often as hourly [Rettig 91]. The test goals were to test every path once, develop and use reusable test procedures, perform all testing under peer review, and reduce the tedium of testing. Programmers were responsible for developing executable test plans, which were reviewed using a detailed test standard. A class `TestManager` was developed to execute a block of code and to complain in the event of an unexpected response. It had several output modes: log to a file, display on a window, start the debug tool. A

TestProcedure method was developed for each application class. It sent many messages to TestManager. The tests were run by entering

```
TestManager testClass: ClassUnderTest
```

Most classes "involved no more than one or two days of coding effort, followed by one or two days of writing test procedures. . . . When we complete a [class] and integrate the new code with the official version of the prototype, the TestManager is invaluable." A master procedure checked all classes, which facilitated testing of the entire system at any point in development. This test suite was rerun as soon as a class and its test procedure were complete.

The team produced roughly 50,000 lines of Smalltalk. Thirty percent of the total effort went into design and test case development, 33 percent into coding, and 33 percent into test and integration. In the course of testing, "we have had less than a dozen errors slip through the testing process and appear in a subsequent module. In my experience, that is remarkable" [Rettig 91, 28].

Windows NT 3.0

At its release, Microsoft Windows NT 3.0 consisted of 40,000 source files containing 5.6 million lines of C code. In response to chronic integration problems during its development, project manager David Cutler focused his attention on the build process and bug prevention. "His cure for bad check-ins called for brute force. He himself would become a sentry for quality, reviewing as many of the seventy-five to one hundred daily check-ins. . . . No amount of rhetoric could equal the example of Cutler's actions. 'If I'm in the build lab, that tells [the developer] I better not check-in ****.' " [Zachary 94, 181]. A complete build took as many as 19 hours on several machines, but a new build was produced every day. The process and the system stabilized after a year, and Cutler moved out of the build lab. "White's group turned out on average a build a day, seven days a week. Changes in the build were usually limited to bug fixes. Check-ins now assumed a ritualized pattern" [Zachary 94, 245]. Further commentary on this project and the institution of the daily build model at Microsoft is offered in [McCarthy 95] and [McConnell 96].

OS/400

A weekly build regimen was used in development of IBM's OS/400 operating system, which included 14,000 C++ classes and 20 million lines of C and C++ code.

A complete build of the project was performed once a week. After a programmer finished a class, the class was compiled and linked against the previous build, and then integrated into the next complete build. Although developers lost time finding defects on the weekly build day, this potential for lost time created a strong incentive to avoid defects within the development ranks since no one wanted to be known as the person who held up a particular week's build [Berg+95, 58].

AT&T

The *Named Stable Bases* pattern advocates High-frequency Integration and cites its application in an AT&T project that "had a nightly build (which was guaranteed only to compile), a weekly integration test build (which was guaranteed to pass system-wide sanity tests), and a (roughly biweekly) service test build (which was considered stable enough for QA's system test)" [Coplien+95, 224–225].

Extreme Programming

Extreme Programming is a highly iterative development process that requires (among other things) that executable test cases be developed with each class. High-frequency Integration, conducted several times per day, is an integral part of the approach. It has been deployed for several large Smalltalk applications.

> On C3 payroll, we use a practice we call Continuous Integration. Developers break their work down into tasks requiring about a day to do. They start from the currently released software, make their changes, run the tests, and integrate the changes into the currently released software. We do that multiple times a day. It's like the daily build times ten. The good news, of course, is that if you could make this work, your big bangs become little bangs, and littler and littler. Since we use Smalltalk, we can integrate in seconds rather than overnight. Since we have about 30,000 Unit Test checks, and a few hundred functional tests checking the whole system, we can be really sure that we didn't break anything. So when we release, we require that all the tests run perfectly, that is, that ZERO defects are shown. . . . Of course, we couldn't start this in the middle. But on the first day, it's not hard to release with all your tests at 100%. There aren't many. You just repeat every day. . . . we have over 2,000 classes, 30,000 methods, and we've been doing this for 2½ years with better results than any of us have ever seen before [Ron Jeffries, posted to the comp.software-eng newsgroup, December 6, 1998].

A published account of the C3 project appears in [Anderson+98]. Due to the nature of Smalltalk development environments, this kind of integration actually imports all other changes into each developer's workspace, rather than exporting changed code into a common repository.

13.3   Bibliographic Notes

Most of the Known Uses reports first appeared in [Binder 96i].

Myers summarizes and compares bottom-up, top-down, sandwich, and big bang integration [Myers 76]. An expanded analysis of Top-down Integration and Bottom-up Integration appears in [Myers 79]. Integration strategies corresponding to the architecture of modular systems are presented and compared in [Yourdon+79]. Beizer compares Bottom-up, Top-down, and Big Bang Integration and presents the backbone approach [Beizer 84]. McCabe presents a call path model based on analysis of intramodule and intermodule control flow and suggests a call path coverage for integration [McCabe+89]. Beizer reviews considerations for integration testing [Beizer 90].

The OOSE methodology offered the first practical approach to integration in object-oriented systems [Jacobson 92]. An advanced approach to dependency analysis and some implications for testing are presented in [Lieborherr+92]. Graham outlines a uses-based, bottom-up integration strategy [Graham+93]. Marick argues that testing should be done at (small) subsystem scope, implying subsystem Big Bang Integration followed by subsystem integration [Marick 95]. A general approach to integration appears in [Siegel 96]. Firesmith's *Test Stubs* and *Dependency-based Testing* patterns suggest how the subjects could be used to develop an integration test plan [Firesmith 96]. Lakos's analysis of C++ dependencies is an excellent guide to design-for-testability and integration test planning [Lakos 96].

Chapter 14   Application Systems

The whole is more than the sum of its parts.

Aristotle

> **Overview**
>
> This chapter presents three patterns for designing an application test suite from use cases. Because use cases are not a complete model of system capabilities, additional test strategies for implementation-specific capabilities are outlined.

14.1 Testing Application Systems

Effective testing at system scope requires a concrete and testable system-level specification. System test cases must be derived from some kind of functional specification. Traditionally, user documentation, product literature, line-item narrative requirements, and system scope models have been used. Use cases, augmented for testing, provide much of the information (but not all) needed to develop a complete system test suite. A complete system test suite also requires the kind of tests outlined in Section 14.3, Implementation-specific Capabilities.

14.1.1 A Cautionary Tale

The attorneys reminded Polly Morphic of the chorus in a Greek tragedy. A year ago, Abraxas's International Funds Transfer System (IFTS) had been the hot-bet technology among the masters of the universe, now represented by these gray wolves.[1] Looking back, it seemed that IFTS was doomed from the start. As chief technical officer, Polly had bet on object technology to beat Abraxas's competition. Once an object "worked," you were pretty much finished—Polly had seen this situation before and was sure her team could handle it again. The task was just as simple as finding enough of the right things to objectify and correctly craft the objects. The Abraxas staff was very good at making objects—development time would be halved, at least. The company's competitors were stuck with increasingly obsolete and brittle 1980s technology. Abraxas would win the time-to-market race. Then, they'd leverage object extensibility to stay ahead.

IFTS development had progressed rapidly. The team took pride in demonstrating correct processing of critical transactions. No further testing was needed: the developers *knew* the objects were right. They'd all *seen* the system working. IFTS was shipped on time, to the delight of all. But as key customers began to increase the use of IFTS, several highly visible failures occurred. Correspondent bank information that appeared to have been recorded correctly caused incorrect transaction processing. Accounts transferred among owners in certain countries produced bizarre results. The incident list grew, even as Abraxas corrected problems. Customer relations became tense, then acrimonious.

IFTS was dumped in less than a year. The final blow came when it was used to steal several hundred million dollars. Subsequent police investigations revealed that an Abraxas programmer had coded an undocumented transaction that circumvented normal audit and authentication. "That saved us a year of faking," he laughed. Within a month, no Abraxas customer was using IFTS.

On returning to her office, Polly knew that the customer's lawyers would be going ahead with the lawsuit. Instead of the planned public stock offering, Abraxas would now surely file for bankruptcy. She couldn't fix the moment when it had all gone too far, but it was clear they'd lost control without knowing it.

14.1.2 Testing Object-oriented Application Systems

The case of Abraxas is fictional, but it tells a common story. Abraxas ignored a fundamental truth of software testing: Individual verification of components

---

1. All names are fictional. Correspondence to any person or organization is coincidental and unintentional.

cannot guarantee a correctly functioning system. System scope failures can result from omissions and from interactions that cannot be produced until all components are exercised in the target environment. And even demonstrating that required capabilities are reliable does not guarantee that a system cannot do what it should not.

Clearly, the fact that an application system has an object-oriented pedigree does not excuse it from system testing. But are unique test design approaches required at system scope as they are at class, cluster, and component scopes? In a word, *no*. System test suites may be developed and run in much the same way as for a conventional implementation. System scope testing is based on requirements and capabilities that are mostly implementation-independent. That is, given the same requirements implemented in Java and Cobol, for example, the test design strategy would be mostly the same.

Some dimensions of system test design are necessarily implementation-specific, however.[2] First, capabilities that are tightly coupled to the implementation are not usually defined in feature-oriented requirements (see Section 14.3, Implementation-specific Capabilities). Second, the test harness must interact with the implementation. If the testable interface is a class API, an IDL binding, or an instantiation of a framework component, test design must reflect the implementation. Third, some system scope faults may be more likely (or unlikely) with an object-oriented implementation. If available, this information should be used. A pathological coupling can occur because adequate object-specific testing has been not been performed at a lower scope. This omission can force consideration of class and cluster scope testing concerns during system testing.

Even allowing for these differences, however, the bulk of the system test design problem is the same for all kinds of software systems. Basic system test design strategies are well established (see the Bibliographic Notes section).

---

2. These capabilities are sometimes referred to as "nonfunctional" requirements. I dislike this term as it is contradictory in the same way that "jumbo shrimp" is. McMenamin and Palmer introduced the notion of **essential capabilities** [McMenamin+84]. An essential capability is one that a system under development must provide to solve the application problem at hand. An essential model is limited to technology-independent capabilities. An **incarnation capability** is required only as a result of choosing a particular implementation technology. Cook and Daniels reinterpret "essential" to mean an implementation-independent model of the problem domain [Cook+94].

Several methodologists argue that these strategies can be applied to object-oriented implementations [Jacobson+92, Graham+93, Graham 94, Ambler 97]. In general, I agree.

Why, then, does a chapter on system testing appear in a book on object-oriented testing? Although system test design is mostly implementation-independent, it is closely tied to the representation of system capabilities. Use cases are the dominant representation of system scope capabilities in object-oriented development. The test design patterns in this chapter show how to develop a system test suite from use cases and outline how it should be augmented.

14.1.3   Application System Test Strategy

As noted in Chapter 13, I assume that object-oriented application systems are developed in several increments. System scope testing should begin after all components in an increment have passed integration testing. The scope of the system is the scope of the increment, so system scope testing may be conducted on each increment. Although release strategies vary, the last increment is typically the first one released to users or customers.

An **application system** is a collection of subsystems that cooperate to support a feature set intended for a user or customer. Testing an application system has three primary goals:

- To reveal bugs that are present only at system scope
- To demonstrate that the SUT implements all required capabilities
- To provide information to answer the question, "Can we ship it yet?"

Systematic, comprehensive testing at application system scope can achieve these goals. Except for trivial applications, these goals cannot be achieved by any other software engineering technique. Walkthroughs, reviews, and inspections on models and code do not exercise the actual system. Even passing a test suite that achieves minimum coverage at component or subsystem scope cannot attain these goals. System scope testing is necessary.

A **requirement** is a capability, feature, or function that the system must provide. A system scope test suite must be derived from a representation of capabilities visible at the system boundary (i.e., the system requirements). System test cases must be derived from an implementation-independent specification of capabilities. Typical sources of this information include the work products created in nearly all software development projects.

- Natural-language, line-item requirements
- System requirements models
- User interface prototypes, layouts, and models
- Functions identified to support function-point sizing and cost estimation
- Organization policy implemented as business objects, stored procedures or triggers, and so on
- Features described in product literature
- Features and procedures in documentation, help screens, or wizards

Complete, consistent, and testable requirements are necessary to develop an effective test suite. Myers' observation is as true today as it was over a quarter century ago: "If you do not have written objectives for your product, or if your objectives are unmeasurable, then you cannot perform system test" [Myers 76, 23]. Use cases can express most (but not all) of the system requirements in object-oriented development. Because UML use cases rely on unconstrained natural language, they are usually not test-ready. Correctly constructed extended use cases are inherently testable (see Section 8.3, Use Case Diagram).

Use cases should be designed to be testable. I recommend that you avoid reworking use cases to make them testable. Instead, develop extended use cases from the outset situation. Otherwise, you should develop extended use cases as soon as the nontestable use cases are available. In either situation, some additional work is necessary, but it pays off immediately by preventing bugs and producing a much better understanding of system requirements.

Procedure 17 outlines an overall approach to application system testing. Three test design patterns are presented here to develop test suites for essential capabilities. Although a test suite that meets the exit criteria of these patterns will provide a comprehensive exercise of an application system, these patterns do not address other important capabilities. The resulting test suite should be augmented with additional tests, as described in Section 14.3, Implementation-specific Capabilities.

1. Develop extended use cases for the entire system and testable, implementation-specific requirements as necessary.

2. Meet unit and integration exit criteria.

3. Develop use case suites per **Extended Use Case Test.**

4. If using **Allocate Tests by Profile:**
    Estimate the relative frequency of each use case.
    Estimate your testing productivity.
    Establish your system testing effort budget.
    Develop test cases in accordance with the resource allocation model.
    Fi

5. Run the test suite, debug, and perform regression testing.

6. Develop and run implementation-specific tests (configuration, performance, and so on).

7. Perform the execute-debug-retest cycle until a reliability objective is met, a stability objective is met, or the time and budget are gone.

8. Release the system.

Procedure 17   General System Test Strategy

14.2   Test Design Patterns

This section presents three patterns that can be used to develop a complete suite for the essential requirements of the SUT:

- *Extended Use Case Test.* Design test cases to exercise all relationships implied by a use case.
- *Covered in CRUD.* Identify operations on problem domain objects in the SUT that are not reached by a use case collaboration and exercise these operations.
- *Allocate Tests by Profile.* Develop a quantity of test cases in proportion to the operational frequency of use cases.

Extended Use Case Test

Intent

Develop an application system test suite by modeling essential capabilities as extended use cases.

Context

Extended Use Case Test applies when most, if not all, of the essential requirements for the SUT can be expressed as use cases. Use cases are not always the model of choice for essential system scope capabilities. For example, consider a complex simulation that runs for weeks on a supercomputer. The setup and inquiry for a simulation run could be modeled with use cases. However, these use cases could only hint at the algorithms used to compute and render the results with animated, high-resolution graphics.

It is possible to develop test cases by imagining specific ideas for a use case and corresponding expected results. Some examples of specific use case ideas appear in Table 14.1. Typically, a *very* large number of specific cases can be enumerated. Unless test points are systematically selected based on the use

TABLE 14.1　Some Use Cases and Scenarios for an Automatic Teller Machine

Use Case	Actor	Possible Input/Output Combinations
Establish Session	Bank customer	(1) Wrong PIN entered once; corrected PIN entered. Display menu.
		(2) PIN OK; customer's bank not online. Display "Try later."
		(3) PIN OK; customer's accounts are closed. Display "Call your bank."
		(4) Stolen card inserted; valid PIN entered. Retain card.
Cash Withdrawal	Bank customer	(1) Requests $50; account open; balance $1,234.56; $50 dispensed.
		(2) Requests $100; account closed.
		(3) Requests $155.39; account open; $150 dispensed.
Cash Replenishment	ATM operator with armed guard	(1) ATM opened; cash dispenser is empty; $15,000 is added.
		(2) ATM opened; cash dispenser is full.

case's implicit constraints and relationships, however, all fundamental relation-ships are unlikely to be exercised. Attempts at enumeration can lead to a large, but inefficient, test suite. Efficient and effective testing requires modeling con-straints and relationships and generating enough test cases to be sure they have been exercised.

Although they are most often used to describe requirements at system scope, use cases may be developed at class, cluster, or subsystem scope. The Extended Use Case Test pattern can be applied at any scope for which a use case can be written.

Fault Model

A use case specifies a family of responses to be produced for specific combina-tions of external input and system state. Extended Use Case Test represents these relationships as a decision table. Consequently, faults in a use case imple-mentation can be modeled as decision table faults (see Chapter 6 for details). A use case implementation is therefore susceptible to the same kinds of faults ex-pected for other implementations of combinational logic:

- Domain faults. The code that deals with a boundary of a condition is incorrect. See *Invariant Boundaries* for details of domain faults.
- Logic faults. The IUT behaves as if *and* logic was specified instead of *or*, and so on.
- Incorrect handling of don't care conditions.
- Incorrect or missing dependency on states established by prior use cases.

Use case implementations are also susceptible to generic system scope faults:

- Undesirable feature interactions
- Incorrect output
- Abnormal termination
- Inadequate response time
- Omitted capability
- Extra capability (a surprise)

The typical implementation of a use case is collaboration: a chain of mes-sages among objects and components. We must exercise all collaborations that support the use case to reach a fault. Assuming that integration testing has demonstrated basic operability for all collaborations in the use case, any remaining fault must be sensitive to some combination of input and state. Exercising the combinations of conditions and boundary values of the operational variables is the most effective approach to triggering a fault. Propagation obstacles depend on the particular structure of the collaboration and its components.

Strategy

Test Model

A discussion of use cases and extended use cases is provided in Section 8.3, Use Case Diagrams. An extended use case includes the following information:

- A complete inventory of operational variables.
- A complete specification of domain constraints for each operational variable.
- An operational relation for each use case.
- The relative frequency of each use case. This value, which is optional, supports *Allocate Tests by Profile* testing.

Extended use cases may be prepared in conjunction with any OOA/D technique that calls for use cases. Operational variables are identified and analyzed to model input/output relationships with a decision table.

Test Procedure

With extended use cases in hand, a test suite is developed in four steps. A simplified version of the Establish Session use case described in Table 14.1 is used to illustrate.

1. Identify the Operational Variables.   Operational variables are factors that vary from one scenario to the next and determine significantly different system responses. They include the following:

- Explicit inputs and outputs
- Environmental conditions that result in significantly different actor behavior
- Abstractions of the state of the system under test (e.g., ATM state: out of service, out of cash, ready, and so on)

The operational variables must include all variables that are explicitly part of the interface that supports the use case. If additional variables are necessary to account for all possible distinct responses, then operational variables that represent the system state and relevant environmental factors should be modeled as well. Objects participating in collaborations that implement the use case are often modeled as operational variables. The relevant states of the objects are specified in each variant.

For example, in the Establish Session use case, four variables determine the ATM's response to a bank customer who inserts a card and enters a PIN: the PIN encoded on the card, the PIN entered by the customer, the response from the customer's bank, and the condition of the customer's account at the bank.

2. Define the Domains of the Operational Variables. The domains are developed by defining the set of valid and invalid values for each variable. For example, the domain of the PIN is four digits with the range 0000 to 9999. Test cases require that valid (and invalid) values are specified. Chapter 6 explains how domain definitions can be used to generate additional test cases for each variant.

3. Develop the Operational Relation. Relationships among the operational variables that determine the distinct classes of system response are modeled. The operational variables are cast into an operational relation. This is a decision table: When all conditions in a row are true, the expected action (the response component of the use case) is to be produced. Each row (column) in the decision table is a **variant**[3]. Each variant must be mutually exclusive; that is, one and only one variant must be true for any possible set of operational variable values. Each significantly different class of output should have a variant. For example, suppose that `CustomerName` is displayed in some responses but not others. These responses are significantly different and would be modeled with different variants. We would not model each possible `CustomerName` (e.g., Jones, Smith, and so on) with its own variant, however. Modeling techniques are discussed in Chapter 6.

---

3. A variant can correspond to a scenario, but there are many reasons that it might not. The operational variables can include environmental factors (e.g., time of day), which are not represented in the SUT. The UML defines a scenario as a "useCaseInstance," whose "realization" *may* be modeled with a Sequence Diagram or Collaboration Diagram. Such scenarios may or may not be modeled—the UML does not require completeness. These diagrams may represent one unconditional message sequence or several conditional sequences. A variant can be represented with an unconditional sequence or as one path possible in a conditional sequence. Unless the conditional expressions in a Sequence or Collaboration Diagram correspond exactly to those in the operational relation, however, there is no reason to expect one-to-one correspondence between scenarios and variants.

Table 14.2 gives a partial operational relation for the Establish Session use case. The first row indicates that when an invalid card is inserted (for example, a department store credit card), the card is immediately ejected and a message is displayed prompting the customer for an ATM card. The second row indicates that "Contact your bank" is displayed and the card is ejected if (1) a valid card is inserted, (2) the entered PIN matches the card PIN, (3) the customer's bank acknowledges the account, and (4) the account is reported as being closed.

4. Develop Test Cases.   Every variant is made true at least once and false at least once. This step requires two test cases for each variant: (1) a *true* test case in a set of values that satisfies all conditions in a variant, and (2) a *false* test case—a change in the input or state values so that at least one condition becomes false. Often, the false case for one variant will qualify as a true case for another variant. Try to choose a *false* case that does not repeat a *true* case for another variant. If an operational variable has a bounded domain, additional tests can be developed with *Invariant Boundaries*. Table 14.3 shows a few test cases developed for the Establish Session use case. This operational relation is logically complete and minimal, so every false case turns out to be a true case for another variant. Chapter 6 presents more test generation techniques. If an operational

TABLE 14.2   Operational Relation for the Establish Session Use Case

	Operational Variables				Expected Result	
Variant	Card PIN	Entered PIN	Customer Bank Response	Customer Account Status	Message	Card Action
1	Invalid	DC	DC	DC	Insert an ATM card	Eject
2	Valid	Matches card PIN	Bank acknowledges	Closed	Contact your bank	Eject
3	Valid	Matches card PIN	Bank acknowledges	Open	Select a transaction	None
4	Valid	Matches card PIN	Bank does not acknowledge	DC	Please try later	Eject
5	Valid	Doesn't match	DC	DC	Reenter PIN	None
6	Revoked	DC	Bank acknowledges	DC	Card invalid	Retain
7	Revoked	DC	Bank does not acknowledge	DC	Card invalid	Eject

TABLE 14.3 Minimal Test Suite for the Establish Session Use Case

| Variant | Operational Variables | | | | Expected Result | |
	Card PIN	Entered PIN	Customer Bank Response	Customer Account Status	Message	Card Action
1	Invalid	DC	DC	DC	Insert an ATM card	Eject
1T	%*@#				Insert an ATM card	Eject
1F	Any *true* test for variants 2–7.					
2	Valid	Matches card PIN	Bank acknowledges	Closed	Contact your bank	Eject
2T	1234	1234	ack	CLSD	Contact your bank	
2F	Any *true* test for variants 1, 3–7.					
3	Valid	Matches card PIN	Bank acknowledges	Open	Select a trans-action	None
3T	1234	1234	ack	OPEN	Select a trans-action	None
3F	Any *true* test for variants 1, 2, and 4–7.					
4	Valid	Matches card PIN	Bank does not acknowledge	DC	Please try later	Eject
4T	1234	1234	nack		Please try later	Eject
4F	Any *true* test for variants 2–7.					
5	Valid	Doesn't match	DC	DC	Reenter PIN	None
5T	1234	1134				
5F	Any *true* test for variants 1–4, 6, 7.					
6	Revoked	DC	Bank acknowledges	DC	Card invalid	Retain
6T	5555		ack		Card invalid	Retain
6F	Any *true* test for variants 1–6, and 7.					
7	Revoked	DC	Bank does not acknowledge	DC	Card invalid	Eject
7T	5555		nack		Card invalid	Eject
7F	Any *true* test for variants 1–6.					

variable has a bounded domain, additional tests can be developed with *Invariant Boundaries*.

Oracle

Expected results are typically developed by inspection. That is, a person considers the test case inputs and develops expected results. Ideally, this individual should have a broad understanding of the required capabilities and the ways that the SUT will be used. When an existing system provides a similar capability, it may be possible to use the existing system to generate part or all of the expected results. See Chapter 18, Oracles.

Automation

The test suite may be implemented with a capture/playback tool or a test harness as required by the external interface for the SUT. Any assertions implemented should be enabled to detect otherwise unobservable failures (see the Built-in Test Oracle section in Chapter 18). The Appendix is a case study about how COTS testing tools were used to support extended use case testing.

Entry Criteria

Development of extended use cases may begin when use cases are developed. Because initial use cases are often subject to many revisions, it may be better to postpone development of the extended use cases until the basic use cases have settled. Testing may begin when the following conditions are met:

✓ Extended use cases have been developed and validated.
✓ The SUT has passed an integration test suite that demonstrates that components required to support the use case are minimally operable.

Exit Criteria

All requirements must be exercised to achieve minimally complete system testing. The *TC* coverage metric provides an indication of the completeness of requirements-based testing [IEEE 982.1].

$$TC = \frac{\text{Number of Implemented Capabilities}}{\text{Number of Required Capabilities}} \times \frac{\text{Total Components Tested}}{\text{Total Number of Components}} \times 100$$

The first expression prevents 100 percent coverage from being obtained when some capabilities are missing. This metric can be adapted to extended use cases.

	Test 1	Test 2	Test 3	Test 4	Test 5	Test 6	Test 7	. . .	Test 9999
Use Case 1				✓					
Use Case 2		✓			✓				
Use Case 3	✓					✓			✓
Use Case 4					✓		✓		
Use Case 5									
. . .									
Use Case 999		✓							✓

FIGURE 14.1   Use case test case traceability matrix.

At a minimum, every variant of an extended use case should be exercised at least once. This requirement suggests the following minimal coverage metric for testing based on use cases:

✓ Variant coverage. At least one true-false test pair is passed for each variant in the extended use case decision table. This test suite is minimally adequate, in the same sense that statement coverage is minimally adequate. This formula may be reinterpreted for testing based on use cases as follows:

$$XUCV = \frac{\text{Number of Implemented Use Cases}}{\text{Number of Required Use Cases}} \times \frac{\text{Total Variants Tested}}{\text{Total Number of Variants}} \times 100$$

✓ Use case/test case traceability. Every use case has a test and this test passes. Figure 14.1 suggests how this use case traceability may be established.

Consequences

Disadvantages

- Methodologists do not agree on the appropriate level of abstraction and degree of specificity for a use case. Test design must resolve the ambiguities. Too much detail or not enough will create extra work for the tester.

- Use cases are not typically used to specify performance, fault tolerance, and so on. These capabilities must be defined and tested, as outlined in Section 14.3, Implementation-specific Capabilities.
- The UML defines *extends* and *includes* constructs for use cases. A composite use case must be flattened to produce a testable model of the inter-use-case dependencies. The alternative is to hope that your choices for tests at the high level exercise all low-level dependencies. See Chapter 8 for details.

Advantages

- Use cases are incorporated in nearly all OOA/D methodologies and widely used.
- Use cases may be developed by analysts and testers who do not have object-oriented programming experience.
- Use cases are often the only requirement documentation available.
- Development of testable use cases leverages (and thereby encourages) investment in good OOA/D.
- Use cases reflect the user/customer point of view. They focus on capabilities that will determine the success or failure of the SUT. In contrast, developers often focus on a particular technical strategy. The customer-oriented focus is often more effective in revealing omissions or inconsistent capabilities.
- Extended use cases provide a systematic approach to developing the information necessary for test design. This information will have to be developed to test any use case. Subjective, nonsystematic test design can miss necessary relationships.
- The extended use case format supports test design based on combinational logic and software reliability engineering. These approaches have been the subject of extensive formal research and widespread application. Extended use cases provide a simple interface to these powerful techniques.
- An extended use case makes explicit all relationships that a use case must implement. The arbitrary narrative that suffices for use cases often results in ambiguous, incomplete, or inconsistent models. Often, development of the extended use case is sufficient to find errors and omissions.
- If the SUT was developed from ambiguous, inconsistent, or incomplete use cases, it will likely be buggy. A test suite developed from such

information will probably be inadequate. Developing extended use cases from the outset is preferable.

- If the implementation has been developed from nontestable use cases, a test suite designed from extended use cases can be expected to reveal design bugs resulting from ambiguous, inconsistent, or incomplete use cases.

Known Uses

Jacobson suggests that four general kinds of tests can be derived from use cases: (1) basic courses, or "the expected flow of events," (2) odd courses, or "all other flows of events," (3) tests of any line-item requirements traceable to each use case, and (4) tests of features described in user documentation traceable to each use case [Jacobson+92]. This approach is carried forward in [Jacobson+99]. The *Use Case Testing* pattern [Firesmith 96] suggests that an acceptance test suite may be prepared from use cases, but does not discuss any details of test design. Siegel advocates deriving a system test suite from use cases and an operational profile, but also does not provide details [Siegel 96].

Boisvert describes the results of a system test suite developed from the use cases of a telecommunications system [Boisvert 97]. I have worked with several clients to apply extended use cases to system testing of high-volume financial applications. The Appendix discusses some of the test automation considerations for *Extended Use Case Test*. The integration of use cases and the operational profile is discussed in [Runeson+98].

Related Patterns

If relative frequencies of each use case are developed, system testing may be conducted under the *Allocate Tests by Profile* pattern. It allows systematic generation of test cases in a manner that will maximize field reliability for a given testing budget. Test suites developed with *Round-trip Scenario Test* can be added to Extended Use Case Test suites.

Covered in CRUD

Intent

Covered in CRUD[4] verifies that all basic operations are exercised for each problem domain object in the system under test.

Context

Test suites developed from individual use cases and Sequence Diagrams cannot guarantee that *all* of the problem domain classes in the system under test have been reached. The Covered in CRUD pattern is a simple technique for identifying such omissions. It applies when many use cases share the responsibility for maintaining problem domain classes.

Fault Model

A **problem domain class** is a representation of an external entity or concept that is necessary for an implementation-independent model of the system under test. For example, `Customer`, `Order`, and `Product` are problem domain classes in an order-processing system; `LinkedList` is not. For each such class, the system must be able to create objects of the class, report on their contents, update the contents as needed, and delete the objects (or any object that is a member of a collection) when necessary. These basic operations are typically required for every problem domain class and implemented by a collaboration that corresponds to a use case. Most collaborations involve a class subset and need not perform all basic operations on every class in the subset.

Because use cases are necessarily partial, we must analyze all basic actions over all use cases to identify a system-wide omission. Suppose that for some class, a basic action (create, read, update, or delete) is not performed by any use case defined for the system. It will be impossible for the system to create, read, update, or delete objects of this class. Similarly, suppose that a test suite does not exercise every basic operation on every problem domain class. The test suite cannot be considered adequate because it does not reach all potentially buggy actions. Some classes may not be required to support all basic operations, and basic operations may be prohibited for some classes. For example, classes that

---

4. CRUD stands for Create, Read, Update, Delete. These basic operations must be provided for all problem domain objects represented in the SUT. The CRUD acronym was popularized by the Information Engineering methodology.

TABLE 14.4   Interpretation of CRUD Coverage Analysis

Use Case Test Coverage of Basic Action	Required Behavior for a Basic Action		
	Required	Not Required	Prohibited
Exercised, passes	Validated	Surprise	Failure
Exercised, throws expected exception	Failure	Validated	Validated
Not exercised	Incomplete test suite: add capability test	Incomplete test suite: add exception test	Incomplete test suite: add exception test

represent static information or information maintained by other systems might be limited to read actions. In this situation, the absence of create, update, and delete actions is required for correct operation. If the SUT implements an action to update these classes, it is buggy. Table 14.4 shows the relationships among the requirements for a basic action and the kind of test cases developed (or not developed) for that action.

Strategy

Test Model

The CRUD coverage matrix is developed as follows:

1. Identify all system use cases.
2. Identify the problem domain classes.
3. Prepare a use case/class matrix. For each use case, determine the action it performs on objects of each class: create, read, update, or delete. Note the action in the matrix. This information may be taken from the Sequence Diagram for the use case, if available. Figure 14.2 shows the general form of the matrix.

	Class 1				Class 2				...	Class n			
	C	R	U	D	C	R	U	D		C	R	U	D
Use Case 1	✓	✓		✓		✓							✓
Use Case 2			✓				✓					✓	
:													
Use Case n	✓				✓			✓		✓	✓		

FIGURE 14.2   Use case/class coverage matrix.

4. Analyze the matrix. After all use case actions have been transcribed, check the actions for each class. Every class should have at least one create, read, update, and delete action. If it does not, develop a test to accomplish the action.

If the test suite does not cover all actions for each class, develop test cases as indicated in Table 14.4. Because this analysis often reveals design omissions, it may be used to validate system models as well. Test cases may be developed with *Extended Use Case Test, Round-trip Scenario Test,* and *Class Association Test.*

Test Procedure

The operations to test may be identified as follows:

1. Develop the matrices as outlined in the preceding steps.
2. Develop and execute an *Extended Use Case Test* suite.
3. Map the *Extended Use Case Test* suite to the matrix.
4. Add test cases to achieve CRUD coverage. These test cases can typically be developed by adding slightly revised versions of the basic use case test suite.

Oracle

See *Extended Use Case Test* and *Class Association Test.*

Automation

This analysis is supported in some CASE tools. It may also be performed manually or with a spreadsheet program. The test suite may be implemented with a capture/playback tool or a test harness as required by the external interface for the SUT.

Entry Criteria

This analysis may be prepared for any set of use cases and problem domain classes. The value of the analysis is limited to the extent that these modes are accurate, complete, and consistent.

Exit Criteria

A test suite achieves CRUD coverage when all basic operations for all problem domain classes are exercised and all test cases pass.

Consequences

With the system model and test suite in hand, this analysis is easily performed. As the risk of an omission increases with the size and complexity of a system, the effectiveness of this analysis likewise increases with the size and complexity of the SUT. It can reveal design omissions in system models and in test suites.

Known Uses

CRUD matrix analysis has been used in many systems analysis methodologies from the 1970s onward [Hien 85].

Related Patterns

This pattern builds on the test suite developed by *Extended Use Case Test*.

Allocate Tests by Profile

Intent

Allocate the overall testing budget to each use case in proportion to its relative frequency.

Context

You are planning to develop an *Extended Use Case Test* suite. You must now answer several general questions before developing and running your test suite:

- How many tests should we select for each variant?
- How should these tests be interleaved?

The operational profile offers a systematic, quantitative technique for answering these questions. Use cases are ranked according to their relative frequency; testing resources are allocated based on this profile. Test cases are then developed for each use case until the budget for that use case is exhausted. This approach maximizes system reliability for a given testing budget.

Fault Model

A fundamental insight motivates testing under the operational profile: The frequency of failures seen by customers/users is directly related to usage frequency.

> Testing driven by an operational profile is very efficient because it identifies failures (and hence the faults causing them) on average, in order of how often they occur. This approach rapidly increases reliability—reduces failure intensity—per unit of execution time because the failures that occur most frequently are caused by the faulty operations used most frequently. Users will also detect failures in order of their frequency, if they have not already been found in test [Musa 93, 28].

Test design is a struggle to exploit meager clues about bugs. Frequency-based testing assumes that we have exhausted available information, but not eradicated all bugs.

The operational profile is well suited to object-oriented systems. Object-oriented systems are typically composed of small components, using mosaic modularity and relying on dynamic binding. Even when a collaboration incorporates adequately tested components and has passed a minimal test suite, we cannot guarantee that all faults for the use case have been reached. A collaboration typically has many participants, whose classes may vary from one scenario to the next. Developing an analytical test model for all of these collaboration possibilities is hopeless. We can quickly exhaust our knowledge about effective testing and still leave many paths uncovered. The next best approximation of the necessary conditions to reach a fault is to test in proportion to the externally determined frequency of input. This approach maximizes the likelihood of reaching and triggering faults that customers/users would be most likely to reach and trigger.

Strategy

Test Model

Assuming that bugs are equally likely to occur over all use case implementations, the use cases most likely to fail are those used most frequently. That is, if a heavily used operation is buggy, the system will fail frequently. If a rarely used operation is buggy, the system will fail infrequently. Selecting tests (and removing bugs) according to usage frequency rapidly decreases failure frequency.

The operational profile lists all use cases in a system and their relative frequencies.[5] For example, suppose that a system has two use cases: *update* and *search*. On average, 90,000 searches and 10,000 updates are accepted per day. The relative frequencies are 0.9 for *search* and 0.1 for *update*.

Although a use case specifies a class of interactions, it does not tell us how often the interaction occurs. The relative frequency or probability of each use case must therefore be estimated or measured. We do not need extreme precision in these estimates, but the estimates must be proportionally correct, from most to least frequent. The sum of the relative frequencies for all use cases must sum to 1.0.

The sorted use cases are a key part of the operational profile strategy. We allocate testing effort to use cases so as to test in proportion to probability. Assuming that the estimated profile is a good model of the actual usage, this strategy maximizes operational reliability for a given testing budget and schedule.[6] A system under test typically includes thousands of individual operations (for example, all object/action pairs in the GUI). A single use case typically

---

5. Musa's terms for the operational profile have been adapted to follow the UML: function = use case, operation = operation, run = scenario = test case.

6. Developing an estimate can be difficult, even impossible. Musa states, however, that reliability is "not greatly affected by errors in specifying the operational profile" [Musa 98, 120]. If the relative ordering of use cases is accurate, errors in estimating the frequency of specific use cases will not have a drastic effect. Errors that result in low testing for high frequency will, however, reduce effectiveness.

involves tens of operations, which are modeled as variants in an extended use case. We should test the variants in each use case.

Effort Allocation. With the operational profile in hand, we can make a rational allocation of testing effort. Suppose that our total budget for system testing and debugging of the ATM software is 1000 hours. Assume, for example, that on average

- It takes one hour to design, set up, and run one test case.
- A test reveals a bug 5 percent of the time.
- It takes four hours to correct a bug.

How many test cases can we run? If we let T be the total number of tests, then

$$T + (0.05 \times 4T) = 1000$$
$$1.2T = 1000$$
$$T = 833$$

Thus we can run approximately 833 test cases. Table 14.5 shows a (partial) example of test budget allocation based on the ATM operational profile.

Test Procedure

1. Prepare an operational profile for the SUT. Rank use cases and operations according to their relative frequency. Then prepare an operational profile: Estimate the relative frequency with which users (actors) per-

TABLE 14.5   Test Case Allocation for ATM

Use Case	Probability	Number of Tests
Establish Session	0.37	308
Cash Withdrawal	0.18	150
Checking Deposit	0.15	125
Savings Deposit	0.12	100
Funds Transfer	0.08	67
Balance Inquiry	0.06	50
Restock	0.02	17
Collect Deposits	0.02	17
Total	1.00	834

form each use case to be tested. Break out use cases where differences in operational variables lead to significantly different usages.

2. Estimate your testing productivity.
3. Establish your system testing effort budget.
4. Allocate testing time (or number of tests) to each use case.
5. Generate test cases for each use case.
6. Choose a strategy to interleave the test cases. The simplest approach is to randomize the interleaving. A *Mode Machine* model, which models use cases as transitions, provides an explicit test sequence.

Effective application of profile-based testing requires good engineering judgment.

- Suppose a use case is rarely used, but we must be certain of correct operation. This can be accomplished with a separate operational profile of critical use cases. Testing effort can be allocated according to risk or relative frequency.
- Suppose a high-frequency use case has a trivial implementation—an unusual event in real systems. You may have over specified your use cases or modeled an operation as a use case. For testing purposes, this use case can be merged with another use case.
- Suppose your profile is dominated by many low-frequency use cases. Again, you may have over specified your use cases or modeled an operation as a use case. For testing purposes, some of these use cases can be merged with other use cases.

See [Musa 98] for a complete discussion of these and other practical concerns.

Oracle
See *Extended Use Case Test*.

Automation
See *Extended Use Case Test*. Sequences of test cases can be randomized in many ways. The *shuffled define-use algorithm* (Chapter 10) can be adapted for this purpose.

Entry Criteria

See *Extended Use Case Test*.

- ✓ Adequate unit and integration testing has been done on the components and subsystems.
- ✓ Sufficient resources have been committed to estimating or measuring the profile for all use cases.

Exit Criteria

The exit criteria in *Extended Use Case Test* apply. This pattern assumes that system testing is done under a limited budget and that testing will cease when the budget is depleted. Except in extreme circumstances, allocating the available testing budget should achieve at least All-Variants coverage.

The operational profile is an integral part of *Software Reliability Engineering* (SRE) [Lyu 96]. SRE encompasses several quantitative models for estimating reliability based on the failure rate observed while testing under the operational profile. These models are used to make an informed "stop testing" decision. The SUT is released when the trend in the observed failure rate becomes sufficiently low and stable. Details of SRE and substantial guidance for application are provided in [Lyu 96] and [Musa 98].

Consequences

The primary disadvantage of frequency-based testing is that it may be difficult or impossible to obtain or estimate a sufficiently accurate operational profile. The *FUD Factor Matrix* (see *Managing the Testing Process for Object-Oriented Systems* [Binder 2000]) shows how to develop a heuristic approximation to the operational profile for allocating testing effort. The effort required to develop the profile is typically low.

Profile-based testing offers several advantages. Testing is often done under a budget constraint (which often shrinks as the project proceeds), so profile-based allocation makes the best use of available testing resources. When reliability estimation is used to support the "stop testing" decision, over testing can be avoided. If cost constraints and schedule pressure require reducing the number of test cases, cutting or reducing low-frequency use cases will have the least effect on overall reliability.

Known Uses

Runeson et al. discuss the integration of use cases and the operational profile [Runeson+98]. Fifty-four experience reports on the application of the operational profile are listed in Appendix H of [Musa 98]. Applications include many telecommunication systems, weapon systems, Microsoft's desktop applications and Windows NT operating system, several embedded systems, the NASA Space Shuttle, and Tandem's Guardian operating system. Additional case studies are presented in [Lyu 96]. The Cleanroom Development approach relies on profile-based testing [Deck 97].

Related Patterns

This pattern builds on the test suite developed by *Extended Use Case Test.*

14.3   Implementation-specific Capabilities

Use cases are an abstract model of system capabilities that do not require any specific implementation. A test suite can be developed from use cases with little attention to the unique characteristics of a specific implementation. Nevertheless, some critical capabilities are not modeled in use cases and are instead more closely tied to an implementation. For example, use cases do not usually specify how to recover data after a disk failure, but the ability to recover from intermittent hardware failures is necessary to ensure high-availability operation.

System testing should exercise *all* capabilities of the system under test. Many effective system scope testing strategies are applicable to object-oriented and component-based implementations (see the Bibliographic Notes section). Therefore, only a brief summary of implementation-specific test patterns is provided here.

For the same reasons that it makes sense to use integration testing to achieve a stable build before beginning system testing, testing based on use cases generally precedes implementation-specific testing. In some circumstances, practical considerations (availability of a person, test tools, computers, and so on), risk management, and technical dependencies may dictate otherwise.

14.3.1   Configuration and Compatibility

Context. Application systems are often designed to run on many target environment configurations or are required to interoperate with many combinations of hardware and software. For example, a process in a distributed system may be expected to run on several different processors. *Compatibility* covers a wide range of "abilities" and may be expressed in terms of configuration combinations that must be supported. For example, compatibility may be required of the SUT and any of the following:

- Existing application systems
- Computer systems containing any approved combination of RAM, disks, CPU, video cards, and other hardware
- Different operating systems and/or versions of a particular OS
- Different GUI systems (e.g., Microsoft Windows, X-Windows) and/or versions of a particular GUI

- Different database management systems and/or versions of a particular database management system
- APIs and interface definition languages
- Data interchange formats

Typically, the SUT is expected to produce the same behavior for all configurations. Allowable differences are often defined for response time, display resolution, or other user-configurable features. Compatibility/configuration testing is widely used. Although Java has minimized platform dependencies, experience has shown that testing on each Java Virtual Machine can reveal incompatibility bugs. In the shrink-wrap software industry, it is common practice to test one application system on thousands of hardware configurations. Developers of portable standards have produced compatibility test suites—for example, Sun's Java compatibility suite and OMG's CORBA compliance suite. Ada compilers are said to be validated once they have passed the extensive test suite known as the Ada Compiler Validation Capability (ACVC).

Strategy.   Define the compatibility and configuration requirements. Identify the variables that define each configuration. Identify allowed deviations, don't care conditions, and unspecified variables. With even a few variables (e.g., CPU speed and RAM), there may be thousands of combinations. Typically, the most challenging problem in configuration testing is selecting a feasible, but test-effective, subset. Good results have been obtained by adapting design-of-experiments techniques to select a feasible number of configurations [Mandl 85, Brownlie+92, Cohen+97]. Once the configuration list has been set, develop a configuration/compatibility test suite that is expected to pass on all configurations. The total setup, run, and evaluation time per test will be multiplied by the number of configurations. This test suite should be automated, simple, and repeatable.

14.3.2   Performance

Context.   Software systems must produce results within acceptable time intervals. At the extremes, acceptable intervals may be measured in weeks or microseconds. Most users of desktop systems will be annoyed with response times longer than a few seconds. High-volume transaction-processing systems must reliably process tens of thousands of transactions per second. In many hard real-time systems, the deadlines to accept and respond to an input are measured

in milliseconds. In all of these applications, the inability to meet the performance objective is no less a bug than incorrect output or a system crash.

Strategy.   Performance requirements are expressed as a time interval in which the
SUT must accomplish something. Section 14.5, Note on Testing Performance
Objectives, suggests some ways to develop quantitative formulations of performance requirements. A system performance requirement can be stated in
terms of response time, throughput, or utilization.

   This objective must be translated into a constraint on software execution
time or resource use, under a stated load. Performance requirements are often
set for average and worst-case performance. Worst-case performance is relevant
for mission-critical systems, for example. Average performance is often the
focus of data-processing systems. The performance objectives must state assumptions for factors that can affect performance, including the target system
configuration: network configuration, CPU speed, RAM, task/job priority,
background load, system resource contention, application resource contention,
transaction/input/interrupt arrival rate. If these assumptions are not clear, performance testing cannot provide reliable results.

   There are several variations of performance testing:

- *Load testing* is usually associated with transaction-processing systems.
  In a client/server system, this testing is often accomplished by using a
  load simulator. A set of transactions is automatically submitted to the
  system at varying rates, simulating the effect of many concurrent users
  entering transactions at client nodes.
- *Volume testing* is usually associated with batch-processing systems. The
  largest available input file is used or a large file is generated. The idea is
  to transmit a high quantity of input under normal system loading.

   Performance testing is discussed in [Beizer 84] and [Perry 95]. Performance
requirements for systems with hard real-time deadlines may be analyzed and
modeled with rate monotonic analysis [Klein+93].

14.3.3   Integrity and Fault Tolerance

Concurrency Testing

Context.   The SUT relies on some form of concurrent execution with shared
resources. With the exception of single-user personal computer operating

systems, all present-day operating systems support concurrent execution. For example, Unix, OS/2, OpenStep, and Windows NT support a similar process/ thread model. Java supports multithreading within the scope of an applet or application. Reliable concurrent execution is difficult to achieve, so testing is warranted. Resource contention resolution, scheduling, deadlock avoidance, priority inversion, and race conditions are common problems. Dependable support for concurrency has been a high priority for Ada development environments for many years. The built-in abilities of Ada 95 (e.g., protected objects) prevent many kinds of basic concurrency bugs.

Strategy.   Identify typical configurations of concurrent execution and typical loading levels. The test suite starts several processes and threads, and then simulates typical input patterns. The processes can be quite simple—for example, the program creates a file, opens it, writes a randomly generated number of records, reads them back, changes the content, writes it back to the file, checks file integrity, and closes the file. GUI scripts can be written to run in loops with randomly generated intervals and inputs to cause process and thread creation and termination. This effort may reveal basic timing problems, faults with re-entrant code, and data integrity faults. Extensive output checking is unnecessary, because this testing is to attempt to cause abnormal termination. Beizer's background testing strategy discusses these issues [Beizer 84]. Passing this level of concurrency testing sets the stage for stress testing.

Stress Testing

Context.   The SUT should have a fail-safe response when subjected to a quantity or rate of input that exceeds design limits. This type of testing is analogous to vehicle crash testing.

Strategy.   A stress test pushes the SUT beyond its design limits. It is designed to cause a failure; for example, when 10 times the maximum input rate is generated. This kind of testing will reveal two kinds of faults: lack of fail-safe behavior and load-sensitive bugs. The stress test suite may increase simultaneous actions and cause resources to be used in unexpected ways. This may reveal faults on "weird paths," in exception handlers, and in restart/recovery features. Stress testing is discussed in [Beizer 84] and [Perry 95]. If it is warranted, components that catch exceptions should be unit tested with *Controlled Exception Test.*

Restart/Recovery Testing

Context. The SUT supports automatic or manual recovery from a failure mode to normal operation. For example:

- When a primary high-speed data link fails, transmission should automatically switch to a low-speed back-up link. When the high-speed link returns to service, the application should automatically reestablish the high-speed link.
- A daily database update runs for 15 hours. In the event of a general system crash, the update should restart from the last commit point, instead of rerunning the entire job.
- A supercomputer simulation runs for several weeks. In the event of a general system crash, the simulation should restart from the last commit point, instead of rerunning the entire job.

Strategy. Induce each failure mode that should lead to automated recovery or restart. *Controlled Exception Test* may be useful for simulating the failure mode. Verify that the expected recovery/restart process is attempted. After the recovery is completed, run a regression test suite to check the degree of repair. This effort may require development of special-purpose code to verify the system integrity.

14.3.4   Human—Computer Interaction

Context. When the capabilities of the SUT require human–computer interaction (HCI), its correct and effective use depends on the software, its relative ease of use, and collateral materials that provide necessary information to human users. All of these items must be evaluated together to identify HCI bugs. HCI bugs can be more than simply annoying. For example, accidental deaths caused by the Therac-25 system were a result of a bug in the operator interface [Leveson 95].

Strategy. Human–computer interaction requirements are complex and may be tested in many ways. The basic strategy, however, is simple:

1. Enumerate the capabilities or features.
2. Define an objective pass/no pass criterion for each capability under test.
3. Run the test.

HCI testing typically relies more on skillful manual testing than on high-volume automated testing [Kaner+93]. Any of several HCI aspects may apply in a particular system.

- *Usability testing* evaluates the ergonomics of an HCI design. Sophisticated usability testing labs can not only record keystrokes, but also measure the physiological and psychological responses of users to UI designs. Usability testing is often done early in development to improve the UI.

- *Security testing* evaluates the ability of the SUT to prevent unauthorized use, computer crime, or sabotage. Basic security features (logon, logoff, set permissions, and so on) are tested in the same way as other features. Additional security testing often involves attempts by security specialists and cooperating hackers to breach the security of the SUT.

- *Localization testing* evaluates the SUT's ability to be configured for use with locale parameters. At minimum, this effort involves translating text displayed on the user interface to several (human) languages. It can require a significant effort if the SUT will be distributed to many countries and localization has not been designed to be testable. Localization testing is discussed in [Kaner+93].

- *Installation testing* evaluates the ability of the installation software and related documentation to correctly transfer and configure the SUT on a host computer. The configuration testing strategy may be applied to choose target platform configurations and combinations of installation options. Deinstallation and the ability to install patches and upgrades should be exercised as well.

- *User documentation testing* evaluates the correctness and completeness of user documentation, help screens, and automated assistants. At a minimum, every procedure or operation in the user documentation should be attempted. The use case test suite, the use case model, and the system requirements should be traced to each feature discussed in the user documentation. This effort may reveal inconsistent, missing, or incomplete documentation items.

- *Operator procedure testing* evaluates the correctness and completeness of documentation, help screens, automated assistants, and ancillary software used by technicians to start, monitor, diagnose, repair, and shut down the SUT. Restart/recovery testing may overlap with operator procedure testing. At a minimum, every procedure in the operator documentation should be attempted.

- *Serviceability testing* evaluates the SUT's ability to accept field upgrades, repairs, or reconfiguration.

After verifying that explicit features can be used safely under nominal circumstances, HCI testing should assume that Murphy's law applies and should therefore attempt as many incorrect, weird, wrong, and oddball situations as possible.

14.4 Post-development Testing

Upon the completion of developer-administered system testing, several other forms of system scope testing may be appropriate. They are noted here for completeness.

- *Alpha test.* An alpha test is typically carried out by an independent test group, often within the same organization as the developer, but reporting to a separate manager or to the project sponsor. The focus is on simulating real-world usage and evaluating overall readiness. This effort is often an intra-company acceptance test.

- *Beta test.* Beta testing is the use of an early release by representative groups of users or customers. A version of the system (which has passed developer-conducted system testing) is distributed to customers who volunteer to participate. The customer installs the system and attempts routine usage under typical operating conditions. Observed problems are then reported to the producer. The system producer typically offers a small incentive for users to participate, but does not make any commitments about correcting observed problems or the reliability of the beta test version. The producer uses the problem information generated to identify and correct bugs and to set the timing and positioning of the general release. Beta testing has been employed with varying success for mass-market desktop systems and computer games. It was a key element of Netscape's business strategy, for instance [Cusumano+98].

- *Acceptance test.* Acceptance testing is system scope testing conducted by a customer to decide whether to accept a system which the customer has commissioned. Payment for development work is often contingent upon passing acceptance testing. The producer and the customer should negotiate the acceptance criterion and acceptance test plan. Guidelines for planning acceptance testing appear in [Perry 95].

- *Compliance test.* The system test suite for some application systems must comply with government regulations and standards. The tests to demonstrate this compliance should be designed as part of the producer's system test suite. It may make sense to develop this test suite so that it can be run on its own.

Good practices for the management of post-development testing and strategies for related test suites are independent of the implementation technology.

14.5   Note on Testing Performance Objectives

Computer system performance can be characterized in terms of throughput, response time, and utilization. Table 14.6 lists the qualitative effect of performance objectives. **Throughput** is the number of tasks completed per unit of time. It measures how much work has been performed in an interval, but it does not suggest what is happening to a single task. **Response time** is the time elapsed between input arrival and output delivery. Average and worst-case values are usually of interest. **Utilization** is the percentage of an interval in which a hardware or software resource is busy. Performance parameters are defined differently for batch-processing, transaction-processing, and real-time systems. Table 14.7 suggests how performance can be characterized for several kinds of systems.

TABLE 14.6   Impact of Performance Objectives

Objective	Benefit	Definition	Example
Throughput	Productivity	Number of tasks accomplished per unit time	Transactions per second
Response time	Responsiveness	Time elapsed between input arrival and delivery of output at sink	Click to display interval
Utilization	Component availability: ability to respond to high load	Ratio of time busy/available for a component over a fixed interval	Server utilization

TABLE 14.7   Performance Objectives

Type of System	Performance Objective
Batch	Batch window; transaction throughput
Interactive	Average response time; worst-case response time
Real-time	Critical interval
Client/server	Average response time; worst-case response time; Server throughput

14.5.1   Batch Systems

The *batch window* is a commonly used performance objective. It defines an elapsed time interval for the completion of a batch job. The window opens when the job can be started, which typically depends on completion of an earlier job or availability of an input file. The window closes when the job must be completed, which is usually determined by an overall processing cycle imposed by an application requirement. For example, a bank can begin posting checking account transactions after the close of business, and it must complete posting before accepting new transactions on the next business day.

Batch windows can be developed from a job dependency chart. The start and finish times can be determined by using the same approach used for PERT charts. We need to know four things for each job: earliest start time, latest start time, earliest finish time, and latest finish time. If some jobs can run in parallel, then the chart can be analyzed to find the critical path (the longest path). There are four types of batch windows:

W_1 Wide window   = latest finish − earliest start
W_2 Median window = earliest finish − earliest start
W_3 Narrow window = latest finish − latest start
W_4 Tight window   = earliest finish − latest start

The start and finish times define the operational window. Two other factors can shrink the operational window:

O Operator action time (e.g., mount tapes, start job)
$p(f)$ Probability of failure, requiring job restart

The batch performance objective BP is the interval in which our batch job must complete all processing. It can be stated in three ways:

Optimistic: $BP_1 < W_i - O$

Conservative: $BP_3 < (W_i - O) / 2$

Compromise: $BP_2 < (W_i - O) / (1 + p(f))$

Performance testing would entail setting up batch runs with average and worst-case input quantities and simulating any other load on the target machine.

14.5.2 Interactive System

An interactive system supports a continuous dialog with a user or users. Each user input requires a response. Response time is therefore scaled to human tolerance. Airline reservation systems, most business transaction-processing systems, and command-line interfaces to operating systems are all examples of interactive processing. The interactive performance objective IP is the interval in which our software must produce a response.

For example, in a two-tier client/server system, the total response time per transaction is the sum of (1) the client CPU time to accept and transmit the transaction, (2) the network transmission time (both ways), and (3) the server CPU time to accept and process the transaction. If there is no load on any part of the system, the response time will be the sum of these times. The processing time at each resource may vary with the size of the transaction and complexity of the processing.

These three resources (client, network, and server) have a finite load capacity, which is reached when the resource is at 100 percent utilization. The expected average queue size is a function of the average arrival rate for requests and the average time to service each request. A rule of thumb is that most resources will begin to queue service requests when utilization reaches 70 percent. A discussion of these dynamics is beyond the scope of this book. However, in setting an interactive performance objective, the utilization level of these resources should be specified. Because IP should be an average, we would have to measure many actual response times observed while the system was placed under the specified load to determine compliance.

14.5.3   Real-time Systems

Real-time deadlines are present when a program must keep pace with an external physical process. The implementation under test must respond while the related physical process occurs, so that the response can control the physical process. From a performance point of view, there are three types of signals:

- A *repeating* input signal has a frequency that defines the response window. It must be accepted before the next pulse arrives.
- An *intermittent critical* signal occurs arbitrarily often, and a response must be given within a fixed interval.
- A *repeating critical* signal has a defined frequency that determines the response window. It must be accepted before the next pulse arrives, and a response must be given within a fixed interval.

The real-time performance objective RP is an interval in which the SUT must produce a response to an input signal. Two factors determine this objective:

S Signaling rate

I Critical interval

The real-time performance constraint depends on the type of input signal:

Repeating $RP_1 < S$

Critical $RP_2 < I$

Repeating critical $RP_3 < $ minimum $[\, S \mid I \,]$

Performance testing requires simulating the external system signal at average and worst-case frequency as well as simulating any other load on the target machine. End-to-end response time is monitored.

Ideally, the monitoring software is not run on the same computer running the system under test. Monitoring adds to the load and can distort performance test results if it runs on the same machine. This task can be carried out on a separate computer that simply passes input and output to the target machine. As each input or output arrives at the monitoring computer, the event is logged. The log is analyzed to get the average performance times. This kind of monitoring usually imposes a straightforward latency that can be backed out of the performance analysis. If it is deemed impossible, the load assumptions should be calibrated to compensate for the monitoring load. Alternatively, a simulation model can be developed based on the measured response time and estimated load.

14.6   Bibliographic Notes

The extended use case-based testing strategy was first described in [Binder 96a] and the use of UML Sequence Diagrams was elucidated in [Binder 98a]. Some material from [Binder 96a] has been used.

Little has been written about system testing for object-oriented implementations. The early consensus claimed that established approaches apply with no loss of generality [Jacobson+92, Graham+93, Graham 94]. These sources suggest using established system testing techniques [Myers 79, Beizer 84]. In OOSE, system testing should exercise at least the "basic course" of all use cases, all allocated requirements, and each operation described in the user documentation [Jacobson+92]. Siegel suggests deriving a system test suite from use cases and an operational profile, but does not provide any details [Siegel 96]. Ambler restates Myers's general strategy in the context of object-oriented development [Ambler 97].

System Testing in General

Myers's general discussion of the goals, strategies, and approaches to system testing still apply [Myers 76, Myers 79], as does Beizer's detailed, definitive presentation of technical considerations [Beizer 84]. Kaner et al. provide a pragmatic list of techniques [Kaner+93]. Perry's process-oriented approach organizes the elements of system testing without discussing details [Perry 95]. Testing applications that use a client/server architecture are described in [Mosely 95].

Software Reliability Engineering

The definitive source is [Lyu 96]. A wealth of practical guidance may be found in [Musa 98]. Both provide extensive bibliographies.

Real-time Systems

Verification and validation for real-time applications is discussed in [LaPlante 93]. Several articles regarding performance analysis of distributed systems can be found in [Shatz 89].

Human–Computer Interaction

Practical considerations for human–computer interaction design and evaluation can be found in [Tognazzini 92].

Performance Analysis

Molly provides a good introduction to performance modeling techniques [Molly 89].

Chapter 15   Regression Testing

I Didn't Change Anything! interj. An aggrieved cry often heard as bugs manifest during a regression test. The canonical reply to this assertion is "Then it works just the same as it did before, doesn't it?" . . . This is also heard from applications programmers trying to blame an obvious applications problem on an unrelated systems software change, for example, a divide-by-zero fault after terminals were added to a network. Upon close questioning, they will admit some major restructuring of the program that shouldn't have broken anything, in their opinion, but which actually hosed the code completely.

The New Hacker's Dictionary

Overview

Regression testing is a necessary part of an effective testing process. This chapter presents general considerations in developing and using regression test suites for object-oriented systems. Five test design patterns are presented that develop black box and white box strategies for regression testing at all scopes.

15.1   Preliminaries

15.1.1   What and Why

Adequate testing of a new or modified component gives us a reason to be confident in the component. It does not, however, give us a reason to have the same confidence in the system in which this component is embedded, even if that system previously passed an adequate test suite. A new or modified component can fail when used with unchanged components. It can cause failures in unchanged components by generating side effects or feature interactions. When this happens, the system under test is said to *regress*. A **baseline** version of a component (or system) has passed a test suite. The **delta version** of a component (or a system) is a changed version that has not passed a regression test. A **delta build** is an executable configuration of the SUT that contains all the delta and baseline components. A **regression test case** is a test case that the baseline has passed and which is expected to pass when rerun on a delta build. A **regression test suite** is composed of regression test cases. A test case that has previously passed but no longer passes reveals a **regression fault**.

Regression testing is typically done during iterative development, after debugging, during production of a new instantiation of a reusable component, as a first step for integration, and to support application maintenance.

* *Rapid iterative development.* With the typically rapid pace of change in object-oriented development, some authors report that regression testing may be done several times each day [Rettig 91, Love 92, Arnold+94, Siegel 94]. The Extreme Programming approach requires that a test be developed for each class and that this test be rerun every time the class changes [Anderson+98]. The *Incremental Testing Framework* is used so that tests may be easily developed and rerun. It is common Extreme Programming practice to rerun all tests several times each day.

* *Development by reuse.* Reuse can be accomplished in many ways, as Table 15.1 shows. If the producer's test suite is available to the consumer, running this test suite on the resultant component may be possible. Chapter 11 suggests several ways in which consumers of reusable components could reuse producer test suites. Table 15.1 summarizes the circumstances in which a consumer might apply a producer's test suite as a regression test suite.

* *Integration.* Regression testing is a good first step of integration testing. Rerunning accumulated test suites as components are added to successive test configurations builds the regression suite incrementally and will reveal regression bugs. This kind of regression testing is an essential part of *High-frequency Integration* and is effective for all other integration patterns. See Chapter 13, Integration.

* *Software maintenance.* There are four general kinds of software maintenance. *Corrective* maintenance refers to changes made to debug a system after a failure has been observed. It usually refers to failures observed after

TABLE 15.1   Test Suites of Reusable Components as Regression Test Suites

Reuse Mechanism	Reusable Component	Typical Test Pattern for Component	Applicability of Producer's Test Suite as Consumer's Regression Test	
			Applied to Consumer's Component	Applied to Consumer's System
Source code augmentation				
Cut and paste	Source code fragments	**Modal Class**, etc.	Possible	NA
White box framework	Superclasses	**New Framework Popular Framework**	High	Possible
Translation time-binding				
Macro substitution	Macro	NA		
Inheritance				
Application-specific	Superclasses	**Polymorphic Server**, etc.	Possible	NA
Foundation class library	Superclasses	**New Framework Popular Framework**	High	NA
Composition				
Application-specific	Server class	**Modal Class**, etc.	NA	Possible
Foundation class library	Server class	**Modal Class**, etc.	NA	Possible
Generic class	Server class	**Generic Class**	High	NA
Link-time/runtime binding				
Executable components	Linkable binary	**Mode Machine**, etc.	NA	Possible

a system has been placed in general release. *Adaptive* maintenance refers to changes made to achieve continuing compatibility with the target environment or other systems (e.g., rewriting a 16-bit Windows GUI to use 32-bit controls without changing any capabilities). *Perfective* maintenance refers to changes designed to improve or add capabilities. *Preventive* maintenance refers to changes made to increase robustness, maintainability, portability, and other characteristics. Regression testing should be carried out in each situation to reveal side effects and bad fixes; the original test suite for changed component(s) and the balance of the system should be rerun.

• *Compatibility assessment and benchmarking.* Some test suites are designed to be run on a wide range of platforms and application systems to establish conformance with a standard or to evaluate time and space performance. In these circumstances, the intent is to reveal platform-dependent differences in performance or functionality. These test suites are a kind of regression testing, but are not intended to reveal regression bugs.

Regression testing is effective for revealing regression faults caused by delta side effects, delta/baseline incompatibilities, and undesirable feature interactions between a baseline and a delta. It is also effective for revealing bugs caused by **bad fixes**. Jones reports that high-technology companies like IBM have "a bad fix injection rate which ranges from less than 2% to more than 20% with modern averages in the 1990s running to about 7%" [Jones 97, 30].[1]

The iterative process employed in object-oriented development demands effective regression testing. Regression faults are introduced when changes are made. The essence of iterative development is changing the code. If regression testing is not done as new increments are developed, regression faults will go unrevealed because the focus is on new features and code. These bugs can complicate or delay subsequent development increments, and will eventually cause field failures. Getting a new subclass working without exercising the superclass is often easy. It may be tempting to assume that the inherited features "just work." But, as noted in Chapter 4, With the Necessary Changes, this assumption is unwarranted without adequate integration and regression testing. Just as all forms of testing promote reuse with tangible evidence of dependability, so too does regression testing. Furthermore, an adequate regression test suite that can be rerun by a consumer provides a convincing demonstration that a component "works out of the box."

Regression testing does *not* reduce the need to develop and run tests of new and changed capabilities at either component or system scope.

- A regression test suite does not contain tests for new or changed capabilities.
- When a test suite can be reused as a regression test suite, it is no longer effective as a primary test suite. Because the baseline has passed all of its test cases, the baseline test suite has revealed all the bugs that it can. It does not become effective until a change is made in the component or in another component in the same system.
- Regression suites typically achieve 40 percent to 60 percent statement coverage [Jones 97, Rothermel+98]. Consequently, they cannot be relied on as the sole means of testing.

---

1. Bad fixes are a chronic problem. Myers observed more than 20 years ago that "Experience shows that modifying an existing program is a more error-prone process (in terms of errors per statement written) than writing a new program" [Myers 79, 20].

- Using an inadequate baseline test suite for regression testing cannot improve the test suite's effectiveness. If a baseline test suite does not achieve adequate coverage, then rerunning it as a regression test suite cannot achieve higher coverage.

Despite these limitations, regression testing plays an important role in revealing bugs. The single most costly bug in software history could have been revealed by regression testing. The software failure in the Ariane 5 rocket controller that lead to in-flight destruction of a payload valued at $350 million[2] was in large part due to an assumption that previously tested code would work when it was reused, obviating the need for regression testing.

> The Ada implementation [of the controller] did generate an assertion violation the very first time Ariane 5 dynamics were applied to it. Unfortunately, the very first time Ariane 5 dynamics were applied to it was at LAUNCH! They were not applied earlier, because the contractor assumed that the Ariane 5 dynamics were the same as the Ariane 4, so why spend the money testing the same conditions already tested earlier? (They were wrong, of course, but they didn't know that at the time.) The other part of the problem was that the *response* to the assertion violation was wrong. The designer assumed the assertion would occur due to a hardware failure, not a software requirements failure, and so the handler shut down the "offending" hardware, rather than attempting some other action (e.g., replacing the out-of-range value with a "safe" value). [Ken Garlington, posted to Usenet news group comp.object, July 15, 1997].

Two errors in test planning contributed to this failure. First, regression testing was not performed on the entire system (including the assumed-good reused code). Second, the components that interacted to cause the failure were not integrated and subjected to system testing.

Although object-oriented technologies offer strong support for reuse, they cannot prevent all regression bugs. Developers of object-oriented systems that rely on reuse cannot take high dependability for granted. Routine and systematic regression testing can, however, help to realize the promise of high dependability through reuse.

---

2. For the June 1996 launch, Ariane 5 was carrying a payload of four satellites. It veered off course 37 seconds after launch and was destroyed by mission controllers. Estimates of the total cost vary from a low of $350 million in a European Space Agency press release to a high of $2.5 billion reported in "From Champagne to Shock: Ariane 5 Explodes," *Florida Today Space Online*, June 4, 1996. Subsequent launches have been successful.

15.1.2 When and How

After an initial test suite has been run, regression testing can be performed on any scope IUT and at any point in its development. At component scope, a delta is produced by changing a baseline component. At system scope, a regression test is run on the delta build, which results after new components or delta(s) have been integrated in a baseline system. Regression testing is indicated in several situations:

- *When a new subclass has been developed.* Rerun the superclass tests on the subclass, besides new tests for the new subclass. (See Considerations for Subclass Testing, Chapter 10.)

- *When a superclass is changed.* Rerun the superclass tests on the superclass and on its subclasses. Rerun the subclass tests. (See Considerations for Subclass Testing, Chapter 10.)

- *When a server class is changed.* Rerun tests for the clients of the changed class plus testing the changed class. (See Considerations for Subclass Testing, Chapter 10.) **Retest Within Firewall** provides a detailed model for determining the effects of this kind of change.

- *When a bug fix has been completed.* If the bug was revealed by a test, rerun the test—it should now pass. Then, rerun tests on any parts of the IUT that depend on the changed code to reveal unintended side effects of the bug fix. **Retest Within Firewall** provides a detailed model for determining the effects of this kind of change.

- *When a new system build has been generated.* A build test suite should pass if the build is successful and there are no egregious bugs. A build test suite typically includes smoke tests and tests that exercise each primary feature of the SUT. It typically does not attempt extensive feature coverage, however.

- *When a new increment is generated for system scope integration testing or system testing.* All of the previous increment test suites that are still valid should be rerun before the newly developed tests for the current increment are run. This effort will reveal bad or missing fixes for past increments, incompatibilities, and unwanted side effects of the new code.

- *When a system has stabilized and the final release build has been generated.* The final build generation may include production-only files, locale-specific code, disabled built-in test code (e.g., assertions), and other changes.

Rerun the entire system test suite on this build generation to reveal inadvertently introduced bugs and omitted items.

The basic procedure for regression testing is the same in all situations.

1. Remove broken test cases from the original test suite (a **broken test case** is one that cannot run on the delta build, usually because of a change to an interface).
2. Choose a full regression test suite or a reduced regression test suite.
3. Set up the test configuration.
4. Run the regression test suite.
5. Take appropriate action for any no pass tests.

15.1.3 Regression Faults

A **regression fault** occurs when both a stable baseline system B and a delta component D pass individually adequate test suites, but fail when used together.[3] D can cause some component in B to fail only if a dependency exists between them. Dependencies occur for many reasons, including activation paths (control flow), object usage paths (data flow), sequential activation constraints, shared object serialization, timing, and resource contention. Regression faults can occur in many ways.

- D has a side effect on B. D allocates, changes the value of, or deallocates a global variable, class variable, persistent object, or database tuple used by B. B fails because the new action of D is inconsistent with B's requirements, assumptions, or contract with respect to this object.
- D is a client of B. D sends a message that violates B's invariant or a precondition. B is not defensive, accepts the incorrect message, and fails.
- D is a server of B. B sends a message to D. D's postconditions have changed or are buggy. D returns a value that causes a violation of B's

---

3. This situation is another example of the anticomposition axiom. See the Test Strategy for Flattened Classes section in Chapter 10.

invariant or a postcondition. *B* either fails or returns an invalid value to another baseline component *C. C* fails.

- *D* is a revised superclass. *B* is a client of *E,* a subclass of *D.* Neither the interface nor contract of *D* or *E* has been changed. The implementation of *D* has changed, however, and the effective behavior of *E* is different. For example, *D* uses a new algorithm that is slower or faster, sends a message to a distributed object introducing nondeterminism, can now throw exceptions, and so on. *E* and *D* have been adequately tested and integrated. Because of the nondeterminism, *B* depends on *E*'s old timing, cannot catch the new exception, or produces an incorrect result. *B* fails.

- *D* is a new subclass of a polymorphic hierarchy that is not LSP-compliant. *B* is a client of *D* and expects the new subtype to be compatible. *D* does not comply with all of the superclass contracts, producing an inconsistent state. *B* attempts to use this object and fails.

- *D* produces a new output that is correct with respect to *D*'s specification. This value is saved in persistent storage, which either (1) triggers an existing (but not revealed) fault in *B,* violates *B*'s contract, and generates an exception, or, causes *B* to violate the contract of another baseline component *C. C* fails. For example, *D* expands the allowed range of a parameter x from 10–99 to 10–100. *B* obtains x from *D,* but continues to treat x == 100 as incorrect. *B* will fail if *D* produces this value.[4]

- *D* is incompatible with *B.* Even if the requirements and the implementation have not changed, if another change materially affects the SUT, a failure can result. The Ariane 5 disaster resulted from an incorrect floating-point conversion. The requirements, the algorithm, and the code did not change.

- An undesirable feature interaction occurs between *B* and *D.*

These faults can occur at intracomponent, subsystem, and system scopes. The preceding scenarios apply when classes, clusters, and components are the baseline system and code changed within that scope is the delta component(s).

To reach a regression fault, a *B* component that depends on a *D* must be activated. Because *D* may introduce (or remove) dependencies, dependency analysis should be developed for each new configuration. To trigger a regression

---

4. If the baseline test suite includes a 1×1 domain test for x (see *Invariant Boundaries*), this fault will be revealed, because the baseline test expects that 100 would be rejected.

fault, an effect of *D* must have been produced before *B* is activated and must be sufficient to cause an incorrect result in *B*'s computation. Reaching the fault in *B* is not sufficient to trigger a failure, as the preceding domain inconsistency shows. Once triggered, *B*'s propagation impedance will typically be the same. That is, if *B* has a high propagation impedance, regression failures are likely to be masked.[5] Conversely, if *B* has a low propagation impedance, regression failures are likely to be observable.[6] Thus running a regression test suite is necessary to reveal regression faults but is not sufficient to reveal all regression faults. There is, of course, no practical means to develop a test suite guaranteed to reveal all regression faults.

15.1.4 Test Automation

Manual regression testing is not a good thing. Although manual testing can be effective for initial testing of some components or systems, it cannot support repeatable and consistent regression testing. As development progresses, components are debugged, refactored, revised, and enhanced. The only way to rerun a manual test is to have a person reenter it and judge the result. Newer components are the typical focus of manual testing—it may be hard for testers to see benefit in the laborious repetition of tests that have already passed. As the number of passed tests increases, so does the time needed to rerun them all. As a project nears completion, testers are faced with two undesirable options: (1) rerun fewer baseline test cases and focus on the tests necessary to validate the final increments, or (2) add more people to enter and judge the increasing number of baseline test cases. Typically, only the first option is acceptable. The percentage of the baseline test suite manually rerun tends to approach zero as the ship date nears. As Beizer observes, "The almost universal experience with attempts at manual regression testing is that it doesn't actually happen. . . . This is a dangerous situation because as a product matures, the incidence of bugs caused by maintenance actions converges to the same rate as all other bugs combined . . . the incidence of maintenance bugs [will rise] to unacceptably high levels" [Beizer 95, 235]. Thus, although manual runs are the best approach for some tests and automated test suites necessarily incur maintenance costs, the

---

5. Propagation impedance is the extent to which the SUT prevents an incorrect result from becoming an observable failure.

6. The changes may increase (decrease) propagation impedance. For example, suppose that a superclass invariant is incorrectly weakened. This change would allow corrupt states, which might have triggered an assertion violation, to go unreported.

ability to rerun some or all of the accumulated baseline test cases under software control is necessary if regression testing is to be done.

The specifics of test automation are discussed in Part IV. Effective automated regression testing requires the following general capabilities:

• *Version control.* The test suites and the SUT must be under configuration management control.

• *Modular structure.* Baseline test suites grow with successive increments and releases. It is often desirable to select or change a subset of the baseline test suite. Organizing test suites (and the test harness) into small modules that correspond to use cases, components, or another reasonable unit of work will facilitate selection and maintenance. On the other hand, a monolithic test suite may be difficult to use and vulnerable to errors.

• *Compare baseline and delta results.* The expected or actual results of each baseline test case must be saved in a form that can be compared with the actual results of each regression test case. Automatic pass/no pass evaluation cannot be achieved without comparing the baseline and delta results. The use of expected results developed for the baseline test case or the actual results produced by its test run depends on the application and the test harness design. Considerations for comparators are discussed in Chapter 18.

• *Smart comparator.* The ability to ignore some output fields while comparing expected and actual results can be useful. For example, suppose the SUT outputs a time stamp that necessarily changes for each run. Comparing for equality would result in a no pass, even if all other outputs were the same. This situation can be avoided if the comparison can ignore this field, check for a valid date, check that the baseline date precedes the delta date, and so on.

• *Shuffling.* Some bugs are sequence-sensitive (see Chapter 7). If baseline tests that should be sequence-independent are always rerun in the same order, we miss an opportunity to reveal sequence bugs. The chance of revealing these kinds of bugs increases if the test harness automatically shuffles the order of the test suite [Siegel 96]. The shuffled define-use algorithm presented in **Nonmodal Class Test**, outlined in Chapter 10, suggests how this goal can be accomplished.

• *Built-in test.* Assertions can check that both client and server objects meet the usage contract. Although assertions cannot detect all bugs, they can perform many useful checks and avoid some test suite maintenance problems.

Test drivers packaged with a class or component can reduce the cost of test maintenance. The details of built-in test is discussed in Chapter 17.

Ideally, regression tests should be run in a completely controllable target environment where only the SUT changes from the baseline to the regression test run. The test harness must therefore be able to reset the entire test configuration to the same state and configuration used in the baseline test. In practice, many factors can result in a less-than-identical test configuration:

- A difference occurs in the test environment—for example, in the hardware, operating system, GUI, DBMS, ORB, compiler, linker, command-line utilities, testing tools, and so on.
- Different content appears in persistent storage used by the SUT—for example, files, databases, object bases, and so on. Resetting to the same state can be difficult or impossible when testers must use existing systems that are maintained by other parties or that are part of a live application.
- The SUT uses nondeterministic objects—for example, collection iterators that do not guarantee that the members of a collection are returned in the same order.
- The SUT uses nonrepeatable, pseudorandom generation—for example, the system clock used as a seed.
- The SUT is sensitive to timing differences in the load or arrival rate of some input determined by an external, noncontrollable system.
- The SUT is sensitive to the sequence of some input determined by an external, noncontrollable system.
- The SUT accepts transactions that require serialization for consistent results, but serialization is not supported, is not enabled, or is provided by a later development increment.
- The SUT uses time- or date-sensitive code.
- The SUT uses noncontrollable external input sources—for example, signals from physical processes, communication lines, actual e-commerce traffic, and so on.

Achieving a controlled test configuration can be quite difficult in a complex, multiplatform test environment. In distributed systems, many of these factors are often not under the control of the tester. Testers should try to identify uncontrollable factors and test cases influenced by them. These tests should be removed from the regression test suite or relegated to smoke test status, because the production of a different result by the delta build does not necessarily reveal a regression fault.

The TOBAC system illustrates some issues in designing automated regression testing tools for object-oriented development [Siepmann+94]. This system is designed to support high-frequency, system scope regression testing for Smalltalk development. If a new method is added, it may produce states that are "inappropriate for the existing methods. Therefore, every change to an object's implementation may require complete retesting of that object" [Siepmann+94, 156]. Object-oriented systems are typically composed of *complex objects,* each of which is a composite obtained by recursively expanding object instance variables. Because test cases must correctly initialize variables, the state of a complex object is very important.

> Defining test cases for complex objects requires first and foremost the ability to create these complex objects and set them to specific states. There are three ways to do this: (1) using only existing methods, (2) defining special creation methods (constructors) only used for testing, (3) building a complex object from its subobjects [Siepmann+94, 155].

If "canned" objects are used to set the system state in a regression test, the effect of changes may be missed or masked. Instead, regression testing requires "fresh" complex objects. TOBAC can construct and store new complex objects every time a test is rerun. "Maintaining a description of how to create a complex object is one of the keys for regression testing of object-oriented software" [Siepmann+94, 157]. A *replacement list* is kept in a test case object. Subclasses may be tested from a test case for superclasses by using the replacement list. Regression testing of a class subclassed from a tested class is simplified. Suppose a test suite is developed that includes class X. Later, subclass X' is subclassed from X. The replacement list allows X' to be tested with the original test suite.

Regression tests run from a GUI capture/playback tool are the workhorses of testing. Test scripts developed for these tools can be quite effective. Unfortunately, they have significant limitations and require ongoing maintenance.

- *Brittleness.* If widgets are added or deleted from a GUI, previously recorded scripts will almost certainly not work. Although COTS capture/playback tools have made significant improvements in this area, most changes in the GUI still require manual recoding of the test script.

- *Timing sensitivity.* The speed of desktop computers and user workstations can easily vary by a factor of 10 or more. A script that is rerun on a faster or slower client machine may fail because the server-side response is no longer synchronized with the state of the GUI.

- *Content sensitivity.* The response of the SUT to GUI inputs typically depends on values stored in a database and other persistence mechanisms. If the test script does not establish the same content, the response for the regression run will probably not be the same as that for the baseline run. The scripts will probably interpret this difference as a no pass test result.

- *Unrecognized widgets.* The widgets in a new release of a GUI (not the application) may not be compatible with scripts recorded for the previous version. Some widgets may not be recognized at all.

Thus, although GUI-based test automation is useful for regression testing, it cannot be assumed that stabilized test suites can be rerun without ongoing maintenance effort. Additional issues related to manual versus automated testing arise. For example, some kinds of tests require tester interaction [Kaner 97].

15.1.5   Test Suite Maintenance

Additions and changes to the SUT call for corresponding changes in its test suite. After several release cycles, a regression test suite can become quite large. Test suite decay is inevitable and occurs for several reasons. Baseline test cases become obsolete as the application's interface, capabilities, and implementation evolve. Some test cases will simply fail to run and must be removed. Redundant test cases can easily occur in large test suites. Testers are often reluctant to remove baseline test cases, however, because of the risk of throwing away a test that would reveal some current or future fault. However, the following kinds of baseline test cases can be (or must be) discarded:

- *Broken test cases.* A baseline test case attempts to use a widget, code segment, component, or an interface that was removed or changed, or the results of the baseline test are compared using an interface or data structure that has changed. The test case fails without being run and must be removed or reworked.

- *Obsolete test cases.* A baseline test case is accepted by the SUT, but is no longer appropriate because requirements have changed. For example, suppose the limits on x change from $1 \leq x \leq 100$ to $1 \leq x \leq 10,000$. The baseline on point tests for the upper boundary of x will still pass, but do not probe the boundary. The baseline off point tests for the upper boundary of x incorrectly require that 101 is rejected. Neither baseline test probes the new boundary.

• *Uncontrollable test cases.* A baseline test case is sensitive to uncontrolled inputs or states. These kinds of tests are of dubious value, as they may not be repeatable even with the initial test cycle. At best, a partially controllable test may be effective as a smoke test, which passes if the test inputs are simply accepted without causing an exception or abnormal termination.

• *Redundant test cases.* Two or more baseline test cases are redundant if their input and output for a specific interface is identical. Identical test cases are not necessarily redundant, however. Tests are sometimes repeated to perform a necessary setup, or to accomplish a time delay, or because coding test cases is easier than developing iterative control in the test driver or script.

A leading aerospace manufacturer used a regression test suite that had grown to 165,000 test cases after several years of use.[7] The elapsed time of the test run had become unacceptable. The solution involved several kinds of analysis and revision. First, the regression test suite was run on an instrumented build. This effort revealed that nearly 90 percent of the test cases were redundant and that many segments of the application were not reached at all. Next, reverse engineering of the application was performed to find out which test cases were still applicable, as available documentation was inadequate. Approximately 3000 new test cases were developed to achieve statement coverage. After the cleanup, some 18,000 test cases remained. Although this situation was extreme, it is not atypical. Jones notes that, in the organizations he studied, "About 30% of the regression test cases were duplicates that could be removed without reducing test effectiveness. About 12% of the regression test cases contained errors of some kind" [Jones 97, 83].

The cleanup outlined in Procedure 18 will keep a regression test suite at a high level of effectiveness and efficiency. This procedure should be carried out at least after every major increment or release. Not only is testing efficiency improved by removing obsolete test cases, but the credibility of the test suite is also improved. If obsolete test cases are not pruned away, the test suite has questionable effectiveness. Suppose some obsolete tests no longer pass, but the tester "knows" to ignore these failures. If pass/no pass of the entire test suite is

---

7. Information from Ross Collard, Seminar on Test Automation, May 1995.

1. Run the baseline test suite on the delta build. Remove or rework broken and obsolete test cases.

2. Correct all revealed bugs. If some low-severity bugs are left unfixed, be sure that the test case documentation explains the discrepancy. Do not remove tests that reveal unfixed bugs.

3. Merge component scope test cases developed for new delta component capabilities with the baseline test suite.

4. Instrument the delta build using a coverage analyzer that maps test cases to segments or paths.

5. Rerun the test suite on the instrumented delta build.

6. Analyze tests that traverse the same entry–exit paths. Are these tests necessary to achieve some state, implement a delay, or support a dependency? If not, remove all but one of the tests whose input and actual output are identical for a segment set, an entry–exit path, or a call path.

7. If some segment, component, or critical interface is not exercised, develop a new test to reach it (unless it is truly unreachable).

8. Rerun the test suite on the uninstrumented delta build. All tests should pass. If not, run and debug the SUT (or the tests) until all tests pass.

9. Check in the revised test suite as the new baseline test suite. If your CM tool supports cross-linking, associate the new baseline test suite with the new baseline build of the SUT.

Procedure 18   Regression Test Suite Maintenance

reduced to *and*ing each individual test case status, then each no pass result must be considered individually to decide whether the entire run is acceptable.

15.1.6   Considerations for Reducing a Test Suite

Even conscientiously maintained test suites can grow quite large. Sometimes, re-running an entire test suite is not practical. A **full regression test** includes every baseline test case. Time and cost constraints may preclude running such a test, in which case a **reduced regression test** can be selected, supporting **selective regression testing**.

A regression test suite is valuable because it is a controlled experiment. By removing test cases, we also eliminate the chance of finding a regression bug in the code this test exercises. If we analyze code dependencies in the delta build, however, we can decide which test cases can be removed without defeating the purpose of regression testing. These approaches are **safe reduction** techniques. A test suite can be reduced in other ways, but these are **unsafe reductions**, without dependency analysis; that is, they can remove test cases that would reveal a regression bug.

Safe Reduction

A 100 percent **safe** regression suite consists of "all tests that could possibly exhibit different output when run on [the delta build]" [Rothermel+94]. Regression strategies can be compared on the basis of four criteria [Rothermel+96]. Each regression testing pattern is evaluated by these criteria in the Consequences section for that pattern.

- **Inclusiveness** is the percentage of baseline tests that *may* show regression faults and that are selected for a reduced test suite. A safe regression test suite is 100 percent inclusive.
- **Precision** is the percentage of baseline test cases in a reduced test suite that *cannot* reveal regression faults and that are *not* selected for the reduced test suite. For example, a regression test suite of 100 test cases that includes one test case that cannot reach changed code is 99 percent precise. A **precise** regression suite does not include any tests that cannot cause different output as these tests can be safely removed.
- **Efficiency** is the cost of identifying a reduced regression test suite.
- **Generality** is the range of application for the selection strategy.

Rothermel and Harrold argue that no test suite can be both safe and 100 percent precise as there is no way to decide exactly which tests will pass or fail for the changed system [Rothermel+96].

> Passing a "safe" regression test suite does not demonstrate the absence of regression bugs or any other kind of bug. It simply means that all baseline test cases that *could* reveal a regression bug have been exercised.

The **Retest Changed Code** and **Retest Within Firewall** patterns produce safe reductions, if the dependency analysis is accurate. The safest reduction is, of course, no reduction at all: **Retest All**.

Unsafe Reduction

Other ways of reducing a test suite are not based on code dependency analysis. These reductions are unsafe because they can omit test cases that might reveal a regression bug.

- *Systematic sampling.* Select every *n*th baseline test case automatically. This approach provides a simple way to control the scope of testing. Suppose testing time is cut by two-thirds, perhaps owing to delays in design or programming. The size of the regression test suite could be reduced in the same proportion by selecting every third test case.

- *Random sampling.* Select baseline test cases automatically, so that, given some *n,* each baseline test case has a 1/*n* chance of being selected for the regression suite. For a large enough baseline, this selection will almost certainly produce a different test suite each time.[8]

- *Coverage-based filtering.* Several COTS coverage analyzers can identify tests that exercise the same components and offer this ability as a feature for reducing regression test suites. For example, suppose that 23 out of 100 tests take path *ABDFHK*. Then, it is argued that 23 of these tests may be dropped from the regression suite. This assumption is highly questionable. Although the tests may take the same path, they may exercise different boundary conditions or take the IUT into a different state on each test. From the cover-

---

8. The *n*th and 1/*n* selections will produce test suites that overlap in terms of test cases to some extent. An every-*n*th selection will produce the same tests each time. A 1/*n* selection will produce the same total number of tests. With a suitable pseudorandom algorithm, a different set of tests can be selected or the same selection can be reproduced.

age information alone, there is no way of knowing which tests can safely be removed.

Reduction by sampling is appealing because it is systematic, can be automated, and is not influenced by subjective bias. For example, suppose a developer concludes that "I know foo always works, so we can skip those tests—I didn't change anything." But suppose that innocent foo is clobbered by a bug in a new object oof. The tests for oof pass, and its bug will be revealed only if foo is exercised. Systematic selection has a low probability of making this kind of mistake, but it can produce an unusable mess if the test cases in the baseline test suite have dependencies. For example, suppose that test case 2134 relies on the objects created and initialized in test case 2118. If test case 2118 is not selected, 2134 will either not run or provide spurious results.

Retest by Profile requires that all use cases be exercised and in the same relative frequency as the full test suite, but with fewer tests per use case. It avoids the bias problem and may avoid some dependency problems, as use case tests should be independent.

What about reducing by suspicion? An independent tester might have a very good idea about which new components are likely to cause trouble or which components depend on some others. This information can be used to choose test cases. *Retest Risky Use Cases* presents this approach.

Despite their seeming appeal, the sampling techniques *Retest by Profile* and *Retest Risky Use Cases* are both unsafe because they are not based on dependency analysis. They are presented here to make clear the choices and consequences of using reduced regression test suites.

15.2 Test Patterns

Five test patterns for selecting regression test suites follow:

- *Retest All.* Rerun all baseline tests.
- *Retest Risky Use Cases.* Choose baseline tests to rerun by risk heuristics.
- *Retest by Profile.* Choose baseline tests to rerun by allocating time in proportion to the operational profile.
- *Retest Changed Segments.* Choose baseline tests to rerun by comparing code changes.

- *Retest Within Firewall.* Choose baseline tests to rerun by analyzing dependencies.
- *Retest All* is the default choice. It is the simplest, and easiest, and it poses the least risk of missing a regression bug. If the time or cost of a full regression run is prohibitive, however, a reduced regression test suite must be selected. *Retest Risky Use Cases* and *Retest by Profile* are black box strategies for selective regression testing. Selection is made by analyzing implementation-independent relationships, requirements, and capabilities, which produces unsafe test suites. *Retest Changed Segments* and *Retest Within Firewall* are white box strategies for partial regression that require analysis of implementation dependencies and produce safe test suites.

Retest All

Intent

Rerun the entire baseline test suite on a delta build.

Context

This pattern is applicable at any scope. It may be used to support iterative development, the instantiation of reusable components, and maintenance. (See Section 15.1.2, When and How.)

Fault Model

A delta component induces a failure because of an incompatibility, side effect, or undesirable feature interaction. (See Section 15.1.3, Regression Faults.)

Strategy

Test Model

The baseline test suite is reused.

Test Procedure

The baseline test suite is rerun after removing broken test cases.

Oracle

The results of the baseline test run provide the oracle. That is, if the SUT produces the same results in the regression run as it did in the baseline run, the test passes.

Automation

See Section 15.1.4, Test Automation.

Entry Criteria

Regression testing may begin when the following conditions are met:

- ✓ The delta components pass component scope testing.
- ✓ A suitable baseline test suite exists.
- ✓ The test environment is restored to the same configuration used to run the original baseline test suite. If this is not feasible, the noncontrolable

components should be noted and the risk they pose to the validity of the test run should be assessed.

Exit Criteria

✓ All no pass test cases reveal bugs whose presence and severity are deemed acceptable.

✓ All remaining test cases pass.

Consequences

Table 15.2 compares the relative cost and risk of regression testing approaches. Retest All has the lowest risk of missing a regression fault, but the highest test cost.

- *Inclusiveness.* All baseline tests are selected. Retest All is safe.

- *Precision.* No tests that could be skipped are skipped. Retest All is the least precise.

- *Efficiency.* Retest All has the lowest cost of analysis and setup but the highest run cost, compared with the partial regression patterns discussed later in this chapter.

TABLE 15.2   Cost and Risk of Regression Testing Patterns Compared

| Regression Testing Activity | Cost and Risk of Regression Testing Patterns | | | | |
	Retest All	Retest Risky Use Cases	Retest by Profile	Retest Within Firewall	Retest Changed Code
Scope	System	System	System	Cluster	Class
Remove broken test cases	¢	¢	¢	¢	¢
Analyze dependencies				¢–$	¢–$
Remove obsolete test cases				¢–$$	¢–$$
Remove redundant test cases				¢–$$	¢–$$
Set up test run	¢¢	¢	¢	¢	¢
Test design cost	Lowest	Low	Low	Highest	High
Test run cost	Highest	Budget limited	Budget limited	Size of firewall	Size of deltas
Evaluate no pass tests	¢¢	¢	¢	¢	¢
Risk of omission	Lowest	Moderate	Moderate	Low	Low
"Safe"?	Yes	No	No	Yes	Yes

Key: ¢ = lowest cost, ¢¢ = low cost, $ = medium cost, $$ = high cost

- *Generality*. Retest All can be applied in nearly any circumstance. The test run is easy to set up and does not require any analysis or special development. It typically can be run by technicians with basic skills.

Running a test suite that has not been maintained is a wasteful and ineffective practice. Periodic pruning of dead and redundant test cases will avoid this waste and the problems discussed in Section 15.1.5, Test Suite Maintenance.

Known Uses

This pattern is used extensively. Jones reports that 70 percent of all U.S. projects studied use regression testing [Jones 97, 403]. Regression testing was a key element of the daily build [Zachary 94]. The continuous integration used in the Extreme Programming approach also relies on regression testing [Anderson+98].

Related Patterns

The test suites used to support **High-frequency Integration** are regression tests, for the most part.

Retest Risky Use Cases

Intent

Use risk-based heuristics to select a partial regression test suite. Run this subset on a delta build.

Context

The available time, personnel, or equipment is not sufficient for a full regression run. How can a subset of a baseline test suite be selected without complicated implementation analysis? This pattern is applicable at any scope. It may be used to support iterative development, the instantiation of reusable components, and maintenance. (See Section 15.1.2, When and How.)

Fault Model

A delta component suffers a failure because of an incompatibility, side effect, or undesirable feature interaction. (See Section 15.1.3, Regression Faults.)

Strategy

Test Model

The following risk criteria can be used to select a subset of a baseline test suite:

- *Suspicious use cases.* Select tests for use cases that depend on components, objects, middleware, or other resources that (1) are individually unstable or unproven, (2) have not been shown to work together before or are unstable, (3) implement complex business rules, (4) have a complex implementation (e.g., are 10 times the code size of all other components), or (5) were subject to high churn during development.
- *Critical use cases.* Select tests for use cases that are necessary for safe, effective operation. For each use case, try to identify the worst-case effects of failure. Skip tests for use cases where a failure can have only a level three or four severity.

The goal is to skip enough noncritical, low-priority, or highly stable use cases to meet a deadline or budget constraint.

Test Procedure

Identify, develop, and run the reduced test suite. (See Section 15.1.2, When and How.)

Oracle

The results of the baseline test run provide the oracle. That is, if the SUT produces the same results in the regression run as it did in the baseline run, the test passes.

Automation

See Section 15.1.4, Test Automation. A modular test suite will facilitate selection and execution of the desired subset.

Entry Criteria

Regression testing may begin when the following conditions are met:

- ✓ The delta components pass component scope testing.
- ✓ A suitable baseline test suite exists.
- ✓ The test environment has been restored to the same configuration used to run the original baseline test suite. If this is not feasible, the noncontrollable components should be noted and the risk they pose to the validity of the test run should be assessed.

Exit Criteria

- ✓ All no pass test cases reveal bugs whose presence and severity are deemed acceptable.
- ✓ All remaining test cases pass.

Consequences

See Table 15.2 (page 775). Retest Risky Use Cases has a moderate risk of missing a regression fault and generally a low cost of analysis and setup.

- *Inclusiveness.* Retest Risky Use Cases is unsafe, because test cases are not selected by analysis of dependencies.
- *Precision.* Some tests that could be skipped may be repeated.

- *Efficiency.* The time and cost associated with testing are constrained. Because selection is based on use cases (requirements) and not implementation dependencies, the analysis can be done without code analyzers or in-depth technical knowledge of the SUT. Estimating the time or cost reduction may be difficult unless baseline time/cost information is available by test segment.
- *Generality.* Retest Risky Use Cases can be applied in nearly any circumstance and at any scope.

Dependencies among test cases must be considered in selecting a reduced test suite.

Known Uses

Reducing test suites by focusing on risks and customer priorities is a common practice [Kaner+93, Bach 97].

Related Patterns

No directly related patterns exist. This pattern may be used to support many testing situations.

Retest by Profile

Intent

Use a budget-constrained operational profile to select a partial regression test suite. Run this subset on a delta build.

Context

The available time, personnel, or equipment is not sufficient for a full regression run. How can a subset of a baseline test suite be selected that provides the greatest dependability within the deadline or budget? This pattern is applicable at any scope. It may be used to support iterative development, the instantiation of reusable components, and maintenance.

Fault Model

A delta component induces a failure because of an incompatibility, side effect, or undesirable feature interaction. (See Section 15.1.3, Regression Faults.) *Allocate Tests by Profile* discusses the relationship between frequency-based testing and reliability.

Strategy

Test Model

If the baseline test suite was developed with *Allocate Tests by Profile*, the number of test cases for each use case can be found by using the total budget for regression testing. As the test suite has already been developed, only the average time needed to run each test case is modeled. The expected bug rate is reduced (we hope!) compared with the bug rate expected for the initial baseline testing cycle. Average debugging time probably will not be reduced. For example, suppose that 100 hours (6000 minutes) are available for regression testing of the ATM example discussed in Chapter 14. Assume that an average of 5 minutes is required to run one test case, a test reveals a bug 0.5 percent of the time, and a bug fix requires an average of 4 hours (240 minutes). Suppose the baseline test suite has 20,000 test cases. How many of these test cases can we run? Stating the units in minutes and letting T be the total number of tests, then

$$T + (0.005 \times 240T)\ 5 = 6000$$
$$1.2T\quad = 6000$$
$$T\quad = 5000$$

For this example, approximately 5000 test cases can be run within the budget constraint. Table 15.3 shows how this test budget is allocated to the system use cases, based on the operational profile. The number of test cases is distributed in proportion to the relative frequency of each use case.

Test Procedure

Identify, develop, and run the reduced test suite. Verify that all critical use cases and use case variants are included in the regression test suite, even if they occur at a low frequency.

Oracle

The results of the baseline test run provide the oracle. That is, if the SUT produces the same results in the regression run as it did in the baseline run, the test passes.

Automation

See Section 15.1.4, Test Automation. A modular test suite will ease selection and execution of the desired subset. Tracebility from use case to test case is essential. A test harness that supports either sampling or randomization can automate the work of selection. In the preceding example, about 25 percent of the baseline test suite is selected. This selection could be accomplished with a 1/4

TABLE 15.3   Allocation of Regression Test Time by Use Case Frequency

Use Case	Probability	Number of Tests
Cash Withdrawal	0.53	2650
Checking Deposit	0.15	750
Savings Deposit	0.14	700
Funds Transfer	0.08	400
Balance Inquiry	0.06	300
Restock	0.02	100
Collect Deposits	0.02	100
Total	1.00	5000

test random selector that gave every test a 25 percent chance of being selected. More sophisticated approaches are possible as well.

Entry Criteria

This pattern requires that the baseline test suite has been developed using *Allocate Tests by Profile*. Regression testing may begin when the following conditions are met:

- ✓ The delta components pass component scope testing.
- ✓ A suitable baseline test suite exists.
- ✓ The test environment has been restored to the same configuration used to run the original baseline test suite. If this is not feasible, the noncontrollable components should be noted and the risk they pose to the validity of the test run should be assessed.

Exit Criteria

- ✓ All no pass test cases reveal bugs whose presence and severity are deemed acceptable.
- ✓ All remaining test cases pass.

Consequences

See Table 15.2 (page 775). Retest by Profile has a moderate risk of missing a regression fault.

- *Inclusiveness.* Retest by Profile is unsafe, as test cases are not selected by analysis of dependencies.
- *Precision.* Some tests that could be skipped may be repeated.
- *Efficiency.* The time and cost to run the tests are constrained. Because selection is based on use cases (requirements) and not implementation dependencies, the analysis can be done without code analyzers or in-depth technical knowledge of the SUT. Estimating the time or cost reduction may be difficult unless baseline time/cost information is available by test segment. If the operational profile has already been established, the cost of the selection analysis should be low.
- *Generality.* Retest by Profile can be applied in many circumstances. As the effectiveness of profile-based testing diminishes at a smaller scope,

this technique is best suited to system scope testing of applications for which an accurate operational profile can be developed.

Dependencies among test cases must be considered in selecting a reduced test suite.

Known Uses

Musa advocates regression testing using the operational profile [Musa 98].

Related Patterns

Allocate Tests by Profile.

Retest Changed Code

Intent

Use code change analysis to select a partial regression test suite. Run this subset on a delta build.

Context

The available time, personnel, or equipment is not sufficient for a full regression run. How can a subset of a baseline test suite be selected using automated code analysis? This pattern is applicable at the class, cluster, or subsystem scope and after maintenance, for reuse, and during iterative development. It may be used to support iterative development, the instantiation of reusable components, and maintenance. (See Section 15.1.2, When and How.)

Fault Model

The delta component induces a failure because of an incompatibility, side effect, or undesirable feature interaction. (See Section 15.1.3, Regression Faults.)

Strategy

Test Model

Implementation-based regression test selection is concerned with finding baseline tests that will reveal regression faults in the delta. A regression fault must be related to a new, modified, or deleted code segment. Baseline tests are selected by comparing each segment in the baseline and delta component. All baseline tests that have reached a changed or deleted segment are selected. Rothermel and Harrold call this approach the "graph walk technique" and show that it is safe [Rothermel+94]. The details of the graph walk algorithm for C++ are presented in [Rothermel+94]. Refinements are discussed in [Rothermel+96] and [Rothermel+98].

   The basic code change model does not consider data flow, control flow, or other dependencies arising from state-based behavior, iteration, or recursion. It does not explicitly consider the effects of inheritance or dynamic binding.

TABLE 15.4 Segment/Test Case Coverage

Coverage Analyzer Output	BlockTest.txt
t1: b1, b3, b6, b7	b1 t1
t2: b1, b4, b8,	b3 t1
t3: b2, b5	b6 t1
	b7 t1
	b1 t2
	b4 t2
	b8 t2
	b2 t3
	b5 t3

Test Procedure

The following steps accomplish the same analysis as the graph walk algorithm using a coverage analyzer, version control tool, and several command-line utilities.

1. Obtain a report from your coverage analyzer that lists code segments by test case for the baseline SUT and test suite, as shown on the left of Table 15.4.

2. Extract pairs with each segment ID and test case ID, as shown on the right of Table 15.4. Parse the output with a Perl script or hand hack it into records. Make a file with these records, as suggested by BlockTest.txt.

3. Use a version control tool to generate a report on the changes between the baseline and the delta, as shown on the left of Table 15.5. Each record defines the segment number and the type of change: *same, new, changed,* or *deleted.* The result is the union of all blocks in both the baseline and delta implementation, with a tag that defines what change has occurred. Parse the report with a Perl script or hand hack this output into records. Make a file with these records, as suggested by BlockChange.txt.

4. Concatenate the test and change files. Sort the result by segment and test case. This sort can be easily accomplished with a few Unix commands.

```
cat BlockTest.txt BlockChange.txt | sort > SortedDelta.txt
```

The resulting file, SortedDelta.txt, is shown in the second column of Table 15.6.

TABLE 15.5   Segment Change Analysis

Version Control Report			BlockChange.txt
Baseline	Delta	Change	b1 same
---------------	----------	------------	b2 deleted
b1	b1	same	b3 changed
b2		deleted	b4 same
b3	b3	changed	b5 changed
b4	b4	same	b6 same
b5	b5	changed	b7 deleted
b6	b6	same	b8 changed
b7		deleted	b9 new
b8	b8	changed	
b9	new		

TABLE 15.6   Regression Test Selection from Sorted List

			Regression Test Plan		
Delta.txt	StoredDelta.txt	Action	t1	t2	t3
b1 same	b1 same				
b2 deleted	b1 t1	Skip			
b3 changed	b1 t2	Skip			
b4 same	b2 deleted				
b5 changed	b2 t3	Select			✓
b6 same	b3 changed				
b7 deleted	b3 t1	Select	✓		
b8 changed	b4 same				
b9 new	b4 t2	Select		✓	
b1 t1	b5 changed				
b3 t1	b5 t3	Select			✓
b6 t1	b6 same				
b7 t1	b6 t1	Skip			
b1 t2	b7 deleted				
b4 t2	b7 t1	Select	✓		
b8 t2	b8 changed				
b2 t3	b8 t2	Select		✓	
b5 t3	b9 new				

5. The list of tests to use and skip can be read from the list or extracted and formatted using another script. The selection rules are simple.

- Tests under *same*—skip.
- Tests under *deleted*—include.
- Tests under *changed*—include.
- Tests under *new*—should be empty.

The baseline test cases selected for the regression test suite are listed in the right column of Table 15.6.

Oracle

The results of the baseline test run provide the oracle. That is, if the SUT produces the same results in the regression run as it did in the baseline run, the test passes.

Automation

See Section 15.1.4, Test Automation. A modular test suite will facilitate selection and execution of the desired subset. The selection process can be automated in many ways. A tool that automates the graph walk technique is described in [Rothermel+94] and [Rothermel+98].

Entry Criteria

Regression testing can begin when the following conditions are met:

- ✓ The delta components pass component scope testing.
- ✓ A suitable baseline test suite exists.
- ✓ The test environment has been restored to the same configuration used to run the original baseline test suite. If this is not feasible, the non-controllable components should be noted and the risk they pose to the validity of the test run should be assessed.

Exit Criteria

- ✓ All no pass test cases reveal bugs whose presence and severity are deemed acceptable.
- ✓ All remaining test cases pass.

Consequences

See Table 15.2 (page 775). Retest Changed Code has a low risk of missing a regression fault.

- *Inclusiveness.* All baseline tests that can produce a different result are selected. Retest Changed Code is safe.
- *Precision.* Although few tests that could be skipped may be included, Retest Changed Code is the most precise of the white box partial regression strategies [Rothermel+98]. Baseline tests that exercise unchanged code are not selected for testing. This approach can reduce testing cost roughly in proportion to the extent of the changes. With many changes, just a few tests will probably be skipped; with just a few changes, however, most of the baseline tests will be skipped. These effects will be more pronounced for complex code. For example, all tests will be reselected for any change in method with only a single path.
- *Efficiency.* The computation is on the order of the size of the baseline test suite times the number of segments in the smaller of the baseline or delta component (the worst-case count can be higher). The direct cost of analysis and setup can be low, if automated. The coverage analyzer and the CM tool carry an indirect cost. This approach may reselect the entire baseline test suite, resulting in a test suite whose total run cost is greater than ***Retest All***. It does not guarantee any particular time and cost reduction. In fact, time or cost constraints may not be met.
- *Generality.* Retest Changed Code is applicable at class scope and requires the programmer to have skills in code analysis and related tools.

Dependencies among test cases must be considered in selecting a reduced test suite.

Known Uses

A research tool was developed to apply the graph walk approach to a C++ system [Rothermel+94]. The algorithm requires a connected flow graph. To analyze a class hierarchy, therefore, a "representative driver" was included for the class under test. Derived classes were flattened to account for interaction effects with base class features. Polymorphic calls were not expanded in the graph. When a polymorphic call was encountered, all tests associated with the node containing the polymorphic interface were selected. It is argued that because the program dependence graphs represent data dependencies, encapsulation will limit the extent of a regression test.

The graph walk algorithm was applied to several commercial systems [Rothermel+98]. The reduction in test suite size varied considerably for each system as well as across baseline/delta pairs of a system. The technique was cost-effective in all but a few unusual cases.

Related Patterns

No directly related patterns exist. This pattern may be used to support many testing situations.

Retest Within Firewall

Intent

Use code dependency analysis to select a partial regression test suite. Run this subset on a delta build.

Context

The available time, personnel, or equipment is not sufficient for a full regression run. How can a subset of a baseline test suite be selected using code dependencies? This pattern is applicable at the class, cluster, or subsystem scope and after maintenance, for reuse, and during iterative development. It may be used to support iterative development, the instantiation of reusable components, and maintenance. (See Section 15.1.2, When and How.)

Fault Model

The delta component induces a failure because of an incompatibility, side effect, or undesirable feature interaction. (See Section 15.1.3, Regression Faults.) Components that are outside the firewall do not depend on the changed component and therefore cannot induce regression faults.

Strategy

Test Model

A **firewall** is a set of components whose test cases will be included in a regression test. "Given one or more classes or objects which have been changed, the firewall encloses the set of modules that must be retested. The firewall is an imaginary boundary that limits retesting for modified software containing possible regression errors introduced during modification" [White+97].

The firewall set is identified by analysis of changes to each component in the SUT and its dependencies on other components. Table 15.7 summarizes the test selection rules. Each pair of components, *A* and *B*, is analyzed. Either or both may be the subject of a change. A change is either a contract change or an implementation change.[9]

---

9. To be consistent with usage in this book, I use *implementation change* instead of "code change" and *contract change* instead of "spec change" as used in [White+97].

TABLE 15.7   Decision Table for Selecting Regression Tests with the Firewall Model

Changes		Dependency,	Retesting Requirement						
A	B	B to A	A	As Sub	A Super	B	Bs Sub	Bs Super	AB
Implementation	None	B uses A†	2			3	3	4	2
		B is a subclass of A	2		4	3	3		4
		B overrides A	2	2					2
		B is a server of A	2						
Contract	None	B uses A†	1			2	3	4	1
		B is a subclass of A	1	2	4				1
		B overrides A	1	1					1
		B is a server of A	0						0
None	Implementation	B uses A†	3	3		2			2
		B is a subclass of A	3	3		2		4	3
		B overrides A	2	3		2			3
		B is a server of A	3			2			2
None	Contract	B uses A†	3	3		1			1
		B is a subclass of A	3	3		1			?
		B overrides A	1	1		1			1
		B is a server of A	2			0			0

† There are four ways that B may use A. See text.

- A contract change alters the external interface of a component and/or the externally visible contract of a class. It may consist of the addition or removal of nonprivate methods, alteration of a nonprivate method argument signature, alteration of the required input values in arguments, a change to a global variable, or alteration of exceptions that clients are expected to catch. If the contract requirements are stated as preconditions, postconditions, and a class invariant, then the contract has a concrete implementation—this idea is a generally accepted good practice, but is given language support only in Eiffel.

- An implementation change is everything else: all other changes to a class's implementation that are not visible to clients under the scoping/encapsulation rules of the particular language used for the system under test. An implementation change does not alter the external interface or the externally visible contract of a class (i.e., its preconditions, postconditions, and invariant).

The dependency relationship between each pair of components, *A* and *B*, is used to select test cases from the baseline test suite. *B uses A* refers to one of four code relationships:

- *B* is a client of *A* (i.e., an object of type *A* is declared in *B*).
- *B* has a pointer to *A*, possibly passed in or used to access members of a collection.
- *B* uses an object of class *A* as an argument in a method parameter.
- *B* is a generic class and uses *A* as a type parameter.

Three other relationships are modeled: *B* is a subclass of *A* (inheritance), *B* is a subclass of *A* and at least one method in *B* overrides a method in *A* (polymorphism), and *B* is an object server of *A*.

The change type and dependency determine which baseline test cases are selected. The columns in Table 15.7 refer to the test suite for *A*, *A*'s superclasses, *A*'s subclasses, *B*, *B*'s superclasses, *B*'s subclasses, and *AB*, the relationship between *A* and *B*. The relationship *AB* refers to local scope integration test cases. For example, suppose *B* is a subclass of *A*. The relationship *AB* then includes all interactions among methods of each class, whose test suite would be developed using **Modal Hierarchy Test**.

For each such relationship, the baseline test cases that apply to *A*, *B*, or *AB* may be reused in one of four ways:

- Level 0: No test cases can be rerun.
- Level 1: The state setup and test messages can be rerun. Expected results must be redeveloped. The sequence of the test cases in this test suite may need to be reworked.
- Level 2: The state setup, test messages, and expected results can be rerun. The sequence of the test cases in this test suite may need to be reworked.
- Level 3: The test cases can be rerun as is.

The procedure is applied to all pairs of classes in the SUT. The numbers in Table 15.7 correspond to these levels. For example, consider class `Account` (*A*) and class `Money` (*B*), which are members of the `FinancialService` cluster analyzed in Chapter 13. `Money` is a server of `Account` (`Account` declares an instance variable amount of type Money). Depending on the kind of changes made, different test cases will be selected.

- Implementation change to Account, no change to Money: Level 2 reuse of the test cases for Account.
- Contract change to Account, no change to Money: No regression testing of Account.
- No change to Account, implementation change to Money: Level 3 reuse of the test cases for Account. Level 2 reuse of the test cases for Money, and all applicable integration tests of Account and Money.
- No change to Account, contract change to Money: Level 2 reuse of the test cases for Account.

Test Procedure

Identify, develop, and run the reduced test suite.

1. Develop a dependency matrix for the classes in the SUT—one row and one column for each class. Record the change type with each row and column header. Record the dependency in the corresponding cell. Table 15.8 shows this matrix for the FinancialService cluster.

2. Apply the decision rules in Table 15.7 to each cell—that is, for each pair of classes. Only the upper or lower triangle must be completed. As classes can be self-referent, complete the diagonal, if applicable.

For example, suppose that only the implementation of class Money has changed. Which test cases should we rerun? We can see that Account and Transaction depend on Money. We apply the decision rules.

- No change to Account, implementation change to Money: Level 3 reuse of the test cases for Account. Level 2 reuse of the test cases for Money, and all applicable integration tests of Account and Money.
- No change to Transaction, implementation change to Money: Level 3 reuse of the test cases for Transaction. Level 2 reuse of the test cases for Money, and all applicable integration tests of Transaction and Money.

3. Create a list of all test suites for each class. Transcribe the testing level for each cell to the corresponding test suite. Table 15.9 shows the transcription of the two dependencies in this example. The analysis shows that TestAccount and TestTransaction should be rerun with no change. TestMoney should be reviewed to verify that the sequence of test messages is still appropriate.

TABLE 15.8   Dependency Matrix for Firewall Analysis

	"B" Components						
	FinancialService	Account	Transaction	AccountNum	Money	Rates	Array
FinancialService		C	C				
Account				C	C		
Transaction					C	C	
AccountNum							
Money							
Rates							G
Array							

Key:
C = Client: B is a client of A "composition"
A = Association: B has a pointer to A
U = Uses: B uses A in an argument
G = Generic: B is a generic and uses A as a type parameter
I = Inheritance: B is a subclass of A
P = Polymorphism: B overrides a method in A
O = Object: B is a server of A

Note: Only C and G types occure in this example.

TABLE 15.9   Selection of Test Cases Within Firewall

	Regression Test Selection by Dependency	
Test Cases	Account, Money	Transaction, Money
TestFinancialService		
TestAccount	3[†]	
TestTransaction		3[†]
TestAccountNum		
TestMoney	2	2
TestRates		
TestArray		

[†]In this example, these test cases also perform integration testing.

Oracle

The results of the baseline test run provide the oracle. That is, if the SUT produces the same results in the regression run as it did in the baseline run, the test passes.

Automation

See Section 15.1.4, Test Automation. A modular test suite will facilitate selection and execution of the desired subset. Several commercial source code analyzers can reliably identify dependencies in large systems, including Discover (Software Emancipation) and Sniff.

Entry Criteria

Regression testing may begin when the following conditions are met:

✓ The delta components pass component scope testing.

✓ A suitable baseline test suite exists.

✓ The test environment has been restored to the same configuration used to run the original baseline test suite. If this is not feasible, the noncontrollable components should be noted and the risk they pose to the validity of the test run should be assessed.

Exit Criteria

✓ All no pass test cases reveal bugs whose presence and severity are deemed acceptable.

✓ All remaining test cases pass.

Consequences

See Table 15.2 (page 775) Retest Within Firewall has a low risk of missing a regression fault. The direct cost of analysis and setup can be low, if the analysis is automated.

- *Inclusiveness.* All baseline tests that can produce a different result are selected. Retest Within Firewall is "safe" [Rothermel+96]. Implicit dependencies are considered that are not modeled in other approaches.
- *Precision.* A few tests that could be skipped may be included.

- *Efficiency.* In the worst case, the section computation is on the order of the size of the baseline test suite times the number of components in the larger of the baseline or delta component. The direct cost of analysis and setup can be low, if automated, but the tools have an indirect cost. The approach does not guarantee any particular time and cost reduction. It is possible that time or cost constraints will not be met.
- *Generality.* Retest Within Firewall is applicable at cluster scope. It requires the programmer to have skills in code analysis and related tools.

Dependencies among test cases must be considered in selecting a reduced test suite.

Known Uses

Leung and White developed the regression firewall approach to select regression suites from functional test cases at system scope. A tool to support application of this model is discussed in [White+93]. White's firewall was applied to object-oriented code by Kung et al., but the group did not consider the effects of contract change or polymorphism and did not present a strategy to select test cases [Kung+95].

Related Patterns

Firesmith's *Dependency-based Testing* sketches analysis of dependency relationships [Firesmith 96].

15.3 Bibliographic Notes

Research by Lee White and his colleagues established basic results for regression testing [Leung+90, White+93]. The firewall approach was developed for procedural code and first appears in [White+93]. Rothermel and Harrold provide a detailed survey and comparative analysis of research in regression testing techniques [Rothermel+96].

The dependencies that can occur in object-oriented software are analyzed in [Wilde+92] and [Wilde+93]. The Demeter model offers a detailed, formal model [Lieberherr+92], which can be applied to test planning [Keszenheimer+94, Keszenheimer+95]. Lakos's criteria for C++ systems show how simple changes in coding conventions and file usage can have major effects on buildability, maintainability, and testability [Lakos 96].

Regression testing in object-oriented development is discussed briefly by [Jacobson+92] and [Jüttner+94c]. A report on the application of the graph walk algorithm to C++ pattern appears in [Rothermel+94]. An automated regression testing environment for Smalltalk is presented in [Siepmann+94]. A report on the application of the firewall approach for a small C++ system is presented in [Kung+95a] and [Kung+95c]. Firesmith discusses how test driver hierarchies can support regression testing [Firesmith 95]. Siegel outlines a general strategy for object-oriented regression testing [Siegel 96]. Rothermel and Harrold's 1998 study of regression testing practices is an excellent, must-read paper [Rothermel+98].

Part IV Tools

Part IV concentrates on the design of test automation for object-oriented implementations. The power and elegance of the object-oriented paradigm are just as useful for test automation as they are for application software. A test automation system can be more complex and larger than the system under test. Clearly, the beneficial effects of the object-oriented paradigm are needed. Object-oriented test automation can be efficient, maintainable, and reusable if both generally accepted good development practices and patterns for effective test automation are employed for design and coding. Key design questions for object-oriented test automation include the following:

- How should test cases be implemented?
- How can test results be represented and evaluated?
- How can we easily control and observe encapsulated state in the implementation under test?
- What role can built-in test play?
- How can we make test cases and test drivers reusable?
- How can test cases and test suites be organized to be easy to develop, run, modify, and reuse?

The chapters in Part IV answer these questions in detail and discuss development of an application-specific test harness.

- Chapter 16, Test Automation. This chapter frames general design issues.
- Chapter 17, Assertions. Assertions are a simple and effective approach to embedding self-checking code in an implementation.

They can prevent and reveal bugs. Chapter 17 shows how class requirements can be analyzed to design assertions. Coding considerations for each of our six languages are developed. The pros and cons of using and shipping asserted code are considered.

- Chapter 18, Oracles. Machine-readable expected results are essential to automated testing. We cannot hope to perform extensive automated testing without the ability to compare actual and expected test results automatically. A test oracle produces the results expected for a test; a comparator checks actual and expected results. This chapter presents a dozen patterns for automated oracles.
- Chapter 19, Test Harness Design. Chapter 19 presents design patterns for test cases, test suites, stubs, test drivers, and test frameworks to control testing at the system scope. Simple and advanced approaches are developed.

The Appendix, BigFoot's Tootsie, is a brief case study about how a suite of commercially available testing tools was used to achieve a high degree of test automation at class, cluster, and system scope.

These chapters are not intended as a complete presentation of test automation. For example, GUI-based testing, environment simulators, concepts and tools for non-GUI test scripting, and automated production of test cases are not discussed. Likewise, design of test case generations is not covered.

Chapter 16   Test Automation

Overview

This brief chapter frames general problems in object-oriented test automation.

16.1 Why Testing Must Be Automated

Test automation is software that automates any aspect of testing of an application system. It includes capabilities to generate test inputs and expected results, to run test suites without manual intervention, and to evaluate pass/no pass.

To be effective and repeatable, testing must be automated. The appropriate extent of automated testing depends on your testing goals, budget, software process, kind of application under development, and particulars of the development and target environment. For example, useful test automation is entirely different for the following systems:

- An embedded vehicle control system written in C++ for an onboard microprocessor communicating over a small LAN and cross-compiled from a desktop workstation
- A multimedia decision support application written in Smalltalk with daily changes to requirements
- A high-volume transaction-processing system written in Java with class wrappers for a relational DBMS running on heterogenous servers with many interfaces to legacy systems

After design and development of a test driver, automated testing has six main steps:

1. Exercise the IUT with the automated test suite.
2. Repair faults revealed by failures.
3. Rerun the test suite on the revised IUT.
4. Evaluate test suite coverage.
5. Enhance the test suite to achieve the coverage goal.
6. Rerun these suites to support regression testing or other forms of testing that require the ability to compare baseline results.

This last step delivers the knock-out punch of automated testing.

Although quantity does not necessarily equate to quality in testing, the test design patterns described in Part III can easily produce too many effective tests for manual testing. How can we run these tests in a timely, efficient, and effective manner? Our only hope is to automate testing as much as possible. Automated testing offers many significant advantages:

- It permits quick and efficient verification of bug fixes. An automated test that has revealed a bug can usually be rerun on the fixed code in seconds, with confidence that the same inputs have been applied and evaluated.

- It can speed debugging and reduce "bad fixes." A developer can rerun a test case to reproduce a problem and then to verify that the bug fix works. Without the ability to replay the test, it can be difficult to decide whether a fix has completely removed the bug.

- The test process information produced by manual testing is often inconsistent and fragmentary. The production of test reports is inconsistent, costly, and slow. In contrast, test automation allows consistent capture and analysis of test results.

- The cost of test automation is typically recovered after two or three projects from increased productivity and the avoided costs associated with buggy software.

- Test automation reduces the risk of depending on the "test genius." Although ability always varies, automated testing can bring greater overall uniformity of results to a testing group.

- Tester productivity is improved. Instead of spending time entering and reentering tests, you have more time to design tests that achieve greater coverage.

- Manual testing is error-prone and tedious. In contrast, an automated test suite will never be distracted by a phone call, type the wrong input, or miss one incorrect character in 10,000 lines of output.

- Regression testing, compatibility testing, portability testing, performance testing, and configuration testing require automated, repeatable test suites. With an automated test suite, you can be sure that the same testing has been done on different versions or configurations of an application. Ten years ago, application systems were rarely targeted for many different platforms. Today, however, applications are commonly developed to support several GUIs, networks, operating systems, and databases. Cross-platform automated testing is the only way to assess operability in this situation with any consistency.

- Automation is necessary to run long and complex tests. Some test sequences can involve hundreds, even thousands, of test messages. This kind of testing is often infeasible with manual setup and evaluation. Being able to repeat exactly a long sequence requires automation.

- Automated comparison is the only repeatable and efficient way to evaluate a large quantity of output. Even the most dedicated tester will become fatigued after scanning pages of output, traces, or dumps.

Jim Hanlon, a colleague and tester par excellence, explains why automation makes sense:

> Anyone who has manually prepared the test cases for a moderately complex system, then applied them to the system under test, and then reported on the results versus expected, quickly realizes not only that a lot of the work involved is tiresome and repetitive, but that there's a lot of work, period. Why can't we have a computer do some of this work? The simple answer is that computers require software: the development of software to automatically test a system can be as big a job as the development of the system's software itself. Another point: there is no *The System;* there are only *System Versions.* Keeping the automatic test system software in synchronism with the SUT requires managerial attention, planning, resource allocation, and more work. Nonetheless, the value of a 10×–1000× magnification of test effectiveness is considerable. [Jim Hanlon, personal communication, May 1999.]

16.2 Limitations and Caveats

Manual testing can be accomplished by using the available user interface (GUI or command line), using a debugger to run an implementation that does not have a direct user interface, or simply running the IUT in various configurations. Although ad hoc, manual testing is often ineffective and inefficient, test automation is not a panacea. Automated testing is expensive and not necessarily the best approach in all situations [Kaner 97]. Manual testing is indicated in some situations.

- A skilled tester using knowledge of product features to improvise some tests can be effective. The tester may develop a "feel" for the behavior of the IUT and try scenarios suggested by the response of the IUT. For example, an unexpected limit on an input may suggest using some unrelated feature at this limit. When testing applications with significant user interaction, the tester can use this knowledge to try features and combinations that might be hard to identify when designing a GUI script. In embedded systems, testers with similar knowledge of the environment and the application can probably devise and run tests by running the system in a test bed and attempting to combine "interesting" loads.

- Automating a test is typically more expensive than just running the application. If no need to repeat the tests is evident, then the additional cost of automation is probably not justified.

- Repeatability is the primary (but not the only) cost justification for automated testing. Test cases, test suites, and test harnesses must be maintained if they are to be repeatable (see Section 15.1.5, Test Suite Maintenance). This work is no less difficult or expensive than maintaining application software. The cost of maintenance may be quite high if the requirements and implementation of the IUT change frequently. If the test automation is not maintained, it will become unusable and the expected return will not be realized.

Combining automated and manual testing is a common and effective practice. Certain testing situations favor mostly manual testing; others favor fully automated testing. There is no single "best" approach. Figure 16.1 shows how manual input generation, production of expected results, test execution, and test evaluation can be combined.

Testing Mode	Test Input Generation	Oracle (Expected Result)	Execution	Oracle (Actual Result Evaluation)
Testing by Poking Around	Manual	Manual	Manual	Manual
Beta Testing	Manual	Manual	Manual	Automated
	Manual	Manual	Automated	Manual
GUI Capture/Playback	Manual	Manual	Automated	Automated
Console Testing	Manual	Automated	Manual	Manual
	Manual	Automated	Manual	Automated
	Manual	Automated	Automated	Manual
	Manual	Automated	Automated	Automated
	Automated	Manual	Manual	Manual
	Automated	Manual	Manual	Automated
	Automated	Manual	Automated	Manual
Automated Test Generation	Automated	Manual	Automated	Automated
	Automated	Automated	Manual	Manual
	Automated	Automated	Manual	Automated
	Automated	Automated	Automated	Manual
Regression Testing	Automated	Automated	Automated	Automated

Note: Shaded rows indicate typical approach.

FIGURE 16.1   Testing modes and extent of test automation.

Table 16.1 lists the patterns presented in Part IV. These elements can provide a high degree of test effectiveness. Choosing the elements that are appropriate is a puzzle that is different for every application system. The remaining chapters will present concepts, techniques, and tools to help you devise the application-specific test automation approach best suited to your project.

TABLE 16.1 Test Automation Design Patterns Presented in This Book

	Patterns	
Built-in Test	Percolation	Perform automatic verification of superclass/subclass contract
Test Case Patterns	Test Case/Test Suite Method	Implement test case or test suite as a method
	Catch All Exceptions	Test exceptions with a handler
	Test Case/Test Suite Class	Implement test case or test suite as an object of test case class
Test Control Patterns	Server Stub	Use a stub implementation of a server object for greater control
	Server Proxy	Use a proxy implementation of a server object for greater control
Driver Patterns	Test Driver Superclass	Use an abstract superclass for all test drivers
	Percolate the Object Under Test	Pass the object under test to the driver
	Symmetric Driver	Driver hierarchy is symmetric to classes under test
	Subclass Driver	Driver is a subclass
	Private Access Driver	Driver uses encapsulation-avoiding features
	Test Control Interface	Driver uses interface extension features
	Drone	Driver is a mixin
	Built-in Test Driver	Driver is implemented as part of an application class
Test Execution Patterns	Command-line Test Bundle	Code test executable to be run from a command line or console
	Incremental Testing Framework	Test suites are based on a simple framework that supports incremental development
	Fresh Objects	Test environment with registration and interface to built-in test in all objects

Chapter 17   Assertions

Trust, but verify.

*Ronald Reagan, speaking
to Mikhail Gorbachev*

Overview

This chapter explains how class/scope assertions support built-in tests. Implementation-based assertions can improve testability and check many kinds of relationships. Just as test design models are necessary to design test suites, implementable models of class requirements are necessary to design assertions. The design-by-contract approach provides the model for responsibility assertions, including method preconditions and postconditions, loop invariants and variants, class invariants, state invariants, state-accepting conditions, and state-resulting conditions.

Assertion idioms are presented for six programming languages. The *Percolation* pattern explains how to code assertions to provide built-in test for a polymorphic server hierarchy. In addition, verification of assertions and their use for test design are considered. A discussion of problems and deployment tradeoffs concludes this chapter.

17.1   Introduction

Built-in test refers to code added to an application that checks the application at runtime. This code does not directly support application requirements. The design and implementation of built-in test is influenced by the following factors:

- *Purpose.* Built-in test (BIT) can check both implementation-specific assumptions and implementation-independent responsibilities.
- *Scope.* Built-in test can check relationships that must hold (1) at method entry and exit and are visible to clients of a class, (2) within the scope of a method activation and hidden from clients, (3) for all methods and states of all class objects, and (4) among superclasses and subclasses.
- *Implementation.* Built-in test is typically implemented using a combination of source code preprocessing, programming language constructs, and dedicated methods.
- *Deployment.* The primary role of built-in test is to support prerelease development. Field-deployed built-in test can be used in combination with exception handling to detect and recover from some anomalous conditions.

The simple presence of built-in test does *not* equate to adequate testing. Having built-in test does not mean self-testing code. Some programming languages—notably Ada 95 and Eiffel—include features that provide excellent support for built-in test. In other languages, the programmer must code built-in test from available mechanisms. In any case, built-in test must be designed and coded, typically by a developer. After the built-in test is coded, a test suite must exercise the IUT to activate the built-in test code.

This book presents three built-in test mechanisms:

1. *Equality methods.* The ability to report whether two objects of the same class are equal is crucial for testing. However, the nuances of object-oriented programming can result in quirky, ambiguous, incomplete, or unreliable equality methods. Considerations for dependable implementation of this seemingly simple operation are discussed in Section 18.3, Comparators.

2. *Message sequence checking methods.* A sequence checking method can be built into a modal class which will detect runtime violations of the class's state specification. This technique is discussed in the Runtime Sequence Checking section (pages 838–840).

3. *Assertions.* The assertion is the workhorse of built-in test for object-oriented code. This chapter focuses on how to design and implement built-in test with assertions. Assertions are not a silver bullet, however. They are contraindicated in some situations and have costs and limitations. Pros and cons are discussed in Sections 17.5 and 17.6.

17.1.1 What Are Assertions?

An **assertion** is a Boolean expression that defines necessary conditions for correct execution. Assertions are like a tireless auditor who constantly checks for compliance with necessary conditions and complains when the rules are broken. They may express implementation-specific constraints or implementation-independent class responsibilities. General uses of assertions include the following:

- Checking any implementation-specific assumption
- Checking conditions that must be true at entry to a method (a precondition)
- Checking conditions that must be true at exit from a method (a postcondition)
- Checking conditions that must be true at all times for an object (an invariant)

These types and others are discussed in detail later in this chapter.

Assertions that support built-in test must be executable. An executable assertion has three parts: a predicate expression, an action, and an enable/disable mechanism. The predicate expression is usually coded the same way as an if-then predicate. An assertion action may be as simple as writing a brief message or as complicated as starting an extensive runtime recovery. Typically, assertion checking is enabled or disabled at translation time by a parameter. The usage cycle of assertions includes several steps:

1. Assertions are coded during development.

2. Assertions are **enabled** or **disabled** at translation time.

3. At runtime, when the IUT reaches an enabled assertion, the **assertion predicate** either evaluates to *true* (the state of the IUT satisfies the assertion) or *false*. If the assertion is true, execution continues.

4. An **assertion violation** occurs when an assertion predicate becomes *false,* meaning that a necessary condition was not met. This situation is sometimes called an "assertion failure." In fact, the assertion has not failed, but rather done its intended job: It has detected an unacceptable situation. The incorrect condition may be caused by a fault in the class under test, in another part of the application system, or in its runtime environment.

5. An assertion violation results in transfer of control to an **assertion action**. The typical default assertion action is to generate a diagnostic message and terminate execution.

Assertions are coded differently in each programming language. The examples that follow use the syntax for the C++ `assert.h` macro. For example,

```
assert(a == b);
```

means that if a is not equal to b, the predefined assertion action is to be taken. Assertion idioms in six languages are presented in Section 17.4, Implementation.

17.1.2 Why Use Assertions?

As with any testing strategy, we should be concerned about effectiveness. What kind of bugs can assertions find? Assertions were effective for detecting a wide range of bugs in a study of post-release failures and assertions [Rosenblum 95]. Approximately half of the functions in this 12 KLOC C system were asserted. Of 19 post-release faults, 8 were revealed by assertion violations and 6 could have been caught by assertions that were not written. Three event sequencing bugs and 2 memory allocation bugs could not have been detected with assertions. The routine and extensive use of assertions is reported as beneficial and cost-effective technique in many leading software development organizations, including IBM and Microsoft (see this chapter's case studies). Figure 17.1 summarizes the bug prevention and detection abilities of assertions.

Adding code to application classes to support testing may seem like a strange idea, especially to developers trying to cope with schedule pressure. Assertions can, however, provide many advantages:

- Assertions prevent errors. Responsibilities, assumptions, and their implications are made explicit and executable. This simple act of articulation often reveals errors and omissions.
- Assertions encourage well-documented code. Although the lack of proper documentation is professionally indefensible and contributes to high software maintenance costs, many programmers and software development managers view any form of nonexecutable documentation

Error Type		BIT Prevents	BIT Detects
Design	Type Inversion	✓	✓(1)
	Gnarly Hierarchy	✓	
	Weird Hierarchy	✓	
	Missing Override	✓	✓
Coding	Incorrect Assertion		(2)
	Incorrect Method		✓
	Incorrect Server		✓

(1) See discussion of type inversion test suite in Chapter 15. (2) See BIT Verification that follows.

FIGURE 17.1   BIT bug prevention/detection capability.

as overhead to be minimized. A full set of responsibility assertions can address both concerns by providing executable and accurate documentation.[1]

- Externally driven unit testing typically lags behind coding and is abandoned when system testing begins. In contrast, assertion checking begins when asserted code is exercised and continues, automatically, until disabled. Assertions typically remain active during the initial system test runs, which extends the effective span of unit testing: it begins sooner and ends later. Thus, assertions provide a low-cost extension to formally developed external test suites. Every time a message is sent to an object with enabled assertions, the message and its results are checked. Frequently used objects often detect assertion violations resulting from unanticipated circumstances. Although this effort is not a substitute for planned testing of an instrumented class, it offers a cheap and effective boost to testing effectiveness.

- Responsibility-based test cases can be derived from responsibility-based assertions even when other program documentation is unavailable or inaccurate.

- "Dumb" errors are caught early and automatically. Without precondition checking, common interface faults (e.g., sending incorrect or inconsistent messages) can easily escape into field systems. For

---

1. Assertions cannot provide complete program documentation, but are much better than none at all. General content requirements for complete program documentation are called out in [IEEE 1016].

example, if boundary conditions for message arguments are asserted in all methods, boundary value testing can be reduced and that budget can be spent on other forms of testing. As a result, test scripts and drivers may be smaller and simpler.

- Automatic test generation can be used without having to pregenerate expected results. Although generating input values automatically is easy, generating the corresponding expected results automatically is usually difficult. Postconditions and invariants partially solve the oracle problem for automatically generated test cases. Properly implemented postconditions and class invariants can detect many (but not all) incorrect results.

- Debugging asserted code is easier. Assertions are a built-in debugging tool that does not require any code modification to use. Precondition assertions (in the methods of server objects) are especially effective at finding bugs in clients during integration. In a survey of debugging practices, in at least half of the reported cases, bugs were difficult to find because of "large temporal or spatial chasms between the root cause and the symptom, and bugs that rendered the debugging tools inapplicable" [Eisenstadt 97, 37]. An assertion violation is likely to occur close to a fault and often well before a failure manifests itself. The resulting reduction in diagnostic time for a single bug could easily pay for the development of hundreds of assertions.

- Assertions encourage reuse and reduce maintenance costs because they can be used to document the contract of a class. Unlike comments or separate nonexecutable design documentation, assertions must be compilable. Compared with noncompilable detailed design representations, they are much more likely to remain current and consistent as code is revised.

Beyond these generally beneficial effects, assertions can deal with several unique testing problems posed by object-oriented code:

- Encapsulated states and hidden variables may be directly checked. This checking cannot be done from a driver unless an antiencapsulation idiom is used (see the discussion of the *Private Access Driver* in Chapter 19). Assertions can detect faults that would not otherwise be propagated as observable failures.

- Incorrect design of a server class is avoided. An assertion violation can reveal a design error or omission when a server precondition flags a legal message as a violation.

- A server precondition violation usually results from a bug in the method that sent the message (the client), not in the asserted method (the server).

- Classes typically send messages to themselves and their superclasses. During class or subclass development, preconditions can catch bugs in intraclass clients.

- During integration of new clients with trusted servers, a server precondition violation usually indicates a bug in a new client. This checking provides interclass client testing. If the server has many different clients, the tester gains considerable leverage because many new clients may be debugged with a few trusted servers.

- A client postcondition violation usually results from a bug in a new server (not in the client). For example, in a distributed object system, a server object can have a different implementation or can reside on different hosts within the activation span of any single client. Suppose a recently modified server returns an incorrect value to a trusted client. The client's postcondition can probably catch the incorrect value (such usage is *not* adequate testing of the new servers, however).

- Client postconditions can detect client and server bugs, even if the servers are not asserted. A postcondition can detect a corrupt state resulting from a buggy client algorithm, incorrect usage of a server, or a buggy server.

- Postcondition checking eases integration of third-party server components and distributed objects of uncertain quality.

- Class and state invariants can detect corrupt states resulting from faults in a method algorithm, a bug in a server object, or an anomalous environmental condition.

- Class and state invariants can detect corrupt states that result from a wild pointer in another object, corrupted global variables, or corrupted class variables.

- Sequence checking and state preconditions can identify attempts by a client to send an illegal message.

- State invariants checked at method exit can identify faults resulting in an incorrect resultant state.

But, you say, assertions can result in cluttered code, can distort the behavior of systems with hard real-time deadlines and severe memory constraints, and are subject to abuses. Yes, this is true. Skip ahead to Section 17.6, Limitations and Caveats, for a full discussion.

17.1.3   Who Uses Assertions?

The use of assertions does not require extraordinary skill or experience. If you can write an if-then-else predicate expression, you can write an assertion. assertions are a practical and effective technique for expressing what a server class will do for its clients and what clients can expect from a server. They may be used by the entire development team.

- Analysts and designers can write them to specify class responsibilities. Assertions are a key part of several OOA/D methodologies, including Syntropy [Cook+94], Fusion [Coleman+94], Object Engineering [Desfray 94], BON [Nerson+94], and Catalysis [D'Souza+99]. UML constraints can be used to document assertions [Rumbaugh+99].
- Developers typically code assertions during class development and are responsible for maintaining them.
- Testers can use assertions to design tests.

Assertions have been used with good results in many projects, including large commercial software products. Microsoft, for example, uses them routinely. Required values for parameters passed into a function, developer's assumptions, and some postconditions are asserted in many application systems [Maguire 93]. The Microsoft Foundation Class library is shipped with user-toggled asserts to help in debugging [Stout 97].

A Million Lines of Built-in Test: OS/400

IBM's project to develop the OS/400 operating system is a highwater mark in object-oriented built-in test. OS/400 was developed from 1992 to 1994 at IBM's Baldridge Award–winning division at Rochester, Minnesota. Roughly half of the total development effort was spent on dedicated test code. This high level of test commitment was apparently a significant factor in the project's success. OS/400 is the multitasking operating system for IBM's AS/400 midrange RISC computer system. This system contains "14,000 thousand [sic] classes, 90,000 thousand [sic] methods, and 2 million lines of C++ integrated into 20 million lines of total code. . . . Including testing and diagnosis code, there are over two million lines of C++ source code, with approximately one million lines shipped to customers" [Berg+95, 54]. About half of the source code (1 million lines) developed for this system was dedicated testing code. Assertions accounted for roughly 40 percent of the test code (many implemented with the Heavyweight Coherence idiom—see the discussion later in this chapter.) The balance was test cases, scaffolding, tools, and `printf` statements. Roughly one-third of the total test code developed had become obsolete by the end of the project.[2]

The report on this project describes several organizational and technical problems, but cost and feasibility of this extensive use of assertions were not among them. In fact, some problems were attributed to insufficient use of built-in test.

> By most measures, the project was a success. At a very basic level, [the system] was built quickly and performed according to specification, a nontrivial accomplishment. As the basis for IBM's System/36E, it is both stable and efficient. Indications are that it will have low long-term maintenance costs, but it is too early to reach definitive conclusions. . . . The experience gained from this project was that the initial development cost was less than it would have been with the use of traditional methods [Berg+ 95, 64].

17.2   Implementation-based Assertions

17.2.1   Assumption Checkers

A programmer must make some assumptions. These assumptions about the state and behavior of the target environment may be either modest or bold. Assertions may be used to define and check implementation assumptions. Like good comments, "An effective assertion does not merely restate something appearing in the program text; unlike the program, it succinctly and unambiguously states an important property of the program in a way that is understandable by anyone who reads it" [Rosenblum 95, 20].

An asserted assumption is a necessary condition for correct execution. It should reflect expectations for normally occurring, typical conditions. Assertions should not be used for input checking or exception handling.

---

2. William Berg, personal communication.

- Input checking is done when unacceptable input is likely because the content, frequency, or sequence of input is not under the control of a system or because its source is not trusted. Unacceptable input is typically disregarded, some form of complaint is made, and normal processing continues. The detection and handling of unacceptable input is an application responsibility.

- Exception handling deals with anomalies in the basic operation of a system: insufficient memory, device failure, divide by zero, and so on. The response typically depends on the severity of the exception. Recovery or restart may be attempted, or the process may terminate. The mechanisms for detection and handling of basic exceptions are language- and platform-specific.

Consider a C++ object pointer, foo. An allocation anomaly resulting in a null pointer could trigger an exception or an assertion action. The following conditional expression might appear in a class that has the explicit responsibility to allocate objects before using them:

```
// Resolve a memory allocation error with an exception
if (foo == NULL) throw memExhaust;
```

If an application cannot be assured of successful allocation (e.g., due to competing processes in the same environment) but must still run, such a check necessarily becomes the responsibility of the class and must be deployed. On the other hand, suppose that the class is a consumer of preallocated objects. Although such a class does not bear the responsibility for ensuring the allocation, checking that the assumed allocation has occurred is prudent. This task may be accomplished with an assertion:

```
// Allocation assumed to be good at this point -- verify the
// assumption.
assert (foo != NULL);
```

This assertion can be disabled by recompiling with the appropriate options when the system is deployed (see Section 17.5, Deployment). If proper exception handling is in place, an allocation anomaly will have predictable results. In contrast, the exception expression cannot be disabled without changing the source code. Assertions should not be used to filter incorrect input or deal with situations where necessary conditions cannot be established due to unusual circumstances (see the discussion of exceptions and contracts in Section 17.3.7). Considerations for using assertions as part of an exception handling scheme are discussed in Section 17.4.2, Assertion Actions.

Preconditions, postconditions, and invariants bracket the computation performed in a method and thereby define class responsibilities. Assertions can check compliance with these entry–exit conditions. However, transient states inconsistent with entry–exit assertions are often necessary. For example, a transient state might occur while handling an exception, iterating a complex numerical algorithm, or populating a complex structure of object associations. Although these transient states may be inconsistent with external constraints, they have their own necessary assumptions and relationships. At some point, a transient state must be made consistent with external constraints. Bugs often occur when a transient state is not reset. What sort of code segment might benefit from transient state assertions?

- Compare assumptions about the transient states of instance variables with their entry–exit constraints. If a variable must temporarily violate an entry–exit constraint, assert the external constraint just after the point where the variable should be rehabilitated.
- Explain the code to someone else or attempt to comment it. If a lengthy explanation is required, consider formulating the explanation as an assertion.

The use of implementation-based assertions is limited only by the imagination of the developer and the programming language in use. Table 17.1 lists some typical implementation-based relationships that may be asserted.

17.2.2 Dark Alleys, Lurking Faults, and Sniffers

An ill effect of a bug must become visible to a tester before it can be removed. Certain kinds of code segments are more likely to hide bugs from human scrutiny and careful testing. A **lurking fault** causes a manifest failure under infrequent, weird, or unlikely conditions. Voas therefore argues that assertions should be placed where faults are most likely to hide [Friedman+95, Voas 99]. A **fault sniffer** is an assertion used when a code segment has a better than average chance of a lurking fault.

TABLE 17.1   Implementation-based Assertion Examples

Implementation Relationship	Example Assertion
Reasonable limits on resources	`assert(NumBuff < 256);`
Incomplete or untested code	`assert(TRUE, "foo isn't complete");`
Constraints and unenforced assumptions on message arguments	`// No more than 24 total hours in day` `assert ((taskHours + slackHours) < 25 );`
Range checking on any scalar variable	`assert (dx <= maxDx && dx > 10000);`
Bounds checking on arrays and other collections	`assert (i <= sizeOfArray);` `assert (x == array[i]);`
Membership in enumerated types or collections	`assert ( !myObject.contains(x) );`
Valid, non-null pointers	`assert (this != NULL);` `assert (anArray[i] != NULL);`
"This Should Never Happen" segment in an if, case, or switch expression	`assert (FALSE);`
Language-specific weaknesses	See Implementation
Redundant or cached values	`// Buffers in use don't exceed allocation` `assert (nBuffAlloc >= buffAllocCount)`
Server object invariants	`// foo is a server object.` `assert (foo.checkInvariant( ));`
Arithmetic relationships	`assert (x >= (a + b - c));`
Items in a collection	`assert ((next == last)||(numItems > 0));`
Structures correct	`assert (p->fred != NULL);` `assert (p->refCount != 0);`
Constraints between arguments and instance/class variables	See Invariants
Constraints and unenforced assumptions on global variables	See Invariants
Constraints among instance/class variables	See Invariants
Constraints between arguments and returned values	See Postconditions
Constraints between instance/class variables and returned values	See Postconditions
Variables that must be the same (or different) at entry and exit	See Postconditions
Valid/invalid states	See State Invariants
Contract of a stub	All or part of the contract offered by the stubbed method
Contract of an abstract superclass method	The generic requirements for all subtypes

Where are these dark alleys that harbor lurkers? Such code segements[3] may be located by mutation testing [Freidman+95] and heuristic analysis. Some heuristics for finding dark alleys follow. As they are based on experience, the quantified criteria are relative benchmarks, not absolutes. However, any of the following situations suggests that faults may be lurking and that a fault sniffer is indicated.

- The size of the input domain (the operands on the right side of an assignment or message input arguments) is very large compared with the size of the output domain (the operands on the left side of an assignment or values returned by a message). For example, the message `Date::getDayOfWeek( )` exhibits this funneling effect. It returns the day of the week (only seven possible output values) given a month, day, and year (approximately 111,600 input values assuming a range of 300 years). This funneling effect may be quantified as the *range/domain ratio (RDR)* [Voas+99]. The *RDR* is simply the size of the output domain divided by the size of the input domain. Voas recommends that assertions be placed within any segment where the *RDR* is 0.001 or less. The *RDR* for `Date::getDayOfWeek` is 0.000063 = 7/111,600, which qualifies.
- The segment depends on boundary conditions defined with five or more variables. High complexity is often associated with lurking special-case faults.
- The segment performs floating- or fixed-point arithmetic on objects or variables that may take on values at opposite extremes of precision (e.g., very large numbers divided by very small numbers).
- You are unsure of the intended logic of a segment, possibly because you are modifying old or unfamiliar code.
- The segment depends on a side effect or result of a method in a superclass with which you are unfamiliar.
- The segment relies on convoluted type conversions (C++ casting) or a polymorphic message that may be bound to many different objects (Smalltalk or Objective-C).
- The segment depends on a globally visible variable.

---

3. Here, *segment* refers to a single statement, a sequential block of statements, or an entire method.

- The segment depends on values returned from an interface to a non-trusted system or to a legacy system whose behavior is lost in the mists of time.

A fault sniffer is useful in detecting a suspect or invalid state, upstream from the funneling that may hide the fault. The sniffer should not be placed after the suspect code segment, but rather *within* it. The relationships to be asserted depend on the specific algorithm and data flow in a particular dark alley.

17.3   Responsibility-based Assertions

17.3.1   Overview

This section presents responsibility-based assertions. The process by which **responsibility-based assertions** are divined from general requirements is not considered here (see the Bibliographic Notes section for general design sources). First, this section develops the contract metaphor for class responsibilities and the related ideas of assertion strength/weakness, public/private contracts, and defensive/cooperative components. After discussing these preliminaries, the development of assertions for each element of a class contract is presented.

- At the method scope: preconditions, postconditions, and loop assertions
- At the class scope: the class invariant and state invariants
- At the flattened class scope: the relationship between superclass and subclass assertions
- At the subsystem scope: the relationship between client objects and server objects

These assertions can express relationships at each scope that are required for correct operation. When implemented, they will automatically check these relationships at runtime, every time the SUT is exercised. If used consistently and systematically, this can provide verification that would be very difficult, time-consuming, and expensive to achieve with externally applied and evaluated test cases.

17.3.2   Responsibilities, Contracts, and Subtypes

The Contract Metaphor

Assertions can provide built-in testing of public class responsibilities and private implementation. **Design-by-contract** is a class design technique that shares some similarities with establishing a legal contract [Meyer 97]. A class contract is an explicit statement of rights and obligations between a client and a server. The contract states what both parties must do, independent of how it is accomplished. Class contracts are typically written from the server's perspective: "If a client promises to provide x when sending a message, then the server promises always to return y in response to such a message."

The elements of a class contract are assertions at method and class scopes, inherited assertions, and exceptions.

- Each server method has a precondition assertion that checks the message sent by the client. Meeting the precondition is the client's responsibility.
- Each server method has a postcondition assertion that checks the resultant state of the object and the response to be provided to the client. A postcondition assertion defines what the server promises to provide after completing any request. Meeting this criterion is the server's responsibility.
- Each class has an invariant that defines all valid combinations of instance variable states and values for the class. The invariant is checked at the same point as the precondition and postcondition.

The design-by-contract approach requires a subclass's contract to be consistent with the contracts of all of its superclasses. As a result of this requirement, subclass objects can be substituted for superclass objects without causing failures or requiring special case code in clients. This concept is known as the **Liskov substitution principle** (LSP). Subclass assertions must implement the *Percolation* pattern (see pages 882–896) to check for conformance with LSP.

Meyer's design-by-contract model does not consider sequential constraints. Although this is not a problem for nonmodal classes, it leaves a significant gap for modal classes. Designing modal classes with the FREE state model is a good thing for the same reasons that design-by-contract offers benefits for nonmodal classes. Asserting the class state model with state invariants and transition conditions provides effective built-in test for the sequential behavior of modal classes. The details of this extension to the general design-by-contract model appear in Chapter 7. There are corresponding requirements for contract assertions:

- Each modal class has a public state invariant for each abstract state or provides methods in its public interface that may be used in a client predicate to determine all behaviorally significant abstract states.
- Every method checks for a legal state/event combination at entry. If the object is in a state for which the message is illegal, then an assertion violation is triggered.
- Every method asserts only one legal state at exit. If the object is in a state that is not a legal resultant state for the current transition, an assertion violation is triggered.

The extent to which a server expects clients to handle exceptions is specified in the class contract. An exception occurs when an object cannot meet its contract (a contract exception) or the runtime environment reports an anomaly to the application process (an environment exception). Server exception handling usually places an additional burden on clients—for example, catching exceptions thrown by a server. This part of a contract is typically not expressed in assertions, but is implicit in the way the application uses available exception-handling mechanisms.

Robust systems must handle environment exceptions. The design of contract exception handling presents some difficult problems—not the least of which is the extent to which assertions should be integrated. Two approaches are possible: defensive and cooperative. A **defensive server** always checks client messages against preconditions and complains when they are not met. The client must be prepared to handle such complaints, which may be implemented as exceptions, returned error codes, or a special object state. A **cooperative server** is designed with the assumption that the client will not send an incorrect message and never checks its assertions. If a cooperative server is sent an incorrect message, the results are unpredictable. In a defensive system, precondition checking is part of the application system and must be tested for deployment. In a cooperative system, contract checking (if present) can be considered built-in test to support development. Meyer's design-by-contract strategy implies a metamorphosis from a defensive to a cooperative approach. During development, all assertion checking is enabled, so objects are defensive. When the application is configured for deployment, most assertion checking is disabled, rendering the objects cooperative [Meyer 97].

Even if a class has been developed without an explicit contract, implicit requirements exist for its usage. These requirements are an implicit contract. Such implicit contracts are often troublesome, as a trenchant Usenet posting suggests:

> The "hidden precondition" situation is quite common when dealing with large libraries. We usually say it's insufficient documentation, which is essentially the same as not stating *all* the preconditions that must be fulfilled (i.e., things that have to be done) before calling a certain routine. This is a common situation with Windows programming, for example. You call a routine and the system blows up for no good reason at all. Until you read a *Knowledge Base* article that states that certain things are "dangerous," or certain ways of doing things are "recommended" [you have no way of knowing the precondition].[4]

Assertions and the UML

The UML view of assertions is abstract and accepts nontestable expressions. "An invariant is a Boolean expression that must be true at all times that no operation is active. It is an assertion, not an executable statement" [Rumbaugh+99, 317]. The truth of such an expression may be evaluated by the reader. Invariants may be represented in a UML Class Diagram with a constraint and an attached stereotype of «invariant». Preconditions and postconditions may be shown as notes attached to operations using the stereotype of «precondition» or «postcondition».

These expressions are not required to conform to any sort of syntax, higher-order rules of well-formedness, or executability. However, the Object Constraint Language (OCL), which is part of the UML standard, can be used to write testable (but not executable) UML assertions [Warmer+99]. OCL provides some useful constructs for modeling—notably, the ability to navigate over associations. Code can be used as well. As we are concerned with executable assertions, code is used here.

Assertion Strength and Weakness

Some rules for using assertions are stated in terms of relative strength or weakness. Assertions can be characterized as strong or weak with respect to a given set of variables. We cannot say anything about the relative strength or weakness of assertions composed from different variables. The values that make an assertion true are said to **satisfy** the assertion. To determine relative strength and weakness, we compare the sets of values that satisfy the assertions in question.

---

4. Joachim Durchholz, posted to Usenet comp.object newsgroup, November 21, 1997.

- A **stronger assertion** is more restrictive: it is true for a subset of the value combinations that make a weaker assertion true. For example, `((x > 1) && (x < 42))` is stronger than `((x > 0) && (x < 100))`. The satisfying value set of a stronger assertion is a subset of the satisfying set of a weaker assertion. Some value combinations that are false for a stronger assertion must be true for a weaker assertion. All of the value combinations that would make a stronger assertion true must also make a weaker assertion true.

- A **weaker assertion** is more general: it is true for a superset of value combinations that make a stronger assertion true. For example, `((x > 0) && (x < 100))` is weaker than `((x > 1) && (x < 42))`. The satisfying value set of a weaker assertion is a superset of the satisfying set of a stronger assertion. Some value combinations that are true for a weaker assertion must be false for a stronger assertion.

- If the satisfying value sets are identical, the assertions in question are equivalent or "the same"—neither is stronger or weaker than the other.

For example, let FALSE and TRUE be Boolean constants with the obvious values. Then `assert(FALSE)` is the strongest possible assertion. It can never be true under any circumstance and will always trigger the assertion action. FALSE corresponds to a null satisfying set. The weakest possible assertion is `assert(TRUE)`. It is always true and will never trigger the assertion action. TRUE corresponds to a universal satisfying set. Figure 17.2 shows the strength spectrum as Venn diagrams.

If the value sets that satisfy some assertions are disjoint or partially intersecting, these assertions are neither stronger, weaker, nor the same. Consider the assertions

```
Assert ((x < 0) && (y == 1));  // (1)
```

and

```
Assert ((x > 0) && (y == 10)); // (2)
```

The satisfying value sets for assertions 1 and 2 do not share any common elements: that is, they are disjoint. Assertion 1 is neither stronger, weaker, nor the same as assertion 2. The partially intersecting value sets satisfying assertions

```
Assert ((x < 2) && (y > 100)); // (3)
```

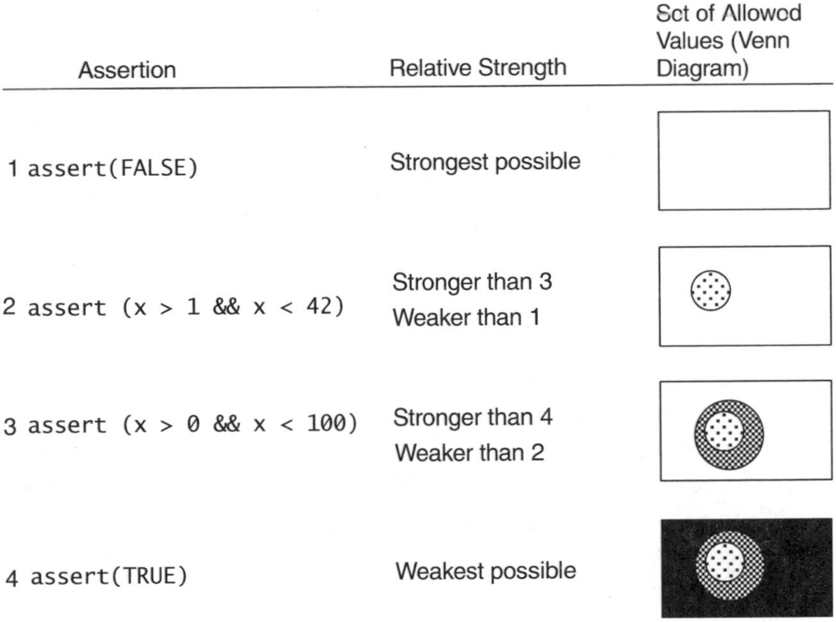

Assertion	Relative Strength	Set of Allowed Values (Venn Diagram)
1 assert(FALSE)	Strongest possible	
2 assert (x > 1 && x < 42)	Stronger than 3 Weaker than 1	
3 assert (x > 0 && x < 100)	Stronger than 4 Weaker than 2	
4 assert(TRUE)	Weakest possible	

FIGURE 17.2 Assertion strength spectrum.

and

```
    Assert ((x > 0) && (y > 100)); // (4)
```

have in common all x, y pairs where x == 1 and y >100. Again, assertion 3 is neither stronger, weaker, nor the same as assertion 4.

Stronger assertions are not more desirable than weaker assertions; weaker assertions are not undesirable. Weaker preconditions allow clients to send a wider range of complying messages; stronger preconditions reduce the acceptable set of message values. Weaker postconditions allow servers to return a wider range of complying messages; stronger postconditions reduce the acceptable set of values that may be returned to the client. The appropriate strength depends on the requirements of the class and its implementation.

The relative strength and weakness of preconditions, postconditions, class invariants, and state invariants are the same as the relative strength and weakness of the predicates appearing in the assertions.

17.3.3 Method Scope

Preconditions

A precondition is an assertion evaluated at entry to a method before any of the code in the method body executes. It expresses constraints on message argument values and object state required for correct execution. For example, the precondition for a floating-point square root function `float sqrt(float x)` is

```
assert (x >= 0.0);
```

This precondition reflects the fact that the square root function is not defined for negative numbers. Unlike the square root functions of many libraries, which throw an exception or ignore an incorrect argument, this function assumes that the client will not send a negative value. Preconditions should reflect both explicit functional requirements and allocation of responsibilities.

Because the client sets the message arguments, meeting a precondition is the client's responsibility. Preconditions can therefore catch client bugs. They can check for problems that might be difficult to produce with a test case—for example, uninitialized variables or incorrect pointers. If the method places no constraints on message content, its effective precondition is

```
assert(TRUE);
```

In an LSP-compliant polymorphic class hierarchy, the precondition for an overriding subclass method must not be stronger than the precondition for the overridden superclass method. The role of preconditions in overridden methods, class invariants, and sequence checking is discussed later in this chapter.

When a precondition assertion is violated, the method cannot guarantee that it will meet its contract. A precondition assertion action should generate an appropriate diagnostic message and may attempt recovery. If processing should continue, control should return to the client without any further execution of the method. The state of the object should not change. If the method is allowed to continue after the assertion violation, the results are unpredictable.

Loops

The conditions for correct loop control may be asserted. Loop control often involves subtle relationships and may depend on side effects of computations in the loop body.[5] The loop invariant and the loop variant assert the conditions for correct loop control.

A **loop invariant** is a Boolean expression that relates the variables used in a loop. It must be true no matter how often the loop iterates. To determine the loop invariant we identify what must be assumed as true before entering the loop and then expand (or contract) this predicate to cover all iterations. Formally, this process is called generalizing the loop postconditions. The loop invariant must be true in the following circumstances:

- After loop control initialization (before the first iteration)
- After each subsequent iteration
- After the final iteration
- If no iteration occurs

Figure 17.3 illustrates these requirements. Loop invariants are typically related to the computation in the loop body. If the loop invariant does not hold, either a bug or a side effect has caused some necessary condition to become false, so the results of the iteration will be incorrect. For example, suppose we have a loop that finds the minimum and maximum values in an array:

```
// nx is number of elements in x

min = x[0];
max = x[0];

for (int i=0; i < nx; ++i) {
    if (x[i] < min ) min = x[i];
    if (x[i] > max ) max = x[i];
};
```

The loop invariant is

```
assert ( min <= max )
```

---

5. The conditions for loop correctness were established in early research on program correctness. Identification of these conditions is typically a difficult puzzle for any nontrivial loop [Gries 81]. Gnarly loop control may also be a symptom of a more general problem in the method algorithm or allocation of class responsibilities. If it is exceedingly difficult to articulate loop conditions, take it as a good (but not conclusive) indication that your basic design is flawed. Jezequel presents pragmatic guidance for developing Eiffel loop assertions [Jezequel 96].

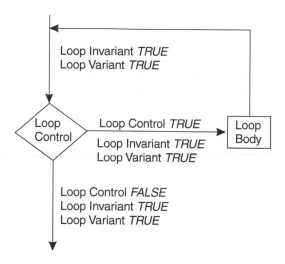

FIGURE 17.3 The loop invariant.

and for all i,

```
x[i] <= max, x[i] >= min
```

That is, if at any time we somehow manage to switch the current minimum and maximum, the code cannot produce a correct result. The asserted loop is

```
min = x[0];
max = x[0];

assert( (min <= max) && (x[0]<= max) && (x[0]>= min));

for (int i=0; i < nx; ++i) {
    if (x[i] < min ) min = x[i];
    if (x[i] > max ) max = x[i];

assert( (min <= max) && (x[i]<= max) && (x[i]>= min));
};
```

We also require that nx does not change. Here, we can see by inspection that nx is not referenced in the loop body, so we can safely assume that it will not change (this assumption reflects the practical necessity of trusting the compiler and the rest of the virtual machine).

A correct loop must iterate the required number of times and must eventually stop. The necessary conditions for loop termination can be asserted by a loop variant. The **loop variant** is a Boolean expression that relates variables in creased or decreased on every iteration. Its predicate must be true while the loop is within bounds and violated if the loop goes out of control. The loop variant is a restatement of the loop control predicate that meets the following conditions:

- It contains an integer expression that is evaluated after each iteration of the loop body.
- The expression is written so that it will never produce a negative value in a correct loop.
- Each successive evaluation of the variant must produce a number smaller than the previous evaluation.

For example, the min/max loop variant is

```
assert ( (nx - i) > 0 );
```

That is, the current index of the array i must always be less than the number of elements nx minus 1 (assuming 0 points to the first element). If the index equals or exceeds the number of elements, the loop control will allow the index to take on incorrect values and will eventually fail. Although nx is not altered in the loop, it could be corrupted by side effects or a pointer error. A function nx( ) could be buggy or nondeterministic. The code with the loop variant assertion is as follows:

```
assert( (min <= max) && (x[0]<= max) && (x[0]>= min));

for (int i=0; i < nx; ++i) {
    if (x[i] < min ) min = x[i];
    if (x[i] > max ) max = x[i];
    assert( (min<=max) && (x[i]<=max) && (x[i]>= min) &&((nx-i)>0));
};
```

When should you assert your loops? The cost of asserting a loop is the additional "think time" needed to articulate the conditions (the coding time is trivial). A good case can be made for this analysis on every loop. If you cannot identify the loop assertions, how can you be sure that your loop will run correctly? An even better case can be made for asserting any loop in which the body modifies the control variables or uses several levels of nesting, as such loops are typically error-prone.

A properly asserted loop reduces the test design and implementation needed to attain loop coverage (see Loop Testing, Chapter 10). With loops whose control variables are encapsulated or otherwise difficult to control, assertions may be the only practical way to gain confidence in loop correctness. If the performance cost is excessive, loop assertions may be disabled after initial class testing passes.

Postconditions

A **postcondition** defines properties that must hold when a method completes. It is evaluated after a method finishes executing and before the message result is returned to the client. Postcondition checking ensures that values bound to the outgoing message arguments are acceptable given the current state of the object and the message that activated it. Stated in terms of design-by-contract, the postcondition verifies that the server's promise is met.

A postcondition usually defines a constraint between message arguments and objects returned to the client. For example, the postcondition for the square root function `float sqrt(float x);` is

```
assert ( abs(x - (sqrt_x * sqrt_x))) < (x * 1.0E-7) );
```

This postcondition uses the reversibility of the square root function: the result times itself should equal the argument. Strict equality is not required; differences in accuracy of less than one part in a million are acceptable. If a method makes no promises about what it produces, the effective postcondition is

```
assert(TRUE);
```

Comparing values at entry and exit may be useful. For example, the postcondition for `Account::debit(amount)` requires that `balance` is decreased by `amount`:

```
assert ( balance == (old_balance - amount) );
```

The variable `old_balance` contains a copy of the value of `balance` at entry to `debit`.

Asserting that the value of an instance variable remains unchanged from entry to exit may be useful. The Eiffel language, for example, uses the `nochange` keyword to designate this relationship. Other languages require a different approach. If the instance variable is a constant, then it should be declared as an immutable: const in C++, static in Java, and so on. If the instance variable is changed in some methods but not others, then the value at entry must be copied and compared to the value at exit.

The postcondition must be evaluated at all explicit and implicit return statements. Note that the postcondition may differ at different exit points. For example, consider the following C++ class fragment:

```
class SomeIts {
public:
    int squashIt(int foo) {
        int old_it;
        old_it = it; // Postcondition needs the value at entry

        if ( foo == it ) {
            assert (TRUE);
            return it;

        } else if ( foo > it ) {
            item = it - foo;
            assert ( (it + foo) == old_it);
            return it;

        } else if ( foo < it ) {
            it = it + foo;
            assert ( (it - foo) == old_it)
            return it;
        }
    }
private:
    int it;
};
```

Clearly, postconditions can ease detection of gross implementation faults due to complexity or simple coding mistakes. Postconditions may seem like overkill, especially in methods implemented in a few lines of code. Even if a method is straightforward and correct in its own simple context, however, it can still fail in ways that are detectable by postconditions.

- Methods typically send messages to many other objects. Messages sent to unstable, distributed, or polymorphic servers of the object under test may be bound to different objects, even within the span of a single activation. These objects may be part of the application under test, serve as wrappers to legacy system components, be provided by a third party, or reside on some remote server thousands of miles away. An incorrect or unexpected response from these server objects can easily result in a postcondition violation, even though the method under test is correct.

- Methods typically send messages to many other objects, including themselves. An incorrect interaction with or side effect of superclass methods can propagate to the method under test.
- Postconditions can help to prevent and detect failures resulting from increased code entropy. As code is debugged or enhanced over time (possibly several decades), it becomes more difficult to ensure its correctness. Initial vigilance wanes. Developer knowledge evaporates. Postconditions can help to maintain continuity and automatically check that the class's contract is preserved for its unchanged clients.

In a polymorphic class hierarchy, the postcondition for an overriding subclass method must be the same as or stronger than the postcondition for the overridden superclass method. Postconditions in overridden methods, class invariants, and transition resultant conditions are discussed later in this chapter.

When a postcondition assertion is violated, the method has not accomplished its intended responsibility. A postcondition assertion action should therefore generate an appropriate message. If processing should continue, the recovery should return the object to a state that conforms to the class invariant.

17.3.4   Class Scope

A **class invariant** specifies properties that must be true of every object of a class. The class invariant must be true after instantiation, upon entry and exit from every method (except in some local call cases), and just before destruction. It must hold for all methods, over all activation sequences, and for any valid value of incoming arguments.

- The complete precondition for a method is `<precondition>` *and* `<classInvariant>`. That is, the class invariant and the precondition must both be true at entry.
- The complete postcondition for a method is `<postcondition>` *and* `<invariant>`. That is, the invariant and the postcondition must both be true at exit.
- In a polymorphic class hierarchy, the invariant for a subclass should not be weaker than the invariant for the superclass.

If all common requirements are factored out of completely specified pre-conditions and postconditions, we obtain the class invariant. The class invariant consolidates conditions that would appear in every precondition or in every postcondition. Removing this redundancy is not essential and, in some circumstances, evaluating the conditions in the precondition or postcondition may be a better tactic. The class invariant defines the boundaries of the domain formed by class instance variables. A state invariant may subdivide this domain, but cannot (validly) extend it.

```
class Account {
    // ...
protected:
    bool invariant( ) const {
    //
    // Last tx date cannot be in the future
    //
    // Must be one of active, frozen, or closed.
    //
        return(   (tx_date <= current_date) &&
                (  ( !isActive && !isFrozen && isClosed) ||
                   ( !isActive && isFrozen && !isClosed) ||
                   ( isActive && !isFrozen && !isClosed)
                )
        );
    }
};
```

This invariant requires that every Account object (1) is either active, frozen, or closed, and (2) cannot contain a predated (future) transaction.

Two special cases occur where runtime invariant checking is suspended. First, if an invariant uses a method of its own class (which also checks the class invariant), an infinite loop will result. Assertion checking should be suspended when the client of a method is an assertion. Second, methods to recover from a corrupt state or other exceptional conditions must be allowed to work for corrupt states. Because the invariant will probably not hold until the recovery is completed, invariant checking is suspended while an object is in recovery mode. Eiffel generates the code to perform both kinds of suspension [Meyer 97]. Designers of hand-coded assertions can prevent the first problem by recoding (e.g., repeat the get method code in the invariant, remove the invariant call from the get method, and so on). The second problem must be resolved for assertions and recovery code to be deployed. For assertions that are not deployed, a simpler course may be to let the assertion violation occur or to disable assertions for particular test runs.

The class invariant is a powerful tool for obtaining correct code, as demonstrated by OS/400. This system did not make extensive use of preconditions and postconditions, but instead relied on invariants. Meyer notes, "Only when I have derived the invariant (for a class that I write) or read and understood it (for someone else's class) do I feel that I know what the class is about" [Meyer 97, 367].

17.3.5 Sequential Constraints

Recall that *state* refers to a set of instance variable value combinations for which the response of a class is the same. A particular combination of instance variable values is the *content* of an object. For example, the class specification for `Account` defines the state *overdrawn* as (`balance < 0.00`). Suppose the content of an `Account` object with instance variables `balance`, `lastTransactionDate`, and `accountNumber` is minus 3471.38, 12/21/1996, and 772910, respectively. This object is in the state *overdrawn*. Any of the large number of content combinations where `balance < 0.00` would also be in the *overdrawn* state.

A modal class has sequentially constrained behavior. That is, not all sequences of messages are acceptable. Legal sequences are defined with respect to states. Constraints on legal sequences of messages and states can be represented with assertions.

- A *state invariant* defines a state, just as a class invariant defines the complete state space of a class.
- An *accepting condition* defines the state(s) in which a method may accept a message.
- A *resulting condition* defines the state that should result after accepting a message in a valid state.

State Invariant

A **state invariant** is an assertion that defines a valid state.[6] The notion of a state invariant is not new. It was a key part of the Ina Jo language for abstract data type specifications [Kemmerer 85], formal object models [Schuman+87], Syntropy [Cook+94], and Catalysis [D'Souza+99]. A state invariant is stronger

---

6. State invariants define states in the FREE model. See Chapter 7.

than (or the same as) the class invariant. A modal class has at least two states and therefore at least two state invariants. For any method in a modal class:

- One and only one state invariant must hold at entry. Every method must have at least one acceptance condition.
- One and only one state invariant must hold at exit. Every method must have at least one resultant condition.

Several relationships between state and class invariants must hold. If no state invariant is defined, the class invariant defines the single legal state. If only one state invariant is defined, it must be identical to the class invariant. With two or more state invariants, several conditions must be met for a correct set of state assertions:

- The class invariant must be the same as or weaker than all state invariants.
- No state invariant may be weaker than the class invariant.
- Only one state invariant may hold for any content combination. Each state invariant defines a unique, mutually exclusive subset of the class state space.
- The domain of the state invariants must completely cover the domain defined by the class invariant—that is, the state invariants are collectively exhaustive.

State invariants greatly simplify state-based testing. Determining the state of the object under test can be cumbersome and unreliable without these assertions. Current state may be determined in two ways without using invariants:

- A driver uses public `get` methods in an expression that defines the state. For example,

```
if (  (acct1234.getBalance( ) < 0.00) &&
        (acct1234.getLastTxDate( ) > 19900101 ) ) {
    // Account overdrawn ...
}
```

- A driver uses an anti-encapsulation idiom (e.g., a `friend` class) to access the implementation and evaluates the content in an expression that defines a state.

```
If ((balance < 0.00) && (lastTxDate > 19900101)) {
   // Account overdrawn
}
```

Both approaches have problems, however:

- The public interface may not offer all of the get methods needed to establish all abstract states.[7]
- The public interface get methods may have side effects or bugs that invalidate the state report.
- Using an anti-encapsulation idiom increases the chance of inadvertent side effects due to bugs in the driver and couples state evaluation with the implementation.
- The state invariant is hard-coded, typically in many places and in many drivers. This is likely to result in inconsistent state invariants, especially the state specification/implementation of the class changes.
- Clients responsible for correct sequential usage of a modal server need to check the state of the server. If the server is widely used, redundant state checking will need to be coded in every client. This coding will be difficult to develop and maintain.

These problems are compounded when the modal behavior is refined in lower levels of a class hierarchy. Implementing each state invariant as a Boolean method solves these problems.

Accepting and Resulting Conditions

An **accepting condition** should be asserted at the same point as a precondition. It checks that an incoming message is acceptable given the current state of the object. A **resulting condition** should be asserted at the same point as a postcondition. It checks that the resultant state is valid state given the accepting state and method. Consider the simple state machine for class TwoState in Figure 17.4. In this two-state machine, method foo does not change state. Method bar always causes a transition. The corresponding invariant assertions are as follows:

---

7. See [Freedman 91] for a detailed theoretical analysis of this problem.

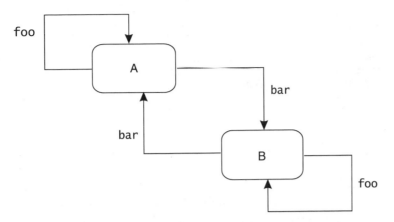

FIGURE 17.4   Relationship of method state invariants to state transitions.

```
class TwoState {
public
   void foo(int x) {
      assert(                          // Accepting condition
         (isStateA() || isStateB())
      );
      int old_x = x;                   // Save content at entry

      // Function body


      assert(                          // Resulting condition
         (isStateA() && wasStateA()) ||
         (isStateB() && wasStateB())
      );
      return;
   }

   void bar(int x) {
      assert(                          // Accepting condition
         (isStateA() || isStateB())
      );
      int old_x = x;                   // Save content at entry


      // Function body

      assert(                          // Resulting condition
         (isStateA() && wasStateB()) ||
         (isStateB() && wasStateA())
      );
      return;
   }
```

```
protected:
   // State Invariants
   bool isStateA( )  const {return (x >= 0);      }
   bool wasStateA( ) const {return (old_x >= 0); }
   bool isStateB( )  const {return (x < 0);       }
   bool wasStateB( ) const {return (old_x < 0);   }
private:
   int x;
}
```

Runtime Sequence Checking

As the preceding examples show, state invariants, accepting conditions, and resultant conditions may be coded like preconditions and postconditions. Payne
et al. present a similar approach to hard-coded sequential constraints [Payne
+97]. Although assertion-based sequence checking is effective, it requires translation of the state specification into assertions and subsequent maintenance of
these assertions. With a large state machine, the number of predicates in such
assertions could become unwieldy.

The entire sequence checking process can be factored out and supported by
several private sequence checking methods.[8] Instead of evaluating hard-coded
conditions, messages are sent to methods that check the three constraints. These
methods would use a state/state table corresponding to the class's state specification implemented as a hash collection `StateTable`.

- `App_Class::legalEvent(methodName)` is a Boolean function that returns *true* when the current state and message correspond to a legal
  transition. If the message is not accepted in this state, it returns *false*.
  `legalEvent` assumes that `currentState` is valid, so `currentState`
  should be asserted before `legalEvent`. If the current `methodname` cannot be obtained at runtime, then the `methodName` must be hard-coded
  in the assertion.

- `App_Class::legalResult` is a Boolean function that returns *true* when
  the current state, message, and entry state correspond to a legal transition. If the resultant state is allowed for the event, it returns *false*.

- `App_Class::legalState` is a Boolean function that returns *true* when
  `currentState` determines that the current contents satisfy a state in-

---

8. Kirani suggests that event (message) sequences can be checked by a private method
using an automata algorithm to determine whether two machines accept the same language
[Kirani+94]. It is not clear just how the second FSM would be computed or content would
be checked.

variant. If the current contents do not satisfy any state invariant, `legalState` returns *false*.

- `App_Class::currentState` is an integer function that returns an index number for the state invariant that holds for the current contents of the object. If no state invariant holds, zero is returned. Each `<StatePredicate>` is simply a Boolean expression over instance variables that defines one state.

- The method `StateTable::transitionExists(methodName, currentState)` returns *true* if the method and state pair are found in the state table hash collection, and *false* otherwise. The hash table may be hard-coded or loaded from a specification repository. This method is defined on the subclass `StateTable`.

- The method `StateTable::resultAllowed(methodName, entryState, currentState)` returns *true* if the method, entry state, and exit state are found in the state table hash collection, and *false* otherwise. This method is defined on the subclass `StateTable`.

At entry, `currentState` and `legalEvent(methodName)` are asserted. The pseudocode for this strategy follows.

```
bool legalEvent(String methodName)
   if !accepted(methodName, currentState)
      return FALSE
   else
      // Side effect, save index of entry state
      entryState = currentState
      return TRUE
   fi
end legalEvent

bool legalState( )
   if currentState == 0
      return FALSE
   else
      return TRUE
   fi
end legalState

bool legalResult(String methodName)
   if !allowed(methodName, entryState, currentState)
      return FALSE
   else
      return TRUE
   fi
end legalResult
```

```
int currentState()
   currentState = 0
   if ( <StatePredicate1> )
      currentState = 1
   else
   if ( <StatePredicate2> )
      currentState = 2
   // ...
   else
   if ( <StatePredicateN> )
      currentState = <n>
   else
      currentState = 0
   fi
end currentState
```

Such a sequence checking method should also:

- Encapsulate the class state specification as a singleton class variable.
- Check superclass sequential constraints using Percolation.
- Provide automatic collection of state coverage information.

An advanced implementation could read the state specification from a CASE repository and generate a checkable model on the fly [Binder 94a].

A full sequence checker can be as large as the control implementation for the state specification for the class under test. If the class under test has an explicit, table-driven implementation of a state machine, then it probably makes more sense to assert the state control implementation itself and not the state machine (design considerations and applicable patterns are discussed in Section 7.2.9, State Machines and Object-Oriented Development). If the class under test depends on its clients to comply with its sequential constraints, however, then a sequence checker will be effective for revealing client bugs. If there are many clients of a cooperative modal class in the system under test, then this kind of sequence checker is the only practical means for verifying the message sequences generated by all of these clients.

17.3.6   Superclass/Subclass Scope

Subcontracts and Type Substitution

Method polymorphism relies on the names and argument signatures of methods in a class hierarchy. The **contract metaphor** suggests that overriding under inheritance is similar to the business relationship between a prime contractor and a subcontractor. A subcontractor is expected to fulfill some part of the prime contractor's promises and to refrain from breaking any of the prime contractor's commitments. The subcontractor is hired to perform a special task that is within the scope of the overall responsibilities of the prime contractor. Similarly, we expect a subclass to accept all valid superclass messages and respond in a way that is consistent with the superclass behavior. The following conditions are necessary to achieve consistent subcontracting.

1.   The precondition of a subclass method that overrides must be the same or weaker than that of the overridden superclass method. The effective subclass precondition is the superclass precondition *or*ed with the explicit subclass precondition.

2.   The postcondition of a subclass method that overrides must be the same as or stronger than that of the overridden superclass method. The effective subclass postcondition is the superclass postcondition *and*ed with the explicit subclass postcondition.

3.   The state space of the subclass must be similarly restricted. The subclass invariant must be the same as or stronger than the invariants of all of its superclasses, with respect to inherited instance variables. The effective subclass invariant is the superclass invariant *and*ed with the explicit subclass invariant. When a subclass redefines the state space by adding instance variables, subclass state invariants (i) must specify valid states with respect to these extended variables, (ii) must be orthogonal to superclass state invariants, and (iii) cannot define a weaker state space with respect to superclass variables that are visible in the subclass.

If met, the first condition guarantees that any message accepted by a superclass method will also be accepted by the corresponding subclass method. The second and third conditions guarantee that the corresponding superclass postcondition and superclass invariant will hold after a message is accepted by a subclass [Liskov+94]. These requirements are sometimes called the *Liskov substitution principle.*[9] The concise statement of LSP is that "the objects of the subtype ought to behave the same as those of the supertype as far as anyone or any program using supertype objects can tell" [Liskov+94, 1811]. A subclass must

---

9. Liskov's papers do not use the term "Liskov substitution principle." This commonly used rubric originated elsewhere.

accept all messages that its superclass will accept and must produce appropriate results once accepted. A subclass that implements the preceding three rules conforms to LSP. The conditions for inheritance under Meyer's design-by-contract approach conform with most of the requirements of LSP. Before showing how assertions can express the necessary conditions for correct subcontracting and detect violations, we consider some possible faults under inheritance.

Buggy Inheritance

Assertions that implement LSP will prevent and detect inheritance bugs. From the contract point of view, a subclass can violate its superclass contract in two ways. First, if the subclass implements a stronger precondition, a message that would be accepted by the superclass may be rejected by the subclass. Second, if the subclass implements a weaker postcondition or invariant, a state that is invalid for the superclass could be computed by the subclass. These conditions are analogous to a subcontractor doing "side deals" or refusing work accepted by the prime contractor. The inheritance problems discussed in Chapters 4 and 10 are listed in Table 17.2. These problems are related to the effects of delocalized plans [Soloway+88] and are endemic to object-oriented development.

> [A] problematic case is precondition inheritance in which the addition of a new precondition in a derived class [should weaken] the effective precondition. Arguably this is an idea that is easily misunderstood: The programmer or code reader might think that a precondition replaces, instead of augments previous preconditions, or even strengthens them [Porat+95, 34].

Most OOA/D methodologies offer heuristics to prevent these problems. The approaches in [Cook+94], [Page-Jones 95], and [Meyer 97] are consistent with the requirements of LSP and design-by-contract. These bugs may be detected with assertions, but subclasses must have access to all assertions of the superclasses. The Eiffel language provides elegant support for this kind of checking. This same kind of checking may be obtained in other languages by using the *Percolation* pattern.

17.3.7   Client/Server Scope

Public and Private Contracts

Contract compliance depends on having access to the elements of a contract. An element becomes visible according to the scoping rules for the programming

TABLE 17.2   Inheritance Bugs

Bug Type	Typical Cause
Incorrect Initialization	Superclass initialization is omitted or incorrect.
Inadvertent Bindings	Incorrect bindings result because of misunderstood name resolution.
Missing Override	A subclass-specific implementation of a superclass method is omitted.
Naked Access	A superclass instance variable is visible in a subclass and subclass methods update these variables directly.
Square Peg in a Round Hole	A subclass is incorrectly located in a hierarchy.
Naughty Children	A subclass either does not accept all messages that the superclass accepts or leaves the object in a state that is illegal in the superclass.
Worm Holes	A subclass computes values that are not consistent with the superclass invariant or superclass state invariants.
Spaghetti Inheritance	Top-heavy multiple inheritance or deep hierarchies (six or more superclasses).
Gnarly Hierarchy	A subclass creates new holes, boundaries, or intersections that are inconsistent with the superclass domain.
Weird Hierarchy	Inheritance is abused as a kind of code-sharing macro to support hacks without regard to the resulting semantics.
Fat Interface	A subclass inherits methods that are inappropriate or irrelevant.

language in use. The typical scope control mechanisms include visibility keywords (`public`, `protected`, `private`), default scoping under inheritance, scoping semantics for globally defined objects and variables, and so on. Table 17.3 summarizes some scope control semantics.

The public elements of a server's contract are the methods, objects, and variables visible to a client. If a client and server have access to global objects or variables, those variables must also be considered as elements of the contract. The public elements of a contract that the server must make visible to a client include the following:

- Preconditions of visible methods
- Visible elements of postconditions
- Visible elements of the invariant
- Visible elements of state invariants

TABLE 17.3   Visibility Determines Contract Scope

Language	Control of Visibility/Scoping
Ada 95	The visibility of data and operations in tagged type (a subclass or superclass) is determined by scope keywords and their placement. A type declared as `private` limits visibility to the type (similarly private in C++). Default visibility is similar to the C++ public. A *child package* has full access to the type.
C++	Class member functions and data members default to `private` (not visible outside of a class) or are declared as `public` (visible at file scope) or `protected` (visible to defining and derived classes). `Friend` functions and classes may access private members. C rules for name control at the file scope apply.
Eiffel	The export keyword determines the visibility of class routines and variables. Export may be unrestricted (the default, or keyword of ANY), limited to specified clients, or NONE (not visible outside of the class). Subclasses always inherit all features and may redefine the export parameters of inherited features.
Java	Java supports four scopes for any member: `private`—within a class, package—within a class and its subclasses, `protected`—within a package, and `public`—all classes in a system.
Objective-C	All methods are public. Instance variable visibility is controlled by the keywords `@public`, `@private`, and `@protected`, with semantics similar to C++. The default is `@protected`; use of `@public` is strongly discouraged. Instance variable encapsulation is enforced at compile time.
Smalltalk	A class interface is globally visible and its implementation is hidden to all clients and subclasses. All variables must be objects and objects may respond only to messages that are part of the class interface.

So, if a Stack class insists that you cannot pop when it is empty, Stack must make a nonEmpty( ) method visible to its clients or provide get methods that allow the client to compute the same result. The same visibility could also be provided by making the related instance variables public or—worse yet—global. The Eiffel compiler enforces adherence to the public contract by flagging precondition references to private variables as an error.

Clearly, both client and server must comply with the server's public contract for correct results. But which contract is relevant for server methods with restricted visibility—for example, private or protected in C++? When should this contract be checked? The elements of a private contract are those parts of a server's implementation not visible to its clients. A private contract:

- Governs intraclass usage of private features.
- Is implementation-specific and concerns concrete state, not abstract state.

- Must support the public contract, but may allow transient states that would be inconsistent with the public contract. Such a transient state might occur while handling an exception, computing a result, or building and populating a complex structure of object associations. These transient states will have their own implementation-specific assumptions, constraints, and so on.

The implementation relationships listed in Table 17.1 suggest assertions for transient states. In Eiffel, transient states do not cause a problem because when a class sends itself a message, assertion checking is suspended. Distinguishing the source of a message in other languages is difficult, so this should be considered when designing services for intraclass usage.

Defensive Contracts?

The purist approach to design-by-contract requires the client to meet the server's preconditions, freeing the server from the responsibility of precondition checking [Meyer 92a]. This idea of a **cooperative** server is at odds with generally accepted practice, which is that a method should always check incoming messages and reject those violating its precondition [Booch 91, Weide 91, Parrish 93b]. This is a **defensive** server. Defensive servers are the better choice.

- Cooperative design means that the same checking code must be repeated in every server and tested. If a precondition violation is a rare occurrence, the checking is better handled as a dedicated exception thrown by the server.
- The server may not provide access to all information necessary to check the precondition, especially if the precondition depends on private variables.
- Suppose a server supports multiple concurrent clients. Even if the clients check preconditions, it is possible that the server's state may change while a client message is queued, resulting in the message not meeting the precondition when it is finally accepted by the server.
- As servers are revised over time or reused in unanticipated contexts, the information or diligence necessary for client checking can be lost.
- Errors can be made in the client code, even when it attempts to observe server preconditions. If there are many clients, the chance of such a bug increases with each client.

In general, defensive systems are easier to test, maintain, and reuse. Defensive precondition checking must be shipped with the application system and therefore may not be an ideal vehicle for all forms of built-in test. See Section 17.5, Deployment.

Exceptions

An exception is a mechanism that has three parts: a recognizer that detects an anomalous condition, a control that activates a handler ("raising" or "throwing" an exception), and a handler that may attempt recovery, notification, or termination. Some exception-handling models force termination of the active method; others allow processing to resume. The design of exception handling is a complex subject beyond the scope of this book (see the Bibliographic Notes section). Exceptions are supported by C++, Java, Eiffel, Ada 95, and some Smalltalk development environments. Each language uses a different approach.

If a server can throw an exception, then it is part of its contract. Clients must know which exceptions can be thrown by their servers and what handling, if any, is expected. Exceptions are as much a part of a contract as preconditions and postconditions. In some circumstances, an exception mechanism is an appropriate implementation for an assertion action. The role of exception handlers in assertions is discussed in Section 17.9.2, Assertion Actions.

From a testing perspective, we should verify that (1) servers generate exceptions when they should and do not generate spurious exceptions, and (2) clients accept and properly handle all exceptions generated by their servers. Class-level assertions are not useful for this kind of testing. Chapter 19 shows how stubs and drivers can be used to exercise exception handling in clients and servers.

17.4 Implementation

17.4.1 A Programmer's Assertion FAQ

The following general considerations are applicable to assertions written in any language.

When should I start coding assertions?

As soon as possible. Don't wait until your classes are coded and stabilized to add assertions. Don't use them as an afterthought to support debugging. Instead, start coding assertions while coding the class interface. Enable assertion checking in your first compile—not as a final pass or only in support of debugging. Stub code can also be asserted as it is developed. Early asserting will prevent many bugs and find more bugs sooner.

What should be asserted?

Assert the class contract and critical assumptions.

- Look for places where fault sniffers might be effective (see the preceding discussion).
- Check preconditions at entry. If you need to refer to values at entry in a postcondition or invariant, copy these values after the precondition is evaluated.
- Check postconditions at exit. If there are multiple exit points (e.g., `return` statements), the postcondition should be asserted at each exit point.
- Check the class invariant whenever a stable abstract state should be present: (1) just before exiting a constructor, (2) just after entering a destructor, (3) at entry, before checking the precondition, and (4) at exit, before checking the postcondition.
- Check state invariants in the same places where you check the class invariant, but only if modal behavior is present.
- Use the *Percolation* pattern to inherit superclass assertion checking (unless you're programming in Eiffel).
- Don't overassert. Asserting the class contract and fault sniffers (if indicated) is usually sufficient.
- Use human intelligence when a constraint isn't easily asserted. For example, display the before and after state of an object and let the developer/tester decide.
- If time does not permit asserting the entire contract, then focus on code that is mostly likely to be buggy. For example, develop precondition checking for a server with many new clients, invariant checking in a complex implementation, and so on.

How should assertions be coded?

Develop assertions with the same diligence you would apply to application coding. Do not view assertions as disposable debugging code. Strive for readability, consistency, and correctness.

- Move conditions common to all preconditions and postconditions to the invariant, unless performance or defensive programming suggests otherwise. If you plan to disable invariant checking, you may want to retain some common checks in the preconditions.

- Do not code assertion predicates (or assertion methods) that have side effects. Do not code predicate expressions that have an embedded assignment operation. If an assertion predicate expression has side effects, then these side effects may be produced when the assertion is enabled and reached. When the assertion is disabled, the side effects will not be produced. The behavior of the system will be different when its assertions are enabled or disabled.

- Precondition predicates may refer only to public methods and public instance variables. As clients are responsible for meeting the precondition, they must have access to this information to meet the conditions.

- A method of a class may be used in an assertion if (1) it has no side effects (it cannot change state or call other methods with side effects), (2) it is trusted and known to be correct, and (3) it cannot loop back on the assertion itself.

- Avoid using the Boolean constant FALSE as an assertion predicate. An acceptable use is a "this should never happen" segment in a switch or `if-elseif` statement.

- Break up long predicates with *and* operators into separate assertion statements. For example, replace

```
assert ( (a == b) || (c != d) &&
      this->isEmpty( ) || this->isFull( )
);
```

with two statements:

```
assert ( (a == b) || (c != d) );
assert ( this->isEmpty( ) || this->isFull( ) );
```

Some people find this coding style offensive and would much rather see a single assertion (there's no accounting for taste). The goal is to produce readable and maintainable code, so choose a convention that achieves this goal in your circumstances. More `assert` statements with simpler predicates will ease debugging.

- When an assertion predicate is based on an obscure relationship or assumption, explain it in a comment.

- Use white space, indentation, and parentheses to avoid errors and enhance readability.

- Check for blind spots. If you have an incorrect understanding of the application, your assertions will probably be incorrect. Explain your code and assertions to someone else. Better still, have the asserted code inspected.

How should assertions be coded in language *x*?

See the language-specific sections later in this chapter.

Should I use assertions to handle input errors and environment exceptions?

In general, no.

- Do not implement application error and exception responsibilities with assertions, unless you are prepared to test and ship them with the application. Unacceptable input should be recognized and rejected by application code or, in Ada 95, with the appropriate built-in features. The default assertion actions in most programming languages do not provide robust exception handling.
- Do not use assertions to check return codes from library functions or system services.

How should I disable assertions before releasing my system?

Very carefully. See Section 7.5, Deployment.

- Do not change application source code to disable assertions. Do not comment out or delete assertion statements. Instead, use a preprocessor or compiler directives to enable/disable assertion checking consistently and automatically.
- Avoid hacks, tricks, or defaults to disable assertion checking. For example, the following postcondition code fragment works correctly when the CHECKASSERTIONS flag is *true*:

```
if ( CHECKASSERTIONS && <AssertionPredicate>) {
    return;
}
throw <AssertionException>;
```

When CHECKASSERTIONS is *false* (e.g., after you've shipped the code), the exception is thrown every time this method is entered. The assertion should have been coded as follows:

```
if ( CHECKASSERTIONS && !<AssertionPredicate>) {
   throw <AssertionException>;
}
return;
```

- In some languages (e.g., Java), a short circuit Boolean expression evaluation is the only practical way to control assertion evaluation. Most optimizing compilers will not generate executable code for an if-then expression whose body cannot be reached. By making a flag like CHECK-ASSERTIONS *false* at compile time, the assertion predicate and the action disappear from the executable. If you must use short circuit Booleans, take care to name variables carefully and comment your code. You can easily cause more bugs than you prevent by inadvertent application use or corruption of the assertion control variable(s), as the preceding example shows.

How should I code postconditions if there are multiple exit points in a method?

Multiple exit points are present when a method has more than one return statement. The postcondition and invariant should be checked at each return. There are three ways to handle this checking:

1. Code the postcondition as a separate Boolean method, and assert it and the invariant at every exit point.
2. Restructure the method algorithm to have a single exit point.
3. In Java, wrap the entire method in a try/finally block (see Section 17.4.7 on Java).

17.4.2   Assertion Actions

When an assertion violation occurs, an assertion action must be produced. The action has two responsibilities: notification and continuation. Figures 17.5 and 17.6 suggest some options. The columns in these figures correspond to a set of actions to be produced. For example, continuation mode 4 attempts to continue execution under the control of a debugger. Continuation and notification modes can be combined in many ways. For example,

- Treat the violation as an input error and continue processing.
- Log the violation, produce a diagnostic dump, and terminate the process.

Continuation Option	Continuation Mode				
	0	1	2	3	4
Terminate	✓				
Continue execution		✓			
Prompt for continue or terminate			✓		
Activate debugger				✓	✓
Attempt recovery					✓

FIGURE 17.5   Assertion continuation options.

Notification Option	Notification Mode				
	0	1	2	3	4
Write to default console	✓	✓	✓	✓	✓
Write to test log		✓	✓	✓	✓
Write a bug report			✓	✓	✓
Generate a stack trace			✓	✓	✓
Generate a dump					✓

FIGURE 17.6   Assertion notification options.

- Use the violation to trigger interactive debugging.
- Log the violation as a successful test case, then continue processing.
- Generate an error message and stop the process (the default for the ANSI C++ `assert`).
- Treat the violation as an exception, then attempt recovery (the default for the Eiffel language).

Unless recovery is attempted, the result of application processing after an assertion violation and its action is usually unpredictable. The effect of the violation may be localized. It may also result in intermittent, low-visibility failures or in an avalanche of spurious output and more assertion violations. Whether this result is just an annoyance or a serious problem depends on the application and the context of the violation. It is typically acceptable during initial development/debugging, problematic in regression testing, and undesirable in a deployed system.

An assertion violation is a successful test run. Unless the assertion is incorrect, a violation is caused by a bug. Advanced assertion actions could include automatic bug reporting. The action could easily write a record to a file to be read by a bug tracking system.

A circular buffer is useful for logging assertion actions. Similar to an endless loop of magnetic tape, a fixed storage space is allocated for logging. Actions are added to the next available section of storage. When the last available location has been used, the next action is logged at the first available location, writing over the oldest entry. In this way, the most recent actions become available for review without allocating and managing storage for a potentially huge number of log entries.

Assertion actions can use existing capabilities for exception handling. In Eiffel, assertions use the built-in exception-handling mechanism. This mechanism can support the design-by-contract approach to developing highly robust applications [Jézéquel 96, Meyer 97]. Use of built-in exceptions is the preferred approach in Ada 95 and Java. In other languages, however, this kind of integration does not exist and may be unwise to attempt. If integration is attempted, support for debugging and robust operation should be separable. Basic error-handling and exception-handling mechanisms do not typically provide useful debugging support when an assertion violation occurs. Nondeployable assertions typically do not require runtime recovery or other forms of software fault tolerance. Handling of unacceptable input and exceptions is necessary for reliable operation and should be subjected to the same design-build-test process as all other deployable application functionality.

> The real problem is in detecting errors and figuring out how to recover from them, not in devising programming language mechanisms to implement the detection procedures. Some programming languages . . . error and exception handling, however, are so complex that they may cause the introduction of errors in the error-handling routines and create more problems than they solve. In general, error-handling mechanisms, like everything else, should be as simple as possible [Leveson 95, 439].

In most systems, the assertion action can be set up to generate a "core" dump. For example, at least one of the following system calls will result in a dump followed by process termination in most Unix systems:

```
abort( );               // Terminate process and generate dump
raise(SIGQUIT);         // Send quit signal to this process
kill(getpid( ), SIGQUIT); // Used on some older systems
```

There is no such facility in some small operating systems—for example,
MS-DOS and some real-time executives. A dump is rarely useful for debugging
unless all other avenues of diagnosis have been exhausted. For an extensive discussion of debugging at this level in the MVS operating system, see [Binder 85].

17.4.3   Nonexecutable Assertions

Code comments and other nonexecutable documentation may include and discuss assertion predicates. Several tools are available to perform static checking
on various forms of nonexecutable assertions. Some generate assertion code,
test cases, or test drivers from the assertion text (see Section 17.7, Some
Assertion Tools).

Cline suggests using commented keyword phrases in C++ class header files
to explain the contract. The PURPOSE line summarizes the transformation accomplished by the method. REQUIRE states or describes the precondition.
PROMISE states or describes the postcondition [Cline+95]. For example,

```
void Account::debit(Money tx_amt) {
   // PURPOSE    Subtract tx_amt from balance
   // REQUIRE    Balance must be greater than $0.00 + tx_amt
   // PROMISE    Balance will be no less than $0.00
}
```

Similar conventions may be followed in any language. Marick provides examples of C++ test design from commented preconditions and postconditions
[Marick 95].

Nonexecutable assertions can express conditions that cannot be easily or
practically checked with assertions. With commentary, they can provide insights into the developer's choices useful for testing and maintenance. The literate programming approach includes both tools and guidance for developing
useful code narratives. The idea is to provide a concise, yet rich, explanation
supported by hypertext tools that embed and expand the commentary in the
code [Cordes+91]. "It is the difference between performing and exposing a
magic trick."[10] Approximately a dozen literate programming tools are available
at no charge via the World Wide Web.

The concerns about increased CPU cycles, code bloat, side effects, and
deployment simply do not arise with nonexecutable assertions. Complete and

---

10. Ross Williams. *FunnelWeb User's Manual*. Technical report, University of Adelaide,
Adelaide, South Australia, Australia, May 1992; *ftp.adelaide.edu.au/pub/funnelweb*

accurate nonexecutable assertions should not hinder design of assertion-based test cases. Of course, none of the mechanisms for runtime checking of executable assertions apply. Because the incremental effort to make an assertion executable is typically negligible, it makes sense to implement assertions in code whenever practical. Comments should be used to amplify or explain considerations that cannot be reflected in code. If you use an assertion tool, the unique capabilities of the tool will determine the appropriate balance.

17.4.4   Ada 95

Ada 83 is a (very) strongly typed, compiled language based on the Abstract Data Type view of modularity. It has built-in support for concurrent tasking and reuse. Ada 95 incorporates the object-oriented programming paradigm by adding inheritance and dynamic binding.

Checking of some relationships is built into Ada 95. The `Normalize_Scalars` pragma provides some support for detecting uninitialized variables. When any of the following anomalous conditions are detected, a specific exception is raised:

- Data values are out of the range defined for a data type.
- An array element index is not within the bounds of its array.
- Package `Text_IO` detects an incorrect range or syntax in I/O values.
- Packages `Sequential_IO` and `Direct_IO` detect input values inconsistent with their designated data type.

This built-in checking obviates the need to assert these conditions. Table 17.4 lists some relationships that may be implemented without assertions.[11] The Ada 95 language definition, however, does not call for assertions or other explicit support for built-in test. Some Ada 95 compilers support general assertion checking. In any case, the programming required for full support of responsibility-based assertions is straightforward.

Assert Pragma

A pragma is a compiler directive that allows the user to specify options for optimization, listing control, and so on. The Ada 95 language specification defines many required pragmas and allows compiler writers to add "implementation-dependent" pragmas. The `Assert` pragma is implementation-

---

11. Suggested by Paul Strachour.

TABLE 17.4   Assertable Relationships That Can Be Checked with Ada 95 Features

Supported by Ada 95 Feature	Assertable Relationship
No	Constraints among arguments
Yes	Constraints on arguments and returned values
Yes	Constraints on arguments and instance/class variables
No	Constraints among instance/class variables
Yes	Constraints on instance/class variables and returned values
No	Variables that must be the same at entry and exit
Yes	Bounds checking on arrays and other collections
Yes	Range checking on scalar types
Yes	Validation for membership in enumerated types or collections
Yes	Pointers that must be non-null
No	"This Should Never Happen" segment

dependent and supported by Ada 95 compilers including GNAT, Aonix, Green Hills, and Intermetrics (the GNAT implementation is considered here). It is similar to the assert macro in C++, but is processed by the compiler and not by a preprocessor. The syntax is

```
pragma Assert (Boolean_EXPRESSION, [static_string_EXPRESSION]);
```

A compiler command-line parameter controls translation of this pragma (Table 17.5). When disabled, all `Assert` pragmas in the compilation stream are treated as comments. Assertion statements are thus enabled/disabled at compile time without source code changes. When enabled, each `Assert` pragma results in code that is equivalent to the following statement:

TABLE 17.5   GNAT Ada 95 Compiler Options Related to Testing

Parameter	Effect
_gnata	Assertions enabled. Pragma `Assert` and `Debug` to be activated.
_gnatb	Generate brief messages to `stderr` even if verbose mode is set.
_gnato	Enable other checks, not normally enabled by default, including numeric overflow checking, and access before elaboration checks.

```
if not Boolean_EXPRESSION then
   System.Assertions.Raise_Assert_Failure
   (static_string_EXPRESSION);
end if;
```

When an assertion violation occurs, the System.Assertions.Assert_
Failure exception is raised. If given, the text in static_string_EXPRESSION is
associated with the exception. If this argument is omitted, a default message is
produced, giving the name of the source file containing the pragma and its line
number.

The Assert pragma allows application code to define assertions without
application-specific compile time parameters, if statements, or checking of runtime parameters. A typical usage follows.

```
package AppClass is
   type AppClass is tagged private;
      procedure Foo(IX: in Integer, IY: in Integer);
private
   type AppClass is tagged
      record
        X: Integer;
        Y: Integer;
      end record;
package body AppClass is

procedure Foo(IX: Integer, IY: Integer) is
declare
   Old_X, Old_Y: Integer;
begin

   pragma Assert ( IX /= IY ); -- Precondition
   Old_X := X;                 -- Save entry value for postcondition
   Old_Y := Y;                 -- Save entry value for postcondition

   -- procedure body
   pragma Assert ((Old_X = X) and (Old_Y > (X+Y)));  --
   Postcondition
end Foo;
```

The Assert pragma works well for basic preconditions and postconditions.
If a postcondition needs to compare values at entry and exit, something like the
local declaration of Old_X and Old_Y is needed. If entry–exit comparison is unnecessary, these kinds of declarations should be omitted. The Assert pragma
alone is not a good implementation for invariants. An invariant should be defined once and checked after initialization, before each precondition, and after
each postcondition. This process requires a separate invariant procedure.

Inline Assertion Procedure

An inline assertion procedure can implement invariants. The same idiom can be used to support general assertion checking for compilers that do not support the Assert pragma. Two procedures are needed.

- A general assertion procedure for preconditions and postconditions. The predicates for these assertions are entry/exit-specific and used in only one place. Thus they may be hard-coded as arguments passed to the assertion procedure. The general assertion procedure may be used by any package.

- A package-specific invariant procedure. The invariant predicate of a package is the same no matter where it is evaluated—and it is evaluated in many places. If the invariant predicate is coded everywhere it is to be evaluated, then many redundant predicate expressions will result. The invariant predicate is therefore defined and evaluated in a separate procedure in its package. This approach prevents the inevitable problems with writing and maintaining redundant code.

This factoring is also necessary to support the *Percolation* pattern.

The general assertion procedure would be coded as follows. The GNAT System.Assertions.Raise_Assert_Failure suggests that the assertion action may be coded, although any appropriate exception or procedure could be used. Procedures are inlined to reduce execution time.

```
procedure CheckAssertion(
   predicate in boolean,    -- Assertion
   msg         in string    -- Violation message
)is
begin
   if CHECK_ASSERTS then
      if not predicate then
         System.Assertions.Raise_Assert_Failure (msg);
      end if;
   else
      null;
   end if;
end CheckAssertion;
pragma INLINE(CheckAssertion);
```

The invariant procedure would be coded as follows:

```
procedure Invariant(
    msg         in string       --Violation message
) is
begin

    if CHECK_ASSERTS then
        if not(  ((X mod 2) = 0) and (( Y mod 2) /= 0 )
                )
        then
            System.Assertions.Raise_Assert_Failure (msg);
        end if;
    else
        null;
    end if;

end Invariant;
pragma INLINE(Invariant);
```

Application procedures would use the assertion procedures as follows.

```
procedure Foo(IX: Integer, IY: Integer ) is
declare
    Old_X, Old_Y: Integer;
begin
    Invariant("AppClass.Foo entry");
    CheckAssertion(        ( IX /= IY ),
                            "AppClass.Foo precondition" );
    Old_X := X;    -- Save entry value for postcondition
    Old_Y := Y;    -- Save entry value for postcondition

    --
    --   procedure body
    --

    Invariant("AppClass.Foo exit");
    CheckAssertion(((Old_X = X) and (Old_Y > (X+Y)),
                    "AppClass.Foo postcondition" );
end Foo;
```

If an initialization section or procedure is defined, the invariant should be asserted at the end of this section.[12]

---

12. Although Ada 95 does not have explicit constructors or destructors, the general rule of asserting the invariant as a constructor postcondition and a destructor precondition applies. Initialization may be performed in the body begin/end block or in a separate procedure. Some support for initialization and deallocation is provided by discriminators and the ada.finalization package, but invariant checking cannot be incorporated with them.

```
package body AppClass is
   --
   -- AppClass implementation
   --

   procedure Invariant (msg in String) is
   begin
      --    Invariant implementation
   end Invariant;
   pragma INLINE(Invariant);

begin -- Initialization section
   --
   -- Initialization code
   --
   Invariant("Initialization Section");
end AppClass;
```

The `invariant` procedure also solves the redundant invariant problem for a compiler that supports the `Assert` pragma.

```
procedure Foo(IX: Integer, IY: Integer ) is
declare
   Old_X, Old_Y: Integer;
begin
   Invariant("AppClass.Foo entry");
   pragma Assert  (   ( IX /= IY ),
                      "AppClass.Foo precondition"
   );
   Old_X := X; -- Save entry value for postcondition
   Old_Y := Y; -- Save entry value for postcondition


   --
   -- procedure body
   --

   Invariant("AppClass.Foo exit");
   pragma Assert  (   ((Old_X = X) and (Old_Y > (X+Y)),
                      "AppClass.Foo postcondition"
   );
end Foo;
```

These basic structures may be adapted and elaborated. For example, instead of a single enable/disable parameter, two parameters could be defined—PREPOST_ENABLED and INVARIANT_ENABLED—to allow for any combination of assertion checking.

17.4.5   C++

C++ is a hybrid, compiled language derived from C. It supports the object-oriented programming paradigm but retains the efficiency and fine-grained control necessary for systems programming applications. The C++ feature set and object model evolved to meet the needs of its original users [Stroustroup 88, Stroustroup 92a]. C++ is strongly typed (with a few exceptions) and provides some compile-time fault detection.

Except for the assert( ) macro, C++ does not offer any direct support for built-in test, although simple and effective built-in test may be obtained by using assert( ). Much more elaborate approaches are possible, like the Heavyweight Coherence idiom discussed later in this section. ANSI C++ includes a built-in exception-handling mechanism (try, throw, catch) that can provide robust operation when properly designed and implemented.

assert.h Macro

The C++ language standard specifies an assert( ) macro. This macro is defined in the standard header file <assert.h> by most C++ compilers. The Gnu gcc implementation of assert.h is typical.

```
# ifndef NDEBUG
    # define _assert(ex) {                                    \
        if (!(ex))                                            \
            {(void) fprintf (stderr,                          \
            "Assertion failed: file \"%s\", line %d\n", \
            __FILE__, __LINE__);
            exit(1);}
        }
    # define assert(ex) _assert(ex)
# else
    # define _assert(ex)
    # define assert(ex)
# endif
```

When assertion expansion is enabled (through the -DDEBUG command-line option), the preprocessor generates source code with the assertion expression. The expanded source is compiled. In the preceding example, the default action is to write the file and line number to stderr and terminate the active process. The -DNDEBUG command-line option disables expansion for most compilers. Although assert is simple and effective, it is often replaced with a locally defined version, usually to provide better control over the assertion action. Several examples follow. Any or all of these examples could be combined and extended. These examples are suggestive, not exhaustive.

1. This variant of the assert macro provides the ability to output messages using the `iostream.h` operators. It will display remarks that might be included in a `printf`, but allows messages to be disabled by recompiling. The `ostream` operators provide improved type safety.

The assert macro directs output to `cerr` instead of `cout`. The formatting behavior of `cout` and `cerr` are the same, but `cout` is buffered and `cerr` is unbuffered. If the process stops before the `cout` buffer is flushed, the buffered messages will not be displayed. Using `endl` or `flush` in a `cout` stream forces the buffer to be written. The output from `cerr` and `cout` can be redirected to different files or devices to separate normal and abnormal messages.

```
#include <iostream.h>
# ifndef NDEBUG
   # define ASSERT(ex, char *msg) {        \
      if (!(ex)) {                         \
         cout  << flush;                   \
         cerr  << endl                     \
            << "Assertion ", #ex,          \
            << " In File " << _FILE_       \
            << " at line " << _LINE_       \
            << " violated. ", msg          \
            << endl;                       \
         exit(1);}
      }
   # define assert(ex) _assert(ex)
# else
   # define _assert(ex)
   # define assert(ex)
   # define ASSERT(ex)
# endif
```

2. You can force the debugger to be activated. The default action of assert is to terminate the process. Even if your code runs under a debugger, the process terminates when it reaches that point. Any potentially useful information is lost.

The following obfuscatory C code causes the debugger to be activated under Windows NT [Feingold 98]:

```
#include <iostream.h>
# ifndef NDEBUG
   # define ASSERT(ex) {
      if (!(ex)) {                    \
         * ((void **) 0) = 0;  \
      }
   # define assert(ex) _assert(ex)
# else
   # define _assert(ex)
   # define assert(ex)
   # define ASSERT(ex)
# endif
```

Assert Template

Stroustroup suggests using template classes and exception handlers for assertions [Stroustroup 94]. For example, an `Assert( )` function template may mimic the assert macro, but avoids the quirks of macro substitution.

```
template <class T>
inline const bool
Assert(T expr, char msg)
{
   if (!NDEBUG) {
      if (!(expr)) {
         cout    << flush;      // Dump anything in app buffer
         cerr    << endl
            << "Assertion "<< #expr,
            << " In File " << _FILE_
            << " at line " << _LINE_
            << " violated. "<< msg
            << endl;
         exit(1);
      }
         return FALSE
   }
   return TRUE;
};
```

The template function may implement the assertion violation action, as shown in the preceding code.

It is also possible to throw an exception, as the following shows.

```
template <class T, class X> inline void Assert(T expr, X x)
{
    if (!NDEBUG) {
        if (!expr) throw x;
    }
}

class AssertionViolation{ /* ... */ };

void f(String& s, int i) {

    Assert (i>=0 && i<s.size(),new AssertionViolation( ));
    // ...
};
```

The Coherence Idiom

In a *coherent* object, the class invariant must hold at entry and exit from every public function [Hurst+95, Cline+95]. Meeting this goal requires that the invariant be checked at all of these points. Instead of an assert statement with a redundant predicate at each point, the invariant is implemented as a protected function. This function is called at each point. Such checking can have a high cost in CPU cycles and memory, however, and it cannot be disabled as easily as an assert.

The Coherence idiom provides a C++-specific solution to these problems. When coherence checking is disabled, references to and the implementation of the invariant are removed by the compiler, so there is no runtime cost in executable size or CPU cycles. The assertion source code remains intact and is easily enabled by recompiling. Although the expansion, inlining, and optimization are assumed to be compiler-independent, verifying the exact results produced in your compiler and target environment would be prudent.

The Coherence idioms do not consider how to check superclass assertions. The *Percolation* pattern shows how superclass assertions may be checked by subclasses.

Lightweight Coherence.   The Lightweight Coherence idiom is presented in [Cline +95].[13] Application classes implement the invariant as a protected, inline,

---

13. See FAQ 225, "How can you ensure an object doesn't get blown away by a wild pointer?", and FAQ 226, "What is behavioral self-testing?"

const member function. Class member functions assert the invariant by calling
this function at entry and exit, on exit from all constructors, and on entry to
the destructor. AppClass shows how these elements collaborate.

```
Class AppClass {
public:
    AppClass ( ) {
        // ctor body
        #ifndef NDEBUG
            invariant( );
        #endif
    }
    ~AppClass( ) {
        #ifndef NDEBUG
            invariant( );
        #endif
        // dtor body
    }

    void foo(int ix, int iy) {
        #ifndef NDEBUG
            invariant( );
        #endif

        // Function body

        #ifndef NDEBUG
            invariant( );
        #endif
        return;
    }
protected:
    inline void invariant( ) const {
        ASSERT(   (mod(x,2)== 0)&&(mod(y,2)!= 0),
                "x and y are inconsistent"
        );
    }
private:
    int x, y;
};
```

When ASSERT is disabled by -DNDEBUG, invariant( ) is empty because the
preprocessor does not expand the assert( ) statements. The compiler will not
generate any executable code for an inline function with an empty function
body. An inline function can be optimized away by a C++ compiler, if it isn't

called. This is why the messages to invariant( ) are bracketed by #ifndef and #endif.

As the preceding example shows, the invariant should be asserted at the following three points:

- Assert the invariant as the last statement in all constructors. A constructor cannot return a value to indicate that it has failed (or succeeded) to create a valid object. Asserting the invariant provides a mechanism to report constructor failure.

- Assert the invariant as the last statement in a destructor. An object can be corrupted even if it is not activated by a wild pointer, for example. Asserting the invariant when the object is destructed will reveal "silent but deadly" bugs.

- Bracket all member functions with invariant checks. This technique is particularly effective in unstable, buggy, or poorly designed environments. Invariant checking provides a good defense against bugs associated with the misuse of friends, public data members, global variables, and wild pointers. These kind of bugs often lead to a corrupt state *after* an invariant has been checked. The invariant checks the assumption that an object remains in the last state in which it placed itself.

Middleweight Coherence.   Precondition and postcondition checking is easily added to Lightweight Coherence. In some postconditions, it is useful to compare the value of a variable at entry with its value at exit. In C++, if entry values are needed for a postcondition, we must copy them at entry. The following example shows how precondition and postcondition assertions would be added to AppClass::foo (the other elements remain the same). Each group of assertion statements is bracketed by #ifndef and #endif so that it can be enabled or disabled.

```
void foo(int ix, int iy) {
   #ifndef NDEBUG
      invariant( );
      ASSERT(  (ix != iy),
            "Precondition violation"
      );
      old_x = x; // Save entry values for postcondition
      old_y = y;
   #endif

   // method body
```

```
    #ifndef NDEBUG
        invariant( );
        ASSERT(  (old_x == x) && (old_y > (x+y))
                "Postcondition violation"
        );
    #endif
    return;
}
```

Heavyweight Coherence.   The heavyweight version of the Coherence idiom provides advanced assertion capabilities under the control of several application-specific `#ifndef...endif` parameters, utility functions, and several class-specific functions [Hurst+95].

- Class-specific enable/disable.
- Public access to the invariant.
- Fine-grained control over the frequency of invariant checking. When enabled, the frequency of checking can be calibrated from none to every assertion in small increments.
- Assertion evaluation and actions supported by general-purpose utility functions.
- Detailed tagging of each assertion.
- Violation logging to a circular buffer, with an option to include a snapshot dump of allocated memory or generate an abend dump.

This idiom was used extensively in the OS/400 project. The developer of a class must code six built-in test components, which use another six utility functions. Each reference to a BIT function is wrapped in an `ifdef` controlled by its own parameter. This approach allows the preprocessor to drop some or all of the source, leading to an empty function, which is removed by the same optimization approach described for the Lightweight Coherence idiom.

Tips and Tricks

Assertions should not have side effects. Member functions that implement assertions should be `const`, and only `const` member functions should be used in assertion expressions.

Be careful to avoid loops if your assertion expressions call member functions. Suppose `invariant( )` calls `empty( )`, and `empty( )` calls `invariant( )`. A practical solution is to skip invariant checking in any function used by an assertion. Use `assert( )` in these functions instead of a function call to `invari-ant( )`.

Use end-of-structure markers to detect pointer bugs [Rosenblum 97]. Suppose a class allocates a 1000-byte block. Any access beyond this address is incorrect. Some pointer bugs can be detected by defining an end-of-block field, placed just after the last field of the block. This field is set to an unusual value—for example, xDEADBEEF. A wild pointer that overruns the block will probably also change the end-of-block field. Include an assertion in the invariant to check the end-of-block field.

```
assert(block[1000] == xDEADBEEF );
```

If the value at entry is needed in a postcondition, copy it at entry to a local variable and wrap the copy in an `ifdef`. See the Middleweight Coherence idiom.

Avoid using `<stdio.h>` functions like `printf`. Use `<iostream.h>` because it improves type safety, accepts user-defined types, and offers simpler formatting. Provide a function to dump concrete state by implementing a friend `operator<<`. For example, the following code performs a formatted dump of an Account object:

```
#include <iostream.h>
class Account{
public:
    friend
        ostream& operator << (ostream& dump, const Account&
        anAccount);
private:
    Money   balance;
    int     accountNumber;
    Stringtitle;
};

ostream& operator << (ostream& dump, const Account& anAccount) {
    return dump     << "Contents of Account object at address "
                    << (void*)&anAccount << endl
                    << "balance "  << anAccount.balance
                    << " number"   << anAccount.accountNumber
                    << " title "   << anAccount.title
                    << endl;
}
```

17.4.6   Eiffel

Eiffel is a strongly typed, pure object-oriented language that supports the design-by-contract approach [Meyer 97]. Responsibility assertions are an integral part of class definitions in Eiffel. Class and routine (method) declarations may include assertions, which are introduced by keyword expressions (keywords are given in bold).

```
class <class declaration>

feature
    <routine interface declaration> is
        require     <precondition predicate>
        local       <local declarations>
        do          <routine body>
        ensure      <postcondition predicate>
        rescue      <exception expression>
        end

feature
-- ...

invariant <invariant predicate>
end
```

Table 17.6 depicts the semantics of the assertion-related keyword expressions. Eiffel supports built-in loop assertions. The check <predicate> expression can be used at any point in the code. Compilation parameters enable/disable assertions by type. All assertions use the same runtime mechanism. When an enabled assertion is reached, the predicate is evaluated for the current contents of the object. If the result is *false,* an assertion exception is raised. If the result is true, execution continues.

The Eiffel assertion strategy provides an elegant implementation of design-by-contract.

- The compiler enforces syntax and correct usage.
- The level of assertion checking is selected at compile time: none, all, or any combination of assertion types.
- All elements of precondition predicates must be visible to clients. Elements of postconditions and invariants may be private.
- Functions (routines that do not change state) may be used in assertion predicates.

TABLE 17.6 Elements of Eiffel Assertion Checking

Assertion Type/Semantics	Eiffel Syntax
Class invariant.	`invariant <predicate>`
Precondition.	`require <predicate>`
Postcondition.	`ensure <predicate>`
Weakened precondition of a redeclared routine (overridden method).	`require else <predicate>`
Strengthened postcondition of a redeclared routine (overridden method).	`ensure then <predicate>`
General-purpose.	`check <predicate>`
Value of \<entityName\> at entry. Typically used in invariant and postcondition predicates.	`old <entityName>`
Value of \<entityName\> must be the same at entry and exit. Typically used in invariant and post-condition predicates.	`nochange <entityName>`
Assertion action. \<expression\> specifies how the Eiffel exception mechanism will be used.	`rescue <expression>`

Loop invariant; variant.	`from <initialization expression>`
	`invariant <predicate>`
	`variant <predicate>`
	`until <predicate>`
	`loop <loop body>`
	`end`

- When enabled, invariants are automatically evaluated at three points: (1) after an object instantiation is complete, (2) at entry to a routine and before checking the precondition, and (3) after the postcondition is checked and just before exit. When an object sends a message to itself, however, the invariant is not checked. This approach allows for transient states computed by private methods that may be inconsistent with the invariant.

- All superclass invariants are automatically *and*ed to a subclass invariant and checked. Superclass preconditions and postconditions are automatically appended and checked in a redeclaring subclass routine via the `require else` and `ensure then` keywords. This process achieves automatic percolation of assertions.

- Two keyword expressions are provided for relationships unique to postconditions. A predicate may qualify variable references with the keyword `old` \<entityName\>, which results in the value of \<entityName\> at

entry—for example, `ensure x = old x * y`. The keyword `nochange`
<entityName> evaluates as *true* or *false* and may be used in a post-
condition. It is *true* if the value of <entityName> is the same as at
entry; it is *false* otherwise. For example, `ensure nochange maxValue`
is *true* when the current contents of `maxValue` are the same as they
were at entry to the routine.

- All assertion actions use the built-in exception mechanism. The exception-handling code in the `rescue` clause of the active object is entered
  when any exception is raised. Exceptions are automatically raised if an
  assertion evaluates to *false* and for other anomalies—for example, divide by zero. It is possible to decide which exception was raised. The
  `retry` keyword causes the routine to be reentered without reinitializa-
  tion. It may be preceded by code in the `rescue` block that attempts to
  correct the cause of the exception. If the `rescue` clause does not `retry`
  a routine, control returns to the `rescue` clause of its client. This backtracking continues up the call stack until either a `retry` repairs the exception or control returns to the operating system, thereby terminating
  the process. Eiffel does not allow a nonexceptional exit from a `rescue`
  under any circumstance. A normal exit can be realized only by using a
  `retry` to reenter the body of the routine to reach the normal exit point.

Most Eiffel environments support useful documentation features, including
the short-flat form that can present only the class contract and shows inherited
features. If these features are used consistently, the extent of an external test
suite can be reduced and extensive use of random generation of test inputs becomes feasible (see the Test Suite Reduction section later in this chapter).

17.4.7   Java

Basic Checking Capabilities

Java is a strongly typed, hybrid object-oriented language designed to support
applications requiring a high degree of platform independence. It has a two-
stage translation: source code is "compiled" into a byte code file that is interpreted at runtime by the Java Virtual Machine. Although Java is very much like
C++ in its syntax and structure, it has significant differences.

- No pointer addressing and pointer arithmetic
- Language-defined classes for strings and arrays
- Only explicit declarations

- Runtime checking of messages for the correct number of arguments of the right type
- Runtime checking/handling of stack overflow
- Automatic memory allocation and garbage collection
- Single inheritance
- Significantly slower computation, other things being equal

Many discussions of differences and relative merits can be found on the World Wide Web.

Java will detect uninitialized variables at compile time. It includes many built-in exceptions and a framework for exception handling. Built-in exceptions are defined for many runtime problems—for example, incorrect file access, missing classes or methods, and bounds checking on array references. Although these features reduce the need to check corresponding implementation assumptions, they do not provide any direct support for general application correctness.

Final Static/Short Circuit Idiom

Java does not support anything like the C++ `assert` construct and, at this writing, does not offer a pragma or preprocessor that could be used to implement assertion checking.[14] Several freeware Perl scripts have been posted to the Web that translate assertion comments into if-then expressions.

Java assertion checking can be implemented with an assertion class and code that uses short circuit Boolean optimization to enable/disable assertion checking [van der Linden 98]. The solution has three parts: the `Assert` class, the `invariant` method (in each application class), and a coding convention for application assertion statements. When checking is enabled, a Boolean expression is sent to the `Assert.check` method. If the expression holds, no action is taken and control returns to the sender. If it is *false,* a noncatchable `ThrowableException` is instantiated and the process terminates after displaying diagnostic information.

The Assert Class.   The `Assert` class is declared as `final`, causing its methods to be inlined and preventing any subclassing. A single `boolean` constant ENABLED is defined in this class. The developer sets ENABLED to `true` to enable assertion

---

14. Assertions were developed for Oak, Java's predecessor. Commenting about the 0.2 version of the Oak language specification, James Gosling notes, "My major regret about that spec is that the section on assertions didn't survive: I had a partial implementation, but I ripped it out to meet a deadline" [Gosling 98].

checking; enabled is set to false to disable checking. Because Assert is
public, all Assert method calls in the public scope of the system under test
will be enabled/disabled. Package scope checking could also be implemented.
Assert.check cannot have side effects on instance variables because it is
static.

```
public final class Assert {
   public static final boolean
      ENABLED = true;    // Assertion checking control
                         // true enables assertion checking
                         // false disables assertion checking

   public static final void check(boolean p, String msg) {
      if (ENABLED && !p) action(msg);
   }

   private static void action(String msg) {
      Date when = new Date(System.currentTimeMillis());
      System.err.println(  "Assertion violation " +
                           ToGMTstring(when) + " " +
                           msg
      );
      Throwable e = new Throwable( );
      e.printStackTrace( );
      System.exit(2);
   }
}
```

ENABLED is a read-only class variable. When ENABLED is true, the compiler
generates byte code for the if-then statement and the action message. This code
is inlined at the site of each Assert.check message in the application system.
When ENABLED is false, the compiler determines that the if-then predicate can
never be true and discards the entire if-then statement. This action results in an
empty method to inline. The compiler will not inline a null Assert.check, so
no byte code is generated for the assertion calls. Thus, when ENABLED is false,
all assertion checking evaporates. The source code is undisturbed (except for
the change to ENABLED) and there is no space, transmit, or CPU cost for the disabled assertion checking. Although the expansion, inlining, and optimization
are assumed to be compiler-independent, verifying exactly what results are obtained with your compiler and target environment would be prudent.

When the assertion predicate evaluates as true, Assert.check bypasses the
action message and returns control to the client. When the predicate evaluates
as false, the action message is sent. With the example implementation of
action, the following will result:

1. The system date and time are gotten and formatted.
2. A tag line, the Greenwich Mean Time (GMT) date and time, and the text given in the assert message are displayed on System.err.
3. An instance of Throwable is instantiated to capture the stack image, which shows the call path that led to the assertion violation.
4. The exception object displays the stack trace on System.err.
5. System.exit is called, resulting in termination of both the applet/ application and the Java Virtual Machine (this action may result in a SecurityException in some browsers). Any nonzero status value indicates a failure. Using a unique status value for an assertion violation may help in first-level debugging.

This action is appropriate during development for nondeployed assertions. The Throwable exception may be inappropriate in deployed applications. No recovery is attempted, and output is displayed that only a Java nerd could love. If assertions will be deployed, then checked exception classes should be designed and implemented with the appropriate throws and catch blocks.

Application Invariant and Assertion Statements.   Application classes may implement invariants, preconditions, and postconditions using the Assert.check message. An example of the general form of an asserted Java class follows.

```
class AppClass {
    private int x,y,old_x,old_y;
    public AppClass( ) {
        // Constructor body
        invariant( );
    }

    public void foo(int ix, int iy) {
        invariant( );
        Assert.check(Assert.ENABLED &&
                (ix != iy),
                "Precondition violation"
        );
        old_x = x;  // Save entry values for postcondition
        old_y = y;

        // method body

        invariant( );
        Assert.check(Assert.ENABLED &&
                (old_x == x) && (old_y > (x+y)),
                "Postcondition violation"
```

```
        );
    }
    protected final boolean invariant( ) {
        returnAssert.check(Assert.ENABLED &&
                ( (x % 2) == 0) && (y % 2)!= 0) ),
                "Invariant violation"
            );
    }
}
```

The Final Static/Short Circuit idiom could support the *Percolation* pattern, providing a full implementation of built-in test of the LSP for Java applications. This would require implementation of preconditions and postconditions as separate protected methods, similar to `invariant( )`.

Multiple Exit Points.   The Java try/finally construct can be used to simplify the coding of postconditions with multiple exit points.

```
class AppClass {
    public AppClass( ) { // Constructor body
        invariant( );
    }

    public int foo(int ix, int iy) {
        invariant( );
        Assert.check(Assert.ENABLED &&
                (ix != iy),
                "Precondition violation"
        );
        old_x = x; // Save entry values for postcondition
        old_y = y;

        try {       // Method body

            if ( ix != iy )
                return ix;
            else
                return iy;
        }

        finally {   // Method Postcondition
            invariant( );
            Assert.check(Assert.ENABLED &&
                    (old_x == x) && (old_y > (x+y)),
                    "Postcondition violation"
            );
        }
    }
}
```

```
protected final boolean invariant( ) {
    returnAssert.check(Assert.ENABLED &&
            ( (x % 2) == 0) && (y % 2)!= 0) ),
            "Invariant violation"
        );
    }
}
```

Override toString.   The `toString( )` method defined for class `Object` should be overridden for each application class. This approach provides a consistent and easy means to inspect the contents of an object. The output of `toString( )` can be displayed or saved to a file. Once saved to a file, basic file comparison utilities (e.g., Unix `diff`) can be used to support automatic regression testing.

17.4.8   Objective-C

Objective-C is a compiled, hybrid object-oriented language. It uses an object model similar to Smalltalk: single inheritance, classes as objects, a high degree of dynamic binding, and the Smalltalk target-action keyword structure for message syntax. The balance of the syntax and semantics are ANSI C, with extensions. A class may be composed of primitive C types (e.g., `char`, `int`, `float`) or objects. In addition, the NeXT Computer Objective-C supports two unique extensions to the basic object model. A *category* is a named collection of method definitions that is similar to aspects of multiple inheritance and the C++ friend. This collection may extend or override methods of an existing class. A category may be bound at compile time or runtime. *Protocols* are a kind of abstract method (interface only), but may be implemented by any class.

Brad Cox developed Objective-C in the early 1980s. The Stepstone compiler and class library enjoyed an early success but were later eclipsed by C++. The Gnu implementation of Objective-C was adopted as the development language for NeXT Computer's NeXTStep and OpenStep operating systems, and subsequently incorporated into Apple Computer's Rhapsody operating system. The Mach kernel used in OpenStep will probably be incorporated with Apple Computer's MacOS. The future of OpenStep is unclear as of this book's publication.

Objective-C provides the same built-in support for type checking, design-by-contract, and fault tolerance as does ANSI C—in other words, next to nothing. Instead, Objective-C provides the speed of C and approximates the Smalltalk object model. This combination is unusually powerful, with the preferred coding style of maximal dynamic binding, producing maintainable, robust Objective-C applications. Some support for built-in test is provided by the assertion checking and exception handling provided in the Rhapsody/OpenStep Foundation Kit.

OpenStep Foundation Kit Assertion Macros

The ANSI C `assert` macro is supported in Objective-C. It may be used or modified as suggested previously for the C++ `assert` macro. Output formatting is limited to `printf` functionality. The `NSAssert` and `NSParameterAssert` macros included in OpenStep's Foundation Kit provide enhanced assertion support for Objective-C developers. They replace the default burp-and-crash behavior of the C `assert` with Foundation Kit exception handling. The syntax is simple:

```
NSAssert(<predicate>, NSString *message);
```

Any valid Objective-C Boolean expression may be given as the `<predicate>`. When `<predicate>` is *false,* an `NSAssertionHandler` object is instantiated for the current thread. This object writes an error message, giving the method and class names (or the function name) that raised the exception along with the text in the `message` parameter. The message text may contain `printf` formatting commands, allowing a maximum of five additional arguments to be supplied for insertion, by using `NSAssert1`, `NSAssert2`, and so on. The `NSParameter-Assert(<predicate>);` works in the same way, but does not allow a message or insert arguments. Instead, the predicate expression is output with the method and class name. These macros are meant for use inside a method. In contrast, the `NSCAssert( )` macro is used inside a function. All assertion macros return `void`.

All variants of `NSAssert` raise an `NSInternalInconsistencyException`. This exception causes the assertion message to be written to the system console and terminates the active process. Assertions are disabled if the preprocessor macro `NS_BLOCK_ASSERTIONS` is defined. A suggestive example of a full set of contact assertions implemented with the Foundation Kit macros follows.[15]

```
@interface AppClass:NSObject
{
    // class interface
}
```

---

15. Thanks to Peter Vandenberk for suggesting this approach.

```
- id   init:(int)ix y:(int) iy;
- void foo ( );
@end

@implementation AppClass:NSObject
{
    @private
        int _x;
        int _y;
}
- init:(int)ix y:(int)iy {

    [super init];
    _x = ix;
    _y = iy;

    invariant (@"foo init");
    return self;
}

- void foo:(int)ix y:(int)iy {

    #ifndef CHECKASSERTS
    // Check preconditions

        invariant(@"foo entry");
        NSAssert((ix != iy),
                    @"Precondition violation"
        );
        _old_x = _x; // Save entry values for postcondition
        _old_y = _y;
    #endif

    // method body

    #ifndef CHECKASSERTS
        invariant(@"foo exit");
        NSAssert((old_x == _x) && (old_y > (_x+_y)),
                    @"Postcondition violation"
        );
    #endif
}

_inline void const invariant(String msg)
{
    // Check type

    NSAssert([self integer] == _x, @"x corrupted");
    NSAssert([self integer] == _y, @"y corrupted");
```

```
    // If x is even, y must be odd

    NSAssert ((mod(_x,2)== 0)&&(mod(_y,2)!= 0),
            @" x or y incorrect"
    );
}
@end
```

17.4.9 Smalltalk

Smalltalk is a pure object-oriented language designed to be intuitive, extensible, and conducive to rapid application development. Extensibility is obtained by weak typing and an interpretive execution strategy. Typically, Smalltalk environments implement a two-stage translation: source code is parsed and translated into a byte code as it is entered. The byte code is interpreted at runtime as needed to create objects and respond to messages. The Smalltalk object model does not support static type checking, abstract classes, or generic classes.

Smalltalk was originally designed to be a self-contained, single-user development environment. This model proved to be a serious limitation for large-scale application development. Today, Smalltalk systems provide multiuser configuration management and effective subsystem partitioning. Some environments support exception handling. No support for assertions is defined in the language or object model, but may be developed, as the following approaches indicate.

Context Assertion Method

In the Smalltalk/V environment, a context method makes a method available to all classes. This capability can be exploited to provide a general assertion protocol that is similar to the C++ assert macro [Weir 95].

```
    !Context methods ! assert self value ifFalse: [ self halt ].! !
```

This message, with the appropriate expression, is used to check preconditions, postconditions, and invariants. For example,

```
    [ anAccount balance != 0 ] assert.
```

Checking is disabled by manually removing the body of the context assert method.

```
    !Context methods !
      assert
      ^ self! !
```

The assert messages in the application source code are undisturbed. Although processing time is reduced because the assert body is null, message overhead is still incurred. The advantage of this approach is simplicity.

Design-by-Contract Extensions

Carillo et al. developed extensions to the Smalltalk/V class browser to support design-by-contract [Carillo+96]. Modifications were made to the class and method definition templates in `ClassHierarchyBrowser` and related Smalltalk system classes. The user may enter block expressions for preconditions, post-conditions, and invariants. Additional code is generated automatically to control the activation of assertions before the class is saved and byte code is generated. Table 17.7 shows how contract elements are defined by the developer and then automatically augmented.

Two template modifications were made. The default browser class definition template presents the following fields:

```
<superclassName> Subclass: <subclassName>
instanceVariableNames:
classVariableNames:
poolDictionaries:
```

This template was modified to prompt for a class invariant. The user defines an invariant by entering a Boolean expression block.

```
<superclassName> Subclass: <subclassName>
instanceVariableNames:
classVariableNames:
poolDictionaries:classInvariant:
```

This block is checked for correct syntax and to ensure that all variables in the block are declared for the class. Slots for `require` (precondition) and `ensure` (postcondition) block expressions were added to the method template. The invariant is stored as a class variable.

```
<messagePattern>
"comment"
|temporaries|
require: [..].
    <Method Body>
ensure: [..].
```

TABLE 17.7 Smalltalk Class Definition with Generated Assertion Code

Action	Code Entered	Augmented Code

Define new class Account, specifying the invariant	Object Subclass: #Account
	instanceEntityNameNames:
	  "balance lastTxDate accountNumber"
	classEntityNameNames: " "
	poolDictionaries: " "
	classInvariant: "[balance > 0]"
		Object Subclass: #Account
		instanceEntityNameNames:
		  "balance lastTxDate accountNumber"
		classEntityNameNames: " "
		poolDictionaries: " "
		classInvariant: "[balance > 0]"

Designate the invariant for the class initialization method	open:amount owner:aString
	"Creates new account with balance = amount"
	
	^((self new)
	  initialize:
	    (Array with:amount with:aString)).
		open:amount owner:aString
		"Creates new account with balance = amount"
		
		^((self new)
		  initialize:
		    (Array with:amount
		    with:aString))
		    checkcInvClass:[].

Define a class method debit, specifying the precondition and postcondition for debit	debit: amount
	"Subtract amount from account"
	
	require: [balance>=amount and:
	[amount<10000]].
	
	balance := balance - amount.
	
	^balance
	
	ensure:
	  [(self old) balance = balance+amount]
		debit:amount
		"Subtract amount from account"
		
		self invariant: [balance > 0].
		
		self require: [balance>=amount and:
		[amount<10000]].
		
		balance := balance - amount.
		
		^self return: [balance]
		
		self ensure:
		  [(self old) balance =
		  balance+amount].

The code generated performs the housekeeping necessary to implement consistent checking and predicable actions for a violation.

- Smalltalk does not have an explicit designator for a constructor method, so the user must designate such methods. If the user designates a method as an initialization method, code to check the invariant is generated. It is acceptable practice in Smalltalk to leave instance variables undefined by the initialization method and defer initialization to other instance methods. In this case, the invariant might fail, so checking may be skipped.
- The `require` and `ensure` blocks are translated into messages sent to `self`.
- An `invariant` method is generated that accepts the invariant expression block as an argument. If the invariant expression is true, the object state is pushed onto `StackObject`. `StackObject` is a stack of `Object-Context` objects, each of which contains a deep copy of the entry contents of an activated object, a reference to the current object, and the postcondition as a block expression.
- A message `return` with the invariant block expression as an argument is generated at the exit of the method. This value is used to evaluate the invariant at exit. When the invariant is *true*, `return` sends a message to pop the current object off `StackObject` and control returns to the caller. If the invariant is *false,* the assertion action is taken.
- When any assertion is *false,* the assertion action is triggered. The entry state of the active object is restored from the stack. An error message is displayed in Window. The user may run the system debugger to diagnose the failure.

These modifications to Smalltalk also support operations with the Eiffel semantics of `old` and `nochange`, loop invariants, and general-purpose assertions. Table 17.7 shows how developer input would be augmented with automatically generated code to support assertion checking.

Percolation

Intent

Implement automatic checking of superclass assertions to support design-by-contract and the Liskov substitution principle.

Motivation

Assertions cannot be inherited in Ada 95, C++, Java, Objective-C, or Smalltalk. Only Eiffel supports assertion inheritance. For example, although we can make a C++ base class `invariant( )` function visible in a derived class, there is no built-in mechanism for checking base class assertions with the proper Boolean operators in a derived class. The Percolation pattern results in a straightforward structure that yields the same checking as built-in assertion inheritance.

Percolation is effective at revealing bugs that result from inheritance and dynamic binding. The likelihood of such bugs increases as class hierarchies are extended, patched, and reused. Some bugs that result from incorrect inheritance structures can be detected if base class assertions are checked in a derived class. Automatic checking of base class[16] assertions is supported only by Eiffel. Recoding base class assertions in derived classes would be time-consuming, error-prone, and inelegant.

The Percolation pattern allows base class invariants, preconditions, and postconditions to be checked in derived class functions without the use of re-dundant code. It respects base class encapsulation by providing a fixed interface to base class assertions without direct access to base class instance variables. It allows loosely coupled, compile-time enabling/disabling of assertion checking.

Applicability

Checking base class assertions in a derived class is useful when the derived class depends on correct and consistent use of base class features. This consideration is especially important in hierarchies that export polymorphic functions. The Percolation pattern provides effective built-in test in any class hierarchy designed to conform with design-by-contract [Meyer 97] or the LSP [Liskov+94, Martin 96]. A class hierarchy that exports polymorphic functions and does not follow the LSP is almost certainly buggy. In hierarchies composed for conven-

---

16. C++ terms are used because the example is in C++. The pattern applies to all other languages as well.

ience or naive reuse without regard for the LSP, the flattened assertions will probably be ambiguous or inconsistent. Percolation will not be useful in this case.

Structure

Figure 17.7 shows the basic structure of Percolation in C++. Although the figure depicts three levels, the pattern can be extended to any number of levels and multiple inheritance.

Participants

The participants in this pattern are protected functions that implement the assertions for all preconditions, postconditions, and invariants in each class in a hierarchy.

Collaboration

The scope of the Percolation pattern is a class hierarchy. Classes outside the hierarchy need not be considered. When a class invariant is checked, all of its base class invariants should be checked as well. Similarly, when the precondition or postcondition of an overridden function is checked, all of its base class preconditions and postconditions should be checked, too. Checking begins at the lowest level (a derived class) and works up the hierarchy, suggesting a percolation action.

This pattern requires that base class assertions are implemented as functions visible to derived class assertion functions. Every derived class assertion function calls its corresponding assertion function in its immediate base class. This approach results in the assertion checking being percolated, one level at a time, until a root class assertion is reached.

The requirements for base class checking can be made explicit by considering flattened assertions. A flattened assertion is obtained by using *and* or *or* to concatenate all corresponding assertions in the hierarchy. Flattened assertions can be described with the following syntax:

```
<derived.pre>    // Derived class local precondition
<flat.pre>       // Flattened precondition
<base.pre>       // Base class precondition
<derived.post>   // Derived class local postcondition
<flat.post>      // Flattened postcondition
<base.pre>       // Base class postcondition
<derived.inv>    // Derived class invariant
```

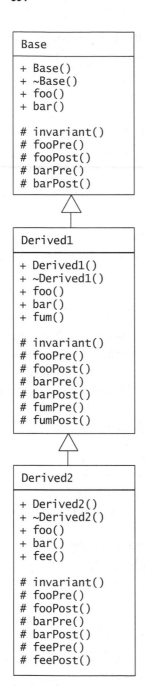

FIGURE 17.7   Percolation Class Diagram.

```
<base.inv>           // Base class invariant
<flat.inv>           // Flattened invariant
<a> ::= <b>          // <a> is composed of <b>
<op><assert>^        // The concatenation of all corresponding base
                     // class assertions, prefixed by op, || (or) or
                     // && (and).
```

Parentheses denote order of evaluation. A flattened invariant can implement the lower/stronger invariant rule in four ways.

```
<flat.inv> ::= <derived.inv> &&<base.inv>^
    // There are nontrivial invariants for derived and base classes.

<flat.inv> ::= TRUE &&<base.inv>^
    // The Derived class invariant is trivial

<flat.inv> ::= <derived.inv> && TRUE
    // All base class invariants are trivial.

<flat.inv> ::= <derived.inv>
    // There is no base class
```

The same principle holds under multiple inheritance. For example, suppose invariants are contributed to a derived class by two base classes, BaseA and BaseB. The flattened invariant is obtained by *and*ing all base class invariants.

```
<flat.inv> ::= <derived.inv> && <baseA.inv>^ && <baseB.inv>^
```

Percolation for preconditions and postconditions depends on how inheritance has been used to compose the function. There are three cases:

1. The highest-level definition of a function (specialization)
2. The automatic inclusion of a base class function in a derived class (extension)
3. The redefinition of a base class function in a derived class (overriding)

Percolation for Defining/Specializing Methods

The first level in which a function is defined requires evaluation of its preconditions, postconditions, and flattened invariant.

```
<flat.pre> ::= <derived.pre> && <flat.inv>
    // There is no base class precondition to inherit.
```

```
<flat.post> ::= <derived.post> && <flat.inv>
    // There is no base class postcondition to inherit.
```

Percolation for Extended Methods

A base class function made available by inheritance must conform to its preconditions, postconditions, and the derived class's flattened invariant. Although the function is inherited, it would be unacceptable for it to create a corrupt derived class state. This task is accomplished by evaluating the flattened invariant of the derived class (which includes the base class's invariant).

```
<flat.pre> ::= <base.pre> && <flat.inv>
    // The flattened base class precondition is inherited and
    // the flattened derived class invariant must hold.

<flat.post> ::= <base.post> && <flat.inv>
    // The flattened base class postcondition is inherited and
    // the flattened derived class invariant must hold.
```

Percolation for Overridden Methods

The flattened invariant must be *and*ed with preconditions and postconditions for a base class function that is redefined in a derived class. Clearly, the derived class functions must conform to the flattened invariant. The three possible cases for a flattened precondition of any overriding derived class function implementation implement the lower/weaker precondition rule:

```
<flat.pre> ::= (<derived.pre> ||<base.pre>^) && <flat.inv>
    // There are preconditions in derived and base classes.

<flat.pre> ::= (TRUE ||<base.pre>^) && <flat.inv>
    // The derived class precondition is trivial.

<flat.pre> ::= (<derived.pre> || TRUE) && <flat.inv>
    // The base class preconditions are trivial, or
    // the base function is abstract.
```

The three possible cases for the flattened postcondition of an overriding derived class function implementation implement the lower/stronger postcondition rule:

```
<flat.post> ::= (<derived.post> &&<base.post>^) && <flat.inv>
    // There are postconditions in derived and base classes.

<flat.post> ::= (TRUE &&<base.post>^) && <flat.inv>
    // The derived class postcondition is trivial.
```

```
<flat.post> ::= (<derived.post> && TRUE)   && <flat.inv>
   // The base class postconditions are trivial.
```

Consequences

The favorable consequences of Percolation include the following:

- Improved readability. Assertions coded in a function body can decrease readability. Percolation reduces code clutter, as only four additional statements appear in each function body (calls to the precondition, postcondition, and to the invariant at entry and exit).
- Reduced time to gain confidence in derived class extensions and modifications by testing. All of the base class's built-in test is automatically activated by testing the derived class.
- The general benefits of built-in test and design-by-contract.

The costs and limitations of Percolation include the following:

- The increased effort to design, implement, and maintain this code.
- The size of the executable and runtime will increase when assertions are enabled.
- Implementation requires an understanding of the LSP and design-by-contract. Developers must apply these principles while coding the class hierarchy. Not only must the assertions represent a well-formed class contract, but the structure of the percolating assertions must also conform to the syntax given earlier, for each general case of inheritance.
- The general limitations and costs of built-in test and design-by-contract apply.

The example implementation cannot distinguish between self as client and external clients. Eiffel does, however, and suspends checking for self-messages. This ability is useful if, for example, a private function computes an intermediate result that is inconsistent with the invariant.

Implementation

Percolation assertions must be hand-coded in most languages. Eiffel implements explicit support for Percolation: base class assertions are automatically inherited and checked with derived class assertions. When a function (routine) is overridden (redeclared), preconditions must be given as `require else <predicate>`. This expression *or*s the derived class precondition with all corresponding base class preconditions. Similarly, postconditions in an overridden function must be stated by `ensure then <predicate>`, which *and*s the derived class postcondition with the corresponding base class postcondition. This requirement applies for all levels of redeclaration.

The functions of each immediate base class must be visible to a derived class to implement Percolation. Default visibility, however, is typically all or nothing. Care must be taken in coding the assertion functions to ensure that the immediate base class is the target of Percolation.

The generic C++ example given here does not show how to exercise a finer degree of control over assertion actions. This programming problem could be solved in many ways.

Sample Code

A generic C++ implementation of Percolation follows. In the example, the functions `foo` and `bar` are overridden, and `fee` and `fum` are examples of the defining and extending cases. Placement of the assertions follows recommendations given earlier: invariant after constructor body, invariant and precondition before function body, invariant and postcondition after function body, invariant before the destructor body. Only a single constructor is shown—the same structure would be implemented for all constructors. The basic elements of this implementation are as follows:

- The standard `<assert.h>` is replaced with `<ASSERT.h>` to allow the assertion to identify itself.

- Each precondition, postcondition, and invariant is implemented as a protected member function. A protected member function makes the base class assertions visible to derived classes without exposing them to clients. These member functions are all type `bool` (returning *true* when the assertion holds, and *false* when it is violated), `inline` (to increase performance and then allow the optimizer to remove the entire function when it is null), and `const` to ensure that there are no side effects. The assertion function body may be implemented only with ASSERT statements. When the assertion expansion is disabled, an empty inline function results. Empty inline functions are completely removed by the compiler's optimization.

- The class to which an `invariant( )` message is bound is assumed to be the class in which the message appears. This assumption is necessary to evaluate the derived class's flattened invariant when a base class function is used by a derived class object.

- The application function must make two calls: first to the invariant function, then to the pre or post-function. If the invariant call was packaged with the pre or post-function, then base class invariants would be called twice (once when the invariant is percolated and a second time when the precondition is percolated).

```
// ASSERT -- macro+function to support extended
            C++ assertion checking
#include <iostream.h>
#ifndef NDEBUG
   #define ASSERT(ex,msg) Assert(ex, msg, #ex, __FILE__, __LINE__)

   inline bool
   Assert( bool condition,
           const char* message,
           const char* expression,
           const char* filename,
           int linenumber )
   {
      if (! condition) {
          cout << flush;
          cerr << endl
               << message
               << expression
               << " In File " << filename
               << " at line " << linenumber
               << " violated. "
               << endl;
          exit(1);
      }
      return true;
   }

#else
   #define ASSERT(ex,msg) /* */
#endif


class Base {
public:

   Base () { /*ctor body */ invariant();}

   virtual void foo() {
      invariant();
      fooPre();
```

```
        // foo body

        invariant();
        fooPost();
        return;
    }

    virtual void bar() {
        invariant();
        barPre();

        // bar body

        invariant();
        barPost();
        return;
    }

    virtual ~Base() {invariant(); /*dtor body */ }

private:
    int baseValue;
    static const int required_BaseValue = 0;
    int fooValue;
    static const int required_fooValue = 0;
    int barValue;
    static const int required_barValue = 0;


protected:

// Base Class Assertions *****************************************
    virtual inline bool invariant() const {
        return ASSERT( (baseValue == required_BaseValue),
                       "Base Invariant"
                     );
    }

    virtual inline bool fooPre() const {
        return ASSERT( (fooValue == required_fooValue),
                       "Base::foo Precondition"
                     );
    }

    virtual inline bool fooPost() const {
        return ASSERT( (fooValue == required_fooValue),
                       "Base::foo Postcondition"
                     );
    }
```

```
            virtual inline bool barPre() const {
                return ASSERT( (barValue == required_barValue),
                                "Base::bar Precondition"
                              );
            }

            virtual inline bool barPost() const {
                return ASSERT( (barValue == required_barValue),
                                "Base::bar Postcondition"
                              );
            }
        };


        class Derived1: public Base {
        public:

            Derived1 () {/*ctor body */ invariant();}
            virtual void foo() {
                invariant();
                fooPre();

                // foo body

                invariant();
                fooPost();
                return;
            }

            virtual void bar() {
                invariant();
                barPre();

                // bar body

                invariant();
                barPost();
                return;
            }

            void fum() {              // Specialization--new member function
                invariant();
                fumPre();

                // fum body

                invariant();
                fumPost();
                return;
            }
```

```cpp
        virtual ~Derived1() {invariant(); /*dtor body */ }

    private:
        int fooD1Value;
        static const int required_fooD1Value = 1;

        int barD1Value;
        static const int required_barD1Value = 1;

        int fumD1Value;
        static const int required_fumD1Value = 1;


    protected:

    // Derived1 Class Assertions *************************************

        inline bool invariant() const {
            return ASSERT( (fooD1Value == required_fooD1Value &&
                            Base::invariant()
                           ),
                           "Derived1 Invariant"
                         );
        }

        inline bool fooPre() const {
            return ASSERT( (fooD1Value == required_fooD1Value ||
                            Base::fooPre()
                           ),
                           "Derived1::foo Precondition"
                         );
        }

        inline bool fooPost() const {
            return ASSERT( (fooD1Value == required_fooD1Value ||
                            Base::fooPre()
                           ),
                           "Derived1::foo Postcondition"
                         );
        }


        inline bool barPre() const {
            return ASSERT( (barD1Value == required_barD1Value ||
                            Base::barPre()
                           ),
                           "Derived1::bar Precondition"
                         );
        }
```

```
        inline bool barPost() const [
            return ASSERT( (barD1Value == required_barD1Value ||
                            Base::barPre()
                            ),
                            "Derived1::bar Postcondition"
                        );
        }

        inline bool fumPre() const {
            // Base class asserts aren't appended to specialization
            return ASSERT( (fumD1Value == required_fumD1Value),
                            "Derived1::fum Precondition"
                        );
        }

        inline bool fumPost() const {
            // Base class asserts aren't appended to specialization
            return ASSERT( (fumD1Value == required_fumD1Value),
                            "Derived1::fum Postcondition"
                        );
        }
};


class Derived2 : public Derived1{
public:

    Derived2 () {/*ctor body */ invariant();}

    virtual void foo() {
        invariant();
        fooPre();

        // foo body

        invariant();
        fooPost();
        return;
    }

    virtual void bar() {
        invariant();
        barPre();

        // bar body

        invariant();
        barPost();
        return;
    }
```

```
        void fee() {    // Specialization
           invariant();
           feePre();

           // fee body

           invariant();
           feePost();
           return;
        }

        virtual ~Derived2() {invariant(); /*dtor body */ }

    private:
       int fooD2Value;
       static const int required_fooD2Value = 2;

       int barD2Value;
       static const int required_barD2Value = 2;

       int feeD2Value;
       static const int required_feeD2Value = 2;


    protected:

    // Derived2 Class Assertions ************************************//

       inline bool invariant() const {
          return ASSERT( (fooD2Value == required_fooD2Value &&
                          Derived1::invariant()
                          ),
                          "Derived2 Invariant"
                       );
       }

       inline bool fooPre() const {
          return ASSERT( (fooD2Value == required_fooD2Value ||
                          Derived1::fooPre()
                          ),
                          "Derived2::foo Precondition"
                       );
       }

       inline bool fooPost() const {
          return ASSERT( (fooD2Value == required_fooD2Value &&
                          Derived1::fooPost()
                          ),
                          "Derived2::foo Postcondition"
                       );
       }
```

```cpp
        inline bool barPre() const {
           return ASSERT( (barD2Value == required_barD2Value ||
                           Derived1::barPre()
                          ),
                          "Derived2::bar Precondition"
                        );
        }

        inline bool barPost() const {
           return ASSERT( (barD2Value == required_barD2Value &&
                           Derived1::barPost()
                          ),
                          "Derived2::bar Postcondition"
                        );
        }

        inline bool feePre() const {
           return ASSERT( (feeD2Value == required_feeD2Value),
                          "Derived2::fee Precondition"
                        );
        }

        inline bool feePost() const {
           return ASSERT( (feeD2Value == required_feeD2Value),
                          "Derived2::fee Postcondition"
                        );
        }

    };
```

Known Uses

Several research systems have been developed to explore automatic verification of type/subtype relationships. The Larch system for specification verification has been extended to C++ and Smalltalk [Leavens, Cheon+94]. Sun et al. show how assertions can be used to express similar correctness constraints for superclasses and subclasses [Sun+95].

Eiffel implements automatic Percolation checking [Meyer 97]. Percolation would be supported in the C++ extensions proposed by Porat and Fertig [Porat+95]. In addition, it is supported in the design-by-contract extensions to Smalltalk/V developed by Carrillo et al. [Carrillo+96]. A weak form of invariant percolation is recommended practice for classes derived from Microsoft Foundation Classes: the message `Base::AssertValid( )` should be sent on entry to derived class member functions [Stout 97].

Percolation is a basic strategy in object-oriented programming. It is used for initialization in Smalltalk and Objective-C: Upon receiving a new message, the super new message is sent to the immediate base class, which in turn sends super new to its base class, and so on. Percolation is also used for dynamic binding in these languages. The search for a method begins in the class of the object that receives a message and continues up the class hierarchy until a method is found that matches the message selector.

A form of Percolation is used in the abstract data type verification techniques developed by Bernot [Bernot+91] and implemented in the LOFT system [Dauchy+93]. An abstract data type can be specified in terms of its own operations. These specification expressions can be recursively evaluated in a process called unfolding. The effect of unfolding a specification expression is much the same as the effect of the sequence of assertion functions that result when an assertion is percolated from a subclass to a superclass.

Related Patterns

The Coherence idiom [Cline+95] provides C++ assertion checking, but does not offer a strategy for Percolation.

17.5 Deployment

17.5.1 Verification of Built-in Test

Assertions, sequence checkers, and all forms of built-in test can be wrong in all of the same ways that application code can be wrong. The general causes are the same: misunderstanding, misinterpretation, omissions, coding errors, configuration errors, and so on. Assertions and application code are usually written by the same person, so a misunderstanding may lead to correlated faults in the code and the assertions [Hurst+95, Voas+99]. There is no magic for obtaining correct assertions. Careful desk checking and inspections are the best preventive measures. Voas observes that this blind spot may be avoided if assertions are identified and coded by different people.

Assertions do not complain when the contract is met or assumptions hold, so assertion bugs may easily hide. Your test suite should therefore include negative assertion tests. Try to identify and execute test cases that cause each assertion to be violated. The considerations for developing domain and combinational test cases apply. Tests of postconditions and invariants may involve concrete state and private contracts, requiring the use of stubs. Such testing will check not only the assertion, but also the assertion action.

When assertions are in routine use, the possibility of assertion bugs should be considered during debugging.

- When an assertion violation is reported, do not immediately rule out the possibility that the assertion is wrong, especially if it has been added or changed recently.
- If a failure occurs in asserted code but does not trigger an assertion action, try to decide why the assertion missed the fault and what other faults it might have missed. Revise the assertion accordingly, and rerun your test suite.
- If a failure occurs in unasserted code, try to devise assertions that would have detected the fault and add them to the code.

The verification of built-in test code relies on the same techniques as any other system under test. Perhaps the only difference is that built-in test code is symbiotic. It must be developed and tested in tandem with its application.

17.5.2   Using Assertions to Design Tests

The simple presence of assertions is *not* equivalent to adequate testing. Code must still be exercised by a test suite that results in the desired coverage. None of the assertion code considered in this chapter can generate test case input. So, while assertions ease testing, they do not preclude the need for test design and execution.

Four scenarios can obtain with respect to assertions:

- The code and design are unasserted; the contract is unarticulated.
- The code uses ad hoc implementation-based assertions, but the contract is unarticulated.
- The contract is asserted, but only at class scope.
- The contract is fully asserted, over all levels.

Procedure 19 describes how to prepare test cases from assertions.

Testers can use assertions to identify domains, equivalence classes, and boundary values. In many cases, preconditions define valid domains for arguments; values rejected by a precondition provide at least one equivalence class for invalid data. Boundary values can be taken directly from the precondition (see Section 10.2.4, *Domain Testing Models*). Output domains can be inferred from postconditions.

Unarticulated Contracts

Assertion strategies can be applied without an articulated contract, however, this chapter focuses on testing with an articulated contract.

Classes are often developed and reused without the benefit of an explicit class contract. However, every class has an implicit contract. Some model of behavior is a prerequisite for any kind of test design. Teasing a complete set of assertions from an undocumented class is an effective reverse-engineering approach. The tester's analysis of the implicit class contract is recorded as preconditions, postconditions, and invariants. The resulting assertions can be entered to test generation tools like ADLT or JavaSpec or used to support the responsibility-based test design techniques discussed in earlier chapters.

1. Write the flattened assertion for the method under test (MUT).
   a. All superclass invariants are ANDed with the CUT's invariant.
   b. The CUT's expanded invariant is ANDed with each precondition and postcondition.
   c. If the MUT overrides a superclass method:
      (1) The superclass preconditions are ORed with the MUT's expanded preconditions.
      (2) The superclass postconditions are ANDed with the MUT's expanded postconditions.

2. Identify at least one negative test case for each logical OR in each precondition and postcondition. Use the Each-Condition/All-Conditions strategy described in Chapter 6.
   a. Attempt to violate (make false) each precondition predicate at least once.
   b. Attempt to reach each postcondition predicate at least once.

3. Develop additional tests to simulate failures in server objects of the class under test that would, in turn, cause postcondition exceptions. Server stubs will be useful.

Procedure 19   Develop Test Cases from Preconditions and Postconditions

Practical Considerations

Testers should consider the following when testing a system with built-in test:

- *Statement coverage.* When assertions are enabled, every assertion statement in every activated method should be covered. If all are not covered, there is a serious bug in the method, its assertions, or both. The action should not be covered, unless a violation occurs. This situation can skew coverage results.

- *Multiple-condition coverage.* If your assertion expressions have multiple Boolean operators, then some coverage tools will report the extent to which multiple-condition coverage is realized for the assertions. If your test suite does not cover all combinations of conditions in an assertion predicate, you should carefully consider the missing cases.

- *You can't assert everything.* Assertions are a good way to check implementation relationships hidden from nonintrusive test drivers. Note, however, that not all relationships of interest can be expressed with assertions. Some form of intrusive evaluation may be necessary. Be sure to develop tests for conditions that cannot be asserted. This effort may require manual inspection of ambiguous situations.

- *Abend testing.* Suppose you disable assertion checking in the deployed system. What will happen if an anomaly occurs that would have been detected by an assertion? Will an abend core dump be produced, as it is in many Microsoft desktop applications? Would this result be acceptable in your deployed system? You can probably get some insight into behavior under anomalous conditions by disabling assertions and running a test suite that would have generated assertion violations. "Cheating" may be necessary—that is, using stubs to force the assertion violations. An abend test will provide an indication of system robustness without assertions.

- *Performance.* Assertion checking consumes processor cycles and uses memory. Full assertion checking can easily double CPU time or elapsed time. The behavior of many systems is time-dependent, even in "real-enough" time systems that do not have hard real-time deadlines. Assertion checking can mask some time-sensitive bugs or induce spurious failures. Unless assertions are to be deployed, full regression testing is warranted after assertion checking is disabled.

Test Suite Reduction

Some kinds of externally applied tests may be omitted if equivalent checking is done by assertions: boundary tests, loop control, and the client side of polymorphic messages. These reductions should not be considered unless the assertions have been verified to provide equivalent checking. In any case, the coverage goal should not be reduced—branch coverage is still the bare minimum for any class, regardless of whether it is asserted.

Under most circumstances, you can omit or reduce test cases for boundary conditions on method arguments that are *explicitly* checked by preconditions and postconditions. In addition, you can omit test cases to exercise boundary conditions on looping and recursion with loop invariants and loop variants. If your code has loops, be sure that each loop body iterates *at least* twice in succession (this requirement is necessary to exercise intraloop data flow). If you have nested loops, this requirement extends to the combinational cases (see Implementation-based Testing, Chapter 10). With a loop variant (which expresses the termination condition), you may omit the test cases for the maximal and overflow iteration. As inducing a maximal iteration is often difficult and time-consuming, such an assertion can significantly reduce testing effort.

You can reduce tests on both the client and server side of a polymorphic message. Coverage of all possible bindings for each message sent to a polymorphic server is difficult even with a small system implemented in type-safe languages. It is infeasible with the dynamic binding model used in Objective-C and Smalltalk [Ponder+94]. Polymorphic server hierarchies that implement the *Percolation* pattern can greatly reduce the testing scope of polymorphism. Unless every message sent to a polymorphic object is bound to all server subtypes and every DU path to the message arguments is covered, we cannot be sure that all clients use the system correctly. Incorrect client usage will be captured by server preconditions, greatly reducing testing needed to exercise these interfaces. Type/subtype faults in a polymorphic server can be found by server testing. In particular, superclass test suites may be applied to subclasses to identify subtype bugs (see *Modal Class Hierarchy Test*). Without percolating assertions, this type of testing becomes more difficult and time-consuming as the depth of inheritance increases.

Complete and correct responsibility assertions make low-cost random generation of test input effective. Although testing with truly random test generation is effective [Hamlet+90], it requires development and evaluation of the expected result for each random test input. Thus, while inputs can be computed at machine speed, the corresponding outputs must often be laboriously hand-calculated. Invariants and postconditions may be substituted for manual production of expected results. You therefore do not have to precompute the expected result for each randomly generated input. Test inputs can be generated and applied at machine speed without using a separate comparator or manual evaluation. As assertions are limited in the extent to which they can detect all failures, this technique is not assured of finding all failures that result from random input generation.

17.5.3   Prerelease Considerations

Built-in test supports several primary development goals: design-time bug prevention, effective testing, and efficient debugging. The design and implementation of built-in test should begin as early as possible. Responsibility-based assertions are an excellent lightweight design representation. Although built-in test is typically disabled before a system is shipped for field use, you should postpone this step as long as possible. Assertions will continue to work for you without any additional effort. Meyer offers some pragmatic guidance for deployment of assertions [Meyer 97].

- Design the application to be robust and reliable in the first place. Use assertions as a kind of safety net—not as the mainstay.
- Never let developers assume that the field system will run with assertion checking turned on.
- Develop and test with at least precondition checking enabled and with invariant and postcondition checking enabled whenever possible.
- Ship the system with precondition checking enabled to support rapid debugging of field-reported failures (this measure requires customer-ready assertion actions).

What should happen when violation occurs? An assertion violation is an application failure in every sense that a no pass test case is an application failure. Assertion violations should be treated in the same way that you would treat a no pass test case. That is, it should be logged as a bug and tracked to resolution. Your assertion action could automatically generate a bug report.

Built-in test should be coded so that it can be disabled by changing compiler parameters and rebuilding the system. The alternative is to make last-minute, line-by-line code changes to a stabilized, tested system. This is highly undesirable for at least three reasons:

- The process of manual revision (deleting or commenting out assertions, and so on) is time-consuming and error-prone.
- The chance of creating new bugs is very high.
- Unless a complete regression test is rerun, the resulting (shipped) system will *not* have been tested.

This approach is like stepping on a rattlesnake: you might live, but your situation will probably become very unpleasant, very quickly. Better to avoid it. Built-in test source code should be packaged with the same configuration item as the released application source code. It is disabled by building the system to be shipped with the necessary compiler parameters. This task is easily accomplished for loosely coupled and tightly coupled built-in test. Embedded built-in test typically cannot be deactivated without code changes. If you use any of the embedded BIT idioms discussed earlier, be sure to limit the origination of messages sent to embedded BIT functions to code that can be deactivated by compiler control. Otherwise, changing this code manually will be necessary.

In some large systems, recompilation and rebuilding can take several days [Lakos 96]. System-wide enabling/disabling of assertions should be considered in planning for system-wide builds in this situation. Developer unit tests with assertions enabled or disabled do not need to be controlled by this schedule, however. Using a configuration management tool, developers can work on a private copy of their code, which can be revised and rebuilt without requiring a complete system build.

Finally, plan for at least two complete regression test runs after rebuilding the deasserted system. The first is to verify that no glitches have been introduced by disabling BIT and that the system meets its space and time constraints. The second is to verify that any bugs found by the first regression run have been corrected and that these corrections have not spawned additional bugs. The first regression test run should not be the first time you conduct performance testing, but it will be the last.

17.5.4   Post-release Considerations

Why not just ship a tested application system with enabled built-in test? The performance penalty of assertions is the most common reason that they are disabled. Additional reasons for not shipping with enabled tests include high confidence in the reliability of the application system (a highly reliable system may not gain much from built-in test in the field) and the lack of robust, safe assertion actions. Disabling built-in test before release has, however, been compared to putting on your seat belt while in the garage and then taking it off when you get on the highway. Several factors argue for shipping built-in test:

- The built-in test in your system uses only safe and robust assertion actions.
- Shipping built-in test avoids the problem of different code being tested than released. This practice obviates the need for an extra round of regression testing on the deasserted system.
- Development debugging capabilities will be present in the field system and may be useful for diagnosing failures in the deployed system. Care must be taken to provide safe and appropriate assertions actions, however.
- Suppose you disable assertion checking in the deployed system. What will happen if an anomaly occurs that would have been detected by an assertion? Will the system just crash? This uncertainty is reduced when assertions with safe actions are shipped.

It is not necessary to disable all built-in test code. Many systems (OS/400, for example) ship with some test code. Built-in test capabilities released with a system are an integral part of it, even if you never intend to display an assertion violation message on a user interface. Table 17.8 summarizes the issues that should be considered in deciding whether to ship asserts.

- *Built-in test responsibilities.* When built-in test code is not shipped, it cannot be used to implement application responsibilities, as the system will not work when it is deasserted. Nonshippable assertions are therefore limited to checking constraints. If assertions are inadvertently used to implement application responsibilities, they must be either shipped or reworked. Conversely, assertions become part of the delivered application when shipped. In this case, it may make sense to use shipped assertions to implement some application responsibilities (e.g., input checking and error handling) besides contract checking.

- *Exception handling for assertion violations.* Many possible actions can be taken when an assertion fails, ranging from the C++ <assert.h> default

TABLE 17.8 Considerations for Built-in Test Deployment

BIT Design Issue	Don't Ship	Ship
Implementation	Embedded BIT must be accessed only from disabled BIT.	May use loose, tight, or embedded BIT.
Responsibilities	BIT cannot implement application responsibilities; must check only correctness constraints.	BIT may play a role in application exception handling.
Robust exception handling used as action	Optional. May be useful for debugging.	Required. Must be considered in the design of application exception handling.
Increased runtime when BIT is enabled	Enabled BIT may distort test results. Performance testing with disabled BIT is required.	Ability to meet response time, batch window, or hard real-time deadlines. Performance testing with BIT enabled is required.
Binary (object code) size	Smaller after BIT is disabled.	May be significantly larger; possible concern with tight RAM/ROM constraints.
Regression testing of the system under development	Required after BIT is disabled.	Second-pass regression testing not needed.
Incremental cost/schedule impact	Additional time to (1) develop repeatable, automated regression test suite; (2) field build with disabled BIT; (3) two additional regression test runs; (4) possible debug time due to weird dependencies.	Additional effort to design and code customer-ready BIT. Additional testing to verify customer-ready exception handling.
Debugging	More difficult after BIT is disabled.	Eases field debugging.
Testability	Decreases after BIT is disabled.	No change.
Maintainability	May be degraded, as asserts can be ignored.	May be enhanced, as asserts cannot be ignored.

burp-and-crash to robust recovery schemes. When assertions are shipped, the assertion action is part of the application functionality; a crude default response is typically inappropriate. If assertions will be shipped, the related exception handling must be designed, coded, and tested as part of the application system. Pay special attention to the content and phrasing of error messages. Although cryptic or sarcastic comments may be amusing to developers, users and customers probably will not appreciate them. If the application is to support different human languages in its interface, assertion messages must be internationalized as well.

- *Performance effects.* Barring pathological cases, the increase in runtime from built-in test should be linear. Suppose an application runs in $n\log(n)$ and the time for each n is 125 milliseconds. Enabling built-in test should not degrade this time to, say, n^2. The time should increase by a constant—for example, by 20 milliseconds for each n to 145 milliseconds. Meyer reports that when precondition checking is enabled for all objects in an Eiffel system, runtime increases an average of 50 percent. About one-fourth of this additional computation is used to evaluate assertion predicates, with the balance being used for housekeeping to support entry/exit checking and assertion actions. When postcondition and invariant checking are enabled in addition to precondition checking, runtime increases from 100 to 200 percent [Meyer 97].

- *Binary (object code) size.* Enabled built-in test will increase binary code size, especially if optional runtime libraries are required. In spite of rapid improvements in the price and performance of RAM, executable size is constrained in many application systems.

- *Regression testing.* If you plan to ship a deasserted system, you should also plan to run a complete regression test on the deasserted code. Nonfunctional changes, such as disabling a built-in test, are a chronic source of bugs owing to weird dependencies. Skipping regression testing after deasserting is foolish at best.[17] The use of nondeployable built-in test therefore implies a commitment to comprehensive and automated regression testing.

- *Incremental cost/schedule effects.* The "don't-ship" approach requires additional effort to disable built-in test, rebuild the system, and run regression tests. It is likely that some debugging will be necessary due to weird dependencies. If built-in test is shipped, the cost of the additional regression testing is avoided but more effort is required to design and code robust built-in test. As this robust built-in test is part of the application, additional testing is warranted to verify its exception handling for assertion violations (proper error messages, restartability, and so on).

---

17. In safety-critical systems, this kind of regression testing is not optional. For example, developers of avionics systems to be certified by FAA standard DO-178 are required to demonstrate object code coverage. *Any* change to the binary code (including deasserting) would require retesting that achieves the same coverage.

- *Testability.* Deasserting a system that is still under test may allow some bugs to go undetected and hamper debugging. Shipping built-in test can ease field debugging.

- *Maintainability.* Inessential software components rot first. As systems evolve, necessary parts are maintained; optional parts are neglected or jettisoned. Thus commented assertions will rot first, followed by loosely coupled, tightly coupled, and finally embedded built-in test.

Finally, what effect on reliability can be expected? One can imagine scenarios where weird dependencies could create additional problems for shipped or disabled BIT. System testing on a deasserted system (a common practice due to performance concerns), however, may allow some bugs to hide that might otherwise be revealed. Other things being equal, there should be no significant effect on field reliability either way. The kinds of faults that can be detected before release by assertions do not depend on whether assertions are shipped. The timing of deasserting in the test process may have an effect, however. Therefore, if built-in test is used, it should be disabled at the latest prudent point in development.

17.6   Limitations and Caveats

Consistent use of built-in test (and other measures to prevent defects and improve testability) can be expected to reduce the overall defect density of the system. However, built-in test is not a replacement for known-good practices for analysis, design, coding, or testing. Like any technical strategy, built-in test has weaknesses and trade-offs that can be resolved with good engineering judgment. None of these problems is insurmountable. They should all be considered when planning and carrying out built-in test during development, however.

Not Feasible for All Systems.   Coding assertions and other forms of built-in test may be practically infeasible in some situations. For example,

- An embedded system is never shut down. Instead, new code is hot-swapped into the runtime environment. The additional effort to verify the deinstrumented code and/or the runtime performance effect (if it is left in) is prohibitive.

- The regulatory, contractual, or technical requirements of a system are such that the built-in test code could not be removed. The additional effort to verify the built-in test code and/or the runtime performance effect is prohibitive.
- The source code is unavailable for any reason.
- The SUT is a legacy system that has been patched beyond all recognition.

Testing Not Obviated.   The beneficial aspects of design-by-contract and built-in test do not reduce the need for execution of an adequate test suite.

- Testing requires execution. Code that contains assertions cannot be considered as tested in any way until it has been exercised by an adequate test suite.
- An asserted class is not necessarily a class with useful built-in test. Assertions can be used for many purposes that do not directly check the class contract. Testers should evaluate the relationships asserted and devise a test model accordingly.
- Exercising asserted code by ad hoc usage is testing-by-poking-around, at best. Suppose a precondition and an invariant contain six relational operators. There are at least 2^6 possible combinations if all of the assertion variables are Boolean, and more if there are interesting domains in the assertion variables (see Chapter 6).
- Many kinds of bugs can hide from assertions.
- The presence of assertions does not prevent bugs in reused code, interfaces to external or legacy systems, or other target environment components.
- The scope and placement of assertions are not necessarily correlated with the operational profile of a system (see Chapter 14). Therefore, operational reliability is not necessarily improved or degraded by assertions. If a rarely used capability is asserted, it will have a relatively small effect on overall reliability.

Assertions Cannot Detect All Bugs.   Even if we could guarantee that no errors would be made in writing assertions, there are limits on the relationships that assertions can express. Assertions cannot express all valid, quantifiable preconditions and postconditions and cannot discriminate among all correct and incorrect values.

They can detect inputs, states, and outputs that are blatantly incorrect, but cannot detect all incorrect output. For example,

- Vague, ambiguous, or subjective conditions are present. A subjective feature that cannot be quantified or expressed as a conditional predicate cannot be asserted—for example, a "fast" response, a "realistic" rendering, a "rich" audio signal.

- The scope of an assertion is a method or class. Necessary conditions at subsystem or system scope are not necessarily the sum of individual assertions. A system can fail even if all of its individual assertions are met. As a result, system testing is necessary even in systems composed of highly reliable components.

- Human semantics can create confusion. We can check a string for valid ASCII alphanumeric characters and even proper spelling. In general, it is impossible to decide automatically that the user should have, for example, entered "The check is in the mail" instead of "The Czech is in the male."

- The developer cannot determine the contract due to missing, incomplete, ambiguous, or incorrect requirements. With the cumulative effect of many changes, this problem becomes more pronounced.

- An incorrect assertion will not report itself as defective. Instead, it will incorrectly complain about a correct result or, more ominously, it will remain silent when a real failure occurs.

- The time and space cost of evaluating some conditions may be prohibitive or may result in undesirable side effects. For example, suppose a precondition for a matrix operation is that the matrix has a nonzero determinant. Computation of the determinant requires iterative summing over all elements of the matrix. Although we might `assert(determinant == 0.0)` after this iteration (which would have its own looping invariants), we could not express the condition with a simple predicate.

- An assertion language that could express all possible relationships of interest would require the ability to directly manipulate sets, sequences, functions, relations, and first-order operators with the semantics of the universal qualifiers "for all" and "there exists" [Meyer 92, Porat+95]. For example, the postcondition for a `stack.pop`

```
ensure (pop ( push( x, old_stack ) ) = stack )
```

cannot be asserted in Eiffel. Tools have been developed and used that support universal quantifiers. In C++, Mueller's functions [Mueller 94] and Nana support these operations, as do the Anna system (Ada) and the Larch specification language (see Section 17.7, Some Assertion Tools).

- Extreme funneling of results may result in trivial conditions. When an algorithm maps a relatively large input domain onto a relatively small output domain, postcondition assertions may be of little interest. For example, consider a Boolean function that maps 32 binary input variables onto a single bit. We could assert that the result must be a valid Boolean (i.e., 0 or 1); unless the postcondition restates the entire combinational function, however, we cannot decide that the output is correct. In this situation, the trivial postcondition is worthless.

In such situations, we must rely on good engineering judgment. Marick suggests simply dumping the input and letting the tester decide correctness [Marick 95].

Distortion of Coverage Analysis. If assertions are limited to expressions placed at entry and exit points, then there should be no effect on the coverage reported by a test run on an instrumented class. If built-in test methods are added to a class, the coverage analyzer may complain that the built-in test code is uncovered.

Costs and Side Effects Related to Execution Space and Time. Assertions typically increase executable size and increase runtime. This can cause several problems:

- In some circumstances, the increased code size may exceed available storage or cause unanticipated, strange behavior.
- If the system has soft or hard real-time deadlines, the execution overhead of built-in test may prevent the IUT from running at all. Increased memory requirements for the executable can result in virtual memory thrashing, which in turn reduces available CPU cycles, which then degrades IUT response time or throughput. If the application is not tested under a high load, this problem can escape the testing process.
- If test runtime doubles, only half as many tests can be run. This could be a serious problem under schedule pressure.

Reducing runtime overhead without completely disabling built-in test is possible. A counter or similar mechanism can be checked before fully evaluating assertions. The full evaluation is skipped if the counter is, for example, not evenly divisible by 7. The frequency of full assertion checking can be scaled be-tween 100 percent and none [Porat+95, Hurst+95]. Another tack is to weaken the contract for the class, so that less expensive assertion checking is required.

Human Factors.   Assertions must be identified and programmed by people. As such, they are subject to social-psychological dynamics.

- Resistance may appear. Despite the ease and effectiveness of assertions, some developers will find them objectionable and will balk at their use.
- Assertions can be wrong. Assertions and code are equally vulnerable to human error. Verification of built-in test presents the same problems as verification of code. If assertions are coded by the same person who codes the implementation, errors in assertions are often similar to er-rors in the implementation—especially errors of omission.
- Going overboard with assertions is possible. Asserting every line of code is overkill.
- Lack of training or poor judgment can lead to excessive, poorly placed, or poorly coded assertions. This practice can result in "ugly," hard-to-read source code, leading to unfounded and unfavorable opinions about assertions.
- Assertions are source code. Their presence means more code to main-tain over the life of a system. As assertions are not an absolute neces-sity, they may be given short shrift as a system matures.
- If an asserted class or method is changed, the assertions also probably need to be changed. Assertions are a living part of the class and must be kept consistent or discarded. Although this "extra" work provides the long-term benefits of built-in test, it can also provide an easy target for short-sighted cost reduction.

These problems are similar to those associated with general software process improvement and may be managed by established strategies [Donaldson+97, Paulk+95, Wiegers 96].

17.7   Some Assertion Tools

Descriptions of the following tools are paraphrased from the developers' Web pages. The URL as of publication follows the description. Remarks were cor-rect as of publication date of this book.

ADLT. Assertion Definition Language (ADL) is a specification language for any C-callable function, library, or system call that may be used for C++ code. Test programs can be automatically generated from ADL specifications by ADLT (the ADL translator). ADLT generates header files (suitable for implementation), test driver code, and documentation from the ADL specification. No generated code is added to the system under test. The ADLT system is available at no cost by FTP. The system includes the source for the ADL translator and run-time library, some precompiled binaries, and documentation.

http://www.sunlabs.com/research/adl/

Anna. ANNotated Ada (Anna) is a language for writing formal specifications for Ada programs. It is based on first-order logic and includes generalized type constraints, virtual checking functions, and behavior specification [Luckham 90]. See [Place+91] for an experience report. A tool set is available that includes necessary Ada extension packages, parsers and pretty-printers, a syntax checker, an analyzer to help in checking specification correctness, a preprocessor that expands the Anna annotations into Ada code, and a specification-aware debugger. The tool set is written in Ada and has been implemented for many platforms.

ftp://anna.stanford.edu/pub/anna http://pavg.stanford.edu/index.html

AssertMate. AssertMate is a code assertion system for Java offered by RST Corporation. Many aspects of AssertMate are discussed in [Payne+98].

http://www.rstcorp.com/tools.html

Eiffel. The Eiffel language offers the most advanced and well-integrated implementation of assertions for object-oriented development. The definitive source is [Meyer 92b]. Several Eiffel compilers with mature development kits are available at very reasonable prices.

JavaSpec. JavaSpec, which is similar to ADLT, is integrated with Sun Microsystems' Java test tool suite. The user writes assertions for Java classes. These assertions define acceptable data values and expected behavior. Once the assertions have been parsed, JavaSpec generates Java driver code for the class that evaluates required behavior and actual results. No generated code is added to the system under test.

http://www.suntest.com

Larch.   Larch is a family of specification languages for research on formal specification of abstract data types [Guttag+85]. The Larch system checks specifications, but does not generate code or test components. Larch is composed of two "tiers" (or layers). The top tier is the language-specific Behavioral Interface Specification Language (BISL), which uses preconditions and postconditions to define interfaces and behavior. BISLs are available for Ada, Smalltalk-80, and C++. The bottom tier is the Larch Shared Language, which is used to describe the abstract domain model and mathematical vocabulary used in the precondition and postcondition specifications. The Larch system is available at no cost by FTP.

http://www.cs.iastate.edu/~leavens/larch-faq.html

Nana.   Nana is a research system that supports C++ assertion checking and program logging with minimal time and space overhead. Limited support is available for specifying "before" state and universal quantifiers. Release 0.75 uses the normal GNU conventions and comes with a small demonstration program. The system is available at no cost by FTP.

http://www.cs.ntu.edu.au/staff/pjm/nana/index.html

17.8   Bibliographic Notes

Implementation Support for Proof of Correctness

Software assertions were first studied in formal specification and verification techniques by Floyd (1967), Hoare (1969), and Hoare and Wirth (1973). An early formulation of invariants appears in [Hoare 72]. Research into programming languages to support these ideas suggested a special kind of module (a "type") that strongly encapsulated its implementation, offering only a single interface composed of operations, and defined behavior only through these exported operations. These modules became known as Abstract Data Types (ADTs) [Liskov+75, Guttag+85, Liskov+86].

The "algebraic" approach to ADTs uses the operations of the type (similar to methods of a class) to specify its behavior. Each operation is expressed in terms of other operations. The "model-based" approach uses assertions. Algebraic and model-based specification are equal in expressive power [Zweben+92]. The research language Alphard supported assertions [Shaw 81]. The CLU language supported an algebraic definition of an ADT [Liskov+86].

Formal development methodologies like VDM, Z, and Inna Jo [Kemmerer 85] adapted correctness ideas for procedural implementations, but followed the model-based definition. The role of Z assertions in testing is considered in [Hayes 86]. A similar approach is considered in [Bartussek+86].

The similarity (and gaps) between ADTs and object-oriented programming suggested how proof notions could be made operational [Olthoff 86]. A formal, object-oriented meta-model using Z preconditions and postconditions, class invariants, and state invariants is given in [Schulman+87]. Meyer's Eiffel language was the first generally available object-oriented language to provide built-in support for assertions [Meyer 88]. Additional historical notes on the use of assertions in specification and programming may be found in [Meyer 97]. Korel shows how test cases can be developed from assertions [Korel+96].

Design-by-Contract

The notions of responsibilities and collaboration are sketched in [Cunningham+86]. The assertion-based, design-by-contract approach and its Eiffel implementation are presented in [Meyer 88]. Wirfs-Brock gives an informal, introductory discussion of the idea of responsibility and class collaboration [Wirfs-Brock+90]. Several OOA/D methodologies define responsibilities with assertions. They are deliverables in the Fusion methodology [Coleman+94], and the Class Relation methodology [Desfray 94]; they are an integral part of the Syntropy approach [Cook+94]. The Business Object Notation (BON) methodology assumes an Eiffel implementation and uses assertions to specify contracts [Nerson+94, Walden 95]. Responsibilities and collaboration are an integral element of the Object Constraint Language (OCL) [Warmer+99], which provides meta-definitions for the UML notation. The discussion in [Meyer 97] provides the definitive statement of Meyer's point of view.

Inheritance and Type Hierarchies

Computer science researchers formalized the intuition that gnarly inheritance is a bad thing and have suggested *monotonic inheritance* as a design criterion [Choi+91]. Some testing implications of the similar, but informally defined, notion of "strict inheritance" are discussed in [MacGregor 93a]. Overbeck uses monotonic inheritance in a formal analysis of the extent to which superclass test cases can be reused to test subclasses [Overbeck 94a]. The definitive analysis of type-subtype design requirements known as the Liskov substitution principle (LSP) appears in [Liskov+94]. Useful explanations and examples of the LSP for C++ are provided in [Coplien 92] and [Martin 95]. Page-Jones' design guidance about LSP-consistent inheritance and polymorphism is both pragmatic and readable [Page-Jones 95]. The role of assertions for preventing incorrect redeclaration is sketched in [Meyer 92] and considered in detail in [Meyer 97].

Software Fault Tolerance and Exception Handling

Meyer advocates cooperative design (clients are responsible for correct usage) [Meyer 88, Meyer 92a]. The defensive design (servers check for correct use) is advocated in [Booch 91] and [Berard 93]. Weide presents a comprehensive analysis of the effect of defensive and cooperative design on reusability [Weide+91]. Cline provides pragmatic and concise guidance for design of exception handling in C++ [Cline+95]. A good summary of exception handling in Java is given in [Campione 96]. General considerations for the design of exception handling in safety-critical systems are presented in [Leveson 95] and [Friedman+95]. The Eiffel exception model is advocated and a critique of Ada is presented in [Meyer 97].

Ada

The use of assertions for Ada 95 and an assertion checking package is discussed in [Culwin 95]. See also the preceding comments about Anna.

C++

The mechanics of the C `assert` macro are essentially unchanged in C++, so most discussions of C assertions apply [Bates 92, Rosenblum 95]. Discussion of C (and some C++) debugging and related coding is discussed in [Thielen 92] and [Spuler 94]. Implementation-based assertions for C++ are discussed in several sources [Thielen 92, Maguire 93, Davis 94, Spuler 94, Hunt 95b]. A complete assertion system for Apple development is presented in [Rosenblum 97]. The implementation of responsibility-based assertions is considered by [Mueller 94], which shows how to implement universal qualifiers (there exists, for all), in the Coherence idiom [Hurst+95, Cline+95], and in the concept definition for the exlC++ compiler [Porat+95]. Payne et al. provide a complete and articulate discussion of the use of assertions in C++ to increase testability, implement design-by-contract, and check state transitions [Payne+97]. Marick lists many strategies for identifying C and C++ assertions and developing test cases from them [Marick 95]. Voas makes the case for C++ fault sniffers in [Voas+99].

Eiffel

Meyer's extensive discussion of the Eiffel implementation of assertions and the design-by-contract notion is must reading for anyone contemplating assertions [Meyer 97]. Although Meyer frequently suggests that testing benefits from assertions, he does not discuss test design. Jézéquel provides a concise, professional-level tutorial that includes a chapter on basic test design and implementation in Eiffel [Jézéquel 96a].

Java

An approach to Java assertions is presented in [Payne+98].

Objective-C

Assertions are briefly discussed in [Cox 92]. Many of the concepts and techniques for C and C++ assertions using the `assert` macro apply to Objective-C.

Smalltalk

The use of Larch for developing specifying Smalltalk class assertions is presented in [Cheon+94]. Carrillo et al. present extensions to the Smalltalk/V class browser to support design-by-contract [Carrillo+96].

Chapter 18   Oracles

> **Overview**
> A test oracle produces the results expected for a test case. This chapter discusses considerations for development of an oracle. Patterns for several kinds of oracles are presented. Design considerations for actual/expected comparators that deal with the special problems of object equality are discussed.

18.1 Introduction

Expected results are essential to test design. Although generating test inputs automatically is relatively easy, we cannot hope to perform extensive automated testing without expected results and the ability to make an automatic comparison of actual and expected results.

A test case passes when the IUT produces an acceptable result. Pass/no pass evaluation is made by comparing the actual result with an expected result established by a trusted source. In testing jargon, an oracle is a trusted source of expected results.[1] "The oracle can be a program specification, a table of examples, or simply the programmer's knowledge of how a program should operate" [Howden+78, 997]. It is a mechanism to evaluate the actual results of a test case as pass or no pass. This evaluation requires a **result generator** to produce the expected results for an input and a **comparator** to check the actual results against the expected results. An oracle is the generation and comparison mechanism, but never the comparator alone.[2] It may be manual, automated, or partially automated. The name is well chosen, as there are several parallels to the Delphic oracle. An oracle can be correct in particulars but misleading about the overall reliability of a system.[3]

A **perfect oracle** would be behaviorally equivalent to the implementation under test and completely trusted. In effect, it would be a defect-free version of the IUT. It would accept every input specified for the IUT and would always produce a correct result. Developing a perfect oracle is therefore at least as difficult as solving the original design problem and imposes the additional constraint of correctness. If a perfect oracle was available and portable to the target environment, we could dispense with the IUT and fulfill the application requirements with the ideal oracle. The perfect oracle, however, is something like a philosopher's stone for software. We cannot guarantee the ability of any algorithm to decide that an output is correct in all possible cases [Manna 78].

This chapter presents design patterns for oracles. The micro patterns cover a wide range of cost and complexity. Considerations for equality evaluation in

---

1. Besides the suggestion of a trusted source of information, there is no connection between this term and the software products of Oracle Corporation.

2. Many approaches to object-oriented testing rely on manual generation of expected results and limited automatic test evaluation [Binder 96i]. Several approaches support interesting solutions to comparators. A few call the comparator itself an oracle.

3. Human oracles were fixtures of the ancient world. Around 700 B.C.E., a temple of Apollo was built in Greece near the remote mountain village of Delphi. The Pythia, priestesses of the temple, were believed to speak for Apollo and were therefore considered a reliable source of prophecies. Movers and shakers of the day consulted the Pythia about making war, marriages, deals, and other matters. Besides the necessary rituals, supplicants paid large sums for this privilege. The Pythia's answers were often riddles. In 550 B.C.E. Croesus, king of Lydia, consulted the Pythia about going to war against the Persians. He set up a cooking configuration (see the chapter epigraph) and then sent messengers to ask the Pythia about it. The Pythia correctly described Croesus's barbeque, *before* the messengers could pose the question. Satisfied with this test, Croesus made an especially large contribution and asked if he should make war on the Persians. The Pythia answered that he would destroy a great empire by attacking. Croesus decided to go to war. His armies were decimated and the Persians conquered Lydia. When Croesus later accused the priestess of lying, she replied that a great empire had indeed fallen—his own. The Delphic oracle remained in business until the temple was sacked by the Christian emperor Arcadius in 398 C.E.

object-oriented programming are developed in Section 18.3, Comparators. Specific techniques for developing expected results or oracle algorithms are not discussed in this chapter. Instead, expected results are developed for nearly all of the test design patterns in Part III, providing examples of techniques to develop specific expected results. This chapter focuses on general patterns for implementing oracles.

18.2 Oracle Patterns

18.2.1 Introduction

Design Considerations

The oracle should be designed as an integral part of a test suite and its test harness. Problems of oracle design include the following:

- Given the responsibilities and implementation of the IUT, how can expected results be produced? Can they be produced at all?
- Is there any advantage to combining (separating) generation of test inputs and expected results?
- Should the expected results be available before, during, or after a test run?
- How can expected and actual results be stored to support regression testing?
- Is evaluation done by direct comparison or by indirect checking?
- What should be the scope of checking? Just the public interface of a class, all of the objects that compose a class, or the entire address space of the process in which the IUT is running?
- Can evaluation be partially manual and partially automatic?
- What is the test run frequency? Would a fast, reliable oracle/comparator cut test cycle time, allowing many more tests to run? Would this improvement in test effectiveness offset any increased cost to develop the faster oracle/comparator?
- What level of precision is required of scalar variables? Is exact equality required to pass? Do you understand exactly how floating-point operations work for the IUT?
- What kind of probes, traces, or accessor methods are necessary to obtain the actual results?

- How much platform independence is necessary? Must the oracle work on many different computers?
- What are the observable output formats—GUI bitmap, GUI widgets, character strings on standard output, file system, database system, network packets, device-level bitstreams, analog (voice, data, audio, video, or other RF signals), mechanical movements, or other physical quantities? On what media: displayed, printed, file, and so on? What kind of encoding—EBCDIC, ASCII, Unicode, or binary?
- Is the observable output persistent or must provisions be made to capture and save it?
- Will the observable results be produced on a single system or must the test harness coordinate collection of results from nodes in a distributed system?
- Will localization (translation between human languages) be required?
- To what extent will the state of the runtime environment (apart from the IUT) need to be evaluated?
- How much time is available to generate and evaluate the results?
- Should expected results be usable by humans? By subsequent test cases? In subsequent regression test runs?

Timing presents interesting problems of its own. A *pretest* oracle requires that inputs be known before the test run. The expected results are precomputed and stored in some form. This approach is useful if the oracle is slower than the IUT and necessary if the test driver must evaluate results. However, pregeneration may be infeasible or impractical. An *on-demand* oracle produces expected results or evaluates actual results in parallel or as soon as the IUT has produced a test result. A *post-test* oracle requires that actual results are stored and evaluated afterward. This offers the greatest flexibility but may make it hard to interleave testing and debugging.

Test validity is a result of several factors. The presence of an oracle alone does not guarantee a valid test. A buggy oracle can cause correct results to be evaluated as no pass (spurious no pass). Time will probably be wasted trying to debug a nonexistent problem and the resulting "fix" may cause further distortions. Or, a test with incorrect actual results can be evaluated as a pass (spurious pass). This kind of error typically goes undetected until a user identifies the supposedly correct output as incorrect. Test validity can be characterized as follows:

- A **valid pass** occurs if and only if (1) the required, actual, and expected results are the same and (2) both the IUT and oracle are correct. The second condition is necessary to distinguish a valid from a coincidental pass.
- A **valid no pass** occurs if and only if (1) the required, actual, and expected results are not the same and (2) the oracle is correct. The second condition is necessary to distinguish a valid from a coincidental no pass.
- A **spurious pass** occurs when a faulty oracle produces an expected result that is the same as an actual result produced by a faulty IUT. The IUT and the oracle have bugs (possibly the same) that produce consistent results.
- A **spurious no pass** occurs when a faulty oracle produces an expected result that is different from the actual result produced by a correct IUT.
- A **coincidental pass** occurs when the IUT is coincidentally correct.
- A **coincidental no pass** occurs when the IUT and the oracle are faulty and the expected and actual results are not the same. The IUT and the oracle have bugs (possibly the same) that produce inconsistent results.

Several conditions can lead to invalid test results. Suppose the IUT is required to compute the function $z = x + y$, where x and y are the inputs and z is the output. The oracle for this function must, therefore, perform or simulate the same computation. Either implementation may be correct or incorrect; for example, $z = x - y$, $z = x \times y$, or $z = x / y$. The oracle and the IUT can be incorrect in exactly the same way (this can easily occur if the same person develops both based on an incorrect understanding of requirements) or may have different bugs. Table 18.1 lists the combinations and associated test validity. Infeasible combinations have been suppressed (if either the IUT or the oracle is correct, neither can have the same fault). The table shows example values for test cases, the required result, the actual result produced by the IUT, and the expected result produced by the oracle.

The design, implementation, and output of an oracle should be verified. As noted earlier, the problem of oracle verification is at least as hard as application verification. From a theoretical perspective, we cannot be completely sure that a valid pass or valid no pass has obtained without also proving the correctness of both the IUT and the oracle. From a practical perspective, the additional effort required for complete certainty would be prohibitively expensive even when technically feasible. The risk of spurious or coincidental results can be

TABLE 18.1   Effect of Oracle on Test Validity

IUT/Oracle Quality				Same Bug?	CC?	Test Case		Results			Test Validity
IUT		Oracle				x	y	Required	Expected	Actual	
Correct	$x+y$	Correct	$x+y$	NA	NA	5	3	8	8	8	Valid Pass
Correct	$x+y$	Faulty	$x*y$	No	No	5	3	8	15	8	Spurious No Pass
Correct	$x+y$	Faulty	$x*y$	No	Yes	2	2	4	4	4	Coincidental Spurious Pass
Faulty	$x-y$	Correct	$x+y$	No	No	5	3	8	8	2	Valid No Pass
Faulty	$x-y$	Correct	$x+y$	No	Yes	0	0	0	0	0	Coincidental Pass
Faulty	x/y	Faulty	x/y	Yes	No	5	3	8	0.6	0.6	Spurious Pass
Faulty	x/y	Faulty	x/y	Yes	Yes	0.5	0.5	1	1	1	Spurious, Coincidental Pass
Faulty	$x*y$	Faulty	$x-y$	No	No	5	3	8	2	15	Coincidental No Pass
Faulty	$x*y$	Faulty	$x-y$	No	Yes	0	0	0	0	0	Spurious, Coincidental Pass

Key: CC = Coincidental Correctness

reduced to an acceptable level by verifying the oracle and meeting the exit criteria of the appropriate test design pattern.

After having faced the oracle design problem many times, I have a few suggestions for tackling this difficult problem:

- If possible, review some expected results produced by your oracle and your assumptions with system users. Values that may look correct to a developer or tester may be subtly incorrect due to some special constraints.
- The more complex the oracle, the greater the chance of spurious test results. Try for the simplest solution.
- If the oracle is specification-based, do not forget to verify the specification. Scrutinize the specification for omissions.

- Try the oracle for test cases that have obvious expected results—for example, all zeros in, all zeros out. Such test cases check the oracle and the comparator.

- If practical and feasible, try using several independent sources. For example, if you are picking values from a table in a reference work, try to find several other reference works that provide the same information. Interleave values from these sources. If you are using an existing system as the oracle, try running the system in different configurations or platforms, varying the time of day, altering the background load, and so on.

- Although writing a program to generate millions of test case inputs is usually not difficult, producing their expected results is often equivalent to developing the SUT. Two of the oracle patterns can partially overcome this limitation. *Built-in Test Oracle* will detect some, but not all, incorrect output from any input. You may be able to use an existing system as a gold standard oracle. Run the existing system with your test inputs. It will automatically produce some or all of your expected results (*Trusted System Oracle*).

- Design-for-testability tip: Consider abandoning a test strategy or test case if it requires a very difficult or costly oracle. Try to use existing code, files, or test suites as much as possible.

- Design-for-testability tip: Consider reworking an application specification or requirement if its oracle would be very difficult or costly to develop.

- Consider a partial or approximating oracle. Don't assume that your oracle must generate complete expected results for every possible input and state. Concentrate on generating outputs that must be correct or that are difficult and/or time-consuming to check by hand.

- Consider using several kinds of oracles to offset weaknesses. For example, you can use an existing system to generate about half of the critical outputs for a new system. You could implement built-in test assertions to check relationships on the newer output.

Choosing an Approach

Oracles are often difficult and expensive to develop. Typical practice is to mix judging (manual test evaluation) with simple automatic evaluation. Table 18.2 compares the fidelity, range, and cost of the various oracles. This classification reflects practical consequences of oracle use in my experience.

TABLE 18.2   Oracles Ranked by Fidelity, Generality, and Cost

	Lower Cost		Higher Cost	
	Narrow Range	Broad Range	Narrow Range	Broad Range
High Fidelity	Smoke Test Reversing	Trusted System Regression Testing Parallel Testing	Generated Implementation Different But Equivalent	Solved Example Voting
Low Fidelity	Built-in Test	Judging	Approximation Simulation Executable Specification	

Fidelity is correspondence between the expected results and actual results. A low-fidelity oracle cannot produce expected results for some possible test inputs, is too slow to allow many tests, or cannot distinguish between all incorrect and correct responses. Built-in test is low fidelity, as assertions cannot detect all incorrect output. A high-fidelity oracle can generate correct and complete results for any test case.

Generality is the range of application. A broad oracle has few constraints; a narrow oracle is appropriate only in limited circumstances. For example, *Solved Example Oracle* is applicable in nearly all circumstances and therefore a broad oracle. *Different But Equivalent Oracle* is a narrow oracle: it is applicable only at class scope, requires an equality operation, and requires the ability to identify and generate many equivalent message sequences.

Cost refers to the expected average cost per test. For example, a trusted system can be used as-is to generate thousands of expected results automatically, so the average cost per test is very low. In contrast, suppose working a few solutions by hand requires several weeks. The average cost per test is very high.

Pattern Summary

The following 15 oracles discussed in this chapter are presented as micropatterns. Each discussion covers the context, solution, and specific consequences in a few paragraphs. Published reports on usage are given where possible. The common issues have been factored out and are discussed in the preceeding sections. The oracle micropatterns are presented in four groups.

Judging.   The tester evaluates pass/no pass by looking at the output on a screen, a listing, using a debugger, or another suitable human interface.

Prespecification. The expected results are determined before the test is run. These results are made available to a comparator.

- *Solved Example Oracle.* Develop expected results by hand or obtain from a reference work.
- *Simulation Oracle.* Generate exact expected results with a simpler implementation of the IUT (e.g., a spreadsheet).
- *Approximation Oracle.* Develop approximate expected results by hand or with a simpler implementation of the IUT.
- *Parametric Oracle.* Use an algorithm to compute parameters from the actual results and compare the actual parameters to specified parameter values.

Gold Standard. A **gold standard oracle** is an existing implementation that is trusted.[4] For example, an existing implementation of the Unix command-line utilities could be considered a gold standard if we were porting these utilities to a different operating system. A legacy application system that has run for years without trouble is another example. Don't forget that this trust is relative. It is likely that a few bugs remain in even the most extensively used systems.

- *Trusted System Oracle.* Run a new test case against a trusted system to generate expected results.
- *Parallel Test Oracle.* Run the same live inputs into the IUT and a trusted system. Compare the output.
- *Regression Test Oracle.* Run an old test suite against a partially new system.
- *Voting Oracle.* Compare the output of several versions of the IUT.

Organic. An **organic oracle** exploits an informational redundancy present in some systems. That is, the IUT, the test case input, and the actual result are sufficient to decide pass/no pass.

- *Smoke Test.* Use the basic operability checks of the runtime environment.
- *Reversing Oracle.* Reverse the IUT's transformation.

---

4. This jargon originates in hardware development: a gold standard or golden implementation is a device that is known to be "good."

- *Built-in Check Oracle.* Use an algorithm to generate fields or objects that encode certain IUT relationships. Compare the pretest encoded value to the post-test encoded value.
- *Built-in Test Oracle.* Implement assertions that define valid and invalid results.
- *Executable Specification Oracle.* Actual input values and output values are used to instantiate the parameters of an executable specification. A specification checker will reject an instantiation that is inconsistent, indicating incorrect output.
- *Generated Implementation Oracle.* Generate a new implementation from a specification; compare output from the IUT and the generated IUT for the same test case.
- *Different But Equivalent Oracle.* Generate message sequences that are different but should have the result; run on separate objects and compare for equality.

18.2.2 Judging

Judging means that a person makes the pass/no pass decision. The tester or user decides whether each test passes. The decision may be based on analysis, subjective evaluation, or both. Judging is appropriate for alpha, beta, and usability testing. There are at least three kinds of judging:

- *Subjective evaluation/testing by poking around.* The test cases are improvised and results assessed on the fly—"run it and see what happens." This kind of testing typically results during ad hoc beta testing. This approach should be used only in these limited circumstances to augment an effective testing process. It cannot be considered as effective testing on its own.

- *Post-test analysis.* The system under test is exercised by a test suite. The test cases either do not specify or provide only a general indication of expected results. The actual results for each test case are recorded and subsequently checked by hand or simulation. Incorrect results can be identified by knowledgeable persons without prespecification of the expected result.

- *Expert user.* The output of some systems defies quantitative evaluation. Suppose we are testing a program that generates high-resolution animated graphics. The aesthetics of the rendering (apart from the correctness of its illumination computations) is a critical aspect of the output. The output must

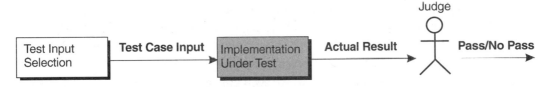

FIGURE 18.1   Judging Oracle.

be seen to be evaluated, and it must be evaluated by a person with the necessary expertise in animation.

Judging is limited by human ability: it is slow and error-prone. Actual results must be formatted to be usable by a judge and presented at a rate suitable for human recognition and consideration. The use of a judge as an oracle tends to be an obstacle to effective regression testing. The judge is likely to try to avoid repeating what is usually perceived as unpleasant and tedious work. Figure 18.1 depicts this process.

Judging is often associated with improvised tests. The use of a judge does not mean, however, that test design and test documentation can be skipped. Developing a complete and systematic plan of attack is important, even if the plan is to improvise. This should be documented in the Test Procedures section of the test plan (see Section 9.3, Documenting Test Cases, Suites, and Plans). The judge should work through the test cases in the plan and produce a log that captures the result of each test. A written log of all tests (planned and improvised) and their results is an essential deliverable for this kind of testing.

18.2.3   Prespecification Oracles

Solved Example Oracle

When expected values cannot be produced by another system and are not available from a trusted reference (e.g., published tables of astronomical conditions), they must be developed by hand. As test cases are designed, each output is prepared manually. The expected results may be incorporated with the test case implementation to support automatic evaluation.

This oracle is useful at any scope, but is generally limited to evaluation of simple processing rules with several output variables. Not all responsibilities require detailed computation. Once the test cases have been developed, determination of the expected results is like an exercise in writing a specification or developing examples for documentation: Given these inputs, what result is required? For example, the expected results for tests designed by *Category-Partition* are often easily defined. Prespecification may be useful for special cases or to augment a different kind of oracle. Suppose an automated oracle is limited or cannot be modified (e.g., we're using an existing system). We would manually develop expected results for tests that can't be generated by this oracle.

Figure 18.2 shows this configuration. This basic technique has been used since the dawn of programming. Most of the expected results in the example test plans in this book were developed by hand.

Simulation Oracle

Expected results are produced using a reduced, simplified, or prototype implementation of the IUT. The essential responsibilities of the IUT can be simulated by a simplified version of the IUT. Figure 18.3 shows this configuration.

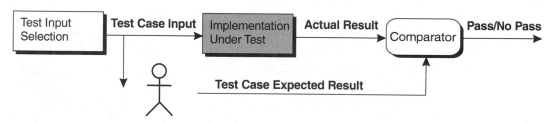

FIGURE 18.2   Solved Example Oracle.

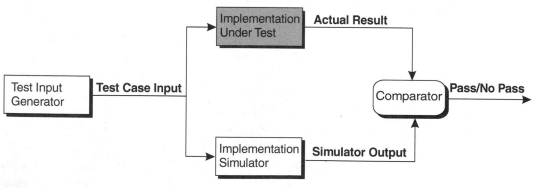

FIGURE 18.3   Simulation Oracle.

Design and coding errors may be made in developing the simulator. A simulator should be designed so that developing and verifying it are (much) easier than they are for the IUT. A spreadsheet can be used to mimic a wide range of computation and searching. Application generation tools can be used to develop complex systems with simple drag-and-drop programming. The essential transformation of a system or function can often be implemented in several hundred lines of code.

A simulation oracle can be useful at any scope. A simulator that interprets a specification language to generate expected results is described in [Brown+ 92]. The use of simulators and prototypes as oracles is suggested in [Beizer 95]. A spreadsheet was used to simulate use case inputs and outputs for a large financial transaction processing system implemented in Java [Pemmaraju 98]. Advanced simulation can be extended to include a complete virtual environment for the SUT, where outputs can be fedback into the environment. Such a closed-loop oracle can be very useful for testing motion-control systems in which both discrete and continuous aspects of output must be evaluated [Jones 90].

Approximation Oracle

Some systems are built to solve unsolved problems or problems for which there is no analytical solution. Complex simulation in mechanical design, weather and economic forecasting, and geological exploration are examples. In such cases, there is no simple technique for checking the output produced by the IUT. Several strategies are suggested in [Weyuker 82].

- Reduce the input/state space. Try tests that are simple (even trivial), but for which the answer can be checked by hand or simulation.
- In some systems, a subject-matter expert may be able to recognize an output that is egregiously wrong or inconsistent.
- There may be constraints on some outputs (e.g., x should never be greater than y) that can be checked.
- Determine the acceptable accuracy of the results. Interpolate.

Code assertions at important steps in the computation. The assertions can check convergence in a numerical algorithm, assumptions about any kind of constraint, the integrity of data structures in use, and so on.

It may be possible to find a subset of the IUT's input that can also be accepted by a similar, trusted system. For example, a reduced model of a complex simulation could be formulated to run on a commercially available general-purpose simulation tool. This may help to establish the bounds of a solution. Figure 18.4 shows how a converter could be used to map from a smaller implementation to the IUT. The smaller implementation would provide the approximate solution to be compared with the IUT's solution. Approximation is indicated for new, complex systems for which no other alternative exists.

Parametric Oracle

A parametric oracle applies a trusted algorithm to compute parameters of interest from the actual results of a test run [Hoffman 99]. If the actual result parameter values comply with those specified for the IUT, the test passes. Suppose the SUT produces data values that can be characterized by one or more statistical parameters. For example, we expect that the stream of digits produced by a pseudorandom number generator can be characterized by the normal distribution. Checking every value the generator can produce might be infeasible. Nevertheless, even if we could, it still would not help us decide whether the generator produced set values that met the required statistical parameters. To evaluate this requirement, statistical parameters, such as mean and standard deviation of the actual results, can be computed by a trusted implementation.

The tests implied by a parametric oracle should not be assumed to be sufficient. For example, suppose the specification for our random number generator also requires that no systematic pattern occur in the sequence of digits produced—for example, 10 increasing values followed by 10 decreasing values. We would need to write a program to analyze the output stream to evaluate this requirement.

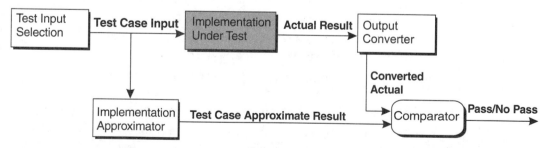

FIGURE 18.4   Approximation Oracle.

18.2.4   Gold Standard Oracles

All of the gold standard oracles use one or more versions of an existing application system to generate expected results. Although they are the same in this respect, the following patterns have important operational differences in the use and configuration of the existing system. For example, it may be possible to install a copy of a trusted system in the test lab, but it would be infeasible to capture all actual input to achieve parallel testing.

Trusted System Oracle

An existing system is **trusted** if it has been used in anger with success. Although more formal and quantitative definitions are possible, the general idea is that an existing system is routinely used with high confidence. This system must also compute many (if not all) of the same functions as the IUT.

A trusted system is used as an oracle by feeding it test inputs for the IUT. The output of the trusted system provides the expected results for the IUT. Figure 18.5 shows this configuration. If the trusted implementation cannot be directly invoked from your test case generator or test driver because it is written in a different language or runs on a different platform, consider writing an object wrapper for it. Expected results can then be automatically produced and compared by the driver. Some data conversion is typically required. These converters are a potential cause of spurious test results and should be carefully verified (yes, even *tested*).

This approach is useful at any scope. A trusted system is often present when a legacy system will be replaced or ported to a new platform. Such systems can be set up to produce expected results for a large quantity of test cases.

As noted earlier, a trusted system can be coupled with a program that performs pseudorandom test data generation. This combination is particularly powerful because a high quantity of test cases with trusted expected results can

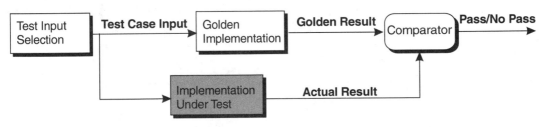

FIGURE 18.5   Trusted System Oracle.

be produced in a short period (runs on the order of millions of complete test cases in few hours are possible). Figure 18.6 shows this configuration.

Parallel Test Oracle

In parallel testing, the same input stream is supplied to a trusted system and to the IUT. The IUT must be a replacement for the trusted system or must have significant similarities. The IUT is expected to produce the same results as the trusted system. If it does not, a bug may have been revealed. Some data conversion between the system input and output is typically required. These converters are a potential cause of spurious test results and should be carefully verified. In practice, this approach often reveals as many bugs in the trusted system as it does in the IUT. Figure 18.7 shows this configuration.

Ideally, the software running in parallel executes on independent computers, so as to avoid spurious test results due to a doubled load and contention for application and system resources. Shared network channels may present similar problems. This issue is particularly important if the results of the SUT or the trusted system are sensitive to timing or resource contention.

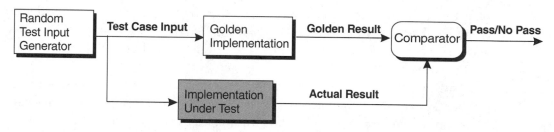

FIGURE 18.6   Trusted System Oracle with random input generation.

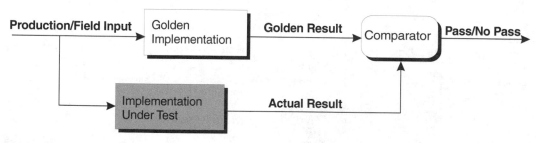

FIGURE 18.7   Parallel Test Oracle.

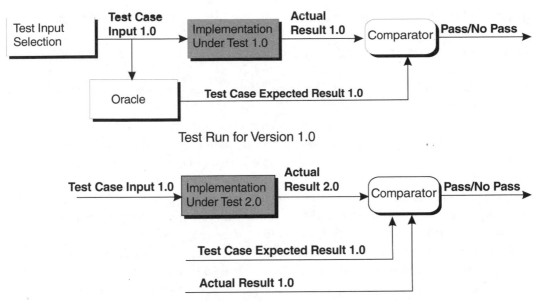

FIGURE 18.8   Regression Test as an Oracle.

If independent platforms are not available, it may make sense to run each system in sequence, save the systems, output to files, and then run a comparator on the output files as a third and final step of the test run.

Regression Test Oracle

Regression testing is discussed in Chapter 15. The actual results of a previous run provide the expected results for the regression run. *Popular Framework Test* shows how existing test suites can be used to verify changes to a framework. Regression testing is useful at any scope and is widely used. Figure 18.8 shows this configuration.

Voting Oracle

A voting oracle is similar to trusted system and parallel testing oracles, but there are two or more golden systems. The same input is presented to all systems, and the results are compared. If all of the results are the same, we can have high confidence that the IUT has produced a correct result. If they disagree (in any combination), all of the actual results must be studied to decide which answer is correct. Although building several different implementations of the same responsibility may not be possible, it may be possible to use several older versions of the trusted system as "voters." Of course, feasibility is limited by differences found among successive versions. Some data conversion between the system input and output is typically required. These converters are a potential cause of spurious test results and should be carefully verified. Figure 18.9 shows this configuration.

Experimental evaluation of n-version programming (in which n independent systems are developed from the same requirements) found that many of the same bugs were produced by independent teams [Knight+86]. This finding suggests that it may be difficult to obtain truly independent systems. Even if the systems are independent, testing can be defeated by minor glitches. In 1981, the first flight of the Space Shuttle *Columbia* was delayed when the fifth backup computer became unsynchronized with the four primary computers [Garman 81]. The four primary systems ran exactly the same software and compared results, in effect voting on the output. If the first pair did not agree, then output of the third would be compared and, if necessary, the output of the fourth. The fifth computer ran a completely different implementation of the same specification, in case the primary software had a bug. The fifth machine had been restarted but, due to a bad fix, had a 1 in 67 chance that it would not synchronize with the four primaries. This case occurred. The backup waited for a synch signal that could not be accepted, while the primaries waited for the fifth machine to acknowledge its readiness.

The Kimera project used an advanced application of a voting oracle to verify compliance of several Java Virtual Machines (JVMs) with the Java Language

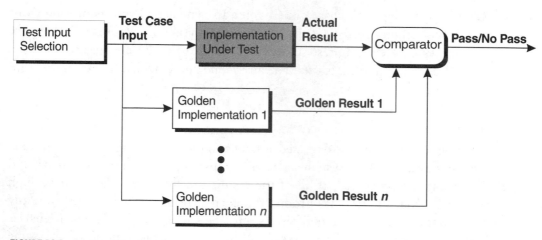

FIGURE 18.9   Voting Oracle.

Specification [Sirer+98]. The test suite was produced by a code generator that produced millions of legal Java classes and test inputs for each generated class. Each class was run on several JVMs and the outputs were compared. This revealed over 100 bugs in the JVMs from Sun, Microsoft, and Netscape and "two dozen weaknesses and deviations from the JVM spec, and ambiguities in the specification."

18.2.5   Organic Oracles

Smoke Test

A smoke test does not require any expected results. Any test case that runs without abnormal termination is considered to have passed. Smoke tests are useful at any scope to establish minimal operability, but they have only limited value.

Some authors argue that white box testing techniques are self-sufficient, implying that the implementation provides a kind of oracle [Smith+92, Kung+93, Kung+94, Parrish+93b, Harrold+94, Siepmann+94]. That is, if the code works for a given test suite, the implementation passes. At best, code-based testing may produce exceptions or outputs that are prima facie evidence of a fault: memory leaks, attempts to use a missing feature, deadlock, livelock, runaway loops, hardware or operating system interrupts (overflow, underflow, divide by zero, and so on), resource allocation errors, or grossly inadequate performance. Aside from these cases, there is no nonsubjective means to decide the correctness of results produced by white box test cases that is not a tautological fallacy.

Built-in Test Oracle

Built-in test refers to assertions and other mechanisms of the IUT that check correctness but do not implement any application responsibilities. An executable class contract (see Chapter 17) can be used to evaluate many relationships of interest. Built-in test is useful at class, cluster, and subsystem scopes. Figure 18.10 shows this configuration.

The Testgraph approach requires that the tester devise and program a state model of the CUT [Hoffman+95]. The model is limited to certain states of interest, but can produce the expected results as each element of a test sequence executes. A specification-based approach is discussed in [Karani 94]. Implementation considerations for a sequence checker are discussed in Runtime Sequence Checking in Chapter 17.

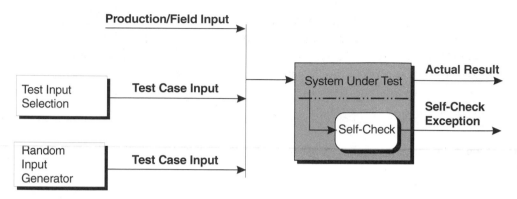

FIGURE 18.10   Built-in test Oracle.

Random selection of test input values has been shown to be effective [Hamlet+90], but a large number of test cases may be required. Although generation of test inputs is usually straightforward, an expected result for each test is still required and presents all the general problems of oracles. Assertions can reduce the need for specific expected results to a certain extent. An assertion can detect out-of-range output and some incorrect, but in-range, inputs. Suppose a method evaluates a function on two parameters and returns a number between 1 and 100. We can easily assert the output interval, but constructing an assertion for all of the relationships between input and output may be difficult. The IUT could produce an incorrect result that would not cause an assertion violation. Thus a large number of test cases could be generated, run, and partially evaluated without having to produce expected results.

Built-in Check Oracle

A built-in check oracle uses an algorithm to generate fields or objects that encode certain IUT relationships. The encoded value is computed before the test run and is typically embedded in a field, data value, or persistent object in the IUT. After the test is run, the same algorithm is used to compute the value on the post-test IUT, which is compared with the pretest encoded value. Different values show that the state of the IUT has changed. The application requirements determine whether a different value or the same value reveals a bug.

The use of redundant information to check for data corruption is a long-standing practice. Identifier numbers (part number, driver's license number, and so on) often include a check digit, which, for example, is obtained by adding the individual numbers of the identifier and appending the least significant digit of this sum to the identifier. Parity checking has long been used to check for memory faults and data-transmission corruption. This requires that at least one checkbit be added to the bit field or bit stream. Data-transmission protocols often include a checksum, which represents the number of bits in a data packet or message.[5] It is common practice in financial systems to add a total record to a batch of transactions. The total record contains the total dollar amount of all transactions in the batch and the number of transactions.

In each case, descriptive data values are added to the basic data, which are assumed to be correct when generated. As the basic data is transmitted or updated, the loss or corruption of a bit, byte, record, or object will cause the basic data and its descriptive values to become inconsistent. A transmission or update is checked by reapplying the same algorithm to the basic data to generate the descriptive data. The newly generated descriptive data is compared with the original descriptive data. An inconsistency shows a bug or data corruption (these schemes are not guaranteed to find all possible kinds of data corruption).

If the data maintained by the SUT can be so described, it may be useful to add the ability to generate a descriptive field or object. Recomputing this value during test evaluation may be simpler and faster than attempting to verify every basic data item. Here, the oracle is the algorithm that generates the descriptive data.

Reversing Oracle

Some computations can be reversed. For example, elementary school students are taught to check a long division answer by comparing the dividend to the product of the quotient and divisor. Similarly, multiplying the result of a square root function by itself should produce a result equal to the original argument, within some limit of precision. Thus no work is needed to produce expected results (test case input values must still be developed). Many transformations cannot be reversed—for example, sorting (the unsorted input can be saved or tagged to support an "undo," but the original order cannot be reconstructed from sorted output alone). Reversible functions are unusual, but when present, should be exploited as oracles. Figure 18.11 shows this configuration.

The relationships of methods in a class may lend themselves to a kind of reversing [Culwin 95]. For example, consider the following code fragment for a Java class Date, which supports date arithmetic for dates between FIRSTDAY

---

5. Algorithms for error-correcting codes and checksums have been extensively studied. Pless provides a quantitative introduction to their design [Pless 98].

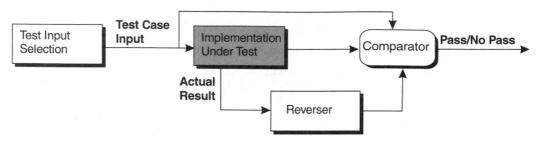

FIGURE 18.11   Reversing Oracle.

and LASTDAY. DAYRANGE is a constant that is to equal the number of days be-tween FIRSTDAY and LASTDAY plus 1.

```
class Date {
    // ...

    Date tomorrow(Date aDay)
          {/* Returns one day after aDay */}

    Date yesterday(Date aDay)
          {/* Returns one before aDay */}

    Date today()
          {/* Returns todays date */}

    Date earlier(Date aDay, int diff)

          {/* Returns the date diff days before aDay /*}

    Date later(Date aDay, int diff)

          {/* Returns the date diff days after aDay /*}

    // ...
}
```

Some required relationships on these methods are reversible. For example, we expect the date one day earlier than one day after today to be today. Assuming d is the object under test, this relationship could be written as

```
assert(d.earlier(later(d.today(),1),1) == d.today());
```

Leaving off the assert syntax and object identifiers for clarity, some addi-tional reversible relationships include the following:

```
earlier( later( today( ),1),1) == today()

tomorrow(earlier(today(),1)) == today()

yesterday(later(today(),1)) == today()

earlier(((today()+1),1) == today()

earlier((FIRSTDAY + DAYRANGE), DAYRANGE) == FIRSTDAY

earlier(LASTDAY, DAYRANGE) + DAYRANGE) == LASTDAY

yesterday(FIRSTDAY) == DateException

tomorrow(LASTDAY) == DateException
```

An advantage of this approach is that no expected results need to be provided, although the relationships must be identified and given a suitable implementation. Research on abstract data type verification has exploited similar relationships [Binder 96i]. The *Different But Equivalent Oracle* also relies on these kinds of relationships.

Executable Specification Oracle

Some research systems have been developed that can take the input and output of the system under test and substitute these values into corresponding parameters of an executable specification. An incorrect output will be rejected by the result checker as inconsistent. Figure 18.12 shows this configuration.

All of these systems verify output at method scope. The test results produced by the CUT are substituted in constraints expressed in a model-based specification [Jia 93]. If the CUT produces results that are within the specified bounds, then the test passes [Korel 96, Peters+98]. This process is similar to using assertions to check input and output, but the specifications and checking are done in a separate system.

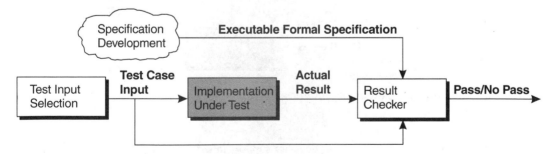

FIGURE 18.12   Executable Specification Oracle.

◆ **Generated Implementation Oracle**

The Specification and Implementation Testing (SITE) system is an automated approach to checking the completeness of abstract data type specifications [Jalote 89, Jalote 92].[6] The purpose of the system is to detect missing "axioms" in an ADT specification. A missing axiom may be due to a coding error or an omission in the problem model represented by the specification. SITE generates an implementation and test cases. The test cases are executed against both the IUT and the generated implementation. If the state of the IUT and the state of the generated implementation are not the same, a bug has been revealed. Figure 18.13 shows this configuration.

SITE uses only syntactic specification elements (the variable definitions and operation signatures, excluding the axioms). It is based on the observation that a complete and consistent set of axioms should not allow the production of an instance (by any sequence of state-changing operations) that cannot be acted on by an accessor operation. If such a state obtains, the specification has been shown to have an omission or inconsistency.

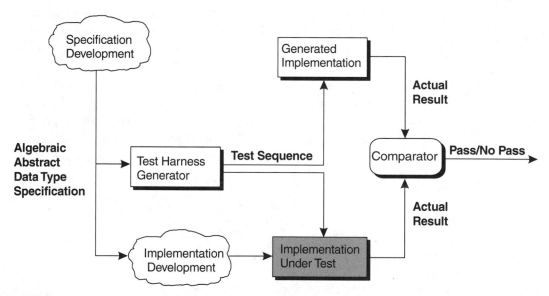

FIGURE 18.13   Generated Implementation Oracle.

---

6. An abstract data type is like a class but does not support inheritance. See [Binder 96i] for an overview of ADTs and related testing strategies.

The strategy is to generate, by simple permutation, sequences of modifiers terminated by an accessor. The number of operations in each sequence is limited to a practically small value. It is argued that test sets composed of short modifier sequences (two or three operations are mentioned) are both computationally feasible and effective for revealing errors. Use of the technique in a classroom setting has demonstrated effectiveness in revealing specification and implementation errors [Jalote 92]. The test case generation algorithm can be summarized as follows:

1. Generate, to a user-selected "depth," all sequences of modifier operations. ("Depth" refers to the number of ADT expressions to be nested in a test case.) A depth of 2 is argued to be practical because most ADT axioms are not more deeply nested, so double nested test cases are sufficient to detect their errors.

2. Permute arguments: substitute external names for inline expansion.

3. Apply each accessor to each member of the set of modifier sequences. Thus 32 test cases are required for 2 accessor operations and 4 modifier operations.

Different But Equivalent Oracle

The ASTOOT (*a Set of Tools for Object-Oriented Testing*) system generates message sequences which should have the same result, but which are different [Doong+94]. For example, we expect an empty stack after repeating the sequence push(i), pop(i) 50 times, and after 50 push(i) followed by 50 pop(i). If an isEqual method is implemented, then no additional oracle is needed for tests whose sequences are different, but the effect should be equivalent. Two instances of the CUT are instantiated (x and y) and placed in the same initial state. Test sequence 1 is sent to x; test sequence 2 is sent to y. Then x is compared to y for equality using the class's isEqual method. If they are not equal, a bug has been revealed. Figure 18.14 shows the configuration. Automation is needed because manual inspection of the state of complex types is slow and difficult. For example, C++ test cases 1 and 2 run a pair of sequences on stack objects sa and sb, which should yield the same result in all four sequences—5 on top with no other items in the stack.

```
// Test case 1

sa = Stack( ); sa.push(5); sa.push(6); sa.pop( );
sb = Stack( ); sa.push(5);
assert (sa == sb);
```

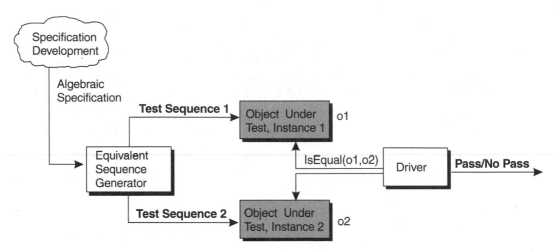

FIGURE 18.14   Different But Equivalent Oracle.

```
// Test case 2

sa = Stack( ); sa.push(5); sa.push(6); sa.pop( ); sa.top( );
sb = Stack( ); sb.top( ); sb.size( );sb.push(5);sb.top( );sb.size( )
assert (sa == sb);
```

Thus the CUT becomes its own oracle. Although there is no need to develop expected results, the expense of finding message-equivalent message sequences must be incurred. The CUT must implement a method that can compare two class instances and determine if they are equivalent (see Section 18.3, Comparators). If functionally equivalent classes have different implementations, it may be difficult to determine equivalence.

The ASTOOT system was used to test two classes written in Eiffel (stack and queue) with known faults. Several thousand test sequences were automatically generated, executed, and evaluated in a few minutes. Experiments were carried out to investigate the effects of variations in sequences: the number of operations from 10 to 100, ranges of data values over three orders of magnitude, and four proportions of add and delete operations. Overall, longer sequences and wider data ranges were reported as being more likely to reveal faults. On average, longer and wider sequences revealed the fault about 50 percent of the time. Shorter, narrower sequences were roughly half as effective.

18.3   Comparators

18.3.1   Introduction

Although evaluating test results by inspection is sometimes necessary, automated comparison is generally the only practical approach. Most of the output from a test run will be correct, so examining page after page of output is difficult for even the most dedicated tester. If the IUT is not designed to support a human–computer interface, the developer will have to examine a trace, analyze a memory dump, or use a debugger to inspect memory. This task is usually even more fatiguing and error-prone than examining a GUI display or report.

Of course, only a small part of the runtime environment is examined for any given test case. We focus on the elements that are directly involved in the IUT. The specific elements to be compared depend on the design of the oracle and a particular test case. They can be instance variables (primitive types and objects), class variables, files, databases, screen captures, event traces, call path traces, system event logs, memory dumps, and so on. The complete context of a test case includes the input, output, pretest and post-test states of the hardware, operating system, system interfaces (e.g., human, sensors, actuators), state of the network, and state of files and databases.

Comparators can be classified into one of three general types: system utilities, smart comparators, and application-specific comparators.

1.   *System utilities.* Expected results and actual results can be written to files. These files can be compared with primitive file comparison utilities like Unix diff. Then, if the actual results file is not the same as the expected results file, we may have found a bug. For example, suppose that we have built a test executable oof that writes a test log to stdout (using C++ <iostream.h>, Ada.streams for Ada 95, and so on). The output of a previous run is found in testOutputFile0.txt. It could be run from a Unix command line such as

```
$ oof < oofTestInputFile.txt > oofTestOutputFile1.txt
$ diff testOutputFile1.txt testOutputFile0.txt
```

These utilities can be invoked from within the Smalltalk environment. The quoted string is passed to the command interpreter interface.

```
[OperatingSystem executeCommand:
'diff testOutputFile1.txt testOutputFile0.txt'] ifTrue "..."
```

Programs like `diff` cannot ignore harmless changes or convert concrete differences for abstract comparison. For example, suppose a time stamp is written to a log file for every run. The value of this field necessarily changes from run to run. A dumb comparator will report that the files are different, which would normally be interpreted as a no pass test run. In fact, we are not interested in this difference. This difficulty can be overcome by editing the actual or expected result file to eliminate the unimportant difference. Although this technique is expedient, a bug in the editing can corrupt the files and lead to spurious test results.

2. *Smart comparators*. A smart comparator provides greater control over the comparison action. For example, the COTS tools File-Aid (Compuware) and DB Tester (Segue) work on a variety of databases. Xdiff (Software Research) works on Unix files. Many of the leading capture/playback tools have a built-in comparator function for the log files they generate. Product offerings change frequently, so some Web searching may be useful to locate a COTS tool that meets your project's requirements.

3. *Application-specific comparators*. Application-specific comparator utilities can be designed and developed to suit any purpose. An application-specific comparator is custom-coded as part of an application-specific driver or as a stand-alone function. Object-oriented programs pose some unique difficulties for production and evaluation of expected results. Comparing objects that represent expected results with the objects under test may require a complex comparator. Method arguments often have a more complex structure than simple character, integer, or floating-point types. Equivalent abstract states may have different concrete states [Meyer 88, Doong+94, Murphy+94, Siepmann+94]. Different objects of the same class may have identical states, so being able to determine object identity in addition to object equivalence is useful [Thielen 92, Davis 94, Siepmann+94]. The balance of this chapter presents considerations for application-specific comparators.

18.3.2   Determining Object Equality

The ability to determine whether two or more objects of the same class are equal is essential for testing. With an equality method, the resultant state of an object under test can be easily compared to an object of the same class that contains the expected value. Without an equality method, we need to develop an inspector/comparator method, code many throwaway `printf` or `cout` statements, or even resort to reading hexadecimal displays of memory produced by a debugger.

Equality methods developed for application purposes may suffice for testing. An example of a straightforward comparator can be found in the JUnit documentation for Java testing. An `equals` method is developed within the test suite cluster for Money objects. The following (including the code) is from [Gamma+98]:

> The `equals` method in `Object` returns true when both objects are the same. However, Money is a value object. Two [Money objects] are considered equal if they have the same currency and value. To test this property we have added a test to verify that Monies are equal when they have the same value but are not the same object. Since `equals` can receive any kind of object as its argument we first have to check its type before we cast it as a Money. As an aside, it is a recommended practice to also override the method `hashCode` whenever you override method `equals`.

```
public boolean equals(Object anObject) {
    if (! anObject instanceof Money)
        return false;
    Money a money= (Money)anObject;
    return aMoney.currency().equals(currency())
        && amount() == aMoney.amount();
}
```

This kind of simple comparator is often sufficient, but suggests how nuances in the determination of equality should be considered before using or developing an equality method to support testing. The programming semantics of the equality operation on primitive arithmetic types is close enough to the mathematical idea of equality so that it is not confusing.[7] The definition of object equality is a result of class-specific requirements and the underlying object model of the implementation language. Table 18.3 summarizes the basic equality operations supported by our six languages. The operations are often overridden with application-specific definitions of equality, as the Junit example shows. With complex classes, the semantics of what is called an equality operation may be fuzzy, rather than strict. A test-worthy equality method should be developed if none exists or available equality methods are inadequate.

The comparator operations implemented in the Tobac tool [Siepmann+94] offer a good list of the responsibilities that an object comparator should

---

7. In mathematics, *equality* expresses an immutable truth about a relationship between variables (see Chapter 8). Equality is defined by two sets whose values are all identical, for example. In programming languages, an equality operator does not make this kind of assertion. It is a command to determine whether two operands are the same (or close enough to being the same) at some point in the execution of a program. I use the software sense of equality here.

TABLE 18.3 Equality and Identity Operators

Language		Content Equality		Object Identity
		Equal	Not Equal	Same
Ada 95		a = b	a /= b	Not supported
C++		a == b	a != b	Application specific
Eiffel		equal(a,b)	a /= b	a = b
Java	Integral types	a == b	a != b	Not supported
	Class instances	Class specific		Object.equals( )
Objective-C		a == b	a != b	Not supported
Smalltalk		a = b		a == b

implement. It should be able to compare any two objects (usually one is the expected result and the other is the actual result) and report the following:

- Objects are equal.
- Objects are identical.
- Objects are equal and identical.
- Objects are partially equal.
- Object is true.
- Object is false.
- Object is nil (i.e., has not been allocated or has been deallocated).

The implementation of these operations must consider deep versus shallow scope, abstract versus concrete state, the effects of aliases and collections, and the effects of type/subtype relationships; it must also define what partial equality means, if applicable. Recent research results demonstrate that the objects exported by the interface of a class are not necessarily sufficient to determine equality [Barbey 97].

18.3.3 Deep and Shallow Equality

In contrast to primitive types composed of data structures based on available hardware (integer, floating point, byte, and so on), object instance variables are typically complex composites of fields and references. A **field** is self-contained; it does not refer to other objects. It may be a primitive, built-in, or user-defined type. A **reference** is a pointer to another object.

Object assignment and copy semantics are different for each programming language, and there are often additional differences among translators of the same language. For example, the Smalltalk assignment method (part of the protocol of `Object`) simply establishes a reference. The expression `target:=source` means "make the object `target` refer to the same object as `source`." The default behavior of the C++ assignment operator is to copy the target object to the source object, but this behavior is typically overridden by application classes. A pointer to the source object may also be created and copied.

The design of an oracle and a comparator often requires saving the state of an object for later analysis. This operation is straightforward with primitive types, files, and databases. It is not so with objects. The structure of the object may be determined at runtime. The copy operation can be nontrivial. Three kinds of copy operations are used:

- *Bitwise copy.* This operation transfers the bit values from the storage allocated for the source variable to the destination variable.
- *Shallow copy.* This operation produces an object that points to the same fields and references as the copied object. The reference variables in the source and target objects are set to the same pointer values, but referenced objects are not copied. Aliases result from shallow copy methods when several different objects point to the same referent.
- *Deep copy.* This operation results in a new target object whose content is identical to the source object. The objects have different identities. The fields and reference structures are the same, but there are pointers to new objects with copied values (new storage is allocated for an identical set of reference variables and the content is copied). Deep copy traverses the entire pointer structure of the source object and creates an exact copy of the structure anchored in the target object. Side effects of this type of operation typically include allocation and initialization if the target object does not exist, and production of garbage when references to other objects are dropped.

Figure 18.15 shows the general semantics of bitwise copy, shallow copy, and deep copy. Each language provides different support for these operations, as follows.

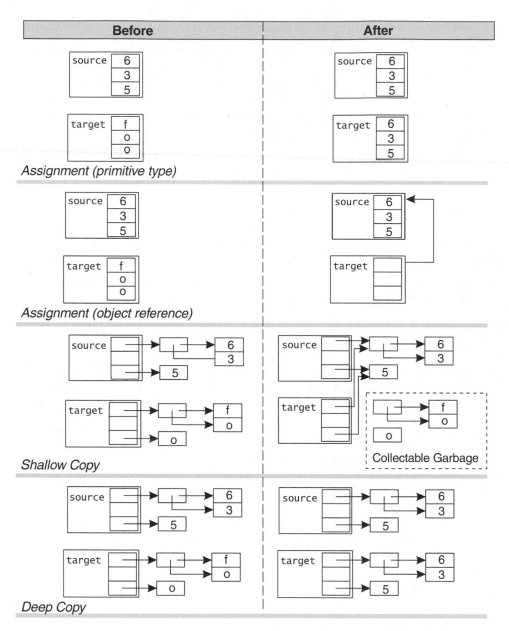

FIGURE 18.15   Assignment and copy semantics.

- In Ada 95, the `Adjust` procedure for `controlled` types can be overridden to implement deep or shallow copy. `Adjust` is called automatically after any assignment to an object of a controlled type.

- A C++ implementation for shallow copy and deep copy is presented in [Stroustroup 92a], and considerations for design and reusability are considered in [Carroll 95].

- All Eiffel classes inherit the functions `clone` (a shallow copy), `deep-clone` (a deep copy), and corresponding `equal` and `deep-equal` functions.

- A `clone` method is defined for the Java `Object` class, and developers are encouraged to implement a `clone` for their classes. The `clone` method for Java Developer Kit collection classes is a shallow copy.

- In Smalltalk, the `Object` methods `shallowCopy` and `deepCopy`[8] are used to create objects that share referents or create new, separate referents.

These variations on copy semantics imply corresponding variations in the evaluation of equality. For example, equality could be defined with respect to referents (pointers), so that two objects with identical dereferenced content but different referents (the result of a deep copy) would compare `notEqual`. Equality could also be defined with respect to dereferenced content and would evaluate the same objects as `Equal`. Several flavors of equality are possible:

- Abstract equality. The public state is the same.
- Alias equality. The symbols refer to (point to) the same object.
- Field equality. The content of fields is equivalent.
- Reference equality. The referents are the same.
- Deep equality. The pointer structure is the same and the dereferenced contents of the objects are the same.
- Supertype/subtype equality. The content of supertype variables is the same in subtype or supertype instances.

One can imagine situations where all flavors of equality would be true and other situations where only some would be satisfied. In using or developing an

---

8. The `deepCopy` method was removed from ParcPlace Smalltalk 4.1 because of frequent problems with cyclic dependencies. The Visual Age and Visual Works Smalltalk `deepCopy` uses `shallowCopy` at the second level (i.e., references are not expanded beyond two pointer links) for similar reasons.

equality method for testing, one must select the equality appropriate to the testing goals and take care not to mix incompatible flavors. Besides selecting the appropriate equality semantics, other considerations apply.

- It is important to verify that the object identifiers are established correctly. The identifiers of the original and copied objects should be different. A deep copy or clone operation should return a new object, not just a pointer to the original object [Barbey 97].
- If an equality method uses other class methods, a buggy or incorrectly used method could result in a false equality report or an undesirable side effect.
- Strict equality may be irrelevant for some content (e.g., audio and video streams).
- The equality operation should not have any side effects. The abstract and concrete states of the objects should be unchanged after being evaluated for equality.

18.3.4   Abstract Content Versus Concrete Content

The abstract content of two objects of the same class is equal if and only if they cannot be distinguished using only the public methods of the class [Freedman 91]. The content of an object is the current value of each of its instance variables; a state is a set of such values. Abstract content can be determined with the public methods of a class, provided that these methods are correct, free of side effects, and do not omit or obscure any significant part of the abstract state. Equality of abstract content is limited to the operations that can be performed with public methods. Nevertheless, objects that have the same abstract content may have different concrete content.

- Consider r1 and r2, which are objects of class Ratio. Ratio is implemented with two integers for its arguments and a double word floating point that contains the dividend of the arguments. Suppose r1 contains {5, 4, +8.0E-1} and r2 contains {100, 80, +7.99999999999E-1}. Are these objects equal?
- Consider two objects of class Account, acct1234 and acct4567. Both have a balance of $1000.00. The object acct1234 has been instantiated to compute a result that is not yet committed to persistent storage; acct4567 has been refreshed from a persistent store and contains infor-

mation necessary to recommit the object to the persistent store. The abstract states are equal, but the concrete state is quite different. Are these objects equal?

- Suppose we are comparing objects that can represent both English and metric units. Does 1 inch = 2.54 cm? 2.540 cm? 2.545 cm? Does 11.9999 inches = 1 foot? Does 28.5 inches = 2 feet, 4.5 inches?

These kinds of differences in abstract and concrete content are common and have implications for testing. First, implementers should carefully consider the semantics and implementation of equality methods. Second, testers should understand just what "equals" means for a particular equality method and decide if it is appropriate for testing. Third, low-level bitwise comparison of the memory allocated to objects typically does not produce meaningful results. The same code, run with the same inputs but under different system loads, may be loaded differently. Even with an identical level of system utilization, if any operating system service is upgraded or changed or the main processor configuration is changed, a low-level comparison will often be meaningless.

18.3.5   Aliases

Every object has a unique identity. In effect, the identity of an object is its memory address, or whatever a particular language uses as a proxy for an address. So, even if two objects of the same class have the same name and hold identical dereferenced values, they have different identities. The Smalltalk message == ("is identical") answers true when two objects are aliases. For example, the message x == y answers true when immediately preceded by x:= y. The Object message = ("is equal") has the same behavior as == but is typically overridden to support subclass semantics. Smalltalk objects may be equal without being identical, but must be equal if they are identical.[9]

18.3.6   Collections

Table 18.4 provides a decision table for comparing collections. In only the last two cases is it necessary to iterate through the elements. Collections compared at deep and shallow levels may produce different results for the reasons noted

---

9. Although it is common Smalltalk practice to override =(isEqual), the object methods == (isIdentical) and ~~ (isNotIdentical) should not be overriden. When = is overriden, a hash method is typically implemented [Skublics 96].

TABLE 18.4   Decision Table for Collection Equality

Object Identity	Class	Number of Elements	Element Content	Result
Same	DC	DC	DC	Equal
Not same	Not same	DC	DC	Not equal
Not same	Same	Not same	DC	Not equal
Not same	Same	Same	Not same	Not equal
Not same	Same	Same	Same	Equal

DC = don't care

earlier. In the worst case, checking for deep equality requires iterating through both collections, comparing pairs of elements.

Clearly, the sequence in which the elements are produced is critical. Not all collection iterator methods are deterministic. A nondeterministic iterator does not guarantee that it will produce members of a collection in the same order for all invocations of the iterator. The output of nondeterministic iterators cannot be directly compared for equality. Instead, the entire collection must be produced from each instance and then ordered according to some reliable criteria (e.g., sorted by key or size). The ordered collections may then be compared member for member.

The members of a collection may point to themselves. If this kind of structure is allowed, some iteration in a deep equality computation may be avoided by keeping a separate collection of member identifiers with a flag to show that a member has been already evaluated.

The Smalltalk = method is not implemented for the collection classes of some leading environments. This probably reflects the fact that a complete comparison of all elements has a high cost in CPU cycles and that simple object identity often suffices.

18.3.7   Type/Subtype Equality

Suppose SavingsAccount is a subclass of Account, and SavingsAccount defines additional instance variables. An equality method is implemented in both Account and SavingsAccount. In C++ and Smalltalk, an equality message will be bound to the class on the left side of the equality operator. So, with objects SavingsAccount and Account, the expressions

```
Account = SavingsAccount            "Smalltalk"

Account == SavingsAccount           // C++
```

will return `true` when the superclass instance variables are equal. The superclass equality method is used in this expression and examines only the superclass variables. Even when `Account` and `SavingsAccount` are in a state that
returns `true` for the preceding statements, however, swapping the operands

```
SavingsAccount = Account            "Smalltalk"

SavingsAccount == Account           // C++
```

may result in a `false` response—that is, the objects are considered not equal.
When the subclass instance is on the left, the subclass equality method is bound
to the expression.

When a superclass object is compared with a subclass object, the absence of
subclass variables may or may not be interpreted as an unequal condition.
Thus, even if the contents of superclass instance variables are the same, a comparison may report they are not equal. This approach may or may not make
sense for a particular class. Suppose `CertificateOfDeposit` is a subclass of
`SavingsAccount` and each overloads ==. Client usage like

```
void foo(Account &acct1, Account &acct2) {

    if ( acct1 == acct2 ) {
        // equal message sent to acct1, acct2 is argument
        // ...
    }
}
```

must be expected, so any combination of base and derived objects may be presented for comparison. The implementations of == should provide a correct response in all cases. In such a hierarchy, the subclass equality operator should
check only subclass instance variables and then send a message to the superclass
to check its variables. With a three-level hierarchy, there are nine possible combinations:

```
Account == Account
Account == SavingsAccount
Account == CertificateOfDeposit
SavingsAccount == Account
```

```
SavingsAccount == SavingsAccount
SavingsAccount == CertificateOfDeposit
CertificateOfDeposit == Account
CertificateOfDeposit == SavingsAccount
CertificateOfDeposit == CertificateOfDeposit
```

In C++ Run Time Type Identification (RTTI) capability is useful in this situation. The static type of a C++ object pointer is determined by the class of the pointer declaration. At runtime, a base class pointer may point to a derived class object. The dynamic type of a pointer designates the current derived class. RTTI can return the current dynamic type to the == function, which can decide whether a legal pair of types is present.

In Java, the informational methods in the reflection package can be used. Ada provides similar methods to return information about type tags. OpenStep Objective-C supports type introspection. For example, the NSObject method isMemberOfClass will evaluate as *true* if anObject is an instance of someClass. Similarly isKindOfClass will evaluate as *true* if anObject inherits from or is a member of someClass.

```
if ( [anObject isMemberClass:someClass] ) { /* ... */ };
if ( [anObject isKindOfClass:someClass] ) { /* ... */ };
```

18.3.8   Partial Equality Methods

If you define an operator that only partially compares two objects, do not name it isEqual or overload ==. Instead, use a name that clearly defines the limited comparison. For example, suppose we wish to compare objects of the class Package in a system that tracks shipments. An actual package can never be "equal" to another package, even if they happen to have the same size, weight, sender, and destination—the packages are distinct and separate items. However, we will probably want to determine whether two packages have the same weight, sameShipDate, sameShipper, and so on. If historical analysis is to be supported (was the package that was in the warehouse three days ago the same one that is on the truck today?), a samePackage operation may be needed.

18.4   Bibliographic Notes

Relatively little has been written about the oracle problem. Howden suggested the term "test oracle" [Howden 78]. Weyuker discussed the limits of oracles

[Weyuker 82]. Development of specification-based oracles is considered in [Richardson 92]. Barbey's strategy for object-oriented testing uses a formal specification that also serves as an oracle [Barbey 97]. This approach draws on similar techniques developed for verification of abstract data types, which also use the ADT specification as an oracle [Bernot+91], [Dauchy+92]. A survey of these techniques appears in [Binder 96i].

Poston lists four kinds of oracles: range checking (similar to assertions), manual projection (prespecification), simulation, and reference testing. Reference testing is the process of judging the actual results and then saving acceptable results to support regression testing [Poston 94]. Beizer suggests using a simple language (e.g., Basic) to program a reduced implementation to generate expected results [Beizer 95]. Hoffman's oracle taxonomy and discussion of approximation, statistical (parametric), and embedded (built-in check) oracles provides practical insights [Hoffman 99].

Chapter 19   Test Harness Design

Overview

This chapter presents patterns to develop the components of a test harness: test cases, test suites, stubs, test drivers, and test control systems. Three test framework patterns are presented.

19.1   How to Develop a Test Harness

A **test harness** is a system that supports effective and repeatable automated testing. The IUT may be a single class, a cluster, a subsystem, or an entire application system. A test harness is the central part of a test environment; related components of a test environment are discussed in the case study in the Appendix. The test harness is the system that starts the IUT, sends test messages to it, and then evaluates test pass/no pass results. It may be implemented in several ways.

- *No harness.* The IUT is run in situ with inputs supplied by simulating actual usage. For example, a tester enters order transactions using a GUI interface; an embedded engine control system is placed in a vehicle and the engine is run. The inputs are supplied and evaluated according to a test plan, but no software other than the application system and its platform is used. The quality and quantity of testing are necessarily limited, and regression testing is nearly impossible.

- *Debugger.* Debuggers can be used as test drivers. It is easy to set or view anything in the IUT, including an encapsulated state. Trace code (`printf`, cout) or special accessor methods are not needed. It may be easier to generate a stack trace, examine the contents of control blocks, and so on. Most debuggers have good integration with source code editors and browsers. I have found it useful to link test scripts and debuggers so that when a test does not pass, the debugger is automatically started. This ability is useful for initial unit scope testing and is disabled for later test runs. A debugger is not a test harness, however. The kind and quantity of testing it can support are limited and it almost certainly will not support automated regression testing.

• *COTS tools.* This chapter presents design patterns for application-specific test tools and does not discuss COTS tools. There is no single COTS product that offers all of the capabilities discussed here. However, COTS tools do provide some of these features—and many more that are better bought than made. The Appendix presents a case study that describes how a test harness was developed using COTS tools.

• *COTS/application-specific tool suite.* It is hard to imagine how any software system could be tested without writing at least some application-specific testware. This chapter will help you to design an effective test harness.

A test harness is software just like an application system. As in any software design problem, you must define reasonable goals, identify requirements, and consider trade-offs among cost, capabilities, and time. You will probably use a combination of COTS tools and application-specific tools. The application-specific tool patterns that follow can help you develop requirements for your test environment. Use this model to evaluate COTS tools to decide what to buy and what to make. Useful guidance is offered in IEEE standards 1062, *Recommended Practice for Software Acquisition,* and 1209, *Recommended Practice for the Evaluation and Selection of CASE Tools.* With hard work and a liberal tool budget, you can achieve an effective, feature-rich test harness by integrating COTS tools and developing application-specific drivers.

Although this chapter necessarily covers a wide range of test harness capabilities, you should not conclude that your test environment must have every one. Start with a small and simple test automation system that meets your immediate needs and learn from it. Add COTS tools and develop your own tools in accordance with your priorities and budget.

1. Choose an integration and regression testing approach first (see Chapter 13, Integration, and Chapter 15, Regression). Your integration strategy

is the main factor in determining what kind of drivers you'll need and how much stubbing is necessary. Your regression testing goals must be supported.

2. Choose a test harness framework. The ***Incremental Testing Framework*** is a good place to start.

3. Choose a test case generation approach. All of the test design patterns in this book can be generated manually. Some can also be generated automatically. Automated test generation is an advanced topic not discussed in this book. If you will be using automated input generators, your test drivers must be designed to accept these inputs. If you are developing tests by hand and then coding drivers and test cases, you don't need to consider this issue.

4. Design interfaces to the oracles, if any. For example, you may be able to use an existing system as an oracle. Identify interface, conversion, and synchronization requirements and design your test harness accordingly.

5 Try a simple driver on a simple component. Use iterative and incremental development to identify problems and special requirements (there are usually quite a few) and to get to a stable test environment in the shortest time. Plan your next increment, develop it, and then stabilize the system.

6. Integrate COTS tools to support your framework. COTS tools typically require time to set up, learn, and get up to speed in a particular environment. Try to avoid a big bang integration. Instead, add one or two tools at a time.

19.1.1 Requirements

Table 19.1 describes some scenarios for test harnesses. The combinations are suggestive (but not exhaustive) and indicate that no single solution exists for every test automation requirement. Some COTS tools are available that will generate a significant proportion of your testware code. These tools are typically not cheap and can be difficult to use, but they reduce the cost and effort of testware development. In a pinch, a debugger can be used as a driver for API-level testing. If the cost of drivers appears too high, consider ***Top-down Integration***. This strategy reduces the number of drivers that need to be developed (but does require many stubs).

TABLE 19.1 Some Common Test Harness Architectures

Driver Type	Typical IUT Scope	Test Driver	Test Case Implementation	Tester's Interface to IUT	Expected Results Implementation	Comparator
API	Class, Class Cluster	TestClass Implementation	Test Case Method	Message	Golden Object, Hard-coded Value	Assertions
			Test Case Object	Message	Golden Object	Pass( ) Method
Console	Class Test Package, Build Group, Process Group	Scripting Language	Command-Line Bundle	Parameters	Parameters, File	Judge
				Parameters	Parameters, File	File Comparator
			File	File	File	File Comparator
			Embedded	API	API	API
GUI Playback	Transaction Processing System	GUI Capture/ Playback	Bitmap Script	x, y coordinates	Captured GUI	Bit String Compare
			Widget Script	Widget Parameters, Script Parameters	Script-specific	Script Services
In Situ, Controlled	Transaction Processing System	User Interface	Manual Procedure	Application-specific	Subjective/ Manual	Judging
	Transformational or Reactive System	GUI Capture/ Playback	Input Multiplexing (parallel runs)	Application-specific	Application-specific	Output Comparator
	Reactive System	Test Control System	Test Control System	Party Line	Application-specific	Output Comparator
In Situ, Uncontrolled	NA	NA	Ad hoc	Application Interface	Subjective	Judging

A harness provides some (and, ideally, all) of the following capabilities:

- Test case/test suite implementation
- Test environment/test case initialization including the IUT, objects in its namespace, and its virtual machine
- Stub generation/stub build control
- Test coverage instrumentation
- The interface to the IUT by which test messages may be sent
- Test execution control
- Automated comparator
- Result logging
- Trace analysis and coverage analysis

A harness may also support related capabilities:

- Automated test input generation
- Extraction or copying input of a stream from an existing system
- Automated production of expected results (an oracle)
- Use of an existing system as an oracle
- Target environment simulator
- Debug support and integrated debugging
- Runtime override of exception handling and exception generation
- Execution time-interval instrumentation
- Resource utilization instrumentation
- Restart, recovery, and selective bypass of failed test cases
- Regression test support: selection of a test suite subset and creation of the necessary test configuration
- Interfaces to upper and lower CASE tools, defect tracking, and project management tools
- Integrated test documentation: plans, test runs, logs, results, metrics analysis, and status reports

A test harness for object-oriented software must deal with several unique problems. It is often difficult to control the pretest state of the IUT. The instance variables of the IUT are encapsulated and often composed of still more uncontrollable objects. The interface of the IUT is typically insufficient for testing purposes. It is good programming practice to encapsulate instance variables, so a test harness must provide other ways to achieve the necessary control. Although existing IUT methods can be used to control state, they often do not provide all access needed and can produce spurious test results if they are buggy. They may not even exist, if their development has been deferred to a later increment or they are part of an abstract class. The same problems occur in setting the test state of message parameter objects. Observing the post-test state of the IUT is often difficult, for the same reasons that controlling the pretest state is difficult.

19.1.2 Architecture

Design presents patterns for developing a test harness are grouped by the main components of a test harness. Each pattern provides answers to the basic design problem for that component.

- *Test cases:* How should test messages be implemented?
- *Test control:* How should the servers of the IUT and its environment be controlled and observed?
- *Test drivers:* How should test code be organized so that it is modular, has a meaningful correspondence to the IUT, and achieves reuse where possible? How can drivers support controllability and observability?
- *Test framework:* How should test cases, test suites, drivers, and a tester interface be organized for an entire application system?

These patterns range from simple to advanced, and can be combined in many ways. Figure 19.1 shows the overall relationship of these components.

19.2 Test Case Patterns

19.2.1 Considerations

The implementation of a test case achieves the necessary pretest state, sends a message to the IUT and evaluates results as pass or no pass. It contains a complete, execution-ready representation of the pretest conditions, the test messages, and expected results. A test case has four main steps: set up, execute, evaluate, and clean up.

1. *Set up*. The test case implementation must set the state of the IUT, the application server objects of the IUT, and the runtime environment as required

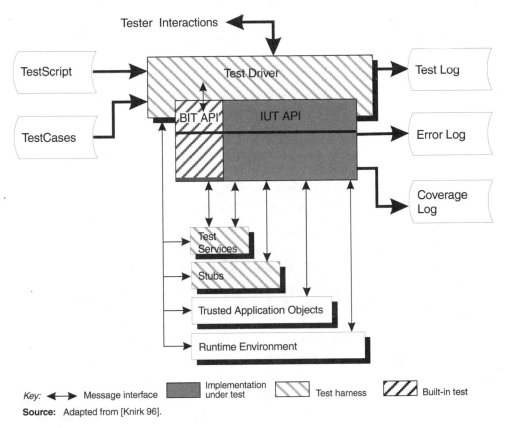

FIGURE 19.1 Test harness architecture.

by the test case. The environment includes system resources required to run the test, possibly on remote computers. For example, a setup includes sending messages to stubs or proxies; sending messages to objects or variables that are parameters in the messages sent to the IUT; loading files, databases, or memory images that are accessed by the IUT; establishing a network connection to a remote object or ORB; or waiting to lock a resource that must be exclusively controlled by the OUT.

If several test cases need the same setup, the setup code should be factored out and implemented as a separate method. The test case implementation must define all variables used in the interface of the IUT and set their initial values.

2. *Execute.* The test case implementation must set values required by the test case. Then, the test message is sent to the IUT.

3.   *Evaluate.* The test case implementation must compare actual results with the expected results: the values returned from the IUT, messages sent to servers of the IUT, exceptions thrown by the IUT, the state of the IUT, and the state of environment. The results are displayed and/or logged.

4.   *Clean up.* Resources are released, deallocated, or restored as needed. Post-test cleanup is performed for two reasons. First, restoring the environment of the IUT to a nominal post-test state increases the range over which the test case can be reused. Of course, if succesor tests depend on the state achieved by a test case no cleanup is needed. Second, unreleased resources could cause a failure of a test run due to insufficient memory or related performance degradation. The specific actions depend on the test design, but typically include the following:

- Closing open network connections, files, or databases
- Committing (or canceling) an open transaction
- Deallocating memory (garage collection)
- Writing a log record
- Resetting counters
- Deleting or removing elements of a collection entered for a test
- Clearing or unloading buffers, stacks, undo history, and so on

In a simple test design, these four steps occur in sequence. If the test design has many steps (**Nonmodal Class Test**), these steps must be interleaved to support the test design.

A test case is the basic unit of work in testing. A **test suite** is a collection of test case sequences that serve a particular testing goal for a particular version of an IUT. A whole–part relationship exists among test cases. A **test log** contains the results of an execution of a test suite.

The simplest possible test case implementation is to hard-code test messages for an API in a driver class. But this approach is hardly good design. Objectification is a good thing because test cases can be more readily inherited and the test protocol can be standardized. Some test capabilities can be reused. Test cases (as objects) can be factored out of the driver and packaged with the class under test. For example, a test suite can be packaged as a collection of test objects and implemented as a class variable. In this way, only one instance of each test object is brought into memory and access can be controlled. If the test object interfaces are designed with a general-purpose driver, a high degree of built-in testing and test efficiency can be obtained.

This section presents several patterns for test case implementation that may be used on a stand-alone basis or as components of a testing framework.

- *Test Case/Suite Method*. Implement each test case as a method or collect several test cases into a test suite. Implement the test suite as a method that activates individual test cases.
- *Test Case/Suite Class*. Implement each test case or test suite as a subclass of an abstract class `TestCase`.
- *Catch All Exceptions*. Include general and specific exception handlers in the test case to verify the IUT's exception handling.

Test Case/Test Suite Method

Intent

Implement an API scope test case as a method of a driver class.

Also Known As

In the *Test Case as Operation* [Firesmith 96] and *Create a Parallel Test Component for Each Production Component* [McGregor+96] patterns, one test case is implemented with one method. The *Test Script as Operation* [Firesmith 96] and *Sequence Test Cases Using Test Scripts* [McGregor+96] patterns show how several related test cases (a test suite) may be implemented with one method.

Motivation

The implementation of a test case must set up, execute, evaluate, and clean up. These steps typically require sending several messages, function calls, remote procedure calls, and so on, to the IUT and elements of its environment. The test design may call for a sequence that is lengthy, repetitive, or determined by a nontrivial algorithm. The test case must be implemented in a language that can access the interface of the IUT and that has sufficient to achieve this test design. The obvious solution is to use the same language as the IUT.

Some versions of this pattern distinguish between methods that implement one or several test cases per method. This distinction is arbitrary, and it often makes sense to bundle several related test cases in a single method.

Applicability

The Test Case/Test Suite Method pattern is useful at class and cluster scope for unit and integration testing when you are developing a driver to exercise a class, a class cluster, or other component that will be tested using its API.

This pattern is a straightforward approach to test case implementation. It is indicated when expediency is a dominant concern. It has disadvantages that diminish its attractiveness when reusability, maintainability, and support for the full range of testing activities are important.

Participants

The components of this pattern are as follows:

- The test case method. It is a member of a test driver class.
- The object under test. It may be defined as a local variable of the method, or as an instance variable of the class that implements the test case method, or it may be passed into the test case method.
- The application environment of the class under test. The test case method may need to send messages or make calls to achieve the necessary pretest state.
- The runtime environment of the class under test. The test case method may need to send messages or make calls to achieve the necessary pretest state.

Figure 19.2 depicts the structure of these components.

Collaborations

A test case method sends messages that achieve the four steps: set up, execute, evaluate, and clean up. A test suite method simply calls other test methods in the desired sequence.

Implementation

A simple test case for the `Triangle` class (Chapter 1) is illustrated in the following code fragments. `CUT` is the class under test, `out` is the object under test, which is an instance of `CUT`, following the *Percolate the Object Under Test* pattern. A local or class scope instance could also be used.

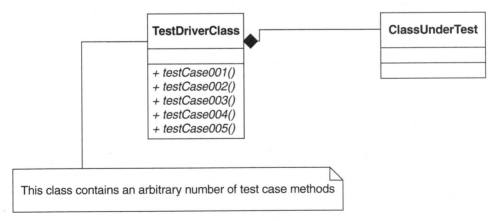

FIGURE 19.2   Structure of Test Case/Test Suite Method pattern.

Make each test case's setup explicit. Avoid assumed values or reusing values established by the last test. This approach makes test cases more reliable, portable, modifiable, and easier to debug. Common setup and cleanup actions can be factored out and implemented as separate methods.

Ada 95

```
procedure Test001 (out: CUT) is
begin
  -- setup scalene triangle, check type
  out.new_line(5,1,5,4)
  out.new_line(1,1,5,1)
  out.new_line(1,1,5,4)
  if(             out.is_scalene and
    not   out.is_isoceles and
    not   out.is_equilateral)
  then
    put_Line ("Test001 Passes");
  else
    put_Line ("Test001 Did Not Pass");
  end if;
end Test001;
```

C++

```
bool test001(CUT out) {
  // Setup scalene triangle, check type
  out.new_line(5,1,5,4);
  out.new_line(1,1,5,1);
  out.new_line(1,1,5,4);
  if (    out.is_scalene() &&
          !out.is_isoceles() &&
          !out.is_equilateral()
  )
      cout << "Test001 Passes"<< endl;
  else
      cout << "Test001 Did Not Pass"<< endl;
}
```

Eiffel

```
feature
test001(out:CUT):BOOLEAN is
  -- Setup scalene triangle, check type
  out.new_line(5,1,5,4)
  out.new_line(1,1,5,1)
  out.new_line(1,1,5,4)
  if(     out.is_scalene and
    not   out.is_isoceles and
    not   out.is_equilateral)
```

```
            then
               io.put_string("Test001 Passes:%N")
            else
               io.put_string("Test001 Did Not Pass:%N")
            end -- if
         end -- test001
```

Java

```
    bool test001(CUT out) {
       // Setup scalene triangle, check type
       out.new_line(5,1,5,4);
       out.new_line(1,1,5,1);
       out.new_line(1,1,5,4);
       if (    out.is_scalene()      &&
               !out.is_isoceles()    &&
               !out.is_equilateral()
       )
          cout << "Test001 Passes";
       else
          cout << "Test001 Did Not Pass";
    }
```

Objective-C

```
    -- (BOOL)test001:(CUT)out {
       // Setup scalene triangle, check type
       [out new_line:5:1:5:4];
       [out new_line:1:1:5:1];
       [out new_line:1:1:5:4];
       if (    [out is_scalene ]     &&   .
               ![out is_isoceles]    &&
               ![out is_equilateral]
       )
          printf "Test001 Passes"\n;
       else
          printf "Test001 Did Not Pass"\n;
    }
```

Smalltalk

```
    test001: out
       "Setup scalene triangle, check type"
       |"local vars?"|
       out new_line: 5,1,5,4
       out new_line: 1,1,5,1
       out new_line: 1,1,5,4
       ( out :is_scalene && (out : ! is_isoceles  &&
               out : !is_equilateral
       )
       ifTrue :[ console : 'Test001 Passes']
       ifFalse : [ console : 'Test001 Did Not Pass']
```

Consequences

Test Case/Test Suite Method has several advantages.

- The implementation is simple and easy to code. No additional framework or helper classes are required.
- It may be used with any kind of API driver class, and it may be inherited and overridden.
- Direct, traceable correspondence of a method to a test case is established, as methods are written in one-to-one correspondence to test cases.
- The full power of the implementation language can be used to automate all aspects of test execution.

The pattern's disadvantages include the following:

- Source code is not a good medium for test documentation. All noncode test design information must be entered as code comments. These comments are typically terse and hard to extract, and they often become inconsistent with the actual test case as the test suite evolves.
- The test code is susceptible to the same problems as application code: hazard of bugs, low maintainability, low portability, and so on.
- The pattern requires programmer skills to design, develop, debug, and maintain.
- The focus is necessarily at a low level of abstraction. A test designer may focus on simple method scope testing to the exclusion of class scope integration. Tests of class scope responsibilities and dependencies can be deemphasized, especially if the class hierarchy has been refactored to meet performance goals.

Reflecting on the test cases as methods used for the IC-Pack 201 library, Cox observes, "The right part was that the `TestTools` developers built what amounts to a database of individual procedures for testing some aspect of a class's behavior in a procedural notation that could be applied directly to the implementation under test. The wrong parts were (a) the determination of which tests should be applied to which classes was solely based on an implementation matter; and (b) it left the specification implicit in the code, rather than capturing it explicitly" [Cox 88, 47].

Known Uses

Nearly every report on API-level testing of object-oriented code uses methods to implement test cases [Cox 88, Love 92, Beck 94, Murphy+94, Weir 95, Firesmith 96, Gamma+98].

Related Patterns

See *Test Case/Test Suite Class*. An arbitrarily large hierarchy of test cases (test suites) can be implemented with the *Composite* pattern [Gamma+95]. Common execution control and reporting can be developed for any test suite (a "whole") and its subordinate test suites and test cases ("parts").

Test Case/Test Suite Class

Intent

Implement test cases or test suites as objects of class `TestCase`.

Also Known As

Test Case as Object [Firesmith 96], *Test Script as Object* [Firesmith 96].

Motivation

The complete definition of a test case [IEEE 829] implies more responsibilities than just the execution of a four-step test sequence.

- Documentation of the test design
- The association of a test case with test runs and versions of the IUT
- Traceability to requirements, detail design, user documentation, and change orders
- Dependencies on other test cases
- Special setup or cleanup instructions

Implementing these capabilities in each test method would be redundant. In addition, implementing a test case as a method statically binds the tests to their driver class. They cannot be factored out and used independently. Implementing test cases as instances of class `TestCase` resolves these problems.

Applicability

This pattern is useful at class and cluster scopes for unit and integration testing: developing a driver to exercise a class, a class cluster, or other component that will be tested using its API. It supports systematic test automation. It is indicated when reusability, maintainability, and support of the full range of testing activities are important.

Participants

The components of Test Case/Test Suite Class are as follows:

- `TestCase`, an abstract superclass that provides a common interface to test case objects and test services.
- `SomeTestCase`, a subclass of `TestCase`. There will be one subclass for each test case.
- The object under test.
- A driver class that declares an instance of `SomeTestCase`.

Figure 19.3 depicts the structure of these components.

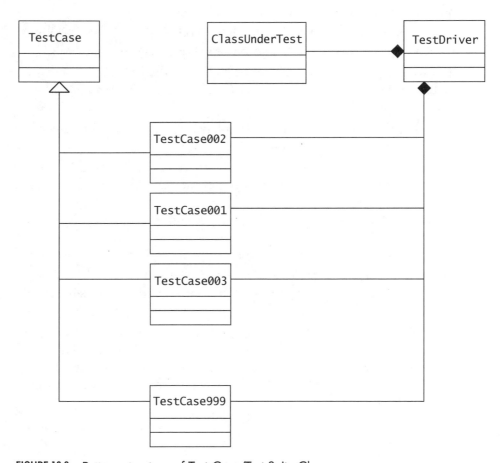

FIGURE 19.3 Pattern structure of Test Case/Test Suite Class.

Collaborations and Implementations

TestCase objects may be used in many patterns. The essence of the Test Case/ Test Suite Class pattern is to locate the test implementation in a method of a subclass of the abstract class TestCase. The considerations discussed in *Test Case/Test Suite Method* apply.

Consequences

The advantages of Test Case/Test Suite Class include the following:

- Traceability and related information are easily represented and may be automatically updated as tests are run and rerun.
- Direct, traceable correspondence of a method to a test case is possible, if each object is written in one-to-one correspondence to test cases.
- Test case subclasses can be inherited and overridden to support symmetric drivers. Compared with *Test Case/Test Suite Method*, however, another level of indirection is added.
- The full power of the implementation language can be used to automate all aspects of test execution.
- The implementation of test cases as objects is a good fit with the architecture of extensible testing frameworks.

The pattern's disadvantages include the following:

- The test code is susceptible to the same problems as application code: the hazard of bugs, low maintainability, low portability, and so on.
- This pattern requires programmer skills to design, develop, debug, and maintain.
- The focus is necessarily at a low level of abstraction and can erode the primacy of responsibility-based test design. Testing based on class scope integration hazards and responsibility-based requirements may be neglected when, for example, the hierarchy is refactored to meet performance goals, but the original tests continue to pass.

Known Uses

The objectification of test cases is discussed in several sources [Seipmann+94, Beck 94, Firesmith 96, Gamma+98].

Related Patterns

An arbitrarily large hierarchy of test cases (test suites) can be implemented with the *Composite* pattern [Gamma+95]. Common execution control and reporting can be developed for any test suite (a "whole") and its subordinate test suites and test case cases ("parts") See ***Incremental Testing Framework*** for an effective use of test case objects.

Catch All Exceptions

Intent

Provide the ability to catch and evaluate all exceptions thrown by the implementation under test.

Motivation

If the CUT throws exceptions, the driver must catch exceptions in each test. If the driver does not catch the exceptions, the exceptions cannot be evaluated. The IUT can fail with respect to an exception in four ways:

- It throws an exception when it should not.
- It throws an incorrect exception.
- It fails to throw an exception when it should.
- It fails to catch an exception thrown by one of its servers.

The test case must catch all exceptions to reveal these bugs, if they exist. If the test case does not, some exception bugs will be missed.

Applicability

This pattern is useful at class and cluster scopes for unit and integration testing. It should be considered when developing a driver to exercise a class, a class cluster, or other component that can throw exceptions as part of its contract.

Participants

The two participants are the test case method with the catch block and the IUT.

Collaborations

Test messages are sent to the IUT. The driver must evaluate whether the occurrence or absence of an exception is a correct response. Because the driver must detect illegal exceptions, the catch block must include a "catchall" construct so that an unexpected exception is caught by the driver and does not percolate beyond it.

Implement each exception test case as a method with a catch block. An exception is an object that contains information related to the anomaly that caused the exception to be thrown.

Implementation

The test case implementation must (1) cause an exceptional condition to occur in the OUT and (2) attempt to catch the resulting exception. If the exception occurs and is otherwise as expected, the test passes. Examples in Ada and C++ follow. The implementation in Eiffel and Java is similar. Although Objective-C does not provide built-in support for exceptions, the OpenStep Foundation Kit ExceptionHandling framework provides basic capabilities.

Suppose that the contract of class DateTime calls for a BadYear exception when an attempt is made to set the year greater than 19999. The following code fragments suggest how to test this behavior.

Ada 95

```
procedure TestDateX is
   Year: Integer;
begin
   Year := 20000;
   SetYear( Year );
exception
   when BadYear => Put_Line(
           "Bad Year Exception Test Passes");
   when others => Put_Line(
           "Bad Year Exception Test NoPass, Invalid Exception");
end TextDateX;
```

C++

Exception handling in C++ is complex, owing to the vagaries of unwinding the stack under dynamic binding. The exception object is programmer-defined. This definition determines which catch block will receive the exception object. In the following example, the ellipsis in the catch block means that all exceptions thrown within the scope of the try block will be sent to this catch block.

```
bool testDateX(CUT out) {
   int year;
   try{
      year = 20000;    // Invalid year, off point
      out.setYear(year);
   }
   catch (...) {
      // Examine the exception object
      return true;    // The test passes
   }
   return false;      // The exception was not thrown,
                      // test does not pass
}
```

Smalltalk

Exception handling is supported in some Smalltalk IDEs. Visual Smalltalk uses a class-based approach. VisualWorks uses an instance- (or signal-) based approach. The test strategy is the same: attempt to force and catch the exception in the driver. The on:do keywords specify the exception handler, as the following fragment shows.

```
TestDatex: out
   ^[out setYear: 20000]
      on: BadDate do:[console : "Bad Year Exception Test Passes"]
```

Consequences

This pattern provides a systematic approach to exercising all exceptions. It increases the coupling of the test driver and the IUT. Changes in the IUT's exception handling will probably require corresponding changes in the test code.

Known Uses

The *Test Messages and Exceptions* pattern suggests using stubs to generate exceptions or exception conditions for the class under test, but does not discuss details of the driver [Firesmith 96]. Code to test exceptions is discussed in [Seipmann+94] (Smalltalk) and [Hoffman+95] (C++).

Related Patterns

See **Controlled Exception Test** for a test design strategy to exercise application- and platform-specific exceptions.

19.3   Test Control Patterns

19.3.1   Considerations

The object-oriented programming paradigm relies on mosaic modularity. That is, object-oriented software systems are composed of many small parts. These numerous parts are connected by explicit interfaces and implicit dependencies. Effective testing of one part or a subsystem of related parts requires the cooperation of the other parts in the system. The parts must be controlled—that is, put into the pretest state required by a test deign. Then, the post-test state must be observed to evaluate the test case. Because encapsulation is also a key element of the paradigm, the available behaviors and collaborations of the system are often insufficient to achieve the desired degree of control and observation.

The test harness must include capabilities to support necessary control and observation. This section presents several patterns that achieve this goal. The simplest approach is to use a **stub**, which is a reduced implementation of a class (or method) of a server object.[1] A server refers to an object that is part of the IUT, which is not necessarily a software component that plays the architectural role of a server.

- *Server Stub* shows how to develop temporary replacements for server methods.
- *Server Proxy* shows how to develop an object that acts like a stub, but can also delegate to a server method. It is based on the *Proxy* pattern [Gamma+95].

---

1. *Stub* is used in a general sense. In particular, it does not refer to a *stub* or *skeleton* in Java remote method invocation (RMI).

Server Stub

Intent

Use a temporary, minimal implementation of a method (a stub) to increase controllability and observability during testing.

Also Known As

Test Stub, Test Messages, and Exceptions [Firesmith 96].

Motivation

Three common problems with the environment of the IUT can hamper testing:

- The state of an object is defined by the values held by its instance variables, which are in turn composed of instance variables. The design of a given test case often requires a certain pretest state, so that instance variable responses correspond to the desired execution. Achieving these states using only the interface of the class under test can be difficult. The variables may be private, and the interface of the CUT may not provide a set method. Even if it does, the instance variables may be complex objects whose component objects cannot be accessed.

  If the instance variables are proxies for objects on remote systems not under the control of the application developer, achieving the required state once may be difficult—let alone cheaply and reliably enough to support iterative testing.

- There are cyclic references between two or more components in the scope of the IUT, such that neither can be controlled or tested independently. For example, in C++, two components are mutually visible via a `#include` directive [Lakos 96].

- A server resource is needed to run a test, but the server isn't available. It may not have been developed yet. For example, the IUT uses hardware or software services that are not yet developed or that are available for testing only at brief scheduled times.

Applicability

This pattern is useful at class and cluster scope for unit and integration testing. Stubs are necessary in the following situations:

- Stubs are used to implement the deferred components in *Top-down Integration*, *Backbone Integration*, *Layer Integration*, *Client/Server Integration*, and *Distributed Services Integration*.
- Stubs are necessary to break cyclic dependencies.
- Stubs can be used to test exception handling in a CUT by generating controllable throwing of exceptions in the servers. See *Controlled Exception Test*.
- Stubs can be used to check the content of messages sent to servers of the IUT. These servers are typically difficult to control and/or observe.

However, stubs should be avoided if possible. The problems with stubs are discussed in the Consequences section. If class/cluster integration follows the *Bottom-up Integration* pattern, few (if any) stubs will be needed to simulate untested methods.

Participants

The components of this pattern are the class under test and its servers. A method stub may be used in the class under test, its superclass or subclasses, any of its servers, and for any component in the test configuration. The structure should be identical to the client/server relationships in the IUT.

Collaborations

A method stub is typically part of a server object of the class under test but may also be a method of the class under test or its superclasses. Stub methods can implement many possible responses, as the following list suggests. This list is not exhaustive and should be used to suit the particular situation.

- Return to the client with no action.
- Return a constant value.
- Return a count of the number of times that the stub has been called.
- Return values that change depending on the number of times that the stub is called.
- Return the minimum and maximum values of arguments sent to the stub.
- Return values read from a file, database, or persistent collection. The values may be constant, selected sequentially, or selected randomly.

- Return values computed by a simplified or reduced algorithm.

- Log or display the values of the input arguments to a file or the test console.

- Log or display the name of the stub and the type of object to which it was bound.

- Monitor system resource utilization: memory allocated and available, the number of active processes, tasks, or threads, average CPU utilization, and so on. Write it to a log file or display it on the test console.

- Send a trace message to a file, standard output, or the test console.

- Send a trace message and prompt to continue. If the prompt is displayed on a GUI, it should use its own widget (i.e., not an application widget).

- Generate a stack dump. Write it to a log file or display it on the test console.

- Wait or loop for a specified period or number of iterations.

- Wait for the occurrence of some event not under the control of the IUT (e.g., on a remote node in a network).

- Simulate exceptions or abnormal conditions.

Object-oriented languages that allow explicit separation of interface and implementation as .h and .cpp files mean that a stub's interface should be identical to the nonstub interface—we need only to substitute the implementation.

Implementation

Stubs are programmed in the same way that ordinary methods are programmed. The interface of the stub class or method is identical to (has the same name and signature as) the application class or method that it replaces.

When stubs are necessary, avoid throwaway code. Try for a minimal implementation: every nonconstructor method is an executable stub.

- Develop swappable build libraries and control inclusion of stubs through build (link) parameters.

- Try to include assertions for the contract of any stubbed method (see Chapter 17). An asserted stub will reveal bugs in its clients. It will help to avoid stub code that significantly diverges from the intended responsibility of the stubbed method as well as spurious test results.

- Develop constructors for a stubbed class. Try to use a default constructor and avoid hard-coding initial values. If this effort is not sufficient, the stub must provide hard-coded assignment of every private instance variable. Depending on name scoping of the driver, you may have to set the values of protected and public variables in the stub.

The implementation of these responsibilities is a straightforward programming task in each of the languages considered here, so no code examples are provided.

Consequences

Stubs have several potential problems. For small methods, the time and effort to develop a stub are often about the same as they are for the actual method.

- If the stub is used by several clients in the same cluster or will be implemented with access to other private data, crafting a stub that supports all test cases may not be possible.
- The time and cost to develop and maintain stubs can be high. In testing a C++ system with more than 1 MLOC, Thuy concludes, "it is difficult and extremely costly to test a component really independently of the components it depends on. That implies replacing those components by stubs, for which the reliability is not guaranteed and for which the costs and delays are very high" [Thuy 92, 6].
- Unwarranted confidence can arise from passing test runs on an IUT with stubbed servers. Stubs are temporary. A test suite that passes with stubbed server objects cannot be considered as adequate for the same client with fully implemented server objects. When stubs are replaced by the application implementation, the test suite that passes with the stubs should be scrutinized for functional holes related to the stubbed responsibilities and revised if necessary. The behavior of the fully implemented object may be quite different from its stub. At a minimum, the client test suite should be rerun on the nonstubbed implementation. Both the code and specification coverage of the client should be rechecked for this build.
- Failure to rebuild the IUT with the full implementation of the stubbed server objects may be an oversight. This situation is not unlike a surgeon leaving an instrument inside a patient.
- A stub typically supports a few test cases—it may or may not be appropriate for other test cases. The test suite for a cluster can have hundreds

of stubbed methods, and possibly thousands of test-case-specific stubs. The task of coding, building, and revising all of these stubs can be time-consuming and error-prone.

- Large complex dependency cycles can overpower stubs. Cycles should be prevented at design time [Thuy 92, Thuy 93, Lakos 96, Barbey 97].

The main alternative to stubbing is to follow an order of development that minimizes or eliminates the need for stubs. See Section 13.1.3, Dependency Analysis and *Bottom-up Integration*.

The main technical advantages of stubs are better control and observation of the servers of the class under test. These characteristics allow for more extensive testing, which may reveal more bugs. Stubs can also isolate interfaces to other systems, which can ease subsequent porting or converting to a different system. A stub implementation of some classes used by the class under test can provide sufficient control over the response of a server object.

- A stub can serve as a placeholder for an uncompleted method, allowing iterative development to proceed.
- Stubs can control the scope of integration during class testing. This is useful when the class under test uses many untested server objects. Without stubs, a problematic big bang integration can result. Client test suites are rerun as a server object, and stubs are gradually replaced with the actual server object implementation.
- Stubs can increase controllability by hard-coding, simulating, or otherwise limiting the behavior of server methods. This ability may be especially useful when testing a class or cluster that must interface with external systems or devices that cannot be easily controlled. A stub that simulates such an interface can provide predictable, repeatable responses to client messages.
- Stubs can increase observability by tracing, dumping, and providing other forms of temporary monitoring in stubbed methods.
- Stubs can simulate the response of a binary component, server object, or virtual machine service that cannot be controlled directly.
- Typically, a class sends messages to its server objects. If server object methods are replaced by stubs, the stubs can check for specific content in the message sent from the object under test. This effort can reveal bugs in delegation.

A stub can also help to deal with practical problems like hardware/software availability. For example, the IUT may use hardware or software services that are not yet developed or that are available for testing only at brief scheduled times. A stub can be used to wrap this interface so that your testing can continue when the server is unavailable, but can be removed or disabled when the server is available.

Known Uses

Considerations for stubs in conventional programming are discussed in [Page-Jones 88], in Ada [Jones 94], and in C++ [Thielien 92, Spuler 94]. Problems with stubs are discussed in [Thuy 92]. Desfray's methodology emphasizes test planning and calls for stubs to emulate deferred Eiffel routines. When a stub is replaced, retesting is needed [Desfray 94]. Jüttner reports that stubs are necessary but should be avoided [Jüttner+94a, Jüttner+94b, Jüttner+94c, Jüttner+95]; Barbey agrees [Barbey 97]. Problems with server stubs in C++ and a tool to generate proxy stubs is described in [Dorman 97].

The C++ and Ada COTS tools from IPL (Cantata and AdaTest) automatically generate stubs.

Related Patterns

Stubs are necessary for most forms of integration. See Chapter 13.

Server Proxy

Intent

Use a temporary implementation of a server class that can delegate messages to the application server methods (a **proxy**) to increase controllability and observability during testing.

Motivation

The motivation for using a proxy is the same as it is for using a stub: you need to control the response of a server object, but cannot easily do so. See *Server Stub*.

   Of course, the same delegation can be accomplished in a server stub. The proxy can, however, define additional methods to support testing—for example, setPassThruMode( ) described below. Suppose that the intent is to "grow" the stub into the application class. Having a separate proxy makes the distinction between the test harness and application.

Applicability

This pattern is useful at class and cluster scopes for unit and integration testing. See *Server Stub*.

Participants

Participants include the class under test, its servers, and a proxy class. A proxy is typically a distinct class that exports the same interface as the server. The structure should be identical to the client/server relationships in the IUT. The proxy class is added between the CUT and the server. The proxy declares an object of the server. See [Gamma+95] for a detailed discussion of the *Proxy* design pattern.

Collaborations

Masking can be controlled by a compile-time or global parameter. The system under test can be built with a stub library or the actual clients. The stubs can perform many kinds of simulation:

   • They can simulate exceptions thrown by an application server or the virtual machine.

- Client proxies can simulate a client process sending messages to server processes in a client/server architecture.

- Server proxies can simulate server response in a client/server architecture.

The *Controlled Exception Test* pattern shows how proxies can be used to test the exception handling of the IUT. The stub conditionally passes the message it receives to the actual implementation.

Implementation

Proxies are programmed in the same way that ordinary methods are programmed. See *Server Stub*. In addition, a proxy must be able to operate in pass-through mode or simulation mode, as this C++ fragment suggests.

```cpp
class A_Server {
    // ...
    void setModePassThru( );
    void setModeSimulate( );
    // ...
};
```

Consequences

The advantages and disadvantages of *Server Stub* apply to Proxy Stub as well. Proxies provide a clearer separation of concerns (test harness versus application) and can support additional test control functions. Because they add another level of indirection, they will increase test runtime and executable size.

Known Uses

The Cantata tool for C++ testing has replaced generation of stubs with the generation of a proxy for C++ [Dorman 97].

Related Patterns

See [Gamma+95] for a detailed discussion of the *Proxy* design pattern. *Controlled Exception Test* relies on a proxy stub. Proxy stubs can be useful in integration under the *Layer Integration*, *Client/Server Integration*, and *Distributed Services Integration* patterns.

19.4   Driver Patterns

19.4.1   Considerations

Design Goals

A **test driver** performs test setup, sends test messages to the object under test, evaluates post-test results as pass/no pass, and handles any necessary cleanup. The design of effective and reusable object test drivers is challenging. There are several key considerations:

- How can we gain sufficient control to set the state of the IUT, its inputs, and its environment for test setup?
- How can we gain sufficient access to the resultant state of the IUT, its outputs, and its environment for test evaluation?
- Do we want automatic test value generation?
- Do we want randomized test value or test sequence selection?
- Do we want pass/no pass evaluation to be fully automatic, manual, or mixed?
- How can we make tests easy to rerun and reuse?
- How can we make superclass tests easy to run in a subclass?
- Must the tested implementation be identical to the released implementation?
- How much code bloat is acceptable?
- If some or all of the test driver ships with the IUT, are the potential misuse and security problems manageable and acceptable?
- What level of additional design, programming, and maintenance is feasible? It is not uncommon for the code volume of a test harness to be two to three times as large as the system under test.

Inheriting Test Suites

Inheritance is a fundamental mechanism of object-oriented programming that has significant implications for testing strategy (see Chapters 4 and 10). The power of inheritance can also be used to develop efficient and effective test suites. Application-specific drivers can use the application class hierarchy as a basis for modular organization of a test suite and to achieve test case reuse. Inheritance can support several test driver design goals:

- It can support reuse by making it easy to do regression testing for a new subclass. It allows a developer to answer the question easily, "Does my new subclass induce any regression faults?"
- It can detect bugs in subclasses that violate the LSP.
- It can reuse superclass test suites in the context of the subclass.
- It can promote superclass reuse by reducing the test effort by reusing test suites and by providing concrete evidence that the superclasses have been adequately tested.

Considerations for test design of inherited features are discussed in Chapter 10. Briefly, the scope of adequate (re)testing under inheritance is controlled by the following factors:

- Passing is not inherited. That is, the fact that superclass methods pass a test run on a superclass object does not guarantee that these methods will pass the same tests when run on a subclass class object. If there are no intraclass dependencies, then method scope retesting of inherited methods may be reduced. Because most of this testing can be automated, however, the incremental cost of running the test will most often be trivial. The analysis needed to determine whether a test can be safely skipped is rarely trivial.
- Rerunning superclass tests on a subclass object can reveal bugs that violate the LSP.
- In any case, the interaction among all subclass features (newly defined and inherited) should be exercised. These tests can be generated by applying the test strategy appropriate to the modality of the class under test. These tests cannot be inherited because the methods do not exist in the superclass.

Table 19.2 suggests what can be inherited and what an adequate test suite would exercise. For example, the test suite for the local integration test of subclass C would be formed by tests of the interactions at the flattened scope of C—that is, tests of the interactions of all inherited and locally defined methods. What can be reused to conduct an adequate test of C? Test suites *TS(A)*, *TS(B)*, and *TS(A'+B)* can be "inherited"—that is, we can pass an object of type C to them. Clearly, we will need to also develop and run tests of the new and overridden features in C, yielding *TS(C)*. None of this guarantees that the inter-

TABLE 19.2 Contribution of Superclass Test Suites to Subclass Testing

Class	Scope	Test Suite Obtained by Inheriting Test Drivers	Test Suite That Must Be Developed for Adequate Testing	Resultant Test Suites
A	Local	—	$TS(A)$	$TS(A)$
	Flattened	—	—	
B	Local	—	$TS(B)$	
	Flattened	$TS(A)$	$TS(A' + B)$	$TS(A), TS(B), TS(A' + B)$ $TS(C)$
C	Local	—	$TS(C)$	
	Flattened	$TS(A), TS(B),$ $TS(A' + B)$	$TS(A'' + B' + C)$	$TS(A), TS(B),$ $TS(A'' + B'),$ $TS(A'' + B' + C)$

X' = The feature set of superclass X visible one level down.
X'' = The feature set of superclass X visible two levels down.
$TS(X)$ = The test suite developed for class X.
$M + N + ... + Z$ = The flattened scope of a set of classes.

actions among the methods of C, B, and A have been exercised. Therefore, the test suite $TS(A'' + B' + C)$ must be developed. Strategies for design of such a test suite are presented in Chapter 10.

Controllability, Observability, and Reuse

Three forces influence the design patterns for all of the test drivers: controllability, observability, and reuse. These forces motivate the drivers presented here. Each driver is a different solution to these forces with different trade-offs.

Controllability.   The interface of an implementation under test often does not provide sufficient access to set the concrete state of instance variables to the desired pretest state. Even if the interface is sufficient, long message sequences may be required to achieve the desired state. This problem is typically solved with a combination of stubs and intrusive access by the driver.

Observability.   The interface of an implementation under test often does not provide sufficient access to determine post-test values of instance variables. Even if the interface is sufficient, long message sequences may be required to assess the resultant state. Assertions placed in the IUT (see Chapter 17) are a good way to check implementation relationships, but they are not always practical. This problem is typically solved with intrusive access by the driver with some assistance from stubs that trace messages sent to the servers of the IUT.

Reuse.   Inheritance is an essential element of the object-oriented programming paradigm. Test drivers should provide an efficient and effective interface with an application class hierarchy. The application hierarchy provides a natural and obvious factoring of the test suite. Just as a good application hierarchy supports modularity and reuse, so too will it support a modular and reusable test suite, if the test suite is symmetric to the application hierarchy. A symmetric test suite supports regression testing and is effective for revealing bugs that are likely to be found in hierarchies. Describing a *Symmetric Driver* for an Objective-C system, Cox noted, "The automatically inherited `TestTools` often detect long-standing bugs that have persisted because nobody thought to verify . . . deeply inherited methods, particularly easily forgotten object-level methods like `copy` and `isEqual:` [which] were overridden to adapt to the peculiarities of the subclasses" [Cox 88, 46].

Reuse is achieved by arranging the test cases to correspond to the hierarchy of the class under test. This organization of test cases is not always ideal, so test suites may be organized on different lines. Controllability and observability are achieved through clever uses of language features. Each approach has different consequences, so no single pattern is right for all applications.

Table 19.3 summarizes the extent to which each driver pattern overcomes the controllability/observability barrier. Each language is best suited to

TABLE 19.3   Scope of Controllability/Observability by Driver Pattern

	Driver Pattern			
Scope	Built-in Test Driver	Private Access	Subclass	Symmetric
Private	Yes	Yes	No	No
Protected	Yes	Yes	Yes	No
Public	Yes	Yes	Yes	Yes
Package	No	No	No	Yes

TABLE 19.4   Driver Patterns and Programming Language Scoping

	Pattern	Mechanism
Ada 95	Private Access Driver	Child unit
C++	Private Access Driver	Friend class
Eiffel	Drone	Descendant class
Java	Built-in Test Driver	Private scoping
Objective-C	Test Interface	Class implements test protocol and test interface as category
Smalltalk	Test Interface	Envy extension
	Built-in Test Driver	Private scoping

certain driver patterns (e.g., a *Private Access Driver* cannot be implemented in Java, but is ideal for C++). Table 19.4 summarizes driver patterns and languages.

19.4.2   Driver Design Patterns

The following test patterns for designing a class/cluster scope test driver are presented here:

- *TestDriver Superclass.* Implement general test services as a driver superclass.
- *Percolate the Object Under Test.* Pass the object under test between drivers to reuse superclass tests.
- *Symmetric Driver.* Implement the drivers as a hierarchy symmetric to the hierarchy of the classes under test.
- *Subclass Driver.* Implement the driver as a subclass of the class under test.
- *Private Access Driver.* Achieve controllability and observability by taking advantage of language-specific mechanisms that defeat encapsulation and support new objects in the expanded scope.
- *Test Control Interface.* Achieve controllability and observability by taking advantage of language-specific mechanisms that defeat encapsulation but do not support new objects in the expanded scope.

- **Drone.** Implement the driver with a mixin class and the class under test.
- **Built-in Test Driver.** Implement the driver as a part of the class under test.

The Part class hierarchy shown in Figure 19.4 provides an example class under test for the patterns.

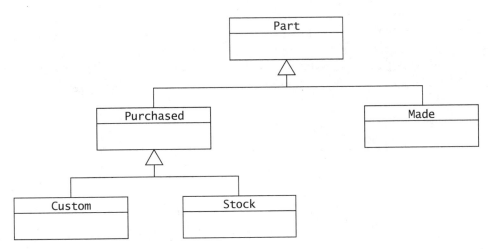

FIGURE 19.4   The Part class hierarchy.

TestDriver Superclass

Intent

Define an abstract superclass `TestDriver` to provide a common interface and test services that can be inherited by class-specific drivers.

Motivation

All of the following test driver patterns use several levels of inherited classes. Each must implement common testing services. If these services were implemented in each subclass, undesirable redundancy would result, and the opportunity to provide a single API for test services would be missed. A single test services superclass can also define a common interface for all test services.

Applicability

Use when developing any of the following inheritance-based drivers.

Participants

Class `TestDriver` implements the following protected methods.[2] Other general test services can be implemented in this way and inherited by test driver classes.

- `startTestCase(Object testCase)`   Generate a test log entry with a test case start date and time.
- `finishTestCase(bool pass)`   Generate a test log entry with a test case finish date and time. Record pass/no pass results.

The `TestDriver` class implements the following private methods:

- `openTestLog( )`   Open the test run log. Record environment variables (e.g., operating system version, `TestDriver` version CPU type, available memory), CPU serial number, and so on.
- `closeTestLog( )`   Close the test run log. Record environment variables (e.g., operating system version, `TestDriver` version CPU type, available memory), CPU serial number, and so on.

Figure 19.5 shows the Class Diagram.

---

2. The class name `TestDriver` is not mandatory.

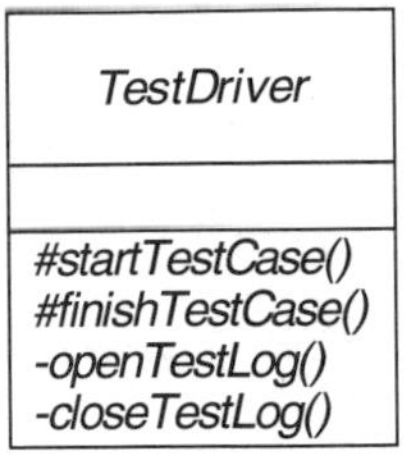

```
┌─────────────────────────┐
│      TestDriver         │
├─────────────────────────┤
│                         │
├─────────────────────────┤
│ #startTestCase()        │
│ #finishTestCase()       │
│ -openTestLog()          │
│ -closeTestLog()         │
└─────────────────────────┘
```

FIGURE 19.5   `TestDriver` superclass.

Collaborations

Test cases and suites are implemented by subclasses of `TestDriver`. These subclasses send messages to `TestDriver`, which accomplishes general test execution services.

Implementation

Implementation examples are not presented here as their development is a straightforward programming task, with many application- and platform-specific variations.

Consequences

Generic test services are implemented once and reused. `TestDriver` provides a common interface that may be used by other classes in a test framework. The usual considerations for superclasses apply.

Known Uses

General test services are implemented with superclasses in the test frameworks described in several sources [Cox 88, Love 92, Beck 94, Murphy+94, Firesmith 96, Gamma+98].

Related Patterns

`TestDriver` is used in all of the following test driver patterns.

Percolate the Object Under Test

Intent

Allow the object under test to be passed between drivers so that superclass tests can be rerun on subclass objects.

Motivation

Applying superclass test suites to a subclass object can reveal many kinds of bugs. Once superclass test suites have been established, how can they be applied to a subclass object without reworking the test code or making redundant copies of the test code?

Applicability

This pattern is useful at class and cluster scopes for unit and integration testing: developing a driver to exercise a class, a class cluster, or other component that will be tested using its application programmer interface. This pattern supports systematic reuse of superclass tests. It is indicated when the IUT has or may have one or more subclasses.

Participants

The components of this pattern are as follows:

- The class that defines the object under test
- The object under test (an instance of the class under test)
- The implementation of the test cases, either methods (*Test Case/Test Suite Method*) or objects (*Test Case/Test Suite Class*)

Collaborations

In statically typed languages (Ada 95, C++, and Eiffel), the object under test may be passed as a parameter to the test case method or a method of the test case object.

- Define the object of the class under test in a `TestDriver`. Do not define the OUT in the `TestCase` object.

- The interface of the `TestCase` object must be polymorphic. It will accept any subclass in the hierarchy under test.
- The `TestDriver` passes the object under test to a `TestCase` object.
- Upon completing its test cases, each `TestCase` object calls its superclass `TestCase`, passing the OUT.

In dynamically typed languages (Java, Objective-C, and Smalltalk), the class under test may be passed as a parameter, and the test driver or test case object can create its own instance.

Implementation

The effects of each test case on subsequent test cases will be either preserved or eliminated, depending on whether the message that passes the OUT uses call-by-value or call-by-reference. Several examples of percolating the OUT are shown in *Symmetric Driver*.

Consequences

The primary advantage of passing the out (or CUT) to the test case implementation is that reusing test cases developed for superclasses of the class under test is simple. Cox notes that this flexibility allows superclass test cases "to be applied to any subclass, and more generally any class that claimed to implement the same specification" [Cox 88, 46].

The disadvantages are due to indirection: the code is not explicit about what object is being tested and additional construction/destruction can add to the test runtime and memory requirements. It can also induce spurious test results owing to side effects of a buggy or inconsistent linkage mechanism. As the rules for resolving runtime references can be convoluted, careful attention must be given to the semantics of the implementation language and its use in a particular harness.

Known Uses

The test drivers developed by Stepstone Corporation to test its ICpak 201 commercial class library used percolation [Cox 88]. The application class hierarchy had a parallel `TestTool` class hierarchy, as shown in Figure 19.9 (see next pattern). The name of the class under test was provided as a parameter to `TestTool` (a common Objective-C idiom). Then, the `TestTool` object simply instantiated this class as the object under test. Test cases were hard-coded in each

`TestTool` object as messages sent to the OUT and were designed to test a particular class. The driver for each subclass exercised all inherited methods for its target subclass and those specialized or refined.

Related Patterns

Some of the general considerations in *Chain of Responsibility* [Gamma+95] apply.

Symmetric Driver

Intent

Implement a driver as a class hierarchy that is symmetric to the hierarchy of the class under test. Each driver class sends a test message to an object of the class under test.

Also Known As

Separate Driver Hierarchy [Firesmith 96] and *Create Hierarchies of Parallel Components* [McGregor+96].

Motivation

See the section Controllability, Observability, and Reuse. A Symmetric Driver implementation inherits superclass test cases providing test reuse.

A practical consideration is where and how to define the object under test. Constructors are not inherited and must be implemented in each subclass. So, if a test case method constructs the OUT, that code cannot be reused for a subclass test.

Applicability

This pattern is useful at class and cluster scope for unit and integration testing of an application class hierarchy implemented in any of the languages discussed here. The hierarchy under test may use either single or multiple inheritance.

A Symmetric Driver implementation uses the public interface of the class under test. The typical obstacles to controllability and observability of a public interface may make some test design patterns infeasible with this driver. For example, lack of controllability might require that millions of add messages be sent to the CUT so as to reach the capacity limit of a collection. If the public interface of the class under test is insufficient or awkward for testing purposes, consider using **Private Access Driver**, **Test Control Interface**, **Drone**, or **Built-in Test Driver** instead.

Participants

There is a test driver class for each class in the application hierarchy. The inheritance relationships are symmetrical. A higher-level superclass, `Test-Procedure`, may be added to the top. This class can provide general testing services (log, dump, trace, and so on) and define a common interface for running tests.

The driver class must define instance variables for every argument in the public interface of the class under test. This definition should be symmetric; for example, TestPart defines instance variables for all arguments in public methods of Part, TestMade defines all arguments in public methods of Made (but not of Part, as those definitions are inherited), and so on.

Figure 19.4, in the Driver Design Patterns section (page 992), shows a simple three-level application class hierarchy. Figure 19.6 shows the corresponding test driver hierarchy. Figure 19.7 shows how the test driver hierarchy could "hard-code" each object under test. This configuration interferes with the reuse of superclass test cases, so it is not recommended. Instead, the object under test should be passed into the driver object. See *Percolate the Object Under Test*. Figure 19.8 (page 1002) shows how a test bundle could be configured with symmetric drivers to support console testing.

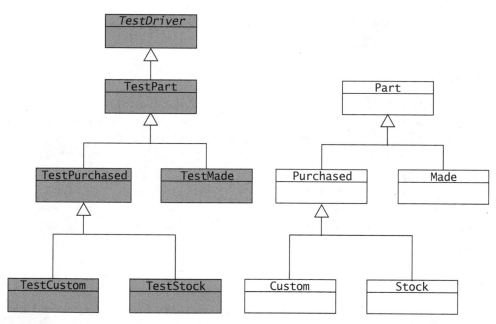

FIGURE 19.6 Symmetric hierarchies.

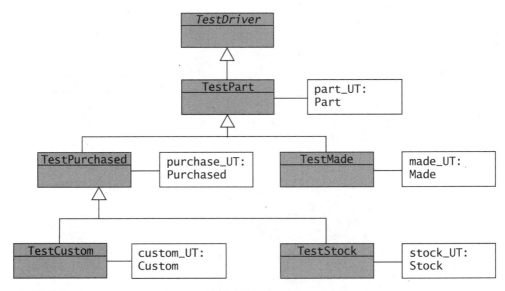

FIGURE 19.7   Symmetric test driver with OUT instantiations.

Collaborations

The client/server test driver is the simplest possible driver arrangement. The object under test is an instance variable. To implement test cases, a message is sent to the object under test. Test cases are typically hard-coded as methods. The driver sets message parameters according to the test plan. For each test, the state of the OUT must be set. The driver may set the OUT state by message sequences. Then, the driver sends messages to the OUT. The resultant state and returned message are evaluated by the driver. The driver/OUT interface can be implemented in several ways.

A debugger can be used to manually set pretest state and inspect post-test state if the interface is insufficient. This effort should be avoided because it is time-consuming, error-prone, and not automatically repeatable. Consider *Private Access Driver* instead.

Implementation

Skeletal Ada 95 and C++ examples of Symmetric Driver follow. Implementation of this class structure is straightforward in Eiffel, Java, Objective-C, and Smalltalk.

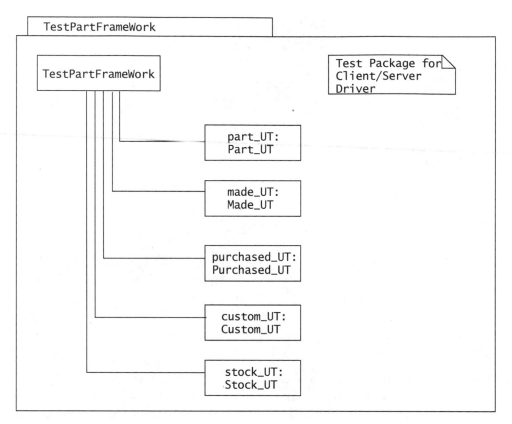

FIGURE 19.8   Symmetric test package.

Ada 95

```
type A is ... -- Root of the class hierarchy under test
   procedure A1( );
   procedure A2( );

type B is new A;
   procedure b3( );
   procedure b4( );

type C is new B;
   procedure C5( );
   procedure C6( );
```

Note that the object under test is passed in as a parameter.

```
type TestA is new TestProcedure;
   procedure TestA01(Iut: A'Class) is
```

```
                begin
                  m = out.a1( );
                  n = out.a2( );
                  assert (m==n);
                  return;
                end TestA01;

            type TestB is new TestA;
               procedure TestB01(Iut: B'Class) is
                  begin
                    P := Iut.a1( );
                    Q := Iut.a2( );
                    assert (p==q );
                    this.testA01(out);
                    return;
               end TestB01;

            type TestC is new TestB;
               procedure TestC01(Iut: C'Class) is
                  begin
                    x = out.a1( );
                    y = out.a2( );
                    assert (x ==y);
                    this.testB01(out);
                    return;
               end TestC01;
```

The test drivers are instantiated and run as a group.

```
     Main {
         A aut; B but; C cut;
         TestC testC;
         TestB testB;
         TestA testA;

         testA.testA01(aut);    -- Run Test Package for A
         testB.testB01(but);    -- Run Test Package for B
         testC.testC01(cut);    -- Run Test Package for C
     }
```

C++

```
     class A {
     public
         A( );
         int a1( );
         int a2( );
     }
```

```
class B: public A {
    B( );
    int b3( );
    int b4( );
}

class C: public B {
    C( );
    int c5( );
    int c6( );
}
```

The corresponding symmetric test drivers follow. Note that the object under test is passed in as a parameter.

```
class TestA public TestProcedure {
public
    TestA( );
    void testa01(A out ) {
        m = out.a1( );
        n = out.a2( );
        assert (m ==n);
        return;
    }
}

class TestB: public TestA {
    TestB( );
    void TestB01(B out) {
        p = out.a1( );
        q = out.a2( );
        assert (p==q);
        this.testA01(out);
        return;
    }
}

class TestC: public TestB {
    TestC( );
    void TestC01(C out) {
        x = out.a1( );
        y = out.a2( );
        assert (x ==y);
        this.testB01(out);
        return;
    }
}
```

Consequences

The main advantage of the Symmetric Driver pattern is that it organizes test cases in direct correspondence to the structure of the classes under test.

- It can support automatic regression testing of all superclass test cases, if a subclass object under test can be passed to the superclass test methods (see *Percolate the Object Under Test*).

- It provides a single point of control for testing a class or the head of a cluster.

- It respects encapsulation and is coupled to only the CUT's public interface.

- A full or partial implementation of the driver can be shipped with the CUT to promote reuse and consumer regression testing. Many translators do not generate object code for nonreferenced source code. If the test driver is not instantiated, no reference to the test methods is generated. In effect, test driver code is treated as comments.

Disadvantages of this pattern include the following:

- Control and observation are limited to the CUT's public interface. Establishing a desired pretest state or inspecting the post-test state may be difficult or impossible.

- Private and protected methods cannot be exercised directly.

- The cost of developing and maintaining an additional, separate class hierarchy will be incurred. If the class hierarchy inheritance changes, the existing test suite must be reworked.

Known Uses

ICpak 201 Test Environment

A suite of test tools was developed to test the Stepstone Corporation's ICpak 201 commercial class library. The application class hierarchy had a parallel TestTool class hierarchy, as shown in Figure 19.9 [Cox 88]. The driver for each subclass could exercise all inherited methods for its target subclass and those specialized or refined.

The name of the class under test was provided as a parameter to TestTool. It allowed an object of any class to be instantiated as the OUT. Test cases were hard-coded in the TestTool as messages sent to the OUT. The response to the

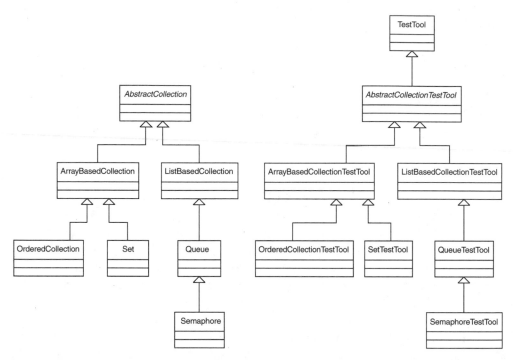

FIGURE 19.9 Cox's TestTool hierarchy.

test messages was evaluated in an assertion that defined the test pass/fail condition. If the test failed, the assertion provided uniform reporting of the failure.

A later report describes additional capabilities [Love 92]. A session recorder automatically logged all developer interactions. The log could be played back to reproduce failures occurring in an interactive session. A test driver generator would automatically generate a "test class" driver for each class and a "test method" for each method. "The result was a parallel hierarchy of class tests that mirrored the original inheritance tree" [Love 92, 192]. The method tester used random number generators to produce argument values. Method testers would check for memory leaks and correct types on returned items.

SAYS

The SAYS methodology calls for a test driver hierarchy that parallels the application class hierarchy. Drivers are specialized from an abstract superclass to provide consistent logging and display of results. The drivers define and initialize the OUT and send a sequence of messages. Drivers "should be able to determine whether the OUT has returned the appropriate value and placed itself in the appropriated state." [McGregor+94b, 75]. Tests are represented as unbundled scripts to promote reusability.

Less extensive reports have also appeared [Rettig 91, Taylor 92, Harrold +92, Wilke 93, Dorman 93, Firesmith 93b, Beck 94, Murphy+94].

Related Patterns

Class as Unit, Class Via Instance, Test Messages and Exceptions [Firesmith 96].

Subclass Driver

Intent

Implement a driver as a subclass of the class under test.

Also Known As

Test Subclasses [Firesmith 96].

Motivation

See the Controllability, Observability, and Reuse section. A subclass driver inherits the nonprivate implementation of the class under test, thereby removing some obstacles to test control and observation. The visibility that is obtained under inheritance is different in each language.

Applicability

This pattern is useful at class and cluster scopes for unit and integration testing. A subclass driver is appropriate for testing an abstract superclass and, with multiple inheritance, can support effective testing of a class hierarchy. There are two reasons for using a subclass driver:

- A subclass driver is ideal for testing an abstract superclass. It can also test deferred features, by providing their implementations in the test driver.
- Subclass drivers may be layered in languages that support multiple inheritance to accomplish test reuse by inheritance.

Beyond two levels of inheritance, this scheme becomes problematic. The problems are discussed in the Consequences section (see page 1012).

Participants

The components of this pattern are the class under test and the driver subclass. Figure 19.10 shows the structure of a test driver for an abstract superclass. Figure 19.11 shows the single inheritance case. Figure 19.12 shows the multiple inheritance case.

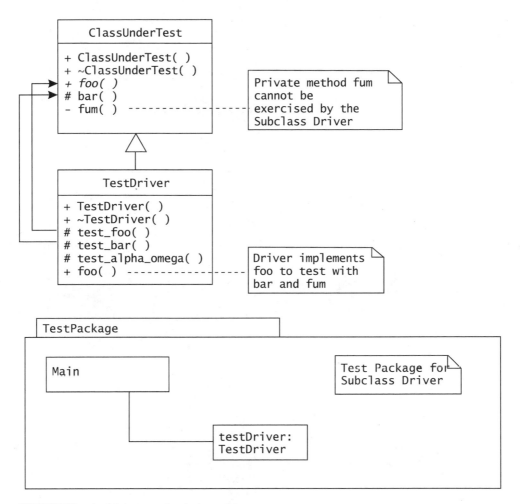

FIGURE 19.10   Architecture of subclass driver.

Collaborations

A two-level subclass driver can be used to provide an implementation for abstract deferred (virtual) methods (in the subclass test driver). The implementation may be a stub or a fully developed implementation. In effect, the driver provides part of the implementation.

Implementation

The parameters passed to the CUT must be instance variables of the driver.

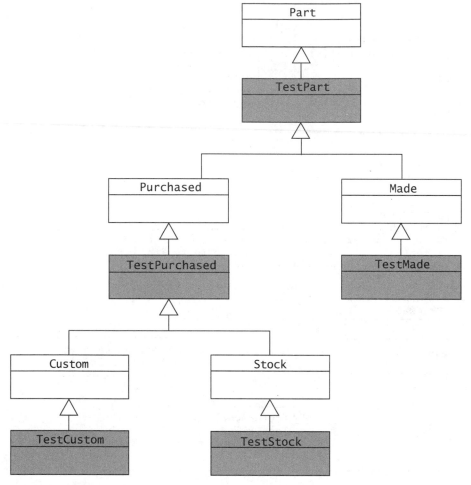

FIGURE 19.11   Subclass drivers with single inheritance.

Ada 95

An Ada 95 **Private Access Driver** provides access to private instance variables without the complications of a subclass driver. The primary use of an Ada subclass driver is therefore to test abstract base types.

C++

A C++ **Private Access Driver** provides access to private instance variables without the complications of a subclass driver. The primary use of a C++ subclass driver is therefore to test abstract base classes.

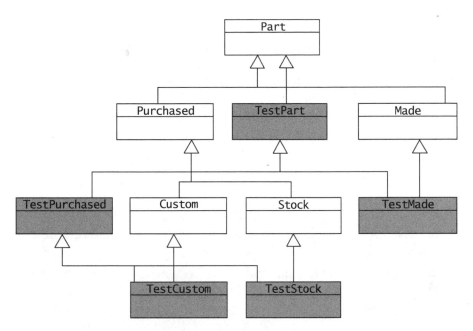

FIGURE 19.12 Subclass drivers with multiple inheritance.

Eiffel

Eiffel subclasses have access to all superclass features. A subclass driver has access to all private variables. As Eiffel supports multiple inheritance, the pattern shown in Figure 19.12 may be used. This choice avoids the snarl that results with a single-inheritance subclass driver.

Java

Java prevents a subclass driver from accessing private instance variables, and its single inheritance would require the ungainly structure shown in Figure 19.11. Subclass drivers are of limited use in Java—primarily, they are employed to produce a testable implementation of an abstract superclass.

Objective-C

Objective-C prevents a subclass driver from accessing private instance variables, and its single inheritance would require the ungainly structure shown in Figure 19.11. Subclass drivers are of limited use in Objective-C—primarily, they are employed to produce a testable implementation of an abstract superclass.

Smalltalk

Smalltalk's encapsulation prevents a subclass driver from providing any benefit, and its single inheritance would require the ungainly structure shown in Figure 19.11. Subclass drivers are of limited use in Smalltalk—primarily, they are employed to produce a testable implementation of an abstract superclass.

Consequences

A subclass driver is a good approach for testing abstract classes and classes with only one or at most two superclasses. It is problematic in other cases.

- In languages that support private scoping (C++, Java, Objective-C, and Smalltalk), private methods and instance variables are still not visible to the driver.
- With single inheritance, a subclass driver becomes a component part of the application class (Figure 19.11). This structure will probably be undesirable in many situations—something like having a crash dummy shipped with every new car. Figure 19.11 shows how subclass drivers must be placed to test an entire hierarchy in single inheritance languages (Java, Objective-C, Smalltalk). This approach is problematic and is not recommended.
- Multiple inheritance provides an escape from some of these problems, as Figure 19.12 shows. Subclass drivers can be placed to test an entire hierarchy in multiple-inheritance languages (Ada 95, C++, and Eiffel). Note, however, that this scheme results in repeated inheritance. For example, TestMade has two paths to Part: TestPart to Part and Made to Part. Although this approach is not as problematic as the single-inheritance case, it is not recommended.

Known Uses

Subclass drivers are mentioned without any details in [Murphy+94] and [Desfray 94]. Firesmith notes that a subclass driver "is commonly used to test abstract classes" without providing details [Firesmith 96].

Eiffel Heir

A driver implemented as an Eiffel subclass allows access to encapsulated features of the CUT [D'Souza+94]. This approach avoids development of built-in tests, use of debug probes, and the need to trust untested accessor methods. The subclass driver does not require any modifications to the CUT, but allows full access to its implementation. Test cases are hard-coded in the example driver. The driver is called from a user interface class, and it accepts a parameter that controls the number of tests to be run. The CUT and arguments are reinitialized for each test.

Private Access Driver

Intent

Use special-purpose language mechanisms that make all elements of a class's implementation visible to a driver to achieve necessary control of pretest state and observation of post-test state.

Also Known As

Voyeur Test Hierarchy [Firesmith 96], *Overcome Information Hiding in Order to Observe State* [McGregor+96].

Motivation

See the Controllability, Observability, and Reuse section. A Private Access Driver inherits superclass test cases and uses special access mechanisms to achieve test control and observation.

Applicability

This pattern is useful at class and cluster scopes for unit and integration testing necessary to support your test design. A Private Access Driver may be developed only in a language that offers the ability to bypass normal scoping/visibility rules, providing visibility of all elements of a class implementation to a client class or subclass. C++ and Ada 95 support such mechanisms.

Private access removes obstacles to setting and determining concrete state. A Private Access Driver uses this mechanism to access methods and instance variables that would otherwise not be visible outside implementation scope. Table 19.4 (page 992) compares inheritance scoping mechanisms.

- The C++ friend class and the Ada 95 child unit support complete access to the implementation of another class and do not impose any restrictions on the content of the private access code.

- Eiffel does not implement a separate mechanism to grant private access. Instead, a subclass always has complete access to all superclass features. Thus, although a Private Access Driver can be constructed in Eiffel, it is an inelegant use of its basic object model. The preferred approach is a **Drone**.

- Java does not implement any such construct. The only way to achieve comparable controllability and observability for a Java class is to implement a **Built-in Test Driver** with inner classes.

- OpenStep Objective-C supports *class categories*. The Smalltalk/ENVY development environment supports *class extensions*. Both constructs allow complete visibility of instance variables of a class, but cannot define any additional instance variables. They cannot support the full range of test code but can be used as a **Test Control Interface**.

Participants

The participants in this pattern are the class under test and the Private Access Driver. Figure 19.13 illustrates this approach for the Part example. Figure 19.14 shows how a test bundle could be configured to support console testing.

Collaborations

A Private Access Driver is supported by translation-time binding. The scoping mechanism allows a Private Access Driver to do anything that could be done within the scope of the class under test. Besides sending and evaluating test messages, a Private Access Driver typically exercises and probes the private features of the class under test.

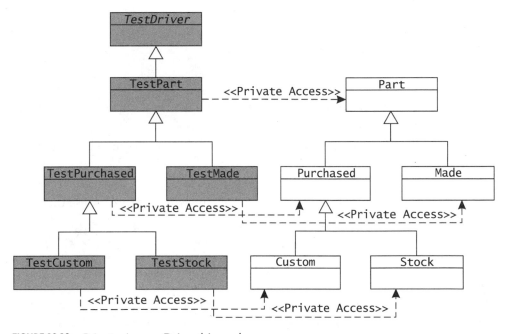

FIGURE 19.13   Private Access Driver hierarchy.

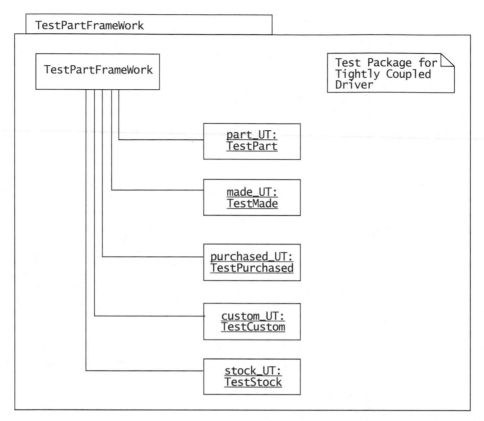

FIGURE 19.14   Test package for Private Access Driver.

- It initializes private instance variables to meet the setup requirements of particular test cases.
- It sends test messages to private methods so that adequate testing of these methods may be achieved.
- It examines private instance variables to assess their consistency with the results reported by the class's public interface and to assess their correctness.

Implementation

Ada 95

Any Ada 95 compilation unit may be declared as a *child* of another, but only a package may have a child unit. All features of the parent package are visible to the child unit: objects, functions, and procedures in the private part of a package, as well as private types in the package specification and body. A *private child unit* (private package P.C is . . .) is similar to a protected member: it is visible within a subsystem (hierarchy), but cannot be *with*ed by an external client.

A child can be added, modified, and removed without a recompilation of the parent packages or clients of the parent. This approach is ideal for test drivers. When a parent private type is changed and recompiled, however, the child unit must be recompiled before it can be used. Inconsistencies in the child package (e.g., it sends a message to a deleted procedure) will be revealed.

```
package ClassUnderTest is . . .    -- Class under test

package TestSuite.ClassUnderTest   -- Private Access Driver
```

C++

The friend should be defined in the same header file as the CUT. This strategy prevents accidental or intentional spoofing of the CUT and reduces coupling. Changes to the CUT will have effects on other files that use this friend. Friendship is not inherited, so each class in the hierarchy must declare its Private Access Driver as a friend.

```
//Test Package using a friend
#include <iostream.h>
using namespace std;

class ClassUnderTest {
    int x, y;
public:
    ClassUnderTest( int i, int j) { x = i; y = j; }

    virtual ~ClassUnderTest( ){ }

    bool areSame( ) { x == y; }
    /*CUT must declare a friend*/
    friend class TestProcedure_ClassUnderTest;
};

class TestProcedure_ClassUnderTest {
    int m, n;
    ClassUnderTest cut;
public:
    bool test001( ) {
        m = 0; n = 0;
        ClassUnderTest cut(m,n);
```

```
        testTrue( x == y);
        testTrue (cut.areSame( ) );
    }
};

int main ( ) {
    TestProcedure_ClassUnderTest testPackage;

    return testPackage.test001( );
}
```

An alternative is to use unchecked casting, which is effective but horribly coupled. Suppose we want to test the date logic in class Account, but the class provides no way to set the date.

```
class Account{
private:
    int balance = 0;
    Date dateOpened;
    int acctId = 0;
};

class AccountStruct{
public:
    int balance = 0;
    Date dateOpened;
    int acctId = 0;
};

int main () {
Date testDate("01/10/2000");
    anAccount Account;
    AccountStruct *testAcct = (AccountStruct *)&Account;
     testAcct->dateOpened = testDate;
}
```

Finally, a truly nasty preprocessor trick may be used to make everything visible at file scope.

```
#define private public
#define protected public
```

This approach makes all protected and private members appear public to the files that use these preprocessor definitions. All other files will continue to see private and protected members, but the files in question will have full access to everything. These files would contain the test driver code.

Eiffel

Eiffel does not implement a private access mechanism. All superclass features are visible to subclasses, however, and a class can limit the extent to which its features are visible to clients outside the hierarchy.

```
class INSPECTOR-- Adapted from [Barbey 97, 81]
feature

viewer: INTERNAL;

Create (object: CUT) is
   local
      i: Integer;
   do
      viewer.Create;
      io.Putstring (viewer.class_name (object));
      io.Putint (viewer.field_count (object));
      from
         i := 1;
      until
         i > viewer.field_count(object)
      loop
         io.Putstring(viewer.field_name (i, object));
         i:= i+1;
      end;
end; -- Create
end -- Inspector
```

Java

Java scoping follows the C++ public/protected/private model for the most part, but does not support private access that allows holes in these boundaries. However, inner classes can be used to achieve the same effect. An inner class is a class declared within the scope of another class. All elements of the inner class are granted the visibility as locally defined elements of the outer class. In this way, the inner class can directly access private variables of the outer class. An example of an inner class is given in ***Built-in Test Driver***.

Objective-C

Objective-C does not directly support private access. The @defs construct can be used to give the effect of private access, as can *class categories* (see ***Test Control Interface***). All methods are public in Objective-C. Variables are either @public (visible everywhere), @protected (visible to a class and its subclasses), or @private (visible at class scope only). The @defs directive may be used to access private or protected instance variables in a driver function or class.[3] The @defs(ClassName) directive produces the declaration list for the designated class. This list can be used to define a struct that corresponds to the object. The struct allows direct access to the implementation. Suppose that we wish to test class Account and need access to a private instance variable dateOpened. We generate the struct with the following directive:

```
struct accountStruct {
   @defs(Account)
}*publicAccount;
```

A pointer publicAccount is established for an Account object. The object definition is cast to obtain the object's pointer.

```
// Create an account object and a pointer
id anAccount;
anAccount = [[Account alloc] init];

// Set the pretest state and allocate a date object
process(anAccount)
Date* dateOpened;

// Cast the struct pointer to the account object
publicAccount = (struct accountStruct *)anAccount;

// account object's private variables are visible
dateOpened = publicAccount->dateOpened;
// . . .
```

Smalltalk

Smalltalk does not support private access. Instance variables are visible within the class that defines them but to no other class or subclass. Temporary variables are allocated for the duration of a method or block activation and are not visible elsewhere. Shared variables are visible at system scope. To achieve access to private instance variables and methods, the test driver is implemented as part of the class *(Built-in Test Driver)* or by using the Envy class extensions to implement a *Test Control Interface*.

---

3. Steve Donelow suggested this idiom and provided the example.

Consequences

A Private Access Driver has several advantages:

- Access to all methods and instance variables is obtained. No obstacles are posed to setting and determining concrete state.
- Test case setup and evaluation will often be simpler. For example, instead of sending several million messages to reach the storage limit of a collection, a simple loop may be used or a previously generated image can be retrieved and copied to a particular location using assembly language. This approach can cut test runtime and make repetition possible. Similar shortcuts can be applied to evaluate the results of large or complex implementation data structures.
- Corrupt states may be induced directly to evaluate exception handling.
- A Private Access Driver avoids risk of a bug in an accessor method providing spurious test results.
- Test drivers can share the same interface.
- The pattern supports test case inheritance.
- In Ada 95, a child unit may be added without any change to the parent package.

Disadvantages of the pattern include the following:

- A Private Access Driver is tightly coupled to implementation. If the implementation changes, the driver should at least be reviewed, if not reworked.
- A Private Access Driver can induce side effects that appear to be application bugs.
- In C++, the friend class declaration must be coded in the class under test. This effort may require reworking existing code. If the declaration will not be shipped, it must be removed. Once removed, the application should be subjected to a regression test. If the regression suite depends on the Private Access Drivers, however, then it will be either non-runnable or of dubious value.
- The access granted to a Private Access Driver can be misused. If the test suites are shipped with the application code, it is possible that

they could be reworked as a Trojan horse to defeat security or as
the basis for a quick-and-dirty hack to correct a bug or implement a
feature.

Known Uses

The Cantata testing tool generates driver classes for C++ as friend classes
[Dorman 93, Dorman 97].

Related Patterns

A *TestDriver Superclass* provides common services and interfaces. If the test
methods or objects implement *Percolate the Object Under Test*, superclass tests
may be automatically run on subclass objects.

Test Control Interface

Intent

Use special-purpose language mechanisms that make all elements of a class's implementation visible to a driver to achieve necessary control of pretest state and observation of post-test state.

Motivation

See the Controllability, Observability, and Reuse section. A Test Control Interface uses special access mechanisms to achieve test control and observation. This interface may be used by another driver.

Applicability

This pattern is useful at class and cluster scope for unit and integration testing. It can provide the test driver for Objective-C and Smalltalk/ENVY implementations with sufficient control.

Participants

The components of this pattern are the class under test, the Test Control Interface, and the test driver. Figure 19.15 shows this approach for the `Part` example.

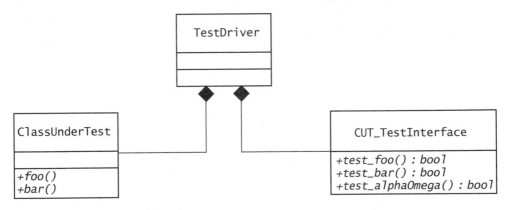

FIGURE 19.15   Test Control Interface.

Collaborations

A Test Control Interface is supported by translation-time binding. Its scoping mechanism allows it to set and get all instance variables within the scope of the class under test.

- It initializes private instance variables to meet the setup requirements of particular test cases.
- It reports the value of private instance variables so that the test case implementation can assess their consistency with the results reported by the class's public interface and make other checks for correct content.

A Test Control Interface does not perform any other testing function.

Implementation

Ada 95

See *Private Access Driver.* A child unit can be used as a Test Control Interface.

C++

See *Private Access Driver.* A friend class can be used as a Test Control Interface.

Eiffel

See *Drone.* Any Eiffel subclass can be used as a Test Control Interface.

Java

Java does not have a construct that can support a full-access Test Control Interface. Java interfaces can provide such access only if the test methods are implemented in the class under test.

Objective-C

The class category supported in the OpenStep Objective-C (Yellow Box) can support a Test Control Interface.

```
#import "ClassUnderTest.h"
@interface ClassUnderTest(ClassUnderTestInterface )
// Test method declarations
-   (BOOL) testFoo;
-   (BOOL) testBar;
-   (void) setState;
-   (void) getState;
@end
```

```
#import "ClassUnderTestInterface.h"
@implementation ClassUnderTest(ClassUnderTestInterface )
//method definitions to implement the test interface
-  (BOOL) testFoo { /*body*/ };
-  (BOOL) testBar { /*body*/ };
-  (void) setState { /*body*/ };
-  (void) getState { /*body*/ };
@end
```

Smalltalk

The Smalltalk/ENVY development environment supports class extensions. A class defines its protocol, methods, instance variables, and comments. A class extension defines additional methods for a class. Classes and class extensions are organized by *applications* or *subapplications*. A class can be extended in a separate application or subapplication by adding new methods to a previously defined class. The Test Control Interface can be defined as a class extension. The class extension is declared as in the test driver.

Consequences

A Test Control Interface has the same advantages and disadvantages as a **Private Access Driver.** It is a third piece of code (besides the driver and the application) to design, develop, debug, and maintain, with corresponding cost and problems. Nevertheless, it provides an easily removed and controllable interface to observe and set state.

Known Uses

Class categories are routinely used in the development of OpenStep drivers.

Related Patterns

A **TestDriver Superclass** provides common services and interfaces. If the test methods or objects implement **Percolate the Object Under Test**, superclass tests may be automatically run on subclass objects.

Drone

Intent

Use multiple inheritance to compose a test package class that combines the driver and the class under test.

Also Known As

Mixin and *Join Test Hierarchies* [Firesmith 96].

Motivation

See the Controllability, Observability, and Reuse section. A Drone uses multiple inheritance to construct a testable class, achieves test control and observation, and inherits superclasses and their test cases.

Applicability

A Drone driver is useful at class and cluster scopes for unit and integration testing. It provides the same controllability and observability as private access, but relies on multiple inheritance instead of language-supported exposure. A Drone is indicated when the test harness code must be removed from the application system before delivery. For example, this step might be required to meet memory utilization constraints or to preclude abuse of the test harness.

Participants

Figure 19.16 shows the structure of a Drone. The components are as follows:

- The hierarchy of classes under test.
- `TestDriver`. This abstract superclass is the root of the mixin hierarchy. It exports the interface for methods `testClass` and `testInstance`. It has `testLog` as a class variable, and it defines an interface for two methods:

`testClass`	Constructs the join instance
`testInstance`	Implements the test messages

- `Test<ClassUnderTest>`. This mixin class implements test cases for a CUT. Test cases are protected. The class inherits superclass test methods and overrides them if needed.

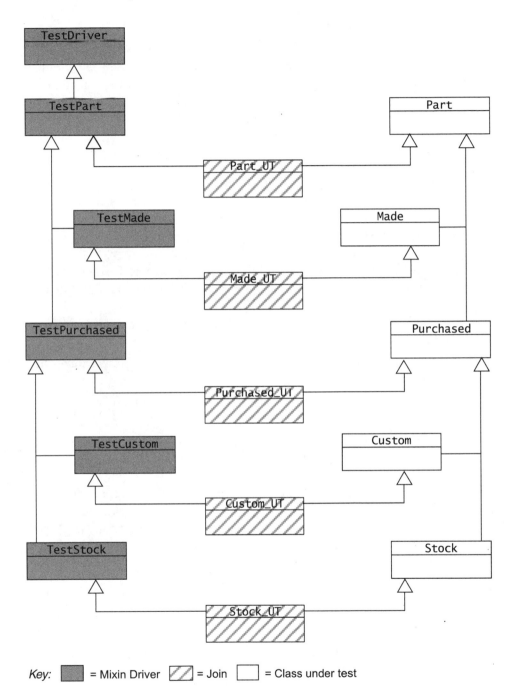

FIGURE 19.16   Drone driver hierarchy.

- Drone<ClassUnderTest>. This join class inherits from the CUT, the test mixin, and the Drone for the superclass. The Drone achieves the same controllability and observability as a subclass of the CUT would. It does not need to inherit from a superclass Drone, because all super-classes of the CUT and the TestDriver are inherited (visible) within the Drone.

Collaborations

A **mixin class** typically does not accomplish much on its own, but makes a common attribute available to disparate clients. It is supplied via inheritance instead of aggregation to take advantage of the greater accessibility that inheritance provides.[4] A **join class** exists to bring two or more superclasses together as a unit, at least one of which is a mixin.

The Drone pattern uses the mixin idiom to produce a test driver that has access to all parts of the class under test without altering the class under test.

- The Test<ClassUnderTest> (mixin) classes implement the test protocol, test case objects, and test execution code.
- The root TestDriver class defines an interface for test activation—the ExecuteTest method.
- The Drone (join) classes inherit from the CUT and the corresponding TestDriver, exposing features in the CUT.
- The Drone class is instantiated—for example, by main( )—and then sent the executeTest.

Testclass constructs the join class, and then sends the testInstance message to the CUT. Errorlog pointer is an input. Errorlog is a class variable, to which the test log writes. TestInstance does actual test cases (setup, send, evaluate). The protected test cases are stored in the mixins. The child joins inherit and override as needed.

---

4. Opinions vary on how to use a mixin. The relationship of a primary class to the mixin is like that of a noun to an adjective. For example, ScrollableWindow is a kind of Window, but either can be rendered as Character, HighResolution, or Animated. Window and its subclass ScrollableWindow are the primary classes and the rendering classes are the mixins, allowing six join classes: CharacterWindow, AnimatedScrollableWindow, and so on. Some authors argue that a mixin should be an abstract class that can contribute only an interface, with the join class providing the implementation. Others view it as an idiom to support reuse of method implementations, interfaces, and instance variables where the is-a-kind-of relationship does not apply.

Implementation

Figure 19.17 shows a test bundle for a Drone. A Drone cannot be implemented in Java, Objective-C, and Smalltalk because they do not support multiple inheritance. In C++, the derived `TestDriver` cannot get private features of the class under test, unless it is also a friend of the class under test or uses the hacks presented in *Test Control Interface*.

Consequences

A Drone driver has most of the advantages of a *Private Access Driver*, and several more.

- The code of the CUT need not be altered in any way.
- The pattern provides a clear separation of concerns between the test drivers and the class hierarchy under test.

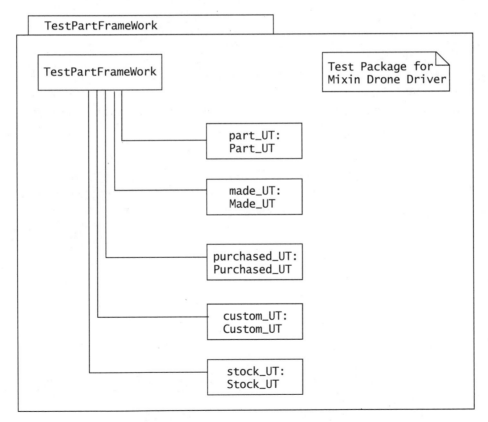

FIGURE 19.17   Test package for Drone driver.

Disadvantages of the pattern include the following:

- In languages that support private scoping (C++, Java, Objective-C, and Smalltalk), private methods and instance variables are still not visible to the Drone driver.
- The shipped class is not tested. Although the code of the CUT is unchanged, an object of the Drone class is exercised, not the CUT. A side effect of the Drone can mask an application bug.
- The join class (the Drone) can induce side effects that appear to be application bugs.
- The join class (the Drone) is tightly coupled to the implementation. If the implementation changes, the driver should at least be reviewed, if not reworked.
- There are two test hierarchies to design, code, debug, and maintain. As this structure is more complex than a single hierarchy, it is more error-prone.

Known Uses

This pattern was used for class and cluster testing of the Switched Multimegabits Data Service (SMDS) [Jézéquel 96a]. SMDS is an Eiffel system. Firesmith mentions its application on C++ systems without providing details [Firesmith 96].

Related Patterns

A *TestDriver Superclass* provides common services and interfaces. If the test methods or objects implement *Percolate the Object Under Test*, superclass tests may be automatically run on subclass objects.

Built-in Test Driver

Intent

Implement a test suite and a test driver wholly contained within the class under test. Provide an interface to activate and exercise the tests.

Also Known As

Built-in Tests [Firesmith 96].

Motivation

See the Controllability, Observability, and Reuse section. Packaging the test suite with a class removes all obstacles to controllability and observability at class scope. The test suite is inherited without requiring a separate hierarchy.

Applicability

This pattern is useful at class and cluster scope for unit and integration testing. The proximity and ease of running a test suite support iterative and incremental development. Built-in Test Driver is indicated in the following circumstances:

- Testing is a significant factor for subsequent reuse. Built-in Test Driver can support consumer reuse by offering concrete evidence of trustworthiness and by providing test suites that the consumer can use for regression testing. This supports the goals of the *Works Out of the Box* process pattern [Foote+98].
- It can contribute to the efficiency and effectiveness of producer development by providing a common test interface.

For some programming languages, Built-in Test Driver is the only way to achieve complete class scope controllability/observability.

- Java does not support mechanisms needed for access to a *Private Access Driver.* Java interfaces and subclasses cannot be used to access private methods and instance variables.
- Many Smalltalk systems do not include capabilities like the ENVY extensions needed to develop a *Test Control Interface.* Subclasses cannot be used to access instance variables.

- Categories and protocols are an OpenStep extension to the Objective-C language that are not supported by all Objective-C compilers. Developing a *Test Control Interface* without these extensions is not possible. Subclasses cannot be used to access private instance variables. The @defs approach is inelegant and error-prone.

The pros and cons of shipping the test code with the implementation are discussed in the Consequences section.

Participants

Figure 19.18 shows the general structure of Built-in Test Driver. All of its components are part of the class hierarchy under test. Each application class exports at least one public selfTest method. Individual test cases may be implemented as methods—for example, test001, test002, and so on. The client of the test interface sends the selfTest message.

Collaborations

The collaboration is much the same as any other driver, although the built-in test suite cannot be run unless the class is instantiated. Three basic collaborations are possible.

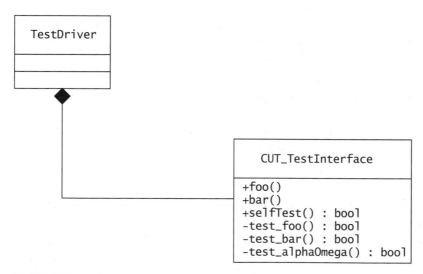

FIGURE 19.18   Built-in Test Driver.

Producer Development Testing

The selfTest message may be sent from any client of the class under test. The client may be:

- A main that instantiates only the CUT
- A main that instantiates a group of classes in a system or subsystem and sends the selfTest message to every one
- A collection class that is part of a tester interface framework, which can selectively run any combination of tests
- Any client of the class, as all such clients can send the selfTest message

The public selfTest method is an implementation of *Test Suite Method*. That is, selfTest simply sends messages to all of the individual test methods. Test cases may be implemented using the *Test Case Method*. Generally, test case methods should be declared as protected, so that they cannot be activated from outside the CUT. Once activated, the test cases are run like any other test case.

Runtime Diagnostics

An instance of the class may test itself. That is, any method of the class via test can send self.selfTest or this.selfTest. This verification could be used in at least two ways. First, the test suite can be viewed as a more extensive kind of invariant checking used to validate that the class and its servers are in a correct state. The additional execution time of this checking would limit the feasible frequency. Second, the built-in test could be run as a self-diagnostic when an exception is thrown by a server or detected by the application code.

Consumer Regression Testing

The superclass test suite can be invoked from consumer subclasses or via any of the preceding client collaborations. For example, this approach can provide a more extensive, but equally simple kind of checking similar to the AssertValid() idiom for Microsoft's C++ Foundation Classes (MFC). When an MFC consumer develops a derived class, it is considered good practice to implement Derived::AssertValid(). The first statement in this function is the message to base class AssertValid().

```
#ifdef _DEBUG
void Derived::AssertValid() const {
    // Assert the base class first
```

```
   CObject::AssertValid();
   // Assertions for derived class invariant...
}
#endif


#ifdef _DEBUG
void Derived::selfTest() {
   CObject::selfTest();
   // Tests cases for the consumer's class ...
}
#endif
```

This code is an example of **Percolation**. Again, the test suite `CObject::_
selfTest()` would typically be more extensive than `AssertValid()` and would
be used with the appropriate frequency.

Implementation

Code bloat can be reduced if the instance variables that are used only by the
test routines are declared as static (C++, Java, and Objective-C) or as class variables (Smalltalk, Objective-C). In addition, compiler directives can be used
to control expansion, leading to nonreferenced code. Compile-time and link-
time optimizers often do not generate any executable code for nonreferenced
symbols.

In Java and OpenStep Objective-C, access to the test methods can be controlled with an interface. The class can respond to an interface that includes (or
does not include) test methods.

Java

Two features of Java may be used to implement a built-in test driver. An "embedded main" establishes the class as a Java application, which allows it to be
run with command-line invocation of Java [Smith 97]. For example:

```
public class ClassUnderTest {

    private int x:
    public void setx(int newx) {
        x = newx;
    }

    /* Test interface */
    public static void main(string argv[]){
        ClassUnderTest out = new classUnderTest( );
        out.setx(0);
        if (x==0) {
            System.out.println("passed");
```

```
        } else {
             System.out.println("failed");
        }
        return;
   }
} // End ClassUnderTest
```

An inner class is a class declared within the scope of another class. All elements of the inner class are granted the visibility as locally defined elements of the outer class. In this way, the inner class can directly access private variables of the outer class. The following example combines the embedded main technique with an inner class.

```
public class ClassUnderTest {
    private int x;
    public void setx(int newx) {
        x = newx;
    }

    public static class BuiltInTest {
        public static void main(String argv[ ]){
            test001();
            return;
        }

        public void test001() {
            ClassUnderTest out = new ClassUnderTest();
            out.setx(0);
            if (x == 0) {
                System.out.println("passed");
            } else {
                  System.out.println("failed");
            }
            return;
        }

    } // End Built-in Test

} // End ClassUnderTest
```

Inner classes can inherit, so it is possible to reuse features defined in an *Incremental Testing Framework* like JUnit, as the following example shows.[5]

---

5. Suggested by Dave Hoag.

```
public class ClassUnderTest {
    private int x;
    public void setx(int newx) {
        x = newx;
    }

    public static class BuiltInTest extends test.Framework.Testcase {

        public static void main(Strig argv[]){
            test.textui.TestRunner.run(suite());
        }

        public Test(String testName){
            super(testName);
        }

        public static test.framework.TestSuite suite( ) {
            test.framework.TestSuite suite =
                                new test.framework.TestSuite();
            suite.addTest(new Test("test setx()"));
            return suite;
        }

        /** Test Case Implementation */

        public void test001() {
            ClassUnderTest out = new ClassUnderTest();
            out.setx(0);
            assert("Test 001 did not pass", x == 0);
        }

    } // End BuiltInTest
} // End ClassUnderTest
```

Consequences

The cost and difficulty of Built-in Test Driver development are roughly the same
as for other driver patterns. Because no additional hierarchy and special access
code are needed, the cost and complexity of the test code can be lower. The advantages of Built-in Test Driver include the following:

- Encapsulation obstacles (at class scope) to controllability/observability
  are eliminated. The need for server stubs may also be reduced, as server
  interfaces are accessible to the driver and the test cases. Stubs may still
  be needed for interfaces that are insufficient for testing purposes and
  that act as servers of the servers.

- If this approach is used consistently, a single test interface can be obtained for the entire application. A single tester interface can therefore run tests on all objects in an application system.

- There is no extra test driver class hierarchy to maintain.

- If superclass test cases are implemented as methods, then they can be reused by subclass test suites or overridden.

- Because the test harness is packaged with the application code, this pattern poses the lowest barrier to test reuse.

- The increased testability and concrete evidence of reliability can promote greater consumer reuse.

Built-in Test Driver also has some disadvantages:

- Bugs in the test cases or test drivers can induce side effects or spurious test results.

- If the test code and application code are developed by the same person, errors (incorrect assumptions) that led to application faults are likely to be carried over to the test implementation. Using a systematic test design approach can offset this risk. If the test suite is designed and developed by a different person, the risk of test blind spots can be reduced.

- The test code can be misused. For example, if it produces a side effect, the side effect might be incorporated as part of the application by a subsequent maintainer. State setting or reporting methods could therefore be used for malicious or criminal purposes.

- The test code may increase executable size ("code bloat") and degrade storage-sensitive performance, increase storage contention, and induce load-related failures in the memory-management services. Unless the tests are run as part of the application system, however, execution time should not have any direct increase.

- If used for Java applets, the test code may increase executable size and will increase the transmit and load time of the applet.

- The test code can skew coverage analysis if the test code is instrumented.

Perceptions and expectations should also be considered. For example, some developers may view adding test code as a disfigurement of their work. Although Built-in Test Driver results in the simplest and smallest driver implementation, inclusion of the driver and test cases with the application source may seem like an increase in the scope and effort of the application. This inaccurate perception may persist even if it can be shown that development of a separate driver necessarily requires more code, is more error-prone, and may be insufficient for testing purposes.

In addition, the presence of a Built-in Test Driver by itself does not provide any greater (or lesser) assurance of reliability. The test code is only as good as the test design and the coverage that it achieves.

Known Uses

Firesmith mentions several applications of this pattern without providing details [Firesmith 96]. RBSC clients doing Java application development have found this pattern to be an effective approach.

Related Patterns

Built-in Test Driver supports the *Works Out of the Box* process pattern [Foote+98]. Considerations for test code implementation can be guided by *Singleton* [Gamma+95].

A *TestDriver Superclass* provides common services and interfaces. If the test methods or objects implement *Percolate the Object Under Test*, superclass tests may be automatically run on subclass objects.

19.5   Test Execution Patterns

A test harness framework must provide several general abilities. We want to run simple or composite test suites and record the results, support controllability and observability for the IUT, and support iterative and incremental development by making it easy to run regression tests. Three patterns for controlling the execution of a test suite are presented:

- *Command Line Test Bundle*. Run a test package from the command line.
- *Incremental Testing Framework*. Support interactive test development and regression testing.
- *Fresh Objects*. Provide the ability to control and observe the servers of the object(s) under test.

Command Line Test Bundle

Intent

Provide a main program or root class so that the test driver(s) and the object(s) under test can be translated to an executable that may run from a command line or similar interface.

Motivation

When the IUT does not have a GUI or other testable interface, the test harness code and the IUT must be translated into an executable file(s) that can be run.

Applicability

Building a test executable is the basic approach for most API-level testing. This pattern may be used with any of the preceeding test drivers.

Participants

The structure of an executable test bundle is shown in Figures 19.8, 19.14, and 19.17. A test bundle typically has several primary components:

- TestMain. This main function or root class allows generation of the object code and is translated into a symbolic entry point for the run-time system.
- The object(s) under test. The objects are defined in the test package so that they can be passed to the drivers. See *Percolate the Object Under Test*.
- The test driver object(s). The test driver class is instantiated.

Collaborations

The operating system invokes the test package executable. The collaboration depends on the structure of the test driver.

Implementation

A few simple suggestive examples follow.

C++

```
int foo(int bar)
{
    // do something
}
//Test driver
#ifdef TEST
#include <assert.h>

int main()
{
    assert ( foo(1) == 100);
    assert ( foo(2) == 200);
    assert ( foo(*garbage) == 0 );
// ...
}
#endif
```

Compile the preceding code as

```
cc -DTEST foo.c
```

The test drivers are instantiated and run as a group.

```
int main( ){
    A aut; B but; C cut;
    TestC testC;
    TestB testB;
    TestA testA;

    testA.testA01(aut);    // Run Test Package for A
    testB.testB01(but);    // Run Test Package for B
    testC.testC01(cut);    // Run Test Package for C
}
```

Java

A Java test driver can be packaged as a main class—in effect, as an application [Smith 97]. JDoc can be used to develop supporting documentation for the test code. The test wrapper could point to some Web pages with additional documentation, coverage reports, and test cases.

```
public class ATestApp {

public static void main ( String [] args ) {

    System.out.print ( args [i] )
```

```
    System.out.println();

    // Test code follows--e.g., and instance of the CUT declared
    // and test messages are sent and evaluated.

  }// end main

} end test package wrapper
```

Consequences

Tests can be run (and rerun) easily. The test bundle must be developed by persons with programming skills. Testers without programming skills can run a test bundle, but probably will not be able to produce them. Test bundles can be packaged into large test suites using any suitable command-line script processor. Typically, a test bundle has a close correspondence to a configuration item, so test bundles can usually be included in a configuration management process. This effort usually supports regression testing. Test bundles are shipped with a reusable framework that can provide a working example to consumers.

Known Uses

Most commercially available test harness generators produce executables that are to be run from the command line. The test executables produced with the *Incremental Testing Framework* are runnable from the command line.

Related Patterns

Works Out of the Box process pattern [Foote+98].

Incremental Testing Framework

Intent

Provide a user interface that supports development and execution of test cases and test suites. Support iterative and incremental testing by providing the ability to define test cases easily, add them to a test suite, and run them. As the test suite grows, make it easy to rerun test suites. Provide a simple framework that can be reused for testing any application.

Also Known As

Tester Interface, Tester Framework [Firesmith 96].

Motivation

A test suite for a small system can easily have tens of thousands of test cases. It is a complex software system in its own right. The test cases should be organized so that they can be easily rerun and adapted as the SUT evolves.

The interleaving of test design and execution with small coding increments (design a little, code a little, test a little) is beneficial. Errors can be revealed soon after they are made, which usually reduces the cost of diagnosis and correction. The increased visibility of testing and the point of view required for test design also help to prevent errors. If the effort to produce and run tests is high, however, less testing will be done. Gamma and Beck observe that "Every programmer knows they should write tests for their code. Few do. The universal response to 'Why not?' is, 'I'm in too much of a hurry.' This quickly becomes a vicious cycle—the more pressure you feel, the fewer tests you write. The fewer tests you write, the less productive you are and the less stable your code becomes. The less productive and accurate you are, the more pressure you feel" [Gamma+98]. A simple, adaptable testing framework can overcome this problem.

Applicability

An Incremental Testing Framework supports unit and integration testing at class and cluster scopes. It is especially well suited to rapid iterative and incremental development.

The implementation uses the public interface of the class under test. The typical obstacles to controllability and observability of a public interface may make some test design patterns infeasible with this driver. For example, its lack of controllability might require that millions of add messages be sent to the CUT to reach the capacity limit of a collection. If the public interface of the class under test is insufficient or awkward for testing purposes, consider using *Private Access Driver*, *Test Control Interface*, *Drone*, or *Built-in Test Driver*.

Participants

Figure 19.19 shows a Class Diagram of the participants.

Framework Classes

The basic framework has three classes: `TestResult`, `TestCase`, and `TestSuite`. `TestResult` records the results of a particular run of a test case or test suite. It has the following responsibilities:

- Add a `DidNotPass` entry to the `DidNotPass` list (the list of successful test cases).[6]
- Add an exception to the list of unexpected exceptions thrown.
- Log the start of a test run.
- Log the start of a test case.
- Log the completion of a test run.
- Report all errors in a test run.
- Report the number of errors in a test run.
- Report all `DidNotPass` entries for a test run.
- Report the number of `DidNotPass` entries for a test run.
- Report the total number of tests executed in a test run.
- Report the status of the entire test run (`AllPass` or at least one `DidNotPass`).

   `TestCase` is an abstract class that provides a common interface for test case setup, execution, evaluation, and cleanup. It has the following responsibilities:

---

6. Several implementations refer to a test case that does not pass as a "failure" and exceptions as "errors" [Beck 94, Gamma+98]. A no pass test that causes the IUT to produce a nonexpected result is a successful test (a bug has been revealed). Similarly, expected exceptions are not bugs, but unexpected exceptions are. I use *unexpected exception* to refer to this kind of bug.

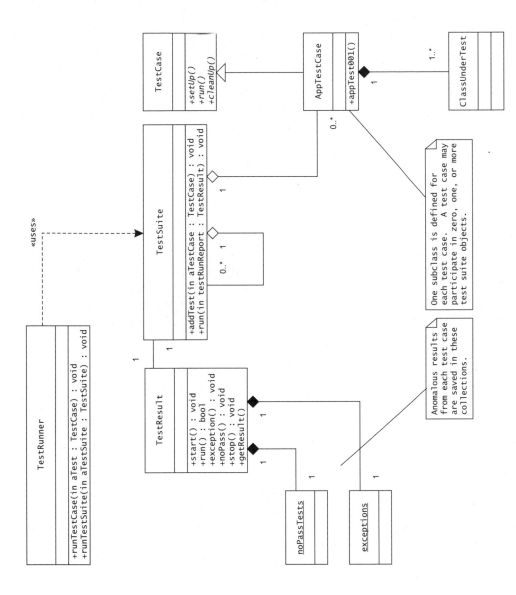

FIGURE 19.19 Incremental Testing Framework: Class Diagram.

1045

- Establish an empty `TestResult` object for a test case.
- Assign a test case name.
- Report the test case name.
- Provide an interface to do test case setup.
- Provide an interface to run the test case and return a `TestResult` object.
- Provide an interface to do test case cleanup.

Some implementations of `TestCase` also provide generic comparators to evaluate actual and expected results and to record `DidNotPass` entry as needed. For example, a method `assertEqual(x, y)` returns true if objects x and y are equal [Gamma+98].

`TestSuite` follows the *Composite* pattern [Gamma+95]. Both `TestSuite` and `TestCase` respond to the `run` message. The members of this collection may be other collections (test suites) or single items (test cases). `TestSuite` will support an arbitrarily large and complex hierarchy of test cases. It has the following responsibilities:

- Add a test case subclass to the suite.
- Add a test suite subclass to the suite.
- Report the number of test cases in the test suite.
- Run all test elements and return a `TestResult` object.

User Components

The user develops several kinds of classes and objects to use this framework. First, subclasses of `TestCase` (generically called `AppTestCase` here) are developed. These subclasses instantiate the OUT and all other objects necessary for each test, including the message parameters for the OUT. The subclass implements the abstract interface in `TestCase` for the setup, evaluation, and cleanup methods. It has the following responsibilities:

- Provide the code to do test case setup.
- Provide the code to do test case cleanup.
- Implement one method for each test case. This method sends messages necessary for setup, sends test messages to the OUT, passes the actual and expected results to the generic comparators, and sends a message to the cleanup method.

Test cases are implemented by methods of the `AppTestCase` class.

In another part of the code, messages are sent to a `TestSuite` object that adds each `AppTestCase`. The Java implementation of the `TestSuite` object uses Reflection to send a `run` message to the test case name, which is the method name that implements the test case.

Collaborations

Figure 19.20 shows a Collaboration Diagram for the Incremental Testing Framework. A test run begins when the `TestRunner` object is executed (for example, in Java, by coding the `main` method in this class so it can run as a command-line application). The test package either loads an existing test suite object or runs the code to add the test cases in the package to the test suite. The `run` message is sent to the test suite object, which creates a new `TestResult` object. The suite sends the `run` message to each test case or test suite. If the

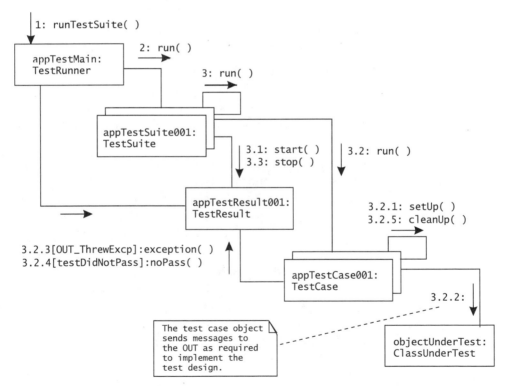

FIGURE 19.20   Incremental Testing Framework: Collaboration Diagram.

element is an `AppTestCase`, then the test case does setup, execution, evaluation, and cleanup, and adds a log entry to the `TestResult` object. If the element is a (different) `TestSuite` object, the `run` message is applied to its elements. After the last test suite element has been run, control returns to the `TestRunner` object. The contents of the `TestResult` object are displayed, showing which tests passed or did not pass.

The code that adds the `AppTestCases` to an `AppTestSuite` can be included in the `TestRunner` object.

Implementation

Complete working implementations of this pattern are freely available on the Internet for C++, Eiffel, Java, and Smalltalk. See the Known Uses section for a summary of these implementations and their URLs. The test cases and test suites are incrementally developed.

1. Create a subclass of `TestCase`, `AppTestCase`, for each test case or group of related test cases.

2. Implement methods in `AppTestCase` for each test case. The name of the method is the test case identifier.

3. If the same setup can be used in more than one test case, factor it out and implement it as a separate method of `AppTestCase`.

4. If the same setup can be used by two or more test cases, implement the setup as a test case, so that it can be invoked as part of the test suite.

5. Organize test cases into test suites. This task is accomplished by passing the name of the test case method to a test suite object. The entries in a test suite are references to `AppTestCase.TestMethodName`. A test suite can contain any combination of methods in an `AppTestCase` and may execute the methods in any order. Sequential dependencies among test cases can be avoided if each test case does a complete cleanup.

6. This pattern is typically used with a tester GUI that supports browsing and test execution. For example, the JUnit implementation of `TestRunner` extends several Java AWT classes to provide a simple user interface to run tests. The user can select either test cases or test suites to run. A progress bar is displayed as the tests run. Colors indicate pass and no pass results.

Consequences

The Incremental Testing Framework has several advantages:

- The implementation of test cases is simple, consistent, and modular. The full power of the implementation language may be used for complex test algorithms.
- The ease of test implementation and execution supports iterative, incremental development.
- The ease of rerunning a test suite makes high-frequency regression testing possible. This can support *High-frequency Integration*.
- The approach will support at least moderately large projects. Known uses include system with tens of thousands of test cases.
- The cost of test case development and maintenance should be roughly the same as that for a *Symmetric Driver*. The explicit test framework should improve productivity by offering a single approach to learn, use, and maintain.

This approach has two main disadvantages:

- The TestCase class relies on the interface of the class under test. Some interesting test design patterns can be stymied by controllability/observability problems. These obstacles may be overcome by incorporating appropriate elements of *Private Access Driver*, *Test Control Interface*, *Drone*, or *Built-in Test Driver*.
- The TestCase class does not provide an explicit mechanism to rerun superclass tests in the context of a subclass. This obstacle may be overcome by incorporating appropriate elements of *Percolate the Object Under Test* and constructing an AppTestCase hierarchy under TestCase to correspond with the hierarchy under test.

Both remedies increase the complexity of the test harness.

The implementations in the Known Uses section do not address test support capabilities such as storage and retrieval of tests, support of regression testing by using the results of past tests, and version control issues. Support for IEEE 829 test documentation items is not considered here, but could be added (as Beale's Eiffel framework shows). Design and implementation of these capabilities is straightforward and should be considered to support a complete and repeatable test process.

Known Uses

Rettig's Test Tools

The `TestManager` is a Smalltalk class that uses hard-coded test cases [Rettig 91]. The test class responds true or false (pass/fail). Several modes may be designated: write a log file, display results in a window, or start debugger. The user enters `TestManager: testClass: ClassUnderTest`. If all tests pass, the driver answers `true`. All such class tests may be invoked from a single `TestProcedure` class. This class was used in daily integration testing on a 50 KLOC Smalltalk application.

Beck's Smalltalk Framework

A simple Smalltalk test driver can be constructed with three classes: `TestCase`, `TestSuite`, and `TestResult` [Beck 94]. `TestCase` instantiates the object under test, sends a message for the desired test, evaluates the result, and then does cleanup. `TestSuite` contains a collection of `TestCases` and records the result of running each `TestCase` in `TestResult`. A `TestCase` subclass is coded for each test case for the CUT. It is suggested that all application classes respond to the message `testSuite`, returning a collection of unit tests for the class. Source code for the Dolphin, Squeak, VisualAge, VisualSmalltalk, and VisualWorks environments is available at

ftp://www.armaties.com/TestingFramework

A C++ port is also available, as is the JUnit Java implementation.

Beale's IEEE 829 Framework for Eiffel

Thomas Beale has developed an Eiffel test framework based on the test documentation specified by IEEE 829. Each test case is implemented as a descendant class of an abstract class `TEST_CASE`, which is collected in a `TEST_SUITE` class. `TEST_CASE` descendants implement the `execute()` function, which exercises the CUT. They can optionally implement the `check_result` function to evaluate pass/DNP. The result is logged. `TEST_ENV` is an abstract class that is subclassed to define common test data sets, procedures, and utilities. Both `TEST_CASE` and `TEST_SUITE` inherit from the specialization of `TEST_ENV` to access these common objects.

JUnit

The JUnit testing framework is a Java implementation of Beck's Smalltalk framework [Gamma+98]. It uses an abstract `TestCase` class that is subclassed to implement a test case or group of related test cases. `TestCase` objects can be collected into a `TestSuite` object that can run all of the test cases. The implementation uses Java Reflection to bind the name of the test case in a test suite collection to an actual `TestCase` object. The framework plays a key role in supporting the Extreme Programming approach of testing and retesting each small increment of code. An article about JUnit and the source code may be found at

http://members.pingnet.ch/gamma/junit.htm

Related Patterns

The recursive containment of test cases or test suites within a test suite is an implementation of the *Composite* pattern [Gamma+95].

Fresh Objects

Intent

Implement consistent built-in test capabilities at component scope with interfaces that provide system scope controllability and observability.

Motivation

How can an entire system of objects that encapsulate their implementation and state be made controllable and observable? Even with a user-controllable interface to class scope tests, achieving sufficient controllability can be difficult, especially in a distributed object environment. Simulating the behavior of a server object that is composed of many levels of other objects may be difficult for a stub.

The following newsgroup query provides an example of these difficulties in testing large systems:

> As I spend more time working with application frameworks (e.g., Borland's OWL or Microsoft's MFC), I've come to notice that unit testing becomes increasingly difficult as one includes more of the class components. Stubbing out the behavior of a complex object requires a very involved set of simulation code.

The poster asks what can be done about this problem.

In a typical test run, the system under test (the class under test, all of its servers, all of their servers, and so on) is loaded and some setup code is run. If necessary, stubs may be used to force needed values in server objects. The residue of preceding test cases in servers may be either useful or problematic. A system whose pretest setup is achieved in this manner is said to be using **canned objects**. In contrast, a system whose pretest setup is achieved by setting every object to a desired state for each test case is said to use **fresh objects**. These terms come from the TOBAC system [Seipmann+94].

Applicability

The Fresh Objects pattern is applicable when a very high degree of testability is required and when the system under test can be designed and implemented from the outset with this capability. All (or most) of the classes in the system must implement several built-in test methods. This pattern will increase development cost and system complexity. It should not be attempted unless the increased testability warrants the expense. The cost of retrofitting the *Fresh Objects* framework to an existing system could be significant. This pattern is best suited for development of new, complex systems with high reliability requirements and low intrinsic controllability and observability.

Participants

The basic framework has two classes: `TestManager` and `TestInterface`.

`TestManager` implements a central registry for all objects in the system under test and provides a single point of control to support testing. It has the following responsibilities:

- Register an object creation (constructor activated). Assumes `self` or `this` sent by registering object.
- Register an object deletion (destructor activated). Assumes `self` or `this` sent by registering object.
- Request that a designated object check its invariant.
- Request that a designated object run a particular test suite on itself.
- List all "live" registered objects.
- List all "dead" registered objects.
- List all registered objects.

`TestInterface` is an abstract class that declares method interfaces to support the following responsibilities:

- Check the class invariant.
- Run a test suite.
- Set the object to a specific concrete state.
- Report the current concrete state of the object.

Collaborations

Fresh Objects provides a standard test API for all classes. There are two main classes. The `TestManager` class (Figure 19.21) provides a single user interface for running tests and a single point of control for test activation on objects in the system under test and system-wide view of object activation. The

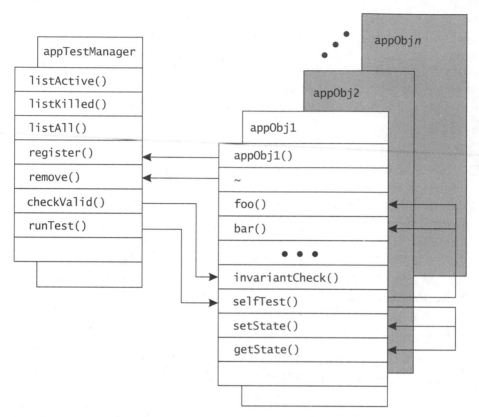

FIGURE 19.21   Fresh Objects: runtime collaboration with `TestManager`.

`TestInterface` class (Figure 19.22) is an abstract superclass for all application classes. It defines a driver, a reporter, which accepts messages from the `TestManager`. Each application class provides an implementation for the methods driver, reporter, and so on.

`TestManager` has the following responsibilities:

- Provide a single user interface for running tests.
- Provide a single point of control for test activation on objects in the system under test.
- Provide a global view of object activation.

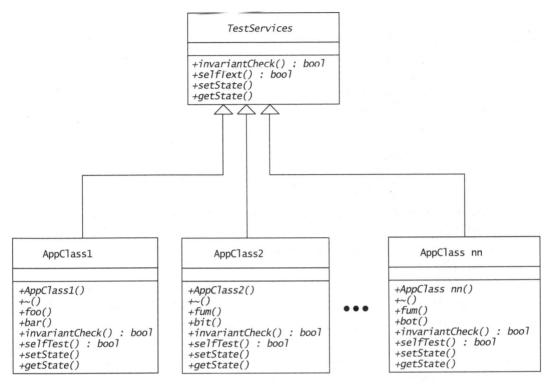

FIGURE 19.22 Fresh Objects: `TestService` class and `Application` classes.

`TestInterface` has the following responsibilities:

- Provide a common interface to built-in test methods in all application classes.
- Implement general-purpose test support features: logging, reporting, and so on.
- Each application class implements the `TestInterface` protocol.

Implementation

A Fresh Objects implementation must deal with two main problems: enabling/ disabling of services and state control.

Enable/Disable

It should be possible to automatically enable or disable the services provided by Fresh Objects. The considerations and techniques presented in Chapter 17 apply. Useful set/reset and reporter functions necessarily violate encapsulation. BIT services should not be used to accomplish application requirements. To prevent inadvertent or willful misuse of BIT services, a safety provision is advisable. Three approaches are possible.

1. *Source code* control uses compiler directives to include or exclude BIT features. Consequently, either a BIT or a non-BIT version of the SUT can be built. This flexibility is problematic in that the tested implementation is not necessarily the released implementation. Horror stories abound regarding systems that inexplicably failed when an apparently innocuous code segment was added or removed. Source code control should be used with care.

2. *Mode control* provides a global parameter to toggle test mode and normal mode. In normal mode, BIT services are disabled. Any BIT invocation is treated as a no-op or an exception. In test mode, BIT services are enabled.

3. *Password control* requires a password of some kind to activate BIT functions. The driver must supply a password value in a parameter defined as part of the BIT interface. A BIT request without the password would be treated as a no-op or an exception.

State Control

A set/reset method places an object in a predefined state. Several approaches are possible. The set/reset method could offer a menu of states with non-controllable instance variable values or controllable values. It could also provide for direct manipulation of instance variables.

Consequences

Fresh Objects offers several advantages:

- It provides a high degree of control over an entire system of objects through a single programmatic or user interface.
- It simplifies more extensive testing, as test cases that would otherwise be difficult to set up or evaluate become feasible.
- It simplifies regression testing, as prior configurations that would otherwise be difficult to set up or evaluate become feasible.

- It supports debugging, as developers can diagnose and evaluate a problem by experimenting with configurations that would otherwise be difficult to set up or evaluate.

Disadvantages of this pattern include the following:

- The additional test code will slow execution of application functions and increase memory requirements during testing.
- The additional test code will result in higher development and maintenance costs.
- Consistent use of the self-registration protocol and the implementation of the application class test methods is required.
- The access provided by Fresh Objects could be abused.
- If the behavior of the IUT depends on classes, frameworks, or other components that do not implement the Fresh Objects pattern, then you may not be able to achieve sufficient control over the entire IUT to justify implementing it in those components you can.

Known Uses

TestableSystem

This approach uses a registration (publisher–subscriber) pattern to test Eiffel applications. Each application object under test registers with a driver object, allowing the driver to send test messages to it [Giltinan 94]. The registry pattern requires that each class contain a registration method. A `TestRepository` class is globally visible to all objects in the SUT. It contains a pointer to every registered object. On creation, an object sends its ID to a test control object, which may then send messages to registered objects (i.e., test cases). On destruction, an object deregisters. The test control class provides a user interface for testing, issues test sequences, and supports queries on registered objects.

Several types of assertions are used with a registration driver. The `TestInstance` method verifies internal consistency by checking the class invariant and postconditions. The `MakeSafe` method turns on precondition checking following construction, class invariant checking before destruction, and heap integrity checking after destruction. The `IsSafe` method checks the class invariant and returns a Boolean.

TOBAC

TOBAC is a Smalltalk test support tool [Siepmann+94]. The system addresses the problem of setting a *complex object* to a known, useful state. The servers of an object are other objects, which in turn are composed of objects, and so on. A complex object is the entire set of objects that make up an object. Placing these objects into the desired state is a nontrivial task. Every object involved in a test (arguments, instance variables, class variables, responses, and exceptions) may need a "recursive" initialization.

The system supports four phases of test execution:

1. *Initialization*: global and class variable.
2. *Complex object creation*: recursively the set state of all members of the complex object.
3. *Execution*: set argument state and send a message to the OUT.
4. *Evaluation*: analyze the resultant state of the complex object to the expected state (this process is referred to as the "Oracle" phase, but no means for producing the expected results is discussed).

TOBAC is implemented by five main classes:

- `ObjectCreator` allows interactive definition of a complex object. The `ObjectCreator` results may be saved and are expressed in a representation that can be refined for regression testing (the TODL language).
- `TestOracle` determines whether the object under examination meets expectations. The expected and actual complex object may be compared for equality, identity, no change (equal and identical), partial change, true, false, or nil. Each object that fails the comparison is reported.
- `TestCase` performs creation, execution, and comparison by sending messages to the OUT. `TestOracle` is invoked for each instance variable, response, and argument.
- `TestSuite` contains a list of test cases. Individual test cases can be used in more than one test suite.
- `TestCaseBrowser` provides a user interface to control test execution. It displays categories, classes, test suite, class hierarchy, and test cases.

Related Patterns

Fresh Objects is a variation on the Publisher–Subscriber pattern [Buschmann +96]. Hunt describes a simple and efficient C++ approach to saving and restoring a flattened object structure that can be used to refresh test state [Hunt 95b].

◆ 19.6 A Test Implementation Syntax

The syntax provided in this section supports the test documentation specified in [IEEE 829] and represents the typical elements of API-level test cases. See the standard for detailed definitions of these items. The notation is SAF (Structured Analysis Form).

=	composed of
–	comment
|	or
+	and
{x}	0 to n instances of x
{x}i,j	i to j instances of x
< >	a composite element

```
Test Case

    = -- IUT Id
      < Symbolic Name + Version Release Identifier >

    + -- Test case ID
      < Symbolic Name + Version Release Identifier >

    + Purpose
    + Test Engineer
    + Revisions
      { Date + Description }

    + Pre-Test Environment
    + Pre-Test IUT State
    + Test Message
    + Expected Response Message
    + Expected Exceptions
    + Expected Output Actions
    + Expected Post-Test IUT State
    + Expected Post-Test Environment


Pre-Test Environment

    = -- Abstract Instantiation
      { < Set Method Values | Assignment Algorithm > }

    + -- Concrete Instantiation
      { < Instance Variable Values | Assignment Algorithm > }
```

```
        + -- Setup Process
          { < Executable Name + Parameters > }


    Pre-Test IUT State

        = < State Identifier | State Invariant Name >

        + -- Abstract Instantiation
          { < Set method Values | Assignment Algorithm > }

        | -- Concrete Instantiation
          { < Instance Variable Values | Assignment Algorithm > }

        | -- Set state Instantiation
          { < Set method Values | Assignment Algorithm > }


    Expected Response Message

        = -- Values
          { < Parameter name + Parameter value > }

        | -- Message Objects report by interface
          { Get method Value }

        | -- Message Objects report by State Reporter
          { Getstate Report }

        | -- Message Objects are inspected
          { Instance Variable Values }


    Post-Test IUT State

        = < State Identifier | State Invariant Name >

        | -- IUT reports by interface
          { Get method Value }

        | -- IUT reports by State Reporter
          { GetState Report }

        | -- IUT is inspected
          { Instance Variable Values }


  Expected Exceptions

      -- Expected Exceptions

      = { < Exception Name > }
```

Test Message

```
= -- Assignment
  { < Parameter name + Parameter value > }

| -- Concrete Instantiation
  { < Instance Variable Values | Assignment Algorithm > }

| -- Abstract Instantiation
  { < Set method Values | Assignment Algorithm > }
```

Expected Output Action

-- Messages produced by the IUT and sent to its servers/sinks

```
= {   < MessageName | FunctionName |
        ProcessName | SystemResourceName >

    + -- Value
      { Parameter name + Parameter value }

    | -- Message Objects report by interface
      { Get method Value }

    | -- Message Objects report by State Reporter
      { Getstate Report }

    | -- Message Objects are inspected
      { Instance Variable Values }
  }
```

Expected Post-Test Environment

-- State of all other objects and system resources of interest.

```
  = -- Object States
      { -- Same as Post-Test IUT State }

  + -- Parameter Values

    { Parameter name + Parameter value }

  + -- Resource Interfaces

    { ResourceInterface
        { Parameter name + Parameter value }
    }
```

```
Test Log

    = Test Log Id

    + Test Case ID

    + Start DateTime

    + Stop DateTime

    + Test Engineer

    + Test System Configuration

    + Run Notes

--  Actual results have same content and structure as setup

    + Actual Response Message
    + Actual Exceptions
    + Actual Output Actions
    + Actual Post-Test IUT State
    + Actual Post-Test Environment

    + -- Test Status
      [     Test Run Blocked
      |     Test Run Passed
      |     Test Run Did Not Pass
      |     Test Run Failed
      ]

    + Test Incident Note
```

19.7   Bibliographic Notes

Beizer's survey of test automation for procedural software is instructive [Beizer 90]. It summarizes more than 50 papers on test automation published from 1975 to 1989. Many of the basic strategies in these papers are applicable to object-oriented software. Summaries of research on test generation for abstract data types in [Binder 96i] may be of interest to tool developers.

Considerations for test drivers of C and C++ implementations are discussed in [Marick 95]. Debugging tools often support features that can be adapted for automated testing. C++ debug considerations are discussed in [Spuler 94] and [Ball 95]. Smalltalk debugging extensions are discussed in [Hinke+93] and [Rochat+93]. Eiffel test design and test drivers are discussed in [Jézéquel 96a].

Some parallels between built-in tests for VLSI and object-oriented software are considered in [Binder 94b]. The history, motivation, features, and impact of IEEE/ANSI Standard 1149.1, *Boundary Scan Architecture for Built-in Test,* are summarized in [Maunder+92]. Cox compares levels of abstraction in VLSI and class libraries in a sketch of some notions about the contribution that built-in testing could make to reuse [Cox 90]. Lakos's C++ testability guidelines are based on the concept of VLSI levels [Lakos 96].

A test harness reference model is presented in [Eickelmann+96]. Considerations for automatic test case generations are developed in [Poston 96]. A complete introduction to process and technical considerations to establish test automation for applications with a GUI is developed in [Dustin+99].

Appendix   BigFoot's Tootsie: A Case Study

Overview

A brief report on integrating a COTS tool suite for large-scale, object-oriented development is presented.

Requirements

What would an ideal COTS tool suite for automated testing and object-oriented development look like? The answer can't be too much different from Tootsie (Total Object-Oriented Testing Support Environment), an environment developed to support automated testing of a large C++ client/server application. The proof-of-concept implementation was started for an RBSC client in October 1995 and completed in March 1996.

BigFoot is a multiplatform client/server system implemented in C++. Clients use Microsoft Foundation Classes for Windows 95 and Windows NT. Server objects wrap a relational DBMS running on multiple Sun/Solaris servers. An ORB provides client/server communication using a distributed object model. BigFoot processing modes include high-volume batch, real-time external links, and GUI-based interactive sessions. The system must provide 7×24 availability. Any incorrect output could have very serious and costly consequences.

The investment in test automation was motivated by short development cycles and the need for high reliability. BigFoot customers frequently produced

---

Note: This appendix first appeared as [Binder 96e].

totally new requirements on very short notice for rapid delivery. To obtain a repeatable reduction in development cycle time, BigFoot relied on systematic reuse and an architecture designed for extensibility. To ensure high reliability and contribute to rapid development, the testing strategy had to support both high-volume regression testing and stringent component testing in compressed time cycles. Testing had to be both highly automated and highly effective.

Tootsie had three main design goals.

1. Effective Tester Interface

The target environment consisted of many technological islands. An effective test tool suite should provide a consistent mechanism for test documentation and execution, no matter the technology of the implementation under test. Access to all test capabilities should be only a few mouse clicks away from code editing, in any platform. We wanted Tootsie's users to be able to perform the following tasks:

- Control all test execution through a single user interface.
- Selectively run and rerun any subset of test cases in an entire test suite.
- Use integrated total-environment configuration management so that any application test package build could be run on any current and prior virtual machine configuration.
- Provide developers (individuals or small teams) with an isolated "sand-box" to minimize interference, code dependencies, and inadvertent wipe-outs.
- Support any build cycle, from daily to monthly.

2. Automate Test Generation

Hand-coding of drivers and stubs for comprehensive and repeatable testing can easily double programming and maintenance effort. Some aspects of test design are very challenging. Others are mechanical enough to be automated. Thus automated generation of test drivers, test cases, and stubs that would allow subsequent manual editing was needed. Tootsie would offer the following capabilities:

- Automatically generate tests from specifications and requirements.
- Automatically test hard-to-control capabilities like exception handling.

- Automatically generate a driver/stub test harness for a class or cluster with control over how much stubbing or integration.
- Support addition of manually prepared tests.
- Support cut-and-paste cloning of tests.
- Support regression testing by automatic impact analysis to select and rerun tests for unchanged components.
- Automate and support development of all scopes of the FREE test design methodology: intraclass, cluster, subsystem, and system.

3. Automate Test Setup and Execution

Effective testing cannot be done without a repeatable and controllable test suite. Repeatable testing is especially important with object-oriented development because adequate testing under most forms of reuse requires rerunning tests of reused components. It can be difficult to set and determine the state of a system of objects, so automated test setup is a necessary part of repeatable testing. Tootsie's test setup and execution would perform the following tasks:

- Control the state of the system under test: set it, reset it, save it.
- Measure coverage of statements, branches, and message interfaces.
- Represent expected results for a test to support automatic pass/fail evaluation.
- Perform automatic pass/fail evaluation.
- Provide automatic capture of test metrics.

Tootsie met these requirements.

OOA/D for Capability-driven Testing

Tootsie supports specification-based testing. In large part, Tootsie's extensive test automation was possible because a complete object model containing more than 300 problem domain classes had been developed for BigFoot. It allowed development of specification-based test suites in parallel with iterative class development. Iterative development mitigates a long-standing obstacle to specification-based testing: stale specifications. If an implementation has been refined without updating its specification, the specification is of little to no use for testing. The tester must interpolate changes to reverse-engineer a testable specification from the implementation.

The stale specification problem is addressed in two ways when an OOA/D repository is the primary source for test suites in interactive/incremental development. First, iterative changes are often small and therefore easier to record. Second, when tests can be automatically generated, there is a strong motivation to keep the specification current, as this effort reduces the developer's test design and test coding work. Automatic test generation, a viable repository, and iterative specification-based development produce a sustainable synergy that leads to higher-quality systems.

Tootsie supports the FREE testing methodology. FREE is specification-based and requires that cartoon-level object modeling technique models be made test-ready. We implemented many testability extensions discussed in Chapter 8.

- Line item requirements. A concise narrative statement of each capability to be provided, with traceability to use cases, classes, and test cases, was written.
- Extended use cases. A use case model included additional items: the operational relation and full integration with system-level, dynamic object-interaction diagrams. The operational relation is a kind of decision table that can support systematic generation of external test cases.
- A FREE state model for each class with sequentially constrained behavior.
- Preconditions and postconditions for each member function.
- State invariants for each class, implemented as Boolean member functions. A state invariant is a Boolean expression that defines the set of values allowed in the state. For example, the state invariant for the overdrawn state in an `Account` object might have the invariant `bool IsOverdrawn{balance<0}`.

Without these extensions, the typical OMT specification is an untestable cartoon. The information is useful for human interpretation but cannot support automated test case generation.

Implementation

A primary design goal for Tootsie was to use off-the-shelf software tools. A very high degree of test automation is possible when off-the-shelf tools are augmented with a systematic approach to built-in testing (parallel driver hierarchies, assertions, set/reset/register in every class, and so on). As most of the application system had been developed, it would have been impractical to retrofit extensive built-in test capabilities. We therefore concentrated on tool-based testing.

Test Control Strategy

A test plan for a system release is made up of many test runs. A test run may include many test cases; a test case may be used in many test runs. A test case has three main phases: set up, execute, and evaluate. The mechanics of these steps are significantly different depending on the implementation and kind of test. Even the simplest testing scenario involves using at least four testing tools, possibly running on different platforms. Without a common interface, the developer would have to learn to use 10 completely different and idiosyncratic tool interfaces, ranging from command-line cryptic to GUI obstructive. Tootsie was designed to present the same interface whatever the test focus (class/cluster, subsystem, or application). This was achieved by using a multiplatform tool that could run any kind of test (Segue's QA/Planner and QA/Partner). At the leaf level of a test plan, the appropriate test tool and implementation under test were designated. This effort provided powerful yet straightforward interfaces to both large test plans (tens of thousands of test cases) and the large collection of tools in Tootsie.

Table A.1 lists the tools that made up Tootsie. Readers should bear in mind that the tools used in Tootsie were selected to support the specific constraints and requirements of BigFoot. They are not necessarily the right choice for other applications. The challenge in developing Tootsie was not so much in selecting the tools, but in providing bridges between these islands and the application islands. In a few cases, interfaces were available from the tool suppliers. For the majority we had to develop interfaces, which typically consisted of ASCII files and Perl scripts (not very exotic, but highly effective and portable).

TABLE A.1 Tootsie's Tool Slots

Tool Slot	Implementation
Line item requirements	DOORS (Zycad)
Extended use cases	DOORS (Zycad)
Object models	Paradigm Plus (Platinum Technologies)
Test case generation	T (IDE, Inc.)
Unit test driver generation	Cantata (QCS/IPL)
Coverage analysis	Cantata (QCS/IPL)
Memory leak checker	BoundsChecker (Nu-Mega)
Regression test support	Discover (Software Emancipation)
Test suite management	QA/Planner (Segue)
GUI and console test driver	QA/Partner (Segue)
Exception test	QC/Sim (Centerline)
Configuration management	Clear Case (Atria)
Problem tracking	QA Plan/Track (Direct Technology)
Extended use case schema	DOORS/DXL (Zycad)
Extended use case export	DOORS/DXL (Zycad)
Database loader/unloader	Perl
Database comparator	Perl

Some Test Automation Scenarios

Testing is not a monolithic activity. Instead, it depends on the scope and technology of the implementation under test. For example, initial unit testing of a server cluster with no user interface needs a driver that can simulate messages sent to the server and simulate (or control) a DBMS wrapped by the cluster under test. These criteria are very much different from what is needed for a unit test of the Windows 95 GUI implemented with a DLL and from what is needed for selection of a regression test suite at the system scope that includes batch, GUI, and performance testing.

In all, there were two dozen testing scenarios for BigFoot. The scenarios differed by platform, client tests, server tests, batch process tests, various scopes of integration sequences, and regression testing. Tootsie's components were configured to support all possible testing scenarios for BigFoot.

For example, a scenario for unit testing of a server class/cluster with Tootsie consists of the following steps (each is actually an activation of a separate test tool). Each step is activated under the control of the QA/Partner.

1. Extract the test parameters for the class from the OOA/D repository.
2. Automatically generate the raw test case values.
3. Generate a test harness (a driver, an object of the class under test, and a code section to instantiate a message for each test case) for the class.
4. Include base class test drivers as appropriate.
5. Generate a controllable stub library for untested objects used by the class under test.
6. Instrument the class under test.
7. Build a test package using the driver, instrumented class, and stub library.
8. Run the database loader.
9. Run the test package.
10. Run the database unloader.
11. Run the database comparator.

The output produced by this scenario includes recording of the test case results in the QA/Partner test script, the coverage report, the stub trace report (if any), the exception log, and the database comparator output. Tootsie provided a consistent interface and control mechanism for developers for any testing scenario. Figure A.1 shows how these tools were arrayed to support this testing scenario.

Tootsie supports a full life-cycle test process using the FREE test design methodology. It is constructed from off-the-shelf testing tools and simple utility programs. Although this approach seemed straightforward to us, none of Tootsie's tool vendors could point to other organizations using the same extent of test automation.

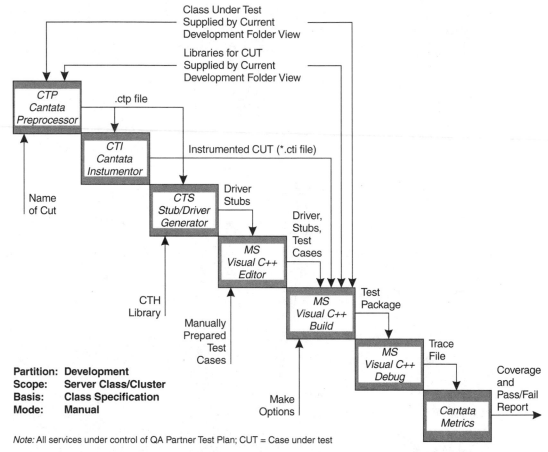

FIGURE A.1   Test automation configuration to support developer class testing scenario.

GLOSSARY

α state. *See* **alpha state.**

β state space. In the **FREE** state model, the set of legal states reachable from the α state; there are three cases of interest: empty, singleton, and *n*-ary. An empty β state is a pathological class which does nothing. A singleton β obtains when a class has no sequential constraints on method activation. This is a nonmodal class. The *n*-ary case obtains when two or more states are needed to represent sequential constraints.

γ state space. In the **FREE** state model, the set of all illegal states, γ, is the complement of β. The union of β and γ is the set of all possible combinations of instance variable values. These special states facilitate production of full cycle testing. In particular, the α state allows explicit modeling of multiple constructors in C++. This is useful when the constructors generate different initial states.

ω state. *See* **omega state.**

abend. An abrupt termination of a program, synonymous with task abort, application crash, or system crash. Abend is IBM jargon for abnormal end. It is pronounced ab-end, to rhyme with "the end." An abend often produces a memory dump, for example, the "blue screen of death" generated by Microsoft operating systems.

abort. (1) In database systems, a generic operation that prevents the commitment of transactions to stable storage. (2) **abend.**

abstract class. A class that provides common features (typically method interfaces) for subclasses and cannot be **instantiated** on its own. This facilitates consistent subclass definition and usage.

abstract data type (ADT). A software module that encapsulates data and operations. Encapsulated data may only be accessed by operations said to be exported from an ADT interface. The operations defined for a type constrain the mapping between input and output parameters in an operation.

abstract state. A state defined over the combinational value set visible to class clients by the class interface.

abstract state in point. Any value combination that places an object of the class in a given abstract state and is not an off point or on point for the state in question.

abstract state off point. A valid state that is (1) not the focus state, and (2) is different from the focus state by the smallest change that results in a different state.

abstract state on point. A state such that the smallest possible change in any of its state variables would result in a state change.

abstract type. *See* **abstract data type.**

acceptance testing. **Formal testing** conducted to determine whether or not a system satisfies its acceptance criteria and to enable the customer to determine whether or not to accept the system [IEEE 610].

accepting condition. An **assertion** that defines the **state**(s) in which a method may be activated. The assertion predicate that should be asserted at the same point as a precondition. The accepting condition checks that an incoming message is acceptable given the current state of the object. *See also* **resulting condition, state invariant, transition.**

accepting state. A state in which some transition is accepted.

accessor. A method that reports the state of an **object.** Syn. **selector, function.**

action. In a **state transition,** the result or output that follows an event. In a **decision table,** the outputs required for a variant.

action section. *See* **decision table.**

actual results. What the IUT produces when a test case is applied to it. This includes messages generated by the IUT, exceptions, returned values, and the resultant state of the IUT and its environment. A test whose actual results are the same as the expected results is said to **pass;** otherwise, it is a **no pass.** A no pass test reveals a bug, and is therefore a successful test, even though the actual results of a no pass test are typically an application failure.

acyclic graph. A graph that does not have any paths that exit and enter the same node, either directly or by traversing several other nodes.

adequacy criterion. A formal specification of the elements of an IUT to be exercised by a test strategy.

adequate. A test suite is adequate if all of the elements indicated by the related **adequacy criterion** have been exercised.

aggregate state. A state defined by subsets of some combinational value set.

alpha-omega path. A path from the alpha to the omega state.

alpha state. The α state is a null state representing the declaration of an object before its construction. This is different from an initial state, which is the first state an object takes after being constructed or initialized.

alpha testing. Simulated or actual operational testing at an in-house site not otherwise involved with software developers [Beizer 90].

alpha transition. An alpha state may only accept a constructor, new, or similar initialization message.

ambiguity. A statement, concept, or representation that has several interpretations. Many statements in natural language are inherently ambiguous. For example, the statement "Time flies like an arrow" has at least three interpretations: (1) as a metaphor: things seem to happen rapidly; (2) as an imperative concerning the measurement of insect speed (i.e., time the flies in the same way you would an arrow); and (3) as an assertion: a type of insect, the time fly, appreciates arrows. Software engineering strives to remove ambiguity.

ancestor. (1) In a directed acyclic graph, if there is a path from node *a* to node *b,* then *a* is an ancestor of *b.* (2) In Eiffel, a superclass.

antecedent. A work product required to begin development of another work products. For example, detail design is an antecedent of programming.

anticomposition. A testing axiom which states that test suites that are individually adequate for segments within a module are not necessarily adequate for the module as a whole.

antidecomposition. A testing axiom which states that the coverage achieved for a module under test is not necessarily achieved for modules which it calls.

antiextensionality. A testing axiom which states that a test suite which covers one implementation of a specification does not necessarily cover a different implementation of the same specification.

anti-requirement. A system behavior (or its absence) that would have highly unfavorable consequences, and therefore must *not* occur.

API. *See* **application programmer interface.**

app. *See* **application.**

applet. A relatively small Java application which can be sent from one computer to another over the Internet. Applets can be of any size, but are usually small to minimize download and excecution time. Typically executed by a browser that implements a Java Virtual Machine. The applet brings its own widgets with it and thus extends the native objects of the browser.

application. (1) *n.* A software program or system which is used to solve a specific problem or a class of similar problems. (2) *v.* The use of a technology or concept for any purpose.

application programmer interface (API). A reusable library of subroutines or objects that encapsulates the internals of some other system and provides a well-defined interface. An API typically (1) makes it easier to use the services of a general-purpose system (e.g., a GUI), (2) encapsulates the subject system providing higher integrity, (3) increases the user's productivity by providing reusable solutions to common problems.

application-specific tool. Software written to support testing of a particular application. Typically not reusable and not available outside of a single development organization.

assertion. (1) A **predicate** expression whose value is either true or false. (2) In C++ and Objective-C, a capability implemented by the `assert()` macro. (3) In Eiffel, a keyword clause and a Boolean expression specify preconditions (the require clause), invariants (the invariant clause), and postconditions (the ensure clause). (4) In Prolog, a horn clause that is always true: a conclusion without a condition.

assertion action. The processing that follows an assertion violation. The typical default assertion action is to generate a diagnostic message and terminate execution.

assertion failure. Deprecated. *See also* **assertion violation.**

assertion predicate. An asserted condition which either evaluates to *true* (the state of the IUT satisfies the assertion) or *false*. If true, execution continues.

assertion violation. The result of an assertion predicate evaluting as *false,* meaning a necessary condition was not met.

asynchronous. Conditions, events, or tasks that occur at irregular intervals, or that are not coordinated at some regularly occurring time interval.

automaton. A mathematical model of automatic computation and, indirectly, of a computer system (pl. *automata*).

availability. The percent of some interval during which a system or a component is operational.

axiom. A statement or assertion on which deductions are based. Assumed to be true, not proven.

bad fix. A bug fix that either does not correct a bug or creates a new bug(s).

baseline. A specification or product that has been formally reviewed and agreed on, that thereafter serves as the basis for further development, and can only be changed through formal change control procedures [IEEE 90a].

baseline version. A component (or system) that has passed a test suite.

basis-path test model. A test model that requires that C different entry–exit paths be covered.

BDD. *See* **binary decision diagram.**

BDD determinant. A root-to-leaf path in a BDD.

behavior. (1) The actual or specified sequences of messages (or events) that a class (component) accepts. (2) All the operations, services, responsibilities, or functions performed by the **methods** of a **class** (object).

behavioral testing. *See* **responsibility-based test design.**

beta test. (1) A form of prerelease system testing. A representative group of users or customers attempts routine usage under typical operating conditions. (2) Testing of a package by an unbiased, incorruptible, independent tester under contract to a software developer, operating under a meager budget and tight schedule [Beizer 90].

binary decision diagram (BDD). An ordered, acyclic graph representation of a Boolean function.

binding. (1) Assignment of a specific value to a variable by evaluation or instantiation. (2) Assignment of a physical address to a symbolic name. (3) Translation of software components into a resultant component (e.g., link-editing programs in an object library to produce a relocatable load module).

binding time. The stage in the process of program translation and execution when a symbolic name is associated with an actual value or address. This may occur when a program is translated (compile-time), linked (link-time), or executed or interpreted (runtime). Static binding is done at compile-time or link-time. Dynamic binding is done at runtime.

black box. A metaphor for a software or hardware component. The only visible aspects of a black box are its external interface and functional specification. Internal details are irrelevant for usage.

black box testing. *See* **responsibility-based test design.**

Boolean algebra. An algebraic system developed in 1847 by George Boole. Variables are binary: they may be either true (1) or false (0). Digital logic and software control flow are based on implementations of this algebra.

Boolean equation. Asserts equality of two Boolean formulas.

Boolean formula. An expression composed of Boolean operators and Boolean variables.

Boolean function. *See* **logic function.**

Boolean operator. (1) In **Boolean algebra,** the operations *and, or, not,* and *exclusive or.* **Logic expressions** are formed by applying these operations to binary (Boolean) variables. (2) In many programming languages, statement operators that implement the rules of Boolean algebra. This evaluation is typically used to control execution.

Boolean values. The values *true* and *false.* The domain and range of Boolean functions.

Boolean variable. A variable that may be only *true* (typically binary 1) or *false* (typically binary 0).

bottom-up. Any technical approach that begins with components and works toward aggregation or abstraction. Similar to inductive logic (reasoning from specific cases to general principles). Compare **top-down.**

boundary. (1) (Of a system) determined by how events are recognized and responses are delivered. Defines the **scope** of its development project. (2) In testing, the set of values that limit an input or output domain.

boundary condition. (1) In **domain analysis,** Boolean expressions on the input variables of the implementation under test. At class scope, the operands in a boundary condition are message parameters and instance. (2) Generally, an input or state that results in a condition that is on or immediately adjacent to a boundary value. For example, if a loop is to terminate after the tenth iteration, the boundary conditions include the ninth, tenth, and possibly the eleventh iteration.

boundary value analysis. A heuristic test value selection strategy where the ranges or limits of inputs are analyzed to choose test cases. Deprecated. Compare **domain analysis.**

bounded state. A state defined over a combinational value set defined by local instance variables, i.e., no recursive expansion is applied.

branch. (1) One of several **segments** that can immediately follow a **predicate** statement after a conditional transfer of control. (2) The transfer of control to a label, statement, instruction, or address other than the next in sequence. (3) A control path. (4) A set of connected nodes and edges in a **tree.**

branch coverage. Achieved when every path from a control flow graph node has been executed at least once by a test suite. This is also known as decision coverage, all-edges coverage, or C2 coverage. Branch coverage improves on statement coverage by requiring that each branch be taken at least once (at least one true and one false evaluation).

branch testing. *See* **branch coverage.**

breakpoint. A **statement** designated to an interactive **debugger,** whose execution will cause the debugger to pause and return control to the user. Many debuggers allow other actions to be automatically done at the breakpoint (e.g., listing a certain range of memory).

broken test case. A test case that cannot run on a **delta build,** usually because of a change to an interface.

bug. An unwanted and unintended property of a program or hardware, especially one that causes it to malfunction. Commonly used to mean defect, error, failure, fault, omission, or surprise.

bug hazard. A circumstance that increases the chance of a bug. Bug hazards arise for many reasons and in many situations.

build. The executable(s) produced by a build generation process, typically providing some related set of capabilities. Compare **version, release.**

build generation. The process of selecting and merging specific versions of source and binary files for translation and linking within a component and among components.

built-in test. Test software that resides in an application.

C metric. A formula for single-entry, single-exit program complexity: $C = e - n + 2,$ where e is the number of edges in the program flow graph and n is the number of nodes [IEEE 982.1].

call. The activation of a task, program, or module effected by a context swap followed by transfer of control to the entry point address of the target routine. Usually, when the called routine reaches an exit, return, or similar statement, the calling routine's context is restored and control is returned to the caller's next statement. Other kinds of exit semantics are possible.

call pair. A client and server that exchange messages.

call path. A sequence of messages, function calls, remote procedure calls, interprocess communication messages, etc., which is possible as a result of intercomponent interfaces.

call trace. An actual set of calls (messages) made along some call path.

canonical. A general, preferred form of some thing.

can't happen. A condition that reflects an assumption that some inputs are mutually exclusive, cannot be produced as input by the environment, or that the implementation is structured in such a way as to prevent evaluation.

capability. (1) Of a system, any feature, function, or other characteristic relevant for its intended use. (2) Of an organization, the relative efficiency and effectiveness of its **software process.**

capacity. In software systems (1) the rate at which input can be accepted, (2) the rate at which output can be produced, (3) the quantity of data that can be stored. *See also* **throughput, response time.**

capture/playback. A general approach to developing **GUI** test scripts for automatic execution. Some sequence of inputs (key strokes and pointing device inputs) is "captured" in a script file. This is accomplished by running the capture tool and the application under test at the same time. The resulting script file records the user inputs, the GUI component to which the input is sent (e.g., characters into a text box, mouse click on a radio button, etc.), and the displayed response or error message. Then, the tool can be asked to play back the script. This causes the application to be started. The script inputs are sent to the same components, and the response of the application is compared to the expected response contained in the script.

cardinality. (1) *See* **multiplicity.** (2) The number of members of a set.

cartoon. A model that is not **test-ready.** Cartoons are useful for sketching, refining, and documenting solutions, but typically cannot support test design without further work.

CASE. Computer-Aided Software Engineering.

case structure. A complex predicate expression that specifies conditional activation for 1 of n mutually exclusive segments.

casting. Type conversion in C++, Java, and Objective-C. *See also* **coercion.**

category. A subset of parameter values that (1) determines a particular behavior or output, and (2) whose values are not included in any other category.

cause–effect graph. A graphical model used to identify and analyze the relationships to be modeled in a decision table.

check-in. (1) In configuration management, the release of exclusive control of a configuration item. For example, after completing edits, a program is checked-in to the source code library. Compare **check-out.** (2) In distributed processing, the release of a lock or similar mechanism on a data item being updated by one site or user.

checklist. A list of specific characteristics, results, or properties needed for some work product. Checklists are particularly useful for avoiding errors of omission in complex systems or procedures. A checklist item should be phrased so that compliance is unambiguous and easily ascertained.

check-out. (1) In configuration management, the granting of exclusive control of a configuration item to a single user. For example, to edit a program, it is checked-out from a source code library. Compare **check-in.** (2) In distributed processing, the granting of a lock or similar mechanism on a data item for access by one site or user.

child. (1) In a directed acyclic graph, if there is an edge from node a to node b, then b is a child of a. (2) An Ada 95 subclass.

choice. A specific test value for a **category.** Any reasonable criteria may be used to make choices.

class. A lexical unit of statements from which **objects** may be created. In object-oriented development, a representation or source code construct used to create objects. Defines public and private attributes, methods, messages, and inherited features. An object is an instance of some class. A class is an abstract, static definition of an object. It defines and implements instance variables and methods. A **subclass** has a name and may designate a **superclass**; it may specify its own instance variables, message patterns, and methods. A subclass inherits, or has access to, the methods and instance variables of its superclass, or superclasses, if multiple inheritance is supported. A subclass may override a superclass with a method that has the same name as a superclass method, providing method polymorphism. Compare **user-defined data type, abstract data type.** Contrast **object.** *See also* **abstract class, class method, class variable, client, collection class, container class, delegation, derived class, destructor, friend, generality, genericity, inheritance, metaclass, multiple inheritance, repeated inheritance, server, specialization, subclass, template class, yo-yo effect.**

class contract. The set of assertions at method and class scope, inherited assertions, and exceptions.

class flattening. Source code analysis that makes the effects of inheritance explicit by source code expansion; a flattened class shows all the features it inherits [Meyer 88].

class invariant. An **assertion** that specifies properties that must be true of every object of a class. The class invariant must be true after instantiation, upon entry and at exit from every method (except in the local call cases), and just before destruction. It must hold for all methods, over all activation sequences, and for any valid value of incoming arguments.

class library. Classes that support reuse by composition, often sharing some common attribute (e.g., data structures like lists, queues, stacks, sets, etc.). Classes in the library can typically be used independently.

class responsibility. *See* **responsibility.**

class under test (CUT). The implementation that is the subject of test design or is being exercised by a test suite.

class variable. Variables that have the same value in all objects of a class.

clear box testing. *See* **implementation-based testing.**

client. (1) In a **client/server system,** a process (logical or physical) that generates requests for service to be processed by a **server.** The client is independent and asynchronous with respect to the server. (2) In OOA, OOD, and OOP, a **class** X is said to be a client of class Y when X defines an instance variable of type Y; Y is said to be a **server** of class X. Client objects are said to activate methods in server objects.

client-/server system. A generic system architecture which is well suited to microprocessor computer systems and local area networks. Data storage and processing are distributed over logical and physical **clients** and **servers.** Functional requirements are typically split into front-end and back-end processes. The front-end (the client) can initiate requests for service and is often packaged with the user interface. The back-end (the server) is reactive. Servers often perform resource-intensive processing, so server processes are typically allocated to high-performance processors.

closed boundary. A boundary operator that includes strict equality, for example `a >= b` or `c == 500`.

cluster head. A single class that uses the others as instance variables or as message parameters. A small cluster can be treated as a single class if the cluster head uses all the constituent class capabilities and the constituents.

coercion. The automatic resolution of a type mismatch. Explicit coercion uses a built-in function (I = IFIX(3.998)). This is more readable, consistent, and general, but places greater responsibility on the programmer. Implicit coercion relies on built-in defaults. The rules are usually complex and need to be learned on a case by case basis. Coercion is said to be *narrowing,* when the mapping goes from a larger domain to smaller domain (real to integer), or *widening,* when the mapping is done from a smaller to a larger domain. In C and C++ coercion are provided by built-in and explicit casts.

coincidental correctness. The production of a correct result from faulty code for certain inputs.

collaboration. The use (activation) of one object by another through **message passing**. A request from a client class to a server class. The server performs a responsibility required by the client so that the client can meet one of its responsibilities. Collaborations are found by examining classes and responsibilities. For each class, ask "Are any other classes needed to satisfy a responsibility?" or "Which other classes needed to use 'my' responsibilities?" Collaborations may be suggested by relationships among classes [Wirfs-Brock 90].

collection class. A **class** (object) that may contain multiple instances of some other class (object). A class whose instances each contain multiple occurrences of some object. In Smalltalk, the classes Bag, Set, and Dictionary.

combination. Any subset of some finite set. The order or arrangement of the subset is not significant. For example, the combinations of the set $\{a, b, c\}$ are a, b, c, ab, bc, ac, and abc (*bac* and *cba*, for example, are considered the same combination.) For a set of n members and any subset of r members, $r \geq n$, there are exactly $n!/r!(n - r)!$ combinations in each subset.

combinational. A function, system, model, circuit, etc., that has only one state—the present values of its inputs. It has no representation of any previous input or output and therefore can only produce output determined by combinations of current input.

combinational circuit. A circuit whose output depends only upon its input at a given time. A special case of a sequential circuit without storage. Previous inputs or outputs are not used to determine current output. May be represented with a **decision table**, **Boolean algebra**, or Karnaugh map. *See also* **KV Matrix**.

combinational logic. The implementation of a Boolean function.

combinational value set. The set of all possible combinations of instance variable values.

combinatorial circuit. *See* **combinational circuit**.

combinatorial. Pertaining to combinatorics; the study of the permutations and **combinations** of elements in finite sets.

combinatorial explosion. The very rapid increase in the time or space of an algorithm or search which has an exponential growth rate. For example, the search space for the game of chess is estimated at 10^{120} possible games. Each player begins with 20 possible moves. The number of possible sequences of moves increases rapidly: 20^2 for the second move, 20^3, 20^4, . . . In only 5 moves, there are 3,200,000 possible sequences.

comparator. A device or program that compares two or more inputs and reports the result. The comparison operation may simply test for an exact equality, or may perform more complex evaluation.

compatibility bug. A revision to the framework breaks a previously working feature: a new feature is inconsistent with an old feature, or a new feature breaks an unchanged application rebuilt with the new framework code.

complaint. An error message of any sort.

complexity. The extent to which the parts of a system interact in nontrivial ways and the number of relevant interactions. There have been many metrics proposed to quantify system complexity. In many important respects **software engineering** is a strategy for dealing with complexity.

component. Any software aggregate that has visibility in a development environment, for example, a method, a class, an object, a function, a module, an executable, a task, a utility subsystem, an application subsystem. This includes executable software entities supplied with an application programmer interface.

component toolkit. A collection of programming utilities that support reuse of a certain component libraries.

component under test (CUT). The implementation that is the subject of test design or is being exercised by a test suite.

compound predicate. A predicate with multiple conditions.

computational complexity. The study of the time (number of iterations) and space (quantity of storage) required by algorithms and classes of algorithms.

concrete state. A state defined over the combinational value set visible to the implementation.

concurrent. Said of tasks that execute at the same time in a multiprogramming or distributed processing system. This typically requires (1) task management: definition, initiation, termination, status inquiry, synchronization, priority setting/changing, and scheduling, and (2) serialization of shared data or other resources. There are many operating systems and several programming languages that provide these capabilities. Key issues include: can a task gain exclusive control over data accessible to other tasks? How is resource contention managed? How susceptible to **deadlock** is the implementation? What is the synchronization protocol? How do tasks communicate? Is the communication highly coupled with synchronization? Are there scaling considerations? Are increments in design/coding/overhead linear with respect to unit increments in the number of tasks to be managed?

condition. (1) A programming language expression that can be evaluated as true or false. (2) An algebraic expression whose value is either true or false. *See also* **logic expression**.

condition section. *See* **decision table**.

confidence. A subjective assessment of the likelihood of unrevealed bugs in an implementation. A qualitative judgment based on available information. Testing provides information that can increase or decrease our confidence. When a responsibility test suite passes and achieves appropriate coverage, we may have increased confidence that the IUT will perform without failure. Confidence can be quantified when testing is conducted under certain controlled conditions. Compare **dependability**.

configuration management. A technical and administrative approach to manage change and control a collection of work products. Steps include: identify and document the functional and physical characteristics of a work product, control changes to those characteristics, record and report change processing and implementation status, and verify compliance with specified requirements [IEEE 610].

configuration testing. Testing conducted to identify legal combinations of hardware and/or software environments that cause the system under test to fail.

conformance-directed. Testing that aims to demonstrate conformance to required capabilities.

conformance-directed testing. Testing that seeks to establish conformance to requirements or specifications.

consistency. The degree of uniformity, standardization, and freedom from contradiction among the documents or parts of a system or component [IEEE 610].

consumer. A person or organization who uses a software component developed by a **producer**.

container class. A **class** whose instances are each intended to contain multiple occurrences of some other **object**. For example, a list, stack, queue, set, or tree.

contract. A definition of the services a supplier class must provide to a client class. Compare **collaboration, delegation**.

contract metaphor. *See* **design-by-contract**.

control. (1) In a user interface, a component of a GUI toolkit. Syn. **widget.** (2) In a software system, the mechanisms that determine the order of actions (computations, input/output, resources allocation, etc.

control flow graph. A flow graph that shows the relationship between program **segments.**

cooperative server. A server designed with the assumption that the client will not send an incorrect message and never checks its assertions.

CORBA. Common Object Request Broker Architecture. *See also* **object request broker.**

correctness. The extent to which a software system meets its requirements and specification.

corrupt state. An incorrect combination of instance variable values. The **class invariant** will evaluate as false if and only if an object is in a corrupt state.

COTS. /kahtz/ Commercial-Off-the-Shelf. Software components or complete systems that are offered for sale to the general public. General-purpose software written to support testing of a wide range of applications. Typically offered for sale by a commercial organization.

coverage. The percent of elements required by a test strategy that have been exercised by a given test suite. When "coverage" is used without quantification, 100 percent is usually understood, e.g., "This test suite achieves branch coverage for member function x" means 100 percent branch coverage has been achieved.

crash. (1) A sudden failure that renders a computer system completely inoperable. (2) Contact between a moving disk platter and a read head.

CRUD. Mnemonic for Create, Read, Update, Delete.

CRUD matrix. A table that lists the operations performed on all **problem domain classes** in the SUT.

cube. A compressed, partial **truth table.**

current state. Refers to the state that is active. A transition is made from the current state to a resultant state.

CUT. *See* **class under test, component under test.**

cycle. (1) A loop in a **directed graph.** (2) A collection of software components that have mutual dependencies. For example, suppose class A uses class B, B uses C, and C uses A.

cyclomatic complexity metric. *See also* **C metric.**

dead code. A segment of a program that cannot be executed under any condition. This may be a result of an **error,** a **kluge,** or an infeasible path.

deadline. In a **real-time system,** the maximum time interval that may elapse between the occurrence of an event requiring service and the production of a response. The event may be: (1) the arrival of an input, (2) the start or end of some time period (e.g., every 5 milliseconds), or (3) an internal state transition (e.g., release of a blocked resource).

deadlock. Occurs when two (or more) tasks block each other. Neither task can proceed until the other is unblocked. For example, task 1 locks resource A, task 2 locks resource B, task 1 requests resource B, task 2 requests resource A. Unless there is some external intervention, both tasks will wait for the other forever.

dead loop. Once a dead loop is entered, no states outside of the loop may be reached. This typically prevents a transition to a final state.

dead state. Once a dead state is entered, the machine effectively ceases to operate. No paths lead out of a dead state, so no other state is reachable from it.

deadly embrace. *See* **deadlock.**

debug. To detect, locate, and correct **faults** in a computer program. Techniques include use of breakpoint, desk checking, dumps, inspection, reversible execution, single-step operation, and traces [IEEE 610]. Debugging is a reaction to a failure observed during test or normal operation, whereas **testing** is a systematic process to reveal faults.

debugger. A software tool used to perform debugging. When run under a debugger, a program can be executed one line at a time, and the contents of all program data storage displayed after each statement. Typical functions include runtime tracing, breakpoints, formatted storage inspection, and the ability to change the contents of registers and main memory. May provide the ability to execute selectively compiled statements (assertions) that can force a breakpoint if the condition is true.

debugging. The work required to diagnose and correct a bug.

decision table. A tabular representation of **combinational logic**. The **condition section** lists conditions and combinations of conditions. Decision variables are inputs or environmental factors referenced in the condition section. A **condition** expresses a relationship among decision variables that must be resolvable to true or false. Each unique combination of conditions and actions (represented as a single row or column) is a **variant**. When all the individual conditions in one variant are true, the corresponding action should be produced. The action section lists responses to be produced when corresponding combinations of conditions are true. Any number of resultant actions may be specified and any combination of actions may be associated with any particular condition variant.

decision tree. A graphic representation of a **decision table**. Each branch represents a state or value of some decision variable. A root-to-leaf branch represents a single case and the action(s) that are to be taken in this case.

decision variables. *See* **decision table**.

declaration. A programming language statement that brings a symbolic name into use. Compare **definition**.

defect. (1) A product anomaly. (2) An output or performance feature (manifest or omitted) that does not meet reasonable customer expectations. (3) An incorrect or missing software component that results in a failure to meet a functional or performance requirement. Any implementation deviation from requirements and specifications; also errors in the specification. Compare **bug, error, fault, failure**.

defect density. The number of defects identified in a product divided by the size of the product component (expressed in standard measurement terms for that product) [SEI 93].

defect prevention. The activities involved in identifying defects or potential defects and preventing them from being introduced into a product [SEI 93].

defect root cause. The underlying reason (e.g., process deficiency) that allowed a defect to be introduced [SEI 93].

defensive server. A server that always checks client messages against preconditions and complains when they are not met. The client must be prepared to handle such complaints, which may be implemented as exceptions, returned error codes, or a special object state. Contrast **cooperative server**.

definition. A programming language statement that declares an object, causes an instance of it to be created, and associates a symbolic name with the object. Compare **declaration**.

delegation. In object-oriented systems, the transfer of a responsibility to another object. This provides some of the code-sharing aspects of inheritance without classes. When a responsibility is delegated, control is passed to a dynamically created independent actor. This new actor has access to the private data of the actor that created it. Compare **inheritance**.

delta. A change to a component within the scope of an increment.

delta build. An executable configuration of the SUT that contains all the delta and baseline components.

delta version. A component (or a system) that has been changed but has not passed a regression test.

demo app. A testable instantiation of a **framework**.

dependability. The extent to which *"reliance can justifiably be placed on the service [a system] delivers.* The service delivered by a system is its behavior *as it is perceptible* by its user(s); a user is another system (human or physical) interacting with the former"* (Laprie's italics) [Laprie+96, 29].

deployment. The release of a system for use by its intended customers or users.

dereferencing. (1) When a variable is used in a statement, it is interpreted as either a *reference* to some address in storage, or the *content* of that address. For example, in *ix = ix + 1* the right side *ix* refers to the content of *ix*. The left side refers to the address of *ix*, meaning that the result of the calculation is to be stored there. Since the content cannot be accessed apart from the address (the reference), the steps to obtain the content are called *dereferencing*. (2) In call by value, this refers to determination of the actual address of passed parameters. (3) In C and C++, the indirection (dereference) operator * is used to obtain the content of a pointer variable (an address), which in turn is implicitly dereferenced to obtain the contents of the pointed-to variable.

derived class. In C++, a class which obtains some or all of its members from a base class. Syn. **subclass**.

design-by-contract. (1) A class design technique that has some similarities to establishing a legal contract [Meyer 97]. A class contract is an explicit statement of rights and obligations between client and server. This contract states what both parties must do, independent of how it is done. The specification of a class contract is given by preconditions, postconditions, and invariants. (2) When trademarked, a proprietary methodology.

destructor. (1) In object-oriented systems, a method that removes an active object. If automatic **garbage collection** is supported, the memory allocated to the object becomes available without explicit deallocation code. (2) In C++, a special member function that accomplishes 1.

deterministic. A system, program, or device whose entire repertoire is predictable. Given any possible state and input, the output and next state can be determined.

developer. A person or organization (also "supplier") that produces software project work products.

directed graph. In **graph theory**, a graph composed of directed edges. A graph where the connections between vertices are shown by arrows. This may represent sequence among vertices (e.g., control flow), precedence or hierarchy (e.g., super- to subclass), etc. *See also* **edge, vertex**.

distinguishing sequence. A sequence of events that generates a unique set of actions.

distributed. Said of computing systems whose components are physically remote, independent, and loosely coupled.

domain. (1) In software testing, the set of values that input or state variables of the IUT may take. The testing usage of domain is derived from the mathematical definition of domain: the set of inputs accepted by a function. (2) In software reuse, "a group or set of systems or functional areas, within systems, that exhibit similar functionality. . . . Domain engineering . . . is the process of defining the scope (i.e., domain definition), analyzing the domain (i.e., domain analysis), specifying the structure (i.e., domain architecture development), building the components (e.g., requirements, designs, software code, documentation) for a class of subsystems that will support reuse" [Kean 97]. An "application domain," which refers to a general class of user problems (e.g., international banking, avionics, word processing, etc.) [Kean 97]. (3) A "problem domain," which is any collection of ideas related by some human purpose, (4) the domain component of an IP address, or (5) the value set of an attribute in database theory [Date 82].

domain analysis. The process of identifying and formalizing constraints on input, state, and output values to select test values.

domain matrix. A tabluar representation of domain variables, boundary conditions, on/off/in points, and test cases.

domain selection criteria. An algorithm or heuristic to choose test points from a domain.

don't care. A condition that, for a particular **variant**, may be either true or false without changing the action. The variant is selected (or suppressed) regardless of the truth value of the don't care condition(s).

don't know. A condition that reflects an incomplete model. The applicability of a condition or a desired outcome may be unknown for many reasons.

driver. A class, main program, or external software system that applies test cases to the component under test.

dynamic. Processing or services performed during task execution.

dynamic polymorphism. Binding (name resolution) that occurs at runtime.

dynamic type checking. **Type checking** done at runtime. In an interpreted language, this occurs as each expression is evaluated. This requires runtime data descriptors. Advantages include (1) no **declarations** are needed, (2) an object's type may be changed during execution, allowing polymorphic functions (as in Ada overloading, or Smalltalk), (3) translation may be faster, (4) the translator does the work of typing. Disadvantages include (1) harder to debug, (2) requires additional memory (possibly a large quantity) for runtime descriptors, (3) checking involves substantial execution overhead, (4) it is less reliable, and (5) the resulting code is less self-documenting.

dynamic verification. Defect prevention accomplished by executing (testing the implementation). Major types of testing include **functional testing, implementation-based test design, heuristic testing,** and **feature-based testing.**

edge. In a **graph,** a connection between **nodes.** In **graph theory,** an abstract entity that represents a relationship between two vertices. May represent any relationship of interest concerning two vertices. Edges are *directed* or *undirected.* An undirected edge represents some relationship between two vertices. A directed edge exits its *initial vertex* and enters its *terminal vertex.* A graph may have many edges. An edge is typically drawn as a line segment (undirected) or an arrow (directed.) Syn. **branch, link, arc.**

element. (1) A member of a set. (2) A variable that holds a single data value as opposed to a collection of values.

elicitation. The process of extracting information about a problem and desired capabilities from the intended users of a system.

embedded system. A system that is an integral component of a larger system. The embedded system is not useful outside the larger system, whose primary purpose is not computational. Embedded systems often control the actions of a larger electromechanical system (e.g., the engine control module (ECM) used in automobiles and trucks or a microcontroller in a home appliance).

encapsulation. Programming language access control mechanisms that determine visibility of names in and among lexical units. The physical details of a data structure, device interface, or other software component are not visible to other modules. Reduces coupling.

With encapsulation, (1) a component can be used without explicit reference to implementation details, and (2) the programmer is effectively prevented from using the hidden details. Compare **information hiding**.

entry node. The node of a flow graph that represents the entry point of a method or module.

entry–exit path. A path in a flow graph from the entry node to the exit node.

equivalence class. A set of input values such that if any value is processed correctly (incorrectly), then it is assumed that all other values will be processed correctly (incorrectly). The conceptual basis for some well-known heuristics for test point selection include **equivalence class partitioning, boundary value analysis.**

equivalence class partitioning. A heuristic **partition** identification strategy. An equivalence class (in Myers's usage) is a partition defined so that if any single test value from the partition passes (or does not pass), then all other values in the partition are expected to pass (or not pass). Deprecated.

equivalence relation. In mathematics, a binary relation that is (1) *reflexive* (holds when the left and right sides are the same: $x = x$), (2) *symmetric* (holds when the left and right sides are swapped: $x = y$ and $y = x$), and (3) *transitive* (holds for over two or more expressions: if $x = y$ and $y = z$, then $x = z$ must hold).

equivalent states. Any two states are equivalent if all possible event sequences applied to these states result in identical output action sequences. That is, if we start in either equivalent state and apply all possible combinations of events up to and including those that result in a final state, we cannot tell which state we had started from by comparing output actions. The notion of equivalence can be extended to any set of states.

error. A human action that results in a software **fault**. Errors, faults, and failures do not occur in one-to-one relation. Many different failures can result from a single fault. The same failure can be caused by different faults. Similarly, a single error may lead to many faults. These categories are generally useful, but somewhat ambiguous. They are all subsumed by the concept of a **bug**.

error guessing. The design of **test cases** by making assumptions about likely **errors**. The assumptions are based on hunches, intuition, general experience, or other subjective conclusions about sources and locations of errors. Syn. **suspicion testing**.

error seeding. The purposeful introduction of faults into a program to test the effectiveness of a test suite or other quality assurance program. Compare **mutation testing**.

essential capability. A capability that must be provided to solve the application problem at hand, regardless of any implementation technology.

event. (1) In a state machine, the simulus that may cause a transition. (2) In the **FREE** state model, either (i) a message sent to the class under test, (ii) a response received from a server or class under test, or (iii) an interrupt or similar external control action that must be accepted by the class under test. An event represents any kind of stimulus that can be presented to an object: a message from any client, a response to a message sent to the virtual machine supporting an object, or the activation of an object by an externally managed interrupt mechanism. Thus an object may change state (accept an event) without receiving a message from an external client. (2) In many GUI environments, any externally generated request for service visible to the application program.

event-to-state format. A **state transition table** in which each event in the model has a row; each state gets one column.

exception. A condition or event that causes suspension of normal program execution. Typically results from incorrect or invalid usage of the virtual machine: device failure, divide by zero, stack overflow, attempting to call a nonexistent program, attempting to open a nonexistent file.

exception handling. The activation of program components to deal with an **exception**. Many programming languages have built-in exception-handling mechanisms: Ada exceptions, C++, Java, try/throw/catch, and Eiffel rescue expressions. Exception handling is typically accomplished by using built-in features and application code. There are two basic strategies. In resume handling, the exception is intercepted at a low level, handled, and execution continues with the next application statement (PL/I uses this approach). In percolation handling, the exception causes transfer to the exception handler, and the exception handler returns control to the module that invoked the module that encountered the exception (Ada C++, Java, and Eiffel use this approach).

executable component. A binary executable that supports reuse with link-time/runtime binding.

exhaustive testing. A test suite that would cause all possible combinations of program values to be executed, over all possible paths. Impossible (except for trivial cases) due to the huge number of test cases required.

exhaustive test suite. A test suite that has a test case for every possible value and sequence of inputs is applied in every possible state of the system under test, causing every possible execution path to be taken. This results in an astronomical number of test cases, even with trivial programs. Exhaustive testing is a practical impossibility.

exit. (1) In many programming languages, a statement that returns control to the caller or the environment. (2) In **structured programming**, the terminal node in a single-entry, single-exit program. (3) In a GUI, an optional action that terminates the active application and closes associated windows.

exit node. The node of a flow graph that represents an exit point of a method or module.

expanded state-to-state format. A **state transition table** in which event/state pairs and action/state pairs are shown in separate cells.

expected result. Specifies what the IUT should produce from the test inputs. This includes messages generated by the IUT, exceptions, returned values, and resultant state of the IUT and its environment. Test cases may also specify initial and resulting conditions for other objects that comprise the IUT and its environment.

explicit variant. A **variant** modeled in a decision table or truth table.

expression. In a programming language, expression evaluation is an aspect of sequence control. The components are data references (operands), implicit syntax or explicit symbols to sequence evaluation, and **operators** that specify a transformation. High-level languages are distinguished from low-level languages by the presence of expressions (among other things). Since intermediate results are "hidden," expressions provide both control and data abstraction over typical assembly languages. The syntax and sequence control semantics of expressions are key design and implementation issues.

extended use case. A use case that supplies information necessary for test design: a complete inventory of operational variables, specification of domain constraints for each operational variable, an operational relation for each use case, and, optionally, the relative frequency of the use case.

extension. A basic mechanism of **inheritance** in which superclass features are replicated and visible at subclass scope. Compare **specialization, overriding**.

failure. The manifested inability of a system or component to perform a required function within specified limits. A failure is evidenced by **incorrect output**, an **abend**, or inability to meet processing deadlines.

failure intensity. The frequency of **failures** in some time interval (e.g., failures per CPU second).

failure rate. The probability that failure will occur after a certain period of usage.

fat interface. A subclass that inherits methods that are inappropriate or irrelevant.

fault. (1) An incorrect statement, step, process, or data definition in a computer program. When a fault is executed it may result in a **failure**. **Errors**, faults, and **failures** do not occur in one-to-one relation. Many different failures can result from a single fault. The same failure can be caused by different faults. Similarly, a single error may lead to many faults. (2) A malfunction or unrecoverable failure in any component of a computer system. (3) An **exception** or **interrupt** that is not a failure, but calls for a specific response. For example, a page fault in a virtual memory system means the page is swapped-out and must be swapped-in to be used.

fault-directed testing. Testing that seeks to reveal implementation **faults**. It is motivated by the observation that conformance can be demonstrated for an implementation that contains faults.

fault efficient. A fault-oriented technique which has a high probability of revealing targeted faults, if they exist.

fault model. Identifies relationships and components of the system under test that are most likely to have faults. It may be based on common sense, experience, suspicion, analysis, or experiment. Each test design pattern has an explicit fault model.

fault sensitivity. The ability of code to hide **faults** from a test suite.

fault sniffer. An assertion used when a code segment has a better than average chance of a lurking fault.

fault spawning. The inadvertent introduction of new faults when a fault is removed. Syn. **bad fix**.

fault tolerant. The capability of a computer system to continue to produce correct results in spite of faults in storage, processors, or peripherals, and, to a limited extent, software failures. Fault tolerance requires (1) rapid detection of and recovery from faults and (2) graceful degradation. For example, Tandem computer systems use a fault-tolerant strategy that combines hardware and software. Identical pairs of tightly coupled computer systems are run with an operating system that provides fast, automatic transfer of executing tasks from the failing system to the standby system.

feature. (1) A function or attribute of a system that is significant to its intended users or customers. (2) in Eiffel, a *routine* (**method**) or an *attribute* (**instance variable**).

feature interaction. A behavior or side effect produced when two or more features are used together. These may be desirable or undesirable. For example, a residential telephone service offers call forwarding (automatically transferring an incoming call).

feature sufficient. A conformance-oriented test suite that exercises all specified features.

fidelity. The correspondence between the expected results and actual results produced by an oracle.

field. A self-contained object or primitive type variable; it does not refer to other objects.

field release. A **release** of a system that is ready to ship.

final state. A state in which the machine stops accepting events.

finite automata. A class of mathematical models that represent computation using a finite number of states.

finite state machine. *See* **state machine**.

fire. The process that occurs when a state machine makes a transition.

firewall. A set of components whose test cases are to be included in a regression test.

focus state. The state specified in a domain boundary.

foo. (1) Used very generally as a sample name for absolutely anything [Raymond 90]. (2) Term of disgust.

foobar. *See* **foo.**

formal language. A language whose semantics are precise.

formal parameter. A variable used to specify a procedure interface. A parameter list argument declared by and visible within a subprogram. Usage is evaluated at translation time. At run time, an actual parameter value is bound by formal parameters when a subprogram is called.

formal review. A formal meeting at which a product is presented to the end user, customer, or other interested parties for comment and approval. It can also be a review of the management and technical activities and of the progress of the project [SEI 93].

formal specification. A system representation that uses a well-defined notation (typically mathematical), in which all elements and operations are defined in a mathematical system.

formal test design. A test strategy whose fault-revealing capability has been established by mathematical analysis.

formal testing. Testing conducted in accordance with test plans and procedures that have been reviewed and approved by a customer, user, or designated level of management. Compare **informal testing** [IEEE 610].

formal verification. The use of **proof of correctness** techniques to assess the compliance of an implementation with its specification.

foundation class library. Supports translation-time reuse by inheritance. Foundation classes typically provide a broad range of related capabilities. The consumer develops subclasses to implement application-specific responsibilities.

framework. An implementation of a reusable domain-specific design. It provides a partial application system. The developer must specialize and develop additional code before the framework becomes a working system.

framework instantiation. A system of subclasses that realizes one possible implementation of the framework.

FREE (Flattened REgular Expression). A state-based testing strategy that focuses on flattened classes.

friend function. In C++, a **member function** that is given special privileges to access the private features of some other class. A friend of a class has access to the private data members of the class.

full regression test. A test run that includes every baseline test case. Time and cost constraints may preclude running a full regression test, in which case a **reduced regression test** can be selected, supporting **selective regression testing.**

function. (1) In **Eiffel**, a routine that computes a value based on the state of the object. (2) In C, a module. (3) A capability or feature provided by a system. (4) In mathematics, a relation in which no two ordered pairs have the same first component. The value of the dependent variable depends on the independent variable(s) in a uniquely specified manner. A function produces values in its range when it is applied to arguments in its **domain.** *See also* **mapping.**

functional cohesion. The unity of purpose (or lack thereof) among two or more functions.

functional testing. The development and execution of test cases developed by analysis of requirements or specifications. No knowledge about the internal structure of the program is used to identify test cases. Syn. **black box testing.**

function points. A product metric based on counting the number of distinct interfaces the system has with its environment (screens, panels, reports, files, transducers, etc.), and the number of external objects represented in the system. Each item (a function point) is weighted according to its relative complexity. The sum of these values is weighted by another value determined by characteristics of the development and operating environment of the system.

Gang of Four (GoF). Refers to the four authors of [Gamma+95], an influential collection of software design patterns.

garbage collection. The process of reclaiming allocated blocks of main memory (garbage) that are (1) no longer in use or (2) not claimed by any active procedure. These areas are returned to the heap and become available for subsequent allocation. May be performed incrementally (e.g., after module termination), or when available storage decreases to a threshold value.

generality. The range of application of a regression test strategy or an oracle.

generalized framework. A **framework** developed by generalizing an antecedent application system.

generic class. A C++ template class, an Eiffel generic class, or an Ada 95 generic. In Ada, type parameters are typically defined for a package or a procedure, not an individual type. The declaration to produce an object of a generic class requires the generic class, a **type argument,** and other declaration elements. The type argument is a name of a class or primitive data type. The compiler generates a new class by substituting the type argument for occurrences of the **type parameter** defined in the generic class.

generic class instantiation. The class that results when a type argument is provided to a generic class.

genericity. The ability to define parameterized classes or templates. Static polymorphism.

glass box testing. *See* **implementation-based test design.**

glitch. A hardware failure, typically intermittent.

GoF. *See* **Gang of Four.**

gold standard oracle. An existing implementation that is trusted to provide correct results and can accept test case inputs to produce expected results.

granularity. The relative degree of detail considered for some facet of a system.

graph. A representation of relationships among things using two simple constructs: **nodes** and **edges.** Nodes are connected to nodes by edges. The nodes and edges of a graph represent a **relation.**

graph theory. The mathematical study and analysis of the properties of graphs. Graphs can represent many aspects of software and systems. Graph models have many applications in computer science and software engineering. *See also* **directed graph, edge, graph, minimum spanning tree, root, topological sort, tree, vertex.**

graph traversal. In **graph theory,** there are several important classes of traversals over edges and vertices.

Begin/end vertices	Edge repeated?	Vertex repeated?	Traversal
any	no	may	walk (edge train, chain)
different	no	may	open walk
different	no	no	path
same	no	may	closed walk
same	no	no	circuit

gray box testing. Combining of **black box** and **white box testing** to reveal omissions and surprises.

guard. (1) A predicate expression associated with an event. In a specification, an expression that represents selective or conditional activation. (2) In a program, a conditional expression that controls activation, especially of a concurrent process or task. (3) In an input file, a special character(s) or other indicator, usually terminating the input stream.

guarded transition. A transition that cannot fire unless (1) the system is in the accepting state for this transition, (2) the guarded event occurs, and (3) the guard predicate evaluates to true.

GUI. /goo-ee/ (1) Graphic User Interface. A human-computer interface that uses full-sceen video display images instead of line-at-a-time alphanumeric display. GUI's rely on direct manipulation and the use of metaphors. (2) An application development toolkit that supports development of (1).

guideline. A description of a process or attributes of a work product that are generally beneficial, but require judgment for effective application.

Heisenbug. A **bug** that disappears or alters its behavior when one attempts to probe or isolate it, suggestive of the behavior of subatomic particles defined by Heisenburg's uncertainty principle.

heuristic. A rule, procedure, approach, or guideline for solving a problem that usually works. "A heuristic . . . is a rule of thumb, strategy, trick, simplification, or any other kind of device which drastically limits search for solutions in large problem spaces. Heuristics do not guarantee optimal solutions; in fact, they do not guarantee any solution at all; *all that can be said for a useful heuristic is that it offers solutions which are good enough most of the time*" [Feigenbaum 63].

heuristic test design. A test strategy that relies on expert judgment or experience to select test cases.

hose. (jargon) To cause a system or some component to become unusable, jumbled, or inoperative. Compare **crash**.

hot spot. A program segment or database component that is heavily used. Some research indicates that, on average, as little as 5 percent of source code accounts for 95 percent of the CPU time.

hybrid test design. The combined use of responsibility-based and implementation-based test design. Synonymous with **gray box testing**.

idiom. A language-specific **pattern**.

illegal event. An otherwise valid event (message) that should not be accepted given some states. If accepted, an **illegal transition** results.

illegal message. An otherwise valid message that should not be accepted given some states; if accepted, an **illegal transition** results.

illegal transition. A bug that allows a message that is not explicitly specified for the current state to be accepted.

implementation. A software artifact, typically a program, an object, or a module, that can be executed. The realization of a specification. A software artifact, as opposed to its requirements, design, or description.

implementation-based test design. The use of source code analysis to develop test cases. Synonymous with structural, glass box, clear box, white box test design.

implementation under test (IUT). The implementation that is the subject of test design or is being exercised by a test suite.

implicant. A term in a sum-of-products Boolean formula that is a sufficient condition for a true output.

implicit type conversion. *See* **coercion**.

implicit variant. A variant that can be inferred but is not given in a decision table.

incarnation capability. A capability that is a consequence of choosing a particular implementation technology.

inclusiveness. The percent of baseline tests that *may* show regression faults and which are selected for a reduced test suite.

incomplete specification. A state machine in which at least one event/state pair is not explicitly defined.

incorrect output. An output value that does not conform to the requirements or specifications for content, format, sequence, or timeliness.

increment. A subset of system components, which typically (but not necessarily) has a corresponding subset of requirements. Increments are typically progressive; the second increment includes and depends on the first, etc. The last increment becomes the delivered (shipped) system.

incremental development. The development of a system by building stand-alone versions and then integrating them. Each version goes through a full development cycle, and is integrated with the previous baseline. This approach is very flexible. Versions can be developed in sequence or in parallel. The version can be defined in many ways: highest-priority functions, highest-risk functions, functional subsystem, cost or time limited. Compare **waterfall model**. *See also* **rapid application development**.

independent verification and validation (IV&V). Verification and validation performed by an organization that is not responsible for developing the product or performing the activity being evaluated.

industrial strength. Said of system that can reliably process a high volume of input. Syn. **robust**.

informal testing. Testing conducted in accordance with test plans and procedures that have *not* been reviewed and approved by a customer, user, or designated level of management [IEEE 610]. Compare **formal testing**.

information hiding. (1) An approach to program design that looks for "secrets" to be kept within one module. A secret is any interface, algorithm, or data structure likely to change, inherently complex, or highly physical. (2) A result of **encapsulation**, either built-in or programmer constructed.

inheritance. (1) A mechanism in object-oriented programming languages that allows one class (the **subclass**) to incorporate the **declarations** of all or part of another class (the **superclass**). It is implemented by three basic mechanisms. **Extension** is the automatic inclusion of superclass features in a subclass. The superclass method implementation and interface are inherited. Some languages support name qualification to distinguish features that have the same name in both super- and subclasses. **Overriding** is the definition of a subclass method with the same name and message arguments as a superclass method. The interface is the same but the method typically has a different implementation. Overriding supports polymorphic classes and abstract superclass methods. **Specialization** is the definition of methods and instance variables that are unique to a subclass. (2) In object-oriented analysis and design, a model that represents an is-a or subtype hierarchy.

initial state. The state in which the first event is accepted. The initial state is specified by the model—it does not need to be entered by a transition.

in point. A value that satisfies all boundary conditions and does not lie on a boundary.

input vector. A specific set of input values. Syn. **test vector**.

input vector number. In combinational logic, the decimal integer equivalent to the input vector bit pattern: 0000 is vector 0, 1001 is vector 9, etc.

inspection. A formal, small group procedure for detailed scrutiny of a technical work product. Inspections have been consistently found to be very cost-effective and efficient for defect prevention. An inspection process has formal entry–exit criteria, defined checklists, captures process and product metrics, and has mandatory follow-up.

instance. (1) An individual case of some set of things. (2) An **object** is an instance of a **class**.

instance-model. A representation constructed using the technique defined by a meta-model. Often, "a model" means an instance-model concerning a specific application.

instance variable. The objects that are defined as a part of a **Class**. In C++, data member.

instance variable domain. The set of discrete values (states) that may be represented by an instance variable.

instantiate. (1) In object-oriented programming, to cause a specific instance of a class to be created, i.e., to construct an object. (2) In a database system, to cause the creation of a data item.

instantiation. The specification or generation of an instance of a data type, a class, or other generic entity.

instrumentation. (1) In testing, the addition of program statements to report which segments have been activated and optionally report on the contents of data structures. (2) In performance analysis, the usage of task resource utilization monitors.

integration. *See* **integration testing**.

integration coverage. An exit criteria for an integration test.

integration test. The scope of an integration test is a complete system or subsystem of software and hardware units. The units included are physically dependent or must cooperate to meet some requirement. Integration testing exercises interfaces among units within scope to demonstrate that the units are collectively operable. Integration testing begins early in the programming of object-oriented software because a single class is typically composed of objects of other classes and inherits features from superclasses.

integration testing. Testing that attempts to reveal component faults that cause intercomponent failures and to demonstrate that an operability threshold has been reached.

interesting test case. A test case that has a good chance of revealing a fault.

interface. (1) The features of a module, program, class, or type that are externally visible and necessary for its activation, e.g., the name of a C function and its formal parameters. (2) Any shared boundary defined by common physical interconnection, signal, and encoding characteristics. The hardware and software that connects one component of a system to another.

interoperability. The relative ease or difficulty of (1) getting the output of one system accepted as input by another system and (2) once accepted, having it interpreted and processed correctly.

intractable. An algorithm that may be feasible in trivial cases, but for which even moderately complex or large input requires prohibitively large quantities of storage or computation.

invalid input. In **testing**, a test case consisting of input which should be rejected. For example, attempting to enter letters into a currency amount field.

isomorphic. (1) Loosely, two things that share the same structure. (2) In graph theory, two graphs with identical incidence relationships, i.e., the number and structure of nodes and edges is the same.

isomorphic test environment. An environment that replicates the structure of the architecture and the capabilities of the target environment, if not its scale.

isomorphism. In **graph theory**, two graphs which are equivalent in structure. Isomorphic graphs may be drawn differently. This requires that (1) vertices correspond one-to-one, (2) edges correspond one-to-one, (3) all vertex-edge-vertex triples correspond one-to-one.

iteration. (1) Repetition of some section of a program, often a loop body. Compare **recursion**. (2) In **structured programming**, an expression that a segment is to be repeated under the control of a predicate.

iterator. A **method** that visits the components of an object and typically returns them to a client.

IUT. *See* **implementation under test**.

join class. *See* **mixin class**.

judging. The pass/no pass decision for a test is made by a person.

Karnaugh-Veitch Matrix. *See* KV Matrix.

KLOC. /kay-lok/ Thousand Lines of Code. *See also* **lines of code**.

kluge. /klooj/ A cobbled-together, ad hoc solution. The devices portrayed in Rube Goldberg cartoons are canonical kluges.

knot. Suppose a program **control flow graph** is drawn such that all backward branches are placed on one half of a sheet (e.g., left) and all forward branches are placed on the other half (e.g., right). A knot is formed if any path crosses another (and cannot be avoided by nesting the nodes). **Structured programming** cannot contain a knot. A program containing a knot is not a structured program.

KV Matrix. **Karnaugh-Veitch Matrix** (also Karnaugh Map, Karnaugh-Veitch Chart) is the basis of a straightforward graphical technique to derive a minimal **logic function**.

late binding. Any **binding** that occurs during runtime.

latent bug. A bug that has been dormant (unobserved) in two or more releases.

lattice. (1) In mathematics, a partially ordered set in which any two elements have both a greatest lower bound and least upper bound. (2) Generally, any network with relatively dense connections among neighboring nodes.

layer. A description of a system or a set of interface services that have a consistent level of abstraction.

lazy evaluation. *See* **short circuit Boolean evaluation**.

legacy system. An existing software system.

legal event. Explicitly allowed: all the transitions shown in the state transition diagram are legal transitions.

level. The relative position of some item in a hierarchy.

lexical. Pertaining to program source code and source code syntax.

lexical scope. The rules used to determine the visibility of variables and procedures in block structured languages. Each procedure defines a scope for its **formal parameters** and **local variables**. This scope is nested within the block that contains the procedure. Syn. **static scope**.

lines of code (LOC). The number of source statements in a software unit or system. Typically applied to programming language statements and may count operating system command statements. Opinions differ on whether to count program white space (comments, pretty-printing commands, etc.). The advantages of this measure are (1) the counting can often be automated, (2) obtaining the data is relatively easy, (3) there are published studies that can be used as benchmarks, and (4) the count is unambiguous. Disadvantages are: (1) programming style can bias the counts up or down, (2) measurements taken in one language cannot be directly compared to those taken in another (500 lines of assembly language are not equivalent to 500 lines of Java), (3) the measurement cannot be taken until development is complete, (4) it may not be meaningful to non-technical managers, and (5) the use of lexical inclusion (included or copied code fragments, reused from a common library) can also skew the counts.

Liskov substitution principle (LSP). A requirement that subclass objects can be substituted for superclass objects without causing failures or requiring special case code in clients.

literal. An occurrence of an individual variable in a Boolean formula.

logical. (1) A requirement, component, or function that is minimally bound to a particular implementation. (2) In some programming languages, features used for evaluation of boolean types and control flow. (3) The abstract features of some component, as opposed to its physical implementation.

logic expression. A statement-based operation defined in **Boolean algebra.** Variables may be either true (binary 1) or false (binary 0).

logic function. A relationship that maps n Boolean input variables to m Boolean output variables. Output values are determined by binding truth values to input variables and applying the function's formula.

logic gate. An electrical circuit that implements a **Boolean function.** The commonly used gates are AND, OR, XOR, Inverter, NAND, and NOR. Logic gates are the building blocks of micro instructions.

logic minimization. A process for deriving an efficient **logic gate** design to implement a set of **Boolean equations,** for example, reducing (A and not B) or (not A and B) to the equivalent (A xor B). The first expression requires three gates and two inverters; the second a single xor gate. Karnaugh maps provide a technique to do this for systems with two, three, or four Boolean variables. Pattern matching algorithms are available for automated reduction of larger numbers of variables, and are commonly used in IC development.

loop invariant. An **assertion** about a loop that is true no matter how many times the loop iterates. It must be true on entry, it must be true for any number of iterations, and it must imply the desired result on exit. The determination of loop invariants is a fundamental (and difficult) aspect of **proof of correctness.** Algorithmic derivation of loop invariants is **undecidable.**

loop variant. An **assertion** on variables increased or decreased on every iteration that is true no matter how many times the loop iterates. It defines a predicate on iteration control variables that must become false if the loop is to terminate. Its predicate must be true while the loop is within bounds and violated if the loop goes out of control.

LSP. *See* **Liskov substitution principle.**

lurking fault. A bug that causes a manifest failure under infrequent, weird, or unlikely conditions.

magic state. A magic state that has no inbound transition but has transitions to other states. In effect, a pathological or extra initial state.

Mandelbug. [From the Mandelbrot set] A bug whose underlying causes are so complex and obscure as to make its behavior appear chaotic or even nondeterministic [Raymond 90].

many-to-many. A multiplicity relationship between two objects such that one instance of either may be associated with many instances of the other.

mapping. (1) The process of identifying correspondence between items in separate groups, or within the same group. (2) A representation of (1). (3) The multiplicity of an association. (4) In mathematics, a function that assigns each element of a domain set (input) to some element in a range set (output). A *one-to-one* mapping assigns every element of the domain to a single unique element in the range. There may be range elements that are not mapped into the domain. An *onto* mapping assigns every element of the range to at least one element in the domain. Several elements of the domain may map to the same element of the range. A *bijective* mapping is both one-to-one and onto. Every element of the domain is mapped to exactly one element in the range and every element of the range is mapped to at least one element in the domain.

Mealy machine. A state machine in which a transition may have an output action and any output action may be used in more than one transition. No output action is associated with state—states are passive. Compare **Moore machine.**

mean-time-between-failures (MTBF). The average interval between failures of some system. May be required, estimated, or observed. *See also* **availability.**

mean-time-to-repair (MTTR). The average interval required for corrective maintenance of some system. May be required, estimated, or observed. *See also* **availability.**

member function. In C++, a function which belongs to a class. *See also* **method.**

message. A mechanism for invocation of a **method,** resulting in binding a specific method to the message name and binding of specific objects to message parameters. A message is overloaded if two or more methods are associated with it.

message dictionary. In Smalltalk, a list of the messages accepted by a class, or names of methods that objects of the class respond to. This is searched to resolve dynamic binding: if the message is found in the class dictionary, then the method associated with the message is activated; if not, the superclass dictionary is searched for a match. This search continues in successively higher superclasses, until a match is found, or the root object does not contain the message. If not found, then the message doesNotUnderstand is sent to the object that originated the message.

message passing. (1) A non-blocking interprocess communication mechanism for the exchange of data among tasks or processors. This is **asynchronous** since no handshake is required between sender and receiver. (2) In typical object-oriented programs a blocking, synchronous procedure call. An object is said to be activated by receipt of a message.

meta. A description of a description or set of descriptions.

meta-class. A class whose instances are classes. In Smalltalk, a class of classes.

meta-model. The definition of a modeling technique: symbols used in its notation, rules for using these symbols, and concepts associated with symbols and compositions of symbols.

method. A lexically contiguous unit of statements that are executed in response to a message. The **protocol** of a class defines the messages it accepts. The protocol of a program is the set of all class protocols.

method interface. The named entry point of a method and optionally a list of formal parameters.

method under test (MUT). The implementation that is the subject of test design or is being exercised by a test suite.

minimal state machine. A state machine that has no equivalent states.

minimum spanning tree. In **graph theory,** a set of edges such that (1) all vertices in the graph are included and (2) the weights on the edges are the minimum of all sets of vertices that meet.

minterm. A formula with a literal for each variable in a function and that evaluates to true for that function. Minterms can be obtained by inspection of a truth table or by expanding the term.

mission critical. An application system whose correct operation is necessary for successful completion of its intended use. A parachute is mission critical in skydiving.

mixin class. A class that typically does not accomplish much on its own, but makes a common attribute available to disparate clients. It is supplied via inheritance instead of aggregation to take advantage of the greater accessibility that inheritance provides. A join class exists to bring two or more superclasses together as a unit, at least one of which is a mixin.

mode. (1) A collection of states. (2) In a user interface, a state of the application (i) which must be canceled or completed before any other action may be initiated, or (ii) in which an action has different results than in some other state. An undesirable UI characteristic. (3) Loosely, one of several distinct sets of capabilities or functions, for example, run mode, operator mode, or debug mode. May imply a relatively longer duration.

model. "A representation intended to explain the behavior of some aspects of [an artifact or activity]. The model is less complex or complete than the artifact or activity modeled. A model is considered an abstraction of reality." [Thayer 90, 533]

model-based framework. A framework developed to support a family of application systems that share a common set of classes. Typically based on a class model which represents a complex, broad scope.

model-based specification. A technique for **abstract data type** specification that defines individual operations by **preconditions** and **postconditions**. This provides a nonprocedural expression of input/output mapping.

module. A contiguous set of programming language statements that (1) is named, i.e., the entry point, (2) can be activated by name, (3) the name must be visible within a program, (4) the name may be visible to other activation mechanisms in other programs, (5) has an exit point, and (6) can send or receive data from other modules. Compare **class, method**.

module interface. The means by which a module is activated, receives data, and transmits data.

monkey. An automatically, randomly generated test case. Dumb: keystroke generation; semi-intelligent: statistical profile of commands; intelligent: uses state machine model to develop test cases.

Moore machine. A state machine in which a transition does not have an output action. Instead, an output action is associated with each state; states are active. Every output action has at least one corresponding state.

mosaic modularity. The use of many small software modules to compose a system. Many of these must be considered to understand system scope behavior.

multiple-condition coverage. Achieved when all true-false combinations of simple conditions are exercised at least once. There are at most 2^n true-false combinations for a predicate statement with n simple conditions.

multiple inheritance. The ability to inherit features from more than one class. For example, this would allow class dog to inherit from both mammal and pet. Not all OOPLs support multiple inheritance (C++ and Eiffel do, Smalltalk does not). Multiple inheritance offers both increased flexibility and increased hazards.

multiplicity. The quantitative constraints on an object-to-object relationship. The number of object x that may be associated with any one instance of object y.

multiplicity parameters. The upper and lower bound on the number of instances of object x that can be associated with one instance of object x. The lower bound is given as an integer, 0, 1, 2, . . . The upper bound is specified as either an integer greater than the lower bound or an indeterminate value.

MUT. *See* **method under test**.

mutation testing. A testing strategy where small variations to a program are inserted (a mutant), followed by execution of an existing test suite. If the test suite detects the mutant, the mutant is "retired." If undetected, the test suite must be revised.

N^2 chart. A graphic representation of N functions or processes and all interfaces among them. Functions are placed on the diagonal of a square matrix, beginning in the upper left corner. Each nondiagonal square represents a different function-to-function interface. N^2

charts can represent many subjects, including abstract or physical systems, work flows, communication networks, and material handling.

name clash. With **multiple inheritance**, a subclass may inherit from two or more parent classes that contain features with the same names. For example, D is derived from classes B and C, and B and C both contain some feature *x*.

name mangling. The assignment of internal names to source code identifiers during compilation or interpreting.

name scope. In a programming language, the conventions that determine how source code units may refer to data and procedure names, especially those defined outside the local scope of a given unit.

narrative requirements. System or component requirements that are given in natural language. Such requirements are typically **ambiguous**.

no pass. The status of a completed test case whose actual results are not the same as the expected results.

node. (1) The elements of a graph that are connected by edges. In graph theory, an object represented in a graph by a point, circle, box, etc. Formally, a **vertex**. (2) A diagram element that represents a processor (UML). (3) In a communication system, any point with two or more communication links which is individually addressable (e.g., a user workstation). (4) Any component of a network or hierarchy.

nominal. A rating of maximum speed or capacity under optimal conditions.

nondeterministic. (1) When a program may execute one of several paths depending on a randomly varying externally determined state or input, the program exhibits nondeterministic behavior. (2) A finite state automation that models several transitions on the same input.

nonreflexive relation. A relation that is not reflexive (i.e., does not allow self-reference).

nonspecific fault model. Any fault will do to prevent conformance. The sufficiency of the testing model with respect to system requirements is crucial to establish conformance.

nonsymmetric relation. A relation that is not symmetric (i.e., does not allow transposition).

nontransitive. A relation that is not transitive—that is, given facts about two member pairs with one common element, we cannot assume the property of interest holds for all the members.

no-op. A *no operation* instruction. A machine instruction that does not perform any action, except to increment the instruction counter.

object. (1) In an **object-oriented programming language**, an instance of a **class** that has a unique symbolic name. An object is statically declared and may be defined at either compile-time or **runtime**. It encapsulates a unique set of instance variable values which persist from one activation to the next. Compared to conventional languages, an object is a composite of variables and modules; it is similar in many respects to a user-defined type. (2) Syn. for **entity**.

object-based. A programming language or system that supports **encapsulation** and **object identity**, but does not support set abstraction, class-based programming, **inheritance**, and **self-recursion**.

object-based programing language. Programming languages whose primary abstraction is encapsulation of modules and data are **object-based**: Ada-83, Modula, etc.

object code. (1) The output of a compiler or assembler. A stream (usually a file) of machine instructions that can be loaded into main memory and executed. (2) A program written in an **object-oriented programming language**.

object code coverage. Coverage measured by instrumentation inserted in the object code generated by the compiler, not in the source code.

object identity. The symbol by which an object may be referenced.

object module. A source code module that has been translated into **object code,** but is not necessarily link-edited or loadable. A separately compiled module.

object-oriented program. An executable assemblage of objects.

object-oriented programming language. A programming language with full support for encapsulation, data abstraction, inheritance, polymorphism, and self-recursion. Ada 95, C++, Eiffel, Java, Objective-C, and Smalltalk are examples of object-oriented languages.

object request broker (ORB). The integrating component of the object management architecture. The ORB defines a standard protocol and offers an API for communication among objects and service requests. The API is accessed by Interface Definition Language (IDL). This language is similar to C++ and provides a generic high-level interface for application-to-application communication. IDL is used to define objects manipulated by the ORB. These objects can be any application system, specifically those not implemented in object-oriented languages.

object type. An entity that encapsulates a data structure and provides methods that act upon the encapsulated values. Syn. **class.**

object under test (OUT). The implementation that is the subject of test design or is being exercised by a test suite.

off point. A value not on a boundary.

omega state. In the FREE state model, the null final state reached after an object has been destructed, deleted, or gone out of scope. The α and ω states facilitate testing of multiple constructors and destructors. The ω state is reached after an object has been destructed, deleted, or gone out of scope. This may be different from an explicitly modeled final state. The omega state allows explicit modeling and systematic testing of destructors, garbage collection, and other termination actions.

omega transition. An event that causes a transition to an omega state, typically an implicit destructor.

omission. A required capability that is not present in an implementation. For purposes of testing, omissions must be defined with respect to required capabilities.

one-to-many. In object-oriented analysis, any relationship between two **classes** or **objects** *A* and *B* such that one instance of *A* can be associated with many instances of *B,* but each *B* is associated with only one *A*. Based on the mathematical concept of onto (into) mapping. The "one" refers to the singleton instance and the "many" to the associated instance. In some contexts, the lower bound on the associated instance is understood to be zero; in others, one. The distinction is not trivial. A lower bound of zero means that an associated instance is optional. A lower bound of one means that an associated instance is mandatory.

on point. A value that lies on a boundary.

opaque. *See* **black box.**

open boundary. A boundary defined by a strict inequality operator, for example, $a > b$ or $c < 500$.

operability threshold. An explicit, demonstrable criterion for minimal part (component) interoperability.

operational definition. An agreed upon procedure for measurement of some aspect of a process or work product that clearly communicates expectations for quality and performance. This requires (1) an objective, unambiguous acceptance criterion for a process or work product based on a metric(s), (2) a validated, repeatable procedure to obtain measurement of the metric, and (3) a decision rule to evaluate compliance with the criterion.

operational profile. A hierarchic model of system usage used for **system testing**. Each unique leaf-level usage (a **scenario**) is assigned a probability and facilitates design of a functional test case. Tests are executed in order of highest probability.

operational relation. A decision table that enumerates relationships among use case input variables that lead to distinctly different classes of response.

operational variable. A variable that participates in determining the response of a use case.

operator. (1) In programming languages, a component of an expression that specifies predefined transformations on expressions or data items: e.g., + − * / ∧. (2) The operation code in a machine instruction. (3) A person who uses a system, typically to perform some kind of system management task.

operator overloading. The association of several distinct operations with a single operator symbol. For example, in C++, the + operator (addition) may be overloaded to perform matrix or vector addition as well as scalar addition on integer and real variables. A kind of **polymorphism**.

oracle. A mechanism to evaluate the actual results of a test case as pass or no pass. This requires a result generator to produce the expected results for an input and a **comparator** to check the actual results against the expected results. An oracle is the generation and comparison mechanism, but never the comparator alone. An oracle may be manual, automated, or partially automated.

ORB. *See* **object request broker.**

order. A relative measure of the time required to compute an algorithm, often expressed by big-oh notation. Formulas for the number of iterations usually have O on the left side. For example, the time to perform a binary search on n sorted items is $O(n) = \log_2 n$.

order of magnitude. A factor of ten. An order of magnitude increase means a tenfold increase, two orders means a hundredfold, three orders means a thousandfold, etc.

organic oracle. An oracle that exploits an informational redundancy present in some systems. That is, the IUT, the test case input, and the actual result are sufficient to decide pass/no pass.

orthogonal. (1) Mutual independence. Factors, relationships, or components that can be considered independently, or that do not overlap. The effect of one does not change the other; the meaning or behavior of one can be understood without reference to another. (2) A property of a design or representation technique which has well-defined non-redundant informational domains with explicit intersections. In a language, the absence of orthogonality results in increased complexity, lack of clarity, and diminished expressive power.

OUT. *See* **object under test.**

overloading. (1) in **object-oriented programming**, a message is said to be overloaded if there are two or more methods associated with it. For example, draw(x), where x can be a circle or a box. The argument signature determines which method is selected. A form of **polymorphism.** (2) The context-dependent action of simple operators in most languages. The + means to add regardless of the data type of the associated operators. In one case, it means a floating-point add, in another, an integer add. Ada extends this idea to the typing that is imposed on function and procedure calls. Thus, given the context, $Y=F(X)$ can invoke different procedures or functions, e.g., an integer $F(X)$ if X is an integer, or a floating-point $F(X)$ if X is a floating point.

override. A subclass may override a superclass with a method that has the same name as a superclass method, providing method **polymorphism.**

overriding. A basic mechanism of **inheritance** in which a new implementation of a superclass method is defined in a subclass. The subclass uses the same interface (name and argument signature) as the superclass method. Compare **extension, specialization.**

parameter. (1) Data items and expressions used in a subprogram interface. There are three subprogram **binding times** that are important in parameter passing protocols: definition (translation time), activation (when called), execution (while running). There are four main methods for parameter transmission: call by reference, call by value, call by value/result, and call by name. The semantics of each transmission method are significantly different. *See also* **formal parameter.** (2) A value that controls or influences a selection or outcome. (3) In statistics, a variable whose specification provides an instance of a general model.

parameter list. The interface to a procedure or module. The data items and expressions included in a module interface. Syn. **argument list.**

parent. In a directed acyclic graph, if there is an edge from node a to node b, then a is the parent of b.

partial correctness. A mathematical proof that a program or a specification will meet its **postconditions** and invariants given that its **preconditions** hold. Termed partial because termination is not proved. Compare **total correctness.** *See also* **proof of correctness.**

partition. Any subset of all possible inputs for an IUT. Synonymous with **subdomain.**

partition testing. Any testing strategy for choosing **partitions** and selecting values from partitions. The input-space of the implementation under test is divided according to some scheme (a partition). A few test data values are selected from each partition. Any available information about the program, its specification, or the development process may be used to define the groups. Most, but not all, testing approaches can be considered partition testing.

parts. Software components at the next lower level of abstraction. For example, the parts of a method are statements and expressions. The parts of a class are methods. The parts of a cluster are classes, and so on.

pass. The status of a completed test case whose actual results are the same as the expected results.

path. (1) A sequence of **segments** through a program. An entry–exit or complete path begins at the program entry point and terminates at the exit point. (2) In **graph theory,** in either a directed or undirected graph $G = (V,E)$ a sequence of nodes $v_1, v_2, \ldots v_n$ such that $[v_i, v_{i+1}]$ are edges in E; a finite, connected sequence of edges and vertices, such that no edge is repeated and no vertex is repeated. (3) A collection of line segments in a diagram (UML). (4) In a state machine, a sequence of transitions: $state_p$, $event_i$, $state_q$, $event_j$, $state_r \ldots$

path coverage. Achieved when every possible entry–exit path has been exercised at least once.

path expression. A string that lists the nodes visited along a path. Loops are represented by segments within parentheses, followed by an asterisk to show that this group may iterate from zero to n times.

path sensitization. The process of determining argument and instance variable values that will cause a particular path to be taken. Results in a **partition** that contains at least one combination of input values necessary to execute a particular path. Path sensitization is undecidable; no algorithm can solve this problem in all cases.

patlet. A less than fully documented **pattern.**

pattern. A generalized solution to a specific recurring design problem. A pattern explains insights that have lead to generally recognized good practices for design and implementation. A pattern has a context, which is the circumstances that determine its applicability. Forces are constituent parts of the context which may occur in varying degrees.

pattern template. A list of subjects (sections) that comprise a pattern.

peer review. *See* **inspection, review, walkthrough.**

perfect oracle. An **oracle** that is behaviorally equivalent to the implementation under test and completely trusted. In effect, a defect-free version of the IUT.

performance. Generally, the amount of time, storage, or cost consumed by an application system. Measured by three key factors: **throughput, response time,** and **availability.**

performance objective. An unambiguous, quantifiable target response time, throughput, utilization, or availability. Expressed as the service rate for some task given a workload, for example, response time under peak load, average load, and worst-case loading. Average or worst-case tolerance depends on the application. Worst-case performance is relevant for mission critical systems like air traffic control. Average performance is often the focus of data processing systems.

performance requirements. The constraints on resources consumed or speed of execution that a system is expected to satisfy.

performance testing. Testing conducted to evaluate the compliance of a system or component with specified performance requirements [IEEE 610]. Performance requirements impose constraints on functional requirements (e.g., the speed, accuracy, or memory usage with which a given function must be performed).

persistence. In object-oriented programming, the ability to preserve object state after program execution terminates, and restore state on subsequent executions. Typically requires that an object be writable/readable on nonvolatile secondary storage with automatic and robust encapsulation while in the persistent state.

persistent object. An **object** that maintains state between activations of the program in which it is created. An object whose lifetime extends beyond the lifetime of the agent that creates it. For example, objects in an OODBMS.

pesticide paradox. The necessary loss of test suite effectiveness. This is similar to the effect of a pesticide to which a few pests develop immunity.

platform. A family of computer systems or operating systems that provide a **target environment** for running application systems. For example, a Unix platform is any computer system that runs the Unix operating system.

polymorphism. A mechanism essential to object-oriented programming languages. In object-oriented programming, the ability to associate one method name with different methods. From the Greek, "having many forms." The same message (expression, method name) can be bound to different methods. Typically requires dynamic binding. *General* polymorphism allows a single method to accept arguments of many types (classes). This is common in functional programming languages. *Ad hoc polymorphism* selects a different method based on the type (class) of the operand. *Parameterized polymorphism* selects a different method based on parameters. The selection mechanism typically uses an inheritance hierarchy to determine bindings. *See* **static polymorphism, dynamic polymorphism.**

popular framework. A **framework** that has become widely used within an organization or by customers of a commercial software provider.

possible sneak path. Any combination of an event and a state which is not explicitly permitted by the state specification for the IUT.

postcondition. An **assertion** that defines properties that must hold when a method completes. It is evaluated after a method completes execution and before the message result is returned to the client. This is ideally stated as a mapping or function between input and output (e.g., $y = x + 1$). For complex functions the acceptable output values can also be expressed as a range, enumeration, or relationship. The activated module is responsible for meeting the postconditions. Contrast **precondition**. *See also* **contract, proof of correctness.**

precision. The percent of baseline test cases in a reduced test suite that *cannot* reveal regression faults and which are *not* selected for the reduced test suite.

precondition. An **assertion** that defines properties that must hold when a method begins execution. It defines acceptable values of parameters and variables upon entry to a module or method. This is typically stated as a range or enumeration. A precondition is similar to mathematical set builder notation: $\{x \mid x$ has the property $P\}$, or the set of x, such that all x have the property P. A precondition can include relationships to constants ($x > 0$) or other variables ($x <> y$). The activating module and modules that own global data are responsible for establishing the preconditions. Contrast **postcondition**. *See also* **contract, proof of correctness.**

predecessor. A task that must be completed to begin a subsequent task.

predicate. (1) A branching statement containing at least one condition: if, case, do while, do until, or for. The evaluation of a predicate selects a segment of code to be executed. (2) A function whose range is the set of Boolean values. (3) A well-formed expression in the predicate calculus that consists of at least one predicate function.

predicate expression. An expression that contains a condition (conditions) that evaluates to true or false.

prime implicant. (1) All outputs for the cube are true (it must be an implicant) and (2) the cube is not a subset of any other cube.

primitive state. A state defined by a value that can be represented with a low-level data type that does not contain any expandable definitions.

private contract. The contract that applies to the intraclass usage of private features. It is implementation-specific.

problem domain class. A representation of an external entity or concept that is necessary for an implementation-independent model of the system under test.

procedural programming language. Programming languages whose primary abstraction is module control flow; e.g., C, Cobol, Fortran, Pascal, and PL/I are procedural languages.

producer. A person or organization who makes a software component available to **consumers**.

production release. A **release** of a system that is ready to ship. Syn. **field release.**

product machine. The states of a product machine are combinations of the states of two or more basic machines.

product term. A string of **literals** connected by the *and* operation in a **Boolean formula.**

program. (1) A load module as defined by the target environment. (2) A set of source code modules that can be processed by a language translator to create (1). (3) In project management, an effort requiring several parallel projects.

program slicing. A program slice with respect to variable x contained in statement n is the minimum set of antecedent statements needed to use x in the execution of statement n. The statements in a slice are related by dataflow. A slice must be executable and if executed must produce the same result for x that would obtain under execution of the full program.

proof of correctness. (1) A formal technique used to prove mathematically that a computer program satisfies its specified requirements. (2) A proof that results from applying the technique in (1) [IEEE 610]. (3) The use of techniques of mathematical logic to infer that a relation between program variables assumed true at program entry implies that another relation between program variables holds at program exit [Adrion 82].

protocol. (1) In data communications, an agreement about automatic procedures for transmitting messages over some channel that specifies how an exchange is started and stopped, how sender and receiver are synchronized, how error detection and correction is performed, and what data format and encoding are used. (2) In Smalltalk, the set of messages that an object will accept and the definition of the type and behavior of each message.

prototyping. Experimentation to determine specific user requirements. It is most often used to design human–computer interaction (HCI), but can be used to obtain other kinds of requirements. It has been very successful at getting early validation of user requirements for HCI. A means to elicit and validate user requirements by a cut-and-fit approach. A software prototype usually lacks many important features of a desired application, but allows an early try-out of the user interface.

proxy. A component that provides an interface but simply delegates all incoming messages to another object.

pseudorandom numbers. A sequence of numbers generated by an algorithm that approximates a truly random sequence. A computed sequence of numbers with statistical properties similar to a sequence generated by a physically random process (e.g., repeated toss of fair coin).

public contract. The contract that applies to the interclass usage of public features. It should be implementation-independent.

public interface. The interface to a class or object which is externally visible.

quality. (1) The degree to which a system, component, or process meets specified requirements. (2) The degree to which a system, component, or process meets customer or user needs or expectations [IEEE 610]. (3) In engineering, the totality of features and characteristics of a product or service that bears on its ability to satisfy given needs [ASQC 1978].

queue. (1) *n.* A line or list of tasks waiting for some resource or service. (2) A data type that follows a queuing discipline. For example, a FIFO (first-in, first-out) queue adds new items only at the end and removes them only from the front. (3) *v.* To be added to or to wait in a queue.

queuing theory. The mathematical modeling and analysis of **queues.**

RAD. /rahd/ *See* **rapid application development.**

range/domain ratio (RDR). The quantity r/d where r is the number of discrete input states (the cardinality of the range) and d is the number of discrete output states (the cardinality of the domain) for a code segment or function [Voas 99].

rapid application development (RAD). A short-cycle approach to the development of data processing applications. It has several elements: (1) joint application development sessions to elicit requirements, (2) **prototyping** conducted by experienced developers for early validation, (3) emphasis on model-based code generation beginning with an upper CASE tool, and (4) some form of a timebox project plan.

rapid prototyping. *See* **prototyping.**

RDR. *See* **range/domain ratio.**

reachability analysis Analysis of a state model to determine which states are reachable.

real-time system. (1) An application in which speed of a response to an input affects subsequent inputs. A required response time interval is called a **deadline**. The consequences of missing a deadline classify such systems: (i) *hard real-time,* missed deadline is a **failure**, (ii) *firm real-time,* hard deadline, but a low probability of missed deadline is acceptable, (iii) *soft real-time,* missed deadline degrades performance but is not a failure. (2) A system that must provide subsecond response time. (3) Loosely, an interactive system.

recursion. (1) A subroutine, program, module, or object that calls itself (direct recursion), or that calls another routine which calls the first routine. Each activation causes a copy of the arguments to be saved. This typically requires creation of a list of unfinished uses in a stack of activation records. Each successive call may make use of the results of the preceding call. Some terminal condition must be specified. When the terminal condition is true, the chain established by the recursive call is retraced. This is useful for searching tree data structures or in algorithms to evaluate mathematically recursive functions. (2) In mathematics, a function whose values are natural numbers derived from natural numbers by a substitution formula that uses the function as an operand. (3) Loosely, anything repetitive and self-referential.

recursive state. A state defined over a combinational value set obtained by expanding (recursively) each instance variable in a class. Also called "object flattening" [Jacobson+92], "the collection of associations for that object" [Martin+92], or "complex objects" [Siepmann+94].

reduced regression test suite. A subset of a regression test suite.

reference. An object that is a pointer to another object.

reflexive relation. A relation in which self-reference is valid. The property of interest holds when applied to each individual entity (i.e., the property of interest holds about every member of the relation).

regression fault. A fault induced by a **delta build**. Revealed by a test case that has previously passed but no longer passes: stable **baseline** system B and a delta component each pass individually adequate test suites, but fail when used together.

regression test case. A test case that the **baseline** has passed and that is expected to pass when rerun on a delta build.

regression testing. Selective retesting of system or component to verify that modifications have not caused unintended effects and that the system still complies with its specified requirements [IEEE 610].

regression test suite. A test suite composed of regression test cases.

regular expression. A string of variables and operators that describes a class of strings. For example, **r.t** corresponds to any string beginning with r and ending with t.

release. A relatively minor set of changes to a system. For example, a set of fixes and performance improvements that do not add to or reduce the stated capabilities of the system. Compare **version**.

repeated inheritance. Repeated inheritance occurs when a common superclass is present in a multiple inheritance network. For example, classes B and C are derived from superclass A, and class D is derived from B and C.

repository. A database of software requirements, specifications, and implementation components.

representation. (1) In system development, a model, notation, plan, or specification of a system or a component as opposed to its implementation. (2) Any technique by which information or knowledge is stored according to a data model or knowledge representation schema.

requirement. Any capability, or feature, function that a system must provide to meet the goals or needs of its intended users.

response matrix. A state machine specification that is a modified form of the **event-state table**. All **events** are listed. Each unguarded event has a row. Each **guarded event** has one row for each truth value combination of its guard and an additional column for each predicate within its guard. The **truth table** of the guard expression is enumerated in these predicate columns.

response time. The time elapsed between input arrival and output delivery. Average and worst-case values are usually of interest.

responsibility. An anthropomorphic metaphor for functions and representation supported by a component. At class scope, aggregate responsibilities are synonymous with the **class contract**. In OOA and OOD, the requirements allocated to a class. Responsibilities are part of the class's **public interface.**

responsibility-based assertion. An assertion that expresses some element of the class's contract or other specification.

responsibility-based test design. The use of specified or expected responsibilities of a unit, subsystem, or system to design tests. Synonymous with specification-oriented, behavioral, functional, or black box test design.

resultant state. A state that is the result of some transition.

result generator. *See* **oracle.**

resulting condition. An **assertion** that defines the **state**(s) in which a method may be exited, given the state in which the method was entered. *See also* **accepting condition, state invariant, transition.**

results-oriented testing. The orchestration of responsibility-based and implementation-based test techniques for effectiveness. Instead of being cast as incompatible opposites or narrow technical specialties, scope-specific test design and execution techniques are organized into a coherent whole.

return. (1) The exit point of a routine. (2) To transfer control back to the caller of a routine. (3) To bind a value to a variable by expression evaluation.

reusability. The relative ease of reusing software components, in whole or in part, for newer applications.

reuse. Making use of existing software components in new applications. Reuse is facilitated by well-designed component interfaces and functions.

review. A meeting at which a work product or set of work products is presented to project personnel, managers, users, customers, or other interested parties for comment and approval [IEEE 610].

risk. Possibility of suffering a loss [SEI 93].

robust. Said of a system that is failure and **fault tolerant,** and supports systems management in a straightforward, efficient, and cohesive manner. A system that handles unexpected states in a way to minimize performance degradation, data corruption, incorrect output, and abends.

root. (1) In a **tree** structure or other hierarchy, the highest or first vertex. A vertex that has no **ancestors** or **parents.** (2) In **graph theory,** the **vertex** in a tree that has no incoming **edges.** (3) In a hierarchic database system, a segment that has no parent segment. (4) A class that has no superclass.

round-trip scenario. A complete stimulus-response path on a sequence diagram. A sequence diagram typically has many round-trip scenarios.

runtime stack. Storage allocated for activation records.

runtime. *See* **binding time.**

safe reduction. A **reduced regression test suite** determined by analysis of code dependencies to decide which test cases can be removed without removing any existing test case that could reveal a **regression fault.**

satisfy. The values that make an assertion true are said to satisfy the assertion.

scenario. An interaction with a system under test that is recognizable as a single unit of work from the user's point of view. This step, procedure, or input event may involve any number of implementation functions.

scope. (1) The collection of software components to be verified. Since tests must be run on an executable software entity, scope is typically defined to correspond to some executable component or system of components. (2) The level of abstraction represented in a state machine. It may be bounded (only abstract values of state variables are considered) or recursive (all levels of abstraction are flattened until only primitive data types remain). (3) In a program, the names visible for a given lexical unit. (4) In project management, the boundary of the work assignment, or the project goals.

segment. In a source program, a set of statements such that if one is executed, all the others must be executed. A set of lexically contiguous statements with no conditionally executed statements. The last statement in a segment must be a conditional (if-then or case), a loop control, or module exit. Program paths are composed of segments.

selective regression testing. The use of a **reduced regression test suite.**

self-recursion. In an object-oriented programming language, the capability to program an **object** to send messages to itself.

self-reference. *See* **self-recursion.**

semantics. (1) In a programming language, definitions of what expressions, statements, and instructions are intended to accomplish. The meaning of a statement is the computation it describes. There is no inherent meaning or significance, unlike natural language. Statements denote the values that are bound to them. Formal approaches to semantics include axiomatic (algebraic) semantics and denotational semantics. Formal semantics are typically of interest to the language developer. Operational semantics are narrative explanations of language capabilities, for example, programmer's reference documentation.

server. (1) An **object** that accepts **messages** from other objects but does not send messages. Contrast **client.** A class X is said to be a client of class Y when X defines an instance variable of type Y; Y is said to be a server of class X. Client objects are said to activate methods in server objects. (2) In a **client/server system,** a process (logical or physical) that accepts requests for service generated by a client. The client is independent and asynchronous with respect to the server. A server typically performs a specialized function, e.g., data storage or high-speed computing.

service. An abstraction of (1) a **method** in an OO language, (2) an operation on a private type in Ada, or (3) an Ada task entry. Each service has an argument signature. The set of signatures constitutes the client interface, or class protocol of the object.

shipped. The act of making a system available for its intended use.

short circuit Boolean evaluation. The implicit branching logic for compound predicate expressions used by many language translators. At runtime, each predicate expression operand is incrementally evaluated. When a sufficient condition to a branch is reached, the branch is taken without evaluating remaining conditions.

show stopper. A severe **failure**, which prevents further use of a program or system. Syn. **abend, abort**.

side effect. A change to the state of an object or variable that is an indirect result of some operation. The postfix increment operator ++ causes a variable reference to have the side effect of being incremented by one. Can occur with call by reference.

silver bullet. A software tool or methodology that purports to solve all or many of the fundamentally hard problems of software development. Allusion to the fiction that only a silver bullet can kill a werewolf.

simple path. A path that contains only one iteration of a loop, if a loop is present in some sequence.

sink. (1) Generally, any destination for data. (2) In data communications, a device that can accept data signals from a channel. It may verify these signals and issue error-control signals.

site failure. In a distributed system, a failure where one site ceases to function without warning and data in volatile storage is lost.

slice. *See* **program slicing**.

SLOC. /ess-loch/ Source Lines of Code. *See also* **lines of code**.

small cluster. The typical focus of class scope testing. A small cluster includes several classes which are so tightly coupled that testing constituent classes in isolation is impractical.

smoke test. A minimal test suite designed to pass if the implementation under test can be run at all.

sneak path. The bug that allows an illegal transition or eludes a guard.

software component. (1) A reusable software module supplied as an executable. The component may be accessed by its defined interface (typically a function call). Components are typically provided as documented libraries of executables that support a particular kind of development. Some commercial examples include JavaBeans (SunSoft), ActiveX/COM (Microsoft), LiveConnect (NetScape), OpenDoc (IBM). (2) Generally, any unit of source or executable code that can be referenced by name.

software design pattern. A pattern whose subject is a recurring software design problem.

software engineering. The application of rigorous techniques and proven heuristics to the problem of software development. Its goal is to produce very high-quality software by minimizing guesswork, bad habits, and superstition from all phases of the software life cycle.

software process. A set of activities, methods, practices, and transformations that people use to develop and maintain software and the associated products (e.g., project plans, design documents, code, test cases, and user manuals) [SEI 93].

software project. The set of all project functions, activities, and tasks, both technical and managerial, required to satisfy the terms and conditions of the *project agreement*. A software project may be self-contained or may be part of a larger project. A software project may span only a portion of the software life cycle [IEEE 610].

software quality assurance (SQA). (1) A planned and systematic pattern of all actions necessary to provide adequate confidence that a software work product conforms to established technical requirements [IEEE 610]. (2) A set of activities designed to evaluate the process by which software work products are developed and/or maintained [SEI 93].

software reliability. The probability of failure-free operation of a program for a specified time in a specified environment.

software reliability model. A model that characterizes software reliability or a related quality as a function of failures or time.

software requirement. A capability expressed in a software requirements specification that is to be provided by the software components of a system.

software testing. *See* **testing.**

spaghetti code. Code with complex control flow, resulting from (1) misuse of GOTO statements, (2) entry or exit to the body of a loop which bypasses the normal loop control statement (especially in nest loops), or (3) multiple exit points from a loop or the program itself. Compare **structured programming.**

spaghetti inheritance. An object-oriented program that contains complex, hard to understand inheritance. *See also* **yo-yo effect.**

specialization. (1) A basic mechanism of **inheritance** in which new methods and instance variables are defined at subclass scope. Compare **extension, overriding.** (2) A class hierarchy that models "kind-of" relationships.

specification-oriented testing. *See* **responsibility-based test design.**

spiral model. A risk-driven approach to managing the software process. A system is developed as a series of versions. The initial version is a minimal prototype. Subsequent versions explore high-risk aspects of the system using a truncated development cycle that builds on previous versions.

SQA. Software quality assurance.

stable system. A system that has sufficient **dependability** to support system scope testing. The threshold for stability is usually set by practical considerations and may be defined by an **operability threshold.**

stage. The activities that begin and end with the development and execution of a test configuration.

state. A set of instance variable value combinations that share some property of interest for the class under test (all inherited instance variables are considered as part of the state variable set, i.e., the class under test is "flattened"). State is defined over sets of instance variable value combinations that are limited to the acceptable results of computations performed by methods. The relationship among instance variables which constitute a state must be expressible as a valid Boolean expression in some object-oriented programming language. Such an expression is a **state invariant.** A state represents some effect of the history of messages accepted by a class. For example, the message `withdraw` would not be accepted in the overdrawn state of account. A state may be either abstract (using only variables exported by the class interface), or concrete (using all class instance variables).

state-based behavior. A response pattern such that identical inputs are not always accepted, and when accepted, may produce different output.

state-based testing. Testing with test cases developed by modeling the system under test as a **state machine.**

statechart. A state machine that uses graphical conventions to represent complex transitions and hierarchical relationships.

state invariant. An **assertion** that defines a **state** as combinations of instance variables. A state invariant must define a subset of the values allowed by the **class invariant,** i.e., it must be no weaker than the class invariant (if only one state is defined, the class invariant and this state variant must be equivalent).

state machine. (1) A system model composed of events (inputs), states, and actions (outputs). Output is determined by both current and past input. The effects of previous inputs are represented by states. (2) A mathematical model that defines the sequence of inputs that can be accepted by an abstract machine. State machines have been used to study many kinds of software problems. Syn. **finite state machine, finite automata.** Compare **combinational.** *See also* **Mealy machine, Moore machine.**

statement. A single line of code, delimited by a statement terminator. For example, in Ada and C++ the code between pairs of semicolons.

statement coverage. A coverage achieved when all the statements in a method have been executed at least once. This is also known as C1 coverage, line coverage, segment coverage, or basic block coverage. Segment and basic block coverage count segments instead of individual statements.

state space. The set of all possible states that an abstract or actual system may assume. The set of all possible combinations of variables visible to a software component.

state-to-state format. A state transition table where rows represent accepting states and columns represent resultant states.

state transition diagram. A graphic representation of a state machine. Nodes represent states. Arrows (directed edges) represent transitions.

state transition table. A tabular representation of a state machine. Rows and columns may be used to represent states, action, or events. Cells in the table show the relationship for the intersection, e.g., an event/accepting state pair.

state variable. (1) A variable that represents a state. (2) Occasionally, a synonym for an **instance variable.**

static binding. Binding accomplished by the language translator prior to execution. *See also* **binding time.**

static polymorphism. Binding that occurs at translation time. For example, Ada 95 types, subtypes, derived types, operators, derived operators, derived subprograms, subprograms from generic instantiations, static types, and tagged types can be bound to two or more objects. C++ templates are another example.

static program structure. The organization of a program as it is written; the bindings performed prior to runtime.

static scope. *See* **lexical scope.**

static type checking. Type checking at a translation time. The programmer (or language defaults) must include the type of each data object, and structure and type of component interfaces in each **declaration.** The number, order, and type of arguments and results must be provided for operations: +, *, sin(), etc. For variables and constants, the operand data type must be declared or determinable. Some languages support user-defined types. Overloaded operators may need several checks. Overloaded operators are replaced with operations specific to the type. Advantages include reduced object module size and overhead, and more reliable readable code. Detailed declarations must be coded and type conversion defaults (**coercions**) may have surprises. A language that relies wholly on static checking is said to be strongly typed. This may be restrictive. For example, since array size is part of a Pascal declaration, variable size arrays are not permitted.

static verification. Defect prevention and removal techniques that do not require implementation execution. Techniques include desk checking, **walkthroughs, inspections, reviews, formal proof,** and use of automatic source code analyzers.

stealth bug. A **bug** that removes information useful for its diagnosis and correction.

stream I/O. Input/output processing that can be viewed as manipulation of a single string of bits, bytes, or characters.

stress testing. Testing conducted to evaluate a system or component at or beyond the limits of its specified requirements [IEEE 610].

strict inheritance. Deprecated. *See* **Liskov substitution principle.**

stronger assertion. A more restrictive assertion; it is true for a subset of the value combinations that make a weaker assertion true. The satisfying value set of a stronger assertion is a subset of the satisfying set of a weaker assertion.

structural testing. *See* **implementation-based test design.**

structured programming. An approach to programming motivated by the practical problems of **spaghetti code.** A structured program is composed of only three constructs: sequence, selection, and iteration (D-structures.) No other control structures are allowed. All program units must have a single entry and exit point. Every node in the program must be on at least one path from the entry to the exit point (the *liveness* criteria). Any computable function can be expressed as a structured program, and any program flow graph can be rewritten with only D-structures. A reorganized program may require flags, and is not necessarily "better" or more efficient. Dijkstra's famous letter to the CACM, titled "Goto Considered Harmful" made the argument that structured programming is qualitatively better because the as-written program is more likely to parallel the as-executed program. In part, a technique to facilitate mathematical proof of correctness.

stub. A skeletal or special-purpose implementation of a software component, used to develop or test a component that is dependent on the stub. A stub may simulate the response of a component that has not yet been implemented.

stuck-at fault model. A fault model often used for combinational digital logic. Stuck-at faults occur when a physical defect (a short or open) causes the input to a gate to remain at logical one or zero, whatever the actual input.

stuck-at-one. *See* **stuck-at fault model.**

stuck-at-zero. *See* **stuck-at fault model.**

subclass. A class that designates a superclass and typically specifies its own instance variables, message patterns, and methods. A subclass inherits, or has access to, the methods and instance variables of its superclass (superclasses if **multiple inheritance** is supported). A subclass may **override** a superclass with a method that has the same name as a superclass method, providing method **polymorphism.** In C++, a **derived class;** in Eiffel, an heir class.

subdomain. A subset of a domain. A partition of a domain defined by **boundary conditions.**

subgraph. A subset of a formal **graph** G, such that all edges and vertices in the subgraph are also in G.

subroutine. An activation mechanism used in many programming languages. A subroutine is a control abstraction. It is a **module** which (1) can be activated by name (called), (2) the language provides built-in support for parameter passing, and (3) which returns control to the caller (the module which contains the call statement). The composition of subroutines and their interfaces is the subject of structured design, **information hiding,** and similar detail design methodologies. Compare **message passing.**

subsume. Test strategy x is said to subsume some other strategy y if all the elements that y exercises are also exercised by x. For example, branch coverage is said to subsume statement coverage, because exercising all branches necessarily exercises all statements.

subsumes hierarchy. An analytical ranking of coverages. No generalizable results about relative bug-finding effectiveness have been reached that correlate with this ranking.

subsystem. A subset of the functions or components of a system. Subsystem components usually share some common attribute or contribute to a common goal.

sum-of-products form. A Boolean formula that consists of product terms related by *or* operators (summing).

superstate. A state may be an aggregate of other states (a superstate) or an atomic, singleton state.

surprise. A capability discovered during testing that is not traceable to requirements or specifications. Spurious functionality or extra code possibly due to (1) gold-plating, creeping elegance, or other forms of programmer creativity, or (2) misinterpretation of requirements or specifications. Compare **omission, fault.**

suspicion. Any commonsense indicators that some component or code is more likely to be buggy than others.

SUT. *See* **system under test.**

sw. Software.

symmetric relation. A relation in which the property of interest is bi-directional for any pair of entities.

system. (1) Generally, a collection of components interconnected to meet some goal or perform related functions. The useful characteristics result from the interconnection, not from the individual components. (2) The operating system and computer system at some particular installation. (3) The operating system at some particular installation. (4) An application at some particular installation.

system integration. (1) A commercial service where a contractor delivers a system to meet customer requirements by acquiring and testing hardware, package software, and custom software. (2) *See* **integration test, system test.**

system life cycle. A view of software systems that recognizes three main stages: development, operation, and retirement. This view is useful for focusing on the dominant issues in each stage.

system test. A test that is exercised on a complete integrated application. Tests are made on capabilities and characteristics that are only present with the entire system. The boundary of the system under test typically excludes the virtual machine which supports it and other application systems to which it has direct or indirect interfaces.

system under test (SUT). The implementation that is the subject of test design or is being exercised by a test suite. The application to be exercised, as distinct from its operating environment.

target environment. The intended operational configuration of a system, usually some family of computer systems and at least one operating system. For example, the target environment for Java is any Java Virtual Machine.

target machine. Syn. **target environment.**

tautology. An **assertion** or **condition** that is always true, no matter what values are substituted for its variables.

template class. In C++, a class that defines the common structure and operations for related types. For example, a template class `Array` could provide definitions for integer, floating-point, and character arrays. The class definition takes a parameter that designates the type.

test. (1) An activity in which a system or a component is executed under specified conditions, the results are observed or recorded, and an evaluation is made of some aspect of the system or component. (2) To conduct an activity as in (1). (3) A set of one or more test cases. (4) A set of one or more test procedures. (5) A set of one or more test cases and procedures [IEEE 610].

testability. (1) The *controllability* and *observability* of a system under test. The relative ease or difficulty of producing and executing an economically feasible test suite to determine whether the SUT (i) conforms to stated requirements and specifications, and (ii) exhibits an acceptably low probability of failure. In general, testable requirements and specifications are specific, unambiguous, and quantitative where appropriate. A testable implementation has components which can be exercised separately to produce repeatable results that can be observed and measured. (2) The degree to which a system or component facilitates the establishment of test criteria and the performance of tests to determine whether those criteria have been met [IEEE 610]. (3) The degree to which a requirement is stated in terms that permit establishment of test criteria and performance of tests to determine whether those criteria have been met [IEEE 610]. (4) The likelihood that a statement or a program will mask a fault given some set of input [Voas 92].

test bed. An environment containing the hardware, instrumentation, simulators, software tools, and other support elements needed to conduct a test [IEEE 610].

test case. A set of inputs, execution conditions, and expected results developed for a particular objective. A representation or implementation that defines a pretest state of the IUT and its environment, test inputs or conditions, and the expected result.

test configuration. A defined and versioned set of drivers, stubs, and a build of the system under test.

test criteria. The criteria that a system or component must meet in order to pass a given test [IEEE 610]. Decision rules used to determine whether a software item or software feature passes or fails a test.

test data. The criteria that a system or component must meet in order to pass a given test [IEEE 610]. Decision rules used to determine whether a software item or software feature passes or fails a test.

test design. The process of producing a suite of test cases using a test strategy. Test design is concerned with three problems: identification of **interesting** test points, placing these test points into a **test sequence**, and defining the **expected result** for each **test point** in the sequence.

test design specification. A document specifying the details of the test approach for a software feature or combination of software features and identifying the associated tests.

test driver. A software component used to invoke a component under test. The driver typically provides test input, controls and monitors execution, and reports results.

test effectiveness. The relative ability of a testing strategy to find bugs.

test efficiency. The relative cost of finding a bug.

test harness. A system of test drivers and other tools to support test execution (e.g., stubs, executable test cases, and test drivers).

testing. The process of operating a system or component under specified conditions, observing or recording the results, and making an evaluation of some aspect of the system or component [IEEE 610]. *See also* **acceptance testing, beta test, configuration testing, functional testing, implementation-based test design, integration testing, performance testing, regression testing, stress testing, system testing, unit testing.**

test log. Contains the results of an execution of a test suite.

test message. The code in a test driver that is sent to a method of the object under test.

test model. A testable representation of the relationships among elements of a representation or implementation. The test model typically highlights elements of the IUT indicated by a fault model.

test plan. A document prepared for human use that explains a testing approach: the work plan, general procedures, explanation of the test design, and so on. It may include test cases and expected results for each test case. The test plan may also address other relevant technical and administrative considerations.

test point. A specific value for test case input and state variables. A test point, which may be used in many test cases, is selected from a domain.

test process. The set of tools, methods, and practices used to test a software product.

test-ready. Said of a model that contains enough information to produce test cases for its implementation automatically. Typically, this requires complete information, consistent usage, and useful integration with other facets of a model and its repository.

test run. The execution (with results) of a test suite(s).

test script. A program written in a procedural script language (usually interpreted) that executes a test suite(s).

test sequence. Two or more test messages which follow one another.

test strategy. An algorithm or heuristic to create test cases from a representation, an implementation, or a test model.

test suite. (1) A related collection of **test cases.** A collection of test case sequences that serve a particular testing goal for a particular version of an IUT. A whole-part relationship exists among test cases. (2) A **test bed** depreciated.

test tools. Software tools that support **testing.** There are eight main types: (1) data utilities, including test data generators, editors, dump formatters, and analyzers; (2) simulators, which configure an environment and generate input in a controlled, repeatable manner; (3) comparators for files and data streams; (4) capture-replay, including script features and regression testers; (5) trace and coverage analyzers; (6) program analyzers: path finder, restructure, animation; (7) interactive debuggers; and (8) upper CASE tools to the extent they can be used to produce test plans from specifications and provide test suite traceability.

theorem. A statement that is accepted as true due to mathematical proof or well-formed logical argument.

thread. In a multiprogramming operating system, a section of a process (task) which may execute independently of other threads within the process.

throughput. The number of tasks (or other unit of work) completed in a given time interval. Indicates how many tasks have been completed in an interval but does not indicate how quickly an individual task has been performed. Compare **response time, utilization.**

top-down testing. An incremental testing strategy. The highest levels of a system are programmed and unit tested first. When the next lower level of the system is programmed, the upper level serves as a test driver.

topological sort. An ordering of the nodes in a directed graph such that all predecessors of every node are listed before the node itself. That is, no item appears until all its predecessors have been listed.

topology. Arrangement or structure of components.

total correctness. A mathematical proof that a program or a specification will meet its **post-conditions** and invariants and will terminate for all possible inputs, given that its **pre-conditions** hold. Compare **partial correctness.**

total failure. In a distributed system, the inability of all sites to perform any normal function.

toy problem. A simple problem contrived for the purposes of demonstration.

trace. The result of instrumentation, showing (e.g., a time-stamped list of module activation).

traceability. (1) The identification of the **antecedent** of a work product. For example, each user requirement should be traceable to a software requirement; each software requirement to an architecture component; each architecture component to a program module specification; each module specification to a source code component. (2) The degree to which a relationship can be established between two or more products of the development process, especially products having a predecessor-successor or master-subordinate relationship to one another [IEEE 610].

transition. In a state machine, an event/state/action/state tuple. In the **FREE** model, a unique combination of (1) state invariants (one for the accepting state and one for the resultant state), (2) an associated event, and (3) optional guard expressions. An action may or may not be associated with a transition. The accepting and resultant states may be the same. Each transition is the result of an event and results in zero or more actions. Only one state may result from any particular transition.

transition function. The mapping of event/state pairs to resultant states.

transition tree. A tree transcribed from a state machine that includes all round-trip paths: transition sequences that begin and end with the same state and simple paths from the initial to final state.

transitive relation. A relation in which the property of interest holds when, for any two pairs of entities that share a common entity, the relationship also holds for both pairs.

translation-time binding. Translation-time reuse is supported by macro substitution, inheritance, and composition. Problems with macros have limited their role in reuse. A class declaration that specifies a superclass accomplishes reuse by inheritance. An instance variable declaration that specifies a class accomplishes reuse by composition.

tree. (1) Generally, any hierarchic organizational scheme that begins at a single point and spreads out into many other points, resembling the trunk, branches, and leaves of a tree. (2) In **graph theory**, a rooted directed graph where there is a unique path from the root node to every other node in the tree.

true singleton. A variant with only one true value. A no-true variant contains only false values; a no-false variant contains only true values.

trusted system. An existing system is trusted if it has been used successfully. More formal and quantitative definitions are possible, but the general idea is that an existing system is routinely used with high confidence.

trustworthiness. If a single failure of a system is unacceptable in that it can lead to catastrophic consequences, the system must be trustworthy before it can be used.

truth table. An enumeration of all possible input and output values for a Boolean function; given n Boolean input variables there are always 2^n rows in its truth table. The function is the essential definition; the table is its enumeration.

type argument. The name of a class or primitive data type. The compiler generates a new class by substituting the type argument for occurrences of the **type parameter** defined in the generic class.

type checking. A feature of some programming languages that prevents mismatches of data types and operations. This automatically eliminates an insidious source of errors at the expense of some flexibility. For example, passing a character variable to a floating-point function is reported as an error by the compiler. For parameter passing and function calls, this means checking for consistency in the corresponding parameters of the caller and called routine, and between the function type and its receiving value. The extent and strictness of type checking varies. Strongly typed languages intercept and reject type mismatches. Weakly typed languages allow many type mismatches. **Static type checking** is done at compile time; **dynamic type checking** at runtime. Some type mismatches are automatically resolved by type **coercion**. *See also* **type-safe language**.

type parameter. A symbolic definition for which a type argument is to be substituted.

type-safe exclusion. Conditions that are defined for a nonbinary decision variable but which can only hold one value at a time.

type-safe language. A programming language where all declarations and uses of variables, function, and other identifiers are subjected to **type checking**. An attempt to mix types will be rejected by the compiler or runtime environment. C++ is a type-safe language. *See also* **coercion**.

undecidable. An assertion or relationship for which it can be shown that no algorithm can exist that could perform the required computation in every possible case.

unit test. A test that exercises a relatively small executable. In object-oriented programming, an object of a class is the smallest executable unit, but test messages must be sent to a method, so we can speak of method scope testing. A test unit may be a class, several related classes (a cluster), or an executable binary file. Typically, it is a cluster of interdependent classes.

unit testing. Testing of individual software units, or groups of related units. A test unit may be a module, a few modules, or a complete computer program.

unsafe reduction. A **reduced regression test suite** determined by heuristics or practical considerations. This may remove existing test cases that could reveal a **regression fault**.

utilization. The percentage of an interval in which a hardware or software resource is busy.

V&V. *See* **validation and verification**.

validation. *See* **validation and verification**.

validation and verification (V&V). An approach to developing high-quality software that combines preventative and corrective measures. Validation asks the question "Has the right thing been built?" "Is the specification correct?" or "Are all user requirements met?" Verification asks the question "Has the thing been built right?" "Does the implementation fully and correctly realize the specification?" or "Do all components exhibit good workmanship, sufficient performance, and conform to applicable standards?" Verification in phase *n* addresses the extent of fulfillment of work defined in phase *n* – 1. Validation addresses the extent of fulfillment of the customer requirements, in any phase. *See also* **static verification, dynamic verification, inspection, walkthrough, review, testing, proof of correctness**.

value. The particular data assigned to an instance of an attribute, **variable**, or **object**.

variant. A unique combination of input conditions in a decision table or truth values in a truth table. *See also* **decision table**.

version. An incremental modification of a system that is significantly different from previous versions in scope, capability, or implementation. For example, the changes needed to support multiple concurrent users instead of a single user or the addition of a forecasting and an EDI interface to an inventory package. Compare **release**.

vertex. In **graph theory**, an abstract entity which may be related to other abstract entities (and itself) by directed or undirected **edges**. A graph may have many vertices. Typically drawn as a circle, box, or point. May represent any property of interest. Syn. **node**.

virtual function. In C++, a member function that may be overidden, allowing method polymorphism.

walkthrough. A group meeting to conduct an informal peer review of a technical work product.

waterfall model. A view of the **software process** that recognizes several distinct phases in software development. The work of each phase must be completed before the next phase can begin.

weaker assertion. A less restrictive assertion; it is true for a superset of value combinations that make a stronger assertion true. The satisfying value set of a weaker assertion is a superset of the satisfying set of a stronger assertion.

weak typing. A programming language that has optional or limited **type checking**. Ant. **strong typing.**

weird dependency. An undocumented, unanticipated, and bizzare interaction among source statements, classes, objects, components, or a runtime environment. *See also* **Mandelbug.**

white box framework. Consumers typically develop implementations for abstract classes provided in the framework and additional application-specific code. After refinement and stabilization, a white box framework may become a black box framework where composition plays a larger role.

white box testing. *See* **implementation-based test design.**

widget. A user interface object in an X Window display.

yo-yo effect. In **object-oriented programming**, an understandability loss due to high span of inheritance and wide span of uses. To understand what's going on in a leaf-level method, you often need to look at inherited method(s) in upper classes, then down, then up, etc. Frequent use of "self" or "this" tends to increase bouncing. Having resolved which "self" is appropriate, another interclass use (in the target of self you've just located) may send you back to the bottom of some other class, where you may need to repeat the upward trace again. The up and down motion suggests a yo-yo.

REFERENCES

[Abramovici+90] Miron Abramovici, Melvin A. Breuer, and Arthur D. Friedman. *Digital systems testing and testable design.* New York: Computer Science Press, 1990.

[Adrion+82] W. R. Adrion, M. A. Branstad, and J. C. Cherniavsky. Validation, verification and testing of computer software. *ACM Computing Surveys* 14(2):159–192, June 1982.

[Agarwal+89] H. Agarwal and Eugene Spafford. Bibliography on debugging and backtracking. *ACM Software Engineering Notes* 14(2):49–56, April 1989.

[Alexander 79] Christopher Alexander. *The timeless way of building.* New York: Oxford University Press, 1979.

[Alford 85] Mack Alford. SREM at the age of eight: the distributed computing design system. *IEEE Computer* 18(4):36–46, April 1985.

[Allen+95] Arthur Allen and Dennis de Champeaux. Extending the statechart formalism: event scheduling & disposition. In *ACM Conference on Object-Oriented Programming Systems, Languages and Applications (OOPSLA),* October 1995.

[Ambler 94] Scott Ambler. Use-case scenario testing. *Software Development* 3(6):53–61, July 1995.

[Ambler 97] Scott Ambler. *Building object applications—patterns, architecture, design, construction, and testing.* New York: SIGS Books, Inc., 1997.

[Anderson+98] Ann Anderson et al. Chrysler goes to extremes. *Distributed Object Computing,* 24–28, October 1998.

[Armstrong+94] James M. Armstrong and Richard J. Mitchell. Uses and abuses of inheritance. *IEE Software Engineering Journal* 9(1):19–26, January 1994.

[Arnold 94] Andre Arnold. *Finite transition systems.* Translated by John Plaice. Englewood Cliffs, N.J.: Prentice-Hall, 1994.

[Arnold+94] Thomas R. Arnold and Willam A. Fuson. Testing "In a Perfect World." *Communications of the ACM* 37(9):78–86, September 1994.

[Ashcroft+71] E. A. Ashcroft and Zohar Manna. Translation of GOTO programs to WHILE programs. In *Proceedings, Congress of the International Federation for Information Processing.* Amsterdam: North-Holland Publishers, 1971.

[Auer 97] Antti Auer. *State testing of embedded software.* Research Papers, Series A25. Oulu, Finland: Department of Information Processing Science, University of Oulu, 1997.

[Bach 97] James Bach. Good enough quality: beyond the buzzword. *IEEE Computer* 30(8):96–98, August 1997.

[Baker 75] Terry F. Baker. Structured programming in a production programming environment. *IEEE Transactions on Software Engineering* SE-1(2):241–252, June 1975.

[Balcer+89] Mark Balcer, William Halsing, and Thomas Ostrand. Automatic generation of test scripts from formal test specifications. In *Proceedings of the Third Symposium on Software Testing, Analysis, and Verification.* New York: ACM Press, December 1989.

[Ball 95] Michael S. Ball. Debugging C++. In *OOP 95'/C++ World Conference Proceedings.* New York: SIGS Conferences, Inc., January 1995.

[Barbey 97] Stéphane Barbey. Test selection for specification-based unit testing of object-oriented software based on formal specifications. Ph.D. diss., Lausanne, Switzerland: Swiss Federal Institute of Technology, Computer Science Department, Software Engineering Laboratory, 1997.

[Barnes 96] John Barnes. *Programming in Ada 95.* Reading, Mass.: Addison-Wesley, 1996.

[Bartussek+86] Wolfram Bartussek and David L. Parnas. Using assertions about traces to write abstract specifications for software modules. In *Software specification techniques.* Reading, Mass.: Addison-Wesley, 1986.

[Basili+87] Victor R. Basili and Richard W. Selby. Comparing the effectiveness of software testing strategies. *IEEE Transactions on Software Engineering* SE-13(12): 1278–1296, December 1987.

[Basili+96a] Victor R. Basili, Lionel C. Briand, and Walcélio L. Melo. How reuse influences productivity in object-oriented systems. *Communications of the ACM* 39(10): 104–116, October 1996.

[Basili+96b] Victor R. Basili, Lionel C. Briand, and Walcélio L. Melo. A validation of object-oriented design metrics as quality indicators. *IEEE Transactions on Software Engineering* 22(10):751–761, October 1996.

[Beck 94a] Kent Beck. Simple Smalltalk testing. *The Smalltalk Report* 4(2):16–18, October 1994.

[Beck+94b] Kent Beck and Ralph Johnson. Patterns generate architectures. In *ECOOP '94: Proceedings of the 1994 European Conference on Object-Oriented Programming.* Cambridge, U.K.: Cambridge University Press, July 1994.

[Beeck 94] Michael von der Beeck. A comparison of statechart variants. In H. Langmaack, W. D. Roever, and J. Vytopil (eds.), *Formal techniques in real-time and fault-tolerant systems.* New York: Springer-Verlag, *Lecture Notes in Computer Science,* 863:128–148.

[Beizer 84] Boris Beizer. *Software system testing and quality assurance.* New York: Van Nostrand Reinhold, 1984.

[Beizer 90] Boris Beizer. *Software testing techniques,* 2nd ed. New York: International Thompson Computer Press, 1990.

[Beizer 95] Boris Beizer. *Black box testing.* New York: John Wiley & Sons, 1995.

[Bender 98] R. Bender. Why a disciplined approach means a competitive approach to software quality, May 1998; *http://www.softtest.com/pages/discipl.htm*

[Berard 93] Edward V. Berard. *Essays on object-oriented software engineering.* Englewood Cliffs, N.J.: Prentice-Hall, 1993.

[Berg+95] William Berg, Marshall Cline, and Mike Girou. Lessons learned from the OS/400 OO project. *Communications of the ACM* 38(10):54–65, October 1995.

[Bernhard 94] Philip J. Bernhard. A reduced test suite for protocol conformance testing. *ACM Transactions on Software Engineering and Methodology* 3(3):201–220, July 1994.

[Bernot+91] Giles Bernot, M. C. Gaudel, and B. Marre. Software testing based on formal specifications: a theory and a tool. *Software Engineering Journal* 6(6):387–405, November 1991.

[Bertolino+97] Antonia Bertolino, Raffaela Mirandola, and Emilia Peciola. A case study in branch testing automation. *Journal of Systems and Software* 38(1):47–59, July 1997.

[Binder 85] Robert V. Binder. *Application debugging: an MVS abend handbook for assembler, Cobol, Fortran, and PL/I programmers.* Englewood Cliffs, N.J.: Prentice-Hall, 1985.

[Binder+92] Robert V. Binder and Jeffrey P. Tsai. KB/RMS: an intelligent assistant for requirement definition. *International Journal of Artificial Intelligence Tools* 1(4): 503–522, 1992.

[Binder 93] Robert V. Binder. Test case design for object-oriented programs: the FREE approach. Chicago: RBSC Corporation. Technical Report, June 1993 (photocopy).

[Binder 94a] Robert V. Binder. Testing object-oriented systems: a status report. *American Programmer* 7(4):22–28, April 1994.

[Binder 94b] Robert V. Binder. Design for testability with object-oriented systems. *Communications of the ACM* 37(9):87–10, September 1994.

[Binder 94c] Robert V. Binder. *The FREE Approach to Testing Object-Oriented Systems.* Technical Report TR 94-001. Chicago: RBSC Corporation, January 1994.

[Binder 95a] Robert V. Binder. The FREE-flow graph: implementation-based testing of objects using state-determined flows. In *Proceedings, 8th annual software quality week.* San Francisco: Software Research, May 1995.

[Binder 95b] Robert V. Binder. Testing objects: myth and reality. *Object Magazine* 5(2):73–75, May 1995.

[Binder 95c] Robert V. Binder. State-based testing. *Object Magazine* 5(4):75–78, July–August 1995.

[Binder 95d] Robert V. Binder. State-based testing: sneak paths and conditional transitions. *Object Magazine* 5(6):87–89, October 1995.

[Binder 95e] Robert V. Binder. Trends in testing object-oriented software. *IEEE Computer* 28(10):68–69, October 1995.

[Binder 96a] Robert V. Binder. Use-cases, threads, and relations: the FREE approach to system testing. *Object Magazine* 5(9):72–79, February 1996.

[Binder 96b] Robert V. Binder. The FREE approach to object-oriented testing: an overview. Chicago: RBSC Corporation; 1996; *http://www.rbsc.com/pages/FREE.html*

[Binder 96c] Robert V. Binder. Off-the-shelf test automation for objects. *Object Magazine* 6(2):26–30, April 1996.

[Binder 96d] Robert V. Binder. An integrated tool suite for high-reliability object-oriented client/server systems. In *Proceedings, 9th Annual Software Quality Week.* San Francisco: Software Research, May 1996.

[Binder 96e] Robert V. Binder. BigFoot's tootsie. *Object Magazine* 6(4):81–87, June 1996.

[Binder 96f] Robert V. Binder. Testing for reuse: libraries and frameworks. *Object Magazine* 6(6):36–40, August 1996.

[Binder 96g] Robert V. Binder. Summertime, and the testin' is easy. . . . *Object Magazine* 6(8):26–27, October 1996.

[Binder 96h] Robert V. Binder. Modal testing strategies for object-oriented software. *Computer* 29(11):97–99, November 1996.

[Binder 96i] Robert V. Binder. Testing object-oriented software: a survey. *Journal of Software Testing, Verification and Reliability* 6:125–252, December 1996.

[Binder 97a] Robert V. Binder. Class modality and testing. *Object Magazine* 7(2):48–54, February 1997.

[Binder 97b] Robert V. Binder. Developing a test budget. *Object Magazine* 7(4):56–58, June 1997.

[Binder 97c] Robert V. Binder. Automated Java testing. *Object Magazine* 7(5):44–50, July 1997.

[Binder 97d] Robert V. Binder. Object-oriented testing: what's new. *Object Magazine* 7(5):21–23, July 1997.

[Binder 97e] Robert V. Binder. Verifying class associations. *Object Magazine* 7(9):18–20, November 1997.

[Binder 98a] Robert V. Binder. How to test UML Sequence Diagram scenarios. *Object Magazine* 7(9):16-19, March 1998.

[Binder 2000] Robert V. Binder. *Managing the Testing Process for Object-Oriented Systems*. Reading, Mass.: Addison-Wesley, 2000.

[Boisvert 97] Jean Boisvert. OO testing in the Ericsson pilot project. *Object Magazine* 7(5):27–33, July 1997.

[Booch 90] Grady Booch. *Software components with Ada: structures, tools, and subsystems*. Redwood City, Calif.: Benjamin/Cummings, 1990.

[Booch 91] Grady Booch. *Object-oriented design with applications*. Redwood City, Calif.: Benjamin/Cummings, 1991.

[Booch 96] Grady Booch. *Object solutions, managing the object-oriented project*. Reading, Mass: Addison-Wesley, 1996.

[Bosman 96] Oscar Bosman. Testing and iterative development: adapting the Booch method. In *Proceedings, 13th International Conference and Exposition on Testing Computer Software*. Silver Spring, Md.: USPDI, June 1996.

[Bourdeau+95] Robert H. Bourdeau and Betty H. C. Cheng. A formal semantics for object model diagrams. *IEEE Transactions on Software Engineering* 21(10):799–821, October 1995.

[Brand+83] Daniel Brand and Pitro Zafiropulo. On communicating finite state machines. *Journal of the ACM* 30(2):323–342, April 1983.

[Briand+98] Lionel C. Briand, Jürgen Wüst, John Daly, and Victor Porter. A comprehensive empirical validation of design measures for object-oriented systems. In *Proceedings of the 5th International Symposium on Software Metrics*. IEEE Computer Society Press, 1998.

[Brooks 75] Frederick P. Brooks, Jr. *The mythical man-month: essays on software engineering*. Reading, Mass.: Addison-Wesley, 1975.

[Brooks 87] Frederick P. Brooks. No silver bullet: essence and accidents of software engineering. *IEEE Computer* 20(4):10–19, April 1987.

[Brown+92] David Brown, R. Roggio, J. Cross, and C. McCreary. An automated oracle for software testing. *IEEE Transactions on Reliability* 41(2):279–295, June 1992.

[Brown+95] Jeffery R. Brown, Larry H. Quandt, and Patricia K. Fuher. Integration strategies for OO software. In *Proceedings, STAR 95*. Jacksonville, Fla.: SQE, Inc., May 1995.

[Brownlie+92] Robert Brownlie, James Prowse, and Mahdav S. Phadke. Robust testing of AT&T PMX/StarMail using OATS. *AT&T Technical Journal* 41–47, May/June 1992.

[Bryant 92] Randal E. Bryant. Symbolic Boolean manipulations with ordered binary-decision diagrams. *ACM Computing Surveys* 24(3):293–318, September 1992.

[Buschmann+96] Frank Buschmann, Regine Meunier, Hans Rohnert, Peter Sommerlad, and Michael Stal. *Pattern-oriented software architecture: a system of patterns*. New York: John Wiley & Sons, 1996.

[Caldiera+98] G. Caldiera, G. Antoniol, R. Fiutem, and C. Lokan. Definition and experimental evaluation of function points for object-oriented systems. In *Proceedings, 5th International Symposium on Software Metrics*. Los Alamitos, Calif.: IEEE Computer Society Press, November 1998.

[Campione+96] Mary Campione and Kathy Walrath. *The Java tutorial: object-oriented programming for the Internet*. Reading, Mass.: Addison-Wesley, 1996.

[Cargill 92] Thomas A. Cargill. *C++ programming style*. Reading, Mass.: Addison-Wesley, 1992.

[Cargill 93] Thomas A. Cargill. C++ gotchas. In *C++ World Conference Proceedings*. New York: SIGS Conferences, Inc., October 1993.

[Cargill 95] Tom Cargill. Short tour testing. *C++ Report* 7(2):60–62, February 1995.

[Carrillo+96] Manuela Carrillo-Castellon, J. Garcia-Molina, E. Pimentel, and I. Repiso. Design by contract in Smalltalk. *Journal of Object-Oriented Programming* 9(7): 23–28, November/December 1996.

[Carroll+95] Martin D. Carroll and Margaret A. Ellis. *Designing and coding reusable C++*. Reading, Mass.: Addison-Wesley, 1995.

[Chan+97] Patrick Chan and Rosanna Lee. *The Java class libraries: an annotated reference*. Reading, Mass.: Addison Wesley Longman, 1997.

[Chang+96] Kuang-Nan Chang, D. Kung, P. Hsia, Y. Toyoshima, and C. Chen. Object-oriented data flow testing. In *Proceedings, 13th International Conference and Exposition on Testing Computer Software*. Silver Spring, Md.: USPDI, June 1996.

[Cheatham+90] Thomas J. Cheatham and Lee Mellinger. Testing object-oriented software systems. In *Proceedings of the 1990 ACM 18th Annual Computer Science Conference*. New York: ACM Press, February 1990.

[Chen+98] Huo Yan Chen, T. H. Tse, F. T. Chan, and T. Y. Chen. In black and white: an integrated approach to class-level testing of object-oriented programs. *ACM Transactions on Software Engineering and Methodology* 7(3):250–295, July 1998.

[Cheon+94] Yoonsik Cheon and Gary T. Leavens. The Larch/Smalltalk interface specification language. *ACM Transactions on Software Engineering and Methodology* 3(3):221–253, July 1994.

[Cherry 96] Terrence C. Cherry. OOPSLA '96 Workshop 27, development of object-oriented frameworks. Postition Paper 13; *http://www-cat.ncsa.uiuc.edu/~yoder/Research/Frameworks/WS27.HTM*

[Chidamber+94] Shyam R. Chidamber and Chris F. Kemerer. A metrics suite for object-oriented design. *IEEE Transactions on Software Engineering* 20(6):476–493, June 1994.

[Chillarege+96] Ram Chillarege. Orthogonal defect classification. In Michael R. Lyu (ed). *Handbook of software reliability engineering*. Los Alamitos, Calif.: IEEE Computer Society Press, 1996.

[Choi+91] Injun Choi and Michael V. Mannino. Graph interpretation of methods: a unifying framework for polymorphism in object-oriented programming. *OOPS Messenger* 2(1):38–54, January 1991.

[Chow 78] Tsun S. Chow. Testing software design modeled by finite state machines. *IEEE Transactions on Software Engineering* SE-4(3):178–186, March 1978.

[Chung+94] Chi-Ming Chung and Ming-Chi Lee. Object-oriented programming testing methodology. *International Journal of Mini- and Microcomputers* 16(2):73–81, 1994.

[Chung 95] In Sang Chung. Methods of comparing test criteria for object-oriented programs based on subsumption, power relation and test reusability. *Journal of Korea Information Science Society* (South Korea) 22(5):693–704, May 1995.

[Clarke+89] Lori A.Clarke, A. Podgurski, D. J. Richardson, and S. J. Zeil. A formal evaluation of data flow path selection criteria. *IEEE Transactions on Software Engineering* 15(11):1318–1332, November 1989.

[Cline+95] Marshall P. Cline and Greg A. Lomow. *C++ FAQs*. Reading, Mass.: Addison-Wesley, 1995.

[CODASYL 78] Conference on Data Systems Languages (CODASYL), Decision Table Task Group. *A modern appraisal of decision tables*. New York: Association for Computing Machinery, 1978.

[Codenie+97] Wim Codenie, K. De Hondt, P. Steyaert, and A. Vercammen. From custom applications to domain-specific frameworks. *Communications of the ACM* 40(10):71–77, October 1997.

[Cohen+97] David M. Cohen, S. R. Dalal, M. L. Fredman, and G. C. Patton. The AETG system: an approach to testing based on combinatorial design. *IEEE Transactions on Software Engineering* 23(7):437–444, July 1997.

[Coleman+92] Derek Coleman, Fiona Hayes, and Stephen Bear. Introducing objectcharts or how to use statecharts in object-oriented design. *IEEE Transactions on Software Engineering* SE-18(1):9–18, January 1992.

[Coleman+94] Derek Coleman, P. Arnold, S. Bodoff, C. Dollin, H. Gilchrist, F. Hayes, and P. Jeremaes. *Object-oriented development: the fusion method*. Englewood Cliffs, N.J.: Prentice-Hall, 1994.

[Comer 95] David J. Comer. *Digital logic and state machine design*. New York: Oxford University Press, 1995.

[Cook+94] Steve Cook and John Daniels. *Designing object systems*. New York: Prentice-Hall, 1994.

[Coplien 92] James O. Coplien. *Advanced C++: programming styles and idioms*. Reading, Mass.: Addison-Wesley, 1992.

[Coplien+95] James Coplien and Douglas Schmidt (eds.). *Pattern languages of program design*. Reading, Mass.: Addison-Wesley, 1995.

[Cordes+91] David Cordes and Marcus Brown. The literate-programming paradigm. *IEEE Computer* 24(6):52–61, June 1991.

[Cox 88] Brad J. Cox. The need for specification and testing languages. *Journal of Object-Oriented Programming* 1(2):44–47, June/July 1988.

[Cox 90] Brad J. Cox. Planning the software industrial revolution. *IEEE Software* 7(6):25–33, November 1990.

[Cox+91] Brad J. Cox and Andrew J. Novobilski. *Object-oriented programming: an evolutionary approach*, 2nd ed. Reading, Mass.: Addison-Wesley, 1991.

[Culwin 95] Fintan Culwin. *Ada: a developmental approach*, 1995; *http://www.scism.sbu.ac.uk/law/lawhp.html*

[Cunningham+86] Ward Cunningham and Kent Beck. A diagram for object-oriented programs. In *ACM Conference on Object-Oriented Programming Systems, Languages and Applications (OOPSLA)*. New York: ACM Press, September 1986.

[Cusumano+98] Michael A. Cusumano and David B. Yoffie. *Competing on Internet time: lessons from Netscape and its battle with Microsoft*. New York: The Free Press, 1998.

[D'Souza+94] Rosario J. D'Souza and Richard J. LeBlanc. Class testing by examining pointers. *Journal of Object-Oriented Programming* 7(4):33–39, July 1994.

[D'Souza+99] Desmond F. D'Souza and Alan Cameron Wills. *Objects, components and frameworks with UML: the Catalysis approach*. Reading, Mass.: Addison Wesley Longman, 1999.

[Dahl+72] O. J. Dahl, E. Dijkstra, and C.A.R Hoare. *Structured programming*. New York: Academic Press, 1972.

[Date 82] Christopher J. Date. *An Introduction to database systems*, 3rd ed. Reading, Mass.: Addison-Wesley, 1982.

[Dauchy+93] P. Dauchy, M-C. Gaudel, and B. Marre. Using algebraic specifications in software testing: a case study on the software of an automatic subway. *Journal of Systems and Software* 21(3):229–244, June 1993.

[Davis 93] Alan M. Davis. *Software requirements: objects, functions, and states*. Englewood Cliffs, N.J.: Prentice-Hall, 1993.

[Davis 94] Stephen R. Davis. Armor cladding C++ classes. C++ *Report* 36–41, September 1994.

[Deck 97] Michael D. Deck. Cleanroom software engineering: myths and realities. In *Proceedings, 10th Annual Software Quality Week*. San Francisco: Software Research, Inc., May 1997.

[DeMarco 79] Tom DeMarco. *Structured Analysis and System Specification*. Englewood Cliffs, N.J.: Prentice-Hall, 1979.

[DeMillo+87] Richard A. DeMillo, W. Michael McCracken, R. J. Martin, and John F. Passafiume. *Software testing and evaluation*. Menlo Park, Calif.: Benjamin/Cummings, 1987.

[Deo 74] Narsingh Deo. *Graph theory with applications to engineering and computer science*. Englewood Cliffs, N.J.: Prentice-Hall, 1974.

[Desfray 94] Philippe Desfray. *Object engineering: the fourth dimension*. Reading, Mass.: Addison-Wesley, 1994.

[Devadas+94] Srinivas Devadas, Abhijit Ghosh, and Kurt Keutzer. *Logic synthesis*. New York: McGraw Hill, 1994.

[Devadas 97] Srinivas Devadas. Lecture notes: Course 6.373—Computer-aided design of integrated circuits. Massachusetts Institute of Technology, Department of Electrical Engineering and Computer Science, June 1997; *http://sobolev.mit.edu/6.373/*

[Dijkstra 89] E. W. Dijkstra. On the cruelty of really teaching computer science. *Communications of the ACM* 32(12):1398–1404, December 1989.

[Donaldson+97] Scott E. Donaldson and Stanley G. Siegel. *Cultivating successful software development: a practitioner's view*. Upper Saddle River, N.J.: Prentice-Hall PTR, 1997.

[Doong+94] Roong-Ko Doong and Phyllis G. Frankl. The ASTOOT approach to testing object-oriented programs. *ACM Transactions on Software Engineering and Methodology* 3(4):101–130, April 1994.

[Dorman 93] Misha Dorman. Unit testing of C++ objects. In *Proceedings, EuroSTAR 93*. Jacksonville, Fla.: SQE, Inc., October 1993.

[Dorman 97] Misha Dorman. C++—It's testing, Jim, but not as we know it. In *Proceedings of the Fifth European Conference on Software Testing, Analysis and Review*, Jacksonville, Fla., November 1997.

[Douglass 98] Bruce Powel Douglass. *Real-time UML: developing efficient objects for embedded systems*. Reading, Mass: Addison Wesley Longman, 1998.

[Dr Dobbs 98] Dr. Dobbs' TechNetCast: an interview with Stan Lippman. Washington, DC: Software Development 98 East, August 18–20, 1998; *http://www.technetcast.com/tnc_sd98e_sl.html*

[Drusinsky+94] Doron Drusinsky and David Harel. On the power of bounded concurrency I: finite automata. *Journal of the ACM* 41(3):517–539, May 1994.

[Dustin+99] Elfriede A. Dustin, Jeff S. Rashka, and John Paul. *Automated software testing: introduction, management, and performance.* Reading, Mass.: Addison Wesley Longman, 1999.

[Dyson+98] Paul Dyson and Bruce Anderson. State patterns. In *Pattern languages of program design 3.* Robert Martin, Dirk Riehle, and Frank Buschmann (eds.). Reading, Mass.: Addison Wesley Longman, 1998.

[Eickelmann+96] Nancy S. Eickelmann and Debra J. Richardson. An evaluation of software test environment architectures. In *Proceedings, 18th International Conference on Software Engineering.* Los Alamitos, Calif.: IEEE Computer Society Press, May 1996.

[Eisenstadt 97] Marc Eisenstadt. My hairiest bug war stories. *Communications of the ACM* 40(4):31–37, April 1997.

[Embley+92] David W. Embley, B. D. Kurtz, and S. N. Woodfield. *Object-oriented systems analysis: a model-driven approach.* Englewood Cliffs, N.J.: Prentice-Hall, 1990.

[Feingold 98] Jason Feingold. Asserting yourself. *Doctor Dobbs Journal* 23(2):10, February 1998.

[Fichman+92] Robert G. Fichman and Chris Kemerer. Object-oriented and conventional analysis and design methodologies: comparison and critique. *IEEE Computer* 25(10):22–39, October 1992.

[Fiedler 89] Steven P. Fiedler. Object-oriented unit testing. *Hewlett-Packard Journal* 40(2):69–75, April 1989.

[Firesmith 93a] Donald G. Firesmith, *Object-oriented requirements, analysis, and logical design: a software engineering approach.* New York: John Wiley & Sons, 1993.

[Firesmith 93b] Donald G. Firesmith. Testing object-oriented software. In *Proceedings of the Eleventh International Conference on Technology of Object-oriented Languages and Systems (TOOLS USA, '93).* Englewood Cliffs, N.J.: Prentice-Hall, 1993.

[Firesmith 95a] Donald G. Firesmith. Object-oriented regression testing. *Report on Object Analysis and Design* 1(5):42–45, January/February 1995.

[Firesmith 95b] Donald G. Firesmith. *Testing object-oriented software* (photocopy), 1995.

[Firesmith 96] Donald G. Firesmith. Pattern language for testing object-oriented software. *Object Magazine* 5(9):32–38, January 1996.

[Firesmith+98] Donald Firesmith, Brian Henderson-Sellers, and Ian Graham. *Open Modeling Language (OML) reference manual.* New York: SIGS Books & Multimedia, 1998.

[Foote+98] Brian Foote and Joseph Yoder. The selfish class. In *Pattern Languages of Program Design 3.* Robert Martin, Dirk Riehle, and Frank Buschmann (eds.). Reading, Mass.: Addison Wesley Longman, 1998.

[Frankl+88] Phyllis. G. Frankl and Elaine J. Weyuker. An applicable family of data flow testing criteria. *IEEE Transactions on Software Engineering* 14(10):1483–1498, October 1988.

[Frankl+93] Phyllis. G. Frankl and Elaine J. Weyuker. A formal analysis of the fault-detecting ability of testing methods. *IEEE Transactions on Software Engineering* 19(3):202–213, March 1993.

[Freedman 91] Roy S. Freedman. Testability of software components. *IEEE Transactions on Software Engineering* 17(6):553–564, June 1991.

[Friedman+95] Michael A. Friedman and Jeffrey M. Voas. *Software assessment: reliability, safety, testability.* New York: John Wiley & Sons, Inc., 1995.

[Fujiwara 85] Hideo Fujiwara. *Logic testing and design for testability.* Cambridge, Mass.: MIT Press, 1985.

[Fujiwara+91] Susumu Fujiwara, G. V. Bochmann, F. Khendek, M. Amalou, and A. Ghedamsi. Test selection based on finite state models. *IEEE Transactions on Software Engineering* 17(6):591–603, June 1991.

[Gamma+95] Erich Gamma, Richard Helm, Ralph Johnson, and John Vlissides. *Design patterns: elements of reusable object-oriented software.* Reading, Mass.: Addison-Wesley, 1995.

[Gamma+98] Erich Gamma and Kent Beck. Test infected: programmers love writing tests. *The Java Report* 3(7):37–50, July 1998.

[Garlan+95] David Garlan, Robert Allen, and John Ockerbloom. Architectural mismatch: why reuse is so hard. *IEEE Software* 12(6):17–26, November 1995.

[Garman 81] John R. Garman. The "Bug" heard 'round the world. *ACM Software Engineering Notes* 6:3–10, October 1981.

[Gause+89] Donald C. Gause and Gerald M. Weinburg. *Exploring requirements: quality before design.* New York: Dorset House, 1989.

[Gill 62] Arthur Gill. *Introduction to the theory of finite-state machines.* New York: McGraw-Hill, Inc., 1962.

[Gill+91] Geoffrey K. Gill and Chris F. Kemerer. Cyclomatic complexity density and software productivity maintainance. *IEEE Transactions on Software Engineering* 17(12):1284–1288, December 1991.

[Giltinan 94] Ty Giltinan. Leveraging inheritance to test objects. In *Proceedings, 3rd International Conference on Software Testing, Analysis, and Review.* Jacksonville, Fla.: SQE, Inc., May 1994.

[Goldberg 91] David Goldberg. What every computer scientist should know about floating-point arithmetic. *ACM Computing Surveys* 23(1):5–48, March 1991.

[Goldberg+95] Adele Goldberg and Kenneth S. Rubin. *Succeeding with objects.* Reading Mass.: Addison-Wesley, 1995.

[Goodenough+75] John E. Goodenough and Susan L. Gerhart. Toward a theory of test data selection. *IEEE Transactions on Software Engineering* 1(1):156–173, January 1975.

[Goodman+95] Steve Goodman, Leo Hsu, and Regina Obe. Implementing state-based testing in Smalltalk. Position paper, Workshop on Smalltalk Testing. *ACM Conference on Object-Oriented Programming Systems, Languages and Applications (OOPSLA),* October 1995.

[Gosling 98] James Gosling. *A brief history of the green project,* October 1998; *http://java.sun.com/people/jag/green/index.html*

[Gourlay 83] John S. Gourlay. A mathematical framework for the investigation of testing. *IEEE Transactions on Software Engineering* SE-9(6):686–709, November 1983.

[Grady 92] Robert B. Grady. *Practical software metrics for project management and process improvement.* Upper Saddle River, N.J.: Prentice-Hall PTR, 1992.

[Graham 94] Ian Graham. *Object-oriented methods,* 2nd ed. Reading, Mass.: Addison-Wesley, 1994.

[Graham+93] J. A. Graham, A. C. T. Drakeford, and C. D. Turner. The verification, validation and testing of object oriented systems. *BT Technology Journal* 11(3):79–88, 1993.

[Green 98] Roedy Green. *Java gotchas.* March 22 , 1998; *http://oberon.ark.com/~roedy/gotchas.html*

[Gries 81] David Gries. *The science of programming.* New York: Springer-Verlag, 1981.

[Guttag+85] John V. Guttag, James J. Horning, and Jeannette M. Wing. The Larch family of specification languages. *IEEE Software* 2(5):24–36, September 1985.

[Hamlet+90] Dick Hamlet and Ross Taylor. Partition testing does not inspire confidence. *IEEE Transactions on Software Engineering* 16(12):1402–1411, December 1990.

[Harel 87] David Harel. Statecharts: a visual formalism for complex systems. *Science of Computer Programming* 8:231–274, 1987.

[Harel 88] David Harel. On visual formalisms. *Communications of the ACM* 31(5): 514–529, May 1988.

[Harel+97] David Harel and Eran Gery. Executable object modeling with statecharts. *IEEE Computer* 30(7):31–42, July 1997.

[Harrold+92] Mary Jean Harrold, John D. McGregor, and Kevin J. Fitzpatrick. Incremental testing of object-oriented class structures. In *Proceedings, 14th International Conference on Software Engineering*. Los Alamitos, Calif.: IEEE Computer. Society Press, May 1992.

[Harrold+94] Mary Jean Harrold and Gregg Rothermel. Performing data flow testing on classes. In *Proceedings of the Second ACM SIGSOFT Symposium on Foundations of Software Engineering*. New York: ACM Press, December 1994.

[Hatley+87] Derek J. Hatley and Imtiaz A. Pirbhai. *Strategies for real-time system specification*. New York: Dorset House, 1987. .

[Hayes 86] Ian J. Hayes. Specification directed module testing. *IEEE Transactions on Software Engineering* SE-12(1):124–133, January 1986.

[Hayes 94] Jane Huffman Hayes. Testing of object-oriented programming systems (OOPS): a fault-based approach. In *Proceedings, Object-Oriented Methodologies and Systems*. E. Bertino and S. Urban (eds.), LNCS 858. New York: Springer-Verlag, 1994.

[Hayes 97] Roger Hayes. Testing Java applets. *Java Developers Journal* 2(3):20–23, 1997.

[Hecht 77] Matthew S. Hecht. *Flow analysis of computer programs*. New York: Elsevier-North Holland, 1977.

[Hein 85] Peter K. Hein. Information system model and architecture generator. *IBM Systems Journal* 24(3/4):213–235, 1985.

[Hellwig 98] Frank Hellwig. Implementing associations. *Dr. Dobbs' Journal* 23(6): 86–91, June 1998.

[Henderson 92] Brian Henderson-Sellers. Modularization and McCabe's cyclomatic complexity. *Communications of the ACM* 35(12):17–19, December 1992.

[Hetzel 88] Bill Hetzel. *The complete guide to software testing*, 2nd ed. Wellesley, Mass.: QED Information Sciences, 1988.

[Hinke+93] Bob Hinke, Vicki Jones, and Ralph E. Johnson. Debugging objects. *The Smalltalk Report* 2(9):4–26, July/August 1993.

[Hoare 72] C.A.R. Hoare. Proof of correctness of data representations. *Acta Informatica* 1(4):271–281, 1972.

[Hoare 85] C.A.R. Hoare. *Communicating sequential processes*. Englewood Cliffs, N.J.: Prentice-Hall, 1985.

[Hoffman+95] Daniel Hoffman and Paul Strooper. The testgraph methodology: automated testing of collection classes. *Journal of Object-oriented Programming* 8(7):35–41, November/December 1995.

[Hoffman 99] Douglas Hoffman. Heuristic test oracles. *Software Testing & Quality Engineering* 1(2):28–32, March/April 1999.

[Holzmann 91] Gerald J. Holzmann. *Design and validation of computer protocols.* Englewood Cliffs, N.J.: Prentice-Hall, Inc., 1991.

[Hong+95a] H. S. Hong, Y. R. Kwon, and S. D. Cha. Testing of object-oriented programs based on finite state machines. In *Proceedings, 2nd IEEE Asia-Pacific Software Engineering Conference.* Los Alamitos, Calif.: IEEE Computer Society Press., 1995.

[Hong+95b] H. S. Hong, J. H. Kim, S. D. Cha, and Y. R. Kwon. Static semantics and priority schemes for statecharts. In *Proceedings, The Nineteenth Annual International Computer Software and Applications Conference (COMPSAC 95).* Los Alamitos, Calif.: IEEE Computer Society Press, 1995.

[Hopcroft+79] John E. Hopcroft and Jeffrey D. Ullman. *Introduction to automata theory, languages, and computation.* Reading, Mass.: Addison-Wesley, 1979.

[Hopper 81] Grace M. Hopper. The first bug. *Annals of the History of Computing* 3:285–286, 1981.

[Horgan+94] Joseph R. Horgan, Saul London, and Michael R. Lyu. Achieving software quality with testing coverage measures. *IEEE Computer* 27(9):60–69, September 1994.

[Horgan+96] Joseph R. Horgan and Aditya P. Mathur. Software testing and reliability. In Michael R. Lyu (ed.), *Handbook of software reliability engineering.* Los Alamitos, Calif.: IEEE Computer Society Press, 1996.

[Howden 76] William E. Howden. Reliability of the path analysis testing strategy. *IEEE Transactions on Software Engineering* SE-2(3):208–215, September 1976.

[Howden+78] William E. Howden and Peter Eichhorst. Proving properties of programs from program traces. In *Tutorial: Software Testing and Validation Techniques*: E. Miller and W. E. Howden (eds.). New York: IEEE Computer Society Press, 1978.

[Howden+93] William E. Howden, Yudong Huang, and Bruce Wieland. Scientific foundations for practical software testing and analysis. In *Conference Proceedings, Quality Week 1993.* San Francisco: Software Research Institute, May 1993.

[Hughes+96] Merlin Hughes and David Stotts. Daistish: systematic algebraic testing for OO programs in the presence of side-effects. *ACM Software Engineering Notes* 21(3):53–61, May 1996.

[Hunt 95a] Neil Hunt. C++ boundary conditions and edge cases. *Journal of Object-Oriented Programming* 8(2):25–29, May 1995.

[Hunt 95b] Neil Hunt. Automatically tracking test case execution. *Journal of Object-Oriented Programming* 8(7):22–27, November/December 1995.

[Hunt 96] Neil Hunt. Unit testing. *Journal of Object-Oriented Programming* 8(9):18–23, February 1996.

[Hurley 83] R. B. Hurley. *Decision tables in software engineering.* New York: Van Nostrand Reinhold, 1983.

[Hurst+95] Jeff Hurst and Robert Willhoft. The use of coherence checking for testing object-oriented code. In *Proceedings, IBM International Conference on Object Technology.* IBM Corporation, June 1994.

[IEEE 610] *ANSI/IEEE standard 610.12-1990: glossary of software engineering terminology.* New York: The Institute of Electrical and Electronic Engineers, 1987.

[IEEE 829] *ANSI/IEEE standard 829-1983: IEEE standard for software test documentation.* New York: The Institute of Electrical and Electronic Engineers, 1987.

[IEEE 830] *ANSI/IEEE standard 830-1984: software requirements specifications.* New York: The Institute of Electrical and Electronic Engineers, 1987.

[IEEE 982.1] *ANSI/IEEE standard 982.1-1988: IEEE standard dictionary of measures to produce reliable software.* New York: The Institute of Electrical and Electronic Engineers, 1989.

[IEEE 1008] *ANSI/IEEE standard 1008-1987: IEEE standard for software unit testing.* New York: The Institute of Electrical and Electronic Engineers, 1987.

[IEEE 1016] *ANSI/IEEE standard 1016-1987: IEEE recommended practice for software design descriptions.* New York: The Institute of Electrical and Electronic Engineers, 1987.

[IEEE 1042] *ANSI/IEEE standard 1042-1987: IEEE guide to software configuration management.* New York: The Institute of Electrical and Electronic Engineers, 1987.

[IEEE 1149] *ANSI/IEEE standard 1149.1-1990: IEEE standard test access port and boundary-scan architecture.* New York: The Institute of Electrical and Electronic Engineers, 1990.

[IEEE 1420.1a] *IEEE guide for information technology—software reuse-data model for reuse library interoperability: asset certification framework.* New York: The Institute of Electrical and Electronic Engineers, 1996.

[Jacobson 95] Ivar Jacobson. The use-case construct in object-oriented software engineering. In *Scenario-based design: envisioning work and technology in system development*, John M. Carroll (ed.). New York: John Wiley & Sons, Inc., 1995.

[Jacobson+92] Ivar Jacobson, Magnus Christerson, Patrik Jonsson, and Gunnar Overgaard. *Object-oriented software engineering.* Reading, Mass.: Addison-Wesley, 1992.

[Jacobson+99] Ivar Jacobson, Grady Booch, and James Rumbaugh. *The unified software development process.* Reading, Mass.: Addison Wesley Longman, 1999.

[Jalote 89] Pankaj Jalote. Testing the completeness of specifications. *IEEE Transactions on Software Engineering* SE-15(5):526–531, May 1989.

[Jalote 92] Pankaj Jalote. Specification and testing of abstract data types. *Computer Language* (UK) 17(1):75–82, 1992.

[Järvinen+90] H.-M. Järvinen, R. Kurki-Suonio, M. Sakkinen, and K. Systä. Object-oriented specification of reactive systems. In *Proceedings of the 12th International Conference on Software Engineering*. IEEE Computer Society Press, March 1990.

[Jeng+94] Bingchiang Jeng and Elaine J. Weyuker. A simplified domain-testing strategy. *ACM Transactions on Software Engineering and Methodology* 3(3):254–270, July 1994.

[Jézéquel 96] Jean-Marc Jézéquel. Object-oriented software engineering with Eiffel. Reading, Mass.: Addison Wesley Longman, 1996.

[Jézéquel+96] Jean-Marc Jézéquel and Bertrand Meyer. Put it in the contract: the lessons of Ariane. *IEEE Computer* 30(1):129–131, January 1997.

[Jia 93] Xiaoping Jia. Model-based formal specification directed testing of abstract data types. In *Proceedings, The Seventeenth Annual International Computer Software and Applications Conference*. Los Alamitos, Calif.: IEEE Computer Society Press, November 1993.

[Johnson 97] Ralph Johnson. Classic Smalltalk bugs, January 12, 1997; *ftp://st.cs.uiuc.edu/pub/Smalltalk/st-docs/classic-bugs*

[Johnson+88] Ralph E. Johnson and Brian Foote. Designing reusable classes. *Journal of Object-Oriented Programming* 1(2):22–35, June/July 1988.

[Johnson+98] Ralph Johnson and Don Roberts. Patterns for evolving frameworks. In *Pattern Languages of Program Design 3*. Robert Martin, Dirk Riehle, and Frank Buschmann (eds.). Reading, Mass.: Addison Wesley Longman, 1998.

[Jones 90] D. W. Jones. Software testing an Ada cruise control. *Journal of Pascal, Ada, and Modula-2* 9(2):53–64, March–April 1990.

[Jones 94] D. W. Jones. Ada in action (with practical programming examples), 2nd ed. (photocopy), 1994.

[Jones 97a] Capers Jones. *Software quality: analysis and guidelines for success.* London: International Thompson Computer Press, 1997.

[Jones 97b] Capers Jones. *The economics of object-oriented software.* Burlington, Mass.: Software Productivity Research, Inc., April 14, 1997.

[Jorgenson+94] Paul C. Jorgenson and Carl Erickson. Object-oriented integration testing. *Communications of the ACM* 37(9):30–38, September 1994.

[Jüttner+94a] Peter Jüttner, S. Kolb, U. Naumann, and P. Zimmerer. A complete test process in object-oriented software development. In *Proceedings, 7th International Software Quality Week.* San Francisco: Software Research, May 1994.

[Jüttner+94b] Peter Jüttner, S. Kolb, U. Naumann, and P. Zimmerer. Experiences in testing object-oriented software. In *Proceedings, 11th International Conference on Testing Computer Software.* Washington, D.C.: USPDI, June 1994.

[Jüttner+94c] Peter Jüttner, Sebald Kolb, and Peter Zimmerer. Integrating and testing of object-oriented software. In *Proceedings, EuroSTAR '94.* Jacksonville, Fla.: SQE, Inc., October 1994.

[Jüttner+95] Peter Jüttner, S. Kolb, U. Naumann, J. Wood, and P. Zimmerer. Integration testing of object-oriented software. In *Proceedings, 8th Annual Software Quality Week.* San Francisco: Software Research, May 1995.

[Kan+95] Stephen H. Kan. *Metrics and models in software engineering quality.* Reading, Mass.: Addison-Wesley, 1995.

[Kaner 97] Cem Kaner. Pitfalls and strategies in automated testing. *IEEE Computer* 30(4):114–116, April 1997.

[Kaner+93] Cem Kaner, Jack Falk, and Hung Quoc Nguyen. *Testing computer software.* 2nd ed. New York: Van Nostrand Reinhold, 1993.

[Kean 97] Liz Kean. *Domain engineering and domain analysis;* January 1997; *http://www.sei.cmu.edu/activities/str/descriptions/deda_body.html*

[Kemmerer 85] Richard A. Kemmerer. Testing formal specifications to detect design errors. *IEEE Transactions on Software Engineering* SE-11(1):32–43, January 1985.

[Keszenheimer+94] Linda M. Keszenheimer and Karl J. Lieberherr. *Incremental testing of adaptive software,* Technical Report NU-CSS-94-22. Boston: Northeastern University, November 1994.

[Keszenheimer+95] Linda M. Keszenheimer and Karl J. Lieberherr. *Testing adaptive software during class evolution.* Technical Report NU-CSS-95-02. Boston: Northeastern University, January 1995.

[Kirani+94] Shekar Kirani and W. T. Tsai. Method sequence specification and verification of classes. *Journal of Object-Oriented Programming* 7(6):28–38, October 1994.

[Klimas 92] Edward Klimas. Quality assurance issues for Smalltalk based applications. *The Smalltalk Report* 1(9):2–7, July/August 1992.

[Knight+86] John. C Knight and Nancy G. Leveson. An experimental evaluation of the assumption of independence in multiversion programming. *IEEE Transactions on Software Engineering* SE-12(1):96–109, January 1986.

[Knirk 96] Wayne D. Knirk. Software testing process improvements. In *Proceedings, 13th International Conference on Testing Computer Software.* Washington, D.C.: USPDI, June 1996.

[Korel+96] Bogdan Korel and Ali M. Al-Yami. Assertion-oriented automated test data generations. In *Proceedings of the 18th International Conference on Software Engineering*. Los Alamitos, Calif.: IEEE Computer Society Press, 1996.

[Krasner+88] Glenn E. Krasner and Stephen T. Pope. A cookbook for using the model-view-controller user interface paradigm in Smalltalk-80. *Journal of Object-oriented Programming* 1(3):26–49, August/September 1988.

[Krishnamurthy 85] E. V. Khrishnamurthy *Introductory theory of computer science.* New York: Springer-Verlag, 1985.

[Krueger 92] Charles W. Krueger. Software reuse. *ACM Computing Surveys* 24(2): 131–183, 1992.

[Kung+93] D. Kung, J. Gao, P. Hsia, J. Lin, and Y. Toyoshima. Design recovery for software testing of object-oriented programs. In *Proceedings of the Working Conference on Reverse Engineering*. Los Alamitos, Calif.: IEEE Computer Society Press, May 1993.

[Kung+94] David Kung, N. Suchak, J. Gao, P. Hsia, Y. Toyoshima, and C. Chen. On object state testing. In *Proceedings, The Eighteenth Annual International Computer Software and Applications Conference*. Los Alamitos, Calif.: IEEE Computer Society Press, November 1993.

[Kung+95a] David Kung, J. Gao, P. Hsia, J. Lin, and Y. Toyoshima. Class firewall, test order, and regression testing of object-oriented programs. *Journal of Object-Oriented Programming* 8(2):51–65, May 1995.

[Kung+95c] David Kung, J. Gao, P. Hsia, Y. Toyoshima, C. Chen, Y. Kim, and Y. Song. Developing an object-oriented software testing and maintenance environment. *Communications of the ACM* 38(10):75–86, October 1995.

[Lakos 96] John S. Lakos. *Large scale C++ software design.* Reading, Mass.: Addison Wesley Longman, 1996.

[Lange+97] Danny B. Lange and Yuchi Nakamura. Object-oriented program tracing and visualization. *IEEE Computer* 30(5):63–70, May 1997.

[Laprie+96] Jean-Claude Laprie and Karama Kanoun. Software reliability and system reliability. In Michael R. Lyu (ed.). *Handbook of software reliability engineering.* Los Alamitos, Calif.: IEEE Computer Society Press, 1996.

[Laycock 92] Gilbert Laycock. Formal specification and testing: a case study. *Journal of Software Testing, Verification, and Reliability* 2(1):7–23, May 1992.

[Leavens 91] Gary T. Leavens. Modular specification and verification of object-oriented programs. *IEEE Software* 8(4):72–80, July 1991.

[Lejter+92] Moises Lejter, Scott Meyers, and Steven P. Reiss. Support for maintaining object-oriented programs. *IEEE Transactions on Software Engineering* 18(12): 1045–1052, December 1992.

[Leung+90] H. Leung and Lee White. A study of integration testing and software regression at the integration level. In *Proceedings, International Conference on Software Maintenance*. Los Alamitos, Calif.: IEEE Computer Society Press, 1990.

[Leveson 95] Nancy G. Leveson. *Safeware: system safety and computers.* Reading, Mass.: Addison-Wesley, 1995.

[Lewis+81] Harry R. Lewis and Christos H. Papadimitriou. *Elements of the theory of computation.* Englewood Cliffs, N.J.: Prentice-Hall, 1981.

[Li+93] Wei Li and Sallie Henry. Object-oriented metrics that predict maintainability. *Journal of Systems and Software* 23(2):111–122, November 1993.

[Lieberherr+89] Karl J. Lieberherr and Ian M. Holland. Assuring good style for object-oriented programs. *IEEE Software* 6(5):38–49, September 1989.

[Lieberherr+92] Karl J. Lieberherr and Cun Xiao. Object-oriented software evolution. *IEEE Transactions on Software Engineering* 19(4):313–343, April 1992.

[Lim 98] Wayne C. Lim. *Managing software reuse: a comprehensive guide to strategically reengineering the organization for reusable components.* Upper Saddle River, N.J.: Prentice-Hall, 1998.

[Liskov+75] Barbara H. Liskov and Stephen N. Ziles. Specification techniques for data abstractions. *IEEE Transactions on Software Engineering* SE-1(3):7–19, March 1975.

[Liskov+86] Barbara Liskov and John Guttag. *Abstraction and specification in program development.* Cambridge, Mass.: MIT Press, 1986.

[Liskov+94] Barbara H. Liskov and Jeannette M. Wing. A behavioral notion of subtyping. *ACM Transactions on Programming Languages and Systems* 16(6): 1811–1841, November 1994.

[Lorenz+94] Mark Lorenz and Jeff Kidd. *Object-oriented software metrics.* Englewood Cliffs, N.J.: Prentice-Hall, 1994.

[Love 92] Tom Love. *Object lessons.* New York: SIGS Books, 1992.

[Luckham 90] David C. Luckham. *Programming with specifications: an introduction to Anna, a language for specifying Ada programs.* Texts and Monographs in Computer Science. New York: Springer-Verlag, October 1990.

[Lyu 96] Michael R. Lyu (ed.). *Handbook of software reliability engineering.* Los Alamitos, Calif.: IEEE Computer Society Press, 1996.

[Mac Lane 86] Saunders Mac Lane. *Mathematics: form and function.* New York: Springer-Verlag, 1986.

[Maguire 93] Scott Maguire. *Writing solid code.* Redmond, Wash.: Microsoft Press, 1993.

[Mandl 85] Robert Mandl. Orthogonal Latin squares: an application of experiment design to compiler testing. *Communications of the ACM* 28(10):1054–1058, October 1985.

[Manna+78] Zohar Manna and Richard Waldinger. The logic of computer programming. *IEEE Transactions on Software Engineering* SE-4(3):199–229, May 1978.

[Marick 95] Brian Marick. *The craft of software testing.* Englewood Cliffs, N.J.: Prentice-Hall, 1995.

[Martin 95] Robert C. Martin. *Designing object-oriented C++ applications: using the Booch method.* Englewood Cliffs, N.J.: Prentice-Hall, 1995.

[Martin 96] Robert C. Martin. The Liskov substitution principle. *C++ Report* 8(3): 30–37, March 1996.

[Martin+98] Robert Martin, Dirk Riehle, and Frank Buschmann (eds.). *Pattern languages of program design 3.* Reading, Mass.: Addison Wesley Longman, 1998.

[Martin+92] James Martin and James J. Odell. *Object-oriented analysis and design.* Englewood Cliffs, N.J.: Prentice-Hall, 1992.

[Maunder+92] Colin M. Maunder and Rodham E. Tulloss. Testability on TAP. *IEEE Spectrum* 29(2):34–37, February 1992.

[McCabe 76] Thomas J. McCabe. A complexity measure. *IEEE Transactions on Software Engineering* SE-2(12):101–111, December 1976.

[McCabe+89] Thomas J. McCabe and C. W. Butler. Design complexity measurement and testing. *Communications of the ACM* 32(12):1415–1425, December 1989.

[McCabe+94] Thomas J. McCabe, L. A. Dreyer, A. J. Dunn, and A. H. Watson. Testing an object-oriented application. *Journal of the Quality Assurance Institute* 8(4): 21–27, October 1994.

[McCarthy 95] Jim McCarthy. *Dynamics of software development*. Redmond, Wash.: Microsoft Press, 1995.

[McClintock 97] Colleen McClintock. The logic of business rules. *Software Development* 5(11):45–50, November 1997.

[McConnell 96] Steve McConnell. Daily build and smoke test. *IEEE Software* 13(4): 144–143, July 1996.

[McGregor 94a] John D. McGregor. Functional testing of classes. In *Conference Proceedings, 7th International Software Quality Week*. San Francisco: Software Research Institute, May 1994.

[McGregor 94b] John D. McGregor. Constructing functional test cases using incrementally derived state machines. In *Conference Proceedings, 11th International Conference on Testing Computer Software*. Washington, D.C.: USPDI, Inc., June 13–16, 1994.

[McGregor+93a] John D. McGregor and Douglas M. Dyer. A note on inheritance and state machines. *Software Engineering Notes* 18(4):61–69, October 1993.

[McGregor+93b] John D. McGregor and Douglas M. Dyer. Selecting functional test cases for a class. In *Proceedings, 11th Annual Pacific Northwest Software Quality Conference*. Portland, Ore., October 1993.

[McGregor+94] John D. McGregor and Tim Korson. Integrating object-oriented testing and development processes. *Communications of the ACM* 37(9):59–77, September 1994.

[McGregor+96] John D. McGregor and Anuradha Kare. Parallel architecture for component testing of object-oriented software. In *Proceedings, 9th Annual Software Quality Week*. San Francisco: Software Research Institute, May 1996.

[McMenamin+84] Stephen M. McMenamin and John F. Palmer. *Essential systems analysis*. New York: Yourdon Press, 1984.

[Mealy 55] George H. Mealy. A method for synthesizing sequential circuits. *Bell System Technical Journal* 34:1045–1079, September 1955.

[Meyer 88] Bertrand Meyer. *Object-oriented software construction*. Englewood Cliffs, N.J.: Prentice-Hall, 1988.

[Meyer 92a] Bertrand Meyer. Applying "design by contract." *IEEE Computer* 25(10): 40–51, October 1992.

[Meyer 92b] Bertrand Meyer. *Eiffel: the language*. Second revised printing. Englewood Cliffs, N.J.: Prentice-Hall, 1992.

[Meyer 97] Bertrand Meyer. *Object-oriented software construction*. Upper Saddle River, N.J.: Prentice Hall PTR, 1997.

[Monarchi+92] David E. Monarchi and Gretchen I. Puhr. A research typology for object-oriented analysis and design. *Communications of the ACM* 35(9):35–47, September 1992.

[Moore 56] Edward P. Moore. Gedanken-experiments on sequential machines. In *Automata studies: annals of mathematical studies* (34). Princeton, N.J.: Princeton University Press, 1956.

[Moreland 94] Clarence C. Moreland. How to design effective tests for C++ class libraries. In *Object Expo Proceedings*. New York: Object Expo, Inc., June 9, 1994.

[Morell 90] Larry J. Morell. A theory of fault-based testing. *IEEE Transactions on Software Engineering* 16(8):844–857, August 1990.

[Morell+92] Larry J. Morell and Lionel E. Deimel. *Unit analysis and testing*. SEI Curriculum Module SEI-CM-9-2.0. Pittsburgh, Penn.: Carnegie-Mellon University, Software Engineering Institute, June 1992.

[Mueller 94] Harald M. Mueller. Powerful assertions for C++. *C/C++ Users Journal* 12(10):21–37, October 1994.

[Murata 89] Tadao Murata. Petri nets: properties, analysis, and applications. *Proceedings of the IEEE* (77):541–580, 1989.

[Murphy 95] Gail Murphy. "Testing Smalltalk Applications"; *http://www.cs.washington.edu/homes/gmurphy/testSTApp.html*

[Murphy+92] Gail Murphy and Pok Wong. Towards a testing methodology for object-oriented systems. Poster paper. ACM *Conference on Object-Oriented Programming Systems, Languages and Applications (OOPSLA)*, September 1992.

[Murphy+94] Gail C. Murphy, Paul Townsend, and Pok Wong. Experiences with cluster and class testing. *Communications of the ACM* 37(9):39–47, September 1994.

[Musa 93] John D. Musa. Operational profiles in software-reliability engineering. *IEEE Software* 10(4):14–32, March 1993.

[Musa 98] John D. Musa. *More reliable, faster, cheaper testing through software reliability engineering.* New York: McGraw-Hill, 1998.

[Myers 76] Glenford J. Myers. *Software reliability: principles and practices.* New York: John Wiley & Sons, 1976.

[Myers 77] Glenford J. Myers. An extension to the cyclomatic measure of program complexity. *ACM SIGPLAN Notices* 10(10):61-64, October 1977.

[Myers 79] Glenford J. Myers. *The art of software testing.* New York: John Wiley & Sons, 1979.

[Nerson+94] Jean-Marc Nerson and Kim Walden. *Seamless object-oriented architectures.* Englewood Cliffs, N.J.: Prentice-Hall, 1994.

[Neumann 90] Peter G. Neumann, moderator. *Forum on risks to the public in computers and related systems.* ACM Committee on Computers and Public Policy, 9(69), February 20, 1990.

[NeXT 95] NeXT Software. *Object-oriented programming and the Objective-C language.* Redwood City, Calif.: NeXT Software, Inc., 1995.

[NIST 95] U.S. Department of Commerce, National Institute of Standards and Technology. *Testability of object-oriented systems.* Report NIST GCR-675. Gaithersburg, M.D.: Computer Systems Laboratory, June 1995.

[NRC 97] U.S. Nuclear Regulatory Commission. *Review guidelines on software languages for use in nuclear power plant safety systems.* Report NUREG/CR-6463, Rev. 1. Rockville, Md., 1997.

[Ntafos 88] Simeon C. Ntafos. A comparision of some structural testing strategies. *IEEE Transactions on Software Engineering* 14(6):868–874, June 1988.

[Odell 95] James Odell. Approaches to finite-state machine modeling. *Journal of Object-oriented Programming* 7(1):14–20, January 1995.

[Offutt+95] A. Jefferson Offutt and Alisa Irvine. Testing object-oriented software using the Category–Partition method. In *Proceedings, TOOLS 17.* Englewood Cliffs, N.J.: Prentice-Hall, 1995.

[Olthoff 86] W. G. Olthoff. Augmentation of object-oriented programming by concepts of abstract data type theory: the ModPascal experience. In *Proceedings, ACM Conference on Object-Oriented Programming Systems, Languages and Applications (OOPSLA).* New York: ACM Press, December 1986.

[OMG 98] OMG Unified Modeling Language Specification. OMG Document Number ad/98-12-02, version 1.2. Framingham, Mass.: Object Management Group, Inc., July 1998.

[Ostrand+88] Thomas J. Ostrand and Marc J. Blacer. The Category–Partition method for specifying and generating functional tests. *Communications of the ACM* 31(6): 676–686, June 1988.

[Overbeck 94a] Jan Overbeck. *Integration testing for object-oriented software.* Ph.D. dissertation, Vienna University of Technology, 1994.

[Overbeck 94b] Jan Overbeck. Testing generic classes. In *Proceedings, EuroSTAR '94.* Jacksonville, Fla.: SQE, Inc., October 1994.

[Overbeck 95] Jan Overbeck. Testing object-oriented software and reusability—contradiction or key to success? In *Proceedings, 8th Annual Software Quality Week.* San Francisco: Software Research, May 1995.

[Page-Jones 88] Meilir Page-Jones. *The practical guide to structured system design,* 2nd. ed. Englewood Cliffs, N.J.: Yourdon Press, 1988.

[Page-Jones 92] Meilir Page-Jones. Comparing techniques by means of encapsulation and connascence. *Communications of the ACM* 35(9):147–151, September 1989.

[Page-Jones 95] Meilir Page-Jones. *What every programmer should know about object-oriented design.* New York: Dorset House, 1995.

[Parrish+93] Allen S. Parrish, Richard B. Borie, and David W. Cordes. Automated flow graph-based testing of object-oriented software modules. *Journal of Systems and Software* 23(2):95–109, November 1993.

[Parrish+94] Allen S. Parrish, David Cordes, and Mohan Govindarajan. Systematic defect removal from object-oriented modules. In *Conference Proceedings, 7th International Software Quality Week.* San Francisco: Software Research, May 1994.

[Parrish+95] Allen S. Parrish and Stuart H. Zweben. On the relationships among the all-uses, all-du-paths, and all-edges testing criteria. *IEEE Transactions on Software Engineering* 21(12):1006–1009, December 1995.

[Paulk+95] Mark C. Paulk, Charles V. Weber, Bill Curtis, and Mary Beth Chrissis. *The capability maturity model: guidelines for improving the software process.* Reading, Mass.: Addison-Wesley, 1995.

[Payne+97] Jeffery E. Payne, Roger T. Alexander, and Charles D. Hutchinson. Design-for-testability for object-oriented software. *Object Magazine* 7(5):33–43, July 1997.

[Payne+98] Jeffery E. Payne, Michael A. Schatz, and Matthew N. Schmid. Implementing assertions for Java. *Doctor Dobbs' Journal* 23(1):40–44, January 1998.

[Pemmaraju 98] Kamesh Pemmaraju. Effective testing strategies for enterprise-critical applications. *Java Report,* December 1998.

[Perry 95] William Perry. *Effective methods for software testing.* New York: John Wiley & Sons, 1995.

[Perry+87] Dewayne E. Perry and W. M. Evangelist. An empirical study of software interface faults—an update. In *Proceedings of the 20th Annual Hawaii International Conference on System Sciences.* New York: ACM Press, January 1987.

[Perry+90] Dewayne E. Perry and Gail E. Kaiser. Adequate testing and object-oriented programming. *Journal of Object-Oriented Programming* 2(5):13–19, January/February 1990.

[Peters+98] Dennis K. Peters and David Lorge Parnas. Using test oracles generated from program documentation. *IEEE Transactions on Software Engineering* 24(3): 161–173, March 1998.

[Peterson 95] Ivars Peterson. *Fatal defect: chasing killer computer bugs.* New York: Vintage Books, 1995.

[Place+91] Patrick Place and William G. Wood. *Formal development of Ada programs using Z and Anna: a case study*, CMU/SEI–91-TR-001. Pittsburgh: Software Engineering Institute, 1991.

[Pless 98] Vera Pless. *Introduction to the theory of error-correcting codes*, 3rd ed. New York: John Wiley & Sons, 1998.

[Ponder+94] Carl Ponder and Bill Bush. Polymorphism considered harmful. *Software Engineering Notes* 19(2):35–37, April 1994.

[Porat+95] Sara Porat and Paul Fertig. Class assertions in C++. *Journal of Object-Oriented Programming* 8(2):30–37, May 1995.

[Poston 87] Robert M. Poston. Preventing the most probable errors in requirements. *IEEE Software* 4(5):81–83, September 1987.

[Poston 94] Robert M. Poston. Automated testing from object models. *Communications of the ACM* 37(9):48–58, September 1994.

[Poston 96] Robert M. Poston (ed.). *Automating specification-based software testing*. Los Alamitos, Calif.: IEEE Computer Society Press, 1996.

[Prather+87] Ronald E. Prather and J. Paul Meyers, Jr. The path prefix software testing strategy. *IEEE Transactions on Software Engineering* SE-13(7):761–766, July 1987.

[Pree 95] Wolfgang Pree. *Design patterns for object-oriented software development*. Reading, Mass.: Addison-Wesley, 1995.

[Purchase+91] Jan A. Purchase and Russell L. Winder. Debugging tools for object-oriented programming. *Journal of Object-Oriented Programming* 4(3):10–27, June 1991.

[Rangaraajan+96] K. Rangaraajan, P. Eswar, and T. Ashok. Retesting C++ classes. In *Proceedings, 9th Annual Software Quality Week*. San Francisco: Software Research, May 1996.

[Rapps+85] Sandra Rapps and Elaine J. Weyuker. Selecting software test data using data flow information. *IEEE Transactions on Software Engineering* SE-11(4):367–375, April 1985.

[Raymond 91] Eric Raymond (ed.). *The new hacker's dictionary*. Cambridge, Mass.: MIT Press, 1991.

[Reed 93] David R. Reed. Program development using C++. In *C++ World Conference Proceedings*. New York: SIGS Conferences, Inc., April 1993.

[Reed 94] David R. Reed. Program development using C++. In *C++ World Conference Proceedings*. New York: SIGS Conferences, Inc., January 1994.

[Rettig 91] Marc Rettig. Testing made palatable. *Communications of the ACM* 34(5):25–29, May 1991.

[Richardson+85] Deborah J. Richardson and Lorie C. Clark. Partition analysis: a method of combining testing and verification. *IEEE Transactions on Software Engineering* SE-11(12):1477–1490, December 1985.

[Richardson+92] Deborah J. Richardson, S. L. Aha, and T. O. O'Malley. Specification-based test oracles for reactive systems. In *Proceedings of the 14th International Conference on Software Engineering*. Los Alamitos, Calif.: IEEE Computer Society Press, May 1992.

[Richardson+93] Deborah J. Richardson and Margaret C. Thompson. An analysis of test data selection criteria using the RELAY model of fault detection. *IEEE Transactions on Software Engineering* 19(6):533–553, June 1993.

[Riehle 98] Dirk Riehle. Bureaucracy. In *Pattern languages of program design 3*, Robert Martin, Dirk Riehle, and Frank Buschmann (eds.). Reading, Mass.: Addison Wesley Longman, 1998.

[Rine 87] David C. Rine. A common error in the object structure of object-oriented design methods. *Software Engineering Notes* 12(4):42–44, October 1987.

[Rine 96] David Rine. Structural defects in object-oriented programming. *Software Engineering Notes* 21(2):86–88, March 1996.

[Rochat+93] Roxie Rochat and Juanita Ewing. Smalltalk debugging techniques. *The Smalltalk Report* 2(9): 1, 18–23, July–August 1993.

[Roper 94] Marc Roper. *Software testing.* London: McGraw-Hill Book Co., 1994.

[Rosenberg+99] Doug Rosenberg and Kendall Scott. *Use case driver object modeling with UML: a practical approach.* Reading, Mass.: Addison Wesley Longman, 1999.

[Rosenblum 95] David S. Rosenblum. A practical approach to programming with assertions. *IEEE Transactions on Software Engineering* 21(1):19–31, January 1995.

[Rosenblum 97] Bruce D. Rosenblum. Improve your programming with asserts. *Doctor Dobbs' Journal* 22(12):60–63, December 1997.

[Rothermel+94] Greg Rothermel and Mary Jean Harrold. Selecting regression tests for object-oriented software. In *Proceedings, Conference on Software Maintenance.* Los Alamitos, Calif.: IEEE Computer Society Press., October 1994.

[Rothermel+96] Greg Rothermel and Mary Jean Harrold. Analyzing regression test selection techniques. *IEEE Transactions on Software Engineering* 22(8):529–551, August 1996.

[Rothermel+98] Greg Rothermel and Mary Jean Harrold. Empirical studies of a safe regression test selection technique. *IEEE Transactions on Software Engineering* 24(6):401–419, June 1998.

[Rumbaugh+91] James Rumbaugh, M. Blaha, W. Premerlani, F. Eddy, and W. Lorensen. *Object-oriented modeling and design.* Englewood Cliffs, N.J.: Prentice-Hall, 1991.

[Rumbaugh+93] James Rumbaugh. Disinherited! examples of misuse of inheritance. *Journal of Object-Oriented Programming* 5(9):22–24, February 1993.

[Rumbaugh+99] James Rumbaugh, Ivar Jacobson, and Grady Booch. *The Unified Modeling Language reference manual.* Reading, Mass.: Addison Wesley Longman, 1998.

[Runeson+98] Per Runeson and Björn Regnell. Derivation of an integrated operational profile and use case model. In *Proceedings, 9th International Symposium on Software Reliablity Engineering.* Los Alamitos, Calif.: IEEE Computer Society Press, November 1998, 70–79.

[Rushby 97] John Rushby. Subtypes for specifications. *ACM Software Engineering Notes* 22(6):4–19, November 1997.

[Sakar+91] S. Sakar and D. S. Rosenblum. Surveyors' forum: runtime checking and debugging of formally specified programs. *ACM Computing Surveys* 23(1):125–127, March 1991.

[Sakkinen 88] Markku Sakkinen. On the darker side of C++. *Lecture notes in computer science,* n 322. New York: Springer-Verlag, 1988.

[Sane+95] Aamod Sane and Roy Campbell. Object-oriented state machines: subclassing, composition, delegation, and genericity. In *ACM Conference on Object-Oriented Programming Systems, Languages and Applications (OOPSLA '95).* New York: ACM Press, 1995.

[Schuman+87] S. A. Schuman and D. H. Pitt. Object-oriented subsystem specification. In *Program specification and transformation.* G.L.T. Meertens (ed.). Amsterdam: Elsevier Science Publishers B.V., 1987.

[SEI 93] Mark C. Paulk, Bill Curtis, Mary Beth Chrissis, and Charles V. Weber. *Capability maturity model for software, version 1.1; CMU/SEI-93-TR-24.* Pittsburgh: Software Engineering Institute, 1993.

[Selic 98] Brian Selic. Recursive control. In *Pattern languages of program design 3*. Robert Martin, Dirk Riehle, and Frank Buschmann (eds.). Reading, Mass.: Addison Wesley Longman, 1998.

[Selic+94] Brian Selic, Garth Gullekson, and Paul T. Ward. *Real-time object-oriented modeling*. New York: John Wiley & Sons, 1994.

[Shatz 93] Sol M. Shatz. *Development of distributed software—concepts and tools*. New York: Macmillan Publishing Company, 1993.

[Shatz+89] Sol M. Shatz and Jia-Ping Wang (eds.). *Tutorial: distributed-software engineering*. Los Alamitos, Calif.: IEEE Computer Society Press, 1989.

[Shaw 84] Mary Shaw. Abstraction techniques in modern programming languages. *IEEE Software* 1(5):10–26, October 1984.

[Shepperd+97] Martin Shepperd and Michelle Cartwright. *An empirical study of object-oriented metrics*. Technical Report No. TR 97/01, Dept. of Computing, Bournemouth University, U.K., 1997.

[Shaler+92] Sally J. Shaler and Steven J. Mellor. *Object-oriented lifecycles: modeling the world in states*. Englewood Cliffs, N.J.: Prentice-Hall, 1992.

[Shopiro 93] Jonathan Shopiro. Tips and tricks to avoid the traps. In *C++ World Conference Proceedings*. New York: SIGS Conferences, Inc., October 18–22, 1993.

[Sidhu+89] Deepinder P. Sidhu and Ting-Kau Leung. Formal methods for protocol testing: a detailed study. *IEEE Transactions on Software Engineering* 15(4):413–426, April 1989.

[Siegel 94] Shel M. Siegel. OO integration testing specification. In *Conference Proceedings, 7th International Software Quality Week*. San Francisco: Software Research, May 1994.

[Siegel 96] Shel Siegel. *Object-oriented software testing: a hierarchical approach*. New York: John Wiley & Sons, 1996.

[Siepmann+94] Ernst Siepmann and A. Richard Newton. TOBAC: a test case browser for object-oriented software. In *Proceedings of the 1994 International Symposium on Software Testing and Analysis*. New York: ACM Press, 1994.

[Silverstein 99] Michael Silverstein. *Testing Smalltalk Applications*. SilverMark, Inc; *http://www.silvermark.com/pubs/sts99/*

[Sirer+98] Emin Gün Sirer, Sean McDirmid, and Brian N. Bershad. Verifying verifiers. *Workshop on Security and Languages, Palo Alto, September 1998; http://kimera. cs.washington.edu/papers/egs-paloalto/ppframe.htm*

[Skubics+96] Suzanne Skubics, Edward J. Klimas, and David A. Thomas. *Smalltalk with style*. Englewood Cliffs, N.J.: Prentice-Hall, 1996.

[Smith 97] Kevin A. Smith. Testing Java applets and applications. In *JavaOne Proceedings*. Mountain View, Calif.: Sun Microsystems, 1997.

[Smith+90] M. D. Smith and D. J. Robson. Object-oriented programming: the problems of validation. In *Proceedings of the 6th International Conference on Software Maintenance*. Los Alamitos, Calif.: IEEE Computer Society Press, November 1990.

[Smith+92] M. D. Smith and D. J. Robson. A framework for testing object-oriented programs. *Journal of Object-Oriented Programming* 5(3):45–53, June 1992.

[Soloway+88] Elliot Soloway, J. Pinto, S. Letovsky, D. Littman, and R. Lampert. Designing documentation to compensate for delocalized plans. *Communications of the ACM* 31(11):1259–1267, November 1988.

[Sommerlad 98] Peter Sommerlad. Manager. In *Pattern languages of program design 3*. Robert Martin, Dirk Riehle, and Frank Buschmann (eds.). Reading, Mass.: Addison Wesley Longman, 1998.

[Sparks+96] Steve Sparks, Kevin Benner, and Chris Faris. Managing object-oriented framework reuse. *IEEE Computer* 29(9):52–61, September 1996.

[Spuler 94] David A. Spuler. *C++ and C debugging, testing, and reliability.* Englewood Cliffs, N.J.: Prentice-Hall, 1994.

[Stout 97] John W. Stout. Front-end bug smashing in C++ and MFC: pointer validation and tracing. *Visual C++ Developers Journal,* January 1997.

[Stroustroup 88] Bjarne Stroustroup. What is object-oriented programming? *IEEE Software* 5(3):10–20, May 1988.

[Stroustroup 92a] Bjarne Stroustroup. *The C++ programming language*, 2nd ed. Reading, Mass.: Addison-Wesley, 1992.

[Stroustroup 92b] Bjarne Stroustroup. *The design and evolution of C++.* Reading, Mass.: Addison-Wesley, 1992.

[Subramanian+92] Girish H. Subramanian, J. Nosek, S. P. Raghunathan, and S. S. Kanitkar. A comparison of the decision tables and trees. *Communications of the ACM* 35(1):89–94, January 1992.

[Sun+95] W. Sun, Y. Ling, and C. Yu. Supporting inheritance using subclass assertions. *Information Systems* (Germany) 20(8):663–685, 1995.

[Szyperski 98] Clemens Szyperski. *Component software: beyond object-oriented programming.* Reading, Mass.: Addison Wesley Longman, 1998.

[Taenzer+89] David Taenzer, Murhty Ganti, and Sunil Podar. Problems in object-oriented software reuse. In *ECOOP '89: Proceedings of the 1989 European Conference on Object-Oriented Programming.* Cambridge, U.K.: Cambridge University Press, July 1989.

[Tai+87] Kuo-Chung Tai and Hsun-Kang Su. Test generation for Boolean expressions. In *Proceedings, The Eleventh Annual International Computer Software and Applications Conference (COMPSAC 87).* Los Alamitos, Calif.: IEEE Computer Society Press, October 1987.

[Taylor 92] David Taylor. A quality-first program for object technology. *Object Magazine* 2(3):17–18, June/July 1992.

[Thayer+90] Richard H. Thayer and Merlin Dorfman, (eds.). *System and software requirements engineering.* Los Alamitos, Calif.: IEEE Computer Society Press, 1990.

[Thielen 92] David Thielen. *No Bugs. Delivering error free code in C and C++.* Reading, Mass.: Addison-Wesley, 1992.

[Thuy 92] Nguyen N. Thuy. Testability and unit tests in large object oriented software. In *Proceedings, 5th International Software Quality Week.* San Francisco: Software Research, May 1992.

[Thuy 93] Nguyen N. Thuy. Design for quality in large object oriented software. In *Conference Proceedings, 6th International Software Quality Week.* San Francisco: Software Research, May 1993.

[Tip 95] Frank Tip. A survey of program slicing techniques. *Journal of Programming Languages* 3(3):121–189, September 1995.

[Tracz 95] Will Tracz. *Confessions of a used program salesman: institutionalizing software reuse.* Reading, Mass.: Addison-Wesley, 1995.

[Trausan-Matu+91] S. Trausan-Matu, J. Tepandi, and M. Barbuceanu. Validation, verification, and testing of object-oriented programs: methods and tools. In *Proceedings of the 1st East European Conference on Object-Oriented Programming.* September 1991.

[Turner 93] Kenneth J. Turner (ed.). Using formal description techniques: an introduction to ESTELLE, LOTOS and SDL. New York: John Wiley & Sons, 1993.

[Turner+95] C. D. Turner and D. J. Robson. A state-based approach to the testing of class-based programs. *Software Concepts and Tools* 16(3):106–112, 1995.

[van der Linden 98] Peter van der Linden. *Java programmers FAQ*, May 1998; *http://www.best.com/~pvdl/javafaq.html*

[Vines 98] Donald H. Vines, Jr. Integration testing of CORBA-based systems. *Distributed Object Computing* 1(6):42–45, June 1998.

[Voas+91] Jeffrey Voas, Larry Morell, and Keith Miller. Predicting where faults can hide from testing. *IEEE Software* 8(2):41–48, March 1991.

[Voas+99] Jeffrey Voas and Lara Kassab. Using assertions to make untestable software more testable. *Software Quality Professional Journal* 1(4), September 1999.

[Walden+95] Kim Walden and Jean-Marc Nerson. *Seamless object-oriented software architecture: analysis and design of reliable systems.* Englewood Cliffs, N.J.: Prentice-Hall, 1995.

[Ward+85] Paul T. Ward and Stephen J. Mellor. *Structured development for real-time systems.* Englewood Cliffs, N.J.: Prentice-Hall, 1985.

[Warmer+98] Jos Warmer and Anneke Kleppe. *The Object Constraint Language: precise modeling with UML.* Reading, Mass.: Addison Wesley Longman, 1998.

[Wasserman 85] Anthony I. Wasserman. Extending state transition diagrams for the specification of human–computer interaction. *IEEE Transactions on Software Engineering* SE-11(8):699–713, August 1985.

[Waters 85] Richard C. Waters. The programmer's apprentice: a session with KBEmacs. *IEEE Transactions on Software Engineering* 11(11):1296–1320, November 1985.

[Watt 90] David A. Watt. *Programming language concepts and paradigms.* New York: Prentice-Hall, 1990.

[Webster 87] Dallas E. Webster. *Mapping the design representation terrain: a survey.* MCC Technical Report STP-093-87, Austin, Tex.: Microelectronics and Computer Technology Corporation, July 1987.

[Wegner 87] Peter Wegner. Dimensions of object-based design. In *ACM Conference on Object-Oriented Programming Systems, Languages and Applications (OOPSLA).* New York: ACM Press, October 1987.

[Weide+91] Bruce W. Weide, William F. Ogden, and Stuart H. Zweben. Reusable software components. In *Advances in computers,* vol. 33, Marshall C. Yovits (ed.). Boston: Academic Press, 1991.

[Weinberg 78] Victor Weinberg. *Structured analysis.* Englewood Cliffs, N.J.: Prentice-Hall, 1978.

[Weir 95] Charles Weir. Code-level testing of Smalltalk applications, 1995; *http://www.cs.ubc.ca/spider/murphy/st_workshop/28-7.html*

[Weizenbaum 76] Joseph Weizenbaum. Computer power and human reason: from judgment to calculation. New York: W. H. Freeman & Co., 1976.

[West 96] Douglas B. West. *Introduction to graph theory.* Englewood Cliffs, N.J.: Prentice-Hall, 1996.

[Weyuker 82] Elaine J. Weyuker. On testing non-testable programs. *Computer Journal* 25(4):465–70, 1982.

[Weyuker 88] Elaine J. Weyuker. The evaluation of program-based software test data adequacy criteria. *Communications of the ACM* 31(6):668–675, June 1988.

[Weyuker+94] Elaine Weyuker, Tarak Goradia, and Ashutosh Singh. Automatically generating test data from a Boolean specification. *IEEE Transactions on Software Engineering* 20(5):353–363, May 1994.

[White 87] Lee J. White. Software testing and verification. In *Advances in computers,* vol. 26, Marshall C. Yovits (ed.). Boston: Academic Press, 1987.

[White+78] Lee J. White and E. I. Cohen. A domain strategy for computer program testing. In *IEEE Workshop on Software Testing and Documentation*. New York: IEEE, December 1978.

[White+80] Lee J. White and E. I. Cohen. A domain strategy for computer program testing. *IEEE Transactions on Software Engineering* SE-6(5):247–257, May 1980.

[White+93] Lee J. White, V. Narayanswamy, T. Friedman, M. Kirschenbaum, P. Piwowarski, and M. Oha. Test manager: a regression testing tool. In *Proceedings, Conference on Software Maintenance*, September 1993.

[White+97] Lee J. White and Khalil Abdullah. A firewall approach for regression testing of object-oriented software. In *Proceedings, 10th Annual Software Quality Week*. San Francisco: Software Research, May 1997.

[Wiegers 96] Karl E. Wiegers. *Creating a software engineering culture*. New York: Dorset House, 1996.

[Wilde+92] Norman Wilde and Ross Huitt. Maintenance support for object-oriented programs. *IEEE Transactions on Software Engineering* 18(12):1038–1044, December 1992.

[Wilde+93] Norman Wilde, Paul Matthews, and Ross Huitt. Maintaining object-oriented software. *IEEE Software* 75–80, January 1993.

[Wilke 93] George Wilke. *Object-oriented software engineering: the professional developer's guide*. Reading, Mass.: Addison-Wesley, 1993.

[Wirfs-Brock+90] Rebecca Wirfs-Brock, Brian Wilkerson, and Lauren Wiener. *Designing object-oriented software*. Englewood Cliffs, N.J.: Prentice-Hall, 1990.

[Woolf 97] Bobby Woolf. The abstract class pattern. In *Proceedings, Pattern Languages of Programming Conference*, September 1997; *http://home.att.net/~bwoolf/Abstract_Class/Abstract_Class.htm* (October 1998).

[Yourdon 89] Edward Yourdon. *Modern structured analysis*. Englewood Cliffs, N.J.: Yourdon Press, 1989.

[Yourdon+79] Edward Yourdon and Larry L. Constantine. *Structured design: fundamentals of a discipline of computer program and systems design*. Englewood Cliffs, N.J.: Prentice-Hall, 1979.

[Zachary 94] G. Pascal Zachary. *Show-stopper! the breakneck race to create Windows NT and the next generation at Microsoft*. New York: Free Press, 1994.

[Zhu+97] Hong Zhu, Patrick A. V. Hall, and John H. R. May. Software unit test coverage and adequacy. *ACM Computing Surveys* 29(4):366–427, December 1997.

[Zweben+92] Stuart Zweben, Wayne Heym, and John Kimmich. Systematic testing of data abstractions based on software specifications. *Journal of Software Testing, Verification and Reliability* 1(4):39–55, 1992.

Index

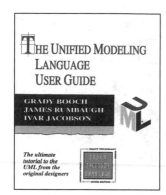

The Unified Modeling Language User Guide

Grady Booch, James Rumbaugh, and Ivar Jacobson
Addison-Wesley Object Technology Series

The Unified Modeling Language User Guide is a two-color introduction to the core eighty percent of the Unified Modeling Language, approaching it in a layered fashion and showing the application of the UML to modeling problems across a wide variety of application domains. This landmark book is suitable for developers unfamiliar with the UML or modeling in general, and will also be useful to experienced developers who wish to learn how to apply the UML to advanced problems.

0-201-57168-4 • Hardcover • 512 pages • ©1999

Surviving Object-Oriented Projects

A Manager's Guide
Alistair Cockburn
Addison-Wesley Object Technology Series

This book allows you to survive and ultimately succeed with an object-oriented project. Alistair Cockburn draws on his personal experience and extensive knowledge to provide the information that managers need to combat the unforeseen challenges that await them during project implementation. *Surviving Object-Oriented Projects* supports its key points through short case studies taken from real object-oriented projects. In addition, an appendix collects these guidelines and solutions into brief "crib sheets" that are ideal for handy reference.

0-201-49834-0 • Paperback • 272 pages • ©1998

Doing Hard Time

Developing Real-Time Systems with UML, Objects, Frameworks, and Patterns
Bruce Powel Douglass
Addison-Wesley Object Technology Series

Doing Hard Time is written to facilitate the daunting process of developing real-time systems. The author presents an embedded systems programming methodology that has been proved successful in practice. The process outlined in this book allows application developers to apply practical techniques—garnered from the mainstream areas of object-oriented software development—to meet the demanding qualifications of real-time programming.

0-201-49837-5 • Hardcover • 800 pages • ©1999

Real-Time UML, Second Edition
Developing Efficient Objects for Embedded Systems
Bruce Powel Douglass
Addison-Wesley Object Technology Series

The Unified Modeling Language is particularly suited to modeling real-time and embedded systems. *Real-Time UML* is the completely updated and UML 1.3 compliant introduction that developers of real-time systems need to make the transition to object-oriented analysis and design with UML. The book covers the important features of the UML, and shows how to effectively use these features to model real-time systems. Special in-depth discussions of finite state machines, object identification strategies, and real-time design patterns, to help beginning and experienced developers alike, are also included.

0-201-65784-8 • Paperback • 384 pages • ©2000

Automated Software Testing
Introduction, Management, and Performance
Elfriede Dustin, Jeff Rashka, and John Paul

This book is a step-by-step guide to the most effective tools, techniques, and methods for automated testing. Using numerous case studies of successful industry implementations, the authors present everything you need to know to successfully incorporate automated testing into the development process. In particular, this book focuses on the Automated Test Life Cycle Methodology (ATLM)—a structured process for designing and executing testing that parallels the Rapid Application Development methodology.

0-201-43287-0 • Paperback with CD-ROM • 608 pages • ©1999

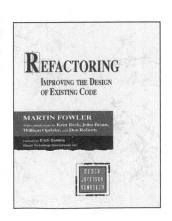

Refactoring
Improving the Design of Existing Code
Martin Fowler with contributions by Kent Beck, John Brant, William Opdyke, and Don Roberts
Addison-Wesley Object Technology Series

Refactoring is the process of changing a software system in such a way that it does not alter the external behavior of the code, yet improves its external structure. In this book, Martin Fowler et al. show you where opportunities for refactoring can typically be found, and how to go about reworking a bad design into a good one. In addition to discussing the various techniques of refactoring, the authors provide a detailed catalog of more than 70 proven refactorings.

0-201-48567-2 • Hardcover • 464 pages • ©1999

UML Distilled, Second Edition

A Brief Guide to the Standard Object Modeling Language
Martin Fowler with Kendall Scott
Addison-Wesley Object Technology Series

Thoroughly revised and updated, this best-selling book is a concise overview that introduces you to the Unified Modeling Language, highlighting the key elements of the standard modeling language's notation, semantics, and processes. Included is a brief explanation of the UML's history, development, and rationale, as well as discussions on how the UML can be integrated into the object-oriented development process. The book also profiles various modeling techniques associated with UML—use cases, CRC cards, design by contract, dynamic classification, interfaces, and abstract classes. The first edition of this classic work was named recipient of *Software Development* magazine's 1997 Productivity Award.

0-201-65783-X • Paperback • 224 pages • ©2000

The Unified Software Development Process

Ivar Jacobson, Grady Booch, and James Rumbaugh
Addison-Wesley Object Technology Series

The Unified Software Development Process goes beyond other object-oriented analysis and design methods by detailing a family of processes that incorporate the complete lifecycle of software development. This new book, representing the collaboration of Ivar Jacobson, Grady Booch, and James Rumbaugh, clearly describes the different higher-level constructs—notation as well as semantics—used in the models. Thus stereotypes such as use cases and actors, packages, classes, interfaces, active classes, processes and threads, nodes, and most relations are described intuitively in the context of a model.

0-201-57169-2 • Hardcover • 512 pages • ©1999

Use Case Driven Object Modeling with UML

A Practical Approach
Doug Rosenberg with Kendall Scott
Addison-Wesley Object Technology Series

This book presents a streamlined approach to UML modeling that includes a minimal but sufficient set of diagrams and techniques you can use to get from use cases to code quickly and efficiently. *Use Case Driven Object Modeling with UML* provides practical guidance that will allow software developers to produce UML models quickly and efficiently, while maintaining traceability from user requirements through detailed design and coding. The authors draw on their extensive industry experience to present proven methods for driving the object modeling process forward from use cases in a simple and straightforward manner.

0-201-43289-7 • Paperback • 192 pages • ©1999

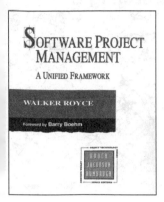

Software Project Management

A Unified Framework
Walker Royce
Addison-Wesley Object Technology Series

This book presents a new management framework uniquely suited to the complexities of modern software development. Walker Royce's pragmatic perspective exposes the shortcomings of many well-accepted management priorities and equips software professionals with state-of-the-art knowledge derived from his twenty years of successful from-the-trenches management experience. In short, the book provides the software industry with field-proven benchmarks for making tactical decisions and strategic choices that will enhance an organization's probability of success.

0-201-30958-0 • Hardcover • 448 pages • ©1998

The Unified Modeling Language Reference Manual

James Rumbaugh, Ivar Jacobson, and Grady Booch
Addison-Wesley Object Technology Series

James Rumbaugh, Ivar Jacobson, and Grady Booch have created the definitive reference to the UML. This two-color book covers every aspect and detail of the UML and presents the modeling language in a useful reference format that serious software architects or programmers should have on their bookshelf. The book is organized by topic and designed for quick access. The authors also provide the necessary information to enable existing OMT, Booch, and OOSE notation users to make the transition to UML. The text also includes an overview of the semantic foundation of the UML in a concise appendix.

0-201-30998-X • Hardcover with CD-ROM • 576 pages • ©1999

Enterprise Computing with Objects

From Client/Server Environments to the Internet
Yen-Ping Shan and Ralph H. Earle
Addison-Wesley Object Technology Series

This book helps you place rapidly evolving technologies—such as the Internet, the World Wide Web, distributed computing, object technology, and client/server systems—in their appropriate contexts when preparing for the development, deployment, and maintenance of information systems. The authors distinguish what is essential from what is incidental, while imparting a clear understanding of how the underlying technologies fit together. Among the essential topics examined in the book are data persistence, security, performance, scalability, and development tools.

0-201-32566-7 • Paperback • 448 pages • ©1998